Neurocomputing 2

Neurocomputing 2
Directions for Research

**edited by James A. Anderson, Andras Pellionisz,
and Edward Rosenfeld**

The MIT Press
Cambridge, Massachusetts
London, England

Printed and bound in the United States of America

Library of Congress Cataloging-in-Publication Data
(Revised for vol. 2)

Neurocomputing.
    Vol. 2: "A Bradford book.
    Contents: 1. Foundations of research - - 2. Directions
for research.
    1. Neural networks.   2. Neural computers.
I. Anderson, James A.   II. Rosenfeld, Edward.
QP363.3.N46   1988   152   87-3022
ISBN 0-262-01097-6 (v.1)
ISBN 0-262-01119-0 (v.2)

Contents

General Introduction
James A. Anderson   xiii

I Network Architecture

1

Introduction   1

(ca. 400 B.C.) Aristotle, "De memoria et reminiscentia," *Aristotle on Memory*, Richard Sorabji (Trans.), Providence, RI: Brown University Press, 1972   5

2

Introduction   11

(1948, 1961) Norbert Wiener, *Cybernetics*, Cambridge, MA: MIT Press, Introduction to first edition, pp. 1–29; Chapter V, "Computing machines and the nervous system," pp. 116–132; Chapter VI, "Gestalt and universals," pp. 133–143; and Chapter VII, "Cybernetics and psychopathology," pp. 144–154   14

3

Introduction   45

(1961) E. R. Caianiello; "Outline of a theory of thought-processes and thinking machines," *Journal of Theoretical Biology* 1: 204–235   48

4

Introduction   65

(1967) K. Steinbuch and E. Schmitt, "Adaptive systems using learning matrices," *Cybernetic Problems in Bionics*, H. L. Oestricher and D. R. Moore (Eds.), New York: Gordon and Breach, pp. 751–768   67

5

Introduction   75

(1968) James A. Anderson, "A memory storage model utilizing
spatial correlation functions," *Kybernetik* 5: 113–119   79

6

Introduction   87

(1972) Kaoru Nakano, "Associatron—a model of associative
memory," *IEEE Transactions on Systems, Man, and Cybernetics*
SMC-2: 380–388   90

7

Introduction   99

(1974) Karl H. Pribram, Marc Nuwer, and Robert J. Baron, "The
holographic hypothesis of memory structure in brain function and
perception," *Contemporary Developments in Mathematical
Psychology, Volume II, Measurment, Psychophysics, and Neural
Information Processing,* David H. Krantz, Richard C. Atkinson, R.
Duncan Luce, and Patrick Suppes (Eds.), San Francisco: W. H.
Freeman, pp. 416–457   102

8, 9

Introduction   123

(1976) D. J. Willshaw and C. von der Malsburg, "How patterned
neural connections can be set up by self-organization," *Proceedings
of the Royal Society of London, B* 194: 431– 445   126
(1980) Shun-ichi Amari, "Topographic organization of nerve
fields," *Bulletin of Mathematical Biology* 42: 339–364   135

10

Introduction   147

(1987) Gail A. Carpenter and Stephen Grossberg, "ART 2:
self-organization of stable category recognition codes for analog
input patterns," *Applied Optics* 26: 4919–4930   151

11

Introduction   163

(1988) Bart Kosko, "Bidirectional associative memories," *IEEE
Transactions on Systems, Man, and Cybernetics* 18: 49–60   165

12

Introduction   177

(1988) Pentti Kanerva, *Sparse Distributed Memory,* Cambridge,
MA: MIT Press, Chapter 4, "Neurons as address decoders," pp.
43–48; Chapter 5, "Search of memory for the best match," pp.
49–52; Chapter 6, "Sparse memory," pp. 53–59; and Chapter 7,
"Distributed storage," pp. 61–77   180

II   Computation and Neurobiology

13

Introduction   199

(1959) J. Y. Lettvin, H. R. Maturana, W. S. McCulloch, and W. H.
Pitts, "What the frog's eye tells the frog's brain," *Proceedings of the
Institute of Radio Engineers* 47: 1940–1951   202

14

Introduction   215

(1972) H. B. Barlow, "Single units and sensation: a neuron doctrine
for perceptual psychology?" *Perception* 1: 371–394   218

15

Introduction   235

(1976) J. T. McIlwain, "Large receptive fields and spatial
transformations in the visual system," *International Review of
Physiology, Neurophysiology II,* Robert Porter (Ed.), 10: 223–247   239

16

Introduction   255

(1985) Nobuo Suga,"The extent to which biosonar information is
represented in the bat auditory cortex," *Dynamic Aspects of
Neocortical Function,* Gerald M. Edelman, W. Einar Gall, and W.
Maxwell Cowan (Eds.), New York: Wiley-Interscience, pp. 315–373   259

17, 18, 19

Introduction   295

(1984) J.–P. Changeux, T. Heidmann, and P. Patte, "Learning by
selection," *The Biology of Learning,* P. Marler and H. S. Terrace
(Eds.), Berlin: Springer-Verlag; pp. 115–133   300
(1984) Gerald M. Edelman and Leif H. Finkel, "Neuronal group
selection in the cerebral cortex," *Dynamic Aspects of Neocortical
Function,* Gerald M. Edelman, W. Einar Gall, and W. Maxwell
Cowan (Eds.), New York: Wiley-Interscience, pp. 653–695   308
(1987) John C. Pearson, Leif H. Finkel, and Gerald M. Edelman,
"Plasticity in the organization of adult cerebral cortical maps: a
computer simulation based on neuronal group selection," *The
Journal of Neuroscience* 7: 4209–4223   335

20

Introduction   351

(1985) A. Pellionisz and R. Llinás, "Tensor network theory of the
metaorganization of functional geometries in the central nervous
system," *Neuroscience* 16: 245–273   356

21

Introduction   383

(1987) Christine A. Skarda and Walter J. Freeman, "How brains
make chaos on order to make sense of the world," *Behavioral and
Brain Sciences* 10: 161–195 (plus many commentators)   386

22

Introduction   421

(1987) Eric I. Knudsen, Sascha du Lac, and Steven D. Esterly,
"Computational maps in the brain," *Annual Review of Neuroscience*
10: 41–65   424

23

Introduction   437

(1988) David Zipser and Richard A. Andersen, "A back-propagation
programmed network that simulates response properties of a subset
of posterior parietal neurons," *Nature* 331: 679–684   440

24

Introduction   447

(1988) Thomas H. Brown, Paul F. Chapman, Edward W. Kairiss,
and Claude L. Keenan, "Long-term synaptic potentiation," *Science*
242: 724–728   451

III   Statistics and Pattern Classification

25, 26, 27

Introduction   459

(1965) Nils Nilsson, *Learning Machines,* New York: McGraw-Hill,
Chapter 1, "Trainable pattern classifiers," pp. 1–13; and Chapter 2,
"Some important discriminant functions: their properties and their
implementations," pp. 15–42   464
(1967) T. M. Cover and P. E. Hart, "Nearest neighbor pattern
classification," *IEEE Transactions on Information Theory* IT-13:
21–27   482
(1974) Bruce G. Batchelor, *Practical Techniques for Pattern
Recognition,* London: Plenum Press, "Methods of pattern
classification," Chapter 3, pp. 35–51   489

28

Introduction   497

(1981) Douglas L. Reilly, Leon N. Cooper, and Charles Elbaum, "A
neural model for category learning," *Biological Cybernetics* 45:
35–41   500

29

Introduction   507

(1987) Charles M. Bachmann, Leon N. Cooper, Amir Dembo, and Ofer Zeitouni, "A relaxation model for memory with high storage density," *Proceedings of the National Academy of Sciences* 84: 7529–7531   509

30

Introduction   513

(1988) Teuvo Kohonen, György Barna, and Ronald Chrisely, "Statistical pattern recognition with neural networks: benchmarking studies," *Proceedings of the IEEE International Conference on Neural Networks, San Diego, 1988,* pp. I-61–I-68   516

31

Introduction   525

(1988) Ralph Linsker, "Self-organization in a perceptual network," *Computer* 21: 105–117   528

32, 33

Introduction   541

(1988) Garrison W. Cottrell, Paul Munro, and David Zipser, "Image compression by back propagation: an example of extensional programming," *Advances in Cognitive Science, Volume 3,* N. E. Sharkey (Ed.), Norwood, NJ: Ablex   546
(1989) Pierre Baldi and Kurt Hornik, "Neural networks and principal component analysis: learning from examples without local minima," *Neural Networks* 2: 53–58   570

IV   Current Applications and Future Problems

34

Introduction   579

(1988) Marvin L. Minsky and Seymour A. Papert, *Perceptrons,* third edition, Cambridge, MA: MIT Press, "Epilog: the new connectionism," pp. 247–280   583

35

Introduction   599

(1988) Jerry A. Fodor and Zenan W. Pylyshyn, "Connectionism and
cognitive architecture: a critical analysis," *Cognition* 28: 3–72   603

36, 37

Introduction   639

(1988) L. D. Jackel, H. P. Graf, W. Hubbard, J. S. Denker, D.
Henderson, and Isabelle Guyon, "An application of neural net chips:
handwritten digit recognition," *Proceedings of the IEEE
International Conference on Neural Networks, San Diego, 1988*, pp.
II-107–II-115   643
(1990) Y. LeCun, B. Boser, J. S. Denker, D. Henderson, R. E.
Howard, W. Hubbard, and L. D. Jackel, "Backpropagation applied
to handwritten zip code recognition," *Neural Computation* 1:
541–551   648

38

Introduction   653

(1988) Teuvo Kohonen, "The 'neural' phonetic typewriter,"
Computer 21: 11–22   656

39

Introduction   669

(1988) Halbert White, "Economic prediction using neural networks:
the case of IBM daily stock returns, *Proceedings of the IEEE
International Conference on Neural Networks, San Diego, 1988*, pp.
II-451–II-459   671

40

Introduction   677

(1988) Ning Qian and Terrence J. Sejnowski, "Predicting the
secondary structure of globular proteins using neural network
models," *Journal of Molecular Biology* 202: 865–884   680

41

Introduction   701

(1989) James A. Anderson, Michael L. Rossen, Susan R. Viscuso,
and Margaret E. Sereno, "Experiments with representation in neural
networks: object motion, speech, and arithmetic," *Synergetics of
Cognition,* H. Haken (Ed.), Berlin: Springer   705

Name Index   717
Subject Index   723

General Introduction
James A. Anderson

Why Another?

In 1988 two of us (Anderson and Rosenfeld) coedited a collection of reprints entitled *Neurocomputing: Foundations of Research*. We have returned with a second volume of papers, which we call *Neurocomputing 2: Directions for Research*. The subtitles tell the story.

In our first volume we tried to present classics from a wide range of the area that we called *neurocomputing*, that complex of theoretical models, cognitive science, neuroscience, and practical devices and applications that tries to understand how the brain and mind work and how to build devices that take some of their inspiration from how we think the brain and mind work. In our first volume, we presented some of the essential foundations of the field.

In this volume we present some classics in neurocomputing, and we also present some papers that, in our opinion, suggest important directions in which the field will evolve in the future and some problems in store. In particular we include a section on neurobiological computation, as well as some serious criticisms of neural networks as computing devices.

Overview

In section I we include some important papers on network architecture. Several of these papers are many years old, but still contain valuable insights and fresh ideas. Some of the more recent papers contain novel and exciting ideas on network organization.

In section II we include a number of papers on neurobiology and computational neuroscience. It is our belief that many of the most valuable *practical* ideas for neurocomputing in the 1990s will come from contemplation and emulation of the "computational" techniques used in the nervous systems of animals. In particular neurobiology gives us unique insights into how to organize and use the computing powers of the *very* large neural networks that will shortly become available because of the imminent availability of neural network VLSI. A physically parallel array of a million model neurons should properly be used in a very different way than a network with one hundred units simulated on a serial computer.

We present in section III, the shortest section, papers discussing and using statistical ideas that have important consequences for neurocomputing. In a rapidly developing field, there is often a desire to establish a unique identity with a completely original set of techniques. In neurocomputing this sometimes manifests itself as a failure to appreciate how close many neural networks are in aspects of their operation to ideas used in the older fields of statistics and pattern recognition. We focus on two such important ideas in section III: nearest neighbor pattern recognition and principal components analysis. Both are highly practical, well understood, and closely related to many simple neural network operations. It is worth knowing about this similarity, why it happens, and how valuable such ideas can be when they are explicitly used by networks.

In section IV we present papers that contain some good news and some bad news about the future of neural networks. The first two papers contain important criticisms of the current state of the art in neural networks: There are some severe intrinsic difficulties with the networks that have been studied up to now, and initial successes should not hide major future problems. It is important to know what the problems are and what shape they take. The good news is that neural networks are being applied to a large number of important practical problems. We include papers describing a few particularly significant recent applications. The papers suggest what works and what does not work when a neural network is applied to a hard problem.

The Generic Neural Network

Almost all neural networks make frequent use of a few basic ideas. For those who are not familiar with the concepts or the jargon, let us briefly review the generic neural network model. (This material is largely taken from the general introduction to *Neurocomputing*: *Foundations of Research*.)

There are very many neurons, or nerve cells, in the human brain, at least ten billion. Each neuron receives inputs from other cells, integrates the inputs, and generates an output, which it then sends to other neurons or, in some cases, to effector organs such as muscles or glands. Neurons receive inputs from other neurons by way of specialized structures called *synapses* and send outputs to other neurons by way of output lines called *axons*. A single neuron can receive on the order of hundreds or thousands of input lines and may send its output to a similar number of other neurons. A neuron is a complex electrochemical device that contains a continuous internal potential called a *membrane potential*, and when the membrane potential exceeds a *threshold*, the neuron can propagate an all-or-none *action potential* for long distances down its axon to other neurons. Synapses come in a number of different forms, but two basic varieties are of particular note: *excitatory* synapses, which make it more likely that the neuron receiving them will fire action potentials, and *inhibitory* synapses, which make the neuron receiving them less likely to fire action potentials.

The most common neural network computing unit is an abstraction of the very complex biological neuron. The generic computing unit performs a two-stage computation. Units connect to each other with connections of varying *strengths*, usually simple numbers. The units driving a unit show varying activities. In the first stage of the computation, the driven unit forms the sum of products of connection strengths between that unit and the activities of the units driving it. It forms, mathematically, the inner product between the set of connection strengths and the input unit activities. The second stage usually consists of a simple nonlinearity, which takes the inner product from the first stage, which can have any value, and operates on it with a sigmoidal or clipping nonlinearity, forming the output of the computing unit.

Neuroscientists usually measure the *activity* of a neuron by its firing frequency, that is, the number of action potentials per second or something closely related to firing frequency. Biological neurons are rarely binary, that is, having only an on or off state as their output.

Outputs are continuous valued, and the neuron acts something like a voltage-to-frequency converter, converting membrane potential into firing rate. Many network models use elements that are continuous valued to some extent. However, a number of neural network models assume that the basic computing elements are binary, that is, can only be on or off. The resulting binary valued systems are valuable and often give useful insights into the behavior of complex networks of whatever type, and are often easier or more convenient to analyze than systems of more complex neurons.

Given our degree of ignorance of nervous system function and the early stages of our modeling efforts, it would be most unreasonable to dismiss one or another assumption made by a modeler as "unbiological" until we see how the resulting system works. And, of course, biological plausibility is significant only if you want to model the brain. If instead we desire to construct a useful device, there is no reason whatsoever to be bound by the way the brain happens to do it.

When the network is functioning, many cells can be active simultaneously. To describe the system at a moment in time, we have to give the activities of all the the cells in the system at that time. This set of simultaneous element activities is represented by a *state vector*, corresponding to the activities of many cells.

Neural networks have lots of computing elements connected to lots of other elements. This set of connections is often arranged in a *connection matrix*. The overall behavior of the system is determined by the structure and strengths of the connections. It is possible to change the connection strengths by various learning algorithms. It is also possible to build various kinds of dynamics into the responses of the computing elements.

Learning

Detailed computations in neural networks are performed largely by the connection strengths, hence the name *connectionist* is frequently used in cognitive science for neural networks used to make models to understand mental operations. There is often a decoupling between the learning phase and the retrieval phase of operation of a network. In the *learning phase* the connection strengths in the network are modified. Sometimes, if the constructor of the network is very clever or if the problem structure is so well defined that it allows it, it is possible to specify the connection strengths a priori. Otherwise it is necessary to modify strengths using one of a number of useful learning algorithms. Learning algorithms have been the heart of neural network research for the past two decades.

Network Operation

In the *retrieval phase* some initial information, in the form of an initial state vector or activity pattern, is put into the system. In most neural networks, if no initial information is provided, nothing useful is retrieved, and the more information that is provided, the more reliable the output information becomes. The initial input pattern passes through the connections to other elements, giving rise to an output pattern. If the system works properly, the output pattern contains the conclusions of the system. Given the complexity of the connections and the fact that many operations are going on simultaneously, it is hard to analyze exactly what is going on in the network. Although programs for traditional computers may be complicated, there is always faith that a program bug has a simple, usually localized cause. This may not be true for a neural network because both information and meaning may be spread out over many connections and many model neurons. This widespread computation leads to a number of intrinsic error mechanisms that are difficult, and probably impossible, to get rid of, given that many of the desirable features of networks (noise and damage tolerance, generalization) arise from the same cause.

Network Structure

There are a number of ways of organizing the computing elements in neural networks. Typically the elements are arranged in groups or layers. Single-layer and two-layer systems, with only an input and an output layer, are easy to analyze and are used extensively, though they often have limitations on what they can compute. More recently learning algorithms have become available that allow the network to develop appropriate connection strengths in multilayer networks. There is currently a great deal of effort devoted to understanding multilayer systems. Such systems are potentially much more powerful than one- and two-layer systems, but they are also more complex and harder to analyze. For example, sometimes there are elements in the middle layers that are neither input nor output neurons, often referred to as *hidden units*.

Representation

In the earliest days of neural networks, major research attention focused on the network structure, assumptions about the properties of the model neurons, and the learning algorithms used to change connection strengths.

Now that we have some idea of what various learning algorithms and network structures can do, there is a growing interest in the problems of representation of information in the network. The mammalian brain often follows very simple rules for representation, for example, arranging visual information into topographic maps on the cortex or mapping the surface of the body onto a cortical map that looks like a distorted map of the body. Presumably the way the brain represents information is useful for the kinds of things the brain does with it.

There is also interest in studying systems that can organize themselves, that is, develop the optimal way of arranging the information they must represent. Our feeling is that problems of representation may prove to be the major area for research in neural networks in the next few years. This is because *all* practical applications of networks are critically dependent on the way the data is represented. A major criticism of neural networks has been the necessity to handcraft the representations to make the systems work. With the proper description of the inputs, many learning algorithms will work adequately. Without the proper description, none may work.

Photocopiers versus Reprint Collections

What is the function of a reprint collection when we have photocopiers? Although this is the age of the photocopier, this also is the age of the information explosion. Who knows what to photocopy? How do you know what might be important when it is far outside your field, or when the books containing it are not in the company library because the company librarian never dreamed that the journal *Cognition* or books on the physiology of cerebral cortex would be of practical interest to engineers.

There is a problem with the time involved in the diffusion of knowledge. Sometimes the relevance of a paper far outside a particular field is hard to see until it is set into context. In truly interdisciplinary areas such as neurocomputing, one should know a fair amount about neuroscience, cognitive science, computer science, and applied mathematics. But, even with effort, it is impossible to keep really current in more than a small area. It can take years, or even decades, for ideas to transfer from neuroscience, say, to the engineers that could use those ideas as a starting point to build practical neurocomputing devices. The information diffusion time constant from cognitive science to engineering is even longer. To many engineers, the last time they encountered psychology (if at all) was as part of an introductory course as a college undergraduate. So to them psychology (and, by extension, cognitive science) is Skinnerian rat learning, salivating dogs, or Dr. Ruth, Leo Buscaglia, or Timothy Leary.

And most cognitive scientists and neuroscientists have very little understanding of the mathematical tools that engineers and physical scientists find essential. How, for example, is it possible to survive in science without knowing what an eigenvalue is?

Neurocomputing

The past few years have seen a more restrained continuation of the early enthusiasm for neural networks after their rediscovery in the mid-1980s. Initial euphoria has died away, and there is now some appreciation of both the strengths and weaknesses of neural networks, as technology, as theory, and as scientific tool. There are now several large neural network meetings, for example, the twice-yearly International Joint Conference on Neural Networks (IJCNN), which unified two separate large conferences associated with the IEEE and the International Neural Network Society (INNS). Close to a majority of the papers at these meetings are concerned with the practical applications of neural network technology.

In the following paragraphs we try to set our choice of papers in perspective. We must admit that the assignment of papers to sections is somewhat intuitive on our part. Some papers could fit quite nicely into other sections. The reader's neural networks can, no doubt, cope with this ambiguity and imprecision. We have tried to briefly describe each paper in the collection in the context of its neighboring papers and of the book as a whole. The individual introductions to the papers and, of course, the papers themselves provide more perspective and details.

Section I: Network Architecture

Scientists and engineers working in exciting and rapidly developing areas often suffer from what has been called *neophilia*, "love of the new," so if something is not the latest word, new, shiny and surprising, it is only of historical interest. Computer science is probably the paradigm of neophilia: By the time hardware is built, it is obsolete. In neurocomputing, neophilia is a particularly dangerous habit, though that does not make it any less prevalent. Because neurocomputing has suffered from long periods of neglect, there are a number of genuinely interesting and important ideas that have simply not been developed yet and that are awaiting rediscovery. We have tried to include a number of such gems in both volumes of *Neurocomputing*.

Section I contains papers concerned with neurocomputing and network architecture at a general level. Our first selection was published over two millennia ago by Aristotle, who discusses memory and makes some modern and still controversial assertions (paper 1). He claims that memory is, first, composed of *sense images*, that is, low-level sensory based representations of the world, and second, that such memories are linked together to form associative structures. We can "compute" by creatively manipulating images and associations between images.

The founder of cybernetics, Norbert Wiener, is represented by several chapters from his famous book *Cybernetics* (paper 2). We have included the introduction to *Cybernetics* because it shows, through historical example, that biology, neuroscience, engineering, and applied mathematics can mutually influence one another in important ways. *Cybernetics*, viewed in the light of the chapters and the introduction, becomes a strong argument for the *practical* utility of true interdisciplinary research.

Caianiello (paper 3) and Steinbuch and Schmitt (paper 4) present important ideas from the first flowering of neural network research. Caianiello presents a *big* theory, in a well-known paper that views neural computation as a whole and looks for resulting large-scale behavior. Some of the analysis and results—for example, the emphasis on long period system oscillations—is strikingly modern. Steinbuch and Schmitt review Steinbuch's *Lernmatrix*, which can serve as a simple and effective pattern classifier and pattern associator.

Anderson presents an early paper (paper 5) that he feels still makes an important point. Because information from *different* memories mixes together to give the value of a particular connection strength, networks intrinsically lose and distort information. This can be a strength or a weakness, depending on how it is viewed. Generalization can be good, loss of accuracy of retrieval can be bad, but the two are different aspects of the same process.

Nakano (paper 6) presents the *Associatron*, an autoassociative network using outer product learning that is used for what look like artificial intelligence computations. Nakano shows how by suitable representations, an autoassociator can answer questions, make generalizations, and can be used as a simple, flexible data base. The rest of the world did not rediscover these techniques until the 1980s.

Fifteen years ago optical holograms offered a novel analogy for memory and brain organization. Although we now think that the brain does not literally build a hologram as such, many of the general ideas discussed by Pribram, Nuwer and Baron (paper 7) can be carried over directly into current neural network research.

One of the most prominent features of cortical organization is the formation of topographic maps to represent sensory data. For example, there are many maps of the visual field in the visual areas, there are maps of the body surface for touch, and so on. If maps are ubiquitous and apparently important, how can they be formed? Both biology and a kind of self-organization seem to play parts, though the proportions vary greatly depending on which biological system is being considered. Two papers, by Willshaw and von der Malsburg (paper 8) and by Amari (paper 9), discuss how a few simple rules can make a network self-organize so it can generate topographic organization. The organizational effects are very robust and are greatly aided by even a small amount of initial biological bias.

Amari's paper is of technical interest because of its interesting use of continuous mathematics to analyze network behavior: Amari works analytically with what is effectively an infinite-dimensional network. Computer simulation or mathematical analysis using many discrete computing elements is the traditional means of studying neural networks.

The next two papers, by Carpenter and Grossberg (paper 10) and by Kosko (paper 11), discuss the two best-known examples of what are often called *resonance* models: adaptive resonance theory (ART 1 and ART 2) and the bidirectional associative memory (BAM). Information is passed back and forth between two levels in a network. The basic idea of both models is that particular learned patterns can give rise to what look like "resonances" in a physical system, so particular patterns are enhanced and modified based on learning. Carpenter and Grossberg present an elaborate network architecture that is capable of self-organizing and that can form "concepts" from its input data. Kosko analyzes a simple network with a similar architecture that gives resonances and stable oscillations. The practical importance of such models is that they are potentially capable of organizing the world presented to them into conceptlike equivalence classes.

The last paper in section I, by Kanerva (paper 12), presents a remarkably simple, ingenious, and elegant way of storing and retrieving information in parallel from a computer memory. Although it is not strictly a neural network, it can easily be realized by a neural network, and it incorporates a number of neural network ideas. Kanerva calls his memory a *sparse distributed memory* because information is stored in many locations and there are many fewer discrete items than memory locations. This unusual memory is well suited to practical applications and is easy to build with current technology.

Section II: Computation and Neurobiology

Real understanding of the nervous system would involve knowing what is being computed as well as the details of the machinery doing it. A field called *computational neuroscience* is in the process of definition, which tries to couple the computation to the machine in a way that illuminates both. (The name was recently popularized by Sejnowski, Koch, and Churchland (1988) in a well-known *Science* article.) The relation between neurobiology and theory has been uneasy in the past, and computational neuroscience is the latest in a series of attempts, going back to McCulloch and Pitts and even earlier, to understand what the nervous system is *doing*.

Neurobiologists typically accuse theorists of being casual with the details of the biology. We don't yet know enough to make models, they say. Neurotheorists, in turn, respond that we don't really need all that detail. Is it necessary, for example, to worry about the dynamics of the fourth voltage-dependent potassium channel to understand what the system is computing? ("Yes!" says the neurobiologist who spent the last decade studying its details. "No!" says the theorist who estimates that it makes a difference of at most a few percent in the frequency of firing of the neuron. "Yes!" says the neurobiologist, who points out that it might be a very important few percent, and the theorist hasn't considered its effects on membrane time constants . . . and so on, with varying degrees of acrimony.)

Computational neuroscience, like *systems neuroscience* and *theoretical neurobiology*—alternate names for pretty much the same thing—tries to strike a balance: Worry about the details to a point, but the resulting system must first be able to perform the biological computation. Practically this usually means most of the details must be thrown away so that the system can be simplified enough to be understood and simulated. After it more or less does the right thing, the details of the computation and the assumptions about the neurobiology can be refined.

One problem with this approach is that, to be done right, it means that there must be knowledge about what a part of the nervous system is *doing*, in addition to how it is constructed. It, perhaps inadvertently, builds an essential role for psychology and cognitive science into computational neuroscience, because in many parts of the mammalian brain *cognition* is the name we give to the results of the computation performed by cerebral cortex. For example, it is ironic that we know surprisingly little about the actual *function* of two of our most carefully studied, modeled, and characterized neural systems—the mammalian cerebellum and the hippocampus. It is hard to comprehend a system when its function is unknown.

We suspect that many of the initial successes of theory combined with neurobiology will come in the areas of sensory information processing—computational vision, for example—where it is easier to guess the nature of the computation being performed. (See the excerpt from Marr, paper 28 in *Neurocomputing: Foundations of Research*.)

The papers we have selected for section II, Computation and Neurobiology, discuss some of the central issues in neuroscience, as well as some of the information processing strategies used to do computation in the mammalian nervous system. There is little mention of invertebrates in this section, largely because we feel that the mammalian nervous system may be specialized for computation using very large populations of neurons, a structure basically similar to the assumptions usually made for neural networks.

The mammalian nervous system, particularly cerebral cortex, has served as the inspiration for most neural networks, which usually start with a mass of undifferentiated, more or less identical computing units that learn from experience. Often these networks contain subgroups of cells with different statistical connection patterns, but each subgroup is usually held to contain many similar units. There are so many cells, the story goes, that the genes cannot specify all the connections in detail, and only statistical connection rules are possible. Cells will develop selectivity due to learning or can have different initial input connection patterns, but cells in a group start by being similar.

Although it is highly questionable how accurate this gross approximation to mammalian cortex actually is, it has even less in common with the invertebrate systems. Invertebrates are equally as fascinating, important, and complex as vertebrates, but many commonly used invertebrate preparations study quite small interacting sets of highly differentiated and individualized neurons. Examples might be the stomatogastric ganglion of lobster or the *Aplysia* abdominal ganglion. The number of cells that are *recognizable* as individuals in simple invertebrate systems is small enough that it is quite conceivable that the genes *can* specify a great deal of wiring.

Another problem that greatly concerns neurobiology is *representation*, and essentially all of the papers in this section discuss this issue. Representation, in neural networks as in artificial intelligence, describes the means for putting information into the system and for getting it out. A neural network contains many different individual computing elements. Information corresponds to a pattern of activation of these elements.

What is the relation between a single element and the information contained in the pattern? One possibility would be that single neurons are very selective. A typical state vector would consist of a single active element. Another possibility is that very many elements are active simultaneously to describe an input. As a simple example, we could represent the twenty-six letters by having a set of twenty-six units. A letter would correspond to a single active unit. This is sometimes caricatured as a *grandmother cell* representation, because in its most extreme form it suggests that somewhere in your brain is a single cell that represents grandmother. When it is active, grandmother is being perceived or thought of.

We could also represent the character as a *distributed* pattern of activity. To represent a letter in a computer requires seven or eight bits. The pattern of all the bits determines the character. A bit can be "on" in the representation of many different letters; there is much less unit selectivity.

In artificial systems one can represent information in any way that is convenient. In neurobiology, however, we have to go look at what the cells are doing. Are lots of cells active or only a few when something interesting is happening? Do cells take random samples of a sensory input, as was suggested in some early perceptron papers, or do they respond to only a few particular "important" aspects of the environment? Are cells with similar responses close together physically? These are experimental questions, and an enormous amount of neuroscience is concerned with them.

One reason that the neurobiology may be particularly relevant for practical applications lies in the details of the representations. Most biologists believe that the way the nervous system does things is *optimal* in many respects. That means that the representation of information in the nervous system is liable to be extremely effective. Therefore a very good place to start in building an artificial system that will see or hear would be to use initial representations that are "brainlike." Carver Mead, the well-known designer of VLSI circuitry, is using this strategy to build silicon chips that mimic the initial processing found in mammalian sensory systems, using the biologically impeccable rationale that this is likely to be the best way to build a sensory front end for an artificial perceiving system (see Mead 1989).

There is also a school of thought, which is, in our opinion, becoming more prominent, that says that engineering time is better spent on getting the representations right for the particular problem to be solved than on developing exceptionally powerful learning algorithms. One can get a correctly functioning network by using a simple network with very good prepro-grammed representations or by using a crude representation of the input data combined with a very powerful learning algorithm. Experience suggest that the first approach usually works more reliably, generalizes better, and is overall more robust. However, the good solutions found will often be quite problem specific. In one sense this should not concern us. For a general purpose digital computer to do anything, it has to have a specific program telling it what to do. Designing the input and output representations in a neural network corresponds in many ways to programming. Perhaps we have invented a new classification of worker, to be called a *representationer*, who does for neural networks what programmers do for digital computers.

We have chosen as the first paper for section II a genuine classic in neurobiology, "What the Frog's Eye Tells the Frog's Brain," by Lettvin, Maturana, McCulloch, and Pitts (paper 13). What the frog's eye seems to report to the brain are matters of biological relevance to the frog, such as the presence of bugs. This immensely influential paper, besides its elegant neurobiological natural history, also suggested that individual neurons were quite selective and were responding to only a few important features of the visual environment. The data representation sent to the brain already contained tremendously enhanced responsiveness to important classes of input items.

In the next paper Barlow (paper 14) explored the question, What does a neuron *mean*? His conclusion was that individual neurons were greatly different from each other and that each neuron was speaking a "word" in a complex language, where each neuronal word was of the rough order of selectivity of a word in a human language. Perception corresponded to the activation of a small number of highly selective units. Barlow concluded that relatively few cells are active for visual perception—hundreds or thousands—a small fraction of the cells, but greater than one.

A sensori-motor representational strategy is suggested by McIlwain (paper 15), based on his studies of the superior colliculus. The colliculus is a brain stem structure that, crudely, directs the eyes to move to "interesting" regions of visual space. The colliculus is a sensori-motor system, with retinal input coming in one side of the structure, and motor output leaving the other. Retinal cells respond to quite restricted regions of visual space. As processing proceeds, cells respond to larger and larger regions of visual space. McIlwain suggests that information about location is not lost, merely rerepresented in a more useful way, and that by assuming a distributed output representation driving the eye muscles, it is possible to get high accuracy using what seem at first to be imprecise elements.

Next Suga (paper 16) provides a wealth of information on how a particularly fascinating biological system processes information: the sonar system of the bat. Because bats fly and must be as light as possible for aerodynamic reasons, information processing is pared down to its essentials. A great deal is known about the physics and engineering of radar and sonar. Therefore it is often possible to compare biological sonar information processing with strategies thoroughly developed and analyzed for artificial systems. For example, the mustache bat studied by Suga, uses such sophisticated sonar techniques as pulse compression and combined Doppler and pulsed sonar.

The next three papers—the first by Changeux, Heidemann, and Patte (paper 17), followed by two papers from the group of Gerald Edelman at Rockefeller University, by Edelman and Finkel (paper 18) and by Pearson, Finkel, and Edelman (paper 19)—present a biologically based class of models that use a network organizing technique called *learning by selection*.

This class of models was suggested by the theory of evolution. Unlike more traditional *instructional* theories, where connection strengths are learned based on what the environment directs, learning by selection assumes that learning proceeds by *selecting* particular response patterns from a preexisting potential set of response patterns. The network contains a great deal of initial variability, and this intrinsic variability provides the material for learning. The analogy, of course, is the more successful reproduction of the fitter individuals from a population of individuals with varying fitness. This class of models is particularly unfamiliar to many physical scientists and engineers because they only work if they are complex, variable, and "noisy," making virtues of what are usually considered to be problems.

Pellionisz and Llinás (paper 20) point out the importance of geometry in the organization of the sensori-motor system. Proprioception and muscle geometry form a loop through the three-dimensional environment. One way to understand the essence of the computation being performed is to realize that one sensory coordinate representation is being transformed to another motor coordinate representation in lawful ways described by geometry. Therefore the powerful mathematical techniques called *tensor theory* can be applied to the problem. Pellionisz and Llinás suggest that one function of the cerebellum is to perform this transformation, and they interpret some aspects of cerebellar physiology in this light. Although the mathematics of tensors are not familiar, the basic ideas are straightforward, and this approach suggests the virtues of looking at *both* the input *and* the output representations in detail instead of the aarbitrary input-output transformations more common in neural network research.

Skarda and Freeman (paper 21) present a model for the early stages of olfactory processing that contains an unusually rich set of ideas. The aim of the neural interactions is to produce a spatially distributed stable state of a complex dynamical system. Because olfaction in the rabbit is synchronized with respiration, Skarda and Freeman propose that the olfactory system forms a dynamical system capable of several modes of operation. As the system evolves, control of several global system parameters shifts the network from *off* to *chaotic oscillation*. When the system classifies odors, the parameters are such that the sensory input drives the system into one of a number of potential stable limit cycle oscillations, corresponding to a particular odor. Skarda and Freeman suggest that chaotic oscillations are used to "randomize" the initial state of the system.

Almost all sensory systems have maps associated with them. Sometimes the maps are based on obvious spatial structure—the visual field, for example—but other times they are built from less obvious structure. Bats, for example, have a map of what amounts to range to target in their cortex, generated from sonar returns. Knudsen, du Lac, and Esterly (paper 22) review the large amount of information known about map-based computation in biological systems and provide a wealth of ideas and references. When an information processing technique is ubiquitous, it must be valuable.

Zipser and Andersen (paper 23) use the powerful network learning algorithm *back propagation* to understand the properties of cells in parietal cortex. When the eyes can move relative to the head, it is hard to understand how we can detect and use stable relations between stationary objects in the world and the body. The retinal image must interact somehow with head position, and part of this interaction seems to go on in one section of parietal cortex. Back propagation can find the statistically optimal representation to be used in so-called *hidden layer* cells that are neither input or output. Zipser and Andersen use back propagation to determine the optimal hidden layer representation and suggest that it is very similar to the way the cells behave in parietal cortex. A neural network learning rule is being used as a statistical probe to study representations.

Brown, Chapman, Kairiss, and Keenan (paper 24) provide a brief review of the neurobiology of modifiable synapses. For decades neural network learning algorithms have *assumed* that learning involves an interaction between the pre- and postsynaptic activity levels in a synapse. Donald Hebb is usually given credit for the clearest formulation of what has become known as the Hebb rule of synaptic modification, but it seems to have been discovered and rediscovered on a number of occasions. (The simplest form of Hebb rule says that a synapse is strengthened only when the presynaptic and postsynaptic cells are simultaneously excited. See *Neurocomputing: Foundations of Research*, paper 4.) When asked for biological evidence for the rule, theorists could only look sheepish and say that it or something just like it had to be there to do any interesting associative learning. Now there is convincing experimental evidence that a Hebb-like synapse is in fact present in the mammalian hippocampus.

Section III: Statistics and Pattern Classification

In many respects neural networks are not *that* different from some of the things that have gone before. It has become clear in the past couple of years that some older techniques from pattern recognition and statistics are similar to some of the ideas developed for neural networks.

We have included several papers that bear on this issue in section III, Statistics and Pattern Classification. Most of the real and potential *applications* of neural networks at this time are as pattern classifiers.

There are two ideas we believe are particularly important to know about. The first is an important set of pattern classification algorithms called *nearest neighbor* techniques. We assume many of the readers of this collection will be interested in making pattern classifiers that are easy to use, quick to learn, and fast and accurate in operation. Therefore it is worth knowing about neural network variants that may work just as well as and be much easier to implement than some of the more powerful learning algorithms. Nearest neighbor algorithms form such a class for many problems.

The first three papers in section III, by Nilsson (paper 25), by Cover and Hart (paper 26), and by Batchelor (paper 27), present some background and important results for nearest neighbor classifiers. The essential idea motivating nearest neighbor classifiers is obvious and is based on our ideas about the way the world is put together, where similar things tend to be given the same name. Suppose we have a group of patterns that are classified into groups; an example might be pixel arrays that represent one or another letter. If a pattern is very similar to a pattern with a known classification, say differing from it in only a few pixels, then it probably has the same classification as the previously classified pattern. Suppose we learn a number of examples of the classifications. When a new pattern is to be classified, we compute the distance between the new pattern and all the classified examples. We give the new pattern the classification of the nearest classified example because that is presumably most like the new pattern.

Computing distances does not at first seem like what a neural network does. But the most common form of a neural network computing element takes an inner product between an input pattern and its connection strengths. As Nilsson shows, only a very small number of assumptions are then required to realize a nearest neighbor classifier with model neurons. Cover and Hart show that nearest neighbor classifiers in fact are very accurate if enough examples can be stored. Batchelor reviews a number of important variants of nearest neighbor architectures and discusses their strengths and weaknesses, as well as the kind of decision regions they form.

In the next paper, Reilly, Cooper, and Elbaum (paper 28) present a well-developed neural network model that implements a useful type of nearest neighbor classifier. This particular network has been of practical utility and has formed the basis of several commercial neural network products.

A paper by Bachmann, Cooper, Dembo, and Zeitouni (paper 29) combines two important neural network ideas into a single model. Many dynamical system neural network models have dynamics that minimize a system energy function. Most learning rules produce system energies of quite complex shape, forming uncontrolled local minima at what may be undesirable places. Bachmann and coauthors suggest that by assuming that classified examples act like electric charges, it is possible to construct an energy surface of more controllable form.

Kohonen, Barna, and Chrisely (paper 30) present a good example of a careful benchmark study of neural network learning algorithms. As a bonus they also describe two simple and effective nearest neighbor variants: LVQ (Learning Vector Quantization) and LVQ2. For many problems the LVQ algorithms learn more rapidly than the more traditional network learning rules.

The second idea from statistics that is coming to greater and greater prominence in neural network theory is the rediscovery of the importance of principal components. The idea behind principal components is simple, though the derivations involved are somewhat technical. We want to know the best and most economical way to represent a set of structured data. Suppose we want to describe a data point with only a fixed number of descriptors, chosen so as to minimize errors in description. The principal components are the particular patterns that minimize error in a linear analysis.

The minimization that principal components perform mathematically turns out to be similar to what many learning algorithms minimize. Most important a connection matrix formed from Hebb synapses is often closely related to the matrix whose eigenvectors are principal components. This means that principal components are liable to appear where they were not at first expected.

Linsker (paper 31) describes a simple self-organizing system designed to model low-level processing in the visual system. The optimization being performed generates model cells whose response properties are related to the first principal component.

The next two papers, by Cottrell, Munro, and Zipser (paper 32), and by Baldi and Hornik (paper 33), are related. Cottrell and colleagues look at a neural network that does image compression: a back propagation network applied to visual images. The input and output of the three-layer network are supposed to be as identical as possible, but all the data have to pass through the bottleneck of a hidden layer with only a few units. Experimentally they found that the space spanned by the hidden units looks very similar to the space described by the first few principal components. Baldi and Hornik analyze mathematically a linearized version of this network and show that, for this simplification, the network is indeed computing the principal component space.

Section IV: Current Applications and Future Problems

Although neural networks are interesting and exciting devices, they cannot do everything. The early enthusiasm for neural networks twenty years ago deflated when it became clear that networks were harder to use than was first thought and that simple networks could not compute some useful things.

At this time there are two serious theoretical criticisms that can be made about neural network research. We have already mentioned the first. Neuroscientists would simply say that there is so much that we don't know about the nervous system that it is premature to try to make realistic models of brain function.

The second criticism is an attack on computational adequacy, the new version of the devastating criticisms that Minsky and Papert provided in 1969 in *Perceptrons*. The first and second papers in section IV, by Minsky and Papert and by Fodor and Pylyshyn, describe computational problems with current neural networks. These criticisms, in our opinion, point out serious problems and should be treated with respect. One way to view them is as challenges. If they can be answered, the answers are liable to greatly extend our understanding of network capabilities and, even more exciting, of how human cognition might work.

Minsky and Papert (paper 34) discuss the current enthusiasm for neural networks and are not very impressed. Their conclusion is that much current work has simply not answered the twenty-year-old criticisms in *Perceptrons* and, worse, often seems to think that these criticisms are no longer relevant. Minsky and Papert say that this is a serious mistake because the fundamental theoretical problems have not gone away merely because everyone now has a workstation on their desk and can do large simulations with ease. Computer power does not make up for lack of answers.

Fodor and Pylyshyn (paper 35) argue convincingly that *some* aspects of human cognition simply cannot be explained by neural networks. Neural networks of almost all types belong to what is sometimes called the *associationist* tradition in psychology. The computational limitations of pure association have been discussed for (literally) centuries. Fodor and Pylyshyn's argument is that it is not possible to explain many aspects of syntax with simple association. More to the point, simple association is such an incredibly inefficient way to compute that no engineer would dream of using it for many kinds of computations that humans can obviously do easily.

Both Minsky and Papert and Fodor and Pylyshyn are perfectly happy to admit that neural networks are useful models to explain many aspects of brain and mind function. They do not want, however, enthusiasm and hype to obscure some fundamental difficulties that will not go away easily.

The last papers present what we think are some interesting applications of neural networks. They demonstrate the various approximations and assumptions that are useful in working on real problems.

Two closely related papers, separated by two years, from an experienced group of investigators at AT&T Bell Laboratories (papers 36 and 37), discuss digit recognition with a neural network. The two papers give a glimpse at a project in progress. Some of the first significant commercial applications of neural networks may involve digit recognition, to read numbers printed on checks or on envelopes. Digit recognition, like speech recognition, is a typical example of a perceptual problem that is so easy for humans that we don't appreciate how hard it really is until we try to do it artificially. One conclusion of the Bell group is that considerable effort should be expended on developing a good set of features for early processing of the pixel array representing a digit. With good engineering design, adapted to the problem, neural networks can provide state-of-the-art digit recognition.

Kohonen (paper 38) discusses speech recognition with a neural network. He uses a self-organizing map-forming network to recognize phonemes. This model is described in detail in paper 30 in *Neurocomputing: Foundations of Research* and is closely related to the map-forming systems discussed by Willshaw and von der Malsburg and Amari in papers 8 and 9 in this volume.

White (paper 39) discusses the predictive problem to which we all want the answer: predicting the behavior of the stock market. Unfortunately, but not really unexpectedly, a neural net does not work. White presents some useful formal network techniques along with some interesting economics.

Qian and Sejnowski (paper 40) try to predict secondary protein structure with a neural network. The order of amino acids linked together determines the way a protein twists itself up. The ability to predict the resulting structure simply from the order of amino acids would be of considerable value. The resulting network works as well as or better than existing methods, but also does not obtain very high accuracy. The numerical experiments performed by Qian and Sejnowski are particularly useful in understanding network operation.

The last paper, by Anderson, Rossen, Viscuso, and Sereno (paper 41), presents three recent network applications in quite different areas: object motion, speech, and arithmetic learning. It is our belief that they suggest a useful direction for practical network applications: simple networks, using large numbers of elements, with representational techniques suggested by the kind of representations used by the nervous system.

Multiple Cultures

A very mixed group is interested in neural networks. Among them are engineers, computer scientists, physicists, cognitive scientists, neurobiologists, and business people. These different groups all have valuable insights to bring to neural network research.

Practical applications are one important driving force for research because it brings new participants and lots of support into the field. Practical applications must work, therefore hard problems must be overcome, not avoided.

Neurobiologists and cognitive scientists have experience with the hardware and software of the one working intelligent system we know. For many years grant proposals would claim that research on the brain or the mind would help us to build brainlike computers. Perhaps that claim is now coming true. Certainly neurobiology gives us many construction hints about how to put together complex systems from simple elements. And cognitive science suggests to us what the software does extremely well and what seems to cause difficulties.

The next few years should be exciting and eventful. Perhaps we really will start building genuine brainlike computers as well as understanding how our own minds and brains work. We would like to think research in neurocomputing, of the kind presented here, will aid that process.

Bibliographic Note

In choosing the papers for this collection, we looked for reasonably self-contained articles. We tried to find the most complete statement of a point of view. On a couple of occasions we have used two or three articles to represent different but related aspects of work in an area. We have also included several review articles for areas that may be unfamilar to some of our readers. Entry points to the literature are particularly difficult to obtain in neurobiology because of the enormous number of published papers and their often specialized and technical nature. In a few cases the original authors have asked us to correct minor errors in their papers, and we have honored their wishes as far as we could.

References

C. Mead (1989), *Analog VLSI and Neural Systems*. Reading, MA: Addison-Wesley.

T.J. Sejnowski, C. Koch, and P. Churchland (1988), Computational Neuroscience. *Science* 241: 1299–1306.

I
Network Architecture

1
Introduction

(ca. 400 B.C.)
Aristotle

"De memoria et reminiscentia,"*Aristotle on Memory*, Richard Sorabji (trans.),
Providence, RI: Brown University Press, 1972

Aristotle is a name almost everyone in science has heard about and whose works almost no one has read. He was the scientist of the Greeks and was immensely influential on Western thought for two thousand years.

The excerpt from his writings that we reprint here is a brief essay on memory. It was translated by Richard Sorabji, who also provided extensive notes and commentary with the translation, placing the work in its historical and philosophical perspective. We recommend the notes highly. But we include this fragment from Aristotle in our collection because it raises some remarkably contemporary *scientific* issues. We can be quite sure that the way the mind and brain work was the same in 500 B.C. as now, so Aristotle is talking about the same system we study today when he, largely introspectively, discusses memory. However, because his culture and assumptions are so different from ours, he comes at things from what is for us an unusual direction. Aristotle's writing is extremely terse and difficult. Sorabji's notes assure us that this is true in the Greek, as well as in the translation.

There are two important scientific statements that Aristotle makes about memory: First, the elementary unit of memory is a *sense image,* and, second, associations and links between memories serve as the basis for higher-level cognition. The text uses the names *memory* for the elementary unit and *recollection* for reasoning by association with elementary units.

It is striking to see how much emphasis Aristotle places on the *sensory* qualities of memory. He sees memories as belonging "to the perceptual part" and believes that "memory involves an image in the soul, which is among other things, a sort of imprint in the body of a former sense image." Memory, specifically, does not consist of abstractions.

Appropriately Aristotle comes up with a remarkably vivid visual image to express this: "For the change that occurs marks in a sort of imprint, as it were, of the sense image, as people do who seal things with signet rings."

Aristotle's position is still controversial. Consider visual imagery, which usually consists of individual past events or of combinations of memories of previously seen objects. Most people have visual imagery to varying degrees of intensity. However, some people seem to have no visual imagery at all, and (sometimes) these people are extremely intelligent and verbal individuals who (sometimes) are influential linguists, psychologists, or philosophers. There is a remarkably persistent and outspoken school of thought that either denies that visual imagery occurs or holds that, if it does occur, it is misleading in that it reflects an underlying symbolic or nonvisual abstract reasoning process that has the visual part along for the ride, so to speak.

The problem is complicated by the fact that visual memory imagery, when it occurs, is rarely an exact veridical reproduction of the sense image, but often contains systematic distortions and omissions, as well as strong signs of participating in higher-level abstract structure. The visual image is of a much lower degree of spatial accuracy and detail than often believed, though there are frequent examples, especially among children, of extremely detailed and accurate images, called *eidetic imagery.*

Kosslyn's book, *Image and Mind* (1981) discusses these issues in detail. As one example most of us have various geographical maps in our visual memories. Is Reno, Nevada east or west of San Diego? Or, on our internal world map, is Paris north or south of Montreal? There is interference between knowledge about the map and more abstract knowledge: Nevada is east of California, Reno is in Nevada, hence it is east of San Diego. Montreal seems northern because it is in Canada and very cold in winter, whereas Paris is warmer and in the heart of western Europe. In fact Paris is north of Montreal, and Reno is west of San Diego.

Kosslyn shows quite convincingly that visualization serves as a useful computational tool. Properly used, it saves storing a huge number of interrelated propositions, and like most computational tools it comes with a set of elementary subroutines such as zoom, translate, scan, and the like. But the degree of spatial accuracy that we think we have in our remembered images is much less than actually seems to be there.

Also there are many kinds of nonvisual remembered sense images. Many people with weak visual imagery may have powerful auditory or kinesthetic imagery and memories, as William James pointed out in the nineteenth century (See Ch. 19, "Imagination," in *Psychology: Briefer Course*).

Aristotle seems to have been aware of these qualifications and difficulties and some others that are less obvious. For example, when we think of a triangle, do we think of the abstract geometrical definition, which fits *all* triangles, or do we think of a specific, imaged triangle? Why *that* triangle? Suppose we need a triangle with a right angle for a proof and happen to think of a triangle with an obtuse angle. Wouldn't this reduce the accuracy and generality of our geometrical reasoning? In understanding a sentence like *The cat is near the mat*, is the cat to the left or right or in back of or in front of the mat? Or is it in all locations at once? How can there be an image of one cat in all locations? and so on.

If memories are sense images, then how do we discriminate between old and new sense images? That is, why do we not hallucinate every time we remember something? Aristotle suggests we attach a temporal tag to the memory, though how this is done is unclear. Aristotle suggests it is another sense image. If the tag is lost, there is a confusion of images and reality, as was the problem with the unfortunate Antipheron of Oreus, mentioned in the manuscript.

However, despite these problems, Aristotle is quite firm that sense images are the content of memory. Given that the elementary units of memory are these sense images, what can you do with them? Aristotle poses the problem with clarity. Given a sense image, how do you remember something else: "How therefore will he remember what is not present?"

Aristotle then discusses how one "computes" with memorized sense images. The word *recollection* is used in the translation to denote this complex process: "Acts of recollection happen because one change is of a nature to occur after another." Clearly Aristotle is proposing an (unexplained) linkage mechanism between memories. He suggests a number of ways that linkage can occur: by temporal succession or by "something similar, or opposite, or neighboring." This notion of linkage of elementary memories is usually given the name *association* in the later psychological literature, and these passages are why Aristotle is often given credit for the first publication in the area.

Once the notion of linkage of images is proposed, Aristotle develops the idea in an unusual manner. He first gives a series of practical hints on how to *use* associative memory. If one wants to retrieve a memory in the middle of an associative chain, Aristotle suggests several ways how it might be done. For example, one tries to choose a place in the chain close to where the desired item might be and then does a linear search up or down the chain. This emphasis on practice partly arose because keeping points in order and not skipping any was critical to an orator or lecturer who generally was not able to use detailed notes.

It is clear that Aristotle sees "recollection" as being a highly dynamic and flexible process: ". . . recollecting is, as it were, a sort of reasoning. . . . a sort of search. And this kind of search is an attribute only of those animals which also have the deliberating part."

The modern scientific idea that comes closest to what Aristotle seems to mean by "recollection" is a simple semantic network, where sense images are linked together to form complex structures. A good deal of reasoning can then be done by using the semantic net to retrieve pertinent information by moving from node to node in the network. The nodes in Aristotle's nets presumably correspond to something like sense images. One of the practical problems with semantic nets is branching, that is, what to do if there is more than one link leaving a node. Aristotle was fully aware of this problem: ". . . it is possible to move to more than one point from the same starting point." Sometimes the memory moves to the wrong branch, providing one mechanism for errors or failures of memory: "So a person is sometimes moved to one place and at other times differently . . ."

Because recollection is a creative process, it offers a computational mechanism for forming new ideas. Perhaps the most famous example of this process in the classical literature, as Sorabji points out in his introduction, is Plato's dialog, *Meno*, where Socrates leads a slave boy to understand geometry by a series of small associative steps. Taken to the limit, properly directed recollection is capable of discovering new truths, using memorized sense images as the raw material.

There is also an extensive, and rather unclear, discussion of how to use the temporal tags attached to the sense images. These tags are important because they prevent normal people from hallucinating, because they allow an entry into memory for retrieval, and because they offer a way of ordering events and estimating time lapses. There are also some wonderful paragraphs in this essay on the pathology of memory, for example, why children, old people, and dwarfs have poor memories.

If one was to summarize Aristotle's discussion from a contemporary neural network point of view, it might look something like this: The elementary units of memory are closely related to sense images (state vectors?). These elementary units are linked together by a number of mechanisms (connection matrices?). It is possible to systematically use these associative structures to perform reasoning and memory access by forming chains and more complex structures built from elementary associations (semantic networks?).

Although Aristotle's suggestions about memory lack what we would now consider to be essential details, the well-specified outline of a perfectly viable computational theory of memory are present in these few pages, written over two thousand years ago.

References

W. James (1894/1962), *Psychology: Briefer Course*. London: Collier-Macmillan.

S. Kosslyn (1981), *Image and Mind*. Cambridge, MA: Harvard University Press.

(ca. 400 B.C.)
Aristotle

"De memoria et reminiscentia,"*Aristotle on Memory*, Richard Sorabji (trans.),
Providence, RI: Brown University Press, 1972

Chapter One

Programme

449ᵇ4   In discussing memory and remembering, it is necessary to say what they are, and how their occurrence is to be explained, and to which part of the soul this affection, and recollecting, belong. For it is not the same people who are good at remembering and at recollecting. Rather, for the most part, slow people are better at remembering, while those who are quick and learn well are better at recollecting.

First main topic. The object of memory. This is the past, not the future or present, nor what is present as an object of perception or theorizing. But after perception or theorizing is over, one can remember, and in doing so, will remember the fact of having perceived or theorized.

449ᵃ9   First, then, one must consider what sort of things the objects of memory are, for this often leads people astray. For it is not possible to remember the future, which is instead an object of judgment and prediction. (There might even be a predictive science, as some people say divination is.) Nor is memory of the present; rather, perception is, for by perception we know neither the future nor the past, but only the present. But memory is of the past. No one would say he was remembering what was present, when it was present, e.g. this white thing when he was seeing it; nor would he say he was remembering the object of his theorizing when he was in the act of theorizing and thinking. Rather he says simply that he is perceiving the one, and exercizing scientific knowledge of the other. But when a person possesses scientific knowledge and perception without actually exercizing them, under these conditions he remembers in the one case that he learned or theorized, in the other that he heard, or saw, or something of the kind. For whenever someone is actively engaged in remembering, he always says in his soul in this way that he heard, or perceived, or thought this before.

Conclusions. Memory is not identical with, but subsequent to, perception and conception. It is a state or affec-

tion connected with these. Only those animals which can perceive the time-lapse can remember.

449ᵇ24   Therefore memory is not perception or conception, but a state or affection connected with one of these, when time has elapsed. There is no memory of the present at the present, as has been said. But perception is of the present, prediction of the future, and memory of the past. And this is why all memory involves time. So only animals which perceive time remember, and they do so by means of that with which they perceive.

Second main topic. To what part of the soul does memory belong? Two reasons why it belongs to the perceptual part. (a) It involves cognizing time. Time must be cognized in the same way as magnitude and change, since these are three interrelated continua. We know, then, from our discussion of cognizing magnitude that the cognition will be by means of images. (b) Memory also involves cognizing the thing remembered. And this too is done by means of images. Any connexion between memory and the intellect is merely incidental.

449ᵇ30   An account has already been given of imagination in the discussion of the soul, and it is not possible to think without an image. For the same effect occurs in thinking as in drawing a diagram. For in the latter case, though we do not make any use of the fact that the size of the triangle is determinate, we none the less draw it with a determinate size. And similarly someone who is thinking, even if he is not thinking of something with a size, places something with a size before his eyes, but thinks of it not as having a size. If its nature is that of things which have a size, but not a determinate one, he places before his eyes something with a determinate size, but thinks of it simply as having size. Now the reason why it is not possible to think of anything without continuity, nor of things not in time without time, is another story. But it is necessary that magnitude and change should be known by the same means as time. And an image is an affection belonging to the common sense. So it is apparent that knowledge of these is due to the primary perceptive part. Memory, even the memory of objects of thought, is not without an image. So memory will belong to thought in virtue of an incidental association, but in its own right to the primary perceptive part.

Corollaries. But for this, memory would not belong to animals lower than man, and perhaps to no mortal animals. Even as it is, it does not belong to those animals which lack perception of time.

450ª15   And this is why some other animals too have memory, and not only men and those animals that have judgment or intelligence. But if memory were one of the thinking parts, not many of the other animals would have it, and perhaps no mortal animals would, since even as it is, they do not all have memory, because they do not all have perception of time. For, as we said before, when someone is actively engaged in memory, he perceives in addition that he saw this, or heard it, or learned it earlier; and earlier and later are in time.

Summary

450ª22   It is apparent, then, to which part of the soul memory belongs, namely the same part as that to which imagination belongs. And it is the objects of imagination that are remembered in their own right, whereas things that are not grasped without imagination are remembered in virtue of an incidental association.

Third main topic. An impasse. Why it arises. Memory involves an image in the soul, which is among other things a sort of imprint in the body of a former sense-image. (A suitable surface is needed in the body to take the quasi-imprint.)

450ª25   One might be puzzled how, when the affection is present but the thing is absent, what is not present is ever remembered. For it is clear that one must think of the affection, which is produced by means of perception in the soul and in that part of the body which contains the soul, as being like a sort of picture, the having of which we say is memory. For the change that occurs marks in a sort of imprint, as it were, of the sense-image, as people do who seal things with signet rings.

450ª32   (And this is also why memory does not occur in those who are subject to a lot of movement, because of some trouble or because of their time of life, just as if the change and the seal were falling on running water. In others, because of wearing down, as in the old parts of buildings, and because of the hardness of what receives the affection, the imprint is not produced. And this is why the very young and the old have poor memory, since they are in a state of flux, the former because they are growing, the latter because they are wasting away. Similarly the very

quick and the very slow are also obviously neither of them good at remembering. For the former are too fluid, the latter too hard. Therefore with the former the image does not remain in the soul, while with the latter it does not take hold.)

The impasse. What it is. How by contemplating and perceiving this image does one remember something quite distinct from it?

450ᵇ11   But then, if this is the sort of thing that happens with memory, does one remember this affection, or the thing from which it was produced? For if the former, we would remember nothing absent; but if the latter, how is it that while perceiving the affection we remember the absent thing which we are not perceiving? And if it is like an imprint or drawing in us, why should the perception of this be the memory of a different thing, rather than of the affection itself? For one who is exercizing his memory contemplates this affection and perceives this. How therefore will he remember what is not present? For at that rate one could also see and hear what is not present.

Solution. One contemplates the image as being of, i.e. as being a copy of, something distinct.

450ᵇ20   Or is there a way in which this is possible and happens? For the figure drawn on a panel is both a figure and a copy, and while being one and the same, it is both, even though the being of the two is not the same. And one can contemplate it both as a figure and as a copy. In the same way one must also conceive the image in us to be something in its own right and to be of another thing. In so far, then, as it is something in its own right, it is an object of contemplation or an image. But in so far as it is of another thing, it is a sort of copy and a reminder. So again when the change connected with the other thing is active, if the soul perceives the image as something in its own right, it appears to come to one as a thought or image. But if one contemplates the image as being of another thing, and (just as in the case of the drawing) as a copy, and as of Coriscus, when one hasn't seen Coriscus, then (not only in the case of the drawing is the experience of so contemplating it different from when one contemplates it as a drawn figure; but also) in the case of the soul, the one image occurs simply as a thought, the other, because it is a copy (as in the case of the drawing), is a reminder.

Corollaries of this solution. The possibility of regarding, or not regarding one's image as a copy helps to explain four phenomena. (a) Doubt as to whether one has memory. (b) Suddenly switching to remembering. (c) Wrongly supposing one has memory. (d) Memorizing.

451ᵃ2 And for this reason, when changes like this are produced in our soul as a result of former perception, we sometimes do not know whether this is happening in accordance with the previous perception, and are in doubt whether it is memory or not.

451ᵃ5 At other times it happens that we have a thought and recollect that we heard or saw something earlier. This happens when one changes from contemplating the image as the thing that it is to contemplating it as being of something else.

451ᵃ8 The contrary also happens, as it did to Antipheron of Oreus and other mad people. For they used to speak of their images as things that had occurred and as if they were remembering them. This happens whenever someone contemplates what is not a copy as if it were.

451ᵃ12 Exercizes safeguard memory by reminding one. And this is nothing other then contemplating something frequently as a copy and not as a thing in its own right.

Retrospect

451ᵃ14 Now, it has been said what memory and remembering are, namely the having of an image regarded as a copy of that of which it is an image, and to which part in us memory belongs, namely the primary perceptive part and that with which we perceive time.

Chapter Two

First main topic. What recollection is not. Recollection is not the recovery of memory, for no memory need have preceded. Admittedly, recollection may be the recovery of scientific knowledge, perception, etc., and so perception or the acquisition of scientific knowledge must have preceded. But it does not follow that memory must have preceded, for perception and the acquisition of scientific knowledge do not presuppose prior memory, nor incorporate within themselves the acquisition of memory, nor are they immediately followed by remembering.

Recollection is not acquisition of memory. For remembering, followed by memory, can precede any act of recollection.

Recollection cannot even be defined simply as the recovery of scientific knowledge, perception, etc., if we want to distinguish it from relearning.

451ᵃ18 It remains to speak about recollecting. First, then, one must take as being the case all that is true in the essays. For recollection is neither the recovery nor the acquisition of memory. For when someone first learns or

experiences something, he does not recover any memory, since none has preceded. Nor does he acquire memory from the start, for once the state or affection has been produced within a person, then there is memory. So memory is not produced within someone at the same time that the experience is being produced within him. Further, at the indivisible and final instant when the experience has first been produced within, although the affection and scientific knowledge are already present in the person who had the experience (if one should call the state or affection scientific knowledge—and nothing prevents us also remembering in virtue of an incidental association some of the objects of our scientific knowledge), none the less remembering itself, does not occur until time has elapsed. For a person remembers now what he saw or experienced earlier. He does not now remember what he experienced now.

451ᵃ31 Further, it is apparent that a person can remember from the start, once he has perceived or experienced something, without having just now recollected it. But when he recovers previously held scientific knowledge, or perception, or that of which we were earlier saying that the state connected with it is memory, this is, and is the time of, recollecting one of the things mentioned. (When one does remember, it results that memory follows.)

451ᵇ6 Nor indeed do these things in all circumstances yield recollection when they are reinstated in a man who had them before. Rather, in some circumstances they do, in others they do not. For the same man can learn and discover the same thing twice. So recollecting must differ from these cases, and it must be that people recollect when a principle is within them over and above the principle by which they learn.

Second main topic. Prerequisites and method of recollection. Prerequisites: images are naturally fitted to occur in a certain order, and will do so, if not of necessity, then by habit.

451ᵇ10 Acts of recollection happen because one change is of a nature to occur after another. If the changes follow each other of necessity, clearly a person who undergoes the earlier change will always undergo the later one. But if they follow each other not of necessity but by habit, then for the most part a person will undergo the later one. It can happen that by undergoing certain changes once a person is more habituated than he is by undergoing other changes many times. And this is why after seeing some things once, we remember better than we do after seeing other things many times.

Method: sometimes one takes a short cut, and chooses a starting-point which (because it is similar, opposite, or neighbouring) will lead one straight to the thing one wishes to recollect. The image corresponding to such a starting-point comes next to, or overlaps with, or is the same as, the image of the thing to be recollected. But for the most part, one has to pass through other images first, before one reaches the image of the penultimate item in the series. Even so, the method of recollecting is the same as when one takes a short cut, if one considers how each item in the series is related to its successor.

451ᵇ16　Whenever we recollect, then, we undergo one of the earlier changes, until we undergo the one after which the change in question habitually occurs.

451ᵇ18　And this is exactly why we hunt for the successor, starting in our thoughts from the present or from something else, and from something similar, or opposite, or neighbouring. By this means recollection occurs. For the changes connected with these things in some cases are the same, in others are together, and in others include a part, so that the remainder which one underwent after that part is small.

451ᵇ22　Sometimes, then, people search in this way. But also when they do not search in this way they recollect, whenever the change in question occurs after another one. And for the most part it is after the occurrence of other changes like those we spoke of that the change in question occurs. There is no need to consider how we remember what is distant, but only what is neighbouring, for clearly the method is the same. (I mean the successor, not having searched in advance, and not having recollected.) For the changes follow each other by habit, one after another.

Method (cont.). The importance of getting a starting-point.

451ᵇ29　And thus whenever someone wishes to recollect, he will do the following. He will seek to get a starting-point for a change after which will be the change in question. And this is why recollections occur quickest and best from a starting-point. For as the things are related to each other in succession, so also are the changes. And whatever has some order, as things in mathematics do, is easily remembered. Other things are remembered badly and with difficulty.

Recollecting and relearning distinguished in light of the above. He who recollects can move on to what follows the starting-point without the help of someone else.

452ᵃ4　And recollecting differs from relearning in that a person will be able somehow to move on by himself to what follows the starting-point When he cannot, but depends on someone else, he no longer remembers. Often a person is unable to recollect, at a given moment, but when he

searches he can, and he finds what is sought. This occurs when he excites many changes, until he excites a change of a sort on which the thing will follow. For remembering is the presence within of the power which excites the changes, and this in such a way that the man moves of himself and because of changes that he possesses, as has been said.

The importance of starting-points (resumed).

452ᵃ12　But one should get a starting-point. And this is why people are thought sometimes to recollect starting from places. The reason is that people go quickly from one thing to another, e.g. from milk to white, from white to air, and from this to fluid, from which one remembers autumn, the season one is seeking.

The middle member of a triplet makes a good starting-point. If unsuccessful with the first triplet, one should skip on to the middle member of the next triplet.

452ᵃ17　In general in every case the middle also looks like a starting-point. For if no sooner, a person will remember when he comes to this, or else he will no longer remember from any position, as for example if someone were to think of the things denoted by A B ΓΔ E Z H Θ. For if he has not remembered at Θ, he will remember at Z for from here he can move in either direction to H or to E. But if he was not seeking one of these, after going to Γ he will remember, if he is searching for Δ or B, or if he is not, he will remember after going to A. And so in all cases.

The possibility just mentioned of moving to alternative destinations from the same starting-point explains why from a given starting-point one sometimes remembers and sometimes does not. Habit may divert one to the wrong destination. Alternatively, so may similarity. The method of recollecting has now been described.

452ᵃ24　The reason why one sometimes remembers and sometimes does not, starting from the same position, is that it is possible to move to more than one point from the same starting-point, e.g. from Γ to Z or Δ. So if a man is moved through something old, he moves instead to something to which he is more habituated. For habit is already like nature. (And this is why what we think of frequently we recollect quickly. For just as by nature one thing is after another, so also in the activity. And frequency creates nature.)

452ᵃ30　But just as among natural events there occur also ones contrary to nature and the result of luck, still more is this so among events that are due to habit, seeing that nature does not belong to these in the same way. So a person is sometimes moved to one place and at other times differently, especially when something draws him away else-where from the one place. For this reason also when we have to remember a name, if we know a similar one, we blunder onto that.

Recollecting, then, happens in this way.

Third main topic. Estimating time-lapses. Remembering involves estimating time-lapses. Different time-lapses, like different spatial magnitudes, are represented by differing small scale models in one's thought.

452ᵇ7   But the main thing is that one must know the time, either in units of measurement or indeterminately. Assume there is something with which a person distinguishes more and less time. Probably it is in the same way as he distinguishes magnitudes. For a person thinks of things large and distant not through stretching out his thought there, as some people say one stretches sight (for even if the things do not exist, he can think of them in the same way), but by means of a change which is in proportion. For there are in the thought similar shapes and changes. How, then, when someone is thinking of larger things, will the fact that he is thinking of them differ from the fact of thinking of smaller things? For everything within is smaller and in proportion to what is without.

452ᵇ15   Perhaps just as one can receive in oneself something distinct but in proportion to the forms, so also in the case of the distances. It is then, as though, if a person undergoes the change AB, BE, he constructs ΓΔ. For the changes AΓ and ΓΔ are in proportion. Why, then, does he construct ΓΔ rather than ZH? Is it that as AΓ is to AB, so is Θ to I? So one undergoes these latter changes simultaneously. But if someone wishes to think of ZH, he thinks in the same way of BE, but instead of the changes Θ, I, he thinks of the changes K, Λ. For these latter are related as is ZA to BA.

Estimating time-lapses (cont.). The image of the thing remembered and the image representing the time-lapse must occur together. One must not wrongly suppose one's image is of a certain thing. One need not know the time-lapse in standard units of measurement.

452ᵇ23   Whenever, then, the change connected with the thing and that connected with the time occur together, then one is exercising memory. But if a person thinks he is doing this, when he is not, then he thinks he is remembering. For nothing prevents him from being deceived and thinking he is remembering when he is not. However, when exercising his memory a person cannot think he is not doing so and fail to notice that he is remembering. For this turned out to be what remembering was. But if the change connected with the thing occurs without that connected with the time, or the latter without the former, one does not remember.

452ᵇ29   The change connected with the time is of two sorts. For sometimes a person does not remember the time in units of measurement, e.g. that he did something or other the day before yesterday but sometimes also he does remember the time this way. None the less, he remembers, even if it be not in units of measurement. And people are in the habit of saying that they remember but don't know when, whenever they do not know the amount of time in units of measurement.

Fourth main topic. Recollecting and remembering. Differences between the two. Recollecting is too like reasoning to belong to animals lower than man.

453ᵃ4   Now, it has been said in what precedes that it is not the same people who are good at remembering and at recollecting. Recollecting differs from remembering not only in respect of the time, but in that many other animals share in remembering, while of the known animals one may say that none other than man shares in recollecting. The explanation is that recollecting is, as it were, a sort of reasoning. For in recollecting, a man reasons that he formerly saw, or heard, or had some such experience, and recollecting is, as it were, a sort of search. And this kind of search is an attribute only of those animals which also have the deliberating part. For indeed deliberation is a sort of reasoning.

Fifth main topic. Recollection involves the body. Evidence of its physiological character: some people become upset when they fail to recollect, and succeed in recollecting after giving up, which needs to be explained by saying that they have set up motion in an organ, and, once set up, the motion will not stop, until what is sought returns.

453ᵃ14   The following is a sign that the affection is something to do with the body, and that recollection is a search in something bodily for an image. It upsets some people when they are unable to recollect in spite of applying their thought hard, and when they are no longer trying, they recollect none the less. This happens most to melancholic people. For images move them most. The reason for recollecting not being under their control is that just as it is no longer in people's power to stop something when they throw it, so also he who is recollecting and hunting moves a bodily thing in which the affection resides. The people who get upset most are those who happen to have fluid around the perceptive region. For once moved, the fluid is not easily stopped until what is sought returns and the movement takes a straight course.

*That a motion, once set up, may be hard to stop explains
various other phenomena.*

453ª26   And this is also why, when cases of anger and of
fear set something moving, they are not halted, even though
the people set up counter-movements in turn, but rather the
anger and fear make counter-movements in the original
direction. And the affection is like names and tunes and
sayings, when one such has come to be very much on
someone's lips. For after the people have stopped, and
without their wishing such a thing, it comes to them to sing
it or say it again.

*Further evidence of the physiological character of rec-
ollection. Defects in memory can be traced to physiological
conditions.*

453ª31   Those also whose upper parts are especially
large and those who are dwarf-like have poorer memories
than their opposites because they have a great weight resting on the perceptive part, and neither from the start are the
changes able to persist within such people and avoid being
dispersed, nor during recollecting does the movement easily take a straight course. The extremely young and the very
old have poor memory because of the movement in them.
For the one group is wasting away, the other growing
rapidly. Further, children at any rate are also dwarf-like
until late in their youth.

Retrospect

453ᵇ7   Now, it has been stated what is the nature of
memory and remembering, and what it is in the soul that
animals remember with, and what recollecting is, and in
what manner it occurs, and through what causes.

2
Introduction

(1948, 1961)
Norbert Wiener

Cybernetics, (Second Edition), Cambridge, MA: MIT Press.
Introduction to the First Edition, pp. 1–29;
Chapter V, "Computing machines and the nervous system," pp. 116–132;
Chapter VI, "Gestalt and Universals," pp. 133–143;
and Chapter VII, "Cybernetics and psychopathology," pp. 144–154

Norbert Wiener is famous for his work on cybernetics, a set of techniques with important practical uses in control theory, communications theory, and statistics, as well as being a fertile source of concepts in biology. It is interesting to see how complementary Wiener's approach to understanding brain function is to the neural network approach represented elsewhere in this collection. We have excerpted three chapters from Wiener's classic book, *Cybernetics,* where Wiener discusses his ideas on brain function.

We have also included the introduction to the first edition of *Cybernetics* because of its considerable historical interest. The introduction, which appeared in 1948, gives a brief intellectual history of Weiner's scientific community over the preceeding few years. It acknowledges assistance from several authors whose papers have appeared in these collections: Warren McCulloch and Walter Pitts, Oliver Selfridge, and Jerry Lettvin. It also contains an eloquent argument in favor of interdisciplinary work. As Wiener puts it, "It is these boundary regions of science which offer the richest opportunities to the qualified investigator." It is striking to see how closely Wiener worked with biologists, engineers, and brain scientists in developing cybernetics and how close he and his peers were to the practical technology and the ideas behind the development of mechanical and electronic computers. (Those of us who have observed science in action for a while have noted, perhaps cynically, that there is much more verbal than financial support for interdisciplinary work on the part of governmental granting agencies and universities.) Wiener also mentions his intellectual indebtedness to his opportunities to travel and work with collaborators in other institutions and the value of small, intensive workshop meetings on a particular topic, all mechanisms equally useful today.

We have chosen for inclusion here the chapters explicitly concerned with brain organization. There is an interesting discussion at the start of Chapter 5, where Wiener discusses the relative efficiency of coding a number by a single analog quantity and by a large number of scales, each with less precision. Wiener shows by a simple argument that a set of scales dividing their various ranges into two coarse parts gives the most efficient coding. This argument corresponds to describing the analog quantity as a binary number, but it also suggests a simple rationale for the neural network representation technique known as *coarse coding* (Hinton, McClelland, and Rumelhart 1986). Coarse coding is a distributed representation, where the pattern of activation of many units, each responding to a wide range of values, represents a quantity, as opposed to a single active unit representing a small range of values. For representing a single value, distributed codings are much more compact.

Wiener is surprisingly terse discussing the biological mechanisms of memory and devotes more space to discussing mechanical ways of storing information in computers — magnetically, in the Williams CRT tubes used in very early computers, or photographically — than to biological memory. But he does suggest two ways of storing biological memory. First, and the way he seems to like best, memory can be stored in the short term in reverberant loops of self-sustaining neural activity. This model suggests to him a mechanism for psychopathology: He conjectures that the longest loops are the most complex and cognitively significant ones. Because they are long, they are liable to disruption. Humans, as the most intelligent and complex animals, have the greatest number of long loops and are more prone to mental illness and malfunction than are lower animals. Examples of loop malfunctions that he gives are obsessive worry (high gain, persistent loops) and stuttering (malfunctioning loops through the brainstem). Second, he suggests a biological mechanism for permanent storage: change in the thresholds of neurons. He goes on to make an uncharacteristic misstatement, when he says that changes in the threshold lead to "changes in the permeability of each synapse to messages." He then goes on to comment, correctly, that storage could take place by "the opening of new paths or the closure of old ones." Dealing with neurobiology at the level of the neuron seems to have caused him a degree of discomfort.

In 1947 Walter Pitts and Warren McCulloch (paper 3 in *Neurocomputing: Foundations of Research*) suggested a means for computing the *invariances* of perception. A version of this idea reappears in the chapter entitled "Gestalt and Universals" in *Cybernetics*. The problem is that every time we see an object, it is likely to be different. In vision, even if the orientation of the object is the same, the retinal image may be larger or smaller, depending on distance from the observer. Yet, within wide limits, the object is recognized. Something about it must be invariant. One way to recognize a transformed object is to memorize lots of different transformed versions of it. Although this strategy is used to some extent in perception, there are too many possible transformations to learn them all. However, for a small number of particularly important transformations, it is easy to propose neural hardware to do it. The particular problem Wiener uses to suggest this mechanism involves a device to turn printed characters into sound. Because type comes in different sizes, Wiener wants to make a system that gives the same sound pattern for different sizes of type. He assumes several layers of computing units driven by photoreceptors. Different layers respond to different sizes; because of the simple arithmetic of magnification, the anatomical connections to accomplish it are straightforward. It was the figure showing the layers and connections (figure 8, ch. 6) that provoked a cortical neuroanatomist to comment that it looked just like layer IV of visual cortex. (Others have found this resemblance much less striking.) This incident must have had a powerful impact on the MIT group, because both McCulloch and Wiener mention it on several occasions. The technical problem is that, if all the layers are going at once, the output will be confused. So Wiener suggests the layers are sequentially scanned. If a character is present, the output it gives will be the same, even though one layer or another might be doing the match, depending on character size. This model requires the presence of an oscillator to do the scanning, and Wiener was fascinated by the oscillations of the EEG (electroencephalograph), sometimes quite narrow band, and which seemed to be a likely candidate for a scanning mechanism. Unfortunately the EEG did not seem to have such a simple interpretation, and, though it is of medical importance, even now its neurological function and its genesis are unclear. (See paper 21 by Skarda and Freeman for a more modern look at the

EEG.) Wiener's fascination with oscillations grows naturally out of his earlier work on Fourier analysis and control theory.

Throughout *Cybernetics* Wiener takes an approach that is somewhat at variance with that common in most of the other papers in this collection. Although Wiener was aware of the importance of single units and their individuality, he usually approaches brain function from the direction of the continuous mathematics of control. In 1947 Wiener used mathematics to find solutions to problems and to develop intuitions about complex systems. Often nowadays, especially in fields such as neural networks that could not exist without computer simulations, one finds mathematics used to justify computer algorithms and not used so much to analyze the behavior of the resulting system. The solutions found by the algorithms, when used, are sometimes mysterious and not what the developers of the algorithm expected.

Neural networks in general show simplicity at high levels combined with bewildering detail at lower levels. Of course the brain shows this as well. (And the bewildering detail at the lower level can be generated from very simple learning rules.) An important theoretical problem is reconciling the immense number of degrees of freedom at low levels with the much smaller number of degrees of freedom that the system may show in operation. Simple techniques of feedback, for example, can control extremely complex systems, even in the absence of detailed information about the inner workings of the controlled system. Wiener's comments in *Cybernetics* remind us of this.

Reference

G.E. Hinton, J.L. McClelland, and D.E. Rumelhart (1986), Distributed representations. In D.E. Rumelhart and J.L. McClelland (Eds.), *Parallel Distributed Processing, Volume I* . Cambridge, MA: MIT Press.

(1948, 1961)
Norbert Wiener

Cybernetics, (Second Edition), Cambridge, MA: MIT Press.
Introduction to the First Edition, pp. 1–29;
Chapter V, "Computing machines and the nervous system," pp. 116–132;
Chapter VI, "Gestalt and Universals," pp. 133–143;
and Chapter VII, "Cybernetics and psychopathology," pp. 144–154

Introduction

This book represents the outcome, after more than a decade, of a program of work undertaken jointly with Dr. Arturo Rosenblueth, then of the Harvard Medical School and now of the Instituto Nacional de Cardiología of Mexico. In those days, Dr. Rosenblueth, who was the colleague and collaborator of the late Dr. Walter B. Cannon, conducted a monthly series of discussion meetings on scientific method. The participants were mostly young scieintists at the Harvard Medical School, and we would gather for dinner about a round table in Vanderbilt Hall. The conversation was lively and unrestrained. It was not a place where it was either encouraged or made possible for anyone to stand on his dignity. After the meal, somebody—either one of our group or an invited guest—would read a paper on some scientific topic, generally one in which questions of methodology were the first consideration, or at least a leading consideration. The speaker had to run the gauntlet of an acute criticism, good-natured but unsparing. It was a perfect catharsis for half-baked ideas, insufficient self-criticism, exaggerated self-confidence, and pomposity. Those who could not stand the gaff did not return, but among the former habitués of these meetings there is more than one of us who feels that they were an important and permanent contribution to our scientific unfolding.

Not all the participants were physicians or medical scientists. One of us, a very steady member, and a great help to our discussions, was Dr. Manuel Sandoval Vallarta, a Mexican like Dr. Rosenblueth and a Professor of Physics at the Massachusetts Institute of Technology, who had been among my very first students when I came to the Institute after World War I. Dr. Vallarta used to bring some of his M.I.T. colleagues along to these discussion meetings, and it was at one of these that I first met Dr. Rosenblueth. I had been interested in the scientific method for a long time and had, in fact, been a participant in Josiah Royce's Harvard seminar on the subject in 1911–1913. Moreover, it was felt that it was essential to have someone present who could examine mathematical questions critically. I thus became an active member of the group until Dr. Rosenblueth's call to Mexico in 1944 and the general confusion of the war ended the series of meetings.

For many years Dr. Rosenblueth and I had shared the conviction that the most fruitful areas for the growth of the sciences were those which had been neglected as a no-man's land between the various established fields. Since Leibniz there has perhaps been no man who has had a full command of all the intellectual activity of his day. Since that time, science has been increasingly the task of specialists, in fields which show a tendency to grow progressively narrower. A century ago there may have been no Leibniz, but there was a Gauss, a Faraday, and a Darwin. Today there are few scholars who can call themselves mathematicians or physicists or biologists without restriction. A man may be a topologist or an acoustician or a coleopterist. He will be filled with the jargon of his field, and will know all its literature and all its ramifications, but, more frequently than not, he will regard the next subject as something belonging to his colleague three doors down the corridor, and will consider any interest in it on his own part as an unwarrantable breach of privacy.

These specialized fields are continually growing and invading new territory. The result is like what occurred when the Oregon country was being invaded simultaneously by the United States settlers, the British, the Mexicans, and the Russians—an inextricable tangle of exploration, nomenclature, and laws. There are fields of scientific work, as we shall see in the body of this book, which have been explored from the different sides of pure mathematics, statistics, electrical engineering, and neurophysiology; in which every single notion receives a separate name from each group, and in which important work has been triplicated or quadruplicated, while still other important work is delayed by the unavailability in one field of results that may have already become classical in the next field.

It is these boundary regions of science which offer the richest opportunities to the qualified investigator. They are at the same time the most refractory to the accepted techniques of mass attack and the division of labor. If the difficulty of a physiological problem is mathematical in essence, ten physiologists ignorant of mathematics will get precisely as far as one physiologist ignorant of mathematics, and no further. If a physiologist who knows no mathematics works together with a mathematician who knows no physiology, the one will be unable to state his problem in terms that the other can manipulate, and the second will be unable to put the answers in any form that the first can understand. Dr. Rosenblueth has always insisted that a proper exploration of these blank spaces on the map of science could only be made by a team of scientists, each a specialist in his own field but each possessing a thoroughly sound and trained acquaintance with the fields of his neighbors; all in the habit of working together, of knowing one another's intellectual customs, and of recognizing the significance of a colleague's new suggestion before it has taken on a full formal expression. The mathematician need not have the skill to conduct a physiological experiment, but he must have the skill to understand one, to criticize one, and to suggest one. The physiologist need not be able to prove a certain mathematical theorem, but he must be able to grasp its physiological significance and to tell the mathematician for what he should look. We had dreamed for years of an institution of independent scientists, working together in one of these backwoods of science, not as subordinates of some great executive officer, but joined by the desire, indeed by the spiritual necessity, to understand the region as a whole, and to lend one another the strength of that understanding.

We had agreed on these matters long before we had chosen the field of our joint investigations and our respective parts in them. The deciding factor in this new step was the war. I had known for a considerable time that if a national emergency should come, my function in it would be determined largely by two things: my close contact with the program of computing machines developed by Dr. Vannevar Bush, and my own joint work with Dr. Yuk Wing Lee on the design of electric networks. In fact, both proved important. In the summer of 1940, I turned a large part of my attention to the development of computing machines for the solution of partial differential equations. I had long been interested in these and had convinced myself that their chief problem, as contrasted with the ordinary differential equations so well treated by Dr. Bush on his differential analyzer, was that of the representation of functions of more than one variable. I had also become convinced that the process of scanning, as employed in television, gave the answer to that question and, in fact, that television was destined to be more useful to engineering by the introduction of such new techniques than as an independent industry.

It was clear that any scanning process must vastly increase the number of data dealt with as compared with the number of data in a problem of ordinary differential equations. To accomplish reasonable results in a reasonable time, it thus became necessary to push the speed of the elementary processes to the maximum, and to avoid interrupting the stream of these processes by steps of an essentially slower nature. It also became necessary to perform the individual processes with so high a degree of accuracy that the enormous repetition of the elementary processes should not bring about a cumulative error so great as to swamp all accuracy. Thus the following requirements were suggested:

1. That the central adding and multiplying apparatus of the computing machine should be numerical, as in an ordinary adding machine, rather than on a basis of measurement, as in the Bush differential analyzer.

2. That these mechanisms, which are essentially switching devices, should depend on electronic tubes rather than on gears or mechanical relays, in order to secure quicker action.

3. That, in accordance with the policy adopted in some existing apparatus of the Bell Telephone Laboratories, it would probably be more economical in apparatus to adopt the scale of two for addition and multiplication, rather than the scale of ten.

4. That the entire sequence of operations be laid out on the machine itself so that there should be no human intervention from the time the data were entered until the final results should be taken off, and that all logical decisions necessary for this should be built into the machine itself.

5. That the machine contain an apparatus for the storage of data which should record them quickly, hold them firmly until erasure, read them quickly, erase them quickly, and then be immediately available for the storage of new material.

These recommendations, together with tentative suggestions for the means of realizing them, were sent in to Dr. Vannevar Bush for their possible use in a war. At that stage of the preparations for war, they did not seem to have sufficiently high priority to make immediate work on them worth while. Nevertheless, they all represent ideas which have been incorporated into the modern ultra-rapid computing machine. These notions were all very much in the spirit of the thought of the time, and I do not for a moment wish to claim anything like the sole responsibility for their introduction. Nevertheless, they have proved useful, and it is my hope that my memorandum had some effect in popularizing them among engineers. At any rate, as we shall see in the body of the book, they are all ideas which are of interest in connection with the study of the nervous system.

This work was thus laid on the table, and, although it has not proved to be fruitless, it led to no immediate project by Dr. Rosenblueth and myself. Our actual collaboration resulted from another project, which was likewise undertaken for the purposes of the last war. At the beginning of the war, the Germam prestige in aviation and the defensive position of England turned the attention of many scientists to the improvement of anti-aircraft artillery. Even before the war, it had become clear that the speed of the airplane had rendered obsolete all classical methods of the direction of fire, and that it was necessary to build into the control apparatus all the computations necessary. These were rendered much more difficult by the fact that, unlike all previously encountered targets, an airplane has a velocity which is a very appreciable part of the velocity of the missile used to bring it down. Accordingly, it is exceedingly important to shoot the missile, not at the target, but in such a way that missile and target may come together in space at some time in the future. We must hence find some method of predicting the future position of the plane.

The simplest method is to extrapolate the present course of the plane along a straight line. This has much to recommend it. The more a plane doubles and curves in flight, the less is its effective velocity, the less time it has to accomplish a mission, and the longer it remains in a dangerous region. Other things being equal, a plane will fly as straight a course as possible. However, by the time the first shell has burst, other things are *not* equal, and the pilot will probably zigzag, stunt, or in some other way take evasive action.

If this action were completely at the disposal of the pilot, and the pilot were to make the sort of intelligent use of his chances that we anticipate in a good poker player, for example, he has so much opportunity to modify his expected position before the arrival of a shell that we should not reckon the chances of hitting him to be very good, except perhaps in the case of a very wasteful barrage fire. On the other hand, the pilot does *not* have a completely free chance to maneuver at his will. For one thing, he is in a plane going at an exceedingly high speed, and any too sudden deviation from his course will produce an acceleration that will render him unconscious and may disintegrate the plane. Then too, he can control the plane only by moving his control surfaces, and the new regimen of flow that is established takes some small time to develop. Even when it is fully developed, it merely changes the acceleration of the plane, and this change of acceleration must be converted, first into change of velocity and then into change of position, before it is finally effective. Moreover, an aviator under the strain of combat conditions is scarcely in a mood to engage in any very complicated and untrammeled voluntary behavior, and is quite likely to follow out the pattern of activity in which he has been trained.

All this made an investigation of the problem of the curvilinear prediction of flight worth while, whether the results should prove favorable or unfavorable for the actual use of a control apparatus involving such curvilinear prediction. To predict the future of a curve is to carry out a certain operation on its past. The true prediction operator cannot be realized by any constructible apparatus; but there are certain operators which bear it a certain resemblance and are, in fact, realizable by apparatus which we can build. I suggested to Professor Samuel Caldwell of the Massachusetts Institute of Technology that these operators seemed worth trying, and he immediately suggested that we try them out on Dr. Bush's differential analyzer, using this as a ready-made model of the desired fire-control apparatus. We did so, with results which will be discussed in the body of this book. At any rate, I found myself engaged in a war project, in which Mr. Julian H. Bigelow and now myself were partners in the investigation of the theory of prediction and of the construction of apparatus to embody these theories.

It will be seen that for the second time I had become engaged in the study of a mechanico-electrical system which was designed to usurp a specifically human function—in the first case, the execution of a complicated pattern of computation, and in the second, the forecasting of the future. In this second case, we should not avoid the discussion of the performance of certain human functions. In some fire-control apparatus, it is true, the original impulse to point comes in directly by radar, but in the more usual case, there is a human gun-pointer or a gun-trainer or both coupled into the fire-control system, and acting as an essential part of it. It is essential to know their characteristics, in order to incorporate them mathematically into the machines they control. Moreover, their target, the plane, is also humanly controlled, and it is desirable to know its performance characteristics.

Mr. Bigelow and I came to the conclusion that an extremely important factor in voluntary activity is what the control engineers term *feedback*. I shall discuss this in considerable detail in the appropriate chapters. It is enough to say here that when we desire a motion to follow a given pattern the difference between this pattern and the actually performed motion is used as a new input to cause the part regulated to move in such a way as to bring its motion closer to that given by the pattern. For example, one form of steering engine of a ship carries the reading of the wheel to an offset from the tiller, which so regulates the valves of the steering engine as to move the tiller in such a way as to turn these valves off. Thus the tiller turns so as to bring the other end of the valve-regulating offset amidships, and in that way registers the angular position of the wheel as the angular position of the tiller. Clearly, any friction or other delaying force which hampers the motion of the tiller will increase the admission of steam to the valves on one side and will decrease it on the other, in such a way as to increase the torque tending to bring the tiller to the desired position.

Thus the feedback system tends to make the performance of the steering engine relatively independent of the load.

On the other hand, under certain conditions of delay, etc., a feedback that is too brusque will make the rudder overshoot, and will be followed by a feedback in the other direction, which makes the rudder overshoot still more, until the steering mechanism goes into a wild oscillation or *hunting,* and breaks down completely. In a book such as that by MacColl,[1] we find a very precise discussion of feedback, the conditions under which it is advantageous, and the conditions under which it breaks down. It is a phenomenon which we understand very thoroughly from a quantitative point of view.

Now, suppose that I pick up a lead pencil. To do this, I have to move certain muscles. However, for all of us but a few expert anatomists, we do not know what these muscles are; and even among the anatomists, there are few, if any, who can perform the act by a conscious willing in succession of the contraction of each muscle concerned. On the contrary, what we will is *to pick the pencil up.* Once we have determined on this, our motion proceeds in such a way that we may say roughly that the amount by which the pencil is not yet picked up is decreased at each stage. This part of the action is not in full consciousness.

To perform an action in such a manner, there must be a report to the nervous system, conscious or unconscious, of the amount by which we have failed to pick up the pencil at each instant. If we have our eye on the pencil, this report may be visual, at least in part, but it is more generally kinesthetic, or, to use a term now in vogue, proprioceptive. If the proprioceptive sensations are wanting and we do not replace them by a visual or other substitute, we are unable to perform the act of picking up the pencil, and find ourselves in a state of what is known as *ataxia.* An ataxia of this type is familiar in the form of syphilis of the central nervous system known as *tabes dorsalis,* where the kinesthetic sense conveyed by the spinal nerves is more or less destroyed.

However, an excessive feedback is likely to be as serious a handicap to organized activity as a defective feedback. In view of this possibility, Mr. Bigelow and myself approached Dr. Rosenblueth with a very specific question. Is there any pathological condition in which the patient, in trying to perform some voluntary act like picking up a pencil, overshoots the mark, and goes into an uncontrollable oscillation? Dr. Rosenblueth immediately answered us that there is such a well-known condition, that it is called purpose tremor, and that it is often associated with injury to the cerebellum.

We thus found a most significant confirmation of our hypothesis concerning the nature of at least some voluntary activity. It will be noted that our point of view considerably transcended that current among neurophysiologists. The central nervous system no longer appears as a self-contained organ, receiving inputs from the senses and discharging into the muscles. On the contrary, some of its most characteristic activities are explicable only as circular processes, emerging from the nervous system into the muscles, and re-entering the nervous system through the sense organs, whether they be proprioceptors or organs of the special senses. This seemed to us to mark a new step in the study of that part of neurophysiology which concerns not solely the elementary processes of nerves and synapses but the performance of the nervous system as an integrated whole.

The three of us felt that this new point of view merited a paper, which we wrote up and published.[2] Dr. Rosenblueth and I foresaw that this paper could be only a statement of program for a large body of experimental work, and we decided that if we could ever bring our plan for an interscientific institute to fruition, this topic would furnish an almost ideal center for our activity.

On the communication engineering plane, it had already become clear to Mr. Bigelow and myself that the problems of control engineering and of communication engineering were inseparable, and that they centered not around the technique of electrical engineering but around the much more fundamental notion of the message, whether this should be transmitted by electrical, mechanical, or nervous means. The message is a discrete or continuous sequence of measurable events distributed in time—precisely what is called a time series by the statisticians. The prediction of the future of a message is done by some sort of operator on its past, whether this operator is realized by a scheme of mathematical computation, or by a mechanical or electrical apparatus. In this connection, we found that the ideal prediction mechanisms which we had at first contemplated were beset by two types of error, of a roughly antagonistic nature. While the prediction apparatus which we at first designed could be made to anticipate an extremely smooth curve to any desired degree of approximation, this refinement of behavior was always attained at the cost of an increasing sensitivity. The better the apparatus was for smooth waves, the more it would be set into oscillation by small departures from smoothness, and the longer it would be before such oscillations would die out. Thus the good prediction of a smooth wave seemed to require a more delicate and sensitive apparatus than the best possible pre-

[1]MacColl, L. A., *Fundamental Theory of Servomechanisms,* Van Nostrand, New York, 1946.

[2]Rosenblueth, A, N Wiener, and J. Bigelow. "Behavior, Purpose, and Teleology," *Philosophy of Science,* **10,** 18–24 (1943).

diction of a rough curve, and the choice of the particular apparatus to be used in a specific case was dependent on the statistical nature of the phenomenon to be predicted. This interacting pair of types of error seemed to have something in common with the contrasting problems of the measure of position and of momentum to be found in the Heisenberg quantum mechanics, as described according to his Principle of Uncertainty.

Once we had clearly grasped that the solution of the problem of optimum prediction was only to be obtained by an appeal to the statistics of the time series to be predicted, it was not difficult to make what had originally seemed to be a difficulty in the theory of prediction into what was actually an efficient tool for solving the problem of prediction. Assuming the statistics of a time series, it became possible to derive an explicit expression for the mean square error of prediction by a given technique and for a given lead. Once we had this, we could translate the problem of optimum prediction to the determination of a specific operator which should reduce to a minimum a specific positive quantity dependent on this operator. Minimization problems of this type belong to a recognized branch of mathematics, the calculus of variations, and this branch has a recognized technique. With the aid of this technique, we were able to obtain an explicit best solution of the problem of predicting the future of a time series, given its statistical nature, and even further, to achieve a physical realization of this solution by a constructible apparatus.

Once we had done this, at least one problem of engineering design took on a completely new aspect. In general, engineering design has been held to be an art rather than a science. By reducing a problem of this sort to a minimization principle, we had established the subject on a far more scientific basis. It occurred to us that this was not an isolated case, but that there was a whole region of engineering work in which similar design problems could be solved by the methods of the calculus of variations.

We attacked and solved other similar problems by the same methods. Among these was the problem of the design of wave filters. We often find a message contaminated by extraneous disturbances which we call *background noise*. We then face the problem of restoring the original message, or the message under a given lead, or the message modified by a given lag, by an operator applied to the corrupted message. The optimum design of this operator and of the apparatus by which it is realized depends on the statistical nature of the message and the noise, singly and jointly. We thus have replaced in the design of wave filters processes which were formerly of an empirical and rather haphazard nature by processes with a thorough scientific justification.

In doing this, we have made of communication engineering design a statistical science, a branch of statistical me-

chanics. The notion of statistical mechanics has indeed been encroaching on every branch of science for more than a century. We shall see that this dominance of statistical mechanics in modern physics has a very vital significance for the interpretation of the nature of time. In the case of communication engineering, however, the significance of the statistical element is immediately apparent. The transmission of information is impossible save as a transmission of alternatives. If only one contingency is to be transmitted, then it may be sent most efficiently and with the least trouble by sending no message at all. The telegraph and the telephone can perform their function only if the messages they transmit are continually varied in a manner not completely determined by their past, and can be designed effectively only if the variation of these messages conforms to some sort of statistical regularity.

To cover this aspect of communication engineering, we had to develop a statistical theory of the *amount of information,* in which the unit amount of information was that transmitted as a single decision between equally probable alternatives. This idea occurred at about the same time to several writers, among them the statistican R. A. Fisher, Dr. Shannon of the Bell Telephone Laboratories, and the author. Fisher's motive in studying this subject is to be found in classical statistical theory; that of Shannon in the problem of coding information; and that of the author in the problem of noise and message in electrical filters. Let it be remarked parenthetically that some of my speculations in this direction attach themselves to the earlier work of Kolmogoroff[1] in Russia, although a considerable part of my work was done before my attention was called to the work of the Russian school.

The notion of the amount of information attaches itself very naturally to a classical notion in statistical mechanics: that of *entropy.* Just as the amount of information in a system is a measure of its degree of organization, so the entropy of a system is a measure of its degree of disorganization; and the one is simply the negative of the other. This point of view leads us to a number of considerations concerning the second law of thermodynamics, and to a study of the possibility of the so-called Maxwell demons. Such questions arise independently in the study of enzymes and other catalysts, and their study is essential for the proper understanding of such fundamental phenomena of living matter as metabolism and reproduction. The third fundamental phenomenon of life, that of irritability, belongs to the domain of communication theory and falls under the group of ideas we have just been discussing.[2]

[1]Kolmogoroff, A. N., "Interpolation und Extrapolation von stationären Zufälligen Folgen," *Bull. Acad. Sci. U.S.S.R.,* Ser. Math. **5,** 3–14 (1941).
[2]Schrödinger, Erwin, *What is Life?,* Cambridge University Press, Cambridge, England, 1945.

Thus, as far back as four years ago, the group of scientists about Dr. Rosenblueth and myself had already become aware of the essential unity of the set of problems centering about communication, control, and statistical mechanics, whether in the machine or in living tissue. On the other hand, we were seriously hampered by the lack of unity of the literature concerning these problems, and by the absence of any common terminology, or even of a single name for the field. After much consideration, we have come to the conclusion that all the existing terminology has too heavy a bias to one side or another to serve the future development of the field as well as it should; and as happens so often to scientists, we have been forced to coin at least one artificial neo-Greek expression to fill the gap. We have decided to call the entire field of control and communication theory, whether in the machine or in the animal, by the name *Cybernetics,* which we form from the Greek χυβερνήτηζ or *steersman.* In choosing this term, we wish to recognize that the first significant paper on feedback mechanisms is an article on governors, which was published by Clerk Maxwell in 1868,[1] and that *governor* is derived from a Latin corruption of χυβερνήτηζ. We also wish to refer to the fact that the steering engines of a ship are indeed one of the earliest and best-developed forms of feedback mechanisms.

Although the term *cybernetics* does not date further back than the summer of 1947, we shall find it convenient to use in referring to earlier epochs of the development of the field. From 1942 or thereabouts, the development of the subject went ahead on several fronts. First, the ideas of the joint paper by Bigelow, Rosenblueth, and Wiener were disseminated by Dr. Rosenblueth at a meeting held in New York in 1942, under the auspices of the Josiah Macy Foundation, and devoted to problems of central inhibition in the nervous system. Among those present at that meeting was Dr. Warren McCulloch, of the Medical School of the University of Illinois, who had already been in touch with Dr. Rosenblueth and myself, and who was interested in the study of the organization of the cortex of the brain.

At this point there enters an element which occurs repeatedly in the history of cybernetics—the influence of mathematical logic. If I were to choose a patron saint for cybernetics out of the history of science, I should have to choose Leibniz. The philosophy of Leibniz centers about two closely related concepts—that of a universal symbolism and that of a calculus of reasoning. From these are descended the mathematical notation and the symbolic logic of the present day. Now, just as the calculus of arith-

metic lends itself to a mechanization progressing through the abacus and the desk computing machine to the ultra-rapid computing machines of the present day, so the *calculus ratiocinator* of Leibniz contains the germs of the *machina ratiocinatrix,* the reasoning machine. Indeed, Leibniz himself, like his predecessor Pascal, was interested in the construction of computing machines in the metal. It is therefore not in the least surprising that the same intellectual impulse which has led to the development of mathematical logic has at the same time led to the ideal or actual mechanization of processes of thought.

A mathematical proof which we can follow is one which can be written in a finite number of symbols. These symbols, in fact, may make an appeal to the notion of infinity, but this appeal is one which we can sum up in a finite number of stages, as in the case of mathematical induction, where we prove a theorem depending on a parameter n for $n = 0$, and also prove that the case $n + 1$ follows from the case n, thus establishing the theorem for all positive values of n. Moreover, the rules of operation of our deductive mechanism must be finite in number, even though they may appear to be otherwise, through a reference to the concept of infinity, which can itself be stated in finite terms. In short, it has become quite evident, both to the nominalists like Hilbert and to the intuitionists like Weyl, that the development of a mathematico-logical theory is subject to the same sort of restrictions as those that limit the performance of a computing machine. As we shall see later, it is even possible to interpret in this way the paradoxes of Cantor and of Russell.

I am myself a former student of Russell and owe much to his influence. Dr. Shannon took for his doctor's thesis at the Massachusetts Institute of Technology the application of the techniques of the classical Boolean algebra of classes to the study of switching systems in electrical engineering. Turing, who is perhaps first among those who have studied the logical possibilities of the machine as an intellectual experiment, served the British government during the war as a worker in electronics, and is now in charge of the program which the National Physical Laboratory at Teddington has undertaken for the development of computing machines of the modern type.

Another young migrant from the field of mathematical logic to cybernetics is Walter Pitts. He had been a student of Carnap at Chicago and had also been in contact with Professor Rashevsky and his school of biophysicists. Let it be remarked in passing that this group has contributed much to directing the attention of the mathematically minded to the possibilities of the biological sciences, although it may seem to some of us that they are too dominated by problems of energy and potential and the methods of classical physics to do the best possible work in the study

[1]Maxwell, J. C., *Proc. Roy. Soc. (London),* **16,** 270–283, (1868).

of systems like the nervous system, which are very far from being closed energetically.

Mr. Pitts had the good fortune to fall under McCulloch's influence, and the two began to work quite early on problems concerning the union of nerve fibers by synapses into systems with given over-all properties. Independently of Shannon, they had used the technique of mathematical logic for the discussion of what were after all switching problems. They added elements which were not prominent in Shannon's earlier work, although they are certainly suggested by the ideas of Turing: the use of the time as a parameter, the consideration of nets containing cycles, and of synaptic and other delays.[1]

In the summer of 1943, I met Dr. J. Lettvin of the Boston City Hospital, who was very much interested in matters concerning nervous mechanisms. He was a close friend of Mr. Pitts, and made me acquainted with his work.[2] He induced Mr. Pitts to come out to Boston, and to make the acquaintance of Dr. Rosenblueth and myself. We welcomed him into our group. Mr. Pitts came to the Massachusetts Institute of Technology in the autumn of 1943, in order to work with me and to strengthen his mathematical background for the study of the new science of cybernetics, which had by that time been fairly born but not yet christened.

At that time Mr. Pitts was already thoroughly acquainted with mathematical logic and neurophysiology, but had not had the chance to make very many engineering contacts. In particular, he was not acquainted with Dr. Shannon's work, and he had not had much experience of the possibilities of electronics. He was very much interested when I showed him examples of modern vacuum tubes and explained to him that these were ideal means for realizing in the metal the equivalents of his neuronic circuits and systems. From that time, it became clear to us that the ultra-rapid computing machine, depending as it does on consecutive switching devices, must represent almost an ideal model of the problems arising in the nervous system. The all-or-none character of the discharge of the neurons is precisely analogous to the single choice made in determining a digit on the binary scale, which more than one of us had already contemplated as the most satisfactory basis of computing-machine design. The synapse is nothing but a mechanism for determining whether a certain combination of outputs from other selected elements will or will not act as an adequate stimulus for the discharge of the next element, and must have its precise analogue in the computing machine. The problem of interpreting the

nature and varieties of memory in the animal has its parallel in the problem of constructing artificial memories for the machine.

At this time, the construction of computing machines had proved to be more essential for the war effort than the first opinion of Dr. Bush might have indicated, and was progressing at several centers along lines not too different from those which my earlier report had indicated. Harvard, Aberdeen Proving Ground, and the University of Pennsylvania were already constructing machines, and the Institute for Advanced Study at Princeton and the Massachusetts Institute of Technology were soon to enter the same field. In this program there was a gradual progress from the mechanical assembly to the electrical assembly, from the scale of ten to the scale of two, from the mechanical relay to the electrical relay, from humanly directed operation to automatically directed operation; and in short, each new machine more than the last was in conformity with the memorandum I had sent Dr. Bush. There was a continual going and coming of those interested in these fields. We had an opportunity to communicate our ideas to our colleagues, in particular to Dr. Aiken of Harvard, Dr. von Neumann of the Institute for Advanced Study, and Dr. Goldstine of the Eniac and Edvac machines at the University of Pennsylvania. Everywhere we met with a sympathetic hearing, and the vocabulary of the engineers soon became contaminated with the terms of the neurophysiologist and the psychologist.

At this stage of the proceedings, Dr. von Neumann and myself felt it desirable to hold a joint meeting of all those interested in what we now call cybernetics, and this meeting took place at Princeton in the late winter of 1943–1944. Engineers, physiologists, and mathematicians were all represented. It was impossible to have Dr. Rosenblueth among us, as he had just accepted an invitation to act as Head of the laboratories of physiology of the Instituto Nacional de Cardiología in Mexico, but Dr. McCulloch and Dr. Lorente de Nó of the Rockefeller Institute represented the physiologists. Dr. Aiken was unable to be present; however, Dr. Goldstine was one of a group of several computing-machine designers who participated in the meeting, while Dr. von Neumann, Mr. Pitts, and myself were the mathematicians. The physiologists gave a joint presentation of cybernetic problems from their point of view; similarly, the computing-machine designers presented their methods and objectives. At the end of the meeting, it had become clear to all that there was a substantial common basis of ideas between the workers in the different fields, that people in each group could already use notions which had been better developed by the others, and that some attempt should be made to achieve a common vocabulary.

[1] Turing, A. M., "On Computable Numbers, with an Application to the Entscheidungsproblem," *Proceedings of the London Mathematical Society*, Ser. 2, **42**, 230–265 (1936).

[2] McCulloch, W. S., and W. Pitts, "A logical calculus of the ideas immanent in nervous activity," *Bull. Math. Biophys*, **5**, 115–133 (1943).

A considerable period before this, the war research group conducted by Dr. Warren Weaver had published a document, first secret and later restricted, covering the work of Mr. Bigelow and myself on predictors and wave filters. It was found that the conditions of anti-aircraft fire did not justify the design of special apparatus for curvilinear prediction, but the principles proved to be sound and practical, and have been used by the government for smoothing purposes, and in several fields of related work. In particular, the type of integral equation to which the calculus of variations problem reduces itself has been shown to emerge in wave-guide problems and in many other problems of an applied mathematical interest. Thus in one way or another, the end of the war saw the ideas of prediction theory and of the statistical approach to communication engineering already familiar to a large part of the statisticians and communication engineers of the United States and Great Britain. It also saw my government document, now out of print, and a considerable number of expository papers by Levinson,[1] Wallman, Daniell, Phillips, and others written to fill the gap. I myself have had a long mathematical expository paper under way for several years to put the work I have done on permanent record, but circumstances not completely under my control have prevented its prompt publication. Finally, after a joint meeting at the American Mathematical Society and the Institute of Mathematical Statistics held in New York in the spring of 1947, and devoted to the study of stochastic processes from a point of view closely allied to cybernetics, I have passed on what I have already written of my manuscript to Professor Doob of the University of Illinois, to be developed in his notation and according to his ideas as a book for the Mathematical Surveys series of the American Mathematical Society. I had already developed part of my work in a course of lectures in the mathematics department of M.I.T. in the summer of 1945. Since then, my old student and collaborator,[2] Dr. Y. W. Lee, has returned from China. He is giving a course on the new methods for the design of wave filters and similar apparatus in the M.I.T. electrical engineering department in the fall of 1947, and has plans to work the material of these lectures up into a book. At the same time, the out-of-print government document is to be reprinted.[3]

As I have said, Dr. Rosenblueth returned to Mexico about the beginning of 1944. In the spring of 1945, I received an invitation from the Mexican Mathematical Society to participate in a meeting to be held in Guadalajara that June. This invitation was reinforced by the Comision

Instigadora y Coordinadora de la Investigación Cientifica, under the leadership of Dr. Manuel Sandoval Vallarta, of whom I have already spoken. Dr. Rosenblueth invited me to share some scientific research with him, and the Instituto Nacional de Cardiología, under its director Dr. Ignacio Chávez, extended me its hospitality.

I stayed some ten weeks in Mexico at that time. Dr. Rosenblueth and I decided to continue a line of work which we had already discussed with Dr. Walter B. Cannon, who was also with Dr. Rosenblueth, on a visit which unfortunately proved to be his last. This work had to do with the relation between, on the one hand, the tonic, clonic, and phasic contractions in epilepsy and, on the other hand, the tonic spasm, beat, and fibrillation of the heart. We felt that heart muscle represented an irritable tissue as useful for the investigation of conduction mechanisms as nerve tissue, and furthermore, that the anastomoses and decussations of the heart-muscle fibers presented us with a simpler phenomenon than the problem of the nervous synapse. We were also deeply grateful to Dr. Chávez for his unquestioning hospitality, and, while it has never been the policy of the Instituto to restrict Dr. Rosenblueth to the investigation of the heart, we were grateful to have an opportunity to contribute to its principal purpose.

Our investigation took two directions: the study of phenomena of conductivity and latency in uniform conducting media of two or more dimensions, and the statistical study of the conducting properties of random nets of conducting fibers. The first led us to the rudiments of a theory of heart flutter, the latter to a certain possible understanding of fibrillation. Both lines of work were developed in a paper,[4] published by us, and, although in both cases our earlier results have shown the need of a considerable amount of revision and of supplementation, the work on flutter is being revised by Mr. Oliver G. Selfridge of the Massachusetts Institute of Technology, while the statistical technique used in the study of heart-muscle nets has been extended to the treatment of neuronal nets by Mr. Walter Pitts, now a Fellow of the John Simon Guggenheim Foundation. The experimental work is being carried on by Dr. Rosenblueth with the aid of Dr. F. García Ramos of the Instituto Nacional de Cardiología and the Mexican Army Medical School.

At the Guadalajara meeting of the Mexican Mathematical Society, Dr. Rosenblueth and I presented some of our results. We had already come to the conclusion that our earlier plans of collaboration had shown themselves to be practicable. We were fortunate enough to have a chance to present our results to a larger audience. In the spring of

[1]Levinson, N., *J. Math. and Physics*, **25**, 261–278; **26**, 110–119 (1947).
[2]Lee, Y. W., *J. Math. and Physics*, **11**, 261–278 (1932).
[3]Wiener, N., *Extrapolation, Interpolation, and Smoothing of Stationary Time Series*, Technology Press and Wiley, New York, 1949.

[4]Wiener, N., and A. Rosenblueth, "The Mathematical Formulation of the Problem of Conduction of Impulses in a Network of Connected Excitable Elements, Specifically in Cardiac Muscle," *Arch. Inst. Cardiol. Méx.*, **16**, 205–265 (1946).

1946, Dr. McCulloch had made arrangements with the Josiah Macy Foundation for the first of a series of meetings to be held in New York and to be devoted to the problems of feedback. These meetings have been conducted in the traditional Macy way, worked out most efficiently by Dr. Frank Fremont-Smith, who organized them on behalf of the Foundation. The idea has been to get together a group of modest size, not exceeding some twenty in number, of workers in various related fields, and to hold them together for two successive days in all-day series of informal papers, discussions, and meals together, until they had had the opportunity to thresh out their differences and to make progress in thinking along the same lines. The nucleus of our meetings has been the group that had assembled in Princeton in 1944, but Drs. McCulloch and Fremont-Smith have rightly seen the psychological and sociological implications of the subject, and have co-opted into the group a number of leading psychologists, sociologists, and anthropologists. The need of including psychologists had indeed been obvious from the beginning. He who studies the nervous system cannot forget the mind, and he who studies the mind cannot forget the nervous system. Much of the psychology of the past has proved to be really nothing more than the physiology of the organs of special sense; and the whole weight of the body of ideas which cybernetics is introducing into psychology concerns the physiology and anatomy of the highly specialized cortical areas connecting with these organs of special sense. From the beginning, we have anticipated that the problem of the perception of *Gestalt,* or of the perceptual formation of universals, would prove to be of this nature. What is the mechanism by which we recognize a square as a square, irrespective of its position, its size, and its orientation? To assist us in such matters and to inform them of whatever use might be made of our concepts for their assistance, we had among us such psychologists as Professor Klüver of the University of Chicago, the late Dr. Kurt Lewin of the Massachusetts Institute of Technology, and Dr. M. Ericsson of New York.

As to sociology and anthropology, it is manifest that the importance of information and communication as mechanisms of organization proceeds beyond the individual into the community. On the one hand, it is completely impossible to understand social communities such as those of ants without a thorough investigation of their means of communication, and we were fortunate enough to have the aid of Dr. Schneirla in this matter. For the similar problems of human organization, we sought help from the anthropologists Drs. Bateson and Margaret Mead; while Dr. Morgenstern of the Institute for Advanced Study was our adviser in the significant field of social organization belonging to economic theory. His very important joint book on games with Dr. von Neumann, by the way, represents a

most interesting study of social organization from the point of view of methods closely related to, although distinct from, the subject matter of cybernetics. Dr. Lewin and others represented the newer work on the theory of opinion sampling and the practice of opinion making, and Dr. F. C. S. Northrup was interested in assaying the philosophical significance of our work.

This does not purport to be a complete list of our group. We also enlarged the group to contain more engineers and mathematicians such as Bigelow and Savage, more neuroanatomists and neurophysiologists such as von Bonin and Lloyd, and so on. Our first meeting, held in the spring of 1946, was largely devoted to didactic papers by those of us who had been present at the Princeton meeting and to a general assessment of the importance of the field by all present. It was the sense of the meeting that the ideas behind cybernetics were sufficiently important and interesting to those present to warrant a continuation of our meetings at intervals of six months; and that before the next full meeting, we should have a small meeting for the benefit of the less mathematically trained to explain to them in as simple language as possible the nature of the mathematical concepts involved.

In the summer of 1946, I returned to Mexico with the support of the Rockefeller Foundation and the hospitality of the Instituto Nacional de Cardiología to continue the collaboration between Dr. Rosenblueth and myself. This time we decided to take a nervous problem directly from the topic of feedback and to see what we could do with it experimentally. We chose the cat as our experimental animal, and the quadriceps extensor femoris as the muscle to study. We cut the attachment of the muscle, fixed it to a lever under known tension, and recorded its contractions isometrically or isotonically. We also used an oscillograph to record the simultaneous electrical changes in the muscle itself. We worked chiefly with cats, first decerebrated under ether anesthesia and later made spinal by a thoracic transection of the cord. In many cases, strychnine was used to increase the reflex responses. The muscle was loaded to the point where a tap would set it into a periodic pattern of contraction, which is called *clonus* in the language of the physiologist. We observed this pattern of contraction, paying attention to the physiological condition of the cat, the load on the muscle, the frequency of oscillation, the base level of the oscillation, and its amplitude. These we tried to analyze as we should analyze a mechanical or electrical system exhibiting the same pattern of hunting. We employed, for example, the methods of MacColl's book on servomechanisms. This is not the place to discuss the full significance of our results, which we are now repeating and preparing to write up for publication. However, the following statements are either established or very probable: that the frequency of clonic oscillation is much less sensitive to changes of the loading conditions than we had expected, and that it is much more nearly determined by the constants of the closed arc (efferent-nerve)-muscle-(kinesthetic-end-body)-(afferent-nerve)-(central-synapse)-(efferent-nerve) than by anything else. This circuit is not even approximately a circuit of linear operators if we take as our base of linearity the number of impulses transmitted by the efferent nerve per second, but seems to become much more nearly so if we replace the number of impulses by its logarithm. This corresponds to the fact that the form of the envelope of stimulation of the efferent nerve is not nearly sinusoidal, but that the logarithm of this curve is much more nearly sinusoidal; while in a linear oscillating system with constant energy level, the form of the curve of stimulation must be sinusoidal in all except a set of cases of zero probability. Again, the notions of facilitation and inhibition are much more nearly multiplicative than additive in nature. For example, a complete inhibition means a multiplication by zero, and a partial inhibition means a multiplication by a small quantity. It is these notions of inhibition and facilitation which have been used[1] in the discussion of the reflex arc. Furthermore, the synapse is a coincidence-recorder, and the outgoing fiber is stimulated only if the number of incoming impulses in a small summation time exceeds a certain threshold. If this threshold is low enough in comparison with the full number of incoming synapses, the synaptic mechanism serves to multiply probabilities, and that it can be even an approximately linear link is possible only in a logarithmic system. This approximate logarithmicity of the synapse mechanism is certainly allied to the approximate logarithmicity of the Weber-Fechner law of sensation intensity, even though this law is only a first approximation.

The most striking point is that on this logarithmic basis, and with data obtained from the conduction of single pulses through the various elements of the neuromuscular arc, we were able to obtain very fair approximations to the actual periods of clonic vibration, using the technique already developed by the servo engineers for the determination of the frequencies of hunting oscillations in feedback systems which have broken down. We obtained theoretical oscillations of about 13.9 per second, in cases where the observed oscillations varied between frequencies of 7 and 30, but generally remained within a range varying somewhere between 12 and 17. Under the circumstances, this agreement is excellent.

[1]Unpublished articles on clonus from the Instituto Nacional de Cardiología, Mexico.

The frequency of clonus is not the only important phenomenon which we may observe: there is also a relatively slow change in basal tension, and an even slower change in amplitude. These phenomena are certainly by no means linear. However, sufficiently slow changes in the constants of a linear oscillating system may be treated to a first approximation as though they were infinitely slow, and as though over each part of the oscillation the system behaved as it would if its parameters were those belonging to it at the time. This is the method known in other branches of physics as that of secular perturbations. It may be used to study the problems of base level and amplitude of clonus. While this work has not yet been completed, it is clear that it is both possible and promising. There is a strong suggestion that though the timing of the main arc in clonus proves it to be a two-neuron arc, the amplification of impulses in this arc is variable in one and perhaps in more points, and that some part of this amplification may be affected by slow, multineuron processes which run much higher in the central nervous system than the spinal chain primarily responsible for the timing of clonus. This variable amplification may be affected by the general level of central activity, by the use of strychnine or of anesthetics, by decerebration, and by many other causes.

These were the main results presented by Dr. Rosenblueth and myself at the Macy meeting held in the autumn of 1946, and in a meeting of the New York Academy of Sciences held at the same time for the purpose of diffusing the notions of cybernetics over a larger public. While we were pleased with our results, and fully convinced of the general practicability of work in this direction, we felt nevertheless that the time of our collaboration had been too brief, and that our work had been done under too much pressure to make it desirable to publish without further experimental confirmation. This confirmation—which naturally might amount to a refutation—we are now seeking in the summer and autumn of 1947.

The Rockefeller Foundation had already given Dr. Rosenblueth a grant for the equipment of a new laboratory building at the Instituto Nacional de Cardiología. We felt that the time was now ripe for us to go jointly to them—that is, to Dr. Warren Weaver, in charge of the department of physical sciences, and to Dr. Robert Morison, in charge of the department of medical sciences—to establish the basis of a long-time scientific collaboration, in order to carry on our program at a more leisurely and healthy pace. In this we were enthusiastically backed by our respective institutions. Dr. George Harrison, Dean of Science, was the chief representative of the Massachusetts Institute of Technology during these negotiations, while Dr. Ignacio Chávez spoke for his institution, the Instituto Nacional de Cardiología. During the negotiations, it became clear that the laboratory center of the joint activity should be at the Instituto, both in order to avoid the duplication of laboratory equipment and to further the very real interest the Rockefeller Foundation has shown in the establishment of scientific centers in Latin America. The plan finally adopted was for five years, during which I should spend six months of every other year at the Instituto, while Dr. Rosenblueth would spend six months of the intervening years at the Institute. The time at the Instituto is to be devoted to the obtaining and elucidation of experimental data pertaining to cybernetics, while the intermediate years are to be devoted to more theoretical research and, above all, to the very difficult problem of devising, for people wishing to go into this new field, a scheme of training which will secure for them both the necessary mathematical, physical, and engineering background and the proper acquaintance with biological, psychological, and medical techniques.

In the spring of 1947, Dr. McCulloch and Mr. Pitts did a piece of work of considerable cybernetic importance. Dr. McCulloch had been given the problem of designing an apparatus to enable the blind to read the printed page by ear. The production of variable tones by type through the agency of a photocell is an old story, and can be effected by any number of methods; the difficult point is to make the pattern of the sound substantially the same when the pattern of the letters is given, whatever the size. This is a definite analogue of the problem of the perception of form, of *Gestalt,* which allows us to recognize a square as a square through a large number of changes of size and of orientation. Dr. McCulloch's device involved a selective reading of the type imprint for a set of different magnifications. Such a selective reading can be performed automatically as a scanning process. This scanning, to allow a comparison between a figure and a given standard figure of fixed but different size, was a device which I had already suggested at one of the Macy meetings. A diagram of the apparatus by which the selective reading was done came to the attention of Dr. von Bonin, who immediately asked, "Is this a diagram of the fourth layer of the visual cortex of the brain?" Acting on this suggestion, Dr. McCulloch, with the assistance of Mr. Pitts, produced a theory tying up the anatomy and the physiology of the visual cortex, and in this theory the operation of scanning over a set of transformations plays an important part. This was presented in the spring of 1947, both at the Macy meeting and at a meeting of the New York Academy of Sciences. Finally, this scanning process involves a certain periodic time, which corresponds to what we call the "time of sweep" in ordinary television. There are various anatomic clues to this time in the length of the chain of consecutive synapses necessary to run around one cycle of performance. These yield a time

of the order of a tenth of a second for a complete performance of the cycle of operations, and this is the approximate period of the so-called "alpha rhythm" of the brain. Finally, the alpha rhythm, on quite other evidence, has already been conjectured to be of visual origin and to be important in the process of form perception.

In the spring of 1947, I received an invitation to participate in a mathematical conference in Nancy on problems arising from harmonic analysis. I accepted and, on my voyage there and back, spent a total of three weeks in England, chiefly as a guest of my old friend Professor J. B. S. Haldane. I had an excellent chance to meet most of those doing work on ultra-rapid computing machines, especially at Manchester and at the National Physical Laboratories at Teddington, and above all to talk over the fundamental ideas of cybernetics with Mr. Turing at Teddington. I also visited the Psychological Laboratory at Cambridge, and had a very good chance to discuss the work that Professor F. C. Bartlett and his staff were doing on the human element in control processes involving such an element. I found the interest in cybernetics about as great and well informed in England as in the United States, and the engineering work excellent, though of course limited by the smaller funds available. I found much interest and understanding of its possibility in many quarters, and Professors Haldane, H. Levy, and Bernal certainly regarded it as one of the most urgent problems on the agenda of science and scientific philosophy. I did not find, however, that as much progress had been made in unifying the subject and in pulling the various threads of research together as we had made at home in the States.

In France, the meeting at Nancy on harmonic analysis contained a number of papers uniting statistical ideas and ideas from communication engineering in a manner wholly in conformity with the point of view of cybernetics. Here I must mention especially the names of M. Blanc-Lapierre and M. Loève. I found also a considerable interest in the subject on the part of mathematicians, physiologists, and physical chemists, particularly with regard to its thermodynamic aspects in so far as they touch the more general problem of the nature of life itself. Indeed, I had discussed that subject in Boston, before my departure, with Professor Szent-Györgyi, the Hungarian biochemist, and had found his ideas concordant with my own.

One event during my French visit is particularly worth while noting here. My colleague, Professor G. de Santillana of M.I.T., introduced me to M. Freymann, of the firm of Hermann et Cie, and he requested of me the present book. I am particularly glad to receive his invitation, as M. Freymann is a Mexican, and the writing of the present book, as well as a good deal of the research leading up to it, has been done in Mexico.

As I have already hinted, one of the directions of work which the realm of ideas of the Macy meetings has suggested concerns the importance of the notion and the technique of communication in the social system. It is certainly true that the social system is an organization like the individual, that it is bound together by a system of communication, and that it has a dynamics in which circular processes of a feedback nature play an important part. This is true, both in the general fields of anthropology and of sociology and in the more specific field of economics; and the very important work, which we have already mentioned, of von Neumann and Morgenstern on the theory of games enters into this range of ideas. On this basis, Drs. Gregory Bateson and Margaret Mead have urged me, in view of the intensely pressing nature of the sociological and economic problems of the present age of confusion, to devote a large part of my energies to the discussion of this side of cybernetics.

Much as I sympathize with their sense of the urgency of the situation, and much as I hope that they and other competent workers will take up problems of this sort, which I shall discuss in a later chapter of this book, I can share neither their feeling that this field has the first claim on my attention, nor their hopefulness that sufficient progress can be registered in this direction to have an appreciable therapeutic effect in the present diseases of society. To begin with, the main quantities affecting society are not only statistical, but the runs of statistics on which they are based are excessively short. There is no great use in lumping under one head the economics of steel industry before and after the introduction of the Bessemer process, nor in comparing the statistics of rubber production before and after the burgeoning of the automobile industry and the cultivation of *Hevea* in Malaya. Neither is there any important point in running statistics of the incidence of venereal disease in a single table which covers both the period before and that after the introduction of salvarsan, unless for the specific purpose of studying the effectiveness of this drug. For a good statistic of society, we need long runs *under essentially constant conditions,* just as for a good resolution of light we need a lens with a large aperture. The effective aperture of a lens is not appreciably increased by augmenting its nominal aperture, *unless the lens is made of a material so homogeneous that the delay of light in different parts of the lens conforms to the proper designed amount by less than a small part of a wavelength. Similarly, the advantage of long runs of statistics under widely varying conditions is specious and spurious.* Thus the human sciences are very poor testing-grounds for a new mathematical technique: as poor as the statistical mechanics of a gas would be to a being of the order of size of a molecule, to whom the fluctuations which we ignore from a larger

standpoint would be precisely the matters of greatest interest. Moreover, in the absence of reasonably safe routine numerical techniques, the element of the judgment of the expert in determining the estimates to be made of sociological, anthropological, and economic quantities is so great that it is no field for a newcomer who has not yet had the bulk of experience which goes to make up the expert. I may remark parenthetically that the modern apparatus of the theory of small samples, once it goes beyond the determination of its own specially defined parameters and becomes a method for positive statistical inference in new cases, does not inspire me with any confidence unless it is applied by a statistician by whom the main elements of the dynamics of the situation are either explicitly known or implicitly felt.

I have just spoken of a field in which my expectations of cybernetics are definitely tempered by an understanding of the limitations of the data which we may hope to obtain. There are two other fields where I ultimately hope to accomplish something practical with the aid of cybernetic ideas, but in which this hope must wait on further developments. One of these is the matter of prostheses for lost or paralyzed limbs. As we have seen in the discussion of *Gestalt,* the ideas of communication engineering have already been applied by McCulloch to the problem of the replacement of lost senses, in the construction of an instrument to enable the blind to read print by hearing. Here the instrument suggested by McCulloch takes over quite explicitly some of the functions not only of the eye but of the visual cortex. There is a manifest possibility of doing something similar in the case of artificial limbs. The loss of a segment of limb implies not only the loss of the purely passive support of the missing segment or its value as mechanical extension of the stump, and the loss of the contractile power of its muscles, but implies as well the loss of all cutaneous and kinesthetic sensations originating in it. The first two losses are what the artificial-limbmaker now tries to replace. The third has so far been beyond his scope. In the case of a simple peg leg, this is not important: the rod that replaces the missing limb has no degrees of freedom of its own, and the kinesthetic mechanism of the stump is fully adequate to report its own position and velocity. This is not the case with the articulated limb with a mobile knee and ankle, thrown ahead by the patient with the aid of his remaining musculature. He has no adequate report of their position and motion, and this interferes with his sureness of step on an irregular terrain. There does not seem to be any insuperable difficulty in equipping the artificial joints and the sole of the artificial foot with strain or pressure gauges, which are to register electrically or otherwise, say through vibrators, on intact areas of skin. The present artificial limb removes some of the paralysis caused by the amputation but leaves the ataxis. With the use of proper receptors, much of this ataxia should disappear as well, and the patient should be able to learn reflexes, such as those we all use in driving a car, which should enable him to step out with a much surer gait. What we have said about the leg should apply with even more force to the arm, where the figure of the manikin familiar to all readers of books of neurology shows that the sensory loss in an amputation of the thumb alone is considerably greater than the sensory loss even in a hip-joint amputation.

I have made an attempt to report these considerations to the proper authorities, but up to now I have not been able to accomplish much. I do not know whether the same ideas have already emanated from other sources, nor whether they have been tried out and found technically impracticable. In case they have not yet received a thorough practical consideration, they should receive one in the immediate future.

Let me now come to another point which I believe to merit attention. It has long been clear to me that the modern ultra-rapid computing machine was in principle an ideal central nervous system to an apparatus for automatic control; and that its input and output need not be in the form of numbers or diagrams but might very well be, respectively, the readings of artificial sense organs, such as photoelectric cells or thermometers, and the performance of motors or solenoids. With the aid of strain gauges or similar agencies to read the performance of these motor organs and to report, to "feed back," to the central control system as an artificial kinesthetic sense, we are already in a position to construct artificial machines of almost any degree of elaborateness of performance. Long before Nagasaki and the public awareness of the atomic bomb, it had occurred to me that we were here in the presence of another social potentiality of unheard-of importance for good and for evil. The automatic factory and the assembly line without human agents are only so far ahead of us as is limited by our willingness to put such a degree of effort into their engineering as was spent, for example, in the development of the technique of radar in the Second World War.[1]

I have said that this new development has unbounded possibilities for good and for evil. For one thing, it makes the metaphorical dominance of the machines, as imagined by Samuel Butler, a most immediate and non-metaphorical problem. It gives the human race a new and most effective collection of mechanical slaves to perform its labor. Such mechanical labor has most of the economic properties of slave labor, although, unlike slave labor, it does not involve the direct demoralizing effects of human cruelty. However, any labor that accepts the conditions of competition with

slave labor accepts the conditions of slave labor, and is essentially slave labor. The key word of this statement is *competition*. It may very well be a good thing for humanity to have the machine remove from it the need of menial and disagreeable tasks, or it may not. I do not know. It cannot be good for these new potentialities to be assessed in the terms of the market, of the money they save; and it is precisely the terms of the open market, the "fifth freedom," that have become the shibboleth of the sector of American opinion represented by the National Association of Manufacturers and the Saturday Evening Post. I say American opinion, for as an American, I know it best, but the hucksters recognize no national boundary.

Perhaps I may clarify the historical background of the present situation if I say that the first industrial revolution, the revolution of the "dark satanic mills," was the devaluation of the human arm by the competition of machinery. There is no rate of pay at which a United States pick-and-shovel laborer can live which is low enough to compete with the work of a steam shovel as an excavator. The modern industrial revolution is similarly bound to devalue the human brain, at least in its simpler and more routine decisions. Of course, just as the skilled carpenter, the skilled mechanic, the skilled dressmaker have in some degree survived the first industrial revolution, so the skilled scientist and the skilled administrator may survive the second. However, taking the second revolution as accomplished, the average human being of mediocre attainments or less has nothing to sell that it is worth anyone's money to buy.

The answer, of course, is to have a society based on human values other than buying or selling. To arrive at this society, we need a good deal of planning and a good deal of struggle, which, if the best comes to the best, may be on the plane of ideas, and otherwise—who knows? I thus felt it my duty to pass on my information and understanding of the position to those who have an active interest in the conditions and the future of labor, that is, to the labor unions. I did manage to make contact with one or two persons high up in the C.I.O., and from them I received a very intelligent and sympathetic hearing. Further than these individuals, neither I nor any of them was able to go. It was their opinion, as it had been my previous observation and information, both in the United States and in England, that the labor unions and the labor movement are in the hands of a highly limited personnel, thoroughly well trained in the specialized problems of shop stewardship and disputes concerning wages and conditions of work, and totally unprepared to enter into the larger political, technical, sociological, and economic questions which concern the very existence of labor. The reasons for this are easy enough to see: the labor union official generally comes

---

[1] *Fortune*, **32**, 139–147 (October); 163–169 (November, 1945).

from the exacting life of a workman into the exacting life of an administrator without any opportunity for a broader training; and for those who have this training, a union career is not generally inviting; nor, quite naturally, are the unions receptive to such people.

Those of us who have contributed to the new science of cybernetics thus stand in a moral position which is, to say the least, not very comfortable. We have contributed to the initiation of a new science which, as I have said, embraces technical developments with great possibilities for good and for evil. We can only hand it over into the world that exists about us, and this is the world of Belsen and Hiroshima. We do not even have the choice of suppressing these new technical developments. They belong to the age, and the most any of us can do by suppression is to put the development of the subject into the hands of the most irresponsible and most venal of our engineers. The best we can do is to see that a large public understands the trend and the bearing of the present work, and to confine our personal efforts to those fields, such as physiology and psychology, most remote from war and exploitation. As we have seen, there are those who hope that the good of a better understanding of man and society which is offered by this new field of work may anticipate and outweigh the incidental contribution we are making to the concentration of power (which is always concentrated, by its very conditions of existence, in the hands of the most unscrupulous). I write in 1947, and I am compelled to say that it is a very slight hope.

The author wishes to express his gratitude to Mr. Walter Pitts, Mr. Oliver Selfridge, Mr. Georges Dubé, and Mr. Frederic Webster for aid in correcting the manuscript and preparing the material for publication.

Instituto Nacional de Cardiología,
Ciudad de México

November, 1947

V Computing Machines and the Nervous System

Computing machines are essentially machines for recording numbers, operating with numbers, and giving the result in numerical form. A very considerable part of their cost, both in money and in the effort of construction, goes to the simple problem of recording numbers clearly and accurately. The simplest mode of doing this seems to be on a uniform scale, with a pointer of some sort moving over this. If we wish to record a number with an accuracy of one part in n, we have to assure that in each region of the scale the pointer assumes the desired position within this accuracy. That is, for an amount of information $\log_2 n$, we must finish

each part of the movement of the pointer with this degree of accuracy, and the cost will be of the form An, where A is not too far from a constant. More precisely, since if $n - 1$ regions are accurately established, the remaining region will also be determined accurately, the cost of recording an amount of information I will be about

$$(2^I - 1)A \tag{5.01}$$

Now let us divide this information over two scales, each marked less accurately. The cost of recording this information will be about

$$2(2^{I/2} - 1)A \tag{5.02}$$

If the information be divided among N scales, the approximate cost will be

$$N(2^{I/N} - 1)A \tag{5.03}$$

This will be a minimum when

$$2^{I/N} - 1 = \frac{I}{N} 2^{I/N} \log 2 \tag{5.04}$$

or if we put

$$\frac{I}{N} \log 2 = x \tag{5.05}$$

when

$$x = \frac{e^x - 1}{e^x} = 1 - e^{-x} \tag{5.06}$$

This will occur when and only when $x = 0$, or $N = \infty$. That is, N should be as large as possible to give the lowest cost for the storage of information. Let us remember that $2^{I/N}$ must be an integer, and that 1 is not a significant value, as we then have an infinite number of scales each containing no information. The best significant value for $2^{I/N}$ is 2, in which case we record our number on a number of independent scales, each divided into two equal parts. In other words, we represent our numbers in the binary system on a number of scales in which all that we know is that a certain quantity lies in one or the other of two equal portions of the scale, and in which the probability of an imperfect knowledge as to which half of the scale contains the observation is made vanishingly small. In other words, we represent a number v in the form

$$v = v_0 + \frac{1}{2} v_1 + \frac{1}{2^2} v_2 + \cdots + \frac{1}{2_n} v_n + \cdots \tag{5.07}$$

where every v_n is either 1 or 0.

There exist at present two great types of computing machines: those like the Bush differential analyzer,[1] which

---

[1]Journal of the Franklin Institute, various papers, 1930 on.

are known as *analogy machines,* where the data are represented by measurements on some continuous scale, so that the accuracy of the machine is determined by the accuracy of construction of the scale; and those, like the ordinary desk adding and multiplying machine, which we call *numerical machines,* where the data are represented by a set of choices among a number of contingencies, and the accuracy is determined by the sharpness with which the contingencies are distinguished, the number of alternative contingencies presented at every choice, and the number of choices given. We see that for highly accurate work, at any rate, the numerical machines are preferable, and above all, those numerical machines constructed on the binary scale, in which the number of alternatives presented at each choice is two. Our use of machines on the decimal scale is conditioned merely by the historical accident that the scale of ten, based on our fingers and thumbs, was already in use when the Hindus made the great discovery of the importance of the zero and the advantage of a positional system of notation. It is worth retaining when a large part of the work done with the aid of the machine consists in transcribing onto the machine numbers in the conventional decimal form, and in taking off the machine numbers which must be written in the same conventional form.

This is, in fact, the use of the ordinary desk computing machine, as employed in banks, in business offices, and in many statistical laboratories. It is not the way that the larger and more automatic machines are best to be employed; in general, any computing machine is used because machine methods are faster than hand methods. In any combined use of means of computation, as in any combination of chemical reactions, it is the slowest which gives the order of magnitude of the time constants of the entire system. It is thus advantageous, as far as possible, to remove the human element from any elaborate chain of computation and to introduce it only where it is absolutely unavoidable, at the very beginning and the very end. Under these conditions, it pays to have an instrument for the change of the scale of notation, to be used initially and finally in the chain of computations, and to perform all intermediate processes on the binary scale.

The ideal computing machine must then have all its data inserted at the beginning, and must be as free as possible from human interference to the very end. This means that not only must the numerical data be inserted at the beginning, but also all the rules for combining them, in the form of instructions covering every situation which may arise in the course of the computation. Thus the computing machine must be a logical machine as well as an arithmetic machine and must combine contingencies in accordance with a systematic algorithm. While there are many algorithms which *might* be used for combining contingencies,

the simplest of these is known as the algebra of logic *par excellence,* or the Boolean algebra. This algorithm, like the binary arithmetic, is based on the dichotomy, the choice between *yes* and *no,* the choice between being in a class and outside. The reasons for its superiority to other systems are of the same nature as the reasons for the superiority of the binary arithmetic over other arithmetics.

Thus all the data, numerical or logical, put into the machine are in the form of a set of choices between two alternatives, and all the operations on the data take the form of making a set of new choices depend on a set of old choices. When I add two one-digit numbers, A and B, I obtain a two-digit number commencing with 1, if A and B are both 1, and otherwise with 0. The second digit is 1 if $A \neq B$, and is otherwise 0. The addition of numbers of more than one digit follows similar but more complicated rules. Multiplication in the binary system, as in the decimal, may be reduced to the multiplication table and the addition of numbers, and the rules for multiplication for binary numbers take on the peculiarly simple form given by the table

$$\begin{array}{c|cc} \times & 0 & 1 \\ \hline 0 & 0 & 0 \\ 1 & 0 & 1 \end{array}$$

(5.08)

Thus multiplication is simply a method to determine a set of new digits when old digits are given.

On the logical side, if O is a negative and I a positive decision, every operator can be derived from three: *negation,* which transforms I into O and O into I; *logical addition,* with the table

$$\begin{array}{c|cc} \oplus & O & I \\ \hline O & O & I \\ I & I & I \end{array}$$

(5.09)

and *logical multiplication,* with the same table as the numerical multiplication of the $(1, 0)$ system, namely,

$$\begin{array}{c|cc} \odot & O & I \\ \hline O & O & O \\ I & O & I \end{array}$$

(5.10)

That is, every contingency which may arise in the operation of the machine simply demands a new set of choices of contingencies I and O, depending according to a fixed set of rules on the decisions already made. In other words, the structure of the machine is that of a bank of relays, capable each of two conditions, say "on" and "off"; while at each stage the relays assume each a position dictated by the positions of some or all the relays of the bank at a previous stage of operation. These stages of operation may be definitely "clocked" from some central clock or clocks, or the action of each relay may be held up until all the relays which should have acted earlier in the process have gone through all the steps called for.

The relays used a computing machine may be of very varied character. They may be purely mechanical, or they may be electro-mechanical, as in the case of a solenoidal relay, in which the armature will remain in one of two possible positions of equilibrium until an appropriate impulse pulls it to the other side. They may be purely electrical systems with two alternative positions of equilibrium, either in the form of gas-filled tubes, or, what is much more rapid, in the form of high-vacuum tubes. The two possible states of a relay system may both be stable in the absence of outside interference, or only one may be stable, while the other is transitory. Always in the second case and generally in the first case, it will be desirable to have special apparatus to retain an impulse which is to act at some future time, and to avoid the clogging up of the system which will ensue if one of the relays does nothing but repeat itself indefinitely. However, we shall have more to say concerning this question of memory later.

It is a noteworthy fact that the human and animal nervous systems, which are known to be capable of the work of a computation system, contain elements which are ideally suited to act as relays. These elements are the so-called *neurons* or nerve cells. While they show rather complicated properties under the influence of electrical currents, in their ordinary physiological action they conform very nearly to the "all-or-none" principle; that is, they are either at rest, or when they "fire" they go through a series of changes almost independent of the nature and intensity of the stimulus. There is first an active phase, transmitted from one end to the other of the neuron with a definite velocity, to which there succeeds a refractory period during which the neuron is either incapable of being stimulated, or at any rate is not capable of being stimulated by any normal, physiological process. At the end of this effective refractory period, the nerve remains inactive, but may be stimulated again into activity.

Thus the nerve may be taken to be a relay with essentially two states of activity: firing and repose. Leaving aside those neurons which accept their messages from free endings or sensory end organs, each neuron has its message fed into it by other neurons at points of contact known as *synapses*. For a given outgoing neuron, these vary in number from a very few to many hundred. It is the state of the incoming impulses at the various synapses, combined with the antecedent state of the outgoing neuron itself, which determines whether it will fire or not. If it is neither firing nor refractory, and the number of incoming synapses which "fire" within a certain very short fusion interval of time exceeds a certain threshold, then the neuron will fire after a known, fairly constant synaptic delay.

This is perhaps an oversimplification of the picture: the "threshold" may not depend simply on the number of synapses but on their "weight" and their geometrical relations to one another with respect to the neuron into which they feed; and there is very convincing evidence that there exist synapses of a different nature, the so-called "inhibitory synapses," which either completely prevent the firing of the outgoing neuron or at any rate raise its threshold with respect to stimulation at the ordinary synapses. What is pretty clear, however, is that some definite combinations of impulses on the incoming neurons having synaptic connections with a given neuron will cause it to fire, while others will not cause it to fire. This is not to say that there may not be other, non-neuronic influences, perhaps of a humoral nature, which produce slow, secular changes tending to vary that pattern of incoming impulses which is adequate for firing.

A very important function of the nervous system, and, as we have said, a function equally in demand for computing machines, is that of *memory,* the ability to preserve the results of past operations for use in the future. It will be seen that the uses of the memory are highly various, and it is improbable that any single mechanism can satisfy the demands of all of them. There is first the memory which is necessary for the carrying out of a current process, such as a multiplication, in which the intermediate results are of no value when once the process is completed, and in which the operating apparatus should then be released for further use. Such a memory should record quickly, be read quickly, and be erased quickly. On the other hand, there is the memory which is intended to be part of the files, the permanent record, of the machine or the brain, and to contribute to the basis of all its future behavior, at least during a single run of the machine. Let it be remarked parenthetically that an important difference between the way in which we use the brain and the machine is that the machine is intended for many successive runs, either with no reference to each other, or with a minimal, limited reference, and that it can be cleared between such runs; while the brain, in the course of nature, never even approximately clears out its past records. Thus the brain, under normal circumstances, is not the complete analogue of the computing machine but rather the analogue of a single run on such a machine. We shall see later that this remark has a deep significance in psychopathology and in psychiatry.

To return to the problem of memory, a very satisfactory method for constructing a short-time memory is to keep a sequence of impulses traveling around a closed circuit until this circuit is cleared by intervention from outside. There is much reason to believe that this happens in our brains during the retention of impulses, which occurs over what is known as the specious present. This method has been imitated in several devices which have been used in computing machines, or at least suggested for such a use. There are two conditions which are desirable in such a retentive apparatus: the impulse should be transmitted in a medium in which it is not too difficult to achieve a considerable time lag; and before the errors inherent in the instrument have blurred it too much, the impulse should be reconstructed in a form as sharp as possible. The first condition tends to rule out delays produced by the transmission of light, or even, in many cases, by electric circuits, while it favors the use of one form or another of elastic vibrations; and such vibrations have actually been employed for this purpose in computing machines. If electric circuits are used for delay purposes, the delay produced at every stage is relatively short; or, as in all pieces of linear apparatus, the deformation of the message is cumulative and very soon becomes intolerable. To avoid this, a second consideration comes into play; we must insert somewhere in the cycle a relay which does not serve to repeat the form of the incoming message but rather to trigger off a new message of prescribed form. This is done very easily in the nervous system, where indeed all transmission is more or less of a trigger phenomenon. In the electrical industry, pieces of apparatus for this purpose have long been known and have been used in connection with telegraph circuits. They are known as *telegraph-type repeaters*. The great difficulty of using them for memories of long duration is that they have to function without a flaw over an enormous number of consecutive cycles of operation. Their success is all the more remarkable: in a piece of apparatus designed by Mr. Williams of the University of Manchester, a device of this sort with a unit delay of the order of a hundredth of a second has continued in successful operation for several hours. What makes this more remarkable is that this apparatus was not used merely to preserve a single decision, a single "yes" or "no," but a matter of thousands of decisions.

Like other forms of apparatus intended to retain a large number of decisions, this works on the scanning principle. One of the simplest modes of storing information for a relatively short time is as the charge on a condenser; and when this is supplemented by a telegraph-type repeater, it becomes an adequate method of storage. To use to the best advantage the circuit facilities attached to such a storage system, it is desirable to be able to switch successively and very rapidly from one condenser to another. The ordinary means of doing this involve mechanical inertia, and this is never consistent with very high speeds. A much better way is the use of a large number of condensers, in which one plate is either a small piece of metal sputtered in to a dielectric, or the imperfectly insulating surface of the dielectric itself, while one of the connectors to these condensers is a pencil of cathode rays moved by the condensers and magnets of a sweep circuit over a course like that of a plough in a ploughed field. There are various elaborations

of this method, which indeed was employed in a somewhat different way by the Radio Corporation of America before it was used by Mr. Williams.

These last-named methods for storing information can hold a message for quite an appreciable time, if not for a period comparable with a human lifetime. For more permanent records, there is a wide variety of alternatives among which we can choose. Leaving out such bulky, slow, and unerasable methods as the use of punched cards and punched tape, we have magnetic tape, together with its modern refinements, which have largely eliminated the tendency of messages on this material to spread; phosphorescent substances; and above all, photography. Photography is indeed ideal for the permanence and detail of its records, ideal again from the point of view of the shortness of exposure needed to record an observation. It suffers from two grave disadvantages: the time needed for development, which has been reduced to a few seconds, but is still not small enough to make photography available for a short-time memory; and (at present [1947]) the fact that a photographic record is not subject to rapid erasure and the rapid implanting of a new record. The Eastman people have been working on just these problems, which do not seem to be necessarily insoluble, and it is possible that by this time they have found the answer.

Very many of the methods of storage of information already considered have an important physical element in common. They seem to depend on systems with a high degree of quantum degeneracy, or, in other words, with a large number of modes of vibration of the same frequency. This is certainly true in the case of ferromagnetism, and is also true in the case of materials with an exceptionally high dielectric constant, which are thus especially valuable for use in condensers for the storage of information. Phosphorescence as well is a phenomenon associated with a high quantum degeneracy, and the same sort of effect makes its appearance in the photographic process, where many of the substances which act as developers seem to have a great deal of internal resonance. Quantum degeneracy appears to be associated with the ability to make small causes produce appreciable and stable effects. We have already seen in Chapter II that substances with high quantum degeneracy appear to be associated with many of the problems of metabolism and reproduction. It is probably not an accident that here, in a nonliving environment, we find them associated with a third fundamental property of living matter: the ability to receive and organize impulses and to make them effective in the outer world.

We have seen in the case of photography and similar processes that it is possible to store a message in the form of a permanent alteration of certain storage elements. In reinserting this information into the system, it is necessary to cause these changes to affect the messages going through the system. One of the simplest ways to do this is to have, as the storage elements which are changed, parts which normally assist in the transmission of messages, and of such a nature that the change in their character due to storage affects the manner in which they will transport messages for the entire future. In the nervous system, the neurons and the synapses are elements of this sort, and it is quite plausible that information is stored over long periods by changes in the thresholds of neurons, or, what may be regarded as another way of saying the same thing, by changes in the permeability of each synapse to messages. Many of us think, in the absence of a better explanation of the phenomenon, that the storage of information in the brain can actually occur in this way. It is conceivable for such a storage to take place either by the opening of new paths or by the closure of old ones. Apparently it is adequately established that no neurons are formed in the brain after birth. It is possible, though not certain, that no new synapses are formed, and it is a plausible conjecture that the chief changes of threshold in the memory process are increases. If this is the case, our whole life is on the pattern of Balzac's *Peau de Chagrin,* and the very process of learning and remembering exhausts our powers of learning and remembering until life itself squanders our capital stock of power to live. It may well be that this phenomenon does occur. This is a possible explanation for a sort of senescence. The real phenomenon of senescence, however, is much too complicated to be explained in this way alone.

We have already spoken of the computing machine, and consequently the brain, as a logical machine. It is by no means trivial to consider the light cast on logic by such machines, both natural and artificial. Here the chief work is that of Turing.[1] We have said before that the *machina ratiocinatrix* is nothing but the *calculus* ratiocinator of Leibniz with an engine in it; and just as modern mathematical logic begins with this calculus, so it is inevitable that its present engineering development should cast a new light on logic. The science of today is operational; that is, it considers every statement as essentially concerned with possible experiments or observable processes. According to this, the study of logic must reduce to the study of the logical machine, whether nervous or mechanical, with all its non-removable limitations and imperfections.

It may be said by some readers that this reduces logic to psychology, and that the two sciences are observably and demonstrably different. This is true in the sense that many psychological states and sequences of thought do not conform to the canons of logic. Psychology contains much that

---

[1]Turing, A. M., "On Computable Numbers with an Application to the Entscheidungsproblem," *Proceedings of the London Mathematical Society,* Ser. 2, **42,** 230–265 (1936).

is foreign to logic, but—and this is the important fact—any logic which means anything to us can contain nothing which the human mind—and hence the human nervous system—is unable to encompass. *All logic is limited by the limitations of the human mind when it is engaged in that activity known as logical thinking.*

For example, we devote much of mathematics to discussions involving the infinite, but these discussions and their accompanying proofs are not infinite in fact. No admissible proof involves more than a finite number of stages. It is true, a proof by mathematical induction *seems* to involve an infinity of stages, but this is only apparent. In fact, it involves just the following stages:

1. P_n is a proposition involving the number n.
2. P_n has been proved for $n = 1$.
3. If P_n is true, P_{n+1} is true.
4. Therefore, P_n is true for every positive integer n.

It is true that somewhere in our logical assumptions there must be one which validates this argument. However, this mathematical induction is a far different thing from complete induction over an infinite set. The same thing is true of the more refined forms of mathematical induction, such as transfinite induction, which occur in certain mathematical disciplines.

Thus some very interesting situations arise, in which we may be able—with enough time and enough computational aids—to prove every single case of a theorem P_n; but if there is no systematic way of subsuming these proofs under a single argument independent of n, such as we find in mathematical induction, it may be impossible to prove P_n *for all n.* This contingency is recognized in what is known as metamathematics, the discipline so brilliantly developed by Gödel and his school.

A proof represents a logical process which has come to a definitive conclusion in a finite number of stages. However, a logical machine following definite rules need never come to a conclusion. It may go on grinding through different stages without ever coming to a stop, either by describing a pattern of activity of continually increasing complexity, or by going into a repetitive process like the end of a chess game in which there is a continuing cycle of perpetual check. This occurs in the case of some of the paradoxes of Cantor and Russell. Let us consider the class of all classes which are not members of themselves. Is this class a member of itself? If it is, it is certainly not a member of itself; and if it is not, it is equally certainly a member of itself. A machine to answer this question would give the successive temporary answers: "yes," "no," "yes," "no," and so on, and would never come to equilibrium.

Bertrand Russell's solution of his own paradoxes was to affix to every statement a quantity, the so-called type, which serves to distinguish between what seems to be formally the same statement, according to the character of the objects with which it concerns itself—whether these are "things," in the simplest sense, classes of "things," classes of classes of "things," etc. The method by which we resolve the paradoxes is also to attach a parameter to each statement, this parameter being the time at which it is asserted. In both cases, we introduce what we may call a parameter of uniformization, to resolve an ambiguity which is simply due to its neglect.

We thus see that the logic of the machine resembles human logic, and, following Turing, we may employ it to throw light on human logic. Has the machine a more eminently human characteristic as well—the ability to learn? To see that it may well have even this property, let us consider two closely related notions: that of the association of ideas and that of the conditioned reflex.

In the British empirical school of philosophy, from Locke to Hume, the content of the mind was considered to be made up of certain entities known to Locke as ideas, and to the later authors as ideas and impressions. The simple ideas or impressions were supposed to exist in a purely passive mind, as free from influence on the ideas it contained as a clean blackboard is on the symbols which may be written on it. By some sort of inner activity, hardly worthy to be called a force, these ideas were supposed to unite themselves into bundles, according to the principles of similarity, contiguity, and cause and effect. Of these principles, perhaps the most significant was contiguity: ideas or impressions which had often occurred together in time or in space were supposed to have acquired the ability of evoking one another, so that the presence of any one of them would produce the entire bundle.

In all this there is a dynamics implied, but the idea of a dynamics had not yet filtered through from physics to the biological and psychological sciences. The typical biologist of the eighteenth century was Linnaeus, the collector and classifier, with a point of view quite opposed to that of the evolutionists, the physiologists, the geneticists, the experimental embryologists of the present day. Indeed, with so much of the world to explore, the state of mind of the biologists could hardly have been different. Similarly, in psychology, the notion of mental content dominated that of mental process. This may well have been a survival of the scholastic emphasis on substances, in a world in which the noun was hypostasized and the verb carried little or no weight. Nevertheless, the step from these static ideas to the more dynamic point of view of the present day, as exemplified in the work of Pavlov, is perfectly clear.

Pavlov worked much more with animals than with men, and he reported visible actions rather than introspective states of mind. He found in dogs that the presence of food causes the increased secretion of saliva and of gastric juice. If then a certain visual object is shown to dogs in the presence of food and only in the presence of food, the sight of this object in the absence of food will acquire the property of being by itself able to stimulate the flow of saliva or of gastric juice. The union by continuity which Locke had observed introspectively in the case of ideas now becomes a similar union of patterns of behavior.

There is one important difference, however, between the point of view of Pavlov and that of Locke, and it is precisely due to this fact that Locke considers ideas and Pavlov patterns of action. The responses observed by Pavlov tend to carry a process to a successful conclusion or to avoid a catastrophe. Salivation is important for deglutition and for digestion, while the avoidance of what we should consider a painful stimulus tends to protect the animal from bodily injury. Thus there enters into the conditioned reflex something that we may call *affective tone*. We need not associate this with our own sensations of pleasure and pain, nor need we in the abstract associate it with the advantage of the animal. The essential thing is this: that affective tone is arranged on some sort of scale from negative "pain" to positive "pleasure"; that for a considerable time, or permanently, an increase in affective tone favors all processes in the nervous system that are under way at the time and gives them a secondary power to increase affective tone: and that a decrease in affective tone tends to inhibit all processes under way at the time and gives them a secondary ability to decrease affective tone.

Biologically speaking, of course, a greater affective tone must occur predominantly in situations favorable for the perpetuation of the race, if not the individual, and a smaller affective tone in situations which are unfavorable for this perpetuation, if not disastrous. Any race not conforming to this requirement will go the way of Lewis Carroll's Bread-and-Butter Fly, and always die. Nevertheless, even a doomed race may show a mechanism valid so long as the race lasts. In other words, even the most suicidal apportioning of affective tone will produce a definite pattern of conduct.

Note that the mechanism of affective tone is itself a feedback mechanism. It may even be given a diagram such as shown in Fig. 7.

Here the totalizer for affective tone combines the affective tones given by the separate affective-tone mechanisms over a short interval in the past, according to some rule which we need not specify now. The leads back to the individual affective-tone mechanisms serve to modify the intrinsic affective tone of each process in the direction of

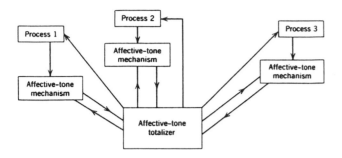

Figure 7

the output of the totalizer, and this modification stands until it is modified by later messages from the totalizer. The leads back from the totalizer to the process mechanisms serve to lower thresholds if the total affective tone is increasing, and to raise them if the total affective tone is decreasing. They likewise have a long-time effect, which endures until it is modified by another impulse from the totalizer. This lasting effect, however, is confined to those processes actually in being at the time the return message arrives, and a similar limitation also applies to the effects on the individual affective-tone mechanisms.

I wish to emphasize that I do not say that the process of the conditioned reflex operates according to the mechanism I have given; I merely say that it *could* so operate. If, however, we assume this or any simular mechanism, there are a good many things we can say concerning it. One is that this mechanism is capable of learning. It has already been recognized that the conditioned reflex is a learning mechanism, and this idea has been used in the behaviorist studies of the learning of rats in a maze. All that is needed is that the inducements or punishments used have, respectively, a positive and a negative affective tone. This is certainly the case, and the experimenter learns the nature of this affective tone by experience, not simply by *a priori* considerations.

Another point of considerable interest is that such a mechanism involves a certain set of messages which go out generally into the nervous system, to all elements which are in a state to receive them. These are the return messages from the affective-tone totalizer, and to a certain extent the messages from the affective-tone mechanisms to the totalizers. Indeed, the totalizer need not be a separate element but may merely represent some natural combinatory effect of messages arriving from the individual affective-tone mechanisms. Now, such messages "to whom it may concern" may well be sent out most efficiently, with a smallest cost in apparatus, by channels other than nervous. In a similar manner, the ordinary communication system of a mine may consist of a telephone central with the attached wiring and pieces of apparatus. When we want to empty a

mine in a hurry, we do not trust to this, but break a tube of a mercaptan in the air intake. Chemical messengers like this, or like the hormones, are the simplest and most effective for a message not addressed to a specific recipient. For the moment, let me break into what I know to be pure fancy. The high emotional and consequently affective content of hormonal activity is most suggestive. This does not mean that a purely nervous mechanism is not capable of affective tone and of learning, but it does mean that in the study of this aspect of our mental activity, we cannot afford to be blind to the possibilities of hormonal transmission. It may be excessively fanciful to attach this notion to the fact that in the theories of Freud the memory—the storage function of the nervous system—and the activities of sex are both involved. Sex, on the one hand, and all affective content, on the other, contain a very strong hormonal element. This suggestion of the importance of sex and hormones has been made to me by Dr. J. Lettvin and Mr. Oliver Selfridge. While at present there is no adequate evidence to prove its validity, it is not manifestly absurd in principle.

There is nothing in the nature of the computing machine which forbids it to show conditioned reflexes. Let us remember that a computing machine in action is more than the concatenation of relays and storage mechanisms which the designer has built into it. It also contains the content of its storage mechanisms, and this content is never completely cleared in the course of a single run. We have already seen that it is the run rather than the entire existence of the mechanical structure of the computing machine which corresponds to the life of the individual. We have also seen that in the nervous computing machine it is highly probable that information is stored largely as changes in the permeability of the synapses, and it is perfectly possible to construct artificial machines where information is stored in that way. It is perfectly possible, for example, to cause any message going into storage to change in a permanent or semi-permanent way the grid bias of one or of a number of vacuum tubes, and thus to alter the numerical value of the summation of impulses which will make the tube or tubes fire.

A more detailed account of learning apparatus in computing and control machines, and the uses to which it may be put, may well be left to the engineer rather than to a preliminary book like this one. It is perhaps better to devote the rest of this chapter to the more developed, normal uses of modern computing machines. One of the chief of these is in the solution of partial differential equations. Even linear partial differential equations require the recording of an enormous mass of data to set them up, as the data involve the accurate description of functions of two or more variables. With equations of the hyperbolic type, like the wave equation, the typical problem is that of solving the equation when the initial data are given, and this can be done in a progressive manner from the initial data to the results at any given later time. This is largely true of equations of the parabolic type as well. When it comes to equations of the elliptic type, where the natural data are boundary values rather than initial values, the natural methods of solution involve an iterative process of successive approximation. This process is repeated a very large number of times, so that very fast methods, such as those of the modern computing machine, are almost indispensable.

In non-linear partial differential equations, we miss what we have in the case of the linear equations—a reasonably adequate, purely mathematical theory. Here computational methods are not only important for the handling of particular numerical cases, but, as von Neumann has pointed out, we need them in order to form that acquaintance with a large number of particular cases without which we can scarcely formulate a general theory. To some extent this has been done with the aid of very expensive experimental apparatus, such as wind tunnels. It is in this way that we have become acquainted with the more complicated properties of shock waves, slip surfaces, turbulence, and the like, for which we are scarcely in a position to give an adequate mathematical theory. How many undiscovered phenomena of similar nature there may be, we do not know. The analogue machines are so much less accurate, and in many cases so much slower than the digital machines that the latter give us much more promise for the future.

It is already becoming clear in the use of these new machines that they demand purely mathematical techniques of their own, quite different from those in use in manual computation or in the use of machines of smaller capacity. For example, even the use of machines for computing determinants of moderately high order or for the simultaneous solution of twenty or thirty simultaneous linear equations shows difficulties which do not arise when we study analogous problems of small order. Unless care is exercised in setting up a problem, these may completely deprive the solution of any significant figures whatever. It is a commonplace to say that fine, effective tools like the ultra-rapid computing machine are out of place in the hands of those not possessing a sufficient degree of technical skill to take full advantage of them. The ultra-rapid computing machine will certainly not decrease the need for mathematicians with a high level of understanding and technical training.

In the mechanical or electrical construction of computing machines, there are a few maxims which deserve consideration. One is that mechanisms which are relatively frequently used, such as multiplying or adding mechanisms, should be in the form of relatively standardized assemblages adapted for one particular use and no other, while those of more occasional use should be assembled for the moment of use out of elements also available for other purposes. Closely related to this consideration is the one that in these more general mechanisms the component parts should be available in accordance with their general properties, and should not be allotted permanently to a specific association with other pieces of apparatus. There should be some part of the apparatus, like an automatic telephone-switching exchange, which will search for free components and connectors of the various sorts and allot them as they are needed. This will eliminate much of the very large expense which is due to having a great number of unused elements which cannot be used unless their entire large assembly is used. We shall find this principle is very important when we come to consider traffic problems and overloading in the nervous system.

As a final remark, let me point out that a large computing machine, whether in the form of mechanical or electric apparatus or in the form of the brain itself, uses up a considerable amount of power, all of which is wasted and dissipated in heat. The blood leaving the brain is a fraction of a degree warmer than that entering it. No other computing machine approaches the economy of energy of the brain. In a large apparatus like the Eniac or Edvac, the filaments of the tubes consume a quantity of energy which may well be measured in kilowatts, and unless adequate ventilating and cooling apparatus is provided, the system will suffer from what is the mechanical equivalent of pyrexia, until the constants of the machine are radically changed by the heat, and its performance breaks down. Nevertheless, the energy spent per individual operation is almost vanishingly small, and does not even begin to form an adequate measure of the performance of the apparatus. The mechanical brain does not secrete thought "as the liver does bile," as the earlier materialists claimed, nor does it put it out in the form of energy, as the muscle puts out its activity. Information is information, not matter or energy. No materialism which does not admit this can survive at the present day.

VI Gestalt and Universals

Among other things which we have discussed in the previous chapter is the possibility of assigning a neural mechanism to Locke's theory of the association of ideas. According to Locke, this occurs according to three principles: the principle of contiguity, the principle of similarity, and the principle of cause and effect. The third of these is reduced by Locke, and even more definitively by Hume, to nothing more than constant concomitance, and so is subsumed under the first, that of contiguity. The second, that of similarity, deserves a more detailed discussion.

How do we recognize the identity of the features of a man, whether we see him in profile, in three-quarters face, or in full face? How do we recognize a circle as a circle, whether it is large or small, near or far; whether, in fact, it is in a plane perpendicular to a line from the eye meeting it in the middle, and is seen as a circle, or has some other orientation, and is seen as an ellipse? How do we see faces and animals and maps in clouds, or in the blots of a Rorschach test? All these examples refer to the eye, but similar problems extend to the other senses, and some of them have to do with intersensory relations. How do we put into words the call of a bird or the stridulations of an insect? How do we identify the roundness of a coin by touch?

For the present, let us confide ourselves to the sense of vision. One important factor in the comparison of form of different objects is certainly the interaction of the eye and the muscles, whether they are the muscles within the eyeball, the muscles moving the eyeball, the muscles moving the head, or the muscles moving the body as a whole. Indeed, some form of this visual-muscular feedback system is important as low in the animal kingdom as the flatworms. There the negative phototropism, the tendency to avoid the light, seems to be controlled by the balance of the impulses from the two eyespots. This balance is fed back to the muscles of the trunk, turning the body away from the light, and, in combination with the general impulse to move forward, carries the animal into the darkest region accessible. It is interesting to note that a combination of a pair of photocells with appropriate amplifiers, a Wheatstone bridge for balancing their outputs, and further amplifiers controlling the input into the two motors of a twinscrew mechanism would give us a very adequate negatively phototropic control for a little boat. It would be difficult or impossible for us to compress this mechanism into the dimensions that a flatworm can carry; but here we merely have another exemplification of the fact that must by now be familiar to the reader, that living mechanisms tend to have a much smaller space scale than the mechanisms best suited to the techniques of human artificers, although, on the other hand, the use of electrical techniques gives the artificial mechanism an enormous advantage in speed over the living organism.

Without going through all the intermediate stages, let us come at once to the eye-muscle feedbacks in man. Some of these are of purely homeostatic nature, as when the pupil opens in the dark and closes in the light, thus tending to confine the flow of light into the eye between narrower bounds than would otherwise be possible. Others concern the fact that the human eye has economically confined its best form and color vision to a relatively small fovea, while its perception of motion is better on the periphery. When the peripheral vision has picked up some object conspicuous by brilliancy or light contrast or color or above all by motion, there is a reflex feedback to bring it into the fovea. This feedback is accompanied by a complicated system of interlinked subordinate feedbacks, which tend to converge the two eyes so that the object attracting attention is in the same part of the visual field of each, and to focus the lens so that its outlines are as sharp as possible. These actions are supplemented by motions of the head and body, by which we bring the object into the center of vision if this cannot be done readily by a motion of the eyes alone, or by which we bring an object outside the visual field picked up by some other sense into that field. In the case of objects with which we are more familiar in one angular orientation than another—writing, human faces, landscapes, and the like—there is also a mechanism by which we tend to pull them into the proper orientation.

All these processes can be summed up in one sentence: we tend to bring any object that attracts our attention into a standard position and orientation, so that the visual image which we form of it varies within as small a range as possible. This does not exhaust the processes which are involved in perceiving the form and meaning of the object, but it certainly facilitates all later processes tending to this end. These later processes occur in the eye and in the visual cortex. There is considerable evidence that for a considerable number of stages each step in this process diminishes the number of neuron channels involved in the transmission of visual information, and brings this information one step nearer to the form in which it is used and is preserved in the memory.

The first step in this concentration of visual information occurs in the transition between the retina and the optic nerve. It will be noted that while in the fovea there is almost a one-one correspondence between the rods and cones and the fibers of the optic nerve, the correspondence on the periphery is such that one optic nerve fiber corresponds to ten or more end organs. This is quite understandable, in view of the fact that the chief function of the peripheral fibers is not so much vision itself as a pickup for the centering and focusing-directing mechanism of the eye.

One of the most remarkable phenomena of vision is our ability to recognize an outline drawing. Clearly, an outline drawing of, say, the face of a man, has very little resemblance to the face itself in color, or in the massing of light and shade, yet it may be a most recognizable portrait of its subject. The most plausible explanation of this is that, somewhere in the visual process, outlines are emphasized and some other aspects of an image are minimized in importance.

The beginning of these processes is in the eye itself. Like all senses, the retina is subject to accommodation; that is, the constant maintenance of a stimulus reduces its ability to receive and to transmit that stimulus. This is most markedly so for the receptors which record the interior of a large block of images with constant color and illumination, for even the slight fluctuations of focus and point of fixation which are inevitable in vision do not change the character of the image received. It is quite different on the boundary of two contrasting regions. Here these fluctuations produce an alternation between one stimulus and another, and this alternation, as we see in the phenomenon of after-images, not only does not tend to exhaust the visual mechanism by accommodation but even tends to enhance its sensitivity. This is true whether the contrast between the two adjacent regions is one of light intensity or of color. As a comment on these facts, let us note that three-quarters of the fibers in the optic nerve respond only to the flashing "on" of illumination. We thus find that the eye receives its most intense impression at boundaries, and that every visual image in fact has something of the nature of a line drawing.

Probably not all of this action is peripheral. In photography, it is known that certain treatments of a plate increase its contrasts, and such phenomena, which are of non-linearity, are certainly not beyond what the nervous system can do. They are allied to the phenomena of the telegraph-type repeater, which we have already mentioned. Like this, they use an impression which has not been blurred beyond a certain point to trigger a new impression of a standard sharpness. At any rate, they decrease the total unusable information carried by an image, and are probably correlated with a part of the reduction of the number of transmission fibers found at various stages of the visual cortex.

We have thus designated several actual or possible stages of the diagrammatization of our visual impressions. We center our images around the focus of attention and reduce them more or less to outlines. We have now to compare them with one another, or at any rate with a standard impression stored in memory, such as "circle" or "square." This may be done in several ways. We have given a rough sketch which indicates how the Lockean principle of contiguity in association may be mechanized. Let us notice that the principle of contiguity also covers much of the other Lockean principle of similarity. The different aspects of the same object are often to be seen in those processes which bring it to the focus of attention, and of other motions which lead us to see it, now at one distance and now at another, now from one angle and now from a distinct one. This is a general principle, not confined in its application to any particular sense and doubtless of much importance in the comparison of our more complicated experiences. It is nevertheless probably not the only process which leads to the formation of our specifically visual general ideas, or, as Locke would call them, "complex ideas." The structure of our visual cortex is too highly organized, too specific, to lead us to suppose that it operates by what is after all a highly generalized mechanism. It leaves us the impression that we are here dealing with a special mechanism which is mot merely a temporary assemblage of general-purpose elements with interchangeable parts, but a permanent sub-assembly like the adding and multiplying assemblies of a computing machine. Under the circumstances, it is worth considering how such a sub-assembly might possibly work and how we should go about designing it.

The possible perspective transformations of an object form what is known as a group, in the sense in which we have already defined one in Chapter II. This group defines several sub-groups of transformations: the affine group, in which we consider only those transformations which leave the region at infinity untouched; the homogeneous dilations about a given point, in which one point, the directions of the axes, and the equality of scale in all directions are preserved; the transformations preserving length; the rotations in two or three dimensions about a point; the set of all translations; and so on. Among these groups, the ones we have just mentioned are continuous; that is, the operations belonging to them are determined by the values of a number of continuously varying parameters in an appropriate space. They thus form multi-dimensional configurations in n-space, and contain sub-sets of transformations which constitute regions in such a space.

Now, just as a region in the ordinary two-dimensional plane is covered by the process of scanning known to the television engineer, by which a nearly uniformly distributed set of sample positions in that region is taken to represent the whole, so every region in a group-space, including the whole of such a space, can be represented by a process of *group scanning*. In such a process, which is by no means confined to a space of three dimensions, a net of positions in the space is traversed in a one-dimensional sequence, and this net of positions is so distributed that it comes near to every position in the region, in some appropriately defined sense. It will thus contain positions as near to any we wish as may be desired. If these "positions," or sets of parameters, are actually used to generate the appropriate transformations, it means that the results of transforming a given figure by these transformations will come as near as we wish to any given transformation of the figure by a transformation operator lying in the region desired. If our scanning is fine enough, and the region transformed has the maximum dimensionality of the regions transformed by the group considered, this means that the transformations actually traversed will give a resulting region overlapping *any* transform of the original region by an amount which is as large a fraction of its area as we wish.

Let us then start with a fixed comparison region and a region to be compared with it. If at any stage of the scanning of the group of transformations the image of the region to be compared under some one of the transformations scanned coincides more perfectly with the fixed pattern than a given tolerance allows, this is recorded, and the two regions are said to be alike. If this happens at no stage of the scanning process, they are said to be unlike. This process is perfectly adapted to mechanization, and serves as a method to identify the shape of a figure independently of its size or its orientation or of whatever transformations may be included in the group-region to be scanned.

If this region is not the entire group, it may well be that region A seems like region B, and that region B seems like region C, while region A does not seem like region C. This certainly happens in reality. A figure may not show any particular resemblance to the same figure inverted, at least in so far as the immediate impression—one not involving any of the higher processes—is concerned. Nevertheless, at each stage of its inversion, there may be a considerable range of neighboring positions which appear similar. The universal "ideas" thus formed are not perfectly distinct but shade into one another.

There are other more sophisticated means of using group scanning to abstract from the transformations of a group. The groups which we here consider have a "group measure," a probability density which depends on the transformation group itself and does not change when all the transformations of the group are altered by being preceded or followed by any specific transformation of the group. It is possible to scan the group in such a way that the density of scanning of any region of a considerable class—that is, the amount of time which the variable scanning element passes within the region in any complete scanning of the group—is closely proportional to its group measure. In the case of such a uniform scanning, if we have any quantity depending on a set S of elements transformed by the group, and if this set of elements is transformed by all the transformations of the group, let us designate the quantity depending on S by $Q(S)$, and let us use TS to express the transform of the set S by the transformation T of the group. Then $Q(TS)$ will be the value of the quantity replacing $Q(S)$ when S is replaced by TS. If we average or integrate this with respect to the group measure for the group of transformations T, we shall obtain a quantity which we may write in some such form as

$$\int Q(TS)\,dT \tag{6.01}$$

where the integration is over the group measure. Quantity 6.01 will be identical for all sets S interchangable with one another under the transformations of the group, that is, for all sets S which have in some sense the same form or *Gestalt*. It is possible to obtain an approximate comparability of form where the integration in Quantity 6.01 is over less than the whole group, if the integrand $Q(TS)$ is small over the region omitted. So much for group measure.

In recent years, there has been a good deal of attention to the problem of the prosthesis of one lost sense by another. The most dramatic of the attempts to accomplish this has been the design of reading devices for the blind, to work by the use of photoelectric cells. We shall suppose that these efforts are confined to printed matter, and even to a single type face or to a small number of type faces. We shall also suppose that the alignment of the page, the centering of the lines, the traverse from line to line are taken care of either manually or, as they may well be, automatically. These processes correspond, as we may see, to the part of our visual *Gestalt* determination which depends on muscular feedbacks and the use of our normal centering, orienting, focusing, and converging apparatus. There now ensues the problem of determining the shapes of the individual letters as the scanning apparatus passes over them in sequence. It has been suggested that this be done by the use of several photoelectric cells placed in a vertical sequence, each attached to a sound-making apparatus of a different pitch. This can be done with the black of the letters registering either as silence or as sound. Let us assume the latter case, and let us assume three photocell receptors above one another. Let them record as the three notes of a chord, let us say, with the highest note on top and the lowest note below. Then the letter capital F, let us say, will record

———————————   Duration of upper note

————————   Duration of middle note

————   Duration of lower note

The letter capital Z will record

————————

————

————————

the letter capital O

————

————   ————

————

and so on. With the ordinary help given by our ability to interpret, it should not be too difficult to read such an auditory code, not more difficult than to read Braille, for instance.

However, all this depends on one thing: the proper relation of the photocells to the vertical height of the letters. Even with standardized type faces, there still are great variations in the size of the type. Thus it is desirable for us to be able to pull the vertical scale of the scanning up or down, in order to reduce the impression of a given letter to a standard. We must at least have at our disposal, manually or automatically, some of the transformations of the vertical dilation group.

There are several ways we might do this. We might allow for a mechanical vertical adjustment of our photocells. On the other hand, we might use a rather large vertical array of photocells and change the pitch assignment with the size of type, leaving those above and below the type silent. This may be done, for example, with the aid of a schema of two sets of connectors, the inputs coming up from the photocells, and leading to a series of switches of wider and wider divergence, and the outputs a series of vertical lines, as in Fig.8. Here the single lines represent the leads from the photocells, the double lines the leads to the oscillators, the circles on the dotted lines the points of connections between incoming and outgoing leads, and the dotted lines themselves the leads whereby one or another of abank of oscillators is put into action. This was the device, to which we have referred in the introduction, designed by McCulloch for the purpose of adjusting to the height of the type face. In the first design, the selection between dotted line and dotted line was manual.

This was the figure which, when shown to Dr. von Bonin, suggested the fourth layer of the visual cortex. It was the connecting circles which suggested the neuron cell bodies of this layer, arranged in sub-layers of uniformly changing horizontal density, and size changing in the opposite direction to the density. The horizontal leads are probably fired in some cyclical order. The whole apparatus seems quite suited to the process of group scanning. There must of course be some process of recombination in time of the upper outputs.

This then was the device suggested by McCulloch as that actually used in the brain in the detection of visual *Gestalt*. It represents a type of device usable for any sort of ground

scanning. Something similar occurs in other senses as well. In the ear, the transposition of music from one fundamental pitch to another is nothing but a translation of the logarithm of the frequency, and may consequently be performed by a group-scanning apparatus.

A group-scanning assembly thus has well-defined, appropriate anatomical structure. The necessary switching may be performed by independent horizontal leads which furnish enough stimulation to shift the thresholds in each level to just the proper amount tomake them fire when the lead comes on. While we do not know all the details of the performance of the machinery, it is not at all difficult to conjecture a possible machine conforming to the anatomy. In short, the ground-scanning assembly is well adapted to form the sort of permanent sub-assembly of the brain corresponding to the adders or multipliers of the numerical computing machine.

Lastly, the scanning apparatus should have a certain intrinsic period of operation which should be identifiable in the performance of the brain. The order of magnitude of this period should show in the minimum time required for making direct comparison of the shapes of objects different in size. This can be done only when the comparison is between two objects not too different in size; otherwise, it is a long-time process, suggestive of the action of a non-specific assembly. When direct comparison seems to be possible, it appears to take a time of the order of magnitude of a tenth of a second. This also seems to accord with the order of magnitude of the time needed by excitation to stimulate all the layers of transverse connectors in cyclical sequence.

While this cyclical process then might be a locally determined one, there is evidence that there is a widespread synchronism in different parts of the cortex, suggesting that it is driven from some clocking center. In fact, it has the order of frequency appropriate for the alpha rhythm of the brain, as shown in electroencephalograms. We may suspect that this alpha rhythm is associated with form perception, and that it partakes of the nature of a sweep rhythm, like the rhythm shown in the scanning process of a television apparatus. It disappears in deep sleep, and seems to be obscured and overlaid with other rhythms, precisely as we might expect, when we are actually looking at something and the sweep rhythm is acting as something like a carrier for other rhythms and activities. It's most marked when the eyes are closed in waking, or when we are staring into space at nothing in particular, as in the condition of abstraction of a yogi,[1] when it shows an almost perfect periodicity.We have just seen that the problem of sensory prosthesis—the problem of replacing the information normally conveyed

[1]Personal communication of Dr. W. Grey Walter, of Bristol, England.

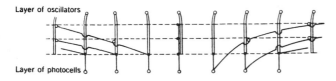

Layer of oscillators

Layer of photocells

Figure 8

through a lost sense by information through another sense still available—is important and not necessarily insoluble. What makes it more hopeful is the fact that the memory and association areas, normally approached through one sense, are not locks with a single key but are available to store impressions gathered from other senses than the one to which they normally belong. A blinded man, as distinguished perhaps from one congenitally blind, not only retains visual memories earlier in date than his accident but is even able to store tactile and auditory impressions in a visual form. He may feel this way around a room, and yet have an image of how it ought to look.

Thus a part of his normal visual mechanism is accessible to him. On the other hand, he has lost more than his eyes: he has also lost the use of that part of his visual cortex which may be regarded as a fixed assembly for organizing the impressions of sight. It is necessary to equip him not only with artificial visual receptors but with an artificial visual cortex, which will translate the light impressions on his new receptors into a form so related to the normal output of his visual cortex that objects which ordinarily look alike will now sound alike.

Thus the criterion of the possibility of such a replacement of sight by hearing is at least in part a comparison between the number of recognizably different visual patterns and recognizably different auditory patterns *at the cortical level*. This is a comparison of amounts of information. In view of the somewhat similar organization of the different parts of the sensory cortex, it will probably not differ very much from a comparison between the areas of the two parts of the cortex. This is about 100:1 as between sight and sound. If all the auditory cortex were used for vision, we might expect to get a quantity of reception of information about 1 per cent of that coming in through the eye. On the other hand, our usual scale for the estimation of vision is in terms of the relative distance at which a certain degree of resolution of pattern is obtained, and thus a 10/100 vision means an amount of flow of information about 1 per cent of normal. This is very poor vision; it is, however, definitely not blindness, nor do people with this amount of vision necessarily consider themselves as blind.

In the other direction, the picture is even more favorable. The eye can detect all of the nuances of the ear with the use of only 1 per cent of its facilities, and still leave a vision of about 95/100, which is substantially perfect. Thus the problem of sensory prosthesis is an extremely hopeful field of work.

VII   Cybernetics and Psychopathology

It is necessary that I commence this chapter with a disavowal. On the one hand, I am not a psychopathologist nor a psychiatrist, and lack any experience in a field where the guidance of experience is the only trustworthy one. On the other hand, our knowledge of the normal performance of the brain and the nervous system, and *a fortiori* our knowledge of their abnormal performance, is far from having reached that state of perfection where an *a priori* theory can command any confidence. I therefore wish to disclaim in advance any assertion that any particular entity in psychopathology, as for example any of the morbid conditions described by Kraepelin and his disciples, is due to a specific type of defect in the organization of the brain as a computing machine. Those who may draw such specific conclusions from the considerations of this book do so at their own risk.

Nevertheless, the realization that the brain and the computing machine have much in common may suggest new and valid approaches to psychopathology and even to psychiatrics. These begin with perhaps the simplest question of all: how the brain avoids gross blunders, gross miscarriages of activity, due to the malfunction of individual components. Similar questions referring to the computing machine are of great practical importance, for here a chain of operations, each covering a fraction of a millisecond, may last a matter of hours or days. It is quite possible for a chain of computational operations to involve 10^9 separate steps. Under these circumstances, the chance that at least one operation will go amiss is very far from negligible, even though, it is true, the reliability of modern electronic apparatus has far exceeded the most sanguine expectations.

In ordinary computational practice by hand or by desk machines, it is the custom to check every step of the computation and, when an error is found, to localize it by a backward process starting from the first point where the error is noted. To do this with a high-speed machine, the check must proceed with the speed of the original machine, or the whole effective order of speed of the machine will conform to that of the slower process of checking. Furthermore, if the machine is made to keep all intermediate records of its performance, its complication and bulk will be increased to an intolerable point, by a factor which is likely to be enormously greater than 2 or 3.

A much better method of checking, and in fact the one generally used in practice, is to refer every operation simultaneously to two or three separate mechanisms. In the case of the use of two such mechanisms, their answers are automatically collated against each other; and if there is a discrepancy, all data are transferred to permanent storage, the machine stops, and a signal is sent to the operator that something is wrong. The operator then compares the results, and is guided by them in his search for the malfunctioning part, perhaps a tube which has burnt out and needs replacement. If three separate mechanisms are used for each stage and single misfunctions are as rare as they are in fact, there will practically always be an agreement between two of the three mechanisms, and this agreement will give the required result. In this case, the collation mechanism accepts the majority report, and the machine need not stop; but there is a signal indicating where and how the minority report differs from the majority report. If this occurs at the first moment of discrepancy, the indication of the position of the error may be very precise. In a well-designed machine, no particular element is assigned to a particular stage in the sequence of operations, but at each stage there is a searching process, quite similar to that used in automatic telephone exchanges, which finds the first available element of a given sort and switches it into the sequence of operations. In this case, the removal and replacement of defective elements need not be the source of any appreciable delay.

It is conceivable and not implausible that at least two of the elements of this process are also represented in the nervous system. We can hardly expect that any important message is entrusted for transmission to a single neuron, nor that any important operation is entrusted to a single neuronal mechanism. Like the computing machine, the brain probably works on a variant of the famous principle expounded by Lewis Carroll in *The Hunting of the Snark:* "What I tell you three times is true." It is also improbable that the various channels available for the transfer of information generally go from one end of their course to the other without anastomosing. It is much more probable that when a message comes in to a certain level of the nervous system, it may leave that point and proceed to the next by one or more alternative members of what is known as an "internuncial pool." There may be parts of the nervous system, indeed, where this interchangeability is much limited or abolished, and these are likely to be such highly specialized parts of the cortex as those which serve as the inward extensions of the organs of special sense. Still, the principle holds, and probably holds most clearly for the relatively unspecialized cortical areas which serve the purpose of association and of what we call the higher mental functions.

So far we have been considering errors in performance which are normal, and pathological only in an extended sense. Let us now turn to those which are much more clearly pathological. Psychopathology has been rather a disappointment to the instinctive materialism of the doctors, who have taken the point of view that every disorder must be accompanied by material lesions of some specific tissue involved. It is true that specific brain lesions, such as injuries, tumors, clots, and the like, may be accompanied by psychic symptoms, and that certain mental diseases, such as paresis, are the sequellae of general bodily disease and show a pathological condition of the brain tissue; but there is no way of identifying the brain of a schizophrenic of one of the strict Kraepelin types, nor of a manic-depressive patient, nor of a paranoiac. These disorders we call *functional,* and this distinction seems to contravene the dogma of modern materialism that every disorder in function has some physiological or anatomical basis in the tissues concerned.

This distinction between functional and organic disorders receives a great deal of light from the consideration of the computing machine As we have already seen, it is not the empty physical structure of the computing machine that corresponds to the brain—to the adult brain, at least—but the combination of this structure with the instructions given it at the beginning of a chain of operations and with all the additional information stored and gained from outside in the course of this chain. This information is stored in some physical form—in the form of memory—but part of it is in the form of circulating memories, with a physical basis which vanishes when the machine is shut down or the brain dies, and part in the form of long-time memories, which are stored in a way at which we can only guess, but probably also in a form with a physical basis which vanishes at death. There is no way yet known for us to recognize in the cadaver what the threshold of a given synapse has been in life; and even if we knew this, there is no way we can trace out the chain of neurons and synapses communicating with this, and determine the significance of this chain for the ideational content which it records.

There is therefore nothing surprising in considering the functional mental disorders as fundamentally diseases of memory, of the circulating information kept by the brain in the active state, and of the long-time permeability of synapses. Even the grosser disorders such as paresis may produce a large part of their effects not so much by the destruction of tissue which they involve and the alteration of synaptic thresholds as by the secondary disturbances of traffic—the overload of what remains of the nervous system and the re-routing of messages—which must follow such primary injuries.

In a system containing a large number of neurons, circular processes can hardly be stable for long periods of time. Either, as in the case of memories belonging to the specious present, they run their course, dissipate themselves, and die out, or they comprehend more and more neurons in their system, until they occupy an inordinate part of the neuron pool. This is what we should expect to be the case in the malignant worry which accompanies anxiety neuroses. In such a case, it is possible that the patient simply does not have the room, the sufficient number of neurons, to carry out his normal processes of thought. Under such conditions, there may be less going on in the brain to load up the neurons not yet affected, so that they are all the more readily involved in the expanding process. Furthermore, the permanent memory becomes more and more deeply involved, and the pathological process which occurred at first at the level of the circulating memories may repeat itself in a more intractable form at the level of the permanent memories. Thus what started as a relatively trivial and accidental reversal of stability may build itself up into a process totally destructive to the ordinary mental life.

Pathological processes of a somewhat similar nature are not unknown in the case of mechanical or electrical computing machines. A tooth of a wheel may slip under just such conditions that no tooth with which it engages can pull it back into its normal relations, or a high-speed electrical computing machine may go into a circular process which there seems to be no way to stop. These contingencies may depend on a highly improbable instantaneous configuration of the system, and, when remedied, may never—or very rarely—repeat themselves. However, when they occur, they temporarily put the machine out of action.

How do we deal with these accidents in the use of the machine? The first thing which we try is to clear the machine of all information, in the hope that when it starts again with different data the difficulty may not recur. Failing this, if the difficulty is in some point permanently or temporarily inaccessible to the clearing mechanism, we shake the machine or, if it is electrical, subject it to an abnormally large electrical impulse, in the hope that we may reach the inaccessible part and throw it into a position where the false cycle of its activities will be interrupted. If even this fails, we may disconnect an erring part of the apparatus, for it is possible that what yet remains may be adequate for our purpose.

Now there is no normal process except death which completely clears the brain from all past impressions; and after death, it is impossible to set it going again. Of all normal processes, sleep comes the nearest to a non-pathological clearing. How often we find that the best way to handle a complicated worry or an intellectual muddle is to sleep over it! However, sleep does not clear away the deeper memories, nor indeed is a sufficiently malignant state of worry compatible with an adequate sleep. We are thus often forced to resort to more violent types of intervention in the memory cycle. The more violent of these involve a surgical intervention into the brain, leaving behind it permanent damage, mutilation, and the abridgment of the powers of the victim, as the mammalian central nervous system seems to possess no powers whatever of regeneration. The principal type of surgical intervention which has been practiced is known as prefrontal lobotomy, and consists in the removal or isolation of a portion of the prefrontal lobe of the cortex. It has recently been having a certain vogue, probably not unconnected with the fact that it makes the custodial care of many patients easier. Let me remark in passing that killing them makes their custodial care still easier. However, prefrontal lobotomy does seem to have a genuine effect on malignant worry, not by bringing the patient nearer to a solution of his problems but by damaging or destroying the capacity for maintained worry, known in the terminology of another profession as the *conscience*. More generally, it appears to limit all aspects of the circulating memory, the ability to keep in mind a situation not actually presented.

The various forms of shock treatment—electric, insulin, metrazol—are less drastic methods of doing a very similar thing. They do not destroy brain tissue or at least are not intended to destroy it, but they do have a decidedly damaging effect on the memory. In so far as this concerns the circulating memory, and in so far as this memory is chiefly damaged for the recent period of mental disorder, and is probably scarcely worth preserving anyhow, shock treatment has something definite to recommend it as against lobotomy; but it is not always free from deleterious effects on the permanent memory and the personality. As it stands at present, it is another violent, imperfectly understood, imperfectly controlled method to interrupt a mental vicious circle. This does not prevent its being in many cases the best thing we can do at present.

Lobotomy and shock treatment are methods which by their very nature are more suited to handle vicious circulating memories and malignant worries than the deeper-seated permanent memories, though it is not impossible that they may have some effect here too. As we have said, in long-established cases of mental disorder, the permanent memory is as badly deranged as the circulating memory. We do not seem to possess any purely pharmaceutical or surgical weapon for intervening differentially in the permanent memory. This is where psychoanalysis and other similar psychotherapeutic measures come in. Whether psychoanalysis is taken in the orthodox Freudian sense or in the modified senses of Jung and of Adler, or whether our psychotherapy is not strictly psychoanalytic at all, our treatment is clearly based on the concept that the stored information of the mind lies on many levels of accessibility and is much richer and more varied than that which is accessible by direct unaided introspection; that it is vitally conditioned by affective experiences which we cannot always uncover by such introspection, either because they never were made explicit in our adult language, or because they have been buried by a definite mechanism, affective. though generally involuntary; and that the content of these stored experiences, as well as their affective tone, conditions much of our later activity in ways which may well be pathological. The technique of the psychoanalyst consists in a series of means to discover and interpret these hidden memories, to make the patient accept them for what they are and by their acceptance modify, if not their content, at least the affective tone they carry, and thus make them less harmful. All this is perfectly consistent with the point of view of this book. It perhaps explains, too, why there are circumstances where a joint use of shock treatment and psychotherapy is indicated, combining a physical or pharmacological therapy for the phenomena of reverberation in the nervous system, and a psychological therapy for the long-time memories which, without interference, might re-establish from within the vicious circle broken up by the shock treatment.

We have already mentioned the traffic problem of the nervous system. It has been commented on by many writers, such as D'Arcy Thompson,[1] that each form of organization has an upper limit of size, beyond which it will not function. Thus the insect organization is limited by the length of tubing over which the spiracle method of bringing air by diffusion directly to the breathing tissues will function; a land animal cannot be so big that the legs or other portions in contact with the ground will be crushed by its weight; a tree is limited by the mechanism for transferring water and minerals from the roots to the leaves, and the products of photosynthesis from the leaves to the roots; and so on. The same sort of thing is observed in engineering constructions. Skyscrapers are limited in size by the fact that when they exceed a certain height, the elevator space needed for the upper stories consumes an excessive part of the cross section of the lower floors. Beyond a certain span, the best-possible suspension bridge which can be built out of materials with given elastic properties will collapse under its own weight, and beyond a certain greater span, *any* structure built of a given material or materials will collapse under its own weight. Similarly, the size of a single telephone central, built according to a constant, non-expanding plan, is limited, and this limitation has been very thoroughly studied by telephone engineers.

In a telephone system, the important limiting factor is the fraction of the time during which a subscriber will find it impossible to put a call through. A 99 per cent chance of success will certainly be satisfactory for even the most exacting; 90 per cent of successful calls is probably good enough to permit business to be carried on with reasonable facility. A success of 75 per cent is already annoying but

[1]Thompson, D'Arcy, *On Growth and Form,* Amer. ed., The Macmillan Company, New York, 1942.

will permit business to be carried on after a fashion; while if half the calls end in failures, subscribers will begin to ask to have their telephones taken out. Now, these represent over-all figures. If the calls go through n distinct stages of switching, and probability of failure is independent and equal for each stage, in order to get a probability of total success equal to p, the probability of success at each stage must be $p^{1/n}$. Thus to obtain a 75 per cent chance of the completioin of the call after five stages, we must have about 95 per cent chance of success per stage. To obtain a 90 per cent performance, we must have 98 per cent chance of success at each stage. To obtain a 50 per cent performance, we must have 87 per cent chance of success at each stage. It will be seen that the more stages which are involved, the more rapidly the service becomes extremely bad when a critical level of failure for the individual call is exceeded, and extremely good when this critical level of failure is not quite reached. Thus a switching service involving many stages and designed for a certain level of failure shows no obvious signs of failure until the traffic comes up to the edge of the critical point, when it goes completely to pieces, and we have a catastrophic traffic jam.

Man, with the best-developed nervous system of all the animals, with behavior that probably depends on the longest chains of effectively operated neuronic chains, is then likely to perform a complicated type of behavior efficiently very close to the edge of an overload, when he will give way in a serious and catastropohic way. This overload may take place in several ways: either by an excess in the amount of traffic to be carried, by a physical removal of channels for the carrying of traffic, or by the excessive occupation of such channels by undesirable systems of traffic, like circulating memories which have increased to the extent of becoming pathological worries. In all these cases, a point will come—quite suddenly—when the normal traffic will not have space enough allotted to it, and we shall have a form of mental breakdown, very possibly amounting to insanity.

This will first affect the faculties or operations involving the longest chains of neurons. There is appreciable evidence that these are precisely the processes which are recognized to be the highest in our ordinary scale of valuation. The evidence is this: a rise in temperature within nearly physiological limits is known to produce an increase in the ease of performance of most if not of all neuronic processes. This is greater for the higher processes, roughly in the order of our usual estimate of their degree of "highness." Now, any facilitation of a process in a single neuron-synapse system should be cumulative as the neuron is combined in series with other neurons. Thus the amount of assistance a process receives through a rise in temperature is a rough measure of the length of the neuron chain it involves.

We thus see that the superiority of the human brain to others in the length of the neuron chains it employs is a reason why mental disorders are certainly most conspicuous and probably most common in man. There is another more specific way of considering a very similar matter. Let us first consider two brains geometrically similar, with the weights of gray and of white matter related by the same factor of proportionality, but with different linear dimensions in the ratio $A : B$. Let the volume of the cell bodies in the gray matter and the cross sections of the fibers in the white matter be of the same size in both brains. Then the number of cell bodies in the two cases bears the ratio $A^3 : B^3$, and the number of long-distance connectors the ratio $A^2 : B^2$. This means that for the same density of activity in the cells, the density of activity in the fibers is $A : B$ times as great in the case of the large brain as in that of the small brain.

If we compare the human brain with that of a lower mammal, we shall find that it is much more convoluted. The relative thickness of the gray matter is much the same, but it is spread over a far more involved system of gyri and sulci. The effect of this is to increase the amount of gray matter at the expense of the amount of white matter. Within a gyrus, this decrease of the white matter is largely a decrease in length rather than in number of fibers, as the opposing folds of a gyrus are nearer together than they would be on a smooth-surfaced brain of the same size. On the other hand, when it comes to the connectors between different gyri, the distance they have to run is increased if anything by the convolution of the brain. Thus the human brain would seem to be fairly efficient in the matter of the short-distance connectors, but quite defective in the matter of long-distance trunk lines. This means that in case of a traffic jam the processes involving parts of the brain quite remote from one another should suffer first. That is, processes involving several centers, a number of different motor processes, and a considerable number of association areas should be among the least stable in cases of insanity. These are precisely the processes which we should normally class as higher, and we obtain another confirmation of our expectation, which seems to be verified by experience, that the higher processes deteriorate first in insanity.

There is some evidence that the long-distance paths in the brain have a tendency to run outside of the cerebrum altogether and to traverse the lower centers. This is indicated by the remarkably small damage done by cutting some of the long-distance cerebral loops of white matter. It almost seems as if these superficial connections were so inadequate that they furnish only a small part of the connections really needed.

With reference to this, the phenomena of handedness and of hemispheric dominance are interesting. Handedness seems to occur in the lower mammals, though it is less conspicuous than in man, probably in part because of the lower degree of organizatioin and skill demanded by the tasks which they perform. Nevertheless, the choice between the right and the left side in muscular skill does actually seem to be less than in man even in the lower primates.

The right-handedness of the normal man, as is well known, is generally associated with a left-brainedness, and the left-handedness of a minority of humans with a right-brainedness. That is, the cerebral functions are not distributed evenly over the two hemispheres, and one of these, the dominant hemisphere, has the lion's share of the higher functions. It is true that many essentially bilateral functions—those involving the fields of vision, for example—are represented each in its appropriate hemisphere, though this is not true for *all* bilateral functions. However, most of the "higher" areas are confined to the dominant hemisphere. For example, in the adult, the effect of an extensive injury in the secondary hemisphere is far less serious than the effect of a similar injury in the dominant hemisphere. At a relatively early age in his career, Pasteur suffered a cerebral hemorrhage on his right side which left him with a moderate degree of one-sided paralysis, a hemiplegia. When he died, his brain was examined, and he was found to be suffering from a right-sided injury, so extensive that it has been said that after his injury "he had only half a brain." There certainly were extensive lesions of the parietal and temporal regions. Nevertheless, after this injury he did some of his best work. A similar injury of the left side in a right-handed adult would almost certainly have been fatal and would certainly reduce the patient into an animal condition of mental and nervous crippledness.

It is said that the situation is considerably better in early infancy, and that in the first six months of life an extensive injury to the dominant hemisphere may compel the normally secondary hemisphere to take its place; so that the patient appears far more nearly normal than he would be had the injury occurred at a later stage. This is quite in accordance with the general great flexibility shown by the nervous system in the early weeks of life, and the great rigidity which it rapidly develops later. It is possible that, short of such serious injuries, handedness is reasonably flexible in the very young child. However, long before the child is of school age, the natural handedness and cerebral dominance are established for life. It used to be thought that left-handedness was a serious social disadvantage. With most tools, school desks, and sports equipment primarily made for the right-handed, it certainly is to some extent. In the past, moreover, it was viewed with some of the superstitious disapproval that has attached to so many minor variations from the human norm, such as birthmarks or red hair. From a combination of motives, many people have attempted and even succeeded, in changing the external handedness of their children by education, though of course they could not change its physiological basis in hemispheric dominance. It was then found that in very many cases these hemispheric changelings suffered from stuttering and other defects of speech, reading, and writing, to the extent of seriously wounding their prospects in life and their hopes for a normal career.

We now see at least one possible explanation for the phenomenon. With the education of the secondary hand, there has been a partial education of that part of the secondary hemisphere which deals with skilled motions, such as writing. Since, however, these motions are carried out in the closest possible association with reading, speech, and other activities which are inseparably connected with the dominant hemisphere, the neuron chains involved in processes of the sort must cross over from hemisphere to hemisphere and back; and in a process of any complication, they must do this again and again. Now, the direct connectors between the hemispheres—the cerebral commissures—in a brain as large as that of man are so few in number that they are of very little use, and the inter-hemispheric traffic must go by roundabout routes through the brain stem, which we know very imperfectly but which are certainly long, scanty, and subject to interruption. As a consequence, the processes associated with speech and writing are very likely to be involved in a traffic jam, and stuttering is the most natural thing in the world.

That is, the human brain is probably too large already to use in an efficient manner all the facilities which seem to be anatomically present. In a cat, the destruction of the dominant hemisphere seems to produce relatively less damage than in man, and the destruction of the secondary hemisphere probably more damage. At any rate, the apportionment of function in the two hemispheres is more nearly equal. In man, the gain achieved by the increase in size and complication of the brain is partly nullified by the fact that less of the organ can be used effectively at one time. It is interesting to reflect that we may be facing one of those limitations of nature in which highly specialized organs reach a level of declining efficiency and ultimately lead to the extinction of the species. The human brain may be as far along on its road to this destructive specialization as the great nose horns of the last of the titanotheres.

3
Introduction

(1961)
E. R. Caianiello

Outline of a theory of thought-processes and thinking machines
Journal of Theoretical Biology 2: 204–235

This paper by E. R. Caianiello describes a *big* theory, where an extremely general approach is taken toward mental function in an attempt to understand it all, or at least a big chunk of it. As Caianiello says, "Our main guiding principle has been the conviction ... that the human brain, tremendous in its complexity, yet obeys, if one looks at the operations of individual neurons, dynamical laws that are not necessarily complicated; and that these laws are such as to engender in large neuronal assemblies collective modes of behavior, to which thought processes are correlated." This large-scale approach has fallen somewhat out of fashion in recent years, though there are other well-known examples of it in neural networks, for example, the work of McCulloch and Pitts (paper 2, in *Neurocomputing: Foundations of Research*).

Caianiello proposes two sets of equations for brain operation, corresponding to different system time scales. The first set of equations is called the *neuronic equations* and corresponds to the immediate dynamics of the neural network. The second set of equations he proposes are called the *mnemonic equations*, which describe the changes in connection strengths in the network with past activity, that is, learning rules.

The model neuron assumed by Caianiello is related to the McCulloch-Pitts neuron. Time in the system is quantized, and the unit has only two allowable states: one and zero. The neuron sums its inputs and changes state if the sum is greater than a threshold. The neuronic equations describe the entire set of neurons, that is, a single neuron is embedded in a nervous system and the emphasis throughout the paper is on patterns of activity shown by the entire set of neurons. The model neurons can receive inputs not only from the immediately past time quantum, but from time quanta many steps in the past, a way of representing effects like refractory period, which may render a cell insensitive for several time quanta. The emphasis throughout the paper is on what Caianiello clearly thinks of as distributed patterns with many active cells.

The mnemonic equations describe how the synapses change with system activity. These equations contain a "Hebb" component in that the rate of change of the connection strength has a term with the product of the pre- and postsynaptic activation, though the expression is complicated by the presence of other terms. Caianiello restricts the magnitude of the connection strength to a maximum value, so that synapses cannot grow indefinitely strong. One common criticism of the simplest versions of Hebb synapses has been that connection strengths can grow in magnitude without limits.

The equations are applied on two different time scales, related by what Caianiello calls the *Adiabatic Learning Hypothesis*, which simply states that learning occurs on a very slow time scale relative to system dynamics, that is, connection strengths coupling elements together do not change as the system changes in time according to the neuronic equations.

This is an intriguing assumption, not least because it is unconsciously accepted in most neural network models. In the standard network model there are a set of connections, with strengths, coupling units together. The input-output relations that the system generates are the computations that the network performs. Learning is what sets the connection strengths during a specific learning period. It is unusual to find a model where the connection strengths change continuously while the system is evolving. Besides complicating the mathematics of system dynamics, there are also some difficult technical problems with system stability if learning occurs rapidly.

However, both the physiological and psychological data indicate a wide range of time scales for learning. The effects described loosely as *adaptation* can occur quickly, as well as more slowly. Many *attentional* effects require what amounts to very rapid connection strength changes (see Crick, paper 34 in *Neurocomputing: Foundations of Research*). The models for short-term plasticity of von der Malsburg and Bienenstock (1986) depend almost entirely on very short-term Hebbian modification as a way to "unify" different parts of a perception. And, interestingly, the physiological short-term plasticity observed in the NMDA synapse (see Brown et al., paper 24) is very rapid. It is sometimes possible to analyze systems with relatively fast learning. One example (of many) of such an analyzed neural network is a paper by Kawamoto and Anderson (1985), which models multistable perception of the Necker cube, the well-known reversing cube illusion.

Caianiello's equations are much too complex to solve in detail. However, it is possible to make a number of qualitative statements about system structure. A major concern in all networks with feedback is system stability. The problem is compounded greatly if learning rules that respond to correlations are used—for example, Hebb synapses—because large groups of neurons will tend to mutually excite each other more and more strongly, and their mutual connection strengths will increase. However, at the same time, mutual excitation gives rise to much of the most interesting behavior of the network and is used as an organizing principle in models such as Hebbian cell assemblies or Edelman's neuronal groups (see papers 18 and 19). Unfortunately a network pathology that is surprisingly easy to obtain in simulation is for very large groups of units to turn on and off in synchrony. This behavior looks something like what is called epilepsy when it happens in the nervous system.

Caianiello suggests several network stability mechanisms, including proper choice of initial connections and adaptation effects that modify the threshold. Cortical pyramidal cells mutually excite each other by way of an extensive network of recurrent collaterals, yet the overall system is remarkably resistant to instability (Shepherd 1979). Biologically there are multiple mechanisms used to maintain system stability including inhibitory gain contol mechanisms that damp excess activity. The poison strychnine, for example, disables one kind of cortical inhibition, causing uncontrolled activity with seizures.

One of the most interesting and unusual aspects of the paper for readers today is the analysis of the network in terms of its reverberations. Caianiello sees the system as operating by a kind of nonlinear reverberatory "Fourier" analysis, inspired by the kinds of nonlinear analysis pioneered by Norbert Wiener (see paper 2). The system develops a number of long time period reverberations at characteristic frequencies. These reverberations can be excited by particular patterns in the input to the system, hence patterns can be represented by their particular combinations of Fourier components.

The discussion in the last section, 5.B.2, of a linearized version of the neuronic equations in terms of eigenvalues and eigenfunctions foreshadows some later neural net models. As described in several papers in section III, principal component analysis involves determining the eigenvectors of what amounts to a Hebbian connectivity matrix. (See Linsker, paper 31; Cottrell, Munro and Zipser, paper 32; and Baldi and Hornik, paper 33; as well as Pellionisz and Llinás, paper 20. See also paper 22 in *Neurocomputing: Foundations of Research*.) Particularly interesting is Caianiello's analysis of developmental learning in terms of eigenvalues, where a network progresses from an "infant" network, through adulthood, to senility based on the qualitative behavior of its eigenvalues.

This paper is striking in its emphasis on the centrality of large-scale system behavior and patterns of activity defined over the entire set of units. Information is never localized, in fact the behavior of individual units is almost never mentioned, only as component parts of groups of active units. This use of system-wide parameters as the critical parameters in the understanding and control of the network is also found in even stronger form in Wiener's work (paper 2) and may be the only satisfactory way of working with extremely complex networks.

In 1989 Caianiello reviewed three decades of his neural network research, beginning with this 1961 paper, in a book chapter. It is a short technical account of both this model and its extensions and contains an extensive list of references to later work. In an interesting brief historical introduction to this review, Caianiello acknowledges his "profound indebtedness" to both Warren McCulloch and Norbert Wiener and comments that Wiener stayed at Caianiello's institution in Naples for a year and a half. Perhaps some of his interest in the significance of long time constant network oscillations and loops of activity arises from that interaction.

References

E.R. Caianiello (1989), A theory of neural networks. In I. Alexsander (Ed.), *Neural Computing Architectures*. Cambridge, MA: MIT Press.

A.H. Kawamoto and J.A. Anderson (1985), A neural network model of multistable perception. *Acta Psychologica* 59: 35–65.

G.M. Shepherd (1979), *The Synaptic Organization of the Brain*, 2nd edition. Oxford: Oxford University Press.

C. v.d.Malsburg and E. Bienenstock (1986), Statistical coding and short term synaptic plasticity: A scheme for knowledge representation in the brain. In E. Bienenstock, F. Fogelman-Soulie, and G. Weisbuch, *Disordered Systems and Biological Organization*. Berlin: Springer.

(1961)

E. R. Caianiello

Outline of a theory of thought-processes and thinking machines
Journal of Theoretical Biology 2: 204–235

Thought-processes and certain typical mental phenomena are schematized into exact mathematical definitions, in terms of a theory which, with the assumption that learning is a relatively slow process, reduces to two sets of equations: "neuronic equations", with fixed coefficients, which determine the instantaneous behavior, "mnemonic equations", which determine the long-term behavior of a "model of the brain" or "thinking machine". A qualitative but rigorous discussion shows that this machine exhibits, as a necessary consequence of the theory, many properties that are typical of the living brain: including need to "sleep", ability spontaneously to form new ideas (patterns) which associate old ones, self-organization towards more reliable operation, and many others. Future works will deal with the quantitative solution of these equations and with concrete problems of construction—things that appear reasonably feasible. With a transposition of names, this theory could be applied to many sorts of social or, more generally, "collective" problems.

1. Introduction

A. Levels of Approach

Attempts at a quantitative understanding and analysis of thought-processes, with or without the explicit aim of devising machines that should reproduce functions typical of the living nervous system, date as far back as Ramon Lull's syllogistic wheels. They have become a recognized and major part of scientific investigation since N. Wiener's celebrated enunciation of the principles of Cybernetics; herein lies indeed clearly, much more than in specialized studies of circuitry or of information theory, the heart and scope of this new science, which aims at synthesis as well as analysis.

The investigation of the mechanism of thought has been undertaken with a variety of methods, ranging e.g. from the study of systems that should mechanize the operations of Aristotelian logic without any requirement of similarity to living structures, to the faithful electronic reproduction of populations of hundreds or thousands of neurons. We shall benefit from all these discussions in that they permit us to reduce the verbal presentation of our own concepts to a bare minimum, since they have made abundantly clear with what cautions and restrictions one should accept for example the very expression "mechanical thought"; otherwise we shall restrict our treatment exclusively to the presentation of our approach to this problem, as we feel that in such a field judgment is passed better *a posteriori* than a *priori*, on the ground of concrete results—which are yet to be borne by any theory, including ours—than of mere opinion.

The present outline of a theory of thought-processes is the result of about three years of discussions with people who have been working with the same premises in various fields of neuroanatomy, mathematics and theoretical physics; it also reflects, of course, the evolution of our own ideas through many discussions with guests and hosts. Our main guiding principle has been the conviction, strengthened by these discussions, that the human brain, tremendous in its complexity, yet obeys, if one looks at the operation of individual neurons, dynamical laws that are not necessarily complicated; and that these laws are such as to engender in large neuronal assemblies collective modes of behavior, to which thought-processes are correlated. A convenient formulation of these laws appears therefore as the primary objective of a research of this nature; it can only be achieved by trial and error by the process, familiar in the physical sciences, of abstracting what seems relevant into a simplified model of the real thing. The present work is one such trial; its novelty is not, of course, in the concepts just mentioned, which are as old as physics itself, although they have not yet gained general acceptance among neurophysiologists, but in the attempt made here to give them a precise and quantitative formulation.

Constant resort to neuroanatomy and neurophysiology, which is the keystone of our approach, appears necessary at two different levels: the "elementary level", which studies the individual neurons and the connections, or synapses, between neurons; the "integrative level", which studies the structure and function of specially connected assemblies of neurons, which may act as a whole and play in the nervous system a rôle similar to that of specialized organs in the body. The integrative level compares with the first as the physics of matter does with that of the atom, and is of course as essential to the understanding of the functions of a brain or of a thinking machine; we firmly believe, against the opposite views which we have heard expressed, that a study at the elementary level is as essential to the second as one type of physics is to the other.

We shall have very little to say here about the integrative approach, in which many more investigations are needed before a satisfactory state of knowledge is achieved, except that our equations, once the appropriate connections among neurons of a given assembly are introduced into them, will permit the quantitative study of its collective behavior as a whole. It is our belief that the subsystems of a brain are quite different, in structure and complication, from the standard circuits of electronics, and that there will be a great deal to learn in this respect from neuroanatomy; also, that a thinking machine built for some special purpose may well need organs, or subsystems, organized quite differently from those of the animal brain, although the same elementary laws will be valid. Our equations are also intended to provide a useful tool both for theoretical study and for experimentation in this respect.

Because of the lack of definite knowledge and of general agreement among specialists on many facts of neuroanatomy and neurophysiology on one hand, and of the great wealth of available observational material on the other, we think it best to present our views as the direct description, reduced to bare essentials, of a *model* of the brain forgoing the detailed analysis of anatomical data from which, in fact, our considerations stem.

B. The Model

By "model" or "machine" we mean exclusively a device *that can actually be built,* and which operates according to mathematical equations that are *exactly known and numerically solvable* to any wanted accuracy. Although this necessarily implies drastic schematizations and simplifications, it is hoped that the features essential to thought-production are retained by the model; successive approximations to reality will require improvements in the structure of the machine and in its operational laws, but at each step one must know exactly what is being done. Without a complete mathematical control of the situation, a machine may perhaps think, but one would hardly know why or how.

Mathematically, our model consists of two sets of equations: the "neuronic equations", which describe the instantaneous operation of the machine; the "mnemonic equations", which describe the growth of memory into it. From these equations it is possible to predict and study the "mental" phenomena which are typical of such a machine: learning, forgetting, re-integration, conditioning, analysis of patterns and spontaneous formation of new patterns, self-organization into reliable operation. An exact mathematical definition is given of each of these phenomena; that they do actually take place is shown, qualitatively but rigorously, from the form of both sets of equations; methods for the quantitative solution of these are in part already

available and will be discussed in a future work. Likewise, although we are actively engaged also in the study of the concrete aspects of the question, we shall limit the present report to an outline of the mathematical theory.

c. Normal Physiological Model

Finally, we wish to emphasize that our machine does not purport to realize necessarily *an anatomical model* of the brain, that is, there need be no one-to-one correspondence between the anatomical neuron and the basic unit of the machine; we are concerned here only with the description of a *physiological model,* in which, as a whole, it is irrelevant whether the functions of a single neuron are taken up by a single unit or by a group of units in the machine, or vice-versa. Likewise, one could reproduce the functions of a circuit containing electronic tubes of various descriptions in terms, say, of a model circuit containing only triodes. We wish to emphasize also that our model intends to simulate the physiology of neurons in their *normal* condition in the living tissue, and not at all the various reactions they exhibit when tortured in the physiologist's laboratory: most of the latter will be as irrelevant to the study of the collective behavior of neuronal assemblies, as is the detailed knowledge of the radiation spectra of Na and Cl ions to the determination of the crystalline structure of the NaCl salt.

2. Symbols

$1(x) =$	unit step function
$\sum =$	Stieltjes integral or summation
$h, k, i, r =$	indices denoting integers (subscripts of superscripts
$R, N =$	fixed integers
$a_{hk}^{(r)}, A_{hk}^{(r)}, b_{hk} =$	real numbers (coupling coefficients)
$s_h =$	real numbers (thresholds)
$t =$	time variable
$\tau =$	a fixed "time quantum"
$u_h(t) =$	piece-wise-constant functions (-0 or 1 in any quantal interval of time)
$v =$	class of all functions $u_h(t)$
$c_i(t) =$	a constellation of neurons at time t
$n_i(t) =$	number of neurons of $c_i(t)$
$E =$	a fixed set of neurons
$M_E, \overline{M}_E =$	classes of solutions of eqs. (2) relative to E
$G(t) =$	group of transformations under which eqs. (2) are invariant
$\mathcal{N} =$	configuration space

$P(t) =$ representative point of system in $\mathcal{N}$

$\mathcal{F} =$ a functional space built over $\mathcal{N}$

$S(t) =$ a frame in $\mathcal{F}$

$\Theta_i, \Theta_{ij}, \ldots =$ patterns presented to, or constructed by, the machine

$f(a_{hk}; \lambda) =$ secular equation with variable λ

$\bar{\lambda}_h =$ eigenvalue of $f(a_{hk}; \lambda) = 0$

$\rho_{hk} =$ small random variation of a_{hk}

$\rho, <\delta\bar{\lambda}_h> =$ average values of ρ_{hk} and of corresponding variation of $\bar{\lambda}_h$

3. Neuronic and Mnemonic Equations

A. General Remarks

1. The present considerations aim at simplicity, rather than at formal elegance; many restrictive assumptions are therefore made which could easily be relaxed, gaining thereby a greater apparent generality in our equations but, in reality, only complication which is better avoided at this early stage. The most evident is the fact that we use throughout summations instead of integrations, although Stieltjes integrals would be in many cases more appropriate to a faithful description of the anatomical situations of interest.

Instead of considering the actual speed of propagation of the neuronic discharge along dendrites and axones, we neglect the first and lump the second together with the synaptic delay into a single time-unit τ; this is a better approximation than it may seem, because in the brain, as is well known, speed in axones is proportional to diameter and, although less generally, diameter to length. We schematize this situation by assuming that a neuron which receives a pulse (either does not fire or) fires after exactly τ sec; or, more generally, that τ denotes some conveniently small "time quantum", of which the neuronic delay times are (not necessarily equal) multiples (our neuronic equations (2), although apparently designed to describe only the first situation, also cover the second).

2. We shall base our treatment on two sets of equations: the *neuonic equations* (N.E.) which have constant coefficients and determine the instantaneous behavior of the system, and the *mnemonic equations* (M.E.) which account for the semi-permanent or permanent changes in the structure of the system caused by its past operation. This is, again, an artificial simplification of the actual situation, which is better described by retaining only the first set of equations, with coefficients taken as "slow" functions of time and past neuronic activity. The approximation thus made is analogous to the Born-Oppenheimer approximation of molecular physics, which consists in studying first the motion of the (much faster) electrons as if the nuclei were fixed, and then the behavior of the latter. It is justified physiologically by the experimental observation that electro-shock, or concussion, cancels all memories of things learnt within a previous time interval of minutes or more, while memories acquired before that time remain unimpaired: this makes it reasonable to assume that the brain takes about that much time to change the dynamical phenomena which we consider here to be the carriers of functional, short-range memories, into semi-permanent or permanent alterations. That the latter actually exist is proved by the fact that they are not suppressed by hybernation or artificially provoked cessation of all neural activity.

We may call this the *adiabatic learning hypothesis* (A.L.H.): the degree of adiabaticity of learning in the brain can be estimated roughly from the remark just made, with the conclusion that the engramming of permanent or semi-permanent memories takes roughly a time of 10^4 to 10^5 sec or more. The determination of the duration of semi-permanent memories in the brain is a task for experimental psychology, and is not discussed here.

The mathematical advantages of uncoupling the actual equations of neural activity into two distinct sets by means of the A.L.H. will be evident: by considering all constants frozen, the resulting N.E. are solvable notwithstanding their utter non-linearity, and in any case their very form leads immediately to many interesting qualitative conclusions, as we shall show later.

3. It is perhaps relevant to emphasize that the equations which we shall take as the basis of our treatment do not certainly contain, in themselves, any striking novelties. They are about what any neurophysiologist would write at once, should he wish to arithmetize, say, the kind of logic that is usually associated with neuronic circuits, or to formulate some reasonable guess about the growth of memory.

What we consider to be the essential point in our whole theory is, rather, the fact that arithmetization is considered here as the *necessary first step*: once equations are written, then, and only then in our opinion, the real groundwork can begin. Furthermore, equations alone mean very little to a mathematician; the detailed prescription of the type of information which is wanted from the solutions of a given equation constitutes a "problem", the formulation and solution of which is, in all cases, the most relevant question. We shall therefore be concerned here essentially with the formulation of problems which arise from these equations and are central to our theory of thought-processes; in so doing, we shall meet interesting and novel mathematical situations, the quantitative study of which is well under way and will be reported in the future. The qualitative discussions of Sections **4** and **5** will suffice for our present purposes.

B. Neuronic Equations

1. We take as the basic component of the machine—which for convenience we call a "neuron", although its functional relation to living neurons need not be 1 : 1—a discriminator with a large number of inputs (dendrites) and a large number of outputs (branching axons). Signals can only travel *unidirectionally,* with infinite speed, from the output of a neuron to the input of the neurons connected to it; when a signal reaches a neuron it is annihilated, unless enough signals arrive with it to cause the neuron to fire a pulse, after a delay τ, simultaneously in *all* its outputs. The intensity of these pulses may vary with the "anatomy" of the neuron, i.e. number of inputs, outputs, location in the machine, etc.; such pulses may be attenuated during propagation, or other phenomena may occur, as is discussed later. As a matter of formal convenience, we normalize all pulses to unit strength and account for larger or smaller strengths by giving suitable values to the coupling coefficients. Finally, a neuron will fire only if the total sum of afferent pulses is greater than its threshold. All coupling coefficients and thresholds are considered to be constant (adiabatic learning approximation).

We define the function:

$$1(x) = \begin{cases} +1 & \text{for } x > 0 \\ 0 & \text{for } x \leq 0 \end{cases} \qquad (1)$$

let $u_h(t)$ denote a function belonging to the class U of piece-wise-constant functions which are either constantly 0 or constantly 1 in any of the intervals $l\tau, (l+1)\tau$ (l integer $\gtreqless 0$); we take then as fundamental equations for the description of the instantaneous behavior of our machine (neuronic equations, N.E.):

$$u_h(t+\tau) = 1\left[\sum_{k,r} a_{hk}^{(r)} u_k(t-r\tau) - s_h \right] \qquad (2)$$

The meaning of the coefficients $a_{hk}^{(r)}$ and s_h is stated below; the anatomy of the machine at a given instant is described entirely by their values. (Taking $\rho_h\tau$ instead of τ at l.h.s. of (2) would not change the structure of these equations: an obvious re-naming of their coefficients would lead back to the form (2).)

2. s_h, usually > 0, is the threshold of the neuron h; the neuron h fires at time $t + \tau$ if its *excitation* at time t (given by the sum in (2)) is greater than s_h.

a_{hk}^{0} ($k \neq h$) is the *coupling coefficient* that transfers the pulse originating from neuron k to neuron h; it contains the *total effect* of the first on the second, *regardless* of the number of synapses between k and h and of the intensity

with which the stimulus coming from k reaches h along each pathway. When $a_{hk}^{(0)} \neq 0$, we say that there is a (unidirectional) *direct channel* between neuron k and neuron h, which causes a *facilitation* $k \rightarrow h$ if $a_{hk}^{(0)} > 0$, or an inhibition $k \rightarrow h$ if $a_h^{(0)} < 0$.

The rôle of the coefficients $a_{hk}^{(r)}$ ($h \neq k$) and $a_{hh}^{(r)}$ is quite different:

$a_{hk}^{(r)}$ ($h \neq k$; r integer > 0) is $\neq 0$ only if it is required that the actual mechanism of stimulation be such that the effect of the pulse from k may reach h, or last on h some time $> \tau$ after k has ceased firing; this would be the case if stimulation were due, say, to some transmitter substance released at the synaptic junction, which would be re-absorbed only after a time $> \tau$. Such a mechanism would account for latency and be related to the well-known dependence of pulse frequency on intensity of stimuli. It may not be a bad approximation, in a model, to take $a_{hk}^{(r)} = 0$ for $h \neq k$, $r > 0$, except perhaps for input elements.

The coefficients $a_{hh}^{(r)}$ express instead the memory that the neuron h retains of each of its firings (in the brain, for about 100 τ sec). For all we know, the characteristic observed shape of the neuronic discharge (as well as many other things) may well be only the result of biological necessity, and to ask that it be closely reproduced in a thinking machine might prove as binding as demanding that moving objects be built with legs rather than wheels. We shall want in any case $a_{hh}^{(r)} \ll 0$ for all values of r from $r = 0$ until $r\tau$ becomes greater than the absolute refractory time of the neuron; for the latter and higher values of r it may be convenient to follow different prescriptions, according as one wishes to study the actual behavior of the brain on this model, or instead to construct a thinking machine for some special purpose.

3. As an example (among the many that might be produced) of the fact mentioned earlier that our N.E. might be a poor description of the anatomy and yet give a faithful description of the physiology of a nervous system, we consider here the situation that would arise if, in a nerve, or bundle of fibers, the electrotonus due to axones which are carriers of pulses should induce firings in other axones of the same nerve which originate from neurons that *have not fired.*

This possibility was not contemplated when writing the N.E. (2). A model which reproduces also this new type of behavior must lead to equations such that signals can be either *transmitted directly* from neuron k to neuron $h,$ or *induced* into the channel $k \rightarrow h$ by the firing of some neighbouring neurons; the neuron h must not be able to discriminate whether the pulse it receives through that channel has a direct or induced nature. Taking for simplicity $a_{hk}^{(r)} = 0$ for $r > 0$ ($h \neq k$), we obtain clearly the wanted equations by replacing $\sum_r a_{hk}^{(r)} u_k(t - r\tau)$ in (2) with

$$a_{hk}^{(0)} u(_k t) + \sum_{k_i \neq k} b_{hk_i}^{(0)} u_{k_i}(t) \tag{3}$$

where $\sum_{k_1 \neq k}$ means sum over the neurons k_i, neighbours of k, the axones of which can act in this way on the channel $k \to h$, and $b_{hk_i}^{(0)}$ are some suitable coefficients.

It is then evident that, renaming the coefficients, one finds again N.E. of type (2). The same can be said for inter-dendritic interference.

C. Mnemonic Equations

1. There is sufficient evidence to prove that memory in the brain is due both to functional processes and to reversible and irreversible alterations of its micro-structure. Very little, if anything, is known for certain beyond this, so that we are forced to rely upon "plausible" hypotheses if we wish to assign the specific laws which determine semi-permanent or permanent physico-chemical changes. We shall not hesitate to do so for the sake of concreteness; we wish however to emphasize that the qualitative analysis of thought-processes which is the purpose of this work does not require precise knowledge of these laws, but only that they share some very general features, which may be assumed with much greater reliability.

Here lies a substantial difference between the brain and the thinking machine: the latter, which is obviously not restricted by the severe limitations of biological necessity, may have mnemonic devices and laws much more efficient than those of Nature, while giving rise to thought-processes (as described by the N.E.) of the same type. We feel also that, as regards memory growth and contrary to the situation that arises in the study of the N.E., a thinking machine of this sort might be of greater use to neurophysiology than vice versa; observations performed on models, which can be built with mnemonic laws changeable at will, might help to shed light on the quantitative aspects of biological phenomena which are extremely difficult to observe directly.

Thought-processes in a portion of the cortex may be ascribed either ₋o excitation of neurons which would be otherwise mostly at rest, or to inhibition of the activity of neurons which would be otherwise unceasingly firing. To the first one would associate mnemonic mechanisms which make firing easier with the progress of learning (this we may call a *facilitatory*, or *positive*, type of memory); the opposite with the second (*inhibitory, or negative memory*). Both types offer interesting possibilities for machine con-

struction; since they obey essentially the same kind of N.E., we refer here throughout only to the first type.

The so-called "genetic", or "anatomical", i.e. permanent inherited memory, corresponds clearly in our description to the fact that, as we shall see, some (actually most) of the coefficients which couple neurons together must be taken initially, and kept throughout, vanishing. Our mnemonic laws will therefore be chosen so that if a coupling coefficient vanishes initially, it stays forever so, while its modulus may grow to maximum value from any given initial non-vanishing value.

In our model, thought-processes will be represented by non-trivial solutions of the N.E.; the machine can also "think" therefore if all coefficients in the N.E. stay forever frozen, i.e. if the machine cannot learn or forget, provided these coefficients have convenient values. The present framework can thus account, as it should, for a clear distinction between "instinctive" and "intelligent" behavior. It is natural to suppose that genetic patterns determine the laws according to which cells duplicate, branch out and anastomize, rather than the actual ultimate detailed anatomy of a tissue (thus, a "gene" carrying the instruction "add + 1" would suffice to generate all integers from zero, while an infinite number of "genes" would be obviously required if each integer should have its distinctive "gene"); then even a few mutations may determine the appearance of neural structures quite at variance with previous patterns, from which the evolutionary laws can secure the selection of the fittest, that is those which possess the most favorable neuronal couplings. Our definition of thought comprises thus two types of performance for which we use the conventional terminology: "instinct", which is learnt genetically, and "intelligence" which arises when these couplings can change during the life of the individual.

2. The quantities s_h, $a_{hh}^{(r)}$ and $a_{hk}^{(r)}$ ($h \neq k$) were seen to play quite different rôles. When assigning their variation with time, we refer henceforth to a machine rather than to the living brain, for the reasons mentioned before.

It is apparent from (1) and (2) that the maximum learning capacity of the machine is already reached by assigning suitable variations only to $a_{hh}^{(r)}$ and $a_{hk}^{(r)}$ Once the mnemonic laws are given for these, changes induced in the s_h appear as the best way of controlling the operation of the machine. We shall return on this point in Section **4** and consider here the s_h as quantities the values of which do not change because of mnemonic laws, but, if at all, through some different mechanism.

The coefficients $a_{hh}^{(r)}$ have already been discussed in B, 2; for the purposes of the present discussion we may assume.

$$a_{hh}^{(r)} = \begin{cases} -\infty & 0 \le r \\ 0 & r > R \text{ (integer)} \end{cases} \tag{4}$$

For $h \ne k$ a convenient law is (for positive, or facilitatory $a_{hk}^{(r)}$):

$$\frac{da_{hk}^{(r)}(t)}{dt}$$

$$= \left\{ \alpha^{(r)} u_k(t-\tau) u_h(t) - \beta^{(r)} 1 \left[a_{hk}^{(r)}(t) - a_{hk}^{(r)}(0) \right] \right\} a_{hk}^{(r)}(t) 1 \left[A_{hk}^{(r)} - a_{hk}^{(r)}(t) \right] \tag{5}$$

where

$\alpha^{(r)} \gg \beta^{(r)} > 0$, $A_{hk}^{(r)} > 0$, and it is imposed that $a_{hk}^{(r)}(t)$ be continuous, with $a_{hk}^{(r)}(0) \le A_{hk}^{(r)}$.

For the sake of concreteness we take (5) as the mnemonic equations (M.E.) of our machine; we also neglect inhibitory (negative) couplings, to which (5) is immediately extended in an obvious manner. We may suppose here, for simplicity, that only coefficients with $r = 0$ survive, and that all $A_{hk}^{(0)} = A$ and all $a_{hk}^{(0)} = a$. We have already emphasized that all that we actually need are M.E. that admit solutions having the same qualitative behavior as those of (5); these we proceed to discuss briefly.

3. We write $a_{hk}(t)$ for $a_{hk}^{(0)}(t)$. The M.E. (5) describe a situation in which $a_{hk}(t)$ never becomes smaller than $a > 0$, nor greater than A. When the latter value is reached, it is retained for ever: the information is engrammed permanently. This is perhaps an oversimplified view of the real situation in the brain; it could be, though, easily modified.

$a_{hk}(t)$ increases if, and only if, the neuron h which is connected by a direct channel to neuron k, fires at time $t + t$ and has received a pulse at time $t - \tau$ from the latter. It decreases slowly afterwards ($\alpha \gg \beta$), until the same situation repeats. Only if a series of such rises occurs, without excessive delays in between, can $a_{hk}(t)$ reach the engramming value A.

There is ample choice of mechanical devices which can reproduce qualitatively this behavior. If it is desired that the machine exhibit a behavior typified by (3), coefficients like $b_{hk}^{(0)}$ might be given constant values, not subject to mnemonic phenomena.

4. Qualitative Discussion

A. Operational Definition of "Thought"

1. We propose now to show that, as was mentioned in the Introduction, a machine that works according to the N.E. (2) and the M.E. (5) will exhibit phenomena which are typical of a nervous system, provided of course the number of its elements is sufficiently large and the initial values

$a_{hk}^{(r)}(0)$ of the couplings among these ("genetic memory") are conveniently chosen (e.g. so as to prevent "epilepsy": cf. c, 4, p. 221).

The most obvious features of the N.E. are non-linearity and unidirectionality of pulse transmission; their solutions describe therefore in any case states of excitation (or "motions", or "modes") that "travel" unidirectionally from neuron to neuron and interfere nonlinearly whenever they meet. This interference is either instantaneous or nearly so, as it happens when summation of pulses at the synapsis of a neuron causes its firing (as described in the r.h.s. of (2)); or delayed, as it happens when pulses, which would otherwise cause the firing of a neuron, cannot do so because they reach that neuron when it is still inhibited by a previous firing, due to different pulses.

2. *We define a thought-process*, operationally, *as a solution of the N.E.*, or, equivalently, as the corresponding "motion" in the machine. It is convenient further to qualify this definition, so as to meet obvious objections.

We may disregard as "trivial" and not consider as "thoughts" solutions that correspond to (say accidental) firings of neurons at a given time, such that no other neurons are induced into firing thereby and all activity ceases immediately afterwards. Any "thought" implies thus the passing of at least one neuronic channel.

3. For any given set E of neurons, all motions of a given duration can be classed either into a set M_E, the motions of which cause at least one neuron in E to fire at least once, or into a set $\overline{M}_E$ of the remaining possible motions. There is thus (and in many ways) the possibility of establishing operational distinctions between "types of thought"; should, for instance, a portion of the machine correspond to the central and one to the autonomic nervous system, the name "thought" could be further restricted thereby to the solutions of the N.E. which affect only the neurons of the first. If, in a different partition, E is the set of neurons the firing of which is associated somehow with consciousness (e.g. because they control a loudspeaker, or some prescribed feed-back mechanism), then all motions of M_E can be taken as representing the "conscious activity", all those of $\overline{M}_E$ the "subconscious activity" of the brain.

It is interesting to remark that, in the latter instance, because of the various possibilities of interference discussed before between the motions of $\overline{M}_E$ and those of M_E, each type of activity influences the other. "Psychoanalysis" reduces for this machine to a simple and well-defined mathematical problem.

B. Problems Connected with the N.E.

1. The N.E. clearly contain, as special cases, the description of all logical networks of the kind beautifully analyzed

in the pioneering work of McCulloch and Pitts. Should their solution be attempted by the obvious method of iteration, they would, for these cases, give just as much—or as little—information as can be gathered from the standard logical switchboard analysis; there is here a clear analogy with the Darboux (better than the Cauchy) problem of the theory of differential equations.

The systematic algebraization of logic, which is the real content of the N.E. (with frozen coefficients), permits us to pose for them much more general questions, which may be treated with a variety of mathematical tools; the logic of the system is seen to play a rôle so to speak similar to that of the constraints which limit position and mobility of a dynamical system; an appropriate treatment of the N.E. will permit, as with the equations of motion of dynamical systems, the search for those long-range collective solutions which, in our scheme, form the basis for a useful analysis of thought-processes.

2. We consider first of all the N.E. with frozen coefficients, in keeping with the A.L.H. Their quantitative discussion poses some interesting and novel mathematical questions, and will probably require the introduction of techniques *ad hoc*; on the other hand, it is evident that in simple cases, such as may correspond to situations involving very few neurons, the N.E. may be solved on inspection. It is also clear that straightforward combinatorics can give useful information on the possible types and multiplicities of the solutions of interest, as defined below; and that this can be translated at once into the customary language of "excitation probabilities", etc. While deferring to future reports for detailed studies on these matters, on which work is in progress, it is fully sufficient for our present purposes to formulate the "problems" which we envisage as most relevant in study of the N.E., and to discuss them briefly at a qualitative level.

The first obvious, and obviously important, remark is that the N.E. are not uniquely determined; their formulation (2) is perhaps deceptively simple. Because of the definition of the function $1(x)$, there is a whole group G of transformations which change a given set of N.E. into an *equivalent* one—having, that is, exactly the same solutions, although not necessarily the same form (thus, $1(x) = 1(2x) = 1(x^3) = 1(\sin x)$, etc.). This fact was already used in the discussion of the threshold values s_h made in Section **3**, c, 2; it shows, for instance, that matrix algebra should be used with caution in handling these questions.

For the same reason, "suitably small" changes of the $a_{hk}^{(r)}$ and s_h will not change the solutions of a set of N.E.: this adds credit to the reliability of the A.L.H. and provides what we may call the *first criterion of stability* of the machine.

3. We shall soon specify what types of "input" and "output" seem most appropriate for a machine of this sort; we are now interested in the "spontaneous" activity of the machine, which we define as that which takes place in it when, at a given time t_0, the machine starts from any given state of excitation and no input pulses are fed into it for $t > t_0$.

In a linear network—it is convenient, for purposes of comparison, to refer to a system of harmonic oscillators with linear couplings—such activity is naturally analyzed in terms of eigensolutions, eigenfrequencies, harmonics; the behavior of a single element is in general not periodic, but simple periodal analysis will resolve it into a sum of periodic normal modes, which have a collective character and may be defined as the motions of quasi-particles (this remark already suffices to eliminate as illusory any attempt at deciding on the existence of periodic motions in the brain through observations performed on one or few neurons). In a non-linear system things become much more involved; e.g. one finds in general, besides harmonics (multiples of a fundamental frequency), also subharmonics (multiples of a fundamental period).

The extreme schematization which is expressed by the form (2) given here to the N.E. has the evident consequence that one can only expect subharmonics; if there are periodic solutions of the N.E., these are *reverberations,* i.e. transfers of excitation from neuron to neuron which may reach anywhere into the machine and, after the closing of suitable multi-channel paths, repeat with a periodicity which is, obviously, some integral multiple of τ.

The consideration of reverberations is central to our approach. There are tremendous numbers of them even in the simplest conceivable models; their types, paths, multiplicities are determined by the coefficients $a_{hk}^{(r)}$ and s_h, of the N.E., and change therefore, because of the M.E., with learning and forgetting.

4. The first mathematical problem is therefore the determination of all the solutions that correspond to reverberations, or free ("spontaneous", "autogenic") modes compatible with the N.E. The minimum duration of a reverberation is clearly determined by the refractory period of the neurons through which it travels; if we assume that "normal" activity (i.e. without special stimulation) of the neurons in the brain uses the total period of the pattern of spike-afterpotentials (~ 100 msec), then the maximum possible frequency (reverberations involving ~ 100 neurons) is about 10 cycles/sec, which coincides with the frequency of the α-waves of the E.E.G. If we assume further that stimulation may force the neurons of the brain into using a refractory time intermediate between the absolute (~ 4 msec) and the total time, then this maximum frequency increases and the number of neurons necessary for the

smallest permissible reverberations decreases. We do not wish to draw any conclusions at this early stage from these remarks, which may be a gross oversimplification of reality; we only state here that they are not in disagreement with observation.

If thresholds and couplings have the values that are observed in the brain, then reverberations certainly involve several tens of neurons. Reverberations, furthermore, should last for ever in an ideal machine, a conveniently long time in a real machine and in the brain. From the first remark it follows that one cannot expect to observe direct evidence of prolonged autogenic activity in a portion of the cortex in ordinary conditions: this would require innumerable microelectrodes stuck into as many neurons for an experiment to be feasible. One would expect, however, from our theory, that if thresholds are sufficiently lowered artificially or the intensity of stimuli increased, then also a very small number of aptly chosen neurons should suffice for a prolonged autogenic reverberation to take place. In a brilliant series of experiments A. Féssard (Symposium on Memory, Naples, 1960) has demonstrated, by using tetanic potentiation, that this actually happens: he recorded reverberations among only four neurons which would last minutes. We regard his results as a crucial, if only partial, confirmation of our theory, which was developed while we were still unaware of his work.

5. Reverberations, as all other notions, interfere non-linearly unless one reverberation never affects in any way the neurons of another, i.e. as we shall say, is *disjoint* from the other. At this point the analogy with a linear network breaks down completely, much to the advantage of our machine, which possesses many more essentially distinct modes of behavior than a linear system. It is still possible to classify *all* possible spontaneous reverberations, for instance according to periodicity, multiplicity (i.e. degeneracy), etc.

The next mathematical problem that arises is the study of the evolution of the state of excitation which was present in the machine at time $t = t_0$, as was discussed in 3, above. It may either coincide with a configuration of excitations which characterizes at t_0 a reverberation, and thereafter continues its periodic behavior; or, more often, *decay,* into a reverberation, or *develop* into a reverberation, or produce *catastrophic behavior,* i.e. lead to total (or nearly total) simultaneous excitation ("epilepsy") of the neurons, which may decay immediately afterwards into rest (cf. the N.E.).

Excluding for the time being the last dramatic alternative, we find here the most interesting situation, as close an analogue as is possible with a non-linear system to harmonic analysis. In a frozen state of knowledge, out of the machine as many distinct responses can be evoked as there are distinct excitable reverberations, or modes; each of

these we may identify with a "pattern" which the machine knows genetically, or has learnt; the "initial configuration" is the pattern which is presented to the machine; the set of (one or more) disjoint reverberations to which the latter gives rise (depending upon the value of the couplings) is the *analysis of that pattern* performed by the machine which corresponds to the state of knowledge it has learnt until that moment.

Apart from learning, we have here the counterpart to what we regard as the essential activity of the mind, the ability to analyze a situation, or shape, or pattern, into a set of already classified patterns. No single element acts as a classifier since the total response of the machine is required for this analysis.

6. The situation described above is manifestly an extreme simplification. The next mathematical problem is in fact that of studying the evolution in time of the total state of excitation of the machine when its "input" is subject to continued external stimulations.

It will also be expedient, of course, whenever dealing with very large assemblies of neurons, to distinguish between "traveling" and "stationary" solutions. We have been considering thus far only the latter, but it is clear that, as soon as distinctive special-purpose "organs" are built into the anatomical structure of the machine, our previous considerations should be restricted mostly to the latter, with pulses travelling from organ to organ as among the boxes of a diagram.

It is also to be expected that there will be a maximum duration, and a maximum complexity, beyond which reverberations cease to be significant for pattern-analysis. This assumption, or requirement, will greatly facilitate the mathematical study of the problem formulated in this section.

7. We have thus far taken, for the sake of simplicity, a perhaps too realistic view of reverberations as modes which are actually connected to fixed chains of neurons. This is not certainly the case when one considers the normal modes of linear networks, and it is therefore of interest also to investigate the possibility of resolving actual motions, which do not have manifest periodicity, into "normal" periodic collective modes (cf. 3, above: the Lissajous figures of linear problems are an example of this behavior); any such latent periodicity would be easily revealed by observations made upon populations of neurons (e.g. with the E.E.G.).

Questions of this nature, and many others, suggest themselves in a quantitative investigation; they need not be considered here in further detail.

C. Rôle of the M.E.

1. In the preceding section we have focused our attention on the operation of the machine when all coupling constants and thresholds are kept fixed, and have found that *reverberations* play a central rôle in its most typical activity, which is *pattern-analysis* in a very general sense. All such statements presuppose already, of course, the existence of favorable conditions, as are expressed for instance by the assumption (A, 1), which prevent epileptic, or catastrophic, behavior; it was also implicitly assumed that the machine is indifferent to the "meaning" (referred to any standards) of what it knows genetically or has learnt during its past activity. While we can reasonably expect that careful engineering and a long series of painstaking adjustments would in the end produce devices capable of some useful performance solely by virtue of conveniently chosen N.E., we are much more interested in machines that can adjust themselves to prescribed tasks by means of some learning mechanism; this should also give the machine a tendency to organize itself into increasingly reliable operation, so as to compensate for minor flaws in the accuracy of its elements.

The M.E. provide, to a large extent, the answer to these questions, as we shall now show. In the course of the same discussion it will become apparent, however, that a machine of this sort is not realistically conceivable unless at least two additional controlling devices are not also explicitly included; the first we identify tentatively with the thalamus, the second, with more assurance, with the reticular system of the brain. The necessity of devices of this sort, if not already suggested in the brain by anatomical and physiological evidence, is made imperative in the machine by the structure of the N.E. and M.E.

Mentioning a "thalamus" takes us, of course, one step nearer to the "sentient" machine than we wish to stay for the time being; we shall therefore restrict this part of our discussion to barest essentials, pointing only to what is relevant for purely "rational" thought.

2. There are many mathematical ways of representing the overall situation and evolution of the machine, each suited to some special purposes. We mention here briefly a few which take the instantaneous state of each neuron as the object of interest.

If the number of neurons in the N.E. is N, then a solution of the N.E. at a time t is representable by means of a one-column matrix with N rows, the element of row h being given by $u_h(t)$; or one can define, equivalently, an N-dimensional *configuration* (or *neuron*) *space* $\mathcal{N}$, which has N axes, on the hth of which the abscissa is $u_h(t)$. The state at time t of the machine is thus represented by the *point*, or *matrix*, or *vector*, $P(t) \equiv \{u_h(t)\} \equiv \overrightarrow{u}(t)$; its evolution in time by the (discontinuous) motion of the point $P(t)$.

All trajectories in $\mathcal{N}$ are invariant under the transformations of the N.E. which belong to the group G defined in B, 2, provided of course that at each time t one takes G as it is determined by the M.E.: now, $G = G(t)$.

$\mathcal{N}$ contains at most 2^N points; a trajectory in $\mathcal{N}$ is a polygonal joining some, or all, of these points. A reverberation is represented in $\mathcal{N}$ by a *closed polygonal* (and lasts at least as long as the coefficients in the N.E. stay frozen).

$P(t)$ changes in $\mathcal{N}$ (i) because it describes the evolution in time of a solution of the N.E., (ii) because the N.E. themselves change, due to the intervention of the M.E. The A.L.H. permits the study of simple phenomena by separating step (i) from step (ii): it allows, that is, that they be performed alternately. Step (ii) becomes necessary as soon as, because of M.E., the N.E. undergo a transformation which does not belong to G.

A qualitative discussion is better stopped here (see, however, Section **5**, A, 2); it should already be clear from what little has been said on this subject, though, that the introduction of spaces of functionals on $\mathcal{N}$ will be of the highest conceptual importance, because then everything becomes again linear, group theory may be resorted to as a valid tool of analysis, each "pattern" is easily made to correspond to a point, and problems such as those of language translation or study of emotive behavior can receive a precise mathematical formulation.

3. The pattern-analysis described in B, 5, presupposes, clearly, that the machine has already formed, either genetically or by learning, some typical responses (or modes, or patterns), in terms of which a pattern presented to it is analyzed. Very little, if anything at all, can be expected from a machine with fixed constants built entirely at random: the most likely thing to occur in such a case is that, unless the experimenter arranges the connections of the machine in a way that is equivalent to giving it a genetic memory, the only resulting effect will be a total loss of information. Also a machine endowed with ability to learn will give, at best, a poor performance, unless the controlling devices mentioned above (1) are included into it, as we shall soon discuss. The best procedure, or at least by far the most economical, appears to be in any case that of borrowing as much as possible from anatomical and physiological information.

Before proceeding further we need say a few words about the kind of "input" and "output" which seems appropriate to a machine of this nature. The notions of input as "that which comes before" and of output as "that which comes after" the machine proper are clearly out of the question; we are interested in what occurs *at all places* and *at all times* in the machine, and a relatively small number of terminal plugs could never tell us readily this much. Adequate inputs and outputs are instead devices out of which (inputs) an afferent lead goes to *each* neuron of the machine, or into which (outputs) an efferent lead comes out of *each* neuron; or, more economically, these leads connect input and output terminals with a *large* number of neurons spread throughout the machine, and connected with all the other neurons so that no relevant information on its behavior is lost. Anatomically, this seems to correspond to some regions of the brain stem for the afferents, for instance, to the thalamus. It is clear that such a device is what can be best desired for many sorts of feed-back operations; to this point we shall return briefly in connection with the learning mechanism.

4. We have excluded, in the discussion made in B, 5, the possibility that a stimulus presented at the input may produce catastrophic, or epileptic behavior. In any real machine constructed with a very large number of elements and connections among these, however, and even with very good engineering and planning, catastrophic behavior is the very first thing to be expected.

Even assuming ideal starting conditions, the intervention of the M.E. will soon change the values of the $a_{hk}^{(r)}(t)$. The maintenance of a reverberation presupposes that, after its cycle is completed, the same situation repeats identically. Unless the ratios of the numbers and weights (as given by the $a_{hk}^{(r)}(t)$) of output *v.* input terminals are kept within very critical limits (cf. the operation of a nuclear reactor), the most likely event to occur is that the initial situation does not repeat exactly after one cycle of reverberation is completed, but more, or fewer neurons are excited than the correct number. In either case a process very similar to a chain reaction might take place immediately, that is, a very fast excitation of all neurons, or a very fast extinction of all activity; more generally, totally uncontrollable phenomena would occur as a rule rather than as an exception.

Whenever learning is involved, and in any case whenever design is not ideally perfect, a controlling mechanism (like the cadmium bars in reactors) is necessary to prevent any such possibility. We saw in Section **3**, C, 2, that we can use, without any loss in the learning capacity of the machine, the neuronic thresholds s_h for this purpose; this is also, clearly, the best choice from a practical point of view.

Any machine that works according to the N.E. and the M.E. necessitates therefore a mechanism which, upon receiving information on its local and general activity at a given time, may alter the thresholds s_h of the neurons, so as to avoid catastrophic conditions at later times. We have described here the function of the reticular system of the brain, as was made clear by the profound physiological investigations of G. Moruzzi & H. W. Magoun. The exis-

tence of such a mechanism will provide the *second criterion of stability* for our machine.

It will also be necessary, of course, to resort to the methods of which Nature avails herself in the brain: most of the $a_{hk}^{(r)}(0)$ will be taken as vanishing, in such a way that a neuron be connected through its efferent terminals mostly to rather distant neurons. Thus, excitations spread out and tend to stay below the epileptic thresholds; if couplings were only with "nearest neighbours", epileptic waves would be the only mode of operation of this machine. Such a choice of initial coupling coefficients will provide the *third criterion of stability.* We may include into this the action of inhibitory couplings also.

5. We can now discuss the operation of the machine from the point of view of the M.E.; learning and forgetting will play an equally important rôle. The cortex of the brain has many, more or less specialized input and output "areas"; we shall refer, generically, only to "input" and "output" and refrain from using the current terminology of "sensory", "motor" and "associative" zones, which presupposes a more detailed structural knowledge than is needed for a qualitative discussion.

We also forgo such obvious things as the convenience that special input devices be constructed so as to perform a preliminary analysis of the figures, or patterns, "shown" them (fed into them; we refer, for concreteness, to a visual input); thus, if a set of homothetic triangles is shown, one may require that the input device transmit to the direct input of the machine only the image of a standardized triangle, plus an information on the value of the homothety parameter. Devices of this sort are not hard to conceive as special organs or extensions of the machine itself, to which they are linked by additional N.E. with fixed coefficients (learning is undesirable at this level). We refer hereafter only to the direct input of the machine, and assume that any such simplification has already been performed somehow.

Without a thalamus, the machine can only learn *by repetition* from habit. Suppose it starts as a *tabula rasa*, i.e. with all couplings having values $a_{hk}^{(r)}(0)$; suppose also, for the sake of simplicity, that a figure may be presented to it any number of times, but each time only for a very short duration. Each presentation will stimulate into firing a number of input neurons which we assume to be sufficiently large to initiate a collective activity, which spreads into the machine as described in A, 1 and B, 3 and 5. Unless the collective motion thus induced is strongly favoured by the genetic memory (i.e. the $a_{hk}^{(r)}(0)$; this ought to be the case for such things as the infant's sucking reflex), nothing much should happen after the virgin machine sees a figure Θ_1 (say, a triangle) for the first time; reverberations will be evoked but, because of the low values of the coefficients

$a_{hk}^{(r)}(0)$, a great many pulses are required to cause the firing of each single neuron, so that periodic, or nearly periodic, modes may be expected to involve a great many neurons and to be quite slow. The activity thus induced will be rather *diffuse*, not yet quite specific; it will last for some time $\gg \tau$ and the coefficients will start changing slowly because of the M.E. The pattern of this motion will be altered as soon as this change requires step (ii) as described in 2: the increase of the coupling constants will tend to favor the creation of pathways through which reverberations are facilitated, i.e. have shorter cycles and require less neurons. Normal biological disturbances, or mechanical variations, spontaneous (e.g. due to the variations of the coefficients caused by the M.E.) or imposed, e.g. by the reticular system, will cause this state of motion eventually to cease; the chance that a single direct channel be used as many times as is required by the M.E. for a permanent engramming of a facilitation is very low; what alterations have been caused by the sight of Θ_1 will be slowly forgotten by the machine.

Clearly, however, the thing is quite different if Θ_1 is shown many times in succession to the machine: then the semi-permanent changes induced by the M.E. will accumulate, until permanent changes are induced that definitely facilitate the "most convenient" reverberations evoked by Θ_1, i.e. those that are quickest and involve the least number of neurons; these we regard as specific to Θ_1. Permanent engramming is favored if the intervals between the exposures of Θ_1 are made shorter, disfavored otherwise; it may however take a very long time (days, or months, or years in an animal), or never occur at all: semi-permanent memories may decay very slowly indeed, and there may also be more stages, with various decay times, before permanent enframming obtains, than is assumed in the form (5) of the M.E.

It is evident that if a series of random figures is shown in succession to the machine, it will learn nothing, except perhaps a response meaning only that "a figure is being shown" (see later for a further discussion of this fact); but if among these random figures a given one Θ_1 is shown repeatedly enough, the machine will "learn" only Θ_1, together with the general response mentioned before.

This discussion is manifestly incomplete; diminishing response because of assuefaction, for instance, is not considered. The reason we do not wish to push it farther is that it appears too easy, rather than too difficult, to answer such questions at a qualitative level—which may be as dangerous as inconclusive. For instance, both the action of inhibitory couplings (which we have arbitrarily disregarded here for the sake of brevity, although their importance cannot be doubted) and of external inhibitions, e.g. from the reticular system may be invoked to explain assuefaction. Even with these restrictions, we hope that the present discussions of the subject may suffice to provide a convenient basis for further elaborations.

6. Learning by repetition, as described in 5 above, does not appear very satisfactory. One may say that the virgin machine has no more reason to wish to learn a triangle than the infant child. The same mechanism, however, makes it easy to explain "learning by punishment and reward", or *conditioning of the first kind* (as we shall say) and to account why the latter is much faster than the first.

The machine must, of course, be sentient to some degree to know whether it is being punished or rewarded. This will mean here that the thalamus has in-built criteria (homeostatic devices) which enable it to "like" or "dislike" what it records. Suppose that this is the case, and that the thalamus can either suppress, or create a state of excitation in the neurons. Then, even when a stimulus is presented only once at the input, the thalamus may evaluate the situation through its homeostats and determine either a quick suppression of it (or of a part of it, e.g. that which produces some specific motor pulses), or that it be reinforced and maintained until permanent engramming is achieved, much more quickly in this way, clearly, than by "external" repetition at long or random intervals.

A thinking machine may perhaps do without this device and method of learning, which becomes of utmost importance only when survival has to be fought for.

7. We have discussed in 5 the situation that occurs if a given figure, or pattern, Θ_1 is presented repeatedly at the input. We consider now what can happen if two distinct patterns Θ_1 and Θ_2 are used.

If the machine has already learned Θ_1, i.e. if it responds to Θ_1 with specific reverberations, when Θ_2 is presented for the first time the situation is not the same as at the origin of time; some facilitations are already formed in the connections, so that the machine, as its first reaction, will show all of the reverberations which Θ_2 may evoke in common with Θ_1, plus extra motions which will slowly be changed into a response distinctive of Θ_2. In other words, if the machine knows already Θ_1, and sees Θ_2 for the first time, its only immediate response will be to tell how much Θ_2 has in common with Θ_1; later on it will learn also Θ_2. Thereafter, it will be able to analyze likewise Θ_2 in terms of Θ_1 and Θ_2; and so on.

This is, at its simplest, the mechanism of pattern-analysis, as it develops with the evolution in time of the machine—its "education". The analysis the machine is capable of performing at time t is determined, because of the A.L.H., solely by the N.E., taken with the values their coefficients have at that time.

8. The most typical and distinctive characteristic of the human mind is, in our opinion, its ability to abstract what is "common" to two, or more, situations or patterns, and to retain the result of this operation as a new pattern, which is entrusted to the memory as if learnt from the outside. Just as pattern-analysis was seen to be the fundamental operation of a machine described by N.E. with frozen coefficients, we proceed now to show that *abstraction* is the other fundamental operation performed by a machine which obeys N.E. and M.E. as well. The same discussion will clarify also the exact meaning to be given to the word "common" used above.

At any time t intermediate between the time t_0 at which a pattern Θ_1 is activated into the machine (e.g. a triangle Θ_1 is shown at the input) and the time t_1 at which the collective motion aroused by that act dies out ($t_1 - t \gg \tau$; no other such activations are supposed to take place, and the mechanism described in 7 above is excluded), there will be $n_1(t - t_0)$ neurons which actually fire, and form the *constellation* (set) $c_1(t - t_0)$ engendered by the activation of Θ_1 at t_0. There will be also, in addition, a constellation $c'_1(t - t_0)$ of $n'_1(t - t_0)$ (in general, $n' > n$) of "penumbral" neurons which *do not fire,* but receive a *subliminal facilitation* from the activation of Θ_1 at t_0.

Suppose now that at some time $t'_0(t_0 < t'_0 < t_1)$ another pattern Θ_2 is activated (a different triangle Θ_2 is shown at the input). The machine may have already learnt Θ_1 in a permanent or semi-permanent way, or not. Define likewise $n_2(t - t'_0)$ and $c_2(t - t'_0)$, etc., and neglect (this is incorrect and could easily be avoided in this discussion without altering its *qualitative* conclusions) the alterations caused by the non-linear interference of these motions at times between t'_0 and t in the constellations $c'_1(t - t_0)$ and $c'_2(t - t'_0)$; suppose that at least for some t between t'_0 and t_1 the intersection of the sets $c'_1(t - t_0)$ and $c'_2(t - t'_0)$ is not void and contains a constellation $c'_{1,2}(t - t'_0)$ of neurons which (would receive only subliminal stimuli from *either* motion, but) *fire* because the non-linear summation of the stimuli from *both* motions exceeds their thresholds: then, $c_{1,2}$ cannot be distinguished from a state of excitation such as would be produced by the presentation (not necessarily at the direct input which this, we recall, has the same structure as the rest of the machine) of a pattern $\Theta_{1,2}$. $\Theta_{1,2}$ can be aroused, clearly, only if Θ_1 *and* Θ_2 are shown at the input, the second after the first, and will result quite differently, in general, from $\Theta_{2,1}$, if the temporal development of both motions and the interference effects between them are treated without the illegitimately oversimplified assumptions which were made here for short.

Although presented here in more outline on purpose, this line of reasoning makes it evident that, because of the non-linearity of the N.E., whenever a pattern is activated while the response to a previous one has not yet died out, the machine can *abstract* something which is "common" to both (the structure of the machine decides what meaning this word should have) and then adjust itself through the M.E. so as to memorize it, permanently or not, not differently from its normal behavior in response to any other pattern.

"Patterns of patterns" of any sort, in any number, may be formed and learnt in this way: chains of abstractions can take place without limitations other than those imposed by the complexity and structure of the machine. We recognize here, in full, the mechanical analogue to the faculty of abstraction of the human mind.

9. Abstraction alone is not enough: it would be highly uneconomical to remember all single instances, once the general concept is grasped. Our machine takes, in this respect, good care of itself. Suppose that, say, a sufficiently large number a of random triangles Θ_i have been shown to the machine, which has learnt them semi-permanently; it has also formed the responses $\Theta_{1,2}, \Theta_{2,1}, \Theta_{1,2,3}, \dots, \Theta_{1,2,3\dots a} \equiv \Theta$ which are common to all subsets of triangles (ordered or not) and memorized these semi-permanently. This memorization is accompanied by a process of facilitation; whereas, before memorization, Θ could be evoked only if *all* the triangles were shown to the machine, after facilitation, the $a_{hk}^{(r)}$ that appear in the N.E. which describe the behavior of the neurons of the constellation $c_{1,2,\dots,a} \equiv c$, have increased their values considerably; suppose, for maximum simplicity, these values to have become so large that each single motion Θ_i gives now to the neurons of c, instead of a subliminal stimulus, an excitation above threshold (if more than one, but less than a, Θ_i were involved at this stage, our argument would only take a few more steps). Then each time *any* triangle Θ_i is presented to the machine, the common response Θ (which can convey, clearly, only the "general concept" of triangle) is always evoked, i.e. the neurons of the "common" constellation c fire and their channels are facilitated some more; on the average, the couplings of each constellations c_i will be susceptible to increase for only $1/a$ of the total time, while those of c will be exposed to facilitating actions for *all* the time—until permanent memory is achieved. Even if at the beginning, say, c_1 had been markedly facilitated, the presentation of more and more patterns which have "something in common" with it (as decided by the machine) will cause the specific response to c_1 to fade into oblivion, while the "abstract", or "common" response is evoked as the first thing, after a convenient learning period.

If we consider now only two stimuli Θ_1 and Θ_2 and assume that Θ_1 *causes* already, say, because of the genetic structure of the machine, *a direct response* (e.g. the food-salivation reflex of Pavlov's dogs), while Θ_2 is ineffective (cf. bell-ringing), then the same mechanism can be clearly extended to account first for the formation of the response $\Theta_{2,1}$ (bell before food, $\neq \Theta_{1,2}$), then, for the fact that Θ_2 alone comes to provoke the same effect as Θ_1 or Θ_2. The temporal behavior given by M.E. of type (5) is perfectly suited to describe the available evidence, which might be used for a determination of the numerical values of some of the constants which appear in (5).

This type of conditioning is manifestly different from that described in 6 above, which requires the intervention of the thalamus: we shall call it *conditioning of the second kind,* or "by information" (the bell just tells the dog that food is coming).

10. We discuss, finally, *re-integration,* which we define as the fact that our machine shall, after learning a pattern, respond to the "incomplete" presentation of that pattern as if it were complete (cf. the familiar oversights of the proof-reader). That this must be the case can be seen now quite trivially: after a number of facilitations have occurred, a smaller number of input stimuli will be required to cause the firing of neurons than were necessary when that pattern was presented for the first time. This also accounts for the children's alterations of new words, which are reduced to combinations of already familiar words; in part, for the fact that a cue suffices to evoke a long string of memories, e.g. verses, etc.

5. Concluding Remarks

A. Time Evolution of Pattern-Analysis

1. The preceding discussion has been, at various places, restricted to situations in which a stimulation, or presentation of a pattern, at the input occurs at given instant, after which it ceases while the machine starts its analysis of it; that is, we have chosen to consider only the "free" modes of motion of the machine, of which the stimulation sets the initial conditions, rather than the evidently prevalent situations in which the machine will perform "forced" motions under the *continued* influence of stimulations which persist and may vary with time.

This simplification is obviously convenient for the purposes of a purely qualitative discussion, as it permits separate examination of the various features of the operation of the machine; nor can forced motions be adequately described without a quantitative analysis of the solutions of the N.E. and M.E. We wish to point out here, however, that this simplifying assumption is, in all likelihood, a much better approximation of reality than it may seem at first.

We can consider a continued stimulation as the presentation to the machine of a *time-series of patterns;* its analysis by the machine is therefore a *serial* operation. Our observation is, that a machine such as the one envisaged by us, with a very large number of elements, can actually transform that serial operation into a *parallel* operation.

Let the patterns presented at the input (or anywhere by the machine to itself: cf. Section **4,** C, 8) at time $0, \tau, 2\tau, 3\tau, \ldots$ be $\Theta_0, \Theta_1, \Theta_2, \ldots$. We recall (Section **3,** B, 2) that each neuron, as described by the N.E., has a *refractory* period which is $> \tau$, and may be $\gg \tau$; we take it here to be $R\tau$, according to the schematization expressed by (4). Θ_0 causes a set S_0 of neurons to fire at time 0; all neurons of S_0 then stay dead for $R\tau$ sec, while other neurons are excited by them at rather distant places (3rd criterion of stability, Section **4,** C, 4) and then remain dead in turn while stimulating other distant neurons, etc. When Θ_1 is presented at time τ, all neurons of S_0 *cannot respond,* and another set S_1 *disjoint* from S_0 fire and excite likewise distant neurons, etc.; and so on for Θ_2 at time 2τ, etc.

All the patterns presented from t_0 until $t = R\tau$ are therefore registered *in parallel* by the machine, which can thus, for example, abstract a concept meaning "motion" with the same mechanism by which it abstracts one meaning "triangularity".

The extent to which this happens is determined, in this simple example, by the value of R. If the reverberations which are significant for pattern-analysis have periods $< R\tau$, then the simplifying assumption made in Section **4** is quite good. In any case, the conversion of serial into parallel operation, and *vice versa,* will emerge as an obvious and important feature in any quantitative discussion of the N.E.

2. It is convenient at this stage to return briefly to the matters mentioned in Section **4,** C, 2, so as to summarize the essentials of the operation of the machine into a few mathematical concepts.

Our machine learns, by the process of abstraction (by virtue of the M.E.), *to perform pattern-analysis* (by virtue of the N.E.). This sentence contains all that is most relevant in our theory; mathematically, it can be expressed as follows.

At a fixed time t, the N.E. have frozen coefficients: A.L.H. A pattern Θ presented at or into the machine at t evokes, in general, a very large number of disjoint modes, or reverberations: this is the "Fourier" analysis performed by the machine, each mode corresponding to a point $\mathcal{Q}$ or an axis in an appropriate functional space $\mathscr{F}$ on $\mathcal{N}$ (the quotes call to mind the profound difference from linear Fourier analysis).

We may also say that each point Q of $\mathscr{F}$ corresponds to one of the *basic concept,* or *words,* which the machine has learnt until t: the N.E. contain, implicitly, all the *knowledge* or *vocabulary* of the machine, in terms of which each new pattern is translated by the machine. (This vocabulary we expect to have a surprisingly different structure from those of Western languages, in which a word is a "point", and a sentence or definition is a "surface constructed point-by-point"; more akin to Chinese or Japanese, in which a word is a "plane" and a sentence or definition a "surface constructed as envelope of planes".)

The second difference from Fourier analysis (the first being non-linearity) is that now the set of fundamental modes, or axes in $\mathscr{F}$ is not *constant,* but *changes in time* because of the M.E. Thus, at a given t a pattern is represented by a point in a given frame S in $\mathscr{F}$ (N.E.); this frame, however, is not fixed, but changes slowly (A.L.H.) in time (M.E.): $S = S(t)$.

This scheme, if correct, has profound implications: for instance, the efficiency of the machine will depend tremendously on the method followed in its education, because to the same external stimulus machines which have been educated differently may offer very quick and simple, or very slow and involved responses.

3. An interesting consequence of our theory is the fact that a machine thus constructed necessitates periods of rest, or "sleep". Indeed, even giving it a tremendously large number of elements, the long duration of reverberations (and induced motions in general), which goes far beyond that of the actual stimulations, will cause, if stimuli are unceasingly offered to it, an ever increasing cumulation of activity; the possibility of co-existence of disjoint reverberations will become less and less, interference will cause "confusion of ideas" and inability to give correct answers even to familiar questions.

A period of "sleep", i.e. cessation of activity through the suave interaction of the reticular system, will permit the gradual extinction first of the less facilitated, then of all other reverberations, and the fading of semi-permanent memories of relatively short duration as well. A more quick and drastic treatment, such as "electroshock", followed by total quiescence for only the period of time which is required for such semi-permanent memories to disappear, will produce the same effect. This reminds one of some Yogi techniques which are said to achieve, in a relatively short time, the same state of rest which follows a full night's sleep.

4. As a final remark, we wish to point out that it might be interesting, in the light of the present considerations, to attempt an analysis of E.E.G.'s in terms of subharmonics instead of the customary one in terms of harmonics of a suitably chosen frequency. The *amplitude* of the E.E.G. recordings should depend strongly on the mechanism described in **5**, A, 1.

B. Self-organization into Reliable Operation

1. In the study of any system containing a very large number of interacting elements built with realistic tolerances—let this be the machine which is being discussed here, or a bee-hive, or the whole socio-political and administrative framework of a nation—the central question is certainly whether this system obeys instantaneous and evolutionary laws which guarantee its spontaneous *convergence in time towards more efficient operation,* or whether the system may rather show *erratic* or *divergent* performance. This question was formulated with full clarity by N. Wiener, who, besides emphasizing the vital importance of it, gave also powerful mathematical tools for its investigation; in his treatment the non-linearity of the interaction laws was rightly stressed as the key to the whole problem.

We can do nothing better than refer the reader to his work for a deeper elaboration of these ideas; it is important, however, here, to show that there is very satisfactory qualitative evidence that a machine obeying *suitable* N.E. and M.E. will satisfy Wiener's principle of self-organization. We shall keep this discussion at a qualitative level by resorting to physical more than to mathematical arguments, and by examining later in detail, instead of the actual machine proposed here, a simplified functional model of it.

That non-linearity of some sort is necessary for self-organization is physically obvious. A linear system (with *frozen* coefficients, or else non-linearity intervenes: cf. A, 2 above) cannot perform a spontaneous transition from one of its states to another (we use the language of quantum mechanics only because of its greater appeal to intuition; of course, the same is true classically); such transitions—without which the system could not choose spontaneously, from our point of view, states with a better (or worse) organization—are only possible if there are *perturbations* to cause them (e.g. the interaction with the electromagnetic field causes the quantum jumps in atoms); furthermore, *the system itself* must originate these perturbations (the electrons of the atom are the source of the electromagnetic field in spontaneous emission), or else its changes of state would be "induced" rather than "spontaneous". The equations of the system must therefore be non-linear in an essential way; such, for instance, as we have in electrodynamics when the electromagnetic field is expressed in terms of electron sources.

Only a non-linear system of this sort can change its state spontaneously; it will not be generally true, however, that its changes are necessarily "for the better". Again, simple examples suffice to prove this statement; leaving aside those, plentiful indeed, which come from societies or civilizations that go bankrupt, we observe that the behavior of a non-linear physical system the energy of which is not restricted by a finite lower bound is certainly catastrophic. We expect therefore that such a system, in order to satisfy Wiener's principle, shall obey additional *necessary* "convergence" conditions—of the type, for instance, that in quantum mechanics secures the existence of a ground state, which we may identify with the "best state for efficient operation". It is our belief that these conditions will amount to satisfying the third criterion of stability (Section **4,** C, 4) and to choosing N.E. with the qualitative behavior exhibited by (5).

The study of the restrictions that this criterion would impose on N.E. (2) and M.E. (5) appears to be a rather straightforward problem, which we add to the list of those which we formulated and set aside in Section **4** for future investigation. A dynamical interpretation of (2) and (5) would be indeed quite natural, as the M.E. (5) just express a non-linear coupling of the N.E. (2) with themselves; we deem it more meritorious, at this stage, to resist the temptation of adapting the available quantum-field-theoretical knowledge to these problems, than to yield to it.

Clearly, the A.L.H. imposes the distinction between two types of non-linearity: that which is expressed by the N.E. (2) and that which is expressed by the M.E. (5). The first is useful, but only the second is necessary for the type of self-organization we are discussing; this statement will appear obvious after the discussion in 2 below, which is dedicated, as was announced, to a simplified version of our problem.

2. We wish to discuss here a *model* of our machine (which we may also regard as another, though less sophisticated, model of the brain; as such it was briefly discussed at an early stage of our work) which consists in a system of N linearly coupled harmonic oscillators, the constants of which obey M.E. of type (5) ($r = o$), under the A.L.H. This was mentioned in Section **4,** B, 3, and is a model of our machine in the sense that, as was said there, "reverberations" correspond in it to normal modes, "subharmonics" to ordinary harmonics, etc. The wealth of solutions of N.E. of type (2) is now lost, because of the linearity of the N.E. of this model; for it the central problem reduces to the determination of the solutions of a secular equation of degree N:

$$f(a_{hk}; \lambda) = 0 \qquad (6)$$

This digression is useful both because it readily provides a qualitative insight into the behavior of a learning machine with respect to self-organization, and because it shows that many different mechanisms may be built, with various degrees of convenience, to produce "thought": the only

essential thing is that they obey *some* N.E., *some* M.E. (*suitable*, but not necessarily of type (2) and (5)), and closely enough the A.L.H.

We wish to compute the average change $< \delta\bar{\lambda} >$ of a solution $\bar{\lambda}$ of (6), when the coefficients a_{hk} of the equations of the system undergo infinitesimal random variations (from a "macroscopic" point of view, small variations due to learning will appear as "random"):

$$a_{hk} \to a_{hk}(1 + \rho_{hk}) = a_{hk} + \delta a_{hk} \qquad (7)$$

such that $< \rho_{hk} > = \rho$.

From:

$$
f(a_{hk} + \delta a_{hk}; \bar{\lambda} + \delta\bar{\lambda})
$$
$$
= \sum_{hk} a_{hk}\rho_{hk} \frac{\partial f}{\partial a_{hk}} + \left(\frac{\partial f}{\partial \lambda}\right)_{\lambda = \bar{\lambda}} \delta\bar{\lambda} = 0
$$
$$(8)$$

we find, on taking averages (since (6) is homogeneous of degree zero in the term λ^N and of degree one in all other terms, with respect to the variables a_{hk}):

$$<\delta\bar{\lambda}> = \frac{(\bar{\lambda})^N}{f'(\bar{\lambda})}\, \rho \qquad (9)$$

which tells us several interesting things. It requires, first of all, that $f'(\delta) \neq 0$, or else $\bar{\lambda}$ would be a degenerate eigenvalue, and even with $\rho = 0$ the degeneracy might be removed just the same by (7). We suppose therefore $f'(\bar{\lambda}) \neq 0$; to gain some insight into the behavior of $< \delta\bar{\lambda} >$ we just suppose here that the roots of (6) are all simple and equally spaced, so that

$$\bar{\lambda}_k = k\lambda_0, \quad (k = 1,2,3,\dots N) \qquad (10)$$

then (9) gives:

$$\left| \frac{<\delta\bar{\lambda}_k>}{\bar{\lambda}_k} \right| = \frac{1}{(N-1)!}\binom{N-1}{k-1}k^{N-1}\rho \qquad (11)$$

whence, for $k = 1$ and $k = N$ ($N \gg 0$):

$$\left| \frac{<\delta\bar{\lambda}_1>}{\bar{\lambda}_1} \right| = \frac{1}{(N-1)!}\, \rho \qquad (12)$$

$$\left| \frac{<\delta\bar{\lambda}_N>}{\bar{\lambda}_N} \right| \sim e^N \rho \qquad (13)$$

For our qualitative purposes, (12) and (13) suffice amply to show that random variations, due to learning as expressed by M.E. of type (5), may alter by a vanishing amount the smaller, by increasingly relevant amounts the larger eigenfrequencies of the normal modes of this model.

If a frequency which is kept long enough unchanged becomes permanent, this model will evolve therefore with learning so as to preserve the modes with small frequency; the modes with higher frequency, as well as those that correspond to degenerate solutions, will change at random without staying long enough at any given value to become permanent. After a "long" time, the system will have shifted spontaneously, because of its learning ability, toward a "ground state", in which there is no degeneracy, but the allowed frequencies stay as close to one another as the maximum and minimum values conceded by the M.E. to the constants will permit; this is the "senile age" of the system, in which no learning is possible because all available memories are already engrammed permanently (cf. (7): all $\delta a_{hk} \equiv 0$). The "infancy" of the system is characterized instead by $\rho > 0$, because for $t > 0$ (when all the $a_{hk}(0)$ have minimum absolute values) they can only increase monotonically: learning is somewhat slower, degeneracies are removed faster. The "adult" age corresponds to the period in which it is mostly $\delta a_{hk} \neq 0$, $\rho = 0$.

This cursory and incomplete glance at the properties of this model is tended only to show in which sense we should expect Wiener's principle to be verified by it: the "reliable" information is that carried by the small eigenfrequencies; when the erratic behavior of the higher frequencies pushes one of them down enough, it may be permanently "engrammed", increasing thus the reliability of the system.

3. The main differences between the machine we study and the model of it discussed in 2 above lie, as regards the validity of Wiener's principle, in the non-linearity of the N.E. (2) and in the 2nd criterion of stability (Section **4**, C, 4). The situation is made worse to some extent than in (2) by this non-linearity; in any case, though, by assuming the number of elements to be large enough, one ought to obtain a preferential decrease of the effect of random learning variations on the faster reverberations (to higher frequencies of the model described in 2 slower reverberations of the machine now correspond), so as to reproduce, although perhaps less dramatically, a situation like that represented in 2 by (12) and (13).

The existence of a thalamus and of a reticular system (2nd criterion of stability) makes instead a tremendous improvement upon the model discussed in 2, which could still satisfy Wiener's principle even though it is not endowed with these homeostatic devices. Conditioning of the first kind and arousal of attention by the thalamus, prevention of too diffuse (and therefore not very meaningful) reverberations by the reticular system, are only examples, clearly, of what controlling devices of such effectiveness may do in the way of forcing the machine into learning important information in a reliable manner. These devices are especially important if the memory is prevalently of *negative*, rather than of *positive* type as is assumed here

(Section **3**, C, 1), because then the machine would have, in its infancy, a tendency towards epilepsy.

Of importance in a discussion of this principle are also, clearly, all the additional special-purpose devices that Nature uses. The machine also is better with these devices, as intermediate links between external inputs and outputs, and inputs and outputs to the machine proper or cortex; their consideration, however, belongs to engineering more than to physics, and would not be relevant at this place. In conclusion, we should like to stress once more our firm conviction that the speediest way to progress in all the problems connected with the actual construction of machines of this sort is humble resort to Nature's own doings, through neuroanatomy and physiology.

c. Further Outlooks

As a final comment, we think it appropriate to remark that the general formalism of N.E., M.E. and A.L.H. which is expounded here seems to us to admit of a far wider range of applicability than that to which it has been restricted in this work. The N.E. in fact, for instance, serve only to express, in a more or less schematic manner, the fact that a decision is taken, after a weighted evaluation of the information which lasts a finite time, by a member of a set; and that such a decision is bound to affect other decisions, etc. We may change their name into that of *decision equations,* call the M.E. *evolution equations,* and take all our considerations over to the study of social or economical or other collective phenomena.

We have pursued this line of thought in several directions for personal amusement, and have soon found, to our surprise, that the qualitative analysis given here for thought-processes applies as well, *mutatis mutandis* (that is, names), to a great many other instances. We believe that, as soon as it becomes possible to agree on a concrete choice of schemes and numbers, quite reasonable predictions may be made in this way about, say, the operation of a stock-exchange, the variation in time of a parameter in feminine fashion, the type of national government that would best obey Wiener's principle, and so on. This we say with at least the same degree of assurance that we have found in the economists who apply the Schrödinger equation to the study of their problems.

Although we have refrained here from a quantitative analysis of the several mathematical problems formulated in the course of this work, the results we have already obtained in this direction seem to justify some optimism; if these expectations are not illusory, then the present formalism might help us to gain a finer knowledge of some physical phenomena that can now be treated only with statistical methods.

This research would not have been possible without the generous and enthusiastic collaboration of Dr. V. Braitenberg, neuroanatomist, among whose merits were certainly not least patience toward this writer's initial ignorance and presumption, and success in eliminating the latter; of Dr. F. Lauria, a young mathematician who dared to place mathematics not too high above common brains; and of many others, to all of whom it is our duty and pleasure to extend our sincerest thanks.

References

Beurle, R. L. (1956). *Phil. Trans.* **B669,** 55.

Braitenberg, V. & Lauria, F. *Nuovo Cim.* Suppl. (In press).

Braitenberg, V., Caianiello, E. R., Lauria, F. & Onesto, N. (1959). *Nuovo Cim.* **11,** 278.

McCulloch, W. S. & Pitts, W. (1943). *Bull. math. Biophys.* **5.**

Moruzzi, G. & Magoun, H. W. (1949). *Electroenceph. clin. Neurophysiol.* **1,** 445.

Wiener, N. (1958). "Nonlinear Problems in Random Theory". Massachusetts Institute of Technology.

4
Introduction

(1967)
K. Steinbuch and E. Schmitt

Adaptive systems using learning matrices
Biocybernetics in Avionics,
H. L. Oestericicher and D. R. Moore (Eds.), New York: Gordon and Breach, pp. 751–768.

During the first flowering of neural networks in the early 1960s, a number of parallel adaptive learning models were suggested. One of them, the learning matrix (*Die Lernmatrix*), was proposed by Steinbuch in 1961 and is capable of both pattern classification and pattern association, though by a mechanism somewhat different from those used by other neural network pattern associators.

The learning matrix is an array of connections that are organized in rows and columns. Input patterns are impressed on the columns. Outputs are read off from the rows. There are modifiable connection strengths between the rows and columns, which can be adjusted over the range between -1 and +1. The output of a row is given by the inner product between the connection strengths and the input activity in the columns. Therefore each row activity corresponds to the output of a single generic neural network neuron. The "neuron" is given a modifiable threshold—which is valuable for many problems—by the technical trick of *augmenting* the state vector, that is, adding an additional column with the fixed input value +1 to the matrix. As the connection strength between that $(n + 1)$st column and a particular row changes, it has the effect of changing the threshold of that unit. (See papers on the perceptron, papers 8 and 11 in *Neurocomputing: Foundations of Research*.)

The simplest version of the learning matrix acts as a pattern classifier, which is still the most common use of a neural network. That is, given a particular input pattern, it figures out which category it belongs to, for example, which letter or digit corresponds to a particular array of pixels. In the learning matrix each row corresponds to a particular category (a particular letter or digit for character classification). During operation an input is presented to the matrix. Attached to the rows is a *maximum detector*, which selects the row with the largest response, giving the categorization determined by the network.

The weights connecting rows and columns can be trained by several mechanisms. Training is *supervised*, that is, a categorized set of examples is used to set the weights. The rule used is a coincidence rule, effectively Hebbian, so that only the weights on the row corresponding to the correct classification are changed.

As Steinbuch and Schmitt point out, the classifications performed by the learning matrix are very similar to those formed by a nearest neighbor, minimum distance classifier (see papers 25, 26, and 27), with the distinction that only a single representative of a category is allowed. If many examples are presented, the learning rule implies that the weights representing a category will be proportional to the average pattern in the category. Steinbuch and Schmitt suggest that by using the matrix in what they call *read out mode*, which reads off the weights in a row, we can get an idea of what this average pattern might be. This can be performed with the *row selector*, which chooses a particular row and reads out its weights.

By combining the read out mechanism with the attachment of an additional learning matrix to the output of the first matrix, it is possible to form what is called a *learning matrix dipole*, which can act as a simple pattern associator.

Suppose we have a single learning matrix operating, so that its output will be represented by a single active row. Suppose we have a *second* matrix attached to the output of the first, with another set of adjustable weights. We train the second matrix so that every time a particular row is active, the pattern we wish to associate with that category is presented to its column inputs. If we use a coincidence learning rule to modify the weights of the second matrix, then the weights of that row will take on the values of the pattern associated with the category. In the future, presentation of an example of the category to the first matrix will generate the associated output pattern at the column outputs of the second matrix.

There are a number of other learning matrix variants. The overall system is closely related in its properties to a number of better known neural network algorithms. The use of abstract rows and columns, instead of explicit computing units with weights, allows operating flexibility, for example, it is natural to read off row and column weights when that is useful, even though such an idea violates some of our intuitions about what model neurons should be doing.

(1967)
K. Steinbuch and E. Schmitt

Adaptive systems using learning matrices
Biocybernetics in Avionics,
H. L. Oestericicher and D. R. Moore (Eds.), New York: Gordon and Breach, pp. 751–768.

Abstract

Of late, learning machines are gaining in practical importance for processes in which the governing mathematical rules are a priori unknown, and/or vary with time. Such systems change their behaviour on the basis of their past experience. During the adaptation stage a mathematical relationship between the input and the output or the adaptive system is established by changing the parameters of an adjustable transformation unit in accordance with a selected criterion of performance.

The adjustable transformation unit can be realized using Learning Matrices. Depending on the complexity of a Learning Matrix structure, binary or non-binary sets of input patterns can be transformed to outputs which may either be represented in an "one out of m-code" or in any binary code or in a set or non-binary output components. In general, the latter transformation may be arbitrary and non-linear.

It is an inherent and advantageous property of Learning Matrix systems that the data are processed in parallel and that the systems are capable of operating in various modes. In the training mode (operating mode 1) some definite training procedure may be implemented. In special cases, adaptation can be performed automatically too, either in one step, or by an iterative procedure using some averaging technique or by other iterative methods.

Learning Matrix systems have been realized by using adaptive hardware and by digital computer simulation. As one special example, a hierarchical adaptive system which is capable of predicting numbers of binary sequences whose statistical properties are not restricted is described.

Adaptive System Model

In recent years much effort has been made to develop technical systems which we generally refer to as "adaptive systems," "learning systems" or "self-organizing systems." Although many definitions of such systems exist, a general description including all of them is yet lacking.

Adaptive systems have practical importance for processes in which the governing mathematical laws are a priori unknown, and/or vary with time. Their purpose is to achieve a practical goal, for example control a non-linear process, or recognize variable input patterns or forecast the weather etc.

In order to explain the principal function of an adaptive system, it is convenient to consider the model in Figure 1.

The relevant data pertaining to the physical conditions of the environment to be adapted are transduced by the sensor unit. It should be noted that certain difficulties are associated with the selection of suitable characteristic data of the process. As this problem is beyond the scope of this paper it will not be dealt with in greater detail.

In order to transform the input signals into the respective output signals a transformation unit is needed, the parameters of which are adjustable. Further, an adaptation algorithm must be provided which should be capable of making adjustments depending on the instantaneous physical situation of the environment and the past experience stored in the system (storage of experience).

The decisions for adjusting the particular elements and for storing or eliminating past experience are controlled by the evaluation unit in such a way that the performance of the system would be improved successively during adaptation, until the desired transformation is established. Out of several possible adaptation criteria one may be selected corresponding to the instantaneous situation. Further, fa-

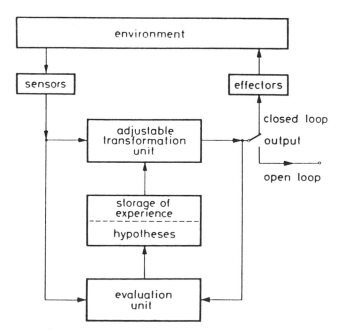

Figure 1   Adaptive System Model

cility must be provided to store past experience, including the possibility "to forget," in cases where the processes are non-stationary. All these possibilities foreseen by the designer will be henceforth called "hypotheses." The larger the number of hypotheses, the higher would be the probability to find a desired solution of the problem provided that convergence can be achieved. Lastly a suitable evaluation criterion for the performance of the system has to be chosen.

In some applications the output of the adaptive system is fed back through effectors (closed loop system), for instance in closed loop control systems. In order to effect a goal directed change of the environment, suitable parameter changes selected by the hypotheses unit must be carried out internally (test signals) depending on the past experience and the state of the external system to be controlled.

On the other hand there exist processes in which the output has no influence on the environment, for instance as in the case of pattern recognition, weather forecasting, or similar applications (open loop system).

It should be noted that this system stands for a general model. In practical systems sometimes the particular units of the scheme are integrated so that they are not distinguishable from one another. In some cases the storage of experience may be contained in the adjustable transformation unit.

Learning Matrices as Adjustable Transformation Unit

Adjustable transformation units can be realized by Learning Matrices. The principle of Learning Matrices, and some of their applications have been published in earlier papers.[1, 2, 3, 4] The essential features concerned with adaptive networks will be described below.

The structure of a single Learning Matrix may be represented as in Figure 2. It consists essentially of adjustable connecting elements ("weights") arranged in the form of a matrix. The columns and rows of the matrix are connected with input and output units which come into action during the various operating modes. Three operating modes are possible.

1. Operating Mode 1 (Training Mode)

The input signals $e_1 \ldots e_n$ derived from the sensors are applied to the columns (Fig. 3). They may be binary or non-binary.

In the latter case, we assume that their values are such that

$$-1 \leq e_\nu \leq +1 \tag{1}$$

If the inputs are binary, then they may take the values +1 or −1 directly.

Further, we suppose that the adjustable connecting elements may be varied between the limits −1 and +1; i.e.

$$-1 \leq \upsilon_{\mu\nu} \leq +1 \tag{2}$$

During the training mode the "weights" of one particular row are adjusted simultaneously. In order to achieve this, a certain row is chosen by the row selector, and the elements are varied by means of coincidence of row and column signals. There are various procedures possible to adjust the elements, based on certain criteria, which will be described later. Each of the possible input sets is assigned to a particular row; each row corresponds to a certain "class".

Besides the n columns corresponding to the n components of the input, it may be seen from Figure 3 that there is an auxiliary column $n +1$ of connecting elements. By

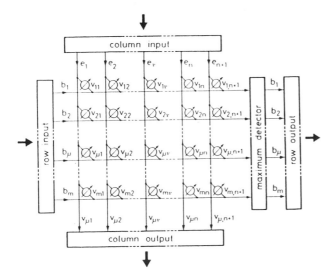

Figure 2 Schematic of the Learning Matrix

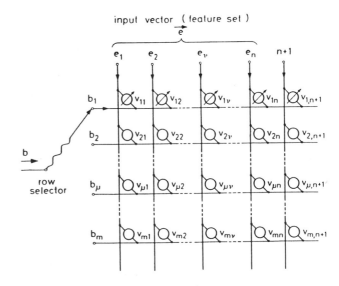

Figure 3 Operating Mode 1 (Training Mode)

means of this, the performance of the system in classifying the various input sets is improved. In the case of binary signals the $(n + 1)^{st}$ column is not necessary, as other means for classifying are provided.

2. Operating Mode 2 (Classifying Mode)

During the operating mode 2 which would be also called classifying mode it is required that the input sets be classified to the respective classes represented by the "weight sets" contained in the various rows.

As is shown in Figure 4 the n components of the first input signal $e^{(i)}$ are applied to the columns $1 \ldots n$, and a constant signal $+1$ to the column $n + 1$. In each of the rows a linear function of the input $e^{(i)}$ is formed by multiplying the "weights" in the columns with the corresponding signal components and summing up along the rows. Thus we obtain a set of linear functions $Z_1(e^{(i)}) \ldots Z_m(e^{(i)})$ at the outputs of the rows, namely

$$Z_\mu(e^{(i)}) = \upsilon_{\mu 1} \cdot e_1^{(i)} + \upsilon_{\mu 2} \cdot e_2^{(i)} + \cdots + \upsilon_{\mu \nu} \cdot e_\nu^{(i)} + \cdots$$

$$+ \upsilon_{\mu n} \cdot e_n^{(i)} + \upsilon_{\mu, n+1}$$

$$\mu = 1, \ldots, m \tag{3}$$

The maximum detector selects and indicates the row with the greatest sum.

It may be seen that any input set $e^{(i)}$ can be represented by an n-dimensional vector in the Euclidean space.

$$e^{(i)} = \left\{ e_1^{(i)}, e_2^{(i)}, \ldots, e_\upsilon^{(i)}, \ldots e_n^{(i)} \right\} \tag{4}$$

Similarly a "weight set" may also be represented by a vector υ_μ, however, with $n + 1$ components.

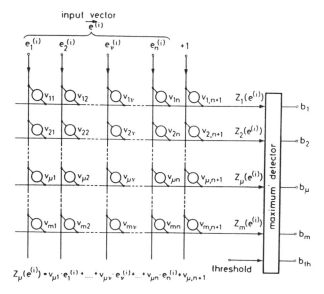

$$Z_\mu(e^{(i)}) = \upsilon_{\mu 1} \cdot e_1^{(i)} + \ldots + \upsilon_{\mu \nu} \cdot e_\nu^{(i)} + \ldots + \upsilon_{\mu n} \cdot e_n^{(i)} + \upsilon_{\mu, n+1}$$

Figure 4 Operating Mode 2 (Classifying Mode)

$$\upsilon_\mu = \left\{ \upsilon_{\mu 1}, \upsilon_{\mu 2}, \ldots, \upsilon_{\mu \nu}, \ldots, \upsilon_{\mu n}, \upsilon_{\mu, n+1} \right\} \tag{5}$$

Further, we define a reduced "weight vector" v_u with n components

$$\upsilon_\mu^* = \left\{ \upsilon_{\mu 1}, \upsilon_{\mu 2}, \ldots, \upsilon_{\mu \nu}, \ldots, \upsilon_{\mu n} \right\} \tag{6}$$

The input sets and the n-dimensional "weight set" υ_μ^* may also be thought of as being represented by the endpoints of the vectors in the n-dimensional space.

Classification is obtained as a result of partitioning the n-dimensional space into regions by a set of hyperplanes which satisfy the following equations:

$$Z_1(e^{(i)}) - Z_2(e^{(i)}) = 0$$
$$Z_1(e^{(i)}) - Z_3(e^{(i)}) = 0$$
$$\cdot$$
$$\cdot$$
$$Z_1(e^{(i)}) - Z_m(e^{(i)}) = 0$$
$$Z_2(e^{(i)}) - Z_3(e^{(i)}) = 0$$
$$\cdot$$
$$\cdot$$
$$Z_2(e^{(i)}) - Z_m(e^{(i)}) = 0$$
$$\cdot$$
$$\cdot$$
$$Z_{m-1}(e^{(i)}) - Z_m(e^{(i)}) = 0 \tag{7}$$

There are $\dfrac{m \cdot (m-1)}{2}$ such equations ($m =$ number of classes) of which, however, not all are necessarily linearly independent of one another. Further, under certain circumstances, some of the hyperplanes represented by Eq. (7) may be redundant.

In the case of n-dimensional input sets the separating hyperplanes have $(n - 1)$ dimensions. Thus, for two-dimensional inputs straight lines are obtained; for three-dimensional inputs we obtain planes.

In vector representation, the Eq. (7) can also be written in the form:

$$e^{(i)} \cdot (\upsilon_1^* - \upsilon_2^*) = (\upsilon_{2, n+1} - \upsilon_{1, n+1})$$
$$e^{(i)} \cdot (\upsilon_1^* - \upsilon_3^*) = (\upsilon_{3, n+1} - \upsilon_{1, n+1})$$
$$\cdot$$

etc. $\tag{8}$

For all cases where the difference of the $(n + 1)^{st}$ "weights" in Eq. (8) is not equal to zero, the separating hyperplanes do not pass through the origin of the Euclidean space. The function of the auxiliary "weights" in the $(n + 1)^{st}$ column is therefore explained. By giving them appropriate values we may obtain a lateral shift of the separating hyperplanes.

As a special case we consider minimum distance classification. Here, an input set is categorized to such a class that the distance between the points corresponding to the input set and to the representative of the class is a minimum. In this case it is necessary to adjust the "weights" of the $(n + 1)^{\text{st}}$ column to values such that

$$\upsilon_{\mu, n+1} = -\frac{1}{2} |\upsilon_\mu^*|^2$$

$$\mu = 1, ..., m \tag{9}$$

To illustrate this special case we consider two-dimensional input sets which are to be classified into four classes. We assume that the class representatives exist as weight vectors stored in four rows of a Learning Matrix. In Figure 5 the points $V_1^*, ..., V_4^*$ denote the endpoints of the weight vectors $\upsilon_1^*, ..., \upsilon_4^*$ in the two-dimensional space. In this case the separating hyperplanes are the perpendicular bisectors of the lines joining the points $V_1^*, V_2^*, V_3^*, V_4^*$. The classes are formed as regions bordered by these separating lines. Input sets are classified according to the regions in which the endpoints of the vectors are located. As may be seen in Figure 5 the separating straight line (indicated by the dotted line S_{24}) between class 2 and class 4 is redundant. This occurs generally when classes are not adjoined.

Further, in some applications it would not be expedient to classify input sets which lie too far away from the nearest class representative. Such input sets can be recognized and indicated by means of an additional variable threshold

input to the maximum detector (Fig. 4). To do this, we can arrange that, in case of binary inputs, the row output b_{th} delivers a signal if a predetermined Hamming distance between an input set and nearest representative is exceeded.

3. Operating Mode 3 (Read Out)

In this mode of operation the components of the representative vector stored in any row are read out at the column outputs (Fig. 6). The components of a certain row are either binary or non-binary. As it will be shown later, even in the case of binary input sets the connecting elements may assume non-binary values. If, in spite of this, binary signals are desired at the column outputs (Fig. 6) a suitable transformation must be performed. For instance according to the following relationship

$$\text{column output} \begin{cases} \upsilon'_{\mu\nu} = +1, & \text{if } \upsilon_{\mu\nu} > 0 \\ \upsilon'_{\mu\nu} = -1, & \text{if } \upsilon_{\mu\nu} < 0 \\ \text{undecided}, & \text{if } \upsilon_{\mu\nu} = 0 \end{cases}$$

4. Learning Matrix-Dipole

The various operating modes of the Learning Matrix provide us with means to construct comprehensive systems for performing adjustable transformations. A so-called Learning Matrix-Dipole consisting of two matrices is shown in Figure 7. The connecting elements of a given row of the two matrices are adjusted simultaneously, whereby, the adaptation laws in the operating mode 1 may be different for the two matrices. When the left matrix operates in the classifying mode, the right one operates in the read-out mode. Thus any binary or non-binary input set of n components can be transformed into any desired output set of M components. This is performed in two stages: In the left

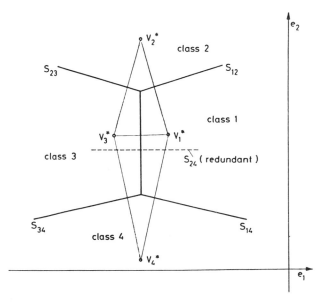

Figure 5 Minimum Distance Classification

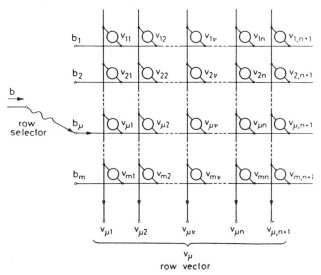

Figure 6 Operating Mode 3 (Read Out)

matrix the *n*-dimensional input set is transformed into a binary output in an "one out of *m*-code," the right matrix transforms this "one out of *m*" binary input into a binary or non-binary *M* component output. In this way non-linear transformations may also be effected.

In the last years Learning Matrices have been realized by suitable hardware and by computer simulation. The most appropriate elements for realizing the connecting elements are tape-wound magnetic cores up to now.

It should be observed that the great advantage of Learning Matrix networks in hardware is the fact that during all operating modes the data are processed in parallel. For this reason a Learning Matrix in hardware operates very much faster than a simulated network of this type by a digital computer.

5. Adapting Techniques

During the training mode the connecting elements of the Learning Matrix are adjusted. This may be done by various procedures.

6. Binary Input Sets

a) one step adjustment

A trivial case is that of one step adjustment. Here, the connecting elements are set in one step to the binary values +1 or −1 depending on the binary inputs. This procedure is useful if the representative of the desired class is known and available to be applied to the input.

b) stepwise adjustment

If this is not the case, then a one step adjustment cannot be applied. The following averaging technique is useful, if the endpoints of the input vectors are clustered around a mean value. During every adjustment step, instead of setting the connecting elements to their full values at

once, they are shifted by a small amount Δv in the appropriate direction. Thus, the "weights" of the matrix are made to act as up and down counters with boundaries at +1 and −1. The rate at which the boundaries are achieved is dependent on the value of Δ_υ which may be controlled according to a suitable criterion ("*h*-input," see ref. 3). For instance, the input sets belonging to a class may be statistically distributed around a mean value. Then, after some adjusting cycles the components of this mean value set would be formed in the connecting elements of the corresponding row.

It must be noted that the lengths of the row vectors are not necessarily equal. In order that the input set be classified correctly in the operating mode 2, the classification must be invariant with respect to the vector length. This can be achieved by increasing all the length to the maximum value $|\upsilon_\mu^*| = \sqrt{n}$ (as all components are either +1 or −1). In this case an input set would be classified to a class to whose representative it bears the smallest angle.

7. Non-Binary Input Sets

a) One step adjustment

If, as in the case of binary input sets, the class representative is available at the input, adaptation can be performed in one step[5]. Here, it is suitable to give the $(n + 1)^{st}$ weights the value in Eq. (9) so that the matrix may act as a minimum distance classifier.

b) Standard average adjustment

For stationary processes, under the condition that the input sets are clustered around a mean value, a standard average technique is useful to perform adaptation. The class representative would be obtained by presenting the cluster of input sets in several steps.

The $(N + 1)^{st}$ adjustment of the μth row vector υ_μ would then be

$$\upsilon_\mu^*(N + 1) = \frac{1}{N + 1} \cdot [N \cdot \upsilon_\mu^*(N) + e(N + 1)] \tag{10}$$

where the *N*'s represent the number of adjustments at which the row μ was selected.

If all clusters have equal diameters, minimum distance classification may be used, whereby equidistant hyperplanes constitute the separating surfaces. Otherwise the adjustment of the $(n + 1)^{st}$ "weights" may facilitate the required shift of the separating hyperplanes to be achieved.

c) Weighted average adjustment

In the case of non-stationary processes, a weighted average technique should be employed in order that events occurring at earlier stages have a weaker effect on an

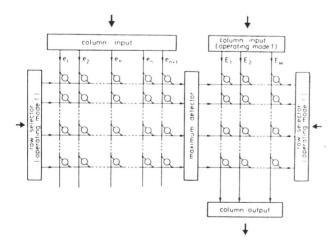

Figure 7   Schematic of Learning Matrix-Dipole

adjustment. For example, the following adjustment law can be applied:

$$\upsilon_\mu^*(N + 1) = \alpha \cdot \upsilon_\mu^*(N) + (1-\alpha) \cdot e(N + 1)$$
$$(0 < \alpha < 1) \tag{11}$$

In this case the $(N + r)^{\text{th}}$ input set is weighted α^{-r} times as strong as the Nth input set. By setting $\alpha = \dfrac{N}{N + 1}$, Eq. (11) reduces to Eq. (10).

A more versatile system may be obtained by controlling the parameter α in Eq. (11) with a suitable evaluation function.

Binary Prediction Using a Learning Matrix-Dipole

As an application of an adaptive system (open loop) illustrated in the model of Figure 1 we consider a device capable of predicting binary sequences. In this system a Learning Matrix-Dipole is used as an adjustable transformation unit.

The complexity of a predicting system depends on the statistical properties of the binary sequences to be processed. We assume that the binary sequences are represented by non-homogeneous Markovian processes, i.e. the lengths (degrees) and the conditional probabilities of the Markovian chains vary with time. In doing this we include all other statistical processes in our system.

An adaptive system designed to process such sequences should adapt itself to

a) the varying lengths of the Markovian chains, and

b) the varying conditional probabilities.

Figure 8 shows a system capable of performing these requirements. It consists, essentially, of a Learning Matrix-Dipole structure. The requirement a) is satisfied by the left matrix which is divided into a set of subsystems $P_1, P_2, \ldots,$ P_n. Markovian chains of length one are adapted in the subsystem P_1, that of length n in the subsystem P_n. The evaluated past experience of the subsystems are stored in the last column ex_{n+1}

Requirement b) can be satisfied by the right-hand matrix which calculates the conditional probability of the oncoming binary number according to several procedures. A column pair (j) is provided for each procedure, whereby in the first column (p_j) the conditional probability is calculated and in the second (ex_j) the experience corresponding to the respective procedure is stored.

The various subsystems of the left matrix and the different procedures in the right one can be looked upon as a set of hypotheses. The hypotheses of the left matrix are primary, and those of the right are secondary; i.e. for predic-

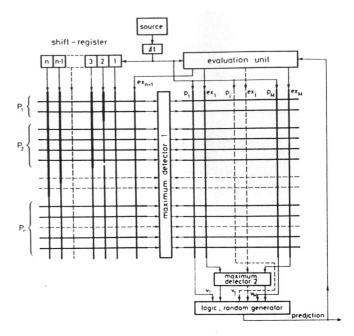

Figure 8 Binary Prediction Using a Learning Matrix Dipole

tion, first, a subsystem, and subsequently a column pair are selected such that the "best" success will be achieved.

The input signals are emitted as a binary sequence from the source. Δt represents some time delay of the oncoming number with respect to its prediction. The input signals to the left matrix are derived from the parallel outputs of a shift-register in which the preceding set of n binary digits are stored. This set constitutes the Markovian chains of variable length $1 \ldots n$. Markovian chains which occur the first time are adapted into the respective subsystems $P_1, \ldots, P_n$ in one step, by automatically selecting a free row of each subsystem, as described in (3). Thus, each row represents a certain Markovian chain. In the same row of the right matrix the conditional probabilities of this chain are formed according to the various procedures which differ from one another in the step amount $\Delta\upsilon$ by which the connecting values are varied. In the first column (p_1), the step-width $\Delta\upsilon$ has a small value which would be useful in the case of stationary processes. In the last column (p_M), $\Delta\upsilon$ has a large value, so that very strong nonstationary processes may be adapted. The adjustment of the connecting elements is as follows. If the number following the Markovian chain is +1 the connecting value is increased by $\Delta\upsilon$, if it is −1 it is decreased by $\Delta\upsilon$.

The performance of the various hypotheses consisting of the subsystems in the left matrix and the M procedures for calculating the conditional probability in the right matrix is evaluated by the evaluation unit when the predicted input signal occurs. The results of the evaluations are stored as experience in the column ex_{n+1} of the left matrix as well

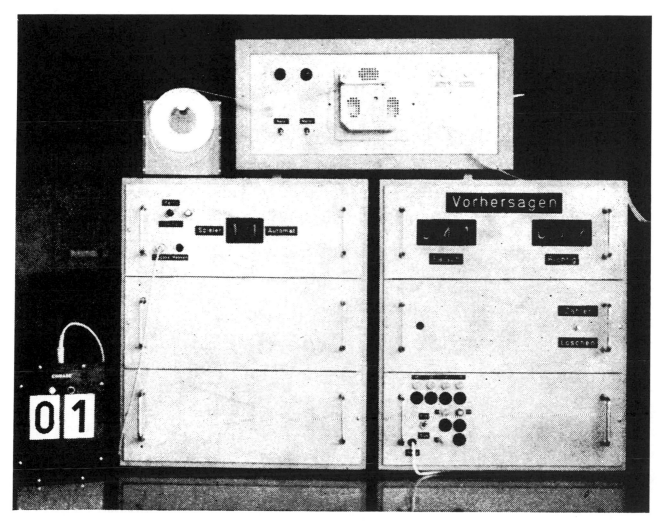

Figure 9 Binary Number Predictor

as in the columns $ex_1 \ldots ex_M$ of the right matrix. This is achieved by increasing the respective connecting values by a fixed amount $\Delta\upsilon$ in the case of correct prediction, and decreasing them in the case of incorrect prediction. Thus, the connecting element with the highest value determines the "best" hypothesis. By variation of the step-width $\Delta\upsilon$, past experience can be eliminated more or less rapidly (as the connecting values are bounded at ±1).

For prediction of the next number, the left matrix works in the classifying mode in which a row, corresponding to the Markovian chain at the input, and to the best subsystem, is selected by the maximum detector 1. The right matrix operates in the read-out mode (operating mode 3). Here, the best hypothesis is selected by the maximum detector 2. The corresponding weight value υ_j is used to predict the number most probably emitted by the source. The prediction would be:

$$
\begin{array}{ll}
+1, & \text{if } \upsilon_j > +\delta \\
-1, & \text{if } \upsilon_j < -\delta \\
\text{indeterminate,} & \text{if } -\delta \le \upsilon_j \le +\delta
\end{array}
$$

(δ represents a certain dead zone)

In the last case a binary number would be generated at random.

Figure 9 shows a realized system of the described structure in hardware. The input signals may be generated by pushing the buttons "0" or "1", or read in by a tape reader. We conducted a large number of experiments with this system and we investigated stationary as well as nonstationary binary sequences consisting of Markovian chains $1 \ldots 4$. To obtain a measure for the performance of the system, the cumulative entropy and the cumulative redundancy of the binary sequences were calculated[6].

An experiment with 121 binary sequences was started containing 700 digits each. The processes were mostly nonstationary. The cumulative redundancy revealed that 73% of the digits may be predicted correctly by an ideal system. With the system in Figure 9, consisting of four subsystems and three procedures for adapting the conditional probabilities, we obtained 69.8% correct predictions.

References

1. Steinbuch, K. Die Lernmatrix, *Kybernetik* **1**, 36–45, January 1961.

2. Steinbuch, K., and Piske, U. A. W. Learning matrices and their applications, *IEEE Trans. on El. Computers, EC-***12**, 846–862, December 1963.

3. Steinbuch, K. Adaptive networks using learning matrices, *Kybernetik*, **2**, 148–152, February 1965.

4. Steinbuch, K., and Widrow, B. A critical comparison of two kinds of adaptive classification networks, *IEEE Trans. on Electronic Computers*, EC-**14**, 737–740, October 1965.

5. Müller, P. Eigenschaften und Aufbau von Lernmatrizen für nichtbinäre Signale, *Kybernetik* **2**, 103, September 1964.

6. Schmitt, E. Untersuchungen an Binärprädiktoren, insbesondere bezüglich ihrer Anpassungsfähigkeit und ihrer Vorhersgeleistung gegenüber Versuchspersonen, *Kybernetik*, **2**, 93–102, September 1964.

7. Nilsson, N. J. "Learning machines", McGraw-Hill, New York (1965).

5
Introduction

(1968)
James A. Anderson

A model for memory using spatial correlation functions
Kybernetik 5: 113–119

(Comments by Anderson). This paper was the first modeling paper I wrote. It is included here because I think some of the ideas it contains are still worth making, though sometimes forgotten. (I was also pleased to see that it was reprinted in the excellent collection edited by Shaw and Palm, *Brain Theory*, included, I hope, for the same reason.)

Last year I had a brief exchange of letters with a foreign philosopher, who informed me that my ideas about concepts were all wrong and that he was pleased to send me his own papers, which showed the right way to work with concepts. (Symbolically!) Among other comments he made were that he never understood why anyone even bothered to do experiments with the higher mammals in neuroscience or psychology because they were so complicated. To understand the brain of humans, it was necessary to start with lower organisms, understand them, and eventually work up to the higher animals, recapitulating evolution, as it were.

Many neuroscientists would agree. A great many wonderful simple systems have been found in "lower" organisms that illuminate one or another aspect of the nervous system. Neuroscientists, however, being biologists, are also well aware that every animal species we look at, even a sponge or a jellyfish, has managed to survive until now, against an array of environmental and biological obstacles. In its totality it may be just as complex as we are, only with the complexity in different places.

From 1964 to 1967 I spent several years working on the nervous system of *Aplysia californica*, a large marine mollusc with a nervous system designed by God for neurophysiologists. The *Aplysia* nervous system is composed of a number of clusters of nerve cells, called ganglia, joined together by large nerve trunks. The nervous system is very rugged and can survive in isolation for hours or even days, with care. Or the ganglia can be stabilized mechanically while still in the animal and the responses of cells to stimuli can be recorded. Molluscan neurons do not have dendrites but make their synaptic connections on the axons, and the cell bodies are pushed to the outside of the ganglion where they sit, waiting for the physiologist's microelectrode, ripe and luscious as orange grapes. (The *Aplysia* nervous system is brightly pigmented.)

Eric Kandel and his collaborators have done world-famous work on the neurobiology of *Aplysia* (see Kandel 1976). One of the best-characterized modifiable synapses is found in *Aplysia*, and some of the biochemical and physiological details of that invertebrate synapse do seem to carry over to mammalian neurons.

However, if you are interested in global nervous system organization as it affects mammalian cognition, *Aplysia* is not the place to look. One major difference between many invertebrates and mammals is what makes invertebrates so attractive to physiologists. There are a small number of cells in a ganglion, a few thousand at most in *Aplysia*, and some of these cells are *identifiable*, that is, they recur from individual to individual in the same location and with the same connections and functions. The individual cell and its connections are genetically hardwired, although connection strengths can change with experience, as Kandel has shown in his extensive experiments on the withdrawal responses.

What this suggested (to me, in 1967) was that there were fundamental differences in the way that one could organize nervous systems. Invertebrates with small numbers of cells had handcrafted neurons, each one of which was designed to fit with other specialized cells to produce behavior. Each cell seemed to show considerable behavioral specificity. They often looked somewhat like grandmother cells, though cells in a group of cells usually cooperated with each other in complex ways to produce behavior. However, there were some examples known of what seem to be genuine *command neurons*, where a single cell has major responsibility for a coordinated behavior. A well-known example of a command neuron is the famous squid giant axon, which controls and coordinates the squid's escape response.

However, the vertebrate, and especially the mammalian, nervous system presented a different picture. In place of handcrafting, there was mass production. Tens of millions of neurons cooperated to bring about any complex behavior. Indentifiable cells in *Aplysia* had different sizes and shapes. But large areas of cerebral cortex looked pretty homogeneous. One layer V pyramidal cell looked about the same as nearby ones. And there were millions of layer V pyramids. Whatever organizational principle was being used must involve activity of many neurons, and the overall activity pattern must be the important thing.

But if a reasonably large number of cells cooperated to produce a behavior and represent information, then the same cell must participate in many different behaviors. Therefore the individual synapses of those cells must also participate in many different associations and behaviors. This is roughly what Karl Lashley was saying in his discussion of nervous system organization (see paper 5 in *Neurocomputing: Foundations of Research*).

Suppose we consider memory. Suppose that what was being stored in memory were large patterns. If very many things were stored, they would start interacting with each other, that is, one memory pattern would interfere with others *in the act of storage*.

I was not a psychologist. And what filters down to graduate students is a caricature of the deep, careful, and highly hedged thinking going on at the tenured faculty level. Because we (the graduate students) knew that frogs saw bugs (Lettvin et al., paper 13) and that Hubel and Wiesel had shown that cats saw lines, there must be more and more complex detectors further along in the brain. Grandmother cells seemed like a real possibility. And with grandmother cells there is no reason to worry about interference between different stored memories because memories are separate, just like (to use another metaphor) files in a file cabinet. And, to an engineer, storing things on top of each other seemed untidy since information was lost irretrievably.

So this paper was an attempt to look at the implications of the other point of view. Suppose that memories, represented as activity patterns, involved activities of many units and that the memories that were stored simply were these patterns. And suppose they all had to be stored in the same storage elements, that is, some part of a storage element's value (a single number) was due to one stored memory, and the rest of its value was due to other memories. Could such a system still work? Could it actually store memories and retain enough information to function as a memory?

The answer was yes, *if* certain restrictions were placed on the functions of memory. Exact retrieval of stored information was likely to be impossible because since it had been mixed up with other information. But it might be possible to do useful things if the right questions were asked. For example, *recognition*, that is, has a new pattern been seen before?

With the proper mathematical techniques, it proved quite easy to get a numerical measure of the familiarity of a new pattern, that is, whether or not it had been seen before. And the signal-to-noise ratio of retrieval could be quite high. A number of interesting effects fell out of this approach. For example, if a number of stored items were similar to each other, then there was constructive interference between them, so the response to a new, similar pattern could be very large. This is the mechansm used to form concepts that is described in Knapp and Anderson (paper 36 in *Neurocomputing: Foundations of Research*). The mathematical techniques were interesting too. Problems very much like this memory were studied in signal detection theory and communications theory, where it was necessary to detect a signal (the desired memory) in the presence of noise (the other stuff). This immediately led to the use of things like inner products and correlation functions and turned memory research into a branch of statistics, rather than to filing cabinet design. And because all the elements are computing at once, the approach is intrinsically parallel, which was perceived of as an intrinsically *good thing*, even in 1968.

A few years later this model was directly applied to the storage of items in memorized lists (Anderson 1973). An argument for some kind of parallelism in memory operation is that it takes about as long to find out if something is present in memory as to find out if it is absent in memory. If list items are separately represented, serially searched, and randomly arranged, then it should take less time for a hit (because half the items are searched, on the average) than for a miss (because all the items must be checked). As the list gets longer, the difference in search time for hits and misses should grow in systematically different ways, but this pattern is not found. So it seemed natural to apply the recognition model to some real psychological data, which appeared to fit reasonably well. This application also lead to my gainful employment as a mathematical psychologist, a not inconsiderable personal benefit. In general psychologists are much more hospitable to unusual ideas and theory than are neuroscientists, who often seem to be so hypnotized by the complexity of the system they are studying that they are incapable of thinking about it.

One procedural point: All the calculations in this paper were done with a mechanical calculator, which was slow, but made delightful noises when it operated and usually gave the right answers.

I still believe that the basic ideas in this paper are more or less correct: First, information is represented as patterns, not by single cells. Second, use of patterns means that interference occurs between stored items, and so information loss must be accepted. Third, memory and cognitive operations in general are statistical. And, fourth, biological computation is quite different from engineering computation, and the right questions must be asked.

References

J.A. Anderson (1973), A theory for the recognition of items from short memorized lists. *Psychological Review* 80: 417–438.

E.R. Kandel (1976), *Cellular Basis of Behavior*. San Francisco, CA: Freeman.

G.L. Shaw and G. Palm (1988), *Brain Theory*. Singapore: World.

(1968)
James A. Anderson

A model for memory using spatial correlation functions
Kybernetik 5: 113–119

Abstract. A model of memory incorporating several unusual features is discussed. It is assumed that stored traces are added together in a common storage array. When the recovery system is presented with an input pattern, three reasonable demands may be made of the storage array for the memory system to be useful: has anything similar to the input pattern been stored previously (recognition); what are the significant differences between the input pattern and the stored pattern (reconstruction); what other stored patterns are similar to the input pattern (association). Methods of meeting these demands are discussed. A numerical example embodying these concepts is presented.

The problem of memory is one of the most vexing and most important problems in modern physiology. By its very nature it is difficult and elusive to study since objective correlates of its function are often subtle. The following work presents some abstract theoretical discussion of a scheme for storing information that may have some, though possibly remote, connection with the physiological and underlying logical structure of the nervous system. A simple numerical model employing the concepts discussed is also presented. Little attempt is made to present any physiological or psychological justification of the assumptions and implications of the model, other than a very general discussion of the motivation behind the model.

It is commonly accepted that a single memory "trace" in higher vertebrates (a trace is defined here as related bits of information that are processed as a group and that tend to act as a whole when operated on by the nervous system) is not stored in a very localized area of the brain, for example, a single cell, but is spatially diffuse. Evidence, discussed and summarized by JOHN (1967) suggests that a single "trace" may be stored in a rather large area of the brain and activity involving this trace incorporates, at the least, thousands of neurons. In any case, it appears certain that a trace, or a significant part of one, is not stored in a single neuron. Since it is known that the cortex is highly interconnected, this suggests that there may be a strong degree of interconnection and interaction between traces. Since we often conceive of traces as being well separated, presumably because this corresponds in some sense to our casual introspection, the idea of dissimilar traces being stored in the same "place", i.e. making use of many of the same neurons, seems unnatural. However let us assume that traces are highly interacting, that different traces make use of many of the same elements, and see what implications this assumption might have.

Let us consider an $m \times n$ array as the permanent memory storage unit in an application of this model. Each element of the array has a numerical value. Let us assume that a "trace" is some pattern of numerical values on an $m \times n$ array. A new trace will algebraically add to the previous values of the storage array and the resultant values of the individual elements of the storage array will be the sum of the value of the element in that location in the new trace and the old element in that location. Formally, if the $i\,j$-th element of the input array is a_{ij} and the $i\,j$-th element of the storage array is b_{ij}, the resultant value in the storage array will be $c_{ij} = a_{ij} + b_{ij}$. The current value of any element is thus a function of the past history of the array.

It is very easy to store information in such a storage unit. The significant problems are involved in the retrieval of the stored information, where there are certain difficulties. In fact, with this model, or any model where there is very strong interaction between traces, the information that can be retrieved is subject to stringent qualifications.

Therefore the basic assumption that will be made in proposing recall schemes is that a trace must be recalled with the assistance of another trace. This views recall as a movement from an input, to an "association" of that input. This is in distinction to a system which might propose an analysis of an input, decomposition into "categories", a search through cross-files using these categories, and reconstruction of the trace by some technique using information stored in the cross files. The scheme proposed here uses a trace as its own index and makes no reference to information stored outside the processing and storage systems.

We may suggest three questions we can reasonably require our storage array and retrieval system to answer.

First, given an input pattern, is anything "similar" stored in the array. This process might be called "*recognition*". Since "similar" is a flexible term, we should be able to propose a precise definition of "similar" and also, be able to measure the degree of "similarity" between the input and stored patterns.

Second, once the presence of a "similar" trace has been recognized, some method should exist for retrieving the previously stored pattern, or, at the least, reconstructing some of the major differences between the new and old patterns. Let us call this process "*reconstruction*".

Third, we might ask, once we have reconstructed one stored trace, presumably one of the more "similar" to the input pattern, are there any other stored traces that are also "similar" to the input pattern. It would be of interest to examine these patterns. Let us call this process "*association*"

The following discussion and proposed recognition and recovery techniques are designed to allow a computer program to be developed using them. Since there are no obvious formal criteria to use in some operations, it will be necessary to develop criteria in the course of the operation of the program. Thus there is a necessarily large uncertainty in some of the discussion since precise definition is not at present possible or desirable.

I. Recognition

This problem may be restated as that of the detection of the presence or absence of a pattern in the presence of a large amount of noise, the noise in this case being the other stored traces. This problem has been extensively studied, both as it applies to communications (LEE, 1960) and as it is applied to psychophysical measurements (GREEN and SWETS, 1966).

The mathematical techniques that are proposed as the most useful techniques for working with the storage array are the spatial correlation functions. If we define the function on an m by n array, the spatial autocorrelation function is defined as

$$\varphi_{11}(x, y) = \sum_{i=1}^{i=m} \sum_{j=1}^{j=n} f_1(i, j) f_1(i+x, j+y)$$
$$(i, j, x, y \text{ are integers})$$

and the spatial cross correlation function is defined by

$$\varphi_{12}(x, y) = \sum_{i=1}^{i=m} \sum_{j=1}^{j=n} f_1(i, j) f_2(i+x, j+y)$$
$$(i, j, x, y \text{ are integers}).$$

Here $f_1(i, j)$ means the $i\,j$-th element of the array. Let us assume $f_1(i, j)$ is the input array and $f_2(i, j)$ is the storage array with many stored traces presumably present. Some constraints on $f_1(i, j)$ and $f_2(i, j)$ will be discussed later. Here let us assume that $f_1(i, j)$ and $f_2(i, j)$ are zero on the average (i.e. have no "DC" component). They are necessarily square-integrable since the arrays are finite. If $f_1(i, j)$ is present along with other patterns in the storage array $f_2(i, j)$, then we may write

$$f_2(i, j) = f_1(i, j) + f_n(i, j).$$

Thus $f_n(i, j)$ is the "noise" present interfering with the recognition of $f_1(i, j)$. We may write

$$\varphi_{12}(x, y) = \sum_{i=1}^{i=m} \sum_{j=1}^{j=n} f_1(i, j) f_1(i+x, j+y)$$
$$+ \sum_{i=1}^{i=m} \sum_{j=1}^{j=n} f_1(i, j) f_n(i+x, j+y).$$

Note that the first term is the autocorrelation of $f_1(i, j)$. If we assume that $f_1(i, j)$ and $f_n(i, j)$ are independent then *on the average* the second term will be zero. Thus if we perform the spatial cross correlation, we will find the autocorrelation of the input function in the presence of a "noise term" which is zero on the average. Thus the problem of recognition becomes the problem of detecting the presence of the autocorrelation of the input function in the spatial cross-correlation. There are several ways of accomplishing this. The simplest and crudest is threshold detection based on the observation that

$$\varphi_{11}(0, 0)$$

is a large positive number. A more complex approach is developed in the next few paragraphs.

Let us consider a more general case than just identity between an input figure and a storage array containing an identical figure. First, let us define "similar" for the purposes of this paper as meaning *partially identical*. Thus we can write

$$f_1(i, j) = f_a(i, j) + f_b(i, j),$$
$$f_2(i, j) = f_a(i, j) + f_c(i, j) + f_n(i, j).$$

We may write the cross-correlation of f_1 and f_2 as

$$\varphi_{12}(x, y) = \sum_{i=1}^{i=m} \sum_{j=1}^{j=n} [f_a(i, j) + f_b(i, j)] [f_a(i + x, j + y) + f_c(i + x, j + y) + f_n(i + x, j + y)].$$

We write a similar expression for $\varphi_{11}(x, y)$, the autocorrelation. Let us define

$$s(x, y) = \varphi_{12}(x, y) - \varphi_{11}(x, y).$$

If we expand the expressions for $\varphi_{11}(x, y)$ and $\varphi_{12}(x, y)$ and collect and cancel terms (a straightforward procedure), we can write

$$s(x, y) = \sum_{i=1}^{i=m} \sum_{j=1}^{j=n} f_1(i, j) [f_c(i + x, j + y)$$
$$- f_b(i + x, j + y)]$$
$$+ \sum_{i=1}^{i=m} \sum_{j=1}^{j=n} f_1(i, j) f_n(i + x, j + y)$$
$$= \varphi_{1(c-b)}(x, y) + \varphi_{1n}(x, y).$$

We wish to obtain some numerical parameter that bears a relation to the "similarity" between an input and a stored figure. This parameter will be used as a decision parameter in the current discussion but we will also wish to use it as a guide during the recovery procedure, and as a measure of "similarity". Unfortunately, there appears to be no such obvious parameter. Two simple, easily calculated functions of the function $s(x, y)$ will serve as points of departure for discussion but computer models designed to test the concepts presented here will try to determine empirically a more satisfactory method.

For the first parameter, P_1, let us simply consider

$$P_1 = \sum_{x=-\infty}^{x=\infty} \sum_{y=-\infty}^{y=\infty} s(x, y) = \sum_{x=-\infty}^{x=\infty} \sum_{y=-\infty}^{y-\infty} (\varphi_{1(c-b)}(x, y) + \varphi_{1n}(x, y))$$

and note that

$$\sum_{x=-\infty}^{x=\infty} \sum_{y=-\infty}^{y=\infty} \varphi_{1n}(x, y) = 0$$

on the average since $f_1(i, j)$ and $f_n(i, j)$ are assumed independent. Then we note that if $f_c(i, j) = f_b(i, j)$ (i.e. if the stored and input functions are identical) the other term is zero. If, on the other hand $f_a(i, j)$ is zero (i.e. the input and stored functions are totally dissimilar) then we may write

$$\sum_{x=-\infty}^{x=\infty} \sum_{y=-\infty}^{y=\infty} s(x, y)$$
$$= \sum_{x=-\infty}^{x=\infty} \sum_{y=-\infty}^{y=\infty} \varphi_{bc}(x, y) - \sum_{x=-\infty}^{x=\infty} \sum_{y=-\infty}^{y=\infty} \varphi_{bb}(x, y)$$

and note that

$$\sum_{x=-\infty}^{x=\infty} \sum_{y=-\infty}^{y=\infty} \varphi_{bc}(x, y) = 0$$

since $f_b(i, j)$ and $f_c(i, j)$ are dissimilar.

Thus we have a measure which acts somewhat as we desire, being zero on the array when the input and stored functions are identical and being non-zero when the two functions are dissimilar. However the behavior of the function is hard to predict between these two extremes. We may also note that P_1 is independent of translations of x and y, i.e. a coordinate transformation in one function of the type $(x' = x - p, y' = y - q)$. This property can seriously limit its usefulness in certain applications.

The second parameter is closely related:

$$P_2 = \sum_{x=-\infty}^{x=\infty} \sum_{y=-\infty}^{y=\infty} (s(x, y))^2.$$

Here we note that if the stored and input functions are identical, if $f_c(i, j) = f_b(i, j)$ (assume $f_a(i, j) = 0$ for convenience in notation), then

$$P_2 = \sum_{x=-\infty}^{x=\infty} \sum_{y=-\infty}^{y=\infty} \varphi_{bn}^2(x, y).$$

If the two figures are totally dissimilar, i.e. if $f_a(i, j) = 0$ and $\varphi_{bc}(x, y) = 0$, then

$$P_2 = \sum_{x=-\infty}^{x=\infty} \sum_{y=-\infty}^{y=\infty} (\varphi_{1(c-b)}(x, y) + \varphi_{1n}(x, y))^2$$
$$- \sum_{x=-\infty}^{x=\infty} \sum_{y=-\infty}^{y=\infty} (\varphi_{b(c-b)}(x, y) + \varphi_{bn}(x, y))^2$$
$$= \sum_{x=-\infty}^{x=\infty} \sum_{y=-\infty}^{y=\infty} (\varphi_{bc}^2(x, y) + \varphi_{bb}^2(x, y) + \varphi_{bn}^2(x, y)$$
$$- 2\varphi_{bc}(x, y) \varphi_{bb}(x, y)$$
$$- 2\varphi_{bb}(x, y) \varphi_{bn}(x, y)$$
$$+ 2\varphi_{bn}(x, y) \varphi_{bc}(x, y)).$$

We note that since $f_b(i, j)$, $f_c(i, j)$ and $f_n(i, j)$ are assumed to be independent, and since $\varphi_{bc}(x, y) = 0$, and since $\varphi_{bb}(x, y)$ is an even function, only the second and third terms are non-zero on the average. We may then collect terms and write

$$P_2 = \sum_{x=-\infty}^{x=\infty} \sum_{y=-\infty}^{y=\infty} (\varphi_{bn}^2(x, y) + \varphi_{bb}^2(x, y))$$

when the two figures are dissimilar. Thus parameter P_2 will be small when the input and stored figures are identical and larger when the input and stored figures are completely dissimilar. This measure also acts somewhat as we would wish a measure of similarity to act. Many other simple measures of similarity are available. We might wish to consider, for example, $\varphi_{12}(x, y)$ and $\varphi_{11}(x, y)$ as functions and attempt to detect the presence of $\varphi_{11}(x, y)$ amidst the noise present in $\varphi_{12}(x, y)$ by use of correlation techniques.

Presumably the final parameter would involve some kind of consensus among the many different measures of similarity.

II. Reconstruction

If we have successfully completed the first part of the recovery procedure, that is, we have "recognized"

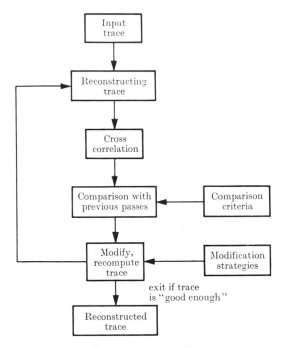

Fig. 1. This figure diagrams the proposed trace recovery procedure. The input is cross-correlated with the permanent memory store ("storage array") and a decision is made as to whether the input pattern is "novel" or not. Threshold criteria are based on past experience. If the input is "recognized" it is subjected to the reconstruction procedure (see Fig. 2) which attempts to determine the pattern present in the permanent memory store. The output of the reconstruction procedure may be used as part of a new input or the original input pattern may be recycled in order to provoke associations

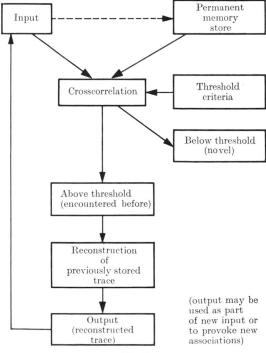

Fig. 2

the presence of a figure similar to the input figure in the array we may next ask for the differences between the input and stored figures. A procedure to accomplish this will be briefly outlined. We assume we are using some parameter found by experience to measure "similarity", for example P_1 or P_2. We start with the input figure. We then perform the spatial cross-correlation and calculate a value for our similarity parameter (Figs. 1 and 2 show block diagrams of this process and the recognition process).

We then make use of what we will call "modification strategies". These are a list of well-defined operations that take the input figure and change it in various "reasonable" ways so as to hopefully make it more like the stored figure. The "reasonable" modification strategies are a function of past experience and would be operations like "lengthen the longest straight line in the figure by two elements" or "close a gap of one element." Then the similarity parameter is recalculated, normalizing the new parameter if necessary to compensate for the change in size of the modified figure. If the similarity parameter has indicated that the modified figure is more similar to the stored figure than the input figure, the modified figure is used as the basis for further modification; if the similarity parameter indicates less similarity, the modification strategy is changed and the initial figure is used as a basis for the application of other strategies. The process will terminate whenever some pre-determined value of similarity parameter is attained or when no modification seems to increase the similarity between the stored and modified figures.

Clearly, much experience must be gained in order to write an effective group of modification strategies and in order to learn to terminate the process at the appropriate time. There are uncertainties in the application of this technique: the process may not terminate with a satisfactory representation of the stored figure, it may prove excessively difficult to write useful strategies, several stored figures may tend to be retrieved together, producing confusion.

III. Association

Possibly the most useful feature of this model is the natural way it allows for the formation of "associations". There are two distinct mechanisms for

Fig. 2. This figure outlines the trace reconstruction procedure. An input, that has been "recognized", i.e. that is similar to a stored trace as determined by the recognition procedure, is cross-correlated with the permanent memory store. Then the original input is modified according to well-defined modification strategies which have been determined by experience to be useful. The modified trace is cross correlated again with the permanent memory store and the results of the first and second correlations are compared according to well-defined comparison criteria. (Parameters that may be used for these comparisons are discussed in the text.) If the modified trace is "more similar" (according to the comparison criteria) to the stored trace than the unmodified trace, the modified trace is used as the basis for further modification. Otherwise the unmodified trace is modified again and the comparisons repeated. When the trace cannot be improved by an application of the modification strategies or when the "similarity parameters" indicate that the modified trace is presumably "good enough" (i.e. similar enough to the original trace present in the permanent memory store), the process terminates. The original trace may have modification strategies applied to it in different permutations in order to produce "associations"

producing "associations", which might be defined in this model as "distinct terminations of the recovery procedure". The first would simply be the result of repeated application of various modification strategies in various orders to the input figure. Each successful application of a modification strategy would eliminate certain possible termination states. Again applying the strategies to the initial input pattern, but in different order would allow different possible outcomes.

The other mechanism for association utilizes the capability of the spatial cross-correlation to detect easily translations of figures since if $f_1'(i, j) = f_1(i + p, j + q)$ then $\varphi_{12}'(x, y) = \varphi_{12}(x - p, y - q)$. Thus if the cross-correlation shows a large positive value removed from point $(x, y) = (0, 0)$ it indicates that a similar figure may be present, merely displaced. A simple coordinate transformation allows the application of all the modification strategies to this new similar figure and the generation of new associations. An example of this is presented in the numerical example.

IV. Other Considerations

It was mentioned briefly that among the constraints on $f_1(i, j)$ and $f_2(i, j)$ were that their average should be zero, (i.e. they should contain no "DC" component). If this were not the case, many of the arguments presented in section I would be invalid, and the calculations would become excessively complex.

There is one other line of argumentation indicating that an average of zero is desirable. Any real system will have elements of finite dynamic range. If the input arrays did not have a zero average, over many stored inputs there would be a tendency for these elements to saturate with time, i.e., the mean of the values of the elements would move to one or the other limit. It is still possible for saturation to take place in a storage system with zero average because the standard deviation of the element values will increase as more and more input patterns are stored. Eventually, as the standard deviation approaches the value of the limits, the system will start to saturate. However this process will show a different dependence on number of stored traces than a process involving a migrating average. As a simple example if each of the elements of the input arrays were to possess a non-zero average of the same sign the limits would be approached linearly (as a first approximation) as the number of stored traces. If the average was zero, the standard deviation would approach the limit as the square root of the number of stored traces, assuming reasonable statistics for element values in the input arrays.

It may be significant that the most direct way of assuring a zero average for an input pattern is to use a very simple inhibitory surround around positive values, as is used in the numerical example in the next section.

V. Numerical Example

In order to test the concepts discussed previously, a simple numerical model was constructed. Since all calculations described were performed on a desk calculator, the amount of data is necessarily limited, however many features of the more complex computer program that is evolving from these simple calculations are present here.

A. Model. The input patterns consisted of line figures drawn on a 14 by 15 array, comprising 210 elements (Fig. 3). Simple, continuous figures, composed primarily of straight lines were used. There was no intensity grading in the figures.

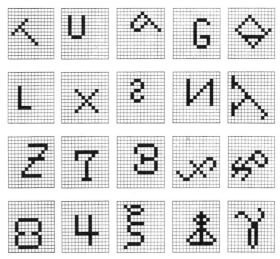

Fig. 3. The storage array used in the numerical example is composed of the sum of these 20 figures, after the figures have been transformed according to the procedures outlined in Section V of the text

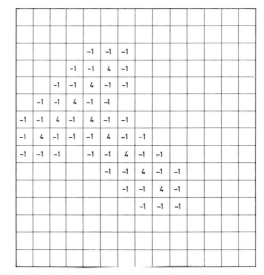

Fig. 4. The function $f_T(i, j)$, corresponding to the stored figure. This figure is identical to the "T" in the upper left hand corner of Fig. 3, after it has been transformed according to the procedures outlined in Part V of the text

Since it was desirable that the average of all the elements in the array be zero on the average, a simple way to do this was used.

Each square in contact with a square containing part of the figure, in contact along an edge or at a corner, is given the value -1. The number of squares containing -1 is divided by the number of squares comprising the figure. The quotient is rounded off to the nearest integer which is placed in each of the

9*

elements making up the figure. Positive values used in this particular study ranged from 2 to 4 depending on the geometry of the figures. Although the average of elements in this case will not automatically be exactly zero it will be small if there is reasonable

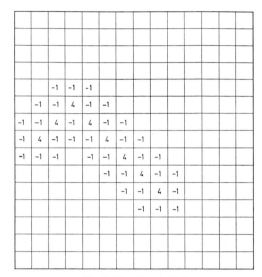

Fig. 5. Function $f_L(i, j)$

-1	-2	-2	-1	-1	-1	-2	-2	-1					
-1	1	1	-3	1	-4	-3	-3	-5	-4	-4	-3	-2	
-1	1	0	-2	-4	-6	15	3	3	5	2	4	-3	
-1	1	3	-8	4	8	-4	0	-6	-3	-1	5	-3	
-1	1	0	-2	9	-5	-2	-4	8	2	8	-2	-4	
-1	-6	-5	6	12	-10	8	1	0	1	-1	0	-6	-2
-1	-5	10	-6	9	0	7	11	6	8	5	4	2	-3
-2	0	5	0	-4	1	4	1	3	-3	-10	8	-1	-3
-3	-1	-4	2	9	3	12	1	8	9	3	0	0	-1
-3	4	-3	6	5	5	8	3	9	-5	-1	5	-4	-1
-3	5	7	-7	-5	-2	14	-5	14	5	-3	-5	-4	-1
-1	4	3	-9	5	1	-4	6	4	4	1	-5	1	-1
-2	-1	-1	2	6	-2	4	-3	3	-3	-4	4	-2	-1
-1	-3	0	0	-1	-3	-1	2	-1	-6	1	-2	-2	
	-1	-2	-2	-1	-1	-2	-2	-2	-2	-1	-1		

Fig. 6. The sum of all 20 figures presented in Fig. 3 after they have been transformed. This function is denoted as $f_2(i, j)$ in the text and is the "permanent memory store" in the numerical example

variation in pattern geometry. If certain restrictions on geometry would be allowed, it would be possible to assure an average of zero. Examples of patterns given numerical values in this way are presented in Fig. 4 and 5. This simple technique also has the advantage, not immediately apparent in this application, that all parts of the figure interact to produce the positive values of the figure. There are important advantages to such a "unification" for the figure then tends to act as a whole in its interactions. If a figure

is made up of separate pieces, it is asking much of a retrieval system to connect pieces that are not clearly related to each other. This is a point that will be investigated further for there is a relation between the richness of possible associations produced by the retrieval mechanism and the closeness of connections of parts of each figure.

The sum of all the patterns shown in Fig. 3 is shown in Fig. 6.

B. Calculations. In order to test the model the pattern "T" presented in Fig. 4 and in unprocessed form in the upper left hand corner of Fig. 3 was used. This pattern of numbers is defined as the function

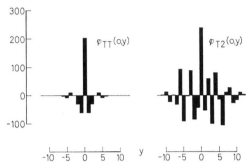

Fig. 7. Graph of the two correlation functions,

$\varphi_{TT}(0, y)$ and $\varphi_{T_2}(0, y)$

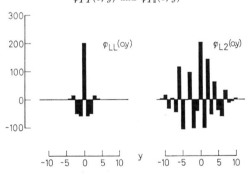

Fig. 8. Graph of the two correlation functions,

$\varphi_{LL}(0, y)$ and $\varphi_{L_2}(0, y)$

Note that both these functions have been multiplied by a constant 1.24 (equals $\varphi_{TT}(0,0)/\varphi_{LL}(0,0)$ in order to compensate for the fact that $f_L(i, j)$ is smaller than $f_T(i, j)$. The rationale for this is discussed in Section V of the text

$f_T(i, j)$. A simple variant of the figure has constructed to see if discrimination between correct and incorrect figures was possible. Fig. 5 shows an incomplete "T", [which will be designated $f_L(i, j)$]. Because of the initial placement of the figures on the array only correlations in the y direction were taken, since there was insufficient room on the array for significant displacements in the x direction. Fig. 7 shows the autocorrelation function, $\varphi_{TT}(0, y)$ and next to it the cross correlation $\varphi_{T_2}(0, y)$, where $f_2(i, j)$ is the storage array presented in Fig. 6. Similarly, Fig. 8 shows $\varphi_{LL}(0, y)$ and $\varphi_{L_2}(0, y)$. The presence of the prominent peak at $(x, y) = (0, 0)$ in both cross correlations suggests that a "similar" figure is present in both cases.

We now proceed, as the first step in the reconstruction procedure, to calculate the two "similarity" parameters, discussed in Section I, as indicators of the degree of closeness of the input figure and the stored figure. The results are tabulated in the Table. Note that it was necessary to compensate for the fact that $f_L(i, j)$ is "smaller" than $f_T(i, j)$. There is no obvious compensation mechanism so the one that was chosen, subject to further experience, was equating the amplitudes of the autocorrelation functions at $(x, y) = (0, 0)$. This value is the sum of the squares of the values of the elements and is proportional, in applications of correlation functions to physical problems, to the total energy of the function. The values of the cross and autocorrelations of $f_L(i, j)$ were multiplied by this compensation factor. Both similarity parameters, P_1 and P_2 indicated that the "most similar" figure was the correct figure $f_T(i, j)$.

Table

A. For $f_1(i, j) = f_T(i, j)$ (Fig. 4)
$$P_1 = -2$$
$$P_2 = 66{,}728$$

B. For $f_1(i, j) = f_2(i, j)$ (Fig. 5)
$$P_1 = 76$$
$$P_2 = 90{,}126 *$$

* $\varphi_{LL}(0, y)$ and $\varphi_{L2}(0, y)$ are multiplied by $\left(= \dfrac{\varphi_{TT}(0,0)}{\varphi_{LL}(0,0)} \right)$ 1.24 as discussed in Part V, Section B.

Even the most elementary calculations involving successive applications of a modification strategy involved far too much computation for a desk calculator.

However if a set of modification strategies had produced the two test patterns, there would have been no difficulty distinguishing the stored pattern from the other using either similarity parameter.

We may also note the presence of a large secondary peak at $(x, y) = (0, 2)$. If we wish to study the possibility of an association being formed from this peak, we may simply transform coordinates and attempt to minimize the similarity parameters with this peak. (Note that parameter P_1 is not changed by a coordinate transformation.) Note that this peak is larger with test pattern $f_L(i, j)$ and smaller, possibly indicating less similarity with *this* stored function, when $f_T(i, j)$ is used. Thus further applications of modifications strategies designed to determine the associations of this peak might start from $f_L(i, j)$ rather than $f_T(i, j)$. Calculation of P_2 with $y' = (y - 2)$ indicates that this guess is correct and that further application of modification strategies should start with $f_L(i, j)$ if we are trying to work with the $(x, y) = (0, 2)$ peak. (If $y' = y - 2$, P_2 for $\varphi_{T2}(0, y') = 161{,}522$ and P_2 for $\varphi_{L2}(0, y') = 142{,}502$.)

Bibliography. 1. GREEN, D. M., and J. A. SWETS: Signal detection theory and psychophysics. New York: John Wiley & Sons, Inc. 1966. — 2. JOHN, E. R.: Mechanisms of memory. New York: Academic Press 1967. — 3. LEE, Y. W.: Statistical theory of communication. New York: John Wiley & Sons, Inc. 1960.

JAMES A. ANDERSON, Ph. D.
Department of Physiology
University of California
Los Angeles, Calif. 90024, U.S.A.

6
Introduction

(1972)
Kaoru Nakano

Associatron—a model of associative memory
IEEE Transactions on Systems, Man, and Cybernetics SMC-12: 380–388

This early neural network paper by Kaoru Nakano describes an associative system, along with some farsighted suggestions about how to use the network effectively for information retrieval and reasoning. The Associatron, the model described, is one of the first published outer product associators. (See papers 14 and 15 in *Neurocomputing: Foundations of Research* for a description of the related linear associator networks.) Large state vectors, representing information to be stored, are autoassociated; that is, the desired output of the network is the same as the input. This has the effect of associating all parts of the state vector with each other. Nakano accomplishes this by storing the outer product of each of the associations to be stored, which he calls an *autocorrelation*. To avoid having to store a separate matrix for each input state vector, he makes the common network assumption that the autoassociations are summed to form a single connection matrix, which becomes the system memory.

Nakano restricts element values in the state vectors to be +1, 0, or −1, and defines a quantizing function to operate on continuous values to accomplish this. This function is necessary because, in common with most neural networks, recall of information will not be exact, and the output of the network must be quantized to ensure that the output vector will also be composed of −1, 0, or +1. The assumption that Nakano makes that is most unlike other simple network models involves this quantizing function. In the simple associative networks the first step in recall is usually to multiply an input state vector by a connection matrix. The generic connectionist computing unit, which Nakano describes in equation 6, takes an inner product between the weights and the input pattern. The continuous output from this stage is often then passed through a nonlinearity. However, Nakano applies the nonlinear quantizing function to the matrix elements themselves (equation 7), so the inner product is taken between the input pattern and a matrix composed entirely of +1's, -1's, and 0's. This assumption must decrease recall accuracy to some extent, but associative recall will still occur, just as it will in other pattern associators.

Although autoassociation might seem to be a limited special case of an associative system, in fact autoassociation is completely general. In section III Nakano shows this. A multiple-layered network architecture, for example, or a heteroassociative system can be constructed by putting blocks of zeros in the connection matrix. The autoassociative terms are blocks of nonzero connection strengths along the main diagonal, and the heteroassociative terms are nonzero blocks off the main diagonal. With proper placement of blocks, complex structures can be realized.

Nakano is concerned with the proper use of an associative system. The most striking property of an autoassociative network is sometimes called *pattern completion*. When *part* of an autoassociated pattern is presented to the network, the *entire* stored pattern can be retrieved. Nakano assumes that an entire correlated set of associated information is associatively interconnected. Therefore any part of the information can be recalled by the presence of other parts. Information in artificial intelligence is often represented as collections of atomic facts, for example pairs or small sets of items linked together. However, as William James (1894/1962, p. 301) commented in the nineteenth century,

. . . the more other facts a fact is associated with in the mind, the better possession of it our memory retains. Each of its associates becomes a hook to which it hangs, a means to fish it up by when sunk beneath the surface. Together, they form a network of attachments by which it is woven into the entire tissue of our thought.

Nakano assumes that each state vector contains a large number of "atomic facts." Clusters of information can be stored this way. Examples he uses are *apple-spherical-red*, *banana-sticklike-yellow*, and so forth. Then presentation of the partial state vector corresponding to *apple* reconstructs *spherical* and *red*, and so on. Autoassociative reconstruction of exactly this type has been applied to the formation of psychological concepts and to linguistic disambiguation, (for example, Anderson and Murphy 1986). When implemented in a large system, it can serve as a simple and quite powerful associative data base that is also capable of doing simple inference, because the network can generalize to novel situations to a limited extent. For example, in an autoassociative data base network containing information on drugs and diseases, a good guess can be made of the appropriate drug to be used to treat a disease whose causative organism was not explicitly stored, based on related information that was learned (Anderson, 1986).

Nakano also applies this strategy to learning a very simple game, but much less successfully. In general games are not good candidates for simple associative neural networks because most games (perhaps to be challenging for the neural networks of humans!) are highly nonlinear and nonmonotonic. However, the very simple game analyzed by Nakano can be learned by a simple associative network. Game playing with neural networks is an area just beginning to be explored. Games that have a large probabilistic (poker) or pattern recognition component (go, backgammon) are the most successfully modeled, and there is currently a neural network backgammon program, designed by Gerald Tesauro, that can beat good human players.

A supportable generalization about game playing with neural networks might be that networks are (potentially) good strategists but poor tacticians. Current computer chess programs gain their power by very fast, deep tree searches, simply looking at as many future board positions as they can compute and choosing the best. Humans search many fewer board positions, but play a strategic game based on memory and intuition, a completely different approach. Neural networks, because they are memory based and can generalize to some extent, should complement current computer chess programs very well, if the networks can be made large enough and if the right representational features can be built into the input to the network. There is ample psychological evidence that human expert chess players see a game position as something like a "sentence" in a "chess language." The position is seen as being composed of "words," perhaps like *Fianchettoed bishop, Queen-side castle, developed King-side rook*, and the like. Nonsense sentences, that is, pieces randomly placed on the board, are remembered no better by chess experts than novices, but experts have far better recall than novices when pieces placed so as to correspond to possible game positions, that is, the positions form grammatical sentences (Chase and Simon 1973).

References

J.A. Anderson (1986), Cognitive capabilities of a parallel system. Ed. E. Bienenstock, F. Fogelman-Soulie, and G. Weisbuch, *Disordered Systems and Biological Organization*. Berlin: Springer.

J.A. Anderson and G.L. Murphy (1986), Psychological concepts in a parallel system. *Physica* 22D: 318--336.

W.G. Chase and H.A. Simon (1973), Perception in chess. *Cognitive Psychology* 4: 55–81.

W. James (1894/1962), *Psychology: Briefer Course*. London: Collier-Macmillan.

(1972)
Kaoru Nakano

Associatron—a model of associative memory
IEEE Transactions on Systems, Man, and Cybernetics SMC-12: 380–388

Abstract—Thinking in the human brain greatly depends upon association mechanisms which can be utilized in machine intelligence. An associative memory device, called "Associatron," is proposed. The Associatron stores entities represented by bit patterns in a distributed manner and recalls the whole of any entity from a part of it. If the part is large, the recalled entity will be accurate; on the other hand, if the part is small, the recalled entity will be rather ambiguous. Any number of entities can be stored, but the accuracy of the recalled entity decreases as the number of entities increases.

The Associatron is considered to be a simplified model of the neural network and can be constructed as a cellular structure, where each cell is connected to only its neighbor cells and all cells run in parallel. From its mechanisms some properties are derived that are expected to be utilized for human-like information processing. After these properties have been analyzed, an Associatron which deals with entities composed of less than 180 bits is simulated by a computer. Simple examples of its applications for concept formation and game playing are presented and the thinking process by the sequence of associations is described.

Manuscript received January 11, 1971; revised July 5, 1971 and February 21, 1972. This work was supported by the Science and Technology Agency of Japan.

The author is with the Faculty of Engineering, University of Tokyo, Tokyo, Japan.

I. INTRODUCTION

THE PURPOSE of this paper is to outline an approach for simulating certain functions of the human brain. It has been known that an association mechanism is essential to information processing in the human brain. Association in the human brain has been studied mainly in the field of psychology. Quite a few semantic models for association have been presented in the past few years. Now biological studies are beginning gradually to reveal the structure of the nervous system, but our present knowledge is still not sufficient to construct the structure artificially, although models of nerve cells have been presented [1], [2].

In this situation, it will be important, from the viewpoint of artificial intelligence, to construct a machine with homogeneous structure where the microscopic behavior of its components gather to form the macroscopic behavior such as pattern recognition, concept formation, game playing, etc. Perceptron [3] and Adaline [4] have this property to some extent, although they do not provide the functions of the lifelike memory and the memory-oriented information processor. Work concerning a rather biological associative memory was presented by Post [5]. His model is a distributed memory device which memorizes triplets of entities and recalls one of these entities from two other entities in the specific triplet. The model would be helpful for realizing lifelike information processing.

Associatron [6], [7], proposed here, is this type of model, but it is different from Post's model in its structure and functions. In this model many bit patterns representing entities are stored in the same region of its structure and any stored entity can be recalled from parts of it. The more parts fed into the memory device, the more accurately the entity will be recalled. The principle is based on the application of the autocorrelation functions. If the autocorrelation function of an entity is held in the memory, it is quite natural that the entity can be reproduced from only a small part of it. Since storing all these autocorrelation functions is too redundant to be practical, they are linearly added in the memorizing process. In this case, if the stored entities are very numerous, entities cannot always be recalled completely, but are expected to be reproduced only probabilistically. This kind of associative memory has the following properties which differ from the conventional memory.

1) Reliability is improved in the sense that the failure of some components of the memory device does not cause the loss of the whole of any entity, but causes only inaccuracy in recalling.

2) Although some uncertainties appear in recalling, they are rather useful for realizing artificial intelligence with flexibility and applicability. This is because strictly logical comparison, for example, is apt to discard useful data which resemble a certain datum. The uncertainty confusing similar data will make the device extract automatically, from a number of entities, the essence useful for a certain job.

3) Information is accessed without any addressing, however large the quantity may be. The speed of access or information retrieval is very high, in the sense that any entity can be accessed by using the relation of meaning without any index.

By these properties, information processing using the Associatron is different from that of conventional computers.

Recently, the thinking process has been studied in detail using so-called heuristic programs. For example, the learning program for the game of checkers [8], [9] is well known. The model in this paper is related to such heuristics in game playing, general problem solving, and possibly to the thinking process itself.

II. PRINCIPLE OF ASSOCIATRON

To realize the function of associative memory previously described, the following method is used. Assume that an entity to be memorized is represented by a two-dimensional array of three-valued elements. Since the geometrical properties will not be dealt with by this model, it is convenient

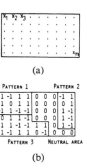

(a)

(b)

Fig. 1. Configuration of an entity. (a) Arrangement of components of x. (b) Example of entity.

to map the array to a row vector

$$x = (x_1, x_2, \cdots, x_n) \qquad (1)$$

where $x_i = -1, 0, 1$. Here the construction of an entity is considered briefly, and will be considered precisely in Section III. An entity is composed of several patterns and of neutral areas as shown in Fig. 1. Fig. 1(a) shows the array of components of vector x, and Fig. 1(b) shows an example of an entity. The entity has patterns 1,2,3 and a neutral area. Each pattern is composed of minus ones, zeros, and ones, and represents a meaning (for example, "apple," "red," or "spherical"), while a neutral area is composed only of zeros. The meaning is dependent upon the location of the elements as well as their values. The elements at a pattern are not necessarily adjacent as in the figure.

Now the memorizing process is considered. Let x^t denote the transposed vector of x. If an $n \times n$ matrix $x^t x$ is memorized in the memory device, the whole of x will be recalled easily from a part of it. When the entities are numerous, it is wasteful to memorize the same number of matrices as x. Therefore, the matrices are added as follows:

$$M = x^{(1)t}x^{(1)} + x^{(2)t}x^{(2)} + \cdots + x^{(k)t}x^{(k)} \qquad (2)$$

where $x^{(1)}, x^{(2)}, \cdots, x^{(k)}$ are k entities. If there exists an efficient method of recalling any entity $x^{(j)}$ using M, it will be reasonable to consider M the inner state of the memory device after k entities are stored.

To recall entities, we first define the quantizing function

$$\phi(a) = \begin{cases} -1, & \text{when } a < 0 \\ 0, & \text{when } a = 0 \\ 1, & \text{when } a > 0. \end{cases} \qquad (3)$$

Suppose that it can also be applied to a vector $u = (u_j)$ and matrix $A = (a_{ij})$ as

$$\phi(u) = (\phi(u_j))$$

$$\phi(A) = (\phi(a_{ij})). \qquad (4)$$

From an input $y = (y_1, y_2, \cdots, y_n)$, the same type of vector as x, the memory device can recall a row vector z as the output, where

$$z = \phi(y\phi(M)). \qquad (5)$$

This equation is used to extract an x from M by majority logic. If y has the same pattern as a stored entity x in a

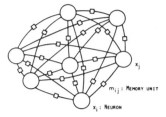

Fig. 2. Associatron as neural network. Any two neurons, x_i and x_j, are connected through memory unit m_{ij}, which corresponds to synapse.

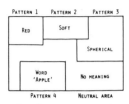

Fig. 3. Explanation of entity, pattern, and concept. Any part of entity can be pattern, but in this case each pattern is chosen to have explicit concept.

certain area and the rest of y is composed of zeros, then it is expected that z is nearly equal to x, even when many entities are memorized. This would enable recalling the whole of a stored entity from a part of it. Consequently, a few patterns previously mentioned can be associated with the rest of the patterns of entity x.

The structure that can realize the process described by (1)–(5) is considered before proceeding to analyze the properties of the process. Fig. 2 depicts the structure, where a circle denotes a component of vector x and a square denotes a component of matrix M; these are named neuron and synapse, respectively, because the structure is similar to a so-called neural network model. The details are as follows.

1) Any pair of neurons x_i and x_j is connected through a synapse m_{ij}.

2) Each neuron has three possible states: -1, 0, and 1.

3) The following operation proceeds in a unit time. For any pair of neurons x_i and x_j, when both are not 0, the product of the values is added to the synapse m_{ij}, which connects these neurons. When x_i is not 0 and x_j is 0, a stimulus whose value is the product of x_i and the quantized value of m_{ij} (namely, $\phi(m_{ij})$) propagates to neuron x_j. At the next state x_j will take the value determined by the majority of all such stimuli that arrived at x_j from other neurons.

In most ordinary models of neural networks, the state of a neuron $x_j(t)$ at time t is described as

$$x_j(t) = \phi \left[\sum_{i=1}^{s} x_i(t-1) \cdot w_{ij} - \theta \right] \quad (6)$$

where s is the number of neurons connected to the specific neuron x_j, θ is the threshold value, and w_{ij} is the weight representing the synaptic conductance from x_i to x_j. In this model the equation

$$x_j(t) = \phi \left[\sum_{i=1}^{s} x_i(t-1) \cdot \phi(m_{ij}) \right] \quad (7)$$

is used for describing the behavior. This means that instead of multiplying m_{ij} directly by x_i, the quantized value $\phi(m_{ij})$ is used and the threshold value θ is taken to be zero so that the probabilities of appearance of 1 and 0 in patterns should be equal. From these equations, and from the preceding items 1)–3), it can be said that the Associatron is a simplified model of a neural network, although it is not similar in detail to the nervous system in a human brain. The extreme simplification might cause a situation where the separation of patterns is not very good; reversed pat-

terns cannot be separated because $x^t x = (-x)^t(-x)$; and the direction of recall in sequential recalling is out of control, as explained in Section VI. The first problem will be solved by increasing neurons, and the other problems by modifying the model. But the modification is not always necessary because the defects are found to be no defects when the model is applied appropriately. Although the principle is similar to the Perceptron in some sense, this model has rather a primitive structure and has functions of both a memory and a learning machine. Therefore, it has properties which enable it to perform more human-like information processing.

III. PROPERTIES OF THE ASSOCIATRON

In this section, properties of memorizing and recalling entities are discussed. It was previously mentioned that an entity is composed of patterns. Here we consider this in more detail, taking the example shown in Fig. 3, whose representation format is the same as that of Fig. 1. Any part of an entity can be a pattern, and any pattern has a concept, either explicit or implicit. An explicit concept is a concept which can be clearly described by a language, while an implicit concept is difficult to describe by a language. An example of an implicit concept will appear in Section IV, namely, the characteristic pattern of board positions considered to be useful for winning in game playing. Thus a concept can be represented by a pattern. In Fig. 3, each pattern is taken to have an explicit concept; that is, pattern 1 has the concept "red," pattern 2 the concept "soft," etc. Moreover, a complex pattern of patterns 1 and 2 has the concept "red and soft," a complex pattern of patterns 1–4 has the concept "apple," and so on. In the Associatron, when entities or combinations of patterns are stored, not only can patterns be recalled, but various concepts are gradually formed.

The following discussion considers the properties of memorizing and recalling. Presume that Q denotes the set of all n-dimensional vectors

$$x = (x_1, x_2, \cdots, x_n) \quad (8)$$

where $x_i = -1, 0, 1$. Now we consider the recalling function $\alpha: Q \to Q$. If $x \in Q$, and α is defined as

$$z = \alpha(x) = \phi(x\phi(M)) \quad (9)$$

then z is also a member of Q. Now, let us introduce the index vector

$$v = (v_1, v_2, \cdots, v_n) \quad (10)$$

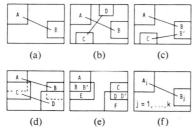

Fig. 4. Various states of memory. (a) State where only one entity, pair of patterns A and B, is stored. (b) Two entities, pairs A–B, C–D are stored. (c) Two entities are stored and one pattern of each entity overlaps. (d) Two entities are stored and overlap partially. (e) State (d) rewritten for analysis. (f) k entities, pairs of two patterns A_j and B_j are stored and mutually overlap.

where $v_i = 0,1$. This vector represents a certain area of the neural network. Defining elementwise multiplication $*$ as

$$v * x = (v_1 x_1, v_2 x_2, \cdots, v_n x_n) \qquad (11)$$

we call $v * x$ the concept of x at the area v. Assume that both x and y are members of Q. If

$$v * x = v * y \qquad (12)$$

then x and y are said to have the same concept at area v. The measure of area v is defined by

$$l(v) = \sum_{i=1}^{n} v_i. \qquad (13)$$

Now it is assumed that the entity x or a pair of patterns A and B is stored in the memory device, as in Fig. 4(a), whose representation is the same as that of Figs. 1 and 3. If the order of the elements of x is changed to put together the elements constructing each of A and B just for simplifying the expression, the entity x is represented by a row vector as

$$x = (A,B,0) \qquad (14)$$

where A and B are row vectors and 0 denotes the zero vector. Then the matrix M, which stores only x, will be

$$M = (A,B,0)^t(A,B,0) = \begin{pmatrix} A^t A & A^t B & 0 \\ B^t A & B^t B & 0 \\ 0 & 0 & 0 \end{pmatrix}. \qquad (15)$$

If the index vectors of A and B are v_A and v_B, respectively, the concept at area v_B of the recalled pattern from $v_A * x$ is

$$v_B * \phi((v_A * x) \cdot \phi(M)) = v_B * \phi(A\phi(A^t A), A\phi(A^t B), 0)$$
$$= (0, A\phi(AB), 0)$$
$$= (0,B,0). \qquad (16)$$

This means that the pattern or concept B is completely recalled from A. Where pairs A–B and C–D are stored independently, as shown in Fig. 4(b), in the same way it can be clarified that a pattern of each pair is completely recalled from another.

In the case of Fig. 4(c), two pairs A–B and C–B' are stored in such a way that patterns B and B' are overlapped. The stored vectors are

$$x = (A,B,0,0) \qquad y = (0,B',C,0). \qquad (17)$$

The matrix is

$$M = \begin{pmatrix} A^t A & A^t B & 0 & 0 \\ B^t A & B^t B + B''B' & B''C & 0 \\ 0 & C^t B' & C^t C & 0 \\ 0 & 0 & 0 & 0 \end{pmatrix}. \qquad (18)$$

The recalling process is as follows:

$$v_B * \alpha(A,0,0,0) = \phi(0, A\phi(A^t B), 0, 0) = (0,B,0,0)$$
$$v_A * \alpha(0,B,0,0) = \phi(B\phi(B^t A), 0, 0, 0) = (A,0,0,0). \qquad (19)$$

In the case of Fig. 4(d), where two pairs A–B and C–D are stored, A and C, B and D partially overlap, respectively. This is rewritten as Fig. 4(e), where the overlapping areas are dealt with as new patterns. From the previous results, it is clear that E and F are indifferent to the recalling $AB \rightarrow CD$, where AB means the complex concept of A and B, etc., so they are eliminated. Therefore, stored vectors can be considered as

$$x = (A,B,C,D,0) \qquad y = (0,B',0,D',0). \qquad (20)$$

The recalling process from AB to CD is as follows:

$$v_{CD} * \alpha(v_{AB} * x)$$
$$= (0,0,\phi(A\phi(A^t C) + B\phi(B^t C)),\phi(A\phi(A^t D)$$
$$+ B\phi(B^t D + B''D')),0)$$
$$= (0,0,C,D,0). \qquad (21)$$

Thus, CD can be completely recalled from AB because only two patterns are overlapped at v_B. When this number is arbitrary, the following argument will hold.

Let k pairs of A_j–B_j be stored as shown in Fig. 4(f). For simplicity of calculation, k is assumed to be an odd number. Also, it is assumed that $l(v_A) = s$ is odd and that the entities are random patterns at areas v_A and v_B. These assumptions do not hold in actual use of the associative memory, but it matters little, because this only causes a small error in the estimation of accuracy of recalling. If k is even, the accuracy when the number of stored entities is k is greater than when it is $k + 1$, and is less than when it is $k - 1$. A similar statement holds for s. In any recalling process, the probability that a memory unit votes for the right state of a neuron for the specific entity stored in the memory device is

$$\frac{k + 1}{2k}. \qquad (22)$$

The probability that the state of a neuron decided by majority is right is represented by the sum of the first $(s + 1)/2$ terms of the binomial expansion of

$$\left(\frac{k + 1}{2k} + \frac{k - 1}{2k}\right)^s. \qquad (23)$$

That is,

$$P = \left(\frac{1}{2k}\right)^s \sum_{i=0}^{(s-1)/2} \binom{s}{i} (k + 1)^{s-i}(k - 1)^i \qquad (24)$$

where $\binom{s}{i}$ is the number of combination. As this summation cannot be written in a simple form, to determine the behavior of this equation the values of P calculated for

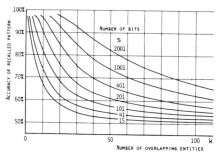

Fig. 5. Accuracy of recalling. $s = l(v_A)$ represents number of bits of input pattern. It is shown that recalled pattern is more accurate as number of stored entities k decreases and s increases.

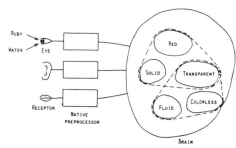

Fig. 6. Assumption about human brain. When ruby is seen, as result of preprocessing, stimulus patterns which represent "red," "solid," and "transparent" appear in brain, etc.

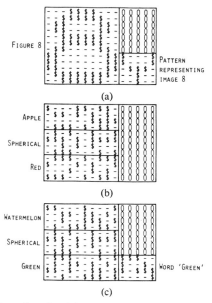

Fig. 7. Examples of entities. (a) Entity representing association of Fig. 8 and its image. This kind of entity is used in pattern recognition experiment. (b), (c) These entities are used in experiments concerning concept formation.

various values of k and s are shown graphically in Fig. 5. From the graph, it is found that completely accurate recalling can be done when the number of stored entities is very small or when the number of bits constructing the input pattern is very large. Many neurons are certainly required for actual information processing. But it should be taken into account that the function of an associative memory is not only the accuracy of memory.

These analyses are based upon the following assumption about a human brain, illustrated by Fig. 6. When information is accepted by a receptor, it causes an appearance of a stimulus pattern in the brain. Since the pattern has been preprocessed by a native preprocessor, it is constructed by a set of smaller patterns which represent various characteristics of the original information. For example, when a ruby is seen, stimulus patterns which represent "red," "solid," and "transparent" appear in the brain, and when water is seen, stimulus patterns which represent "colorless," "fluid," and "transparent" appear there. The purpose of the Associatron is to deal with these patterns associatively, but not to construct a pattern classifier or to simulate a human eye. Therefore, the use of random vectors does not limit the function of this model.

Characteristics of information processing using an associative memory are shown in the following sections.

IV. COMPUTER SIMULATION AND SOME EXPERIMENTAL RESULTS

The Associatron composed of 180 neurons was simulated by a digital computer. The neurons were arranged in 12 rows and 15 columns. Fig. 7 shows some examples of the computer output format of entities, where \$, −, and 0 correspond to 1, −1, and 0, respectively. Using this simulated model, a few experiments were performed. To evaluate the results, the correlation coefficient between a stored pattern and the recalled pattern is used. Assume that both patterns A and B consist of n bits, and that corresponding elements of patterns are a_i and b_i, respectively. The correlation coefficient is defined as

$$r = \frac{1}{n} \sum_{i=1}^{n} a_i b_i. \qquad (25)$$

$r = 1$ means that A and B are the same. When $r = 0$, they are indifferent, and when $r = -1$, one is the complement

of the other. Although input patterns for recalling should also be memorized, for convenience of evaluation of the behavior of the memory they are not memorized in these experiments.

Example 1

The figures 0–9 are represented as 10×12 bit patterns and their images as 5×6. After figures F0, F1, $\cdots$, F9 had been stored with corresponding images I0, I1, $\cdots$, I9, the images were recalled from the figures, and correlation coefficients between proper patterns of images and the recalled ones are calculated. The result is shown in Fig. 8(a), where $\bar{r}$ is the average of the r's. The input patterns with 10-percent noise (10 percent of the bits are chosen at random and are reversed from 1 to −1, or −1 to 1) are used in Fig. 8(b). This shows that this memory device is scarcely affected by 10-percent noise. Next, to make use of memorized information about the form of the figures themselves, each figure was recalled from the figure with

STORED PAIRS FIGURE-IMAGE	F→I	F→I Noise10%	F→F Noise10%	I→F	ADDITIONAL STORED PAIRS	F→I
F1-11	$r=1.00$	1.00	1.00	0.82		0.80
F2-12	0.60	0.47	0.72	0.65	F-I of	0.67
F3-13	0.53	0.47	0.83	0.69	$r\leq0.6$	0.67
F4-14	0.87	0.80	1.00	0.49	IN (a)	0.63
F5-15	0.67	0.67	0.85	0.80		0.53
F6-16	0.47	0.33	0.68	0.70	F2-12	0.40
F7-17	1.00	1.00	0.78	0.84	F3-13	0.67
F8-18	0.80	0.89	0.93	0.87	F6-16	0.73
F9-19	0.36	0.40	0.82	0.69	F9-19	0.80
F0-10	0.60	0.60	0.78	0.78	F0-10	0.73
	$\bar{r}=0.69$	$\bar{r}=0.68$	$\bar{r}=0.84$	$\bar{r}=0.73$		$\bar{r}=0.66$

(a) (b) (c) (d)   (e)

Fig. 8. Pattern recognition. First, figures 1,2,···,9,0 are stored with their images. (a) Device recalls from figures to their images. (b) Device recalls from figures with 10-percent noise to their images. (c) Device recalls from figures with 10-percent noise to original figures. (d) Opposite of (b), device recalls from images to figures. (e) Pairs of figure and image, for which r is smaller than 0.6 in experiment (a), are memorized additionally. After that, device recalls from figures to their images.

MEMORIZE	RECALL	
STORED TRIPLETS		(ACCURACY)
1. Apple-Spherical-Red	Apple → Spherical, Red	($r=1.00$)
2. Watermelon-Spherical-Green	Watermelon → Spherical, Green	($r=1.00$)
3. Banana-Sticklike-Yellow	Banana → Sticklike, Yellow	($r=1.00$)
4. Wooden box-Boxlike-Yellow	Wooden box → Boxlike, Yellow	($r=1.00$)
5. Cucumber-Sticklike-Green	Cucumber → Sticklike, Green	($r=1.00$)
6. Brick-Boxlike-Red	Brick → Boxlike, Red	($r=1.00$)
	Spherical, Red → Apple	($r=0.78$)
	Spherical, Green → Watermelon	($r=0.75$)
	Sticklike, Yellow → Banana	($r=0.78$)
	Sticklike, Green → Cucumber	($r=0.78$)
	Boxlike, Yellow → Wooden box	($r=0.88$)
	Boxlike, Red → Brick	($r=0.88$)

Fig. 9. Memorizing and recalling. Six triplets in left column are memorized beforehand. Device recalls from things to their colors and shapes, and vice versa. Accuracy of recalling is evaluated by correlation coefficient r between recalled pattern and its original pattern.

10-percent noise. The result is shown in Fig. 8(c). Since 10-percent noise corresponds to $r = 0.80$, recalled patterns ($r = 0.84$) are more accurate than input ones. Fig. 8(d) shows the result of recalling from images to figures. In the experiment shown in Fig. 8(e), after pairs of a figure and its image (for which $r \leq 0.6$ in the experiment of Fig. 8(a)) were stored one more time to improve the separation of figures, images are recalled from figures. Although $\bar{r}$ decreases, compared with that in Fig. 8(a), r is homogenized and the recognition power is considered to be increased.

In this example, visual patterns are directly stored and recalled as shown in Fig. 7(a), but this application is not preferable. The reason was described in the preceding section. Recognition using the patterns without any preprocessing is easily effected by positioning, circulation, and variation of size. Therefore, effective use of this model will be shown in the following examples.

Example 2

Three areas A, B, and C, each of which consists of 40 neurons, are taken on the neural plane. Each of the names of 6 things, 3 colors, and 3 shapes is coded into a 40-bit pattern. A thing, its color, and its shape are stored at areas A, B, and C, respectively. After 6 triplets are stored, the memory device is made to recall the color and the shape from a thing and vice versa. The results are shown in Fig. 9. The device recalls the color and the shape completely from the thing but the accuracy of reverse recalling is about 92 percent.

An experiment concerning simple concept formation was also accomplished. In this case, for example, red things and

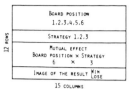

Fig. 10. Allocation of entity in game playing. Entity is composed of four patterns representing board position (40 bits), strategy (20 bits), mutual effect (40 bits), and result (20 bits), each of which is coded at random.

the word "red," such as apple-red-spherical-word "red," brick-red-boxlike-word "red," blood-red-fluid-word "red," are shown to the memory device. At first, the memory device might take the word "red" for "spherical," but as it is trained, it comes to associate "red" with the word "red."

Example 3

When the associative memory device is applied to games, a set of patterns effective for winning the game is expected to be extracted automatically. The following game is used for demonstration of learning process in the associative memory. There are n chips on the board initially. Two players take any number of one to three chips alternately from these chips. The player who is forced to take the last chip loses the game. The restriction is that each player must not take the number which the opponent took at the previous move. For simplicity, presume that there are only six chips on the initial board. To make the Associatron play the game, first the components of vector or an entity are assigned as shown in Fig. 10 to patterns of the board position, the move, the mutual effect of the board position and the move, and the image of the result. Learning is performed in such a way that, after a game is over, all sets of patterns of board position, strategy, mutual effect, and the result which have appeared in the game are memorized one by one. The player with the associative memory (Player A) at every move recalls the image of the result from the board position, a possible strategy, and their mutual effect. The strategy from which the image of "win" is recalled is taken. If the images are the same through possible strategies, one strategy is chosen at random. In this simple way, Player A is expected to make progress in developing his skill in the game, utilizing the property of the associative memory. For example, suppose that the player cannot win at the board position of four chips whatever strategy he may take. The memory is expected to recall the image of "win" from board position four, regardless of other patterns. In this experiment, it is assumed that the opponent player (Player R) chooses one of the possible strategies at random. In training after each game, for the opponent's move the image of the result is reversed from "win" to "lose" and vice versa and is used. Therefore, Player A makes progress using his opponent's strategies, too. Eighteen games have been played (each player alternately plays the first move and Player A learns during the games) and the result is that the winners are, in order of time, R, A, A, A, A, A, A, A, A, R, A, A, A, R, R, A, R, and A; that is, Player A wins 13 times while

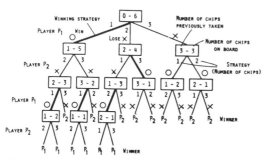

Fig. 11. Game tree of game used for demonstration of Associatron.

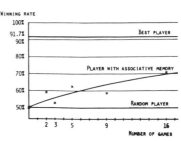

Fig. 13. Graphical expression of learning. Macroscopically, graph increases with number of games, that is, learning progresses. Points plotted show that, microscopocally, skill is not necessarily improved in each game.

Board	Stra-tegy	After nth game					Best Player
		2	3	5	9	16	
0 - 6 -	1	×	○	○	○	○	○
	2	×	○	×	○	×	○
	3	×	×	×	×	×	×
1 - 5 -	2	×	×	–	–	–	×
	3	×	×	×	×	×	×
2 - 4 -	1	×	○	○	×	×	○
	3	×	×	×	×	×	×
3 - 3 -	1	○	○	○	○	○	○
2 - 3 -	1	○	○	×	○	△	○
	2	△	○	○	○	○	○
	3	△	○	○	○	○	○
1 - 3 -	2	○	○	×	○	△	○
	3	×	○	△	○	○	×
3 - 2 -	1	×	×	○	○	△	○
	2	×	×	×	○	○	×
1 - 2 -	2	×	×	×	×	×	×
	3	×	×	×	×	×	×
Winning rate %		58.3	54.2	62.5	58.3	70.9	91.7

○ : Win
× : Lose
△ : Neither
– : Reverse image of 'Win'

Fig. 12. Learning process in game playing. 2 – 3 – 1 ○ means, for example, that if player with associative memory takes one chips at board position of three chips resulted from opponent's taking two chips, he thinks he will win game.

Player R wins 5 times. Examination of the game tree of Fig. 11 yields the best player's strategy at every board position. Strategies of the player are examined after a certain number of games, as shown below. At every possible board position, a check is made as to which image of "win" or "lose" Player A recalls from the board position, possible strategy at the board, and their mutual effect. The result of the examination is shown in Fig. 12. The winning rate of Player A to Player R is shown, too. Fig. 13 shows it graphically. From the graph, it is found that the associative memory can learn how to play the game well.

V. Hardware Realization

The hardware can be constructed as an iterative circuit shown in Fig. 14(a). Since the matrix M in (2) is symmetrical, only half of the $n \times n$ memory units are required. The memory unit is represented by a simple automaton operating synchronously. Assume that the notation is assigned as in Fig. 14(b), and the automaton is described as shown in the following equations:

$$S(t + 1) = S(t) + X_1(t)X_2(t)$$

$$Y_1(t + 1) = \phi(S(t))X_2(t) + X_3(t)$$

$$Y_2(t + 1) = \phi(S(t))X_1(t) + X_4(t)$$

$$Y_3(t + 1) = X_1(t)$$

$$Y_4(t + 1) = X_2(t) \qquad (26)$$

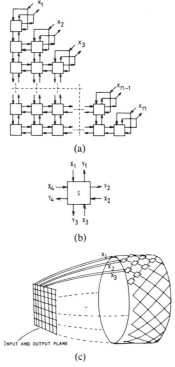

(a)

(b)

(c)

Fig. 14. Hardware realization. (a) Associatron constructed as iterative circuit. (b) Element of iterative circuit is simple automaton whose function is described by (25). (c) Triangular structure of (a) changed to cylindrical structure.

where S corresponds to the multivalued memory unit. For the value of the unit, a few levels are enough to operate the device specifically. In the present memory unit, there are seven levels: $-3, -2, -1, 0, 1, 2, 3$. Changing slightly the arrangement of memory units of Fig. 14(a), we can get the cylindrical structure shown in Fig. 14(c). The structure is fully homogeneous and wiring is simple because the memory unit is connected to only its four neighbor units, except for the lines for power supply, so that it is expandable to a large-scale device.

In this way, a memory device with 25 neurons, that is, 325 memory units, has been constructed for trial. Fig. 15(a) shows the appearance of the device and Fig. 15(b) shows the memory units. Each memory unit is composed of 20

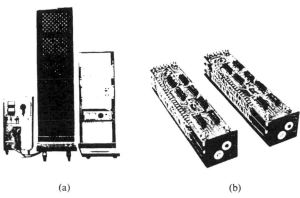

(a)   (b)

Fig. 15. Associatron made for trial purposes. (a) External appearance of device. It consists of 325 memory units, that is, 25 neurons. (b) Memory units. Element has function of automaton described by (25) and is composed of 20 integrated-circuit elements.

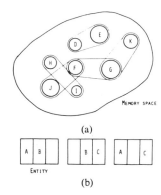

(a)

(b)

Fig. 16. Model for thinking. (a) Couples mean associations of two patterns which actually have been stored. Chain from J to K is formed through experience. (b) When these three entities are memorized, sequential recalling follows loop $A \to B \to C \to A$.

integrated-circuit elements. Any entity can be set in the input register with 25 input switches. The output can be transferred to the input register manually or automatically. If some of 25 selecting switches are turned on, corresponding bits of the input register are obtained from the input switches instead of the output register. Thus, the recalled pattern can be immediately modified and be used as the next input. Although this device is very small in number of neurons, it is effective for some experiments in the sense that it can recall patterns, sequentially returning the output to the input with or without modification each time. The importance of this type of experiment is demonstrated in the next section.

VI. THINKING WITH ASSOCIATIONS

If the recalling process is repeated in the method where the recalled pattern is used as the next input, a chain of associations may be traced. The process is considered to be a thinking process rather than one of recalling the stored entities because the structure of the associations was not directly memorized but has been formed in the memory through experience from a piece of associations, as in the example shown in Fig. 16(a). In this figure, pairs $D–E$, $F–G$, $H–I$, $J–F$, and $G–K$ are memorized in different times, and, from input J, the device can recall F,G,K sequentially.

Though the real thinking process may be far more complicated, here we consider the simplest loop $A \to B \to C \to A$ by setting

$$x = (A,B,0) \qquad y = (0,B,C) \qquad z = (A,0,C) \quad (27)$$

where $l(v_A) = l(v_B) = l(v_C) = 60$. After a number of such loops have been stored, an initial input of $u = (A',0,0)$ is used to recall patterns sequentially, where A' is an arbitrary pattern. In the case that the stored loops number less than six, the sequence of recalling falls into one of the loops shown in Fig. 17(a), that is, the loops can be completely separated. This coincides with the results of theoretical evaluation. When the number of loops is larger, merging, metamorphosis, and extinction of the loops take place as shown in Fig. 17(b)–(d). Merging means that two or

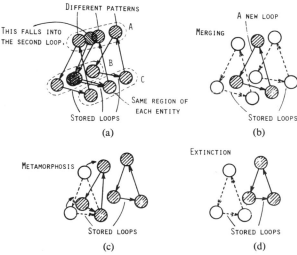

Fig. 17. Structure of associations. (a) Stored loops do not affect each other mutually; that is, loops can be completely separated through recalling. Sequential recalling from arbitrary pattern falls into one of the loop. (b) Stored loops merge into new loop and original loops are not held in memory. (c) Component patterns of certain loop are slightly changed. (d) This loop is extinguished.

more stored loops merge into a new loop. Metamorphosis means that the component patterns of a certain loop are changed by the effect of other loops. Extinction means that a certain stored loop ceases to exist in the memory due to the effect of other loops.

The behavior of the associative memory concerning the thinking process is now being analyzed.

VII. CONCLUSION

Information processing based on associative memory was studied. The model proposed, named Associatron, memorizes entities distributively and recalls them associatively. Consequently, it has different properties from conventional memory devices. Those properties were analyzed and found useful for realizing machine intelligence. The ability of Associatron increases as the number of neurons increases. A few examples, using the model simulated by a digital computer, showed that pattern recognition, concept formation, and game playing with learning are possible. In the example of game playing, it is found that the application of the method is not restricted to a special game, because it fully utilizes the properties of associative memory and the method itself is very primitive and simple. Hardware of an Associatron with 25 neurons uses integrated-circuit elements.

Although consideration is limited to "static" properties, or the properties of simple recalling of the model in this paper, Section VI suggests that "dynamic" properties, or sequences of associations, are more important. Dynamic information processing means that recalling is repeated automatically, even if input does not enter into the device each time, and that, through the process, information is processed. If refractory time and time delay in synapses are added to the model, dynamic information processing might be realized. The model will possibly be a cue toward revealing the relation between so-called reverberation in the nervous system and information processing in the human brain.

ACKNOWLEDGMENT

The author wishes to express his thanks to Prof. J. I. Nagumo for his guidance and encouragement.

REFERENCES

[1] W. S. McCulloch and W. H. Pitts, "A logical calculus of the ideas immanent in nervous activity," *Bull. Math. Biophys.*, vol. 5, pp. 115–133, Dec. 1943.
[2] E. R. Caianiello, "Outline of a theory of thought processes and thinking machines," *J. Theoret. Biol.*, vol. 1, pp. 204–235, Apr. 1961.
[3] F. Rosenblatt, "The perceptron—a probabilistic model for information storage and organization in the brain," *Psychol. Rev.*, vol. 65, pp. 386–407, 1958.
[4] B. Widrow, "Generalization and information storage in networks of adaline 'neurons'," in *Self-Organizing Systems*, M. C. Yovits *et al.*, Eds. Washington, D.C.: Spartan, 1962, pp. 435–461.
[5] P. B. Post, "A lifelike model for association relevance," in *Proc. Int. Joint Computer Conf. Artificial Intelligence*, May 1969.
[6] K. Nakano, "'Associatron' and its applications," presented at the Conf. Information Theory, Inst. Electron. Commun. Eng. Japan, Sept. 1969.
[7] K. Nakano and J. Nagumo, "Studies on associative memory using a model of neural network," presented at the Conf. Medical Electronics, Inst. Electron. Commun. Eng., Japan, June 1970.
[8] A. Samuel, "Some studies in machine learning using the game of checkers," *IBM J. Res. Develop.*, vol. 3, pp. 210–229, July 1950.
[9] ——, "Some studies in machine learning using the game of checkers II—recent progress," *IBM J. Res. Develop.*, vol. 11, p. 601, Nov. 1967.

7
Introduction

(1974)
Karl H. Pribram, Marc Nuwer, and Robert J. Baron

The holographic hypothesis of memory structure in brain function and perception
Contemporary Developments in Mathematical Psychology, Volume I I,
David H. Krantz, Richard C. Atkinson, R. Duncan Luce, and Patrick Suppes (Eds.),
San Francisco: W. H. Freeman, pp. 416–457

The mammalian brain is a largely parallel device, with many neurons working simultanously. The remarkable power of the resulting computation is due to the effective way that the results from individual units are coordinated so that there arises a good resulting consensus answer.

Neuroscientists and psychologists are always searching for models, analogies, and metaphors from other parts of science. Many significant recent advances in the brain sciences have arisen because ideas from physics and engineering were incorporated into the common lore of the brain sciences: signal processing, information theory, and the theory of computation are examples.

The search for metaphors to explain brain function, as has frequently been pointed out, goes far back into the history of science: In the seventeenth century hydraulic analogies were used, because many of the most complex and flexible systems known were complex hydraulic systems. (There were clearly not little gears and cogs in the brain, the other complex mechanical system known at the time. After all you couldn't see them, and the brain was wet.) From the late nineteenth to the early twentieth century, the telephone was the favorite source of ideas: To connect a stimulus to a response, you needed an automated telephone exchange. (Using a tiny operator to make connections would involve what philosophers like to call an infinite regress.) And the middle twentieth century gave us the digital computer, the metaphor that still dominates the thinking of many about intelligent systems, both inside and outside of neuroscience.

If we consider that one essential feature of the brain is that it is a highly interconnected parallel computing device, one source of physical analogies is immediately apparent: optics. Optical devices are parallel because they can operate on the entire wavefront at once. It is natural to think of them in terms of their input-output relations. And, best of all, electromagnetic waves interact linearly in free space. This means total connectivity is easy to obtain because waves from different parts of the image pass through each other. Every point of an input image can affect every point of an output image without interference.

Until about 1960 optics seems not to have been considered seriously as a scientific brain metaphor. However the invention of the laser, and the subsequent popularity of the hologram, changed that.

Karl Lashley (see paper 5 in *Neurocomputing: Foundations of Research*) had found that large amounts of cortex could be damaged, with surprisingly little damage to memory. This and other similar experiments had suggested that information was spread out over cortex in some way. Traditional photography stores an image as a copy of that image. If part of the photograph is lost, then that part of the image cannot be reconstructed. Gabor, in 1947, had suggested a novel form of information storage that he named a *hologram*, which acted differently. Holograms store not the image of an object but the wavefront arising from that object, a much different thing. There are many ways to do this. Basically what is needed is a reference beam and a storage medium (like photographic film) that responds to the intensity of the incident light. Suppose the intensity of the sum of a *reference* wave and an incident wave is stored on a film or other medium. This interaction between two waves is called an interference pattern. The paper provides a lucid description of how the interference pattern, when illuminated by the reference wave, will give rise to a copy of the incident wave.

Holograms have a number of unusual properties that are now familiar to us because they can be seen, among other places, on millions of credit cards. Because they actually construct the wavefront, they appear three-dimensional, and moving the head will cause the hologram to move as real object would. But the property that immediately caught the attention of brain modelers was the way they responded to damage. If part of the film storing the hologram was destroyed, it did not destroy part of the image. The *entire* image was still present, though there was some loss of quality. This was a good qualititive match to what was felt to happen with cortical brain damage: The function was still there, but the brain didn't work as well overall. And the defect was more a result of the size of the damage than what particular part was removed.

Effects like this led to a number of attempts to use holograms to model brain function. And even earlier Lashley had suggested the possiblity of the storage of interference patterns rather than images in his 1950 paper. However, it was immediately obvious that there were difficulties in the direct applications of optical holographic theory. For one thing the brain did not have electromagnetic waves to carry information from point to point, but used nerve fibers with limited connectivity. The source and nature of the reference beam presented a few problems. Was it an actual reference, generated by pacemakers internal to the brain, or could one part of a pattern be used to cue the other parts, giving a useful kind of optical holographic autoassociator? Electromagnetic waves are characterized by both frequency and phase information. The problem of what to do about phase could not be avoided because phase information gave rise to the interference that was essential in constructing holograms. Also the functions that holograms had to perform in a psychological context were much more varied and complex than simple retrieval of stored information. Mechanisms for effects such as memory search, memory decay, psychological (as opposed to optical) interference, and so on had to be proposed.

It was clear that a number of major modifications would have to be made before the ideas behind optical holograms could form a satisfactory brain model. Pribram, Nuwer, and Baron review attempts to use holographic theory to explain brain function and give some of their own suggestions about the connection between optical and neural holograms. They are quite candid about the difficulties of the approach and are unusually open to theoretical ideas other than their own.

In the years since this paper was written, it is fair to say that direct application of holographic theory to brain modeling has not fared well. However, it is worth pointing out that if the word holography is used in a broad sense to describe an information storage system where one pattern is mixed together with another pattern (for example, input and output patterns), and the resulting interaction is stored as intensities or, in the neural network jargon, as connection strengths, then one has a reasonable description of many neural network models.

Whatever their theoretical applicability, holograms may make a direct contribution to the technology of neural networks. Because of the natural similarity between a parallel, highly interconnected optical system and a parallel, highly interconnected neural system, there has been a great deal of recent work attempting to realize neural networks optically. One example is given by Farhat, Psaltis, Prata, and Eung (paper 39 in *Neurocomputing: Foundations of Research*). And the holographic storage of information in suitable crystals may be the ultimate neural net memory technology. So perhaps the major influence will run backward: The brain will suggest to engineers the appropriate way to use parallel optical computing devices rather than the other way around.

(1974)
Karl H. Pribram, Marc Nuwer, and Robert J. Baron

The holographic hypothesis of memory structure in brain function and perception
Contemporary Developments in Mathematical Psychology, Volume I I,
David H. Krantz, Richard C. Atkinson, R. Duncan Luce, and Patrick Suppes (Eds.),
San Francisco: W. H. Freeman, pp. 416–457

Why a Holographic Hypothesis?

Introduction
Recently a growing number of theorists have invoked the principles of holography to explain one or another aspect of brain function. Historically the ideas can be traced to problems posed during neurogenesis when the activity of relatively remote circuits of the developing nervous system must become integrated to account for such simple behaviors as swimming. Among others, the principle of chemical 'resonances' that 'tune' these circuits has had a long and influential life (see, e.g., Loeb, 1907; Weiss, 1939). More specifically, however, Goldscheider (1906) and Horton (1925) proposed that the establishment of tuned resonances in the form of interference patterns in the adult brain could account for a variety of perceptual phenomena. More recently, Lashley (1942) spelled out a mechanism of neural interference patterns to explain stimulus equivalence and Beurle (1956) developed a mathematically rigorous formulation of the origin of such patterns of plane wave interferences in neural tissue. But it was not until the advent of holography with its powerful damage-resistant image storage and reconstructive capabilities that the promise of an interference pattern mechanism of brain function became fully appreciated. As the properties of physical holograms became known (see Stroke, 1966; Goodman, 1968; Collier, Burckhardt, & Lin, 1971), a number of physical and computer scientists saw the relevance of holography to the problems of brain function, memory, and perception (e.g., van Heerden, 1963; Julesz & Pennington, 1965; Westlake, 1968; Baron, 1970; Cavanagh, 1972).

The purpose of the present chapter is threefold: (a) to summarize the neurological evidence that makes holographic processing, storage (temporary or permanent), and image reconstruction a plausible analogy to students of brain function; (b) to present a mathematical network model for the holographic process as a demonstration that optical systems are not necessary for its realization; and (c) to examine the evidence sustaining or negating the neurological assumptions involved in this and alternate realizations.

The Anatomical Problem
One of the best established, yet puzzling, facts about brain mechanisms and memory is that large destructions within a neural system do not seriously impair its function. Various controlled experiments have been performed to investigate this puzzle. Lashley (1950) showed that 80 percent or more of the visual cortex of a rat could be damaged without loss of the ability to correctly respond to patterns; Galambos, Norton, and Frommer (1967) have severed as much as 98 percent of the optic tracts of cats with similar negative results; and Chow (1968) has combined the two experiments into one simultaneous assault, again with little effect on visual recognition behavior. In man, of course, hemianopia and other large scotomata also fail to impair the recognition mechanism. Even small punctal irritative lesions peppered throughout the cortical mantle of monkeys and shown to disrupt its electrical activity leave response to visual patterns intact (Kraft, Obrist, & Pribram, 1960).

These findings have been interpreted by everyone to indicate that the neural elements necessary to the recognition and recall processes must be distributed throughout the brain systems involved. The questions that arise are (a) how is the distribution effected, (b) how does recognition occur, and (c) how are associated events recalled by the network?

An answer that is often given is to consider the input systems of the neuraxis to be composed of large numbers of randomly connected neural elements (Rosenblatt, 1962) and to show either by computer simulation or by mathematical analysis that in a random network of neurons, replication and distribution of signals can occur. Unfortunately for this explanation, the anatomical facts are largely otherwise. In the visual system, for instance, the retina and cortex are connected by a system of fibers that run to a great extent in parallel. Only two modifications of this parallelity occur.

1. The optic tracts and radiations that carry signals between the retina and cortex constitute a sheaf within which the retinal events converge to some extent onto the lateral geniculate nucleus of the thalamus from where they diverge to the cortex. The final effect of this parallel network is that each fiber in the system connects ten retinal outputs to about 5,000 cortical receiving cells.

2. In the process of termination of the fibers at various locations in the pathway, an effective overlap develops (to about 5° of visual angle) between neighboring branches of the conducting fibers.

Equally striking and perhaps more important than these exceptions, however, is the interpolation at every cell station of a sheet of horizontally connected neurons in a plane perpendicular to the parallel fiber system. These horizontal cells are characterized by short or absent axons but spreading dendrites. It has been shown in the retina (Werblin & Dowling, 1969) and to some extent also in the cortex (Creutzfeldt, 1961), that such spreading dendritic networks may not generate nerve impulses; in fact, they usually may not even depolarize. Their activity is characterized by hyperpolarization that tends to organize the functions of the system by inhibitory rather than excitatory processes. In the retina, for instance, no nerve impulses are generated prior to the ganglion cells from which the optic nerve fibers originate. Thus, practically all of the complexity manifest in the optic nerve is a reflection of the organizing properties of depolarizing and hyperpolarizing events, not of interactions among nerve impulses.

Some Neurophysiological Considerations

Two mechanisms are therefore available to account for the distribution of signals within the neural system. One relies on the convergence and divergence of nerve impulses onto and from a neuronal pool. The other relies on the presence of lateral (mostly inhibitory) interactions taking place in sheets of horizontal dendritic networks situated at every cell station perpendicular to the essentially parallel system of input fibers. Let us explore the possible role of both of these mechanisms in explaining the results of the lesion studies.

Evidence is supplied by experiments in which conditions of anesthesia are used that suppress the functions of small nerve fibers thus leaving intact and clearly discernible the connectivity by way of major nerve impulse pathways. These experiments have shown that localized retinal stimulation evokes a receptive field at the cortex over an area no greater than a few degrees in diameter (e.g., Talbot & Marshall, 1941). Yet, the data that must be explained indicate that some 80 percent or more of the visual cortex including the foveal region can be extirpated without marked impairment of the recognition of a previously learned visual pattern. Thus, whatever the mechanisms, distribution of input cannot be due to the major pathways but must involve the fine fibered connectivity in the visual system, either via the divergence of nerve impulses and/or via the interactions taking place in the horizontal cell dendritic networks.

Both are probably to some extent responsible. It must be remembered that nerve impulses occurring in the fine fibers tend to decrement in amplitude and speed of conduction thus becoming slow graded potentials. Further, these graded slow potentials or minispikes usually occur in the same anatomical location as the horizontal dendritic inhibitory hyperpolarizations and thus interact with them. In fact, the resulting micro-organization of junctional neural activity (synaptic and ephaptic) could be regarded as a simple summation of graded excitatory (depolarizing) and inhibitory (hyperpolarizing) slow potential processes.

These structural arrangements of slow potentials are especially evident in sheets of neural tissue such as in the retina and cortex. The cerebral cortex, for instance, may be thought of as consisting of columnar units that can be considered more or less independent basic computational elements, each of which is capable of performing a similar computation (Mountcastle, 1957; Hubel & Wiesel, 1968). Inputs to the basic computational elements are processed in a direction essentially perpendicular to the sheet of the cortex, and therefore cortical processing occurs in stages, each stage transforming the activation pattern of the cells in one of the cortical layers to the cells of another cortical layer. Analyses by Kabrisky (1966) and by Werner (1970) show that processing by one basic computational element remains essentially within that element, and therefore the cortex can be considered to consist of a large number of essentially similar parallel processing elements. Furthermore, the processing done by any one of the basic computational elements is itself a parallel process (see, for example, Spinelli, 1970), each layer transforming the pattern of activity that arrived from the previous layer by the process of temporal and spatial summation, the summation of slow hyper- and depolarizations in the dendritic microstructure of the cortex. Analyses by Ratliff (1965) and Rodieck (1965) have shown that processing (at least at the sensory level) that occurs through successive stages in such a layered neural network can be described by linear equations. Each computational element is thus capable of transforming its inputs through a succession of stages, and each stage produces a linear transformation of the pattern of activity at the previous stage.

Holography

Optical Computing

The problem that thus confronts us is essentially this: how can the relationships between neural activity become distributed and stored (temporarily or more permanently) by a neural network in which such patterns are transmitted and transformed through several successive stages in which processing is an essentially linear parallel process?

Fortunately for neurophysiology, physicists have been concerned with such systems for a long time: optical devices are parallel transmission systems, and during the past 25 years their processing characteristics have been studied intensively. One property of optical processing initially called it to our attention. As we shall see, records can be produced in which the input becomes distributed throughout the storage medium. This makes the record resistant to damage, and, in fact, loss of all but a small portion does not destroy its image reconstructing potential.

Most of us are familiar with the image-generating aspects of optical systems. A camera records on photographic film a copy of the light intensities reflected from the objects within the camera's field of view. Each point on the film stores the intensity (the square of the amplitude) of the light that arrives from a corresponding point in the field of view, and thus the film's record 'looks like' the visual field. What have been studied more recently are the properties of records made when a film does not lie in an image plane of an optical system. When a piece of film is exposed to coherent light that is reflected and scattered by objects in the visual field, there is no ordinary image produced on the film. In fact, the film becomes so blurred that there is no resemblance whatever between the pattern that is stored on the film and the visual field itself. However, when properly illuminated, the film reconstructs the wavefronts of light that were present when the exposure was made. As a result, if an observer looks toward the film, it appears as if the entire visual scene were present behind it. The reconstructed image appears exactly as it did during the exposure, complete in every detail and in three dimensions! The light waves from each point of the visual field had interacted to produce an interference pattern at the film, and it is this interference pattern that was stored throughout the film. Interference patterns give rise to the remarkable characteristics of optical information storage as we shall show.

Even before the practical demonstration of the use of interference patterns in the reconstruction of images, Gabor (1948) had mathematically proposed a way of producing images from photographic records. Gabor began with the intent to increase the resolution of electron microphotographs. He suggested that a coherent background wave and the waves refracted by the tissue could produce interference patterns that would store both amplitude and spatial phase information. Then, in a second step, these stored patterns could be used to reconstruct an image of the original tissue. Gabor christened his film record a *hologram* because it contains all necessary information to reconstruct the whole (hol-) image. The use of this term

for that type of photographic record has since become common.

As the art and science of holography developed, it became clear that a variety of methods described by a number of mathematical procedures could result in holograms. This chapter briefly describes two elementary types—the Fresnel and the Fourier—and provides a network realization of the Fourier holographic process. Other types of holograms have been found useful: they go by names such as Reflection, Volume, Phase, Color, Pulsed-laser, Incoherent, and Digital holograms. All are basically similar to the elementary Fourier and Fresnel types but have special properties that make them especially useful in one or another application. The following exposition is therefore meant to provide only a guideline to holographic processing by presenting the requirements necessary for a holographic hypothesis of memory storage in brain function.

Lensless Optical Holography

The problem faced when trying to store a wavefront of light on photographic film is that film does not store the amplitude or phase distributions (patterns) of light, but instead it records only the intensity (amplitude squared) distribution. The image that is stored on the film is a static representation of the dynamic wavefront of light that arrived during the exposure process, but the stored image has no phase information. As a result, it is impossible to recreate the dynamic pattern of light from which the image was made. Holography offers a way to overcome this problem by recording on film the interference pattern formed by two different wavefronts of light. As we shall show, if the intensity pattern formed by the interference (superposition) of two different wavefronts of light is recorded on the film, sufficient information is retained to enable a reconstruction of either wavefront when only the other one is present at a later time.

Let us suppose than an object, say O_A, is placed near a piece of film and illuminated by a coherent source of light. The wavefront produced at the film by light that is scattered from the object will be denoted by A. The ideal situation would result if film could store the wavefront A. However, when the film is exposed and developed, the image recorded by the film is proportional to the intensity pattern $|A|^2 = AA^*$, not the desired pattern A. As we mentioned earlier, the wavefront A cannot be reconstructed from AA^* alone. Several different holographic techniques have been studied that enable a wavefront of light to be stored, and we shall discuss four of them now.

One technique that has been widely discussed in the literature consists not only of illuminating the object O_A with a plane coherent wavefront of light, but at the same time reflecting some of the coherent light by a plane mirror directly toward the film. The second wavefront of light is called a reference wave and will be denoted by R. When the two different arrival patterns A and R interact, the superposition (algebraic sum of electric and magnetic components) given by $A + R$ is formed. Because A and R are generated by the same light source, they have the same frequency. A stable interference pattern is formed, and the film records the intensity of the interference pattern given by $(A + R)(A + R)*$. If the film is transparent, A and R continue to propagate independently, and we call these output portions of the wavefronts the output patterns or departure patterns.

Now suppose the film is developed and replaced in the optical system. Also suppose that the object O_A is removed so that only the reference wave R is allowed to illuminate the film. The departure pattern is given by the product of the incoming wavefront attenuated at each point by the transmission coefficient of the film at that point. The departure pattern is therefore given by $R(A + R)(A + R)*$, which can be expanded mathematically to

$$R(|A|^2 + |R|^2) + A|R|^2 + A^* R \cdot R.$$

The first term of the expansion describes the reference wave R attenuated by an amount $|A|^2 + |R|^2$ The second term describes a reconstructed copy or the desired wavefront A attenuated by an amount $|R|^2$. This wavefront has all the properties of the original wavefront present during the exposure process. As a result, a person looking toward the film would 'see' the object O_A. Because O_A is not present, the reconstructed image is called a 'ghost image,' and since the reconstructed wavefront is an exact copy of A, the ghost image appears in three dimensions and has all other properties that could be seen during the exposure. The last term describes noise, which is introduced into the system by the holographic process. The film is called a hologram and the wavefront A is said to be stored. (Note that if A could have been stored directly, the noise term would not have been produced and the reconstructed image could have been formed directly from the stored image.)

Now let us suppose that the mirror rather than the object had been removed during the reconstruction process. The departure pattern would have been given by $A(A + R)(A + R)* = A(|A|^2 + |R|^2) + R|A|^2 + R^*A \cdot A$. In this case, the reference wave is reconstructed (the second term), the wavefront A attenuated (the first term), and again noise is produced. There is thus a natural symmetry between the two wavefronts in the system.

Recognition Holography

The second type of holography discussed is a slight modification of the first type. Rather than using a plane mirror to produce the reference wave, let us use a spherical mirror

that focuses the reflected light onto a point P in front of (on the output side of) the film. When the hologram produced by this system is developed and replaced in the system, two different departure patterns result depending on how the hologram is illuminated. If the object is removed and the hologram is illuminated only by light reflected by the mirror, the wavefront A is reconstructed. Both the focused wavefront and a noise term are also produced. If the object is used to illuminate the hologram and the mirror removed, the focused wavefront is reconstructed, and a bright spot of light is focused at the point P. A light detector placed at P could be used to detect the bright spot, and since a bright spot is produced only when object O_A is present in the system, the detector can be used to 'recognize' the presence of the object O_A. This optical system can be used for the recognition of three-dimensional objects.

Association Holography

The third lensless system described is similar to the two previous systems. This time, however, the mirror is replaced by a second object, say O_B. See Figure 1. When objects O_A and O_B are illuminated by a coherent light source, two wavefronts A and B are produced. If a film is exposed to the interference pattern produced by A and B and given by $A + B$, the film will record the static pattern $(A + B)(A + B)*$.

Now let us see what happens if the film is developed and placed exactly where it was during the exposure. Assume that object O_A is removed. If O_B is illuminated, the arrival wavefront that reaches the film is B, and the static distribution of transmission coefficients on the film is given by $(A + B)(A + B)*$. The departure wavefront is given by $B(A + B)(A + B)^* = B(|A|^2 + |B|^2) + A|B|^2 + A^*B \cdot B$. The first term shows that the wavefront B is transmitted, the second term shows that the wavefront A is also reconstructed, and the third term shows that noise is produced.

If the objects do not cause light to be focused on the film, the intensity distributions $|A|^2$ and $|B|^2$ are nearly uniform across the film even over small (millimeter) distances. However, the interference pattern $(A + B)$ gives rise to an intensity pattern that varies considerably over small distances, and the resulting stored pattern $(A + B)(A + B)*$ resembles a very complex diffraction grating. It is precisely for this reason that the departure pattern is a reconstruction of the wavefront of A that is not present during the reconstruction process.

Figures 1 and 2 illustrate the holographic association process. Figure 2 shows the exposure process. Light is reflected from two objects, a wide block O_A in the background, and a tall block O_B in the foreground. Both objects are illuminated by a single coherent monochromatic plane wave generated by a laser. After exposure, the film is

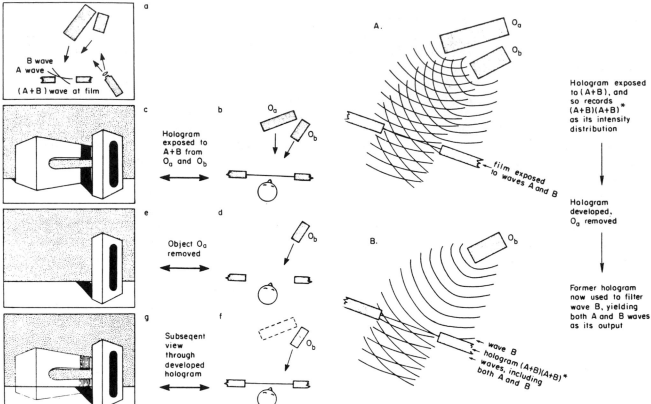

Figure 1 A hypothetical holographic experiment. The apparatus for a Fresnel hologram is shown in (a). The view as the film is being exposed is shown in (b) and (c); the view after the film and one object are removed in (d) and (e); and the view after the developed hologram is returned, in (f) and (g), demonstrating the ghost image of the missing object. (Adapted from Collier & Pennington, 1966.)

Figure 2 Diagram of waves in creation (A) and reconstruction (B) processes. Note how in (B) the filtering of B through hologram $(A + B)(A + B)^*$ results in waves including both A and B.

developed and replaced exactly where it was during the exposure process. Now, however, the object O_A is 'seen' so that the film is exposed to light which is reflected only from the tall block O_B. Because the departure wavefront A is reconstructed by the hologram, the object is 'seen' by an observer even though it is no longer present. Again the reconstructed wavefront is an exact copy of the departure pattern that was present during the exposure, so the object appears in three dimensions and has all other properties that could be seen during the exposure.

The three lensless holographic processes described above are among many similar techniques used for producing holograms. Holograms can be produced by exposure to objects that are either near the film (near-field holograms) or far away from the film (far-field holograms). The optical far-field transforms used above are known as Fresnel transforms. However, both the near-field and far-field lensless holograms—i.e., those produced with scattered wavefronts as reference waves (e.g., the third system)—are usually referred to as Fresnel holograms. Holograms pro-

duced with infinitely far-field transforms are called Fourier holograms.

One optical system of the Fourier type, using a plane coherent reference wave produced by lenses, is of special interest to the neurotheorist because a direct analogy can be drawn between it and a layered neural network. Because it is this analogy that we wish to pursue, the mathematical properties of the system are described in somewhat greater detail.

The Fourier Holographic Process

The Lens System
The system of interest consists of two spherical lenses arranged so that the second focal plane of the first lens is coincident with the first focal plane of the second lens. This is shown in Figure 3. The three focal planes of the two lenses are also of interest to this analysis and will be called the *input plane, transform* or *memory plane,* and *output plane* of the system.

It is well known that when a photographic image is placed in one focal plane of a spherical lens and illuminated by a plane, coherent light wave, the Fourier transform of

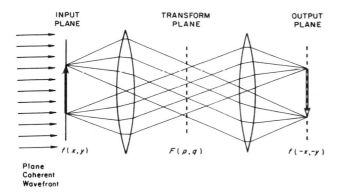

INPUT PLANE   TRANSFORM PLANE   OUTPUT PLANE

$f(x,y)$ $F(p,q)$ $f(-x,-y)$

Plane Coherent Wavefront

Figure 3 Fourier transforming property of a lens. Note how the second lens effects a second 'reverse' transform, causing an image in the output plane like the original object in the input plane.

the image is produced in the other focal plane of the lens. (For a nice proof of this result, see Preston, 1965.) For the optical system pictured in Figure 3, this transformed image occurs in the transform plane. The transformed image also lies in the first focal plane of the second spherical lens and therefore the Fourier transform of the transformed image appears in the third focal plane or output plane of the system. An elementary theorem of Fourier analysis tells us that the resulting output image of the system is precisely the input image, only it appears upside down and backwards.

This process may be stated more precisely as follows. In an optical system, wavefront patterns are of two distinctly different types: *static* and *dynamic*. The static patterns are the stored photographic images that are described in terms of their transmission coefficients for light as a function of position on the photographic film. We will let (x, y) represent the geometric coordinates of position and $f(x, y)$ represent the transmission coefficient at the point (x, y). The function $f(x, y)$ on a piece of film represents a static storage pattern for the optical system. The dynamic or active patterns are the wavefronts of light that are processed and transformed by the optical systems. The specific transformations that occur in an optical system depend on the components (lenses, prisms, etc.), their placement, and the properties of the light waves used. For the optical system being described, Fourier transformation results because of the choice of spherical lenses, their arrangement, and the use of coherent light. Let $F(p, q)$ be the Fourier transform of $f(x, y)$. Then for the optical system of Figure 3, $F(p, q)$ is imaged in the transform plane. The variables p and q represent the position of the image in the transform plane. If we denote by $\rightarrow$ the process of Fourier transformation, then we write

$$f(x, y) \rightarrow F(p, q)$$

to represent the first stage of processing, and

$$F(p, q) \rightarrow f(-x, -y)$$

to represent the second stage.

Now consider the process that occurs at the photographic film itself. A light wave of uniform intensity, say A, illuminates the image $f(x, y)$. The intensities of the departure wavefront are attenuated by the presence of the input film. In fact, the intensity at point (x, y) is proportional to the transmission coefficient of the film at that point. The static storage pattern is converted to a dynamic processing pattern with amplitude distribution proportional to the spatial distribution of transmission coefficients of the image. This conversion is multiplicative. Thus, if the amplitude of the arrival pattern at point (x, y) is A, then the amplitude of the departure pattern in front of the image at point (x, y) is $Af(x, y)$.

Now let us suppose that an actual photographic image of the transform $F(p, q)$ could be placed in the transform plane of the optical system. Also suppose that the transform image could be illuminated by a plane coherent wavefront. (A uniform illumination across the transform plane can easily be produced by placing a point source of light in the center of the input plane.) The departure pattern produced by the film would have an intensity distribution $F(p, q)$ and the image $f(-x, -y)$ would be produced in the output plane. We find that both images $f(x, y)$ and $F(p, q)$ contain exactly the same information, the only difference is in the way in which information is coded. In fact, a film record of the transformed image, if made with a plane reference wave, is a Fourier hologram of the input image and from now on we refer to these transform images as holograms. They are the 'memories' of the optical system.

As described earlier, the static images are intensity distributions whereas the dynamic images are amplitude and phase distributions. Static distributions can be represented by positive real functions whose value is less than unity (light is not produced and the phase of transmitted light is not changed by a piece of film), whereas dynamic patterns are represented by arbitrary complex (in the mathematical sense) quantities. In general, the Fourier transform of a positive real image is a complex quantity and therefore cannot be stored directly as a static pattern. To produce a hologram of the image $f(x, y)$, we cannot simply expose a piece of film in the transform plane. However, by taking the superposition of the desired wavefront and a plane reference wave, a hologram is produced in which the desired information is not lost. This is illustrated in Figures 4 and 5. The details of this process are similar to the lensless case, which was described earlier using a plane reference wave, and may be pursued in detail elsewhere by the

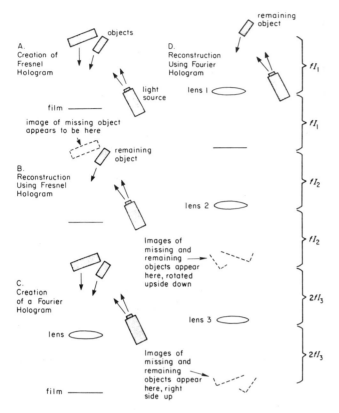

Figure 4 Comparison of apparatus and images in creation and reconstruction using Fresnel- and Fourier-type holograms. Note that the third lens in (D) is optional, and simply inverts the first reconstructed image.

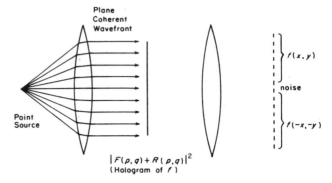

Figure 5 Reconstruction of $f(x, y)$ using Fourier holography. Here the plane wave $R(p, q)$ acts as the second, reference wave in capturing $F(p, q)$ on the hologram. $R(p, q)$ is the Fourier plane image of an *off-centered* point source. Reconstruction is effected here through use of an *on-center* point source. This trick separates $f(x, y)$ from $f(-x, -y)$ in the output plane.

interested reader (Stroke, 1966; Tippett, Berkowitz, Clapp, Koester, & Vanderburgh, 1965).

A second theorem from Fourier theory is important to the discussion that follows. When the Fourier transform $F(p, q)$ of an image $f(x, y)$ is multiplied by the complex conjugate of the Fourier transform $G(p, q)*$ of a second image $g(x, y)$, and the Fourier transform of the product taken, the result is the cross correlation of the two initial images. This is important because cross correlation is a measure of the similarity of the original two images. A measure of similarity is precisely what is required for recognition.

For our optical system, if the hologram $(G(p, q) + R(p, q))(G(p, q) + R(p, q))*$ is placed in the transform plane while the image $f(x, y)$ is placed in the input plane, the departure pattern that results just after the hologram is the product of the two functions $F(p, q)$ and the hologram. The result that follows from the above theorem is that the cross correlation of the functions $f(x, y)$ and $g(x, y)$ is produced in the output plane. See Figure 5. If the two images are similar, a bright spot appears in the output plane and the brightness of the spot indicates how similar the two images are. The system instantaneously cross correlates

two spatial patterns. In fact, this technique has been applied successfully to the instantaneous recognition of human faces! (In general, a thresholding light detector is placed in the output plane to determine whether or not a given input image should be 'recognized.') The reader should note that the hologram is formed from the interference pattern between the desired transform $G(p, q)$ and a plane coherent wavefront $R(p, q)$. The result is that both the cross correlation and convolution functions of the two images are formed in the output plane. Figure 6 illustrates the formation of these functions by the optical system, and Figure 7 gives a geometric interpretation of the cross correlation and convolution functions. Also note the similarity between this system and recognition holography described earlier.

There is another property of the Fourier transform of an image that is of interest to the neurophysiologist. Each point of the transform indicates the presence of specific spatial frequencies that are present in the input image. If, for example, the input image is a simple sinusoidally varying intensity pattern of spatial frequency p, then the Fourier transform at position $F(p,0)$—or $F(0,p)$ depending on the orientation of the image—would have intensity proportional to the brightness of the image, and the rest of the transform would have zero intensity. By analyzing the Fourier transform of an input image, one can determine its exact spatial components.

The analysis of the optical system is similar to the analyses both of conventional optical holography in which Fourier or Fresnel holograms are produced and of van Heerden's (1963) method of information storage in solids. There are also analogies between cross correlation in the optical system described here and in recognition (and in fact association) techniques both in van Heerden's system

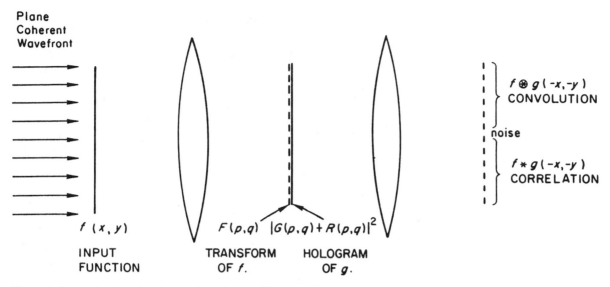

Figure 6 Results from illuminating a Fourier hologram with a wave, $F(p, q)$, which is not the same as the waves which created the hologram, $G(p,q)$ and $R(p, q)$. Convolution and correlation functions are formed in the output plane.

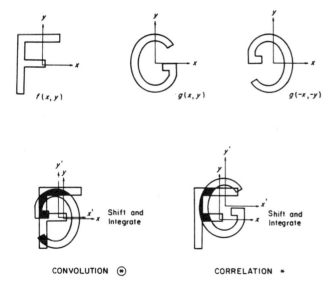

Figure 7 Geometric interpretations of the convolution and correlation functions. Note how the convolution involves a rotated version of one function, while the correlation does not.

and in conventional holography. The reader is directed for the details to the references cited.

A Mathematical Network Model

Enough of the formal attributes of the holographic optical systems that we have found to have the essential properties for storage, recognition, and recall. What needs to be done to make holography into a useful metaphor for students of brain function in memory and perception is to see whether the lens system, or even an optical system, is necessary to the accomplishment of the holographic process.

We found earlier that there are both static (storage) and dynamic (processing) patterns in the optical system. We found that optical processing occurs because of the geometry and components of an optical system. We found how static and dynamic information patterns interact, and finally we found that a system in which there are two stages of linear information processing is capable of storing, recognizing, and recalling visual information. We now draw an analogy between each of these quantities in optical systems and corresponding quantities in computer simulated systems.

There are both static (storage) and dynamic (processing) patterns in our network model. The static patterns are sensitivity values of the junctional contacts between two cells. (For convenience we call our mathematical processing elements 'cells' and the loci of changes of sensitivity values 'junctions.') The junctions are assumed to be distributed throughout the volume of the assembly of cells. The contribution that a unit (not to be confused with a processing unit) of transmissivity has toward the rate of activation of the postjunctional cell may differ depending on the geometric position of its arrival. We therefore define the *local sensitivity* at point (x, y, z) of a cell to be a measure of the effective contribution toward activation that is produced at position (x, y, z) from prejunctional cells. Static patterns are described by giving for each cell (p, q) of the network the local sensitivity function $k_{pq}(x, y, z)$. Local sensitivity values are a function of the junctional microstructure of contacts among the cells.

In our model, dynamic or processing patterns are the patterns of activation in collections of processing cells. We assume for simplicity that the activation of a cell depends only on the average value of local sensitivity throughout its junctional microstructure. (This assumption is made here for expository purposes only. In a more comprehensive model by Baron, 1970, this assumption is not made.) We define the *sensitivity* of unit (p, q), denoted by K_{pq}, to be the volume integral over the microstructure of the local sensitivity function. That is,

$$K_{pq} = \iiint k_{pq}(x, y, z)\, dx\, dy\, dz.$$

These sensitivity values correspond to the transmission coefficients of the optical systems. Memories, the static stored patterns, are preserved in these sensitivity values as we now show.

The dynamic patterns process information from one collection of cells to another. Dynamic patterns are described by giving the rate of activation and inhibition of the junctional contacts of each cell in the collection as a function of time. Dynamic patterns must be real-valued functions of time.

There is also a direct analogy between the transformations of the optical system as specified by its geometry and components, and the transformations of the network model. In the network model, patterns of excitation are transformed as they propagate from one layer of cells to another because of the *coupling coefficients* between cells. If, for example, one cell excites another at a high rate, the coupling between the two cells is high and positive. If the one cell tends to inhibit another, the coupling is negative. Coupling coefficients are functions of pairs of cells and must be specified for every connected pair of cells of a network.

Static and dynamic patterns interact in the network model in much the same way that they do in optical systems. In an optical system, light travels in a straight line and the 'coupling' is determined geometrically by the precise distance the light has to travel from its origin to its destination. In the optical system described above, the irradiating light wave is coherent, and therefore the phase of light transmitted from each point is the same. If the distance a light ray travels is a multiple of the wavelength, that ray adds; if the distance is an odd multiple of half the wavelength, the ray subtracts. These correspond to maxi-

mum excitatory and inhibitory coupling in the network model, respectively. See Figure 8. Because the distance that the light has to travel varies systematically across the transform plane, the Fourier transform of the input pattern is formed in the transform plane. As noted, in the network model 'coupling' is determined by the amount of activity occurring in pairs of cells of an ensemble.

In the optical system, if the superposition of all light waves has amplitude A at point (x, y) and the film at point (x, y) has transmission coefficient $f(x, y)$, then the output pattern has amplitude $Af(x, y)$. In the network, if the spatial summation of all activity results in a net excitatory quantity A at cell (p, q) in the network, the contribution of activity to the next cell is determined by A and by the sensitivity K_{pq} of the receiving cell. The quantity A is not determined by coherence properties and it is at this point that a geometric analogy with the optical system fails. If the interactions between static and dynamic processes are multiplicative (which we will later propose) the analogy is direct, and the contribution from all prejunctional cells toward the activation of postjunctional cell (p, q) is given by AK_{pq}.

The resulting properties, storage, recognition, and recall depend on specific architecture, coupling coefficients, and sensitivity values, and are now to be studied in detail.

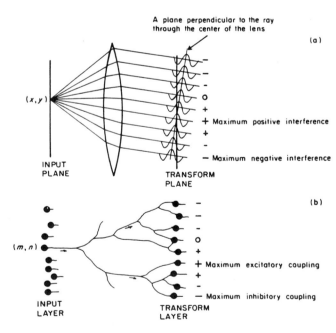

Figure 8 Correspondence between optical and neural systems. The couplings in the neural system may be considered with respect to some positive baseline. Thus an 'inhibitory' coupling is in reality just the decrease in excitation below baseline level, and still could be excitatory in physiological terms.

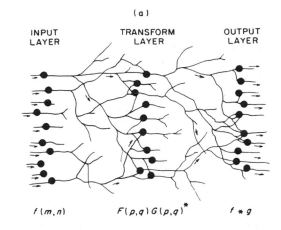

Achieving the Fourier Transformation

Consider the three-layered network illustrated in Figure 9a. We will call the cells in the three layers the *input cells, transform* or *memory cells,* and *output cells,* respectively. The activation patterns in these three collections of cells will correspond directly to the dynamic patterns which occur at the input, transform, and output planes of the optical system of Figure 3.

In order to make an analogy between the optical system and the network of Figure 3, we will need to choose a standard labeling scheme for the cells of the three collections. We will begin by assuming that cells are labeled with a two-dimensional system of variables. Thus a particular cell in a collection may be the $(4, 6)$th cell, or in general, we consider the (m, n)th cell. The activity of the (m, n)th cell at time t will be given by $f(m, n)(t)$. This corresponds to the dynamic input image $f(x, y)$ of the optical system.

For each pair of connected cells we must specify the coupling coefficient between that pair of cells. For the (m, n)th cell in the input layer and the (p, q)th cell in the transform layer we will designate by c_{pq}^{mn} the coupling coefficient. (Superscripts refer to prejunctional cells, and subscripts refer to postjunctional cells.) We assume that the coupling coefficients do not depend on the geometric position (x, y, z) in the network. We must also designate a local sensitivity function $k_{pq}(x, y, z)$ for each cell (p, q) of the transform layer. (For the analysis that follows, the only cells for which the local sensitivity values are of interest are the cells of the transform or memory layer. We will therefore assume for simplicity that the local sensitivity values of all other cells have value 1 and may therefore be omitted from the discussion.)

This network model corresponds to one basic computational element: one collection of cells that are closely coupled together. Our assumption is more precisely that every cell of the input layer makes connections to every cell of the transform layer, and every cell of the transform layer makes connections to every cell of the output layer. We will designate by $f(m, n)(t)$, $F(p, q)(t)$, and $f'(m', n')t$ the dynamic activity patterns in the input, transform, and output layers, respectively at time t. Since we designate by c_{pq}^{mn} the coupling coefficient between the (m, n)th input cell and the (p, q)th transform cell, then the net amount of excitation less the amount of inhibition provided by all input cells at any point in the transform layer of the network is given by

$$\sum_{(m,n)} c_{pq}^{mn} f(m, n)(t). \tag{1}$$

The rate of activation of the (p, q)th transform cell is given by

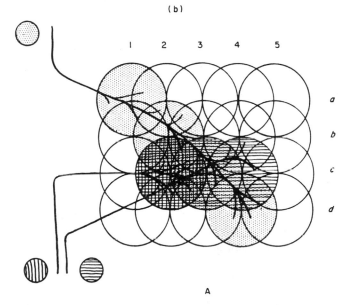

Figure 9 In part a a neural network is described schematically. The network is analogous to the optical diagram of Figure 3. Part b represents a more realistic diagram of microstructure of synaptic domains in cortex. The ensemble of overlapping circles represented the junctions between branches of input axons and cortical dendrites. (Redrawn after Scheibel & Scheibel in Pribram, 1971.)

$$F(p, q)(t) = \iiint k_{pq}(x, y, z) \sum_{(m,n)} c_{pq}^{mn} f(m, n)(t) \, dx \, dy \, dz, \tag{2}$$

where integration would be over the volume containing all prejunctional connections of the transform unit. (In each case, if the rate of activation is negative, we assume the cell is inhibited and will not transmit at all.) Because the coupling coefficients do not depend on position, the integration can be performed and Equation 2 reduces to

$$F(p, q) = K_{pq} \sum_{(m,n)} c_{pq}^{mn} f(m, n)(t). \tag{3}$$

(In a somewhat more complicated model presented by Baron, 1970, the effective coupling between prejunctional and postjunctional cells during storage and recall depends systematically on time and geometric position (x, y, z) in the network. The result is that the local sensitivity values cannot be averaged. The addition of this 'timing mechanism' enables the network to store and recall patterns that vary as a function of time. Thus, for example, storage recognition and recall of verbal (auditory) information is possible.)

In the optical system, specific transformations resulted because of the geometry and components of the specific system. Under the analogy, transformations that result in the network depend directly on the coupling coefficients, c_{pq}^{mn}. We assume that the coupling coefficients are chosen so that the network Fouriers-transforms the input image. To see how this might be done, we need only to look at the specific equations for Fourier transformation in optical systems. For the optical system, the Fourier transform is given by

$$F(p, q) = \iint \exp\big((px + qy)2\pi i\big)f(x, y)\, dx\, dy. \tag{4}$$

If the system is discrete rather than continuous, Equation 4 becomes

$$F(p, q) = \sum_{x=1}^{m} \sum_{y=1}^{m} M^{-1} \exp\big((px + qy)2\pi i/M\big)f(x, y), \tag{5}$$

where M^2 is the number in discrete points of the image.

For our network model, if we could choose the coupling coefficients in the analagous way, that is,

$$c_{pq}^{mn} = M^{-1} \exp\big((mp + nq)2\pi i/M\big), \tag{6}$$

the network would Fourier-transform the input pattern. However, we are not at liberty to use mathematically complex quantities. (Our early assumption was that dynamic patterns are nonnegative real functions.) In order to build a network model that resembles a biological neural network that will preserve the Fourier transform, we must preserve negative and complex quantities. In all optical systems described, negative and complex quantities were preserved by storing the intensity distribution of the superposition of the desired signal with a second (reference) light wave. Because coherent light was used as a source of illumination, a stable interference pattern resulted whose intensity distribution enabled recall (reconstruction) of the stored pattern. One possible mechanism for a neural network to encode negative and complex quantities is to allow independent neurons to convey the positive and negative, real and imaginary components of the desired signal. This approach was used by Baron (1970). Another possible method is to have the cells activated at a background rate (which represents an actual value of 0), and to assume that inhibitory effects reduce a cell's activity to below background firing. These slow rates would represent negative quantities. The real and complex components of the transform would still have to be preserved by independent cells. Several researchers have also considered coherent neural activity in direct analogy with the optical system. In each case an internal signal is used to insure coherence. See for example Westlake (1968), Swigert (1967), and Barrett (1969).

The Neural Hologram
We note that the assumed neural processing that underlies this formalism is relatively simple. Chemical transmitters are released at synaptic junctions between presynaptic and postsynaptic cells. These chemical transmitters diffuse across the synaptic cleft and modify the resting potential of the postsynaptic cell. The local modifications to the resting potential near the synaptic junctions propagate to some extent away from the junctions. Excitatory transmitters cause depolarizations; inhibitory transmitters cause hyperpolarizations in the dendritic microstructure of the postsynaptic cell. Excitatory and inhibitory contributions sum by spatial summation, and the result is a small contribution to the activation of that cell. The contribution to depolarization from any junction is determined by the local sensitivity at that junction that depends in turn on its membrane properties (see below). The local fluctuations, slow potentials, or minispikes interacting with the junctional microstructure, propagate toward the soma and cause it to depolarize at a rate given by Equations 2 or 3. The result is a linear transformation of the input depolarization pattern $f(m, n)(t)$ to the transform pattern $F(p, q)(t)$ through one stage of neural processing.

In the optical system, the exposure of an undeveloped piece of film to an optical pattern sensitizes the film so that development at a later time causes points that are exposed to bright light (light with a large amplitude) to become black upon development, and points that are exposed to dim light (or no light at all) to remain transparent. If one then makes a 'positive' image of the film, the result is that the transmission coefficients of points that received light having a high intensity will become high, and the transmission coefficients of points that received no light at all will become low. This is the optical hologram or 'memory trace' of the optical system. By analogy, we suggest that in the model during the 'exposure' period the local sensitivity values become altered in regions that receive a large net amount of activation and become altered in the opposite direction in regions that received a small net amount of activation. Some neurons store the 'real' part of the transform, other neurons store the 'imaginary' part. In particular, we propose that the local sensitivity values for the 'real' half of the population of junctions become proportional to the net (excitatory less inhibitory) amount of the activation that arrived during the exposure period, while for the 'imaginary' half we propose the opposite, i.e., deactivation (inhibition less excitation) occurs. That is,

$$K_{pq} \text{ is set proportional } \sum_{(m,n)} (c_{pq}^{mn})^* f(m, n)(t), \tag{7}$$

where $f(m, n)(t)$ is the pattern to be stored. Because the net amount of arriving activation has a spatial distribution (Eq. 1) that is precisely the conjugate Fourier transform of the dynamic input pattern, the resultant distribution of local sensitivity values corresponds to one term of the optical Fourier hologram and it is for this reason that we call these 'memory traces' a neural hologram.

In short, a *neural hologram* is the pattern of sensitivity values that correspond to one element of an optical Fourier hologram and it is a function of the junctional microstructure of the memory units. The sensitivity values of a neural hologram preserve the conjugate Fourier transform of the patterns of excitation and inhibition that are initiated by the input.

Recognition and Recall

We have shown that Fourier transformation can be performed by a single stage of incoherent neural processing, at least in principle. We now extend our analogy between the optical system shown in Figure 3 and the three-layered network shown in Figure 9a. We assume that the transformation that occurs between the memory layer and the output layer is also a Fourier transformation. That is, the dynamic activation pattern of the output layer is the Fourier transformation of the dynamic pattern of the memory layer. Once this happens, there are predictable patterns of activity in the output cells, and this activity takes on two distinctly different forms.

For an arbitrary input pattern (i.e., the encoded form of the sensory stimulus), the output pattern is the cross correlation of the input pattern with the pattern represented by the local sensitivity values. In this case, the system gives a strong signal when the input pattern is similar to the stored pattern. This is the recognition process. In the optical system of Figure 3, the recognition signal appears as a bright spot in the output plane of the system. By analogy, the recognition signal for a memory node is the rapid firing of a small group of cells in the output layer. The sensitivity pattern has a 'focusing' effect on the surrounding activity, and when the input pattern is similar to the stored pattern, the recognition information is gathered at a group of cells. The activity in such cells could easily be monitored by other networks and used for selecting the memory nodes from which to later recall information. This process is completely analogous to recognition holography as described earlier, and to the cross-correlation process of the lens system.

By contrast, the output pattern has a completely different nature when the cells of the transform layer are excited in a uniform way. If the memory cells are uniformly excited, that is, by a single cell whose coupling coefficients are the same to all memory cells, the uniform activation is modified by the sensitivity values of the memory cells and the result is that each memory cell fires at a rate that is proportional to its sensitivity value. In this case, their pattern of depolarization is a reactivation of the stored pattern. It is, in fact, the conjugate Fourier transform of the pattern that is stored. The output pattern is in this case a copy of the original pattern of departure activity that was input when the local sensitivity values were established. The output pattern is a recalled copy of the stored information.

Alternate Models

The Fourier process is not the only process our formalism can usefully describe. Equation 3 gives the pattern of activity of the units in the memory layer in terms of the input pattern $f(m, n)(t)$, the coupling coefficients c_{pq}^{mn}, and the sensitivity values k_{pq}. The coupling coefficients that enabled the network to Fourier-transform the dynamic patterns of activity were an arbitrary choice, and in principle any choice of coupling coefficients could be made. In order for the network to be able to store information, the input transformation should not lose information. It must have an inverse. If the sensitivity values of the memory units preserve the transformed pattern and the transformation between the memory units and the output units produces the inverse transformation, then a uniform excitation of the memory cells will cause the stored pattern to be recalled.

However, if the network is to adequately recognize input information, the recognition signal should be much stronger when the stored pattern arrives than when an arbitrary different pattern arrives. It is well known that for a linear system (Turin, 1960), the best possible recognition signal is achieved when the transfer function of the system is the complex conjugate of the Fourier transform of the pattern to be recognized divided by the frequency spectrum of the noise. This is precisely the result achieved by the holographic model presented in this chapter. (We have assumed for simplicity that there is no systematic noise in the network. If noise is present in the system, the sensitivity values must be divided by the spectrum of the noise.) Thus, although other linear transformations can support the storage and recall processes, they are not as ideally suited for recognition as the Fourier processes.

A very recent neural holographic model was proposed by Cavanagh (1972) in direct analogy with the associative holographic system described earlier. Cavanagh proposes that two independent collections of input units contact the memory units, and that two independent collections of output units carry the departure patterns from each computational element of the system. The initial input patterns, say *a* and *b* are converted to the transformed patterns *A* and *B* by the first layer of processing, and the intensity pattern $(A + B) (A + B)^*$ is stored by the sensitivity values of the memory units. (The patterns *A* and *B* correspond to the arrival patterns *A* and *B* in the associative holography system described earlier.) The coupling between the memory units and the output units is assumed to have two properties: if no information is stored in the memory units, the departure patterns in the two collections of cells correspond to the arrival patterns. If, however, consolidation had occurred when arrival patterns *A* and *B* were present, then at a later time, input pattern *a* alone will cause the departure pattern *b* to be reconstructed, and vice versa. Thus, if *a* is present in the input, a 'ghost image' of *b* is automatically generated, and this reconstruction process is instantaneous. No search procedure or external control is necessary.

In contrast to our model, Cavanagh has demonstrated explicitly the two collections of input units that correspond to the two wavefronts of light used in optical holography. Also in contrast to our model, Cavanagh proposes that intensity values are stored rather than the real and complex quantities of the transformed image. The essential point is that many models can be suggested, and each one captures one or more of the essential features of optical holography. At present, each model must be considered as a suitable alternative to the other, and until more direct experimental evidence is at hand, no model can be used to preclude another.

Many models fall into the class of neural holographic storage models, and it is this general class of models we are trying to describe here.

Neural Processes

Storage Properties

Network models of the holographic processes have accomplished several aims:

1. they have shown that optical systems are not required for holographic transformations to be realized; and

2. by keeping in mind some simple characteristics of nervous tissue, they have spelled out requirements for (a) temporary or permanent modification of any one layer of neurons by way of changes in the static patterns of sensitivity values within a junctional microstructure, and (b) processing between layers of neurons by specification of the coupling coefficients between them.

Let us begin by citing evidence consonant with the requirements for neural modification (storage, temporary, or permanent) demanded by the model. The model suggests that the arrival patterns to a unit—a neuron and its dendrites—produce a microstructure of slow potentials (depolarizations and hyperpolarizations) in the form of an interference pattern on that neuron's dendritic and somatic membranes. Eccles, Ito, and Szentagothai (1967) have described the mechanism of production of such interference patterns in the cerebellar cortex. At the regions of greatest constructive interference, changes are produced in the membrane's sensitivity to excitation and inhibition. Whenever new arrival patterns similar to the original occur, perturbations of these sensitive areas are produced. Thus the likelihood of depolarization and conduction in that cell are greater than when nonsimilar inputs arrive. It is precisely this, and *only* this, property that we have shown to be necessary for neural holography to be possible.

There is good reason to believe that a similar process occurs at the cerebral cortex. Benevento, Creutzfeldt, and Kuhnt (1973) have suggested on the basis of intracellular recordings that all input to the cortex results in excitatory (depolarizing) processes while the effects of horizontal interactions are essentially inhibitory (hyperpolarizing). Extracellular recordings, testing the effects of double simultaneous visual stimulation in our laboratory, are most readily interpreted in the same way (Phelps, 1972). These results give some justification to the emphasis given in our strictly holographic model to a single process by which depolarization and hyperpolarization affect changes in sensitivity values. Neither hyper- nor depolarization per se are therefore considered agents for membrane modification.

That this effect is restricted in locus is not unlikely: a rough inverse square law for the effects of slow graded potentials has been assumed by model builders since Beurle (1956) and has sufficient backing of evidence (e.g., Phelps, 1972) to be taken seriously.

The holographic storage hypotheses require that the modified synaptic sensitivity be proportional either to the input signal strength (our model) or to the square of the input signal strength (Cavanagh). This could be accomplished in the following way. Permanent or some reversible semipermanent change to a membrane would be proportional to the square of the voltage difference between neighboring input patterns of electrical activity, since perturbation in the postsynaptic domain is a function of the differences in distribution of hyper- and depolarizations produced by the arrival of input patterns of presynaptic potentials, resulting in voltage differences *parallel* to the postsynaptic membrane. A testable physical description of such a mechanism has been developed by Richard Gauthier for the special, though not unusual, case of two synapses from different axons forming adjacent junctions into a dendritic or somatic membrane. The interactions between excitatory and inhibitory processes can be conceived to occur somewhat like this: with no synaptic input to the membrane, there is a resting electric potential across the membrane, with the voltage gradient or electric field lines perpendicular to the membrane surface (Fig. 10a). Suppose that in neighboring terminals the input to the presynaptic terminals causes the postsynaptic junctions to become locally depolarized and hyperpolarized, respectively (Fig. 10b). The effect is to produce a pair of horizontally oriented electric dipoles at the surfaces of the cell membrane, which superimpose their electric fields on the vertical fields already present (Julesz, 1971; Barrett, 1969; Pribram, 1971). The net effect is to produce significant electric fields or voltage gradient components that are parallel to the surface of the membrane. We propose that these transient horizontal components of electric field trigger structural (e.g., conformational) changes in the membrane that outlast these horizontal fields. The induced structural changes in the membrane which in themselves may be reversible could then set off further biochemical processes leading to long-lasting ion permeability changes.

When either synapse is activated again, these structural or permeability changes can cause the effects (i.e., postsynaptic potentials) of one synaptic input to diffract and mimic the effects of the other, as if the latter were present. Thus the activation of one synapse produces the effects of acti-

vating both. The contribution of any such pair of synaptic inputs is small, but when many identical effects throughout the microstructure of a synaptic domain are summed, the physiology of the network would be significantly affected. While this example concerns two adjacent synapses, it is important to keep in mind that the process also applies to the more remote effects that sets of synapses within a domain can have on each other through the interactions of the slow potential activity induced in the membrane of the postsynaptic cell.

These membrane changes should be detectable with present technology. Short- and long-term changes in sensitivity of a local area of membrane to excitation can be tested by means of intracellular recordings using large invertebrate neurons. In such preparations, cells whose membranes are repeatedly exposed to pairs of input patterns should come to produce equivalent output patterns even when only one input is received. In more complex neural aggregates such a demonstration has already been achieved (Chow, 1964; Dewson, Chow, & Engle, 1964).

The long-lasting modifications of membrane structure are most likely to occur postsynaptically. Although at a somewhat grosser level, evidence has recently been produced that in fact such postsynaptic changes do occur.

Recent evidence from electron micrography comparing the cortex of rats raised in deprived and enriched environments clearly shows the importance of the postsynaptic membrane in modifications of neural structure by experience. These studies show that though the number of synapses per unit volume of the cortex is greater in the deprived rats, a characteristic thickening of the postsynaptic membrane occurs in many of the synapses of the enriched rats (Rosenzweig, Bennett, & Diamond, 1972). Thus a homogeneous network becomes modified into a patterned one.

Processing Properties

Given plausibility for temporarily or more permanently storing the static pattern required by the models, what about the coupling parameters that provide their processing determinants? Let us start with the receptors of the visual system, the rods and cones of the retina—upon which a true visual image is produced by the optical lens system of the eyeball. Each rod and cone can be thought of as an omatidium—a relatively discrete independent intensity transducer of a small part of the total retinal image mosaic.

Now for a moment we turn to the various interactions that occur in the deeper layers of the retina as inferred from the output of the ganglion cell layer that has been studied so extensively by making extracellular microelectrode recordings from the optic nerve. Two major quantitative descriptions are of special interest here. The first details the mathematical description of the receptive field character-

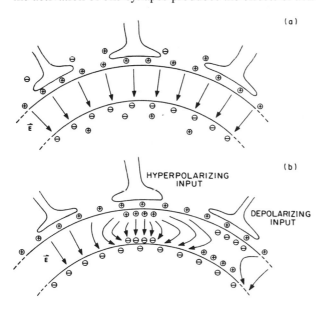

Figure 10 Membrane electrical fields. The upper figure (a) shows the field when undisturbed. The lower figure (b) shows the field when inputs arrive, demonstrating the consequent horizontal components of the field within the membrane. (From Richard Gauthier, personal communication, 1972.)

istics of ganglion cell responses. It is well known (Kuffler, 1953) that the ganglion cell responses are of two types—'on' cells characterized by increased firing of the central portion of the receptive field to onset of illumination, and 'off' cells characterized by increased firing to the offset of illumination. Both 'on' and 'off' cells show a roughly concentric arrangement of their receptive fields: an inhibitory or excitatory penumbra surrounds the center. These surrounds have been shown due to lateral inhibition—hyperpolarizations that are produced in the horizontal and amacrine networks that lie perpendicular to the input-output fibers of the retina. Mathematical descriptions of the relationships obtained in these receptive field configurations are reviewed by Ratliff (1965) and Rodieck (1965). Most of these descriptions involve a convolution of luminance change of the retinal input with inferred inhibitory characteristics of the network to compose the observed ganglion-cell receptive field properties. In short, a set of convolutional integrals has been found to adequately describe the transformations that occur between the retinal receptor mosaic and the ganglion cell output from the eye to the brain.

The second quantitative description comes from Enroth-Cugell and Robson (1966). In their account they have demonstrated in the range of ganglion-cell receptive fields a variety of relationships between center and surround, a finding also emphasized by Spinelli (1966). Enroth-Cugell, Robson, etc., then showed that they could explain this variety on the assumption of an opponent mechanism—separate excitatory (depolarizing) and inhibitory (hyperpolarizing) retinal processes, each process displaying an essentially Gaussian distribution.

Where do these separate excitatory and inhibitory processes take place? Dowling and Boycott (1965) have shown that, prior to the ganglion cell layer, few if any retinal neurons generate nerve impulses. All interactions are performed by way of slow potentials. These are of two opposing types—depolarizing excitations and hyperpolarizing inhibitory effects. Intracellular recordings (Svaetichin, 1967) have suggested that the excitatory potentials are generated along the input transmission paths (bipolar cells) of the retina while the inhibitory potentials are due to the horizontal layers (amacrine and horizontal cells) that cross the transmission channels. This 'lateral' inhibitory process has been studied extensively and made the basis for quantitative descriptions of sensory interaction by Hartline (see Ratliff, 1965) and by von Bekesy (1959) in their treatment of the Mach band phenomenon. The equations they invoke are similar to those used by Rodieck in his description of ganglion-cell receptive fields.

The gist of these experimental analyses is that the retinal mosaic becomes decomposed into an opponent process by depolarizing and hyperpolarizing slow potentials and transforms into more or less concentric receptive fields in which center and surround are of opposite sign. Sets of convolutional integrals fully describe this transformation.

The next cell station in the visual pathway is the lateral geniculate nucleus of the thalamus. The receptive field characteristics of the output from neurons of this nucleus are in some respects similar to the more or less concentric organization obtained at the ganglion cell level. Now, however, the concentric organization is more symmetrical, the surround usually has more clear-cut boundaries and is somewhat more extensive (e.g., Spinelli & Pribram, 1967). Furthermore, a second penumbra of the same sign as the center can be shown to be present though its intensity (number of nerve impulses generated) is not nearly so great as that of the center. Occasionally, a third penumbra, again of opposite sign, can be made out beyond the second (Hammond, 1972).

Again, a transformation has occurred between the output of the retina and the output of the lateral geniculate nucleus. Each geniculate cell acts as a peephole 'viewing' a part of the retinal image mosaic. This is due to the fact that each geniculate cell has converging upon it some 10,000 ganglion cell fibers. This receptive field peephole of each geniculate cell is made of concentric rings of opposing sign, whose amplitudes fall off sharply with distance from the center of the field. In these ways the transformation accomplished is like very near-field optics.

Pollen, Lee, and Taylor (1971), though supportive of the suggestion that the visual mechanism as a whole may function in a Fourier-like manner, emphasize that the geniculate output is essentially topographic and punctate, is not frequency specific, and does not show translational invariance—i.e., every illuminated point within the receptive field does not produce the same effect. Further, the opponent properties noted at the retinal level of organization are maintained and enhanced at the cost of overall translational invariance. Yet a step toward a discrete transform domain has been taken since the output of an individual element of the retinal mosaic—a rod or cone receptor—is the origin of the signal transformed at the lateral geniculate level.

When the output of lateral geniculate cells reaches the cerebral cortex, further transformations take place. One set of cortical cells, christened 'simple' by their discoverers (Hubel & Wiesel, 1968), has been suggested to be characterized by a receptive field organization composed by a literally linelike arrangement of the outputs of lateral geniculate cells. This proposal is supported by the fact that the simple-cell receptive field is accompanied by side bands of opposite sign and occasionally by a second side band of the same sign as the central field. Hubel and Wiesel proposed that these simple cells thus serve as line detectors in the first stage of a hierarchical arrangement of pattern detectors. Pollen et al. (1971) have countered this proposal on the basis that the output from simple cells varies with contrast luminance as well as orientation and that the receptive field is too narrow to show translational invariance. They argue, therefore, that an ensemble of simple cells would be needed to detect orientation. They suggest that such an ensemble would act much as the strip integrator used by astronomers to cull data from a wide area with instruments of limited topographic capacity (as is found to be the case in lateral geniculate cells). Whether in fact strip integration occurs, the linelike arrangement could be conceived as a preparatory step in Fresnel, Fourier or other frequency-type processing—now a slit rather than a peephole 'views' the retinal mosaic.

But it is not necessary to view simple cells as way stations in a hierarchy—these cortical units clearly have functions in their own right. A series of ingenious studies by Henry and Bishop (1971) have confirmed that these simple cells are exquisitely tuned to the *edges* (luminance contrast) of lines in the visual receptive field independent of line width. Some are tuned to the leading, some to the trailing edges. Responses are of two types, excitatory and inhibitory, and very often show opponent properties: i.e., when the edge is moved in one direction across the receptive field the effect (e.g., excitation) is the converse of that (e.g., inhibition) produced when the edge is moved in the opposite direction. These investigators have shown that this effect is binocularly activated. Only when the excitation zones are in phase is an output signal generated. This occurs exclusively when the image on the two retinas superimposes—i.e., when 'objects' are in focus. Thus, simple cells act as gates that let pass only binocularly fused information.

Another class of cortical cells has generated great interest. These cells were christened 'complex' by their discoverers, Hubel and Wiesel, and thought by them (as well as by Pollen) to be the next step in the pattern recognition hierarchy. Some doubt has been raised (Hoffman & Stone, 1971) because of their relatively short latency of response as to whether all complex cells receive their input from simple cells. Whether their input comes directly from the geniculate or by way of simple cell processing, however, the output from complex cells of the visual cortex displays transformations of the retinal input, characteristic of the holographic domain.

A series of elegant experiments by Fergus Campbell and his group have suggested that these complex cortical cells are spatial-frequency sensitive elements. Initially, Campbell showed that the response of the potential evoked in man and cat by repeated flashed exposure to a variety of gratings of certain spacing (spatial frequency), adapted not only to that fundamental frequency but also to any component harmonics present. He concluded therefore that the visual system most be encoding spatial frequency (perhaps in Fourier terms) rather than the intensity values of the grating. He further showed that when a square wave grating was used adaptation was limited to the fundamental and its third harmonic as would be predicted by Fourier theory. Finally, he found neural units in the cat's cortex that behaved as did the gross potential recordings.

Pollen (1973) has evidence that suggests that these spatial-frequency sensitive units are Hubel and Wiesel's complex cells, although both his work and that of Maffei and Fiorentini (1973) have found that simple cells have the properties of spatial frequency filters, in that they are broadly sensitive to a selective band of spatial frequencies. In addition, the latter investigators have found that the simple cells can transmit contrast and spatial phase information in terms of two different parameters of their response: contrast is coded in terms of impulses per second and spatial phase in terms of firing pattern.

The receptive field of complex cells is characterized by the broad extent (when compared with simple cells) over which a line of relatively indeterminate length but a certain orientation will elicit a response. Pollen demonstrated that the output of complex cells was not invariant to orientation alone—number of lines and their spacing appeared also to influence response. He concluded, therefore, as had Fergus Campbell, that these cells were spatial frequency sensitive and that the spatial frequency domain was fully achieved at this level of visual processing. Additional corroborating evidence has recently been presented from the Pavlov Institute of Physiology in Leningrad by Glezer, Ivanoff, and Tscherbach (1973), who relate their findings on complex (and hypercomplex) receptive fields as Fourier analyzers to the dendritic neurostructure of the visual cortex much as we have done here.

There is, however, still another set of problems that must be disposed of before the conception of a spatial frequency transformation of the retinal image by cortex can be accepted. These problems deal with the tuning characteristics of each spatial frequency sensitive element and the extent of retinal image which this element transforms. The evidence to date suggests that each simple cell is rather broadly tuned, but that the receptive fields of complex cells are narrower in their tuning characteristics. Richards and Spitzberg (1972), among others, have suggested the pattern recognition mechanism be considered analogous to that which obtains for color where stepwise recombination of opponent processes sharpens broadly tuned receptor characteristics into a magnificent tool for subtle color perception. We have already detailed the evidence that shows opponent processes to exist at various levels of the visual pattern transformation mechanism. What remains to be done is to show quantitatively how by combinations of opponent processes, sharper tuning characteristics of the spatial frequency mechanism can be achieved.

The problem is not much different for obtaining the greater visual angle over which the spatial frequency mechanism must operate. Some combinational process must occur—the question is, where and how. Evidence pertaining to this point is presented toward the end of this chapter, but first let us take leave from the transform process and look again into the distribution mechanism without which the brain lesion effects cannot be explained.

A Limiting Specification

We thus have evidence that neural transformations occur in the visual system that could, given appropriate storage, result in Fresnel-like (simple cell) and Fourier-like (complex cell) holograms. But all problems are not yet out of the way. Perhaps the most critical current question that is posed by the holographic hypothesis of memory storage is the question of the extent to which input becomes distributed at any one stage of processing. As indicated in an earlier part of this chapter, visual inputs even to the complex cell level of the cortex still represent only a few degrees of visual space. Obviously, input does not become distributed over the whole brain in one pass, if ever. What are the limits on distribution that would yet allow one to use the hologram as a model? This question may not have a single answer and probably depends on the coding and control mechanisms available to the organism for this purpose at any given moment. There is considerable evidence from verbal learning experiments that rehearsal accomplishes internal distribution of the events rehearsed (Voss, 1969; Trabasso & Bower, 1968). Neisser (1967) points out that retinal translation should destroy the congruence necessary for recognition were a simple point-to-point template involved—and it does not. Moyer (1970) on the other hand, in a series of experiments, has shown that recognition at a nonexposed retinal locus is impaired when a complex unfamiliar pattern is presented tachistoscopically once to a restricted retinal locus. Even a single repetition of the exposure with no change of locus will, however, significantly enhance recognition at a distant locus. Rehearsal is obviously a potent source of distribution of information.

Another way of approaching this question is to ask just how much replication and how much distribution is demanded by the holographic hypothesis. Pollen's data suggest that in the visual cortex only small regions of visual space become encoded. However, Hubel and Wiesel (1968) describe considerable overlap of receptive fields within a single penetration for cells at the same orientation and preferred slit width. How this overlap becomes usefully integrated is an experimental question under present laboratory study (Pribram, 1974) and is discussed to some extent in the final section of the chapter.

The evidence cited above thus gives strong support to the concept that local regions of the cortex are responsible for storing the memories of experience. Does this contradict the results of the ablation studies cited earlier? No, for it is quite possible as already noted, that the proposed system, in response to rehearsal, stores multiple copies of the same experience in remote regions of the cortex, and that each of these records is a complete description of the given event. Evidence that in fact such multiple copies occur has been obtained: small macroelectrodes were implanted over the visual cortex of monkeys and electrical activity recorded in a discrimination experiment. In randomly distributed locations over the visual cortex, localized electrical activity was reliably found to be related to either the stimulus or the response (or reinforcement) events in the experiment (Pribram, Spinelli, & Kamback, 1967).

Let us suppose that the strictly holographic transformations are a local phenomenon, and that integration of information across the cortex is done either by a hierarchical summing onto the next level of connectivity, or by a parallel processing mechanism via subcortical connections. These alternatives are being explored experimentally at present (see Pribram, 1974, for review). Since the hierarchical alternative is almost universally espoused, it needs little explanation. Let us for a moment therefore consider the advantages of parallel processing mechanisms that make the experimental investigation worthwhile.

Relation to Control Processes

An essential distinction between a hierarchical serial process and a parallel process is that the latter allows control functions to be exercised before or at the transform or memory plane rather than after transformations and storage have been accomplished. In their operations, control functions can influence several biological memory processes that are independent of the particular storage model, yet each one can crucially affect the way in which the memory store operates. They are the following.

1. Permanence: Are the memory traces permanent (they never change once they are made), or are they temporary (the same memory location can store a different pattern at later times)?

2. Modifiability: Are the memory traces adaptive—do they change slowly after the initial consolidation process? If so, when are the modifications allowed to occur?

3. Consolidation: Do the memory traces become permanent upon a single presentation of the input pattern, or do they slowly become established upon repeated presentations of the same input information? If the latter is true, what are the control processes to insure that only the proper memory traces are allowed to consolidate at any given time?

4. Interference: If more than a single presentation of the input pattern is necessary, how sensitive is the nascent memory trace to interference?

5. Decay: Are the memory traces actually 'permanent' after they are established, or do they slowly degrade as a function of time? If they degrade, what is the rate of degradation? How does degradation affect recognition and recall?

Several memory *control functions* can operate on these storage functions. These control functions are not particular to the holographic model and in fact are not part of the holographic model. They are the following.

1. Start-stop: When will a particular memory location begin the 'exposure' process, and when will it finish? This start-stop process may be considered for a particular memory location, or it may be considered for all the memory locations in a memory store.

2. Selection: For a memory store, the question may be restated: why will one memory location store the current input information rather than another? The memory may be stored initially on the basis of innate competences of the neural tissue involved and later on the basis of changes in competence produced by experience. Or, memory locations may be arbitrarily (pseudorandomly) selected initially and then input deliberately channeled to compatible sites on the basis of temporal or conceptual contiguity.

3. Recognition threshold: An input is judged as 'recognized' when it evokes associated memories. The implication is that whenever memories are called forth from an associative (content addressable) store, then the effects of an earlier similar input must indeed already be in the memory store. How similar must similar be to become recognized by the memory? The simulation of the holographic process developed here proposes that a cross correlation take place in parallel with all stored memory. Then if any region of any cross correlation exceeds some arbitrary threshold, the input is considered recognized. How is that threshold established and altered?

4. Recall: If storage is truly associative, recall occurs to the extent that an input evokes the effects of earlier associated inputs. How are the limits placed on such evocation? A control mechanism must be present that is able to decide

which of the memory locations that have been addressed are to be used in further processing.

The above questions and comments are typical concerning the relationship between memory and its control functions and some of these have been touched on by Spinelli (1970) in the discussion of "Occam." What is important to understand is that the general holographic hypothesis is strictly a model of the interaction between storage and input processing and does not address these decisional questions. However, the holographic hypothesis does propose that these decisional properties involving storage, recognition, and recall occur by way of a content addressable parallel-processing mechanism. We therefore consider briefly the evidence that, in fact, the organization and processing of memory occurs in a content addressable parallel-processing system.

There are a growing number of experiments that are designed to determine whether or not the recognition of a stimulus and the retrieval of related (associated) information are sequential or parallel processes. Results presented by Sternberg (1969) and more recently by Atkinson and Juola (1974) suggest in fact that both sequential and parallel processes are involved. It is generally believed true that there is an initial sequence of processes that encode the stimulus information into the form used by the memory stores. There next appears to be an initial addressing of memory that results in a 'familiarity index' for the stimulus involved. This is the recognition signal or correlation value produced by an associative memory store. The reaction time studies indicate that this is a parallel process—that the encoded stimulus pattern is presented simultaneously to all memory locations (nodes or basic computational elements) of the memory stores.

On the other hand, the experiments indicate that once the familiarity of a stimulus item is obtained, additional information can only be recalled by a secondary sequential search of memory. This secondary search process locates specific items from among those which are related to the stimulus. The sequential search appears to be restricted to those memory locations that contain information associated with the stimulus—memory locations that recognized the encoded stimulus pattern. Furthermore, these experimental results imply that individual memory locations may be accessed independently and their stored information recalled.

Summary

Our studies of holographic processes have detailed possible mechanisms for the distributed memory required by the results of experiments on brain function. Several issues became clarified. Holography depends on two separable functions: (a) storage of interference patterns or their equivalents; (b) patterns created by superposition or other Fresnel- or Fourier-like input processing. A network model of one limiting case of holography—the Fourier Hologram—has been accomplished using elements and junctional characteristics plausibly like those in neural networks. Other models have also been touched upon. In addition, evidence has been adduced that, in fact, holographic storage and spatial frequency—Fourier-like—processing occurs in the visual system.

Thus the advantages of a holographic memory as a model for brain function in perception can be fruitfully pursued with vigor. Aside from the property of distributed storage, holographic memories show large capacities, parallel processing, and content addressability for rapid recognition, associative storage for perceptual completion and for associative recall. The holographic hypothesis serves therefore not only as guide to neurophysiological experiment, but also as a possible explanatory tool in understanding the mechanisms involved in behaviorally derived problems in the study of memory and perception.

Acknowledgments

We wish to thank Richard Gauthier, Erich Sutter, Arthur Lange, and Charles Stromeyer for their assistance and critical comments which enlivened considerably the writing of this paper.

References

Atkinson, R. C., & Juola, J. F. Search and decision processes in recognition memory. In D. H. Krantz, R. C. Atkinson, R. D. Luce, and P. Suppes (Eds.), *Contemporary developments in mathematical psychology.* Vol. 1. San Francisco: Freeman, 1974.

Baron, R. J. A model for cortical memory. *J. of Mathematical Psychology,* 1970, **7,** 37–59.

Barrett, T. W. The cortex as interferometer: The transmission of amplitude, frequency and phase in cortical structures. *Neuropsychologia,* 1969, **7,** 135–148.

Benevento, L. A., Creutzfeldt, O. C., & Kuhnt, U. Significance of intracortical inhibition in the visual cortex: Data and model. *Nature,* 1973, in press.

Beurle, R. L. Properties of a mass of cells capable of regenerating pulses. *Philosophical Transactions of the Royal Society of London, Ser. B,* 1956, **240,** 55–94.

Cavanagh, J. P. Holographic processes realizable in the neural realm: Prediction of short-term memory and performance. Unpublished doctoral dissertation, Carnegie-Mellon University, 1972.

Chow, K. L. Bioelectrical activity of isolated cortex, III. Conditioned electrographic responses in chronically isolated cortex. *Neuropsychologia,* 1964, **2,** 175–187.

Chow, K. L. Visual discrimination after ablation of optic tract and visual cortex in cats. *Brain Res.,* 1968, **9,** 363–366.

Collier. R. J., Burckhardt, C. B., & Lin, L. H. *Optical holography.* New York: Academic Press, 1971.

Collier, R. J., & Pennington, K. S. Ghost imaging by holograms formed in the near field. *App. Phys. Lett.,* 1966, **8,** 44.

Creutzfeldt, O. D. General physiology of cortical neurons and neuronal information in the visual system. In M. B. A. Brazier (Ed.), *Brain and behavior.* Washington, D.C.: American Institute of Biological Sciences, 1961.

Dewson, J. H., III, Chow, K. L., & Engle, J., Jr. Bioelectrical activity of isolated cortex, II. Steady potentials and induced surface-negative cortical responses. *Neuropsychologia,* 1964, **2,** 167–174.

Dowling, J. E., & Boycott, B. B. Neural connections of the retina: Fine structure of the inner plexiform layer. *Quant. Biol.,* 1965, **30,** 393–402.

Eccles, J. C., Ito, M., & Szentagothai, J. *The cerebellum as a neuronal machine.* New York: Springer, 1967.

Enroth-Cugell, C., & Robson, J. G. The contrast selectivity of retinal ganglion cells of the cat. *J. Physiol.,* 1966, **187,** 517–552.

Gabor, D. A new microscopic principle. *Nature,* 1948, **161,** 777–778.

Galambos, R., Norton, T. T., & Frommer, C. P. Optic tract lesions sparing pattern vision in cats. *Experimental Neurology,* 1967, **18,** 8–25.

Glezer, V. D., Ivanoff, V. A., & Tscherbach, T. A. Investigation of complex and hypercomplex receptive fields of visual cortex of the cat as spatial frequency filters. *Vision Res.,* 1973, **13,** 1875–1904.

Goldscheider. A. Über die materiellen Veränderungen bei der Assoziationsbildung. *Neurol. Zentralblatt,* 1906, **25,** 146.

Goodman, J. W. *Introduction to Fourier optics.* San Francisco: McGraw-Hill, 1968.

Hammond, P. Spatial organization of receptive fields of LGN neurons. *J. Physiol.,* 1972, **222,** 53–54.

Henry, G. H., & Bishop, P. O. Simple cells of the striate cortex. In W. D. Neff (Ed.), *Contributions to sensory physiology.* New York: Academic Press, 1971.

Hoffman, K. P., & Stone, J. Conduction velocity of afferents to cat visual cortex: A correlation with cortical receptive field properties. *Brain Res.,* 1971, **32,** 460–466.

Horton, L. H. *Dissertation on the dream problem.* Philadelphia: Cartesian Research Society of Philadelphia, 1925.

Hubel, D. H., & Wiesel, T. N. Receptive fields and functional architecture of monkey striate cortex. *J. Physiol.,* 1968, **195,** 215–243.

Julesz, B. *Foundations of cyclopean perception.* Chicago: University of Chicago Press, 1971.

Julesz, B., & Pennington, K. S. Equidistributed information mapping: An analogy to holograms and memory. *J. Opt. Soc. Am.,* 1965, **55,** 604.

Kabrisky, M. *A proposed model for visual information processing in the human brain.* Urbana: University of Illinois Press, 1966.

Kraft, M. S., Obrist, W. D., & Pribram, K. H. The effect of irritative lesions of the striate cortex on learning of visual discrimination in monkeys. *J. Comp. Physiol. Psychol.,* 1960, **53,** 17–22.

Kuffler, S. W. Discharge patterns and functional organization of mammalian retina. *J. Neurophysiol.,* 1953, **16,** 37–69.

Lashley, K. S. The problem of cerebral organization in vision. In, *Biological symposia.* Vol. 7. *Visual mechanisms.* Lancaster, Pa.: Jacques Cattell Press, 1942.

Lashley, K. S. In search of the engram. In, *Society for experimental biology (Great Britain): Physiological mechanisms in animal behavior.* New York: Academic Press, 1950.

Loeb, J. *Comparative physiology of the brain and comparative psychology.* Science Series. New York: Putman, 1907.

Maffei, L., & Fiorentini, A. The visual cortex as a spatial frequency analyzer. *Vision Res.,* 1973, **13,** 1255–1267.

Mountcastle, V. B. Modality and topographic properties of single neurons of cat's somatic sensory cortex. *J. Neurophysiol.,* 1957, **20,** 408–434.

Moyer, R. S. On the possibility of localizing visual memory. Unpublished doctoral dissertation, Stanford University, 1970.

Neisser, U. *Cognitive psychology.* New York: Appleton-Century-Crofts, 1967.

Phelps, R. W. Inhibitory interactions in the visual cortex of the cat. Unpublished doctoral dissertation, Stanford University, 1972.

Pollen, D. A. Striate cortex and the reconstruction of visual space. In, *The neurosciences study program,* III. Cambridge, Mass.: MIT Press, 1973.

Pollen, D. A., Lee, J. R., & Taylor, J. H. How does the striate cortex begin the reconstruction of the visual world? *Science,* 1971, **173,** 74–77.

Preston, K., Jr. Use of the Fourier transformable properties of lenses for signal spectrum analysis. In J. T. Tippett, D. A. Berkowitz, L. C. Clapp, C. J. Koester, and A. Vanderburgh (Eds.), *Optical and electro-optical information processing.* Cambridge, Mass.: MIT Press, 1965.

Pribram, K. H. *Languages of the brain.* Englewood Cliffs, N.J.: Prentice-Hall, 1971.

Pribram, K. H. Why is it that sensing so much we can do so little? In, *The neurosciences study program,* III. Cambridge, Mass.: MIT Press, 1974.

Pribram, K. H., Spinelli, D. N., & Kamback, M. C. Electrocortical correlates of stimulus response and reinforcement. *Science,* 1967, **157,** 94–96.

Ratliff, F. *Mach bands: Quantitative studies in neural networks in the retina.* San Francisco: Holden-Day, 1965.

Richards, W., & Spitzberg, R. Spatial frequency channels: Many or few? *J. Opt. Soc. Am.,* 1972, **62,** 1394.

Rodieck, R. W. Quantitative analysis of cat retinal ganglion cell response to visual stimuli. *Vision Res.,* 1965, **5,** 583–601.

Rosenblatt, F. *Principles of neurodynamics: Perceptrons and the theory of brain mechanism.* Washington, D.C.: Spartan Books, 1962.

Rosenzweig, M., Bennett, E., & Diamond, M. Brain changes in response to experience. *Scientific American,* 1972, **2,** 22.

Spinelli, D. N. Visual receptive fields in the cat's retina: Complication. *Science,* 1966. **152,** 1768–1769.

Spinelli, D. N. Occam, a content addressable memory model for the brain. In K. H. Pribram and D. Broadbent (Eds.), *The biology of memory.* New York: Academic Press, 1970.

Spinelli, D. N., & Pribram, K. H. Changes in visual recovery function and unit activity produced by frontal and temporal cortex stimulation. *Electroenceph. Clin. Neurophysiol.,* 1967, **22,** 143–149.

Sternberg, S. Memory-scanning: Mental processes revealed by reaction-time experiments. *American Scientist,* 1969, **57,** 421–457.

Stroke, G. W. *An introduction to coherent optics and holography.* New York: Academic Press, 1966.

Svaetichin, G. Horizontal and amacrine cells of retina-properties and mechanisms of their control upon bipolar and ganglion cells. *Act. Cient.,* 1967, **18,** 254.

Swigert, C. J. Computational properties of a nerve and nerve net model. Unpublished doctoral dissertation, University of California, Berkeley, 1967.

Talbot, S. A., & Marshall, U. H. Physiological studies on neural mechanisms of visual localization and discrimination. *Amer. J. Ophthal.,* 1941, **24,** 1255–1264.

Tippett, J. T., Berkowitz, D. A., Clapp, L. C., Koester, C. J., & Vanderburgh, A. (Eds.) *Optical and electro-optical information processing.* Cambridge, Mass.: MIT Press, 1965.

Trabasso, T., & Bower, G. H. *Attention in learning theory and research.* New York: Wiley, 1968.

Turin, G. L. An introduction to matched filters. *IRE Transactions on Information Theory,* 1960, **6,** 311–329.

van Heerden, P. J. A new method of storing and retrieving information. *Applied Optics,* 1963, **2,** 387–392.

von Bekesy, G. Synchronism of neural discharges and their demultiplication in pitch perception on the skin and in hearing. *J. of Acoustical Society of America,* 1959, **31,** 338–349.

Voss, J. F. Associative learning and thought: The nature of an association and its relation to thought. In J. F. Voss (Ed.), *Approaches to thought.* Columbus, Ohio: Meredith, 1969.

Weiss, P. *Principles of development.* New York: Holt, 1939.

Werblin, F. S., & Dowling, J. E. Organization of the retina of the mud puppy, *Necturus maculosus,* II. Intracellular recording. *J. Neurophysiol.,* 1969, **32,** 339–355.

Werner, G. The topology of the body representation in the somatic afferent pathway. In, *The neurosciences study program,* II. New York: Rockefeller University Press, 1970.

Westlake, P. R. Towards a theory of brain functioning: A detailed investigation of the possibilities of neural holographic processes. Unpublished doctoral dissertation, University of California, Los Angeles, 1968.

Introduction

(1976)
D. J. Willshaw and C. von der Malsburg

How patterned neural connections can be set up by self-organization
Proceedings of the Royal Society of London, B 194: 431–445

(1980)
Shun-ichi Amari

Topographic organization of nerve fields
Bulletin of Mathematical Biology 42: 339–364

Papers in both volumes of *Neurocomputing: Foundations of Research* have been concerned with topographic mapping in neural networks. Everywhere one looks in the brain, there are maps of sensory surfaces: multiple maps of the visual field in the cortex, a visual field map in the superior colliculus, a map of the body surface onto the somatosenory cortex, and so on.

The two papers presented here discuss *map formation*, that is, how one layer of cells can be connected to another in an ordered way. The paper by Willshaw and von der Malsburg suggests a basic system architecture and learning rules, and the later paper by Amari further analyzes this approach mathematically. In *Neurocomputing: Foundations of Research* a well known and frequently used model for map formation by Kohonen was presented (paper 30) that uses similar mechanisms to the papers presented here.

Biological mapping relations are initially sketched in during the early development of the nervous system. It is not certain how this is done. (See Udin and Fawcett 1988 for a review of the neurobiology that contains references for some of the following comments.) There are several major theories, each with some experimental support. Different structures may use one technique or the other, or perhaps multiple mechanisms are involved. One suggestion is that there are chemical signals—that is, addresses—on the target structure that are actively searched for by the growing connections. Another suggestion is that axons grow out in temporal sequence and innervate the target structure in order. Or axons could physically maintain neighborhood relationships as they grow. Or the structure could even self-organize from zero, that is, based strictly on network learning rules and system interactions, though this is very unlikely to be the unique mechanism.

Once a map is formed, however, there is no doubt that some systems can show considerable plasticity in the maps in response to various environmental events. Some of this plasticity might be explainable by the kinds of learning rules and self-organization studied in neural networks. For example, a particularly striking example of plasticity is seen in goldfish in the connections between the retina and the optic tectum. As discussed by McIlwain (paper 15), there is a topographic map of the visual world onto the surface of the tectum. If, say, half of the tectum is destroyed, after regeneration the *entire* visual field will be mapped onto *half* the tectum. Somehow all the topographic map relations are maintained, even though the actual connections from cell to cell have changed markedly.

However, sometimes results do not conform to such a nice picture, and plasticity does not occur. Even in the tectum, if a small plug of tectum is removed, rotated, and then replaced, there will be a small permanent region where the map is also rotated. And sometimes plasticity will occur in one structure in a sensory pathway and not occur in other structures in the same pathway. Some Siamese cats have severe miswiring of the visual system, apparently caused by mistakes in connection from the eyes to the lateral geniculate body. (Note that the miswiring occurs and is not corrected, suggesting chemical or other cues are being used in the initial connections.) Some axons do not cross over properly. In normal animals, except for a narrow vertical strip that includes the fovea, one half visual field is represented in one hemisphere, and the other half visual field is represented in the other hemisphere. In one class of miswired cats, a point of the visual field *and its mirror image on the other side of the vertical strip* can be mapped onto the same point in cortex, apparently causing severe conflict between different images. There are substantial behavioral visual defects produced by this miswiring that do not seem to be correctable by plastic mechanisms. Yet other visual projections in the same aberrant animals seem to be correctly connected.

With these cautionary comments made, we can think about the theoretical questions discussed by Amari and by Willshaw and von der Malsburg. Although they are concerned with using a self-organizing neural network as the major mechanism of map formation, there is no doubt that such a system could work well to tune the results of other mechanisms.

The basic idea in both models is the same and remarkably simple: There are two sheets of elements connected, one projecting to the other. There is a short-range excitatory mechanism and a long-range inhibitory mechanism in both sheets. These local mechanisms are critically important in self-organization. Suppose the connections between the two sheets are quite diffuse, and the connections are modifiable using the usual Hebb rule, which learns in response to correlations between pre- and postsynaptic activities. To prevent connection strengths from becoming too large, Willshaw and von der Malsburg require that the total connection strength on a unit must not exceed a certain value; Amari relaxes this assumption somewhat. Assume that a few presynaptic cells are active. If these cells are close together in the first sheet, their local mutual excitation will cause considerable localized activity; if the active presynaptic units are far apart, the long-range inhibition will damp their activity. In the postsynaptic sheet the same effect will occur: Cells close together will tend to become very active by mutual excitation. These two clumps of high activity, one presynpatic and the other postsynaptic, will cause increased coupling in the Hebb synapses connecting the sheets. This is the basic self-organizing mechanism: local active presynaptic groups will lead to local active postsynaptic groups. Connection strengths outside the local groups will drift to zero as learning progresses.

Because local groups are composed of a number of cells, depending on the size of the excitatory regions, cells can participate in many groups. This gives a mechanism for global organization of the connections because there are no discontinuities; groups must grade into one another. Therefore the postsynaptic sheet will reflect the topography of the presynaptic sheet because local relations must be maintained. Willshaw and von der Malsburg comment that even a little preexisting global organization in the postsynaptic sheet would serve as an extremely effective nucleus for the network-based global self-organization. They do a number of computer simulations to test the idea. The simulations demonstrate the basic self-organization mechanism quite convincingly.

Amari uses the same basic idea with a much more formal and traditional approach, using mathematical analysis. Willshaw and von der Malsburg use a network composed of the customary discrete neural network neurons. Amari, however, uses continuous mathematics— one could say that there are an infinite number of cells in the network. This is an interesting approximation for networks, because it throws away the highly prized individuality developed by neurons and emphasizes functional commonalities over the entire set. Therefore it is particularly useful for understanding the global properties of undifferentiated networks, which is the way Amari uses it. Amari's architecture is a continuous version of Willshaw and von der Malsburg's: local excitation, long-range lateral inhibition and Hebbian connection between presynaptic and postsynaptic structures, one-dimensional continuous *neural fields* in Amari's model. It is now possible to set up integral and differential equations for interactions between one part of the field and the other, as well as the modification rules for changing the coupling between fields. The mathematical manipulations Amari uses involves a series of approximations and averaging steps. The paper contains some observations about the activities shown by neural fields with local excitation and longer-range inhibition: activity areas tend to center at maxima of the input activity. This is intuitive, but not trivial to show. Amari also discusses briefly what happens if there are several areas of activity. He then shows how the responses of the local connectivity of the fields interact when two fields are connected together: We want, for self-organization, the structure of the presynaptic field to organize the postsynaptic field.

Amari makes a particularly interesting series of observations describing what happens when one part of the presynaptic field is much more frequently stimulated than other parts of the presynaptic field. There seems to be a relative expansion of the representation of that part on the postsynaptic field, for "good resolution," as Amari puts it. This result is in qualitative agreement with the kinds of results found for cortex by several experimenters. (See the experiments described by Edelman and Finkel in paper 18.)

These two papers suggest that simple mechanisms may give rise to robust self-organization. The key assumptions seem to be that Hebb synapses exist, coupling units together that can respond to the correlations in activity between the units, and that locally excited groups of units can be formed to drive the organization. The much more complex Darwinian self-organizing models, for example, *neuronal group selection* models (see papers 17, 18, and 19), show some of the same organizational results. It is likely that the assumptions made in these complex models contain the essential core analyzed by Amari and by Willshaw and von der Malsburg.

References

S.B. Udin and J.W. Fawcett (1988), Formation of topographic maps. In W.M Cowan, E.M. Shooter, C.F. Stevens, and R.F. Thompson (Eds.), *Annual Review of Neuroscience* 11: 289–327.

(1976)
D. J. Willshaw and C. von der Malsburg

How patterned neural connections can be set up by self-organization
Proceedings of the Royal Society of London, B 194: 431–445

An important problem in biology is to explain how patterned neural connections are set up during ontogenesis. Topographically ordered mappings, found widely in nervous systems, are those in which neighbouring elements in one sheet of cells project to neighbouring elements in a second sheet. Exploiting this neighbourhood property leads to a new theory for the establishment of topographical mappings, in which the distance between two cells is expressed in terms of their similarity with respect to certain physical properties assigned to them. This topographical code can be realized in a model employing either synchronization of nervous activity or exchange of specific molecules between neighbouring cells. By means of modifiable synapses the code is used to set up a topographical mapping between two sheets with the same internal structure. We have investigated the neural activity version. Without needing to make any elaborate assumptions about its structure or about the operations its elements are to carry out we have shown that the mappings are set up in a system-to-system rather than a cell-to-cell fashion. The pattern of connections develops in a step-by-step and orderly fashion, the orientation of the mappings being laid down in the earliest stages of development.

1. The Retino-tectal Projection and Systems-matching in Lower Vertebrates

Many parts of the vertebrate nervous system are known to interconnect in a topographically ordered, or continuous, fashion. The maps so formed are in many cases two dimensional: in higher vertebrates there is a map of the retina on the surface of the striate cortex (Talbot & Marshall 1941), and on the surface of the superior colliculus (Apter 1945; Cooper, Daniel & Whitteridge 1953). In lower vertebrates optic nerve fibres go mainly to the superior colliculus, here called the optic tectum, which is also retinotopically organized (Gaze 1958). We also mention the two dimensional somatotopic organization of the somatosensory cortex (Rose & Mountcastle 1959) and of the motor cortex (Woolsey 1952) and, as an exmaple of maps between central structures, the ordered intertectal projection in amphibia (Gaze, Keating, Székely & Beazley 1970). The preservation of the tonotopic organization of the cochlea in the auditory pathway (Rose, Galambos & Hughes 1959) provides an example of a one dimensional mapping.

A system which has been investigated in great experimental detail is the ordered projection of the retina onto the contra-lateral tectum in amphibia and fishes. In these animals it has been possible to perform various surgical manipulations on the retina and the tectum and to investigate by behavioural, histological and electrophysiological means the retinotectal projection produced after successful regeneration of the optic nerve (Gaze 1970). If one can suppose that the mechanisms arranging nerve connections during embryogenesis are also operative during regeneration then such experiments provide a way of discovering and testing theories for the formation of nerve connections in this system. Many of the experiments carried out are of the 'mismatch' type (discussed by Prestige & Willshaw 1975), in which a portion of retina or tectum (or both) is removed from an adult animal. The results of these experiments indicate that in many cases 'systems-matching' (Gaze & Keating 1972) takes place during regeneration, that is, the whole of the retina (or what remains of it after surgery) maps in a continuous fashion and in a predictable orientation across the whole of the tectum (or what remains of it). Recent work has shown that the retino-tectal system also displays systems-matching during development. In experiments on *Xenopus laevis,* Gaze, Keating & Chung (1974) found that from an early stage the whole of the visual field is projected in topographical order over the entire tectum, which order is maintained as the retina and tectum develop to maturity. Since retina and tectum grow in different ways and at different rates it was concluded that the only way the systems could remain matched throughout development was for the synaptic relations between retina and tectum to be constantly changing.

A number of theories for the establishment of topographical mappings during development or regeneration have been put forward (Weiss 1928; Sperry 1943; Gaze, Jacobson & Székely 1965; Prestige & Willshaw 1975). Perhaps the best known of these is Sperry's theory of neuronal specificity. He proposed that during embryogenesis each retinal ganglion cell and each tectal cell acquires a unique chemical label and that during regeneration or development pairs of pre- and postsynaptic cells with matching specificities are able to couple together. The mismatch experiments are explained in the context of this theory by making the additional assumption that the effect of the surgery is to cause the cells to be systematically relabelled, thus enabling new pairs of cells to be matched. In their paper, Prestige & Willshaw (1975) drew the distinction between two types of theory employing sets of labels to set up topographical mappings. In one of them, the Sperry-type, the search for a partner is carried out by each axon independently. In the other one axons compete for sites, and vice versa, by means of which certain forms of systems-matching can be accomplished. Neither type, however, uses the fact that the prospective partners of neighbouring presynaptic cells are themselves neighbours in the postsynaptic array. As a consequence, such mechanisms are more general than they need to be; all possible one-to-one mappings can be set up using them, not just the topographical ones.

We therefore arrived at the hypothesis that the observed one-to-one correspondence between pre- and postsynaptic cells is not determined genetically and that the ontogentic mechanism is made up of two independent parts. The one part ensures that as a result of an optimizing process neighbouring presynaptic cells come to connect with neighbouring postsynaptic cells. If this condition is obeyed for all pairs of neighbouring cells the resulting mapping will be a topographical one. The other part is concerned with the determination of the position, size and orientation of the final mapping by means of boundary and initial conditions in a way that leads to systems-matching. The boundary conditions may vary from case to case, especially in the experiments mentioned above, so that the same genetical program for the topographic part can in different situations lead to quite different retinal points being connected to a given tectal location, without the need for relabelling.

After having made this division of the ontogenetical problem into a microscopic mechanism leading to topographic order and macroscopic boundary conditions, we now propose a specific model for the microscopic mechanism in which use is made of the concepts of neural excitation and inhibition and of self-organization with the help of modifiable synapses.

2. A Model Working by Self-organization

We shall talk about two two dimensional sheets of elements, intended to represent a pre- and a postsynaptic sheet of nerve cells. The presynaptic elements are able to put out axons and make synapses with elements of the postsynaptic sheet, thereby building up a mapping between the two sheets. The basic requirement of the model is for distances between cells to be encoded in the system. This can be done

in two ways: either in terms of the relative concentrations of certain molecules which are being continuously transferred between adjacent cells or by having a system where electrical activity between adjacent cells is correlated. This introductory paper is not an appropriate place to discuss both models in detail. However, we would like to have a specific model in mind, for only then are we able to make firm predictions about its behaviour. General theories, often containing hidden assumptions, are frequently open to various interpretations. Following an earlier suggestion (Lettvin; cited in Chung 1974), we shall discuss the neural activity model. It should be born in mind, however, that a molecular realization is an alternative possibility. We discuss this point elsewhere (Malsburg & Willshaw 1976, in preparation).

Our model is based on the idea that the geometrical proximity of presynaptic cells is coded in the form of correlations in their electrical activity. These correlations can be used in the postsynatpic sheet to recognize axons of neighbouring presynaptic cells and to connect them to neighbouring postsynaptic cells, hence producing a continuous mapping.

The first problem is to produce correlations between activity in neighbouring cells. By 'neural activity' we here mean spike activity measured in, say, impulses per second. (In fact, the exact nature of the activity is not critical to our argument.) We start by assuming that there are short range excitatory connections between the cells in a sheet so that activity in neighbouring cells becomes mutually reinforced. To prevent activity from spreading too far we must also provide longer range inhibitory interconnections. (Such a scheme of interconnections has already been used by one of us in a model for orientation specificity in the striate cortex (Malsburg 1973).) As a result, if the cells which are active happen to be grouped together they fire strongly, whereas widely dispersed activity is relatively weak. We now assume that the two sheets are interconnected by modifiable synapses of the correlation type, as used in theoretical work by Hebb (1949), and many others (Marr 1969; Willshaw, Buneman & Longuet-Higgins 1969; Malsburg 1973), being facilitated in proportion to the product of the activities in the appropriate pre- and postsynaptic cells. Finally, to drive the system, we assume that at any one time, as a result of some random process, a few presynaptic cells are spontaneously active. These will fire most stongly if clustered together, and the response evoked in the post-synaptic layer will also be at its strongest if due to cells closely grouped together. Since the stronger a cell fires the greater the modification of its synapses, the synapses of tight clusters of presynaptic cells evoking activity in tight postsynaptic clusters will be selectively reinforced. We also insist that to prevent a steady build-up in

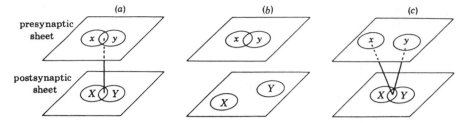

Figure 1 Ways in which the two clusters of cells, *x* and *y*, in the presynaptic sheet can connect with the two postsynaptic clusters, *X* and *Y*, respectively. We denote the cells common to clusters *x* and *y* by (*x* ∩ *y*) and the synapses between *x* and *X* by (*x* → *X*)

Configuration (*a*) is favoured more then (*b*) for two reasons: since *x* and *y* overlap they share axons and thereby synapses. It is therefore unlikely that *X* and *Y* occupy disconnected regions on the postsynaptic surface. Secondly, the synapses ((*x* ∩ *y*) → (*X* ∩ *Y*)) in (*a*) are reinforced by the occurrence of *x* and by the occurrence of *y*.

For small separations of *x* and *y* configuration (*c*) is unstable: the action of the lateral inhibition ensures that *x* and *y* are never active at the same time and so synapses (*x* → (*X* ∩ *Y*)) and (*y* → (*X* ∩ *Y*)) compete against each other, to the benefit of neither set of synapses. For larger separations of *x* and *y* configuration (*c*) is excluded by the mode of growth of the mapping, which is discussed in §3.

all synaptic strengths, leading to instabilities, the total strength associated with each postsynaptic cell is limited. Thus when some synapses increase in strength others are made to decrease. Apart from the modification of existing synapses, we also need a facility for forming new synapses to offset the loss of the seldom modified synapses, which, over time, drift to zero strength. One way of doing this is to assume that axons are continually putting out branchlets to contact neighbouring cells, such contacts being withdrawn if not immediately reinforced.

For the self-organizing component of the model the initial pattern of connections can be random; no form of preference of fibres for cells need to be introduced at this stage. Over a sufficient period of time the axonal arborizations, initially spread out over the entire postsynaptic surface, gradually narrow down until small clusters of presynaptic cells come to be exclusively connected with small clusters of cells located somewhere in the post-synaptic sheet. We shall be referring to this refining of diffuse patterns of connections as the process of *organization*. In particular, overlapping presynaptic clusters will be connected to overlapping postsynaptic clusters (see figure 1), and if this is true for all overlapping clusters the two sheets will be interconnected in a topographically ordered fashion.

3. Boundary and Initial Conditions; Orientation of the Map

The mechanism which was described in the last section acts on a local level. All macroscopic features of the emerging mapping, such as its size and orientation, have to be determined by boundary conditions. Special care must also be taken that the development of the mapping does not get trapped in local optima, which could result if map formation started at different centres, producing extensive but incompatible part-maps. Further improvement could then only be made by partial destruction and reorientation of some of the part-maps, which cannot be carried out by a microscopic mechanism.

The problem of local optima is solved by initially restricting development to one region of nucleation, from which a continuous mapping then spreads out over the whole of both surfaces.

The other question is how to determine genetically the final orientation of the mapping. There is nothing in the local mechanism to specify one orientation rather than another, and if no systematic trends are introduced in the initial pattern of connections then the final orientation of the map is the result of chance. On the other hand, a slight but systematic bias within the initial connections towards a certain orientation will suffice to determine which end of the presynaptic array connects to which of the postsynaptic array. Such a bias could be established by a trace of spatial order within the afferent fibres or by weak preferences of some fibres for particular postsynaptic regions. It is enough if this initial bias is present within the nucleating region because the orientation of this region will impose itself on the rest of the projection developing later on. This paper is not attacking the question of *how* orientation information is produced by the nervous system; the point here is that since the maps observed do have definite orientation this information *must* be provided genetically, and it would be most efficient to specify the orientation of the nucleating region only. We therefore introduce the idea of *polarity markers,* namely that the cells of a particular small presynaptic region initially establish contact, in the required orientation, with a small postsynaptic region. It should not be thought, however, that with the polarity markers we are invoking precise preprogrammed cellular specificity, and thereby introducing redundancy of principle. Precise cellular specificity fails as an explanation of systems-matching. The weak specificity introduced here contains only enough information to specify orientation; the chosen presynaptic region can make initial connections with any small postsynaptic region, not just that region to be connected to it in the final mapping.

The condition for maintaining just one nucleation region in the postsynaptic sheet is that organization must proceed by the catalysing action of organized cells on their neighbours via lateral excitation, and in no other way. In other words, spontaneous organization of isolated cells must be suppressed, although these cells can be fired by presynaptic activity that happens to activate many of their dispersed afferent fibres. There are several ways of doing this. For example, synapses could be modified according to a function of pre- and postsynaptic activity which disfavours small signals, or the random fluctuations could be kept within bounds by slowing down the speed of organization. In our simulations we have adopted the first solution, and have a *modification threshold,* which the pre- and post-synaptic activity must exceed before modification can take place. The threshold is set so that postsynaptic activity induced by correlated activity from as yet unorganized presynaptic cells is not reinforced.

Map formation resulting from the growth of a nucleation region ensures that disconnected presynaptic regions are not connected to the same postsynaptic region despite the fact that the limited range of inhibition permits several presynaptic clusters to be active at the same time. A postsynaptic cell C, which is in the process of organization, is activated almost exclusively by lateral excitation from already organized neighbouring cells. These in turn can only be activated by their 'correct' presynaptic region. At the same time, presynaptic clusters from random positions will also be active, and although they do modify synapses, their total effect, taken over the ensemble of possible stimuli, is small, since the total synaptic strength available to C is limited and so the different modifications interfere with each other. The 'correct' synapses, however, are strengthened with each stimulation, and will in the end win out.

4. Computer Simulation Experiments

We have so far attempted to explain our proposed mechanism entirely by qualitative arguments. A good test of the logic of the arguments is to produce a formal demonstration of their feasiblility. It is fairly easy to write down a set of coupled differential equations to describe the relevant events, but these are not soluble by analytical methods. We therefore wrote computer programs to give us numerical solutions for a model system. The simplifications we made in doing this were:

1. Limitations of computing time and space meant that we could only simulate small systems; the number of cells in a sheet varied between 36 and 64.

2. To save computing time weak diffuse activity in the presynaptic sheet was ignored.

3. We employed a simplified idea of a synapse: we assumed that initially each axon not marking polarity made a contact of roughly equal strength with each postsynaptic cell and that during organization all the synapses were retained, despite the fact that many of them had zero strength.

None of these assumptions is a serious oversimplification, although an extra argument is needed to interpret assumption (3) for a larger, physiologically more realistic, system. We discuss this point in the next section. We did an extra calculation to check the validity of assumption (2).

To enable the reader to repeat our calculations we have listed in the appendix the steps taken in our calculations and the parameter values used.

We first calculated how 36 presynaptic cells, arranged as a 6×6 square sheet, would develop a projection onto an identical square of 36 postsynaptic cells. Four pairs of cells were chosen to mark polarity. The 72 cells involved are marked by filled circles (•) in figure 2.

To depict a particular mapping between the two sheets we calculated, weighting by the appropriate synaptic strengths, the mean coordinates of the presynaptic cells connected to each postsynaptic cell. These coordinate positions were then plotted on a map of the presynaptic sheet, now regarded as a continuum. This way of presenting our results is closely analogous to the electrophysiological maps of the tectum projected on to the visual field favoured by neurophysiologists (Gaze 1970). (The analogy is not exact since we do not have a counterpart to the projection of retina onto visual field.) Figure 3a shows the map obtained after 15 000 trials. Note that the polarity markers have shifted from their initial positions, showing that they are only there to give the map the desired orientation, and so their positions are not rigidly determined. The choice of cells to mark polarity is relatively free. Choosing, for example, the four cells in the middle of the presynaptic surface (as we have done here) does not oblige us to take the corresponding middle four postsynaptic cells as their respective partners.

To demonstrate the model's systems-matching properties we now show the results of three manipulations, in which cells were added to one or both sheets of a system which had already attained an ordered mapping and then the way the enlarged system rearranged its connections was followed for a few more thousand trials. In each case the starting configuration was that shown in figure 3a, and to avoid introducing

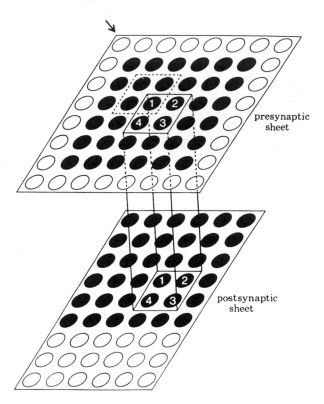

Figure 2 The two sheets which are to interconnect. Filled circles (•) represent the members of the two 6 × 6 sheets involved in the mappings for figures 3a and 4. The pairs of polarity markers used for 3a are labelled 1, 2, 3, 4; for figure 4 the same postsynaptic polarity markers were chosen, but this time their partners are the four cells enclosed by the dotted line drawn on the presynaptic sheet. The cells added in the calculations for figures 3b, c and d are denoted by unfilled circles (O). The arrow indicates the corner of the presynaptic sheet to be placed top left in the maps of figures 3 and 4.

bias, once again the new cells were all given synapses, of roughly equal strength, with all cells from the opposite sheet. The three manipulations were:

1. We increased the number of postsynaptic cells from 36 to 54 by adding 3 rows of 6 cells to make a 6 × 9 oblong sheet, leaving the presynaptic sheet unchanged.

2. The 6 × 6 sheet of presynaptic cells was enlarged by adding a band of cells around the outside to make an 8 × 8 sheet. The postsynaptic sheet was left unchanged.

3. Both sheets were enlarged, to 64 and 54 cells respectively, as described in (1) and (2) above.

The cells added in these manipulations are marked by unfilled circles in figure 2.

Figures 3b, c and d show the three new mappings obtained in this manner. The most striking point about all four maps shown is that the topographical ordering is in each case perfect; each pair of neighbouring postsynaptic cells

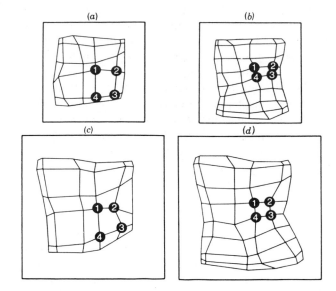

Figure 3 Maps of postsynaptic cells drawn on the presynaptic sheet for various model systems. In each diagram the thick black line tracing out a square denotes the boundary of the presynaptic sheet, oriented with the corner marked by the arrow in figure 2 placed top left. For each postsynaptic cell the centre of the cluster of presynaptic cells connected to it was plotted out. Points associated with neighbouring post-synaptic cells were then joined by a straight line. Since only cluster centres were plotted, the postsynaptic maps so constructed are necessarily smaller than the appropriate presynaptic sheets; the half-width of the distribution of presynaptic cells connected to a given postsynaptic cell never exceeded 9/10 of the presynaptic cell interspacing. Postsynaptic polarity marker positions are indicated as in figure 2.

(a) The mapping between the two 6 × 6 sheets which has developed after 15 000 trials. Figures 3b, c and d show the new mappings obtained after performing on the system in the state shown in 3a the three manipulations described in the text. (b) The mapping between 36 presynaptic and 54 postsynaptic cells after 9 000 trials. (c) The mapping between 64 presynaptic and 36 postsynaptic cells after 10 000 trials. (d) The mapping between 64 presynaptic and 54 postsynaptic cells after 15 000 trials.

is mapped onto neighbouring points on the presynaptic surface. To see how the mapping changes size as the relative sizes of the two sheets alter, the reader should observe the location of the small area marked out by the four postsynaptic polarity markers. In figures 3a and 3c this area is situated in the bottom right-hand quarter. In figures 3b and 3d we find that it has shrunk and has moved up to accommodate the new post-synaptic cells coming in at the bottom.

To emphasize that the polarity markers specify only the relative orientation of the two sheets, and not individual connections, we show in figure 4 another sequence of maps of the development of a topographical projection between two 6 × 6 sheets. The postsynaptic polarity markers were those used in the previous calculations, but this time we took their partners from the diagonally opposing quarter of the other sheet, that is, the quarter indicated in figure 2 by the arrow. Various stages in the growth of the mapping are shown. We only plotted out the positions of those postsynaptic cells which had established organized connections. After 5000 trials, only the polarity markers and a few neighbours have established definite contact, in the region of the presynaptic polarity markers (figure 4a). As time goes on, the map enlarges and gets shifted down and to the right (figure 4b). By 30 000 trials all positions can be mapped out (figure 4c), and by 50 000 trials a stable and orderly map is seen (figure 4d).

In the simulations described so far we assumed that each stimulus consisted of a single cluster of activity. In reality there will be more than one cluster present; each postsynaptic cell can simultaneously receive input from disconnected presynaptic regions, and so one-to-one maps might not result. To investigate this we did an extra simulation, similar to that which gave the map shown in figure 3a. The

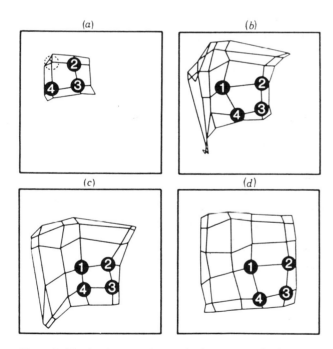

Figure 4 The development of a mapping between two 6 × 6 sheets in the case when the two sets of polarity markers occupied non-corresponding regions on the two surfaces. Conventions as in figure 3. Only the positions of those postsynaptic cells which had established definite contacts were plotted.

(a) By 5 000 trials only the polarity markers and their neighbours had established definite contact. The mapping set up by this stage is between cells in the top left hand quarter of the presynaptic sheet and those in the bottom right hand quarter of the postsynaptic sheet. (b) After 20 000 trials. To accommodate the new cells which have established contact, albeit in a disorganized manner, the map of the postsynaptic sheet has shifted down and to the right. (c) By 30 000 trials positions of all postsynaptic cells could be plotted out, but the map is distorted. (d) After 50 000 trials. A stable and ordered map is produced.

polarity markers used were the four middle cells in each sheet, and this time the typical stimulus was activity in two pairs of adjacent cells, each pair being randomly chosen from the presynaptic sheet. As time went on, although synapses were modified by dispersed activity, the strong effects from the 'correct' cells eventually won out, and by 15 000 trials a perfectly ordered mapping, comparable with that of figure 3a, had developed. This calculation, together with the arguments already given, justifies our decision to ignore dispersed presynaptic activity in our main body of simulations.

5. Physiological Considerations

With the present computer techniques, only small numbers of cells can be simulated, and so one must attempt to extrapolate from our calculations to real size systems.

We made no attempt to represent the complex three dimensional geometry of axonal growth. This led to the unrealistic assumption, in the computer model, that each pair of pre- and postsynaptic cells is interconnected, although their synapse may be of zero strength. In reality this large number of synapses can be reduced drastically, for the following reason.

Owing to the lateral excitation within the postsynaptic sheet, two fibres can influence each other without sharing contact with the same postsynaptic cell. If each axon ramifies on a small scale in the way that we have suggested, then in the synaptic modification procedure the axonal branches will be moved around as some synapses grow and some decay. Therefore, each presynaptic cell need not have a contact with each postsynaptic cell. However, the number of contacts made at the start must suffice to bring each axon within sensing range of its target area. The sensing range S is determined by and roughly equal to the range of the postsynaptic lateral excitation. It can be several times the radius T of the target area, which gives the precision in the final mapping. The region in which an axon must have some contacts if it is to home in on its target area has an area πS^2. Therefore, each axon must initially make at least $N/\pi S^2$ contacts at random among N postsynaptic cells. Although there are at present many unknowns, it is instructive to give a numerical example. Taking N to be 10^6, and arbitrarily setting T at 10 and S four times as great (meaning that approximately 3200 regions can be distinguished), the number of contacts each axon must initially make is about 200. Certainly, our calculation gives a pessimistic estimate since an axon can also be attracted to its target area through the mediation of the axon of a neighbouring presynaptic cell. This reduces further the initial density of contacts required.

The inhibition in the postsynaptic layer is merely there to stop the excitation from spreading too far, and so its range must be slightly greater than the range of excitation.

6. Conclusions

The purpose of this paper is to show that it is possible to devise a theory for the establishment of ordered neural connections displaying systems-matching properties which exploits the already existing order within the two sheets of cells to be matched. Our theory of self-organization can be viewed as marking one end of a spectrum of possible theories, at whose other extremity stand the theories of neuronal specificity. In these theories emphasis is laid on the labelling of cells and a set of relabelling rules to cater for new conditions, whereas there is little or no interaction between cells in the same sheet. In our theory such interactions play a crucial rôle, and the amount of labelling is no more than the minimum required for correct orientation of the map. A simpler type of mechanism, such as one assigning unique and unmodifiable labels to cells, is incapable of explaining systems-matching.

The prime value of our paper is to show that such theories of self-organization do in fact work, and they should now be taken seriously. They have the advantage of requiring only an extremely small amount of information to be specified genetically, and we have not had to make embarrassing assumptions about regulation, that is, relabelling of cells according to global observations to make mappings possible under new conditions. The computer simulations are intended to demonstrate the logical consistency of our assumptions, and should be regarded primarily as an aid to thought.

By working our theory through we have been able to make a number of generalizations, which are independent of the precise details of implementation of our neural activity model.

1. The mapping develops in a step-by-step and orderly fashion.

2. The axonal arborizations initially ramify diffusely over the postsynaptic surface and then become more restricted in extent as the mapping develops.

3. Whereas the pattern of connections reflected in the final map is not laid down straightaway, the orientation of the map is already fixed at the earliest stages of development.

4. Provision of the correct starting conditions, that is, the correct polarity markers, is essential for successful development of the map; inconsistent orientation information leads to peculiar maps. This leads to the speculation that the remarkable series of maps obtained in the transrepolarization experiments (Hunt & Frank 1975) reflects the working out of a set of mutually incompatible polarity markers arising from putting together incompatible hemiretinae. We are at present exploring this possibility.

Appendix

Here is a description of the calculations performed on the computer.

The strength of the synaptic connection between cell i in a sheet of M presynaptic cells and cell j in a sheet of N postsynaptic cells is specified by the entry s_{ij} in the $M \times N$ matrix s. The activity H_j^* in postsynaptic cell j is determined by its membrane depolarizaton H_j, and is calculated according to a linear threshold model of a nerve cell (Malsburg 1973). At time t, cell j is deemed to fire if its depolarization exceeds a fixed threshold value Θ. Its activity $H_j^*(t)$ is defined as

$$H_j^*(t) = \begin{cases} H_j(t) - \theta & \text{if } H_j(t) > \theta, \\ 0 & \text{otherwise} \end{cases}$$

The calculate the membrane depolarization we assume that its rate of change $\partial H_j / \partial t$ is proportional to the sum of the excitatory effects of active presynaptic cells, the excitation and inhibition supplied by nearby active postsynaptic cells and a decay term due to losses in the membrane itself. It is helpful to define the quantities $A_i^*(t)$, e_{kj} and i_{kj}. The variable $A_i^*(t)$ used to describe the state of the presynaptic cells, has value 1 if cell i is active at time t and 0 otherwise. The time independent parameters e_{kj} and i_{kj} specify the short range excitation and inhibition exerted by postsynaptic cell k on postsynaptic cell j.

We can then write a set of N coupled equations.

$$\frac{\partial H_j(t)}{\partial t} + \alpha H_j(t)$$
$$= \sum_i A_i^*(t) s_{ij}(t) + \sum_k H_k^*(t) e_{kj} - \sum_k H_k^*(t) i_{kj}$$

for $j = 1, 2, 3, \ldots, N$.

The first sum represents the contributions from the presynaptic cells; the other two are the excitatory and inhibitory contributions from the postsynaptic cells. The parameter α is the membrane time constant. To ensure that cells which do not mark polarity have initially no particular preference for any cell in the opposite sheet, all initial values of the entries in s are chosen from a set of random numbers normally distributed about a positive mean. The numbers are then adjusted to give synapses between polarity marker cells above-average strengths. The following procedures are carried out for each successive trial, during which the postsynaptic cells are stimulated by a given set of presynaptic cells.

1. A small cluster of c presynaptic cells is chosen at random from the whole set of overlapping clusters of that size covering the presynaptic sheet. These cells constitute the input to the postsynaptic sheet during this trial. (This is where we assume that dispersed patterns of activity that can also occur have no significant effect.)

2. For each of the N postsynaptic cells a stationary solution for its membrane depolarization is found by iterating the set of coupled equations until the mean change in depolarization per unit of time becomes less than 0.5%.

3. Only those synapses between cells firing sufficiently strongly are strengthened. The increase in strength Δs_{ij} of synapse s_{ij} is given by

$$\Delta s_{ij} = h A_i^* H_j^*$$

provided that H_j^*, as calculated in step 2, exceeds the modification threshold ε, and where the constant h sets the speed of organization.

4. The synaptic strengths are then renormalized so as to keep the mean strength associated with each postsynaptic cell at a constant value S, thus

$$\frac{1}{M}\sum_{i=1}^{M} s_{ij} = S \quad \text{for } j = 1, 2, \ldots, N$$

The parameters c, α, θ, h, ε, S and the entries in the matrices i and e are constants, whose values have to be found by trial and error. The values used in the main body of calculations were

$$c = 2, \quad \theta = 10.0, \quad \alpha = 0.5, \quad h = 0.016, \quad \varepsilon = 2.0, \quad S = 2.50$$

A postsynaptic cell could influence other postsynaptic cells up to a distance 3 units away, the distance between the two cells with coordinates (x, y) and (x', y') being defined as the sum $|x - x'| + |y - y'|$. The postsynaptic excitatory and inhibitory constants took the following values

distance between cells j and k	1	2	3
e_{kj}	0.05	0.025	–
i_{kj}	–	–	0.06

For the initial values in the matrix s a set of MN random numbers were first chosen from a normal distribution of mean 2.50 and standard deviation 0.14. The values of the entries designating synapses between polarity markers were then increased fivefold, and then all the numbers were normalized, as in step (4) given above.

For the extra simulation to investigate the disruptive effect of dispersed presynaptic activity, the stimuli used were chosen equiprobably from the set of 1800 pairs of pairs of neighbours which can be formed from the members of a 6×6 sheet. Under these conditions, four instead of two presynaptic cells were active per trial, and to cater for this θ and ε were doubled, to take the values 20.0 and 4.0, and h was decreased to 0.005. All other parameters retained the values given above.

We would like to thank Dr G. Rager, Dr M.C. Presitge and Dr T. Poggio for their helpful comments on earlier drafts of this paper. D.J.W. wishes to acknowledge the financial support of the Alexander von Humboldt-Stiftung. Computing facilities were provided by the Gesellschaft für wissenschaftliche Datenverarbeitung, Göttingen. We are very grateful to Frau C. Rauschenbach for drawing all the figures.

References

Apter, J.T. 1945 Projection of the retina on superior colliculus of cats. *J. Neurophysiol.* **8**, 123–134.

Chung, S.H. 1974 In search of the rules for nerve connections. *Cell* **3**, 201–205.

Cooper, S., Daniel, P.M. & Whitteridge, D. 1953 Nerve impulses in the brain stem and cortex of the goat. *J. Physiol., Lond.* **120**, 514–527.

Gaze, R.M. 1958 The representation of the retina on the optic lobe of the frog. *Qu. J. exp. Physiol.* **43**, 209–224.

Gaze, R.M. 1970 *The formation of nerve connections.* London: Academic Press.

Gaze, R.M., Jacobson, M. & Székely, G. 1965 On the formation of connections by compound eyes in *Xenopus. J. Physiol., Lond.* **176**, 409–417.

Gaze, R.M. & Keating, M.J. 1972 The visual system and 'neuronal specificity'. *Nature, Lond.* **237**, 375–378.

Gaze, R.M., Keating, M.J. & Chung, S.H. 1974 The evolution of the retinotectal map during development in *Xenopus. Proc. R. Soc. Lond.* B **185**, 301–330.

Gaze, R.M., Keating, M.J., Székely, G. & Beazley, Lynda 1970 Binocular interaction in the formation of specific intertectal neuronal connections. *Proc. R. Soc. Lond.* B **175**, 107–147.

Hebb, D.O. 1949 *The organisation of behaviour.* New York: Wiley.

Hunt, R.K. & Frank, E. 1975 Neuronal locus specificity: trans-repolarisation of *Xenopus* embryonic retina after the time of axial specification. *Science, N.Y.* **189**, 563–565.

Malsburg von der, C. 1973 Self-organization of orientation sensitive cells in the striate cortex. *Kybernetik* **14**, 85–100.

Marr, D. 1969 A theory of cerebellar cortex. *J. Physiol., Lond.* **202**, 437–470.

Prestige, M.C. & Willshaw, D.J. 1975 On a role for competition in the formation of patterned neural connections. *Proc. R. Soc. Lond.* B **190**, 77–98.

Rose, J.E., Galambos, R. & Hughes, J.R. 1959 Microelectrode studies of the cochlear nuclei of the cat. *Bull. John Hopkins Hosp.* **104**, 211–251.

Rose, J.E. & Mountcastle, V.B. 1959 Touch and kinesthesis. In *Handbook of physiology* (eds Field, J., Magoun, H.W. & Hall, V.E.), vol. 1. Washington D.C.: American Physiological Society.

Sperry, R.W. 1943 Visuomotor coordination in the newt (*Triturus viridescens*) after regeneration of the optic nerve. *J. comp. Neurol.* **79,** 33–55.

Talbot, S.A. & Marshall, W.H. 1941 Physiologcial studies on neural mechanisms of visual location and discrimination. *Am. J. Ophthal.* **24,** 1255–1264.

Weiss, P. 1928 Eine neue Theorie der Nervenfunktion. *Die Naturwissenschaften* **16,** 626–636.

Willshaw, D.J., Buneman, O.P. & Longuet-Higgins, H.C. 1969 Non-holographic associative memory. *Nature, Lond.* **222,** 960–962.

Woolsey, C.N. 1952 pattern of localization in sensory and motor areas of the cerebral cortex. In *The biology of mental health and disease.* New York: Hoeber 1952.

(1980)
Shun-ichi Amari

Topographic organization of nerve fields
Bulletin of Mathematical Biology 42: 339–364

The vertebrate nervous system has topographic interconnections in many parts, known for example as retinotopy, somatotopy, etc. It is plausible that modifiable synapses play an important role in forming and refining these connections together with the sensory experiences. To elucidate the mechanism of topographic organization, we propose a simple model consisting of two nerve fields connected by modifiable excitatory synapses. The model also includes modifiable inhibitory synapses. The behavior of the model is described by a set of simultaneous non-linear integro-differential equations. By analyzing the equations, we obtain the equilibrium solution of topographic connections. It is also proved that a part of the presynaptic field which is frequently stimulated comes to be mapped on a large area of the postsynaptic field so that it has a good resolution.

1. Introduction

It is known that the vertebrate nervous system has topographic interconnections in many parts. One example is shown in the connections from the retina to the striate cortex or to the optic tectum (retinotopy). Another example is found in the somatosensory cortex or in the motor cortex on which the sensors or effectors scattered on the body are mapped topographically (somatotopy). It is also remarked that such parts as fingers occupy a large area on the cortex so that they have good resolution. Arbib (1972) has pointed out the importance of "somatotopically organized layers" in the brain.

Much attention has been paid to the mechanism of forming such well-organized connections (Sperry, 1951; Gaze and Keating, 1972; Prestige and Willshaw, 1975; Hope *et al.*, 1976). Experimental studies have been made on the retino-tectum connections (see, e.g., Gaze, 1970). It was found that, when a part of the retina or of the tectum (or both) is removed, regeneration of connections takes place even after the original connections are completed such that the whole part of the remaining retina is mapped on the whole part of the remaining tectum in a topographic manner (Yoon, 1971, 1972; Sharma, 1972; etc.). It is therefore suggested that not only genetic specification, but also modifiable synapses play an important role in forming or refining topographic connections.

Willshaw and Malsburg (1976) proposed a mathematical model of such a topographic formation on the basis of

Malsburg's model of synaptic modificaition (Malsburg, 1973). They showed by computer simulation that their model really has an ability of forming topographic mapping between two neural fields. The present paper proposes a revised version of their model, and gives a mathematical analysis of the model by considering (i) dynamics of excitation patterns in neural fields and (ii) dynamics of synaptic modification of nerve systems. The model is analyzed on the basis of neural field theory (Amari, 1977a; Kishimoto and Amari, 1979) as well as neural theory of self-organization (Amari, 1977b; Amari and Takeuchi, 1978).

We treat the equation of a one-dimensional neural field of lateral-inhibitory connections together with the dynamical equation of synaptic modification between presynaptic and postsynaptic fields. We add an equation for modifying the inhibitory synapses which inhibit every part of the field. Under some simplifications, we succeed in obtaining the equilibrium solution of these non-linear simultaneous integro-differential equations. The equilibrium solution gives topographic connections. Moreover, the solution proves that a part of the presynaptic field which is frequently stimulated is mapped on a relatively large area of the postsynaptic field such that it has a good resolution on the map.

The present model shows that a neural system can learn from topological information on sensory signals, because the neural field is self-organized according to the correlation of sensory signals (see also Zeeman, 1962).

2. Fundamental Equations

(A) Structure of the model
We shall propose a simple model to analyze the characteristics of topographic organization. The model consists of two neural fields. One is the presynaptic field, whose neurons put out axons and make synaptic connections with neurons in the other (postsynaptic) field. The synaptic connections are assumed to be modifiable, so that the connections are modified depending on the excitation patterns or the presynaptic and postsynaptic fields. A map is formed in this manner from the presynaptic field to the postsynaptic field. The law of synaptic modification is

Hebbian such that synaptic connections are strengthened when the post- and presynaptic neurons are excited at the same time.

Every part of the postsynaptic field receives an additional constant inhibitory input through modifiable synapses. The modifiable inhibitory synapses replace the unnatural synaptic conservation law in the original Willshaw and Malsburg model (see Amari and Takeuchi, 1978). The postsynaptic field is subject to its own dynamics by recurrent connections of a lateral inhibition type. The recurrent connections are fixed and homogeneous.

Let the fields be one-dimensional for simplicity's sake. Let x and y be, respectively, the position coordinates of the post- and presynaptic fields. Let $s(x, y, t)$ be the intensity of synaptic connections at time t from neurons at position y of the presynaptic field to those at position x of the post-synaptic field. It depends on time t, because it is modifiable. Let $-s_0(x, t)$ be the intensity of modifiable inhibitory synapse at position x at time t of a common constant inhibitory input of intensity 1. Let $w(x, x')$ be the intensity of the fixed recurrent connections within the postsynaptic field from neurons at position x' to those at x (see Fig. 1). Since the field is homogeneous, we can put

$$w(x, x') = w(x - x').$$

We also assume the symmetricalness of the field such that

$$w(x) = w(-x). \tag{1}$$

Since the connections are lateral-inhibitory, $w(x)$ is positive for small $|x|(|x| < x_m)$, and negative for large $|x|(|x| > x_m)$, having a shape shown in Fig. 2. It is assumed to be a negative constant for $|x| > x_c$.

(B) Dynamics of excitation in the field

We consider the following neural dynamics of a neuron pool: The average potential $u(t)$ of a neuron pool changes in proportion to the sum S of all the stimuli given to it, while it tends to decay to the resting potential $-h$ with time constant τ. The dynamics is then given by

$$\tau \frac{\mathrm{d}}{\mathrm{d}t} u(t) = -u(t) + S(t) - h.$$

The output activity (the average pulse emission rate) of the neuron pool is given by $f[u(t)]$, where f is a non-linear monotonically non-decreasing function called the output function. See, e.g. Amari (1972, 1974), Amari *et al.* (1977) etc. for statistical neurodynamics or dynamics of neuron pools.

The field equation can be set up as follows. Let $u(x, t)$ denote the average potential of the neurons at position x at time t. Then, the output activity at x is given by $f[u(x, t)]$. The neurons at position x receive stimuli of total intensity

$$\int w(x - x') f[u(x', t)] \mathrm{d}x'$$

from the outputs of all positions x' of the field. They also receive stimuli of intensity

$$\int s(x, y, t) a(y, t) \mathrm{d}y$$

from the presynaptic field, where $a(y, t)$ is the activity of the neurons at position y at time t of the presynaptic field. The intensity of the inhibitory input is $-s_0(x, t)$, because the activity of the inhibitory input is 1. We hence have the neural field equation

$$\tau \frac{\partial u(x, t)}{\partial t} = -u(x, t) + \int w(x - x') f[u(x', t)] \mathrm{d}x'$$

$$+ \int s(x, y, t) a(y, t) \mathrm{d}y - s_0(x, t) - h. \tag{2}$$

(C) Equation of synaptic modification

We use the following law of synaptic modification: The intensity of synaptic connection increases in proportion to

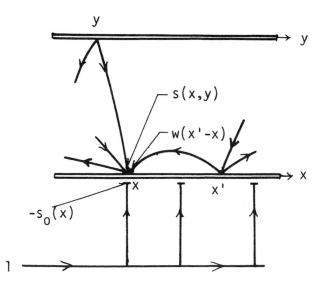

Figure 1   Connection of neural fields

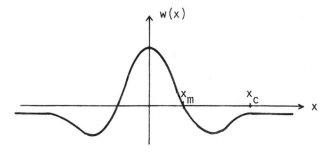

Figure 2   Shape of lateral inhibition

the presynaptic activity when the modification process is activated, while it decays with a large time constant. The modification process is activated when the output of the postsynaptic neurons is positive. See Amari (1977b) for a more general treatment of synaptic modification. Let $1(u)$ be the unit step function defined by

$$1(u) = \begin{cases} 0, & u \leq 0, \\ 1, & u > 0. \end{cases}$$

Then, the equations of synaptic modification are written as

$$\tau' \frac{\partial}{\partial t} s(x, y, t) = -s(x, y, t) + ca(y, t)1[u(x, t)], \tag{3}$$

$$\tau'' \frac{\partial}{\partial t} s_0(x, t) = -s_0(x, t) + c'1[u(x, t)], \tag{4}$$

where the time constants τ' and τ'' are large compared with τ in equation (2), and c and c' are constants.

(D) Mathematical simplifications

The behavior of the model net is described by a set of simultaneous non-linear integro-differential equations (2), (3) and (4). It is, however, difficult to solve them. We make the following simplifications, which make the equations tractable without changing their essential characteristics.

We first assume that the input activity pattern $a(y, t)$ given to the presynaptic field changes slowly compared with the time constant τ of the field equation (2). Let $u(x; a, s, s_0)$ be the equilibrium solution of equation (2) corresponding to a stationary input activity distribution $a(y)$, where synaptic intensity functions $s(x, y)$ and $s_0(x)$ are assumed to be fixed. Then, $u(x; a, s, s_0)$ is the solution of the integral equation

$$u(x) = \int w(x - x')f[u(x')]dx'$$
$$+ \int s(x, y)a(y)dy - s_0(x) - h, \tag{5}$$

which is obtained from (2) by putting $\partial u/\partial t = 0$. When the input activity distribution $a(y, t)$ changes slowly, the potential distribution $u(x, t)$ can be considered to change in a quasi-equilibrium manner as

$$u(x, t) = u[x; a(y, t), s(x, y, t), s_0(x, t)].$$

Since the time constants τ' and τ'' of the synaptic modifications are much larger than the time constant τ of the neural excitation, we can disregard the time change of s and s_0, while $u(x, t)$ converges to its equilibrium state.

In general, the presynaptic activation pattern $a(y, t)$ is a random time sequence, representing the nature of the environment from which the neural field receives stimulus signals. We may consider the following typical environ-

ment, in which an activation pattern $a(y)$ is chosen randomly from a set of all the possible input patterns and applied to the presynaptic field for a time duration which is longer than the time constant τ of the neural excitation but is much shorter than the time constants τ' and τ'' of synaptic modification. The activation pattern $a(y)$ is chosen each time independently, so that the piecewise constant time sequence $a(y, t)$ constitutes a typical sample from this ergodic information source. Given an $a(y)$, the potential distribution of the postsynaptic distribution converges quickly to

$$u(x) = u(x; a, s, s_0). \tag{6}$$

The equations of the synaptic modification then take the following form

$$\tau' \frac{\partial s(x, y, t)}{\partial t} = -s(x, y, t) + ca(y)1[u(x; a, s, s_0)],$$

$$\tau'' \frac{\partial s_0(x, t)}{\partial t} = -s_0(x, t) + c'1[u(x; a, s, s_0)],$$

for the period when $a(y)$ is applied.

Since every input activation pattern $a(y)$ is chosen independently and is applied repeatedly, we may replace the right-hand sides of the above equations by their average overall possible $a(y)$s. We then have the averaged processes

$$\tau' \frac{\partial s(x, y, t)}{\partial t} = -s(x, y, t) + c\langle a(y)1[u(x; a, s, s_0)]\rangle, \tag{7}$$

$$\tau'' \frac{\partial s_0(x, t)}{\partial t} = -s_0(x, t) + c'\langle 1[u(x; a, s, s_0)]\rangle,, \tag{8}$$

where $\langle \ \rangle$ denotes the average over $a(y)$. The averaged process gives a good approximation of the original process, provided τ' and τ'' are sufficiently large. Geman (1979) gave recently a mathematical foundation to this averaging. The averaged processes are used in Amari (1977b) as a technique of treating general neural learning processes (see also Amari and Takeuchi, 1978).

In order to obtain the equilibrium solution $u(x; a, s, s_0)$ explicitly, we approximate the non-linear output function $f(u)$ by the step function $1(u)$. Each portion of the postsynaptic field is then either in the quiescent state with output 0 or in the excited state with output 1. The dynamics of lateral-inhibition type fields has been studied in detail under this simplification by Amari (1977a). This does not oversimplify the essential features of the field dynamics (Kishimoto and Amari, 1979).

3. Results from Neural Field Theory

We recapitulate and extend here some of the results from neural field theory (Amari, 1977a, see also Amari and Arbib, 1977). Consider a one-dimensional neural field with lateral-inhibitory recurrent connections of weight function $w(x)$. When the field receives a stationary input of intensity distribution $S(x)$, the field equation is

$$\tau\frac{\partial u(x,t)}{\partial t} = -u(x,t) + \int w(x-x')1[u(x',t)]dx' + S(x) - h. \tag{9}$$

where the output function f is replaced by the step function $1(u)$.

Let us consider a potential distribution $u(x)$ which is positive on an interval of the field and negative outside the interval. We call such a distribution $u(x)$ a local excitation, because excitation is concentrated on an interval. Given an input distribution $S(x)$, we first look for the equilibrium solution $u(x)$ of equation (9), which is a local excitation.

THEOREM 1. *The excited region of a stable equilibrium solution of local excitation locates at an interval including a maximum of $S(x)$.*

Proof. Assume that there exists a local excitation equilibrium solution $u(x)$ whose excited region is an interval (x_1, x_2). We then have

$$1[u(x)] = \begin{cases} 1, & x_1 < x < x_2 \\ 0, & \text{otherwise.} \end{cases}$$

The equilibrium solution $u(x)$ satisfies

$$u(x) = \int w(x-x')1[u(x')]dx' + S(x) - h$$
$$= \int_{x_1}^{x_2} w(x-x')dx' + S(x) - h \tag{10}$$

which is derived from equation (9) by putting $\partial u/\partial t = 0$. It also satisfies

$$u(x_1) = u(x_2) = 0 \tag{11}$$

because of the continuity of $u(x)$. By putting

$$W(x) = \int_0^x w(x')dx' \tag{12}$$

we have

$$\int_{x_1}^{x_2} w(x_1-x')dx' = \int_{x_1}^{x_2} w(x_2-x')dx'$$
$$= W(x_2 - x_1)$$

because of the symmetry of the connections [i.e. $w(x) = w(-x)$]. We then have from (11)

$$S(x_1) = S(x_2).$$

Now assume that a local excitation exists on an interval $(\tilde{x}_1, \tilde{x}_2)$, where $S(\tilde{x}_1) > S(\tilde{x}_2)$. Then the neurons at $\tilde{x}_1$ receive an amount of stimuli larger than that the neurons at $\tilde{x}_2$ receive. This implies that the excited region cannot stay there but moves to the left as a whole. An excited region generally moves in the direction of increasing the input stimuli $S(x)$. It stops at a maximum of $S(x)$, around which $S(x_1) = S(x_2)$ is satisfied. Hence, the excited region of a stable equilibrium local excitation solution locates at an interval including a maximum of $S(x)$.

When $S(x)$ has a unimodal and symmetric shape, the length $l = x_2 - x_1$ of the excited region of the equilibrium solution $u(x)$ can be determined as follows. Let x_0 be the position of the maximum $S(x)$.

THEOREM 2. *The length l of the equilibrium local excitation solution satisfies*

$$S(x_0 + l/2) = h - W(l). \tag{13}$$

Proof. Let l be the length of the excited region of the solution $u(x)$. Since $S(x)$ is symmetric with respect to x_0

$$S(x_0 + x) = S(x_0 - x),$$

the excited region of $u(x)$ is $(x_0 - l/2, x_0 + l/2)$. Since

$$\int w(x_0 + l/2 - x')1[u(x')]dx'$$
$$= \int_{x_0-l/2}^{x_0+l/2} w(x_0 + l/2 - x')dx' = W(l),$$

we have equation (13) from

$$u(x_0 + l/2) = 0.$$

We next show the existence of the equilibrium solution of local excitation. Since $w(x)$ is of lateral-inhibition type, its integral $W(x)$ has a shape shown in Fig. 3. Let W_m be

$$W_m = \max_{x>0} W(x) = W(x_m).$$

Then $W(x)$ is monotonically increasing for $x > 0$ until it attains to W_m. It is monotonically decreasing thereafter. We assume

$$\lim_{x\to\infty} W(x) = -\infty,$$

which implies that the inhibitory connections exist between the neurons at any large distance.

When

$$W_m > h > 0$$

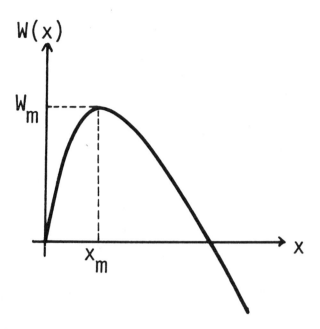

Figure 3 Integral $W(x)$ of $w(x)$

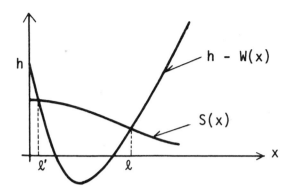

Figure 4 Lengths l and l' of local excitation

$$W_1 = \int_0^{x_0} w_1(x)\mathrm{d}x.$$

The positive part $w_1(x)$ of $w(x)$ can be realized by direct recurrent connections among the neurons in the field. The negative part $-w_0$, which is constant over the entire field, is realized through an inhibitory neuron pool. The pool is excited with an activity proportional to the number of the excited neurons in the field and it in turn inhibits every part of the field with a constant weight w_0. The inhibitory interactions hence have a time lag larger than the excitatory interactions. However, we neglect such a time lag, when we treat an equilibrium solution.

We have so far treated solitary local excitations only. Here we treat the mutual interactions among local excitations. When a local excitation exists, it inhibits the other part of the field through the recurrent connection $w(x)$. The intensity of inhibition depends on the distance from the excited region. Its distribution is in general of the shape shown in Fig. 5. The intensity gradually decreases in region A as the distance becomes large. It then increases gradually in region B. In region C, the intensity of inhibition is kept constant. The regions A, B and C are determined depending on the shape of lateral-inhibition $w(x)$ and the length of the local excitation. Roughly speaking, A is nearly equal to the range where $w(x)$ is decreasing ($|x| < x_m$), B is nearly equal to the range where $w(x)$ is increasing ($x_m < |x| < x_c$), and C the range where $w(x)$ is kept constant ($|x| > x_c$).

When a local excitation exists in the region A of another local excitation, they mutually attract, because the intensity of inhibition is bigger in the far sides of the local excitations than in the near sides. Hence, they tend to unite into one local excitation. When one local excitation exists in the region B of another local excitation, they repulse to each other. When local excitations exist in the region C, they have no direct interaction of attraction or repulsion, so that they can behave rather independently.

holds, equation (13) has a unique positive solution l with $W'(l) = w(l) < 0$, because $S(x_0 + x/2)$ is non-negative and monotonically decreasing for $x > 0$, while $h - W(x)$ is monotonically decreasing for $0 < x < x_m$, monotonically increasing for $x > x_m$, and $h - W(x_m) < 0$ (see Fig. 4 where x_0 is made equal to 0). Equation (13) has another solution l' with $w(l) > 0$, if $S(0) < h$. However, the equilibrium local excitation with the length l' is unstable, and the equilibrium with the length l is stable (Amari, 1977a).

When $S(0) < h$, especially when $S(x) = 0$, the field has the quiescent stable equilibrium solution $u_0(x) < 0$ with no excited region. It should be noted, on the other hand, that even when $S(x) = 0$ equation (13) has a solution l with $w(l) < 0$ if $s(0) < h$. This implies that the field is bistable, and once a local excitation is aroused, the field has an ability of retaining it persistently even after the stimuli $S(x)$ ceases to exist. The excitation will be eliminated by fatigue or by receiving another input stimulus.

We give a simple example of $w(x)$ for later use,

$$w(x) = w_1(x) - w_0 \tag{14}$$

where $w_1(x)$ is a unimodal non-negative even function with

$$w_1(x) > 0 \quad |x| < x_0$$
$$w_1(x) = 0 \quad |x| \geq x_0$$

and w_0 is a positive constant. We have in this case

$$W(x) = W_1 - w_0 x, \quad (x > x_0) \tag{15}$$

where

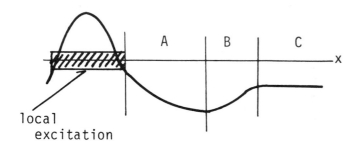

Figure 5   Distribution of inhibitory stimuli from a local excitation

4. Preliminary Considerations on the Formation of Topographic Map

Before analyzing the field equations exactly, we will give some preliminary and intuitive consideration to the mechanism of the formation of the topographic map.

(A) Autocorrelation of input activation patterns

It is more likely that two nearby points of the presynaptic field are activated together than two distant points are activated. This is because the environmental information is highly correlated according to the topology of the outer world. The correlation of presynaptic activity patterns $a(y)$ at points y_1 and y_2 is given by

$$\langle a(y_1)a(y_2)\rangle,$$

where $\langle\ \rangle$ denotes the average over all possible $a(y)$. This is large when y_1 and y_2 are close, and it becomes small rapidly as $|y_1 - y_2|$ increases, converging to a small constant.

The formation of topographic map has one of its bases in this correlational nature of input activity patterns (Willshaw and Malsburg, 1976). Assume that the activation of a point y in the presynaptic field causes a set of local excitations in the postsynaptic field. When two points y and y' are activated at the same time, local excitations aroused thereby interact with each other by the field dynamics. If there is a pair of two nearby local excitations caused by y and y', respectively, they attract to each other and tend to unite into one large local excitation. This in turn suppresses other excitations by lateral-inhibition. Since two nearby points are frequently activated together, they are apt to be mapped on neighboring regions of the postsynaptic field by self-organization. On the other hand, two distant points y and y' are activated relatively seldom at the same time, so that they may be mapped on different regions. Moreover, when the aroused local excitations are not near, they have no direct interactions of attraction or repulsion. Hence, self-organization of $s(x, y)$ at two distant points y_1 and y_2 proceeds relatively independently.

The above consideration allows us to assume the case in which the presynaptic field is activated locally, as

Willshaw and Malsburg (1976) did. In other words, we treat the case where the neurons at around one point only are activated at one time. The activated point y_0 is chosen independently each time. Hence, the input activation pattern can be approximated by

$$a(y) = a\delta(y - y_0),$$

where δ is the delta-function, and a is the intensity of activation which may be determined randomly. This is equivalent to assume that the autocorrelation function $\langle a(y)a(y')\rangle$ can be approximated by the delta-function $\delta(y - y')$.

Let $p(y)$ be the frequency that point y is chosen, and let $q_y(a)$ be the probability density function of the intensity a of the activation at y (it may depend on y). Let

$$u(x) = u(x; y_0, a, s, s_0)$$

be the equilibrium potential distribution of the postsynaptic field, when the neurons at y_0 are activated with intensity a. Since the average overall $a(y)$s reduce to the average over all positions y_0 and intensities a, we have

$$\langle a(y)1[u(x; a(y), s, s_0)]\rangle$$
$$= p(y_0)\langle a1[u(x; y_0, a, s, s_0)]\rangle_{y_0}$$

where $\langle\ \rangle_y$ denotes the average over a with respect to the density $q_y(a)$. Similarly, we have

$$\langle 1[u(s; a(y), s, s_0)]\rangle = \int p(y)\langle 1[u(x; y, a, s, s_0)]\rangle_y dy.$$

The averaged equations of self-organization then reduce to

$$\tau'\frac{\partial s(x, y, t)}{\partial t} = -s(x, y, t) + cp(y)\langle a1[u(x; y, a, s, s_0)]\rangle_y,$$

$$\tau''\frac{\partial s_0(x, t)}{\partial t} = -s_0(x, t) + c'\int p(y)\langle 1[u(x; y, a, s, s_0)]\rangle_y dy.$$

In the equilibrium state, $\partial s(x, y, t)/\partial t = 0$ and $\partial s_0(x, t)/\partial t = 0$ should be satisfied. Hence, we have the equilibrium equations,

$$s(x, y) = cp(y)\langle a1[u(x; y, a, s, s_0)]\rangle_y, \tag{16}$$

$$s_0(x) = c'\int p(y)\langle 1[u(x; y, a, s, s_0)]\rangle_y dy, \tag{17}$$

$$u(x; y, a, s, s_0) = \int w(x - x')1[u(x'; y, a, s, s_0)]dx'$$
$$+ as(x, y) - s_0(x) - h. \tag{18}$$

We will solve these fundamental equations to show that the topographic map really corresponds to an equilibrium of the equations.

(B) Role of modifiable inhibitory synapses

We have shown that two nearby points are apt to be mapped on overlapping regions of the postsynaptic field. However, there must exist another mechanism which prevents the connections from growing and spreading without limit. Otherwise, every point is mapped on the whole postsynaptic region. This mechanism is realized by modifiable inhibitory synapses, and a point is mapped on a limited interval of the postsynaptic field. Moreover, it is also due to this mechanism that a frequently stimulated part of the presynaptic field is mapped on a wider range of the postsynaptic field so that this part has a fine resolution.

We have shown that a local excitation in the lateral-inhibition neural field moves in the direction of increasing stimulus. Hence, when inhibition $s_0(x)$ exists, a local excitation tends to move in the direction of decreasing $s_0(x)$, and the synaptic connections follow gradually the motion of the local excitation. Hence, $s_0(x)$ plays a role of "pressure" at point x, and synaptic connections move from high pressure part to low pressure part.

As can be seen from equation (4), the "pressure" $s_0(x)$ at x increases in proportion to the frequency of excitation of neurons at x. Let a point y be mapped to neurons around x (i.e. the activation of y causes a local excitation around x). When y is frequently activated, the neurons around x are frequently excited and the pressure $s(x)$ becomes large. This in turn makes the connections from y to x expand further to occupy a larger part of the postsynaptic field. The pressure distribution $s_0(x)$ thus tends to become uniform. We will prove that $s_0(x)$ is constant in the equilibrium.

The role of modifiable $s_0(x)$ is elucidated by the following example. Let us consider topographically connected fields shown in Fig. 6. When part B of the presynaptic field is cut and removed, the corresponding part B' of the postsynaptic field loses inputs to it, so that the part is not excited for a while. Then, $s_0(x)$ decreases on this part, while it is still high on part A'. Then, the connections from A to A' begin to expand gradually through part B' by the pressure difference of $s_0(x)$. Thus a new topographic map is formed from A to the whole part of A' and B', as is shown by the dotted lines in Fig. 6.

(C) Role of initial connections

We will prove in the next section that the fundamental equations have a stable topographic equilibrium solution. However, this might not be the only equilibrium solution. If there are other stable equilibrium solutions, it depends on the initial connections $s(x, y, 0)$ and $s_0(x, 0)$ which equilibrium is really attained. Assume, for example, that a point y is mapped by the initial connections on two regions, one around $x' = y/2$ and the other around $x'' = 1 - y/2$ of the postsynaptic field (Fig. 7, where $0 \leq y \leq 1$, $0 \leq x \leq 1$). Then, it is unlikely that the global topographic map is formed by self-organization from these initial connections. The final map seems to be one homeomorphic to the initial one. There is indeed an experiment in which, when a part of retina or tectum is cut out, rotated by an angle, and then reconnected where it was, the topographic map does not recover, unless the angle is small (see, e.g. Gaze et al., 1965).

This suggests that, if the initial connections are completely random, a global topographic map cannot be formed, but a collection of local topographic maps. Hence, some genetic specification seems to be necessary to organize the topographic map, though it may be rough and largely random. Willshaw and Malsburg (1976) showed that, if four presynaptic points have initially strong and tight connections to four points of the postsynaptic field, a topographic map can be organized around these initial strong connections, propagating gradually in the whole region, where other connections are initially weak and random. This seems to be true for our model.

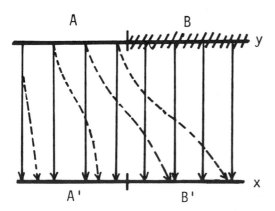

Figure 6   Regeneration of topographic map after removal of B

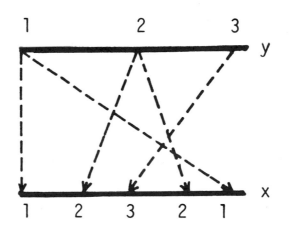

Figure 7   Non-topographic map

(D) Learning of topological structure

The formation of a topographic map can be regarded as learning of topological structures, at least locally, of stimulus signals. Here, the topology is defined by the mutual correlation of signals. Hence, if two points y_1 and y_2 are always activated at the same time (Fig. 8a), the presynatpic field has a topology shown in Fig. 8b. In this case, it is difficult to get a topographic or homeomorphic map from the presynaptic field to the postsynaptic field. Hence, three pieces of the presynaptic field will be mapped separately, and the topography is realized only locally. The equilibrium solution is not unique in this case.

The two dimensional topology is ampler. When the presynaptic field has the topology of ring, a homeomorphic map will be induced on the postsynaptic field, preserving the topology. Since the topology of the presynaptic field is defined by the signal correlation, many other topologies can be induced on the field by giving suitably correlated signals. It is an interesing problem to know the ability of realizing these topologies in the neural field by self-organization. The problem is closely related to that studied by Zeeman (1962).

5. Equilibrium State of Topographic Organization

(A) Topographic map and spread function

Let us look for the equilibrium solution $s(x, y)$, $s_0(x)$ of (16), (17) and (18), which realizes a topographic map. After the synaptic weights have converged to the solution $s(x, y)$ and $s_0(x)$, let a point y of the presynaptic field be activated. Then, a local excitation is aroused in the postsynaptic field. Let $x = m(y)$ be the position of the center of the local excitation, and let $l_y(a)$ be the length of the local excitation, where a denotes the intensity of the activation given at point y. The mapping

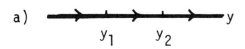

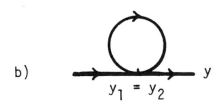

Figure 8 An example of topology defined on the presynaptic field

represents the projection from the presynaptic field to the postsynaptic one. Since we look for the topographic map, we assume that $m(y)$ is a monotonically increasing differentiable function. We call $l_y(a)$ the spread function at point y.

Let us define a pulse function of length l by

$$i(x, l) = \begin{cases} 1, & |x| < l/2, \\ 0, & |x| \geq l/2. \end{cases}$$

Then, the equilibrium solution $u(x; y, a, s, s_0)$ of the field when a point y is stimulated with an intensity a, can be written as

$$1[u(x; y, a, s, s_0)] = i\,[x - m(y), l_y(a)], \tag{19}$$

because it has the excited region at around $x = m(y)$ with a length $l_y(a)$.

On the other hand, we have from (16) and (17)

$$s(x, y) - cp(y)\langle ai[x - m(y), l_y(a)]\rangle_y, \tag{20}$$

$$s_0(x) = c'\int p(y)\langle i[x - m(y), l_y(a)]\rangle_y dy, \tag{21}$$

where $\langle\;\rangle_y$ denotes the average over a with the distribution $q_y(a)$ at point y. Hence, the equilibrium s and s_0 can be obtained, if we know $m(y)$ and $l_y(a)$.

When a point y_0 is stimulated with an intensity a, a local excitation is aroused in the postsynaptic field according to equation (9), where

$$S(x) = s(x, y_0)a - s_0\,(x).$$

Since the excitation is aroused at $x_0 = m(y_0)$, $S(x)$ takes its maximum at $x = x_0$. Since $s(x, y_0)$ is symmetrical with respect to $x = x_0$ as is seen from (20), this implies that $s_0(x)$ takes its extremum at $x = x_0$. Since the same argument holds for every x_0, we have

$$s_0(x) = \text{const} = c_1.$$

Moreover, the length $l_y(a)$ of the excitation satisfies (13), so that we have

$$h - W[l_y(a)] = as[m(y) + l_y(a)/2, y] - c_1. \tag{22}$$

(B) Resolution of the map

Before obtaining $m(y)$ and $l_y(a)$, we define a quantity which represents the distinguishability of two adjacent stimuli when they are mapped on the postsynaptic field. Let $(y, y + dy)$ be a small interval of the presynaptic field. It is mapped on the interval $(m(y), m(y) + m'(y)dy)$ of the postsynaptic field, where m' is the derivative of m. Let

$$l(y) = \langle l_y(a)\rangle_y = \int q_y(a)l_y(a)da \tag{23}$$

be the average length of excitations caused by stimulating y. Then, there exist at most $m'(y)dy/l(y)$ local excitations of the average length in the interval of length $m'(y)dy$ without mutually overlapping. Hence, we define the resolution $r(y)$ at y of the presynaptic field by

$$r(y)dy = \frac{m'(y)}{l(y)} \, dy, \tag{24}$$

which is the number of different stimuli in the interval $(y, y + dy)$ projected on mutually disjoint local excitations in the postsynaptic field. In otherwords, $1/r(y)$ gives the acuity at y, where the acuity is the minimal distance of distinguishing two adjacent stimuli.

Now we assume that $l_y(a)$ is small. We then have

THEOREM 3. *The resolution function is given by*

$$r(y) = \frac{c'}{c_1} p(y), \tag{25}$$

that is, the resolution becomes fine in proportion to the frequency of stimulation.

Proof. We have

$$\int p(y)i[x - m(y), l]dy = \int_{|x - m(y)| < l/2} \frac{p(y)dy}{}.$$

By transforming y to

$$z = m(y)$$

this integral can be written as

$$\int_{x - l/2}^{x + l/2} \frac{p[m^{-1}(z)]}{m'[m^{-1}(z)]} \, dz.$$

When l is small, this can be approximated by $lp(y)/m'(y)$ where $y = m^{-1}(x)$. Under this approximation, we have from equation (21)

$$s_0(x) = c' \frac{p(y)}{m'(y)} \langle l_y(a) \rangle = c' \frac{p(y)}{m'(y)} l(y) = c_1,$$

from which follows equation (25).

It is interesting that the resolution depends on the frequency only, and not on the intensity distribution of stimuli. The spread function $l(y)$ depends on the intensity distribution, as will be shown later.

(C) Equilibrium solution
The map $m(y)$ can be obtained by integrating

$$m'(y) = \frac{c'}{c_1} p(y)l(y), \tag{26}$$

where c_1 can be determined by the boundary condition, if we know $l(y)$ or $l_y(a)$. The synaptic weight function

$s(x, y)$ is then obtained from equation (20). To obtain $l_y(a)$, we define the monotonically non-increasing function

$$Q_y(a) = \int_a^\infty zq_y(z)dz. \tag{27}$$

Let $R_y(a)$ be the montonically non-decreasing version of $aQ_y(a)$ defined by

$$R_y(a) = \max_{0 \le z \le 0} zQ_y(z). \tag{28}$$

Since $aQ_y(a)$ is bounded, $R_y(a)$ is also a bounded function of a. These functions depend on the distribution $q_y(a)$. We give a simple example.

EXAMPLE. When $q_y(a)$ is the uniform distribution over $(0, 2\bar{a}_y)$ we have

$$q_{y(a)} = \begin{cases} \dfrac{1}{2\bar{a}_y}, & 0 < a < 2\bar{a}_y, \\ 0, & \text{otherwise}, \end{cases}$$

where $\bar{a}_y$ is the average intensity of stimuli at y. We then have

$$Q_y(a) = \begin{cases} \dfrac{1}{4\bar{a}_y}(4\bar{a}_y^2 - a^2), & 0 < a < 2\bar{a}_y, \\ 0, & \text{otherwise}, \end{cases}$$

and

$$R_y(a) = \begin{cases} \dfrac{1}{4\bar{a}_y}a(4\bar{a}_y^2 - a^2), & 0 < a < \dfrac{2}{\sqrt{3}}\bar{a}_y, \\ \dfrac{4}{3\sqrt{3}}\bar{a}_y^2, & a \ge \dfrac{2}{\sqrt{3}}\bar{a}_y. \end{cases}$$

The graph of $R_y(a)$ is given in Fig. 9.

THEOREM 4. *The spread function $l_y(a)$ is given by the solution l which satisfies $w(l) < 0$ of the equation*

$$W(l) = c_1 + h - cp(y)R_y(a) \tag{29}$$

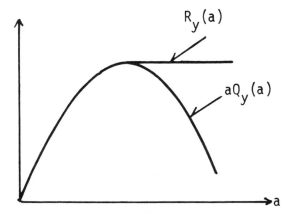

Figure 9. Example of $R_y(a)$

Proof. We first evaluate

$$\langle ai[x - m(y), l_y(a)]\rangle_y$$

$$= \int aq_y(a)i[x - m(y), l_y(a)]da = \int_A aq_y(a)da$$

where the domain A of the integral is given by

$$A = \{a \mid |x - m(y)| \ l_y(a)/2\}.$$

We presume that $l_y(a)$ is a monotonically non-increasing function of a, taking the maximum value l_c for $a \geq a_c$ where a_c may be infinitely large (Fig. 10). Let $\bar{l}_y^{-1}$ be the inverse function of l_y. It is defined for $0 \leq l \leq l_c$, and satisfies

$$l_y[l_y^{-1}(l)] = l.$$

The relation

$$l_y^{-1}[l_y(a)] = a \tag{30}$$

also holds for $0 \leq a < a_c$. However for $a \geq a_c$, $\bar{l}_y^{-1}[l_y(a)]$ is indefinite, taking any value not smaller than a_c. Since A can be written as

$$A = \{a \mid a > l_y^{-1}(2|x - m(y)|)\},$$

we have

$$\int_A aq_y(a)da = Q_y\{l_y^{-1}[2|x - m(y)|]\},$$

by which equation (20) is rewritten as

$$s(x,y) = cp(y)Q_y\{l_y^{-1}[2|x - m(y)|]\}. \tag{31}$$

Since the input $S(x)$ of the postsynaptic field, when the neurons at y are activated with intensity a, is given by

$$S(x) = as(x, y) - c_1,$$

we have from equation (13) of Theorem 2 that the length $l_y(a)$ of the local excitation satisfies

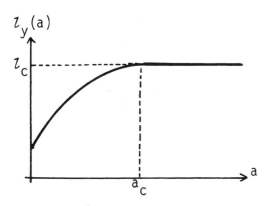

Figure 10 Shape of spread function $l_y(a)$

$$cp(y)aQ_y\{\bar{l}_y^{-1}[l_y(a)]\} - c_1 = h - W[l_y(a)],$$

where $x_0 = m(y)$ and

$$S[x_0 + l_y(a)/2] = cp(y)aQ_y\{\bar{l}_y^{-1}[l_y(a)]\}$$

are taken into account. When $a \geq a_c, \bar{l}_y^{-1}(l_y(a))$ in the right hand side is indefinite. This term should be determined such that $l_y(a)$ is monotonically non-increasing, as we have presumed in the beginning. This requirement is satisfied by defining

$$aQ_y\{\bar{l}_y^{-1}[l_y(a)]\} = R_y(a). \tag{32}$$

The theorem is thus proved. The critical value a_c is the point which maximizes $aQ_y(a)$.

For the example where $w(x)$ is given by equation (14), we obtain $l(y)(a)$ and $l(y)$ explicitly as

$$l_y(a) = d_1 + d_2 p(y)R_y(a),$$

$$l(y) = d_1 + d_2 p(y)\langle R_y(a)\rangle,$$

where

$$d_1 = \frac{W_1 - h - c_1}{w_0}, \quad d_2 = \frac{c}{w_0}.$$

When the intensity a is uniformly distributed, we have

$$l(y) = d_1 + \frac{13}{18}d_2 p(y)\bar{a}_y^2$$

This shows how the average spread of excitation depends on the frequency $p(y)$ and the average intensity $\bar{a}_y$ of stimuli given at a point y.

The map $m(y)$ is obtained by integrating equation (26). The connection $s(x, y)$ is obtained from equation (31). It should be noted that

$$s(x, y) = 0$$

when

$$|x - m(y)| > \frac{1}{2}\max_a l_y(a) = \frac{1}{2}l_c.$$

Therefore, a point y is connected to a finite range only of the postsynaptic field.

Concluding Remarks

1. We have proved that our equations have the equilibrium solution corresponding to the topographic map. However, this does not imply that the genetic information has little to do with formation of the map. It probably plays an important role, and the modifiable synapses play a supplementary role, refining the map. The nerve fields can thus

adapt to the sensory information of the environment or the removal of a part of the field. We have shown the mathematical analysis of a possible mechanism of the topographic organization by a very simple model. In order to fit the real data, we should refine the model further by adding some auxiliary mechanisms to the model.

2. Local topographic maps are easily formed by the mechanism of the present paper. However, it is difficult to form a global topographic map from completely random initial connections. The genetic information should play a role in forming the initial connections (see also Willshaw and Malsburg, 1976).

3. We have treated only one-dimensional fields. It is straightforward to extend the model to two-dimensional cases. However, the mathematical analysis becomes much more difficult. There may be many interesting phenomena peculiar to the two-dimensional case, because the two-dimensional topology is far richer than the trivial one-dimensional topology. It is also interesting to extend the model such that the connections $w(x)$ are also modifiable. In this case, the topological structure of environmental information can be mapped in the field as its inner structure (cf. Zeeman, 1962).

4. The modifiable inhibitory synapses play a fundamental role in our model. They are strengthened when both the pre- and postsynaptic neurons are excited. This is contrary to the Perceptron type modification, where they are strengthened when the excitation of the postsynaptic neuron is blocked by inhibition. Different types of neurons may have different synaptic modification rules. However, the modifiable inhibitory synapses of the present type seem to play important roles in the neural system (see also Wilson, 1975; Amari and Takeuchi, 1978; Kohonen and Oja, 1976, etc.)

5. We have analyzed the limiting case of the pointwise stimulaion of the presynaptic field. We found that, when $a(y)$ is not the delta function but has some finite spread, interesting phenomena occur under some conditions. The topographic map is also formed in this case in the global sense. However, the map has microstructures such that both X and Y are divided into microregions, and the neurons in a microregion have the same receptive field. This might have some relation to the columnar microstructures in the cerebral cortex. This will be published elsewhere (Takeuchi and Amari, 1979).

Literature

Arbib, M. A. 1972. *The Metaphorical Brain.* New York: Wiley.

Amari, S. 1972. "Characteristics of Random Nets of Analog Neuron-like Elements." *IEEE Trans., Systems, Man and Cybernetics,* **SMC-2,** 643–657.

———. 1974. "A Method of Statistical Neurodynamics." *Kybernetik* **14,** 201–215.

———. 1977a. "Dynamics of Pattern Formation in Lateral-inhibition Type Neural Fields." *Biol. Cyberent.* **27,** 77–87.

———. 1977b. "Neutral Theory of Association and Concept-formation." *Biol. Cybernet.* **26,** 175–185.

——— and Arbib, M. A. 1977. "Competition and Cooperation in Neural Nets." *Systems Neuroscience* Ed. J. Metzler, 119–165. New York: Academic Press.

——— and Takeuchi, A. 1978. "Mathematical Theory on Formation of Category Detecting Nerve Cells." *Biol. Cybernet.* **29,** 127–136.

———, Yoshida, K. and Kanatani, K. 1977. "A Mathematical Foundation for Statistical Neurodynamics." *SIAM J. Appl. Math.* **33,** 95–126.

Gaze, R. M. 1970. *The Formation of Nerve Connections.* London: Academic Press.

———, Jacobson, M. and Szekely, G. 1965. "On the Formation of Connections by Compound Eyes in *Xenopus.*" *J. Physiol.* **176, 409–417.**

——— and Keating, M. J. 1972. "The Visual System and 'Neuronal Specificity'." Nature, Lond. 237, 375–378.

Geman, S. 1979. "Some Averaging and Stability Results for Random Differential Equations." SIAM J. Appl. Math. 36, 86–105.

Hope, R. A., Hammond, B. J. and Gaze, R. M. 1976. "The Arrow Model—Retinotectal Specificity and Map Formation in the Goldfish Visual System." Proc. R. Soc. B 194, 447–466.

Kishimoto, K. and Amari, S. 1979. "Existence and Stability of Local Excitations in Neural Fields." J. Math. Biol. 7, 303–318.

Kohonen, T. and Oja, E. 1976. "Fast Adaptive Formation of Orthogonalizing Filters and Associative Memory in Recurrent Networks of Neuron-like Elements." Biol. Cybernet. 21, 85–95.

Malsburg, C. von der. 1973. "Self-organization of Orientation Sensitive Cells in the Striate Cortex." Kybernetik 14, 85–100.

Prestige, M. C. and Willshaw, D. J. 1975. "On a Role for Competition in the Formation of Patterned Neural Connections." Proc. R. Soc. B 190, 77–98.

Sharma, S. C. 1972. "Reformation of Retinotectal Connections after Various Tectal Ablations in Adult Goldfish." Exp. Neurol. 34, 171–182.

Sperry, R. W. 1951. "Mechanism of Neural Maturation." Handbook of Experimental Psychology, Ed. S. S. Steven, pp. 236–280. New York: Wiley.

Takeuchi, A. and Amari, S. "Formation of Topographic Maps and Columnar Microstructures in Nerve Fields." Biol. Cybernet. (in press).

Willshaw, D. J. and Malsburg, C. von der. 1976. "How Patterned Neural Connections can be Set up by Self Organization." Proc. R. Soc. B 194, 431–445.

Wilson, H. R. 1975. "A Synaptic Model for Spatial Frequency Adaptation." J. Theoret. Biol. 50, 327–352.

Yoon, M. 1971. "Reorganization of Retinotectal Projection Following Surgical Operations on the Optic Tectum in Goldfish." Expl. Neurol. 33, 395–411.

———, 1972. "Transposition of the Visual Projection from the Nasal Hemi-retina onto the Foreign Rostral Zone of the Optic Tectum in Goldfish." Expl. Neurol. 37, 451–462.

Zeeman, C. 1962. "The Topology of the Brain and Visual Perception." Topology of 3-Manifolds and Related Topics, Ed. M. K. Fort, pp. 240–256, Englewood Cliffs: Prentice-Hall.

10
Introduction

(1987)
Gail A. Carpenter and Stephen Grossberg

ART 2: Self-organization of stable category recognition codes for analog input patterns
Applied Optics 26: 4919–4930

This paper is taken from a special issue on neural networks of *Applied Optics*. It was written by Gail Carpenter and her husband, Stephen Grossberg. It, and the next paper, by Bart Kosko (paper 11) are well-known examples of what are sometimes called neural network *resonance* models. A 1976 paper by Grossberg (paper 19 in *Neurocomputing: Foundations of Research*) described some of the early ideas behind this approach, and many papers from the Boston University Center for Adaptive Systems have developed these ideas in detail (see Grossberg 1987).

ART stands for *adaptive resonance theory*. Some impressive claims are made for ART. There are two versions of ART described in this paper—ART 2 is a more complex evolution of the earlier ART 1, but both function as self-organizing categorizers. Suppose we have an environment that contains "structure," that is, suppose we have some natural categories of patterns, but these patterns are always seen in noisy form, and the categories are not known ahead of time. The ART model will adaptively respond to the category structure and group similar items together with the same output response. Carpenter and Grossberg place great importance on network and category stability, that is, the resulting categories have to be stable over time and not change as additional information is learned by ART. Also, when a novel pattern appears, it must be recognized as novel and used as the start of a new category. And the network itself must be stable.

There are now a number of different neural network models that have been suggested or used for self-organizing systems, where the environmental categories are not known ahead of time. Most neural network models are well suited to self-organization because they respond strongly to similarity, that is, similar patterns tend to give similar responses. So, for example, even the simplest associative networks will form *prototypes*, a type of unsupervised category formation (paper 36 in *Neurocomputing: Foundations of Research*). Self-organizing maps are discussed by Willshaw and von der Malsburg and Amari (papers 8 and 9) and by Kohonen (paper 30, *Neurocomputing: Foundations of Research*) and self-organizing systems are discussed by Rumelhart and Zipser (1986).

The problem of detecting existing structure in a natural environment is well known to psychologists because it describes the problem faced by a child. A quotation from William James (1894/1961, p. 29), famous among developmental psychologists, describes the situation:

. . . the numerous inpouring currents of the baby bring to his consciousness . . . one big blooming buzzing Confusion. That Confusion is the baby's universe; and the universe of all of us is still to a great extent such a Confusion, potentially resolvable, and demanding to be resolved, but not yet actually resolved into parts.

We now know that a baby is an immensely competent organism, with its sensory systems prewired to a remarkable degree to pick up the kind of structure that has proved useful to the species in the past. As William James (1894/1961 ch. 1, p. 17) also comments, "Mind and world in short have been evolved together, and, in consequence are something of a mutual fit." The biological problem may be much more constrained, and therefore easier, than the general problem of self-organization from nothing. For example, a much less elaborate self-organizing system, using an energy-minimizing attractor network, can be used to cluster and identify radar transmitters because it is known ahead of time roughly what kinds of things the system will be seeing (Anderson, Gately, Penz, and Collins 1990).

We must be candid and admit that Grossberg has a reputation for writing difficult papers. This is partly because he tries to make a network perform multiple, tightly interlocking functions simultaneously. This can be seen in the ART models, where the network has two distinct functional sections: The first is an information-processing part, which operates on detailed patterns of input activity that are processed by a relatively straightforward set of neural networks. The second is a set of control networks that decide what is different enough to be learned as a new category and that operates by using widely distributed scalar control signals. The two networks interact strongly.

The information processing section uses a two-layer network: an input layer and one higher-level set of units. Carpenter and Grossberg refer to the higher level functional units as *nodes*. The top layer contains what Grossberg has called *gated dipole fields*, a nonlinear lateral inhibitory network acting like a winner-take-all (WTA) network in operation. A WTA network has a final stable state composed of only one active unit. The aim of the system is to develop grandmother cells at the higher level with all the strengths and weaknesses of such a localized representation.

When an input pattern comes in, it activates the top layer. The top layer projects back to the input layer. The goal of top-layer learning is to match the input pattern at the input layer, using the top-down connections. If there is a close or exact match, the resulting larger amplitude input pattern activates the top again, and there is a feedback loop, leading ultimately to the presence of a pattern in the first layer and a single active node representing the category at the top layer. If there is a mismatch between input and the response to that input from the top layer, a stable pattern does not emerge because of destructive interference between the input pattern and the pattern coming from the top layer. The name *resonance* refers to the positive interaction between input and top-down patterns, which must nearly match for the resonance to occur.

Carpenter and Grossberg have therefore built system dynamics into the ART network by allowing feedback, and the resulting dynamical system seeks "resonant" long-lasting stable points. There are many nonlinear neural networks that operate in this fashion, and some stability results for large classes of them can be found in Cohen and Grossberg 1983.

To be useful, a categorization system must make the following kind of decision: A pattern has been seen before. A new pattern appears that is "close to" a learned pattern. Is it an example of the old category or a new category? In general this is not an easy decision, and it is one that is governed by several things. First, the representation of the data must code similar things to be close in state space. Second, some idea of expected variability must be built into the system. And, third, the distribution of examples of the category must itself have certain properties, for example, it would be hard for such a system to learn, as a single category, examples from a widely separated bimodal distribution.

These problems are handled in ART by an elaborate set of nonlinear controls. In attractor models it is usually possible to control the size of the attractor basin (that is, the set of points attracted into a stable point) by manipulating a small number of control parameters of the system. If there is a near match of a new input to a learned category, the system must decide if the new pattern is indeed a category member. The acceptability of a new pattern in the ART models is governed in large part by a parameter called *vigilance* which is a measure of distance between the old category center and the new pattern. If the pattern is accepted, then the new pattern can be learned as an example of an old category. This sometimes has the effect of readjusting the center of the category.

If the pattern is not acceptable as a new example of an old category, then other potential old categories can be checked, though the parallel search through old categories involves complex network dynamics.

If there is no match, then the ART model makes an unusual step, which is possible because of the grandmother cell top-layer representation. It effectively constructs a *new node* to represent the new category by taking an "uncommitted" node and changing its weights so as to learn the new category. One other example in the network literature for what amounts to the construction of new units to represent new categories is the useful practical pattern recognition system described by Reilly, Cooper, and Elbaum (paper 28).

The information-processing strategy of ART works somewhat like the nearest neighbor classifiers described by Batchelor or Cover and Hart (papers 26 and 27). The weights of the top-level grandmother nodes correspond to a prototype pattern, and the size of the region representing the category is controlled by the vigilance parameter. What makes the ART models unusual and ambitious is the attempt to handle both information processing and control with neural networks as part of the same system.

Because of the importance of the problems that ART deals with, both ART 1 and ART 2 have been considered for practical applications by a number of engineering groups. The general finding seems to be that it is difficult to get ART 2 to work as a whole, though ART 1, because of its use of binary vectors and its similarity to nearest neighbor categorizers, is much easier to implement. The category structure of both ARTs is very sensitive to the vigilance parameter. Because of the grandmother cell representation, ART is somewhat inflexible in its categorization. However, humans can readjust category sizes quickly and without difficulty, being able to group a set of animals as cats and dogs, as mammals, or as Siamese cats, German shepherds, and so on, depending on the task.

The considerable appeal of ART lies in its attempt to do the whole job of categorization in a single system, and it gives an idea of the kinds of global mechanisms that may be necessary when a nervous system forms and uses categories.

References

J.A. Anderson, M.T. Gately, P.A. Penz, and D. Collins (1990), Radar signal categorization using a neural network. *Proceedings of the IEEE* Vol.: pp.

M.A. Cohen and S. Grossberg (1983), Absolute stability of global pattern formation and parallel memory storage by competitive neural networks. *IEEE Transactions on Systems, Man and Cybernetics* SMC-13: 815–826.

S. Grossberg (1987), *Neural Networks and Natural Intelligence*. Cambridge, MA: MIT Press.

W. James (1894/1961), *Briefer Psychology*. London: Collier-Macmillan.

D.E. Rumelhart and D. Zipser (1986), Feature discovery by competitive learning. In D.E. Rumelhart and J.L. McClelland (Eds.), *Parallel Distributed Processing, Volume 1*. Cambridge, MA: MIT Press.

(1987)
Gail A. Carpenter and Stephen Grossberg

ART 2: Self-organization of stable category recognition codes for analog input patterns
Applied Optics 26: 4919–4930

Adaptive resonance architectures are neural networks that self-organize stable pattern recognition codes in real-time in response to arbitrary sequences of input patterns. This article introduces ART 2, a class of adaptive resonance architectures which rapidly self-organize pattern recognition categories in response to arbitrary sequences of either analog or binary input patterns. In order to cope with arbitrary sequences of analog input patterns, ART 2 architectures embody solutions to a number of design principles, such as the stability-plasticity tradeoff, the search-direct access tradeoff, and the match-reset tradeoff. In these architectures, top-down learned expectation and matching mechanisms are critical in self-stabilizing the code learning process. A parallel search scheme updates itself adaptively as the learning process unfolds, and realizes a form of real-time hypothesis discovery, testing, learning, and recognition. After learning self-stabilizes, the search process is automatically disengaged. Thereafter input patterns directly access their recognition codes without any search. Thus recognition time for familiar inputs does not increase with the complexity of the learned code. A novel input pattern can directly access a category if it shares invariant properties with the set of familiar exemplars of that category. A parameter called the attentional vigilance parameter determines how fine the categories will be. If vigilance increases (decreases) due to environmental feedback, then the system automatically searches for and learns finer (coarser) recognition categories. Gain control parameters enable the architecture to suppress noise up to a prescribed level. The architecture's global design enables it to learn effectively despite the high degree of nonlinearity of such mechanisms.

I. Adaptive Resonance Architectures

Adaptive resonance architectures are neural networks that self-organize stable recognition codes in real time in response to arbitrary sequences of input patterns. The basic principles of adaptive resonance theory (ART) were introduced by Grossberg.[1] A class of adaptive resonance architectures, called ART 1, has since been characterized as a system of ordinary differential equations by Carpenter and Grossberg.[2,3] Theorems have been proved that trace the real-time dynamics of ART 1 networks in response to arbitrary sequences of binary input patterns. These theorems predict both the order of search, as a function of the learning history of the network, and the asymptotic category structure self-organized by arbitrary sequences of binary input patterns. They also prove the self-stabilization property and show that the system's adaptive weights oscillate at most once, yet do not get trapped in spurious memory states or local minima.

The authors are with Boston University, Center for Adaptive Systems, 111 Cummington Street, Boston, Massachusetts 02215.

This paper describes a new class of adaptive resonance architectures, called ART 2. ART 2 networks self-organize stable recognition categories in response to arbitrary sequences of analog (gray-scale, continuous-valued) input patterns, as well as binary input patterns. Computer simulations are used to illustrate system dynamics. One such simulation is summarized in Fig. 1, which shows how a typical ART 2 architecture has quickly learned to group fifty inputs into thirty-four stable recognition categories after a single presentation of each input. The plots below each number show all those input patterns ART 2 has grouped into the corresponding category. Equations for the system used in the simulation are given in Secs. V–VIII.

ART networks encode new input patterns, in part, by changing the weights, or long-term memory (LTM) traces, of a bottom-up adaptive filter (Fig. 2). This filter is contained in pathways leading from a feature representation field (F_1) to a category representation field (F_2) whose nodes undergo cooperative and competitive interactions. Such a combination of adaptive filtering and competition, sometimes called competitive learning, is shared by many other models of adaptive pattern recognition and associative learning. See Grossberg[4] for a review of the development of competitive learning models. In an ART network, however, it is a second, top-down adaptive filter that leads to the

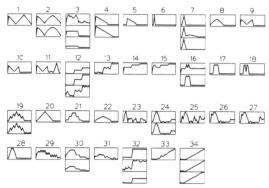

Fig. 1. Category grouping of fifty analog input patterns into thirty-four recognition categories. Each input pattern I is depicted as a function of i ($i = 1\ldots M$), with successive I_i values connected by straight lines. The category structure established on one complete presentation of the fifty inputs remains stable thereafter if the same inputs are presented again.

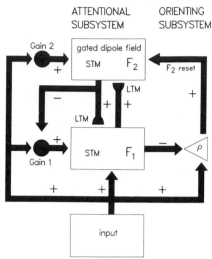

Fig. 2. Typical ART 1 architecture. Rectangles represent fields where STM patterns are stored. Semicircles represent adaptive filter pathways and arrows represent paths which are not adaptive. Filled circles represent gain control nuclei, which sum input signals. Their output paths are nonspecific in the sense that at any given time a uniform signal is sent to all nodes in a receptor field. Gain control at F_1 and F_2 coordinates STM processing with input presentation rate.

crucial property of code self-stabilization. Such top-down adaptive signals play the role of learned expectations in an ART system. They enable the network to carry out attentional priming, pattern matching, and self-adjusting parallel search. One of the key insights of the ART design is that top-down attentional and intentional, or expectation, mechanisms are necessary to self-stabilize learning in response to an arbitrary input environment.

The fields F_1 and F_2, as well as the bottom-up and top-down adaptive filters, are contained within ART's attentional subsystem (Fig. 2). An auxiliary orienting subsystem becomes active when a bottom-up input to F_1 fails to match the learned top-down expectation read-out by the active category representation at F_2. In this case, the orienting subsystem is activated and causes rapid reset of the active category representation at F_2. This reset event automatically induces the attentional subsystem to proceed with a parallel search. Alternative categories are tested until either an adequate match is found or a new category is established. The search remains efficient because the search strategy is updated adaptively throughout the learning process. The search proceeds rapidly, relative to the learning rate. Thus significant changes in the bottom-up and top-down adaptive filters occur only when a search ends and a matched F_1 pattern resonates within the system. For the simulation illustrated in Fig. 1, the ART 2 system carried out a search during many of the initial fifty input presentations.

The processing cycle of bottom-up adaptive filtering, code (or hypothesis) selection, read-out of a top-down learned expectation, matching, and code reset shows that, within an ART system, adaptive pattern recognition is a special case of the more general cognitive process of discovering, testing, searching, learning, and recognizing hypotheses. Applications of ART systems to problems concerning the adaptive process-

ing of large abstract knowledge bases are thus a key goal for future research.

The fact that learning within an ART system occurs only within a resonant state enables such a system to solve the design trade-off between plasticity and stability. Plasticity, or the potential for rapid change in the LTM traces, remains intact indefinitely, thereby enabling an ART architecture to learn about future unexpected events until it exhausts its full memory capacity.

Learning within a resonant state either refines the code of a previously established recognition code, based on any new information that the input pattern may contain, or initiates code learning within a previously uncommitted set of nodes. If, for example, a new input were added at any time to the set of fifty inputs in Fig. 1, the system would search the established categories. If an adequate match were found, possibly on the initial search cycle, the LTM category representation would be refined, if necessary, to incorporate the new pattern. If no match were found, and the full coding capacity were not yet exhausted, a new category would be formed, with previously uncommitted LTM traces encoding the STM pattern established by the input.

The architecture's adaptive search enables it to discover and learn appropriate recognition codes without getting trapped in spurious memory states or local minima. In other search models, such as search trees, the search time can become increasingly prolonged as the learned code becomes increasingly complex. In an ART architecture, by contrast, search takes place only as a recognition code is being learned, and the search maintains its efficiency as learning goes on.

Self-stabilization of prior learning is achieved via the dynamic buffering provided by read-out of a learned top-down expectation, not by switching off plasticity or restricting the class of admissible inputs. For example, after the initial presentation of fifty input patterns in the simulation illustrated by Fig. 1, learning self-stabilized. In general, within an ART architecture, once learning self-stabilizes within a particular recognition category, the search mechanism is automatically disengaged. Thereafter, that category can be directly activated, or accessed, with great rapidity and without search by any of its input exemplars.

The criterion for an adequate match between an input pattern and a chosen category template is adjustable in an ART architecture. The matching criterion is determined by a vigilance parameter that controls activation of the orienting subsystem. All other things being equal, higher vigilance imposes a stricter matching criterion, which in turn partitions the input set into finer categories. Lower vigilance tolerates greater top-down/bottom-up mismatches at F_1, leading in turn to coarser categories (Fig. 3). In addition, at every vigilance level, the matching criterion is self-scaling: a small mismatch may be tolerated if the input pattern is complex, while the same featural mismatch would trigger reset if the input represented only a few features.

Even without any search, as when vigilance is low or the orienting subsystem is removed, ART 2 can often establish a reasonable category structure (Fig. 4). In this case, however, the top-down learned expectations assume the full burden of code self-stabilization by generating the attentional focus to dynamically buffer the emergent code. Although mismatch of bottom-up and top-down patterns at F_1 can attenuate unmatched

features at F_1, such a mismatch does not elicit a search for a more appropriate F_2 code before learning can occur. Such learning will incorporate the unattenuated F_1 features into the initially selected category's recognition code. In this situation, more input trials may be needed before the code self-stabilizes; false groupings may occur during the early trials, as in category 1 of Fig. 4(a); and the flexible matching criterion achieved by variable vigilance is lost. Nonetheless, the top-down expectations can actively regulate the course of learning to generate a stable asymptotic code with desirable properties. For example, despite the initial anomalous coding in the example of Fig. 4(a), Fig. 4(b) shows that a stable category structure is established by the third round of inputs in which the false groupings within category 1 in Fig. 4(a) have been corrected by splitting grossly dissimilar inputs into the separate categories 1 and 7.

The top-down learned expectations and the orienting subsystem are not the only means by which an ART network carries out active regulation of the learning process. Attentional gain control at F_1 and F_2 also contributes to this active regulation (Sec. II). Gain control acts to adjust overall sensitivity to patterned inputs and to coordinate the separate, asynchronous functions of the ART subsystems. Gain control nuclei are represented as large filled circles in the figures.

II. ART 1: Binary Input Patterns

Figure 2 illustrates the main features of a typical ART 1 network. Two successive stages, F_1 and F_2, of the attentional subsystem encode patterns of activation in short-term memory (STM). Each bottom-up

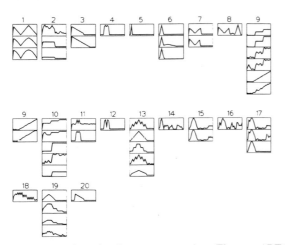

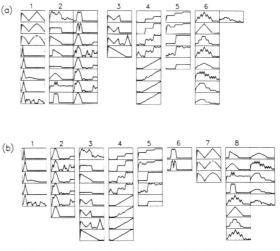

Fig. 4. Category learning by an ART 2 model without an orienting subsystem. (a) The same ART 2 system as used in Figs. 1 and 3, but with vigilance level set equal to zero, has here grouped the same fifty inputs into six recognition categories after one presentation of each pattern. Without the full ART 2 system's ability to reset on mismatch, transitory groupings occur, as in category 1. (b) By the third presentation of each input, a coarse but stable category structure has been established.

Fig. 3. Lower vigilance implies coarser grouping. The same ART 2 system as used in Fig. 1 has here grouped the same fifty inputs into twenty recognition categories. Note, for example, that categories 1 and 2 of Fig. 1 are here joined in category 1; categories 14, 15, and 32 are here joined in category 10; and categories 19–22 are here joined in category 13.

or top-down pathway between F_1 and F_2 contains an adaptive LTM trace that multiplies the signal in its pathway. The rest of the circuit modulates these STM and LTM processes. Modulation by gain 1 enables F_1 to distinguish between a bottom-up input pattern and a top-down priming or template pattern, as well as to match these bottom-up and top-down patterns. In particular, bottom-up inputs can supraliminally activate F_2; top-down expectations in the absence of bottom-up inputs can subliminally sensitize, or prime, F_1; and a combination of bottom-up and top-down inputs is matched according to a 2/3 Rule which activates the nodes within the intersection of the bottom-up and top-down patterns (Fig. 5). Thus, within the context of a self-organizing ART architecture, intentionality (or the action of learned top-down expectations) implies a spatial logic matching rule. Carpenter and Grossberg[3] prove that 2/3 Rule matching is necessary for self-stabilization of learning within ART 1 in response to arbitrary sequences of binary input patterns.

The orienting subsystem generates a reset wave to F_2 when the bottom-up input pattern and top-down template pattern mismatch at F_1, according to the vigilance criterion. The reset wave selectively and enduringly inhibits active F_2 cells until the current input is shut off. Offset of the input pattern terminates its processing at F_1 and triggers offset of gain 2. Gain 2 offset causes rapid decay of STM at F_2, and thereby prepares F_2 to encode the next input pattern without bias.

An ART 1 system is fully defined by a system of differential equations that determines STM and LTM dynamics in response to an arbitrary temporal sequence of binary input patterns. Theorems characterizing these dynamics have been proved in the case where fast learning occurs; that is, where each trial is long enough for the LTM traces to approach equilibrium values.[3] Variations of the ART 1 architecture exhibit similar dynamics. Hence the term ART 1 designates a family, or class, of functionally equivalent architectures rather than a single model.

III. ART 2: Analog Input Patterns

ART 2 architectures are designed for the processing of analog, as well as binary, input patterns. A category representation system for analog inputs needs to be able to pick out and enhance similar signals embedded in various noisy backgrounds, as in category 16 of Fig. 1.

Figure 6 illustrates a typical ART 2 architecture. A comparison of Figs. 2 and 6 illustrates some of the principal differences between ART 1 and ART 2 networks. For ART 2 to match and learn sequences of analog input patterns in a stable fashion, its feature representation field F_1 includes several processing levels and gain control systems. Bottom-up input patterns and top-down signals are received at different locations in F_1. Positive feedback loops within F_1 enhance salient features and suppress noise. Although F_1 is more complex in ART 2 than in ART 1, the

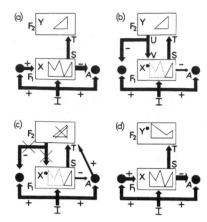

Fig. 5.   Search for a correct F_2 code.   (a) The input pattern I generates the specific STM activity pattern X at F_1 as it nonspecifically activates A.   Pattern X both inhibits A and generates the output signal pattern S.   Signal pattern S is transformed into the input pattern T, which activates the STM pattern Y across F_2.   (b) Pattern Y generates the top-down signal pattern U which is transformed into the template pattern V. If V mismatches I at F_1, a new STM activity pattern X^* is generated at F_1. The reduction in total STM activity which occurs when X is transformed into X^* causes a decrease in the total inhibition from F_1 to A.   (c) Then the input-driven activation of A can release a nonspecific arousal wave to F_2, which resets the STM pattern Y at F_2.   (d) After Y is inhibited, its top-down template is eliminated, and X can be reinstated at F_1. Now X once again generates input pattern T to F_2, but since Y remains inhibited T can activate a different STM pattern Y^* at F_2. If the top-down template due to Y^* also mismatches I at F_1, the rapid search for an appropriate F_2 code continues.

LTM equations of ART 2 are simpler.

How the signal functions and parameters of the various ART 2 architectures can best be chosen to categorize particular classes of analog input patterns for specialized applications is the subject of ongoing research. In particular, since ART 2 architectures are designed to categorize arbitrary sequences of analog or digital input patterns, an arbitrary preprocessor can be attached to the front end of an ART 2 architecture. This property is being exploited to design a self-organizing architecture for invariant recognition and recall using laser radar, boundary segmentation, and invariant filter methods to generate preprocessed inputs to ART 2.[5-8]

IV. ART 2 Design Principles

ART 2 architectures satisfy a set of design principles derived from an analysis of neural networks that form recognition categories for arbitrary sequences of analog input patterns. ART 2 systems have been developed to satisfy the multiple design principles or processing constraints that give rise to the architecture's emergent properties. At least three variations on the ART 2 architecture have been identified that are capable of satisfying these constraints. Indeed, the heart of the ART 2 analysis consists of discovering how different combinations of network mechanisms work together to generate particular combinations of desirable emergent properties. That is why theoretical ablation experiments on ART 2 architectures have proved to be so useful, since they reveal which emergent properties are spared and which are lost in reduced architectures.

In each ART 2 architecture, combinations of normalization, gain control, matching and learning mechanisms are interwoven in generally similar ways. Although how this is done may be modified to some extent, in all the ART 2 variations that we have discovered, F_1 needs to include different levels to receive and transform bottom-up input patterns and top-down expectation patterns, as well as an interfacing level of interneurons that matches the transformed bottom-up and top-down information and feeds the results back to the bottom and top F_1 levels. How the particular F_1 levels shown in Fig. 6 work will be described in Secs. IX–XII. Alternative ART 2 models are illustrated in Sec. XIII and in Ref. 5.

We now describe the main ART 2 design principles.

A. Stability-Plasticity Trade-Off

An ART 2 system needs to be able to learn a stable recognition code in response to an arbitrary sequence of analog input patterns. Since the plasticity of an ART system is maintained for all time, and since input presentation times can be of arbitrary duration, STM processing must be defined in such a way that a sustained new input pattern does not wash away previously learned information. Section XII shows how removal, or ablation, of one part of the F_1 internal feedback loop in Fig. 6 can lead to a type of instability in which a single input, embedded in a particular input sequence, can jump between categories indefinitely.

B. Search-Direct Access Trade-Off

An ART 2 system carries out a parallel search in order to regulate the selection of appropriate recognition codes during the learning process, yet automatically disengages the search process as an input pattern becomes familiar. Thereafter the familiar input pattern directly accesses its recognition code no matter how complex the total learned recognition structure may have become, much as we can rapidly recognize our parents at different stages of our life even though we may learn much more as we grow older.

C. Match-Reset Trade-Off

An ART 2 system needs to be able to resolve several potentially conflicting properties which can be formulated as variants of a design trade-off between the requirements of sensitive matching and formation of new codes.

The system should, on the one hand, be able to recognize and react to arbitrarily small differences between an active F_1 STM pattern and the LTM pattern being read-out from an established category. In particular, if vigilance is high, the F_1 STM pattern established by a bottom-up input exemplar should be nearly identical to the learned top-down $F_2 \rightarrow F_1$ ex-

pectation pattern in order for the exemplar to be accepted as a member of an established category. On the other hand, when an uncommitted F_2 node becomes active for the first time, it should be able to remain active, without being reset, so that it can encode its first input exemplar, even though in this case there is no top-down/bottom-up pattern match whatsoever. Section IX shows how a combination of an appropriately chosen ART 2 reset rule and LTM initial values work together to satisfy both of these processing requirements. In fact, ART 2 parameters can be chosen to satisfy the more general property that learning increases the system's sensitivity to mismatches between bottom-up and top-down patterns.

D. STM Invariance Under Read-Out of Matched LTM

Further discussion of match-reset trade-off clarifies why F_1 is composed of several internal processing levels. Suppose that before an uncommitted F_2 node is first activated, its top-down $F_2 \rightarrow F_1$ LTM traces are chosen equal to zero. On the node's first learning trial, its LTM traces will progressively learn the STM pattern that is generated by the top level of F_1. As noted above, such learning must not be allowed to cause a mismatch capable of resetting F_2, because the LTM traces have not previously learned any other pattern. This property is achieved by designing the bottom and middle levels of F_1 so that their STM activity patterns are not changed at all by the read-out of these LTM traces as they learn their first positive values.

More generally, F_1 is designed so that read-out by F_2 of a previously learned LTM pattern that matches perfectly the STM pattern at the top level of F_1 does not change the STM patterns circulating at the bottom and middle levels of F_1. Thus, in a perfect match situation, or in a situation where a zero-vector of LTM values learns a perfect match, the STM activity patterns at the bottom and middle F_1 levels are left invariant; hence, no reset occurs.

This invariance property enables the bottom and middle F_1 levels to nonlinearly transform the input pattern in a manner that remains stable during learning. In particular, the input pattern may be contrast enhanced while noise in the input is suppressed. If read-out of a top-down LTM pattern could change even the base line of activation at the F_1 levels which execute this transformation, the degree of contrast enhancement and noise suppression could be altered, thereby generating a new STM pattern for learning by the top-down LTM traces. The STM invariance property prevents read-out of a perfectly matched LTM pattern from causing reset by preventing any change whatsoever from occurring in the STM patterning at the lower F_1 levels.

E. Coexistence of LTM Read-Out and STM Normalization

The STM invariance property leads to the use of multiple F_1 levels because the F_1 nodes at which top-down LTM read-out occurs receive an additional input when top-down signals are active than when they are not. The extra F_1 levels provide enough degrees of computational freedom to both read-out top-down LTM and normalize the total STM pattern at the top F_1 level before this normalized STM pattern can interact with the middle F_1 level at which top-down and bottom-up information are matched.

In a similar fashion, the bottom F_1 level enables an input pattern to be normalized before this normalized STM pattern can interact with the middle F_1 level. Thus separate bottom and top F_1 levels provide enough degrees of computational freedom to compensate for fluctuations in base line activity levels. In the absence of such normalization, confusion between useful pattern differences and spurious base line fluctuations could easily upset the matching process and cause spurious reset events to occur, thereby destabilizing the network's search and learning processes.

F. No LTM Recoding by Superset Inputs

Although read-out of a top-down LTM pattern that perfectly matches the STM pattern at the F_1 top level never causes F_2 reset, even a very small mismatch in these patterns is sufficient to reset F_2 if the vigilance parameter is chosen sufficiently high. The middle F_1 level plays a key role in causing the attenuation of STM activity that causes such a reset event to occur.

An important example of such a reset-inducing mismatch occurs when one or more, but not all, of the top-down LTM traces equal zero or very small values and the corresponding F_1 nodes have positive STM activities. When this occurs, the STM activities of these F_1 nodes are suppressed. If the total STM suppression is large enough to reset F_2, the network searches for a better match. If the total STM suppression is not large enough to reset F_2, the top-down LTM traces of these nodes remain small during the ensuing learning trial, because they sample the small STM values that their own small LTM values have caused.

This property is a version of the 2/3 Rule that has been used to prove stability of learning by an ART 1 architecture in response to an arbitrary sequence of binary input patterns.[3] It also is necessary for ART 2 to achieve stable learning in response to an arbitrary sequence of analog input patterns (Sec. XII). In the jargon of ART 1, a superset bottom-up input pattern cannot recode a subset top-down expectation. In ART 1, this property was achieved by an intentional gain control channel (Fig. 2). In the versions of ART 2 developed so far, it is realized as part of the F_1 internal levels. These design variations are still a subject of ongoing research.

G. Stable Choice Until Reset

Match-reset trade-off also requires that only a reset event that is triggered by the orienting subsystem can cause a change in the chosen F_2 code. This property is imposed at any degree of mismatch between a top-down $F_2 \to F_1$ LTM pattern and the circulating F_1 STM pattern. Thus all the network's real-time pattern processing operations, including top-down $F_2 \to F_1$ feedback, the fast nonlinear feedback dynamics within F_1, and the slow LTM changes during learning

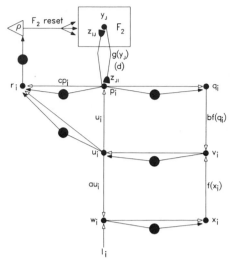

Fig. 6. Typical ART 2 architecture. Open arrows indicate specific patterned inputs to target nodes. Filled arrows indicate nonspecific gain control inputs. The gain control nuclei (large filled circles) nonspecifically inhibit target nodes in proportion to the L_2 norm of STM activity in their source fields [Eqs. (5), (6), (9), (20), and (21)]. When F_2 makes a choice, $g(y_J) = d$ if the Jth F_2 node is active and $g(y_J) = 0$ otherwise. As in ART 1, gain control (not shown) coordinates STM processing with an input presentation rate.

must be organized to maintain the original $F_1 \to F_2$ category choice, unless F_2 is actively reset by the orienting subsystem.

H. Contrast Enhancement, Noise Suppression, and Mismatch Attenuation by Nonlinear Signal Functions

A given class of analog signals may be embedded in variable levels of background noise (Fig. 1). A combination of normalization and nonlinear feedback processes within F_1 determines a noise criterion and enables the system to separate signal from noise. In particular, these processes contrast enhance the F_1 STM pattern, and hence also the learned LTM patterns. The degree of contrast enhancement and noise suppression is determined by the degree of nonlinearity in the feedback signal functions at F_1.

A nonlinear signal function operating on the sum of normalized bottom-up and top-down signals also correlates these signals, just as squaring a sum $A + B$ of two L_2-normalized vectors generates $2(1 + A \cdot B)$. Nonlinear feedback signaling hereby helps to attenuate the total activation of F_1 in response to mismatched bottom-up input and top-down expectation patterns, as well as to contrast enhance and noise suppress bottom-up input patterns. Figure 8(e) shows that the absence of nonlinearity in the F_1 feedback loop can lead to all subpatterns of a pattern being coded in the same category in conditions of low vigilance.

I. Rapid Self-Stabilization

A learning system that is unstable in general can be made more stable by making the learning rate so slow that LTM traces change little on a single input trial. In this case, many learning trials are needed to encode a fixed set of inputs. Learning in an ART system needs to be slow relative to the STM processing rate (Sec. V), but no restrictions are placed on absolute rates. Thus ART 2 is capable of stable learning in the fast learning case, in which LTM traces change so quickly that they can approach new equilibrium values on every trial. The ART 2 simulations in this article were all carried out in fast learning conditions, and rapid code self-stabilization occurs in each case. Self-stabilization is also sped up by the action of the orienting subsystem, but can also occur rapidly even without it (Figs. 4 and 8).

J. Normalization

Several different schemes may be used to normalize activation patterns across F_1. In this paper we used nonspecific inhibitory interneurons (schematized by large black disks in Fig. 6). Each such normalizer uses $O(M)$ connections where M is the number of nodes to be normalized. Alternatively, a shunting on-center off-surround network could be used as a normalizer,[9] but such a network uses $O(M^2)$ connections.

K. Local Computations

ART 2 system STM and LTM computations use only information available locally and in real time. There are no assumptions of weight transport, as in backpropagation, nor of an *a priori* input probability distribution, as in simulated annealing. Moreover, all ART 2 local equations have a simple form (Secs. V–VIII). It is the architecture as a whole that endows the model with its desirable emergent computational properties.

V. ART 2 STM Equations: F_1

The potential, or STM activity, V_i of the ith node at any one of the F_1 processing stages obeys a membrane equation[10] of the form

$$\epsilon \frac{d}{dt} V_i = -AV_i + (1 - BV_i)J_i^+ - (C + DV_i)J_i^- \qquad (1)$$

($i = 1 \ldots M$). Term J_i^+ is the total excitatory input to the ith node and J_i^- is the total inhibitory input. In the absence of all inputs, V_i decays to 0. The dimensionless parameter ϵ represents the ratio between the STM relaxation time and the LTM relaxation time. With the LTM rate $O(1)$, then

$$0 < \epsilon \ll 1. \qquad (2)$$

Also, $B \equiv 0$ and $C \equiv 0$ in the F_1 equations of the ART 2 example in Fig. 6. Thus the STM equations, in the singular form as $\epsilon \to 0$, reduce to

$$V_i = \frac{J_i^+}{A + DJ_i^-}. \qquad (3)$$

In this form, the dimensionless Eqs. (4)–(9) characterize the STM activities, p_i, q_i, u_i, v_i, w_i, and x_i, computed at F_1:

$$p_i = u_i + \sum_j g(y_j)z_{ji} \qquad (4)$$

$$q_i = \frac{p_i}{e + \|\mathbf{p}\|}, \qquad (5)$$

$$u_i = \frac{v_i}{e + \|\mathbf{v}\|}, \qquad (6)$$

$$v_i = f(x_i) + bf(q_i), \qquad (7)$$

$$w_i = I_i + au_i, \qquad (8)$$

$$x_i = \frac{w_i}{e + \|\mathbf{w}\|}, \qquad (9)$$

where $\|\mathbf{V}\|$ denotes the L_2 norm of a vector $\mathbf{V}$ and where y_j is the STM activity of the jth F_2 node. The nonlinear signal function f in Eq. (7) is typically of the form

$$f(x) = \begin{cases} \dfrac{2\theta x^2}{(x^2 + \theta^2)} & \text{if } 0 \le x \le \theta, \\ x & \text{if } x \ge \theta, \end{cases} \qquad (10)$$

which is continuously differentiable, or

$$f(x) = \begin{cases} 0 & \text{if } 0 \le x < \theta, \\ x & \text{if } x \ge \theta, \end{cases} \qquad (11)$$

which is piecewise linear. The graph of function $f(x)$ in Eq. (10) may also be shifted to the right, making $f(x) = 0$ for small x, as in Eq. (11). Since the variables x_i and q_i are always between 0 and 1 [Eqs. (5) and (9)], the function values $f(x_i)$ and $f(q_i)$ also stay between 0 and 1. Alternatively, the signal function $f(x)$ could also be chosen to saturate at high x values. This would have the effect of flattening pattern details like those in category 17 of Fig. 1, sitting on the top of an activity peak.

VI. ART 2 STM Equations: F_2

The category representation field F_2 is the same in ART 2 as in ART 1 (Ref. 3). The key properties of F_2 are contrast enhancement of the filtered $F_1 \to F_2$ input pattern, and reset, or enduring inhibition, of active F_2 nodes whenever a pattern mismatch at F_1 is large enough to activate the orienting subsystem.

Contrast enhancement is carried out by competition within F_2. Choice is the extreme case of contrast enhancement. F_2 makes a choice when the node receiving the largest total input quenches activity in all other nodes. In other words, let T_j be the summed filtered $F_1 \to F_2$ input to the jth F_2 node:

$$T_j = \sum_i p_i z_{ij} \qquad (12)$$

($j = M + 1 \ldots N$). Then F_2 is said to make a choice if the Jth F_2 node becomes maximally active, while all other nodes are inhibited, when

$$T_J = \max\{T_j : j = M + 1 \ldots N\}. \qquad (13)$$

F_2 reset may be carried out in several ways, one being use of a gated dipole field network in F_2. When a nonspecific arousal input reaches an F_2 gated dipole field, nodes are inhibited or reset (Sec. VIII) in proportion to their former STM activity levels. Moreover this inhibition endures until the bottom-up input to F_1 shuts off. Such a nonspecific arousal wave reaches F_2, via the orienting subsystem, when a sufficiently large mismatch occurs at F_1.

When F_2 makes a choice, the main elements of the gated dipole field dynamics may be characterized as

$$g(y_J) = \begin{cases} d & \text{if } T_J = \max\{T_j : \text{the } j\text{th } F_2 \text{ node has not been reset on the current trial}\}, \\ 0 & \text{otherwise.} \end{cases} \tag{14}$$

Equation (14) implies that Eq. (4) reduces to

$$p_i = \begin{cases} u_i & \text{if } F_2 \text{ is inactive,} \\ u_i + dz_{Ji} & \text{if the } J\text{th } F_2 \text{ node is active.} \end{cases} \tag{15}$$

VII.   ART 2 LTM Equations

The top-down and bottom-up LTM trace equations for ART 2 are given by

$$\text{top-down } (F_2 \to F_1): \frac{d}{dt} z_{ji} = g(y_j)[p_i - z_{ji}], \tag{16}$$

$$\text{bottom-up } (F_1 \to F_2): \frac{d}{dt} z_{ij} = g(y_j)[p_i - z_{ij}]. \tag{17}$$

If F_2 makes a choice, Eqs. (14)–(17) imply that, if the Jth F_2 node is active, then

$$\frac{d}{dt} z_{Ji} = d[p_i - z_{Ji}] = d(1-d)\left[\frac{u_i}{1-d} - z_{Ji}\right], \tag{18}$$

$$\frac{d}{dt} z_{iJ} = d[p_i - z_{iJ}] = d(1-d)\left[\frac{u_i}{1-d} - z_{iJ}\right], \tag{19}$$

with $0 < d < 1$. For all $j \neq J$, $dz_{ji}/dt = 0$ and $dz_{ij}/dt = 0$. Sections IX and XI give admissible bounds on the initial values of the LTM traces.

VIII.   ART 2 Reset Equations: the Orienting Subsystem

Since a binary pattern match may be computed by counting matched bits, ART 1 architectures do not require patterned information in the orienting subsystem (Fig. 2). In contrast, computation of an analog pattern match does require patterned information. The degree of match between an STM pattern at F_1 and an active LTM pattern is determined by the vector $\mathbf{r} = (r_1 \ldots r_M)$, where for the ART 2 architecture of Fig. 6,

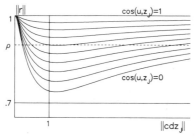

Fig. 7.   Graph of $\|\mathbf{r}\|$ as a function of $\|cd\mathbf{z}_J\|$ for values of cos $(\mathbf{u}, \mathbf{z}_J)$ between 0 and 1 and for $c = 0.1$ and $d = 0.9$. F_2 reset occurs whenever $\|\mathbf{r}\|$ falls below the vigilance parameter ρ.

$$r_i = \frac{u_i + cp_i}{e + \|\mathbf{u}\| + \|c\mathbf{p}\|}. \tag{20}$$

The orienting subsystem is assumed to reset F_2 whenever an input pattern is active and

$$\frac{\rho}{e + \|\mathbf{r}\|} > 1, \tag{21}$$

where the vigilance parameter ρ is set between 0 and 1.

For simplicity, we will henceforth consider an ART 2 system in which F_2 makes a choice and in which e is set equal to 0. Thus $\|\mathbf{x}\| = \|\mathbf{u}\| = \|\mathbf{q}\| = 1$. Simulations use the piecewise linear signal function f in Eq. (11).

IX.   Match-Reset Trade-Off: Choice of Top-Down Initial LTM Values

Vector $\mathbf{r}$ gives rise to all the properties required to satisfy the match-reset trade-off described in Sec. IV. Note first that, when the Jth F_2 node is active, Eq. (20) implies that

$$\|\mathbf{r}\| = \frac{[1 + 2\|c\mathbf{p}\| \cos(\mathbf{u},\mathbf{p}) + \|c\mathbf{p}\|^2]^{1/2}}{1 + \|c\mathbf{p}\|}, \tag{22}$$

where $\cos(\mathbf{u},\mathbf{p})$ denotes the cosine of the angle between the vector $\mathbf{u}$ and the vector $\mathbf{p}$. Also, by Eq. (15), the vector $\mathbf{p}$ equals the sum $\mathbf{u} + d\mathbf{z}_J$, where $\mathbf{z}_J \equiv (\mathbf{z}_{J1} \ldots \mathbf{z}_{JM})$ denotes the top-down vector of LTM traces projecting from the Jth F_2 node. Since $\|\mathbf{u}\| = 1$, the geometry of the vector sum $\mathbf{p} = \mathbf{u} + d\mathbf{z}_J$ implies that

$$\|\mathbf{p}\| \cos(\mathbf{u},\mathbf{p}) = 1 + \|d\mathbf{z}_J\| \cos(\mathbf{u},\mathbf{z}_J). \tag{23}$$

Also,

$$\|\mathbf{p}\| = [1 + 2\|d\mathbf{z}_J\| \cos(\mathbf{u},\mathbf{z}_J) + \|d\mathbf{z}_J\|^2]^{1/2}. \tag{24}$$

Equations (22)–(24) imply that

$$\|\mathbf{r}\| = \frac{[(1+c)^2 + 2(1+c)\|cd\mathbf{z}_J\| \cos(\mathbf{u},\mathbf{z}_J) + \|cd\mathbf{z}_J\|^2]^{1/2}}{1 + [c^2 + 2c\|cd\mathbf{z}_J\| \cos(\mathbf{u},\mathbf{z}_J) + \|cd\mathbf{z}_J\|^2]^{1/2}}. \tag{25}$$

Both numerator and denominator equal $1 + c + \|cd\mathbf{z}_J\|$ when $\cos(\mathbf{u},\mathbf{z}_J) = 1$. Thus $\|\mathbf{r}\| = 1$ when the STM pattern $\mathbf{u}$ exactly matches the LTM pattern $\mathbf{z}_J$, up to a constant multiple.

Figure 7 graphs $\|\mathbf{r}\|$ as a function of $\|cd\mathbf{z}_J\|$ for various values of $\cos(\mathbf{u},\mathbf{z}_J)$. The Jth F_2 node remains active only if $\rho \leq \|\mathbf{r}\|$. Since $\rho < 1$, Fig. 7 shows that this will occur either if $\cos(\mathbf{u},\mathbf{z}_J)$ is close to 1 or if $\|\mathbf{z}_J\|$ is close to 0. That is, no reset occurs if the STM vector $\mathbf{u}$ is nearly parallel to the LTM vector $\mathbf{z}_J$ or if the top-down LTM traces z_{Ji} are all small. By Eq. (18), $\mathbf{z}_J$ becomes parallel to $\mathbf{u}$ during learning, thus inhibiting reset. Reset must also be inhibited, however, while a new category is being established. Figure 7 shows that this can be accomplished by making all $\|\mathbf{z}_j\|$ small before any learning occurs; in particular, we let the top-down initial LTM values satisfy

$$z_{ji}(0) = 0, \tag{26}$$

for $i = 1 \ldots M$ and $j = M + 1 \ldots N$.

Condition (26) ensures that no reset occurs when an uncommitted F_2 node first becomes active. Hence learning can begin. Moreover, the learning rule (18) and the LTM initial value rule (26) together imply that z_J remains parallel to u as learning proceeds, so $\|r(t)\| \equiv 1$. Thus no reset ever occurs during a trial in which an uncommitted F_2 node is first activated.

X. Learning Increases Mismatch Sensitivity and Confirms Category Choice

Figure 7 suggests how to implement the property that learning increases sensitivity to mismatches between bottom-up and top-down patterns. Figure 7 indicates that, for fixed $\cos(u, z_J)$, $\|r\|$ is a decreasing function of $\|cd z_J\|$ for $\|cd z_J\| \le 1$. In fact, in the limit as $c \to 0$, the minimum of each curve approaches the line $\|cd z_J\| = 1$. By Eqs. (18) and (26), $\|z_J\| < 1/(1 - d)$ and $\|z_J\| \to 1/(1 - d)$ during learning. Therefore implementation of the property that learning increases mismatch sensitivity translates into the parameter constraint

$$\frac{cd}{1 - d} \le 1. \tag{27}$$

The closer the ratio $cd/(1 - d)$ is chosen to 1 the more sensitive the system is to mismatches, all other things being equal.

Parameter constraint (27) helps to ensure that learning on a given trial confirms the initial category choice on that trial. To see this note that, if an established category is chosen, $\|z_J\|$ is close to $1/(1 - d)$ at the beginning and end of a fast learning trial. However $\|z_J\|$ typically decreases and then increases during a learning trial. Therefore if $cd/(1 - d)$ were >1, the reset inequality (21) could be satisfied while $\|z_J\|$ was decreasing. Thus, without (27), it would be difficult to rule out the possibility of unexpected F_2 reset in the middle of a learning trial.

XI. Choosing a New Category: Bottom-Up LTM Initial Values

Section IX dicusses the fact that the top-down initial LTM values $z_{ij}(0)$ need to be chosen small, or else top-down LTM read-out by an uncommitted node could lead to immediate F_2 reset rather than learning of a new category. The bottom-up LTM initial values $z_{ij}(0)$ also need to be chosen small, but for different reasons.

Let $z^J \equiv (z_{1J} \ldots z_{MJ})$ denote the bottom up vector of LTM traces that project to the Jth F_2 node. Equation (19) implies that $\|z^J\| \to 1/(1 - d)$ during learning. If $\|z^J(0)\|$ were chosen greater than $1/(1 - d)$, an input that first chose an uncommitted node could switch to other uncommitted nodes in the middle of a learning trial. It is thus necessary to require that

$$\|z^J(0)\| \le \frac{1}{1 - d}. \tag{28}$$

Inequality (28) implies that if each $z^J(0)$ is uniform, each LTM trace must satisfy the constraint

$$z_{ij}(0) \le \frac{1}{(1 - d)\sqrt{M}} \tag{29}$$

for $i = 1 \ldots M$ and $j = M + 1 \ldots N$. Alternatively, random numbers or trained patterns could be taken as initial LTM values. If bottom-up input is the sole source of F_2 activation, at least some $z_{iJ}(0)$ values need to be chosen positive if the Jth F_2 node is ever to become active.

Choosing equality in (29) biases the ART 2 system as much as possible toward choosing uncommitted nodes. A typical input would search only those nodes with which it is fairly well matched, and then go directly to an uncommitted node. If no learned category representation forms a good match, an uncommitted node will be directly accessed. Setting the initial bottom-up LTM trace values as large as possible, therefore, helps to stabilize the ART 2 network by ensuring that the system will form a new category, rather than recode an established but badly mismatched one, when vigilance is too low to prevent recoding by active reset via the orienting subsystem. Thus construction of the instability example in Fig. 8(c) requires, in addition to the removal of the orienting subsystem and the internal feedback at F_1, that the initial bottom-up LTM trace values be significantly less than the maximum allowed by condition (29).

XII. Stability-Plasticity Trade-Off

ART 2 design principles permit arbitrary sequences of patterns to be encoded during arbitrarily long input trials, and the ability of the LTM traces to learn does not decrease with time. Some internal mechanism must therefore buffer established ART category structures against ceaseless recoding by new input patterns. ART 1 architectures buffer category structures by means of the 2/3 Rule for pattern matching (Fig. 5). During matching, an F_1 node in ART 1 can remain active only if it receives significant inputs both bottom-up and top-down. ART 1 implements the 2/3 Rule using an inhibitory attentional gain control signal that is read out with the top-down LTM vector (Fig. 2).

ART 2 architectures implement a weak version of the 2/3 Rule in which, during matching, an F_1 node can remain active only if it receives significant top-down input. It is possible, however, for a node receiving large top-down input to remain stored in memory even if bottom-up input to that node is absent on a given trial. The corresponding feature, which had been encoded as significant by prior exemplars, would hence remain part of the category representation although unmatched in the active exemplar. It would, moreover, be partially restored in STM. During learning, the relative importance of that feature would decline, but it would not necessarily be eliminated. However, a feature consistently absent from most category exemplars would eventually be removed from the category's expectation pattern z_J. The ART 2 matching rule implies that the feature would then not be relearned; if present in a given exemplar, it would be treated as noise.

All parts of the F_1 feedback loop in Fig. 6 work together to implement this ART 2 matching rule. The five simulations in Fig. 8 illustrate the roles of different components of the ART 2 system. Each column shows the ART 2 response to a sequence of four input patterns (A, B, C, and D) presented in the order $ABCAD$ on trials 1–5 and again on trials 6–10. The ART 2 system dynamics established on the second round are stable, and thus would be repeated indefinitely if the same input sequence was repeated. Parameters c and d are held fixed throughout. The simulations explore the role of the remaining parameters, a, b, θ, and ρ.

Figure 8(a) shows a simulation with parameters a, b, and θ in a normal range, but with the vigilance parameter, ρ, set so high that the four inputs establish four categories. Two graphs are depicted for each trial: the top graph shows the input pattern ($I = A$, B, C, or D) and the bottom graph shows the LTM expectation pattern ($\mathbf{z}_J$) at the end of the trial. The category number is shown beside the graph of $\mathbf{z}_J$. On trial 1, input A establishes category 1. Note that pattern A is contrast enhanced in LTM, due to the fact that the pattern troughs are below the noise level defined by the signal threshold θ [Eqs. (7) and (11)]. In fact, θ is set equal to $1/\sqrt{M}$. This is the level at which uniform patterns are treated as pure noise but any nonuniform pattern can be contrast enhanced and stored in STM.

On trial 2, pattern B, which shares all its features with A, first searches category 1. The high vigilance level leads to F_2 reset, and B establishes the new category 2. On trial 3, pattern C also searches category 1; having nothing in common with pattern B, it then goes directly to an uncommitted node and establishes category 3. When A is again presented on trial 4, it directly accesses its original category 1. On trial 5, pattern D searches category 3, then category 1, then establishes the new category 4. Learning is stabilized on the first trial. Thus, on the second set of trials, A, B, C, and D choose the same categories as before, but without any search. Hereafter, each input directly accesses its category node. The bottom portion of the column summarizes the category structure established on trials 6–10. Pattern A is shown twice because it is presented twice every 5 trials. The categorization is stable, or consistent, in the sense that each pattern recognizes its unique category every time it appears.

For the four remaining simulations in Figs. 8(b)–(e), the vigilance parameter ρ is chosen so small that no search can ever occur. Whatever category is chosen first by the bottom-up input must accept and learn the matched F_1 STM pattern for as long as the input remains active. By eliminating reset by choosing vigilance low, one can directly test how much top-down matching can accomplish on its own. For example, in Fig. 8(b), low vigilance enables pattern B to be accepted on trial 2 into the category 1 that was established by pattern A on trial 1. By the weak 2/3 Rule, the critical feature pattern learned in response to B causes the collapse of LTM traces that do not correspond to B. When pattern A is presented again on trial 4, it is recoded into the category 2 that was established by pattern C on trial 3, since A is more similar to the critical feature pattern established by pattern C than to the critical feature pattern established jointly by pattern B and itself. Thereafter, the code is stable

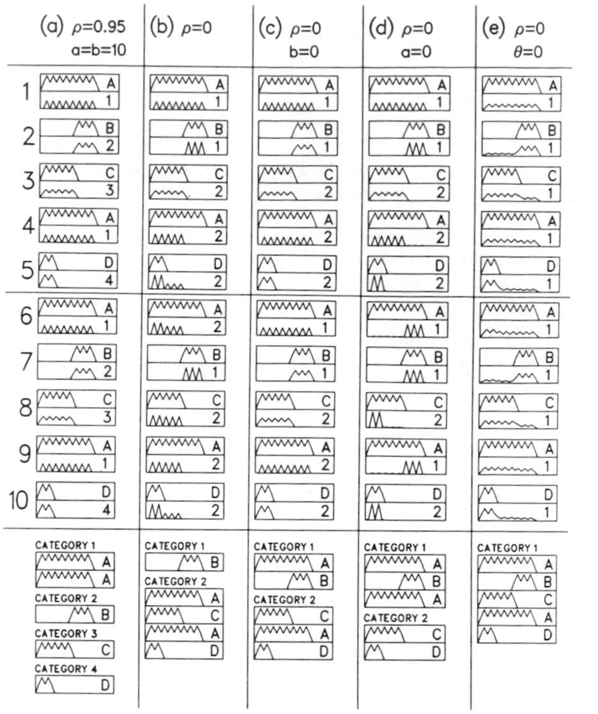

Fig. 8. ART 2 matching processes. The ART 2 system of Fig. 6 was used to generate the five simulations shown in columns (a)–(e). Each column shows the first ten simulation trials, in which four input patterns (A, B, C, D) are presented in order $ABCAD$ on trials 1–5, and again on trials 6–10. Details are given in the text (Sec. XII). (a) The full ART 2 system, with $\rho = 0.95$, separates the four inputs into four categories. Search occurs on trials 1–5; thereafter each input directly accesses its category representation. Parameters $a = 10$, $b = 10$, $c = 0.1$, $d = 0.9$, $\theta = 0.2$, and $M = 25$. The initial $z_{ij}(0)$ values, 1, are half of the maximum, 2, allowed by constraint (27). The piecewise linear signal function (11) is used throughout. (b) Vigilance is here set so low ($\rho = 0$) that no search can ever occur. The coarse category structure established on trials 6–10 is, however, stable and consistent. All system parameters except ρ are as in (a). (c) With $b = 0$, the ART 2 system here generates an unstable, or inconsistent, category structure. Namely, input A goes alternatively to categories 1 and 2, and will continue to do so for as long as the sequence $ABCAD$ repeats. All parameters except b are as in (b). Similar instability can occur when d is close to 0. (d) With $a = 0$, the ART 2 matching process differs from that which occurs when a is large; namely, the input pattern I is stronger, relative to the top-down pattern $\mathbf{z}_J$, than in (b). All parameters except a are as in (b). Similar processing occurs when d is small (~ 0.1) but not close to 0. (e) With $\theta = 0$, the F_1 signal function f becomes linear. Without the noise suppression/contrast enhancement provided by a nonlinear f, the completely different inputs B and D are here placed in a single category. All parameters except θ are as in (b).

under periodic presentation of the sequence $ABCAD$.

Note, however, that patterns A and D are classified together, whereas B is not, even though B is more similar to A than is D. This is a consequence of eliminating reset and of fast learning during periodic presentation. In particular, the critical feature pattern learned on trial 10 illustrates the tendency for D to attenuate LTM traces outside its range. Were this tendency strengthened by increasing contrast or changing presentation order, D would have also been classified separately from A. This simulation thus shows how the ART 2 system can self-stabilize its learning in the absence of reset. In combination with Fig. 8(a), it also illustrates how active reset and search can generate stable categories which better reflect the similarity relationships among the input patterns.

Figure 8(b) also illustrates some finer details of ART 2 matching properties. Here, the F_1 feedback parameters a and b [see Eqs. (7) and (8) and Fig. 6] are large enough so that a feature once removed from the category representation (z_J) is not reinstated even if present in a category exemplar (I). Thus on trial 4, features present in the right-hand portion of pattern A are not encoded in the LTM pattern of category 2, due to the weak 2/3 Rule. However on trial 5, features absent from pattern D but initially coded in z_J are nevertheless able to remain coded, although they are weakened. Since these features are again present in the exemplars of category 2 on trials 6, 8, and 9, they are periodically restored in LTM.

Finally, compare trial 7 in Fig. 8(b) with trial 7 in Fig. 8(a). In each case pattern B has been established as the sole exemplar of a category. However in Fig. 8(b) category 1 had contained pattern A on one previous trial. Memory of pattern A persists in the contrast-enhanced LTM pattern in Fig. 8(b). If the input set were more complex, this difference in learning history could possibly lead to subsequent differences in category structure.

Figure 8(c) illustrates that unstable coding can occur when the feedback parameter b is set equal to zero. Pattern A is placed in category 1 on trials 1, 6, etc.; and in category 2 on trials 4, 9, etc. It jumps to a new category every time it appears. With fast learning, previous LTM patterns are washed away by subsequent input patterns. Failure of the weak 2/3 Rule on trials 4, 6, 9, etc., combined with the absence of the orienting subsystem and with the small initial bottom-up LTM values, leads to the instability. A large class of similar input sequences that share the subset–superset relationships of patterns A, B, C, and D also leads to unstable coding. However, if the class of input patterns were suitably restricted or if slow learning is imposed on each trial, satisfactory results could still be obtained. Similar unstable dynamics occur if the top-down $F_2 \to F_1$ feedback parameter (d), instead of the internal F_1 feedback parameter (b), is chosen small (see Fig. 6).

Figure 8(d) illustrates how the lower feedback loop of the F_1 circuit in Fig. 6 also buffers learned category representations against unstable recording by bottom-up inputs. In this simulation, parameter a is set equal to 0. Similar dynamics occur if the top-down $F_2 \to F_1$ feedback parameter (d) is small, but not so small that instability occurs. Setting a equal to 0 (or making d small) has the effect of weakening the importance of the $F_2 \to F_1$ expectation feedback relative to the bot-tom-up input. In Fig. 8(d), therefore, the weak 2/3 Rule is partially violated. Note in particular the slight reinstatement on trials 4, 6, 8, and 9 of features present in I but not z_J at the start of the trial. An ART 2 system with a large and d close to 1 is better protected against potential instability than is the system of Fig. 8(d).

Finally, Fig. 8(e) illustrates the role of nonlinearity in the F_1 feedback loop of ART 2. Here, the threshold parameter θ is set equal to 0 [Eq. (11)] so that the signal function f in Eq. (7) and Fig. 6 is linear. Level F_1 therefore loses the properties of contrast enhancement and noise suppression. Even though the feedback parameters a, b, and d are all large, trial 2 shows that mismatched features in I, while attenuated, are never eliminated. The result is that, given the zero vigilance value, completely mismatched patterns, such as B and D, can be placed in the same category because they are parts of the superset pattern A that established the category.

XIII. Alternative ART 2 Architectures

Two alternative ART 2 models are shown in Figs. 9 and 10. In Fig. 9, the orienting subsystem pattern (r) is also part of F_1. In this model, $q = p - u$ so that $q = dz_J$ if the Jth F_2 node is active. Thus r directly computes the cosine of the angle between u and z_J. In contrast, vector r in the F_2 model of Fig. 6 indirectly computes this angle by computing the angle between u and p, which is a linear combination of u and z_J. In addition the nonlinear signal function f appears twice in the lower F_1 loop in Fig. 9; in Fig. 6, f appears once in each F_1 loop, so that all matched input pathways projecting to any given node have the same signal function. Dynamics of the two ART 2 systems are similar. Equations for the ART 2 model of Fig. 9 are given in Ref. 5.

The ART 2 model in Fig. 10 is also similar to the one in Fig. 6, except here the input vector I is the output of a preprocessing stage that imitates the lower and upper loops of F_1. This allows I itself to be used as an input to the orienting subsystem, rather than the vector u, which is more like the architecture of ART 1 (Fig. 2). The advantage of this is that I does not change when F_2 becomes active, and so provides a more stable input to the orienting subsystem throughout the trial than does u in Fig. 6. Figure 11 summarizes one category structure established by the ART 2 system of Fig. 10. All parameters, including vigilance, are the same in the simulations of Fig. 3 and 11. The input patterns depicted in Fig. 11 are the result of preprocessing the inputs of Fig. 3. Table I shows which categories of Fig. 3 correspond to categories in Fig. 11. Except for categories 1 and 7 of Fig. 3, which are each split into two in Fig. 11, the category structure generated by the two models is identical.

We wish to thank Cynthia Suchta and Carol Yana-kakis for their valuable assistance in the preparation of the manuscript.

This research was supported in part by the Air Force Office of Scientific Research (AFOSR F49620-86-C-

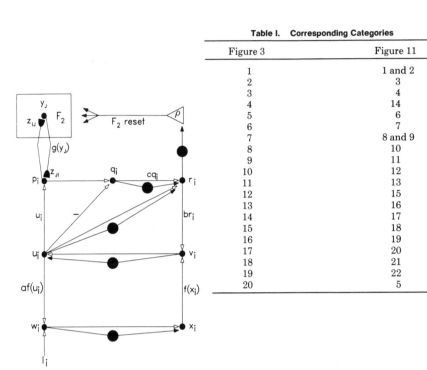

Table I.	Corresponding Categories
Figure 3	Figure 11
1	1 and 2
2	3
3	4
4	14
5	6
6	7
7	8 and 9
8	10
9	11
10	12
11	13
12	15
13	16
14	17
15	18
16	19
17	20
18	21
19	22
20	5

Fig. 10. Alternative ART 2 architecture.

Fig. 9. Alternative ART 2 architecture.

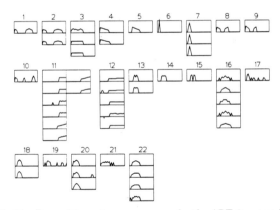

Fig. 11. Recognition category summary for the ART 2 system in Fig. 10. System parameters and vigilance level are the same as in Fig. 3, which was generated using the ART 2 model of Fig. 6. Because of the constant I input to the orienting subsystem, the ART 2 system of Fig. 10 is here seen to be slightly more sensitive to pattern mismatch at a given vigilance level, all other things being equal.

0037 and AFOSR 85-0149), the Army Research Office (ARO DAAG-29-85-K-0095), and the National Science Foundation [NSF DMS-86-11959 (G.A.C.) and NSF IRI-84-17756 (S.G.)].

Gail Carpenter also works in the Department of Mathematics of Northeastern University.

References

1. S. Grossberg, "Adaptive Pattern Classification and Universal Recoding, II: Feedback, Expectation, Olfaction, and Illusions," Biol. Cybern. **23,** 187 (1976).

2. G. A. Carpenter and S. Grossberg, "Category Learning and Adaptive Pattern Recognition: a Neural Network Model," in *Proceedings, Third Army Conference on Applied Mathematics and Computing*, ARO Report 86-1 (1985), pp. 37–56.

3. G. A. Carpenter and S. Grossberg, "A Massively Parallel Architecture for a Self-Organizing Neural Pattern Recognition Machine," Comput. Vision Graphics Image Process. **37,** 54 (1987).

4. S. Grossberg, "Competitive Learning: from Interactive Activation to Adaptive Resonance," Cognitive Sci. **11,** 23 (1987).

5. G. A. Carpenter and S. Grossberg, "ART 2: Stable Self-Organization of Pattern Recognition Codes for Analog Input Patterns," in *Proceedings First International Conference on Neural Networks*, San Diego (IEEE, New York, 1987).

6. G. A. Carpenter and S. Grossberg, "Invariant Pattern Recognition and Recall by an Attentive Self-Organizing ART Architecture in a Nonstationary World," in *Proceedings First International Conference on Neural Networks*, San Diego (IEEE, New York, 1987).

7. K. Hartley, "Seeing the Need for ART", Sci. News **132,** 14 (1987).

8. P. Kolodzy, "Multidimensional Machine Vision Using Neural Networks," in *Proceedings, First International Conference on Neural Networks*, San Diego (IEEE, New York, 1987).

9. S. Grossberg, *Studies of Mind and Brain: Neural Principles of Learning, Perception, Development, Cognition, and Motor Control* (Reidel, Boston, 1982).

10. A. L. Hodgkin and A. F. Huxley, "A Quantitative Description of Membrane Current and Its Applications to Conduction and Excitation in Nerve," J. Physiol. London **117,** 500 (1952).

11
Introduction

(1988)
Bart Kosko

Bidirectional associative memories
IEEE Transactions on Systems, Man and Cybernetics 18: 49–60

The bidirectional associative memory, known commonly as BAM, is, along with the adaptive resonance (ART) models, (Carpenter and Grossberg, paper 10), the best known of what are currently called *resonance* models in neural networks. This paper also contains an instructive example of the analysis of a simple neural network.

The basic idea of both resonance models is that information, represented as activity patterns, is passed back and forth between two groups of cells until an overall stable system state (or stable limit cycle) is reached. Learning in the network has the goal of making sure that the stable states are appropriate. The ART models contain, in addition, a complex set of internal control structures, usually other networks, to control automatically network learning, retrieval, and dynamics. The BAM model was deliberately constructed to be as simple as possible and still contain the essential desirable features of resonance. Therefore the BAM model is far simpler in structure than ART and much easier to understand and analyze because it assumes learning and dynamics are explicitly controlled by the network designer.

Kosko's BAM model is a pattern associator with feedback dynamics. It is a system composed of two groups of units, with a projection from the first group to the second and a projection from the second to the first. Kosko specifically wants to model associations between pairs of patterns, A and B, and the architecture is designed to accomplish this. Traditional pattern associators place pattern A on the first set, pattern B on the second set, and modify connection strengths between A and B so that later, when pattern A occurs on the first set, pattern B will appear at the second set. Such a system forms unidirectional associations, so that pattern A gives rise to B, but, unless specifically learned, B will not give rise to A. Let us assume that there is a set of connections from the second set of units to the first, and that these backward connections associate B with A. Suppose A is input to the first set of units. Then a pattern close to B will be produced at the second set. When this pattern is then fed back to the first set, something like A will be produced, serving as a new input to the upward association. If the system works correctly, the patterns will cycle: At one step a pattern close to A will appear on the first group of units, and at the next step a pattern close to B will appear on the second set of units. These cycling patterns will be stable and may be a closer approximation to the true stored B, say, than the initial first pass through the system.

If one assumes nonlinearities in the system, for example, clipping or thresholding, or partial connectivity between the groups of units, then analysis of the system can get complex. However, one important BAM architecture can be analyzed by the use of the system energy (Lyapunov) functions, popularized by Hopfield. Suppose we assume that the backward connections are the matrix *transpose* of the upward connections. (*Transpose* in a matrix interchanges rows and columns.) For the stability analysis Kosko assumes that the pattern elements are binary, that is, either on or off, depending on whether their input activities are above or below a threshold. Because this is a feedback system, amplitude information will get distorted anyway. Then, using an energy analysis, with a Lyapunov function similar to Hopfield's, Kosko shows that a BAM composed of a matrix and its transpose is stable, for any connection matrix.

In the case of outer product (Hebbian) associators, it is easy to see that the transpose will be a good thing to use. Because the outer product associators are storing associations between patterns f and g in the form gf^T, the transpose matrix will store the association between g and f because that outer product will be fg^T.

Kosko makes an interesting technical point. Many nonlinear, energy minimizing models are autoassociators (for example, the Hopfield networks and the BSB model; papers 22, 27, 35 in *Neurocomputing: Foundations of Research*). The BAM could be viewed as an autoassociator with large blocks of the matrix being set to zero. Then both patterns A and B could be assumed to be part of the same state vector, and both the Lyapunov function used and the analysis can be seen to be closely related to the Hopfield model. Cohen and Grossberg (1983) discuss stability for a large class of nonlinear feedback models.

Although related to the ART models in its use of a metaphorical resonance between two groups of units, the actual networks are different in detail. One major difference is that the ART models, by design, restrict one group of units (their top layer of nodes) to a grandmother cell representation, so that learned input patterns activate only *one* unit in the other group of units. Activity of this unit in the ART formalism represents a class or category. Kosko makes no such assumption about the form taken by the patterns on the groups of units. Dynamical system models with stable points of any form could in general represent categories as stable points and their associated basins of attractions.

Kosko also provides an appendix discussing the often noted but rarely emphasized observation that binary units used in networks work better in almost all circumstances if their values are taken as +1 and −1 rather than 0 and 1.

Reference

M.A. Cohen and S. Grossberg (1983), Absolute stability of global pattern formation and parallel memory storage by competitive neural networks. *IEEE Transactions on Systems, Man and Cybernetics* SMC-13: 815–826.

(1988)

Bart Kosko

Bidirectional associative memories

IEEE Transactions on Systems, Man and Cybernetics 18: 49–60

Abstract —Stability and encoding properties of two-layer nonlinear feedback neural networks are examined. Bidirectionality, forward and backward information flow, is introduced in neural nets to produce two-way associative search for stored associations (A_i, B_i). Passing information through M gives one direction; passing it through its transpose M^T gives the other. A bidirectional associative memory (BAM) behaves as a hetero-associative content addressable memory (CAM), storing and recalling the vector pairs $(A_1, B_1), \cdots, (A_m, B_m)$, where $A \in \{0,1\}^n$ and $B \in \{0,1\}^p$. We prove that *every* n-by-p matrix M is a bidirectionally stable heteroassociative CAM for both binary/bipolar and continuous neurons a_i and b_j. When the BAM neurons are activated, the network quickly evolves to a stable state of two-pattern reverberation, or resonance. The stable reverberation corresponds to a system energy local minimum. Heteroassociative information is encoded in a BAM by summing correlation matrices. The BAM storage capacity for reliable recall is roughly $m < \min(n, p)$. No more heteroassociative pairs can be reliably stored and recalled than the lesser of the dimensions of the pattern spaces $\{0,1\}^n$ and $\{0,1\}^p$. The Appendix shows that it is better on average to use bipolar $\{-1,1\}$ coding than binary $\{0,1\}$ coding of heteroassociative pairs (A_i, B_i). BAM encoding and decoding are combined in the adaptive BAM, which extends global bidirectional stability to realtime unsupervised learning. Temporal patterns $(A_1, \cdots, A_m)$ are represented as ordered lists of binary/bipolar vectors and stored in a temporal associative memory (TAM) n-by-n matrix M as a limit cycle of the dynamical system. Forward recall proceeds through M, backward recall through M^T. Temporal patterns are stored by summing contiguous bipolar correlation matrices, $X_1^T X_2 + \cdots + X_{m-1}^T X_m$, generalizing the BAM storage procedure. This temporal encoding scheme is seen to be equivalent to a form of Grossberg outstar avalanche coding for spatiotemporal patterns. The storage capacity is $m = m_1 + \cdots + m_k < n$, where m_j is the length of the jth temporal pattern and n is the dimension of the spatial pattern space. Limit cycles $(A_1, \cdots, A_m, A_1)$ are shown to be stored in local energy minima of the binary state space $\{0,1\}^n$.

I. Storing Paired and Temporal Patterns

HOW CAN paired-data associations (A_i, B_i) be stored and recalled in a two-layer nonlinear feedback dynamical system? What is the minimal neural network that achieves this? We show that the introduction of bidirectionality, forward and backward associative search for stored associations (A_i, B_i), extends the symmetric unidirectional autoassociators [30] of Cohen and Grossberg [7] and Hopfield [24], [25]. *Every* real matrix is both a discrete and continuous bidirectionally stable associative memory. The bidirectional associative memory (BAM) is the minimal two-layer nonlinear feedback network. Information passes

Manuscript received December 3, 1986; revised November 3, 1987. This work was supported in part by the Air Force Office of Scientific Research under Contract F49620-86-C-0070, and by the Advanced Research Projects Agency of the Department of Defense, ARPA Order 5794.

The author is with the Department of Electrical Engineering, Systems, Signal, and Information Processing Institute, University of Southern California, Los Angeles, CA 90089.

IEEE Log Number 8718862.

forward from one neuron field to the other by passing through the connection matrix M. Information passes backward through the matrix transpose M^T. All other two-layer networks require more information in the form of backward connections N different from M^T. The underlying mathematics are closely related to the properties of adjoint operators in function spaces, in particular how quadratic forms are essentially linearized by real matrices and their adjoints (transposes).

Since every matrix M is bidirectionally stable, we suspect that gradually changes due to learning in M will result in stability. We show that this is so quite naturally for real-time unsupervised learning. This extends Lyapunov convergence of neural networks for the first time to learning.

The neural network interpretation of a BAM is a two-layer hierarchy of symmetrically connected neurons. When the neurons are activated, the network quickly evolves to a stable state of two-pattern reverberation. The stable reverberation corresponds to a system energy local minimum. In the learning or adaptive BAM, the stable reverberation of a pattern (A_i, B_i) across the two fields of neurons seeps pattern information into the long-term memory connections M, allowing input associations (A_i, B_i) to dig their own energy wells in which to reverberate.

Temporal patterns are sequences of spatial patterns. Recalled temporal patterns are limit cycles. For instance, a sequence of binary vectors can represent a harmonized melody. A given note or chord of the melody is often sufficient to recollect the rest of the melody, to "name that tune." The same note or chord can be made to trigger the dual bidirectional memory to continue (recall) the rest of the melody backwards to the start—a whistling feat worthy of Mozart or Bach! Limit cycles can also be shown to be energy minimizers of simple networks of synchronous on–off neurons.

The forward and backward directionality of BAM correlation encoding naturally extends to the encoding of temporal patterns or limit cycles. The correlation encoding algorithm is a discrete approximation of Hebbian learning, in particular, a type of Grossberg outstar avalanche [9]–[12].

II. Every Matrix is Bidirectionally Stable

Traditional associative memories are *unidirectional*. Vector patterns $A_1, A_2, \cdots, A_m$ are stored in a matrix memory

M. Input pattern *A* is presented to the memory by performing the multiplication *AM* and some subsequent nonlinear operation, such as thresholding, with resulting output *A'*. *A'* is either accepted as the recollection or fedback into *M*, which produces *A''*, and so on. A stable memory will eventually produce a fixed output A_f. If the memory is a proper content addressable memory (CAM), then A_f should be one of the stored patterns $A_1, \cdots, A_m$. This feedback procedure behaves as if input *A* was unidirectionally fed through a chain of *Ms*: $A \to M \to A' \to M \to A'' \to M \to \cdots \to A_f \to M \to A_f \to \cdots$.

Unidirectional CAM's are *autoassociative* [28]–[30]. Pieces of patterns recall entire patterns. In effect, autoassociative memories store the redundant pairs (A_1, A_1), $(A_2, A_2), \cdots, (A_m, A_m)$. In general, associative memories are *heteroassociative*. They store pairs of different data: $(A_1, B_1), (A_2, B_2), \cdots, (A_m, B_m)$. A_i and B_i are vectors in different vector spaces. For instance, if A_i and B_i are binary and hence depict sets, they may come from the respective vector spaces $\{0,1\}^n$ and $\{0,1\}^p$. If they are unit–interval valued and hence depict fuzzy sets [38], they may come from $[0,1]^n$ and $[0,1]^p$.

Heteroassociative memories are usually used as "one-shot" memories. *A* is presented to *M*, *B* is output, and the process is finished. Hopefully, *B* will be closer to stored pattern B_i than to all other stored patterns B_j if the input *A* is closest to stored pattern A_i. Kohonen [28]–[30] has shown how to guarantee this for matrix memories by using pseudoinverses as optimal orthogonal projections. For instance, *M* will always recall B_i when presented with A_i if all the stored input patterns A_i are orthogonal.

What is the minimal nonlinear feedback heteroassociative memory that stores and accurately recalls binary associations (A_i, B_i)? Consider the chain $A \to M \to B$. Suppose *A* is closer to A_i than to all the other stored input patterns A_j. Suppose the memory *M* is sufficiently reliable so that the recollection *B* is relatively close to B_i. Suppose further that *M* is an *n*-by-*p* matrix memory. We would like to somehow feedback *B* through the memory to increase the accuracy of the final recollection. The simplest way to do this is to multiply *B* by some *p*-by-*n* matrix memory (then threshold, say), and the simplest such memory is the transpose (adjoint) of M, M^T. Whether the network is implemented electrically, optically, or biologically, M^T is locally available information if *M* is. Any other feedback scheme requires additional information in the form of a matrix *p*-by-*n* matrix *N* distinct from M^T. This gives the new chain $B \to M^T \to A'$, where, hopefully, *A'* is at least as close to A_i as *A* is. We can then reverse direction again and feed *A'* through *M*: $A' \to M \to B'$. Continuing this *bidirectional* process, we produce a sequence of paired approximations to the stored pair (A_i, B_i): $(A, B), (A', B'), (A'', B''), (A''', B'''), \cdots$. Ideally, this sequence will quickly converge to some fixed pair (A_f, B_f), and this fixed pair will be (A_i, B_i) or nearly so.

A *bidirectional associative memory* (BAM) behaves as a heteroassociative CAM if it is represented by the chain of recollection:

$$A \to M \to B$$
$$A' \leftarrow M^T \leftarrow B$$
$$A' \to M \to B'$$
$$A'' \leftarrow M^T \leftarrow B'$$
$$\cdot$$
$$\cdot$$
$$\cdot$$
$$A_i \to M \to B_i$$
$$A_i \leftarrow M^T \leftarrow B_i$$
$$\cdot$$
$$\cdot$$
$$\cdot$$

This BAM chain makes explicit that a fixed pair (A_f, B_f) corresponds to a stable network reverberation or resonance, in the spirit of Grossberg's adaptive resonance [5], [6], [16]–[20]. It also makes clear that a fixed point A_f of a symmetric autoassociative memory is a fixed pair (A_f, A_f) of a BAM. On the contrary, a BAM, indeed any heteroassociator, can be viewed as a symmetrized augmented autoassociator with connection matrix made up of zero block diagonal matrices, and with *M* and M^T nonzero off-diagonal matrices, and $C_i = [A_i | B_i]$.

The fixed or stable points of autoassociative (autocorrelation) memories are often described as rocks on a stretched rubber sheet. An input pattern then behaves as a ballbearing on the rubber sheet as it minimizes its potential energy subject to frictional damping. Hecht–Nielsen [21] even defines artificial neural systems or neurocomputers as *programmable* dissipative dynamical systems. BAM fixed points are harder to visualize. Perhaps a frictionally damped pendulum dynamical system captures the back-and-forth operations of $A \to M$ and $M^T \leftarrow B$, or perhaps a product–space ball bearing rolling into product–space potential energy wells.

A pair (A, B) defines the *state* of the BAM *M*. We prove stability by identifying a Lyapunov or *energy* function *E* with each state (A, B). In the autoassociative case when *M* is symmetric *and* zero diagonal, Hopfield [24], [25] has identified an appropriate *E* by $E(A) = -AMA^T$ (actually, Hopfield uses half this quantity). We review Hopfield's [24], [35], [37] argument to prove unidirectional stability for zero–diagonal symmetric matrices in asynchronous operation. We will then generalize this proof technique to establish bidirectional stability of arbitrary matrices. Equation (21) generalizes this proof to a spectrum of asynchronous BAM update strategies.

Unidirectional stability follows since if $\Delta E = E_2 - E_1$ is caused by the *k*th neuron's state change, $\Delta a_k = a_{k2} - a_{k1}$; then *E* can be expanded as

$$E(A) = -\sum_{i \neq k} \sum_{j \neq k} a_i a_j m_{ij} - a_k \sum_j a_j m_{kj} - a_k \sum_i a_i m_{ik} \tag{1}$$

so that taking the difference $E_2 - E_1$ and dividing by Δa_k

gives

$$\frac{\Delta E}{\Delta a_k} = -\sum_j a_j m_{kj} - \sum_i a_i m_{ik}$$

$$= -AM_k^T - AM^k \qquad (2)$$

where M_k is the kth row of M, M^k is the kth column. If M is symmetric, the right side of (2) is simply $-2AM^k$. AM^k is the input activation sum to neuron a_k. As in the classical McCulloch–Pitts [34] bivalent neuron model, a_k thresholds to $+1$ if $AM^k > 0$, to -1 if $AM^k < 0$. Hence Δa_k and AM_k agree in sign, and hence their product is positive (or zero). Hence $\Delta E = -2\Delta a_k(AM^k) < 0$. Since E is bounded, the unidirectional procedure converges on some A_f such that $E(A_f)$ is a local energy minimum.

The unidirectional autoassociative CAM procedure is in general unstable if M is not symmetric. For then the term AM_k^T in (2) is the output activation sum from a_k to the other neurons, and, in general, $AM_k^T \neq AM^k$. If the magnitude of the output sum exceeds the magnitude of the input sum and the two sums disagree in sign, $\Delta E > 0$ occurs. The unidirectional CAM procedure is no longer a nearest neighbor classifier. Oscillation occurs.

We propose the potential function

$$E(A, B) = -1/2\,AMB^T - 1/2\,BM^TA^T \qquad (3)$$

as the BAM system energy of state (A, B). Observe that $BM^TA^T = B(AM)^T = (AMB^T)^T = AMB^T$. The last equality follows since, trivially, the transpose of a scalar equals the scalar. Hence (3) is equivalent to

$$E(A, B) = -AMB^T. \qquad (4)$$

This establishes that the BAM system energy is a well-defined concept since $E(A, B) = E(B, A)$ and makes clear that the Hopfield autoassociative energy corresponds to the special case when $B = A$. Analogously, if a two-dimensional pendulum has a stable equilibrium at the vertical, then the energy of the pendulum at a given angle is the same whether the angle is measured clockwise or counterclockwise from the vertical. Moreover, the equality $E(A, B) = E(B, A)$ holds even though the neurons in both the A and B networks behave asynchronously.

The BAM recall procedure is a nonlinear feedback procedure. Each neuron a_i in neuron population or field A and each neuron b_j in B independently and asynchronously (or synchronously) examines its input sum from the neurons in the other population, then changes state or not according to whether the input sum exceeds, equals, or falls short of the threshold. Hence we make the neuroclassical assumption that each neuron is either on $(+1)$ or off $(0$ or $-1)$ according to whether its input sum exceeds or falls short of some numerical threshold; if the input sum equals the threshold, the neuron maintains its current state. The input sum to b_j is the column inner product

$$AM^j = \sum_i a_i m_{ij} \qquad (5)$$

where M^j is the jth column of M. The input sum to a_i is,

similarly,

$$BM_i^T = \sum_j b_j m_{ij} \qquad (6)$$

where M_i is the ith row (column) of $M(M^T)$. We take 0 as the threshold for all neurons. In summary, the threshold functions for a_i and b_j are

$$a_i = \begin{cases} 1, & \text{if } BM_i^T > 0 \\ 0, & \text{if } BM_i^T < 0 \end{cases} \qquad (7)$$

$$b_j = \begin{cases} 1, & \text{if } AM^j > 0 \\ 0, & \text{if } AM^j < 0 \end{cases}. \qquad (8)$$

When a paired pattern (A, B) is presented to the BAM, the neurons in populations A and B are turned on or off according to the occurrence of 1's and 0's $(-1$'s) in state vectors A and B. The neurons continue their asynchronous (or synchronous) state changes until a bidirectionally stable state (A_f, B_f) is reached. We now prove that such a stable state is reached for any matrix M and that it corresponds to a local minimum of (3).

E decreases along discrete trajectories in the phase space $\{0,1\}^n \times \{0,1\}^p$. We show this by showing that changes Δa_i and Δb_j in state variables produce $\Delta E < 0$. Note that $\Delta a_i, \Delta b_j \in \{-1, 0, 1\}$ for binary state variables and $\Delta a_i, \Delta b_j \in \{-2, 0, 2\}$ for bipolar variables. We need only consider nonzero changes in a_i and b_j. Rewriting (4) as a double sum gives

$$E(A, B) = -\sum_i \sum_j a_i b_j m_{ij}$$

$$= -\sum_{i \neq k} \sum_j a_i b_j m_{ij} - a_k \sum_j b_j m_{kj}$$

$$= -\sum_i \sum_{j \neq k} a_i b_j m_{ij} - b_k \sum_i a_k m_{ik}. \qquad (9)$$

Hence the energy change $\Delta E = E_2 - E_1$ due to state change Δa_k is

$$\frac{\Delta E}{\Delta a_k} = -\sum_j b_j m_{kj} = -BM_k^T. \qquad (10)$$

We recognize the right side of (10) as the input sum to a_k from the threshold rule (7). Hence if $0 < \Delta a_k = 1 - 0 = 1$, then (7) ensures that $BM_k^T > 0$, and thus $\Delta E = -\Delta a_k(BM_k^T) < 0$. Similarly, if $\Delta a_k < 0$, then (7) again ensures that a_k's input sum agrees in sign, $BM_k^T < 0$, and thus $\Delta E = -\Delta a_k(BM_k^T) < 0$. Similarly, the energy change due to state change Δb_k is

$$\frac{\Delta E}{\Delta b_k} = -\sum_i a_i m_{ik} = -AM^k. \qquad (11)$$

Again we recognize the right side of (11) as the negative of the input sum to b_k from the threshold rule (8). Hence $\Delta b_k > 0$ only if $AM^k > 0$, and $\Delta b_k < 0$ only if $AM^k < 0$. In either case, $\Delta E = -\Delta b_k(AM^k) < 0$. When $\Delta a_i = \Delta b_j = 0$, $\Delta E = 0$. Hence $\Delta E < 0$ along discrete trajectories in $\{0,1\}^n \times \{0,1\}^p$ (or in $\{-1,1\}^n \times \{-1,1\}^p$), as claimed.

Since E is bounded below,

$$E(A, B) \geqslant -\sum_i \sum_j |m_{ij}|, \qquad \text{for all } A \text{ and all } B, \quad (12)$$

the BAM converges to some stable point (A_f, B_f) such that $E(A_f, B_f)$ is a local energy minimum. Since the n-by-p matrix M in (3) was an arbitrary (real) matrix, *every matrix is bidirectionally stable*.

III. BAM ENCODING

Suppose we wish to store the binary (bipolar) patterns $(A_1, B_1), \cdots, (A_m, B_m)$ at or near local energy minima. How can these association pairs be *encoded* in some BAM n-by-p matrix M? In the previous section we showed how to *decode* an arbitrary M but not how to construct a specific M. We now develop a simple but general encoding procedure based upon familiar correlation techniques.

The association (A_i, B_i) can be viewed as a meta-rule or set-level logical implication: IF A_i, THEN B_i. However, bidirectionality implies that (A_i, B_i) also represents the converse meta-rule: IF B_i, THEN A_i. Hence the logical relation between A_i and B_i is symmetric, namely, logical implication (set equivalence). The vector analogue of this symmetric biconditionality is correlation. The natural suggestion then is to *memorize* the association (A_i, B_i) by forming the correlation matrix or vector outer product $A_i^T B_i$. The correlation matrix redundantly distributes the vector information in (A_i, B_i) in a parallel storage medium, a matrix. The next suggestion is to *superimpose* the m associations (A_i, B_i) by simply adding up the correlation matrices pointwise:

$$M = \sum_i A_i^T B_i \quad (13)$$

with dual BAM memory M^T given by

$$M^T = \sum_i \left(A_i^T B_i \right)^T = \sum_i B_i^T A_i. \quad (14)$$

The associative memory defined in (13) is the emblem of linear associative network theory. It has been exhaustively studied in this context by Kohonen [27]–[30], Nakano [36], Anderson *et al.* [2]–[4], and several other researchers. In the overwhelming number of cases, M is used in a simple one-shot feedforward linear procedure. Consequently, much research [22], [23], [30] has focused on preprocessing of stored input (A_i) patterns to improve the accuracy of one-iteration synchronous recall. In contrast, the BAM procedure uses (13) and (14) as system components in a nonlinear multi-iteration procedure to achieve heteroassociative content addressability. The fundamental biconditional nature of the BAM process naturally leads to the selection of vector correlation for the memorization process.

However, the nonlinearity introduced by the thresholding in (7) and (8) renders the memories in (13) and (14) unsuitable for BAM storage. The candidate memory binary patterns $(A_1, B_1), \cdots, (A_m, B_m)$ must be transformed to bipolar patterns $(X_1, Y_1), \cdots, (X_m, Y_m)$ for proper mem-

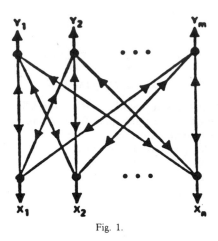

Fig. 1.

orization and superimposition. This yields the BAM memories

$$M = \sum_i X_i^T Y_i \quad (15)$$

$$M^T = \sum_i Y_i^T X_i. \quad (16)$$

Note that (A_i, B_i) can be *erased* from $M(M^T)$ by adding $X_i^T Y_i^c = -X_i^T Y_i$ to the right side of (15) since the bipolar complement $Y_i^c = -Y_i$. Also note that $X_i^{cT} Y_i^c = -X_i^T - Y_i = X_i^T Y_i$. Hence encoding (A_i, B_i) in memory encodes (A_i^c, B_i^c) as well, and vice versa.

The fundamental reason why (13) and (14) are unsuitable but (15) and (16) are suitable for BAM storage is that 0's in binary patterns are ignored when added, but -1's in bipolar patterns are not: $1 + 0 = 1$ but $1 + (-1) = 0$. If the numbers are matrix entries that represent synaptic strengths, then multiplying and adding binary quantities can only produce excitatory connections or zero-weight connections. (We note, however, that (13) and (14) are functionally suitable if *bipolar* state vectors are used, although the neuronal interpretation is less clear than when (15) and (16) are used.)

Multiplying and adding bipolar quantities produces excitatory and inhibitory connections. The connection strengths represent the frequency of excitatory and inhibitory connections in the individual correlation matrices. If e_{ij} is the edge or connection strength between a_i and b_j, then $e_{ij} \gtreqless 0$ according as the number of $+1$ ijth entries in the m correlation matrices $X_i^T Y_i$ exceeds, equals, or falls short of the number of -1 ijth entries. The magnitude of e_{ij} measures the preponderance of 1's over -1's, or -1's over 1's, in the summed matrices.

Coding details aside, (15) encodes (A_i, B_i) in M by forming discrete *reciprocal outstars* [8]–[12], in the language of Grossberg associative learning; see Figs. 1 and 2. Grossberg [8] has long since shown that the outstar is the minimal network capable of perfectly learning a spatial pattern. The reciprocal outstar framework provides a fertile context in which to interpret BAM convergence.

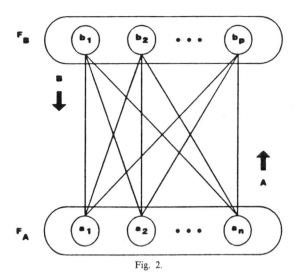

Fig. 2.

The neurons $\{a_1, \cdots, a_n\}$ and $\{b_1, \cdots, b_p\}$ can be interpreted as two symmetrically connected *fields* [5], [6], [15], [16], [20] F_A and F_B of bivalent threshold functions. BAM convergence then corresponds to a simple type of *adaptive resonance* [5], [6], [16]–[20]. Adaptive resonance occurs when recurrent neuronal activity (short-term memory) and variable connection strengths (long-term memory) equilibrate or resonant. The resonance is adaptive because the connection strengths gradually change. Hence BAM convergence represents nonadaptive resonance since the connections m_{ij} are fixed by (15). (Later, and in Kosko [31], we allow BAM's to learn). Since connections typically change much slower than neuron activations change, BAM resonance may still accurately model interesting distributed behavior.

Let us examine the *synchronous* behavior of BAM's when M and M^T are given by (15) and (16). Suppose we have stored $(A_1, B_1), \cdots, (A_m, B_m)$ in the BAM, and we are presented with the pair (A, B). We can initiate the recall process using A first or B first, or using them simultaneously. For simplicity, suppose we present the BAM with the stored pattern A_i. Then we obtain the signal–noise expansion

$$A_i M = \left(A_i X_i^T\right) Y_i + \sum_{j \neq i} \left(A_i X_j^T\right) Y_j \qquad (17)$$

or, if we use the bipolar version X_i of A_i, which, as established in the Appendix, improves recall reliability on average, then

$$X_i M = \left(X_i X_i^T\right) Y_i + \sum_{j \neq i} \left(X_i X_j^T\right) Y_j$$

$$= n Y_i + \sum_{j \neq i} \left(X_i X_j^T\right) Y_j$$

$$\approx \left(c_1 y_1^i, c_2, y_2^i, \cdots, c_p y_p^i\right), \qquad c_k > 0. \qquad (18)$$

Observe that the signal Y_i in (18) is given the maximum positive amplification factor $n > 0$. This exaggerates the

bipolar features of Y_i, thus tending to produce B_i when the input sum $X_i M$ is thresholded according to (8).

The noise amplification coefficients, $x_{ij} = X_i X_j^T$, *correct* the noise terms Y_j according to the Hamming distances $H(A_i, A_j)$. In particular,

$$x_{ij} \gtreqless 0, \qquad \text{iff } H(A_i, A_j) \lesseqgtr n/2. \qquad (19)$$

This relationship holds because x_{ij} is the number of vector slots in which A_i and A_j agree, $n - H(A_i, A_j)$, minus the number of slots in which they differ, $H(A_i, A_j)$. Hence

$$x_{ij} = n - 2H(A_i, A_j), \qquad (20)$$

which implies (19). If $H(A_i, A_j) = n/2$, Y_j is zeroed out of the input sum. If $H(A_i, A_j) < n/2$, and hence if A_i and A_j are close, then $x_{ij} > 0$ and Y_j is positively amplified in direct proportion to strength of match between A_i and A_j. If $H(A_i, A_j) > n/2$, then $x_{ij} < 0$ and the *complement* Y_j^c is positively amplified in direct proportion to $H(A_i, A_j^c)$ since $Y_j^c = -Y_j$. Thus the correction coefficients x_{ij} convert the additive noise vectors Y_j into a distance-weighted signal sum, thereby increasing the probability that the right side of (18) will approximate some positive multiple of Y_i, then threshold to $B_i(Y_i)$. This argument still applies when an arbitrary vector $A \approx A_i$ is presented to the BAM.

The BAM storage capacity is ultimately determined by the noise sum in (18). Roughly speaking, this sum can be expected to outweigh the signal term(s) if $m > n$, where m is the number of stored pairs (A_i, B_i), since n is the maximum signal amplification factor. Similarly, when presenting M^T with B, the maximum signal term is pX_i; so $m > p$ can be expected to produce unreliable recall. Hence a rough estimate of the BAM storage capacity is $m < \min(n, p)$.

The BAM can be confused if like inputs are associated with unlike outputs or vice versa. Continuity must hold for all i and j: $1/nH(A_i, A_j) \approx 1/pH(B_i, B_j)$. The foregoing argument assumes continuity. It trivially holds in the autoassociative (A_i, A_i) case.

Synchronous BAM behavior produces large energy changes. Hence few vector multiplies are required per recall. This is established by denoting $\Delta A = A_2 - A_1 = (\Delta a_1, \cdots, \Delta a_n)$ in the energy change equation

$$\Delta E = -\Delta A M B^T = -\sum_i \sum_j \Delta a_i b_j m_{ij}$$

$$= -\sum_i \Delta a_i \sum_j b_j m_{ij}$$

$$= -\sum_i \Delta a_i B M_i^T. \qquad (21)$$

which is the sum of pointwise energy decreases $-\Delta a_i B M_i^T$, and similarly for $\Delta B = B_2 - B_1$. This argument also shows that simple asynchronous behavior, as required by the Hopfield model [24], can be viewed as special case of synchronous behavior, namely, when at most one Δa_k is nonzero per iteration. More generally, this argument shows [31] that any subset of neurons in either field can be updated per iteration—subset asynchrony.

Let us examine a simple example of a BAM construction and synchronous operation. Suppose we wish to store the following four nonorthogonal associations:

$$A_1 = (1 \quad 0 \quad 1 \quad 0 \quad 1 \quad 0 \quad 1 \quad 0 \quad 1 \quad 0 \quad 1 \quad 0 \quad 1 \quad 0 \quad 1)$$
$$A_2 = (1 \quad 1 \quad 0 \quad 0 \quad 1 \quad 1 \quad 0 \quad 0 \quad 1 \quad 1 \quad 0 \quad 0 \quad 1 \quad 1 \quad 0)$$
$$A_3 = (1 \quad 1 \quad 1 \quad 0 \quad 0 \quad 0 \quad 1 \quad 1 \quad 1 \quad 0 \quad 0 \quad 0 \quad 1 \quad 1 \quad 1)$$
$$A_4 = (1 \quad 1 \quad 1 \quad 1 \quad 0 \quad 0 \quad 0 \quad 0 \quad 1 \quad 1 \quad 1 \quad 1 \quad 0 \quad 0 \quad 0)$$

$$B_1 = (1 \quad 1 \quad 1 \quad 1 \quad 0 \quad 0 \quad 0 \quad 0 \quad 1 \quad 1)$$
$$B_2 = (1 \quad 1 \quad 1 \quad 0 \quad 0 \quad 0 \quad 1 \quad 1 \quad 1 \quad 0)$$
$$B_3 = (1 \quad 1 \quad 0 \quad 0 \quad 1 \quad 1 \quad 0 \quad 0 \quad 1 \quad 1)$$
$$B_4 = (1 \quad 0 \quad 1 \quad 0 \quad 1 \quad 0 \quad 1 \quad 0 \quad 1 \quad 0),$$

where $m = 4$, $n = 15$, $p = 10$. The first step is to convert these binary associations into bipolar associations:

$$X_1 = (1 \quad -1 \quad 1 \quad -1 \quad 1 \quad -1 \quad 1 \quad -1 \quad 1 \quad -1 \quad 1 \quad -1 \quad 1 \quad -1 \quad 1)$$
$$X_2 = (1 \quad 1 \quad -1 \quad -1 \quad 1 \quad 1 \quad -1 \quad -1 \quad 1 \quad 1 \quad -1 \quad -1 \quad 1 \quad 1 \quad -1)$$
$$X_3 = (1 \quad 1 \quad 1 \quad -1 \quad -1 \quad -1 \quad 1 \quad 1 \quad 1 \quad -1 \quad -1 \quad -1 \quad 1 \quad 1 \quad 1)$$
$$X_4 = (1 \quad 1 \quad 1 \quad 1 \quad -1 \quad -1 \quad -1 \quad -1 \quad 1 \quad 1 \quad 1 \quad 1 \quad -1 \quad -1 \quad -1)$$
$$Y_1 = (1 \quad 1 \quad 1 \quad 1 \quad -1 \quad -1 \quad -1 \quad -1 \quad 1 \quad 1)$$
$$Y_2 = (1 \quad 1 \quad 1 \quad -1 \quad -1 \quad -1 \quad 1 \quad 1 \quad 1 \quad -1)$$
$$Y_3 = (1 \quad 1 \quad -1 \quad -1 \quad 1 \quad 1 \quad -1 \quad -1 \quad 1 \quad 1)$$
$$Y_4 = (1 \quad -1 \quad 1 \quad -1 \quad 1 \quad -1 \quad 1 \quad -1 \quad 1 \quad -1).$$

Next the four vector outer-product correlation matrices $X_1^T Y_1$, $X_2^T Y_2$, $X_3^T Y_3$, and $X_4^T Y_4$ are formed and added pointwise to form the BAM matrix $M = X_1^T Y_1 + \cdots + X_4^T Y_4$:

$$\begin{pmatrix}
4 & 2 & 2 & -2 & 0 & -2 & 0 & -2 & 4 & 0 \\
2 & 0 & 0 & -4 & 2 & 0 & 2 & 0 & 2 & -2 \\
2 & 0 & 0 & 0 & 2 & 0 & -2 & -4 & 2 & 2 \\
-2 & -4 & 0 & 0 & 2 & 0 & 2 & 0 & -2 & -2 \\
0 & 2 & 2 & 2 & -4 & -2 & 0 & 2 & 0 & 0 \\
-2 & 0 & 0 & 0 & -2 & 0 & 2 & 4 & -2 & -2 \\
0 & 2 & -2 & 2 & 0 & 2 & -4 & -2 & 0 & 4 \\
-2 & 0 & -4 & 0 & 2 & 4 & -2 & 0 & -2 & 2 \\
4 & 2 & 2 & -2 & 0 & -2 & 0 & -2 & 4 & 0 \\
0 & -2 & 2 & -2 & 0 & -2 & 4 & 2 & 0 & -4 \\
0 & -2 & 2 & 2 & 0 & -2 & 0 & -2 & 0 & 0 \\
-2 & -4 & 0 & 0 & 2 & 0 & 2 & 0 & -2 & -2 \\
2 & 4 & 0 & 0 & -2 & 0 & -2 & 0 & 2 & 2 \\
0 & 0 & -2 & -2 & 0 & 2 & 0 & 2 & 0 & 0 \\
0 & 0 & -2 & 2 & 0 & 2 & -4 & -2 & 0 & 4
\end{pmatrix}$$

lects the respective stored pairs (A_1, B_1), (A_2, B_2), (A_3, B_3), (A_4, B_4). This is expected since the A_i matches correspond to the correct specification of 15 variables, while the B_i matches only correspond to the correct specification of 10 variables.

Then $(A_1, B_1), \cdots, (A_4, B_4)$ are stable points in $\{0,1\}^{15} \times \{0,1\}^{10}$ with respective energies -56, -48, -60, and -40.

This BAM illustrates rapid convergence and accurate pattern completion. If $A = (1 \quad 0 \quad 1 \quad 0 \quad 1 \quad 0 \quad 1 \quad 0 \quad 0 \quad 0 \quad 0 \quad 0 \quad 0 \quad 0 \quad 0) \approx A_1$, with $H(A, A_1) = 4$, then B_1 is recalled in one synchronous iteration, and thus (A_1, B_1) is retrieved from memory since (A_1, B_2) is stable. If $B = (1 \quad 1 \quad 0 \quad 0 \quad 1 \quad 0 \quad 0 \quad 0 \quad 0 \quad 0) \approx B_3$, with $H(B, B_3) = 3$, then (A_3, B_3) is recalled in one iteration. Any of the blended pairs (A_1, B_4), (A_2, B_3), (A_3, B_2), (A_4, B_1) recol-

IV. CONTINUOUS AND ADAPTIVE BIDIRECTIONAL ASSOCIATIVE MEMORIES

The BAM concepts and convergence proof discussed earlier pass over to the continuous or physical case. We prove that if the agggregate real-valued activation to the ith neuron in F_A and jth neuron in F_B, denoted a_i and b_j, are transformed by bounded monotone-increasing signal functions $S(a_i)$ and $S(b_j)$, then every matrix is bidirectionally stable. Hence $S' = dS(x)/dx > 0$. When the signal functions take values in $[0,1]$, the output state vectors

$S(A) = (S(a_1), \cdots, S(a_n))$ and $S(B) = (S(b_1), \cdots S(b_p))$ are fuzzy sets [38]. Then BAM convergence often corresponds [31], [32] to minimization of a nonprobabilistic fuzzy entropy [33].

Suppose a_i and b_i are governed by the additive [16] dynamical equations

$$\dot{a}_i = -a_i + \sum_j S(b_j) m_{ij} + I_i \tag{22}$$

$$\dot{b}_j = -b_j + \sum_i S(a_i) m_{ij} + J_j. \tag{23}$$

This dynamical model is a direct generalization of the continuous Hopfield circuit model [25], [26], which is itself a special case of the Cohen–Grossberg theorem [7]. In (22) the term $-a_i$ is a passive decay term, the constant I_i is the exogenous input to a_i, and similarly for $-b_j$ and J_j in (23). Proportionality constants have been omitted for simplicity. The constant inputs I_i and J_j can be interpreted as sustained environmental stimuli or as patterns of stable reverberation from an adjoining neural network. The time scales are roughly that the (short-term memory) activations a_i and b_j fluctuate orders of magnitudes faster than the (long-term memory) memory traces m_{ij} and the applied external inputs I_i and J_j. Hence a reasonable approximation of realtime continuous BAM behavior is got by assuming all m_{ij}, I_i, J_j constant.

As in the Cohen–Grossberg [7] framework, many more nonlinear models than (22), (23) can be used. To prove stability of the additive model (22), (23), we follow the example of the Cohen–Grossberg theorem and postulate that the dynamical system (22), (23) admits the global Lyapunov or energy function

$$E(A, B) = \sum_i \int_0^{a_i} S'(x_i) x_i \, dx_i - \sum_i \sum_j S(a_i) S(b_j) m_{ij}$$

$$- \sum_i S(a_i) I_i + \sum_j \int_0^{b_j} S'(y_j) y_j \, dy_j - \sum_j S(b_j) J_j. \tag{24}$$

The total time derivative of E is

$$\dot{E} = -\sum_i S'(a_i)\dot{a}_i \left[-a_i + \sum_j S(b_j) m_{ij} + I_i \right]$$

$$- \sum_j S'(b_j)\dot{b}_j \left[-b_j + \sum_i S(a_i) m_{ij} + J_j \right]$$

$$= -\sum_i S'(a_i)\dot{a}_i^2 - \sum_j S'(b_j)\dot{b}_j^2$$

$$\leqslant 0 \tag{25}$$

upon substituting the right sides of (22) and (23) for the terms in braces in (25). Since E is bounded and M is an arbitrary n-by-p matrix, (25) proves that every matrix is continuously bidirectionally stable. Moreover, since $S' > 0$, the energy function E reaches a minimum if and only if $\dot{a}_i = \dot{b}_j = 0$ for all i and all j.

For completeness, we summarize here recent results on *adaptive* BAM's [31]. Since during learning the weights m_{ij} change so much more slowly than the activations a_i and b_j

change, and since fixed weights always produce global stability, if the weights are slowly varied in (22), (23) we can expect stability in the learning case.

The minimal [31] unsupervised correlation learning law is the *signal Hebb law* [10], [12]:

$$\dot{m}_{ij} = -m_{ij} + S(a_i) S(b_j).$$

Hence the signal Hebb law learns an exponentially weighted average of sampled signals. Hence m_{ij} is bounded and rapidly converges. Note that if the signals S are in the bipolar interval $[-1, 1]$, this learning law asymptotically converges to the bipolar correlation learning scheme discussed in Section III. The biological plausibility of the signal Hebb law stems from its use of only locally available information. A learning synapse m_{ij} only "sees" the information locally available to it: its own strength m_{ij} and the signals $S(a_i)$ and $S(b_j)$ flowing through it. (The synapse also "sees" the instantaneous changes $dS(a_i)/dt$ and $dS(b_j)/dt$ of the signals [32].) Moreover, the synapse must, in general, learn from one or few "data passes," unlike feedforward supervised schemes where thousands of data passes are often required.

A global bounded Lyapunov function for the adaptive BAM is

$$E(A, B, M) = F + 1/2 \sum_i \sum_j m_{ij}^2$$

where F denotes the bounded energy function (24) of the continuous BAM. Then

$$\dot{E} = -\sum_i \sum_j \dot{m}_{ij} \left[S(a_i) S(b_j) - m_{ij} \right] - \sum_i S'\dot{a}_i^2 - \sum_j S'\dot{b}_j^2$$

$$= -\sum_i \sum_j \dot{m}_{ij}^2 - \sum_i S'(a_i)\dot{a}_i^2 - \sum_j S'(b_j)\dot{b}_j^2$$

$$\leqslant 0$$

upon substituting the signal Hebb law for the term in braces. Again, since $S' > 0$, $\dot{E} = 0$ iff $\dot{a}_i = \dot{b}_j = \dot{m}_{ij} = 0$ for all i and j. Hence every signal Hebb BAM is globally stable (adaptively resonates [5], [17], [18]). (This theorem extends to any number of BAM fields interconnected with signal Hebb learning laws.) Stable reverberations across the nodes seep pattern information into the memory traces m_{ij}. Input associations dig their own energy wells in the network state space $[0,1]^n \times [0,1]^p$.

The adaptive BAM is the general BAM model. The energy function (24) is only unique up to linear transformation. It already includes the sum of squared weights m_{ij}^2 as an additive constant. Note that in (24) memory information only enters through the quadratic form, the sum of products $m_{ij} S(a_i) S(b_j)$. Time differentiation of these products leads to the terms that eliminate both the feedback terms (path-weighted sums of signals) in (22), (23) and that eliminate the learning component $S(a_i) S(b_j)$ of the signal Hebb learning law when the adaptive BAM energy function E is differentiated and rearranged. Hence for Lyapunov functions of the Cohen–Grossberg type (such as (24)) that use a quadratic form to eliminate feedback sums and do not include memory information in its other terms, *only* the signal Hebb learning law is globally stable. This learning law cannot be changed without making further assumptions, in particular, without changing the activation dynamical models (22), (23). A structurally different Lyapunov function must otherwise be used. This argument holds [31] for all dynamical systems that can be written in the Cohen–Grossberg form [7].

V. Temporal Associative Memories (TAM's)

Temporal patterns are ordered vectors, functions from an index set to a vector space. We assume all temporal patterns are finite and discrete. We, therefore, can represent them as a list of binary or bipolar vectors, vector-valued samples. (A_1, A_2, A_3, A_1) is such a temporal pattern where

$$A_1 = (1 \quad 0 \quad 0 \quad 1 \quad 0 \quad 0 \quad 1 \quad 0 \quad 0 \quad 1)$$
$$A_2 = (1 \quad 1 \quad 0 \quad 0 \quad 1 \quad 1 \quad 0 \quad 0 \quad 1 \quad 1)$$
$$A_3 = (1 \quad 0 \quad 1 \quad 0 \quad 1 \quad 1 \quad 1 \quad 0 \quad 1 \quad 0)$$
$$A_1 = (1 \quad 0 \quad 0 \quad 1 \quad 0 \quad 0 \quad 1 \quad 0 \quad 0 \quad 1).$$

This temporal pattern (array) might represent a musical chord progression where tag bits are added to indicate sustained tones and to discriminate repeated tones. A_1 is appended to the sequence (A_1, A_2, A_3) to convert the sequence into an infinite loop in the sense that A_i is always followed by A_{i+1}. This loop can intuitively correspond to a music box that plays the same tune over and over and over.

How can (A_1, A_2, A_3, A_1) be encoded in a parallel distributed associative matrix memory M? How can a temporal structure be stored in a static medium so that if $A \approx A_i$, then $A_{i+1}, A_{i+2}, \cdots$ are sequentially recalled?

Consider your favorite musical piece or motion picture. In what sense do you remember it? All at once or serially? For concreteness consider the Elizabethan song Greensleeves. How do we remember Greensleeves when we hum or play it? Suppose you are asked to hum Greensleeves starting from some small group of notes in the middle of the song. You probably would try to recollect the small group of notes that immediately precede the given notes. These contiguous groupings might enable you "pick up the melody," enabling you to recall the next contiguous group, then the next, and so on with increasingly less mental effort. Hence we might conjecture that the temporal pattern $(A_1, \cdots, A_m)$ can be memorized by memorizing the local contiguities $A_1 \to A_2$, $A_2 \to A_3$, $\cdots$. Alternatively, this can be represented schematically as the unidirectional conjecture

$$A_1 \to A_2 \to \cdots A_i \to A_{i+1} \to \cdots.$$

This local contiguity conjecture suggests a simple algorithm for encoding binary temporal patterns in an n-by-n matrix memory. First, as in the BAM encoding algorithm, the binary vectors A_i are converted to bipolar vectors X_i. Second, the contiguous relationship $A_i \to A_{i+1}$ is memorized as if it were the heteroassociative pair (A_i, A_{i+1}) by

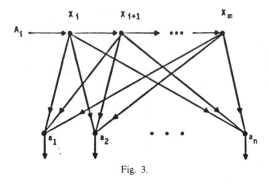

Fig. 3.

forming the correlation matrix $X_i^T X_{i+1}$. Third, the contiguous relationships are added pointwise as in the BAM algorithm to give M:

$$M = X_m^T X_1 + \sum_i^{n-1} X_i^T X_{i+1}. \tag{26}$$

Suppose $A_i(X_i)$ is presented to M. Suppose $(1/n)H(A_i, A_j) \approx (1/n)H(A_{i+1}, A_{j+1})$ tends to hold as in the bidirectional case. Then

$$X_i M = n X_{i+1} + \sum_{j \neq i} \left(X_i X_j^T \right) X_{j+1}$$
$$\approx \left(c_1 x_1^{i+1}, c_2 x_2^{i+1}, \cdots, c_n x_n^{i+1} \right), c_k > 0 \tag{27}$$

as in the BAM signal-noise expansion (18). Hence in synchronous unidirectional threshold operation, $X_{i+2}(A_{i+2})$ tends to be recalled in the next iteration, X_{i+3} in the next iteration, and so on until the sequence is completed or begins anew. Similarly, if $A_i(X_i)$ is presented to the dual bidirectional memory M^T, the melody should proceed backwards to the start:

$$X_i M^T = X_i \left(X_{i-1}^T X_i \right)^T + \sum_{j \neq i} X_i \left(X_{j-1}^T X_j \right)^T$$
$$= n X_{i-1} + \sum_{j \neq i} \left(X_i X_j^T \right) X_{j-1}$$
$$\approx \left(d_1 x_1^{i-1}, d_2 x_2^{i-1}, \cdots, d_n x_n^{i-1} \right), \qquad d_k > 0. \tag{28}$$

A similar approximate argument holds in general when $A \approx A_i$. Since n is the maximal signal amplification factor in (27) and (28), we obtain the same rough maximal storage capacity bound for an m-length temporal pattern as we obtained in the BAM analysis: $m < \min(n, n) = n$. More generally, the memory can store at most k-many temporal patterns of length $m_1, \cdots, m_K$, provided $m_1 + m_2 + \cdots + m_k = m \ll n$.

The neural network interpretation of this temporal coding and recall procedure is a simple type of Grossberg *outstar avalanche*. Grossberg [9]–[12] showed long ago through differential analysis that, just as an outstar is the minimal network capable of learning an arbitrary spatial pattern, an avalanche is the minimal network capable of learning an arbitrary temporal pattern. An avalanche is a cascade of outstars; see Fig. 3.

Outstar bursts are sequentially activated by an axonal cable. In the present case this cable is forged with the contiguous correlation matrices $X_i^T X_{i+1}$. When a spatial pattern A_i is presented to M, the X_i outstar sends an X_i pattern pulse to the neurons $a_1, \cdots, a_n$. The neurons threshold this pulse into A_{i+1}. While the X_i pulse is propagating to the neurons, the axonal cable transmits an X_i command to the X_{i+1} outstar. An X_{i+1} pattern pulse is then sent to the neurons, and an X_{i+1} command is sent along the cable to the X_{i+2} outstar, and so on until all the outstars have fired. Hence the successive synchronous states of the neurons $a_1, \cdots, a_n$ replay the temporal pattern $(A_i, A_{i+1}, \cdots, A_m)$. If the axonal command cable forms a closed loop, the infinite temporal pattern $(A_i, \cdots, A_m, A_1, A_2, \cdots, A_i, \cdots)$ will be recalled in a music-box loop.

Grossberg [9]–[12] uses a differential model to prove that practice makes avalanches perfectly learn temporal patterns. Neurons (nodes) and synapses (edges) are continuous variables governed by differential equations, and the temporal pattern is a continuous vector-valued function approximated with arbitrary accuracy by discrete samples. The key term in the node equation for a_j is the vector dot product $A_i M^j$ (supplemented with a passive state decay term). The key term in the edge equation for $e_{i,i+1}$ is a lagged Hebb product $a_i(t) a_{i+1}(t+1)$ (supplemented with a forget or passive memory decay term) where t is a time index. Equations (7) and (8) are discrete approximations to Grossberg's neuron equation. Moreover, the hyperplane-threshold behavior of (7) and (8) approximates a sigmoid or S-shaped function that is required to dynamically quench noise and enhance signals. Equation (26) is a discrete vector approximation of the lagged Hebbian law in Grossberg's edge, or learning, equation. The memory capacity bound $m < n$ obviates a passive memory decay term and other dynamical complexities but at the price of restricting the pattern environments to which the model can be applied.

We also note that, as Grossberg [10]–[12], [15] observes, a temporal pattern generally involves not just *order* or contiguity information but *rhythm* information as well. The simple temporal associative memory constructed by (26) ignores rhythm. Once a limit cycle is reached, for instance, it cannot stop "playing." More generally, the speed with which successive spatial patterns are read out across the neurons should vary. Grossberg shows that the simplest way to achieve this is to append a command cell atop the outstar cells. The command cell nonspecifically excites or inhibits current activation of outstar cells according to contextual cues, as if a hormone were nonspecifically released into the bloodstream. This architecture is called a *context modulated* outstar avalanche. By reversing the direction of arrows, the dual instar avalanche can recognize learned spatiotemporal patterns.

We now extend BAM energy convergence to temporal associative memories (TAM's). What is the energy of a temporal pattern? We cannot expect as easy an answer as in the BAM case. For we know, just by examining the encoding scheme (26), that the same memory matrix M can house limit cycles of different lengths. We must, therefore, limit our analysis to local behavior around a given limit cycle of length m. The bivalent synchronous TAM recall procedure guarantees convergence to such a limit cycle in at most 2^n iterations. Consider the simplest temporal pattern (A_1, A_2). A natural way to define the energy of this pattern would be

$$E(A_1, A_2) = -A_1 M A_2^T$$

as in the BAM case. Then $E(A_1, A_2) = E(A_2, A_1)$. Now suppose the temporal pattern, the limit cycle, is (A_1, A_2, A_3). Then there are three two-vector sums to consider: $E(A_1, A_2)$, $E(A_2, A_3)$, and $E(A_1, A_3)$. The third energy sum violates the contiguity assumption of temporal encoding. The energy of the sequence can then be defined as the sum of the remaining two:

$$E(A_1, A_2, A_3) = -A_1 M A_2^T - A_2 M A_3^T - A_3 M A_1^T.$$

Then $E(A_1, A_2, A_3) = E(A_3, A_2, A_1)$ since $E(A_1, A_2) = E(A_2, A_1)$ and $E(A_2, A_3) = E(A_3, A_2)$. This leads to a general definition of temporal pattern energy:

$$E(A_1, A_2, \cdots, A_m) = -A_m M A_1^T - \sum_{i=1}^{m-1} A_i M A_{i+1}^T \quad (29)$$

with the property that $E(A_1, \cdots, A_m) = E(A_m, \cdots, A_1)$. Let P denote the temporal pattern $(A_1, \cdots, A_m)$. Then we can rewrite (29) as

$$E(P) = -A_{k-1} M A_k^T - A_k M A_{k+1}^T - \sum_{\substack{i \neq k \\ i \neq k-1}} A_i M A_{i+1}^T \quad (30)$$

where time slice A_k has been exhibited for analysis and the "loop" energy term $-A_m M A_1^T$ has been omitted for convenience and without loss of generality. Observe that the input to a_i at time k, a_i^k, is $A_{k-1} M^i$ in the forward direction, $A_{k+1} M_i^T$ in the backward direction, just as with bidirectional networks. The *serial* synchronous operation of the algorithm is essential to distinguish these directions. At time k in the forward direction A_k is active but A_{k+1} is not. Similarly, at time k in the backward direction A_k is active but A_{k-1} is the null vector. One neural network interpretation is a m-level hierarchy of neuron fields or slabs. The fields are *interconnected* to contiguous fields, field A_k to fields A_{k-1} and A_{k+1}, but have no *intraconnections* among their neurons.

Suppose the energy change $E_2 - E_1$ is due to changes in the kth iteration or kth field, $A_{k2} - A_{k1}$. Then by (30)]

$$\Delta E = -A_{k-1} M \Delta A_k^T - \Delta A_k M A_{k+1}^T$$
$$= -A_{k-1} M \Delta A_k^T - A_{k+1} M^T \Delta A_k^T$$
$$= -\sum_i \Delta a_i^k A_{k-1} M^i - \sum_i \Delta a_i^k A_{k+1} M_i^T$$
$$\leqslant 0.$$

This inequality follows since, first, in the forward direction Δa_i^k and $A_{k-1} M^i$ agree in sign for all i by (8) and $A_{k+1} = \mathbf{0}$, and second, in the backward direction Δa_i^k and $A_{k+1} M_i^T$ agree in sign for all i by (7) and $A_{k-1} = \mathbf{0}$.

Energy decrease can also be seen by examining the equivalent unidirectional autoassociative block matrix TAM defined by the connection matrix T:

$$T = \begin{pmatrix} 0 & M & 0 & \cdots & 0 & 0 \\ 0 & 0 & M & \cdots & 0 & 0 \\ 0 & 0 & 0 & \cdots & 0 & 0 \\ \vdots & \vdots & \vdots & & \vdots & \vdots \\ 0 & 0 & 0 & & M & 0 \\ 0 & 0 & 0 & & 0 & M \\ M & 0 & 0 & \cdots & 0 & 0 \end{pmatrix}.$$

For instance, field A_2 receives the input $[A_1|0|\cdots|0]T = [0|A_1M|0|\cdots|0]$, or A_1M, for short. This input sum forces the vector of state changes ΔA_2, whose components agree in sign with the input sum term by term. If A_2 experiences some nonzero state change, then $\Delta E = -A_1M\Delta A_2^T < 0$. Note that if $A = [A_1|A_2|\cdots|A_m]$, then $-ATA^T$ equals the limit–cycle energy $E(P)$ in (30). This argument shows that at each TAM iteration an energy function is locally minimized just as fast as if it were a single synchronous BAM iteration. It may take more than m steps to stabilize, but such trajectories should be infrequent. The local synchronous energy drops are too great.

Finally, we note again that E is bounded below for all m-length limit cycles P:

$$E(P) \geqslant -m \sum_i \sum_j |m_{ij}|.$$

Hence the TAM algorithm converges to temporal patterns or limit cycles P in $\{0,1\}^n$ that are local energy minima. Since M was arbitrary, every square matrix is temporally stable.

The thrust of this result is energy minimization, not stability. Energy minimization assures quick convergence and arbits potential temporal encoding and decoding schemes. Stability is assured with or without energy minimization because since temporal updates are synchronous, recall must stabilize on some limit cycle in at most 2^n iterations. The first term of the stable limit cycle is the first recalled spatial vector that is recalled twice. The iteration-ordered spatial vectors that occur between the first and second appearance of this repeated spatial vector define the rest of the limit cycle.

As illustration, let us encode the previous temporal pattern (A_1, A_2, A_3, A_1). We form the TAM matrix M by adding the three contiguous correlation matrices

$$M = X_1^T X_2 + X_2^T X_3 + X_3^T X_1$$

which yields

Then $A_1M = (4 \quad 4 \quad -4 \quad -4 \quad 4 \quad 4 \quad -6 \quad -4 \quad 4 \quad 4)$ $\rightarrow (1 \quad 1 \quad 0 \quad 0 \quad 1 \quad 1 \quad 0 \quad 0 \quad 1 \quad 1) = A_2$ by the hyperplane threshold law (8). We can measure the energy of this recollection as in the BAM case by $E(A_1 \rightarrow A_2) = -A_1MA_2^T = -24$. Next $A_2M = (6 \quad -10 \quad 6 \quad -2 \quad 2 \quad 2 \quad 8 \quad -6 \quad 2 \quad -6) \rightarrow (1 \quad 0 \quad 1 \quad 0 \quad 1 \quad 1 \quad 1 \quad 0 \quad 1 \quad 0) = A_3$ with $E(A_2 \rightarrow A_3) = -26$. Next $A_3M = (6 \quad -10 \quad -2 \quad 6 \quad -6 \quad -6 \quad 8 \quad -6 \quad -6 \quad 2) \rightarrow (1 \quad 0 \quad 0 \quad 1 \quad 0 \quad 0 \quad 1 \quad 0 \quad 0 \quad 1) = A_1$ with $E(A_3 \rightarrow A_1) = -22$. Hence $E(A_1, A_2, A_3, A_1) = -72$. Hence presenting any of the patterns A_1, A_2, or A_3 to M recalls the remainder of the temporal sequence.

In this example the energy sequence $(-24, -26, -22)$ contains an energy *increase* of $+4$ when A_3 triggers A_1. We expect this since we are traversing a limit cycle in the state space $\{0,1\}^n$. This is also consistent with the principle of temporal stability since we are only concerned with different sums of contiguous energies. Consider, for example, the bit vector $A = (1 \quad 0 \quad 0 \quad 1 \quad 0 \quad 0 \quad 0 \quad 0 \quad 0 \quad 0)$, with $H(A, A_1) = 2$. Then A recalls A_2 since $AM = (2 \quad 2 \quad -2 \quad -2 \quad 2 \quad 2 \quad -4 \quad -2 \quad 2 \quad 2) \rightarrow (1 \quad 1 \quad 0 \quad 0 \quad 1 \quad 1 \quad 0 \quad 0 \quad 1 \quad 1) = A_2$, but $E(A \rightarrow A_2) = -12 > -24 = E(A_1 \rightarrow A_2)$. Suppose now $A = (1 \quad 1 \quad 0 \quad 0 \quad 1 \quad 1 \quad 0 \quad 0 \quad 0 \quad 0)$, with $H(A, A_2) = 2$. Then $AM = (4 \quad -8 \quad 4 \quad 0 \quad 0 \quad 6 \quad -4 \quad 0 \quad -4) \rightarrow (1 \quad 0 \quad 1 \quad 0 \quad 1 \quad 1 \quad 1 \quad 0 \quad 0 \quad 0) = A'$ (recalling that neurons with input sums that equal the zero threshold maintain their current on–off state), with $H(A, A_3) = 1$ and $E(A \rightarrow A') = -14 > -26 = E(A_2 \rightarrow A_3)$. Finally, $A'M = (5 \quad -7 \quad -3 \quad 5 \quad -5 \quad -5 \quad 5 \quad -5 \quad -5 \quad 3) \rightarrow (1 \quad 0 \quad 0 \quad 1 \quad 0 \quad 0 \quad 1 \quad 0 \quad 0 \quad 1) = A_1$ and $E(A' \rightarrow A_1) = -18 > -22 = E(A_3 \rightarrow A_1)$.

Accessing the backward TAM memory M^T with A_1 gives $A_1M^T = (2 \quad -4 \quad 4 \quad -4 \quad 4 \quad 4 \quad 4 \quad -4 \quad 4 \quad -4) \rightarrow (1 \quad 0 \quad 1 \quad 0 \quad 1 \quad 1 \quad 1 \quad 0 \quad 1 \quad 0) = A_3$ with $E(A_1 \rightarrow A_3) = -22$, as expected. Next, $A_3M^T = (4 \quad 6 \quad -10 \quad -2 \quad 2 \quad 2 \quad -6 \quad -6 \quad 2 \quad 10) \rightarrow (1 \quad 1 \quad 0 \quad 0 \quad 1 \quad 1 \quad 0 \quad 0 \quad 1 \quad 1) = A_2$ with $E(A_3 \rightarrow A_2) = -26$. Next, $A_2M^T = (6 \quad -2 \quad -10 \quad 6 \quad -6 \quad -6 \quad 2 \quad -6 \quad -6 \quad 10) \rightarrow (1 \quad 0 \quad 0 \quad 1 \quad 0 \quad 0 \quad 1 \quad 0 \quad 0 \quad 1) = A_1$ with $E(A_2 \rightarrow A_1) = -24$. Hence a backwards music-box loop (A_1, A_3, A_2, A_1) is recalled with total energy -72.

Appendix
Binary versus Bipolar Coding

The memory storage techniques discussed in this paper involve summing correlation matrices formed from bipolar vectors. Given the memory matrix M and input vector

$$\begin{pmatrix} 3 & -1 & -1 & -1 & 1 & 1 & -1 & -3 & 1 & 1 \\ -1 & -1 & 3 & -1 & 1 & 1 & 1 & 1 & 1 & -3 \\ -1 & -1 & -1 & 3 & -3 & -3 & 1 & 1 & -3 & 1 \\ -1 & 3 & -1 & -1 & 1 & 1 & -3 & 1 & 1 & 1 \\ 1 & -3 & 1 & 1 & -1 & -1 & 3 & -1 & -1 & -1 \\ 1 & -3 & 1 & 1 & -1 & -1 & 3 & -1 & -1 & -1 \\ 1 & 1 & -3 & 1 & -1 & -1 & -1 & -1 & -1 & 3 \\ -3 & 1 & 1 & 1 & -1 & -1 & -1 & 3 & -1 & -1 \\ 1 & -3 & 1 & 1 & -1 & -1 & 3 & -1 & -1 & -1 \\ 1 & 1 & 1 & -3 & 3 & 3 & -1 & -1 & 3 & -1 \end{pmatrix}.$$

$A = (1 \quad 0 \quad 0 \quad 1 \quad 0 \quad 1)$, should we vector multiply A and M or $X = (1 \quad -1 \quad -1 \quad 1 \quad -1 \quad 1)$ and M? Should we, in general, use binary or bipolar coding of state vectors?

Bipolar coding is better on average. The argument is based on the expansion

$$AM = \left(AX_j^T \right)Y_j + \sum_{i \neq j} \left(AX_i^T \right)Y_i \qquad (31)$$

where $H(A, A_j)$ is the Hamming distance between A and A_j, the number of vector slots in which A and A_j differ, $H(A, A_j) = \min_i H(A, A_i)$, and X_i is the bipolar transform of binary A_i — X_i is A_i with 0's replaced with -1's. In words, A is closest to A_j of all the stored input patterns A. The first term on the right side of (31) is the signal term and the second term is the noise term. The parenthetic terms are dot products $a_i = AX_i^T = X_i A^T$. Hence (31) can be written as a linear combination of stored output patterns

$$AM = a_j Y_j + \sum_{i \neq j} a_i Y_i. \qquad (32)$$

We want a_j to amplify Y_j and a_i to "correct" Y_i. If $H(A, A_i) > n/2$, then A is closer to the complement of A_i, A_i^c, than to A_i. Hence we want $a_i < 0$ so that Y_i will be transformed into Y_i^c. If $H(A, A_i) < n/2$, A is closer to A_i than A_i^c, so we want $a_i > 0$. If $H(A, Ai) = n/2$, A is equidistant between A_i and A_i^c, so we want $a_i = 0$. These requirements hold without qualification if M is a sum of autocorrelation matrices, and thus $Y_i = X_i$. For correlation matrices we are implicitly assuming that $H(A_i, A_j) \approx H(B_i, B_j)$—that if stored inputs are close, the associated stored outputs are close.

If we vector multiply M by X, the bipolar transform of A, we get

$$XM = x_j Y_j + \sum_{i \neq j} x_i Y_i \qquad (33)$$

where $x_i = XX_i^T$. We again require that $x_i \gtreqless 0$ according as $H(A, A_i) \lesseqgtr n/2$.

Bipolar coding is better than binary coding in terms of strength and sign of correction coefficients. We shall show that an average 1) $x_i < a_i$ when $H(A, A_i) > n/2$; 2) $x_i > a_i$ when $H(A, A_i) < n/2$; and 3) $x_i = 0$ always when $H(A, A_i) = n/2$. We show this by showing that on average $X * X_i - A * X_i \gtreqless 0$ if and only if $H(A, A_i) \lesseqgtr n/2$, where the asterik " $*$ " denotes the dot product XA_i^T. We shall let I denote the vector of 1's, $I = (1 \quad 1 \cdots 1)$.

We first observe that $X_i * X_j$ can be written as the number of slots in which the two vectors agree minus the number in which they differ. The latter number is simply the Hamming distance $H(A_i, A_j)$; the former, $n - H(A_i, A_j)$. Hence

$$X_i * X_j = n - 2H\left(A_i, A_j \right). \qquad (34)$$

From this we obtain the sign relationship

$$X_i * X_j \gtreqless 0, \qquad \text{if and only if } H\left(A_i, A_j \right) \lesseqgtr n/2. \qquad (35)$$

Although we shall not use the fact, it is interesting to note that the Euclidean norm of any bipolar X is $\sqrt{n}$ while the

Euclidean norm of the binary vector A is $\sqrt{|A|}$, where $|A| = A * I$, the cardinality or number of 1's in A. Hence $\cos(\phi) = \text{correlation}(X_i, X_j) = X_i * X_j/n$, where ϕ is the angle between X_i and X_j in R^n. The denominator of this last expression can be interpreted as the product of the standard deviations of X_i and X_j. Here X_i is a zero–mean binomial random vector with standard deviation given by the Euclidean norm value $\sqrt{n}$.

Suppose that X_i and X_j are random vectors. We assume that the expected number of 1's in any random bipolar/bipolar vector is $n/2$. The only question is how those 1's are distributed throughout $X(A)$. We use

$$A_j * X_i = A_j * (2A_i - I)$$
$$= 2A_i * A_j - |A_j| \qquad (36)$$

to eliminate the term $2A_i * A_j$ in the expansion

$$X_i * X_j - A_i * X_j = (X_i - A_i) * X_j$$
$$= ((2A_i - I) - A_i) * (2A_j - I)$$
$$= 2A_i * A_j + n - |A_i| - 2|A_j|$$
$$= A_j * X_i + n - |A_i| - |A_j|$$
$$\approx A_j * X_i + n - n/2 - n/2$$
$$= A_j * X_i. \qquad (37)$$

The sign of $A_j * X_i$ depends on the distribution of 1's in A_i and A_j. This information is summarized by the Hamming distance $H(A_i, A_j)$. Consider the kth slot of A_j and X_i. The farther apart A_i and A_j, the greater the probability $P\{ A_j^k = 1 \text{ and } X_i^k = -1 \}$ since this probability is equivalent to $P\{ A_j^k = 1, A_i^k = 0 \}$. We can model A_j^k and X_i^k as independent random variables with success/failure probabilities $P\{ A_j^k = 1 \} = P\{ A_j^k = 0 \} = P\{ X_i^k = 1 \} = P\{ X_i^k = -1 \} = 1/2$, but this is valid for all k only if $H(A_i, A_j) = n/2$.

In general, we only impose conditions on the joint distribution $P\{ A_j, X_i \}$. We simply require that the joint distribution obey $P\{ A_j^k = 1, X_i^k = 1 \} = P\{ A_j^k = 0, X_i^k = -1 \}$ and $P\{ A_j^k = 1, X_i^k = -1 \} = P\{ A_j^k = 0, X_i^k = 1 \}$, and that it be driven by the Hamming distance $H(A_i, A_j)$ in a reasonable way. The latter condition can be interpreted as $P(A_j^k = 1, X_i^k = 1) \gtreqless 1/4$ if and only if $H(A_i, A_j) \lesseqgtr n/2$, and $P(A_j^k = 1, X_i^k = -1) \lesseqgtr 1/4$ if and only if $H(A_i, A_j) \lesseqgtr n/2$. Then on average $A_j * X_i \gtreqless 0$ if and only if $H(A_i, A_j) \lesseqgtr n/2$. Hence by (37), on average $X_i * X_j \gtreqless A_i * X_j$ if and only if $H(A_i, A_j) \lesseqgtr n/2$, as claimed.

ACKNOWLEDGMENT

The author thanks Clark Guest, Robert Hecht-Nielsen, and Robert Sasseen for their comments on the theory and application of bidirectional associative memories.

REFERENCES

[1] S. Amari, K. Yoshida, and K. Kanatani, "A mathematical foundation for statistical neurodynamics," *SIAM J. Appl. Math*, vol. 33, no. 1, pp. 95–126, July 1977.

[2] J. A. Anderson, "Cognitive and psychological computation with neural models," *IEEE Trans. Syst. Man. Cyber.*, vol. SMC-13, no. 5, Sept./Oct. 1983.

[3] J. A. Anderson and M. Mozer, "Categorization and selective neurons," in *Parallel Models of Associative Memory*, G. Hinton and J. A. Anderson, Eds. Hillsdale, NJ: Erlbaum, 1981.

[4] J. A. Anderson, J. W. Silverstein, S. A. Ritz, and R. S. Jones, "Distinctive features, categorical perception, and probability learning: Some applications of a neural model," *Psych. Rev.*, vol. 84, pp. 413–451, 1977.

[5] G. A. Carpenter and S. Grossberg, "A massively parallel architecture for a self-organizing neural pattern recognition machine," *Comput. Vis., Graphics, Image Processing*, vol. 37, pp. 54–116, 1987.

[6] ____, "Associative learning, adaptive pattern recognition, and co-operative–competitive decision making by neural networks," *Proc. SPIE: Hybrid, Opt. Syst.*, H. Szu, Ed., vol. 634, pp. 218–247, Mar. 1986.

[7] M. A. Cohen and S. Grossberg, "Absolute stability of global pattern formation and parallel memory storage by competitive neural networks, *IEEE Trans. Syst. Man. Cybern.*, vol. SMC-13, pp. 815–826, Sept./Oct. 1983.

[8] S. Grossberg, "Some nonlinear networks capable of learning a spatial pattern of arbitrary complexity," *Proc. Nat. Acad. Sci.*, vol. 60, pp. 368–372, 1968.

[9] ____, "On the serial learning of lists," *Math. Biosci.*, vol. 4, pp. 201–253, 1969.

[10] ____, "Some networks that can learn, remember, and reproduce any number of complicated space–time patterns, I," *J. Math. Mechan.*, vol. 19, pp. 53–91, 1969.

[11] ____, "On learning of spatiotemporal patterns by networks with ordered sensory and motor components, I," *Stud. Appl. Math.*, vol. 48, pp. 105–132, 1969.

[12] ____, "Some networks that can learn, remember, and reproduce any number of complicated space–time patterns, II," *Stud. Appl. Math.*, vol. 49, pp. 135–166, 1970.

[13] ____, "Contour enhancement, short term memory, and constancies in reverberating neural networks," *Stud. Appl. Math.*, vol. 52, pp. 217–257, 1973.

[14] ____, "Adaptive pattern classification and universal recoding, I: Parallel development and coding of neural feature detectors," *Biol. Cybern.*, vol. 23, pp. 121–134, 1976.

[15] ____, "A theory of human memory: Self-organization and performance of sensory-motor codes, maps, and plans," in *Progress in Theoretical Biology*, vol. 5, R. Rosen and F. Snell, Eds. New York: Academic, 1978.

[16] ____, "How does a brain build a cognitive code?" *Psych. Rev.*, vol. 1, pp. 1–51, 1980.

[17] ____, "Adaptive resonance in development, perception, and cognition," in *Mathematical Psychology and Psychophysiology*. S. Grossberg, Ed. Providence, RI: Amer. Math. Soc., 1981.

[18] ____, *Studies of Mind and Brain: Neural Principles of Learning, Perception, Development, Cognition, and Motor Control.* Boston, MA: Reidel Press, 1982.

[19] S. Grossberg and M. Kuperstein, *Neural Dynamics of Adaptive Sensory-Motor Control: Ballistic Eye Movements.* Amsterdam, The Netherlands: North-Holland, 1986.

[20] S. Grossberg and M. A. Cohen, "Masking fields: A massively parallel neural architecture for learning, recognizing, and predicting multiple groupings of patterned data," *Appl. Opt.*, to be published.

[21] R. Hecht-Nielsen, "Performance limits of optical, electro-optical, and electronic neurocomputers," *Proc. SPIE: Hybrid, Opt. Syst.*, H. Szu, Ed., pp. 277–306, Mar. 1986.

[22] Y. Hirai, "A template matching model for pattern recognition: Self-organization of template and template matching by a disinhibitory neural network," *Biol. Cybern.*, vol. 38, pp. 91–101, 1980.

[23] ____, "A model of human associative processor (HASP)," *IEEE Trans. Syst. Man. Cybern.*, vol. SMC-13, no. 5, pp. 851–857, Sept./Oct. 1983.

[24] J. J. Hopfield, "Neural networks and physical systems with emergent collective computational abilities," *Proc. Nat. Acad. Sci. USA*, vol. 79, pp. 2554–2558, 1982.

[25] ____, "Neurons with graded response have collective computational properties like those of two-state neurons," *Proc. Nat. Adad. Sci. USA*, vol. 81, pp. 3088–3092, 1984.

[26] J. J. Hopfield and D. W. Tank, "'Neural' computation of decisions in optimization problems," *Biol. Cybern.*, vol. 52, p. 141, 1985.

[27] T. Kohonen, "Correlation matrix memories," *IEEE Trans. Comput.*, vol. C-21, pp. 353–359, 1972.

[28] ____, *Associative Memory: A System-Theoretical Approach.* Berlin: Springer-Verlag, 1977.

[29] T. Kohonen, E. Oja, and P. Lehtio, "Storage and processing of information in distributed associative memory systems," in *Parallel Models of Associative Memory*, G. Hinton and J. A. Anderson, Eds. Hillsdale, NJ: Erlbaum, 1981.

[30] T. Kohonen, *Self-Organization and Associative Memory.* Berlin: Springer-Verlag, 1984.

[31] B. Kosko, "Adaptive bidirectional associative memories," *Appl. Opt.*, vol. 26, no. 23, pp. 4947–4860, Dec. 1987.

[32] ____, "Fuzzy associative memories," in *Fuzzy Expert Systems*, A. Kandel, Ed. Reading, MA: Addison-Wesley, 1987.

[33] ____, "Fuzzy entropy and conditioning," *Info. Sci.*, vol. 40, pp. 165–174, 1986.

[34] W. S. McCulloch and W. Pitts, "A logical calculus of the ideas immanent in nervous activity," *Bull. Math. Biophys.*, vol. 5, pp. 115–133, 1943.

[35] R. J. McEliece, E. C. Posner, E. R. Rodemich, and S. S. Venkatesh, "The capacity of the Hopfield associative memory," *IEEE Trans. Inform. Theory*, vol. IT-33, pp. 1–33, July 1987.

[36] K. Nakano, "Associatron—A model of associative memory," *IEEE Trans. Syst. Man. Cybern.*, vol. SMC-2, pp. 380–388, 1972.

[37] D. Psaltis and N. Farhat, "Optical information processing based on an associative-memory model of neural nets with thresholding and feedback," *Opt. Lett.*, vol. 10, no. 2, pp. 98–100, Feb. 1985.

[38] L. A. Zadeh, "Fuzzy sets," *Inform. Contr.*, vol. 8, pp. 338–353, 1965.

Bart Kosko (M'85) received the B.A. degrees in philosophy and economics from the University of Southern California, Los Angeles, the M.A. degree in applied mathematics from the University of California, San Diego, and the Ph.D. degree in electrical engineering from the University of California, Irvine.

He is currently with the Department of Electrical Engineering, Systems, Signal and Information Processing Institute, at the University of Southern California.

Dr. Kosko is the Associate Editor and Technology News Editor of *Neural Networks*. He was organizing and program chairman of the IEEE First International Conference on Neural Networks (ICNN-87) in June 1987 and is program chairman of ICNN-88.

12
Introduction

(1988)
Pentti Kanerva

Sparse Distributed Memory, Cambridge, MA: MIT Press
Chapter 4, "Neurons as address decoders," pp. 43–48;
Chapter 5, "Search of memory for the best match," pp. 49–52;
Chapter 6, "Sparse memory," pp. 53–59; and
Chapter 7, "Distributed storage," pp. 61–77

We have excerpted four chapters from a wonderful short book, *Sparse Distributed Memory* by Pentti Kanerva. This book describes, with great lucidity, a strikingly original model for memory storage that has strong connections to ideas often used in neural networks.

Let us consider how to store information in a computer memory. We have some data, let us suppose, in the form of a long binary word, and we want to put it somewhere so we can retrieve it later. We must now ask a question that exposes a cultural gulf between a psychologist, say, and a computer scientist: "What do we retrieve the data *for*?" A computer scientist would say, "We want to get back exactly what we put in, because we could potentially use any part of that data, and it has to be exact." So we will put the data in a memory location, one of a large number of storage locations, make a note of where we put it in a table somewhere, and then, when we need the data, find it and use it. This approach places a heavy burden on the index, that is, finding the desired location, but it makes no particular assumptions about the contents of the memory or what the data might be needed for.

One class of memory operations, particularly important for psychological function, is not well served by this approach. In many, probably the majority of neural network models, it is assumed that both the input and outputs of the are represented by *distributed activity patterns*. There are a large number of computing elements, and each element has its own activity level. To represent information, a list of element activities is required. Such simultaneous patterns of many elements are called *state vectors*, and the data that psychological operations usually wish to retrieve or store are these state vectors. Because in some sense these state vectors represent psychological reality, there is an implicit assumption made that small differences in the state vectors *usually* do not make a major, discontinuous change in the meaning carried by the state vector. As an example, consider the complex pattern of visual activation on the retina, or in cerebral cortex corresponding to a robin that the observer has never seen before. If a few elements in this very large state vector representing the new robin happen to be different from previously seen robins, as of course will usually be the case in the real world, what the state vector represents has not changed, it still represents a robin. Nearby things are likely to have the same classification and behave the same way.

It is the practical value of nearness that nearest neighbor algorithms exploit effectively (see papers 25, 26, and 27). The importance of nearness also suggests a number of useful memory operations. One that is central to the operation of the Kanerva memory is the operation *best match*: Given a new state vector, where is the stored memory that most closely matches the new data? The most obvious, and most general, way to answer this question simply involves checking all the stored information for the best match. However, this can involve a very large number of operations.

There is a very different way of solving best match in a single step. To use one of Kanerva's examples, suppose we have 100 bits in the data we wish to store or retrieve. That means there are 2^{100} different possible binary vectors that could be stored. Suppose we assume an enormous memory of 2^{100} memory locations. Then suppose we put the memory in its own location: that is, we use the contents of the state vector as its location in memory. Then checking for an exact match with stored data becomes trivial. Simply see if that memory location is occupied. And best match becomes a matter of looking at nearby locations: there are 100 one-bit differences, 9,900 two-bit differences, and so on. Of course 2^{100} corresponds to a truly astronomical number of memory locations. Perhaps we don't need this many locations. If we assume that there are relatively few memories compared with the size of the state space, then, as says (p. 51), "... *if we construct the memory as we store the words of the data set*, we need only one location ... for each word of the data set." In Kanerva's terminology the memory is *sparse*, that is, most memory locations are unoccupied.

This insight now gives rise to a different way of looking at the problem. Suppose the hardware designer gives us, instead of 2^{100} locations, a random set of only 220 100-bit location designators, assumed to be randomly distributed across all the 2^{100} possible words. These prewired locations are called *hard locations* by Kanerva. Suppose we want to store a data word. One way to would be to find the *nearest* hard location to the value of the word and put the word to be stored in this nearest location. If the distribution of locations is uniform, there should be a location close to the contents of the word to be stored. A simple version of the best match retrieval operation is the same as before. When a word is to be checked for best match, the contents of the nearest hard location that contains something is most likely to contain the best match.

Kanerva discusses at length a number of variants on this insight. Suppose we looked at all locations within some distance around the word to be checked for the best match. We can compute the *probability* that the answer is correct, that is, that we retrieved the appropriate information. However Kanerva shows in chapter 6 that simply looking at some radius around the word to be checked does not work very well.

To make the memory work better, the storage procedure has to be modified. Instead of storing a *single* example of the word to be stored, we store *multiple* examples, that is, we put copies of the input data into all the hard locations within a radius of the word to be stored. Kanerva calls this technique *distributed storage*. However there is an immediate problem: We are likely to store information from several data words on top of each other, creating interference between different stored words. Kanerva suggests several ways to cope with this problem. All involve making an additional assumption of some kind about the information stored in the hard locations. Suppose each hard location does not store a single word, but rather multiple words, each corresponding to one of the words stored by the act of multiple storage.

Perhaps the most intuitive way to see what is going on is to assume that an input word is an exact match to a stored word. Suppose that the radius that is to be checked for matches contains 1,000 hard locations. In the act of storing the word, a copy of the input word was put into each of those 1,000 locations within the radius of the nearest hard location. There are usually other, unrelated words from other stored data also stored at some of these locations. However, the most common word will be the stored exact match because the radius of storage and the radius of retrieval are coincident, and all the words within the radius will contain a copy of the stored word. The other, interfering words will not be so frequent because their radius is centered somewhere else.

If the word to be checked and the stored word are not exactly the same, we can still claim that the number of examples of the stored word within the radius will be greatest because the two circles—storage and retrieval—will be nearer to coincidence than other stored words. One can also store the sums of the stored words, instead of keeping the stored words distinct, and the same arguments will still hold.

Kanerva also proposes and analyzes a simple iterative technique for constructing the location of the best match, as long as the input and the best match are not too far apart. Suppose the average data word, generated from the input word, is now used as the input word for *another* averaging step. If the target word and the input word are not too far apart, the resulting average data word will be closer to the target word than the original input data. Repeated iterations will eventually converge to the location of the target word.

The notion of distributed storage also allows for storage of other kinds of data in the stored word, in addition to the part that is used to determine the memory location. Large blocks of data can potentially be retrieved by these statistical techniques, based on retrieval using similarity to the part of the data used to construct the memory location.

What is worth emphasizing is the simplicity, elegance, and practical reliability of these sparse, distributed storage systems, as long as the requirement for theoretically perfect accuracy in retrieval is discarded. Kanerva shows that retrieval based on these systems is adequate for many purposes, and the amount of error potentially introduced in storage can be computed easily. This model is not, strictly speaking, a neural network, but can be realized quite easily in a less abstract, more networklike form. Kanerva has an earlier discussion in his book about the use of simple, neurallike elements as address decoders, which could be used as part of the hard location hardware.

The lack of connections between processing units leads to an important practical point. In many neural networks the number of connections scales as the square of the number of elements. For those interested in building network hardware this rapid increase in connections causes serious difficulties. The theoretical simplicity of the sparse distributed memory makes it exceptionally easy to build. And as a bonus Kanerva shows that the storage capacity is a linear function of the number of hard locations, therefore, it will scale well to large systems.

Although our excerpt describes only a few of the basics of the model as a memory, in the rest of the book, Kanerva uses this theoretical framework for a series of fascinating speculations on the organization of the human mind.

(1988)
Pentti Kanerva

Sparse Distributed Memory, Cambridge, MA: MIT Press
Chapter 4, "Neurons as address decoders," pp. 43–48;
Chapter 5, "Search of memory for the best match," pp. 49–52;
Chapter 6, "Sparse memory," pp. 53–59; and
Chapter 7, "Distributed storage," pp. 61–77

Chapter 4   Neurons as Address Decoders

My thesis is that certain classes of neurons should have their input coefficients (and their thresholds) fixed over the entire life of an organism. For reasons that will soon be made clear, I shall call such neurons *address-decoder neurons*. According to this interpretation, the n-tuple of input coefficients determines an n-bit address—a pattern to which the neuron responds most readily—and the threshold controls the size of the region of similar address patterns to which the neuron responds. This interpretation of the neuron function as an address decoder is the first major insight of this study.

In the remainder of this chapter, the input coefficients of a neuron are assumed to be constant in time, whereas the threshold is allowed to vary. Different neurons, by and large, are assumed to have different input coefficients.

Let us look first at a simple linear threshold function $U(x)$ of four variables, with weights $1, -1, -1,$ and -1 and threshold 0:

$$U(x) = 1 \text{ iff } u(x) \geq 0,$$

where $u(x) = x_0 - x_1 - x_2 - x_3$. Table 4.1 shows the entire function. The fourth column gives the distances between the points of the space and 1000. Notice that the function $U(x)$ is 1 whenever this distance is no more than 1. If the threshold were increased from 0 to 1, the function $U(x)$ would be 1 only when $x = 1000$.

Input Coefficients and the Address of a Neuron

The *address, a,* of a neuron with input coefficients w, where $w = \langle w_0,...,w_{n-1} \rangle$, is defined as the n-bit input pattern that maximizes the weighted sum. The maximum occurs when the inhibitory inputs are zeros and the excitatory inputs are ones, and so the ith bit of the address is

$$a_i = \begin{cases} 1 & \text{if } w_1 > 0 \\ 0 & \text{if } w_1 < 0 \end{cases}$$

(we assume for now that all weights are nonzero). The *maximum weighted sum, $S(w)$,* is then the sum of the positive coefficients:

$$S(w) = \sum_{w_i > 0} w_i.$$

The point opposite the neuron's address, a, yields the *minimum weighted sum, $s(w)$,* which is the sum of the negative coefficients:

$$s(w) = \sum_{w_i < 0} w_i.$$

For brevity, we let S stand for the maximum sum $S(w)$ and let s stand for the minimum sum $s(w)$. (See figure 4.1.) In the example at the beginning of the chapter (and in table 4.1), the input coefficients are $1, -1, -1,$ and -1, the maximum weighted sum is 1 and the pattern corresponding to it

Table 4.1   The linear function $u(x) = x_0 - x_1 - x_2 - x_3$ and the threshold function $U(x)$ with threshold 0.

x	$u(x)$	$U(x)$	$d(1000, x)$
0000	0	1	1
0001	−1	0	2
0010	−1	0	2
0011	−2	0	3
0100	−1	0	2
0101	−2	0	3
0110	−2	0	3
0111	−3	0	4
1000	1	1	0
1001	0	1	1
1010	0	1	1
1011	−1	0	2
1100	0	1	1
1101	−1	0	2
1110	−1	0	2
0111	−2	0	3

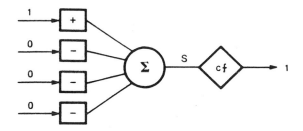

Figure 4.1 The address of a neuron.

(the neuron's address) is 1000, and the minimum weighted sum is −3 and the pattern corresponding to it is 0111.

The Threshold and the Response Region of a Neuron

When the threshold c is in the range $s < c \leq S$, the output of the neuron is 0 for some addresses (input patterns) and 1 for others. If the threshold is above S, the output is always 0; if it is below s, the output is always 1.

By a proper choice of the threshold, a neuron responds to just one address; that is, when the threshold is S (the maximum for the weighted sum), the neuron responds only to its own address and acts like an address decoder of a conventional computer memory.

What, exactly, happens when the threshold decreases from S to s? First, consider the simple case where all positive weights have value 1, all negative weights have value −1, and no weight is 0. Let a be the address of a neuron, let P be the number of positive weights, let Q be the number of negative weights ($P + Q = n$), let d be a distance ($d \geq 0$), and let $c = S - d$ be the threshold. Then $S = P$ and $s = -Q$. Let the threshold c decrease from S to s. This corresponds to letting the distance d increase from 0 to n. Then, for any given d, the neuron responds to all the addresses that are within d bits of the neuron's address a. These addresses form a region around a, called the *response region* of the neuron, with point a at the center of the region. The exact size of the region (the number of points) as a function of distance d is the size of the circle $0(d,a)$ and is equal to $N \cdot N(d)$, where $N(d)$ is the distribution function for the space $\{0,1\}^n$ (see the subsections on "Distribution of the Space N" and "Distribution of a Circle" in chapter 1). Thus, for small values of d the response region grows slowly with d, but in the neighborhood of $d = n/2$ the region grows very rapidly to include most of the address space.

If the firing of a neuron is taken to mean that a pattern has been recognized, a neuron is best thought of as a pattern-recognition device for a single pattern (point) rather than for some linearly separable set of patterns. This pattern is the neuron's address, and it is common to all nonempty, linearly separable sets that are obtained from a given set of input coefficients by varying the threshold. If the neuron's address a is thought of as a prototype or target pattern and an address x is thought of as a sample pattern, the neuron "recognizes" x if x is sufficiently close to (or within the distance $s - c$ of) the neuron's address. The comparison is indifferent to the location of the mismatched bits; only their number matters.

Here the threshold, c, serves as a gauge. To accept (or recognize) only closely matching patterns—that is, patterns that differ from the target pattern by only a small number of bits—c must be almost as high as the maximum weighted sum, S. When the threshold is lowered, more and more patterns are recognized. In the example at the beginning of this chapter, threshold 1 would make the function 1 only for the pattern 1000, threshold 0 makes it 1 for all patterns within one bit of 1000, threshold −1 would make it 1 for all patterns within two bits of 1000, and threshold −2 would make it 1 for all patterns but 0111. A neuron thus seems suited for pattern classification by the *nearest-neighbor method*, which assigns a test pattern to the stored pattern that is most similar to the test pattern. This property of neurons will be used in constructing a best-match machine in the next chapter.

Unequal Weights and Weighted Distance

This section is included for completeness. Its purpose is to show that unequal input weights do not affect the nature of the theory. The remainder of this study is then carried out with the simplifying assumption that all input weights are 1s and −1s.

Assume that the input weights can have values other than 1 and −1. The response region is still centered around the neuron's address, but in general there is no single distance d that would describe the border of the region. However, if some point x is in the response region of a neuron, so are all the points between x and the neuron's address. With unequal input weights, the absolute value of a coefficient is a measure of an input's relative importance to the firing of a neuron.

A slightly more general notion of distance is useful in dealing with unequal weights. Define the *weighted distance* between points x and y as

$$\sum_{i=0}^{n-1} |w_i|\, |y_i - x_i|.$$

Notice that $|y_i - x_i|$ is 0 or 1 according to whether the ith coordinates of x and y agree or differ (it is the exclusive-or function). The weighted distance can also be thought of as a *generalized Hamming distance*,

$$\sum_{i=0}^{n-1} |y'_i - x'_i|,$$

in the n-dimensional space obtained by mapping the zeros and ones of an address z to zeros and $|w_i|$'s of z' as follows:

$$z_i' = |w_i|z_i.$$

Geometrically, instead of the points of the space being at the vertices of an n-dimensional cube with sides of length 1, they are the vertices of an n-dimensional (rectangular) parallelepiped with sides of length $|w_i|$, and the generalized Hamming distance between two points is the length of the shortest path between them along the edges of the parallelepiped. (See figure 4.2.)

Multiplying the weights and the threshold by a positive constant does not affect the behavior of a neuron. Therefore, we will assume that the weights are normalized to make their absolute values add to n,

$$\sum_{i=0}^{n-1} |w_i| = n.$$

which makes $S - s = n$. When the absolute weights are equal and nonzero, the weighted distance is the Hamming distance.

The size of the response region (the number of points), as a function of the weighted distance, is approximately normal, with mean $n/2$ and variance

$$\frac{1}{4}\sum_{i=0}^{n-1} w_i^2.$$

(The normal approximation of the binomial distribution, which we get when the absolute weights are equal, is a special case of this. In both cases we have the sum of n independent random variables.) Thus, as the threshold decreases from S to s, the response region grows in much the same way as it does in the case of equal absolute weights. The unevenness of weights simply makes the distribution flatter and the growth of the region about the (mean) distance $(S - s)/2 (= n/2)$ less sudden.

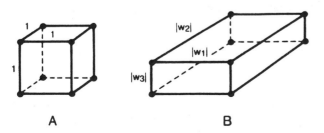

Figure 4.2 Equal (A) and unequal (B) input weights

We will now relax the condition that all weights be nonzero. An input with a zero coefficient means simply that the neuron is indifferent to the value of that input; it could just as well be removed. When some of the coefficients are zeros, the neuron's address is no longer uniquely defined in the n-dimensional address space. However, the response region for all values of the threshold is well defined, and the region corresponding to the maximum weighted sum S could be used as the address of the neuron. It is a subspace of the original space.

The address-decoder function of a neuron is robust. The strength of a synapse is relatively unimportant, for a neuron's address is affected by two things only: the adding or removing of inputs and the change of sign of an input coefficient. The first is manifested in the growth of new synapses and the deletion of old ones. If such changes are not numerous in comparison with the total number of (input) synapses of a neuron, the neuron's address will not be affected greatly. The second would change the neuron's address more drastically; however, as far as is known, synapses do not change from excitatory to inhibitory or vice versa, as the outputs of any one neuron are either all excitatory or all inhibitory. A change of sign is possible but would require the insertion of an intermediate neuron of the opposite kind between the two neurons that form the original synapse. All in all, it does not seem likely that an input coefficient would change sign. This would be a further constraint on perceptron-convergence learning.

In adopting the linear-threshold model, we have ignored the possible effects of the geometry of the dendrites and the positions of the synapses on them and on the cell body. Even if such effects were pronounced, the neuron would still act as an address decoder according to our definition. Only the shape of the response region would be affected.

Chapter 5   Search of Memory for the Best Match

The Problem of the Best Match

This chapter is a bridge from the neuron model to the memory model. As the first application of the unifying principle, which states that the data stored in memory are addresses to the memory, I will describe a computer—the *Best-Match Machine*—that is well suited for solving a problem that is hard for a conventional computer. The construction of the Best-Match Machine gives an idea of what the final memory model of this study is like.

Consider the problem of finding the best match to a test word in a data set of stored words. Minsky and Papert discuss this in their book *Perceptrons* (1969) under the heading "Time vs. Memory for Best Matching: An Open Problem" (pp. 222–225). The problem is the following: Describe a filing scheme for storing a set X of words (a data set of n-bit binary numbers; I have changed their nomenclature to conform with mine) so that one can retrieve, in minimum time, the stored word ζ that is the best match to a test word z. (The Greek letters ξ, η, and ζ will be used for words of the data set, with the target word denoted by ζ.) "Best match" means closest to in Hamming distance. The data set is assumed to fall randomly on the 2^n possible words (the data set has no particular structure), and the test words, likewise, are a random sample of the 2^n words. The question is: How does retrieval time depend on memory size?

Minsky and Papert conclude on a rather pessimistic note. They find an encouraging solution only when memory size is at least $2^n n$ bits—that is, when there is an n-bit storage location for every possible n-bit word. Filing the data X consists of storing at each address the word of X that matches the address the best. Retrieval is then reduced to reading just one word, or n bits, from the location addressed by the test word.

The effort that goes into filing the data set is not dealt with in *Perceptrons*. The filing for the above scheme requires the accessing of all of memory, and much of it more than once. The following might be a reasonable filing scheme: First store the words of the data set at locations addressed by the words themselves. Then, for each word ξ of the data set, compute all the words of N that are one bit away from ξ and write ξ in locations addressed by these distance-1 words, unless a location is already occupied (assume that each memory location has an extra location-occupied bit). Repeat this for distances 2, 3, and so on until all of memory is filled. Various criteria can be used to stop the checking of further locations around the word ξ. For example, if all addresses at distance d from ξ are found to be occupied (because they are closer to other words in the data set), further checking around ξ is unnecessary. In any case, with n but a modest 100, the memory will have 2^{100} (about 1,000,000,000,000,000,000,000,000,000,000) locations. So it would take less time to check each word of a trillion-word data set against each word of a trillion-word test set than to load the 2^{100}-location memory in the first place.

What I wanted to dramatize with this example is that conventional computer architecture does not seem to be suited for dealing with the problem of the best match. So let us examine how we might build a memory from neuronlike components to cope with the problem.

The Best-Match Machine

We have seen that a neuron can function as an address-decoder for a storage location. A proper choice of the threshold makes a neuron respond to, or decode, just one address, and further lowering of the threshold makes it decode a set of addresses centered around that one address.

Consider a memory with N locations, where $N = 2^n$. Let each location have the capacity for one n-bit word (e.g., 2^{100} 100-bit words, just as in the example above), and let the address decoding be done by N address-decoder neurons of the kind discussed in chapter 4. (We will henceforth refer to an address-decoder neuron by its address x.) Set the threshold of each neuron x to its maximum weighted sum, $|x|$, and use a common parameter d to adjust all thresholds when accessing the memory. The effective threshold of neuron x will then be $|x| - d$, which means that the location x is accessible every time that the address x is within d bits of the address presented to the memory (i.e., the address held by the address register; see figure 2.1). With $d = 0$ we have a conventional random-access memory—the kind that, in the preceding section, proved unsuited to the problem of the best match. Assume, further, that each location has a special location-occupied bit that can be accessed in the same way as the regular datum bits. Writing a word to a location sets the location-occupied bit. Assume also that only occupied locations can be read.

To file the data, start by setting $d = n$ and issue a command to clear the location-occupied bit. This single operation marks all of memory as unoccupied, regardless of the value of the address register. Then set $d = 0$ and write each word ξ of the data set with ξ itself as the address. Notice that each write operation affects only one location: the location ξ. Filing time is thus proportional to the number of words in the data set.

Finding the best match for a test word, z, involves placing z in the address register and finding the least distance d for which there is an occupied location. We can start the search by setting $d = 0$ and incrementing d by one successively until an occupied location is found. This method gives average search times that are proportional to the number of address bits, or slightly less than $n/2$, because the nearest occupied location can be expected to be just under $n/2$ bits from z. A binary search on d would be even faster, terminating in $\log_2(n)$ steps.

The apparent need for an enormously large memory seems like a serious objection to this solution. With 100-bit words, 2^{100} locations would be needed. But *if we construct the memory as we store the words of the data set,* we need only one location (and one address decoder) for each word of the data set. None of the unoccupied locations need be present. This aspect of *sparseness,* in a different form, together with the storing of addresses as data, carries over to later memory models.

The reader may feel cheated by my solution, thinking that I made up the rules of the game as I went along, to suit my purposes. But that brings up the exact point I want to make: that the architecture of a computer determines what the computer is good for.

In addition to the problem of the *best* match, Minsky and Papert discuss time versus memory for an *exact* match. Their measure of time is the number of bits retrieved from memory, and the best solution, in a certain sense, is hash coding (a technique known to programmers). I have used the number of memory cycles as the measure, but neither it nor the number of bits retrieved really measures computation if we maintain that the accessing of memory is a form of computing, the amount of which depends on memory size. More is said about this in the next section.

The problem of the best match is a mathematician's problem. To solve it, even with the Best-Match Machine, requires that the machine be reliable (deterministic). If there is any slack, as there usually is in biological systems, the best match is no longer guaranteed. But a somewhat unreliable Best-Match Machine would still find a *good* match, and that is usually sufficient in emulating biological systems. The hash-coding solution for finding an exact match breaks down completely if the computer memory is unreliable. So here, again, the neuron memory shows its robustness in the kinds of tasks that it might be asked to perform.

The Best-Match Machine with Different Data

To solve the problem of the best match, we stored the word ξ of the data set in location ξ. In the learning of sequences, we want to store some other word η in location ξ. If the Best-Match Machine is used in that way, what is retrieved by reading with the address x? We will only touch on this question here; we will return to it in chapter 8.

Let us assume that the data set contains word pairs $\langle \xi_i, \eta_i \rangle$, where the first word, ξ_i, is the address of the location in which the second word, η_i, is stored. Let us assume further that no two words are to be stored in the same location (i.e., $\xi_i \neq \xi_j$ for $i \neq j$; notice that the data in the best-match problem can be expressed as pairs $\langle \xi_i, \xi_i \rangle$). Reading from memory with address x will then find the occupied location that is closest to x (say, ξ_j), and will retrieve its contents, η_j (that is, the word that is stored at the address that matches x the best). If the pairs $\langle \xi_i, \eta_i \rangle$ themselves are thought of as a *partial* function $W: N \to N$, with $W(\xi)_i = \eta_i$, the Best-Match Machine extends the function into a *total* function by defining $W(x)$ as the value of the function at the nearest point where the partial function is defined.

A Note on Serial and Parallel Computing

The notions of serial and parallel computing have come up in the discussion. I want to clarify these notions and dispose of some common misconceptions.

We tend to think of the operation of a computer as serial because instructions are obeyed sequentially. However, many components of a computer are parallel processors. Parallelism is most striking in decoders such as instruction, device, and memory-address decoders, as has already been pointed out. Although by design the decoding usually results in a unique selection, we should appreciate the fact that this selection involves a great deal of parallel computation. The selection function is evaluated by every element that is capable of responding; however, by design the value of the function is 1 (for 'select') for just one element and 0 for all the others. Accordingly, *the mere accessing of memory should be regarded as computing*, the amount of which increases with memory size.

Computer programmers are familiar with the trade-off between run time and memory size. I suggest that the trade-off is really between serial and parallel computing. When the use of more memory actually allows us to write a faster program, we are, in fact, taking advantage of *parallel computing by the address decoders*. In contrast, a Turing machine is truly sequential, and with it we immediately notice the effect of memory size (i.e., the length of the active portion of the tape) on the amount of computing (number of steps, run time) required to access the memory. Similarly, increasing the size of the alphabet or the number of states of a Turing machine often allows us to write faster and more compact Turing-machine algorithms for a given task. But again, the use of a larger alphabet or a larger state space involves choosing from a greater number of alternatives. In any physical realization, that means more (parallel) computing in the form of decoding.

Chapter 6   Sparse Memory

We have seen thus far that a random-access memory is suited for pattern matching provided that linear threshold functions are used for address decoding, and that neurons can therefore serve as address decoders for such a memory. In this and the next chapter, we will see that the memory is practical and that the address-decoder neurons can be set in advance to their particular address patterns.

We will start with the foremost problem of the theory: the vastness of the address space N. There is no way to construct a random-access memory that has, say, $2^{1,000}$ storage locations. Even 2^{100} locations would be too many to fit into the human brain, as 2^{100} molecules of water would more than fill it (the number of neurons in the nervous system is "only" about 2^{36}). With such a vast address space, most of the addresses cannot be represented by an address decoder and a storage location. However, there is hardly the need for $2^{1,000}$ locations, because a human lifetime is too short to store anywhere near $2^{1,000}$ independent entities (a century has fewer than 2^{32} seconds).

A word could be stored in memory by writing it in a free storage location and at the same time providing the location with the appropriate address decoder. This possibility was mentioned in the discussion of the Best-Match Machine, and it is how a content-addressable computer memory works. However, the content-addressable memories of today's computers do not retrieve data on the basis of the similarity of the location's address to the retrieval cue, as is required by our model. (Recall that, in a content-address-able memory, an exact match with a designated part of a stored word causes the location to be selected; that part functions as the address of the location.) A neuron as an address decoder would select a location on the basis of similarity of address. However, it would then be necessary to set the neuron's address, once and for all, at the time of writing in the storage location, and that is a very difficult task to be accomplished with neurons. It would require first the identification of a free location (which in itself is an addressing problem) and then the setting of an address decoder for it (which would be complicated because synapses do not change from excitatory to inhibitory, or vice versa).

The alternative that I will explore here has the following characteristics:

> The storage locations and their addresses are given from the start, and only the contents of the locations are modifiable.

> The storage locations are very few in comparison with 2^n (the memory is sparse).

> The storage locations are distributed randomly in the $\{0, 1\}^n$ address space.

I shall call such a memory a *sparse* random-access memory.

We have already seen that linear threshold functions are ideal for address decoding and that neurons act like linear threshold functions. But neurons are also suitable for storing data. We will see that the storage of data in a location could be realized by a set of counters. An address-decoder neuron with fixed input synapses and modifiable output synapses could function as a storage location.

Concepts Related to Sparse Memory

Multiset N' of Hard Locations

The storage locations N' of a sparse memory—more precisely, the addresses of the locations—are a uniform random sample, with replacement, of the address space N. They will be called simply *locations*. To emphasize that they are physical locations of a sparse memory, they will also be called *hard* locations. Logically, the hard locations N' are a multiset; however, since only very sparse memories are considered here—say, 2^{-980} (i.e., 2^{20} hard locations out of $2^{1,000}$ possible locations)—repetitions of an element can be ignored, and so the hard locations can be thought of as a set. The prime symbol (') on a lowercase letter will be used to indicate elements of N', so that x' refers to a hard address. The symbol N' will also be used for the number of (hard) locations of the sparse memory.

Distance to a Hard Location

Hard locations will be referred to by their addresses—for example x'. By the *distance* from a point y (the address y) to a location x' is meant the distance $d(y, x')$ between the two addresses. Similarly, by the distance between two locations is meant the distance between their addresses.

Nearest N'-Neighbor, x'

The element of N' most similar to the element x of N is called the *nearest N'-neighbor* of x and is denoted by x' (x' is the hard location nearest to x). That x may have several nearest neighbors in N' is irrelevant to the discussion that follows. If X is a subset of N, then X' denotes the set of nearest N'-neighbors of elements of X:

$$X' = \{x' \mid x \in X\}$$

Distance to the Nearest Location, $d(x, x')$

The distribution of distances from points of N to their nearest N'-neighbors can be derived from the distribution of N. The distances in N are distributed according to $N(d)$:

$$N(d) = \Pr\{d(x, y) \le d \mid x, y \in N\}.$$

The distribution of $d(x, x')$, denoted here by $N'(d)$, where

$$N'(d) = \Pr\{d(x, x') \le d\},$$

can then be obtained as follows: The probability that none of N' independent random points of N is within d bits of x is $[1 - N(d)]^{N'}$, so the probability that at least one is within d bits of X is given by

$$N'(d) = 1 - [1 - N(d)]^{N'}.$$

This can be rewritten as

$N'(d) = 1 - [1 - N'N(d)/N']^{N'},$

which is approximated by

$N'(d) \cong 1 - \exp\{- N'N(d)\}.$

The approximation is excellent when N' is large and $N(d)$ is small—say, $N' > 1,000$ and $N(d) < 1/N'$, as they are here. When $N(d) = 1/N'$, we have that $N'(d) \cong 1 - e^{-1} = 0.63$, which means that, with probability 0.63, a circle containing $1/N'$ of N contains at least one hard location. (On the average, the circle contains one location.) Solving for $N(d)$ in terms of $N'(d)$ gives

$N(d) \cong -\ln[1 - N'(d)]/N',$

from which we can compute percentiles of $N'(d)$:

$N'^{-1}(p) \cong N^{-1}[- \ln(q)/N'],$

where $0 \le p \le 1$ and $q = 1 - p$. For example, the median for the distance $d(x, x')$ is $N^{-1}[- \ln(0.5)/N']$. The normal distribution function with mean $n/2$ and standard deviation $\sqrt{n}/4$ can be used for $N(d)$. Selected points of the distribution $N'(d)$ are given in table 6.1.

As an example of a sparse memory, consider one with an address space $\{0,1\}^{1,000}$ and with 1,000,000 hard loctions:

Table 6.1 Distribution of distance to nearest storage location $N'(d)$, in a 1,000-dimensional memory with 1,000,000 locations.

d	$N'(d)$	z[a]	$N(d)$[b]
388.8	0.000001	−7.03	10^{-12}
394.0	0.00001	−6.71	10^{-11}
399.4	0.0001	−6.36	10^{-10}
405.2	0.001	−6.00	10^{-9}
411.3	0.01	−5.61	10^{-8}
417.9	0.1	−5.19	10^{-7}
421.0	0.25	−5.00	3×10^{-7}
423.7	0.5	−4.83	7×10^{-7}
425.9	0.75	−4.69	0.000001
427.6	0.9	−4.58	0.000002
429.9	0.99	−4.43	0.000005
431.3	0.999	−4.35	0.000007
432.2	0.9999	−4.28	0.000009
433.1	0.99999	−4.23	0.000012
433.7	0.999999	−4.19	0.000014

a. z is the number of standard deviations that d is below the mean distance 500: $z = (d - 500)/15.8$.
b. $N(d)$ is the distribution of the space N: $N(d) = \Pr\{d(x,y)\} \cong F(z)$.

$N = \{0,1\}^{1,000}$ and $N' = 1,000,000 \cong 2^{20}$. A hard location would then represent one millionth of the space, or 2^{980} addresses, on the average. A circle with a radius of 425 bits contains a millionth of the space. From table 6.1 we see, for example, that the median distance to the nearest (hard) location is 424 bits (423.7, to be exact), and that only once in about 10,000 is the nearest location within 400 bits of a point. In 98 percent of the cases the distance from a point to the nearest hard location falls between 411 and 430 bits. In what follows, we will assume for simplicity that the distance from a *random* point of N to the hard location nearest to it is the median distance of 424 bits.

The Nearest-Neighbor Method in Sparse Memory

The rest of this chapter is an abortive attempt at using a sparse memory to solve the best-match problem. This attempt is included because it is the most obvious thing to try and because, as we will see in the next chapter, it fails for the very reason that distributed storage works.

Let X be a random data set of 10,000 words of $\{0, 1\}^{1,000}$. It is to be stored in a sparse memory that has 1,000,000 hard locations, and the object is to find the stored word that matches a test word the best.

The strategy most like the one used with the Best-Match Machine is to store each word ξ of X in the hard location nearest to ξ—namely, in ξ'. To find the best match to z, one would read the occupied hard location nearest to z. But that location would not, in general, contain the best match, or even a good match. In fact, storing ξ in the nearest hard location does not help much at all, as is shown by the following example.

Assume that the test word is z, that ζ is the element of X most similar to z, and that the distance between the two is 200 bits (which means that ζ is actually quite similar to z, so we would definitely want to find ζ; the parameter values of the example—1,000,000 locations, a 10,000-word data set, and $d(z,\zeta) = n/5 = 200$—have been selected with the later discussion of distributed storage in mind). There are two questions to ask: What is the probability that the occupied hard location nearest to z contains ζ (i.e., that the location in fact is ζ')? How similar to z, on the average, is the word of X contained in that location? (Notice that the location need not be z'—the hard location nearest to z—as z' can be empty.)

The word ζ has been stored in the location nearest to it, ζ' (which, according to the discussion at the end of the preceding section, is about 424 bits from ζ). Thus, we assume that $d(\zeta, \zeta') = 424$ bits; see figure 6.1. The average distance between z and ζ' is then given by the third side of the triangle z, ζ, ζ', with known sides z, ζ and ζ, ζ' as

$d(z,\zeta') \cong 200 + 424 - 2 \cdot 200 \cdot 424/1{,}000 = 454$ bits.

We can expect to find approximately 0.0017 of N', or 1,700 hard locations, within 454 bits of z (0.001 of the space lies within 451 bits of a point according to table 1.2). About 0.01 of them, or 17 locations, are occupied by elements of X, and so, in a sense, ζ' is one of 17 locations. Its being the location nearest to z would therefore have a probability somewhere around 1/17,

$\Pr\{z'' = \zeta'|d(z,\zeta) = 200\} \cong 1/17,$

where z'' is the nearest X'-neighbor of z.

The probability of obtaining the best match with the nearest-neighbor method is low. In the example it is about 1/17—which, by the way, does not mean that examining the 17 occupied locations nearest to the test word z would guarantee that the best-matching word ζ would be found, although the probability of its being among the 17 is high. Nevertheless, it is reasonable to examine occupied locations in successively larger circles around z and compare their contents with z, although only rarely would the best match be guaranteed without the examining of at least half of memory (one need not look farther than twice the distance to the most similar word found so far).

The real weakness of the nearest-neighbor method becomes evident when data other than the addresses themselves are stored in memory—that is, if, instead of ζ, some other word η of N is stored in location ζ'. In terms introduced at the end of chapter 5, the data set then consists of pairs $\langle\xi,\eta\rangle$ instead of pairs $\langle\xi,\xi\rangle$, and for a test word z we want to find the word η that is paired with the ξ that matches z the best. The problem now is that the contents of location ξ' give no clue as to how close ξ is to z. Consequently, the probability of success in the example would be about 1/17, and there would be no way to tell by reading from memory whether the outcome is a success or a failure, or, in philosophers' terms, knowing whether one knows. (In the best-match case it is possible to tell.)

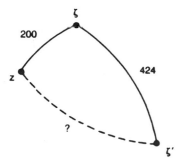

Figure 6.1 The distance from z to the location ζ', where the best-matching word ζ is stored. The "unknown" distance $d(z,\zeta')$ is approximately 454 bits

We can get an idea of how poor the method is (in 16 cases out of 17) by finding out how dissimilar are two addresses u and v that refer to the same hard location, that is, when $u' = v'$. Assume that $d(u,u') = d(v,u') = 424 \cong$ the median distance between a point of N and its nearest neighbor in N'. The mean length of the third side $\{u,v\}$ of the triangle $\{u,u',v\}$ is a good estimate of the distance $d(u,v)$. It is given by $2a(1-a/n)$ (see "The Third Side of a Triangle" in chapter 1), and for $a = 424$ and $n = 1{,}000$ it is 488 bits, or a mere 0.75 standard deviation from the indifference distance (488 bits encompass slightly less than 1/4 of the space). This means that, as a rule, the contents of the nearest occupied location are unrelated to the retrieval cue.

I will conjecture that any simple method that either writes a word of the data set in just one location or reads from just one location of a sparse memory with preset addresses will not work. The reason is that the *contents of memory locations can be similar over sufficiently large, contiguous areas of N* (over 0.00001 of N, say) *only if they are similar over all of N*, that is, if they are essentially constant. This is a simple consequence of how the points of N are distributed: Any two points at indifference distance $n/2$ from each other have a common neighbor (in fact, many of them) that is very close to both in a probabilistic sense (the proportion of the space that lies within $n/4$ bits of a point is exceedingly small).

The following example demonstrates the above conclusion: Assume that the memory has 1,000-bit addresses ($n = 1{,}000$), that the contiguous areas are circles that cover but a billionth of the address space, and that the "similar" 1,000-bit words stored within any such circle differ from one another by at most 100 bits. The circles have a radius of 405 bits, according to table 1.2. If we now take an arbitrary address x and the union of the circles (with 405-bit radii) that include x, we get a circle of addresses with its center at x and with a radius of 810 bits. This larger circle includes almost all of the address space N (it excludes much less than a billionth), and the words stored within it differ from one another by at most 200 bits (since they differ from the word stored at x by at most 100 bits). The surface of a three-dimensional sphere fails to suggest this conclusion.

Chapter 7 Distributed Storage

The idea of distributed storage is that many storage locations participate in a single write or read operation—in marked contrast to conventional computer memories, in which only one location is active at once. Somewhat surprisingly, this gives the memory the appearance of a random-access memory with a very large address space and with data retrieved on the basis of similarity of address.

More specifically, if the word η is stored at the address ξ, then reading from ξ retrieves η, and, what is more important, reading from an address x that is sufficiently similar to ξ retrieves a word y that is even more similar to η than x is to ξ (the similarities are comparable because the addresses to the memory and the data are elements of the same metric space, N).

The first of the postulates for sparse memory given at the beginning of chapter 6 stated that "the storage locations and their addresses are given from the start, and only the contents are modifiable." Nothing was said about the threshold that controls the range of addresses to which an address decoder responds. In chapter 6, as with the Best-Match Machine of chapter 5, the threshold was allowed to vary, and it provided the mechanism for searching memory for the nearest occupied location. With distributed storage, even the thresholds of the address decoders can be fixed. This simplifies the construction of the memory further, leaving the contents of the locations as the only things that need to be modified.

The mathematical feasibility of distributed storage is the main result of this study. It will be demonstrated first with reference to the problem of the best match, but the result applies in general. We shall also have occasion to estimate the capacity of the memory, that is, the maximum number of words that can be stored successfully in a memory of a given size (meaning that the words can be retrieved later). Certain properties of the data retrieved from memory can be interpreted as the philosophers' notion of knowing that one knows, and certain states of a search as the psychologists' notion of a tip-of-the-tongue state. Such interpretations are given at the end of this chapter.

Concepts Related to Distributed Storage

In what follows, frequent reference will be made to an example of a sparse memory with a thousand dimensions and a million hard locations ($n = 1,000$ and $N' = 1,000,000$). The following notation will be used: Words of the data set stored in the memory will be designated by letters of the Greek alphabet. The only other use of the Greek letters is for addresses used in writing (i.e., for centers of write circles—to be discussed in this chapter). Latin letters will stand for general points of the (address) space N. When appropriate, z will stand for a test word and ζ for the target word (the word of the data set most similar to z—the one for zeroing in).

Access Radius, r, and Access Circle, $O'(x)$

We shall require that when the memory is addressed with x, the locations closest to x are accessed. More specifically, all the locations within a given distance r of x will either store or provide data, depending on whether the memory is being written into or read from. This defines the access circle $O'(r,x)$ as the hard locations in the circle $O(r,x)$. Since the access radius r will be constant throughout the discussion, it is convenient to abbreviate $O(r,x)$ to $O(x)$ and $O'(r,x)$ to $O'(x)$. The access circle then is the (multi)set of hard locations given by

$$O'(x) = N' \cap O(x).$$

We say that the (hard) location y' is *accessible* from x if y' is no farther than r bits from x—that is, if y' is in the access circle $O'(x)$. In our example, assume that $1/1,000$ of N (and of N' on the average) is accessed at once. A circle with a radius of 451 bits covers $1/1,000$ of the space (see table 1.2), and so the access radius $r_{0.001}$ is 451 bits. The mean number of hard locations in an access circle is then 1,000.

Most locations in the access circle are quite far from the center of the circle. The location closest to the center is 424 bits from the center, on the average (the median distance to the nearest location is 423.7 bits according to table 6.1). The average (median) distance from the center to the 1,000 or so locations of the access circle is 448 bits (a circle with 448-bit radius encloses 0.0005 of the space according to table 1.2), which is only three bits short of the maximum distance of 451 bits.

Access Overlap, $I'(x,y)$

The set of hard locations accessible from both x and y is given by

$$I'(x,y) = O'x \cap O'(y).$$

The mean number of locations in this access overlap depends on the size of the access circle and on the distance $d(x,y)$ between the centers of the overlapping circles, as figure 1.2 suggests. Table 7.1 gives this number for our sample memory, and figure 7.1 shows it graphically. The outstanding fact is that, for the values of r that interest us here, the size of the overlap falls rapidly as the distance between the centers increases.

Contents of a Location, $C(x')$

We need to specify what a storage location will contain. Let us start with the generous assumption that it can contain the multiset of all the words that have ever been written in it. This is a drastic departure from computer memories in which the old word in a location is replaced by a newly written word. We shall postpone questions of how to construct memory locations of unlimited capacity, both because it is easier to develop the theory when we assume unlimited capacity and because in the end we make do with a relatively small capacity.

Table 7.1 Mean number of hard locations in access overlap of two circles with radii $r_{0.001} = 451$ in a 1,000-dimensional memory with 1,000,000 locations.

d^a	Number of locations	d	Number of locations	d	Number of locations	d	Number of locations	d	Number of locations
0	1000	21	619	60	400	160	146	360	13
1	894	23	603	65	376	170	132	370	11
2	894	25	588	70	361	180	119	380	10
3	842	27	573	75	339	190	107	390	8
4	842	29	559	80	326	200	97	400	7
5	803	31	546	85	307	210	87	410	6
6	803	33	533	90	295	220	78	429	5
7	770	35	521	95	277	230	70	430	4
8	770	37	509	100	267	240	62	440	4
9	743	39	497	105	251	250	55	450	3
10	743	41	486	110	241	260	49	460	2
11	718	43	475	115	228	270	44	470	2
12	718	45	465	120	219	280	39	480	2
13	695	47	455	125	206	290	34	490	1
14	695	49	445	130	198	300	30	500	1
15	674	51	435	135	186	310	26	510	1
16	674	53	426	140	179	320	23	520	1
17	655	55	417	145	169	330	20	530	0
18	655	57	408	150	162	340	18	540	0
19	636	59	400	155	152	350	15	550	0

a. d is the distance, in bits, between the centers of the two circles.

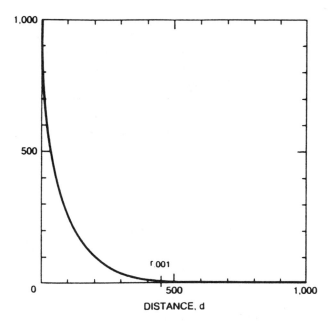

Figure 7.1 Mean number of hard locations in the access overlap of table 7.1 as a function of the distance between the centers of the two circles.

Writing in x'

Writing the word η *in* hard location x' means including it in the multiset of words $C(x')$ contained in x',

$$C(x') := C(x') \uplus [\eta].$$

Writing with Address ξ, or Writing at ξ

Writing the word η *at* ξ means writing η *in* all the (hard) locations accessible from ξ. All told, $|O'(\xi)|$ copies of η are stored in memory. In the example, η is written in the approximately 1,000 locations closest to ξ.

Data at x, $D(x)$

The data *at* x are the pooled contents of the locations accessible from x (i.e., the multiunion of the contents):

$$D(x) = \underset{y' \in O'(x)}{\uplus} C(y').$$

These are the words retrieved by reading with the address x.

Two comments must be made about the pooled data $D(x)$: First, if the word η has been written with the address

STORAGE LOCATIONS

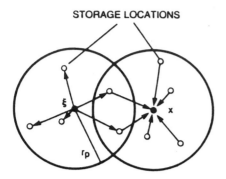

Figure 7.2 Writing at ξ and reading at x.

ξ, the multiset $D(x)$ contains $|O'(x) \cap O'(\xi)|$ copies of η, one from each location accessible from both x and ξ (see figure 7.2). Second, most of the words in $D(x)$ have been written with addresses quite dissimilar to x. In our example, most of them have been written with addresses that are more than 488 bits from x (12 bits short of the indifference distance, which is less than one standard deviation), as can be shown by a calculation identical to the one on page 58. A similar calculation applied to the 448-bit median distance from the center of an access circle to the locations in the circle (see p. 62) gives 494 bits as a *typical* distance from the center of the read circle to the centers of the write circles that contribute to the pooled data.

Reading at x

Reading at x means taking a representative (an element of N) of the data at x. The selection of the representative is a statistical problem that will be dealt with in the next section.

Word at x

The word at x, $W(x)$, is a properly chosen representative of the data at x. It is what reading at x yields.

The Feasibility of Distributed Storage: Finding the Best Match

The feasibility of distributed storage is shown by showing that a sequence of successively read words converges in the right way. This is done most easily with reference the best-match problem by showing that the convergence is to the best-matching word of the data set. We will see that the conditions for convergence are (1) that not too many words have been stored in memory and (2) that the first reading address (i.e., the test pattern) is sufficiently close to the address with which the target word was written (i.e., the target pattern).

To our earlier assumptions, $n = 1,000$, $N' = 1,000,000$, and $r = r_{0.001} = 451$, we add the assumption that the data

set X has 10,000 words. Since each write operation adds a word to each of about 1,000 locations, storing the entire data set means that some 10^7 words are stored in memory, or an average of 10 words per location. This gives our first estimate for the capacity of a storage location: A location should be able to store at least 10 words. Reading will pool the data of about 1,000 locations, yielding a multiset D of about 10,000 words. To summarize: $|X| = 10,000$, $|O'(x)| \cong 1,000$, $|C(x')| \cong 10$, and $|D(x) \cong 10,000$ (x is a random point of N).

For the problem of the best match, storing the data set X is analogous to storing it in the Best-Match Machine of chapter 5; that is, the word ξ of X is written at ξ. But instead of one copy of ξ being stored, 1,000 copies are—one in each location accessible from ξ. After the entire data set has been stored, location x' will contain the multiset of words of X that are accessible from x', or

$$C(x') = X \cap O(x').$$

Representative of the Pooled Data, $W(x)$

Assume that the test word is z and that the word of X most similar to z is ζ. We start by reading at z, which means that the contents of the locations accessible from z are pooled into the multiset of data $D(z)$. How should the representative of $D(z)$ be chosen? I will describe three possible methods first and then settle on a fourth.

The first method would be to examine each element of $D(z)$ and take the one *most similar to* z. It guarantees success if the best-matching word of X is similar to z (say, within 200 bits of it). However, the method can be dismissed on two grounds: First, the pooled data $D(z)$ will be very large. In our example, $D(z)$ will have as many words as the data set X itself, so that nothing would be gained by storing the data set in a random-access memory. Second, the method does not generalize beyond the best-match problem—that is, to cases in which a word unrelated to ζ is written at ζ—because the contents of a location would then bear no relation to the location's address.

The remaining three methods are statistical and are based on the *frequency* of words in the multiset of pooled data. The number of copies of the word ξ in the pooled data $D(z)$ is given by the size of the access overlap when writing at ξ and then reading at z; therefore, it is $|O'(z) \cap O'(\xi)|$. (See figure 7.2, and remember that ξ has been written at ξ.) The closer the circle centers z and ξ are to each other, the more the circles overlap (see figure 7.1). Thus, if ζ is the word of X most similar to z, we can expect ζ to be the most frequent word in the pooled data $D(z)$. Reading at z in the second, third, and fourth methods is then done by taking, respectively, the most frequent word of the pooled data, a random word of the pooled data, and a word of N that is an archetype of the pooled data.

Taking the *most frequent word* in $D(z)$ is sound in principle, but the computational task of deciding which 1,000-bit word is most frequent among some 10,000 words seems insurmountable. This second method is therefore judged to be impractical.

In the third method we would take a *random word* of the pooled data $D(z)$. But notice that the 10,000 or so words of $D(z)$ contain at most about 1,000 copies of ζ (if $z = \zeta$). If the distance from z to ζ is 200 bits, there are only about 95 copies of ζ among the 10,000 (see table 7.1). Thus, the probability of selecting at random the right element would be no more than 1/10, and usually it would be much less (it would be about 1/100 if $d(z, \zeta) = 200$).

The second and third methods appear to require that the words be stored intact in the memory locations; that is, they do not seem amenable to compressed forms of storage. This drawback is overcome by the fourth method.

The fourth and final method is to compute an element of N that is an *archetype* of the pooled data $D(z)$ but not necessarily an element of it. A natural candidate is an average of the words of $D(z)$. The simplest average is obtained by applying the *majority rule* to each bit, or coordinate, independently of the others. This average is the best representative of $D(z)$ in the sense that it is the word of N with the smallest mean distance to the words of $D(z)$. *Reading at z henceforth refers to taking the average of the pooled data* $D(z)$.

The ith bit of the average is given by summing over the ith bits of the words in the pooled data and then thresholding with half the size of the pooled data:

$$W_i(z) = 1 \text{ iff } \sum_{\xi \in D(z)} \xi_i \geq |D(z)|/2.$$

Notice that only sums—and not the individual words—are needed to compute the average word. This simplifies greatly the construction of the memory, as we will see later.

The above bit sum can be written as

$$\sum_{\xi \in D(z)} \xi_i = \sum_{\xi \in X} |O'(z) \cap O'(\xi)| \xi_i$$

to show that the size of the overlap of the write and read circles serves as a weight in computing the average. It is by virtue of such weighting that the element of X most frequent in $D(z)$, and hence most similar to z, might be recovered.

The average of the pooled data, as defined above, is a satisfactory representative of the data so long as the words written in memory are a random sample of N, in which case zeros and ones are equally probable. This assumption is not necessary for the development of the theory, but for simplicity we will adhere to it in the remainder of this chapter.

Convergence to the Best-Matching Word

Under the proper conditions, a sequence of words read from memory starting with the address z converges to the word ζ of X that matches z the best. Specifically, the memory is first read at z to obtain the word $z(1)$; it is then read at $z(1)$ to obtain the word $z(2)$, and so forth, generating the sequence of words $z(0),..., z(i), ...,$ where $z(0) = z$ and $z(i) = W(z(i-1))$ for $i = 1, 2, ...$ This manner of reading is called *iterated reading starting at z*.

What happens when we read at ζ if we have previously written the word ζ at ζ? Can we recover ζ? When the word ζ was written, one copy of it was written in each of the locations in the access circle $O'(\zeta)$, for a total of about 1,000 copies. Reading at ζ retrieves all of them but also about 10,000 copies of words other than ζ. (Reading at a previously written address retrieves about 11,000 words, whereas reading at a random address retrieves about 10,000 words.) However, the other words come mostly in ones or in very small groups, because the intersection of the read circle $O'(\zeta)$ with the write circle $O'(x)$, for most x in N (and in X), is about 0.001 of $O'(\zeta)$, or just one hard location. Against such background noise, the weight of 1,000 is sufficient for the retrieval of ζ (or for its reconstruction, whichever way one wants to look at the computing of the average).

A detailed analysis of the average is given in appendix C. The statistics for a single bit of the average (say, the ith coordinate) work out as follows: The data set X has 9,999 words other than ζ. Each of them occurs once, on the average, in the approximately 10,000 words of the pooled data $D(\zeta)$, and hence their ith coordinates resemble 10,000 Bernoulli trials with a 0.5 probability of an outcome's being 0 (or 1). The sum of such trials has a mean of 5,000 and a standard deviation of 50. Adding to it 1,000 copies of the ith bit of ζ brings the mean sum to 5,500. It is 5,000 if the bit is 0 and 6,000 if it is 1. So we will be measuring a 500-unit deviation from the mean with a standard deviation of 50, which makes the probability of guessing the bit correctly not less than $1 - 1/10^{22}$. The probability of guessing all 1,000 bits correctly and thus retrieving ζ is then the 1,000th power of that, $(1 - 1/10^{22})^{1,000} \cong 1 - 1/10^{19}$, or a near certainty, allowing us to say that the word recovered by reading at ζ indeed is ζ, or $W(\zeta) = \zeta$.

Next consider the problem of finding, for a test word z, the word ζ of X that is most similar to z (i.e.. finding the best match). Assume that the distance $d(z,\zeta)$ between the two is 200 bits. The claim is that reading at z yields a word that is closer to ζ than z is. The word ζ now has a weight of $|O'(z) \cap O'(\zeta)|$, which, according to table 7.1, is about 97. The 10,000 or so other words of X, again, have a weight of about 1 each. By an argument similar to the one above, we will be measuring a 48.5-unit deviation from the mean with a standard deviation of 50. A bit of the read word $W(z)$ will then match the corresponding bit of z with probability 0.83, and the expected distance from $W(z)$ to ζ will be $1,000 - 830 = 170$ bits, or 30 bits less than the original distance 200. Repeating the procedure with $W(z)$ gives $W(W(z))$, which is but 100 bits from ζ, and two more iterations suffice to reproduce ζ. (The next distance to ζ would be about 4 bits, and the one after that zero.)

Table 7.2 shows how the new distance to the target, $d(W(z),\zeta)$, depends on the old distance, $d(z, \zeta)$. A slightly more accurate (and larger) estimate of the variance of a bit sum has been used in computing this table (the variance is derived in appendix C), and so the values in the table are not exactly the same as those in the previous paragraph. Figure 7.3 plots the data of table 7.2.

Iterated reading fails to converge to the best-matching word if the original distance, $d(z,\zeta)$, is too large. In the example, a test word more than 210 bits from the target will not, as a rule, find its target. For example, according to table 7.2, $d(z,\zeta) = 220$ yields $d(W(z),\zeta) = 236$, which yields $d(W(W(z)),\zeta) = 274$, which yields $d(W(W(W(z))),\zeta) = 350$, which yields ... $\cong 500$, and so this sequence diverges. (Notice that these values, as well as those given two paragraphs above, are rounded mean values and thus give only a general idea of how an actual sequence might converge or diverge.) Converging and diverging sequences are illustrated in figure 7.4.

Table 7.2 Transformation of distance to target by reading with access radius $r_{0.0001}$ from a 1,000-dimensional memory with 1,000,000 locations after 10,000 write operations.

Distance							
Old	New	Old	New	Old	New	Old	New
0	0	180	135	250	305	400	474
70	0	185	148	260	325	410	478
80	1	190	160	270	344	420	482
90	3	195	173	280	361	430	485
100	7	200	186	290	376	440	487
110	12	205	199	300	391	450	489
120	21	<u>209</u>	<u>209</u>	310	404	460	491
130	33	210	212	320	416	470	493
140	48	215	224	330	426	480	494
150	67	220	236	340	436	490	495
155	77	225	249	350	444	500	496
160	87	230	260	360	452	520	498
165	99	235	272	370	458	540	499
170	110	240	283	380	464	560	499
175	123	245	294	390	470	580	500

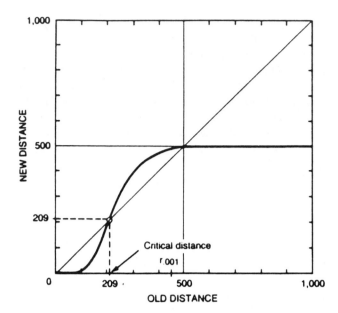

Figure 7.3 New distance to target as a function of old distance.

Further Concepts and Properties of Distributed Storage

The key properties of storage have been demonstrated here with reference to data of the form $\langle \xi, \xi \rangle$, meaning that the word ξ is written at ξ. They will be summarized and further amplified below. More general forms of data will be discussed in the next chapter.

Signal Strength

Signal strength is defined here as the weight of the target word ζ in the pooled data $D(z)$ obtained by reading at z. It equals the size of the overlap of the read circle with the target write circle, $|O'(z) \cap O'(\zeta)|$. Signal strength as a function of the distance between the read address and the target address is shown in table 7.1. Maximum signal strength (obtained by reading at the write address, $z = \zeta$) is the number of locations in the access circle (approximately pN', where p is the portion of the space covered by the access circle). The maximum signal strength of the example is 1,000. The average signal strength is $p^2 N'$ ($= 1$ in the example). Notice that writing a given word k times at a given address results in a k-fold signal strength for that word.

Noise

Noise is defined here as the standard deviation of the ith bit-sum in the data pooled at a random point of N. In the example its value is 50. In appendix C, where different but equivalent definitions of writing and reading are used (the

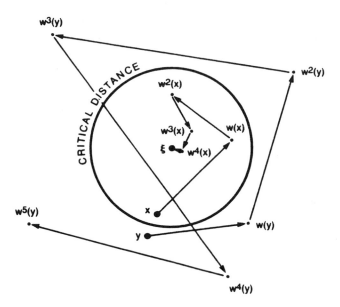

Figure 7.4 Converging and diverging sequences.

values for signal and noise there are twice what they are above), noise is approximately $\sqrt{p^2 N' T}$ where T is the size of the data set that has been stored in memory. The ratio of signal strength to noise, or simply the signal-to-noise ratio, is a normalized quantity. It will be denoted by R. The maximum signal-to-noise ratio, in the terms of appendix C, is therefore

$$R_{max} \cong \frac{pN'}{\sqrt{p^2 N' T}}$$

$$= \sqrt{N'/T} \ .$$

Whenever this ratio is high enough (in the example of the previous section it is 10), a word written at ξ is recovered, with high probability, by reading at or near ξ.

Fidelity

Fidelity at z, denoted by P, is defined here as the probability that a bit of the read word, $W(z)$, matches that of the target word, ζ. From this definition it follows that

$$P = \Pr \left[W_i(z) = \zeta_i \right]$$

$$\cong F(R)$$

where F is the normal distribution function. The probability that $W(z)$ is the target word is then the nth power of fidelity.

Maximum fidelity is obtained by reading at the target address. In the example, the fidelity at 200 bits from the target is 0.83 and the maximum fidelity is somewhere around $1 - 1/10^{22}$. The quantity $1 - P$ tells us how far, on the average, the read word $W(z)$ is from the target. This relation has been given in table 7.2 and figure 7.3. Wherever in figure 7.3 the function is below the 45° line, the read

word $W(z)$ is closer to the target, on the average, than is the original word z.

Convergence and Divergence

The convergence of a sequence of successively read words is the key property of distributed storage. It means that the current estimate of the target word can be improved by reading from memory. It also means that successively read words get closer and closer to one another until they are identical. The stationary condition for a *divergent* sequence is characterized by adjacent words' being approximately orthogonal to one another (and to the target). By chance, an initially diverging sequence can converge to a random word of the data set X. Such convergence (which will be called *chance convergence*) is characterized by a very long expected time to convergence.

Critical Distance

A sequence of read words converges only if the initial address is sufficiently close to the target. The distance beyond which divergence is more likely than convergence will be called the *critical distance*. In the example it is 209 bits (see table 7.2). As more words are stored in memory, the critical distance decreases until it reaches zero, and thereafter it vanishes, meaning that stored words are no longer retrievable (nowhere is there convergence).

The critical distance is the distance at which there is probability 0.5 that the word read from memory is closer to the target word than the reading address is. A very good estimate of the critical distance can be obtained by finding the distance at which the arithmetic mean of the new distance to the target equals the old distance to the target—that is, by solving $1 - P(d) = d/n$ for d, where $P(d)$ is fidelity as a function of distance. This distance is indicated in figure 7.3 by the intersection of the distance function with the 45° line at $d = 209$ bits.

Rates of Convergence and Divergence

When the reading address is at about the critical distance from the target, the probability of getting closer to the target by reading from memory is about 0.5. Successively read words can then bounce back and forth and remain at about the critical distance for some time. However, once the distance to the target differs clearly from the critical distance, convergence to the target or divergence to random indifferent points is rapid (fewer than ten iterations. as a rule).

In contrast, the expected time of chance convergence is extremely long. In the example, the probability that a random point of N is within the critical distance of 209 bits of the nearest point of X is something like 10^{-50}, and so the expected time of chance convergence to some point of

X is somewhere around 1050 iterations. Therefore, the comparison of adjacent terms of a sequence soon reveals whether the sequence will converge or (initially) diverge. These very long times to chance convergence are possible only with very large memories and proportionally large data sets written in them. With small memories and data sets, starting at a random point results in a relatively rapid convergence to a point or a cycle.

We have seen that reading near a previously written address brings us closer to the target address. It is instructive to see how the words found by reading at two nearby addresses compare with one another when the addresses are far from any previously written address. This corresponds to reading at two random points of $\{0,1\}^n$ that are near each other. The result is that the two sequences are orthogonal to one another after only two or three read iterations. For the sample memory, this is seen in table 7.3; if, for example, the initial reading addresses are but one bit apart, the words that are read are 132 bits apart, on the average. Further reading with the addresses that are 132 bits apart yields a pair of words that are over 430 bits apart, on the average, and one more reading yields a pair of words that are orthogonal to one another. (Table 7.3 is derived in appendix D.)

Memory Capacity

Memory capacity is defined here as the size of the data set for which the critical distance is zero. A memory filled to capacity is said to be *full,* and a memory filled beyond capacity is said to be *overloaded.* If the word ξ has been written at ξ in a full memory, the probability of reading ξ

at ξ is, by definition, 0.5. In an overloaded memory the probability is less than 0.5. In either case, if the memory is read at a point x just one bit from ξ, the probability of reading ξ is quite small, and a sequence of successively read words diverges rapidly.

Memory capacity can now be estimated by setting the nth power of the maximum fidelity to $\frac{1}{2}$ and solving for T. From

$$[F(\sqrt{N'/T})]^n = \frac{1}{2}$$

we get the capacity

$$T = N'/H(n),$$

where $H(n) = [F^{-1}(1/2^{1/n})]^2$. Thus, the capacity is proportional to the number of hard locations N'. For $n = 1{,}000$ we have $H(n) = 10.22 \cong 10$, so the capacity in our example is about one-tenth the number of hard locations. Table 7.4 gives memory capacity as a fraction of the number of hard locations N' for selected values of n. The capacity of the sample memory, with its 1,000,000 hard locations, is slightly less than 100,000.

Capacity of a Storage Location

We can now get an idea of how many words a single location must store. Filling memory beyond capacity means that words that have been written only once can no longer be retrieved. They are forgotten because of increased noise. It therefore seems unnecessary for storage locations to have a larger capacity than is needed to fill the memory to near capacity. How much is that?

Table 7.3 Distance between two read chains in reading with access radius $r_{0.001}$ from a 1,000-dimensional memory.

Old distance	New distance	R[a]
0	0	1.00
1	132	0.92
2	157	0.88
5	199	0.81
10	237	0.74
20	283	0.63
50	355	0.44
100	415	0.26
200	470	0.09
500	500	0.00

a. R is the correlation of the bit sums corresponding to the old distance.

Table 7.4 Capacity of sparse distributed memory with N' storage locations.

n (number of dimensions)	c (capacity as a multiple of N')	$1/c$
100	0.165	6.1
200	0.137	7.3
500	0.112	9.0
1000	0.098	10.2
2000	0.087	11.5
5000	0.076	13.2
10,000	0.069	14.5
20,000	0.063	15.8
50,000	0.057	17.6
100,000	0.053	18.9

If a memory of N' locations is filled to its capacity T and if the access radius is r_p, the total number of words in memory is about TpN', and the average number per location is TpN'/N', which equals pT. For $n = 1,000$ and for p small, the capacity is somewhat less than $N'/10$, so let us use $T = N'/10$. A location of a full memory would then contain about $pN'/10$ words. In our example, that would be 100 words. Recall that the average word of the pooled data can be computed from n bit-sums. Therefore, a bit location can be realized as a counter that is incremented by 1 to store 1 and decremented by 1 to store 0. If zeros and ones are equally probable, the mean sum will be zero and the standard deviation will be $\sqrt{pT}$. For the sample memory, the standard deviation is $\sqrt{100} = 10$ and so a bit location that can store the integers $-40, ..., 40$ will suffice (only occasionally will it overflow before the memory is full). The range of values can be reduced to perhaps as little as $-10, ..., 10$ by reducing the size of the write circle and by not attempting to fill the memory to capacity. This would guarantee convergence for all recently stored items, as the following example shows.

When the capacity of a location is limited, the location will eventually overflow. This means that there is an attempt to increment a bit counter that has reached its maximum value or to decrement one that has reached its minimum value. Let us assume that in such cases the counter remains unchanged. It is interesting to see how such a memory performs.

I will discuss only the extreme case in which a bit counter has but two values: 0 and 1. Writing a 0 decrements the count to 0; writing a 1 increments it to 1. In other words, a bit location stores only the last bit written, just as it does in a conventional computer memory. The difference is that writing a word now stores it in more than one location (in about 1,000 locations in our example).

Assume that the word ξ is written at ξ and that immediately thereafter the memory is read at ξ. The 1,000 or so copies of ξ are retrieved, and nothing else, and no doubt the word read would be ξ. If instead the memory is read at another address, x, then

$$|O'(x) \cap O'(\xi)|$$

copies of ξ are read, together with about

$$1,000 - |O'(x) \cap O'(\xi)|$$

words other than ξ. By a method used for the best-match problem, we can estimate that the signal strength is

$$|O'(x) \cap O'(\xi)| / 2,$$

the noise is

$$\sqrt{(1,000 - |O'(x) \cap O'(\xi)|) \cdot \frac{1}{2} \cdot \frac{1}{2}},$$

and the critical distance to ξ is about 380 bits, meaning that a word just written would be read easily. However, subsequent writing will replace the 1,000 copies of ξ as follows: A location survives one write operation with probability $q = 1 - p$ ($= 0.999$), and so the probability that it survives T write operations is q^T. Signal strength for the word ξ after T write operations is then q^T times the original signal strength, or

$$q^T |O'(x) \cap O'(\xi)| /2.$$

In our example this means that when ξ is 2,300 write operations "old," reading at ξ retrieves ξ with probability 0.5 (the critical distance to ξ has been reduced to zero).

In accordance with our definition of memory capacity, we might say that this memory has a capacity of 2,300 words. Notice, however, that much younger words are retrieved readily. For example, the critical distance to a word that is 1,000 write operations old is about 240 bits. A similar calculation shows that reducing the access radius from $r_{0.001}$ to $r_{0.0001}$ increases the capacity to about 11,400 words. A word would then be written in about 100 locations. Reducing the radius much below that would increase the capacity further but would reduce the critical distance, even for newly written words, to such a low value as to do away with useful convergence. As the access circle decreases, the storage scheme begins to resemble that in the nearest-neighbor method in sparse memory, which was criticized in chapter 6.

In this memory, forgetting is caused by gradual loss of signal strength in addition to increased noise, because here new data replace old.

Interpretations

Certain properties of the memory model could be interpreted as counterparts of psychological phenomena. They are not necessarily unique to this memory model, but they are illustrated clearly by it.

Fast convergence—fewer than ten memory reads versus endless millions —could be used as an indication of knowing that one knows. That is, one can start with a retrieval cue, and immediately the successively read words begin to get closer to one another. If one looks at a single bit, it settles down, whereas if the sequence diverges, the bit behaves randomly with each new read.

Related to this is the tip-of-the-tongue state, or the feeling that one is close to recalling an item. The model has something corresponding to it, namely, being about the critical distance (209 bits in the example) from the nearest stored item. At that point the rate of convergence is slow.

The memory provides another internal measure of distance to the target: the magnitudes of the pooled bit sums.

When the read address is near the target address, these sums are far from their mean values, and vice versa. A circuit that measures deviations of the bit sums from their means is realized easily with neurons, although its construction is not pursued here. The output of such a circuit could be interpreted as the subjective feeling of knowing how close to the target one is.

Rehearsal (e.g., piano practicing) would write an item many times in memory and so would increase its signal strength and hence the critical distance to that item. A well-rehearsed item would therefore be retrieved with fewer retrieval cues than an item stored only once.

A full or overloaded memory could support momentary feelings of familiarity that would fade away rapidly, as if one could not maintain attention.

If the capacity of storage locations is sufficiently small, the memory could never be filled to capacity, and the most recently stored items could always be retrieved. Forgetting would increase with the length of time (i.e., the number of intervening write operations) that an item has been stored in memory.

Distributed storage could explain the nonspecific effects of brain damage. There can be noticeable physical damage with little apparent effect on performance. If the damage is extensive but not total in any critical area, the effect is the lowering of the general level of performance rather than a total loss of particular abilities (or memories). This could be explained by the fact that copies of each memory item are stored in multiple locations. The distribution of the space $\{0,1\}^n$ is such that, no matter how the locations are arranged physically in a three-dimensional space, the ones within $r_{0.001}$ bits of a reference address (in n-dimensional space) cannot, as a rule, be in any one restricted region of the three-dimensional space, but are distributed all over it. Reduction in the number of locations N' (the death of neurons) reduces the critical distance for all stored items, so that increasingly exact cues are needed to recognize or recall stored items.

II
Computation and Neurobiology

13
Introduction

(1959)
J. Y. Lettvin, H. R. Maturana, W. S. McCulloch, and W. H. Pitts

What the frog's eye tells the frog's brain
Proceedings of the Institute of Radio Engineers 47: 1950–1961

Really famous scientific papers tell a beautiful and memorable story. This is one of them. The title is one of the best known in neuroscience, and, as a good title should, it expresses succinctly the philosophy of the experimenters and what they did.

Although it is a paper that is entirely neurophysiology, it comes from a special issue of the *IRE Proceedings* on the nervous system. In 1959, as now, many believed there was a natural connection between engineering and brain organization.

The cast of characters was notable: McCulloch and Pitts were famous for their papers on brain theory (see papers 2 and 3 in *Neurocomputing: Foundations of Research*). Maturana later became a philosopher. And Jerry Lettvin was an MIT legend, a charismatic neurophysiologist who was admired and trusted by MIT undergraduates, and an innovative and influential researcher. (Though he published relatively little, much of his immense scientific impact was communicated through brilliant lectures and conversations.)

For many years, Lettvin's laboratory was located in ramshackle Building 20 at MIT, a World War II temporary building that had been constructed for the Radiation Laboratory. It is still standing as of 1990, though there are persistent rumors, as there have been for a generation, that it will soon be torn down for more permanent construction. Although it looked terrible, Building 20 produced more than its share of landmark research. Among other prominent inhabitants at various times were Noam Chomsky, the Communications Biophysics Laboratory, part of the Research Laboratory of Electronics, and the Tech Model Railroad Club (TMRC, also known as the Toy Train Club). For the impressive contributions of TMRC to computer culture, see *Hackers* by Steven Levy (1984). On their way to dropping out of MIT, many of the legendary hackers were deeply involved with TMRC. The complexities of switching model trains around a track are similar to the complexities of switching electrons around logic circuits.

One advantage of a temporary building one step away from destruction is ease of modification: If a hole in the wall is needed *here*, it can be drilled immediately because no one cares much about cosmetics or structural damage. And in fact most of the laboratories in Building 20 were functional and highly productive, though rarely the kind of place to be shown with pride to visitors from the granting agencies.

For many years Lettvin's laboratory in the easternmost wing of Building 20 had a sign reading "Experimental Epistemology Laboratory" on the door. That was exactly the aim of this paper: We see what our nervous system lets us see. The frog (and human) perceptual systems are tuned to what is important for behavior. The close connection between nervous system and behavior has recently given rise to a field of study called *neuroethology*, and this paper can be viewed as an early contribution to the field. (It, and later work, is discussed in books on neuroethology; see, for example, Ewart 1980 and Camhi 1984. Ewart extensively describes detailed behavioral and physiological experiments on the toad visual system, which is similar to that of the frog in many respects.) The basic technical findings of the paper, though obviously extended since 1959, have held up well.

The visual system of the frog is quite specialized, and the paper begins with a brief description of frog hunting behavior. One observation is that the frog only senses moving prey and "will starve to death surrounded by food if it is not moving." The anatomy of the visual system is like that of other vertebrates: An image is cast on the retina, light and dark patterns give rise to neural activity patterns, which are transmitted to the brain of the frog over the optic nerve, which contains perhaps a half million nerve fibers. The central part of the frog visual system consists primarily of the *optic tectum* (usually called the *superior colliculus* in mammals). The colliculus in mammals still plays an important role in orientation and eye movements, but the bulk of detailed visual processing has been moved to visual cortex (see McIlwain, paper 15).

The superior colliculus only knows what the retina tells it, hence the title of the paper. In 1959 it was known that the retina was not simply sending a pixel array of light and dark to higher levels, but was making a much more complex statement about what was going on in the image. The effects of lateral inhibition in the retina were well known, for instance, as was the great motion sensitivity of retinal cells in some animals.

Lettvin's electrodes were recording activity from fibers in the optic nerve. The experimenters took some care to make sure that the frog saw a "natural" environment. An aluminum hemisphere was placed in front of the eyes, and a frog's-eye view of a swamp was pasted to the hemisphere. Stimuli were moved around from the outside using magnets. As a deliberate point of experimental design, vast quantities of detailed data were not taken. There was an interactive interplay between the experimenters and the frog's eye. The attempt was to understand the "language" of the optic nerve, rather than to characterize stimulus and response down to the last photon and action potential. The casualness about the details of data caused some unhappiness among more conservative neuroscientists, but there seems to be no doubt now that this was the right approach to take at the time.

The key result reported in that paper was that the frog eye was sending a highly processed signal to the frog brain and that the processing was closely (and obviously) coupled to the behavior of the frog. One could say that the right way to view the visual system was not as doing information processing but as producing behavior. Computers process information, but brains make animals do the right thing.

The experimenters found four qualitatively different classes of fibers in the frog optic nerve: first, *sustained contrast detectors* that respond to sharp edges that contrast with the background. Second, they found *net convexity detectors* that respond best to small objects passing through their receptive field, which is a few degrees. They respond best not to straight edges but to sharply curved edges and to edges that make jerky movements. Third, they found *moving edge detectors* that respond to moving edges over a rather wide area of the visual field and, fourth, *net dimming detectors* that respond to decrease in light intensity. Only the last class of cells responds to overall intensity. All the other classes require structure in the image before they will respond. The optic nerve fibers are responding not to points of light but to complex features of the environment.

Perhaps the most striking (and famous) of the cell classes is the second, the net convexity detectors. These units have become known as *bug detectors* because the object that best excites them is a buglike moving object. Considering the prey of the frog, the presence of bug detectors showed a remarkable adaptive specialization of the frog retina for overall frog behavior. This result created a mild sensation when the paper appeared. One unintended result of this finding was what might be called "instant brain model," where it was "obvious" that the brain worked by having more and more selective detectors: first bug detectors then, higher up, mosquito detectors, bee detectors, dragonfly detectors, and so on. This brain model was widely accepted (dangerously, sometimes unconsciously accepted), and a great many laboratories looked for very selective higher-level detectors in frogs and elsewhere, with indifferent success. The *reductio ad absurdum* of this approach is the *grandmother cell*, which responds when and only when grandma is seen or thought of and at no other time. (See Barlow, paper 14 for a thoughtful discussion of what the relation between the nervous system and perception might be.)

It was obvious to the experimenters, however, that a bug excited a large number of bug detectors simultaneously. After all their receptive fields were quite large (3° or so), and there were lots of bug detectors, so a bug could not help but excite a large number of them. Also the experimenters found that the four different fiber types made connections to different layers of the colliculus. So there are four separate sheets of parallel connections made, each in spatial register with the other, each sheet signalling a different kind of data about the input. The frog seems not to be forming grandmother cells, but distributed representations of particular important aspects of the environment, involving significant numbers of active units. The mammalian superior colliculus has a somewhat similar architecture, with spatially selective cells at the input feeding much more broadly tuned units on the motor side of the structure. This need not cause lack of selectivity in response and in fact is well suited for driving the output motor neurons.

In any case the perceptual world of the frog must be quite different from ours. It has no interest in form in and of itself; ordinarily the higher levels of the frog brain look at a blank TV screen. Only when an event occurs that is interesting and important to the frog is there something that disturbs the silence. To humans this may seem like an impoverished existence. A frog artist might not work on canvas or paper, but with moving drawings—cartoons. However, if there were frog physicists, perhaps they would have more truthful intuitions about subatomic particles than primates have: essence of bugness.

References

J.M. Camhi (1984), *Neuroethology: Nerve Cells and the Natural Behavior of Animals*. Sunderland, MA: Sinauer.

J.-P. Ewart (1980), *Neuroethology: An Introduction to the Neurophysiological Fundamentals of Behavior*. Berlin: Springer.

S. Levy (1984), *Hackers: Heroes of the Computer Revolution*. Garden City, NY: Anchor/Doubleday.

(1959)

J. Y. Lettvin, H. R. Maturana, W. S. McCulloch, and W. H. Pitts

What the frog's eye tells the frog's brain
Proceedings of the Institute of Radio Engineers 47: 1950–1961

Summary—In this paper, we analyze the activity of single fibers in the optic nerve of a frog. Our method is to find what sort of stimulus causes the largest activity in one nerve fiber and then what is the exciting aspect of that stimulus such that variations in everything else cause little change in the response. It has been known for the past 20 years that each fiber is connected not to a few rods and cones in the retina but to very many over a fair area. Our results show that for the most part within that area, it is not the light intensity itself but rather the pattern of local variation of intensity that is the exciting factor. There are four types of fibers, each type concerned with a different sort of pattern. Each type is uniformly distributed over the whole retina of the frog. Thus, there are four distinct parallel distributed channels whereby the frog's eye informs his brain about the visual image in terms of local pattern independent of average illumination. We describe the patterns and show the functional and anatomical separation of the channels. This work has been done on the frog, and our interpretation applies only to the frog.

INTRODUCTION

Behavior of a Frog

A FROG hunts on land by vision. He escapes enemies mainly by seeing them. His eyes do not move, as do ours, to follow prey, attend suspicious events, or search for things of interest. If his body changes its position with respect to gravity or the whole visual world is rotated about him, then he shows compensatory eye movements. These movements enter his hunting and evading habits only, *e.g.*, as he sits on a rocking lily pad. Thus his eyes are actively stabilized. He has no fovea, or region of greatest acuity in vision, upon which he must center a part of the image. He also has only a single visual system, retina to colliculus, not a double one such as ours where the retina sends fibers not only to colliculus but to the lateral geniculate body which relays to cerebral cortex. Thus, we chose to work on the frog because of the uniformity of his retina, the normal lack of eye and head movements except for those which stabilize the retinal image, and the relative simplicity of the connection of his eye to his brain.

The frog does not seem to see or, at any rate, is not concerned with the detail of stationary parts of the world around him. He will starve to death surrounded by food if it is not moving. His choice of food is determined only by size and movement. He will leap to capture any object the size of an insect or worm, providing it moves like one. He can be fooled easily not only by a bit of dangled meat but by any moving small object. His sex life is conducted by sound and touch. His choice of paths in escaping enemies does not seem to be governed by anything more devious than leaping to where it is darker. Since he is equally at home in water and on land, why should it matter where he lights after jumping or what particular direction he takes? He does remember a moving thing providing it stays within his field of vision and he is not distracted.

Anatomy of Frog Visual Apparatus

The retina of a frog is shown in Fig. 1(a). Between the rods and cones of the retina and the ganglion cells, whose axons form the optic nerve, lies a layer of connecting neurons (bipolars, horizontals, and amacrines). In the frog there are about 1 million receptors, $2\frac{1}{2}$ to $3\frac{1}{2}$ million connecting neurons, and half a million ganglion cells [1]. The connections are such that there is a synaptic path from a rod or cone to a great many ganglion cells, and a ganglion cell receives paths from a great many thousand receptors. Clearly, such an arrangement would not allow for good resolution were the retina meant to map an image in terms of light intensity point by point into a distribution of excitement in the optic nerve.

There is only one layer of ganglion cells in the frog. These cells are half a million in number (as against one million rods and cones). The neurons are packed together tightly in a sheet at the level of the cell bodies. Their dendrites, which may extend laterally from $50\,\mu$ to $500\,\mu$, interlace widely into what is called the inner plexiform layer, which is a close-packed neuropil containing the terminal arbors of those neurons that lie between receptors and ganglion cells. Thus, the amount of overlap of adjacent ganglion cells is enormous in respect to what they see. Morphologically, there are several types of these cells that are as distinct in their dendritic patterns as different species of trees, from which we infer that they work in different ways. The anatomy shown in the figures is that found in standard references. Further discussion of anatomical questions and additional original work on them will appear in a later publication.

Physiology as Known up to This Study

Hartline [2] first used the term *receptive field* for the region of retina within which a local change of brightness would cause the ganglion cell he was observing to discharge. Such a region is sometimes surrounded by an annulus, within which changes of brightness affect the cell's response to what is occurring in the receptive field,

* Original manuscript received by the IRE, September 3, 1959. This work was supported in part by the U. S. Army (Signal Corps), the U. S. Air Force (Office of Sci. Res., Air Res. and Dev. Command), and the U. S. Navy (Office of Naval Res.); and in part by Bell Telephone Labs., Inc.
† Res. Lab. of Electronics and Dept. of Biology, Mass. Inst. Tech., Cambridge, Mass.
‡ Res. Lab. of Electronics, Mass. Inst. Tech., Cambridge, Mass., on leave from the University of Chile, Santiago, Chile.
‖ Res. Lab. of Electronics, Mass. Inst. Tech., Cambridge, Mass.

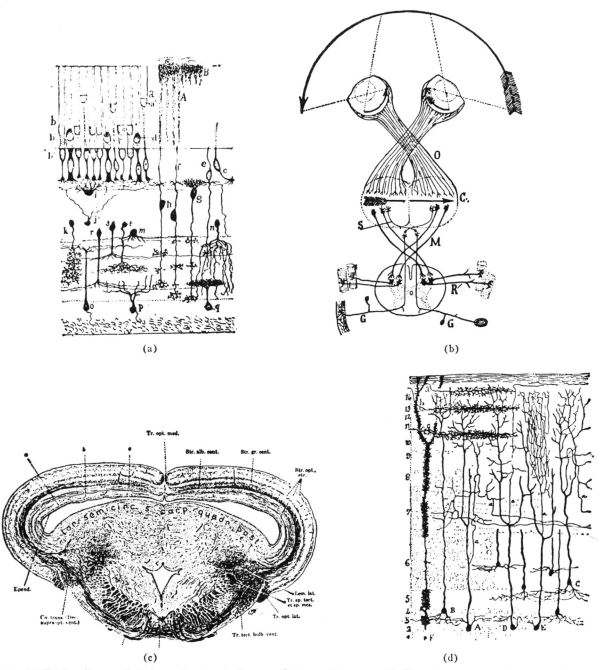

(a)

(b)

(c)

(d)

Fig. 1—(a) This is a diagram of the frog retina done by Ramon y Cajal over 50 years ago [9]. The rods and cones are the group of elements in the upper left quarter of the picture. To their bushy bottom ends are connected the bipolar cells of the intermediate layer, for example, *f*, *g*, and *h*. Lateral connecting neurons, called *horizontal* and *amacrine* cells, also occur in this layer, for example, *i*, *j* and *m*. The bipolars send their axons down to arborize in the inner plexiform layer, roughly the region bounded by cell *m* above and the bodies of the ganglion cells, *o*, *p* and *q*, below. In this sketch, Ramon has the axons of the bipolar cells emitting bushes at all levels in the plexiform layer; in fact, many of them branch at only one or two levels.

Compare the dendrites of the different ganglion cells. Not only do they spread out at different levels in the plexiform layer, but the patterns of branching are different. Other ganglion cells, not shown here, have multiple arbors spreading out like a plane tree at two or three levels. If the terminals of the bipolar cells are systematically arranged in depth, making a laminar operational map of the rods and cones in terms of very local contrast, color, ON, OFF, etc., then the different shapes of the ganglion cells would correspond to different combinations of the local operations done by the bipolars. Thus would arise the more complex operations of the ganglion cells as described in the text. (b) This is Ramon y Cajal's diagram of the total decussation or crossing of the optic nerve fibers in the frog [9]. He made this picture to explain the value of the crossing as preserving continuity in the map of the visual world. *O* is the optic nerve and *C* is the *superior colliculus* or *optic tectum* (the names are synonymous). (c) This is Ariens-Kapper's picture of the cross section of the brain of a frog through the colliculus, which is the upper or dorsal part above the enclosed space. (d) This is Pedro Ramon Cajal's diagram of the nervous organization of the tectum of a frog. The terminal bushes of the optic nerve fibers are labelled *a*, *b*, and *c*. *A*, *B*, *C*, *D* and *E* are tectal cells receiving from the optic nerve fibers. Note that the axons of these cells come off the dendrites in stratum **7**, which we call the *palisade* layer. The endings discussed in this paper lie between the surface and that stratum.

although the cell does not discharge to any event occurring in the annulus alone. Like Kuffler [4], we consider the receptive field and its interacting annulus as a single entity, with apologies to Dr. Hartline for the slight change in meaning. Hartline found three sorts of receptive field in the frog: ON, ON-OFF, and OFF. If a small spot of light suddenly appears in the receptive field of an ON-cell, the discharge soon begins, increases in rate to some limit determined by the intensity and area of the spot, and thereafter slowly declines. Turning off the spot abolishes the discharge.

If the small spot of light suddenly appears or disappears within the field of an ON-OFF cell, the discharge is short and occurs in both cases.

If the spot of light disappears from the field of an OFF cell, the discharge begins immediately, decreases slowly in frequency, and lasts a long time. It can be abolished promptly by turning the spot of light on again.

For all three sorts of field, sensitivity is greatest at the center of each field and least at the periphery.

Barlow [3] extended Hartline's observations. He observed that the OFF cells have an adding receptive field, *i.e.*, the response occurs always to OFF at both center and periphery of that field, and that the effect of removing light from the periphery adds to the effect of a reduction of light at the center, with a weight decreasing with distance.

The ON-OFF cells, however, have differencing receptive fields. A discharge of several spikes to the appearance of light in the center is much diminished if a light is turned on in the extreme periphery. The same interaction occurs when these lights are removed. Thus, an ON-OFF cell seems to be measuring inequality of illumination within its receptive field. (Kuffler [4] at the same time showed a similar mutual antagonism between center and periphery in each receptive field of ganglion cells in the eye of a cat, and later Barlow, Kuffler and Fitzhugh [5] showed that the size of the cat's receptive fields varied with general illumination.) Barlow saw that ON-OFF cells were profoundly sensitive to movement within the receptive field. The ON cells have not been characterized by similar methods.

These findings of Hartline and Barlow establish that optic nerve fibers (the axons of the ganglion cells) do not transmit information only about light intensity at single points in the retina. Rather, each fiber measures a certain feature of the whole distribution of light in an area of the receptive field. There are three sorts of function, or areal operation, according to these authors, so that the optic nerve looks at the image on the retina through three distributed channels. In any one channel, the overlap of individual receptive fields is very great. Thus one is led to the notion that what comes to the brain of a frog is this: for any visual event, the OFF channel tells how much dimming of light has occurred and where; the ON-OFF channel tells where the boundaries of lighted areas are moving, or where local inequalities of illumination are forming; the ON channel shows (with a delay) where brightening has occurred. To an unchanging visual pattern, the nerve ought to become fairly silent after a while.

Consider the retinal image as it appears in each of the three distributed channels. For both the OFF and ON channels, we can treat the operation on the image by supposing that every point on the retina gives rise to a blur about the size of a receptive field. Then the OFF channel tells, with a long decay time, where the blurred image is darkened, and the ON channel tells with a delay and long decay where it is brightened. The third channel, ON-OFF, principally registers moving edges. Having the mental picture of an image as it appears through the three kinds of channel, we are still faced with the question of how the animal abstracts what is useful to him from his surroundings. At this point, a safe position would be that a fair amount of data reduction has in fact been accomplished by the retina and that the interpretation is the work of the brain, a yet-to-be unravelled mystery. Yet the nagging worries remain: why are there two complementary projections of equally poor resolution? Why is the mosaic of receptors so uselessly fine?

Initial Argument

The assumption has always been that the eye mainly senses light, whose local distribution is transmitted to the brain in a kind of copy by a mosaic of impulses. Suppose we held otherwise, that the nervous apparatus in the eye is itself devoted to detecting certain patterns of light and their changes, corresponding to particular relations in the visible world. If this should be the case, the laws found by using small spots of light on the retina may be true and yet, in a sense, be misleading. Consider, for example, a bright spot appearing in a receptive field. Its actual and sensible properties include not only intensity, but the shape of its edge, its size, curvature, contrast, etc.

We decided then how we ought to work. First, we should find a way of recording from single myelinated and unmyelinated fibers in the intact optic nerve. Second, we should present the frog with as wide a range of visible stimuli as we could, not only spots of light but things he would be disposed to eat, other things from which he would flee, sundry geometrical figures, stationary and moving about, etc. From the variety of stimuli we should then try to discover what common features were abstracted by whatever groups of fibers we could find in the optic nerve. Third, we should seek the anatomical basis for the grouping.[1]

This program had started once before in our laboratory with A. Andrew [6], [7] of Glasgow who unfortunately had to return to Scotland before the work got well under way. However, he had reported in 1957 that he found elements in the colliculus of the frog that were sensitive to movement of a spot of light (a dot on an oscilloscope screen) even when the intensity of the spot was so low that turning it on and off produced no response. In particular, the elements he observed showed firing upon movement away from the centers of their receptive fields, but not to centripetal movements. As will appear later, this sort of response is a natural property of OFF fibers.

(ACTUAL) METHODS

Using a variant of Dowben and Rose's platinum black-tipped electrode described in another paper of this issue, we then began a systematic study of fibers in the optic nerve. One of the authors (H. R. M.) had completed the electron microscopy of optic nerve in frogs [8], and with his findings we were able to understand quickly why certain kinds of record occurred. He had found that the optic nerve of a frog contains about half a million fibers (ten times the earlier estimates by light microscopy). There are 30 times as many unmyelinated axons as myelinated, and both kinds are uniformly distributed throughout the nerve. The axons lie in small densely packed bundles of five to 100 fibers with about 100 Å between axons, each bundle surrounded by one or more glial cells [8]. But along the nerve no bundle maintains its identity long, for the component fibers so braid between bundles that no two fibers stay adjacent. Thus the place a fiber crosses one section of the nerve bears little relation to its origin in the retina and little relation to where it crosses another section some distance away.

Fibers are so densely packed that one might suppose such braiding necessary to prevent serious interactions. On the other hand, the density makes the recording easier. A glial wall surrounds groups rather than single fibers, and penetration of the wall brings the tip among really bare axons each surrounded by neighbors whose effect is to increase the external impedance to its action currents, augmenting the external potential in proportion. Thus, while we prefer to use platinum black tips to improve the ratio of signal to noise, we recorded much the same population with ordinary sharp microelectrodes of bright Pt or Ag. The method records equally well from unmyelinated and myelinated fibers.

We used *Rana pipiens* in these experiments. We opened a small flap of bone either just behind the eye to expose the optic nerve, or over the brain to expose the superior colliculus. No further surgery was done except to open the membranes of connective tissue overlying the nervous structure. The frog was held in extension to a cork platform and covered with moist cloth. An animal in such a position, having most of his body surface in physical contact with something, goes into a still reaction—*i.e.*, he will not even attempt to move save to pain, and except for the quick small incision of the skin at the start of the operation our procedure seems to be painless to him. With the animal mounted, we confront his eye with an aluminum hemisphere, 20 mils thick and 14 inches in diameter, silvered to a matte grey finish on the inner surface and held concentric to the eye. On the inner surface of this hemisphere, various objects attached to small magnets can be moved about by a large magnet moved by hand on the outer surface. On our hemisphere, 1° is slightly less than an eighth of an inch long. In the tests illustrated, we use as stimulating objects a dull black disk almost 1° in diameter and a rectangle 30° long and 12° wide. However, in the textual report, we use a variety of other objects. As an indicator for the stimulus, we first used a phototube looking at an image of the hemisphere taken through a camera lens and focussed on the plane of a diaphragm. (Later we used a photomultiplier, so connected as to give us a logarithmic response over about 4 decades.) Thus we could vary how much of the hemisphere was seen by the stimulus detector and match that area in position and size against the receptive field of the fiber we were studying. The output of this arrangement is the stimulus line in the figures.

FINDINGS

There are four separate operations on the image in the frog's eye. Each has its result transmitted by a particular group of fibers, uniformly distributed across the retina, and they are all nearly independent of the general illumination. The operations are: *1) sustained contrast detection; 2) net convexity detection; 3) moving edge detection; and 4) net dimming detection.* The first two are reported by unmyelinated fibers, the last two by myelinated fibers. Since we are now dealing with events rather than point excitations as stimuli, receptive fields can only be defined approximately, and one cannot necessarily distinguish concentric subdivisions. The fibers reporting the different operations differ systematically not only in fiber diameter (or conduction velocity) but also in rough size of receptive field, which ranges from about 2° diameter for the first operation, to about 15° for the last. The following description of these groups is definite.

1) Sustained Contrast Detectors

An unmyelinated axon of this group does not respond when the general illumination is turned on or off. If the sharp edge of an object either lighter or darker than the background moves into its field and stops, it discharges promptly and continues discharging, no matter what the shape of the edge or whether the object is smaller or larger than the receptive field. The sustained discharge can be interrupted (or greatly reduced) in these axons by switching all light off. When the light is then restored, the sustained discharge begins again after a pause. Indeed the response to turning on a distribution of light furnished with sharp contrast within the field is exactly that reported by Hartline for his ON fibers. In some fibers of this group, a contrast previously within the field is "remembered" after the light is turned off, for they will keep up a low mutter of activity that is not present if no contrast was there before. That this is not an extraordinary sensitivity of such an element in almost complete darkness can be shown by importing a contrast into its receptive field after darkening in the absence of contrast. No mutter occurs then. This memory lasts for at least a minute of darkness in some units.

In Fig. 2 we see the response of such a fiber in the optic nerve. We compare these responses with full·illumi-

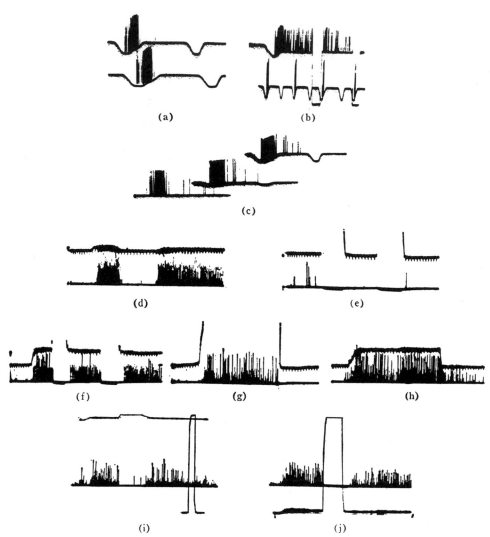

Fig. 2—Operation 1)—contrast detectors. The records were all taken directly with a Polaroid camera. The spikes are clipped at the lower end just above the noise and brightened on the screen. Occasional spikes have been intensified by hand for purposes of reproduction. The resolution is not good but we think that the responses are not ambiguous. Our alternate recording method is by means of a device which displays the logarithm of pulse interval of signals through a pulse height pick-off. However, such records would take too much explanation and would not add much to the substance of the present paper. (a) This record is from a single fiber in the optic nerve. The base line is the output of a photocell watching a somewhat larger area than the receptive field of the fiber. Darkening is given by downward deflection. The response is seen with the noise clipped off. The fiber discharge to movement of the edge of a 3° black disk passed in one direction but not to the reverse movement. (Time marks, 20 per second.) (b) The same fiber shown here giving a continued response when the edge stops in the field. The response disappears if the illumination is turned off and reappears when it is turned on. Below is shown again the asymmetry of the response to a faster movement. (Time marks, 20 per second.) (c) The same fiber is stimulated here to show asymmetrical response to the 3° black object moved in one direction, then the reverse and the stimuli are repeated under a little less than a 3-decade change of illumination in two steps. The bottom record is in extremely dim light, the top in very bright light. (Time marks, 20 per second.) (d) In the bottom line, a group of endings from such fibers is shown recorded from the first layer in the tectum. A black disk 1° in diameter is moved first through the field and then into the field and stopped. In the top line, the receptive field is watched by a photomultiplier (see text) and darkening is given by upward deflection. (Time marks, 5 per second for all tectal records.) (e) OFF and ON of general illumination has no effect on these fibers. (f) A 3° black disk is moved into the field and stopped. The response continues until the lights are turned OFF but reappears when the lights are turned ON. These fibers are nonerasable. (g) A very large black square is moved into the field and stopped. The response to the edge continues so long as the edge is in the field. (h) The 3° disk is again moved into the field and stopped. When it leaves, there is a slight after-discharge. (i) A 1° object is moved into the field, stopped, the light is then turned off, then on, and the response comes back. The light is, however, a little less than 300× dimmer than in the next frame. Full ON and OFF are given in the rectangular calibration on the right. (j) The same procedure as in Fig. 2(i) is done under very bright light. The return of response after reintroducing the light seems more prolonged—but this is due only to the fact that, in Fig. 2(i), the edge was not stopped in optimal position.

nation (a 60-watt bulb and reflector mounted a foot away from the plane of the opening of the hemisphere) to those with less than 1/300 as much light (we put a variable resistance in series with the bulb so that the color changed also). We are struck by the smallness of the resulting change. In very dim light where we can barely see the stimulating object ourselves, we still get very much the same response.

2) Net Convexity Detectors

These fibers form the other subdivision of the unmyelinated population, and require a number of conditions to specify when they will respond. To our minds, this group contains the most remarkable elements in the optic nerve.

Such a fiber does not respond to change in general illumination. It does respond to a small object (3° or less) passed through the field; the response does not outlast the passage. It continues responding for a long time if the object is imported and left in the field, but the discharge is permanently turned off (erased) by a transient general darkness lasting 1/10 second or longer. We have not tried shorter obscurations.

The fiber will not respond to the straight edge of a dark object moving through its receptive field or brought there and stopped. If the field is about 7° in diameter, then, if we move a dark square 8° on the side through it with the edge in advance there is no response, but if the corner is in advance then there is a good one. Usually a fiber will respond indefinitely only to objects which have moved into the field and then lie wholly or almost wholly interior to the receptive field. The discharge is greater the greater the convexity, or positive curvature, of the boundary of the dark object until the object becomes as small as about ½ the width of the receptive field. At this point, we get the largest response on moving across that field, and a good, sustained response on entering it and stopping. As one uses smaller and smaller objects, the response to moving across the field begins to diminish at a size of about 1°, although the sustained response to coming in and stopping remains. In this way we find the smallest object to which these fibers respond is less than 3 minutes of arc. A smooth motion across the receptive field has less effect than a jerky one, if the jerks recur at intervals longer than ½ second. A displacement barely visible to the experimenter produces a marked increase in response which dies down slowly.

Any checked or dotted pattern (in the latter case, with dots no further apart than half the width of the receptive field) moved as a whole across the receptive field produces little if any response. However, if any dot within the receptive field moves differentially with respect to the background pattern, the response is to that dot as if it were moving alone. A group of two or three distinct spots enclosed within the receptive field and moved as a whole produce less direct response to movement and much less sustained response on stopping than if the spots are coalesced to a single larger spot.

A delightful exhibit uses a large color photograph of the natural habitat of a frog from a frog's eye view, flowers and grass. We can move this photograph through the receptive field of such a fiber, waving it around at a 7-inch distance: there is no response. If we perch with a magnet a fly-sized object 1° large on the part of the picture seen by the receptive field and move only the object we get an excellent response. If the object is fixed to the picture in about the same place and the whole moved about, then there is none.

Finally, the response does not depend on how much darker the object is than its background, so long as it is distinguishably so and has a clear-cut edge. If a disk has a very dark center and merges gradually into the grey of the background at the boundary, the response to it is very much less than to a uniform grey disk only slightly darker than the background. Objects lighter than the background produce almost no response unless they have enough relief to cast a slight shadow at the edge.

All the responses we have mentioned are relatively independent of illumination, and Fig. 3 taken as described in the caption shows the reactions to a 3° object and the large rectangle under some of the conditions described.

General Comments on Groups 1) and 2)

The two sorts of detectors mentioned seem to include all the unmyelinated fibers, with conduction velocities of 20 to 50 cm. The two groups are not entirely distinct. There are transition cases. On one hand, some convexity detectors respond well to very slightly curved edges, even so far as to show an occasional sustained response if that edge is left in the field. They may also not be completely erasable (though very markedly affected by an interruption of light) for small objects. On the other hand, others of the same group will be difficult to set into an indefinitely sustained response with any object, but only show a fairly long discharge, acting thereby more as detectors of edges although never reacting to straight edges. Nevertheless the distribution of the unmyelinated axons into two groups is very marked. Any fiber of either group may show a directional response—i.e., there will be a direction of movement that may fail to excite the cell. For the contrast fibers, this will also appear as a nonexciting angle of the boundary with respect to the axis of the frog. Such null directions and angles cancel out in the aggregate.

3) Moving-Edge Detectors

These fibers are myelinated and conduct at a velocity in the neighborhood of 2 meters per second. They are the same as Hartline's and Barlow's ON-OFF units. The receptive field is about 12° wide. Such a fiber re-

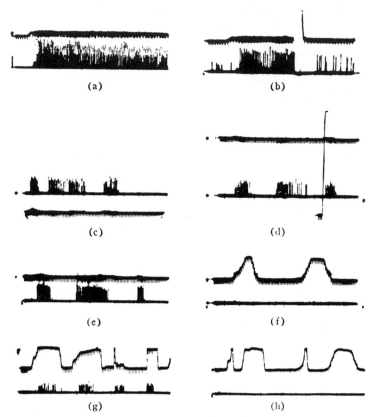

Fig. 3—Operation 2)—convexity detectors. The photomultiplier is used, and darkening is an upward deflection. (a) These records are all from the second layer of endings in the tectum. In the first picture, a 1° black disk is imported into the receptive field and left there. (b) The same event occurs as in Fig. 3(a), but now the light is turned off then on again. The response is much diminished and in the longer record vanishes. These fibers are erasable. (c) The 1° disk, is passed through the field first somewhat rapidly, then slowly, then rapidly. The light is very bright. (d) The same procedure occurs as in Fig. 3(c), but now the light has been dimmed about 300×. The vertical line shows the range of the photomultiplier which has been adjusted for about 3½ decades of logarithmic response. (e) A 1° black disk is passed through the field at three speeds. (f) A 15° black strip is passed through at two speeds edge leading. (g) A 15° black strip is passed through in various ways with corner leading. (h) The same strip as in Fig. 3(g) is passed through, edge leading.

sponds to any distinguishable edge moving through its receptive field, whether black against white or the other way around. Changing the extent of the edge makes little difference over a wide range, changing its speed a great one. It responds to an edge only if that edge moves, not otherwise. If an object wider than about 5° moves smoothly across the field, there are separate responses to the leading and trailing edges, as would be expected from Barlow's formulation. These fibers generally show two or three regularly spaced spikes, always synchronous among different fibers to turning the light on or off or both. The response to moving objects is much greater than to changes in total illumination and varies only slightly with general illumination over a range of 1/300. The frequency of the discharge increases with the velocity of the object within certain limits (see Fig. 4).

4) Net Dimming Detectors

These are Hartline's and Barlow's OFF fibers. But they have some properties not observed before. They are myelinated and the fastest conducting afferents,

clocked at 10 meters per second.[2] One such fiber responds to sudden reduction of illumination by a prolonged and regular discharge. Indeed, the rhythm is so much the same from fiber to fiber that in recording from several at once after sudden darkening, the impulses assemble in groups, which break up only after many seconds. Even then the activity from widely separated retinal areas seems to be related. We observe that the surface potential of the colliculus shows a violent and prolonged oscillation when the light is turned off. This oscillation, beginning at about 18 per second and breaking into 3 to 5 per second after several seconds, seems to arise from these fibers from the retina; the same record is seen when the optic nerve is severed and the recording electrode placed on the retinal stump. See Fig. 5.

The receptive field is rather large—about 15°—and works as Barlow describes. Darkening of a spot produces less response when it is in the periphery of the field than when it is at the center. The effect of a mov-

[2] The even faster fibers, with velocities up to 20 meters per second, we presently believe to be the efferents to the retina, but although there is some evidence for this, we are not yet quite certain.

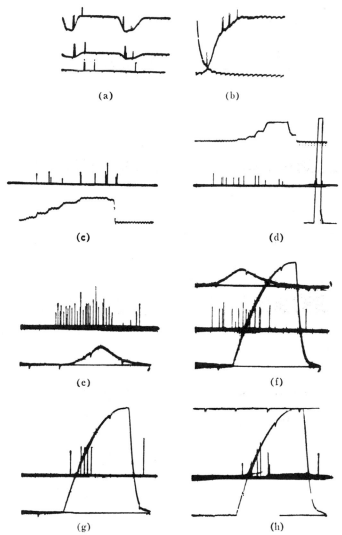

Fig. 4—Operation 3)—moving-edge detectors. The first two pictures are taken from a single fiber in the optic nerve. (a) Shows a 7° black disk moving through the receptive field (the photocell was not in registration with the field). There is a response to the front and back of the disk independent of illumination. There is about a 300/1 shift of illumination between top and bottom of the record. Darkening is a downward deflection with the photocell record. (Time marks, 5 per second.) (b) OFF and ON of general lighting. (Time marks, 50 per second.) Note double responses and spacing. (c) This and succeeding records are in the third layer of endings in the tectum. Several endings are recorded but not resolved. Darkening is an upward deflection of the photomultiplier record. The response is shown to the edge of a 15° square moved into and out of the field by jerks in bright light. (d) The same procedure occurs as in Fig. 4(c), but in dim light. Calibration figure is at the right. (e) The response is shown to a 7° black disk passed through the receptive fields under bright light. The sweep is faster, but the time marks are the same. (f) The same procedure as for Fig. 4(e), but under dim light. The OFF and ON of the photomultiplier record was superimposed for calibration. (g) OFF and ON response with about half a second between ON and OFF. (h) Same as Fig. 4(g), but with 2 seconds between OFF and ON.

ing object is directly related to its size and relative darkness. The response is prolonged if a large dark object stops within the field. It is almost independent of illumination, actually increasing as the light gets dimmer. There is a kind of erasure that is complementary to that of group 2). If the general lighting is sharply dimmed, but not turned off entirely, the consequent prolonged response is diminished or abolished after a dark object passes through the receptive field. In this case, the reasons for erasure are apparent. Suppose one turns off the light and sets up a prolonged response. Then the amount of light which must be restored to in-

terrupt the response gets less and less the longer one waits. That is, the sensitivity of the OFF discharge to the ON of light increases with time. If we darken the general lighting only by a factor of 100, we also get a prolonged discharge. However, if we turn off the light completely a few seconds after the 100/1 dimming and then turn it back on to the same dim level, the discharge is increased by the second dimming and is completely or almost completely abolished by the relighting. The effect of moving a dark object through the field after dimming is to impose a second dimming pulse followed by brightening as the object passes.

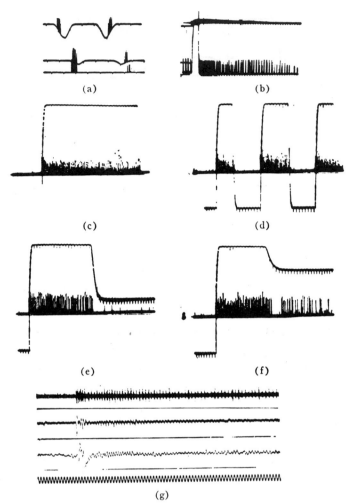

(a)   (b)

(c)   (d)

(e)   (f)

(g)

Fig. 5—Operation 4)—dimming detectors. (a) This and the next frame are taken from a single fiber in the optic nerve. Here we see the response to a 7° black disk passing through the receptive field. The three records are taken at three illumination levels over a 300:1 range. In the phototube record, darkening is a downward deflection. (Time marks, 5 per second.) (b) OFF and ON of light. The OFF was done shortly after one sweep began, the ON occurred a little earlier on the next sweep. The fiber is silenced completely by the ON. (Time marks, 5 per second.) (c) In this and the next three frames, we are recording from the fourth layer of endings in the tectum. This frame shows the response to turning OFF the general illumination. (d) OFF and ON of light at regular intervals. (e) OFF then ON of the light to a lesser brightness. (f) OFF then ON of the light to a still lesser brightness. The level to which the ON must come to abolish activity decreases steadily with time. (g) The synchrony of the dimming detectors as described in the text. At the top are three or four fibers recorded together in the optic nerve when the light is suddenly turned off. The fibers come from diverse areas on the retina. In the second line are the oscillations recorded from the freshly cut retinal stump of the optic nerve when the light is suddenly turned off. In the third line are the oscillations recorded on the surface of the tectum, the visual brain, before the nerve was cut. Again the light is suddenly turned off. The last line is 20 cps. These records of synchrony were obviously not all made at the same time, so that comparing them in detail is not profitable.

Others

Lastly, there is a small group of afferent fibers which does not seem to have distinct receptive fields. They each measure the absolute degree of darkness over a wide area with a long time constant. That is, the frequency of discharge is greater the darker it is. They have a complement in that some of the moving edge detectors have a resting discharge of very low frequency if the illumination is extremely bright.

DISCUSSION

Let us compress all of these findings in the following description. Consider that we have four fibers, one from each group, which are concentric in their receptive fields.

Suppose that an object is moved about in this concentric array:

1) The contrast detector tells, in the smallest area of all, of the presence of a sharp boundary, moving or still, with much or little contrast.

2) The convexity detector informs us in a somewhat larger area whether or not the object has a curved boundary, if it is darker than the background and moving on it; it remembers the object when it has stopped, providing the boundary lies totally within that area and is sharp; it shows most activity if the enclosed object moves intermittently with respect to a background. The memory of the object is abolished if a shadow obscures the object for a moment.

3) The moving-edge detector tells whether or not there is a moving boundary in a yet larger area within the field.

4) The dimming detector tells us how much dimming occurs in the largest area, weighted by distance from the center and by how fast it happens.

All of the operations are independent of general illumination. There are 30 times as many of the first two detectors as of the last two, and the sensitivity to sharpness of edge or increments of movement in the first two is also higher than in the last two.

RESULTS IN THE TECTUM

As remarked earlier, the optic nerve fibers are all disordered in position through the nerve. That is, the probability that any two adjacent fibers look at the same region in the retina is very small. However, when the fibers terminate in the superior colliculus they do so in an orderly way such that the termini exhibit a continuous map of the retina. Each optic nerve crosses the base of the skull and enters the opposite tectum [Fig. 1(b)] via two bundles—one rostromedial, the other caudalateral. The fibers sweep out over the tectum in the superficial neuropil in what grossly appears to be a laminated way [Fig. 1(c)]. The detail of ending is not known, and there is some reason to think Pedro Ramon's drawing [9] is too diagrammatic [Fig. 1(d)], however well it fits with our data.

In any case, the outer husk of neuropil, roughly about half the thickness of the optic tectum, is formed of the endings of the optic fibers mixed with dendrites of the deeper lying cells, and in this felting lie few cell bodies.

We have found it singularly easy to record from these terminal bushes of the optic fibers. That is, if an electrode is introduced in the middle of one bush, the external potential produced by action currents in any branch increases in proportion to the number of branches near the electrode. Since the bushes are densely interdigitated everywhere, it is not difficult to record from terminal arbors anywhere unless one kills or blocks them locally, as is easily done by pressure, etc.

One may inquire how we can be sure of recording from terminal arbors, and not from cells and their dendrites. The argument is this. First, there are about four layers of cells in the depths of the tectum [Fig. 1(d)], and only their dendrites issue into the superficial neuropil wherein lie very few cells indeed. There are about 250,000 of these cells in all, compared to 500,000 optic fibers. In the outer thickness of the tectum, among the terminating fibers, almost every element we record performs one of the four operations characterizing the fibers in the nerve, and has a corresponding receptive field. Now as the electrode moves down from the surface in one track, we record 5 to 10 cells in the deepest half of the tectum. Not a single cell so recorded shows activity even remotely resembling what we find in the superficial neuropil. Among the cells, none show optic nerve operations, and the smallest receptive fields we find are over 30° in

diameter. If the active elements in the upper layers are cells (one will see about 20 to 30 active elements in one electrode track before reaching the cell layer), which cells can they be? Or if they are dendrites, to what neurons do they belong? We regard these considerations as conclusive enough.

Figs. 2–5 show that the four operational groups of fibers terminate in four separate layers of terminals, each layer exhibiting a continuous map of the retina (we confirm Gaze's diagram of the projection [10]) and all four maps are in registration. Most superficial lie the endings for the contrast detectors, the slowest fibers. Beneath them, but not so distinctly separate, are the convexity detectors. Deeper, and rather well separated, are the moving-edge detectors admixed with the rare and ill-defined axons that measure the actual level of darkness. Deepest (and occasionally contaminated with tectal cells or their axons) lie the dimming detectors. Thus the depth at which these fibers end is directly related to their speed of conduction.

Such an arrangement makes experiment easy, for all the fibers of one operation performed on the same field in the retina end in one place in the tectum and can be recorded as a group. It is very useful to see them this way, for then the individual variations among similar units cancel one another and only the common properties remain. We made the tectal records shown in the accompanying figures with a single electrode in two penetrations (to get decent separation of contrast and convexity detectors which lie just below the pia), to show how clear-cut the arrangement is.

CONFIRMATION OF SPERRY'S PROPOSAL

The existence of a fourfold map of the retina in the tectal neuropil led us, naturally, to repeat Sperry's initial experiment on the regeneration of cut optic nerve [11]. Since the nerve is as scrambled as it can be originally, we saw no point in turning the eye around 180° but simply cut one nerve in a few frogs, separated the stumps to be sure of complete severance, and waited for about 3 months. At the end of this time, after it was clear that the cut nerves were functioning again, we compared the tectal maps of the cut and uncut nerves in some of them. We confirmed (as did Gaze [12]) Sperry's proposal that the fibers grew back to the regions where they originally terminated in mapping the retina [13]. But we also found a restoration of the four layers with no error or mixing. In one frog, after 90 days, the fibers had grown back best at the entrance of the two brachia to the colliculus, and least at the center, yet there were no serious errors. The total area of retina communicating with one point of the collicular neuropil (i.e., the sum of the receptive fields of the fibers recorded from that point) had increased three or four times, from a diameter of about 15° to a diameter of about 30°. But there was no admixture of fibers with receptive fields in widely separated regions. In another frog, after 120 days, the area seen from one point was barely twice normal.

GENERAL DISCUSSION

What are the consequences of this work? Fundamentally, it shows that the eye speaks to the brain in a language already highly organized and interpreted, instead of transmitting some more or less accurate copy of the distribution of light on the receptors. As a crude analogy, suppose that we have a man watching the clouds and reporting them to a weather station. If he is using a code, and one can see his portion of the sky too, then it is not difficult to find out what he is saying. It is certainly true that he is watching a distribution of light; nevertheless, local variations of light are not the terms in which he speaks nor the terms in which he is best understood. Indeed, if his vocabulary is restricted to types of things that he sees in the sky, trying to find his language by using flashes of light as stimuli will certainly fail. Now, since the purpose of a frog's vision is to get him food and allow him to evade predators no matter how bright or dim it is about him, it is not enough to know the reaction of his visual system to points of light. To get useful records from individual receptors (the rods and cones), assuming that they operate independently and under no reflex control, this stimulus may be adequate. But when one inspects responses that are a few nervous transformations removed from the receptors, as in the optic nerve, that same choice of stimulus is difficult to defend. It is equivalent to assuming that all of the interpretation is done further on in the nervous system. But, as we have seen, this is false.

One might attempt to measure numerically how the response of each kind of fiber varies with various properties of the successions of patterns of light which evoke them. But to characterize a succession of patterns in space requires knowledge of so many independent variables that this is hardly possible by experimental enumeration of cases. To examine the effect of curvature alone we should have to explore at least the response to all configurations of three spots moving in a large variety of ways. We would prefer to state the operations of ganglion cells as simply as possible in terms of whatever *quality* they seem to detect and, instead, examine the bipolar cells in the retina, expecting to find there a dissection of the operations into combinations of simpler ones performed at intermediate stages. For example, suppose that there are at least two sorts of rods and cones, one increasing its voltage with the log of light at one color, the other decreasing its voltage with the log of light at some other color. If bipolars connect to several contiguous rods or cones of opposing reactions and simply add voltages, some bipolars will register a large signal only if an appropriate contrast occurs. We have in fact found something of the sort occurring, for it seems that the inner plexiform layer of the retina is stratified to display several different local properties, one layer indicating local differences in intensity of light. Some of Svaetichin's [14] data can be adduced

here. The different dendritic distribution of the ganglion cells, as in Fig. 1(a), may signify that they extract differently weighted samples of simple local operations done by the bipolars, and it is on this that we are now working.

But there is another reason for a reluctance to make accurate measurements on the activity of ganglion cells in the intact animal. A significant efferent outflow goes to the retina from the brain. We now know to a certain extent how the cells in the tectum handle the four inputs to them which are described in this paper. There are at least two distinct classes of these cells, and at least one of them issues axons back into the optic nerve. We have recorded this activity there. Such axons enter the retina and we think some effects of their activity on the sensitivity of ganglion cells are noticeable.

The way that the retina projects to the tectum suggests a nineteenth century view of visual space. The image on the retina, taken at the grain of the rods and cones, is an array of regularly spaced points at each of which there is a certain amount of light of a certain composition. If we know the position of every point and the values of light at every point, we can physically reconstruct the image, and looking at it understand the picture. If, however, we are required to establish continuities within the picture only from the numerical data on position and light at independent points, it becomes a very difficult task. The retina projects onto the tectum in four parallel sheets of endings, each sheet mapping continuously the retina in terms of a particular areal operation, and all four maps are in registration. Consider the dendrite of a tectal cell extending up through the four sheets. It is looking at a point in the image on the retina, but that point is now seen in terms of the properties of its neighborhood as defined by the operations. Since the overlap of receptive fields within any operation is very great, it now seems reasonable to erect simple criteria for finding continuities. For example, if an area over which there is little change in the fourfold signature of a moving object is bounded by regions of different signature, it seems likely that that area describes the image of a single object.

By transforming the image from a space of simple discrete points to a congruent space where each equivalent point is described by the intersection of particular qualities in its neighborhood, we can then give the image in terms of distributions of combinations of those qualities. In short, every point is seen in definite contexts. The character of these contexts, genetically built in, is the physiological synthetic *a priori*. The operations found in the frog make unlikely later processes in his system of the sort described by two of us earlier [15], for example, dilatations; but those were adduced for the sort of form recognition which the frog does not have. This work is an outgrowth of that earlier study which set the question.

Conclusion

The output from the retina of the frog is a set of four distributed operations on the visual image. These operations are independent of the level of general illumination and express the image in terms of: 1) local sharp edges and contrast; 2) the curvature of edge of a dark object; 3) the movement of edges; and 4) the local dimmings produced by movement or rapid general darkening. Each group of fibers serving one operation maps the retina continuously in a single sheet of endings in the frog's brain. There are four such sheets in the brain, corresponding to the four operations, and their maps are in registration. When all axonal connections between eye and brain are broken and the fibers grow back, they reconstitute the original retinal maps and also arrange themselves in depth in the original order with no mistakes. If there is any randomness in the connections of this system it must be at a very fine level indeed. In this, we consider that Sperry [11] is completely right.

We have described each of the operations on the retinal image in terms of what common factors in a large variety of stimuli cause response and what common factors have no effect. What, then, does a particular fiber in the optic nerve measure? We have considered it to be how much there is in a stimulus of that quality which excites the fiber maximally, naming that quality.

The operations thus have much more the flavor of perception than of sensation if that distinction has any meaning now. That is to say that the language in which they are best described is the language of complex abstractions from the visual image. We have been tempted, for example, to call the convexity detectors "bug perceivers." Such a fiber [operation 2] responds best when a dark object, smaller than a receptive field, enters that field, stops, and moves about intermittently thereafter. The response is not affected if the lighting changes or if the background (say a picture of grass and flowers) is moving, and is not there if only the background, moving or still, is in the field. Could one better describe a system for detecting an accessible bug?

Acknowledgment

We are particularly grateful to O. G. Selfridge whose experiments with mechanical recognizers of pattern helped drive us to this work and whose criticism in part shaped its course.

Bibliography

[1] H. R. Maturana, "Number of fibers in the optic nerve and the number of ganglion cells in the retina of Anurans," *Nature*, vol. 183, pp. 1406–1407; May 16, 1959.

[2] H. K. Hartline, "The response of single optic nerve fibres of the vertebrate eye to illumination of the retina," *Amer. J. Physiol.*, vol. 121, pp. 400–415; February, 1938.
Also, "The receptive fields of the optic nerve fibers," *Amer. J. Physiol.*, vol. 130, pp. 690–699; October, 1940.

[3] H. B. Barlow, "Summation and inhibition in the frog's retina," *J. Physiol.*, vol. 119, pp. 69–88; January, 1953.

[4] S. W. Kuffler, "Discharge patterns and functional organization of mammalian retina," *J. Neurophysiol.*, vol. 16, pp. 37–68; January, 1953.

[5] H. B. Barlow, R. Fitzhugh, and S. W. Kuffler, "Change of organization in the receptive fields of the cat's retina during dark adaptation," *J. Physiol.*, vol. 137, pp. 338–354; August, 1957.

[6] A. M. Andrew, "Report on Frog Colliculus," Res. Lab. of Electronics, Mass. Inst. Tech., Cambridge, Quarterly Progress Rept., pp. 77–78; July 15, 1955.

[7] A. M. Andrew, "Action potentials from the frog colliculus," *J. Physiol.*, vol. 130, p. 25P; September 23–24, 1955.

[8] H. R. Maturana, "The Fine Structure of the Optic Nerve and Tectum of Anurans. An Electron Microscope Study," Ph.D. dissertation, Harvard University, Cambridge, Mass.; 1958.

[9] Pedro Ramon Cajal, "Histologie du Systeme Nerveux," Ramon y Cajal, Maloine, Paris, France; 1909–1911.

[10] R. M. Gaze, "The representation of the retina on the optic lobe of the frog," *Quart. J. Exper. Physiol.*, vol. 43, pp. 209–214; March, 1958.

[11] R. Sperry, "Mechanisms of neural maturation," in "Handbook of Experimental Psychology," S. S. Stevens, Ed., John Wiley and Sons, Inc., New York, N. Y.; 1951.

[12] R. M. Gaze, "Regeneration of the optic nerve in *Xenopus laevi*," *J. Physiol.*, vol. 146, p. 40P; February 20–21, 1959.

[13] H. R. Maturana, J. Y. Lettvin, W. S. McCulloch, and W. H. Pitts, "Physiological evidence that cut optic nerve fibers in the frog regenerate to their proper places in the tectum," *Science*; 1959 (in press).

[14] G. Svaetichin and E. F. NcNichol Jr., "Retinal mechanisms for chromatic and achromatic vision," *Ann. N. Y. Acad. Sci.*, vol. 74, pp. 385–404; November, 1958.

[15] W. S. McCulloch and W. H. Pitts, "How we know universals. The perception of auditory and visual forms," *Bull. Math. Biophysics*, vol. 9, pp. 127–147; June, 1947.

14
Introduction

(1972)
H. B. Barlow

Single units and sensation: a neuron doctrine for perceptual psychology?
Perception 1: 371–394

Consider the scientific life of a neurophysiologist who records single units from the brain of a mammal. The experiment starts at 7:30 A.M. with anesthesia, initial preparation, and surgery. It is usually necessary to place a cannula in a vein for administration of anesthetic and drugs and to perform a tracheotomy so the animal can be artificially respirated. The animal is placed in a *stereotaxic apparatus*, a piece of finely crafted stainless steel hardware that allows precise placement of an electrode in the nervous system. The coordinate system is usually referred to the openings of the ear canals—ear bars are placed in the ear canals to support the animal's head and provide the reference. Every laboratory has a *stereotaxic atlas* for the animal it is working with, so the location of the part of the nervous system experimenters want to record from can be approximately located. Depending on the experiment, sometimes it is necessary to place stimulating electrodes or gross recording electrodes in various locations, set up one or more microelectrode drives, and often to provide visual, auditory, or other sensory stimuli. The part of the nervous system of interest must be exposed by removing the covering bone. Of course every nervous system is different, so there is almost always a bit of hunting around to find the exact area for that particular animal. In a visual experiment the animal's eyes are opened, its pupils are dilated, corrective lenses are used if necessary, optical geometry is adjusted, and a *tangent screen* where images are presented is placed in the field of view. There are several highly trained people involved with the experiment at all times. With luck, and if the experiment is simple, it might be possible to start microelectrode recording just after lunch. More typically the first recordings that generate useful data are not obtained until later in the day or early evening. A neurophysiological experiment on higher mammals can run continously for several days, 24 hours a day, using rotating shifts of experimenters. Some parts of the brain—especially the brainstem— are extremely sensitive, and the slightest error, or even no obvious error at all, will immediately kill the animal.

The object of this effort is to place a small *microelectrode*, a micron or less in size at the tip, in close proximity to a single neuron. It is hard to do. After all the preliminary effort, the experimental team will have recorded and characterized only a few dozen cells at most. Because so few cells are recorded and studied compared with the number present, there are severe sampling problems. There is a strong bias toward recording from large cells and cells with certain geometries. Things can get missed. In one case in 1984 an entire new, quite large, class of cells, the so-called color blob cells, were discovered in the most intensively studied part of the brain, primary visual cortex (Livingstone and Hubel 1984).

Does the knowledge obtained justify the effort of recording it? This influential paper by Barlow discusses the relation of single units to the operation of the brain. Rumor has it that at least one well-known neurophysiology laboratory required incoming graduate students to read this paper so they would know how to interpret what they were seeing.

This paper is designed to be speculative and provocative. Barlow discusses the relation between single units and "subjective perception." The paper is really a discussion of what in neural networks would be called *representation*, that is, how the sensory world is represented by activities of the units in the system. Representational issues are just as critical to neural network operation as they are to understanding what the brain is doing. Barlow organizes his conclusions as a series of dogmas:

First, he argues that single cells are truly the right thing to study and are at the right level of complexity to make the connection to behavior. Therefore, there is real meaning and importance to the data neurophysiologists labor so hard to obtain, and the effort is important. It might instead be held that what is important are the collective activities shown by small groups of neurons, or computations that are so widespread that a single neuron is of almost no consequence. Barlow argues that this is not so and that perception is arranged around the properties of single units, and the rest of his dogmas make this claim more specific.

Second, Barlow says that the wiring of the brain is such as to code a sensory input with "the minimum number of active neurons." That is, "at the higher levels, fewer and fewer cells are active, but each represents a more and more specific happening in the sensory environment." If many units are active when something interesting is going on, the representation is called *distributed*. If only one unit is active to represent the interesting thing, the representation is often caricatured as a *grandmother cell* representation (that is, a cell that is active when, and only when, grandma is seen or thought of). Many of the quantitative discussions in this paper are concerned with the degree of distribution of the representation. Barlow suggests that perhaps "1,000 active neurons represent the visual scene," out of tens of millions of neurons present. Barlow has a strong bias toward a sparse representation.

After a brief detour, in the fourth dogma, Barlow returns to coding. In perhaps the best-known phrase from this often quoted paper, he says that a single active higher-level unit, "corresponds to a pattern of external events of the order of complexity of a word." Because multiple high-level cells are active, perception becomes a sentence in a high level language of sensory analysis, spoken by a few cells. Barlow suggests that these "words" are combined much like symbols could be, presaging some later heated debates in connectionism about symbolic and associative cognitive computation (see Fodor and Pylyshyn, paper 35).

Barlow insists throughout on a small degree of distribution of representation. Partly this is because it allows a more flexible combination of "words" to represent complex reality. And partly this is because of some practical considerations like damage resistance and neuron dynamic range. A descriptor often used among neurophysiologists is the "pontifical" neuron, that is, the neuron that makes the decisions and tells other units what to do—a slightly more dignified grandmother cell. Although some invertebrates do indeed have command neurons that act in exactly this way for certain behaviors, the much larger mammalian cerebral cortex does not seem to contain command neurons. Barlow suggests that instead of a single pontiff, there is a "college of cardinals," where each high-level cardinal expresses a part of the command. Because there are a great many higher-level units, Barlow points out that the college of cardinals outnumbers the congregation. But only a few speak at a time, so there is rarely confusion of doctrine.

There is another important technical issue here that is not quite so obviously brought out in this paper, though it is in a later review paper (Barlow 1985) and a more technical paper

(Barlow and Foldiak 1989) on the same topic. The coding chosen by Barlow—a college of cardinals—is the end stage of a *decorrelation* process. In the retina nearby cells are quite likely to see similar light intensities because physical objects have extent. Lateral inhibition in a network (paper 23 in *Neurocomputing: Foundations of Research*) can be viewed as an edge enhancer, but it also serves to make nearby cells less similar in their properties because one cell will inhibit the other and only one will fire at a time. The ultimate end of this decorrelation process is the highly selective cells postulated by Barlow, where cells are *very* different from each other, that is, different neural words and therefore uncorrelated. Note the difference between this result and an approach based on a direct application of map relationships, such as Kohonen's maps, where nearby cells tend to be similar in responses. In the nervous system there is a balance struck between (efficient) decorrelation and (inefficient) redundancy. Some of these important issues are raised by Linsker (paper 31).

The third and fifth dogmas are less important for neural network research. The third dogma states that cell selectivity contains a large component developed from experience. There is a large and contentious literature on the environmental modifiability of visual cortical cells that Barlow is alluding to, described at some length in papers by von der Malsburg and by Bienenstock, Cooper, and Munro (papers 17 and 26) in *Neurocomputing: Foundations of Research*. The fifth dogma makes the claim, also made by almost all neural net models, that increased unit activity corresponds to increased certainty that a feature is present in the environment.

It is the feeling of many in neural network research that representation of information is the most important aspect of neural network design. The exact details of the network learning algorithms or network architecture are of interest, but unless the data representation is right, nothing will work. This is the problem that Barlow is addressing. Not surprisingly neurophysiologists were thinking about these issues long before neural network designers. And the brain had been organized to solve efficiently problems of representation relevant to behavior long before either neurophysiologists or network designers existed. There is a balance between distribution and localization in representation, compounded by the limited dynamic range, fragility, cost of connectivity, and noisiness of biological computing elements. What we see in the nervous system is some kind of optimal tradeoff between all these considerations. This paper provides a speculative discussion of these critically important ideas in the context of a biological computing system, but all these ideas have exact corollaries in artificial neural network design and can be ignored only with peril.

References

H.B. Barlow (1985), The Twelfth Bartlett Memorial Lecture: the role of single neurons in the psychology of perception. *The Quarterly Journal of Experimental Psychology* 37A: 121–145.

H.B. Barlow and P. Foldiak (1989), Adaptation and decorrelation in the cortex. In C. Mall, R. M. Durbin, and G. J. Mitchison (Eds.), *The Computing Neuron*. Reading, MA: Addison-Wesley.

M. S. Livingtone and D. H. Hubel (1984), Anatomy and physiology of a color system in the primate visual cortex. *Journal of Neuroscience* 4: 309–356.

(1972)
H. B. Barlow

Single units and sensation: a neuron doctrine for perceptual psychology?
Perception 1: 371–394

Abstract

The problem discussed is the relationship between the firing of single neurons in sensory pathways and subjectively experienced sensations. The conclusions are formulated as the following five dogmas:

1. To understand nervous function one needs to look at interactions at a cellular level, rather than either a more macroscopic or microscopic level, because behaviour depends upon the organized pattern of these intercellular interactions.
2. The sensory system is organized to achieve as complete a representation of the sensory stimulus as possible with the minimum number of active neurons.
3. Trigger features of sensory neurons are matched to redundant patterns of stimulation by experience as well as by developmental processes.
4. Perception corresponds to the activity of a small selection from the very numerous high-level neurons, each of which corresponds to a pattern of external events of the order of complexity of the events symbolized by a word.
5. High impulse frequency in such neurons corresponds to high certainty that the trigger feature is present.

The development of the concepts leading up to these specutative dogmas, their experimental basis, and some of their limitations are discussed.

1 Introduction

In this article I shall discuss the difficult but challenging problem of the relation between our subjective perceptions and the activity of the nerve cells in our brains. Results obtained by recording from single neurons in sensory pathways have aroused a lot of interest and obviously tell us something important about how we sense the world around us; but what exactly have we been told? In order to probe this question, ideas that fit current knowledge as well as possible must be formulated, and they must be stated clearly enough to be tested to see if they are right or wrong; this is what I have tried to do. The central proposition is that our perceptions are caused by the activity of a rather small number of neurons selected from a very large population of predominantly silent cells. The activity of each single cell is thus an important perceptual event and it is thought to be related quite simply to our subjective experience. The subtlety and sensitivity of perception results

from the mechanisms determining when a single cell becomes active, rather than from complex combinatorial rules of usage of nerve cells.

In order to avoid vagueness, I have formulated this notion in five definite propositions, or dogmas, and the reader who wishes to see the trend of this article can glance ahead (to page 380). Some of the dogmas will be readily accepted by most people who hope to find a scientific basis for human thought processes, but I felt they required statement and discussion in spite of their widespread tacit acceptance. Others are more original, will be challenged by many, and have the nature of extrapolations from the current trend of results rather than conclusions reasonably based upon them. Before these dogmas are stated the developments that have led to them will be briefly reviewed. The literature is extensive, and much of it will have been incorporated into the reader's common knowledge. My aim, therefore, is to pick out the conceptual turning points in order to show the direction we are headed. After stating the dogmas, criticisms and alternatives will be discussed in an attempt both to justify them and to clarify them further.

2 Recording from Single Neurons

2.1 Peripheral Nerves

In the twenties and thirties methods were developed for amplifying and recording the weak transient electrical potentials associated with the activity of nerve fibres, and Adrian and his colleagues used these methods to record the all-or-none impulses of single nerve fibres connecting the sense organs to the brain (Adrian, 1926a, 1926b; Adrian and Zotterman, 1926a, 1926b; Adrian, 1928). They showed, for example, that each fibre coming from the skin responded to a particular type of stimulus, such as pressure, temperature change, or damage, applied to a specific region or receptive field. The frequency of the impulses depended upon the intensity of the stimulus, but it was clear that the character of the sensation (touch, heat, or pain) depended upon the fibre carrying the message, not the nature of the message, since this consisted of trains of similar impulses in all fibres. Nerves had long been recognized as the link between physical stimulus and sensation so these results provided physiological flesh and blood to the skeleton that anatomical studies had revealed a long time earlier.

Most of the results confirmed another ancient idea, namely Müller's doctrine of specific nerve energies: the specificity of different sensations stems from the responsiveness of different nerve fibres to different types of stimulus. The chemical senses proved to be a little different (Pfaffman. 1941, 1955; Ganchrow and Erickson, 1970), but in spite of the fact that they did not quite fall in line, the concept that resulted from two decades of recording from peripheral fibres and following their connections in the brain was of a simple mapping from sense organs to sensorium, so that a copy of physical events at the body surface was presented to the brain (Bard, 1938; Marshall *et al.,* 1941 Adrian, 1941, 1947). Some modification was recognized to occur, for sensory nerves usually adapt to a constant stimulus, and therefore signal sudden changes of stimulus energy better than sustained levels. Neighbouring receptive fields and modalities were also known to overlap, but when the activity of neurons at higher levels in sensory pathways was recorded it became obvious that something was happening more complex and significant than could be fitted into the concept of simple mapping with overlap and adaptation.

2.2 Sensory Neurons of the Retina

Starting with Granit (Granit and Svaetichin, 1939; Granit, 1947) and Hartline (1938; 1940a, 1940b) in the retina, and Galambos and Davis (Galambos and Davis, 1943; Galambos, 1944; Galambos and Davis, 1948) at the periphery of the pathway for hearing, a generation of physiologists has studied sensory neurons in the central nervous system; all this obviously cannot be reviewed here, but we shall concentrate on the results that expanded the conceptual frame built on the earlier work. Previously it was possible for physiologist to be satisfied with describing how the sense organs and their nerves present a picture of the external world to the brain, and they were happy to leave it to the psychologists to discuss what happened next) but these next things started to happen around the physiologist's micro-electrodes, and he has to join the discussion.

The realization that physiological experiments can answer questions of psychological interest first dawned on me personally when I was working on the frog's retina. A vigorous discharge can be evoked from retinal ganglion cells by stimulating the appropriate region of the retina—the ganglion cell's "receptive field" (Hartline, 1940a); but if the surrounding region is simultaneously stimulated the response of the cell is diminished or completely abolished

(Barlow, 1953). This phenomenon is called lateral inhibition, or peripheral suppression, and such a physiological mechanism had already been postulated in order to account for simultaneous brightness and Mach bands (Mach, 1886; Fry, 1948). Thus the physiological experiment was really providing evidence in support of a psychological hypothesis.

The invasion of psychological territory did not stop at this point. If one explains the responsiveness of single ganglion cells in the frog's retina using hand-held targets, one finds that one particular type of ganglion cell is most effectively driven by something like a black disc subtending a degree or so moved rapidly to and fro within the unit's receptive field. This causes a vigorous discharge which can be maintained without much decrement as long as the movement is continued. Now, if the stimulus which is optimal for this class of cells is presented to intact frogs, the behavioural response is often dramatic: they turn towards the target and make repeated feeding responses consisting of a jump and snap. The selectivity of the retinal neurons, and the frog's reaction when they are selectively stimulated, suggest that they are "bug detectors" (Barlow, 1953) performing a primitive but vitally important form of recognition.

This result makes one suddenly realize that a large part of the sensory machinery involved in a frog's feeding responses may actually reside in the retina rather than in mysterious "centres" that would be too difficult to understand by physiological methods. The essential lock-like property resides in each member of a whole class of neurons, and allows the cell to discharge only to the appropriate key pattern of sensory stimulation. Lettvin *et al.* (1959) suggested that there were five different classes of cell in the frog, and Levick, Hill and I (Barlow *et al.*, 1964) found an even larger number of categories in the rabbit. We called these key patterns "trigger features", and Maturana *et al.* (1960) emphasized another important aspect of the behaviour of these ganglion cells: a cell continues to respond to the same trigger feature in spite of changes in light intensity over many decades. The properties of the retina are such that a ganglion cell can, figuratively speaking, reach out and determine that something specific is happening in front of the eye. Light is the agent by which it does this, but it is the detailed pattern of the light that carries the information, and the overall level of illumination prevailing at the time is almost totally disregarded.

It is true that Ingle (1968, 1971), Grüsser and Grüsser-Cornehls (1968), and Ewert (1970) have shown that it is too simple to suppose that feeding automatically and inevitably follows the activation of a certain class of retinal ganglion cells by their trigger features; higher coordinating mechanisms are also involved. Just as light is only an intermediate agent allowing a retinal ganglion cell to detect its trigger feature, so these optic nerve impulses must doubtless be regarded as intermediate agents enabling the higher centres to perform their tasks. We shall proceed to discuss these problems, but we have gained two important concepts from the frog's retina: it transmits a map, not of the light intensities at each point of the image, but of the trigger features in the world before the eye, and its main function is not to transduce different luminance levels into different impulse frequencies, but to continue responding invariantly to the same external patterns despite changes of average luminance.

2.3   Sensory Neurons of the Cerebral Cortex

The function of the visual area of the mammalian cerebral cortex is obviously more relevant to the problem of our own subjective perceptions than is the frog's retina, and Hubel and Wiesel (1959) early discovered examples of selectivity for pattern in the responsiveness of cells in the visual cortex of cats. They found that a light or dark line, or a dark-light border, was required to evoke a vigorous response even in the simplest first-order cells. Furthermore the stimulus had to be at a rather precise orientation and position in the visual field and in addition it usually had to be moving, often in a specific direction. Hubel and Wiesel (1962) also made a distinction between these cells and other classes with more elaborate stimulus requirements, which they believed corresponded to cells at later stages of information processing. They called these "complex" and "hypercomplex" units, and showed that they had properties suggesting that the input to each was from the simpler category of cells. The fascination of this analysis depends to a large extent upon successfully following the way units become selective for more and more complex properties at each stage. Some doubts have been cast on their hierarchical scheme (Stone, 1972), but it certainly gave new insight into how higher levels of categorization are developed from lower levels.

As well as the hierarchical concept, this work provided evidence for a new type of invariance. In the cat, as in the frog, the retina is mainly responsible for ensuring that the message sent to the brain is not much perturbed by changes in ambient illumination. In the cortex Hubel and Wiesel (1962) found that some of the higher level neurons responded to the same trigger feature over a considerable range of positions. The modality specificity of peripheral neurons indicates how one can, for instance, detect warmth at any point on the body surface, and we now see that the organized pattern specificity of a set of cortical neurons can in the same way produce positional invariance for pattern perception. This was previously one of the great puzzles, and, although we certainly do not understand how recog-

nition is invariant for position, size, and perspective transformations, at least a start has been made.

Later experiments have shown that the primary neurons of the visual cortex are more specific in one respect than Hubel and Wiesel originally thought. They showed that most neurons are fed by inputs from both eyes, and they emphasized that the dominance of ipsi- or contra-lateral eye varied from cell to cell. Now it can be shown that a binocular stimulus often has to be very precisely positioned in both eyes in order to evoke the most vigorous response (Barlow *et al.*, 1967; Pettigrew *et al.*, 1968), and a more important variable than dominance emerges from the exact relative positions in the two eyes. Consider what must happen when the eyes are converged on some point in front of the cat and appropriate visual stimuli are presented; it is easy to position this stimulus correctly for either eye by itself but if it is to be correctly positioned for both, it will have to be at some specific distance from the cat. When the precise positioning for different units is studied, it is found that this specific distance for optimal response varies in different units in the same cortex, and among units serving the same region of visual space. Conversely, the selection of units which are activated provides the cat with some information about the distances of the various stimulus objects. In uncovering this aspect of the pattern selectivity of sensory neurons we again get the sense that a central neuron is reaching out to discover something important about what is happening in the real objective world. One even wonders if the line and edge detectors of Hubel and Wiesel may not have, as their main function, the linking together of information about the same object in the two retinal images in order to determine the object's most important coordinate—its distance from the animal. At all events, as in the case of the frog's bug-detector, the importance of the information abstracted from the retinal images gives some insight into the purpose or direction of the physiological mechanisms.

Something is known about these first steps of information processing in the visual cortex; what about the later stages? Results suggesting greater and greater specificity of response requirements have been obtained, and a nice example is the unit described by Gross *et al.* (1972) in the infero-temporal cortex of macaques; this responded best to stimulation by a figure with many of the specific characteristics of a monkey's hand, and the requirements of one such unit are well documented. Work in this area is not easy to repeat, for one can readily see that it is largely a matter of chance to find a trigger feature of this order of complexity. Also, the possibility that cells may retain to adulthood the modifiable properties of immature cells that will be described later makes the prospect of investigating the sensory association areas an intimidating one.

Cortical neurons receive selective excitatory and inhibitory inputs from other neurons and thereby possess selective responsiveness for some characteristics and invariances for changes in other characteristics. This seems to have the potentiality of being a powerful information processing system.

3 Single Units and Psychophysics

The neurophysiological discoveries outlined above of course made a deep impression on those investigating sensation psychophysically, but although there are many superficial points of contact it has not proved easy to link sensations securely to specific patterns of neurophysiological activity. The topics I have chosen are again ones which seem to have implications about how we conceptualize this neuropsychic relationship.

3.1 Lateral Inhibitions and Simultaneous Contrast

The relation between lateral inhibition in the retina and simultaneous contrast has already been mentioned, but there is a large gap between the physiological level and the subjective effects shown in textbook illustrations, and it is too big to be bridged by a single simple statement. It is quite easy to show that frog and cat retinal ganglion cells demonstrate relevant effects, since their antagonistic surrounds (Barlow, 1953; Kuffler, 1953) make their responses depend upon contrast rather than absolute luminance. Hence on-centre cells respond to spots we would call white, off-centre cells to spots we would call black, even when the so-called black spot has a higher luminance than the white spot (Barlow *et al.,* 1957). But subjective contrast effects also hold for conditions where one cannot make such easy comparisons, for instance at the centre of an area which is much too large to fill the centre of a retinal receptive field. Of course, one can postulate some "filling in" process (Yarbus, 1965), but the necessity of introducing ad hoc assumptions makes many explanations of subjective effects in terms of single units unconvincing.

The concept that enables one to escape this difficulty is to concentrate on the informational flow rather than on the direct subjective-physiological comparison. Information discarded in a peripheral stage of processing cannot be accurately added back centrally, and in the present case it helps to talk about "attenuating low spatial frequencies" instead of "signalling spatial contrast". To say that some of the low-frequency attenuation of the whole visual system is performed by the opposed centre-surround organisation of the retinal ganglion cell (Campbell and Green, 1965; Enroth-Cugell and Robson, 1966) is more accurate than to say that all simultaneous contrast effects originate there.

3.2 Colour

In the field of colour vision De Valois has looked for relationships between various psychophysically measurable aspects of colour and the properties of single unit responses recorded at the level of the lateral geniculate nucleus. The main results provided a startling confirmation of Hering's long-standing hypothesis about the reciprocal organisation of colour systems (Svaetichin and MacNicholl, 1958; De Valois, 1960; Hurvich and Jameson, 1960; Wagner *et al.,* 1960), but the details are important. He has been able to establish neuro-psychic parallels using what may be called the "lower envelope" or "most sensitive neuron" principle. A monkey's ability to discriminate hue and saturation (De Valois *et al.,* 1966, 1967) is very close to what one would expect if the monkey only pays attention to the most sensitive of the optic nerves conveying information about these qualities of the stimulus. Thus the psychophysical performance follows the lower envelope of the performance of individual fibres. It is particularly interesting to see that a continuous psychophysical function, hue discrimination as a function of wavelength, is served by a different type of neuron in different ranges; over the long wavelength range the red-green opponent system was much more sensitive to wavelength shift, whereas the blue-yellow system was more sensitive at short wavelengths.

This result again fits in with the concept that neurophysiology and sensation are best linked by looking at the flow of information rather than simpler measures of neuronal activity. For instance it might be suggested that sensation follows the average neural activity, and it would be easy to justify this on the neurophysiological grounds that post-synaptic potentials are usually additive. However, this oversimple suggestion is proved false by the fact that psychophysical hue discrimination does not follow the average response of the red-green and blue-yellow systems, but instead follows the lower envelope. Now when two noisy channels are both conveying information about a signal, the channel with the highest signal/noise ratio dominates the situation; the low signal/noise ratio channel can be used to improve performance slightly, but it is a very small contribution except where its signal/noise ratio is nearly as high as that of the more sensitive channel. Thus the "most-sensitive neuron" principle again fits the concept that, to link neurophysiological activity and sensation, one should look at the flow of information.

3.3 Touch

Another example is given by the work of Montcastle and his colleagues (Talbot *et al.,* 1968), in which they studied the responses at a number of levels to vibratory stimuli, applied to the glabrous skin of the hand. First they recorded from cutaneous afferants in the monkey, then the cortical responses in the same species, finally they made psychophysical measures of sensory responses in humans to the same stimuli. As with the work on colour, they established that the sensory response depends simply upon the category of nerve fibre with the lowest threshold.

The fact that the subjective sensation in both the colour and touch system seems to follow the lower envelope of the responses of the various types of sensory neurons may give an important clue to the way in which these neurons represent sensations. It is as if the screen on which sensations appear is completely blank until a sensory pathway is activated, but when this happens a point lights up and becomes instantly visible. This is not what one would expect if there was a lot of ongoing activity in all pathways, or if the magnitude of the signal was linear function of intensity, nor is it what one would expect if sensation depended in a complex combinatorial way upon the activity of many units. Rather it suggest the concept that the magnitude of the signal directly represents the signal/noise ratio for then the insignifcant signals will automatically be small, and the neurons firing most will automatically be the most sensitive. This concept receives some support in the next section and is taken up in the fifth dogma and its discussion.

3.4 Adaptation After-effects

The fact that one is almost unaware of the constant pressure applied to the skin by the chair one is sitting on presumably results, at least in part, from the rapid decline in frequency of the volley of sensory impulses initiated by contact (Adrian, 1928). Central neurons that respond to specific patterns of sensory input also give a decreased response when the pattern is sustained or repeatedly presented, though there have actually been surprisingly few investigations of this effect. These adaptation, habituation, or fatigue effects lead to plausible explanations for many well-known sensory illusions.

For example the rate of discharge in the directionally selective neurons of the rabbit retina declines if a stimulus is continuously moved through the receptive field in the preferred direction, and following cessation of movement the maintained discharge is found to be suppressed (Barlow and Hill, 1963). The resulting imbalance between neurons signalling opposite directions seems to provide a ready explanation of the apparent reversed movement of stationary objects following prolonged inspection of moving objects (the so-called "waterfall effect"), and provides another example of an ancient psychophysical hypothesis (Wohlgemuth, 1911) being confirmed neurophysiologically. One must bear in mind that these neural effects were described in the rabbit's retina, whereas in the human, as

in the eat and monkey, neurons are probably not directionally selective until the level of the visual cortex (Barlow and Brindley, 1963), but the same type of explanation may well apply to neurons at this level.

It has been suggested that one can make inverse inferences from the existence of an after-effect to the presence of neurons with particular selective responses. This is no place to argue whether the after-effects of adaptation to gratings imply a Fourier-type analysis (Blakemore and Campbell, 1969), or whether they can be satisfactorily accounted for by families of different-sized neurons with conventional Hubel-Wiesel-type receptive fields, but there is certainly room for argument, and this makes selective adaptation a difficult tool to use to discover later stages of information processing.

Instead, I think the importance of sensory adaptational effects, and of the corresponding neurophysiological phenomena, lies in the support both these phenomena lend to the concept put forward at the end of the last section. If sensory messages are to be given a prominence proportional to their informational value, mechanisms must exist for reducing the magnitude of representation of patterns which are constantly present, and this is presumably the underlying rationale for adaptive effects.

3.5 Noisiness or Reliability of Single Units

It used to be commonly held that nerve cells were unreliable elements, much perturbed by metabolic or other changes and perhaps also by random disturbances of more fundamental origin (McCulloch, 1959; Burns, 1968). The fairly high degree of reliability that the nervous system achieves as a whole was explained by the supposed redundancy of neural circuits and appropriate rules for averaging and combining them. Developments in the study of human vision at the absolute threshold and of the absolute sensitivity of retinal ganglion cells in the cat now indicate that nerve cells are not intrinsically unreliable and that noise often originates externally.

Signal detection theory has familiarized psychologists with the problem of detecting signals in the presence of noise (Tanner and Swets, 1954; Green and Swets, 1966), and I think the assumed prevalence of internally generated noise was a major reason why this was thought to be an important new approach. But psychophysical studies have actually shown that the senses and the brain can operate with astonishing intrinsic reliability. Noise may always be present, but to an amazing extent it originates outside the nervous system. This was originally implied by the results of Hecht et al. (1942) on the absolute threshold of vision) they showed that about 100 quanta at the cornea, leading to 10 or less absorptions in the retina, were sufficient to give a sensation of light. But their most revolutionary finding was that the frequency-of-seeing curve, describing the breadth of the threshold zone, is mainly accounted for by quantum fluctuations, not internal sloppiness or random variations of the threshold criterion as had previously been thought. That is not to say that "intrinsic retinal noise" or "dark light" is non-existent or unimportant, for it is probably the main factor determining how many quanta are required for reliable detection (Barlow, 1956). It now appears probable that this originates in the photoreceptors and, in some subjects at least, is low enough to allow the conscious detection of the sensation caused by absorption of a single quantum (Sakitt, 1972); similar sensations occur in the absence of light stimuli, but at a lower frequency. In addition, the subjects can apparently discriminate between the sensory messages resulting from 2, 3, 4, etc. quantal absorptions, each being detected progressively more clearly and reliably.

This psychophysical work shows that the human brain, acting as a whole, can distinguish between the disturbances caused by small numbers of quantal absorptions. These must of course originate from single molecular events in single cells, but possibly the disturbance is thereafter diffused through many cells and abstracted in some way from a redundant neural representation. It therefore becomes very interesting to go into the neurophysiology and find how the absorption of a few quanta is signalled

A sensitive example of a retinal ganglion cell of the cat, with its associated bipolar cells, receptors, amacrine and horizontal cells, will give a readily detectable discharge of impulses to as few as 2 or 3 quanta of light absorbed in the retina (Barlow *et al.*, 1971). Such a stimulus will give rise to an average of 5 to 10 extra impulses. Thus a single quantal absorption causes as many as 3 extra impulses, two quanta cause about 6 impulses, and so on. The addition of 3 impulses to the maintained discharge is detectable on average, though, like the absorption of a single quantum in the human, it cannot be reliably detected on a single trial. There is of course some intrinsic noise, as shown by the maintained discharge, but its level is extraordinarily low when one considers that a single ganglion cell is connected to more than 100 rods containing a total of some 10^{10} molecules of rhodopsin, each poised ready to signal the absorption of a quantum. The important point is that quantitative knowledge of the noise level and reliability of single retinal ganglion cells enables one to see that the performance of the whole visual system can be attributed to a single cell: averaging is not necessary.

Individual nerve cells were formerly thought to be unreliable, idiosyncratic, and incapable of performing complex tasks without acting in concert and thus overcoming their individual errors. This was quite wrong, and we now realise their apparently erratic behaviour was caused by our igno-

rance, not the neuron's incompetence. Thus we gain support from this neuropsychical comparison for the concept of a neuron as a reliable element capable of performing a responsible role in our mental life, though we need not of course go to the other extreme and assume that mental errors are never caused by malfunctioning, ill-educated, or noisy neurons.

4 Modifiability of Cortical Neurons

The most recent conceptual change about the neural basis of our sensations has arisen from a reinspection of the origin of the selective responsiveness of cortical neurons.

4.1 Evidence for Modifiability

Hubel and Wiesel (1963) at first thought they had shown that the whole of the elaborate organization responsible for the selectivity of neurons in the primary visual cortex was developed solely under genetic control. They reported that they found codical neurons with normal adult-type specificity of responsiveness in young kittens which had not opened their eyes, or which had been deprived of visual experience by suture of their eyelids. In later investigations (Wiesel and Hubel, 1963, 1965; Hubel and Wiesel, 1965) they found that abnormal visual experience, such as unilateral eye-suture, or prevention of simultaneous usage of the eyes by alternating occlusion or surgically induced strabismus, caused the development of an abnormal population of cortical cells. In accordance with their earlier findings they attributed this to a disruption of the preformed organization, and they discovered the very important fact that abnormal experience only modifies the cortex if it occurs during a particular "sensitive" period—about 3 to 12 weeks in cats (Hubel and Wiesel, 1970).

Recent developments have extended these seminal findings, but they lead to somewhat different conclusions about the relative importance of experience and genetic factors in determining the selectivity of cortical neurons. First it was shown that kittens brought up with the two eyes exposed to different stimuli, one to vertical stripes, the other to horizontal, had a corresponding orientation selectivity of the receptive fields connected to each eye (Hirsch and Spinelli, 1970, 1971). This was confirmed in kittens exposed only to vertically or horizontally striped environments) these had no neurons sensitive to horizontally or vertically oriented stimuli respectively (Blakemore and Cooper, 1970). Evidence has been obtained that cats raised with a vertical displacement of the images in one eye induced by prisms also have abnormal vertical disparities of the pairs of receptive fields of cortical neurons connected to both eyes (Shlaer, 1971). Again, the cortex of a kitten exposed only to bright dots, with no contours or edges, contained units of an abnormal type responding well to small spots of light and showing little of the customary preference for lines (Pettigrew and Freeman, forthcoming). Furthermore it appears that a very brief period of exposure, as little as an hour, can have very pronounced effects on the subsequent selectivity of neurons in the visual cortex (Blakemore and Mitchell, 1973).

Such results could still possibly have been explained by disruption of the innately-determined highly-specific connections that were originally thought to underlie response specificity, but a reexamination of the properties of cortical neurons of kittens with no visual experience shows that they do not actually have fully-developed adult-type specificity (Barlow and Pettigrew, 1971). This is certainly the case with regard to disparity selectivity and, although there is directional preference and may be some weak orientation selectivity, they are not as narrowly selective as adult cells (Pettigrew, forthcoming). The anatomy of the developing cortex shows that only a small fraction of the normal complement of synapses is present before the critical period, and it is hard to believe that the cells could have adult properties (Cragg, 1972). It will take more work to determine the limits within which the pattern selectivity of cortical neurons can be modified, but the results already make it impossible to believe Hubel and Wiesel's original claim that many cells of the visually inexperienced kitten have the full adult-type selectivity.

4.2 Type of Modification Caused

It is instructive to look at the way in which experience modifies selectivity. In all cases the cortex of animals whose visual experience has been modified lacks neurons selectively responsive to patterns of excitation which a normal animal receives, but which have been excluded by the experimental modification. Thus unilateral lid suture led to a cortex with very few neurons excitable from the lid-sutured eye; likewise, alternating occlusion or strabismus, which decreases the probability of simultaneous excitation of corresponding neurons in the two eyes, decreased the proportion of neurons responding to both eyes. The same is true of the kittens reared in striped environments, or with a vertically deviating prism over one eye, or in an environment with point sources but no lines; in all these cases the rule holds that neurons are found for patterns of excitation that occur in the modified environment, but normally occurring types of selectivity are rare or absent if the patterns they would respond to have not been experienced in the modified environment.

This rule seems to amount to a striking confirmation of the speculation (Barlow, 1960) that a prime function of sensory centres is to code efficiently the patterns of excitation that occur, thus developing a less redundant represen-

tation of the environment. Previous examples of redundancy-reducing codes could be explained as genetically determined features of neural connectivity, but the above discoveries are definite examples of a modified code developed in response to a modified environment.

If on this page we have begun the correct story for simple cells of area 17, one can see that a book has been opened with regard to the properties of cells higher in the hierarchy, which are presumably themselves experience dependent and are fed by information from these experience-dependent neurons at the lower cortical levels. Even a small degree of modifiability would be extraordinarily significant in a hierarchically organized system, just as, in evolution, weak selection pressure is effective over many generations.

5   Current Concept of the Single Neuron

The cumulative effect of all the changes I have tried to outline above has been to make us realise that each single neuron can perform a much more complex and subtle task than had previously been thought. Neurons do not loosely and unreliably map the luminous intensities of the visual image onto our sensorium, but instead they detect pattern elements, discriminate the depth of objects, ignore irrelevant causes of variation, and are arranged in an intriguing hierarchy. Furthermore, there is evidence that they give prominence to what is informationally important, can respond with great reliability, and can have their pattern selectivity permanently modified by early visual experience. This amounts to a revolution in our outlook. It is now quite inappropriate to regard unit activity as a noisy indication of more basic and reliable processes involved in mental operations; instead, we must regard single neurons as the prime movers of these mechanisms. Thinking is brought about by neurons, and we should not use phrases like "unit activity reflects, reveals, or monitors thought processes", because the activities of neurons, quite simply, *are* thought processes.

This revolution stemmed from physiological work and makes us realize that the activity of each single neuron may play a significant role in perception. I think that more clearly stated hypotheses are now needed about these roles in order to allow our psychological knowledge and intuitions about our perceptions to help us plan future experiments.

6   Five Propositions

The following five brief statements are intended to define which aspect of the brain's activity is important for understanding its main function, to suggest the way that single neurons represent what is going on around us, and to say how this is related to our subjective experience. The statements are dogmatic and incautious because it is important that they should be clear and testable.

6.1 First Dogma

A description of that activity of a single nerve cell which is transmitted to and influences other nerve cells, and of a nerve cell's response to such influences from other cells, is a complete enough description for functional understanding of the nervous system. There is nothing else "looking at" or controlling this activity, which must therefore provide a basis for understanding how the brain controls behaviour.

6.2 Second Dogma

At progressively higher levels in sensory pathways information about the physical stimulus is carried by progressively fewer active neurons. The sensory system is organized to achieve as complete a representation as possible with the minimum number of active neurons.

6.3 Third Dogma

Trigger features of neurons are matched to the redundant features of sensory stimulation in order to achieve greater completeness and economy of representation. This selective responsiveness is determined by the sensory stimulation to which neurons have been exposed, as well as by genetic factors operating during development.

6.4 Fourth Dogma

Just as physical stimuli directly cause receptors to initiate neural activity, so the active high-level neurons directly and simply cause the elements of our perception.

6.5 Fifth Dogma

The frequency of neural impulses codes subjective certainty: a high impulse frequency in a given neuron corresponds to a high degree of confidence that the cause of the percept is present in the external world.

7 First Dogma: Significant Level of Description

This dogma asserts that a picture of how the brain works, and in particular how it processes and represents sensory information, can be built up from knowledge of the interactions of individual cells. At the moment single-unit electrical recording is the only tool with temporal and spatial resolution adequate to locate the effect of a particular sensory stimulus in a particular cell. Other tools (biochemical, electron microscopy, etc.) can obviously provide essential information about these interactions, but the dogma

may be criticized more fundamentally; it may be suggested that the whole problem should be approached at a different level. One could attack from either side, suggesting either that one should look at grosser signs of nervous activity, such as the weak extracellular potentials that result from the activity of many neurons, or that one should approach the problem at a more microscopic level, studying synaptic and molecular changes.

Interest in evoked potentials and electroencephalography has waned partly because their study led to slow progress compared with single-unit recording, but also because the rationale for their use was undermined. A prime reason for attending to these macroscopic manifestations of nervous activity was the belief that individual cells were too unreliable to be worthy of attention singly, and hence it was better to look at a sign of activity that resulted from many of them. Here, it was thought, may be a property of a group of cells analogous to temperature or pressure as a property of a collection of molecules that individually behave randomly. The demonstration that single nerve cells have diverse and highly specific responsiveness to sensory stimuli, and are astonishingly reliable, showed the fallacy of this analogy.

The search for a molar property of a mass of working nerve cells is certainly not worthless. Physiologists, and all biologists for that matter, tend to be emotionally divided into globalists and atomists. The globalists are amazed at the perfection of functioning of the whole animal, and they observe that the atomists' analytical investigations of living matter always leave unexplained many of the most remarkable attributes of the intact animal. As a result the globalist can play a crucially important role in pointing out where the atomists' explanations are incomplete. Now the brain does much more interesting things than produce weak extracellular potentials: it controls behaviour, and this is surely the global product that, at our present state of understanding, really does appear greater than the sum of its parts. It would be no use looking at single neurons if it will be forever impossible to explain overall behaviour in terms of the actions and interactions of these subunits; if that were so, the globalists' despair would be justified. On the other hand it is precisely because rapid progress has been made that this article is being written; it no longer seems completely unrealistic to attempt to understand perception at the atomic single-unit level.

The second criticism, that one should approach the problem at a more microscopic level, is really only answerable by saying, *"Go ahead and do it"*, for undoubtedly there is much to be learned at a synaptic and molecular level. But the important question here is whether lack of this knowledge will impede a major advance in our conception of how the brain works. The dogma asserts that it is the intercellular actions interactions that possess the elaborate organization responsible for behavior; hence it asserts that knowledge at a more-microscopic intracellular level is not a prerequisite for understanding such organization.

8 Second Dogma: The Economical Representation of Sensory Messages

The main task in this section is to discern the principles that underlie the changes in characteristic responsiveness of single units at successive levels in sensory pathways. The aim is to understand how sensory information is represented or "displayed". The successive levels to be considered will be peripheral photoreceptors and cutaneous afferents; retinal ganglion cells of the cat, frog, or rabbit, the latter of which seem to exemplify a more complex type of processing; and the visual cortex of cats. Obviously these are not an ideal series for comparisons and extrapolations, but they are the best we can do.

The discussion initially revolves around three issues: changes in the degree of specificity and generality of the stimuli to which the cells respond; changes in the number of parallel categories of selectively sensitive cells that carry the information; and changes in the number of the cells that one may expect to be activated by normal visual scenes. What emerges is that, at the higher levels, fewer and fewer cells are active, but each represents a more and more specific happenings in the sensory environment.

8.1 Specificity and Generality of Responsiveness

The pattern specificity of sensory neurons is the aspect that is most widely emphasized: it was spectacular to discover single neurons in the retina responding to movement of the image in a specific direction, cortical neurons responding only to slits of light at a particular orientation, and a unit in the infero-temporal cortex that responds best to a monkey's hand. But the invariance of the response to changes in the stimulus is equally remarkable. A retinal unit continues to respond to direction of motion in spite of many decades of change in input luminance or contrast, in fact in spite of reversal of contrast (Barlow, 1969a). At the cortical level a complex cell insists that a stimulus is appropriately oriented, but will respond in spite of wide variations of position (Hubel and Wiesel, 1962). And the monkey-paw unit similarly retains its pattern specificity over a large part of the visual field (Gross et al., 1972).

In talking about these properties of sensory neurons actual examples are perhaps more informative than the words specific and general. A single receptor containing a red-sensitive pigment is specific in the sense that long-wavelength light must be present at a particular part of the image in order to excite it, and it is general in the sense that

all images with this property will excite it. In contrast to this type of specificity and generality, the high-level neurons are no longer limited to purely local attributes of the image. They are selective for pattern, which requires that a considerable region of the image is taken into account. But there are other aspects of their specific selectivity that also need to be considered.

8.2 Number of Selective Categories

At the level of receptors there are a small number of different sensory modalities picking up, in parallel, information from different positions. This is the case both for the half dozen types of cutaneous sensation, and for the smaller number of retinal receptor types responding to the visual image. At the level of ganglion cells the number of sub-modalities or selective categories has greatly increased. Consider the rabbit, where there are the following (Barlow et al., 1964; Levick, 1967); two concentric types (on- and off-centre); four on-off type directionally selective (for movements up, down, antero-posterior, and postero-anterior); three directions for slow, on-type, directionally selective; one type sensitive to fast movement; one type sensitive to "uniformity"; and, confined to the visual streak, two types of orientation-selective neurons, neurons selective for slow-moving small objects, and neurons selective for edges. This makes a total of 15 different selective categories. In addition there must be units signalling colour, since the rabbit shows behavioural evidence for it, but these have not yet been found in the retina.

Now move up to the simple cells in area 17 of cat cortex. These vary in position, orientation, disparity, and size, as well as being selective for light bars, dark bars, or edges. The evidence is not sufficient to say how many distinct selective categories these form, but for each of the first three variables the resolution of a single neuron is good, in the sense that small departures from the preferred position, orientation, or disparity cause large decreases of response amplitude (Bishop, 1970). These variables already define four dimensions, and we have not yet considered size specificity, velocity specificity, nor the additional complexities of light, dark, or edge detectors, and of course colour. There are certainly several orders of magnitude more neurons in the primary projection area than there are input fibres, or resolvable points in the visual field, and it is abundantly clear that the number of selective categories has increased enormously. Activity of a particular neuron signifies much more than the presence of light at a particular locus in the visual field; its activity signifies a great deal about the nature of the pattern of light at that locus.

The fact that many parallel communication channels are used in the nervous system has been widely recognised, but here we see an enormous expansion of the number of parallel paths, and this occurs without much redundant reduplication of channels, for each neuron seems to have a different specific responsiveness. It is as if, at high levels, the size of the alphabet available for representing a sensory message was enormously increased. Perhaps it would be better to say that, if the activity of a low-level neuron is like the occurrence of a letter, that of a high-level neuron is like the occurrence of a word—a meaningful combination of letters. But to understand this better we must look at the third aspect of the way sensory messages are represented at different levels, namely the proportion of neurons that are usually active. If the pattern of activity caused by a visual scene has, on average, K neurons active out of the total of N neurons, then we have seen above that N increases at high levels; can one say anything about how K changes?

8.3 Number of Active Cells

If one considers the retinal cones under typical photopic conditions, the vast majority must be partially active. They may be nearer the depolarized than the hyperpolarized limit of their dynamic range, but the majority will be somewhere well within it. For the retinal ganglion cells of a cat the situation is a little different; while a few units, those corresponding to the brightest and dimmest parts of the scene, will be vigorously active, the majority, corresponding to the parts of the scene near the mean luminance, will be discharging at rates close to their maintained discharge level, which in its turn is near the low-frequency end of their dynamic range. Thus there will be a lot of units with low degrees of activity and a few which are vigorously active. Recoding in the retina changes the distribution of activity so that low impulse frequencies are common, high impulse frequencies rare.

Now consider the rabbit, with its more elaborate retinal processing, and greater richness of pattern-feature signalling neurons. It is characteristic of the more specific of these neurons that they have a very low maintained discharge, and are extremely hard to excite until their exact trigger feature has been found. One flashes lights, waves wands, and jiggles "noise figures" in the appropriate part of the visual field for many minutes, maybe hours, before finding the right combination for excitation. It is reasonably certain that the right combination does not occur often in the natural environment either, and therefore these units must spend only a small fraction of the time in an active state. Low impulse frequencies are even commoner, high impulse frequencies even rarer, than in cat retina.

For the cat cortex this trend is carried further, and one can see another aspect emerging. If one takes a small region of the visual field, it either does contain a bright bar, dark bar, or edge, or, much more likely, it does not. Thus, like the rabbit units, the cells with these specific responsivities

must be only infrequently active. But in addition, on the rare occasions when one of the appropriate trigger features is present, it is one of a set which tend to be mutually exclusive: a bright bar cannot be a dark bar, and it can have only one orientation and disparity. The stimulus selects which cell to activate from a range of many possible cells, and it is pretty well impossible to activate simultaneously more than a small fraction of this number.

The picture developing is that at low levels visual information is carried by the pattern of joint activity of many elements, whereas at the upper levels of the hierarchy a relatively small proportion are active, and each of these says a lot when it is active. But, although we clearly see that the proportion active, K/N, decreases, we cannot tell whether it decreases as rapidly as N increases, and thus we still do not know how K itself changes. The second dogma goes beyond the evidence, but it attempts to make sense out of it. It asserts that the overall direction or aim of information processing in higher sensory centres is to represent the input as completely as possible by activity in as few neurons as possible (Barlow, 1961, 1969b). In other words, not only the proportion but also the actual number of active neurons, K, is reduced, while as much information as possible about the input is preserved.

By how much can one reasonably expect K to be reduced? One requires the concepts of channel capacity and redundancy from information theory (Shannon and Weaver, 1949; Woodward, 1953) to make a rough estimate. Some reduction can be accomplished without any loss of information simply by the increase of N. K/N is the probability of a fibre being active, and, if it is the same for all neurons, the information capacity of a set of N neurons, either active or not active, is $-K \log_2(K/N) - (N-K)\log_2[(N-K)/N]$. If K/N is small, the second term contributes little; the capacity then is, approximately, the number of active neurons times the information provided by each active neuron, and this increases directly as the negative logarithm of the probability of it being active, $-\log(K/N)$. Hence the number active can be reduced as N increases without loss of information capacity, but by itself this does not allow K to be reduced very much: for instance, if we suppose that 1/4 of the 2×10^6 optic nerve fibres are active and that there are 10^8 cortical neurons receiving this information, then one finds that $1 \cdot 5 \times 10^5$ cortical neurons must, on average, be active in order to have the same information capacity as the 5×10^5 active optic nerve fibres. But this applies only to capacity, and a substantial reduction in K is possible on the basis of another principle.

Visual information is enormously redundant, and it has been suggested previously that sensory coding is largely concerned with exploiting this redundancy to obtain more economical representation of the information. If the argument is correct, the number of active neurons can be reduced, but it is very difficult even to guess how big a reduction in K such recoding can achieve; if it is $1/10$ up to the cortex, and another factor of $1/10$ achieved in visual I, II and III, one would end up with about 1000 active fibres carrying the information provided by 5×10^5 active optic nerve fibres; though the reductions might be substantially greater or less, this is the order of magnitude of the reduction contemplated.

According to dogma, these 1000 active neurons represent the visual scene, but it is obvious that each neuron must convey an enormously larger share of the picture than, say, one point out of the quarter million points of a television picture. Perhaps a better analogy is to recall the 1000 words that a picture is proverbially worth; apparently an active neuron says something of the order of complexity of a word. It seems to me not unreasonable to suppose that a single visual scene can be represented quite completely by about 1000 of such entities, bearing in mind that each one is selected from a vast vocabulary and will in addition carry some positional information.

9 Third Dogma: Selectivity Adapted to Environment

9.1 Evolutionary Adaptation
Some economies of the type indicated above can be achieved by exploiting forms of redundancy which are present in all normal environments. Levels of sensory stimulation do not range at random over the whole scale of possible values, and it makes sense to regard adaptation of peripheral receptors as a measure to achieve economy by signalling changes from the mean instead of absolute values. Similarly in most situations neighbouring points on a sensory surface are more likely to be similar than distant points, and it thus makes sense to regard contrast enhancement by lateral inhibition as another economy measure. The argument can be carried on to cover the redundancy-reducing value of movement, edge, or disparity detectors (Barlow, 1969b), but, if these are genetically-determined redundancy-reducing codes, they must be fixed once and for all during development, and they could only work for redundant properties of all sensory environments. The hypothesis becomes more interesting when one considers the possible mechanisms for achieving economy by exploiting the redundancy of particular sensory scenes, for this requires storage of information and plasticity of the neural structures involved.

9.2 Reversible Adaptation
The neural changes of dark and light adaptation may be regarded as a simple example of reversible plasticity achieving this end. The luminance corresponding to zero impulses is affected by the past history of illumination and by the surrounding luminances in such a way that the majority of fibres are responding at low frequencies. But, even though this involves definite changes in the synaptic transfer properties of retinal neurons, the statistical characteristic of visual images that enables this to achieve economy is always the same, namely the fact that the distribution of luminances is grouped around local and temporal mean values, so that small deviations from the mean are commoner than large deviations (Barlow, 1969a). Hence the most commonly occurring luminances require fewest impulses.

9.3 Permanent Adaptation
The effects permanently impressed on the visual system during the sensitive period are the first example of plasticity for a particular type of redundancy. The distribution of orientational selectivity of primary neurons is biased in favour of the orientations the individual experienced during this critical time. If the analogy of a neuron's signal resembling the utterance of a word is recalled, this result suggests that the kitten's cortex only develops words for what it has seen. This could be brought about by either selection or modification: are the dictionary words there, only the ones experienced becoming permanently connected; or do the cells themselves determine that a frequently experienced pattern, such as lines of a particular range of orientations, are events for which words are desirable? The evidence favours modification, and the idea to which it leads of the successive hierarchical construction of a dictionary of meaningful neurons has enormous appeal. For the present we can only justify the third dogma by saying the evidence suggests such a dictionary may be built up, though we are far from being able to look into its pages by physiological methods. In the next section we turn to the subjective view of this dictionary.

10 Fourth Dogma: Origin of Perceptions

10.1 Personal Perceptions
In order to delimit more accurately what this dogma does and does not say it may be useful to define and separate three mysteries of perception. The first is the personal, subjective, aspect of my experience of, say, the red pencil with a blue eraser in my hand. There does not seem to be anything that could be said about the activity of nerve cells accompanying this experience that would in any way "ex-

plain" the aspect of it that is mysterious, personal, and subjective. I think this part of the experience is something that one must be content to leave on one side for the moment, but it is important that this part of subjective experience almost always accompanies electrical stimulation of a peripheral sensory nerve, and usually accompanies electrical stimulation of the sensory areas of the brain, for this implies that the full subjective experience, including this mysterious personal element, accompanies the neural events of sensation, however these are caused. This fact strongly suggests that it is no waste of time to look into these neural events: beauty is a mysterious attribute of a work of art, but that does not imply that you cannot create a beautiful painting by non-mysterious material means.

10.2 Conscious Perception

The second mystery is that we are not consciously aware of much that goes on in our brains, so the inverse of the fourth dogma is certainly not true: not every cortical neuron's activity has a simple perceptual correlate. Even at high mental levels much neural business is conducted without conscious awareness, and my own belief is that the conscious part is confined to experiences one communicates to other people, or experiences one is contemplating communicating to other people. This immediately introduces a social element into individual consciousness, for communication is impossible without a channel being open to a recipient. However, for present purposes we need only point out that interesting aspects of consciousness of this sort are by no means incompatable with the fourth dogma. An element of perception can possess a simple neural cause without it necessarily being the case that all simple neural events cause perception. There is therefore plenty of room for social, historical, or moral influences on perception, because these can influence the selection of the neural events that enter conscious perception.

10.3 Validity of Perceptions

The third mystery about perceptions is why they are generally "true": why are they so extraordinarily useful in guiding our actions and helping us to make decisions? This is the aspect that the second and third dogmas help one to understand. The economical and fairly complete representation of visual scenes by a reasonably small number of active neurons makes it much easier to visualize how they can be used for these purposes. The key point is that the active neurons carry the bulk of the information, and the vast number of inactive ones need not be taken into consideration. The difficulty of detecting among our sense impressions the entities we use for rational thought has always been baffling: "water", "men", "sheep", and even the simple letter "A" represent particular logical functions

of activity among the sensory neurons, but the number of possible logical functions is so vast that we are mystified how particular ones are realized, or why particular ones are selected for realization. The representation suggested by the second and third dogmas would allow relatively simple logical combinations to have properties approaching those required for the literal symbols of Boole (1854), the subjects of our conceptions. By using such symbols together with operational signs he founded mathematical logic, but the title of his major work, *"The Laws of Thought"*, clearly states his claim that his inquiries had "probable intimations concerning the nature and constitution of the human mind". It is gratifying to approach closer to an intuitively plausible neural realization of what he symbolized.

The notion that what we sense is a point by point representation of the physical signals impinging on our body has been rejected for psychological and philosophical reasons (see Boring, 1942), and more recent physiological evidence clearly supports this rejection. But this same evidence suggests that it should be replaced, not by return to a subjectively constructed phenomenology (Dreyfus, 1972), nor by the notion that we sense the world in terms of rigidly preordained "structures", but by the deeper and more adaptive ideas of dogmas two and three; our sensorium is presented with a fairly small number of communications, each representing the occurrence of a group of external events having a word-like order of complexity, and, like words, having the special property that they lead to an economical representation of these physical events.

11 Fifth Dogma: Signaling Subjective Certainty

There is one way in which the properties of neurons do not match up to the way Boole used symbols, for he insisted on their binary nature, or "duality". This is the property Aristotle called the principle of contradiction, and without it Boole's symbolic representation of logic would have been impossible. In contrast to this duality the response of a sensory nerve cell to its trigger feature consists of a volley of impulses lasting 1/10 to 1 second, during which time the neuron can discharge any number of impulses between zero and nearly 1000. Therefore the response is graded, and it is not legitimate to consider it as a Boolean binary variable. The essential notion expressed in the fifth dogma is that a neuron stands for an idealization of reality whose complement can be formulated as a null hypothesis, and it is this that has the required Boolean logical property of duality. The idealizations should not be thought of as Kantian or Platonic, but rather as abstractions that model reality in the manner suggested by Craik (1943). The ideal populations of a statistician come even closer, for the parameters of such distributions model reality, and they are used to calculate whether or not a particular sample belongs within it. The process of idealizing the complement of the trigger feature will be clarified by a simple example.

Suppose we have a sensory neuron whose trigger feature is a simple physical event, such as the increase of light intensity at a specific position in the visual field. We are examining the suggestion that the graded responses this neuron gives to visual stimuli represent some function of the degree of certainty that the light did in fact increase, estimated from the physical events accessible to the neuron. For simplicity assume that a record is available of the total numbers of quanta absorbed in the receptive field of the sensory neuron during successive periods of about $1/10$ second duration up to and including the period about which it is to signal centrally. It is in principle possible to calculate the probability of occurrence of the observed number of quantal absorptions on the hypothesis that there was no change in the light intensity, and this is the test a statistician would apply to determine whether or not the trigger feature was present. On this view impulse frequency signals some function of the significance level of a test of this sort, low probabilities corresponding to high impulse frequencies. Notice that the trigger feature is "an increase of light", the idealization is "there was no increase", and this idealization is based on observation of what has recently happened and therefore incorporates a model of the recent past.

The responses actually obtained to varying intensities of incremental stimulus fit quite well into this scheme (Barlow, 1969a), as do some less obvious features. The low-frequency maintained discharge could well represent the results, of low significance, obtained by testing the null hypothesis when no stimulus has been applied. Although individual fibres would not reach significance, information about quantal absorptions would be retained, and changes insignificant singly could be combined centrally to reach significance.

In the above example a high value of P and low impulse frequency would result from a shadow falling on the receptive field. The detection of this shadow might be of great survival significance for the animal, but the on-centre unit's trigger feature, null hypothesis, and statistical tests would be a poor way of detecting and signalling this important event. A different type of unit is required whose null hypothesis should be "There has been no *decrease* in the quantal absorption rate"; these would fire when the hypothesis is disproved by the quantal absorption rate dropping below the normal range of variation. Obviously these are the off-centre units, and it seems that the existence of complementary "on" and "off" systems fits the notion quite well. When there are a large number of neurons with trigger features that cannot coexist, as in area 17, these correspond to a large number of mutually exclusive hypotheses to be tested.

The fifth dogma clearly requires more development and testing, but it provides a possible answer to the question "What variable corresponds to impulse frequency in a high level sensory neuron?" Furthermore the answer ties it to a rather definitely felt subjective quantity—the sense of certainty.

12 Criticisms and Alternatives

Single-unit recording hints at this probabilistic, adaptive, many-levelled, system for processing and displaying sensory information, but can we believe that what we perceive is the activity of a relatively small selection of upper-level units of this hierarchy? This is certainly a big jump beyond the present physiological evidence. We do not know how perspective transformations are disregarded, enabling us to perceive the same object irrespective of our angle of view nor do we understand the mechanisms underlying size constancy, yet these mechanisms must intervene between the highest neurons we know about and quite simple perceptions. I think we have seen enough of what can be achieved in a few stages of neural image processing to believe that a few more stages could reach the point where a single neuron embodies, by virtue of its peripheral connections and their properties, elementary percept, but let us examine an alternative and the evidence adduced in its support.

12.1 Combinatorial or Holographic Representations

The key suggestion about the organization of sensory processing that the second dogma asserts is that the information is carried by progressively fewer active neurons at progressively higher levels in the hierarchy. The brain receives complex patterns of activity in nerve fibres from the sensory receptors, and it generates complex patterns of outgoing commands to the muscles. It could be held that the patterns are equally complex at all the intervening stages as well, and this would mean that the significance of a single unit's activity would be virtually undecipherable without knowing what was going on in a host of other units. Certainly one would make little progress in understanding a computer's operation by following the status of a single bit in its central processor, so this criticism is partly met by pointing to the success that has been achieved in the visual system by looking at the activity of units singly, one at a time. But we should also look critically at the main evidence advanced in favour of the combinatorial or holographic scheme.

12.2 Mass Action and Resistance to Damage

The main argument that has been levelled against the view that individual cells play an important role in perception and in favour of a holographic representation is the reported fact that large parts of the cortex can be damaged with only minor resultant changes in behaviour or learning (Lashley, 1929, 1950). This led to Lashley's doctrine of "cerebral mass action", but repetition of the original experiments and refinements in methods of testing, some of it by Lashley himself, have considerably weakened the original evidence in its favour (Zangwill, 1961). However, it certainly is remarkable that a mechanism with as much interdependence between its parts as the brain can function at all after it has been extensively damaged. A computer would not usually survive brain surgery or gunshot wounds, and it is therefore worthwhile considering the implications of the fact that the cortex is relatively immune to quite extensive injury.

The whole of a visual scene can be reconstructed from a small part of a hologram, with only slight loss of resolution and degradation of signal/noise ratio (Gabor et al., 1971), so it has been claimed that the cortex must operate by some analogous principle in order to account for its resistance to damage. What is not widely appreciated is the fact that holography differs from ordinary image-recording photography not only in principle, but also in the materials used, for it requires photographic emulsions with resolutions of the order of the wavelength of light (Gabor et al., 1971). With such materials a good quality 35 mm picture could easily be reproduced and repeated in every 1 mm^2 of the plate, and a plate containing such a reduplicated image would have to be pulverized into tiny pieces to prevent reconstructibility of the original from every fragment. The mass-action-like resistance to damage of the hologram is partly due to the enormous informational capacity of the materials that are required; immunity to damage is easy to achieve when such high redundancy is permissible, and this argument carries little weight in favour of holographic views of nervous operation.

Codes can be given error-correcting properties much less wastefully, and the argument can be turned around to favour the representation hypothesized in dogmas two and three. Because the few active cells have a fixed significance, and because the inactive ones are thought to carry so little information that they can be neglected, the only result of removing part of the cortex would be to eliminate some of the active neurons, and hence some of the perceptual entities, when a given scene is viewed. The "meaning" of the active units in the undamaged cortex would remain the same, and might provide a sufficient basis for decision and action. This is very different from the situation where a neuron's activity has totally different significance de-pending upon the pattern of activity of which it forms a part, for if any of this pattern was in a damaged region the significance of activity in the undamaged part would be altered. Hence damage immunity is really an argument for neurons having an invariant meaning not dependent upon the activity of other neurons.

It should also be pointed out that very limited replication of "percept neurons" would give considerable damage immunity: if a given neuron is replicated half a dozen times in different cortical regions there is a good chance of at least one of them surviving an extensive cortical ablation. This sixfold redundancy is enormously less than the holographic scheme possesses, and it can be concluded that the mass action argument rebounds against the extensive combinatorial usage of neurons and actually favours the hypothesis of this article.

12.3 Pontifical Cells

Sherrington (1941) introduced the notion of "one ultimate pontifical nerve-cell, . . . the climax of the whole system of integration" and immediately rejected the idea in favour of the concept of mind as a "million-fold democracy whose each unit is a cell". Those who like the notion of perception as a cooperative or emergent property of many cells dismiss the suggestion that the activity of a single neuron can be an important element of perception by saying that, carried to its logical conclusion, it implies there must be a single "pontifical cell" corresponding to each and every recognizable object or scene. First, notice that the current proposal does not say that each distinct perception corresponds to a different neuron being active, if perception is taken to mean the whole of what is perceived at any one moment; it says there is a simple correspondence between the elements of perception and unit activity. Thus the whole of subjective experience at any one time must correspond to a specific combination of active cells, and the "pontifical cell" should be replaced by a number of "cardinal cells". Among the many cardinals only a few speak at once; each makes a complicated statement, but not, of course, as complicated as that of the pontif if he were to express the whole of perception in one utterance.

Two important difficulties arise from the notion of pontifical cells; first, if a separate neuron is needed for each of our perceptions, there are not enough to account for their almost incredible variety; second, the activity of a single isolated element would not convey anything of a perception's great richness, the connection between one perception and others. The "grandmother cell" might respond to all views of grandmother's face, but how would that indicate that it shares features in common with other human faces, and that, on a particular occasion, it occurs in a specific position surrounded by other recognizable objects? Our perceptions simply do not have the property of being isolated unique events as one would expect if each corresponded to the firing of a unique neuron. Instead, they overlap with each other, sharing parts which continue unchanged from one moment to another, or recur at later moments in different contexts. I think the "cardinal cell" representation surmounts these problems without any difficulty; if a critic can say how many different perceptions we are capable of, and how rich a network of relatedness exists between these perceptions, then one might be able to estimate how many cardinals' voices were required to represent these perceptions. But there is a misleading feature of the ecclesiastical analogy.

Most organizational hierarchies are pyramids: there are many members of the church, fewer priests, only a select number of cardinals, and a single pope. The hierarchy of sensory neurons is very different. It is true that there are more retinal receptors than ganglion cells, but the number of cortical neurons in area 17 is certainly orders of magnitude greater than the number of incoming fibres. The numbers at succeding levels may be somewhat fewer, but a high proportion of the nerve cells in the brain must be capable of being influenced by vision, so if the hierarchical organization is pyramidal it is inverted rather than erect, divergent rather than convergent. If one uses the term "cardinal cell", one must be sure to remember that the college of these cardinals outnumbers the church members and must include a substantial fraction of the 10^{10} cells of the human brain.

After-Thoughts

It is sufficiently obvious that these propositions are incomplete, that there are aspects of the sensory problem left untouched, and that the dogmas go considerably beyond the evidence. I have said, in essence, that the cells of our brain are each capable of more than had previously been supposed, and that what their activities represent may be more simply related to the elements of our conscious perceptions than had previously been thought. But clever neurons are not enough. The simplest computer program with its recursive routines and branch points has more subtlety than the simple hierarchy of clever neurons that I have here proposed as the substrate of perception.

I think one can actually point to the main element that is lacking. We have seen that some properties of the environment can be represented, or modelled, in a system of the type proposed; I feel that a corresponding model is also needed for our own motor actions and their consequences. Such motor and sensory models could then interact and play exploratory games with each other, providing an internal model for the attempts of our ever-inquisitive per-

ceptions to grasp the world around us. A higher-level language than that of neuronal firing might be required to describe and conceptualize such games, but its elements would have to be reducible to, or constructible from, the interactions of neurons.

The five dogmas do not impede developments in this direction. My claim for them is that they are a simple set of hypotheses on an interesting topic, that they are compatible with currently known facts, and that, if any are disproved, then knowledge in this field will be substantially advanced.

Acknowledgements.

This essay was started many years ago when Gerald Westheimer suggested to me that, if a single-neuron dogma of the power and generality of "DNA codes protein" could be found, it might speed progress of neuropsychology as much as Crick and Watson speeded up molecular biology. Since then I have been helped by the discussion of these ideas with a group of neurophysiologists and psychologists organized in Berkeley by M. F. Land, and by many useful suggestions from B. Sakitt. I think the single neuron revolution is having a powerful effect in sensory psychology, but I still wish it could be expressed in a single dogma.

References

Adrian, E. D., 1926a, "The impulses produced by sensory nerve-endings", Pt.1, *J. Physiol.,* **61**, 49–72.

Adrian, E. D., 1926b, "The impulses produced by sensory nerve-endings, Pt.4, Impulses from pain receptors", *J. Physiol.,* **62**, 33–51.

Adrian, E. D., 1928, *The Basis of Sensation* (Christophers, London; also Hafner, New York, 1964).

Adrian, E. D., 1941, "Afferent discharges to the cerebral cortex from peripheral sense organs", *J. Physiol.,* **100**, 159–191.

Adrian, E. D., 1947, *The physical background of perception* (Clarendon Press, Oxford).

Adrian, E. D., Zotterman, Y., 1926a, "The impulses produced by sensory nerve-endings, Pt.2, The response of a single end-organ", *J. Physiol.,* **61**, 151–171.

Adrian, E. D., Zotterman, Y., 1926b, "The impulses produced by sensory nerve-endings, Pt.3, Impulses set up by touch and pressure", *J. Physiol.,* **61**, 465–493.

Bard, P., 1938, "Studies on the cortical representation of somatic sensitivity", *Harvey Lectures 1938* (Academic Press, New York), pp.143–169.

Barlow, H. B., 1953, "Summation and inhibition in the frog's retina", *J. Physiol.,* **119**, 69–88.

Barlow, H. B., 1956, "Retinal noise and absolute threshold", *J. Opt. Soc. Amer.,* **46**, 634–639.

Barlow, H. B., 1960, "The coding of sensory messages" in *Current Problems in Animal Behaviour,* Eds. W. H. Thorpe, O. L. Zangwill (Cambridge University Press, Cambridge), pp.331–360.

Barlow, H. B., 1961, "Possible principles underlying the transformations of sensory messages" in *Sensory Communication,* Ed. W. A. Rosenblith (MIT Press, Cambridge, Mass. and John Wiley, New York), pp.217–234.

Barlow, H. B., 1969a, "Pattern recognition and the responses of sensory neurons", *Ann. N. Y. Acad. Sci.,* **156,** 872–881.

Barlow, H. B., 1969b, "Trigger features, adaptation, and economy of impulses", in *Information Processing in the Nervous System,* Ed. K. N. Leibovic (Springer-Verlag, New York), pp.209–226.

Barlow, H. B., Blakemore, C., Pettigrew, J. D., 1967, "The neural mechanism of binocular depth discrimination", *J. Physiol.,* **193,** 327–342.

Barlow, H. B., Brindley, G. S., 1963, "Interocular transfer of movement after-effects during pressure binding of the stimulated eye", *Nature,* **200,** 1346–1347.

Barlow, H. B., FitzHugh, R., Kuffler, S. W., 1957, "Change of organization in the receptive fields of the cat's retina during dark adaptation", *J. Physiol.,* **137,** 338–354.

Barlow, H. B., Hill, R. M., 1963, "Evidence for a physiological explanation of the waterfall phenomenon and figural after-effects", *Nature,* **200,** 1345–1347.

Barlow. H. B., Hill, R. M., Levick, W. R., 1964, "Retinal ganglion cells responding selectively to direction and speed of image motion in the rabbit", *J. Physiol.,* **173,** 377–407.

Barlow, H. B., Levick, W. R., Yoon, M., 1971, "Responses to single quanta of light in retinal ganglion cells of the cat", *Vision Research,* **11,** Suppl. 3, 87–102.

Barlow, H. B., Pettigrew, J. D., 1971, "Lack of specificity of neurones in the visual cortex of young kittens", *J. Physiol.,* **218,** 98–100.

Bishop, P. O., 1970, "Beginning of form vision and binocular depth discrimination in cortex", in *The Neurosciences: Second Study Program,* Ed. F. O. Schmitt (Rockefeller University Press, New York), pp.471–485.

Blakemore, C., Campbell, F. W., 1969, "On the existence of neurones in the human visual system selectively sensitive to the orientation and size of retinal images", *J. Physiol.,* **203,** 237–260.

Blakemore, C., Cooper, G. F., 1970, "Development of the brain depends on the visual environment", *Nature,* **228,** 477–478.

Blakemore, C., Mitchell, D. E., 1973, Enviromental modification of the visual cortex and the neural basis of learning and memory", *Nature,* **241,** 467–468.

Boole, G., 1854, *An Investigation of the Laws of Thought* (Dover Publications Reprint, New York).

Boring, E. G., 1942, *Sensation and perception in the history of experimental psychology* (Appleton Crofts, New York).

Burns, B., 1968, *The uncertain nervous system* (Edward Arnold, London).

Campbell, F. W., Green, D. G., 1965, "Optical and retinal factors affecting visual resolution", *J. Physiol.,* **181,** 576–593.

Cragg, B. G., 1972, "The development of synapses in cat visual curtex", *Investigative Ophthalmology,* **11,** 377–385.

Craik, K. J. W., 1943, *The Nature of Explination* (Cambridge University Press, Cambridge).

De Valuis, R. L., 1960, "Color vision mechanisms in the monkey", *J. Gen. Physiol.* **45,** Suppl., 115–128.

De Valois, R. L., Abramov, I., Jacobs, G. H., 1966, "Analysis of response patterns of LGN cells", *J. Opt. Soc. Am.,* **56,** 966, 977.

De Valois, R. L., Abramov, I., Mead, W. R., 1967, "Single cell analysis of wavelength discrimination at the lateral geniculate nucleus in the macaque", *J. Neurophysiol.,* **30,** 415–433.

Dreyfus, H. L., 1972, *What Computers Can't Do* (Harper and Row, New York).

Enroth-Cugell, C., Robson, J. G., 1966, "The contrast sensitivity of retinal ganglion cells of the cat", *J. Physiol.,* **187,** 517–552.

Ewert, J. P., 1970, "Neural mechanisms of prey-catching and avoidance behavior in the toad *(Bufo bufo L.)"*, *Brain Behav. Evol.,* **3,** 36–56.

Fry, G.A. 1948, "Mechanisms subserving simultaneous brightness contrast contrast", *Am. J. Optum.,* **25,** 162–178.

Gabor, D., Kock, W. E., Stroke, G. W., 1971, "Holography", *Science,* **173,** 11–23.

Galambos, R., 1944, "Inhibition of activity in single auditory nerve fibers by acoustic stimulation", *J. Neurophysiol.,* **7,** 287–303.

Galambos, R., Davis, H., 1943, "The response of single auditory-nerve fibres to acoustic stimulation", *J. Neurophysiol,.* **7,** 287–303.

Galambos, R., Davis. H., 1948, "Action potentials from single auditory-nerve fibres?" *Science,* **108,** 513.

Ganchrow, J. R., Erickson, R. P., 1970, "Neural correlates of gustory intensity and quality", *J. Neurophysiol.,* **33,** 768–783.

Granit, R., 1947, *The Sensory Mechanisms of the Retina* (Oxford University Press, Oxford).

Granit, R., Svaetichin, G., 1939, "Principles and technique of the electrophysiological analysis of colour reception with the aid of microelectrodes", Upsala Läkaref Färh., **65,** 161–177.

Green, D.M., Swets, J. A., 1966, *Signal Detection Theory and Psychophysics* (John Wiley, New York).

Gross, C. G., Rocha-Miranda, C. E., Bender, D. B., 1972, "Visual properties of neurons in inferotemporal cortex of the macaque", *J. Neurphysiol.,* **35,** 96–111.

Grüsser, O. J., Grüsser-Cornehls, U., 1968, "Neurophysiologische Grundlagen visueller angeborener Aulösemechanismen beim Frosch", *Zeitschrift für vergleichende Physiologie,* **59,** 1–24.

Hartline, H. K., 1938, "The response of single optic nerve fibres of the vertebrate eye to illumination of the retina", *Am. J. Physiol.,* **121,** 400–415.

Hartline H. K., 1940a "The receptive fields of optic nerve fibers", *Am. J. Physiol.,* **130,** 690–699.

Hartline, H. K., 1940b, "The effects of spatial summation in the retina on the excitation of the fibers of the optic nerve", *Am. J. Physiol.,* **130,** 700–711.

Hecht, S., Shlaer, S., Pirenne, M., 1942, "Energy, quanta, and vision", *J. Cen. Physiol.,* **25,** 819–840.

Hirsch, H. V. B., Spinelli, D. N., 1970, "Visual experience modifies distribution of horizontally and vertically oriented receptive fields in cats", *Science,* **168,** 869–871.

Hirsch, H. V. B., Spinelli, D. N., 1971, "Modification of the distribution of receptive field orientation in cats by selective visual exposure during development", *Exp. Brain Res.,* **13,** 509–527.

Hubel, D. H., Wiesel, T. N., 1959, "Receptive fields of single neurones in the cat's striate cortex", *J. Physiol.,* **148,** 574–591.

Hubel, D. H., Wiesel, T. N., 1962, "Receptive fields, binocular interaction, and functional architecture in the cat's visual cortex", *J. Physiol.,* **160,** 106–154.

Hubel, D. H., Wiesel, T. N., 1963, "Receptive fields of cells in striate cortex of very young, visually inexperienced kittens", *J. Neurophysiol.,* **26,** 994–1002.

Hubel, D. H., Wiesel, T. N., 1965, "Binocular interaction in striate cortex of kittens reared with artificial squint", *J. Neurophysiol.,* **28,** 1041–1059.

Hubel, D. H., Wiesel, T. N., 1970, "The period of susceptibility to the physiological effects of unilateral eye closure in kittens", *J. Physiol.,* **906,** 419–436.

Hurvich, L. M., Jameson, D., 1960, "Perceived color, induction effects, and opponent-response mechanisms", *J. Gen. Physiol.,* **43,** Suppl., 66–80.

Ingle, D., 1968, "Visual release of prey-catching behaviour in frogs and toads", *Brain, Behaviour and Evolution,* **1,** 500–518.

Ingle, D., 1971, "Prey-catching behaviour of anurans toward moving and stationary objects", *Vision Research,* Suppl. No.3, 447–456.

Kuffler, S. W., 1953, "Discharge patterns and functional organization of mammalian retina", *J. Neurophysiol.* , **16,** 37–68.

Lashley, K. S., 1929, *Brain Mechanisms and Intelligence: a Quantitative Study of injuries to the Brain* (University of Chicago Press, Chicago).

Lashley, K. S., 1950, "In search of the Engram physiological mechanisms in animal behaviour", in *Symposium of the Society for Experimental Biology,* Ed. J. F. Danielli and R. Brown (Cambridge University Press, Cambridge).

Lettvin, J. Y., Maturana, H. R., McCulloch, W. S., Pitts, W. H., 1959, "What the frog's eye tells the frog's brain", *Proc. Inst. Rad. Eng.,* **47,** 1940–1951.

Levick, W. R., 1967, "Receptive fields and trigger features of ganglion cells in the visual streak of the rabbit's retina", *J. Physiol.,* **188,** 285–307.

Mach, E., 1886, *The Analysis of Sensations, and the Relation of the Physical to the Psychical* Translation of first edition (1886) revised from fifth German edition by S. Waterlow (Open Court, Chicago and London, 1914) Ed. C. M. Williams. (Also Dover Publications, New York, 1959.)

Marshall, W. H., Woolsey, C. N., Bard, P., 1941 ,"Observations on cortical somatic sensory mechanisms of cat and monkey", *J. Neurophysiol.,* **4,** 1–24.

Maturana, H. R., Lettvin, J. Y., McCulloch, W. S., Pitts, W. H., 1960, "Anatomy and physiology of vision in the frog *(Rana Pipiens)*", *J. Gen. Physiol.,* **43,** Suppl. No.2, *Mechanisms of Vision,* 129–171.

McCulloch, W. S., 1959, "Agatha Tyche: of nervous nets—the lucky reckoners", in *Mechanisation of Thought Processes: Proceedings of a Symposium Held at the National Physical Laboratory, Vol.2* (HMSO, London), pp.611–634.

Pettigrew, J. D. (forthcoming), "The effect of visual experience on the development of stimulus specificity by kitten cortical neurons".

Pettigrew, J. D., Freeman, R. (forthcoming), "Visual experience without lines: Effect on developing cortical neurones".

Pettigrew, J. D., Nikara, T., Bishop, P. O., 1968, "Binocular interaction on single units in cat striate cortex: simultaneous stimulation by single moving slit with receptive fields in correspondence", *Exp. Brain Res.,* **6,** 391–410.

Pfaffman, C., 1941 , "Gustatory afferent impulses", *J. Cell. Comp. Physiol.,* **17,** 243–258.

Pfaffman, C., 1955, "Gustatory nerve impulses in rat, cat, and rabbit", *J. Neurophysiol.,* **18,** 429–440.

Sakitt, B., 1972, "Counting every quantum", *J. Physiol.,* **222,** 131–150.

Shannon, C. E., Weaver, W., 1949, *The mathematical theory of communication* (University of Illinois Press, Urbana).

Sherrington, C. S., 1941, *Man on His Nature* (Cambridge University Press, Cambridge).

Shlaer, R., 1971 "Shift in binocular disparity causes compensatory change in the cortical structure of kittens", *Science,* **173,** 638–641.

Stone, S., 1972, "Morphology and physiology of the geniculocortical synapse in the cat: The question of parallel input to the striate cortex", *Invest. Ophthal.,* **11,** 338–346.

Svaetichin, G., MacNichol, E. R., Jr., 1958, "Retinal mechanisms for chromatic and achromatic vision", *Ann. N. Y. Acad. Sci.,* **74,** 385–404.

Talbot, W. H., Darian-Smith, I., Kornhuber, H. H., Mountcastle, V. B., 1968 "The sense of flutter-vibration: Comparison of human capacity with response patterns of mechano-receptive afferents from the monkey hand", *J. Neurophysiol.,* **31,** 301–334.

Tanner, W. P., Jr., Swets, J. A., 1954, "A decision making theory of visual detection", *Psychol. Review,* **61,** 401–409.

Wagner, H. G, MacNichol, E. R., Wolbarsht, M. L., 1960, "The response properties of single ganglion cells in the goldfish retina", *J. Cen. Physiol.,* **43,** Suppl., 115–228.

Wiesel, T. N., Hubel, D. H., 1963, "Single cell responses in striate cortex of kittens deprived of vision in one eye", *J. Neurophysiol.,* **26,** 1004–1017.

Wiesel, T. N., Hubel, D. H., 1965, "Comparison of the effects of unilateral and bilateral eye closure on cortical unit responses in kittens", *J. Neurophysiol.,* **28,** 1029–1040.

Wohlgemuth, A., 1911, "On the after-effect of seen movement", *Brit. J. Psychol.,* Monograph, Suppl., **1,** 1–17.

Woodward, P. M., 1953, *Probability and Information Theory with Applications to Radar* (Pergamon Press, Oxford).

Yarbus, A. L., 1965, *Eye Movements and Vision,* Translated from Russian by Basil Haigh (Plenum Press, New York).

Zangwill, O. L., 1961, "Lashley's concept of cerebral mass action", in *Current Problems in Animal Behaviour,* Eds. W. H. Thorpe, O. L. Zangwill (Cambridge University Press, Cambridge).

15
Introduction

(1976)
J. T. McIlwain

Large receptive fields and spatial transformations in the visual system
International Review of Physiology, Neurophysiology II, Robert Porter (Ed.), 10: 223–248

This paper by James T. McIlwain is written by a neurophysiologist for neurophysiologists. However, it contains an example of a simple distributed neural computation of considerable behavioral importance. This geometrical computation is of interest as well because it stands on their heads many intuitive feelings about how spatial computations might be done. Many of McIlwain's ideas about representation of information in the visual system are the same as what is called "coarse coding" in the context of artificial neural networks. (Hinton, McClelland, and Rumelhart 1986).

The superior colliculus is a midbrain structure that serves as a primarily visual, though actually multisensory, integrating center for the *visual grasp reflex*. The visual grasp reflex centers the image of an interesting or novel object or event on the retina. Moving the eyes to look at the location of an unexpected noise would be a typical example.

Physically the eyes of vertebrates are a simple optical system that uses a lens to project an image onto the retina at the back of the eyeball. The optical quality of the visual apparatus is such that the vertebrate eye has good spatial acuity only near the visual axis. Many eyes have specialized areas of the retina, usually along the optical axis (the *fovea* in our eye), where the receptor density is very high. In other areas the receptor density is much lower — the density of the receptors and spatial acuity are closely related.

The implication of this is that if we want to look at something carefully, we must move our eyes, heads, and/or bodies so that the part of the retinal image we want to analyze carefully is placed on the high-resolution portion of the retina. In mammals an elaborate subsystem of the nervous system is devoted to moving the eyes to the desired part of the environment.

The superior colliculus has an important role in control of eye movements. It is a layered structure. Crudely the input from the retina enters at the top layer, and the motor output leaves from the bottom layer. In common with most parts of the brain that receive sensory input, there is a topographic map of the visual field on the surface of the colliculus. This was first discovered by Julia Apter in the 1940s, and the presence of this map was influential on the thinking of Pitts and McCulloch in their 1947 paper on geometrical transformations in the nervous system (paper 3 in *Neurocomputing: Foundations of Research*). Also in common with most sensory maps (see papers 16 and 22), the map is highly distorted, with a much larger area of the map corresponding to the high-resolution parts of the retina.

The eye movement computation is closely bound to the map. If the surface of the superior colliculus is electrically stimulated, the eyes will move so as to bring the high resolution part of the retina to the location on the map corresponding to the stimulation. It is as if the electrical stimulation is perceived as something important, and the eyes move to take a closer look at it.

One way to do this would be to have a fine-grained map of the visual field. A point of maximum activation is precisely localized on the map, and the eyes are directed to that point. However, this is *not* what is done. The visual *receptive fields* (the area of visual space that affects the discharge of a cell) at the input layer to the colliculus are quite small and localized. However, receptive fields in the colliculus markedly *increase* in size moving toward the output, being many times larger in the lower layers. It is as if the high spatial precision present in the input is being deliberately thrown away. As McIlwain points out, however, information is not being lost, merely rearranged. From a spatially localized code the information has been rerepresented as what is sometimes known in neurophysiology as an *ensemble code*, where it is the *pattern* of many cells discharging that gives rise to the representation of sensory information. The importance of ensemble codes in sensory systems was clear to Lord Adrian in the 1920s and there is overwhelming evidence for them in essentially all sensory systems, including vision, olfaction, audition, somasthetic senses (touch), and taste.

Ensemble codes are most often now called *distributed* codes in neural networks. Ensemble codes are particularly congenial to most neural network implementations because they correspond to unconstrained points in a high dimensionality state space — that is, a single event corresponds to the pattern of activity of many different computing units. Obviously a point is just as precisely located no matter how it is described in state space: that is, whether it is constrained to lie along a coordinate axis, with a single nonzero value in its state vector, or whether it can be in any location in space and must be described by many nonzero values in the state vector.

One argument for distributed codes (for example, for coarse coding) is that fewer numbers of elements are required. Sometimes this is the case: one could represent an ASCII character as one active element in a state vector of 256 possible characters. Or one could equally well represent it as one of 256 possible patterns of eight bits. The first is localized; the second code is distributed. However, in the colliculus the number of cells before and after the rerepresentation are about the same, so there must be a computational gain from the rerepresentation.

The gain seems to be the ability to integrate information from many locations and from other sensory and cortical locations. After all "interest" is a complex quantity, and a lot of computation is required to get even a first guess at what the interesting points in the visual field are, so the eyes can be directed there for a better look.

McIlwain introduces the important idea of the *point image*, which is the set of units that see a point of light in the visual field. In a widely distributed representation the number of cells in the point image can be very large. This set of units takes up a certain amount of space in the neural structure. Both colliculus and cerebral cortex are uniform, a fairly homogeneous neural substrate, with sensory inputs impressed on them, in the case of the colliculus as a distorted two-dimensional map. The fascinating possibility exists that the point images of different points in the visual field are the same size, which suggests that about the same number of cells always see a point in the visual field. There is some evidence for this, and there is a closely related notion of a hypercolumn, due to Hubel and Wiesel, that suggests that every point in space is looked at by a complete set of cortical "analyzers," even though the analyzers may look at a large area of visual space in one region of cortex and a small area in another area.

It is somewhat as if the colliculus or cortex is a homogeneous analyzer with constant structure, and the selectivity and precision it displays arises primarily from the detailed pattern of the afferents impinging on it. Because the spread of the dendrites of cells in the colliculus is anatomically constant, and the input map is highly distorted, it is possible to predict that the receptive fields of individual cells will also become systematically distorted as they increase in size in lower layers, while the actual anatomical structure remains uniform.

But if we have spread out information about precise localization in space onto many neurons, how can we get spatial precision back again, so we can make the correct eye movement? That is, what is the appropriate *output* representation? McIlwain describes a simple distributed output representation that will do the job. The mechanics of moving the eyeball around are quite straightforward. The extraocular muscles for an eye movement either move the eyes up and down (one set) or left and right (another set). Suppose the output layer of the colliculus is connected to these extraocular muscles. A region of the colliculus that receives inputs from a part of the visual field that is up and to the right from the center of gaze, will connect to motor units that *primarily* are connected to the muscle groups that drive the eyes up and to the right. If the visual field location is primarily to the right of the center of gaze, the cells in the output layer connect primarily to the muscle system driving the eyes to the right.

Suppose a very large number of cells are weakly connected to the motor system. Then suppose a point of light appears in the visual field, and the animal wants to move its eyes to that point. Because of the distribution of information about the point, many cells in the output of the colliculus are activated, each cell (or small group of cells) having a slightly different proportion of connections to the up-down and right-left systems, that is, tending to move the eyes in a different direction appropriate to their location on the map. The overall motor output will be the sum of all these directions, given by many cells. This average output direction can be highly accurate, even though most of the cells that have been activated do not by themselves move the eyes in the right direction.

There are some experimental tests of this idea. Suppose that the computation merely looked for peak activation on the colliculus. If part of the colliculus away from the peak was inactivated, the peak would not be moved. But, in a distributed output code, if part of the colliculus was inactivated, it would make a difference in the resulting eye movements because a large group of cells would not contribute to the movement. Moreover we could predict in which direction the error would be made, depending on where the inactivation occurred. This experiment was done by Lee, Rohrer, and Sparks (1988), and the results strongly support the idea of a distributed output code, summing up movement contributions from many units, though the exact details of the output code are still not entirely clear.

This biological structure suggests an attractive architecture for any neural network, real or artificial: a simple, repetitive structure of uniform design performing a distributed computation and that is programmed by the details of the connections of the input and output maps.

References

G.E. Hinton, J.L. McClelland, and D.E. Rumelhart (1986), Distributed representations. In D.E. Rumelhart and J.L. McClelland (Eds.), *Parallel Distributed Processing, Volume I*. Cambridge, MA: MIT Press.

C. Lee, W.H. Rohrer, and D.L. Sparks (1988), Population coding of saccadic eye movements by neurons in the superior colliculus. *Nature* 332: 357–360. (See also Sejnowski's commentary on this paper in *Nature*'s, "News and Views," p. 332 in the same issue.)

(1976)
J. T. McIlwain

Large receptive fields and spatial transformations in the visual system
International Review of Physiology, Neurophysiology II, Robert Porter (Ed.), 10: 223–248

Introduction

Long before the development of electrophysiology and formulation of the receptive field concept, anatomical and clinical studies firmly established the idea that the visual pathways preserve the spatial arrangement of the retina. According to Polyak (1), those who entertained this idea believed "that such an anatomical arrangement might be a factor responsible for the exquisitely spatial character of the sense of sight" (p. 335). Modern anatomical and physiological analyses have amply confirmed the high degree of spatial order in the primary visual pathways, supporting the concept that stimulus position could be coded in the physical location of the responding visual neurons. This place coding hypothesis is particularly compelling when neurons with very small receptive fields are found in retinotopically organized brain structures.

Receptive field analysis of single visual neurons in cat and primate quickly revealed that cells having the smallest receptive fields are located in parts of the retina and brain subserving the central few degrees of the visual field where spatial vision is most acute. This was consistent with the idea that neural connections in the central retina preserve the spatial arrangement of the receptor mosaic with maximum fidelity (2). The findings also reinforced the view that fine spatial information is transmitted by cells with small receptive fields.

A complementary perspective on this situation is that most of the visual field is subserved by cells having relatively large receptive fields. In the retina (3–10), lateral geniculate nucleus (LGN) (11–14), striate cortex (15–19), and superior colliculus (20–32) of cat and primate, receptive field size is observed to increase more or less monotonically with eccentricity from the fovea or area centralis. Moreover, all receptive fields, regardless of their location in the visual field, appear to increase in size as one probes progressively further along the visual pathway. This process may be observed within the striate cortex, if one holds with Hubel and Wiesel (16) that the large-field complex cells represent a stage of visual processing beyond the small-field simple cells. The phenomenon of progressive receptive field enlargement is even more striking as observations are made in areas 18 and 19 (33–36) and in yet more

distant cortical stations such as the suprasylvian and splenial gyri of the cat (37–40) and the temporal cortex of the primate (41–43).

The receptive fields of cells in the retinotectal pathway exhibit the same apparently inexorable increase in size (22, 23, 25–27, 31, 32, 44–47), prompting Goldberg and Wurtz (22) to conclude that ". . . a major function of the superficial gray and optic layers of the monkey superior colliculus seems to be the construction of cells with large receptive fields. . ." (p. 556). Extra-geniculate regions of the thalamus, which are related anatomically to tectal and cortical visual areas, also contain cells with characteristically large receptive fields (48–53).

The fact that large receptive fields are the rule rather than the exception in many parts of the visual system suggests that their story may be as interesting and important as that of the tiny receptive fields of the fovea and its primary projection. This review begins with a survey of current interpretations of the function of such large-field cells. There follows a discussion of certain geometric factors involved in the synthesis of large receptive fields and their implications for spatial transformations in the visual system. The last section considers a recent suggestion about how large-field cells in the superior colliculus may encode the retinal location of stimuli. The discussion focuses on studies of the cat and primate visual systems.

Current Interpretations of Large-field Visual Neurons

The discovery of visual cells with large receptive fields within a neural structure poses an obvious question: Can the discharge of such cells convey information about the retinal location of the stimuli to which they respond? Since this question is addressed by all current conceptions of the functional roles of large-field cells, it will serve as the focal issue of the following discussion.

Spatial Information Lost
Perhaps the most common assumption is that large-field visual cells cannot transmit precise spatial information at all. Since identical discharge patterns may be evoked by stimuli in different parts of the receptive field, the output

of the cell is ambiguous as to the exact location of the stimulus. Thus, Goldberg and Wurtz (22) concluded from their study that large-field cells in the macaque's superior colliculus "can only crudely indicate the location of a stimulus" (p. 556). Similar views about large collicular fields have been expressed by others (23, 31, 32, 44, 54). Considerations such as this may have prompted Kuffler's (55) concern that the "receptive field" concept could lose its usefulness if receptive fields were found to be very large.

It seems likely that some visual cells with large receptive fields are not concerned with analysis of spatial detail or with the exact spatial location of stimuli. Thus, cells in the pretectum, which probably mediate the pupillary response to light, would be expected to integrate retinal illumination over large areas (24, 56–60). Also, the spatial distribution of retinal illumination may not be important to visually responsive cells in the brainstem reticular formation which are involved in general arousal mechanisms (61). On the other hand, some visual regions, richly endowed with large-field cells, appear from other evidence to be mediating rather precise spatial transactions. In these cases, of which certain examples will be discussed below, it is difficult to avoid the conclusion that large-field cells are sometimes capable of encoding fine spatial information.

Feature Detector Hypothesis

Many visual cells in the central nervous system, though possessed of large receptive fields, are particularly sensitive to specific parameters of the stimulus. For instance, complex cells of the striate cortex often respond preferentially to oriented lines located at various positions within a large receptive field (16, 62). Cells in the inferotemporal gyrus of the macaque which have huge receptive fields may exhibit highly specific "trigger features" (42). These and similar observations have led to the notion that certain classes of central neurons detect specific features of the retinal image, as was suggested originally for neurons of the frog's retina (63). A large receptive field, according to this view, would imply that the neuron signals the presence of a particular stimulus feature, but is unconcerned with its exact position. Hubel and Wiesel (16), discussing complex cells of striate cortex, observe that "their responsiveness to the abstraction which we call orientation is thus generalized over a considerable retinal area" (p. 146). A similar theme has been pursued in discussions of large-field cells which respond preferentially to other aspects of the retinal image such as its size, shape, direction, and velocity of movement (23, 32, 37, 42–44, 53, 60, 64).

It may be observed that this conception, although positing a function for large receptive fields, does not answer the question of how the retinal location of the feature is coded. Presumably, this is accomplished by other neurons

with smaller receptive fields. Furthermore, this interpretation rests on the idea that single neurons serve as detectors or extractors of specific stimulus features. In its extreme form this hypothesis holds that the discharge of some neural elements carries a fixed significance for perception, so that the perception of, say, a vertical edge simply reflects the discharge of certain neurons which respond selectively to vertical edges. Such neurons would be "labeled lines" for the feature "vertical edge" (65). The feature detector hypothesis has been advocated (66–68) and criticized (69–71) with equal vigor.

Because a feature-detecting role is so often ascribed to large-field cells, it is germane to recall several arguments which have been raised against the basic hypothesis. One frequently cited objection is that few if any visual neurons increase their discharge as a function of only one stimulus parameter (18, 69, 70, 72, 73). Since the increased discharge can have more than one interpretation, it is ambiguous. A second objection is that cortical neurons are often broadly tuned, so that widely separated values of the presumed trigger parameter produce equivalent discharge rates (73, 74). Combinatorial or ensemble processes, which could resolve the ambiguity (74), are not permitted in the pure feature detector model (66), since this would violate the axiom that a single cell's discharge has an immutable significance for perception. Related uncertainties arise from as yet unsettled questions about the inherent variability of the cell's selectivity for a given feature (18, 75–82), and the degree to which anesthetic agents contribute to this apparent specificity (18, 82–85). Another discomforting observation is that the foveal representation in the primate's striate cortex has relatively fewer narrowly tuned neurons than the parafoveal representation (18, 72, 86). Since form vision is most acute near the center of gaze, one might expect the highly tuned feature detectors to be most prominent in the foveal projection area of the cortex.

Erickson (73) reminds us that the feature detector hypothesis attempts to extend Müller's doctrine of specific nerve energies (87, 88) to the functional level of single nerve cells. Such attempts have been pursued most vigorously in the area of somesthesis, where debate continues over neuronal specificity theories and pattern theories of the submodalities (see Melzack and Wall (89) for review). It is of interest that Müller took pains to distinguish between the idea of a specific nerve energy (quality, modality) and the propensity of a nerve to be activated by a given stimulus, a property which he called "specific irritability" (87). Although he was unsure of the substrate of the unique sensation associated with a given nerve, suggesting that it was either in the "nerve itself or in the parts of the brain and spinal cord with which it is connected" (88) (p. 1072), he clearly believed that this "specific energy" did not arise from the "specific irritability" of the peripheral sensory organ. In current terminology, Müller concluded that the optic nerve is a labeled line for vision, and that the fixed perceptual significance of its activity does not arise from the photoreceptors' selectivity for light quanta. This may be contrasted with the current tendency to attribute feature detector properties to single neurons *because* of their stimulus preferences or "specific irritabilities."

Ensemble Coding Hypothesis

Unlike the experimenter, whose attention is restricted to the activity of the one or two cells discharging near his microelectrode, the brain has immediate access to all the cells responding to a sensory input. In fact, these cells *are* the brain, or a considerable fraction of it. Recognition of this led long ago to the idea that sensory information could be represented in the pattern of discharge in populations of neurons. For instance, Adrian, Cattel, and Hoagland (90) invoked the process, often called ensemble or distributed coding, to explain how cutaneous afferents of the frog could encode the position of a point stimulus:

There is no reason to suppose that the widespread distribution of the sensory endings of a single fiber will necessarily interfere with the exact localization of a stimulus. Owing to the overlapping of the area of distribution of different fibers the stimulation of any point on the skin will cause impulse discharges in several fibers and the particular combination of fibers in action, together with the relative intensity of the discharge in each, would supply all the data needed for localization (p. 384).

This idea has been used in the literatures of somesthesis (90–94), olfaction (95, 96), gustation (97, 98), and audition (99) to account for the apparent ability of neurons with large or broadly tuned receptive fields to mediate fine discriminations along some sensory dimension. The concept is also central to models of distributed or holographic memory which have appeared in recent years (100–107). Erickson (73) points out that Thomas Young exploited the idea in his classic explanation of how small regions of retina encode many different wavelengths using a limited number of sensitive elements. Although several recent discussions emphasize the possibility of ensemble coding in visual function (69, 86, 108–110), it is perhaps fair to say that an early concern for the importance of patterns of neural activity in the retina (111) and visual cortex (112) has been supplanted by current interest in the stimulus specificities of single visual neurons.

The concepts of ensemble coding and neuronal feature detection are joined in the so-called Fourier or spatial frequency theory of visual analysis, which has attracted wide attention in recent years.[1] According to one form of this theory, visual cells are differentially responsive to sinusoidal luminance contours of specified periodicity. Hence, the cells act as spatial filters and their pattern of discharge represents the spatial spectral composition of part of the retinal image. Large receptive fields arise quite naturally in such systems because a cell's frequency selectivity is in part related to the size of its receptive field (35, 114, 115). Although the discharge of a given cell has a fixed significance in terms of a preferred spatial frequency, its output is relatively meaningless without reference to the activity of other cells. This may be contrasted with the pure feature detector models in which the familiar elements of perception, such as oriented edges, correspond isomorphically to the discharge of individual neurons. An ensemble code of the spatial frequency variety would represent the presence and position of the edge in the discharge of many cells. Other combinations of feature detection and ensemble coding have been proposed (74).

It is one thing to speculate that large-field visual cells may participate in some process of ensemble coding and quite another to understand how such codes are interpreted, or as Perkel and Bullock (65) put it, "Who reads ensemble codes?" These authors and others (116) point out that there is, in fact, no need to postulate a process, analogous to decoding, which "reads" the ensemble code and returns the message to its original form. An external observer might simply see the pattern of neural activity undergo repeated transformations, some contingent upon past experience, until it emerged as behavior.

The study of ensemble coding in populations of visual cells requires knowledge of the spatial distribution of neural responses to visual stimuli. Although several investigators have considered the problem in its mammalian context (117–120), few experimental studies have dealt with it directly. It has been suggested (121) that a major obstacle to research on the question is the great success enjoyed by the technique of receptive field analysis, which generally asks, "Here is a cell, what and where are the stimuli which it sees?" To approach the problem of ensemble coding, the question must be inverted: "Here is a stimulus, where are the cells which see it?" The distribution of cells which see a particular stimulus depends on geometric factors which are intimately related to the construction of large receptive fields, and the following section examines some of these.

---

[1]Consideration of the extensive physiological and psychophysical literature which has grown up around this theory is beyond the scope of this review. The reader will find detailed discussion and references in a recent review by Sekuler (113).

242
Chapter 15

Ingredients of Large Receptive Fields: Some Geometric Factors and Their Implications

Dendritic Fields and Afferent Maps: The Convergence Perspective

Convergence processes in the retina occur in the familiar spherical coordinate system of visual space, where distance across the retina may be directly and simply related to visual angle. The magnification in this system is space invariant, in the sense that a degree of visual angle is equivalent to the same distance across the retina at all points. In the primary central visual pathways, the linear distance allotted to a given visual angle (the Magnification Factor of Daniel and Whitteridge (122)) is space variant, decreasing with distance from the projection of the primate's fovea or the cat's area centralis. This fact has important consequences for the synthesis of large receptive fields in the central nervous system and for the spatial organization of central neural structures containing large-field cells. Of particular interest are the potential interactions of dendritic field size with this space variant magnification and certain of these effects are illustrated in Figure 1.

The cells of Figure 1*A* lie directly beneath one another on a line normal to the surface of a hypothetical central visual structure. The dendritic fields increase in diameter with depth in this structure, which is assumed to receive a point-to-point afferent projection from the retina. The afferent terminals rise perpendicular to the surface through the dendritic fields of the resident neurons. In Figure 1, *B* and *C*, this set of neurons is shown embedded in two different visual nuclei, one considerably larger than the other. In Figure 1*B*, the retina projects to an extensive area and the scale of the afferent map is relatively large compared to the dimensions of the cells' dendritic fields. The visual nucleus of Figure 1*C* is small and the dendritic fields of the cells occupy sizeable portions of the afferent map.[2]

If we assume that the input is purely excitatory, the receptive fields mapped with a point stimulus might appear as in Figure 1, *D* and *E*. Several effects may be seen. The receptive fields of identical cells differ in size if their dendrites sweep out regions of the afferent map representing visual space at different magnification. This situation may be contrasted with the retina, where cells with identical dendritic fields tend to have receptive field centers of comparable size (3, 9, 123). It may also be seen that the receptive fields of cells located immediately above or below one another are centered near the same point only when the dendrites are small relative to the scale of the map.

[2]The relative spacings of the iso-eccentricity lines in the polar coordinate system of Figure 1, *B* and *C*, were measured from the 270° meridian of Figure 5 in Daniel and Whitteridge (122).

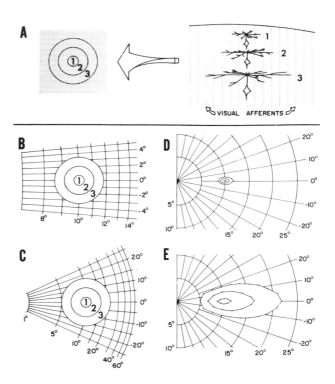

Figure 1 Relationships among dendritic trees, afferent maps, and receptive fields. *A, right,* neurons 1, 2, and 3 viewed from the side. *Dotted lines,* visual afferents ascending to surface through dendritic trees. *Left,* schematic representation of dendritic trees of same cell trio viewed from surface of visual structure. *Stipple,* termination of point-to-point afferent projection from retina. *B* and *C,* dendritic trees of neurons 1, 2, and 3 in two regions where the afferent visual maps differ in scale. *D* and *E,* receptive fields resulting from excitatory action of afferents on cell trios in B and C. Fields obtained by projecting the concentric profiles of *B* and *C* into the coordinate systems of *D* and *E,* respectively. Graphic projection executed on grids of higher resolution than those illustrated.

When this condition is met, cells lying along a line normal to the surface appear to form topographically organized cell columns. When the dendritic field dimensions are large with respect to the scale of the afferent map, as in Figure 1*C*, neighboring cells no longer have receptive fields nested concentrically in visual space. Depending on the coordinate system of the afferent map, cells with concentrically nested receptive fields may not even lie along straight lines drawn through the neural tissue. Note also that, as receptive field diameter increases, the location of the receptive field center becomes a poorer estimator of the retinal origin of the afferent fibers projecting to the vicinity of the cell body. In the case of Figure 1*C*, a map of the afferent projection based on the average field center position would be biased significantly by the inclusion of large-field cells. The visual coordinates assigned to the recording site would reflect a more eccentric origin of the retinal afferents than was actually the case.

The situation in Figure 1*B* may be compared roughly to that of the cat's or monkey's striate cortex, where the total area of the map is large relative to the dimensions of the neural elements (122, 124). The residual scatter in receptive field position reported for cell columns oriented normal to the cortical surface appears to be more or less random about some average center position (16, 17, 125). Consistent drifts across the visual field are revealed only when the electrode traverses a series of neighboring columns. The eccentrically nested receptive fields of Figure 1*C* are similar to those found in the cat's superior colliculus (25) where many cells have dendritic arborizations which are relatively large with respect to the scale of the afferent map (126).

Colonnier (127) has suggested that the oriented receptive fields of striate cortex neurons may reflect regular asymmetries in the dendritic fields of cortical cells, such as are seen in Golgi preparations cut tangential to the cortical surface. This possibility appears to have received little further attention, but it is clear that dendritic geometry must be considered in the context of the afferent map and any anisotropies which it exhibits.

The interaction of dendritic field dimensions and scale of the afferent map may have an interesting consequence in structures receiving two or more topographically organized visual projections, such as the superior colliculus. Degeneration studies following punctate lesions suggest that a small region of the colliculus is innervated from restricted and topographically corresponding regions of retina and striate cortex (128). On the other hand, electrical recordings from single cells in the cat's colliculus reveal that neighboring neurons have quite disparate receptive fields and may be driven electrically from cortical areas differing greatly in size (54). In fact, the cortical area in functional connection with the collicular cell appears to be that which "sees" the same region of the visual field. This somewhat curious finding is easy to understand in terms of the factors operating in Figure 1. Because the colliculus is relatively small, the retinal and cortical connections of a given collicular cell are determined as much by the size of the cell's dendritic tree as by the location of its perikaryon. Thus, neighboring cells of different size may make quite incongruent connections within the space of corticotectal and retinotectal afferent terminals. Since these afferent projections to the superficial gray layer are retinotopically organized and in register, the cortical connections to a given cell will be highly correlated with its own visual receptive field, but not necessarily with the cortical connections and receptive fields of its neighbors.

Yet another consequence of dendritic dimension is suggested by the hypothetical situation of Figure 1*C*, in which the dendrites of the largest neuron ramify in regions of the

afferent map differing considerably in magnification factor. Consider the effects which a small visual stimulus might have on this neuron. Because of the space variant magnification of the afferent projection, the stimulus would activate a larger region of the afferent map when presented near the visual axis than when introduced into the peripheral visual field. From this, one might expect the stimulus to produce a brisker response at the central edges than at the peripheral edges of the receptive field. This is observed in studies of large-field cells of the cat's superior colliculus (25, 44).

Point Images and Receptive Field Images: The Divergence Perspective

Fischer's Relationship
The illustrations used in the preceding discussion assumed that the retina projects in point-to-point fashion to some hypothetical central visual structure. It is well known that real retinal ganglion cells have overlapping receptive fields of finite dimensions, so no point in visual space is "represented" by a single ganglion cell or optic tract axon. This is true even of the primate's midget ganglion cells which are said to receive their input from single cones (1, 2). Since the point spread function[3] of the eye is large with respect to the diameters and separation of foveal cones (1, 2, 129), several cones are illuminated by a point stimulus and a given cone is illuminated from neighboring points in a finite region of visual space. Electrical recordings made from ganglion cells presumably in the midget cell pathway reveal receptive fields with finite dimensions and a center-surround organization (131).

Since a point in the visual field is "seen" by more than one retinal ganglion cell, a point stimulus will produce a distribution of ganglion cell activity, which can be called the neural *point image* (25).[4] Fischer (132) has proposed that the point image in the space of retinal ganglion cells in the cat exhibits an interesting invariance property. He argues that any point on the retina falls within the field centers of a constant *number* of ganglion cells, because the rate at which ganglion cell density decreases with distance from the area centralis is just matched by the concomitant increase of receptive field center diameter. In consequence, the collection of optic nerve axons viewing a point through their receptive field centers will occupy a cross-sectional *area* of the nerve which is roughly invariant with translation of the point. Fischer's relationship acquires added significance from recent findings that the afferent axons

---

[3] The point spread function of an optical system describes the distribution of light in the image of a luminous point object (138).
[4] Fischer (117) uses the German word Punktbild to describe the distribution of excitation in a population of ganglion cells due to activity of a single photoreceptor.

which are decisive in determining responses in the LGN are those which have been stimulated through their receptive field centers (133–135). This implies that the component of the retinal point image which is relayed to cortex is largely that which occupies a constant area of the optic nerve.

Is it possible that such translation invariance of the neural point image is preserved in the geniculocortical projection and that the volume of cortex receiving information from a point in the visual field is independent of the location of the point? This would indeed be an interesting consequence of receptive field enlargement and might confer advantageous properties on the visual system. For instance, if the afferent neural activity concerning a visual point were distributed to a large enough region of cortex, the point could be viewed by cells representing a full spectrum of feature selectivities and preferences (orientation, color, etc.). Furthermore, a neighboring visual point, separated from the first by a vanishingly small distance, could also be served by a full analytic array of the same dimensions, provided that the various tuned sensory elements were appropriately distributed. Thus, a complete range of feature-selective cortical neurons would survey each point in the visual field. Neighboring visual points would, of course, share cortical elements to a degree determined by the magnification factor, since this would dictate how far apart the cortical point images would be located. An idea closely related to this has been proposed by Hubel and Wiesel (17) and is discussed below.

The data on which Fischer based his conclusions did not distinguish between the retinal neurons which project to the tectum and those which participate in the retino-cortical pathway. The numerically dominant input to striate cortex is via the sustained or X-cell population (3, 11, 36, 136–139), so it is of interest to know whether Fischer's relationship holds for this class of cells. One form of the relationship states that

$$R = (k/d \cdot \pi)^{1/2}$$

where R is receptive field center radius, d is ganglion cell density, and k is the number of cells whose field centers contain a given retinal point. R and d are functions of eccentricity. Since $d^{-1/2}$ estimates the distance between neighboring ganglion cells (i.e., the reciprocal of linear density (140)), this expression requires that receptive field diameter be a linear function of cell spacing, if k is to be constant at all values of eccentricity.

Figure 2A shows how inter-cell distance varies with eccentricity for X-cells of the cat's retina. The points represent the reciprocal square roots of the X-cell densities given in Figure 7 of Fukuda and Stone (137). The distribution is well described by the straight line ($r = 0.99$). Figure

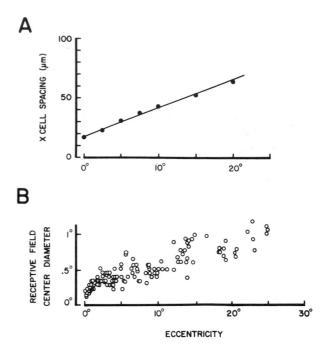

Figure 2 Relationship of cell spacing and receptive field center diameter to eccentricity in retinal X-cells of the cat. A, ordinate: inter-cell spacing estimated as reciprocal square roots of area densities given by Fukuda and Stone (137). *Abscissa,* distance from area centralis. From *ordinate:* X-cell receptive field center diameter. *Abscissa,* distance from area centralis. From Stone and Fukuda (9), courtesy of American Physiological Society.

2B, from Stone and Fukuda (9), shows that, except for the immediate vicinity of 0°, the center diameters of X-cells increase approximately linearly with eccentricity, a finding also reported by others (3, 6). Therefore, cell spacing and field center diameter are approximately linear functions of eccentricity and thus of each other, supporting Fischer's proposal for the case of X-cells.[5]

Translation Invariance and Receptive Field Images
Is there any evidence, then, that the point image in the primary visual pathway retains some kind of translation invariance as it ends in the striate cortex? The number of geniculocortical afferents terminating beneath a unit surface area of striate cortex appears to be approximately constant, at least in the primate (142), so if the point image were to form in an invariant number of LGN relay cells it might occupy a constant area of the terminal projection into cortex. Unfortunately, the connectional geometry of the LGN is not known in sufficient detail to permit a direct estimation of the size of the point image in the postsynaptic

---

[5]The observation that ganglion cell spacing varies linearly with eccentricity was first made by Weymouth (141) using data from the human retina. The same relationship for extrafoveal retina of the monkey may be observed in Figure 5 of Rolls and Cowey (140).

elements. However, another kind of evidence bearing on this question has been obtained in a recent study of the macaque's striate cortex. Hubel and Wiesel (17) report that a microelectrode must move a relatively constant distance of 2–3 mm parallel to the cortical surface before an entirely new region of visual field is represented in the receptive fields of the recorded cells. Within this 2–3 mm distance, the electrode crosses several organizational modules which the authors call *hypercolumns*. A hypercolumn comprises a set of adjacent cell columns or slabs in which the cells' preferred stimulus orientations rotate 180° as the set is traversed. The term also refers to a pair of adjacent right and left eye dominance columns. The orientation hypercolumns and the eye dominance hypercolumns are co-extensive and hence are the same size, 0.5–1.0 mm thick. From these findings, Hubel and Wiesel (17) propose that "a 2–3 mm region of cortex can be said to contain by a comfortable margin the machinery it needs to analyze the region of visual field which it subserves" (p. 303).

This idea and that of the space invariant point image, suggested by Fischer's relationship, are clearly related, so we may ask if the evidence obtained by Hubel and Wiesel supports the latter concept. The question may be approached through a relationship illustrated in Figure 3 and discussed in more detail elsewhere (25). In Figure 3*A*, a point stimulus has produced a small region of activity (*filled circles*) in a hypothetical class of cortical neurons. This point image is assumed to be centered at the coordinates α,ε corresponding to the location of the point stimulus in visual space. For simplicity of illustration, it is also assumed that all cells in the point image are excited, though not necessarily to the same degree. The cell designated by the heavy line lies at the extreme edge of the cortical point image, which is equivalent to saying that the point stimulus at α,ε lies at the edge of the cell's receptive field. Because of the conjugate relationship between point image center and point stimulus location, the centers of all point images having this cell at their very edges will lie at map coordinates corresponding to the boundaries of the cell's receptive field. A line connecting these coordinates is the geometric projection of the receptive field's boundaries onto the cortical sensory map or the *receptive field image* in that coordinate system (25). Figure 3*C* shows that, if the point images in this cell class are circular and of constant diameter, the receptive field images for the class have exactly the same size and shape as the point images. This reciprocity also obtains when the point images are not circular, as long as their orientation with respect to the index cell is constant and the map projection of the point stimulus occurs at some fixed location in the point image's profile (Figure 3*D*). The geometry of this relationship imposes a 180° rotation in going from point images to recep-

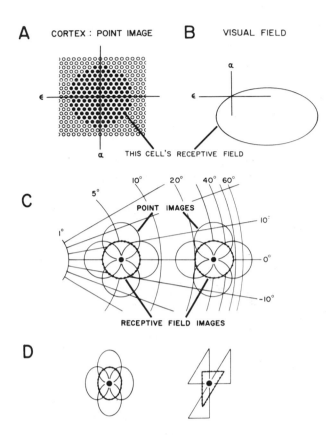

Figure 3 Reciprocity of receptive field images and point images. *A, schematic point image* in a class of cortical cells. *Filled circles*, excited cells. *Open circles*, quiescent cells. *B*, receptive field of cell at margin or cortical point image. Coordinates α, ε refer to conjugate loci in visual field and cortical sensory map. *C*, two cells (*filled circles*) located in different regions of cortical map. Each cell lies at margin of four identical circular point images (*light profiles*). *Dark profile*, locus of centers of all such point images having these cells at their margins. Coordinates of this profile correspond to those of receptive field. *D*, reciprocity of non-circular point images and receptive field images. Receptive field image (*dark profile*) obtained by sliding point image (*light profile*) around cell (*filled circle*), keeping cell at edge of point image and point image in same orientation. During this maneuver any fixed point in the point image describes a locus which has the shape of the point image.

tive field images and vice versa, which becomes evident when these profiles are not symmetric (Figure 3*D*). Were the receptive field images for a cell class heterogeneous in size over a small region of tissue, the boundaries of the point image would be related to the largest receptive field images and the point image would contain quiescent members of the class. An observation of particular interest here is that, if the point image is translation invariant in a class of cells such as those of Figure 3, the receptive field images for the class will also be translation invariant.

In their study of the macaque's striate cortex, Hubel and Wiesel (17) observed that average receptive field size and cortical magnification factor vary inversely across the cortex, which causes the "cortical projection of the boundaries of an average cortical receptive field" (p. 304) to enclose a relatively constant area of about 0.66 mm^2. In other words, the area of the receptive field image of the "average receptive field" is invariant with translation, a finding which is clearly consistent with the possibility that the area of the point image in the cortex is also translation invariant (Figure 3).

Unfortunately, several reservations about such an inference come immediately to mind. First, the point image, as defined above, refers to a distribution of neural activity in a population of cells which actually respond to a point stimulus. Although a point image will form in classes of cortical cells which respond to point or spot stimuli, such as simple cells and corticotectal complex cells of the cat (16, 143) and cells in layer IVc of the primate (34), the notion would appear to have little concrete meaning for populations of neurons which respond poorly to point-like stimuli. In this case, it may prove useful to broaden the definition of point image to designate the locus of all cells whose receptive fields contain a given point in the visual field. Knowledge of this would permit one to locate the set of cells potentially capable of responding to some stimulus at a given visual point.

A second difficulty arises with respect to the meaning of the receptive field image or the "cortical projection of the boundaries" of a receptive field. A key assumption in the scheme of Figure 3 is that the cortical sensory coordinates corresponding to the location of the point stimulus occur at a fixed position in the point image. It is not clear to what degree this assumption is valid in striate cortex, particularly in view of the scatter of receptive fields belonging to neighboring cortical cells (34). The continued separation in cortex of visual inputs from the two eyes also complicates the picture. In the macaque, the separation is most pronounced in layer IVc, where the smallest receptive fields are observed (17, 144). Thus, a point stimulus viewed binocularly may normally yield two point images in this layer, rather than one. Hubel and Wiesel (17) excluded cells from this layer when they demonstrated the reciprocal relationship between average receptive field size and magnification factor. The situation in deeper and more superficial layers may be comparable to the scheme of Figure 3, since the separation of binocular inputs is less marked in these regions and the representation of the visual field does not exhibit the discontinuities which are evident in layer IVc (125, 144).

Visual Acuity and Translation Invariant Point Images

These difficulties indicate that caution is required when making inferences from receptive field images. For this reason it is encouraging to find an old observation, which does not involve receptive field measurements at all, yet suggests that the boundaries of cortical point images may exhibit translation invariance. Daniel and Whitteridge (122) called attention to the fact that when the minimal angle of resolution (minimum separable), as measured at various eccentricities for the human eye, is plotted on the visual map of the monkey's striate cortex, the distance between the plotted points is the same at all eccentricities. Subsequent reports (140, 145) indicate that this relationship holds if the monkey's or the human's minimum separable are plotted on their own cortical visual maps. Daniel and Whitteridge (122) suggested that "presumably two peaks of excitation would have to be separated by this distance and by the corresponding number of cortical cells for them to give rise to separate sensations" (p. 218). It is also possible that when the neural images of two point stimuli overlap sufficiently, the points are no longer discriminable as separate. In other words, visual acuity tests of the minimum separable type may measure the capacity of the nervous system to resolve two overlapping neural point images in striate cortex. The observations of Daniel and Whitteridge (122) and others (140, 145) suggest that the critical overlap occurs when the point images are centered about the same distance apart, wherever they occur in the cortex. It follows that the diameter of the point images in the critical cell class must vary little with translation, since otherwise the degree of overlap and consequently the "resolvable" separation would depend on the location of the point images in the cortical map.

Point Images and Hypercolumn Clusters

We have seen how Fischer's relationship leads to the notion of a translation invariant region of cortex which receives input from a point in the visual field and that this idea, though still speculative, is nonetheless consistent with certain experimental observations. Hubel and Wiesel (17) have proposed that a cluster of hypercolumns also has the property of translation invariance and comprises a full array of neuronal elements for analyzing visual stimuli. One would like next to ask how a point image and a cluster of hypercolumns differ, since both concepts refer to translation invariant cortical regions which may function as analytic modules. They clearly differ with respect to their reference elements in the visual field. The hypercolumn cluster surveys a finite region of visual space which must vary in size as a function of its location, because of the space variant magnification factor of cortex. The point image is referred to a point in visual space, which has by definition no dimensions, only location.

A less obvious distinction between the two ideas lies in their conception of the operational fabric of the visual cortex. From Figure 3 one sees that the size of the point image in a cell class is reflected in the dimensions of the receptive field images of the member neurons. If a given cortical region contains several classes of neurons with receptive fields of different dimensions, then there may exist multiple point images of different size within that region. Since complex cells generally have larger receptive fields than simple cells (16, 62), receptive field images and point images could be larger in the former than in the latter class. Also, the size of the point image in the space of afferent terminals is a function of the dimensions of the receptive fields of the afferent neurons (25). Thus, if a given visual area receives input from two classes of afferents having, respectively, small and large receptive fields, the point images in the two afferent systems can occupy regions of different size. For instance, a point stimulus on the cat's retina may influence a larger region of striate cortex via the Y-cell than via the X-cell projections, since at any eccentricity retinal and geniculate Y-cells have larger receptive field centers than do X-cells (3, 9, 11). These possibilities are linked by recent evidence that the input to complex cells is through the Y-cell system, whereas simple cells are activated principally by X-cell inputs (36). Furthermore, there is evidence that LGN axons terminate in cortical layers V and VI (146, 147) as well as in layer IV, thus providing a structural basis for distinct point images in the afferent input to various cortical strata.

The receptive field image of the "average cortical receptive field" was estimated by Hubel and Wiesel to have an area of 0.66 mm (2, 17). This would imply an "average" point image of the same area, perhaps a square about 0.8 mm on a side. Thus, the "average" point image inferred in this way would be approximately the thickness of a single hypercolumn (17). On the other hand, Hubel and Wiesel estimated that the translation invariant hypercolumn cluster was 2–3 mm in diameter, because "a certain constant distance along the cortex, amounting to 2–3 mm, must be traversed in order to obtain a shift in field position comparable to the size of the fields plus their scatter" (p. 303). Their observation implies that even the largest receptive fields mapped at two cortical loci will not overlap if the recording sites are about 2–3 mm apart. In a system like that of Figure 3, this would mean that the receptive field images, and consequently the point images, for the class of cortical cells with the largest receptive fields are about 2–3 mm in diameter, are translation invariant and span several hypercolumns. In contrast, the "average" receptive field image, and by inference the "average" point image, span only one hypercolumn. This again raises the possibility that point images of different size form in different classes of cortical cells.

The picture of cortical organization which emerges from this development of Fischer's relationship differs from that of a mosaic of cell columns extending through the cortical thickness (16, 34). While the columnar perspective emphasizes the anatomical arrangement of cells which respond to similar stimulus features, the point image notion suggests that neighboring loci in the visual field may be surveyed by discrete sets of neurons in some cell classes and by strongly overlapping sets of other cell classes. The elements of cortical organization derived from this perspective need not be constrained by walls running normal to the surface from pia to white matter, nor are cells located directly above and below one another necessarily linked in an invariant functional relationship.

Note Added in Proof In two papers which have appeared since submission of this manuscript, Albus (162, 163) develops arguments virtually identical with those offered here. He concludes that "Each retinal point...is functionally represented by the same number of cortical cells, irrespective of its position within the retina." (Ref. 162, p. 176).

Large Receptive Fields and Sensory-Motor Transformations in the Superior Colliculus

Although point stimuli may elicit neural responses which display invariant properties under translation, such stimuli are generally of less interest than the complex patterns associated with form vision. There are instances, however, in which the response of the visual system to punctate stimulation may reveal significant details of functional organization. One such case is the highly integrated visual orienting response to a novel stimulus, which, it will be argued, is mediated by large-field cells.

The role of the superior colliculus in visual orienting behavior has been studied actively in the last two decades and reviews of this extensive literature are available (148–150). Of interest here is the evidence that saccadic eye movements, which are part of the visual orienting response, may also be elicited by focal electrical stimulation of the colliculus in cat and primate (29, 151–155). These electrically evoked saccades deflect the visual axes toward the region of visual space represented in the sensory projection to the stimulus site (29, 151, 152, 154). This congruence of the sensory and motor maps of the colliculus supports the view that the colliculi are involved in the production of saccadic eye movements to novel stimuli, a process called "foveation" by Schiller and Koerner (28).

In primates, the direction and amplitude of the electrically evoked saccades are relatively independent of the initial position of the eyes (29, 151, 152), but there has been some controversy as to whether this is true in the cat (152, 153). A recent report by Straschill and Rieger (154) suggests that saccades elicited by stimulation in the superficial gray layer of the cat's superior colliculus resemble those of the primate in being independent of initial eye position.

The output pathway from superficial gray to brain stem oculomotor systems very probably involves cells of the deeper collicular strata (148, 156). Hence, the conclusion seems virtually inescapable that the discharge of these cells encodes the equivalent retinal location of the electrical stimulus applied to the colliculus. Yet the experimental evidence indicates that these cells have large receptive fields (22, 23, 29, 44, 46, 157). Furthermore, to the extent that the colliculus mediates saccadic eye movements to novel visual stimuli, these same cells must be capable of encoding retinal location, despite their large receptive fields. The hypothesis sketched below (25) suggests that the key to the puzzle lies in the requirements of the oculo-motor system, in this instance the ultimate consumer of the collicular output.

The anatomy of the oculomotor system requires that the neural message evoked by a novel visual stimulus eventually take the form of a distribution of activity in twelve sets of motoneurons serving as many extraocular muscles. Single unit recording in the motor nuclei indicates that the amplitude of the resulting saccade is correlated with the duration of the motoneuronal discharge (158, 159). The direction of the saccade must be determined by the relative amount of activity in the different sets of motoneurons. Thus, the saccadic system requires information from the colliculus about the amplitude or duration of the required saccade and about the distribution of activity to the several extraocular muscles.

The results of focal electrical stimulation indicate that there exist distinct spatial gradients in the functional connections made by the colliculus to subdivisions of the oculomotor system. Systems moving the eyes upward, presumably via the superior rectus and the inferior oblique muscles, are increasingly represented toward the medial border of the colliculus, since a stimulating electrode moved in this direction evokes saccades of increasing vertical amplitude (29, 151–154). One form which this functional gradient might take is illustrated in Figure 4*B* on an outline of the cat's superior colliculus. A population of cells with pre-motor connections to the brainstem "up-system" forms the majority cell type in the medial part of the colliculus (*upward directed arrows*). Analogous pre-motor representations of the systems moving the eyes downward and laterally are located in Figure 4*B* as suggested by the stimulation studies. These distributions may be compared to the sensory map in Figure 4*A*. The pre-motor cells of Figure 4*B* are assumed here to be in the superficial gray layer, since this stratum provides spatially organized visual input to the deeper output layers (148, 160).

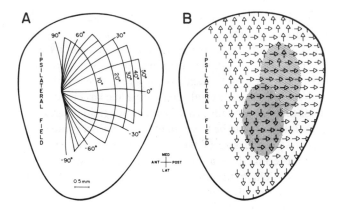

Figure 4 Sensory-motor relationships in the cat's superior colliculus. *A*, polar representation or visual projection to cat's left superior colliculus (25). 0 ° is horizontal meridian. *B*, hypothetical distribution or pre-motor cells in superficial gray layer. Cells symbolized by downward and upward directed arrows connected to systems moving the eyes downward and upward, respectively. Arrows pointing to right signify cells connected to systems which deflect eyes laterally and to the right. *Stippled ellipses,* two point images in the superficial gray layer involving the class of cells having the largest receptive fields.

It has been shown (25) that a point stimulus can potentially excite cells within an oval zone of the cat's superficial gray layer about 1.5 mm (antero-posterior) by 2.5 mm (mediolateral) in size. Cells with the largest receptive fields are excited throughout the zone, which is centered on the coordinate projection of the point stimulus in the sensory map. Within the central part of the colliculus, the largest receptive field images, and consequently the largest point images, are relatively invariant with translation (25). If we assume that the pre-motor cells have the largest receptive fields in the superficial gray layer, then a point stimulus in the right lower visual quadrant might activate cells in the lower of the two overlapping shaded zones in Figure 4*B*. Note that the resultant pre-motor signal from this sample of cells is predominantly "down" and "to-the-right," the appropriate direction for a saccade. Displacement of the point stimulus upward and toward the right results in excited populations of pre- motor cells which include increasingly larger contingents of "up" and "to-the-right" elements and fewer "down" elements (*upper shaded oval zone*). If the conflicting signals of the "up" and "down" elements are summed algebraically by brainstem mechanisms, such an arrangement of large-field pre-motor cells would transform a point stimulus into an output signal containing finely graded amplitude and directional information. The distribution of the excited population formats the output signal to suit the anatomy of the oculomotor system and the signal is independent of the initial position of the eyes. Precise information about stimulus position, not evident in the sensory receptive fields, is nonetheless present in the topography of the motor connections made by the large-field neurons.

This sketch of how large-field cells might encode spatial information does not incorporate many known facts about collicular physiology. For instance, the variation in excitability across receptive fields must surely result in a non-uniform distribution of excitation in the collicular point image. There are also other ways to build directional and amplitude gradients into the collicular networks. The scheme of Figure 4 has arranged the pre-motor elements so that no net signal occurs when a point stimulus appears in the area centralis, but this is only one of many possible explanations for the absence of saccades under these conditions. Further brainstem processing must be assumed to convert the amplitude signal (number of active cells) to a duration of discharge in the motor-neurons and to coordinate the action of yoked extraocular muscles. Nevertheless, a neural device such as this would be consistent with earlier views that ensemble codes are particularly suited to sensory-motor transformations (65) and with the suggestion of Wurtz and Goldberg (161) that ". . . ensembles of these (collicular) cells could transmit information fine enough for guidance that our analysis of single cell discharge patterns would miss" (p. 447).

Summary and Conclusions

In the cat's or primate's visual system, neuronal receptive fields increase in size as they occur farther from the center of gaze. Although this is usually attributed to increasing size of the receptive fields of afferent fibers, other important factors are the dimensions of the dendritic trees of the central neurons and the local scale of the afferent maps in which they reside. The decrease in central magnification factor which parallels the growth of receptive field size may mean that a relatively invariant amount of neural tissue receives input from any point in visual space. Assessment of this potential invariance and its functional significance depends importantly on establishing concrete structural referants for the sensory coordinate maps of central visual pathways, since there appear to exist reciprocity relationships between neural point images and receptive field images. It may be hoped that developments in this area will eventually permit reconstruction of the neural activity patterns resulting from complex visual stimuli.

Large receptive fields occur with increasing frequency in more central stations of the visual pathway and it is difficult to avoid the conclusion that this sometimes reflects spatial transformations supporting complex visual functions. Several hypotheses about such transformations are reviewed here. For the most part, these theories deal with visual neuronal activity in a purely sensory context,

often from a strongly psychophysical point of view. It is also possible to consider large-field cells solely as participants in a sequence of neural transformations which map a sensory event into a behavioral event. A simple example from the superior colliculus illustrates how the significance of large receptive fields may be more apparent from the putative pre-motor functions of the cells than from their sensory behavior. Although it may be unwarranted to extrapolate from this situation to higher visual functions, the example nonetheless supports the view that one is at a serious disadvantage, when interpreting the output signals of central visual neurons, if the neural systems receiving that output are not understood (33, 65).

Acknowledgments

I thank Kent M. Chapman, James A. Anderson, and Menasche Nass for helpful criticism. Support of the United States Public Health Service (Grant NS 09997) and an A. P. Sloan Research Fellowship in Neurophysiology are gratefully acknowledged.

References

1. Polyak, S. (1975). The Vertebrate Visual System. University of Chicago Press, Chicago.

2. Polyak, S. (1941). The Retina, 389 pp. University of Chicago Press, Chicago.

3. Cleland, B.G., and Levick, W.R. (1974). Brisk and sluggish concentrically organized ganglion cells in the cat's retina. J. Physiol. (Lond.) 240:421.

4. Enroth-Cugell, C., and Robson, J.G. (1966). The contrast sensitivity of retinal ganglion cells in the cat. J. Physiol. (Lond.) 187:517.

5. Fischer, B., and May, H.V. (1970). Invarianzen in der Katzenretina. Gesetzmässige Beziehungen zwischen Emfindlichkeit, Grösse und Lage receptiver Felder von Ganglionzellen. Exp. Brain Res. 11:448.

6. Hammond, P. (1974). Cat retinal ganglion cells: size and shape of receptive fields. J. Physiol. (Lond.) 242:99.

7. Hubel, D.H., and Wiesel, T.N. (1960). Receptive fields of optic nerve fibers in the spider monkey. J. Physiol. (Lond.) 154:572.

8. Ikeda, H., and Wright, M.J. (1972). Differential effects of refractive errors and receptive field organization of central and peripheral ganglion cells. Vision Res. 12:1465.

9. Stone, J., and Fukuda, Y. (1974). Properties of cat retinal ganglion cells: a comparison of W-cells with X- and Y-cells. J. Neurophysiol. 37:722.

10. Wiesel, T.N. (1960). Receptive fields of ganglion cells in the cat's retina. J. Physiol. (Lond.) 153:583.

11. Hoffmann, K.-P., Stone, J., and Sherman, S.M. (1972). Relay of receptive-field properties in dorsal lateral geniculate nucleus of the cat. J. Neurophysiol. 35:518.

12. Hubel, D.H., and Wiesel, T.N. (1961). Integrative action in the cat's lateral geniculate body. J. Physiol. (Lond.) 155:385.

13. Sanderson, K.J. (1971). Visual field projection columns and magnification factors in the lateral geniculate nucleus of the cat. Exp. Brain Res. 13:159.

14. Wiesel, T.N., and Hubel, D.H. (1966). Spatial and chromatic interactions in the lateral geniculate body of the rhesus monkey. J. Neurophysiol. 24:1115.

15. Joshua, D.E., and Bishop, P.O. (1970). Binocular single vision and depth discrimination. Receptive field disparities for central and peripheral vision and binocular interactions of peripheral single units in cat striate cortex. Exp. Brain Res. 10:389.

16. Hubel, D.H., and Wiesel, T.N. (1962). Receptive fields, binocular interaction and functional architecture in the cat's visual cortex. J. Physiol. (Lond.) 160:106.

17. Hubel, D.H., and Wiesel, T.N. (1974). Uniformity of monkey striate cortex: a parallel relationship between field size, scatter and magnification factor. J. Comp. Neurol. 158:295.

18. Poggio, G.F. (1972). Spatial properties of neurons in striate cortex of unanesthetized macaque monkey. Invest. Opthalmol. 11:368.

19. Wilson, J.R., and Sherman, S.M. (1974). Receptive field characteristics in cat striate cortex: changes with visual eccentricity. Soc. Neurosci. 4:480.

20. Cynader, M., and Berman, N. (1972). Receptive field organization of monkey superior colliculus. J. Neurophysiol. 35:187.

21. Dreher, B., and Hoffman, K.-P. (1973). Properties of excitatory and inhibitory regions in the receptive fields of single units in the cat's superior colliculus. Exp. Brain Res. 16:333.

22. Goldberg, M.E., and Wurtz, R.H. (1972). Activity of superior colliculus in behaving monkey. I. Visual receptive fields or single neurons. J. Neurophysiol. 35:542.

23. Hoffmann, K.-P. (1970). Retinotopische Beziehungen und Struktur rezeptiver Felder im Tectum opticum und Praetectum der Katze. Z. Vergl. Physiol. 67:26.

24. Kadoya, S., Wolin, L.R., and Massopust, L.C., Jr. (1971). Photically evoked unit activity in the tectum opticum of the squirrel monkey. J. Comp. Neurol. 142:495.

25. McIlwain, J.T. (1975). Visual receptive fields and their images in superior colliculus of the cat. J. Neurophysiol. 38:219.

26. McIlwain, J.T., and Buser, P. (1968). Receptive fields of single cells in the cat's superior colliculus. Exp. Brain Res. 5:314.

27. Rosenquist, A.C., and Palmer, L.A. (1971). Visual receptive field properties of cells of the superior colliculus after cortical lesions in the cat. Exp. Neurol. 33:629.

28. Schiller, P.H., and Koerner, F. (1971). Discharge characteristics of single units in superior colliculus of the alert rhesus monkey. J. Neurophysiol. 34:920.

29. Schiller, P.H., and Stryker, M. (1972). Single unit recording and stimulation in superior colliculus of the alert rhesus monkey. J. Neurophysiol. 35:915.

30. Sterling, P. and Wickelgren, B.G. (1969). Visual receptive fields in the superior colliculus of the cat. J. Neurophysiol. 32:1.

31. Updyke, B.V. (1974). Characteristics of unit responses in superior colliculus of the Cebus monkey. J. Neurophysiol. 37:896.

32. Humphrey, N.K. (1968). Responses to visual stimuli of units in the superior colliculus of rats and monkeys. Exp. Neurol. 20:312.

33. Hubel, D.H., and Wiesel, T.N. (1965). Receptive fields and functional architecture in two non-striate visual areas (18 and 19) of the cat. J. Neurophysiol. 28:229.

34. Hubel, D.H., and Wiesel, T.N. (1974). Sequence regularity and geometry of orientation columns in the monkey striate cortex. J. Comp. Neurol. 158:267.

35. Pollen, D.A., and Ronner, S.F. (1975). Periodic excitability changes across the receptive fields of complex cells in the striate and parastriate cortex of the cat. J.Physiol. (Lond.) 245:667.

36. Stone, J., and Dreher, B. (1973). Projection of X- and Y-cells of the cat's lateral geniculate nucleus to areas 17 and 18 of visual cortex. J. Neurophysiol. 36:551.

37. Dow, B.M., and Dubner, R. (1969). Visual receptive fields and responses to movement in an association area of cat cerebral cortex. J. Neurophysiol. 32:773.

38. Dow, B.M., and Dubner, R. (1971). Single unit responses to moving visual stimuli in the middle suprasylvian gyrus of the cat. J. Neurophysiol. 34:47.

39. Kalia, M., and Whitteridge, D. (1973). The visual areas in the splenial sulcus of the cat. J. Physiol. (Lond.) 232:275.

40. Hubel, D.H., and Wiesel, T.N. (1969). Visual area of the lateral suprasylvian gyrus (Clare-Bishop area) of the cat. J. Physiol. (Lond.) 202:251.

41. Dubner, R., and Zeki, S.M. (1971). Response properties and receptive fields of cells in an anatomically defined region of the superior temporal sulcus in the monkey. Brain Res. 35:528.

42. Gross, C.G., Rocha-Miranda, C.E., and Bender, D.B. (1972). Visual properties of neurons in inferotemporal cortex of the macaque. J. Neurophysiol. 35:96.

43. Zeki, S.M. (1974). Functional organization of a visual area in the posterior bank of the superior temporal sulcus of the rhesus monkey. J. Physiol. (Lond.) 236:549.

44. Gordon, B. (1973). Receptive fields in deep layers of cat superior colliculus. J. Neurophysiol. 36:157.

45. Sprague, J.M., Marchiafava, P.L., and Rizzolatti, G. (1968). Unit responses to visual stimuli in the superior colliculus of the unanesthetized, mid-pontine cat. Arch. Ital. Biol. 106:169.

46. Stein, B.E., and Arigbede, M.O. (1972). Unimodal and multimodal response properties of neurons in the cat's superior colliculus. Exp. Neurol. 36:179.

47. Straschill, M., and Hoffmann, K.-P. (1969). Functional aspects of localization in the cat's tectum opticum. Brain Res. 13:274.

48. Godfraind, J.-M., Meulders, M., and Veraart, C. (1969). Visual receptive fields of neurons in pulvinar, nucleus lateralis posterior and nucleus suprageniculatus thalami of the cat. Brain Res. 15:552.

49. Godfraind, J.-M., Meulders, M., and Veraart, C. (1972). Visual properties of neurons in pulvinar, nucleus lateralis posterior and nucleus suprageniculatus thalami in the cat. I. Qualitative investigation. Brain Res. 44:503.

50. Mathers, L.H., and Rapisardi, S.C. (1973). Visual and somatosensory receptive fields in the squirrel monkey pulvinar. Brain Res. 64:65.

51. Suzuki, H., and Kato, H. (1969). Neurons with visual properties in the posterior group of the thalamic nuclei. Exp. Neurol. 23:353.

52. Veraart, C., Meulders, M., and Godfraind, J.-M. (1972). Visual properties of neurons in pulvinar, nucleus lateralis posterior and nucleus suprageniculatus thalami in the cat. II. Quantitative investigations. Brain Res. 44:527.

53. Wright, M.J. (1971). Responsiveness to visual stimuli of single neurons in the pulvinar and lateral posterior nuclei of the cat's thalamus. J. Physiol. (Lond.) 219:32P.

54. McIlwain, J.T. (1973). Retinotopic fidelity of striate cortex-superior colliculus interactions in the cat. J. Neurophysiol. 36:702.

55. Kuffler, S.W. (1952). Neurons in the retina: organization, inhibition and excitation problems. Cold Spring Harbor Symp. Quant. Biol. 17:281.

56. Cavaggioni, A., Madarasz, I., and Zampollo, A. (1968). Photic reflex and pretectal region. Arch. Ital. Biol. 106:227.

57. Harutiunian-Kozak, B., Kozak, W., and Dec, K. (1968). Single unit activity in the pretectal region of the cat. Acta Biol. Exp. Warsaw 28:333.

58. Harutiunian-Kozak, B., Kozak, W., and Dec, K. (1970). Analysis of visually evoked activity in the pretectal region of the cat. Acta Neurobiol. Exp. 30:233.

59. Smith, J.D., Ichinose, L.Y., Masek, G.A., Watanabe, T., and Stark, L. (1968). Midbrain single units correlating with pupil response to light. Science 162:1302.

60. Straschill, M., and Hoffmann, K.-P. (1969). Response charactcristics of movement detecting neurons in pretectal region of the cat. Exp. Neurol. 25:165.

61. Bell, C., Sierra, G., Buendia, N., and Segundo, J.P. (1964). Sensory properties of units in mesencephalic reticular formation. J. Neurophysiol. 27:961.

62. Pettigrew, J.D., Nikara, T., and Bishop, P.O. (1968). Responses to moving slits by single units in cat striate cortex. Exp. Brain Res. 6:373.

63. Maturana, H.R., Lettvin, J.Y., McCulloch, W.S., and Pitts, W.H. (1960). Anatomy and physiology of vision in the frog (Rana pipiens). J. Gen. Physiol. 43: Suppl. 2, 129.

64. Zeki, S.M. (1974). Cells responding to changing image size and disparity in the cortex of the rhesus monkey. J. Physiol. (Lond.) 242:827.

65. Perkel, D.H., and Bullock, T.H. (1968). Neural Coding. Neurosci. Res. Prog. Bull. 6, No. 3.

66. Barlow, H.B. (1972). Single units and sensation: a neuron doctrine for perceptual psychology. Perception 1:371.

67. Blakemore, C. (1974). Developmental factors in the formation of feature extracting neurons. In F.O. Schmitt and F.G. Worden, (eds.), The Neurosciences, Third Study Program, p. 105. MIT Press, Cambridge, Mass.

68. Ganz, L., and Fitch, M. (1968). The effect of visual deprivation of perceptual behavior. Exp. Neurol. 22:638.

69. Hoeppner, T.J. (1974). Stimulus analyzing mechanisms in the cat visual cortex. Exp. Neurol. 45:257.

70. Spinelli, D.N., and Barrett, T.W. (1969). Visual receptive field organization of single units in the cat's visual cortex. Exp. Neurol. 24:76.

71. Uttal, W.R. (1971). The psychobiological silly season—or what happens when neuro-physiological data become psychological theories. J. Gen. Psychol. 84:151.

72. Bartlett, J.R., and Doty, R.W., Sr. (1974). Response of units in striate cortex of squirrel monkey to visual and electrical stimuli. J. Neurophysiol. 37:621.

73. Erickson, R.P. (1968). Stimulus coding in topographic and non-topographic afferent modalities. Psychol. Rev. 75:447.

74. Erickson, R.P. (1974). Parallel "population" neural coding in feature extraction. In F.O. Schmitt and F.G. Worden (eds.), The Neurosciences, Third Study Program, p. 155. MIT Press, Cambridge, Mass.

75. Bear, D.M., Sasaki, H., and Ervin, F.R. (1971). Sequential changes in receptive fields of striate neurons in dark adapted cats. Exp. Brain Res. 13:256.

76. Donaldson, I.M.L., and Nash, J.R.G. (1975). Variability of the relative preference for stimulus orientation and direction of movement in some units of the cat visual cortex (areas 17 and 18). J. Physiol. (Lond.) 245:305.

77. Henry, G.H., Bishop, P.O., Tupper, R.M., and Dreher, B. (1973). Orientation specificity and response variability of cells in the striate cortex. Vision Res. 13:1771.

78. Horn, G., and Hill, R.M. (1969). Modifications of receptive fields of cells in the visual cortex occurring spontaneously and associated with bodily tilt. Nature 221:186.

79. Rose, D., and Blakemore, C. (1974). An analysis of orientation selectivity in the cat's visual cortex. Exp. Brain Res. 20:1.

80. Sasaki, H., Saito, Y., Baer, D.M., and Ervin, F.R. (1971). Quantitative variation in striate receptive fields of cats as a function of light and dark adaptation. Exp. Brain Res. 13:273.

81. Schwartzkroin, P.A. (1972). The effect of body tilt on the directionality of units in cat visual cortex. Exp. Neurol. 36:498.

82. Ikeda, H., and Wright, M.J. (1974). Sensitivity of neurons in visual cortex (area 17) under different levels of anesthesia. Exp. Brain Res. 20:471.

83. Lee, B.B. (1970). Effect of anesthetics upon visual responses of neurons in the cat's striate cortex. J. Physiol. (Lond.) 207:74P.

84. Pettigrew, J.D. (1974). The effect of visual experience on the development of stimulus specificity by kitten cortical neurons. J. Physiol. (Lond.) 237:49.

85. Robertson, A.D.J. (1965). Anesthesia and receptive fields. Nature 205:80.

86. Spinelli, D.N., Pribram, K.H., and Bridgcman, B. (1970). Visual receptive field organization of single units in the visual cortex of monkey. Int. J. Neurosci. 1:67.

87. Müller, J. (1826). Über die phantastischen Gesichtserscheinungen, p. 6, Hölscher, Coblenz.

88. Müller, J. (1842). Elements of Physiology, Vol. 2, p. 1072. W. Baly (translator). Taylor and Walton, London.

89. Melzack, R., and Wall, P.D. (1962). On the nature of cutaneous sensory mechanisms. Brain 85:331.

90. Adrian, E.D., Cattel, M., and Hoagland, H. (1931). Sensory discharges in single cutaneous nerve fibers, J. Physiol. (Lond.) 72:25.

91. Hahn, J.F. (1971). Stimulus response relationships in first order sensory fibers from cat vibrissae. J. Physiol. (Lond.) 213:215.

92. Mountcastle, V.B. (1966). The neural replication of sensory events in the somatic afferent system. In J.C. Eccles (ed.), Brain and Conscious Experience, p. 85. Springer, New York.

93. Sinclair, D.C. (1955). Cutaneous sensation and the doctrine of specific energy. Brain 78:584.

94. Tower, S.S. (1940). Unit of sensory reception in cornea. J. Neurophysiol. 3:486.

95. Gesteland, R.C., Lettvin, J.Y., and Pitts, W.H. (1965). Chemical transmission in the nose of the frog. J. Physiol. (Lond.) 181:525.

96. O'Connell, R.J., and Mozell, M.M. (1969). Quantitative stimulation of the frog olfactory receptors. J. Neurophysiol. 32:51.

97. Ganchrow, J.R., and Erickson, R.P. (1970). Neural correlates of gustatory intensity and quality. J. Neurophysiol. 33:768.

98. Pfaffman, C. (1944). Gustatory afferent impulses. J. Cell. Comp. Physiol. 17:243.

99. Whitfield, I.C. (1967). The Auditory Pathway, p. 147. Edward Arnold, London.

100. Anderson, J.A. (1972). A simple neural network generating an interactive memory. Math. Biosci. 14:197.

101. Cooper, L.N. (1973). A possible organization of animal memory and learning. *In* B. Lundquist and S. Lundquist (eds.), Nobel Sym. Med. Nat. Sci., Collective Properties of Physical Systems, p. 252. Academic Press, New York.

102. Van Heerden, P.J. (1968). The Foundations of Empirical Knowledge. N.V. Vitgeverij Wistik, Wassenaar.

103. Julesz, B., and Pennington, K.S. (1965). Equidistributed information mapping: an analogy to holograms and memory. J. Opt. Soc. Amer. 55:604.

104. Kabrisky, M. (1966). A Proposed Model for Visual Information Processing in the Human Brain. University of Illinois, Urbana.

105. Longuet-Higgens, H.C. (1968). The non-local storage of temporal information. Proc. Roy. Soc. Lond. Ser. B **171**:327.

106. Pribram, K., Nuwer, M., and Baron, R. (1974). The holographic hypothesis of memory structure in brain function and perception. Contemp. Dev. Math. Psychol. 2:416.

107. Westlake, P.R. (1970). The possibilities of neural holographic processes within the brain. Kybernetik 7:129.

108. Burns, B.D. (1968). The Uncertain Nervous System, p. 28. Edward Arnold, London.

109. Ewert, J.-P., and Borchers, H.-W. (1971). Reaktionscharakteristik von Neuronen aus dem Tectum opticum und Subtectum der Erdkröte *Bufo bufo* (L). Z. Vergl. Physiol. 71:165.

110. Mandl, G. (1970). Localization of visual patterns by neurons in cerebral cortex of the cat. J. Neurophysiol. 33:812.

111. Hartline, H.K. (1940). The receptive fields of optic nerve fibers. Amer. J. Physiol. 130:690.

112. Marshall, W.H., and Talbot, S.A. (1942). Recent evidence for neural mechanisms in vision leading to a general theory of sensory acuity. Biol. Symp. 7:117.

113. Sekuler, R. (1974). Spatial Vision. Annu. Rev. Psychol. 25:195.

114. Legendy, C.R. (1975). Can the data of Campbell and Robson be explained without assuming Fourier Analysis? Biol. Cybernet. 17:157.

115. MacLeod, I.D.G., and Rosenfeld, A. (1974). The visibility of gratings: spatial frequency channels of bar-detecting units. Vision Res. 14:909.

116. Uttal, W.R. (1973). The Psychobiology of Sensory Coding, p. 208. Harper and Row, New York.

117. Fischer, B. (1972). Optische und neuronale Grundlagen der visuellen bildübertragung: Einheitliche mathematische Behandlung des retinalen Bildes und der Erregbarkeit von retinalen Ganglienzellen mit Hilfe der Linearen Systemtheorie. Vision Res. 12:1125.

118. Kaji, S., Yamane, S., Yoshimura, M., and Sugie, N. (1974). Contour enhancement of two-dimensional figures observed in the lateral geniculate cells of cats. Vision Res. 14:113.

119. Marko, H. (1969). Die Systemtheorie der homogenen schichten. I. Mathematische Grundlagen. Kybernetik 6:221.

120. von Seelen, W. (1970) Zur Informationsverarbeitung im visuellen System der Wirbeltiere. I. Kybernetik 7:43.

121. Uttal, W.R. (1969). Emerging principles of sensory coding. Perspect. Biol. Med. 12:344.

122. Daniel, P.M., and Whitteridge, D. (1961). The representation of the visual field on the cerebral cortex in monkeys. J. Physiol. (Lond.) 159:203.

123. Boycott, B.B., and Wässle, H. (1974). The morphological types of ganglion cells of the domestic cat's retina. J. Physiol. (Lond.) 240:397.

124. Bilge, M., Bingle, A., Seneviratne, K.N., and Whitteridge, D. (1967). A map of the visual cortex in the cat. J. Physiol. (Lond.) 191:116P.

125. Hubel, D.H., and Wiesel, T.N. (1968). Receptive fields and functional architecture of monkey striate cortex. J. Physiol. (Lond.) 195:215.

126. Sterling, P. (1971). Receptive fields and synaptic organization of the superficial gray layer of the cat superior colliculus. Vision Res. Suppl. 3:309.

127. Colonnier, M. (1964). The tangential organization of the visual cortex. J. Anat. 98:327.

128. Garey, L.J., Jones, E.G., and Powell, T.P.S. (1968). Interrelationships of striate and extrastriate cortex with the primary relay sites of the visual pathway. J. Neurol. Neurosurg. Psychiat. 31:135.

129. Gubisch, R.W. (1967). Optical performance of the human eye. J. Opt. Soc. Amer. 57:407.

130. Westheimer, G. (1971). Optical properties of vertebrate eyes. *In* M.G.F. Fuortes (ed.), Handbook of Sensory Physiology, Vol. 7, p. 449. Springer, Berlin, New York.

131. Gouras, P. (1968). Identification of cone mechanisms in monkey ganglion cells. J. Physiol. (Lond.) 199:553.

132. Fischer, B. (1973). Overlap of receptive fields centers and representation of the visual field in the cat's optic tract. Vision Res. 13:2113.

133. Hammond, P. (1972). Chromatic sensitivity and spatial organization of LGN neuron receptive fields in cat: cone-rod interactions. J. Physiol. (Lond.) 225:391.

134. Hammond, P. (1973). Contrasts in spatial organization of receptive fields at geniculate and retinal levels: centre, surround and outer surround. J. Physiol. (Lond.) 228:115.

135. Maffei, L., and Fiorentini, A. (1972). Retinogeniculate convergence and analysis of contrast. J. Neurophysiol. 35:65.

136. Cleland, B.G., Dubin, M., and Levick, W.R. (1971). Sustained and transient neurons in the cat's retina and lateral geniculate nucleus. J. Physiol. (Lond.) 217:473.

137. Fukuda, Y., and Stone, J. (1974). Retinal distribution and central projections of Y-, X- and W-cells of the cat's retina. J. Neurophysiol. 37:749.

138. Fukuda, Y., and Saito, H. (1972). Phasic and tonic cells in the cat's lateral geniculate nucleus. Tohuku. J. Exp. Med. 106:209.

139. Singer, W., and Bedworth, N. (1973). Inhibitory interaction between X- and Y-units in the cat LGN. Brain Res. 49:291.

140. Rolls, E.T., and Cowey, A. (1970). Topography of the retina and striate cortex and its relationship to visual acuity in rhesus monkeys and squirrel monkeys. Exp. Brain Res. 10:298.

141. Weymouth, F.W. (1958). Visual sensory units and the minimal angle of resolution. Amer. J. Ophthalmol. 46:102.

142. Clark, W.E. LeGros (1941). The laminar organization and cell ocntent of the lateral geniculate body in the monkey. J. Anat. 75:419.

143. Palmer, L.A., and Rosenquist, A.C. (1974). Visual receptive fields of single striate cortical units projecting to the superior colliculus in the cat. Brain Res. 67:27.

144. Hubel, D.H. Wiesel, T.N., and LeVay, S. (1974). Visual field representation in layer IVc of monkey striate cortex. Soc. Neurosci. 4:264.

145. Cowey, A., and Rolls, E.T. (1974). Human cortical magnification factor and its relation to visual acuity. Exp. Brain Res. 21:447.

146. Rosenquist, A.C., Edwards, S.B., and Palmer, L.A. (1974). An autoradiographic study of the projections of the dorsal lateral geniculate nucleus and the posterior nucleus in the cat. Brain Res. 80:71.

147. Rossignol, S., and Colonnier, M. (1971). A light microscopic study of degeneration patterns in cat cortex after lesions of the lateral geniculate nucleus. Vision Res. Suppl. 3:329.

148. Ingle, D., and Sprague, J.M. (1975). Sensorimotor function of the midbrain tectum. Neurosci. Res. Prog. Bull. 3:169.

149. McIlwain, J.T. (1972). Central vision: visual cortex and superior colliculus. Annu. Rev. Physiol. 34:291.

150. Sprague, J.M., Berlucchi, G., and Rizzolatii, G. (1973). The role of the superior colliculus and pretectum in vision and visually guided behavior. In R. Jung (ed.), Handbook of Sensory Physiology, Vol. 7/III/B, 27. Springer, Berlin.

151. Robinson, D.A. (1972). Eye movements evoked by collicular stimulation in the alert monkey. Vision Res. 12:1795.

152. Schiller, P.H. (1972). The role of the monkey superior colliculus in eye movement and vision. Invest. Ophthalmol. 11:451.

153. Straschill, M., and Rieger, P. (1972). Optomotor integration in the superior colliculus of the cat. In J. Dichgans and E. Bizzi (eds.), Cerebral Control of Eye Movements and Motion Perception, p. 130. Karger, Basel.

154. Straschill, M., and Rieger, P. (1973). Eye movements evoked by focal stimulation of the cat's superior colliculus. Brain Res. 59:211.

155. Syka, J., and Radil-Weiss, T. (1971). Electrical stimulation of the tectum in freely moving cats. Brain Res. 28:567.

156. Kanaseki, T., and Sprague, J.M. (1974). Anatomical organization of pretectal nuclei and tectal laminae in the cat. J. Comp. Neurol. 158:319.

157. Wurtz, R.H., and Goldberg, M.E. (1972). Activity of superior colliculus in behaving monkey. III. Cells discharging before eye movements. J. Neurophysiol. 35:575.

158. Fuchs, A.F., and Luschei, E.S. (1970). Firing patterns of abducens neurons of alert monkeys in relationship to horizontal eye movement. J. Neurophysiol. 33:382.

159. Robinson, D.A. (1970). Oculomotor unit behavior in the monkey. J. Neurophysiol. 33:393.

160. Kawamura, S., Sprague, J.M., and Niimi, K. (1974). Corticofugal projections from the visual cortices of the thalamus, pretectum and superior colliculus in the cat. J. Comp. Neurol. 158:339.

161. Wurtz, R.H., and Goldberg, M.E. (1972). The primate superior colliculus and the shift of visual attention. Invest. Ophthalmol. 11:441.

162. Albus, K. (1975). A quantitative study of the projection area of the central and the paracentral visual field in area 17 of the cat. I. The precision of the topography. Exp. Brain Res. 24:159.

163. Albus, K. (1975). A quantitative study of the projection area of the central and the paracentral visual field in area 17 of the cat. II. The spatial organization of the orientation domain. Exp. Brain Res. 24:181.

16
Introduction

(1985)
Nobuo Suga

The extent to which biosonar information is represented in the bat auditory cortex
Dynamic Aspects of Neocortical Function,
Gerald M. Edelman, W. Einar Gall, and W. Maxwell Cowan (Eds.),
New York: Wiley-Interscience, pp. 653–695

Some of the readers of this volume will be practical people who are interested in making neural networks do practical things. This long integrative paper by Nobuo Suga is full of facts and ideas on how a real neural network in the bat performs a well defined but complex task: sonar detection of flying insects. Simply viewed as a collection of useful hints for neural network signal processing, this paper is essential reading for engineers. However, it also contains fascinating bits of natural history about a nearly miraculous organism.

Bats are extremely common, but may never be seen unless you know where to look. There are a huge number of bat species, with greatly differing behaviors. Suga has spent much of his career studying the mustache bat, primarily found in Central America, which has an advanced biological sonar system.

One reason the bat sonar system is so interesting is that an immense amount of costly engineering research and development has been devoted to sonar and radar in the past fifty years (by humans). We know a great deal about useful signal processing techniques. A good introduction to radar fundamentals is Skolnik 1980.

The mustache bat emits an extremely loud, short, ultrasonic signal and detects the return echo from flying insects. Once a target is detected, the bat flies toward it, intercepts it in the air, catches the insect in its tail membrane, and flips the insect into its mouth. This whole process can take under a second. The bat cry is sufficiently loud at close range to cause permanent damage to human ears, if we could hear it. As the bat closes on the target, the cries become shorter and more frequent. A bat can reliably detect insects up to perhaps ten feet away. The bat can also detect stationary objects using sonar, an essential ability because most bats hunt at night. There is also a problem with interference from other emitters. How bats avoid getting confused and hitting the walls of caves when they exit their caves in vast numbers at dusk is a difficult problem. Suga speculates a bit about how this might be done near the end of the paper.

As in any radar or sonar system, the initial problem for the bat is to tailor the emitted signal so that the return signal can be best used to determine needed information. The cry of the mustache bat is complex, and it uses two distinct signal types to form two quite distinct sonar processing pathways, each giving different information about the target.

In a *continuous wave* (CW), sonar or radar, the transmitter emits a continuous signal and listens for the return. CW radar gives no information about the position of the object; however, if the target is moving relative to the source, the Doppler effect causes a frequency shift in the echo.

In a *pulsed radar*, a brief pulsed signal is emitted. The return echo is detected, and the time delay between the two gives the distance to the target. Because radar transmitters often have limited peak power, sometimes a technique called *pulse compression* is used. Here a relatively long emitted signal is swept in frequency in what is called a *chirp*. The echo will have the same chirped form. Proper signal processing at the receiver can "compress" the long pulse so it acts, in terms of time resolution, like a much shorter, much higher intensity pulse.

The mustache bat's cry is tailored so as to contain components of both classes of signal. There is a long *constant frequency* (CF) portion, which seems to act as a Doppler radar, and there is a chirp at the end of the cry, which seems to act as a pulsed radar, using a chirped signal with pulse compression. Suga calls the chirp the *frequency modulated*, or FM, part of the cry.

Because signal processing requirements are so different for the two types of radar, parts of the signal seems to be handled by different, specialized parallel pathways in the bat. An architecture where different aspects of a biological signal are handled by independent, parallel systems seems to be common. In the visual system, for example, there is now good evidence that there are at least two, perhaps more, anatomically and physiologically distinct processing pathways, so that form, color, and object motion are handled by distinct regions of the brain (DeYoe and Van Essen 1988). Where, or whether, the different pathways get stuck together again to form our (illusion?) of a unified perception is an open question. In any case Suga provides evidence for parallel, anatomically distinct pathways in the bat cortex.

The details of each parallel pathway are fascinating and are discussed in considerable depth. In some cases transmitter and receiver cooperate in a wonderfully flexible way. For example, one problem with Doppler radar signal processing is that a powerful transmitter is only a centimeter away from a very sensitive receiver. A weak return very close in frequency to the transmitted signal must be detected. In the mustache bat's cry maximum signal energy is found around 60 to 63 kHz. One way to handle interference would be to have a set of very narrow filters to analyze the return. In common with good engineering design, the bat uses filters in series: a narrow bandwidth from the peripheral auditory system is further sharpened and shaped in the cortex. The observed Q's (a measure of bandwidth) of the tuning curves actually seen in the bat peripheral auditory system can be as high as 200 in the region around 61 kHz (figure 4). It is not completely clear how such narrow bandwidths are achieved, but there may be some mechanically resonant structures in the peripheral auditory apparatus. In the auditory cortex further improvement of the filter occurs. The narrowest bandwidth cell observed in cortex has a best frequency of 61.5 kHz and a bandwidth of 0.3 kHz, with "essentially infinite" skirt slopes, giving very good narrow band pass filter characteristics.

There are separate regions of auditory cortex to process the frequency modulated part of the cry (the chirp) and the constant frequency part (the Doppler sonar) of the cry. In the region of cortex concerned with the constant frequency portion, there is an extremely large number of cells, about 30 percent of the cells in the cortical region, responsive to the frequency range around 61 kHz (figure 7). A huge number of cortical analyzers are devoted to this small frequency band, presumably to process the Doppler return. Notice, by the way, that this large group of cells seems to have a local mapping topography imposed on the more global tonotopic map, in that neurons responsive to the center of the frequency band (61.5 kHz) are central to the region and neurons away from the center (63 kHz) are on the circumference of the region. Because the bat can control the frequency of its cry to some extent, the bat will change the emitted frequency until the return echo falls in the center of the most analyzed range. Some of the behavioral significance of the Doppler sonar involves the velocity modulation of the return due to the wingbeats of a flying insect as well as overall target velocity. Wing beat frequency and amplitude can serve as means of characterizing insects.

Some topographic maps may be organized so as to impose a global transformation on the input. This has been conjectured to occur in mammalian visual cortex (Schwartz 1984). However, sometimes the mapping transformation may be determined only by a simpler rule: If you want to analyze a particular aspect of a signal, use lots of cells to do it. It is as if each cell adds a roughly constant increment of information to the resulting computation, so more cells mean better information. Relative importance to function of an aspect of a signal can be read from relative size of the responding area on the map.

There is another portion of the bat cortex concerned with analyzing the chirp (the FM part of the cry) that does have significant global organization. In pulsed radar or sonar the parameter of interest is the time it takes for the signal to reach the target and for the echo to return. This time delay determines target distance. Because chirped signals are used by the bat, computing the time delay is not just a matter of starting and stopping a clock. A complex correlational filter must be used to determine an accurate time delay between cry and echo. The bat is able to do this calculation. But, more intriguing, the bat forms a topographic cortical map of target range. Many neurons in this cortical region respond to a fixed "best delay" in milliseconds between cry and echo. There is a quite linear map of best delay (BD) on the cortical surface. As the bat nears the target, a region of activity will sweep from one end of the region to the other.

Suga presents example after wonderful example of effective signal processing in the bat. Because bats are flying animals, it is a reasonable assumption that everything in the brain is there because it is useful. Therefore the kind of signal processing techniques used may very well be close to the best way to do it in a parallel neural network, using the design experience of several hundred million years of evolution. One of the major sources of funding for research on bat sonar is, not surprisingly, the U. S. Navy.

Some interesting countermeasures are taken by prey as well. Some insects listen for bat cries and then, depending on the amplitude of the cry, either turn and go away from the bat, or, if the bat is close, the insects start evasive maneuvers, for example, power diving toward the ground (Roeder 1962).

There do seem to be some simple general design rules that emerge from contemplation of the bat signal processing system: First, a real problem is not simple. There is no "wonder network" that will do everything. The effectiveness of the bat system is due to careful attention to detail, using multiple special purpose systems, each well suited to do part of the job. For example, a selective filter in the peripheral auditory system is further sharpened centrally. One simple step does not do the job; multiple stages are used, each cooperating with the others. Second, there are distinct parallel pathways, each optimized for one aspect of the computation. Third, systematic topographic maps are the most common strategy used to organize sensory information in the bat cortex. Sometimes global organization is present over a large region — the range map — and sometimes global organization is subservient to the need for very large numbers of analyzers for one aspect of a signal — analyzing the Doppler return. Maps are sometimes the result of quite complex computations. Fourth, there is a complex interplay between distributed and localized codes. The simple existence of topographic maps shows a degree of localization. Yet Suga finds that many cells in a region will respond to signals. Not all cells respond, but not only one either. The number that respond is presumably the result of some kind of optimization.

We view this paper as a design handbook on how to solve a real problem with a neurocomputer.

References

E.A. DeYoe and D.C. Van Essen (1988), Concurrent processing streams in monkey visual cortex. *Trends in the Neurosciences* 11: 219–226.

K.D. Roeder (1962), The behavior of free flying moths in the presence of artificial ultrasonic pulses. *Animal Behavior* 10: 300–304.

E.L. Schwartz (1984), Anatomical and physiological correlates of visual computation from striate to infero-temporal cortex. *IEEE Transactions on Systems, Man, and Cybernetics* SMC-14: 257–271.

M.I. Skolnik (1980), *Introduction to Radar Systems*, 2nd Ed. New York: McGraw-Hill.

(1985)
Nobuo Suga

The extent to which biosonar information is represented in the bat auditory cortex
Dynamic Aspects of Neocortical Function,
Gerald M. Edelman, W. Einar Gall, and W. Maxwell Cowan (Eds.),
New York: Wiley-Interscience, pp. 653–695

Abstract

In the auditory cortex, multiple cochleotopic (tonotopic) representation is prominent. Its functional significance has been little known, although tonotopic representation per se has been the principal concern of investigations of the functional organization of the central auditory system for the last 40 years. To explore functional organization beyond tonotopy, the neurophysiology of hearing must be studied in relation to the acoustic signals and auditory information important to a species. For the mustached bat, biosonar information is essential for survival. Experiments performed with synthesized biosonar signals indicate that the functional organization of the auditory system of this species reflects the properties of complex biosonar signals, acoustic behavior, and specialization of the cochlea. Furthermore, they indicate that the multiple cochleotopic representation found in the auditory cortex is related to systematic representation of different types of biosonar information, such as target velocity, subtended angle, and range. Among our findings, the following are particularly important: (1) Complex acoustic signals are processed by specialized neurons that are tuned to particular information-bearing parameters (IBPs) or combinations of IBPs. These neurons may be thought of as IBP filters that can act as "cross-correlators." (2) Different types of IBP filters are clustered separately in identifiable areas of the cerebral cortex. (3) Within each cluster, IBP filters that differ from one another in tuning properties are arranged to represent values of IBPs systematically. (4) The biologically more important values of an IBP are overrepresented by the large number of IBP filters tuned to them in order to achieve higher resolution. (5) IBP filters have particular bandwidths; that is, individual specialized neurons can be activated by stimuli with different values of IBPs. Therefore, each signal is expressed by the spatiotemporal pattern of activity of many specialized neurons.

In the past 40 years, almost all neurophysiological studies on the functional organization of the auditory system have focused on cochleotopic (tonotopic) representation and have explored intriguing multiple cochleotopic representations in the central auditory system. Detailed studies with pure-tone stimuli on cochleotopic representation are valuable because of its relation to the basic layout of functional organization. Such studies, however, are insufficient to explore the functional organization of the auditory cortex and to explain how auditory information is represented by neural activity. (For instance, the tonotopic representa-tion shown in Figure 7 does not indicate how auditory information is represented by the auditory cortex.)

An appropriate method for exploring functional organization beyond cochleotopic representation is to study the responses of single neurons to acoustic stimuli that mimic the sounds used by a species that are important to it. My coworkers and I have adopted this neuroethological method for our research on the auditory system of the mustached bat, *Pteronotus parnellii rubiginosus,* from Panama. We have examined the properties of the bat's biologically important sounds and have used these sounds as stimuli. We have measured the "filter properties" of neurons by varying the individual parameters characterizing these sounds, and we have examined the spatial distribution in the auditory system of neurons with different filter properties.

Such neuroethological studies on bats have demonstrated the following:

1. The peripheral auditory system has evolved not only for the detection of biologically important sounds, but also for frequency analysis of the sound to fulfill species-specific requirements.

2. The central auditory system contains several functional subdivisions specialized for processing different types of auditory information important to a species.

3. The larger area within each subdivision is devoted to processing information more important to a species.

4. Certain subdivisions are occupied by neurons that are specialized for the extraction of particular types of auditory information carried by two components in complex sound.

5. The functional organization of the auditory cortex is quite different among different species, reflecting differences in the properties of the acoustic signals used by them. Organization is also different among individuals within the same species when their acoustic signals are slightly different in physical properties.

My coworkers and I have already written several review articles on the research carried out in my laboratory (Suga, 1978, 1981a,b, 1982; Suga et al., 1981, 1983a,b). Therefore, the aim of this chapter is to integrate, for neurobiologists and speech scientists, our previous work and the data we have recently obtained. Because the functional organization of the central auditory system of the mustached bat reflects clearly the complexity of biosonar signals, acoustic behavior (in particular, Doppler-shift compensation), and the specialization of the peripheral auditory system, I shall first review all three. Without an appropriate introduction, the neural representations of different types of biosonar information superimposed on multiple cochleotopic representation in the cerebrum would be poorly understood.

Biosonar Information Available to the Mustached Bat

The types of biosonar information available to bats depend on the properties of the bats' biosonar signals and receptors. For prey (flying insect) capture and short-range navigation, the mustached bat emits ultrasonic orientation sounds (biosonar signals or pulses), each of which consists of a long constant-frequency (CF) component followed by a short frequency-modulated (FM) component. Since each orientation sound contains four harmonics (H_{1-4}), there are eight components that can be defined (CF_{1-4}, FM_{1-4}). In the emitted sound, the second harmonic (H_2) is always predominant and the frequency of CF_2 is about 61 kHz. In FM_2, the frequency sweeps down from about 61 kHz (the CF_2 frequency) to 49 kHz (Figure 1A). H_3 is 6–12 decibels (dB) weaker than H_2, while H_1 and H_4 are 18–36 and 12–24 dB weaker than H_2, respectively (see Figure 31). Many species of moths have ears that are most sensitive to frequencies between 20 and 40 kHz (Fenton, 1980). They show evasive behavior when they detect the orientation sounds of bats (Roeder, 1962). Since H_1 (24–31 kHz) in the orientation sound of the mustached bat is suppressed, probably by antiresonance of the vocal tract, the bat can approach these moths closely before being detected (Suga and O'Neill, 1979).

Echoes eliciting behavioral responses in the mustached bat always overlap temporally with the emitted signal. As a result, biosonar information must be extracted from a complex sound containing up to 16 components. The CF component is an ideal signal for target detection and the measurement of target velocity because the reflected sound energy is highly concentrated at a particular frequency. The mustached bat uses CF_2 at about 61 kHz for this purpose and performs a unique behavior called *Doppler-shift compensation*, which is described below. The short FM component, on the other hand, is more appropriate for ranging, localizing, and characterizing a target because of the wide distribution of its sound energy over many frequencies. Different parameters of echoes received by the bat carry different types of information about a target (Figure 1D).

During target-directed flight, the duration of the orientation sound shortens from 30 to 7 msec and the emission

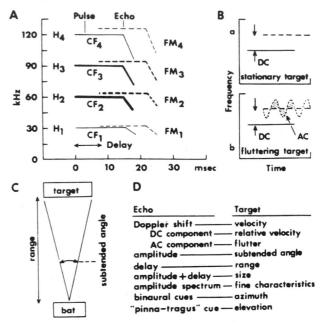

Figure 1 Biosonar signals of the mustached bat, *Pteronotus parnellii rubiginosus*, and the information carried by its signals. **A**: Schematized sonagram of the mustached bat orientation sound *(solid lines)* and the Doppler-shifted echo *(dashed lines)*. The four harmonics (H_{1-4}) of both the orientation sound and the echo each contain a long CF component (CF_{1-4}) and an FM component (FM_{1-4}). Thickness of the lines indicates the relative amplitude of each harmonic in the orientation sound: H_2 is the strongest, followed by H_3 (6–12 dB weaker than H_2), H_4 (12–24 dB weaker than H_2), and H_1 (18–36 dB weaker than H_2). **B**: When the mustached bat flies toward or near a stationary object, the frequency of the echo becomes higher than the emitted sound by the Doppler effect *(graph a)*. This steady shift is called the DC component of the Doppler shift. When the bat flies toward a fluttering target, for example, a flying moth, the Doppler shift of the echo consists of a DC component proportional to relative velocity and the periodic frequency modulation (FM) proportional to the speed of wing beat *(graph b)*. This periodic FM is called the AC component of the Doppler shift. The AC component is complicated because the insect's four wings are moving in complex patterns and in different phase relationships relative to the bat. **C**: Target size is determined from both target range and subtended angle. **D**: Relationship between echo properties and target properties. (From Suga, 1982.)

rate increases from 5/sec to 100/sec. The shortening of the sound's duration is due mainly to shortening of the CF component. Such changes in the signal cause a decrease in information carried by the CF component but an increase in information carried by the FM component. Echo amplitude and delay from the emitted sound also change systematically during target-directed flight.

One of the fascinating acoustic behaviors of the mustached bat is Doppler-shift compensation. When the bat flies toward or near targets, it reacts to Doppler-shifted echoes resulting from its approach by reducing the frequency of its emitted sounds, that is, by compensating for Doppler-shift, which is proportional to the target's relative velocity. This Doppler-shift compensation stabilizes the echo at a predetermined frequency. The mustached bat emits an orientation sound with the CF$_2$ at about 61 kHz when there are no Doppler-shifted echoes. When a Doppler-shifted echo returns, say, at 63 kHz, the bat reduces the frequency of subsequent orientation sounds by nearly 2 kHz, so that the Doppler-shifted echo is stabilized at or just above 61 kHz. Because of the compensation, the CF$_2$ of the Doppler-shifted echo is kept mainly within a range of 61–63 kHz. The frequency of the CF signal is different among subspecies and among individuals of the same subspecies.

The compensation occurs when the mustached bat is flying near or toward stationary objects (Schnitzler, 1970), or is passively moved (Henson et al., 1980). When the bat pursues a flying insect, it initially lengthens the duration of the orientation sound from about 20 to 28–37 msec, and then quickly but systematically shortens the duration down to 6–8 msec during the approach and terminal phases (Novick and Vaisnys, 1964). This increase in duration during the initial approach phase increases the information carried by the CF component. When the bat flies toward a landing platform or is passively moved, however, the initial lengthening does not occur (Schnitzler, 1970; our unpublished observations). If an initial increase in duration takes place only during insect pursuit, then perhaps it is related to maximizing the wing-beat information carried by the AC component of the Doppler shift (Figure 1B, part b). In the mid-approach and terminal phases, the duration of the orientation sound gradually shortens so that the bat receives less and less information about the beating wings. Such acoustic behavior suggests that the bat can identify whether the target is stationary or fluttering prior to or during the early portion of the approach phase, and that processing of the relative velocity information carried by the DC component is difficult when mixed with the AC component, particularly during the late approach and terminal phases. In the horseshoe bat, *Rhinolophus ferrumequinum*, Doppler-shift compensation occurs *only* for the bat's own flight speed and not for the flying speed of the insects (Schnitzler and Ostwald, 1981). Presumably, this is also true for the mustached bat.

Specialization of the Peripheral Auditory System for Detection and Analysis of Biosonar Signals

In the mustached bat, the cochlea is very large relative to the skull. Its basal turn, where ultrasonic signals are analyzed, is enormous (Figure 2B). The basilar membrane of the cochlea, on which there are about 7100 sensory hair cells, is 12.2 mm long. Electrophysiological studies on the peripheral auditory system of this species have clearly

demonstrated that it is remarkably specialized for the detection and frequency analysis of sound at and around 61.0 kHz, the CF2 of the echo when stabilized by Doppler-shift compensation (see Suga, 1978, for a review).

The receptor potential (cochlear microphonic response or CM) typically appears only during the presentation of a tonal stimulus, and its envelope is usually very similar to that of the stimulus (Figure 3A, traces 1 and 6, B, traces 1 and 6). For stimuli at and around 61 kHz, however, the envelope of the CM differs from that of the stimulus (Figure 3A, traces 2–5, B, traces 2–5). This CM envelope indicates that the cochlea has a sharply tuned local resonator. The resonance frequency of the local resonator is 61.1 ± 0.43 kHz ($n = 16$). The exponential rise and decay of the CM due to the sharply tuned local resonator has a time constant of 1.07 ± 0.03 msec. When the cochlea is stimulated by a 0.4-msec tone burst, the ringing CM is much larger and longer than the CM observed during the stimulus (Figure 3B, traces 3 and 4). This suggests the possibility that an unknown active process in the hair cell is related to the ringing.

The threshold curve of a CM recorded from the round window of the cochlea is sharply tuned to 61.0 kHz (Figure 4A). The sharp threshold curve and ringing are not affected by removal of the ossicular chain from the middle ear, also indicating that the sharply tuned local resonator is in the cochlea.

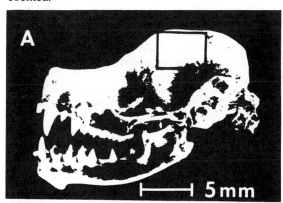
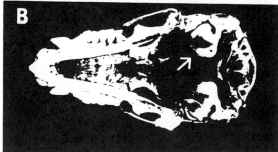

Figure 2 The skull of the mustached bat. **A**: Lateral view; the rectangle corresponds to that in Figure 7. **B**: Ventral view. Arrow indicates the huge cochlea. (From Suga, 1979.)

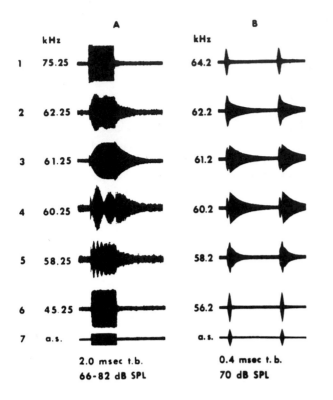

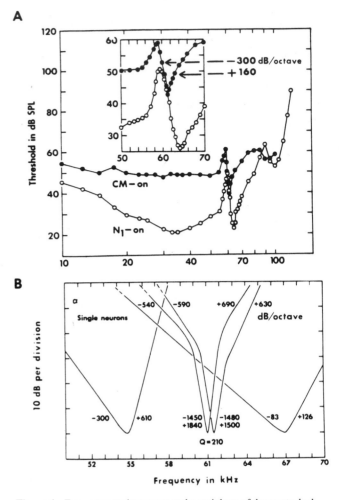

Figure 3 Receptor potentials (cochlear microphonic responses) recorded from the round window of the mustached bat cochlea. **A**: The envelope of the cochlear microphonic response (CM) differs from that of an acoustic stimulus *(a.s.)* at certain frequencies. The duration and rise–decay time of tone burst stimuli *(t.b.)* are 2.0 and 0.05 msec, respectively. The amplitudes of the tone bursts are between 66 and 82 dB SPL. Their frequencies in kHz are shown to the left of each record. Note the prominent transient in the CM in *3*, indicating the presence of a sharply tuned local resonator in the cochlea. When the frequency of a tone burst stimulus is slightly different from the frequency of the resonator, 61.2 kHz, the CM due to the stimulus and the CM due to the local resonator overlap and produce beats *(4* and *5)*. This phenomenon clearly indicates that the sharply tuned local resonator at 61.2 kHz is in the cochlea and oscillates at its resonance frequency semi-independently from the areas tuned to neighboring frequencies. **B**: CM to 0.4-msec tone bursts at 70 dB SPL. The rise–decay times of the tone bursts are both 0.2 msec. The bottom trace shows the tone bursts. The frequencies of the tone bursts are indicated to the left of each CM trace. Note the long-lasting CMs following the cessation of the stimuli. The frequencies of these after-responses are the same, 61.2 kHz, regardless of the stimulus frequency. (From Suga and Jen, 1977.)

Figure 4 Frequency-tuning curves at the periphery of the mustached bat auditory system. **A**: Frequency-tuning curves of CM-on and N_1-on responses based on data recorded from the round windows of four bats. (N_1 is the summated cochlear nerve fiber response.) Since the curves are sharply tuned to either 61 or 64 kHz, respectively, the curves between 50 and 70 kHz were measured from eight bats and then averaged and plotted on expanded coordinates as shown in the inset (Suga and Jen, 1977). **B**: Frequency-tuning curves (excitatory areas) of peripheral neurons. Each of these curves is the average of the frequency-tuning curves of many single neurons tuned to either 54.5, 61.0, 61.5, or 67.0 kHz. Note the extremely steep slopes of the curves with a best frequency of 61.0 or 61.5 kHz. The slopes are given in decibels per octave next to each curve. The quality factor *(Q)* of the tuning curve at 61 kHz is 210. *Q* is the best frequency divided by the bandwidth at 3 dB above minimum threshold. (From Suga, 1978.)

Single cochlear nerve fibers tuned to either 30, 61, or 92 kHz have sharper tuning curves than those tuned to other frequencies (Figure 5C). In particular, neurons tuned to 61 kHz show remarkably sharp tuning curves (Figure 4B). The low- and high-frequency slopes of their tuning curves between the minimum threshold and 30 dB above it are −1450 and +1850 dB/octave, respectively. The quality factor (Q) is 210 (Figure 4B), and Q-10 dB is 85 on the average (Figure 5C). (Q and Q-10 dB are, respectively, the best frequency divided by the bandwidths of a tuning curve at 3 and 10 dB above a minimum threshold.) Since 30.5, 61.0, and 91.5 kHz are the average frequencies of the first, second, and third harmonics of the long CF component in the orientation sound, and since the CF component of 61.0 kHz is predominant and is used for Doppler-shift compensation, the cochlea of the mustached bat is remarkably specialized for fine frequency analysis of the predominant

components in biosonar signals (Suga et al., 1975; Suga and Jen, 1977). Such specialization of the inner ear becomes dramatically clear when comparing the data obtained from different species of bats using different types of biosonar signals (Figure 5).

The population of peripheral neurons tuned to 61–63 kHz is probably disproportionately large compared with the population of neurons tuned to any other 2-kHz frequency band, as the former is much more frequently recorded than the latter (Suga and Jen, 1977). The density of neurons innervating sensory hair cells shows an intriguing variation along the basilar membrane (Henson, 1973) that is presumably related to the disproportionate representation of 61–63-kHz frequencies by peripheral neurons.

Because its Doppler-shift compensation stabilizes the echo CF component to be analyzed by a group of sharply tuned neurons, the mustached bat has certain advantages in

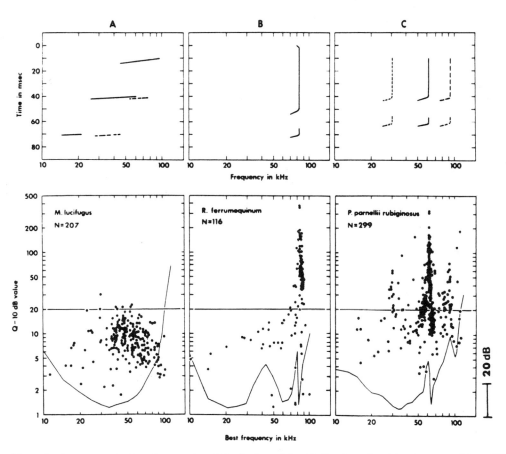

Figure 5 Sonograms of orientation sounds and distributions of $Q = 10$ dB values of peripheral neurons of three different species of bats: *Myotis lucifugus* (**A**), *Rhinolophus ferrumequinum* (**B**), and *Pteronotus parnellii rubiginosus* (**C**). The quality factor, $Q = 10$ dB, is the best frequency divided by the bandwidth at 10 dB above a minimum threshold. The distribution of $Q = 10$ dB values (·) as a function of best frequency shows a clear peak in *R. ferrumequinum* and *P. parnellii rubiginosus*. Note that the peak appears at the frequency of the predominant CF component of the orientation sound: 83 kHz in B and 61 kHz in C. In C, small peaks are also noticeable at 30 and 91 kHz, which are the frequencies of CF_1 and CF_2 of the orientation sound. The curves in the lower graphs represent the N_1 or behavioral frequency-tuning curves of these bats. The 20 dB scale for these curves is shown near the lower right corner. (Based on data obtained by Suga, 1973; Long and Schnitzler, 1975; Suga et al., 1976; Suga and Jen, 1977.)

target detection and velocity analysis. First, sharp tuning increases the signal-to-noise ratio by reducing the masking effect of loud emitted sounds (and also non-Doppler-shifted echoes) on weak Doppler-shifted echoes. Second, fine frequency analysis allows greater resolution of relative velocity and also facilitates detection of the wing beats of flying insects.

Cochlear nerve fibers sharply tuned to between 60 and 63 kHz are extremely sensitive to minor sinusoidal frequency modulations (SFMs). (In our experiments, SFMs have been used as simplified forms of the AC components of Doppler shifts in the echoes from flying insects because each of the parameters characterizing an SFM can be easily described and systematically and independently varied.) They can encode a modulation as small as 0.01%, that is, a 6.1-Hz frequency shift of the 61-kHz carrier (Figure 6A). Furthermore, the summated cochlear nerve fiber response (N_1) also clearly synchronizes with frequency modulations as small as 0.01%, indicating that a large number of peripheral neurons can encode the minute frequency modulations easily caused by flying insects (Figure 6C). The DC component of the Doppler shift is represented by the location of the activated peripheral neurons, whereas the AC component is expressed by a spatiotemporal pattern of neural activity varying synchronously with wing beat.

Representation of Different Types of Biosonar Information in the Subdivisions of the Auditory Cortex

When the bat emits sounds, its ears are self-stimulated. To mimic such vocal self-stimulation, we delivered an electronically synthesized orientation sound from one loudspeaker (artificial vocal apparatus) placed anteroventrally to the bat, thus stimulating both ears to the same extent. To mimic an echo, a similarly synthesized echo was delivered from another loudspeaker (artificial target) mounted on an acoustic perimeter (hoop) 160 cm in diameter. The individual parameters carrying different types of information important for echolocation (biosonar) were systematically varied. For instance, different target ranges were simulated by changing echo delay. Different target sizes were mimicked by modifying echo amplitude. Different target motions in the radial direction were introduced by shifting echo frequency. Different azimuthal target motions were introduced by moving the "echo" loudspeaker horizontally. The beating wings of an insect were mimicked by modulating echoes in frequency and amplitude.

To study the response properties of cortical auditory neurons as a function of a certain stimulus parameter, we used microelectrodes to record action potentials from single neurons in the cerebral cortices of mustached bats. The animals were lightly anesthetized with sodium pentobarbi-

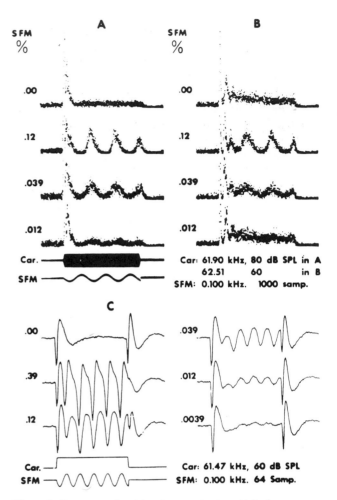

Figure 6 Responses of peripheral neurons to sinusoidally frequency-modulated tone bursts that grossly simulate echoes from beating insect wings. **A** and **B**: Peristimulus-time (PST) histograms of the responses of two neurons with best frequencies of 61.80 (A) and 61.74 kHz (B). The carrier sound (Car.) was set at 61.90 kHz and 80 dB SPL in A and 62.51 kHz and 60 dB SPL in B. The modulation rate was 100 Hz (*SFM*). The modulation depth, which is the peak frequency deviation from the carrier expressed in percent, is shown to the left of each histogram. The number of stimulus repetitions for each PST was 1000 in order to produce a smooth envelope of the histogram for comparison with the waveform of the *SFM*. The bin width was 50 μsec. **C**: Summated auditory nerve responses (N_1) to frequency-modulated tone bursts. The prominent N_1-off response is evoked by the off-response of CM, which is shown in Figure 3A, track 3. The carrier sound was set at 61.47 kHz and 60 dB SPL. The modulation rate was 100 Hz. The modulation depth (%) is shown to the left of each response. The number of stimulus repetitions was 64 and bin width was 100 μsec. Note that the responses were synchronized with frequency modulation as small as 0.01%. These recordings were made from anesthetized mustached bats. (From Suga and Jen, 1977.)

tal. If not anesthetized, they were given a neuroleptic, analgesic Fentanyl–Droperidol mixture and local anesthetic was applied to the surgical wounds. Individual bats were used over several days. Most of the detailed data that brought us to the conclusions and interpretations presented here have been described in O'Neill and Suga (1982), Suga and Manabe (1982), and Suga et al. (1983a,b).

The auditory cortex of the mustached bat is 0.9 mm thick and is about 14.2 mm^2 in its other dimensions, which is very large relative to the size of its brain. In the following, I shall describe multiple cochleotopic (tonotopic) representation in the cortex (Figure 7). Cochleotopic representation itself, however, is insufficient to describe the functional organization of the auditory cortex in its entirety; thus, I shall also describe representations of different types of biosonar information in three physiologically distinct areas: DSCF, CF/CF, and FM-FM. In these areas, certain response properties of single neurons arranged orthogonally to the cortical surface are nearly identical. In this sense, there is *columnar organization*. Along the cortical surface, however, response properties vary systematically and form axes for systematic representation of particular types of biosonar information. As will be described below, the DSCF area is organized along coordinates of frequency versus amplitude and is devoted to processing information carried by the CF$_2$ of the Doppler-shifted echo (Suga, 1977). The CF/CF area examines the CF$_2$ and CF$_3$ of the echo in relation to the CF$_1$ of the orientation sound (Suga et al., 1979) and represents Doppler shift, that is, the target velocity in the radial direction (Suga et al., 1981). The FM-FM area examines the FM$_{2-4}$ of the echo with reference to the FM$_1$ of the orientation sound and represents target range (O'Neill and Suga, 1979, 1982; Suga and O'Neill, 1979). There are a few other areas whose functional organization remains to be studied further. I shall describe our experiments on these less well-defined areas because they also appear to be important for processing biosonar information.

Tonotopic Representation Reflecting the Properties of Biosonar Signals, Acoustic Behavior of the Species, and the Specialization of the Cochlea

One of the main topics in auditory neurophysiology has been the projection of the cochlea to the central auditory system. Tonotopic (cochleotopic) representation reflects the specialization of the cochlea or, more precisely, the properties of acoustic signals used by each species and the acoustic behavior of the species. Here, tonotopic representation means that best frequencies of neurons are significantly correlated with the locations of neurons in the brain.

Research on tonotopic representation in the primary auditory cortex (AI) has an interesting history. Since the

first demonstration by Woolsey and Walzl (1941), tonotopic representation has been found in several different species of mammals. Among these, the data obtained from dogs (Tunturi, 1944) have been cited most frequently. In the mid-1960s, however, tonotopic representation in cats was denied (Evans et al., 1965; Goldstein et al., 1970). In the mid-1970s, studies on the distribution of best frequencies in the AI were performed in cats (Merzenich et al., 1975) and monkeys (Merzenich and Brugge, 1973; Imig et al., 1977), and the controversy about tonotopic representation subsided. In the little brown bat, *Myotis lucifugus,* (Suga, 1965b) and the mustached bat (Suga and Jen, 1976; Suga and Manabe, 1982), tonotopic representation in the AI is clearly present.

In the AI of the little brown bat, there appears to be systematic tonotopic representation. The frequency axis is oriented caudorostrally, as in the cat. Sounds of 30–50 kHz appear to be somewhat overrepresented (Suga, 1965b). Such minor disproportionate tonotopic representation is also found in the cat (Merzenich et al., 1975). It is probably related to uneven organization at the periphery and to the uneven energy distribution over the frequencies of the sounds important for each species.

In the mustached bat, the AI is sandwiched between nonprimary auditory cortices (Figure 7B). There is a clear tendency for high-frequency-sensitive neurons to be located anteriorly and low-frequency-sensitive neurons to be located posteriorly, as in the AI of other mammals. However, tonotopic representation in the mustached bat is unique in four frequency ranges:

1. Neurons sensitive to 50–60 kHz, that is, neurons processing information carried by the FM$_2$ component, are virtually nonexistent or very small in population on the main tonotopic axis, but are displaced anterodorsally into the FM-FM area. The FM-FM area is large and shows vague tonotopic representation.

2. Neurons sensitive to 61–63 kHz, that is, neurons processing information carried by the CF$_2$ component, occupy about 30% of the AI, although the total frequency representation ranges from 7 to 120 kHz. Since orientation sounds are quite distinct from communication sounds and since the animal responds to positively Doppler-shifted echoes by reducing the frequency of subsequent orientation sounds, the 61–63-kHz tuned area is undoubtedly the area specialized for processing the CF$_2$ component of Doppler-shifted echoes from moving targets. Accordingly, this 2.3 mm^2 area is called the Doppler-shifted CF processing area or simply the DSCF area. In the DSCF area, 61.0-kHz-sensitive neurons are located near the center and 63.0-kHz-sensitive neurons along the circumference. Thus the frequency axis is radial.

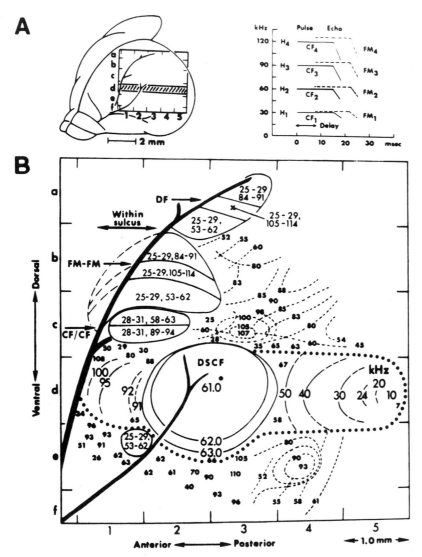

Figure 7 Dorsolateral view of the mustached bat's brain (A) and the distribution of best frequencies along the tangential plane of the auditory cortex (B). **A**: The branching lines represent the branches of the median cerebral artery. The long branch is on the sulcus. The area surrounded by the rectangle is shown in B. The data obtained from the shaded band are presented in Figure 8A. **B**: Numbers and lines represent iso-best-frequency contours. Orderly tonotopic representation is clear in the areas with solid contour lines, but not so systematic in the areas with dashed contour lines. In the areas where contour lines overlap, neurons are tuned to different frequencies. In the areas where contour lines are not drawn, the tonotopic representation, if present, is obscure. Some of the best frequencies obtained in these obscure areas are shown. The area surrounded by the dotted line is the primary auditory cortex (AI), which contains the DSCF area at the center. The FM-FM and CF/CF areas are probably a part of the AI as well. In each of the subdivisions of the FM-FM, CF/CF, and DF areas and a tiny area anteroventral to the DSCF, two different frequency bands are represented. The areas dorsal or ventral to AI are nonprimary auditory cortices.

3. Neurons sensitive to 70–90 kHz, that is, neurons processing information carried by the FM₃ component, are virtually nonexistent along the main tonotopic axis, but are displaced dorsally into the FM-FM area.

4. Neurons sensitive to 91–95 kHz, that is, neurons processing information carried by the CF₃ component, are disproportionately large in population in the area anterior to the DSCF area.

5. Each subdivision of the FM-FM and CF/CF areas of the AI receives the projection for two different frequency bands, for example, 25–29 and 53–62 kHz. The primary auditory cortex itself thus shows multiple representation of certain frequency bands, if the CF/CF and FM-FM areas are truly a part of the primary auditory cortex.

Because of these unique features, the distribution of best frequencies along the anteroposterior axis of the primary auditory cortex shows prominent discontinuity at two locations. The disproportionate and systematic representation of 61–63 kHz sounds in the DSCF area is truly dramatic (Figure 8). The amplitude spectra of most communication sounds are quite different from those of orientation sounds (Suga and Jen, 1976; Suga, unpublished) and can hardly be correlated with the unique features of tonotopic representation listed here. As described in the following sections, these unique features are indeed related to the specialization of the bat's auditory system for processing biosonar signals.

Tonotopic representation in the auditory cortex is clearly different from species to species according to the amplitude spectra of their species-specific signals (Suga, 1981a,b). Tonotopic representation also differs among individuals within the same species; it is "private," reflecting minor differences in the amplitude spectra of the signals essential for survival. For instance, if a mustached bat emits a CF signal with a resting frequency of 60.5 kHz, its DSCF area represents sounds chiefly between 60.5 and 62.5 kHz. If the resting frequency of another mustached bat is 61.5 kHz, its DSCF area represents sounds mainly between 61.5 and 63.5 kHz (Suga and O'Neill, 1980; Suga et al., 1983a,b).

Multiple tonotopic representation in the auditory cortex is present in the mustached bat, as it is in other mammals (Figure 7). The frequencies in each of the four harmonics of the biosonar signals are represented as follows. The frequencies in H₁ are represented within the posterior part of AI, the CF/CF area, and the FM-FM area. Those in H₂ are represented in the DSCF, CF/CF, and FM-FM areas and in the area ventrolateral to AI. Those in H₃ are represented in the anterior part of AI, the CF/CF area, the FM-FM area, and the areas dorsal, anteroventral, and ventroposterior to the DSCF area. The frequencies in H₄ are represented in the anterior edge of AI, the FM-FM area, and the area dorsal to the DSCF area.

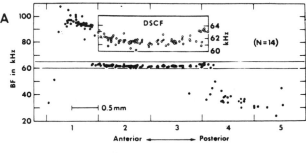

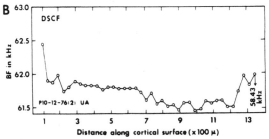

Figure 8 Changes in best frequency (*BF*) along the anteroposterior axis of the primary auditory cortex of the mustached bat. **A**: Distribution of BFs within a 500-μm-wide band along the anteroposterior axis of the primary auditory cortex (the shaded area in Figure 7A). Since the change in BF along the axis of the DSCF area (*middle portion*) is small, the distribution of the BFs in this area is shown in the inset with a larger frequency scale. Note the overrepresentation of 61–63 kHz in the DSCF area and the discontinuities in the frequency axis at both sides of the DSCF area. In the DSCF area, the BF changes from 63 to 61 kHz and then back to 63 kHz along the anteroposterior axis. The data are pooled from 11 anesthetized and 3 unanesthetized mustached bats. (Based on Suga and Jen, 1976; Suga and Manabe, 1982; Asanuma et al., 1983). **B**: Change in BF during a single oblique electrode penetration across the DSCF area of an unanesthetized mustached bat. (From Suga and Manabe, 1982.)

In the CF/CF and FM-FM areas where representations of different parts of the cochlea overlap, tonotopic representation is vague and responses of neurons to single tones are weak. However, when two signal elements are delivered in an appropriate frequency, amplitude, and temporal relationship, their responses are facilitated and the response latency becomes shorter and more constant. The areas that consist of such *combination-sensitive neurons* are "uninteresting" in terms of responses to pure tones, but these areas are extremely interesting in terms of responses to biologically significant complex sounds (Suga et al., 1978, 1979; O'Neill and Suga, 1979; Suga and O'Neill, 1979). In a sense, multiple tonotopic representation indicates that the auditory cortex has "frequency-labeled circuit boards" reflecting the anatomical organization of the sensory epithelium. The following sections describe neurophysiological studies that have explored the functional significance of multiple tonotopic representation in the mustached bat in relation to one of the bat's behaviors, echolocation.

Representation of Target Velocity in the DSCF and CF/CF Areas

As detailed earlier, when the target is a flying insect, its echo is modulated in frequency and amplitude by the beating of its wings. The Doppler shift in the echo consists of a DC component due to the change in distance between the bat and the insect and an AC component caused by the insect's wingbeats (Figure 1B).

A mechanoreceptor system has neurons that are sensitive to either the DC or AC components of mechanical stimuli. In the somatosensory cortex of the monkey, slowly and rapidly adapting neurons are clustered in alternating bands (Kaas et al., 1981). Therefore, the question arises as to how cortical auditory neurons processing target velocity information respond to the DC and AC components, and whether there are functional subdivisions for processing the DC or AC components separately.

The DC component is expressed by the frequency difference between the emitted sound and the Doppler-shifted echo. The frequency information of the emitted sound is available to the bat in the form of vocal self-stimulation and perhaps efferent copy, about which little is currently known. The frequency information contained in the Doppler-shifted echo is available regardless of whether Doppler-shift compensation is performed. With compensation, however, the measurement of echo frequency becomes much more accurate, because the echo frequency is then analyzed by a group of filters in the cochlea that are unusually sharply tuned to sounds between 60 and 62 kHz (Suga et al., 1975; Suga and Jen, 1977). The DC component is expressed by two groups of activated neurons with different best frequencies. It is also possible that the DC component is eventually expressed by a group of activated neurons that selectively respond to a pair of sounds separated in frequency by a particular Doppler shift.

The AC component can be expressed by synchronous discharges of each neuron and by synchronous alternation of excitation among different groups of neurons with different best frequencies. It is also possible that the AC component is eventually expressed by activated neurons that selectively respond to sounds with particular depths and rates of frequency modulation.

Representation of the DC Component of a Doppler Shift

The DSCF Area. In the DSCF area, the majority of neurons are very sharply tuned to particular preferred frequencies (best frequencies) between 61 and 63 kHz, the commonest frequencies of the CF_2 of Doppler-shifted ech-

oes. These neurons are systematically arranged according to their best frequencies and form a radial frequency axis along the cortical surface (Figure 9). Along the frequency axis, best frequency changes at a rate of 20–30 Hz per neuron, that is, velocity information is represented by increments of 5.6–8.4 cm/sec per neuron. Therefore, the representation of target velocity information is very fine (Suga and Jen, 1976; Suga and Manabe, 1982).

Frequency resolution is directly related to the sharpness of the frequency-tuning curve. Extremely narrow frequency-tuning curves of peripheral neurons are further sharpened in the central auditory system by lateral inhibition (Figure 10). In the narrowest curve obtained so far, the best frequency is 61.51 kHz and the bandwidth remains at about 0.3 kHz over a broad amplitude range. The slope of the frequency-tuning curve is essentially infinite in a significant number of cortical neurons. These neurons act as narrow-band frequency detectors irrespective of stimulus amplitude. Since many neurons have an "excitatory" frequency-tuning curve *(excitatory area)* much narrower than those of peripheral neurons and bounded by "inhibitory" frequency-tuning curves *(inhibitory areas),* frequency representation in the DSCF area is improved by lateral inhibition (Suga and Manabe, 1982). The neural mechanism for the sharpening of frequency-tuning curves, which was first demonstrated in cats (Katsuki et al., 1959), starts to operate in the cochlear nucleus (Suga et al., 1975). The neuronal mechanism for the sharpening of cortical representation of a sensory signal was first proposed for the somatosensory system (Mountcastle, 1957).

The CF/CF Area. The DSCF area is devoted to the fine and systematic representation of the frequency and amplitude of the CF_2 in the Doppler-shifted echo. We have also examined whether the auditory cortex has an area where neurons are sensitive to particular differences in frequency between orientation sounds and Doppler-shifted echoes, that is, particular Doppler shifts. To represent a Doppler shift systematically, two frequency axes are needed. There are obviously no such coordinates in the cochlea. In the CF/CF area, however, neurons are tuned to particular combinations of two CF components (Figures 11 and 12) and form such frequency coordinates (Figure 13; Suga et al., 1979, 1981).

The CF/CF area contains two major types of neurons, CF_1/CF_2 and CF_2/CF_3, both of which respond poorly to individual signal elements but show remarkable facilitation when the CF_1 of the orientation sound (pulse) is combined with the CF_2 or CF_3, respectively, of an echo (Figure 11). Note that one of the essential signal elements for the facilitation of CF/CF neurons is the weakest component of the pulse, CF_1. For maximal facilitation, a precise fre-

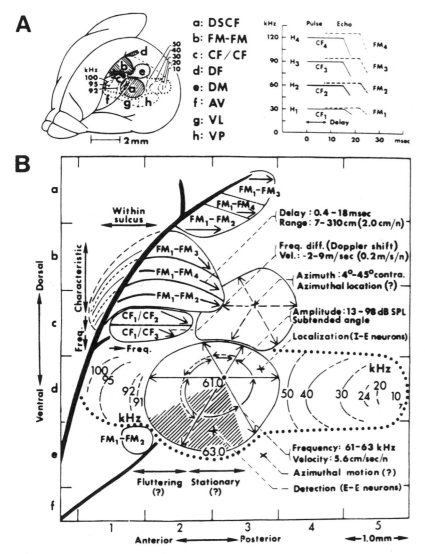

Figure 9 Functional organization of the auditory cortex of the mustached bat. **A:** Dorsolateral view of the left cerebral hemisphere. The areas within the dashed lines comprise the auditory cortex. DSCF, FM-FM, CF/CF, DF, and DM areas (*a, b, c, d,* and *e,* respectively) are specialized for the systematic representation of biosonar information. The branches of the median cerebral artery are shown by the branching lines. The longest branch is on the sulcus. **B:** Graphic summary of the functional organization of the auditory cortex. The tonotopic representation of the primary auditory cortex and the functional organization of the DSCF, FM-FM, CF/CF, and DM areas are indicated by lines and arrows. The DSCF area has axes representing either target velocity information (echo frequency: 61–63 kHz) or subtended target angle information (echo amplitude: 13–98 dB SPL) and is divided into two subdivisions suitable for either target detection *(shaded)* or target localization *(unshaded).* These subdivisions are occupied mainly by excitatory-excitatory (E-E) or inhibitory-excitatory (I-E) neurons, respectively. The FM-FM area consists of three major types of FM-FM facilitation neurons (*FM₁-FM₂, FM₁-FM₃,* and *FM₁-FM₄*), which form separate clusters. Each cluster has an axis representing target ranges of 7–310 cm (echo delay: 0.4–18 msec). The dorsoventral axis of the FM-FM area probably represents fine target characteristics. The CF/CF area consists of two major types of CF/CF facilitation neurons (*CF₁/CF₂* and *CF₁/CF₃*), which aggregate in independent clusters. Each cluster has two frequency axes and represents target velocities of −2–9 m/sec (echo Doppler shift: −0.7 to +3.2 kHz for CF₂ and −1.1 to +4.8 kHz for CF₃). The DF area and a part of the VL area receive nerve fibers from the FM-FM area. The DF area consists of three clusters of FM-FM facilitation neurons, but the VL area contains only a cluster of FM1-FM2 facilitation neurons. FM-FM and CF/CF neurons are tuned to particular combinations of two signal elements in a complex sound and respectively extract target range and velocity information. The DM area appears to have an azimuthal axis representing the azimuthal location of the target. In the VP area, azimuthal-motion-sensitive neurons have been found. The functional organization of the VL and VP areas remains to be studied further. (Based on data obtained by Suga, 1977; Manabe et al., 1978; Suga and O'Neill, 1979; Suga et al., 1979, 1981, 1983a,b; O'Neill and Suga, 1982; and Suga and Manabe, 1982.)

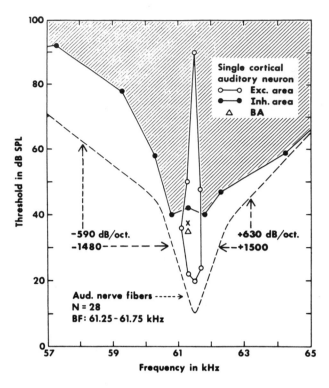

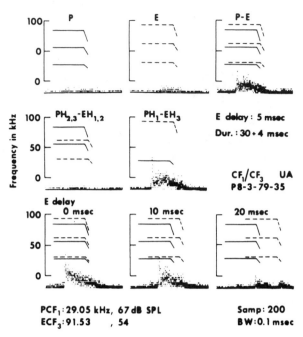

Figure 10 The excitatory *(open circles, unshaded)* and inhibitory *(solid circles, shaded area)* areas of a single neuron in the DSCF area. Since the rate of spontaneous discharge was not high enough for the inhibitory area to be measured with a single tone stimulus, a conditioning tone burst was delivered prior to an excitatory tone burst fixed at 61.3 kHz and 37 dB SPL *(X)*. The conditioning sound was changed in frequency and amplitude to measure the inhibitory area, in which excitation evoked by the 61.3 kHz tone burst was inhibited by the conditioning sound. The inhibitory area is on both sides of the excitatory area and greatly overlaps it. The neuron showed phasic on-responses followed by inhibition to tone bursts within the excitatory area that overlapped the inhibitory area. But it showed tonic on-responses to tone bursts within the excitatory area that did not overlap the inhibitory area. The best amplitude of the neuron was 33 dB SPL *(triangle)*. For comparison, the average of the excitatory areas of 28 single cochlear nerve fibers with best frequencies between 61.25 and 61.75 kHz is shown *(dashed line)*. The slopes of the curve are given in decibels per octave. Note that the excitatory area of the cortical neuron is much narrower at higher stimulus amplitudes than are those of the peripheral neurons. The sharpened excitatory area results from lateral inhibition. (From Suga, 1982.)

Figure 11 PST histograms of responses of a tonic CF_1/CF_3 facilitation neuron to pulse *(P, solid lines)*, echo *(E, dashed lines)*, P–E pairs, and different combinations of elements in the P–E pair. Each PST histogram is shown together with a schematized sonagram of the stimulus in its true time relationship with the response. Facilitation occurs only to combinations of P–E, PH_1–EH_3, and PCF_1–ECF_3, not to P alone, E alone, or to combinations other than these three. The essential components for facilitation are PCF_1 and ECF_3. The CF_3 component must be Doppler-shifted by 4.38 kHz relative to three times the CF_1 frequency to elicit the maximum facilitation. FM components do not play a role in the response. E delay is 5 msec in the upper two rows. In the bottom row, responses are shown to P–E pairs with echo delays of 0, 10, and 20 msec. Facilitation occurs as long as the echo delay is less than 20 msec and some overlap of the CF components of P and E remains. The latency of the response follows the shifting of E relative to P. Frequencies *(kHz)*, amplitudes *(dB SPL)* and durations *(Dur.)* of the essential signal elements are listed in the figure. ("Dur: 30 + 4" means that the CF and FM components are 30 and 4 msec long, respectively.) BW, bin width of the PST histograms; Samp., number of stimulus representations for each PST. U A indicates that the data were obtained from an unanesthetized bat. (From Suga et al., 1983b.)

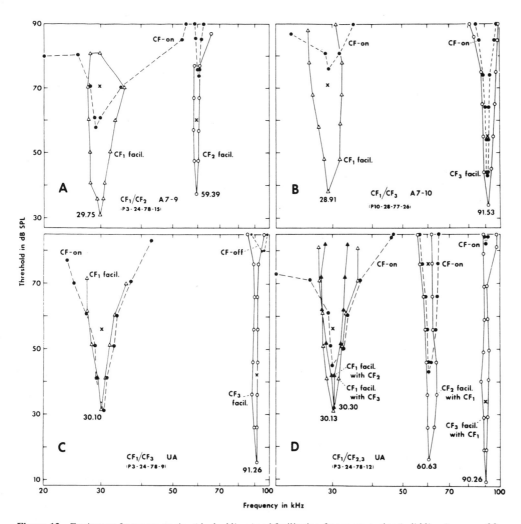

Figure 12 Excitatory-frequency-tuning *(dashed lines)* and facilitation-frequency-tuning *(solid lines)* curves of four neurons (A–D) denoting excitatory and facilitation areas. An excitatory area was measured by delivering a 34-msec-long single CF tone, while a facilitation area was measured by delivering a 34-msec-long CF tone (conditioning tone) simultaneously with another 34-msec-long CF tone (test tone) at a fixed frequency and amplitude. A: CF_1/CF_2 facilitation neuron. The test sound used to measure the CF_1 facilitation area was 59.39 kHz and 60 dB SPL; for the CF_2 facilitation area, it was 29.75 kHz and 70 dB SPL. These fixed values are indicated by the ×-marks in A. **B** and **C:** Two CF_1/CF_3 facilitation neurons. **D:** $CF_1/CF_{2,3}$ facilitation neuron. The test sounds used for the data in B, C, and D are indicated by ×-marks like those in A. Note the extremely sharp facilitation areas for CF_2 and CF_3. (From Suga et al., 1979, by permission of the AAAS.)

quency relationship between the two combined elements is critical. Frequency-tuning curves for facilitation are not particularly sharp for CF_1, but are extremely sharp for CF_2 and CF_3. The latter curves are narrow even at high stimulus levels (Figure 12). Consequently, they are called *level-tolerant* frequency-tuning curves. The tuning of many of these neurons to deviations in the frequency of CF_2 or CF_3 from an exact harmonic relationship with CF_1 suggests that their primary function is to represent the magnitude of echo Doppler shift (which can be calculated by the equations $D = CF_2 - 2CF_2$ or $CF_3 - 3CF_1$, where D is the magnitude of a Doppler shift in kHz and CF_1, CF_2, and CF_3 are best facilitation frequencies of CF_1/CF_2 and CF_1/CF_3 neurons).

The CF/CF area consists of two rostrocaudally elongated bands containing either CF_1/CF_2 or CF_1/CF_3 neurons, which are located dorsally and ventrally, respectively (Figure 9). In both bands, the best facilitation frequency of CF_1 is represented along the rostrocaudal axis, while those for CF_2 and CF_3 are represented along the dorsoventral axis (Figure 13A). (These frequency axes are based on the best facilitation frequencies of single neurons. When tonotopic representation in the CF/CF area was studied in the traditional way with single CF tones, the poor responses of the neurons to such stimuli misrepresented the nature of this area.) This frequency-versus-frequency coordinate system systematically represents Doppler-shift magnitude, that is, the DC component of a Doppler shift. Iso-Doppler-shift

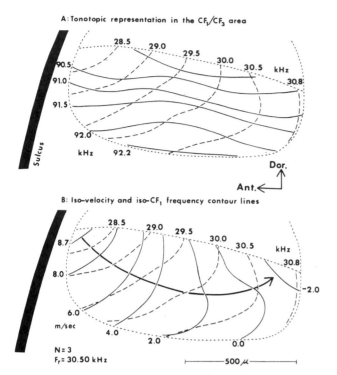

A: Tonotopic representation in the CF₁/CF₃ area

B: Iso-velocity and iso-CF₁ frequency contour lines

Figure 13 Functional organization of the CF₁/CF₃ area. **A:** Iso-best-facilitation-frequency contour lines for CF₁ *(long-dashed lines)* and CF₃ *(solid lines)*. These contour lines are based on data obtained from three unanesthetized mustached bats. **B:** Isovelocity contour lines *(solid)* are shown together with the iso-best-facilitation-frequency contour lines for CF₁ *(long-dashed)*. The long arrow is the axis representing Doppler shift, that is, target velocity (8.7 to −2.0 m/sec) in the radial direction. Note the overrepresentation of speeds of 0.0–4.0 m/sec. The figure indicates, for example, that when the bat emits an orientation sound with a CF₁ of 30.5 kHz (resting frequency), neurons in the CF₁/CF₃ area are best activated by targets moving with relative velocities of −1.2–2.0 m/sec. When the frequency of the CF₁ is reduced to 29.5 kHz, however, they are stimulated best by targets moving with relative velocities of 3.4–6.1 m/sec. Isovelocity contour lines similar to the above have also been found in the CF₁/CF₂ area. (From Suga et al., 1981.)

(isovelocity) contour lines are oblique to both frequency axes, and the velocity representation ranges from 8.7 to −2.0 m/sec (Figure 13B). Since the bat does not fly backward, the area representing velocities of 0 to −2 m/sec probably responds to echoes from insects and conspecifics flying away from the echolocating bat. Velocities of 0–4 m/sec are somewhat overrepresented. The relative speed of a target may be predominantly within this range in the approach and terminal phases of echolocation. There is also a possibility that the area tuned to 0 m/sec is for the detection of orientation sounds emitted by conspecifics because in that area the frequencies of all CF components for optimal facilitation are in exact harmonic relationship.

Since the response properties of CF/CF neurons are very important in terms of neural mechanisms for processing

complex sound, their response properties in the amplitude and time domains are summarized below. Most CF/CF neurons are tuned to particular amplitude relationships between the combined CFs (Figure 14), so they may play a role in target characterization, even though the CF signal is not particularly suited to this task. In many CF/CF neurons, a decrease in the threshold of response by facilitation is prominent. It can be as large as 76 dB, which corresponds to an approximately 6300-fold increase in sensitivity (Suga et al., 1983a,b).

CF/CF facilitation neurons are equally sensitive to 0–10 msec echo delays, and their responses to orientation sound–echo pairs are similar regardless of echo delay when it is within this range. Therefore, they are not suitable for processing distance information, unlike FM-FM neurons, which are described later. The responses of CF/CF neurons start to deteriorate when the echo delay becomes longer than 10 msec. At a delay longer than 20 msec, the facilitation becomes very poor and the facilitation threshold becomes high, even though the two signal elements still overlap significantly (Figure 11). Such response properties of the neurons act as a kind of time gate for echo processing; it is reset by the beginning of each successive orientation sound (Suga et al., 1981). The greater horseshoe bat, *Rhinolophus ferrumequinum,* performs Doppler-shift compensation only when the echo delay is less that 15 msec (Schuller, 1974). The neurophysiological data described earlier show an interesting correlation with this behavior.

Representation of the AC Component of Doppler Shift
Neurons in the DSCF area are very sharply tuned to CF₂ at particular frequencies (Figure 10; Suga and Manabe, 1982), and those in the CF/CF area are sharply tuned and respond strongly to CF₂ or CF₃ at particular frequencies only when combined with CF₁ (Figure 12). They are, therefore, suitable for processing the DC component of a Doppler shift and representing it along the frequency axis or axes (Figures 9 and 13; Suga et al., 1983a,b).

How is the AC component of a Doppler shift represented in these areas? If all or almost all neurons in the DSCF and CF/CF areas show discharges synchronized with the AC component, one may conclude that these areas represent the wing beat of an insect both by synchronous discharges of individual neurons and by synchronous changes in the locus of excitation along the frequency axis. If, on the other hand, there are neurons that are selectively sensitive to either the AC or the DC component, we must ask whether these two possible types are physically segregated. One of our hypotheses was that the DSCF area was devoted primarily to processing the AC component and the CF/CF area to processing the DC component. The data suggest, how-

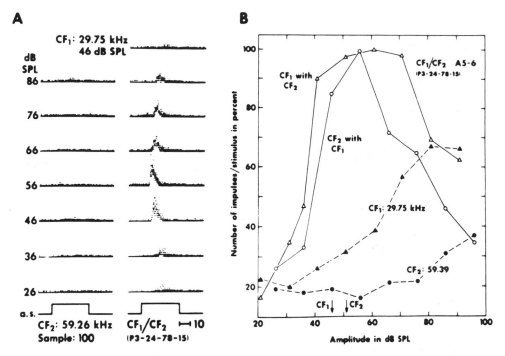

Figure 14 Impulse-count functions of a CF₁/CF₂ facilitation neuron tuned to a certain amplitude relationship between CF₁ and CF₂ components. **A:** PST histograms displaying responses of a CF₁/CF₂ facilitation neuron. The response to CF₁ alone is shown at the top of the right column. The responses to CF₂ alone and to CF₂ with CF₁ are shown in the left and right columns, respectively. The acoustic stimuli (a.s.) were 34 msec in duration and 0.5 msec in rise–decay time. The CF₁ was 29.75 kHz and 46 dB SPL; the CF₂ was 59.26 kHz and 26, 36, 46, 56, 66, 76, or 86 dB SPL. Each PST histogram shows neural activity for 100 presentations of the same sound or sounds. Note that the shortest latency and the largest magnitude of facilitation response was evoked by a 56 dB SPL CF₂ paired with the CF₁. **B:** Impulse-count functions of the CF₁ alone, CF₂ alone, CF₁ with CF₂ of 51 dB SPL, and CF₂ with CF₁ of 46 dB SPL. The number of impulses per stimulus was counted for 200 msec after the onset of the 34-msec-long tone burst delivered 100 times. The 200-msec period was long enough to include any possible change in discharge rate evoked by the stimulus. Note the importance of stimulus amplitude for maximum facilitation. The data were obtained from a lightly anesthetized mustached bat between 5 and 6 hr after Nembutal administration. (From Suga et al., 1979, by permission of the AAAS.)

ever, that both areas are concerned with the representation of both AC and DC components (Suga et al., 1983a,b).

The DSCF Area. In the DSCF area, 46% of the neurons have response properties clearly representing the wing beat of an insect through discharges synchronized with wing motion (Figure 15). In experiments, the AC component of a Doppler shift was mimicked with sinusoidal frequency modulation (SFM) of the carrier at a rate of 100 Hz. The depth of the SFM is important for good phase-locking. In 92% of these "AC-sensitive" neurons, best SFM depths ranged between 0.16 and 1.6%, which corresponded to 97.6 and 976 Hz shifts, respectively, in a 61.0-kHz carrier. The SFM depth evoked by the wing beat of an insect may commonly fall within this range. For instance, flying moths can produce a frequency shift as large as 800 Hz in a 61-kHz carrier (Goldman and Henson, 1977). Some neurons in the DSCF area are very sensitive to frequency modulations as small as 0.05% (31-Hz frequency shift in a 61-kHz carrier) occurring at a rate of 100/sec. There is no doubt that wing beat information is expressed by rhythmic changes in the discharge rate of neurons synchronous with the wing beat.

About 54% of the DSCF neurons, however, have no response properties suitable for detecting the AC component of a Doppler shift. Therefore, the DSCF area consists of two populations of neurons. These two types of neurons tend to aggregate separately in the cortical plane. The sizes and locations of the aggregates are different from animal to animal (Suga et al., 1983a,b). It is not yet known whether they are aggregated into two functional divisions for separate processing of the echoes from flying or stationary targets.

The CF/CF Area. In the CF/CF area, 35% of the neurons show clear phase-locked responses, while 65% show no or poor phase-locked responses. The spatial distribution of these two types in the CF/CF area has not yet been studied. The neurons showing clear or good responses are interesting because they require the CF₁ of the orientation sound to be paired with either the CF₂ or CF₃ of an echo (Figure 16). The depth of SFM is important for good phase-locking (Figure 17). The best SFM depth is different from neuron to neuron, ranging between 0.52 and 5.2%.

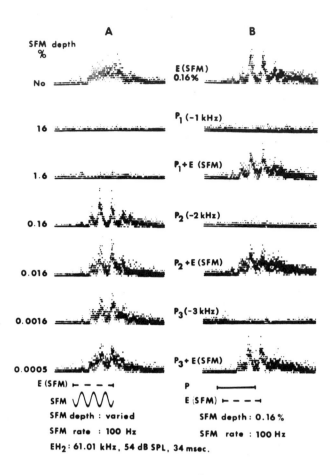

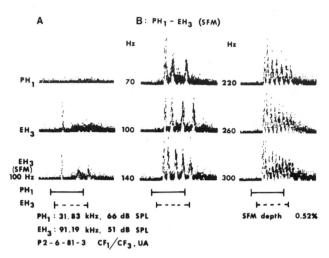

Figure 16 PST histograms displaying responses of a CF_1/CF_3 facilitation neuron to SFM sounds. **A:** From the top, responses are shown to PH_1 alone, EH_3 alone, and EH_3 with SFM. Note the very poor phase-locked response to the EH_3 with SFM. PH_1, first harmonic of a pulse *(solid bar)*; EH_3, third harmonic of an echo *(dashed bar)*. The SFM rate was 100 Hz. **B:** Responses to a PH_1–EH_3 (with SFM) pair. The SFM rates are varied from 70 to 300 Hz, indicated to the left of each histogram. Note that good phase-locked responses to the SFMs of the echo are evoked only when PH_1 is simultaneously presented. The parameters of PH_1 and EH_3 are shown at the bottom left. The duration of these signals was 34 msec. The SFM depth was 0.52%. The mustached bat was unanesthetized. (From Suga, 1983a.)

Figure 15 PST histograms displaying responses of a single DSCF neuron to AC components of Doppler-shifted echoes. **A:** Responses of a single DSCF neuron to an echo ($E = H_1 + H_2 + H_3$) alone that was sinusoidally frequency-modulated *(SFM)* at a rate of 100 Hz and at different depths from 0.0005% to 16%. The H_2 of the E was fixed at 61.01 kHz and 54 dB SPL, which were the best frequency and amplitude of the neuron, respectively. The response to the echo without the SFM is shown at the top. The best SFM depth was 0.16%. Note the absence of response to the E with a large SFM depth. **B:** The effect of pulses ($P = H_1 + H_2 + H_3$) of different fundamental frequencies (P_1, P_2, and P_3) on the response to an echo with an SFM of 100 Hz and 0.16%. In terms of the H_2 component of E, P_1, P_2, and P_3 are 1, 2, and 3 kHz lower than E, respectively. From the top, responses are shown to E with SFM alone, P_1 alone, $P_1 + E$ (with SFM), and so on as indicated. P_2 reduces the phase-locked discharges to the SFM. The properties of the carrier and SFM are specified at the bottom. Each histogram is derived from 200 responses. The animal was unanesthetized. (From Suga, 1983a.)

The rate of SFM does not appear to be critical for phase-locked responses of DSCF and CF/CF neurons. They respond well to SFMs with rates between 70 and 300 Hz, although their responses are somewhat better between 100 and 180 Hz (Figure 16).

In both the DSCF and the CF/CF areas, wing-beat information can be expressed by periodic changes in both the impulse discharges of single neurons and the location of neural activity along the frequency axis. However, the positional change in neural activity is not uniform across frequency contour lines. It is complicated because (1) some neurons are insensitive to periodic frequency modulation, (2) individual neurons are sensitive to different modulation depths, and (3) frequency modulations evoked by beating wings are also associated with amplitude modulation. Furthermore, the frequency modulations actually evoked by flying insects are far more complicated than the SFMs used in our experiments (Suga et al., 1983a,b).

As will be described, target range information is eventually represented by the location of activated neurons tuned to particular distances, that is, particular time intervals between two acoustic events, rather than by the interval between two grouped discharges evoked by an orientation sound and an echo (Suga and O'Neill, 1979). Consequently, there is also a possibility that wing-beat information is eventually expressed by a place mechanism,

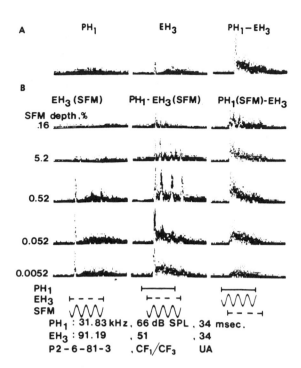

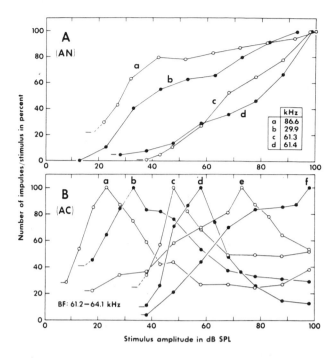

Figure 17 PST histograms displaying responses of a CF$_1$/CF$_3$ facilitation neuron to SFM sounds. **A:** Responses to PH$_1$ alone, EH$_3$ alone, and a PH$_1$–EH$_3$ pair, all without SFM. Note the facilitation of response evoked by the PH$_1$–EH$_3$ pair. **B:** The left column represents the responses to the EH$_3$s presented singly with different SFM depths from 16 to 0.0052% (indicated to the left). The center column shows the responses to PH$_1$–EH$_3$ pairs in which the EH$_3$s were frequency-modulated at different depths. Note the remarkable phase-locked responses only at the SFM depth of 0.52% and the very poor response at the SFM depth of 16%. The right column represents the responses to PH$_1$–EH$_3$ pairs in which the PH$_1$s were frequency-modulated at different depths. Note that the phase-locked response was evoked only by the SFM depth of 16% and that it was very poor. The frequency of phase-locking was double the SFM rate when the SFM depth was larger than 5.2%. The parameters of PH$_1$ and EH$_3$ are listed at the bottom. The mustached bat was unanesthetized. (From Suga, 1983b.)

Figure 18 Impulse-count functions of four single cochlear nerve fibers (**A**) and six single neurons in the DSCF area (**B**). Each normalized curve represents the number of impulses per 50-msec-long tone burst as a function of stimulus amplitude. The data are expressed as a percentage of the maximum response. The frequency of the tone burst was the best frequency of each neuron. The best frequencies or the range of best frequencies of the neurons sampled are shown in each graph. The short horizontal bar at the left end of each curve represents the level of background discharges of a given neuron. Note that the DSCF neurons are tuned to particular stimulus amplitudes. (From Suga and Manabe, 1982.)

in which activated neurons respond selectively to sounds with particular SFM depths and rates. We have not found such neurons in either the DSCF or CF/CF area. Perhaps another cortical area is specialized for processing wingbeat information.

Representation of the Subtended Target Angle in the DSCF Area

The size of a target is determined by its range and subtended angle (Figure 1C). Target range is directly related to echo delay, whereas subtended target angle is largely related to echo amplitude, although several other factors are also involved. For simplicity, we may consider that the representation of the subtended target angle is equivalent to the representation of echo amplitude.

At the periphery, auditory neurons increase the number of impulses per stimulus monotonically with the stimulus

amplitude up to amplitudes of over 80 dB in some neurons (Figure 18A, line b). There is no anatomical basis for the representation of echo amplitude. In the DSCF area, however, neurons are tuned to amplitude as well as frequency (Figures 18B and 19). They respond maximally to particular preferred stimulus amplitudes (best amplitudes) and are systematically arranged according to their best amplitudes, forming a circular amplitude axis (Figure 20). The representation of stimulus amplitude by the location of activated neurons is called *amplitopic representation* (Suga, 1977). The overlap of inhibitory areas with the excitatory area produces not only a sharper excitatory area, but also a particular amplitude-sensitivity curve (Figure 10; Suga, 1965b, 1977). The neural mechanisms for amplitopic representation are systematic changes in both the extent of lateral inhibition and the minimum threshold for excitation (Suga and Manabe, 1982).

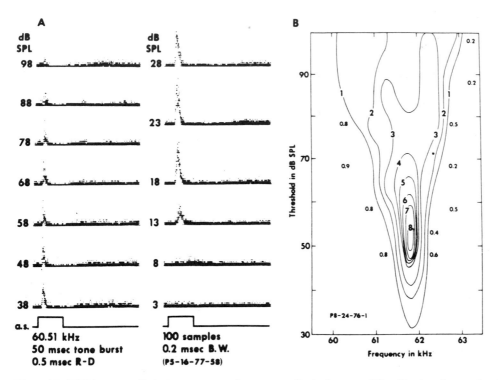

Figure 19 PST histograms displaying nonmonotonic responses of a single neuron (**A**) and iso-impulse-count contours of another single neuron (**B**) in the DSCF area. **A**: The acoustic stimulus *(a.s.)* was a 50-msec-long tone burst of 60.51 kHz, which was the best frequency of this neuron. The amplitude of the tone burst is indicated by the figure to the left of each PST histogram. The minimum threshold and best amplitude of the neuron were 8 and 23 dB SPL, respectively. Each histogram represents the response of the neuron to an identical stimulus delivered 100 times at a rate of 1.5/sec. Note the clear inhibition following the on-response at stimulus levels higher than 28 dB SPL. Nonmonotonic responses result from lateral inhibition (Suga, 1982). **B**: Iso-impulse-count contours of a single neuron tuned to a sound of 51 dB SPL and 61.8 kHz. Numbers indicate the numbers of impulses evoked by 50-msec-long tone bursts. (From Suga and Manabe, 1982.)

Since the DSCF area has frequency versus amplitude coordinates, it can express the amplitude spectrum of a sound through the spatial pattern of neural activity. This amplitude-spectrum representation is apportioned according to the biological importance of the sound; the DSCF area overrepresents a sound of 61.5–62.0 kHz and 30–50 dB SPL. Lateral inhibition is associated with the sharpening of excitatory areas and the production of amplitude selectivity, and probably enhances the contrast of the amplitude-spectrum representation in the DSCF area (Suga and Manabe, 1982).

Representation of Target Range in the FM-FM Area
The primary cue for target ranging is the delay of the echo from the emitted orientation sound. At the periphery, the echo delay (target range) is encoded by the interval between the responses of neurons to the orientation sound and the echo. There are no anatomical components or locations representing range information. In the FM-FM area, however, most neurons respond poorly or not at all to the orientation sound or the echo presented separately, but respond vigorously to orientation sound–echo pairs with specific echo delays between 0.4 and 18 msec (Figures 21A and 22). As such, they are sensitive to particular target ranges (O'Neill and Suga, 1979, 1982; Suga and O'Neill, 1979; Suga et al., 1978).

Two classes of range-sensitive neurons were found: tracking and range-tuned neurons. In tracking neurons, the best echo delay (best delay), that is, the best target range (best range), for response to an echo following the orientation sound becomes shorter and delay-tuning becomes narrower when the repetition rates of paired sounds increase and the durations of individual sounds become shorter, as in the biosonar signals emitted during target-directed flight (Figure 23A). Because of these changes in response, tracking neurons are not suited to processing target range information. But they are suited to tracking a target, and can respond continuously to an echo from an approaching target while simultaneously rejecting echoes from more distant objects that are also approaching but are not the targets of primary interest. This type of neuron is rare in the FM-FM area.

In range-tuned neurons, best delay is constant regardless of the repetition rate and duration of a pair of sounds;

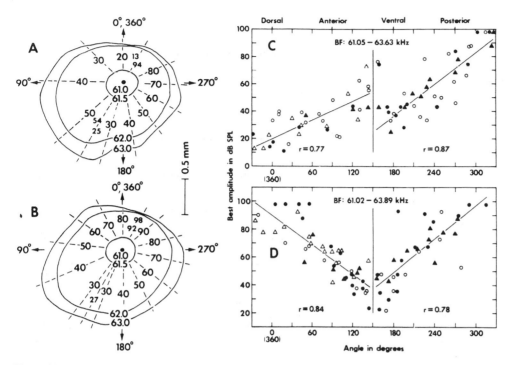

Figure 20 Amplitopic representation in the DSCF area. **A** and **B**: The largest circle represents the boundary of the DSCF area, in which the iso-best-frequency (*BF*) and iso-best-amplitude (BA) contours are shown by solid and dashed lines, respectively. The BF in kilohertz and BA in decibels of SPL are shown respectively by three-digit and two-digit numbers. The averaged BA contour maps are composed from the data shown in C and D. The contours for 64.0 kHz, not shown, are just outside the ventral part of the 63.0 kHz contour. It should be noted that the BF and BA contour maps of individual bats are not as regular as the average ones. **C** and **D**: Each graph shows data obtained from four bats, indicated by four different symbols. The ordinates represent BAs in decibels of SPL and the abscissas represent the angles around the center of the DSCF area in degrees. The angle is expressed counterclockwise, starting from the dorsal part of the DSCF area (see A and B). The correlation coefficient (*r*) is shown below each regression line. The BF range of neurons sampled is also shown in each graph. The amplitopic representations in C and D are called N- and V-types, respectively. Thus far, 6 animals have shown the N-type and 12 the V-type. (From Suga, 1977.)

consequently, they respond to the target only when it is within a certain narrow fixed range (Figures 22, 23B, and 24). Range-tuned neurons are specialized for processing echoes from targets at particular ranges. They are predominant in the FM-FM area and are arranged systematically according to their best ranges. Thus they form a neural axis representing target ranges of 7–310 cm (Figure 25). This is called *odotopic representation*. Target ranges between 50 and 140 cm are overrepresented by the FM-FM area, and best range varies at a rate of 2.0 cm per neuron along the range axis. Neurons tuned to distances of more than 200 cm are relatively few (Figure 25), and appear to take a limited role in ranging because of their broad delay-tuning curves (Figure 23B). Several species of bats show the first sign of the approach phase of echolocation at a distance of about 2.3 m for a wire obstacle of 0.3 cm diameter (Grinnell and Griffin, 1958); they can discriminate distance differences of 1.2–2.5 cm (Simmons, 1971). Our neurophysiological data thus show an interesting correlation with behavioral data.

About 25% of FM-FM neurons are tuned to echo delays shorter than 4 msec (69 cm target range) and respond vigorously to each such orientation sound-echo pair when the pairs are delivered at a rate of 100/sec (Figure 22C). Therefore, the auditory cortex is involved in information processing even during the terminal phase of echolocation.

For the excitation of range-sensitive neurons, the essential elements in the orientation sound-echo pairs are the first harmonic FM component (FM_1) in the orientation sound and one or more higher harmonic FM components (FM_{2-4}) in the echo. CF components have no significant effect on the excitation of FM-FM neurons (Figure 21A). Neurons responding to (or examining) FM_1–FM_3, FM_1–FM_4, or FM_1–FM_2 pairs form three major clusters that are arranged in a dorsal to ventral fashion in almost all brains studied. Odotopic representation has been demonstrated in each cluster (Figure 25).

Since the response properties of FM-FM neurons are very important with regard to overall neural mechanisms for processing complex sound, their response properties in the frequency and amplitude domain are summarized

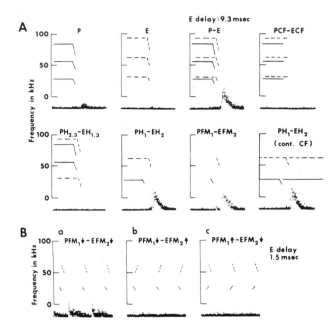

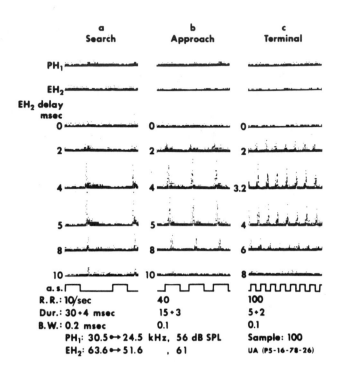

Figure 21 **A and B:** PST histograms displaying the responses of single FM₁–FM₂ facilitation neurons to pulse *(P)*, echo *(E)*, and pulse-echo *(P − E)* pairs of different harmonic complexity. Above each PST histogram is the schematized sonagram of the delivered stimulus. Solid lines represent P and its components; dashed lines represent E and its components. CF and FM durations were 30 and 4 msec, respectively. The essential components for facilitation were PFM₁ and EFM₂. Therefore, the neuron showed facilitation of response to P–E, PH₁–EH₂, and PFM₁–EFM₂ pairs, but no facilitation to any other complex sound that did not contain both PFM₁ and EFM₂. The histogram at the bottom right of A shows that the facilitation evoked by the PFM₁–EFM₂ pair was not masked by two continuous CF tones. There was a strong facilitative response to PFM₁–EFM₂ when both FMs were sweeping down from high to low frequency like those in natural sounds (panel *a* in B). However, there was no response when the stimulus consisted of a downward-sweeping PFM₁ and an upward-sweeping EFM₂ (panel *b* in B) or an upward-sweeping PFM₁ and a downward-sweeping EFM₂ (panel *c* in B). Note that the frequencies swept in b and c were the same as shown in a. EFM₂ was delayed by 9.3 msec (A) or 1.5 msec (B) from PFM₁; these were the best delays for these neurons. The repetition rate of the paired stimuli was 3/sec (A) or 40/sec (B). The frequency sweep and amplitude of PFM₁ were 31.2 to 25.2 kHz, 56 dB SPL in A and 30.2 to 24.2 kHz, 47 dB SPL in B. The frequency sweep and amplitude of EFM₂ were 62.3 to 50.3 kHz, 38 dB SPL in A and 63.7 to 51.7 kHz, 42 dB SPL in B. The number of presentations for each PST was 200. The data were obtained from unanesthetized bats. (From Suga et al., 1983b.)

Figure 22 PST histograms of responses of an FM₁–FM₂ facilitation neuron to PH₁–EH₂ stimulus pairs as a function of echo delay. Stimuli were delivered at repetition rates and durations simulating the search (**A,** 10/sec and 34 msec long), approach (**B,** 40/sec and 18 msec long), and terminal phases (**C,** 100/sec and 7 msec long). The top two PSTs in each column show the responses to the PH₁ and EH₂, which are essential harmonics in the P-E pair for facilitation, presented alone. All other PSTs show the responses to pairs of PH₁ and EH₂ sounds at various echo delays. Maximal responses occurred at 3.2–4.0 msec echo delay at each repetition rate. Beneath each column is shown a time marker (*a.s.*) of the PH₁ in the stimulus or stimulus pair. R.R., repetition rate of stimulus; Dur., duration of the CF and FM components in milliseconds; B.W., bin width of the PST histograms in milliseconds; Sample, number of stimulus repetitions presented for each PST histogram. UA indicates an unanesthetized preparation. Frequency and amplitude of essential harmonics are given at the bottom in kilohertz and decibels of SPL. (From O'Neill and Suga, 1982.)

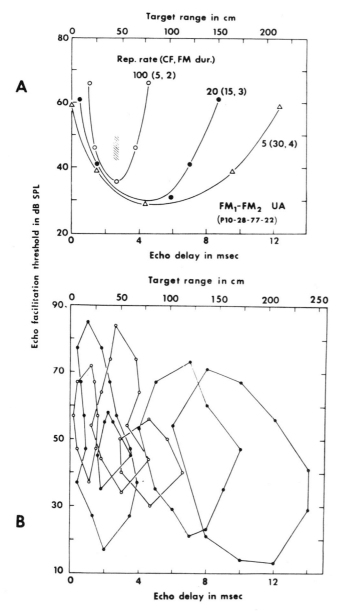

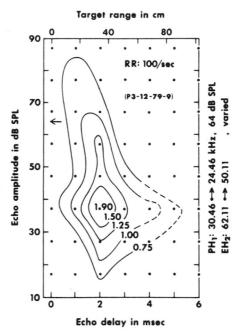

Figure 24 Iso-impulse-count contours representing the response magnitude of a range-tuned neuron (FM_1–FM_2 facilitation) plotted on coordinates of echo amplitude versus echo delay (or target subtended angle versus target range). The outermost contour line (0.75 impulses per paired stimulus) represents the delay-tuning curve when the definition of threshold is an echo evoking a just noticeable response (about a 20% increase above the background discharge rate). When the definition is changed to 1.0 impulse per paired stimulus, the delay-tuning curve shrinks as indicated by the 1.0 line, and similarly for other thresholds. This neuron is tuned to a target located 34 cm in front of the bat that returns an echo of 37 dB SPL. Since the neuron was tuned to a target a short distance away, the pulse-echo pair for this plot was delivered at a rate of 100/sec, mimicking the terminal phase of target-directed flight. The essential components for excitation were the H_1 of the pulse (PH_1) and the H_2 of the echo (EH_2). PH_1 consisted of a 5-msec CF of 30.46 kHz followed by a 2-msec FM sweeping from 30.46 to 24.46 kHz, at an amplitude of 64 dB SPL. EH_2 consisted of a 5-msec CF of 62.11 kHz followed by a 2-msec FM sweeping from 62.11 to 50.11 kHz, at an amplitude that was varied in increments of 10 dB. Note that the maximum response was evoked when the EH_2 was Doppler-shifted by 1.19 kHz. This Doppler shift is one that could be generated by the relative motion of a target at a speed of 3.4 m/sec. Individual dots indicate where an average number of impulses per paired stimulus was obtained by presenting the identical paired stimulus 200 times. The contour lines are drawn on the basis of these data points. The dashed parts of the contour lines indicate where the response to each paired stimulus was not reliably observed because of background noise associated with animal movement. The bat was not anesthetized. (From Suga and O'Neill, 1979, by permission of the AAAS.)

Figure 23 Delay(range)-tuning curves of FM-FM facilitation neurons recorded from unanesthetized mustached bats. **A:** A tracking neuron (FM_1–FM_2 facilitation) shows broad delay-tuning with echo facilitation thresholds of 29–30 dB SPL and best delays of 3.8–5.0 msec (target range, 65–85 cm) for search *(open triangles)* and early approach *filled circles)* phases. During the terminal phase *(open circles)*, the delay-tuning curve becomes much narrower, the threshold increases to about 36 dB SPL, and the best delay shortens to about 2.5 msec (43 cm distance). The orientation sound (P) was fixed, but the echo (E) was varied in amplitude and delay. The essential elements in the P–E pair for facilitation were PFM_1 and EFM_2. The repetition rates of the paired stimuli and the durations of the CF and FM components in each harmonic for the three different phases are shown near the individual curves. For instance, "100 (5,2)" means that the repetition rate was 100 pairs/sec and the CF and FM durations were 5 and 2 msec, respectively. The shaded area indicates the best echo amplitude for facilitation in the terminal phase. (From Suga et al., 1978.) **B:** Delay-tuning curves of seven range-tuned

→

neurons measured at stimulus repetition rates of either 40/sec *(filled circles)* or 100/sec *(open circles)*. These curves demonstrate that populations of delay-tuned neurons can parcel out echo delays, that is, target ranges. The smaller the best delay, the narrower are the delay-tuning curves. The elliptical delay-tuning curves indicate that the neurons are tuned not only for echo delay but also for echo amplitude. They show absolutely no facilitation of response to strong echoes. (From O'Neill and Suga, 1982.)

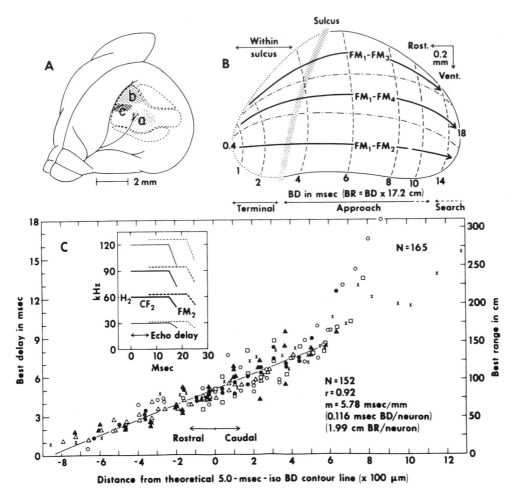

Figure 25 Odotopic representation in the FM-FM area. **A:** The left cerebral hemisphere of the mustached bat. The large auditory cortex *(dotted lines)* contains at least three areas specialized for processing biosonar information: *a,* DSCF; *b,* FM-FM; and *c,* CF/CF. The branched lines are arteries. There is a sulcus below the largest branch. **B:** The FM-FM area consists of three major clusters of delay-sensitive neurons: FM_1–FM_2; FM_1–FM_3; and FM_1–FM_4 facilitation neurons. Each cluster shows odotopic representation. Iso-best-delay contours and range axes are schematically shown by dashed lines and solid arrows, respectively. Best delays *(BDs)* of 0.4 and 18 msec correspond to best ranges *(BRs)* of 7 and 310 cm, respectively. Range information in the search, approach, and terminal phases of echolocation is represented by neural activity at different locations on the cerebral hemisphere. **C:** Relationship between BD and distance along the cortical surface. The data were obtained from six cerebral hemispheres, indicated by six different symbols. The regression line represents an average change in BD with distance along the cortical surface. Since the 5-msec iso-BD contour line always crosses the central part of the FM-FM area along the exposed surface of the cortex, the 5msec BD on the regression line is used as a reference point to express distance. The slope of the regression line corresponds to 0.12 msec BD per neuron, that is, 1.99 cm BR per neuron. Note that the time axis of the FM-FM area is used for representating the time interval between two acoustic events. The inset in C is a schematized sonagram of an orientation sound and a Doppler-shifted echo in the approach phase of echolocation. All the data were obtained from unanesthetized bats. (From Suga and O'Neill, 1979, by permission of the AAAS.)

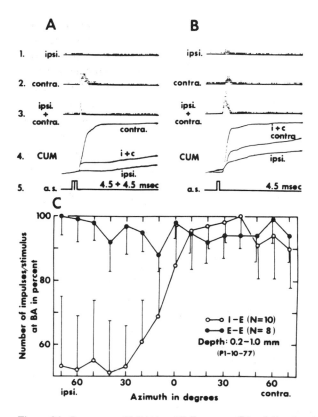

Figure 26 Responses of I-E (A) and E-E neurons (B) and directional sensitivity curves of neurons in I-E and E-E columns (C) in the DSCF area. **A** and **B:** Each PST histogram represents the sum of responses of a single neuron to an identical tone burst or an identical pair of tone bursts delivered 50 times. *1, 2,* and *3* are, respectively, the PST histograms of responses to the ipsilateral, contralateral, and ipsilateral-plus-contralateral stimuli; *4* shows cumulative *(CUM)* histograms of the responses above; *5* shows the envelopes of full-wave-rectified acoustic stimuli *(a.s.).* In 3, the ipsilateral and contralateral stimuli were delivered successively (A) or simultaneously (B). The ipsilateral and contralateral stimuli were, respectively, 64.59 kHz–68 dB SPL and 64.46 kHz–38 dB SPL (A) and 62.27 kHz–28 dB SPL and 62.27 kHz–43 dB SPL (B). The duration of the tone bursts was 4.5 msec. **C:** Impulses per stimulus discharged by either I-E or E-E neurons as a function of azimuth. The stimulus was fixed at the best frequency and best amplitude of each neuron. The best frequency and best amplitude were determined with 50-msec-long tone bursts delivered from the loudspeaker placed in front of the animal. Each circle and vertical line represents the mean and standard deviation. The number of neurons studied between 0.2 and 1.0 mm in depth was 10 in the I-E column *(open circles)* and 8 in the E-E column *(filled circles).* (From Manabe et al., 1978, by permission of the AAAS.)

below. Most FM-FM neurons are optimally excited by a positively Doppler-shifted echo FM, but display broad frequency-tuning to FM sounds. Therefore, these neurons have poor resolution of target velocity information. Some FM-FM neurons are excited only when the FM signals sweep downward, as in natural orientation sound emission (Figure 21B; Suga et al., 1983a,b). [In the inferior colliculus of the little brown bat, *Myotis lucifugus,* there are different types of neurons in terms of responses to CF tones, FM sounds, and noise bursts. Some "FM-specialized" neurons respond only to downward-sweeping FM sounds (Suga, 1968, 1969). Complex response properties of some FM-FM neurons can be explained by interaction among such FM-specialized neurons.]

Delay-tuning curves of most FM-FM neurons are elliptical because they do not show facilitation in response to intense echoes (Figures 23B and 24). They *are* facilitated by particular amplitude relationships between the two FM sounds, so it is possible that they play an important role in target characterization. The FM_1 best amplitudes for facilitation are clustered somewhat around 63 dB SPL, whereas FM_2, FM_3, and FM_4 best amplitudes for facilitation show large variations among neurons. In many FM-FM neurons, facilitation causes a large decrease in threshold up to intensities of 89 dB, which corresponds to an increase in sensitivity of up to 28,000-fold (Suga et al., 1983a,b).

FM_1–FM_4 range-sensitive neurons are theoretically better suited for the fine characterization of small targets than FM_1–FM_2 range-sensitive neurons, because FM_4 has a much shorter wavelength and a broader bandwidth than FM_2. Most range-sensitive neurons are tuned not only to a specific echo delay, but also to a particular echo amplitude (Figure 24). These neurons respond best to targets with particular cross-sectional areas at particular distances (Figure 1D). Furthermore, FM-FM neurons respond best when echoes are Doppler-shifted by approaching targets, as has been described. The response properties of these neurons are, as a result, quite complex (O'Neill and Suga, 1979, 1982; Suga and O'Neill, 1979; Suga et al., 1983a,b). The functional organization of the FM-FM area and the response properties of range-sensitive neurons suggest that the distribution of neural activity perpendicular to the *range* axis within the cortical plane represents the fine structure (amplitude spectra) of all the FM components of an echo including target characteristics such as shape and size.

Representation of Target Characteristics

One of the important target characteristics that insectivorous bats must determine is whether the target, such as a flying insect, is fluttering or stationary. A fluttering target can be represented by the spatiotemporal change in neural activity synchronized with wing fluttering or by the responses of neurons that are insensitive to the carrier itself but sensitive to the frequency modulation caused by wing fluttering. In the DSCF and CF/CF areas, the spatiotemporal pattern of neural activity changes synchronously with flutter, as described above. We have not yet thoroughly examined the second possibility, although we know that the auditory system contains FM-specialized neurons that respond selectively to FM sounds (Suga, 1973).

Other target characteristics such as shape and size are more related to the fine structure of the echo FM than to the echo CF. The amount of information carried by a signal increases with the width of the frequency band. Therefore, target characteristics are theoretically best represented in the area where the FM signals are processed. Neurons in the FM-FM area, you will recall, are tuned to particular echo amplitudes, most probably to particular amplitude spectra of the FM components of an echo. Since wavelength is shorter for higher harmonics, FM_1–FM_4, FM_1–FM_3, and FM_1–FM_2 neurons are theoretically better suited to, in that order, fine characterization of small targets. The distribution of neural activity along the axis perpendicular to the range axis may represent target characteristics (Figure 9B).

Representation of Auditory Space

Interaural amplitude (intensity) and time (phase) differences systematically vary with azimuth and are cues for sound localization in the horizontal plane. For sound localization in the vertical plane, the pinna, which modifies the waveform of an acoustic signal containing higher frequencies, is essential (Batteau, 1967). In many species of bats, the tragus is large and sticks up in front of the external auditory meatus. The importance of the tragus in vertical sound localization has recently been demonstrated (Lawrence and Simmons, 1982).

The auditory system has no sensory epithelium upon which the auditory space in front of an animal is projected. For systematic representation of auditory space, the central auditory system must "create" neurons that are sensitive to binaural cues and to the cues provided by the pinnae, and must systematically arrange them according to the values characterizing their tuning to these cues. Owls are superb in localizing sound sources and have an auditory space map in the midbrain (Knudsen and Konishi, 1978). Echolocating bats have specialized hearing and may also have such a map.

Two Types of Binaural Neurons in the DSCF Area.
Since the DSCF area is disproportionately large, one might ask whether there is a functional organization above and beyond the frequency versus amplitude coordinates. Almost all neurons in this area are excited by contralateral

stimuli and are either excited or inhibited by ipsilateral stimuli. Such cells are called E-E and I-E neurons, respectively (Figure 26A,B). Each electrode penetration orthogonal to the auditory cortex is characterized not only by best frequency and amplitude, but also by E-E or I-E binaural interaction or binaural interaction that varies systematically with depth. Thus the DSCF area consists of at least three types of binaural columns. E-E neurons are poorly directional and are equally sensitive to all sound sources in front of the animal between left 30° and right 30°. On the other hand, I-E neurons are directionally sensitive, being tuned to particular contralateral angles between 29° and 42° (Figure 26C). E-E neurons or columns are located mainly in the area corresponding to low best amplitudes, whereas I-E neurons or columns are distributed mainly in the area corresponding to high best amplitudes (Figure 9B). In other words, neurons more sensitive to weak echoes integrate (or even multiply) signals from both ears for the effective detection of a target. Neurons sensitive to stronger echoes, on the other hand, are suitable for processing directional information about a target. Thus, the DSCF area not only has coordinates of frequency versus amplitude, but also consists of two functional subdivisions, one suitable for target detection and the other for target localization (Manabe et al., 1978). (It should be noted that the E-E and I-E neuron clusters are actually the bands across the iso-best-frequency contour lines and that such organization has also been found in the cat's auditory cortex.) The best azimuths of I-E neurons are, on the average, 36° contralateral (standard deviation: 4.2°, $n = 16$). There is no systematic representation of azimuth within the I-E neuron cluster.

Distribution of Best Azimuths of Neurons in the DM and VP Areas.
The dorsomedial (DM) and ventroposterior (VP) areas are parts of the nonprimary auditory cortex (Figure 9A). Neurons in the DM area are mainly tuned to sounds between 80 and 110 kHz, and those in the VP area are tuned to 80- to 115-kHz sounds and/or 55- to 61-kHz sounds (Figure 7). These neurons are sensitive to particular directions between contralateral 4° and 46° in azimuth and between 20° down and 10° up in elevation. In the DM area, best azimuths (BAZs) of neurons change with their loci in the cortical plane somewhat systematically (Figure 27A). In the VP area, such a change in BAZ is also noticed, although it is less systematic than in the DM area. In both the areas, best elevations (BELs) of neurons are not related to their cortical loci.

The directional sensitivity curves of DM neurons in terms of threshold are so broad that it is not certain whether the DM area actually has an azimuth axis important for sound localization. Directional sensitivity curves in terms of impulse count, however, are sharply tuned to particular

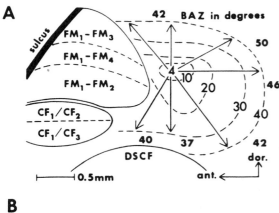

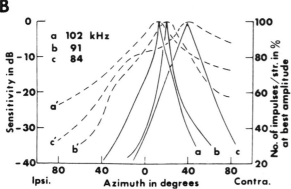

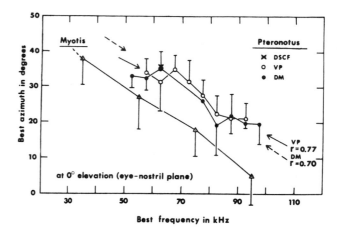

Figure 27 Distribution of best azimuths *(BAZs)* of neurons along the surface of the dorsomedial (DM) area of the mustached bat auditory cortex (A) and directional sensitivity curves of three DM neurons (B). **A:** Iso-BAZ contours are somewhat circular, representing the contralateral auditory field from 4° to 40° in azimuth. The azimuth axis is radial. The BAZs were measured with tone bursts at the best frequencies of individual neurons. The higher the best frequency, the smaller the BAZ. The DM area shares borders with the DSCF, FM-FM, and CF/CF areas. **B:** Directional sensitivity curves based on threshold *(dashed lines)* are broadly tuned to particular azimuths. Directional sensitivity curves based on number of impulses per stimulus *(solid lines)* are sharp. These solid curves were obtained by delivering a tone burst fixed at the best frequency and best amplitude of the individual neuron measured at 0° azimuth. (From Kujirai and Suga, 1983.)

azimuths when these are measured with a tone burst at the best amplitude of each neuron (Figure 27B). The BAZs of neurons with regard to the number of impulses may vary with stimulus amplitude. The conclusion that the DM area has an azimuth axis is thus a tentative one (Kujirai and Suga, 1983).

The distribution of BAZs is similar to that of best frequencies. There is a clear tendency for higher best frequencies to be associated with smaller BAZ degrees (Figure 28). Such a relationship has also been found in the little brown bat, *Myotis lucifugus* (Figure 28; Shimozawa et al., 1974).

Azimuthal-Motion-Sensitive Neurons in the VP Area. When an echo source moves in azimuth rather than in elevation or in depth (distance), the interaural amplitude (intensity) and time (phase) differences change

Figure 28 The relationship between best frequencies and best azimuths of neurons in DSCF, ventroposterior *(VP)*, and dorsomedial *(DM)* areas of the auditory cortex of the mustached bat. The mean and standard deviations of the best azimuth are expressed by a symbol *(x-mark, or open circles,* or *filled circles)* and a bar. The higher the best frequency, the smaller the best azimuth. The correlation coefficient *(r)* is 0.77 for the VP neurons and 0.70 for the DM neurons (Kujirai and Suga, 1983). The data obtained from the little brown bat, *Myotis lucifugus (triangles),* show the same relationship as those obtained from the mustached bat. (From Shimozawa et al., 1974.)

markedly. In the VP area of the auditory cortex (Figure 9A), neurons have been found that are sensitive to a sound (echo) source moving in azimuth at tested speeds of 3–30°/sec, but not to motion in the vertical plane or in depth. These azimuthal-motion-sensitive neurons respond weakly to acoustic stimuli delivered from a stationary loudspeaker and show a very broad frequency-tuning curve. When the loudspeaker is moved in azimuth, however, their responses become vigorous and tonic and their response thresholds lower by 3–55 dB (Figure 29). They do not respond to the azimuthal movement of a silent loudspeaker. These neurons are presumably sensitive to a change in interaural amplitude difference produced by the moving loudspeaker.

For a tone burst delivered from a loudspeaker moving sinusoidally in azimuth at a rate of 0.5/sec and with a peak-to-peak amplitude of 10°, azimuthal-motion-sensitive neurons show broad frequency-tuning curves that frequently show low thresholds at the frequencies of the CF components in echoes (Figure 29C). They are thus suitable for detection of a moving sound source, that is, a target moving relative to the bat. Azimuthal-motion-sensitive neurons show no facilitation response to combinations of elements in biosonar signals, so they do not process echoes in relation to an emitted orientation sound (Figure 29B).

At one point in our research, we recorded several azimuthal-motion-sensitive neurons in three bats. Thereafter, however, we somehow could not record the same type

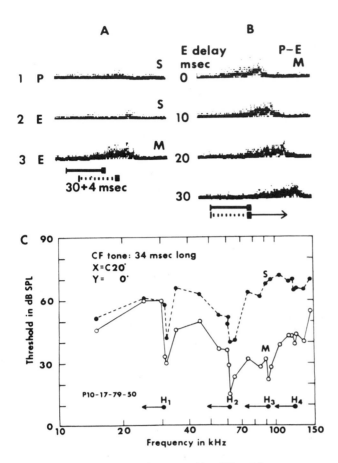

Figure 29 PST histograms of responses (A and B) and frequency-tuning curves (C) of an azimuthal-motion-sensitive neuron. **A:** 1 and 2 respectively represent poor responses to a stationary loudspeaker *(S)* delivering either an orientation sound *(P, solid bar at the bottom)* or an echo *(E, dashed bar at the bottom);* 3 represents a strong response to a moving loudspeaker *(M)* delivering the echo. Note the long latency of response and the gradual increase in the magnitude of response as the echo is delivered from the moving sound source. **B:** The response to the echo from the moving loudspeaker is not affected by the orientation sound from the stationary loudspeaker, regardless of echo delay *(0, 10, 20,* and *30 msec).* In A and B, the durations of the CF and FM components of the stimuli were 30 and 4 msec, respectively. The CF_1s of the orientation sound and the echo were 29.65 and 30.32 kHz, and their amplitudes were 70 and 49 dB SPL, respectively. Each histogram is the sum of the responses to 200 identical stimuli. C: Excitatory frequency-tuning curves (excitatory areas) of an azimuthal-motion-sensitive neuron measured with a 34-msec-long CF tone delivered from either a stationary *(S)* or moving *(M)* loudspeaker. The loudspeaker was placed at 20° contralateral and 0° elevation when it was stationary. 0° elevation includes the eye-nostril line. When it was moved, its azimuthal location varied sinusoidally from contralateral 15° to 25° at a rate of 0.5/sec. The threshold for the moving sound source *(open circles)* is much lower than for the stationary one *(closed circles)* at higher frequencies. The frequencies of four harmonics *(H_{1-4})* in the orientation sound are indicated by closed circles (CF components) and arrows (FM components). Note the lowest threshold at the frequency of the CF component of H_2.

of neuron. Because of this, we wondered whether such neurons actually do exist or whether they were an artifact. Azimuthal-motion-sensitive neurons have been found in the cat's primary auditory cortex (Sovijärvi and Hyvärinen, 1974), but it is not yet known whether they are clustered within a particular part of the cortex.

Representation of Overall Biosonar Images in the Cerebral Cortex

As reviewed above, different types of biosonar information related to different attributes of a target are represented in different functional subdivisions of the auditory cortex. Our present research is on the origin and destination of biosonar information represented in these subdivisions. The problem of destination is related directly to the problems of what the upper limit in specialization (complexity of response properties) of a single neuron is and how the overall target image is recognized by the brain.

For recognition of acoustic signals, information about signals should be stored in the brain and should be compared with incoming signals, that is, the acoustic signals should, theoretically, be cross-correlated with stored information. In our electrophysiological studies, we have measured the filter properties of auditory neurons by varying biologically important parameters. That the neurons can be treated as filters is a theoretical advantage, since a filter acts as a kind of cross-correlator. Auditory neurons are filters that correlate acoustic signals with their filter properties, that is, stored information, and the degree of correlation is expressed by the magnitude of the output of the filters. In other words, neurons are maximally excited only when the properties of acoustic signals perfectly match their filter properties. All neurons in the auditory system, including peripheral ones, act as filters. Specialized neurons expressing the outputs of neural circuits tuned to particular information-bearing parameters (IBPs) may be called "IBP filters" (Suga, 1979). (An IBP is that limited part of a continuum that carries information important for the species in nature. A particular IBP can be quite different in its biological significance for different species of animals.)

One of our working hypotheses is that the recognition of the overall acoustic image is directly related to the spatio-temporal patterns of neural activity occurring within the DSCF, CF/CF, and FM-FM areas. An alternative hypothesis is that recognition is directly related to neural activity in a special area in which the outputs of all the subdivisions specialized for processing different types of biosonar information are integrated. If all the possible combinations of different types of biosonar information listed in Figure 1D have to be represented in such an integration area, it would have to be large and have multiple dimensions.

Accordingly, it can hardly exist in the brain. If there is such an integration area, it must be organized to represent the overall acoustic image in a categorical manner.

To examine these two hypotheses, neuroanatomy has been incorporated with neurophysiology. Tritiated amino acid or horseradish peroxidase injected into either the DSCF or FM-FM area indicates that these areas are connected differently with several other areas of the brain (Fritz et al., 1981; Olsen, 1982). The DSCF area receives most of its ascending input from a distinct dorsomedial part of the ventral division of the ipsilateral medial geniculate body (MGB). The DSCF area projects ipsilaterally to the MGB and pontine motor nuclei and bilaterally to the amygdala, which is crucial for prey imaging and feeding. The corticocortical connections are very sparse.

The FM-FM area receives a heavy projection from the dorsal division and the ventromedial part of the ventral division of the ipsilateral MGB. It projects bilaterally to the dorsal fringe area, the ventrolateral nonprimary auditory cortex, and the pericentral and external nuclei of the inferior colliculus (Figure 30). It projects ipsilaterally to the superior colliculus, the pretectal nucleus, and the pontine motor nuclei. The FM-FM area is reciprocally connected with the contralateral FM-FM area and the ipsilateral claustrum. The parts of the pontine nuclei that receive a projection from the FM-FM area are different from the parts that receive a projection from the DSCF area.

Thus far, the system for processing target velocity information seems separated from that for processing target range information. It is not yet known whether there is an area or a nucleus where the integration of these two eventually takes place.

We have been studying some of the target areas of the FM-FM area electrophysiologically. The dorsal fringe (DF) area contains FM-FM facilitation neurons and has a time axis (Suga, 1983). Part of the ventrolateral nonprimary auditory cortex also contains FM-FM neurons (Asanuma et al., 1983), and there are also FM-FM neurons in the claustrum (D. Wong et al., unpublished data). The response properties of all of these FM-FM neurons are similar to those in the FM-FM area, except that facilitation within the non-FM-FM areas is less prominent and fluctuates more than it does within the FM-FM area. Therefore, we have increased the complexity of the acoustic stimuli in our experiments. We have used complex acoustic stimuli mimicking a series of biosonar signals and echoes during target-directed flight, but we have not yet found any further specialization in the response properties of neurons beyond that already established for neurons in the FM-FM area. We do believe, however, that different clusters of FM-FM neurons must be related to different functions. At the present stage of our research, we are inclined to think that, as far as the cerebral hemisphere is concerned, the spatiotemporal pattern of neural activity occurring in the different subdivisions of the auditory cortex is related to the recognition of the overall target image.

Protection of the Cortical Representation of Biosonar Information from Jamming by Orientation Sounds of Conspecifics

Many species of microchiropterans are colonial. Hundreds or even thousands of bats roost in a single cave. They are frequently found in narrow, elongated passages where they must fly in opposite directions without colliding. One of

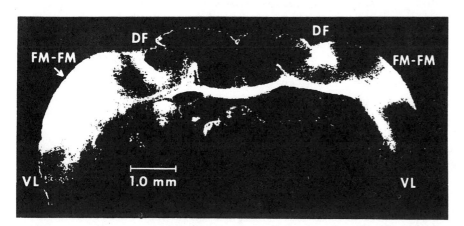

Figure 30 Frontal sections of the mustached bat's brain after an injection of tritiated amino acids (proline and leucine) into the left FM-FM area *(arrow)*. Terminal labeling is found in the dorsal fringe area *(DF)* and a part of the ventrolateral area *(VL)* of the nonprimary auditory cortex in both hemispheres. It is also found in the contralateral FM-FM area. In the right hemisphere, labeled fibers projecting to the VL area are clearly shown. (From E. G. Jones, S. P. Wise, and N. Suga, unpublished data.)

the important problems in echolocation is how bats are protected from the jamming effect of biosonar sounds produced by conspecifics. More specifically, how is the cortical representation of biosonar information protected from the jamming effect? We can enumerate seven possible mechanisms for the reduction of jamming: (1) the sharp directionality of the orientation sound; (2) the sharp directional sensitivity of the ear and binaural hearing; (3) the signature of orientation sounds used by individual bats; (4) auditory time gates; (5) heteroharmonic combinations; (6) the sequential processing of echoes; and (7) efferent copy originating from the vocalization system. All these mechanisms could work simultaneously for successful echolocation. Three mechanisms (nos. 3, 4, and 5) are related to our experiments on the DSCF, FM-FM, and CF/CF areas, and have been discussed in our previous review articles (Suga et al., 1981, 1983a,b).

The resting frequencies of the CF_2 components of the orientation sounds ranged between 59.80 and 62.00 kHz (mean and standard deviation: 60.87 ± 0.48 kHz) in 77 bats from a single location in Panama. Such differences in frequency may function as signatures of individuality and thereby reduce jamming. Interestingly, tonotopic representation in the DSCF area also differs between individuals and matches their CF_2 resting frequency. For example, when a bat's resting frequency is about 60.5 kHz, its DSCF area typically represents frequencies between 60.5 and 62.5 kHz. On the other hand, if the resting frequency is about 61.5 kHz, the DSCF area represents frequencies mainly between 61.5 and 63.5 kHz (Suga and O'Neill, 1980; Suga et al., 1983a,b). Additional quantitative studies on these signatures remain to be performed.

The auditory time gate for sampling echoes and for excluding sounds produced by conspecifics is another mechanism for the reduction of jamming. Neurons in the FM-FM area act as a kind of auditory time gate because they are tuned to particular echo delays between 0.4 and 18 msec. Likewise, neurons in the CF/CF area show clear facilitation of response only when the echo delay is shorter than 20 msec. Thus, the bat's auditory cortex has an echo acceptance gate that opens at the beginning of each emitted orientation sound and closes after a short period of time. The duration of this auditory time gate is shorter in range-tuned neurons with short best delays than in those with long best delays. In tracking neurons, it becomes shorter at higher rates and shorter durations of orientation sound (Suga et al., 1978; O'Neill and Suga, 1979). Therefore, the duration of the auditory time gate in the FM-FM area can vary during target-directed flight.

In the past, we thought that biosonar information was obtained by processing the stronger harmonics in the echo in relation to the corresponding harmonics in the emitted

sound (Figure 31A,B). We did not expect to find that one of the critical components for excitation of neurons in the FM-FM and CF/CF areas was the first harmonic the weakest component, in the orientation sound. One functional role of the sensitivity of FM-FM and CF/CF neurons to heteroharmonic combinations is to reduce jamming by sounds produced by conspecifics in echolocation (Suga and O'Neill, 1979). For a better understanding of this mechanism, consider the following two hypothetical cases. When the energy of the first harmonic is not radiated at all, but rather is dissipated by bone conduction, the bone-

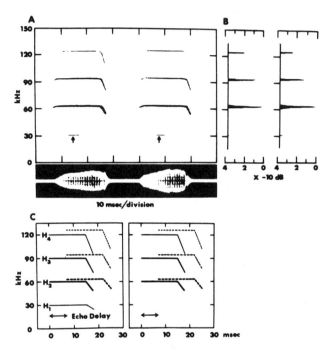

Figure 31 Sonagrams of orientation sounds (biosonar signals or pulses) emitted by the mustached bat flying in a hallway 8.5 feet high, 7 feet wide, and 60 feet long. **A:** Sonagram *(upper figure)* and envelope *(lower figure)* of two orientation sounds. Since the faint harmonics were hardly evident in the original sonagram, they were retouched. These sounds were recorded with a Brüel & Kjaer microphone (4135), Hewlett-Packard amplifier (465), and Ampex tape recorder (FR 100; 60 inches/ sec tape speed). The microphone was placed at the center of the hallway. The sounds were analyzed with a Kay spectrum analyzer (7030A) after a reduction of tape speed for playback down to 7.5 inches/sec. **B:** The amplitude spectra of the CF components *(arrows in A)* of the sounds shown in A. The first harmonic is the weakest of the four harmonics (about 35 dB weaker than the second harmonic), but it is one of the essential signal elements for facilitation of responses of CF/CF and FM-FM neurons. **C:** Schematized sonagram of two orientation sound-echo pairs. When the bat emits an orientation sound, the first harmonic stimulates the animal's own ears by bone conduction, causing the CF/CF and FM-FM neurons to be conditioned to respond to an echo with an appropriate amount of Doppler shift or delay *(left sonagraph)*. If the first harmonic is not radiated at all *(right sonagraph)*, no combination of orientation sounds and/or echoes produced by conspecifics would evoke a facilitation response in CF/CF and FM-FM neurons of the bat that hears such sounds. H_{1-4} are the first to fourth harmonics.

conducted first harmonic stimulates the cochleae and conditions neurons in the FM-FM and CF/CF areas to be excited by echoes returning with short time delays. It is thus essential for the facilitation response of these neurons that the animal itself produce an orientation sound. The combinations of components produced by conspecifics do not excite these neurons (Figure 31C) and as a result, jamming of echolocation by conspecifics is reduced. In the opposite condition, when the first and higher harmonics are equally intense in the emitted sound, there is no such reduction of jamming. The first harmonic of the sound used by the mustached bat falls between these two extreme situations, because it is broadcast to some extent (Figure 31A,B). Therefore, the reduction of jamming in this species by heteroharmonic combinations is not ideal.

For echolocation, bats emit strong orientation sounds. If such sounds strongly stimulated their ears, detection of echoes from targets at short distances would be impaired. Consequently, the protection of echo detection from jamming caused by self-vocalized sounds is important for echolocation. Since different species of bats use different types of orientation sounds, they have different mechanisms specialized for the attenuation of vocal self-stimulation and for the detection of biosonar information (Suga, 1981b).

Protection of the neural representation of auditory information from noise is not a problem special to echolocation, but a problem common to all acoustic communication. Some of the mechanisms enumerated above have been considered to be important for detection of communication sounds in the midst of noise.

"Parallel–Hierarchical" Processing

In mammals, any auditory signal carried by the cochlear nerve fibers ascends from the cochlear nucleus to the auditory cortex of the cerebrum through many intermediate nuclei. At each level of the central auditory system, the auditory signal is represented in several places because of multiple projections from the cochlea. These multiple levels and multiple projections indicate that different types of auditory information or different attributes of the signal are processed both hierarchically and in parallel. Furthermore, the properties of complex acoustic signals and the auditory information carried by them dictate that processing of complex sounds should be both parallel and hierarchical.

In the mustached bat, for instance, velocity information carried by the CF component of biosonar signals and range information carried by the FM component should be processed in parallel, because the CF and FM components differing in frequency stimulate different portions of the basilar membrane. Velocity information carried by the CF_2

component is processed in one of the subsystems that is disproportionally large from the cochlea through the auditory cortex. As summarized in this article, different types of biosonar information are represented in different areas of the cerebral cortex, and the representation of certain types of information in the FM-FM and CF/CF areas is based on the complex response properties of combination-sensitive neurons. Therefore, cortical representation must be the result of *parallel–hierarchical processing*. (In lower auditory nuclei such as the dorsal cochlear nucleus and the pericentral nucleus of the inferior colliculus, specialized neurons similar to those observed at higher levels may yet be found. Such a finding, however, would not necessarily contradict this notion, because these lower nuclei receive efferent nerve fibers originating in the higher auditory nuclei.)

An important question, then, is the extent to which biosonar information carried by complex sounds is processed by subcortical auditory neurons. For amplitopic representation, it is absolutely necessary to have neurons tuned to particular stimulus amplitudes. Such "nonmonotonic" neurons are common in the inferior colliculus (Grinnell, 1963; Suga, 1965a) and even in the cochlear nucleus; they have an excitatory area sandwiched between inhibitory areas (Suga et al., 1975). Thus neurons of the type necessary to produce amplitopic representation are in the subcortical nuclei, but amplitopic representation has not yet been demonstrated in these nuclei.

To accommodate Doppler-shift representation, the brain should have a neural circuit that integrates responses of neurons tuned to two different frequencies and evokes facilitation of response. It is not yet known whether subcortical nuclei have neurons comparable to CF/CF neurons or are organized by frequency-versus-frequency coordinates. Interesting preliminary data, however, have recently been obtained from the mustached bat: (1) Some inferior collicular neurons are tuned to two harmonically related frequencies, but they do not show facilitation of response to paired stimuli (W. E. O'Neill, personal communication); and (2) some medial geniculate neurons show facilitation of response when two elements in the complex biosonar signals are delivered together (Olsen and Suga, 1983). These data suggest that complexity in the response properties of neurons increases in higher auditory nuclei.

For odotopic representation, the brain should have a neural circuit to facilitate responses to echoes following orientation sounds with particular delays. The response properties of FM-FM neurons are quite complex; they are tuned not only to a particular echo delay, but also to a particular echo amplitude. Some FM-FM neurons respond only to a combination of downward-sweeping FM sounds. Doppler shift is also influential in their excitation. Such response properties are not readily explained by interaction among primary and primarylike auditory neurons. It is also unlikely that these properties have resulted from neural interaction taking place only within the auditory cortex; they are most likely the result of neural interaction in various subcortical areas.

Responses of subcortical neurons to FM sounds have been studied best in the inferior colliculus of the little brown bat, *Myotis lucifugus,* which emits short FM sounds for echolocation (Suga, 1965a, 1968, 1973). Experiments were performed with three types of acoustic stimuli that mimicked the basic properties of the three types of information-bearing elements found in sounds produced by many different species of animals, including humans. These three are CF tones (comparable to formants), FM sounds (comparable to transitions), and noise bursts (NB, comparable to fills). The little brown bat has three types of neurons, each of which is specialized to respond selectively to one type of stimulus: CF-, FM-, and NB-specialized neurons (Suga, 1969).

FM-specialized neurons (about 3% of inferior collicular neurons) respond primarily or exclusively to FM sounds. For instance, an FM-specialized neuron has no excitatory area for CF tones, but it responds to downward-sweeping FM sounds. The neuron may not respond at all to upward-sweeping FM sounds and noise bursts, regardless of their amplitudes, or it may be more sensitive to upward-sweeping FM sounds than to downward-sweeping ones (Figure 32D). In other neurons the preferred sweep direction varies with sweep range (Figure 32E). For the excitation of FM-specialized neurons, the direction, range, speed, and functional form of the frequency sweep are very important factors. Since some FM-specialized neurons show the best response to FM sounds similar to orientation sounds, the brain obviously has neurons specialized for selective response to species-specific orientation sounds and their echoes (Suga, 1965a, 1968). Why do FM-specialized neurons respond selectively to FM sounds in spite of the absence of an excitatory area? The lack of excitatory response of the FM-specialized neurons to a CF tone stimulus does not indicate a complete lack of reaction. When a CF tone is delivered prior to a downward-sweeping FM sound, the response to the FM sound is inhibited. By changing the frequency and amplitude of the CF tone, it is possible to measure the area within which the response to the FM sound is inhibited. Interestingly, each of the FM-specialized neurons has a large inhibitory area and responds to an FM sound sweeping across this area. In other words, stimulation of the inhibitory area with the FM sound excites the neuron (Figure 32D–F). Although seemingly paradoxical, this result can be explained by a neural network model of disinhibition (Suga, 1965b, 1973).

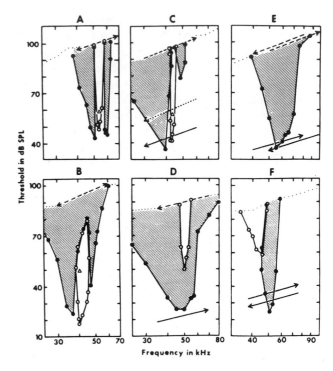

Figure 32 Excitatory *(unshaded)* and inhibitory *(shaded)* areas and thresholds for FM sounds *(arrows)* of six inferior collicular neurons (A–F) of the little brown bat, *Myotis lucifugus.* **A:** A CF-specialized neuron. **B:** A CF-specialized neuron with an upper threshold. **C:** An asymmetrical neuron that responded to downward-sweeping but not to upward-sweeping FM sounds. **D–F:** Three FM-specialized neurons that responded vigorously to FM sounds, but did not respond or responded poorly to CF tones. The excitatory areas were measured with 4-msec-long single tones. The inhibitory areas were measured with a conditioning tone (4 msec long) delivered immediately prior to a test sound (4 msec long) that was fixed in frequency and amplitude. The conditioning tone within the inhibitory areas inhibited the responses to the test sounds, which were CF tones in A–C *(triangles)* and FM sounds in D–F. The uppermost dotted line shows the frequency-response curve of the condenser loudspeaker. The arrow shows the direction and range of frequency sweep of a 4-msec-long FM sound. The threshold of a neuron for this sound is represented by the vertical position of the solid arrow. If a neuron did not respond to an FM sound at any amplitude, it is shown by a dashed arrow on the frequency-response curve of the loudspeaker. If a neuron showed an upper threshold for an FM sound, it is shown by a dotted arrow. (From Suga, 1965a, 1968, 1969.)

Other interesting neurons with respect to responses to FM sounds are the asymmetrical neurons (about 21% of inferior collicular neurons), which have an excitatory area and a large inhibitory area. Their responses to FM sounds sweeping across the excitatory area depend on the sequence in which the excitatory and inhibitory areas are stimulated by the sounds. Thus, they are sensitive to a particular direction of frequency sweep (Figure 32C).

CF-specialized neurons (about 9% of inferior collicular neurons) have a very narrow excitatory area sandwiched between large inhibitory areas. They do not respond to FM sounds swept across the excitatory area because the sounds always stimulate both the excitatory and the inhibitory areas. These neurons also fail to respond to a noise burst that simultaneously stimulates these two areas (Figure 32A,B). The properties of these neurons can be easily explained by a neural network model of lateral inhibition (Suga, 1965b, 1973).

Briefly summarized, the inferior colliculus contains different types of neurons specialized for responding to particular types of signal elements. The population of such specialized neurons is much larger in the auditory cortex than it is in the inferior colliculus (Suga, 1965b). Neural network models that explain the response properties of FM-specialized neurons consist of either asymmetrical neurons (Suga, 1965a, 1973) or asymmetrical and CF-specialized neurons. The response properties of some FM-FM facilitation neurons may be explained by neural network models consisting of FM-specialized neurons. In the mustached bat, FM-FM facilitation neurons have recently been found in the MGB (Olsen and Suga, 1983), but they have not yet been found in the inferior colliculus, which contains FM-sensitive or FM-specialized neurons (O'Neill, 1983). We hypothesize, therefore, that hierarchical processing is incorporated within subsystems for parallel signal processing. In this sense, signal processing in the auditory system is parallel–hierarchical.

Auditory Information Sent to the Vocalization System

The echolocation system is an acoustic communication system specialized for communication with the environment. It consists of the auditory and motor systems. The activity of the vocalization system is modified by the auditory information carried by echoes. The mustached bat changes the frequency of the CF component of its orientation sound depending on the frequency of a Doppler-shifted echo (target relative velocity) and changes the rate and duration of its sound emission depending on echo delay (target range). Very little is known, either anatomically or physiologically, about how the auditory system is coupled

to the vocalization system, but some findings that are interesting enough to be studied further are described below.

The vocalization center for the emission of orientation sounds appears to be in the midbrain, because only electrical stimulation of the lateral part of the central gray matter or the dorsal part of the reticular formation in the midbrain can elicit species-specific orientation sounds (Suga et al., 1973). Interestingly, the orientation sounds elicited by electrical stimulation of the vocalization center become louder when a masking sound is delivered. Such a "vocal response" is strongest in response to a sound that most closely resembles an important component in the orientation sound (Figure 33).

The changes in electrically evoked vocalization in the presence of acoustic stimuli indiate that the bat may have attempted to echolocate with the electrically evoked sounds. When the acoustic stimuli were delivered, echoes from objects in front of the bat (e.g., a loudspeaker) may have been masked. The animal may have increased the amplitude and the number of orientation sounds in order to detect echoes, thus overcoming the masking sound. In this situation, the vocal response to the masking sound should theoretically be related to the properties of the sound, the information-bearing elements in the emitted CF-FM signals, and the properties of the auditory neurons used for echo analysis. The tuning curve for the vocal response is very sharp, and centered at about 62 kHz. The threshold for downward-sweeping FM sounds is much lower than that for upward-sweeping FM sounds. These properties of the vocal response indicate that the response is mediated by two particular types of auditory neurons, one with a very narrow tuning curve centered at about 62 kHz, and the other with a greater sensitivity to downward-sweeping FM sounds than to pure tones or upward-sweeping FM sounds (Suga et al., 1974).

Specialized Neurons for Information Processing

During the past 20 years, auditory neurons specialized for responding to particular types of acoustical stimuli have been found in neurophysiological studies of various species (see review articles by Suga, 1973, and Symmes, 1981). In most of these studies, four major weaknesses are apparent: (1) The filter properties of specialized neurons defining their selectivity and level tolerance were not examined, so that the evidence supporting specialization was not strong; (2) the proportion of specialized neurons in the total population of neurons studied was usually so small that their significance was questionable; (3) the neural representation of biologically important signal variations by specialized neurons was unexplored or unclear; and (4) the locations of individual types of specialized neurons

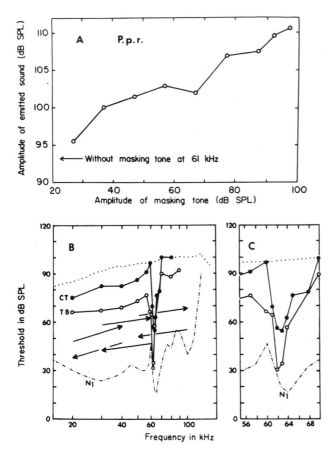

Figure 33 Vocal responses of the mustached bat to masking sounds.
A: Electrically elicited orientation sounds from the mustached bat
(P.p.r., Pteronorus parnelli rubiginosus) increase in amplitude when the
amplitude of 61.0-kHz masking tone bursts is increased. This is called
the "vocal response." The arrow indicates the amplitude of the electrically elicited sounds in the absence of masking tone bursts. To elicit vocalization, a short train of electrical pulses was applied to the dorsal part
of the midbrain reticular formation near the boundary between the inferior and superior colliculi. Each masking tone burst was 2.0 msec long
and was delivered at a rate of 250/sec. **B:** Thresholds of vocal responses
to different types of masking sounds. TB, threshold curve of the vocal
response to 2.0-msec long CF tone bursts (masking tone) delivered at a
rate of 250 pulses/sec; CT, threshold curve of the vocal response to a
continuous CF tone (masking tone). Each arrow indicates the direction
of the frequency sweep in a 2.0-msec-long FM sound (masking sound)
by its head, the range of the frequency sweep by its length, and the
threshold of the vocal response to the FM sound by its vertical position.
A threshold curve for N_1 response is also presented for comparison
(dashed lines). The uppermost dotted line indicates the frequency-
response curve of the loudspeaker. **C:** A section of the threshold curves
in B is shown on an expanded frequency axis. Note differences in
threshold among responses to different types of masking sounds. (From
Suga et al., 1974.)

were not identified, so that it was not possible to examine
their response properties further or to determine their anatomical connections.

These weak points have been overcome in the studies on
the auditory cortex of the mustached bat. Among our findings, the following are essential in understanding the neural
processing of complex acoustic signals in general:

1. Complex acoustic signals are processed by specialized
neurons that are tuned to particular IBPs or combinations
of IBPs. These neurons may be thought of as IBP filters that
act as cross-correlators.

2. Different types of IBP filters are clustered separately in
identifiable areas of the cerebral cortex.

3. Within each cluster, IBP filters differ from one another
in tuning properties and are arranged to represent IBPs
systematically. Thus, they form an axis or coordinate system within the cluster.

4. More significant parts of an IBP are overrepresented
by larger numbers of IBP filters within the cluster for higher
resolution.

5. IBP filters have particular bandwidths; that is, different
specialized neurons can be activated by stimuli that have
different values of IBPs. Therefore, each signal is expressed by the spatiotemporal pattern of activity of many
specialized neurons.

Biological signals commonly show some variation. If
such signal variation is biologically important, it should be
clearly represented by the auditory system. Determining how
biologically important signal variations are represented by
neurons specialized for responding to particular types of
acoustic signals has been a problem. The DSCF, FM-FM,
and CF/CF areas each contain neurons tuned to different IBP
values characterizing a particular signal variation. These
neurons (IBP filters) are arranged to represent systematically
a particular signal variation by the spatial distribution of
neural activity. Thus, one answer to the question of why
different types of neurons are grouped in separate clusters is
that the separate clustering of different types of neurons is
necessary for the systematic representation of biologically
significant signal variations; systematic representation in
each cluster can be easily incorporated with lateral inhibition
for increased contrast in the representation. Systematic representation of an IBP is based on the neural networks needed
to produce an array of specialized neurons tuned to individual
values of IBPs, and may yield an advantage in the interfacing
of the sensory system with the motor system by reducing the
complexity of wiring.

Generalization of the Neural Mechanisms Found in the Mustached Bat

In the mustached bat, the majority of the auditory cortex is devoted to processing biosonar infomation. There are, however, significantly large areas whose functions have not yet been elucidated. Since this species forms large colonies and uses several different types of complex sounds for communication, we expect that some cortical areas are devoted to processing communication sounds. In order to generalize the neural mechanisms for processing complex sound found in the mustached bat to other species, data comparable to those reviewed here need to be obtained for other animals. Unfortunately, such data are not yet available.

In humans, the dominant cerebral hemisphere contains areas specialized for the recognition and production of speech sounds. Since there is an obvious limitation on neurophysiological studies of the human brain, several attempts have been made to explore the functional organization of the cerebral auditory cortex for processing complex sounds in cats and monkeys. There has been, however, only slight success beyond discovering tonotopic representation in these animals. Functional organization beyond tonotopic representation has thus far been explored successfully only in animals with remarkably specialized acoustic behavior: the mustached bat and the barn owl (Knudsen and Konishi, 1978). The data obtained from these animals indicate that the auditory system has evolved for effective processing of auditory information important for each species. Therefore, the functional organization of the cerebral speech areas in humans could not be explored without direct studies. Insight, however, can be obtained from comparative studies on those animals that use complex acoustic signals and are specialized in acoustic behavior. The elements of sounds used by bats for echolocation and communication are clearly analogous to those used by other animals for communication, although the bat's sounds are different from the others in frequency and biological significance. Therefore the studies of the bat auditory system will promote our understanding of the neural processing of complex communication sounds in general.

The sonogram of a vowel shows several formants (CF components), which are called F_1, F_2, and F_3, the lowest frequency being F_1. Vowels are recognized by combinations of F_1, F_2, and F_3. The formant frequency varies among speakers to some extent, and this variation is biologically important. Vowels are thus expressed by identifiable loci or areas on the coordinates of F_1 versus F_2 frequencies and F_1 versus F_3 frequencies (Figure 34C). Does the human brain have such coordinates, enabling it to represent vowels by the loci of the activated neurons? We have no answer

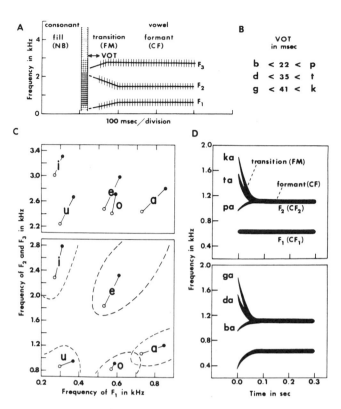

Figure 34 Information-bearing elements in human speech sounds. **A:** A schematized sonagram of a monosyllabic sound shows four types of information-bearing elements: the fill or noise-burst component (NB); transition or frequency-modulated component (FM); formant or constant-frequency component (CF); and the voice-onset time (VOT) or time interval between two acoustic events. F_1, F_2, and F_3 are the first, second, and third formants, respectively. **B:** The phonetic boundary of VOT is 22 msec for the consonants "b" and "p," 35 msec for "d" and "t," and 41 msec for "g" and "k." For example, when the VOT is shorter than 22 msec, a monosyllabic sound is recognized as "ba." When it is longer than 22 msec, however, it is recognized as "pa." (Based on Lisker and Abramson, 1964.) **C:** The relationship among the frequencies of the first, second, and third formants of five vowels (a, e, i, o, and u). The average frequencies of the formants are different between male (open circles) and female (filled circles) speakers. The areas surrounded by dashed lines in the lower figure represent formant frequencies for unanimous classification of vowels by listeners. (Based on Peterson and Barney, 1952.) **D:** Schematized sonagrams of monosyllabic sounds: "a" changes into "pa" or "ta" or "ka" through addition of different FM components to F_2; "pa," "ta," and "ka" respectively become "ba," "da," and "ga" through addition of an FM component to F_1. (Based on Liberman et al., 1957.)

to this question, but we can point out that the CF/CF area of the mustached bat's brain has such frequency-versus-frequency coordinates for representing the information carried by a pair of CF signals. In terms of neural mechanisms, it is not important at all whether these CF signals are harmonically related or not or whether their frequencies are ultrasonic or not, because CF/CF neurons are tuned to particular combinations of two activated locations along a tonotopic axis.

For the recognition of many nonvowel phonemes and combinations of phonemes (e. g., words), transitions (FM components) are very important. When an FM component is added to the F_2 of "a," for instance, the sound is perceived as either "pa," "ta," or "ka," depending on the properties of the FM component. When a second FM component is added to the F_1 of "a," it is recognized as either "ba," "da," or "ga" (Figure 34D). This example demonstrates that combinations of FM components or, more generally, combinations of information-bearing elements are very important for speech recognition. Does the human brain have several aggregates of neurons that are specialized for examining different combinations of information-bearing elements? We cannot answer this question, but we can point out that the brain of the mustached bat contains several aggregates of combination-sensitive neurons that are systematically arranged in each aggregate to represent a certain type of auditory information. It should be noted that the functional organization of each aggregate is subject to an important principle: More important and more frequently occurring information or combinations of signal elements are represented by larger numbers of neurons. Voice-onset time (VOT) is a very important cue for the discrimination of voiced consonants from voiceless consonants (Figure 34B). Does the human brain have a neural axis to represent VOTs? Again, we cannot answer this question, but we can point out that the FM-FM area of the mustached bat's brain has a time axis to express the time interval between two acoustic events.

The data obtained from the auditory cortex of the mustached bat constitute the first strong neurophysiological support for the hypothesis that complex speech sounds are processed by neurons examining combinations of information-bearing elements in the sounds. The data that have been accumulated in my laboratory will be very valuable for comparative neuroanatomy and the neurophysiology of hearing. They will enable us to show the possible upper limit in the specialization of the auditory system for processing certain types of auditory information, and to suggest particular experiments for exploration of neural mechanisms of speech processing in the specialized auditory system of humans.

Epilogue

A Note on Hemispheric Asymmetry. In the mustached bat, a large proportion of the auditory cortex is devoted primarily to processing biosonar information (Figure 9). Therefore, one might ask whether one hemisphere is devoted to processing biosonar signals and the other to processing communication sounds. There is no sign of such asymmetry; what has been found in one hemisphere has also been found in the other. However, hemispheric asymmetry or difference in the shapes, sizes, and locations of functional areas does exist. For instance, the distributions of best FM frequencies and best delays for facilitation of FM-FM neurons are not the same between the left and right FM-FM areas of a single bat (Figure 35).

Acknowledgments

This work has been supported by research grants from the National Science Foundation and the Public Health Service (the current PHS research grant is RO1-NS-17333). I thank my past and present coworkers for their contributions to the research on mustached bats: A. Asanuma, J. Horikawa, P. Jen, K. Kujirai, T. Manabe, W. E. O'Neill, H. Niwa, J. Ostwald, T. Shimozawa, J. A. Simmons, I. Taniguchi, and D. Wong.

References

Asanuma, A., D. Wong, and N. Suga (1983) Frequency and amplitude representations in anterior primary auditory cortex of the mustached bat. *J. Neurophysiol.* **50**:1182–1196.

Batteau, D. W. (1967) The role of the pinna in human localization. *Proc. R. Soc. Lond. [Biol.]* **168**:158–180.

Evans, E. F., H. F. Ross, and I. C. Whitfield (1965) The spatial distribution of unit characteristic frequency in the primary auditory cortex of the cat. *J. Physiol. (Lond.)* **179**:238–247.

Fenton, M. B. (1980) Adaptiveness and ecology of echolocation in terrestrial (aerial) systems. In *Animal Sonar Systems*, R. G. Busnel and J. F. Fish, eds., pp. 427–446, Plenum, New York.

Fritz, J. B., J. Olsen, N. Suga, and E. G. Jones (1981) Connectional differences between auditory fields in a CF–FM bat. *Soc. Neurosci. Abstr.* **7**:391.

Goldman, L. J., and O. W. Henson, Jr. (1977) Prey recognition and selection by the constant frequency bat, *Pteronotus p. parnellii. Behav. Ecol. Sociobiol.* **2**:411–419

Goldstein, M. H., Jr., M. Abeles, R. L. Daly, and J. McIntosh (1970) Functional architecture in cat primary auditory cortex: tonotopic organization. *J. Neurophysiol.* **33**:188–197.

Grinnell, A. D. (1963) The neurophysiology of audition in bats: intensity and frequency parameters. *J. Physiol. (Lond.)* **67**:38–66.

Grinnell, A. D., and D. R. Griffin (1958) The sensitivity of echolocation in bats. *Biol. Bull. (Woods Hole)* **114**:10–22.

Henson, M. M. (1973) Unusual nerve-fiber distribution in the cochlea of the bat *Pteronotus p. parnellii* (Gray). *J. Acoust. Soc. Am.* **53**:1739–1740.

Henson, O. W., Jr., M. M. Henson, J. B. Kobler, and G. D. Pollack (1980) The constant frequency component of the biosonar signals of the bat, *Pteronotus parnellii parnellii.* In *Animal Sonar Systems,* R. G. Busnel and J. F. Fish, eds., pp. 913–916, Plenum, New York.

Imig, T. J., M. A. Ruggero, L. M. Kitzes, E. Javel, and J. F. Brugge (1977) Organization of auditory cortex in the owl monkey *(Aotus trivirgatus). J. Comp. Neurol.* **171**:111–128.

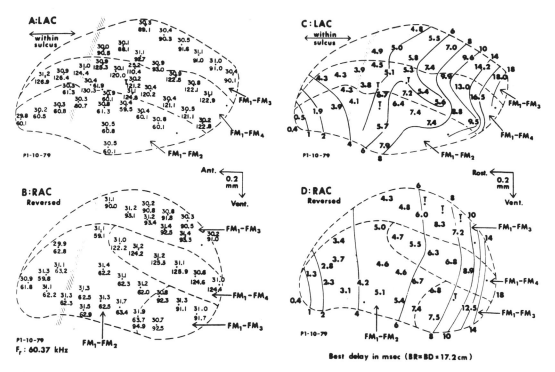

Figure 35 Distributions of best facilitative frequencies (A and B) and best delays (C and D) of FM_1–FM_n facilitation neurons in the tangential plane of the FM-FM areas in the left (*LAC;* see Figure 9) and right *(RAC)* hemispheres of a single mustached bat. For ease of comparison, the RAC is reversed to appear similar to the LAC. Each filled circle represents the projected recording site of neural responses. **A** and **B:** The pair of numbers around each filled circle represents the starting frequencies of the pair of best FM stimuli for facilitation. (The starting frequencies are the same as the frequencies of the CF components that would be associated with the FM components for best facilitation.) Suggested borders of separate clusters containing either FM_1–FM_2, FM_1–FM_3, or FM_1–FM_4 facilitation neurons are derived not only from the data presented in this chapter, but also from several other comparable studies. The area to the left of the hatched bar represents an unfolded view of the area within the sulcus separating the temporal cortex from the frontal cortex. No systematic tonotopic representation is apparent (Suga et al., 1983). **C** and **D:** The numbers represent the best delays *(BDs)* of the neurons whose best FM sounds for facilitation are shown in A and B. Iso-BD contours are drawn by interpolating between recording sites on the maps to indicate how BD increases in the rostrocaudal direction in each hemisphere and within each cluster. Note the disproportionately large area representing BDs of 2–8 msec. BR, best range. (From O'Neill and Suga, 1982.)

Kaas, J. H., M. Sur, and J. T. Wall (1981) Modular segregation in monkey somatosensory cortex. *Trends Neurosci.* **4**:13–14.

Katsuki, Y., T. Watanabe, and N. Maruyama (1959) Activity of auditory neurons in upper levels of brain of cat. *J. Neurophysiol.* **22**:343–359.

Knudsen, E. I., and M. Konishi (1978) A neural map of auditory space in the owl. *Science* **200**:795–797.

Kujirai, K., and N. Suga (1983) Tonotopic representation and space map in the non-primary auditory cortex of the mustached bat. *Auris Nasus Larynx* **10**:9–24.

Lawrence, B. D., and J. A. Simmons (1982) Echolocation in bats: the external ear and perception of the vertical positions of targets. *Science* **218**:481–483.

Liberman, A. M. (1957) Some results of research on speech perception. *J. Acoust. Soc. Am.* **29**:117–123.

Lisker, L., and A. S. Abramson (1964) A cross-language study of voicing in initial stops: acoustical measurements. *Word* **20**:384–422.

Long, G. R., and H. U. Schnitzler (1975) Behavioral audiogram from the bat, *Rhinolophus ferrumequinum. J. Comp. Physiol.* **100**:211–219.

Manabe, T., N. Suga, and J. Ostwald (1978) Aural representation in the Doppler-shifted-CF processing area of the primary auditory cortex of the mustached bat. *Science* **200**:339–342.

Merzenich, M. M., and J. F. Brugge (1973) Representation of the cochlear partition on the superior temporal plana of the macaque monkey. *Brain Res.* **50**:275–296.

Merzenich, M. M., P. L. Knight, and G. L. Roth (1975) Representation of cochlea within primary auditory cortex in the cat. *J. Neurophysiol.* **38**:231–249.

Mountcastle, V. B. (1957) Modality and topographic properties of single neurons of cat's somatic sensory cortex. *J. Neurophysiol.* **20**:408–434.

Novick, A., and J. R. Vaisnys (1964) Echolocation of flying insects by the bat, *Chilonycteris parnellii. Biol. Bull. (Woods Hole)* **127**:478–488.

Olsen, J. F. (1982) The tonotopic organization of the auditory geniculocortical and corticopontine projections in a CF-FM bat. *Soc. Neurosci. Abstr.* **8**:349.

Olsen, J. F., and N. Suga (1983) Combination-sensitive neurons in the auditory thalamus of the mustached bat. *Soc. Neurosci. Abstr.* **9**:768.

O'Neill, W. E. (1983) Response properties and disproportionate representation of FM sensitive neurons in the inferior colliculus of the CF-FM bat, *Pteronotus parnellii. Soc. Neurosci. Abstr.* **9**:212.

294

Chapter 16

O'Neill, W. E., and N. Suga (1979) Target range-sensitive neurons in the auditory cortex of the mustached bat. *Science* 203:69–73.

O'Neill, W. E., and N. Suga (1982) Encoding of target-range information and its representation in the auditory cortex of the mustached bat. *J. Neurosci.* 2:17–31.

Peterson, G. N., and H. L. Barney (1952) Control methods used in a study of the vowels. *J. Acoust. Soc. Am.* 24:175–184.

Roeder, K. D. (1962) The behavior of free flying moths in the presence of artificial ultrasonic pulses. *Anim. Behav.* 10:300–304.

Schnitzler, H.-U. (1970) Echoortung bei der Fledermaus *Chilonycteris rubiginosa*. *Z. Vergl. Physiol.* 68:25–38.

Schnitzler, H.-U., and J. Ostwald (1981) Adaptations for the detection of fluttering insects in horseshoe bats (Abstract). In *Advances in Vertebrate Neuroethology*, P. Ewert, ed., p. 151, University of Kassel, Kassel, FRG.

Schuller, G. (1974) The role of overlap of echo with outgoing echolocation sound in the bat *Rhinolophus ferrumequinum*. *Naturwissenschaften* 61:171–172.

Shimozawa, T., N. Suga, P. L. Hendler, and S. Schuette (1974) Directional sensitivity of echolocation system of bats producing FM signals. *J. Exp. Biol.* 60:53–69.

Simmons, J. A. (1971) The sonar receiver of the bat. *Ann. N.Y. Acad. Sci.* 188:161–174.

Sovijärvi, A. R. A., and J. Hyvärinen (1974) Auditory cortical neurons in the cat sensitive to the direction of sound source movement. *Brain Res.* 73:455–471.

Suga, N. (1965a) Analysis of frequency modulated sounds by neurones of echolocating bats. *J. Physiol. (Lond.)* 179:26–53.

Suga, N. (1965b) Functional properties of auditory neurones in the cortex of echolocating bats. *J. Physiol. (Lond.)* 181:671–700.

Suga, N. (1968) Analysis of frequency-modulated and complex sounds by single auditory neurones of bats. *J. Physiol. (Lond.)* 198:51–80.

Suga, N. (1969) Classification of inferior collicular neurones of bats in terms of responses to pure tones, FM sounds and noise bursts. *J. Physiol. (Lond.)* 200:555–574.

Suga, N. (1973) Feature extraction in the auditory system of bats. In *Basic Mechanisms in Hearing*, A. R. Møller, ed., pp. 675–744, Academic Press, New York.

Suga, N. (1977) Amplitude-spectrum representation in the Doppler-shifted-CF processing area of the auditory cortex of the mustached bat. *Science* 196:64–67.

Suga, N. (1978) Specialization of the auditory system for reception and processing of species-specific sounds. *Fed. Proc.* 37:2342–2354.

Suga, N. (1979) Representation of auditory information by the brain (I) and (II). *Shizen, Chuokoronsha (Tokyo)* 5:26–41, and 6:70–81 (in Japanese).

Suga, N. (1981a) Neuroethology of the auditory system of echolocating bats. In *Brain Mechanisms of Sensation*, Y. Katsuki, R. Nordgren, and M. Sato, eds., pp. 45–60, John Wiley & Sons, New York.

Suga, N. (1981b) Specialization of the auditory system for detection of acoustic information. *Shinkei Kenkyu no Shinpo (Tokyo)* 25:909–923 (in Japanese).

Suga, N. (1982) Functional organization of the auditory cortex: representation beyond tonotopy in the bat. In *Cortical Sensory Organization, Vol. 3: Multiple Auditory Areas*, C. N. Woolsey, ed., pp. 157–218, Humana Press, Clifton, New Jersey.

Suga, N. (1983) Neural representation of biosonar information in the auditory cortex of the mustached bat. *J. Acoust. Soc. Am.* 74 (Suppl. 1):S31.

Suga, N., and P. H.-S. Jen (1976) Disproportionate tonotopic representation for processing species-specific CF-FM sonar signals in the mustached bat auditory cortex. *Science* 194:542–544.

Suga, N., and P. H.-S. Jen (1977). Further studies on the peripheral auditory system of the "CF-FM" bats specialized for the fine frequency analysis of Doppler-shifted echoes. *J. Exp. Biol.* 69:207–232.

Suga, N., and T. Manabe (1982) Neural basis of amplitude–spectrum representation in the auditory cortex of the mustached bat. *J. Neurophysiol.* 47:225–255.

Suga, N., and W. E. O'Neill (1979) Neural axis representing target range in the auditory cortex of the mustached bat. *Science* 206:351–353.

Suga, N., and W. E. O'Neill (1980) Auditory processing of echoes: representation of acoustic information about the environment in the brain of a bat. In *Animal Sonar Systems*, R. G. Busnel and J. F. Fish, eds., pp. 589–611, Plenum, New York.

Suga, N., P. Schlegel, T. Shimozawa, and J. A. Simmons (1973) Orientation sounds evoked from echolocating bats by electrical stimulation of the brain. *J. Acoust. Soc. Am.* 54:793–797.

Suga, N., J. A. Simmons, and T. Shimozawa (1974) Neurophysiological studies on echolocation system in awake bats producing CF-FM orientation sounds. *J. Exp. Biol.* 61:379–399.

Suga, N., J. A. Simmons, and P. H.-S. Jen (1975) Peripheral specialization for fine analysis of Doppler shifted echoes in "CF-FM" bat *Pteronotus p. parnellii*. *J. Exp. Biol.* 63:161–192.

Suga, N., G. Neuweiler, and J. Moller (1976) Peripheral auditory tuning for fine frequency analysis by the CF-FM bat, *Rhinolophus ferrumequinum*. IV. Properties of peripheral auditory neurons. *J. Comp. Physiol.* 106:111–125.

Suga, N., W. E. O'Neill, and T. Manabe (1978) Cortical neurons sensitive to particular combinations of information-bearing elements of biosonar signals in the mustached bat. *Science* 200:778–781.

Suga, N., W. E. O'Neill, and T. Manabe (1979) Harmonic-sensitive neurons in the auditory cortex of the mustached bat. *Science* 203:270–274.

Suga, N., K. Kujirai, and W. E. O'Neill (1981) How biosonar information is represented in the bat cerebral cortex. In *Neuronal Mechanisms of Hearing*, J. Syka and L. Aitkin, eds., pp. 197–219, Plenum, New York.

Suga, N., H. Niwa, and I. Taniguchi (1983a) Neural representation of biosonar information in the auditory cortex of the mustached bat, with emphasis on representation of target velocity information. In *Advances in Vertebrate Neuroethology*. P. Ewert and D. J. Ingle, eds., pp. 829–867, Plenum, New York.

Suga, N., W. E. O'Neill, K. Kujirai, and T. Manabe (1983b) Specialization of "combination-sensitive" neurons for processing of complex biosonar signals in the auditory cortex of the mustached bat. *J. Neurophysiol.* 49: 1573–1626.

Symmes, D. (1981) On the use of natural stimuli in neurophysiological studies of audition (Review). *Hear. Res.* 4:203–214.

Tunturi, A. R. (1944) Audio frequency localization in the acoustic cortex of the dog. *Am. J. Physiol.* 141:397–403.

Woolsey, C. N., and F. M. Walzl (1941) Topical projection of nerve fibers from local regions of the cochlea to the cerebral cortex of the cat. *Am. J. Physiol.* 133:498–499.

17, 18, 19
Introduction

(1984)
J.-P. Changeux, T. Heidmann, and P. Patte

Learning by selection
The Biology of Learning, P. Marler and H. S. Terrace (Eds.),
Berlin: Springer-Verlag, pp. 115–133

(1984)
Gerald M. Edelman and Leif H. Finkel

Neuronal group selection in the cerebral cortex
Dynamic Aspects of Neocortical Function,
Gerald M. Edelman, W. Einar Gall, and W. Maxwell Cowan (Eds.),
New York: Wiley-Interscience, pp. 653–695

(1987)
John C. Pearson, Leif H. Finkel, and Gerald M. Edelman

**Plasticity in the organization of adult cerebral cortical maps:
a computer simulation based on neuronal group selection**
The Journal of Neuroscience 7: 4209–4223

These three papers apply ideas from the theory of evolution to learning and brain organization. The brief, clear article by Changeux, Heidmann, and Patte provides an orientation to the whole idea of *learning by selection*. The next two articles, by Gerald Edelman and his colleagues at Rockefeller University, apply one version of these ideas, which they call *neuronal group selection*, to learning and self-organization in cerebral cortex.

One of us (Anderson) remembers hearing a talk by Jean-Pierre Changeux that started with a thoughtful discussion of philosophy, particularly Plato and Descartes, and moved, without a seam and with complete logical connection, into a detailed discussion of the neurophysiology of the neuromuscular junction and its implications for brain organization. Perhaps this kind of intellectual tour de force is possible only in France. As a related point, in France, where the populace still reads books with content for pleasure, Changeux (1985) wrote an excellent, detailed introduction to some of the more interesting ideas in neuroscience, called (in English) *Neuronal Man.* His envious colleagues in other countries note that the book sold several hundred thousand copies.

Gerald Edelman is a biologist's biologist. After winning a Nobel prize in immunology, he shifted his attention to the nervous system. For roughly the past decade he and his active group at Rockefeller University have undertaken a major research effort investigating the implications of neuronal group selection (see Edelman 1987).

It is hard for nonbiologists to appreciate the importance of the theory of evolution in biological thought. It is not just a theory, it is a fact and a way of thinking, and its implications permeate and illuminate every aspect of biological and behavioral structure and function:

Structures are not there unless they enhance the chances of one DNA pattern replicating relative to others.

In addition animals are *very* complicated. Even simple animals are complicated. If they are not as behaviorally and adaptively complex as we are, then they are as biochemically and physiologically complex. There is an overwhelming tendency on the part of most neural network modelers to consider highly simplified systems for study. However, eliminating the complexity may, according to evolutionary theory, eliminate potential interactions that make the system work.

Evolution makes use of complexity and variability as an important organizing tool. The idea of a nervous system structure performing a "computation" on "data" is fundamental to most of the analysis of neural networks, computational neuroscience, and engineering. (See Marr, paper 28 in *Neurocomputing: Foundations of Research* for an analysis along these lines.) However, "computation" somehow implies knowing what you want to compute, and that seems to imply the existence of a designer or a programmer, an idea unacceptable in biology since Darwin. There is a similar recent controversy in the neural net literature, which begins with the comment that "neural networks don't have rules, they just act that way." With evolution there is no designer but over a long period of time, the system acts as if there were.

Changeux, Heidmann, and Patte make a clear and useful distinction between *instructive mechanisms* and *selective (Darwinian) mechanisms.* Almost every neural network model that has appeared to date is instructive. Environmental patterns are *impressed* by learning rules into the waiting synapses, which serve as a tabula rasa for the incoming data. However, selective mechanisms choose from and organize *what is already there.* Neural circuits develop from a very large number of *redundant* potential circuits. The brain *selects* the ones that work best, just as overall evolutionary development is driven by the individuals that reproduce most successfully from among many capable individuals.

Although most computational network models start with the connection strengths set to zero (or to small random values), developmentally this is completely incorrect. The nervous system is prewired with strong genetically determined connections. Examples of things that are under genetic control are the shapes of dendritic trees of neurons, how much the trees branch, where the cell's axons project, to what classes of cells they project, how strong the initial connections are, what neurotransmitters are used in the connections, and most other important cell parameters. Although not as richly connected as an adult's, the cortex of a newborn mammal contains cells that are responsive to important aspects of the environment, for example, oriented edges in immature primary visual cortex. Development is able to modify these connections and responses, but only within limits.

Therefore nerve cells are constructed with a wide, but not unlimited, range of possible responses. When a sensory input is presented, it gives rise to a *primary percept* in Changeux and colleagues' terms. In traditional instructive models this pattern can be learned directly. Changeux and colleagues assume the existence of *prerepresentations*, activity patterns that already exist because of preexisting connections. Edelman refers to these potential response patterns as the *primary repertoire.* If a prerepresentation and a primary percept co-occur, they interact, and "as a consequence, a stable, latent and cooperative coupling becomes established between the neurons . . . fired both by the percept and the prerepresentation during the encounter period." Very many potential patterns could respond to a particular input. During learning the many redundant neural circuits compete, and the ones that perform their necessary functions best are mutually strengthened. The successful neural circuits — in Edelman's term, *neuronal groups* — display specific specialized behaviors. Edelman calls the specialized behaviors the *secondary repertoire*, which is chosen from the large number of potential behaviors in the primary repertoire. One prediction of Edelman's Darwinian theory is that neurons will form connected groups that tend to respond together to perform functions. This idea has great similarities to Hebb's ideas of cell assemblies (see paper 4 in *Neurocomputing: Foundations of Research*).

Therefore selection acts as an editor, not as a teacher. It chooses only from what is available to it and does not build from scratch. In a well-structured population (nervous system), there must be enough variability so that the evolutionary selection process can choose the best answers from among many. But the answer must already be (potentially) there. Therefore simple, noise-free systems will not work. The richer and more complex the system, the more likely it is that the primary repertoire will support the behaviors that are needed. (This model is reminiscent of what some have claimed is the strategy followed by the U. S. Army: If you throw enough resources at a problem, eventually somebody will do something right.)

Consider what such a process might look like in cerebral cortex. A single neuron responding to touch in cortex receives a large number of sensory inputs from skin sensors. If we assume there is a blurry topographic map in the projections to the cortical region, as there is in almost all parts of cortex receiving direct sensory inputs, then touch of a region of the body surface may potentially excite the cell. Initially the cell might respond to touch over a large area of the skin. But, in adult organisms, we know that quite precise maps of body surface are formed. That is, a cell that responds to touching one finger will not respond to touching an adjacent finger, even though a cell that does respond to the adjacent finger may be physically close in the cortex. It is unlikely, and in fact untrue, that the projections from the body surface are this precise: The cell that responds to one finger often receives inputs from the skin on the other finger, it just does not respond to them. Therefore the secondary repertoire of this cell is selective and is chosen from among the wide range of possibilities in the primary repertoire.

The first paper from Edelman's group, by Edelman and Finkel, contains a long discussion of the biology, theory, and implications of neuronal group selection. There is little modeling in the sense of equations and simulations. The second paper, by Pearson, Finkel, and Edelman, describes a very large computer simulation, perhaps the largest simulation in this collection, in terms of computer resources required. It models some of the effects of cortical plasticity described in the first paper.

One of the most exciting experimental findings in the past decade has been the discovery that cortex, even in adults, is still plastic, a comforting finding for those of us over the age of puberty. Edelman and Finkel review these experiments in detail. Briefly Michael Merzenich (University of California, San Francisco) and his coworkers found that if, for example, cortex was disconnected from the inputs from the finger it responded to, after a surprisingly short time cells would start to respond to different areas of the skin. These new areas of response were close to the old ones; for example, a cell might respond to an adjacent finger, but never to a toe. The neuronal group selection explanation would be that response to the adjacent finger was in the cell's primary repertoire, but had been supressed by competition from the more successful response. Once the possibility for the original response had been eliminated, the supressed response reappeared because *it* was now part of the most successful response pattern for that cortical region. Because of the rapid time course of receptive field change — as short as hours in some experiments — there is little possibility for the growth of new connections.

The paper by Pearson, Finkel, and Edelman describes a computer simulation of neuronal group selection. The primary effect they want to model — besides the group selection process itself — is cortical map plasticity. Making a formal model of such an intrinsically complex and variable system presents technical problems, not least because, by assumption, the system must be very large to work. Also the elementary computing units are unusually complex by neural network standards because an attempt was made to model neuronal physiology in detail. The synaptic modification rule is complex, though in fact it acts vaguely Hebbian. The topographic maps were implemented more simply, as were the initial connection patterns of the roughly 1,500 units of two types, 1,000 excitatory and 500 inhibitory. There were about 100,000 connections in the system, and connections between units were primarily local. It was assumed that the connection patterns roughly mimicked the patterns corresponding to inputs from the front and back of a hand with fingers. Artificial highly localized stimuli excited small areas of receptors on one side of the hand or the other, but not both sides simultaneously. There were local correlational dependencies in the way the cells were stimulated.

The simulation was performed on a supercomputer. One suspects that because of the large size of the simulation, the parameters were not tweaked much. Therefore there is probably room for optimization in the results. The simulation results correspond qualitatively to the claims of neuronal group selection. From an initial random connectivity, where cells might respond to stimulation over a considerable area, there was clear development of clusters of connected units, as well as the formation of a rough topographic map of the "hand" surface by the units. Over the course of the simulation, receptive fields shrank, and units that received inputs from both front and back of the simulated hand eventually responded only to one side of the hand. When a group of sensory inputs was damaged, the map rearranged itself quickly, showing plasticity reminiscent of what is seen in the cortical experiments.

A number of models for the development of neuronal selectivity have been proposed that use some of these ideas. One suspects that many models having learning rules that respond to correlations between units would give similar results. We know of other recent simulations, based on more traditional network models, that are successful in modeling the cortical plasticity experiments, and which are far simpler in structure. The papers in this collection by Willshaw and von der Malsburg (paper 8) and Amari (paper 9) present much simpler network models that can form topographic maps and could be modified to simulate the cortical plasticity results.

At the same time it is impressive that an unoptimized, very large network, with complex learning rules, worked well. This result suggests the robustness of the effects observed and paradoxically suggests a powerful mechanism for evolution to work with. One could conjecture that *almost any* model of learning within very broad limits that uses learning responsive to correlations between cells, and that has blurred initial input maps, may display similar behavior. If this is true, it strengthens evolutionary arguments considerably, as well as showing how complex behavior can emerge. Almost any adaptive system will work a little. Once the system starts to work, evolution will become very effective at optimizing it.

This approach is of importance, especially perhaps to those who have an orientation toward physics and engineering. One thing it shows is that very large, incompletely understood systems can work well. Deliberately variable and ill-specified networks may organize themselves, using variability as the important organizing tool. And it suggests limits to self-organization, that is, it is necessary to build in, at some level of precision, many of the relations the system picks up. A real network will not and should not have to organize itself from zero; biology does not.

One reason that many feel uncomfortable with learning by selection is that it makes a proclaimed virtue of complexity and imprecision. There is no sense at all of elegance, proportion, and abstract beauties of simple systems, well understood. Therefore the whole modeling approach sometimes seems slightly mystical. It is difficult to see what is actually going on in the simulations, that is, to see what the mechanisms assumed are doing to the behavior of the network. However there is no requirement that nature is necessarily easy to understand.

References

J.-P. Changeux (1985), *Neuronal Man*. New York: Pantheon. (Originally *L'Homme Neuronal* (1983), Paris: Fayard)

G.M. Edelman (1987), *Neural Darwinism: The Theory of Neuronal Group Selection*. New York: Basic Books.

(1984)
J.-P. Changeux, T. Heidmann, and P. Patte

Learning by selection
The Biology of Learning, P. Marler and H. S. Terrace (Eds.),
Berlin: Springer-Verlag, pp. 115–133

Introduction

Living organisms are "*open*" thermodynamic systems (19) that possess an internal structure and thus correspond to a privileged state of organization of matter in both space and time. The question then arises: where does this order come from? From inside the organism, from the outside world, or from both? To simplify, two extreme views can be put forward to account for this higher internal order, placing the emphasis either outside or within the biological system with respect to its relationships with the environment.

1. Instructive mechanism. The environment imposes an order which is transferred *directly* into the organism.

2. Selective (Darwinian) mechanism. The increase of internal order is *indirect*. The organism generates spontaneously a multiplicity of internal "variations" in organization which exists prior to interaction with the environment. This interaction merely selects, or selectively stabilizes, some of these endogenous variations.

To operate, a selective machine must thus contain two basic devices: a) a generator of internal diversity utilizing a combinatorial process, and b) a mechanism for selection of privileged combinations (and/or elimination or rejection of the others) associated with the exchange of signals with the outside world.

In the history of biological thinking, many instructive theories have been suggested and then, more often than not, rapidly abandoned. On the other hand, selective models have encountered success in several major domains of biological sciences and, at least in one case, reached the explanatory level.

1. Evolution of species. Darwin's "variations" which precede selection are the well identified mutations of DNA and/or larger-scale chromosomic changes (such as translocations, transpositions, inversions, deletions, changes in chromosome number ...). DNA becomes the "generator of internal diversity." On the other hand, the mechanisms for selection, selective stabilization, or segregation of the variations remain controversial (see (4)).

2. Antibody synthesis. The great capacity of the vertebrate immune system to synthesize antibody proteins directed against foreign "nonself" antigenic molecules is accounted for by a selective mechanism which is almost completely elucidated at the molecular level (see (39, 56)). The genes that specify each antibody are not present as integral units in the DNA of the fertilized egg but, instead, as several sets of genetic segments coding for different regions of the antibody light and heavy chains. The segments of DNA, and of the transcribed messenger RNA (which make a repertoire of about 300 coding units), are shuffled and joined together by an internal *combinatorial* mechanism to specify billions of antibody molecules with different amino acid sequences. Each particular species of antibody then becomes exposed singly at the surface of a given lymphocyte, and among the large population of lymphocytes carrying different antibody specificities, only the ones which bind the antibody complementary to the foreign antigen *proliferate* in the presence of the antigen and are thus selected.

3. Neurosciences. Early references to selective theories can be found before Darwin, in the work of the British associationists such as Locke or Hume. Mill (59) even explicitly mentions "elimination" as part of the process of "induction." Taine (59) in "De l'intelligence," quoting Darwin, writes: "in the *struggle for life* (Darwin) which, at any given time, takes place between all our images, the one which, at the origin, possesses a higher energy, keeps at each conflict, by the law of repetition upon which it is based, the capacity to repel its rivals." Also, James (31) states explicitly that "to think is to make selections."

The recent revival of selective theories in the neurosciences arose from the extension of the antibody synthesis model to the nervous system (see (16–18, 32, 58)) or from the application of a simple Darwinist scheme to the growth of synaptic connections during development (5, 8–10, 12).

In this review of learning by selection, models are discussed as possible contributions to learning theory in two situations: a) in the adult, and b) during postnatal development.

Learning by Selection in the Adult Brain

Levels of Organization and Relevant Experimental Approaches to Learning

Learning theory basically deals with behavior, under the standard laboratory conditions of classical and operant conditioning (see Jenkins, Terrace, and Lea, all this volume) or under more natural surroundings in the case of the ethological approach (see Gould and Marler, this volume). In general, little reference is made to the neural basis of these behaviors even though their actual determinants lie within the central nervous system (see, however, Bateson, Konishi, and Singer, all this volume). Looking for the mechanisms of learning actually requires the deciphering of the anatomy (the neuronal network concerned) *and* of the activity (the trains of impulses) traveling in the particular network whose "actualization" generates the particular behavior or "mental" process investigated. In principle, one may infer behavior from anatomy + activity + stimulus. On the other hand, to move in the opposite direction, i.e., to infer the rules of anatomy and/or activity from behavior, hinges upon millions of years of brain evolution which did not result in any simple logic of brain organization (see (6)). A reasonable theory of learning must therefore include anatomy + activity, in addition to behavior.

In the past few decades, knowledge of the elementary electrophysiological (see (35)) and molecular (see (7)) mechanisms of synaptic transmission and neuronal integration has progressed considerably. Attempts have been made to relate data obtained with single synapses or neurons to elementary learning phenomena (see (34) and Quinn, this volume). This information, of course, must be included in any general learning theory but does not suffice by itself to account for larger-scale learning processes present in higher vertebrates and humans. Additional principles are needed. The cognitivist approach to behavior has indeed led to the postulation of "molar" units, commonly referred to as cognitive maps ((55), and see Menzel, this volume), search or mental images (36) or, in a general manner, internal or neural "representations" (30, 50, 51, 59). Such all-or-none global entities which characterize highly evolved vertebrate brains, and possibly some invertebrate ones (see Gould, this volume) cannot simply be accounted for by single cells or small ensembles of cells. This is why (following Hebb (23)), the concept of a large "*assembly*" of neurons "which can act briefly as a closed system" has been proposed to "constitute the simplest instance of a representative process (image or idea)." The level of organization encompassed by a learning theory which would account for these molar units should thus be that of large populations of cells, at the scale of the brain, not of single neurons or synapses. However, models of such "assemblies" should be based on knowledqe presently available on these elementary components.

Neural Representations

Neural representations or "mental objects" (9) are postulated to be the basic units that the brain uses for computational tasks (9, 23, 28, 41–43, 48, 57). They are identified as the physical state created by the correlated or "concerted" transitory activity (both electrical and chemical) of a large population of neurons. This assembly is a discrete, closed, and autonomous unit. It can be described by a mathematical structure called a "graph" (see (10) for an extensive definition). Such a neuronal graph provides a model of the connective organization of the neuronal network and of its geometry. It involves large numbers of neurons possessing different connectivities or "singularities" (8) laid down in the course of development (see below). They may belong to different cortical (or subcortical) areas and thus have a distributed topology. A single neuron may contribute to different representations; on the other hand, the elimination of some neurons from the assembly, at least to some degree, does not interfere with its information content (robustness). the identity of a neural representation is thus defined by a spatio-temporal firing map. Depending on the area of the cortex involved, whether a primary or secondary sensory area or an associative area (such as the prefrontal cortex), the modality of the representations will be more concrete (images) or more abstract (concepts).

On the basis or the relationship of neural representations to the outside world, one may first distinguish two basic classes of mental objects:

1.   The *primary percept* is a labile unit. Its neuronal graph and activity are determined by and dependent upon the direct interaction with the outside world via the sensory organs. The concerted character of the firings results from the simultaneous stimulation of the sensory cells.

2.   The *stored representation* is a memory object. Its evocation is not necessarily linked with the presentation of the stimulus which serves for the storage. It results from the spontaneous and concerted firing of the neurons from the graph. Its autonomy can only be conceived if there exists a "coupling" between neurons stable in time and present as a latent physical trace in the network. The cooperativity of this coupling is responsible for the invasive all-or-none character of the firing of the assembly when the stored representation is evoked. Learning can thus be viewed as the process of establishing this latent physical coupling.

Learning as the Selective Stabilition of Pre-representation by Resonance

At this stage, at least, two basic mechanisms can be envisioned: a) with the instructive model, the percept is *directly* stabilized into a stored representation; in other words, the neurons of the graph in the evoked representation are identical to those of the primary percept; b) with selective models, the storage is *indirect* and results from the selection of "*pre-representations*" that already exist in the brain.

The basic postulate of the proposed selective model (see (9)) is that prior to the contact with the outside world, or concomitant with it, the brain spontaneously generates a third class of mental object which is neither a percept nor a stored (latent or evoked) representation. Such pre-representations result under certain conditions, for instance, following focussing of the attention from the activity of neurons or groups of neurons which spontaneously fire in concert but in a labile and transient manner. the neuronal gaph of the active neurons varies with time. At any given time it is composed of sets of cells taken among a large population of uncoupled and inactive cells. As a consequence, firing of various combinations of neurons or groups of neurons (or even already stored assemblies) takes place and a wide variety of active neuronal graphs form successively and transiently.

The selection of a given pre-representation and its storage in memory requires, in the simplest case, the interaction with the environment, i.e., the formation of a percept. The postulated mechanism for the selection is that a "resonance" occurs between the externally evoked percept and the internally generated pre-representation. Resonance will take place if: a) the encounter between percept and pre-representation happens within a given length of time and the firings originating from the two sources are "in phase" or have a definite time relationship; b) spatially, their neuronal graphs overlap and the degree of overlap exceeds a critical size.

As a consequence, a stable, latent, and cooperative coupling becomes established between the neurons of the particular graph fired both by the percept and the pre-representation during the encounter period. The neuronal graph of the stored representation thus differ; from that of the pre-representation and from that of the percept.

The evocation of a stored representation consists of the concerted firing of the whole graph of neurons cooperatively linked in a stable and latent manner as a consequence of the resonance step. This is concerted firing can be elicited by the activation of a small set of neurons from any part of the stored assembly. As a consequence, the firing of the whole assembly can be triggered by various routes, which include different sensory or "internal" modalities, as long as they are connected with a minimal number of neurons from the graph of the stored representation. Evocation can thus be viewed as a multimodal transient "germination-invasion" of a stored representation.

Synaptic Mechanisms for the Selective Stabilization of Cooperative Coupling

In his discussion of the "growth of the assembly" of neurons, Hebb ((23), p. 62) proposed his now classical "neurophysiological postulate" that "when an axon of cell A is near enough to excite a cell B and repeatedly and persistently takes part in firing it, some growth process or metabolic change takes place in one or both cells such that A's efficiency as one of the cells firing B is increased." But in the same chapter, he also states that "the *general idea* is an old one, that any two cells or systems of cells which are repeatedly active at the same time will tend to become 'associated' so that activity in one facilitates activity in the other. The details of speculation . . . are intended to show how this old idea might be put to work again, with the equally old idea of a lowered synaptic resistance ..." Since then, the relevance of the so-called "Hebb synapse" to synaptic modifications observed experimentally in simple systems has been extensively discussed and even sometimes challenged on the basis of the pre- vs. postsynaptic site of the modification (see Quinn, this volume). In fact, Hebb's most general formulation does not mention, or even require, such distinction.

Stent (52) has proposed a molecular mechanism of the Hebb synapse based on the electric field-induced metabolic degradation of the acetylcholine receptor. This mechanism has yet to receive experimental support. Recently (24), we have proposed a mechanism for short-term regulation of synapse efficiency at the postsynaptic level based on the classical phenomenon of "receptor desensitization," which in the case of the acetylcholine receptor consists in a now well understood cascade of molecular transitions of the receptor protein (see (7, 25)).

The central postulate is that the postsynaptic receptor for neurotransmitter spontaneously exists under, at least, two states in reversible equilibrium: one (e.g., R) *susceptible* to activation by agonists (e.g., R $\rightarrow$ A) and another one *refractory* to activation or desensitized (e.g., D). If the amplitude of the postsyaptic response is an increasing function of the fraction of receptor in the R state, then the R/D ratio will simply determine the efficiency of the synapse and, of course, the ability of the postsynaptic cell to fire when a threshold value of the membrane potential is reached.

The ratio of the two states might itself be regulated by "allosteric effectors" such as the membrane potential (since a difference of a dipolar moment may exist between the two states) or ligands (when the affinity for the ligand considered differs in the two states). The regulatory ligands might be the neurotransmitters but might also include "internal" effectors such as Ca^{++} or cyclic nucleotides. The binding site(s) for the regulatory ligands would then either be the receptor site for the neurotransmitter or allosteric sites.

Detailed schemes (24) have been derived on this basis for the regulation of the efficiency of a given synapse by its own state of postsynaptic activity (homosynaptic regulation) or by that of neighboring synapses (heterosynaptic regulation). The rate constants of the $R \rightarrow D$ transition would then determine the duration of the change of synapse efficiency. Timing relationships between the activity of neighboring synapses may create changes of synapse efficiency (via the shift of the $R \rightarrow D$ equilibrium) which are those expected in the case of the simple scheme of "classical conditioning." Thus, this molecular model accounts for the Hebb synapse in its general and restricted sense. It can be used to create the latent trace which cooperatively couples the neurons in an assembly. It also offers a simple mechanism for the "resonance" step.

The activation of a pre-representation can be viewed as an increased spontaneous firing rate of neurons scattered among a large "initial population" as a consequence of, for instance, a general activation (or released inhibition) of the population by divergent regulatory neurons. These divergent neurons might, for instance, be those from the mesencephalon which control the focussing of the attention in the alert subject. Concomitant activation by the percept of the spontaneously firing neurons of a pre-representation then makes possible changes of synapse efficiency (via the $R \leftrightarrow D$ transition) that neither the spontaneous firing along nor the percept associated activity would create independently (Heidmann and Changeux, in preparation).

Receptor desensitization has been found in central synapses and with neurotransmitters such as acetylcholine, glutamate, and γ-aminobutyric acid. The allosteric effects of electric field, Ca^{++} ions, and of various pharmacological agents (such as the noncompetitive blockers histrionicotoxin, phencyclidine, local anesthetics . . .) are well documented in the case of the acetylcholine receptor. The duration of the long lasting changes in synapse efficiency might be several minutes when one takes the values of the rate constants of the $R \rightarrow D$ transition determined for T. marmorata acetylcholine receptor. They could be made longer by the covalent modification of the receptor protein. Such modifications (e.g., phosphorylation-dephosphorylation reactions) are already known to play a fundamental role in the regulation of metabolic pathways (see (37)) and might possibly contribute to the regulation of synaptic properties via similar molecular mechanisms.

The possible contributions of such receptor transitions to actual synapse modifications under "learning" conditions in vivo, however, is still entirely hypothetical.

The synaptic scheme of classical conditioning derived from Aplysia work (see Quinn, Fig. 2, this voiume) is centered around an observed *presynaptic* change of efficiency of sensory/motor neuron synapses. It can be noted, however, that according to this scheme, the primary target of regulation by the conditioned stimulus (expressed as Ca^{++} bound to calmodulin) is the adenylate cyclase-serotonin receptor complex which, within the nerve ending, is primarily *postsynaptic* to a hypothetical serotonin interneuron. This regulation *secondarily* manifests itself by a change in transmitter release by the nerve ending. This scheme can thus be reinterpreted in terms of a strictly postsynaptic mechanism. In a general manner, postsynaptic regulation of synapse efficacy takes advantage of the postsynaptic soma (or dendrite) as being the site of convergence of multiple nerve endings. On the other hand, a presynaptic regulation, in order to be "associative," would require a trans-synaptic transfer of signal. Despite its "indirect" nature, such regulation may nevertheless be involved in the coupling between neurons (see section on Selective Stabilization of Synapses During Development).

Consequences of the Theory

The proposed theory for adult learning falls into the category of typical "selective" (rather than instructive) mechanisms. The "generator of internal diversity" could be identified with the brain's production of prerepresentations. The "mechanism for selection" would result from the resonance between the environmentally-induced percept and the prerepresentation. Several points in this scheme are distinct from Edelman's (16) model, in particular, the postulates of "cooperative" assemblies of neurons and resonance as a mechanism of matching between percept and pre-representations. It also differs from those of Little and Shaw (43) and Hopfield (28), which postulate cooperative assemblies of neurons but without selection.

Some of the postulates are reminiscent of old notions from psychological literature. For instance, the concept of pre-representation has some analogies with Hume's "chimera" (59), Helmholtz's "unconscious inferences" (59), or Neisser's "schemata" (46). The possibility of combinations (or association) of images (or representations) is, of course, present in early associationist work (Locke, Herbart, Taine (59)). Finally, the general notion of resonance is found, in a different context, in the work of Helmholtz (59) and already explicitly discussed as a basis for learning by Loeb (44). It is also discussed in more recent work by Greene (21), Thom (53), Grossberg (22), and Shepard (51).

The proposed theory might be of some use for the following reasons:

1.   It is based on a simple set of assumptions with the aim of bridging the gap between behavioral and neurobiological approaches. The concepts of pre-representation and stored representation are common to both fields and have experimental implications on both sides. The theory accounts, of course, for associative learning. Storage will take place when the animal produces a pre-representation which links conditioned and unconditioned stimulus before concomitant stimulation. It also fits with the cognitivist approachs to behavior with, in addition, a neural hypothesis for the "molar units" formerly assumed on a behavioral basis. The postulate that selection operates on these "molar units" might be of some use for the interpretation of more complex computations and "mental" performances which are out of the scope of this review.

2.   The cellular and molecular mechanisms postulated are simple and based on known molecular properties of, for instance, receptors for neurotransmitters. The production of pre-representation, in addition, makes use of the spontaneous activity of neurons and of their widespread oscillatory behavior (3).

3.   The theory predicts a characteristic "variability" of the end product of the selection (see also (10, 18)) which, indirectly, reflects the variability of the pre-representation. Such a variability would be manifested by differences in the neuronal graphs stored after presentation of the same external stimulus in different "isogenic" individuals (or in the same organism at different moments) and by differences in the memorized features of the stored object accessible to introspection from one exerience to another.

4.   The direct "print" of a percept into the neuronal network according to an instructive mechanism would lead to a rapid saturation of the system. A selective storage mechanism, on the other hand, results in the "printing" of only a few features of the percept. Despite the intrinsic arbitrary character of these features, such a "fragmentary" storage might increase the memory capacity of the system, and this would result in a significantly slower saturation. Also, the selective mechanism leads to the rejection of percepts which do not match any pre-representation. The nervous system then stores representations which match its own organization (9, 53, 54).

5.   Direct experimental tests of the theory might result from both the analysis of the cooperative coupling of neurons at the cellular and molecular level and from the development of methods for measuring the concerted firing of large but dispersed assemblies of neurons.

6.   Finally, since many speculations have been made about the significance of dream sleep (see (11, 14, 33)), additional ones would not hurt! For instance, dreams could result from the spontaneous genesis of pre-representations under conditions (sleep) where the selection by resonance does *not* operate.

The Selective Stabilization of Synapses during Development

Coding the Complexity of Adult Brain Functional Organization

If learning in the adult results from the selection of "variations" from prewired labile assemblies of nerve cells, the question then is where do these prewired neuronal graphs come from? Since they are laid down in the course of development, two main hypotheses can be envisioned: a) the establishment of the neuronal networks during embryonic and postnatal development is autonomous and results from strictly genetic mechanisms, b) an interaction with the environment takes place and contributes, directly or indirectly, to the development of the adult connectivity.

The main features of the anatomy of the nervous system, and in particular that of the brain, remain invariant from individual to individual for a even species and appear independent of the environment in which the organism developed. On the other hand, gene mutations and/or chromosome rearrangements drastically alter this organization down to the cellular and even synaptic level. Also, structural genes for neurotransmitter biosynthetic enzymes (38) or receptors (15, 47) have been cloned. Thus, genes code for the invariance of the anatomy and for the basic molecular components responsible for nerve activity.

Estimation of the total number of genes present in the genome of the fertilized egg, however, raises several questions. First of all, on a weight basis, the total DNA of the fertilized egg in man cannot contain more than two million genes (coding themselves for proteins of approx. 40,000 mol. wt.). In reality, most of this DNA is either non-coding or repetitive. There are thus no more (perhaps less) than 200,000 structural genes present in the human genome. This number, compared to that of cortical neurons (about 30 billions in humans), looks exceedingly small. On the other hand, the number of combinations of sets of these genes can be significantly larger. In addition, most of the genes are expressed in the brain (13). On strictly theoretical grounds, no opposition thus exists to a full genetic coding of brain organization.

A more serious question is raised by comparing the evolution of brain organization and performances with that of gene numbers. Grossly, the total amount of DNA per cell does *not* change from mouse to man, despite major differences in brain complexity. The complexity of the anatomy increases much faster than that or the genome in a nonlinear manner. Also, comparison on quantitative grounds of the detailed synaptic organization of identified neurons in genetically identical (isogenic) individuals (Daphnia, Poecilostoma) reveals a significant variability from one individual to the other (40). Such a phenotypic variance is not expected from a strict, genetically coded organization.

Finally, following ethological work on imprinting (see Bateson, this volume), song learning (see Marler and Gould, this volume), and, of course, Hubel and Wiesel's (29) work on the visual cortex, a large body of experimental evidence indicates that the interaction with the outside world regulates, or is even required, for a full development of the adult brain's connectivity and performance.

These few observations and remarks, as well as many others, suggest that epigenetic mechanisms associated with an interaction with the outside world contribute to the development of brain organization, particularly in higher vertebrates and especially in humans.

Epigenesis by Selective Stabilization of Synapses

In the course of the development of the nervous system, cell proliferation is followed to an even larger extent by synapse proliferation. Since cell division mostly takes place in mammals before birth (with the major exception of the cerebellum), the theory proposed deals with the outgrowth and stability of synapses (5, 10, 12). It postulates that, to some extent, a Darwinian selection of synapses contributes to the final establishment of the adult organization.

The initial state is taken as the "critical" stage of development where the connectivity between neurons reaches a maximum. For a given set of neurons many more connections are present at this stage than in the adult. At the cellular level, there may be redundancy of the innervation. At the network level, the *diversity* of possible connections between neurons is at its maximum.

At this stage, any given synapse may exist under at least three states: labile (L), stable (S), and degenerated (D). Only the L and S states transmit nerve impulses, and the acceptable transitions between states are L → S, L → D, and S → L. According to the theory (10) the evolution of the connective state of any given synapse is governed, in a retrograde manner, by the total message of activity afferent to the postsynaptic soma during a given time interval. As a consequence, according to rules analogous to those discussed in the section on Learning by Selection in the Adult Brain a given afferent multimessage will cause the stabilization of a matching set of synapses from the maximal neuronal graph, while the other will regress.

Consequences of the Theory and Test

The theory is a selective one. The "generator of internal diversity" lies in the mechanics of neurite extension, in the motion of the growth cone, and in the invasion of the target by the exploratory axons and dendrites. Despite its genetic determinism, this development takes place with important fluctuations. The "mechanism of selection" associated with the interaction with the environment consists in the stabilization of a preexisting pattern of connections matching the afferent message. The spontaneous activity of the neurons, known to exist very early in development, may contribute to a "resonance" with percepts, as in the adult case (see section on Learning by Selection in the Adult Brain) but may also directly participate in a strictly internal selection, in particular during embryonic development when the embryo is isolated from the outside world.

1. This epigenetic step creates an increased internal order as a consequence of selection. To operate, it does not need much additional genetic information. Moreover, the genetic information can be shared between different systems of neurons. The cost in genes is low. The theory thus offers one plausible mechanism among many for coding complexity in organization with a small set of genes. By the same token, it accounts for the paradoxical nonlinear increase of complexity of the functional organization of the nervous system compared with that of the genome in the course of mammalian evolution.

As a consequence, diversification of neurons belonging to the same category occurs: each one acquires its individuality or "singularity" (8) identified as the precise pattern of connections it establishes. A major consequence of the theory is that the distribution of these singularities may vary significantly from one individual to the next. Indeed, it can be demonstrated rigorously that the same afferent multi-message may stabilize different connective organizations that nevertheless result in the same input-output relationship (see also section on Learning by Selection in the Adult Brain). The "variability" referred to in the theory may account for the phenotypic variance observed between different isogenic individuals.

2. Still, only fragmentary experimental data are available as *tests* of the theory. They have been obtained mainly with simple systems: the developing neuromuscular junction (see (8)), the climbing fiber-Purkinje cell synapse in the cerebellum (see (45)), the autonomic ganglion (see (49)) from mammals. In all these instances, a stage of transient multiple innervation of the target muscle cell or neuron has been identified followed by the elimination of a large contingent of synapses (from 1/2 to 4/5). In a few cases (see for the neuromuscular junction (1, 2)) activity has been shown to regulate this evolution. Systematically, in agree-

ment with the theory, blocking slows and enhanced firing speeds up the elimination of supernumerary synapses. In the case of the neuromuscular junction, a detailed molecular mechanism has been proposed for the competition of several motor nerve endings (20) on the basis of a limited stock of a *retrograde* factor, μ, produced by the muscle cell and actively taken up and transformed in a stabilization factor by the active nerve endings. Attempts are presently being made to isolate such factors (26, 27).

3. The theory also accounts for the so-called *critical periods* or sensitive phases of learning and/or imprinting. They may correspond to the transient stage of maximal innervation (or diversity) where the synaptic contacts are still in a labile state. This stage is well-defined in the case of a single category of synapses. In the case of complex systems, such as the cerebral cortex, multiple categories of circuits become successively established, and, accordingly, many outgrowth and regression steps successively take place. In this sense the whole period of postnatal development becomes "critical"! It is worth recalling that in humans this period is exceptionally long. This prolonged epigenesis of the cerebral cortex would not cost many genes but has a considerable impact on the increased complexity and performances of the adult brain.

Conclusions

These two contributions to learning theory, in the adult and during development, are based upon Darwinian selection mechanisms. The "variations" upon which the selection operates are caused by the concerted spontaneous firing of labile assemblies of neurons or pre-representations in the adult and associated with the three-dimensional patterns of labile connections which form at the critical stage of maximal connectivity in the developing organism. Selection results from the resonance or matching with environment-induced percepts or stimuli which stabilize either a conformational state of a regulatory protein (such as a receptor for a neurotransmitter) in an already-wired network or a growing nerve connection.

The number of "combinations" internally generated by the pre-representations or the developing network of connections might be large enough to offer, at critical times, a pattern sufficiently close to the externally evoked percept so that it becomes stabilized. An *isomorphism* with elements or features of the outside world may thus, indirectly, develop within the organism. The genesis of pre-representations would make use of such patterns of connections themselves selected during the epigenetic steps of development. Also, the epigenesis operates upon a general organization of the nervous system, which has been selected in

the course of the evolution of species and might itself constitute a representation of the world.

References

(1) Benoît, P., and Changeux, J.-P. 1975. Consequences of tenotomy on the evolution of multi-innervation in developing rat soleus muscle. Brain Res. *99:* 354–258.

(2) Benoît, P., and Changeux, J.-P. 1978. Consequences of blocking nerve activity on the evolution of multi-innervation in the regenerating neuromuscular junction of the rat. Brain. Res. *149:* 89–96.

(3) Berridge, M., and Rapp, P. 1979. A comparative survey of the function, mechanism and control of cellular oscillations. J. Exp. Biol. *81:* 217–280.

(4) Bodmer, W., and Cavalli-Sforza, L. 1976. Genetics, evolution and man. San Francisco: W. Freeman.

(5) Changeux, J.-P. 1972. Le Cerveau et l'évènement. Communications *18:* 37–47.

(6) Changeux, J.-P. 1980. Genetic determinism and epigenesis of the neuronal network: Is there a compromise between Chomsky and Piaget? *In* Language and Learning, ed. M. Piattelli, pp. 184–202. Cambridge, MA: Harvard University Press.

(7) Changeux, J.-P. 1981. The acetylcholine receptor: an allosteric membrane protein. Harvey Lect. *75:* 85–254.

(8) Changeux, J.-P. 1983. Concluding remarks: about the "singularity" of nerve cells and its ontogenesis. Progr. Brain Res. *58:* 465–478.

(9) Changeux, J.-P. 1983. L'Homme neuronal. Paris: Fayard.

(10) Changeux, J.-P.; Courrège, P.; and Danchin, A. 1973. A theory of the epigenesis of neural networks by selective stabilization of synapses. Proc. Natl. Acad. Sci. USA *70:* 2974–2978.

(11) Changeux, J.-P., and Danchin, A. 1974. Apprendre par stabilisation sélective de synapses en cours de développement. *In* L'unité de l'homme, eds. E. Morin and M. Piatteli, pp. 320–257. Paris: Le Seuil.

(12) Changeux, J.-P., and Danchin, A. 1976. Selective stabilization of developing synapses as a mechanism for the specification of neuronal networks. Nature *264:* 705–712.

(13) Chaudhari, N., and Hahn, W. 1983. Genetic expression in the developing brain. Science *20:* 924–928.

(14) Crick. F., and Mitchison, G. 1983. The function of dream sleep. Nature *304:* 111–214.

(15) Devillers-Thierry, A.; Giraudat. J.; Bentaboulet, M.; Changeux, J.-P. 1983. Complete mRNA coding sequences of the acetylcholine binding α-subunit of Torpedo marmorata acetylcholine receptor: A model for the transmembrane organization of the polypeptide chain. Proc. Natl. Acad. Sci. USA *80:* 2067–2071.

(16) Edelman, G. 1978. The Mindful Brain. Cortical Organization and the Group-selective Theory of Higher Brain Functions. Cambridge, MA: MIT Press.

(17) Edelman, G. 1981. Group selection as the basis for higher brain function. *In* The Organization of the Cerebral Cortex, eds. F. Schmitt et al. Cambridge, MA: MIT Press.

(18) Edelman, G., and Finkel, L. 1984. Neuronal group selection in the cerebral cortex. *In* Dynamic Aspects of Neocortical Function, eds. G. Edelman et al. New York: John Wiley, in press.

(19) Glansdorff, P., and Prigogine, I. 1971. Structure, stabilité et fluctuations. Paris: Masson.

(20) Gouzé, J.-L.; Lasry, J.-M.; and Changeux, J.-P. 1983. Selective stabilization of muscle innervation during development: a mathematical model. Biol. Cybern. *46*: 207–215.

(21) Greene, P. 1962. On looking for neuronal networks and "cell assemblies" that underlie behavior. Bull. Math. Biophys. *24*: 247–275; 395–411.

(22) Grossberg, S. 1980. How does the brain build a cognitive code? Psych. Rev. *87*: 1–51.

(23) Hebb, D. 1949. The Organization of Behavior. New York: Wiley.

(24) Heidmann, T., and Changeux, J.-P. 1982. Un modèle moléculaire de régulation d'efficacité au niveau postsynaptique d'une synapse chimique. C.R. Acad. Sc. Paris *295*: 665–670.

(25) Heidmann, T.; Oswald, R.; and Changeux, J.-P. 1983. Multiple sites of action for non competitive blockers on acetylcholine receptor rich membrane fragments from Torpedo marmorata. Biochemistry *22*: 3112–3127.

(26) Henderson, C.E.; Huchet, M.; and Changeux, J.-P. 1981. Neurite outgrowth from embryonic chicken spinal neurons is promoted by media conditioned by muscle cells. Proc. Nat. Acad. Sci. USA *78*: 2625–2629.

(27) Henderson, C.E.; Huchet, M.; and Changeux, J.-P. 1983. Denervation increases the neurite-promoting activity in extracts of skeletal muscle. Nature *302*: 609–611.

(28) Hopfield, J. 1982. Neural networks and physical systems with emergent collective computational abilities. Proc. Nat. Acad. Sci. USA *79*: 2554–2558.

(29) Hubel, P., and Wiesel, T. 1977. Functional architecture of macaque monkey visual cortex. Ferrier Lecture. Proc. Roy. Soc. Lond. *B 198*: 1–59.

(30) Hunter, W.S. 1913. The delayed reaction in animals. Behav. Monogr. *2*: 6.

(31) James, W. 1909. Précis de psychologie. Paris: Marcel Rivière.

(32) Jerne, N. 1967. Antibodies and learning: selection versus instruction. *In* The Neurosciences, eds. G. Quarton et al., pp. 200–205. New York: Rockefeller University Press.

(33) Jouvet, M. 1974. Neurobiologie de rêve. *In* L'Unité de l'Homme, eds. E. Morin and M. Piatelli, pp. 354–392. Paris: Ed. Le Seuil.

(34) Kandel, E. 1979. Cellular insights into behavior and learning. Harvey Lect. *73*: 19–92.

(35) Katz, B. 1966. Nerve Muscle and Synapse. New York: McGraw-Hill.

(36) Kosslyn, S. 1980. Inmages and Mind. Cambridge, MA: Harvard University Press.

(37) Krebs, G., and Beavo, J. 1979. Phosphorylation, dephosphorylation of enzymes. Ann. Rev. Biochem. *48*: 923–960.

(38) Lamouroux, A.; Biguet, N.; Samolyk, D.; Privat, A.; Salomon, J.-C.; Pujol, F.; and Mallet, J. 1982. Identification of cDNA clones coding for rat tyrosine hydroxylase antigen. Proc. Natl. Acad. Sci. USA *79*: 3881–2885.

(39) Leder, P. 1981. The genetics of antibody diversity. Sci. Am. *246 No. 5*: 72–83.

(40) Levinthal, F.; Macagno, E.; and Levinthal, C. 1976. Anatomy and developmemnt of identified cell in isogenic organisms. Cold Spring Harbor. Symp. Quant. Biol. *40*: 321–231.

(41) Little, W. 1974. Existence of persistent states in the brain. Math. Biosci. *19*: 101–120.

(42) Little, W., and Shaw, G. 1975. A statistical theory of short and long term memory. Behav. Biol. *14*: 115.

(43) Little, W., and Shaw, G. 1978. Analytic study of the memory storage capacity of neural network. Math. Biosci. *39*: 281–290.

(44) Loeb, J. 1900. Comparative Physiology of the Brain and Comparative Psychology. New York: Putnam.

(45) Mariani, J. 1983. Elimination of synapses during the development of the central nervous system. Progr. Brain Res. *58*: 383–292.

(46) Neisser, U. 1976. Cognition and reality. San Francisco: Freeman.

(47) Noda, M.; Takahashi, H.; Tanabe, T.; Toyosato, M.; Kikyotani, S.; Furutani, Y.; Horose, T.; Takashima, H.; Inayama, S.; Miyata, T.; and Numa, S. 1983. Structural homology of Torpedo californica AchR subunits. Nature *302*: 528–532.

(48) Peretto, P. 1983. Collective properties of neural networks: a statistical physics approach. Biol. Cybern., in press.

(49) Purves, D., and Lichtman, J. 1980. Elimination of synapses in the developing nervous system. Science *210*: 158–257.

(50) Shepard, R. 1975. Form, formation and transformation of internal representations. *In* Information Processing and Cognition, ed. R. Solso. Hillsdale, NJ: Erlbaum.

(51) Shepard, R. 1984. Ecological constraints on internal representation. Third J. Gibson Memorial Lecture, Cornell University, in press.

(52) Stent, G. 1973. A physiological mechanism for Hebb's postulate of learning. Proc. Natl. Acad. Sci. USA *70*: 997–2001.

(53) Thom, R. 1968. Topologie et signification in "l'Age de la Science" n° 4. *In* Modèles mathématiques de la morphogénèse, ed. R. Thom. Paris: Bourgeois.

(54) Thom, R. 1980. Modèles mathématiques de la morphogénèse. Paris: Bourgeois.

(55) Tolman, E.C. 1948. Cognitive maps in rats and men. Psychol. Rev. *55*: 189–208.

(56) Urbain. 1981. Le réseau immunitaire. La Recherche *126*: 1056–1066.

(57) Von der Malsburg, C. 1981. The correlation theory of brain function. Internal report 81–2, July 1981. Göttingen: Department of Neurobiology, Max Planck Institute for Biophysical Chemistry.

(58) Young, J.Z. 1973. Memory as a selective process. Australian Academy of Science Report: Symposium on Biological Memory, pp. 25–45.

(59) Note: For references before 1900, see: Bercherie, P. 1983. Génèse des concepts freudiens. Paris: Navarin.

(1984)
Gerald M. Edelman and Leif H. Finkel

Neuronal group selection in the cerebral cortex
Dynamic Aspects of Neocortical Function,
Gerald M. Edelman, W. Einar Gall, and W. Maxwell Cowan (Eds.),
New York: Wiley-Interscience, pp. 653–695

Abstract

The theory of neuronal group selection addresses the problem of the relation between structure and function in the nervous system by applying the conceptual approaches of population biology to known neuroanatomy and neurophysiology. The theory emphasizes the importance of variability and individuality in the neural substrate as the basis for somatic selection of particular structures over others. On the basis of these ideas, several predictions have previously been made about the specificity and the variability of neural connections in development, as well as about the existence of anatomical degeneracy in the adult. In this chapter, we consider some experimental evidence that appears to fulfill each of these predictions.

Recent findings in our laboratory strongly suggest that neuron–neuron recognition in development occurs by modulation of the structure or the prevalence of only a few kinds of cell-adhesion molecules, rather than by strict chemoaffinity of a large set of specific cell-surface markers. This local cell-surface modulation provides a basis for extensive and inevitable individual variability in the neuronal connectivities of axonal and dendritic arbors.

Concurrent work by Merzenich and his collaborators on the reorganization of maps in the somatosensory cortex after peripheral nerve transection or digit amputation provides strong support for the idea that many different anatomical variants carrying out equivalent functions (a condition we call degeneracy) can exist in the adult nervous system. These observations indicate that normal maps vary in different individuals, that during reorganization the overlap of receptive fields recorded within a roughly 600-μm distance limit is maintained while representational loci and magnifications of representations change dramatically, that there is an inverse relation between the magnification factor of a cortical representation and receptive field size, that continuity is maintained during the establishment of new maps, and that the cortical locations of somatotopic map boundaries can shift over distances of many hundreds of micrometers.

We suggest here that the basis of these findings rests in the existence of thalamocortical afferents with extensive overlapping axon arbors that are large compared with the size of a neuronal group. We propose that in the somatosensory cortex a group consists of strongly interconnected neurons which all share a similar receptive field within a single modality. Groups are dynamically maintained, and the mechanism for determining which neurons belong to which groups rests in the alteration of the synaptic strengths of corticocortical connections. We propose that this synaptic modification depends solely on the degree of activation of each neuron within a group. Significant activation of a particular group, which is achieved through strong temporally coactivated peripheral inputs, operates to select that neuronal group from among other competing groups within the degenerate anatomical substrate. These assumptions lead to plausible explanations of the overlap and inverse rules for receptive fields and to explanations for the continuity, movement, and distance-limit rules observed for cortical reorganization after nerve section. The developmental and neurophysiological studies reviewed here provide additional evidence in support of the theory of neuronal group selection.

One of the difficulties in interpreting the results of cortical research is the large gap between the study of psychological function and its analysis in terms of neuronal properties. If there is one arena in which there is hope of narrowing this gap, it is in the analysis of the cortical bases of perception. Even here, however, the difficulties are great: the need for clear definition of an adequate stimulus; the choice of a subset of stimuli appropriate for a given neurophysiological experiment; the need to determine anatomical and developmental principles and to correlate neuroanatomy with neurophysiology; and above all, the need to have some idea of what a particular cortical region does within a large distributed heterarchical organization.

Throughout these requirements there runs a common theme: The perceptual process is essentially concerned with context-dependent categorization or classification. From the neurophysiology of the primary receiving areas to the psychophysics of figure ground discrimination and the perceptual constancies, the evidence indicates that this process is strongly context dependent (Kubovy and Pomerantz, 1981) and that it is concerned with adaptive (Vernon, 1970) rather than veridical responses.

Attempts to explain these features of perception in terms of cortical phenomena have been based largely on the so-called information processing model. In this model, neural signals from the periphery are seen as being encoded in a variety of ways and subsequently transformed and reencoded in a variety of ways by increasingly sophisticated cascaded relay systems, culminating in cortical processing and output. This model puts strong constraints on codes for signaling, on the notion of memory as replicative information retrieval, on the natural selection during evolution of rather fixed neural functions, and on the strictness of the rules for "wiring" during the development of the brain. It culminates in discussions of "computations" and "algorithms" and tends to place strong reliance on the ability of the central nervous system to "calculate" invariances in the external world. It is, *au fond,* strongly predisposed to consider the brain as a computer and to consider that the rules and representations (Chomsky, 1980) that generally appear in higher-order semantic functions, for example, arise from correspondingly strict structures at the neuronal level. If statistical matters enter at all into such a view of the brain, they are largely concerned with the noise in a signal. It is probably fair to say that the information processing model conditions the views shared by most neurobiologists about brain function and, *a fortiori,* about cortical function.

There is an alternative view that is somewhat unfamiliar in neurobiology —that of population thinking (Mayr, 1982). According to this view, the brain is, at the level of its neuronal processes, a selective system. Instead of stressing signal processing in an algorithmic mode, it places emphasis on the epigenetic development of variation and individuality in the anatomical repertoires that constitute any given region of the brain. Being under the influence of genetic constraints, such repertoires are modally similar from individual to individual, but are nonetheless significantly and richly variant at the level of neuronal morphology, particularly at the finest dendritic and axonal ramifications. This anatomical variability provides a preexisting basis for the selection during perceptual experience of those networks that respond to a given input. Such selection occurs at synapses, but is not selection for individual neurons; rather, it is for those *groups* of neurons whose connectivities and responses are adaptive.

At first blush, this view (Edelman, 1978, 1981; Edelman and Reeke, 1982) does not seem to have the attractive simplicity of the information processing model. How could cogent neural and behavioral responses be elicited from such variable structures without preestablished codes? And could not classical and operant learning paradigms along with evolutionarily adapted algorithms better account for perceptual as well as other kinds of behavior? What is the advantage of such neural Darwinism over the information processing model?

The chief difficulty of the information processing model is its inability to remove the "homunculus" (or his relatives) from the brain. Who or what decides what *is* information? And how are "programs" constructed that are capable of context-dependent pattern recognition in situations never before encountered? Processors of information must have "information" defined for them *a priori,* just as the Shan-

non measure of information must specify *a priori* what the probability is of receiving any given signal. Such categorization can only be made by an organism *a posteriori* (i.e., after having already defined the categories of received signals), and it is this successful adaptive categorization that constitutes pattern recognition. In making such assumptions, information processing models are forced to assume a position similar to the argument of creation from design (Mayr, 1982) which dominated biological thinking prior to Darwin.

Selection theories of brain function avoid the problem of the homunculus by having the environment act dynamically on the potential orderings already represented by neural structures rather than requiring these structures to respond solely to "information" in the environment. The purposes of this chapter are to show that cogent neural responses can be elicited from such a dynamically varying system and to discuss some aspects of an increasing body of evidence that supports selection theories. Before considering that evidence, it is necessary to give a brief description of the theory of neuronal group selection. Further details may be obtained by consulting earlier publications (Edelman, 1978, 1981; Edelman and Reeke, 1982).

Neuronal Group Selection

The theory of neuronal group selection is based on the idea that among the neural networks subserving a specific function, there exists a significant number of nonidentical or variant subnetworks each of which could respond to a particular input more or less well. This is the central notion of degeneracy—the existence of functionally similar but nonisomorphic variants of neural structures (Edelman, 1978). There are three fundamental features of the theory: (1) Variation in connectivity is introduced epigenetically during development, largely by processes of selection, to create different repertoires of neuronal groups; (2) a second selection process, which takes place during experience, occurs by means of modification of synaptic strengths and leads to selection of particular functioning groups within the degenerate ensemble of anatomically variant groups; and (3) temporal correlation of the responses of interacting groups within different regions occurs by means of reentrant signaling.

According to the theory, *primary repertoires* of neuronal groups are established during development, with their local anatomy determined by cell type and by the primary processes (Cowan, 1978) of development. While structures in a given area of the brain are modally alike in their anatomy and are constrained by genetic programs, enormous epigenetic variation occurs at the level of fine axonal and dendritic ramifications and connections. The developmental process leads to degenerate networks of neuronal groups whose dendritic trees and axonal arbors spread over relatively wide areas with a great degree of overlap. The existence of this overlapping arborization does not gainsay the fact that specific contacts may be made with particular cell types or the fact that these contacts may even be restricted to localized regions of certain neurons.

During experience, that is, after receipt of input signals that are filtered and abstracted by sensory transducers, feature extraction networks, and feature correlators, certain neuronal groups are *selected* over others in a competitive fashion. The competition is based on the variation in their structures and on the synaptic rules guiding the temporal interactions of neurons within a group. This competitive process leads to the formation of a *secondary repertoire* of selected neuronal groups which is dynamically maintained by synaptic alterations.

In describing the mechanism by which a secondary repertoire is selected out of the primary repertoire, the theory of neuronal group selection is concerned with explaining the process of functional expression of selected parts of the variant anatomical substrate. Variability in the primary repertoire must occur in such a fashion that significant *functional* variability can occur within the secondary repertoires—variability that is ultimately manifested in the perception and behavior of the animal. In contrast, while it is conceivable that a highly specified, hard-wired, computerlike, neuronal system could still show considerable functional variation in the execution of a program, it is difficult to see how, *in the absence of a programmer,* this variation could be particularly versatile, alterable, or context dependent.

Because of its primary assumption that there must be epigenetic variability (Edelman, 1978), one of the predictions of group selection theory is that there will not be a highly multifarious and specific set of chemoaffinity markers for cell–cell interactions during development of the brain. Instead, it has been proposed that such interactions occur by local cell-surface modulation (Edelman, 1976) of a small set of cell-adhesion molecules (possibly only a few for neurons and a few for glia) (Edelman, 1983). In contrast to strict chemoaffinity, such local modulation must lead not only to characteristic modal anatomical patterns, but also to an inescapable variation in anatomy. As reviewed below, there is now a mounting body of evidence obtained both *in vitro* and *in vivo* to suggest that this is indeed the case.

How do the various neuronal groups in a complex chain of linked structures like those found in the visual or somatosensory system coordinate their responses around a given input object? According to the theory, the selection of groups is coordinated and reinforced via reentrant anatomical connections mediating phasic reentrant signaling. An anatomical example is the thalamocortical and corticothalamic radiation. Phasic reentry operating in a highly parallel system obviates the storage of time and place markers such as those that are required in a parallel computer system. Reentry allows linkage among systems of neuronal groups operating in parallel in real time. In fact, it has been shown in a computer-based model that specific linkages of this type between two sets of groups can lead to the emergence of new associative functions not originally present in either set of groups (Edelman and Reeke, 1982).

This theory has been described in greater detail elsewhere (Edelman, 1978; Edelman and Reeke, 1982). Its self-consistency (but not its applicability to the nervous system or its correctness) has been shown by the successful functioning of a selective network automaton ("Darwin II") that was explicitly designed on the basis of its assumptions (Edelman and Reeke, 1982).

A number of predictions of the theory, as well as certain potential conditions which would restrict its validity, have been proposed. These predictions include the following: (1) Cell–cell recognition in neural development occurs as described by modulation theories (Edelman, 1976; Edelman, 1983), that is, via the selective interaction of developmental primary processes with only a few kinds of molecules to give rise to rich local variation as well as to the characteristic modal anatomical patterns in the large. (2) The anatomical substrate in a given region is highly degenerate, and functional maps organize via the selection of a much less degenerate secondary repertoire; this selection occurs by means of synaptic changes within and among neuronal groups (Edelman, 1981). (3) Reentrant connections operate phasically both to coordinate neuronal groups and to create new interactive functions (Edelman and Reeke, 1982) in the absence of a specific neural code.

Evidence is now accumulating to support the first two predictions; less is known concerning the third. We shall review the evidence here, placing the major emphasis on rearrangements observed in the somatosensory cortex after peripheral lesions, a body of data that supports the second prediction. We will also extend some of the tenets of the group selection theory by providing a more detailed model to account for some specific aspects of the dynamic reorganization of the somatosensory cortex. Our remarks will be restricted to group selection in the cortex and are not necessarily directly relevant to selection in other parts of the central nervous system. Before discussing these issues in detail, it will be revealing to consider the nature of both variability and degeneracy in the nervous system.

Variability, Degeneracy, and the Origins of Neuronal Diversity

A key condition on any selective theory is that there be a source of diversity and individuality within a population. The alternative view is the essentialist position—that categories are real and immutable (Mayr, 1982). Within the nervous system, this would be equivalent to the assertion that individual neurons are fixed in function and hard-wired and that their interactions are strongly prespecified, for example, by genetically determined individual cell markers that govern cell position and interactions with other neurons. A minor variant of essentialism might be called "irrelevantism"—the position that any deviations in these neural patterns are just noise, an inescapable but nonfunctional byproduct of the developmental dilemma. The position taken here, as already stated, is contrary to this. We assert that variation in neuronal structures plays a central role in higher brain function.

What is the origin of this variation and what is its significance? The variation originates as a result of the modulation of a very small set of cell-adhesion molecules and the interaction of these modulated molecular forms with the primary processes of development (Edelman, 1976, 1983). According to this view, neuron–neuron and neuron–glia interactions are not mediated by a large set of strictly determined chemoaffinity markers. Instead, the structures, the binding strengths, and the prevalences at the cell surface of a limited set of neural cell-adhesion molecules are altered during development. These alterations lead to different patterns of connections as they interact with the processes of cell division, cell migration, and cell differentiation, and they also ultimately determine the pattern of cell death insofar as cell death is a consequence of failure to make appropriate connections (Cowan, 1978). The interaction of these primary processes under the varying restraint of local cell surface modulation is the origin of epigenetic variation. The significance of this process is that it provides the necessary rich repertoire of variants for later selective events during experience. To understand how this modulation operates, we must discuss the neural cell-adhesion molecule (N-CAM).

Neuron–Neuron Adhesion during Development

A major sialoglycoprotein present on the surface of all neurons (and developing striated muscles) appears to be responsible for neural adhesion and recognition in the nervous system (Edelman, 1983). Some salient features (Hoffman et al., 1982) of this molecule are given in Table 1. It is worth summarizing the possible relation of this molecule and its functions to the origin of connectional diversity. N-CAM is present on all nerve cells, regardless

of their states of differentiation, from the time of formation of the neural plate to the adult state. In certain cells, for example, neural crest cells (Thiery et al., 1982), it undergoes large developmental changes in its expression at the cell surface. During the development of other cells, it is converted from an embryonic form having charge heterogeneity to several adult forms with relative charge homo-

Table 1 Functional and Molecular Characteristics of N-CAM

Function:	Present during earliest organization of neuraxis; responsible for neurite fasciculation, neuron–myotube interaction, and orderly layering in developing retina and brain. A failure of conversion to less heterogeneous, less charged, adult form is correlated with connectional disorders in *staggerer* mutants. Binding is second-order homophilic—molecules on different cells bind without intervention of another kind of molecule or ligand.
Location:	Integral membrane protein present in neurons, and in myoblasts and myotubes of striated and cardiac muscle.
Subunit size:	M_r = 120,000-polypeptide chain plus variable amounts of covalently attached carbohydrate, bringing M_r to 200,000–250,000 (see "Charge" below).
Carbohydrate content:	26%. Very high sialic acid content: 13 mol/100 mol amino acids but only 1.4 mol galactose/100 mol amino acids. Fucose, mannose, and galactose at levels resembling those in other glycoproteins. 99% of sialic acid removed by neuraminidase, but only at very slow rates. Forms with less sialic acid (e.g., A-forms) bind more strongly to each other.
Charge:	Isoelectric behavior, pI = 5.0–5.5. Highly diffuse pattern in sodium dodecyl sulfate (SDS)–acrylamide gel electrophoresis from apparent M_r = 200,000–250,000. Converts to sharp doublet at M_r = 140,000 after neuraminidase treatment (removal of sialic acid).
Structural features:	Amino terminus, NH_2–leu–gln–val; carboxyl terminus, lys–ala–COOH; same in both embryonic (E) and adult (A) forms. Spontaneous cleavage to fragment of M_r = 65,000 at 37° in low-salt buffer, inhibited by 0.5 M NaCl; this fragment possibly reflects a compact binding domain at NH_2 terminus. Conversion of E- to A-forms at different times in different parts of brain. A-forms have 8% sialic acid and bands at M_r = 140,000 and 180,000 on SDS–acrylamide gel electrophoresis. E- and A-forms have closely similar peptide maps, CNBr fragments, and identical electrophoretic patterns after neuraminidase treatment.

Source: Edelman, 1983

geneity (Rothbard et al., 1982; Edelman, 1983). N-CAM has been shown to be responsible for neurite fasciculation (Rutishauser et al., 1978), for orderly retinal layering (Buskirk et al., 1980), and for nerve–muscle interactions (Grumet et al., 1982). It has been found in a variety of vertebrate species, and is structurally different from molecules of similar function found in nonnervous tissue such as the liver (Bertolotti et al., 1980; Gallin et al., 1983).

For the present purposes, the most striking property of this molecule is its conversion at the cell surface from the embryonic (E) form to several adult (A) forms (Edelman and Chuong, 1982; Rothbard et al., 1982). As mentioned above, the E-form is heterogeneous in charge and molecular weight; the microheterogeneity is attributable to extraordinarily large amounts of sialic acid present in a linkage that is unusually resistant to cleavage by neuraminidase. In the perinatal period (7–21 days) of the mouse, the molecule is converted to three A-forms (Table 1) (Edelman and Chuong, 1982; Rothbard et al., 1982). These forms have lower amounts of sialic acid and each is relatively homogeneous in charge. Sialic acid is not necessary for binding; in fact, its presence on the molecule reduces the rate of binding of reconstituted vesicles containing the molecule. Thus, the presence of the E-form may lower the free energy of binding of N-CAM on one cell to N-CAM on another, probably because of charge repulsion, and the E-to-A conversion should result in higher average binding strengths (Edelman, 1983).

In the *staggerer* mutant of the mouse, E-to-A conversion is indefinitely delayed in the cerebellar cortex and slightly delayed in the cerebral cortex (Edelman and Chuong, 1982). This suggests that one of the main defects accompanying the connectional defects in this granuloprival mutant is a failure to stabilize cell–cell adhesion, possibly at spines of Purkinje cells. The data also suggest that small conversion delays such as those found in the cortex do not radically alter the gross histology.

The presence of N-CAM as the ubiquitous neuron–neuron recognition molecule, the E-to-A conversion and its significance for binding, and the results of the experiments on mutant mice all provide strong evidence to support a modulation theory of cell–cell recognition (Edelman, 1976; Edelman, 1983). Additional evidence for modulation comes from the experiments indicating that the appearance of N-CAM at the cell surface is altered in a fashion that is functionally correlated with the migration of neural crest cells and their aggregation to form ganglia (Thiery et al., 1982). For the present purposes, there are three conclusions that are of particular interest: (1) Patterns in neuron–neuron recognition and neuron–glia recognition (for another CAM mediates that process, see Edelman, 1983) result from interactions of the primary processes of

development (division, migration, differentiation, and death) with various modulated forms of adhesion molecules having different binding strengths or different amounts at the cell surface (Edelman, 1983). (2) The variation introduced as a result of this interaction is epigenetic. (3) No two nervous systems so constructed can be identical.

While these conclusions do not prove the *functional* significance of those variations in anatomy that are a consequence of local cell-surface modulation, they do shed light on the origin of variability and are entirely consistent with the original predictions of the neuronal group selection theory. Having considered some of the developmental origins of variability, we can now profitably ask what types of variability exist.

Anatomic Variability and Degeneracy

Certainly most neurobiologists would agree that variation is not hard to find in the cortex, or even in such highly regular structures as the cerebellum (Chan-Palay et al., 1981, 1982). The problem is to define and categorize the variations, to determine their quantitative distribution and their significance at various levels of function, and, as suggested above, to analyze those mechanisms by which they are generated. In view of the two stages of selection inherent in neuronal group selection (developmental and experiential), it is also important to make a clear distinction between local structural variation (microanatomy) and dynamic variations in cell and synaptic states.

Unfortunately, little has been done to study the populational or numerical aspects of neuroanatomy in well-controlled situations. But as seen in Table 2, one can at least suggest reasonable candidates for levels at which variation may be expressed. A population of neurons may vary in structural or functional characteristics. Microanatomically, neurons of a given type may differ in the locations, shapes, and sizes of their somata and in their dendritic and axonal arborization patterns and connections. Biochemically, they may vary in their intracellular structures, axoplasmic flows, transmitter types, and membrane receptors and channels. These differences may in turn be reflected in variant receptive field characteristics and electrical properties.

In our present discussion, we leave out a detailed consideration of any dynamic neuronal variation (Bindman and Lippold, 1981) or any variation in neurotransmitters. These variations are without a doubt of importance in selection of both the primary and the secondary repertoires. Complex variants of chemical synapses can arise during development and can persist even in such highly regular tissues as the cerebellum (Chan-Palay et al., 1981, 1982). Variations related to sexual dimorphism may also play a role, for example, in the formation of callosal connections

Table 2 Sites and Levels of Neuronal Variation

A. Variation in genetic traits and developmental primary processes [cell division, migration, adhesion (see Table 1), differentiation, and death]
B. Variation in cell morphology
  1. Cell shape and size
  2. Dendritic and axonal arborizations
    a. Spatial distribution
    b. Branching order
    c. Length of branches
    d. Number of spines
C. Variation in connection patterns
  1. Number of inputs and outputs
  2. Connection order with other neurons
  3. Local vs. long-range connections
  4. Degree of overlap of arbors
D. Variation in cytoarchitectonics
  1. Number or density of cells
  2. Thickness of individual cortical layers
  3. Relative thickness of supragranular, infragranular, and granular layers
  4. Position of somata
  5. Variation in columns
  6. Variation in strips or patches of terminations
  7. Variation in anisotropy of fibers
E. Variation in transmitters
  1. Between cells in a population
  2. Between cells at different times
F. Variation in dynamic response
  1. In synaptic chemistry and size of synapse
  2. In electrical properties
  3. In excitatory/inhibitory ratios and locations of these synapses
  4. In short- and long-term synaptic alteration
G. Variation in neuronal transport
H. Variation in interactions with glia

(de Lacoste-Utamsing and Holloway, 1982). Clearly there is a great need to quantitate the populational distributions of both the static and the dynamic neural variations that are qualitatively illustrated in Table 2.

None of this exercise would be of particular value, however, unless the variability were related to function. One of the most intriguing problems concerning the relation between function and microscopic anatomic variability, is posed by the variability in cortical maps. We choose this as one of the main issues to be discussed in this chapter for a number of reasons: (1) It ties anatomical variability to functional variability; (2) it focuses attention on the interaction of populations of neurons; and (3) it is intimately concerned with input–output relations and therefore directs attention to the play between local degeneracy and reentrant circuits (Edelman, 1978, 1981). To set the stage for later discussions of map organization, our purposes here are to emphasize the degeneracy, in the connections of the primary repertoire, to consider the manifestations of connectional diversity, and to show how this diversity relates to maps.

We suggest that, for the nervous system to be able to deal adaptively with the rich classificatory challenges inherent in perception of the real world, there must be a great deal of degenerate variability in the primary repertoire. A major example of this degeneracy is provided by the surprising amount of divergence found in the terminal arborizations of afferents in many different regions of the nervous system. For instance, individual pyramidal motor neuron axons are found to terminate over several spinal segments (Shinoda et al., 1981, 1982); retinotectal afferents can spread over up to one-fourth of the developing tectum (Meyer, 1980; J. T. Schmidt, personal communication); X-cell axons distribute widely over the lateral geniculate nucleus (LGN) (Sur and Sherman, 1982); and the arbors of individual LGN fibers in turn cover an entire ocular dominance column in area 17 (Gilbert and Wiesel, 1979). Finally, thalamocortical axons in the primary auditory cortex may extend over much of the 2- to 3-mm-wide isofrequency dimension (see Merzenich et al., this volume). We emphasize, however, that despite this degeneracy, the physiological or functional effects of these afferents are restricted in such a way that they effectively drive only certain neurons and only over a small fraction of their fields of distribution.

Cortical cells are known to receive hundreds to thousands of afferent inputs, synapsing all over their somata and dendritic trees. Yet the vast majority of these afferents are never involved in mediating the receptive fields of individual cortical neurons. Classically, these observations have been attributed to "convergence and divergence" in the nervous system, and to the existence of subthreshold inputs. This leaves the mechanism of their control a mystery, and their functional significance at best an enigma. From the point of view of group selection, however, it is this degenerate anatomical substrate that serves as the battleground for an ongoing "Darwinian" competition among neuronal groups that occurs in somatic (as opposed to evolutionary) time. The evidence for the existence of such competition will be discussed later in this chapter.

Variability in Functional Maps

The widespread occurrence of shifted overlap between afferent terminals supports one of the strong predictions of group selection theory, namely, that the underlying anatomy in the cerebral cortex is arranged in an overlapping and degenerate fashion (Edelman, 1981). This implies the following: (1) Within the primary repertoire there are variant groups of cells that can carry out the same group functions more or less well; (2) degeneracy can serve, in a similar fashion to redundancy, to offset the problem of unreliability in a distributed system, and goes beyond redundancy in dealing with the "unreliability" engendered by novel situations; (3) even after the group selection that occurs during experience, the primary repertoire may still contain functionally equivalent or even potentially more effective cell groups than those in the secondary repertoire; and (4) cell groups may be subject to competitive exclusion.

These implications have been considered in a previous discussion (Edelman, 1981) of representation and mapping. It was suggested that features of a topographic map must be maintained at at least one level of representation in the brain. If such an invariance were not present, then within any temporally extended neural representation it would be difficult to establish correspondences to the spatiotemporal locus or continuity of an object. This is particularly true in a reentrant system. Such a map need not be isomorphic; it can be at best "point to area" or "area to area." Maps must nevertheless maintain some degree of continuity corresponding to the characteristics of primary sensory inputs, for they serve during early sensory processing as inner representations to which later, higher-order processing can be referred by reentry. But these representations need be neither unique nor one-to-one—it has previously been pointed out, for example, that shifted overlap in the somatosensory cortex is indicative of degeneracy at the level of maps (Edelman, 1981).

According to this view, the existence of maps has the following significance:

1.   A first representation is generated in the cortex that maps the multidimensional properties of an object onto the two-dimensional cortical sheet. This translates physical properties of a real-world object into neural properties in certain regions. Although this map has the property of local continuity, it does not need to be isomorphic with the collection of object features.

2.   The cortical region or domain of a map is not uniquely defined (although its boundaries are determined ultimately by input projections). Instead, the extents and positions of regions of the map must reflect the outcome of functional competition during group selection.

3.   The main function of the map is to provide a reference for higher-order input–output relationships in a reentrant system. That is, inasmuch as other regions of the nervous system, and of the cortex in particular, must carry out routines involving multimodal input, abstractions, and map-free routines, a place must be maintained for continual reference to continuity properties. This place is the map and its constituent domains within the primary receiving areas. But this also strongly implies that in a reentrant degenerate system, map-to-map interactions must be dynamically maintained and rearranged.

Recent experiments by Merzenich and his collaborators (Kaas et al., 1981; Merzenich et al., 1983a,b; 1984b) have provided very strong support both for this view and for the more general aspects of the theory of neuronal group selection. Their studies represent a detailed analysis of densely mapped regions (every 100–150 μm) of areas 3b and 1 in the somatosensory cortex of adult owl and squirrel monkeys. The paradigm involved making extremely careful maps of these areas in individual normal monkeys for comparison and then remapping the same cortical areas after one of the following procedures had been performed: (1) transection of peripheral nerves such as the median nerve, either allowing or preventing conditions for regeneration; that is, the nerve was either transected and tied to prevent regeneration or transected and reconnected to promote regeneration of the nerve; (2) amputation of single or adjacent digits (usually digit 2 or 3); (3) functional alteration without transection by bandaging, applying casts, or finger-tapping protocols; or (4) local cortical ablations.

The results of these studies compel a reassessment of cortical mapping in terms of neuronal group selection. The key observation was that cortical maps rapidly reorganize following nerve transection or digit amputation in adult monkeys. The reorganization involves changes in (1) receptive field sizes and overlaps, (2) the peripheral loci represented at specific cortical loci, (3) the locations of column boundaries, and (4) the locations of representational discontinuities. Equally compelling is the observation that individual normal monkeys have different maps and that following transection or amputation, map reorganization takes place in an individual manner in different monkeys. This reorganization involves lesion-induced territorial expansions of regions serving unaltered nerves and is not restricted to areas served by the transected nerves. Before considering the far-reaching implications of these findings, we shall describe them in somewhat greater detail.

Map Reorganization

Immediately after transection of the median nerve, an incomplete new representation arises within a part (but not all) of the cortical area that formerly represented the median nerve field (Merzenich et al., 1983a). Over the next several months, this new representation gradually changes so that the skin site represented at any cortical location changes with time after the nerve transection (Merzenich et al., 1983b). This suggests that the receptive field recorded at any cortical site is but one of the many possible receptive fields that, under different conditions, could be expressed at that cortical site. In the new maps, receptive fields originally located at a particular cortical site may occasionally be represented at various distances up to several millimeters away from that site; thus, the same receptive field can be expressed anywhere over a relatively wide area of cortex. As the maps are restructured, basic topography is always maintained, so that at all times continuity and global somatotopy are preserved. Although there is movement of borders (such as those between representations of glabrous and dorsal skin, and even between representations of hand and face), the borders remain sharp. For example, cells on one side of a border might respond exclusively to glabrous inputs, while those on the other side might respond exclusively to stimulation of skin on the dorsum of the hand.

During reorganization, the representations of different hand surfaces (e.g., the hypothenar pad, the insular pad, the dorsal digits) innervated by other nerves with bordering skin fields expand and contract in different sequences (Merzenich et al., 1983b). Within weeks, the radial nerve captures more of the previous median nerve territory in area 3b than does the ulnar nerve, but in area 1 the ulnar nerve captures more territory than does the radial. By 2–3 weeks,

reoccupation of the median field is complete, yet the map continues to reorganize internally for months (Merzenich et al., 1983b). When allowed to regenerate after resuturing, the median nerve initially forms a fragmented, disorganized, multiple representation. In time, the representation congeals and organizes to regain limited somatotopy (Merzenich et al., 1984a) and reoccupies much the same area that it occupied before transection.

In normal maps of the hand in area 3b, glabrous regions are centrally represented (Figure 1), and dorsal representations are principally located along the medial and lateral margins of the hand representation (Merzenich et al., 1978). However, the normal map usually also contains small islands of dorsal representation scattered within the sea of glabrous digital-surface representations. After median nerve transection, a larger dorsal representation immediately arises in the former median glabrous field; the new representation is predominantly arranged around, and in topographic continuity with, the normal dorsal islands (Merzenich et al., 1983b). This supports the notion that the anatomical basis for this larger representation was always

NORMAL MAP VARIATION - Examples

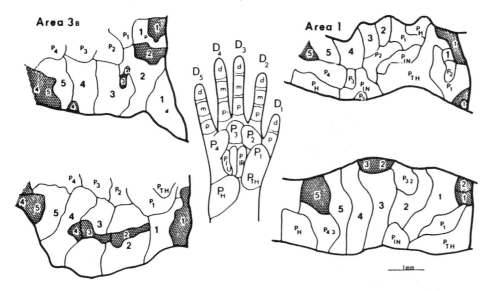

Figure 1 Normal map variations. On the owl monkey hand (*center insert*), D₁–D₅ refer to digits; d, m, and p refer to distal, medial, and proximal phalanges; P₁–P₄. are the palmar pads; Pᴴ is the hypothenar pad; and Pᴛʜ is the thenar pad. The two maps to the left show the internal topography of area 3b in two different adult owl monkeys, and the two maps to the right show that of area 1 in two different adult squirrel monkeys. The variability in the internal organization of area 1 is greater than that recorded in area 3b, but is very significant in both fields. In these examples, note (1) the tremendous differences in the areas of representation of digits in the two area 1 maps; (2) the separation of the representations of digits 1 and 2 in one area 1 map (*top*) and their contiguous placement in the other; (3) the double and reversed representation of the first palmar pad and the thenar eminence recorded in area 1 in one monkey (*top*) and the more normal arrangement recorded in the other (many other differences are apparent on close examination of these maps); (4) the split representation of digit 1 in area 3b in one monkey (*top*), not seen in the other; (5) the significant difference in territory of representation of digit 1 in area 3b between the two monkeys; and (6) the differences in representation of dorsal digital surfaces in area 3b. (From Merzenich et al., 1984.)

present but was effectively suppressed from organizing. Note that the novel dorsal map arises immediately only in the original territory of representation of the glabrous digits, and not in the former region of representation of the palm, in which the normal representation does not have an islandlike "dorsal within glabrous" mapping.

After median nerve transection, large silent areas in which cells cannot be activated by any peripheral stimulation are also seen in the former representational area of the nerve. However, adjacent to these areas are cortical sites that are activated by new receptive fields. The location of the silent areas shifts with time (Figure 2), generally shrink-

ing but occasionally shifting to a region that had earlier been active after transection (Merzenich et al., 1983b). After multiple amputations of adjacent digits, some silent areas remain and never completely fill in (Merzenich et al., 1983c). This indicates that the range of the anatomical basis for potential alternative maps is restricted to those representations of body sites that were reasonably close to the original representation.

Several semiquantitative measurements were made both of receptive field representation and overlap and of distance limits during reorganization. The larger the area of cortex devoted to a body part (the greater the magnification

TIME SEQENCE POST-SECTION MAPS

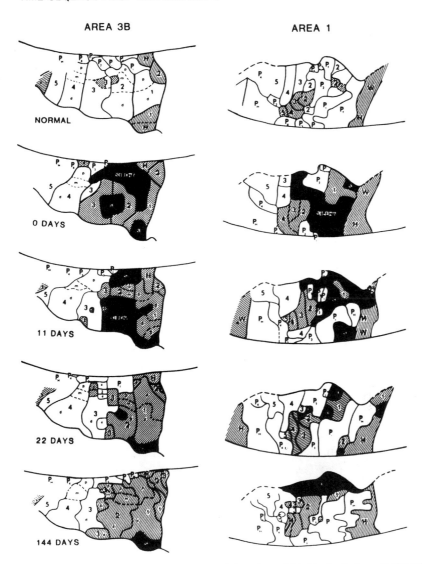

Figure 2 Cortical maps of the hand in area 3b (*left*) and area 1 (*right*) of a single squirrel monkey that was studied before, immediately after, and 11, 22, and 144 days after median nerve cut. Regions not drivable by cutaneous stimulation are shaded black; the representations of the dorsum are hatched; 1–5 refer to digits; H, hand; W, wrist; P, various palmar pads; other abbreviations as in Figure 1. (From Merzenich et al., 1983b.)

factor of the representation), the smaller were the receptive fields on that body part. Conversely, smaller cortical representations yielded larger receptive fields. Thus two-point discrimination, which improves with smaller receptive field size, may be attributable to the size of the cortical representation (Laskin and Spencer, 1979; Merzenich et al., 1983a, 1984b). Of particular significance is the fact that the percentage overlap of the areas of the receptive fields of two cortical cells is a monotonically decreasing function of the cortical separation of the cells (Figure 3). There is reason to believe that the function decreases in a stepwise manner (Merzenich et al., 1983b), reaching zero overlap at critical separations of approximately 600 μm in normal animals (Sur et al., 1980). Of particular significance for competition models of group selection is the fact that, for the first week or two after nerve transection, receptive field overlap is greatly increased, the slope of the decreasing function is several times shallower than normal, and neurons 2 mm or farther apart can have overlapping receptive fields (Figure 3).

Finally, three appears to be a distance limit of approximately 600 μm over which expansion of a representation can take place. After amputation, a silent cortex area that extends over more than 600 μm in radius can never be completely reoccupied. Together with the observation that

the sites of representations can effectively move up to millimeter distances, this is another indication that the anatomical basis for these translocated representations must have preexisted in a suppressed form in the near vicinity. In any detailed model, the 600-μm limit common to both the expansion and the overlap of receptive fields must be specifically explained.

Several empirically defined rules have been formulated (Merzenich et al., 1984a) on the basis of these observations on somatosensory map reorganization. It should be emphasized that these are new mainly with regard to the reorganizational process; several of them resemble principles already known to neurophysiologists.

1. *The Movement Rule*: Sites of representation of particular localized skin surfaces can move hundreds of microns, and can differ severalfold in areal extent. Representational borders remain sharp throughout this process of movement.

2. *The Continuity Rule*: As the representations of uncut nerves expand into silenced cortical areas, they maintain topographic continuity.

3. *The Distance Limit Rule*: The distance limit for reorganization (as shown by amputation of adjacent digits) is roughly 600-μm on either side of the cortical map border

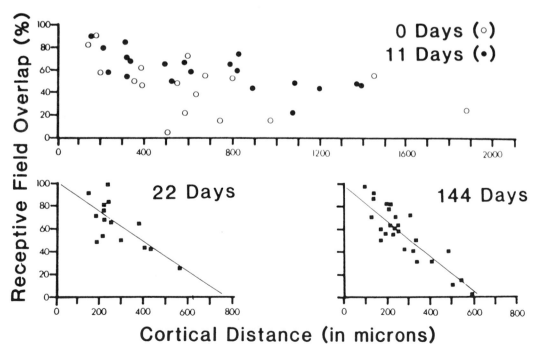

Figure 3 Percentage overlap of receptive fields versus distance between cortical recording sites immediately after median nerve cut and 11, 22, and 144 days later. Receptive fields were on the backs of the middle and proximal phalanges of digits 1–3 and recording was in the area of former median nerve cortical representation. Note that the slope of the graph becomes less steep after transection, but that by 144 days the normal 600-μm limit is restored. (From Merzenich et al., 1983b.)

originally present between the representations of the deprived and normal skin.

4. *The Overlap Rule*: The percentage overlap of the receptive fields of two cortical neurons decreases as the separation between them in the cortex increases. The receptive fields of neurons located more than about 600 μm apart do not overlap at all.

5. *The Inverse Rule*: As representations expand in the cortex, their receptive field sizes decrease in area.

These reorganizational rules suggest that each region of the cortex is organized in such a way that it could support any one of many different possible maps. In view of the topographic continuity at a very refined level of representation, and given the overlap and distance limits, one may conclude that adjacent regions of anatomic input must overlap extensively. At the same time, however, the order of input from the thalamus and ultimately from the periphery is still maintained.

It is important to note that there is no evidence for any sprouting taking place either peripherally or centrally after nerve transection and tying. In fact, even if sprouting were to occur, it could not account for these observations. Changes in the map occur immediately after transection and continue for months, whereas sprouting would follow a different time course. Different types of changes occur in area 3b versus area 1 despite the similarity of their peripheral inputs. Finally, related map changes are normally seen in areas 1 and 3b after noninvasive procedures such as finger-tapping, and it is difficult to postulate sprouting in these cases.

The central conclusion compelled by these facts, a conclusion directly supportive of the theory of neuronal group selection, is as follows: From the degenerate anatomical substrate (or primary repertoire), a dynamic process must select particular neuronal groups to form the functional map (Merzenich et al., 1984a). This dynamism is indicated by the movements of representations and by the reestablishment of receptive field structure after transection. Indeed, evidence has been reviewed (Merzenich et al., 1984a) that indicates that normal (unlesioned) map structure is also dynamically maintained in adult primates. The results suggest that maps are reorganized by selection over a degenerate network and also that preexisting cortical anatomy provides a substrate for limited territorial competition. In other words, following development, there is a degenerate anatomical substrate upon which selection operates competitively to create a functional map from a manifold of possible maps. The major determinant of the competitive selection process appears to be significant neuronal activity resulting from coactivation of the overlapping afferents (Merzenich et al., 1984a). What are the

limits and the mechanisms of such competition? In the next part, we turn our attention to this and related problems.

Mechanisms of Group Confinement, Group Selection, and Group Competition

To account for the data reviewed above, three classes of models can be considered. The first assumes that the receptive field of a cell and any change in that receptive field are exclusively and strictly determined by the afferent input. Cortical maps could thus be viewed as mirrors of experience, capable of reflecting to a greater or lesser extent that environmental experience by means of, for example, alterations at Hebb synapses. This is typical of the instructive, hierarchical, information processing approach and such models would have trouble explaining the overlap rule, the maintenance of sharp borders despite the movement of the location of a cortical representation, and the persistence of thalamocortical synaptic strengths months after nerve transection (Cronholm, 1951). The second class of models postulates the existence of two or more simultaneously fixed and organized underlying maps, only one of which is expressed at any given time in any given region. These maps may arise from disparate sources such as lemniscal and nonlemniscal (dorsal column nuclei versus anterolateral funiculus) pathways. This model cannot by itself account for the inverse rule, the distance limit on reorganization, or the rich variability in possible map changes.

The class of models that we favor assumes that the expressed map emerges as a result of a group-selective competitive process acting upon a degenerate anatomical substrate capable of giving rise to numerous possible maps. We believe that this model can explain all of the data and can specifically account for the five rules of reorganization. The fundamental challenge to the model is to explain the overall process of group selection, that is, how a map is selected out of the degenerate primary repertoire.

In this model, a neuronal group in the cerebral cortex is functionally defined as an ensemble of cohesively interconnected cells which together determine their individual receptive field properties. Most cells in a group will express a similar receptive field. Anatomically, groups are related to cortical columns (Mountcastle, 1978) in that columns are made up of groups; however, groups must always be viewed in conjunction with their dynamic function. Group dynamics depend on both input and internal connectivity, and together these determine which of the afferents received by the group will mediate the group receptive field.

The fundamental operation of neuronal groups is to compete for domination of cell activity. Domination is achieved by strengthening of the synaptic connections between cells in the group and any particular cell that is to be captured by that group. As new cells are brought into the group, the balance of afferent inputs and internal connectivity is altered, and the newly constituted group may require different patterns of input for significant activation. As long as significant activation is achieved, the group can continue to consolidate its "hold" on cells. But other groups are constantly competing for the same cells, and any weakening of connections due to decreased activation puts the group at risk either of losing a few cells or, in the extreme case, of being divided and conquered. In this model, both thalamocortical and corticocortical synapses may be modifiable, but the burden of accounting for movement in cortical maps falls mainly on modifiable intracortical connections. This is not to say that changes do not occur at different levels of the nervous system; indeed the accumulating evidence (e.g., Devor and Wall, 1981), as well as the notion of reentry (Edelman, 1978, 1981), suggests that such changes *must* occur at every level. But at least at the cortical level, we suppose that the most significant changes occur at intrinsic connections rather than at extrinsic connections.

More specifically, we suggest that there are three processes that give rise to cortical maps. The first concerns the limitation of group size, which we call *group confinement*. The primary repertoire consists of degenerate corticocortical connections, which are predominantly oriented vertically (Mountcastle, 1978), an anatomical fact accepted since Lorente de Nó (1938) and consistent with established developmental events (Rakic, 1977). Local inhibitory horizontal connections serve to funnel any activity into restricted cortical domains. As we shall show, this has the

effect of limiting the expansion and contraction of cohesively connected cortical groups. The second process, *group selection,* arises from the distribution of afferent arbors, each of which spreads over a limited cortical region and extensively overlaps with neighboring arbors. Across these degenerate arbors, the play of coactivated and uncorrelated peripheral stimuli leads to selection of groups according to a synaptic modification rule. The final and highest-level process, *group competition,* concerns the competitive interactions among those groups that arise from confinement and are then selected. We propose that a set of hierarchical competition rules determines the readjustment of territorial control among different groups. These competition rules include historical effects, as is reflected by the proposal that functioning extant groups can strongly influence the selection of new groups.

We now consider in order the three processes that we propose to be necessary to account for map formation: group confinement, group selection, and group competition (Figure 4).

Group Confinement
We conjecture that the average size of a group in the hand representation of somatosensory area I (SI) is in the range of 50–100 μm. A 50-μm-diameter group would include 288 ± 25 cell bodies and a 100-μm-diameter group would include 1152 ± 98 cell bodies through the depth of the cortex based on Rockel et al.'s (1980) data on cell density in the macaque somatosensory cortex. We choose the value 50–100 μm because it represents the upper bound for separated locations in the cortex with identical receptive fields (Sur et al., 1980; Merzenich et al., 1984a); group size may

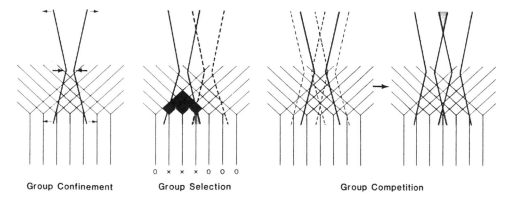

Group Confinement   Group Selection   Group Competition

Figure 4 The three components of map formation according to neuronal group selection theory. Ascending Y-shaped figures represent thalamic afferents; hourglass figures represent groups with narrow waists in layer IV. Group confinement (*far left*) restricts activity to local areas by the interplay of excitation in supra- and infragranular layers with inhibition in layer IV; see Figures 5 and 6 for details. Coactive input (*left center*), denoted by the "x"s, selects the group on the left since it contains a region (*blackened*) that receives coactive input but not uncorrelated input (denoted by "0"s) from the adjacent afferents; see Figure 8 for details. Group competition (*right*) between three previously selected group leads, in this hypothetical case, to dissolution of the central group (perhaps due to lack of overlap of its receptive field with those of the surrounding groups).

vary somewhat in other brain regions. Nonetheless, a group extends over only a fraction of the extent of the arborization of a thalamic afferent. The size of a group depends on all three of the processes mentioned, but before selection and competition of groups can occur, the size of the group must be confined to a limited region. Confinement reflects the existence of a stable size range for groups due to the interplay of excitatory and inhibitory corticocortical connections in different laminae. To appreciate these phenomena, we must review some cytoarchitectonics of the somatosensory cortex.

A schematic depiction of known interconnections of neurons in SI is shown in Figure 5. Connections are presumed to be excitatory or inhibitory on the basis of their vesicular and synaptic morphology (see Shepherd, 1979). The first significant fact is that the majority of synapses in SI are from intrinsic fibers. Jones and Powell (1970) have estimated there are 30 times more intrinsic connections than extrinsic connections, and White and Hersch (1982) found that, even in layer IV, only 20% of synapses degenerate after thalamic lesions. The vast majority of these intrinsic fibers are oriented vertically and link cells in different laminae. Of the seven common types of nonpyramidal cells classified by Jones (1975), four send their axons vertically. The spiny star stellates, with somata in layer IV, send a narrow column of vertical axons to excite pyramidal cells in all layers; and the double bouquet dendritiques with somata in layers II and III send short axonal branches upward and longer branches down to the pyramidals of layers IV and V. Two other cell types have shorter vertically oriented axons.

Horizontally oriented axons are less numerous. Pyramidal cells give off excitatory axonal collaterals in layers I, III, and V–VI that are nonspecifically oriented in the horizontal plane (Jones et al., 1978). The only other horizontal connections are inhibitory and oriented anteroposteriorly; they originate in two types of nonpyramidal cells. One sends long branches through all layers, whereas the other is shorter and confined to layer II (Jones, 1975).

Within layer IV, the predominant cell type is the nonspiny stellate, the major recipient of thalamic afferents (White, 1978). These cells have small, 100-μm dendritic fields and a "ball of string" 300-μm axonal field largely confined to layer IV that inhibits 300 to 500 adjacent cells. In rat visual cortex (Peters and Fairen, 1978), such cells inhibit the somata and the basal or apical dendrites of layer III and V pyramidals, respectively.

As shown in Figure 5, thalamic afferents excite nonspiny stellates and, to a lesser degree, spiny stellates in layer IV (White, 1978). These afferents also excite pyramidal cells in layers VI, IV, and III. Cells in IV and the supragranular

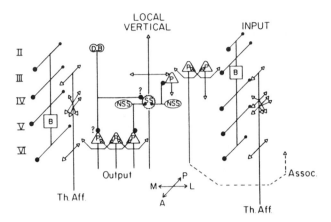

Figure 5 Schematic diagram of known synaptic relationships between various cells in somatosensory cortex (see text for references). Diagram is artificially arranged, with input, interlaminar connections, and output cells displayed separately. Darkened circles represent inhibitory connections; open triangles represent excitatory connections. The question mark signifies that it is not certain whether the synapse is excitatory or inhibitory; however, evidence obtained by Somogyi et al. (1981) in visual cortex indicates that such cells are GABAergic. Local inhibitory cells and chandelier cells are not shown. Th. Aff., thalamic afferent; P, pyramidal cell; SS, spiny (star) stellate cell; NSS, nonspiny stellate cell; B, basket cell; DB, double bouquet dentritique cell; Assoc., corticocortical association fibers. Arrows at bottom of figure: M, medial; L, lateral; A, anterior; P, posterior.

layers also receive excitatory commissural and interarea afferents.

We accept the postulate that pyramidal cells, particularly in the supragranular layers, receive excitatory connections on their spines from other pyramidal cells and from the layer IV spiny stellates (Szentágothai, 1975; Winfield et al., 1981). In conjunction with the thalamic afferents, these excitatory interconnections provide the "cell-catching" mechanism of the group. Pyramidal cells that receive significant excitation (from thalamic, commissural, and associational afferents as well as from other nearby pyramidal cells and from spiny stellates directly below) are activated and strengthen their connections to the pyramidal cells that they excite in turn. Local inhibitory cells sharpen the dy-

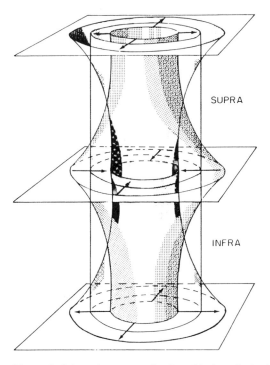

Figure 6 Schematic conceptualization of the hypothesized process of group confinement. Three different group configurations are demarcated by the three surfaces. A group will tend to expand in the supragranular layers due to excitatory horizontal connections. This expansion leads to increased inhibition in layer IV leading to constriction of the group. However, constriction of the group in supragranular layers leads to expansion in layer IV. The intermediate cylinder represents an equilibrium configuration for the group. The infragranular portion is depicted as symmetrical with the supragranular, but in reality probably differs due to the existence of direct supragranular input.

namic response by lateral inhibition. As depicted in Figure 6, the supra- and infragranular layers are sites of excitatory group expansion. However, layer IV, the predominant thalamic recipient, is dominated by the inhibitory nonspiny stellates. As larger regions of layer IV are excited by thalamic input and by the increasing amounts of excitation in other layers, increasing inhibition is generated in IV, which tends to lead to tamponade of the source of excitation. The dynamic equilibrium that occurs between granular level "contraction" and supra- and infragranular "expansion," inextricably linked by predominant vertical connectivity, results in the formation and confinement of the group.

This inhibitory funneling of activity in layer IV may be responsible for the finding by Poggio and Mountcastle (1963), and also by Laskin and Spencer (1979), that peripheral stimulation by a secondary stimulus within the receptive field can lead to a distribution of cortical inhibition nearly identical to the distribution of excitation. Gardner and Costanzo (1980a,b) have found this inhibition to extend over a larger area than the excitation, to occur at longer poststimulus latencies, and to persist for longer durations.

Whatever the case, this inhibition clearly could serve as a mechanism for confining the spread of cortical excitation due to concentrated peripheral stimulation.

There are two other influences of inhibition on the process of confinement that deserve brief mention. First, excitation of a group requires the coordinated flow of activity between the laminae. Uncorrelated activity may disturb the sequencing of excitation, for example, by inhibiting layer IV at a time when returning excitation from supragranular layers tends to excite it. The combined inputs from thalamic, associational, and callosal afferents terminating in layer IV and supragranular layers give rise to separate spike trains. Lack of correlation among these inputs would destroy the phasic sequencing of reentrant connections. Inhibition arising from out-of-phase inputs may then alter the distributions of activity necessary for synaptic change. Second, similar phenomena could occur by means of local inhibition present in the supragranular layers. The inhibiting cells may have different latencies and durations of activity from those of the excitatory cells. Uncorrelated inputs would likely suppress each other, whereas simultaneous inputs could enhance or sharpen each other. At present, however, it is difficult to assess the relative contributions of such processes.

Group confinement is an intrinsic property of the cortex, but group selection depends on both the anatomy and the spatiotemporal properties of the input. The temporal overlap of inputs depends mostly on the pattern of stimulation, but the spatial overlap of the inputs requires convergence of stimulated afferents to a local region. For this reason, before we can discuss group selection, we must consider how the afferents to the cortex are distributed with respect to each other.

Arborization and Overlap

Horseradish peroxidase (HRP) fillings of thalamic afferents to the somatosensory cortex in the cat by Landry and Deschênes (1981) revealed axonal arborizations (Figure 7) quite similar to those observed in the visual cortex (Gilbert and Wiesel, 1979). Single afferents usually give off collaterals before reaching the cortex; each collateral ramifies in a bushy termination of approximately 400 μm diameter. Often two bushy regions from the same collateral are aligned mediolaterally and are separated by a less dense region constituting a gap of about equal size (Landry et al., 1982). Other collaterals may end in bushes some distance away, usually in the anteroposterior directions, but occasionally in another cytoarchitectonic area. Thus terminals from a single afferent in area 3b in this species are spread densely over about 0.5–1 mm^2 of the cortex, with other regions of collateral innervation some distance away. There may be significant anatomical differences between cat and monkey. Pons and colleagues (1982), working in area 3b of the owl monkey, have found, in general, somewhat smaller arbors without distant collateral branches. Our basic argument will be unchanged by these differences.

It is difficult to ascertain the degree of anatomic overlap between separate afferent arbors. There is currently no quantitative information regarding the density of cortical innervation. Degeneration studies shed some light on the matter. Small thalamic lesions in the cat (Kosar and Hand, 1981) lead to the formation of anteroposteriorly oriented strips of degeneration 80–120 µm wide and 2500–3000 µm long. In the monkey (see Jones, 1981), using different techniques, strips of different dimensions have been found. Nonetheless, the relative dimensions indicate a marked anteroposterior anisotropy in the afferent terminations. In several different monkey genera, strips of degeneration seen after transection of commissural or interareal association fibers are 500–1000 µm wide and of varying lengths (Jones, 1975).

Another source of information for estimating overlap, albeit in a specialized region, is the mouse barrel fields. Barrel C-1 has an average area of 56,603 µm^2 (Pasternak and Woolsey, 1975) and receives input from the 162 peripheral fibers innervating vibrissa C-1 (Lee and Woolsey, 1975). Assuming that convergence and divergence through the intervening synaptic relays keep the number of inner-

vating fibers to within the same order of magnitude, we get an approximately 20-µm spacing between adjacent afferents. This calculation assumes that the afferents are regularly spaced, and so does not apply to the barrel fields themselves, but it suggests what the innervation density might be in other cortical regions. It should also be stressed that these examples come from different species, and interspecies differences must ultimately be taken into account. Nevertheless, two major conclusions of great significance for group selection emerge from this anatomy: (1) There is significant overlap between afferent axonal arborizations, perhaps greater in some directions than in others; and (2) every cortical cell receives synapses from a large number of afferents, especially considering the possible interactions of widespread axonal arbors with large dendritic trees. To explain how a precise map is selected against the background of this extensively degenerate anatomical substrate, we must consider the distribution of activity across the cortex leading to group selection.

Group Selection

Group confinement assures that group size will not exceed certain limits, but in itself provides little specificity. To achieve specificity for group selection, we must invoke temporally coactivated inputs to the cells of a group. Figure 8 shows a highly idealized set of overlapping cortical afferents. The branches marked "X" receive coactivated stimulation from peripheral receptors, leading to coactivation of neurons all across the hatched area. Adjacent afferents marked "0" are not coactivated; thus all neurons outside the darkened region receive uncorrelated activity. Despite the wide arborization of the afferent terminals, there is only a small cortical region that experiences maximal coactivation but minimal uncorrelated activity. Only

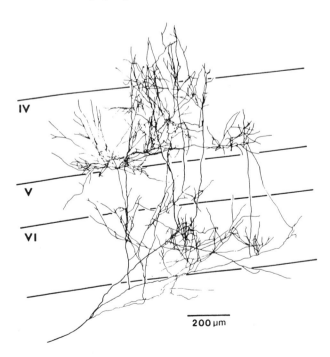

Figure 7 HRP injection in the cat of a thalamic afferent to area 3b. The receptive field was on digit 5. The arbor spreads over an area of approximately 1 mm^2 of cortex in this section. (From Landry and Deschênes, 1981).

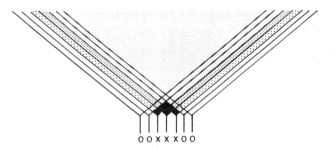

Figure 8 Highly idealized representation of overlapping thalamic afferent arbors. Afferents marked "X" receive coactivated stimulation, whereas those marked "0" receive uncorrelated stimulation. The three densities of stippling indicate regions in which one, two, or three coactivated afferents overlap. The darkened region receives coactivated input, but no uncorrelated input.

groups situated within this region are strongly selected by the coactive stimuli.

Group selection results from synaptic modification induced by the intense activation of cells within a group. The threshold for synaptic modification (see Appendix) must be assumed to lie somewhere within the distribution of activity produced by significant coactivated stimulation. It is the time sequence of activity, in addition to its magnitude, that leads to synaptic modification. The temporal constraints on input are determined in the particular example given in the Appendix by the implicit decay constants for the control variables in the synaptic model —namely calcium and transmitter concentration. Let us now consider that synaptic model.

Synaptic Alteration. The theory of neuronal group selection is compatible with a variety of synaptic models in much the same way that systems of natural selection could conceivably occur with a variety of genetic rules. The major requirement is that there be a mechanism for both increasing and decreasing synaptic strengths to change the contributions of neurons to groups, much as gene frequencies within a population are subject to change. One possible model, described as a suitable example in the Appendix, treats synaptic strength as a variable (as opposed to a constant correlation coefficient) under control by the cell. Synaptic strength depends on the efficacy of both presynaptic and postsynaptic processes, but we propose that modification of the efficacy of these processes depends exclusively on events in the respective cells, not directly on events in the cell across the synaptic cleft. For the present model we consider only presynaptic modifications; we shall show these are sufficient to account for group selection.

The model makes two assumptions. First, the modification of presynaptic efficacy depends on the activity of just the presynaptic cell. Kandel's laboratory (Hawkins et al., 1983) has provided direct experimental evidence on the relationship of activity to synaptic modification. They find, in *Aplysia,* that postsynaptic activity is neither necessary nor sufficient to induce changes in synaptic strength, whereas presynaptic activity alone does lead to such changes. The second main assumption of the present model is that, at least to some degree, all presynaptic terminals of a cell are modified in concert (i.e., all those synapses to which the given cell contributes the presynaptic terminal are strengthened in concert).

The fundamental property arising from the assumptions of the model is the following: Significant activity leads to strengthened synaptic efficacy, lesser amounts of activity lead to weakened efficacy, but minimal or no activity leaves efficacy unchanged. What exact level of activation

is considered "significant" may vary from cell to cell, and depends on the spatiotemporal properties of the stimuli and specific cell parameters. Among these cell parameters are the implicit decay rates of activity. Equally significant activity may arise from different patterns of input and, depending on recent history, the same imput pattern can have different effects; therefore, there is no neural code. Instead, the decay parameters will tend to allow only highly temporally coactivated inputs to result in significant levels of activation.

There is an associated plasticity property that derives from the model: Stronger synapses are less plastic, weaker synapses are more plastic. This avoids the problem of saturation of synaptic efficacy (Sinclair, 1981), and it allows for rapid changes in efficacy under novel conditions (see Appendix).

The Mechanism of Selection. In the Appendix, we discuss how strong coactive stimulation can lead to an increase and uncorrelated stimulation to a decrease of synaptic strength on the cellular level. But it should be emphasized that the link between cortical anatomy, the synaptic modification rule, and group selection is dependent on the effects of correlation at the group level. If the cells within a group fire in a coactive fashion, then they each receive coactivated inputs via corticocortical connections from all other group members. Conversely, differences in cell firing patterns lead to uncorrelated corticocortical inputs. This will eventually lead to increasing homogeneity in the distribution of activity within a group.

There are also corticocortical connections from other groups that may or may not be coactivated with the group activity. Here we encounter what might appear to be a paradox of the model. From the cellular point of view, strengthening all of the connections of a cell in concert may lead to stronger connections with unrelated groups. But from the group point of view, input from unrelated groups is likely to be uncorrelated, and will tend to weaken the internal connections of the recipient group, not to strengthen them. Selection therefore must occur at the group level, with all of the sources of input to the group playing a role.

A group will be selected only if it is localized to the region of high percentage overlap of the afferents mediating its receptive field. This is the region referred to above as receiving maximal coactivated and minimal uncorrelated stimulation. As the number of afferents receiving coactivated stimulation increases, the area of cortex receiving coactivated stimuli also increases. But the distribution of coactivated activity over the cortical surface becomes progressively more peaked and less uniform (until the area exceeds roughly 600 μm in diameter, at which point the distribution flattens out again due to the lack of afferent overlap). This increase in coactivation is matched by a corresponding decrease in uncorrelated activity in the region. These two effects could combine with the highly nonlinear group dynamics to yield a restricted cortical region with a large ratio of coactive to uncorrelated input.

The anatomical basis of these dynamics, like that of group confinement, must relate to the connection scheme depicted in Figure 5. The mutual lateral inhibition mediated by the nonspiny stellate cells in layer IV will serve to suppress all but the local area of maximal activity. Only those spiny stellate cells situated within this localized region will vertically excite a shaft of pyramidal cells in the supra- and infragranular layers.

A possible problem arises in postulating that a group is on the order of 50 μm in diameter, for there are no apparent anatomical structures of this size. But the region of high percentage overlap of afferents involved in mediating the receptive field of cells in the group may be of this dimension. As a rough calculation, for example, let the group have a receptive field mediated by 75 thalamic afferents with 600-μm-diameter arbors, each of which overlaps anatomically with its neighbors by 95%. Then the region in which all 75 fibers are overlapped (interdigitated) is about 50 μm. This region would be somewhat larger if we were to consider the area in which only a major subset, rather than the entire set, of these afferents overlap.

It is crucial to note that when we speak of an area of periphery being stimulated, receptor density must be taken into consideration. All receptive field measurements must be scaled with respect to receptor density, so that, for example, equivalent stimuli on the fingertips are markedly smaller than those on the back. It is also important to keep in mind that the average cortical receptive field includes the contributions of many individual receptors. For example, Meissner's corpuscles, which mediate rapidly adapting cutaneous pressure sensation, are spaced at approximately 200-μm intervals in the human fingertip (Quilliam, 1975). Corresponding receptive fields of mechanoreceptive fibers in the median nerve of the monkey average 3.7 mm^2 in area (Talbot et al., 1968). Given that the average cortical receptive field corresponding to these receptors is roughly 10 mm^2 (Merzenich, 1983a), each cortical receptive field encompasses a territory containing roughly 250 receptors. It is amusing to note that in the fovea of the macaque an average receptive field encompasses 240 cones (Dow et al., 1981; see Dow et al., this volume).

Of course, the arborization pattern depicted in Figure 8 is highly idealized. Real arbors would commonly have patches of higher and lower terminal density on branches of varying sizes and orientations that interdigitate in nonuniform ways. Furthermore, we have assumed that the recipient cortical cells are homogeneously and isotropically arrayed, with identical dendritic trees. Obviously, groups receive a distribution of connections that only approximates this simple idealized version in the statistical limit. In any event, whatever inhomogeneities and anisotropies exist only serve to skew the selection of the preexistent groups and do not affect the basic argument. Finally, it should be mentioned that we have not considered the role of the geometry of dendritic trees, having confined our analysis to the axonal arborizations. Clearly, both types of ramifications play a crucial role, and this simplified approach has, in effect, lumped both together.

Group Competition

We now consider the last of the three processes responsible for map organization, group competition. Our treatment will be necessarily briefer than the previous discussions, as the details of competitive interactions (i.e., who wins under what circumstances) are exquisitely dependent on the environment in which the competition takes place. Group competition is, nevertheless, perhaps the most important single process in determining what the actual map will look like. We will therefore consider those general properties that pertain to most competitive interactions in the cortex.

As different stimuli are successively encountered, we suggest that, in addition to group confinement and selection, a Darwinian competition occurs between various groups for cortical representation space (Figure 4). In general, within the constraints of peripheral innervation density, groups with smaller receptive fields have the competitive edge, as they receive coactivated stimulation most frequently. We surmise that there must be a set of hierarchy rules according to which groups can compete with other groups. A self-consistent set would include, for example, the following: (1) Group expansion beyond a certain size or contraction below a certain size is unstable; (2) groups whose receptive fields overlap within certain limits with those of neighboring groups are favored; (3) cells that are at greater distances from those in the rest of the group are in greater danger of being captured by other groups; (4) extant groups have an advantage over incipient groups; (5) receptor density constrains the receptive field of a group, and thus its competitiveness; and (6) the most competitive groups are those that are associated with the most frequently stimulated peripheral locations.

Explaining the Reorganizational Rules

We are now in a position to explain the reorganizational rules (Merzenich et al., 1984) on the basis of the processes of group confinement, group selection, and group competition.

The Movement Rule

Movement of map boundaries is accounted for in two ways. Local fluctuation of borders occurs as a result of trading of cells between groups. This can occur even across a major border such as the hand/face border (Merzenich et al., 1983b, 1984b). Larger movements, however, are likely to result from the more extreme case of dissolution of a group. Under normal circumstances, an individual group may occasionally be completely taken over by neighboring groups because of changing peripheral stimulation, but the map will undergo only minor shifting, such as is seen normally in area 1. To reorganize a map completely requires a major change in input, such as that produced by nerve transection. The new map may then either express the same arbors in different portions of their extent, or instead may express a distant collateral branch (this can account for the instances of large shifts in representational sites). Any regrowth of peripheral nerves will form a very similar map, due to the similarity in the driving peripheral stimulation. But the map that organizes without new afferents, as in the case in which the nerve is tied to prevent regeneration, will differ radically from the original map.

The sharpness of internal map boundaries, despite their capacity for movement, is an emergent property of the competition between discrete groups with limited receptive field overlap. The receptive field of a group is essentially maintained, except for size changes, regardless of whether cells are being gained or lost through competition. The receptive field is thus (by definition) a property of the group, independent of its cellular constituents. Thus representations and borders will be kept sharp until the group is competed out of existence, at which point the extant groups will determine the new map borders. If single cells, instead of groups, mediated map organization, every vagary of receptive field shifting would be reflected in the fine structure of the map. Groups can appear and disappear—neurons cannot.

The compact nature of the receptive field results from the process of group selection. Adjacent body locations are most likely to give rise to intersecting axonal arbors and are also most likely to be concurrently stimulated. Groups with receptive fields that straddle a boundary on the body, even if selected, would be outcompeted by adjacent groups that receive more temporally and spatially overlapped inputs. Since receptors for different modalities have different temporal characteristics, and cells driven from these afferents reflect these properties (M. Sur, personal communication), groups will rarely express more than one modality.

The Continuity Rule

The necessary condition for the continuity rule is the extensive spread of arbors, which enables a given receptive field to be represented at various different locations over the cortex. Yet continuity actually results from intergroup competition. At each stage of reorganization of the map there are extant groups which assure a continuous representation through group competition. As the groups change, the map changes, but group interactions always maintain overlap of receptive fields (see overlap rule). Although groups can form with multiple or nonadjacent receptive fields, only maps exhibiting local continuity will avoid the significant intergroup inhibition that leads to weakening of group connections.

The Distance Limit Rule

The next reorganizational rule places a distance limit of approximately 600 μm on the area over which reoccupation can occur. This distance represents the average limit of the anatomical spread of axonal arbors and it is therefore not coincidental that it is related to the nonoverlap distance implied by the overlap rule. In the normal animal, glabrous and dorsal afferents spread over the same expanse of cortex (Figure 9A). Any given patch of cortex only expresses one type of group—glabrous or dorsal. Since they are rarely coactivated, the groups expressing each are segregated, with the more commonly activated glabrous representation getting more cortical area. On the fingers, however, where the dorsum is frequently stimulated and coactivation occurs more commonly, the dorsal digits do show a representation in the midst of the glabrous representation in the normal animal.

If the median nerve is cut (Figure 9B), the glabrous representation of the lateral aspect of the hand is removed. The cortex still has dense dorsal input throughout this region, and reorganizes accordingly. If one or more fingers are amputated, however (Figure 9C), *both* dorsal and glabrous input are removed. The only remaining inputs are the spreading axonal arbors from adjacent remaining fingers and palm, which overlap into the deafferented cortical region. But these arbors cannot extend more than about 600 μm, and an amputation creating a larger defect occupying a cortical zone with a radius greater than 600 μm can never be completely reoccupied. This explains the relationship between the 600-μm receptive field overlap condition and the reorganizational distance limit. Of course, it is possible, but unlikely, that some distant afferent could send a collateral into the deafferented region, in which case it could also possibly be expressed there.

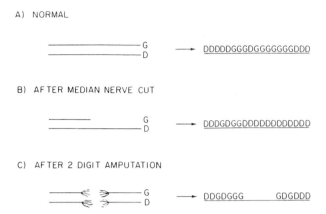

Figure 9 Different categories of experiments done by Merzenich and his collaborators. **A**: The hand region of the somatosensory cortex contains superposed representations of both dorsal (*D*) and glabrous (*G*) surfaces. In the normal map, the glabrous skin is usually represented centrally and the dorsal skin represented at the lateral and medial margins except for a few small islands within the glabrous representation. **B**: After transection of the median nerve, a representation of the dorsum of the fingers arises in the site of the former glabrous representation. **C**: After amputation, both dorsal and glabrous inputs are removed, and two-digit amputation leaves a deafferented region that cannot be completely reoccupied.

The Overlap Rule

The overlap rule is the most profound of the reorganizational rules. It has two aspects. First, the percentage overlap of receptive fields depends only on the distance between the neurons recorded in the cortex and is effectively independent of receptive field size. Second, this dependence of overlap on cortical separation decreases monotonically to zero overlap beyond approximately 600 μm.

Receptive field overlap is maintained by group competition. Such competition is a relative interaction; it does not depend on the absolute strength of either group. Receptive field size, on the other hand, depends primarily on the amount of coactivated input via selection, and is merely modified by group competition. For example, suppose that adjacent cortical groups had overlapping receptive fields but that one receptive field was much larger than the other. Then the percentage overlaps of the two receptive fields with each other would be different. Group competition would act to restore the normal percentage overlap, and the resulting groups would have more equal receptive fields.

The approximately 600-μm limit on receptive field overlap is directly attributable to the anatomic spread of afferent terminals together with the average size of dendritic fields. The apparent monotonic decrease of receptive field overlap with increasing cortical separation (Sur et al., 1980; Merzenich et al., 1984a) results from two factors. First, the overlap function is piecewise continuous since all cells across the extent of a group have close to 100%

receptive field overlap. Second, to guarantee monotonicity, adjacent groups must be partially ordered so that overlap decreases successively. We argue that if the receptive field of a group were chosen randomly from among the afferents that it receives, then providing enough afferents were chosen (to avoid sampling error), receptive field overlap would closely approximate the anatomical overlap of afferents between groups (by the law of large numbers). As a result, receptive field overlap would decrease monotonically with distance in the cortex, regardless of receptive field size, as a statistical property of the afferent arborizations. However, the actual receptive fields are not determined randomly—they are biased by coactivated peripheral stimulation. Closer groups will tend to share a larger proportion of these coactive inputs. Thus, based on the statistical sampling of afferents received and the likelihood of certain subsets firing together, receptive field overlap will decrease with distance. In addition, although we suppose that all groups within a stripe interact, it may well be that closer groups interact to a greater degree.

This explanation of the overlap rule is similar, from a formal point of view, to the analysis by May and MacArthur (1972) of the relationship between niche overlap and the amount of environmental variability in the competitive exclusion of species. Their model supports the conjecture that "environmental fluctuations will put a limit to the closeness of species packing compatible with an enduring community, and that species will be packed closer or wider as the environmental variations are smaller or larger." According to this treatment, providing that environmental fluctuations are not too severe, species packing is limited by a value roughly proportional to the standard deviation of the niche breadth. Thus, species occupying adjacent niches have limited overlap. Furthermore, the percentage overlap between adjacent niches is always the same (one standard deviation) regardless of niche size (May and MacArthur, 1972). This is the analogue of the overlap rule. We are currently preparing a similar mathematical treatment of the present model. To some extent, this treatment suggests that a logical extension of the idea of group selection in neuronal populations rests in a set of ideas similar to those of ecologists, a kind of neuroecology.

Parenthetically, the conjecture that the standard deviation of the niche breadth is usually approximately equal to the packing distance may be related to the finding in the visual cortex (Hubel and Wiesel, 1977) that the amount of scatter in receptive fields is approximately equal to the receptive field size.

Inverse Rule

The final reorganizational rule is the inverse rule, which states that the magnification factor of a cortical represen-

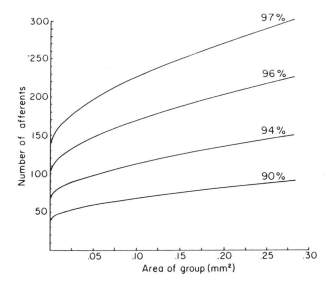

Figure 10 Graph of calculated number of different afferents contacting a group versus area of the group. The calculation assumed that afferents densely cover a 600-μm-diameter circular area and overlap with each other by the percentage shown on each curve. Note that the curves change very slowly outside the region near the origin. The postulated areas of most groups lie in this region, which shows the largest increase of afferents for any increase in group area. Note that a group whose diameter is 50 μm has an area of 0.002 mm^2 and is thus at the extreme left of the graph.

tation varies inversely with the size of its receptive fields. It takes a greater number of smaller receptive fields to cover a given area of periphery, provided that they overlap by the same fixed percentage as do larger receptive fields. Thus, smaller receptive fields are associated with a larger number of groups. This greater number of groups will occupy a larger region of cortex if group size changes relatively little compared with the change in receptive field size. That this is the case can be argued as follows.

First, as shown in Figure 10, as group size increases, the number of different afferents contacting the group changes appreciably only for groups that are small compared to the arborization size. Beyond this size limit, there is little selective advantage to changing group size. Second, the inhibitory funneling of activity in layer IV (group confinement) discussed previously prevents most groups from expanding, even before strong selective processes are applied. In fact, it is implied by our previous discussion of group selection that the smaller the associated receptive field, the larger the size of the group (due to the localized region of overlap of afferents carrying coactivated input). Therefore, the smaller the receptive field of a group, the larger the magnification factor.

The inverse rule, in a way, seems to follow from the overlap rule. However, we conjecture that the origin of the inverse rule lies in the inverse relation, that holds on the

average, between the frequency with which points on the skin are costimulated and the size of the region in which they lie. This would lead either to a greater number of groups with small receptive fields or to a lesser number of groups with large receptive fields. Which type of group is selected depends on what type of stimulation is prevalent.

Organization of Global Map Structure

None of the local processes we have discussed so far can fully account for the complexities of global map organization. However, neuronal group selection does bear on two aspects of map structure in general: the development of somatotopic or topographic organization, and the existence of stripes or columns. Indeed, we speculate that these two phenomena are related.

Somatotopy

While local continuity is selected for by the inhibitory mechanisms discussed previously, we have discussed no mechanism to account for global somatotopy. Although somatotopy must be allowed for in the primary repertoire, in that afferents must reach the appropriate general area, the final topography evolves only later, out of group competition. We assume that the somatotopic organization is similar to that in other developmental systems. For example, during regeneration of the retinotectal projection in amphibians, individual retinal afferents initially spread over wide areas of the tectum, but provided their activity is not blocked (e.g., with tetrodotoxin), they eventually retract branches, hone down, and contact a much more restricted tectal area (Fujisawa et al., 1982; Schmidt, 1982). Crude topography is impossible unless the afferent originally contacted the appropriate tectal quadrant, but the final topography arises from some form of competition among afferent branches for postsynaptic sites.

We predict that maps will exhibit the tremendous variability engendered by the outcome of this competitive process of selection. Selection always results in a map with local continuity (although sharp discontinuities are allowed), but many such maps can potentially be formed from the primary repertoire. Some support for this contention is found in the results of Merzenich and his colleagues (Merzenich et al., 1983b) showing that the normal sequence of digits (1, 2, 3, 4, 5) or phalangeal segments (proximal, medial, distal) in the cortical map appears to undergo several reversals (e.g., 1, 2, 3, 4, 3, 4, 5), but always preserves local continuity. In particular, after cortical lesions, multiple representations of a digit segment often appear, always in a locally continuous but globally disordered fashion. Thus, the somatotopy of the expressed map is a product of selection acting upon a degenerate anatomical substrate that is at best locally continuous.

Stripes

Finally, several comments about stripes may be of relevance. There appears to be a general tendency of afferents to terminate in stripes at various levels of the nervous system (Hand and Van Winkle, 1977; Friedman and Jones, 1980; Constantine-Paton, 1981). There is suggestive evidence that, in at least some regions of SI, afferent stripes are primarily oriented anteroposteriorly while efferent stripes are primarily oriented roughly mediolaterally (Jones et al., 1975; Jones and Wise, 1977). However, the relative orientations of the stripes of various different classes of afferents and efferents have not yet been delineated (Jones, 1981).

Nevertheless, if, in general, afferent and efferent stripes are organized separately, then it appears that the stripe cannot be the "input output" unit. The unit of map organization must be a subunit of a stripe; it must extend through all cortical lamina and participate in both an afferent and an efferent strip simultaneously; and it must be able to effect significant changes in the inputoutput match by altering its structure. This unit is what we have defined as a neuronal group. One may reasonably object that columns, stripes, strips, bands, patches, and so on are different structures and, in particular, that separate columns exist within a strip. This does not appear to be the usual interpretation, although the need for a columnar subunit has been discussed (Mountcastle, 1978).

The data reviewed suggest that the existence of stripes may be related to three anatomical factors. First, the thalamic afferents may terminate in bitufted bushes within alternating stripes (Gilbert and Wiesel, 1979; Landry et al., 1982). Second there may exist a class of corticocortical fibers that mediate interactions among nearby stripes (Rockland and Lund, 1982). The paucity of mediolaterally oriented inhibitory fibers [there has been only one report of an example (Szentágothai, 1975) suggest that pyramidal cell collaterals contacting inhibitory cells may mediate stripestripe inhibition. But then the shift in orientation between afferent and efferent stripes discussed above would imply that these fibers would need to have different orientations in the different cortical layers. Although there are some reports of layer-specific anisotropy (Hoeltzell and Dykes, 1979), such fibers are not presently known. The third fact relating to stripes is that both the ocular dominance columns in area 17 (Hubel and Wiesel, 1977) and the RA/SA bands in area 3b (Sur et al., 1981) intersect cytoarchitectonic borders orthogonally. Whether this reflects a more general rule remains to be seen. It may result either from the selective orientation of the above-mentioned inhibitory connections or from decreased corticocortical connectivity across the cytoarchitectonic border, making cell capture across the border more difficult. If the latter is the case, neuronal groups would tend to minimize their contact with such borders, and stripes would thus appear to approach the border orthogonally.

Regardless of how stripes arise (Whitelaw and Cowan, 1981; von der Malsburg and Cowan, 1982), the question remains as to whether they have any functional significance. While all cells within a group express a similar receptive field, groups within a stripe have overlapped receptive fields of the same submodality on the same body part. We conjecture that the typical width of cortical stripes, 5001000 e mum, is due to the width of afferent arbors. Consider the case in which adjacent cortical stripes represent two different classes of input (e.g., different modalities or different body regions) and a separate afferent population mediates input to alternate stripes. Any given afferent will contribute to only one of the two different alternating stripe classes. Thus, in order to be expressed, an afferent must have at least part of its arbor within the borders of an appropriate stripe. If stripes were much wider than arbors, then afferents might land deep within an inappropriate stripe and be unable to reach any axonal branches to the adjacent appropriate stripes. To prevent this, related groups with overlapping receptive fields will occupy contiguous regions limited in extent to 5001000 e mum in at least one dimension. If both dimensions of these regions were so limited, the resulting pattern would resemble a checkerboard (Hubel and Wiesel, 1977) rather than stripes. However, this checkerboard geometry would involve extensive border contact between adjacent regions; for example, each square would be completely surrounded by squares of the opposite type with disparate receptive fields. Since adjacent groups with nonoverlapping receptive fields are at a selective disadvantage, this geometry would not be favored. Note that stripes should tend to be as wide as possible (approximately the width of an arbor) so as to allow the largest possible number of groups per stripe. A stripe geometry thus optimizes the two desired properties of (1) minimizing border contact between groups with nonoverlapping receptive fields and (2) expressing every afferent in some group. Stripes may therefore be a unit of organization within which neuronal groups interact to form a topographic map.

Conclusion

The basic argument developed in this chapter is that group selection within a degenerate anatomical substrate leads to dynamic expression of maps corresponding to environmentally relevant structures. A cortical group is a cooperative, self-organizing unit whose mechanism of formation constrains all cells within it to share a common receptive field. Group size can vary, but is limited by the vertically mediated dynamic balance between a propensity to contract in layer IV and a tendency to expand in other layers (group confinement). Afferent expression requires that interconnected cortical cells receive connections from afferents that are simultaneously stimulated. The choice of exactly which afferents will be expressed depends on the temporal coactivation of peripheral inputs stimulating these afferents through the various relays, and it operates under the constraints of previously established corticocortical synaptic efficacies (group selection). Every stimulus acts to alter the competitive balance between groups (group competition). The functional map represents the combined effects of group confinement, group selection, and group competition. It is perhaps worthwhile to point out that this realizes the effect of a Hebb-like rule for map formation without assuming information transfer on the synaptic level or an actual Hebb rule. According to the theory of neuronal group selection, a cortical map then exists as the optimal construction by which multidimensional inputs interact to give selected outputs under temporal modulation by local and reentrant circuits. The degeneracy implied by this mechanism and the reentrant interaction of maps with other cortical regions may provide the necessary bases for the context-dependent pattern recognition that is essential for the perceptual process.

Appendix: A Synaptic Model Consistent with Group Selection

The main purpose of presenting the model illustrated below is to show that a detailed example consistent with group selection and known neurophysiology can be constructed. In line with the assumptions of neuronal group selection theory, it is presumed that an individual neuron cannot and does not transmit information from its presynaptic terminals to those of postsynaptic cells by correlated firing in the fashion of a Hebb synapse. Instead, correlation is accomplished at the level of neuronal groups with reentry.

The basic premise of the model is that each neuron is a complex metabolic feedback-controlled unit that attempts to regulate its synaptic strengths in the presence of perturbative activity. Such activity is not viewed as conveying any semantic meaning, but rather merely as a mechanism for modifying the internal metabolic set points of cells. Three types of modification occur: (1) transient local fluctuations of synaptic strength in direct response to activity; (2) semipermanent modifications of local synaptic strengths in response to large transient deviations; and (3) permanent modifications of all synapses of the cell, in

concert, in response to large prolonged deviations of the synaptic strengths of many of its synapses.

Although modification of both the pre- and postsynaptic terminals of a cell may occur, this simple model treats only the presynaptic alterations in the amount of neurotransmitter released by various inputs. Postsynaptic alterations could easily be included—but the crucial point is that whatever alterations occur in most cases depend only on the activity of the individual cell, not on correlation of activity across a particular synapse. For simplicity, we shall neglect most of the complex biochemical machinery of the cell (i.e., the levels of cAMP, protein kinases, transmitter enzymes, etc.) known to be involved in synaptic function. We consider only two generic dependent variables, the calcium concentration $c_{ij}(t)$ at time t in the presynaptic terminal of cell j connected to cell i, and the transmitter level $p_{ij}(t)$ in the same terminal.

Activity leads to fluctuations of the calcium and transmitter concentrations within a presynaptic terminal. The amount of exocytotic release of transmitter depends on the levels of both calcium and transmitter, and therefore fluctuates with activity. The sizes of these deviations in the amount of transmitter release determine whether synaptic strength is to be increased, decreased, or unchanged. Thus, the object is to describe how these deviations depend on activity using equations that reflect known cellular physiology, and then to analyze how the pattern of activity leads to modifications of synaptic strength.

Activity causes calcium influx in an amount dependent on the state of facilitation or habituation of the synapse. The first term in equation (1) is this voltage-dependent calcium current, I_{Ca}. The internal calcium concentration is decreased by a saturable calcium pump. The second term in (1) is the form of such a pump used by Parnas and Segel (1980). Thus, we take calcium concentration to be regulated according to the equation

$$\frac{d}{dt}c_{ij}(t) = I_{Ca}[V_j(t)] - \frac{\lambda \cdot (c_{ij}(t) - c_{ij}^{\circ})}{\kappa + (c_{ij}(t) - c_{ij}^{\circ})} \tag{1}$$

where $V_j(t)$ is the amount of depolarization of cell j (the independent variable), λ and κ are constants for each cell that determine the calcium kinetics (Parnas and Segel, 1980), and c_{ij}° is the set level for calcium concentration.

Transmitter concentration is regulated to a level set by the combined effects of synthesis, transport, and degradation. The first term in equation (2) describes the regulation of transmitter level by feedback control. Transmitter levels are decreased by exocytotic release as described by the second term in (2). Thus,

$$\frac{d}{dt}p_{ij}(t) = \alpha \cdot [p_{ij}^{\circ} - p_{ij}(t)] - \delta \cdot \xi_{ij}(t) \tag{2}$$

where p_{ij}° is the set level for transmitter concentration, α is a constant of the transmitter kinetics of the neuron, $\xi_{ij}(t)$ is the amount of transmitter releasable at time t in response to activation, and δ is assumed to be a constant in the presence of activity and equal to zero in the absence of activity, although more generally δ may be a continuous nonlinear function of the calcium current I_{Ca} or of the voltage $V_j(t)$ (Llinás, 1979).

Synaptic strength depends on the amount of transmitter released by activation as well as on events in the cleft and the postsynaptic receptor response. For simplicity, none of these latter effects is treated directly and only presynaptic morphology, the variable $R_{ij}(t)$, is considered. Although the calcium level, the transmitter level, and the state of the synapse may vary independently, they all have a joint effect on the release of transmitter. To express the parallel nature of this interaction, we let the synaptic strength be given by

$$\xi_{ij}(t) = \left[\frac{1}{c_{ij}(t)} + \frac{1}{p_{ij}(t)} + \frac{1}{R_{ij}(t)} \right]^{-1} \tag{3}$$

with any proportionality constants absorbed into the units of measurement.

The degree of depolarization of cell i is determined by its summed postsynaptic response to bound transmitter, in particular, whether the response is excitatory or inhibitory. This postsynaptic component of synaptic efficacy can be treated directly (Finkel and Edelman, 1984). It is subject to modification over time depending on the pattern of local and heterosynaptic inputs. However, in the present model, we merely represent the net postsynaptic effect by the constant σ_{ij}. Thus, if the potential has a decay constant ϵ, and the voltage $V_i(t)$ is measured relative to the resting membrane potential, then

$$\frac{d}{dt} V_i(t) = \delta \cdot \sum_j \sigma_{ij} \cdot \xi_{ij}(t) - \epsilon \cdot V_i(t) \tag{4}$$

Note that we neglect any voltage differences within the neuron; however, these could easily be incorporated. The exact functional form of these equations is somewhat arbitrary; our interest is not in the detailed form of the transient fluctuations of synaptic strengths but rather in the more permanent changes they induce. These changes are effected by modifying the set level of the transmitter concentration.

Figure 11A shows one possible local semipermanent synaptic alteration. The normal set levels (or resting levels) of calcium c_{ij}° and transmitter p_{ij}° along with that of the state of the synaptic morphology R_{ij}° determine the set level ξ_{ij}° of the synaptic strength.

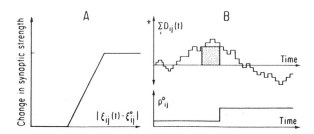

Figure 11 Modification of synaptic strength. **A:** Hypothetical graph of the magnitude of the semipermanent change in synaptic strength versus the absolute value of the deviation of the synaptic strength from its set level. The sign of the change is given by the sign of $D_{ij} = \xi_{ij}(t) - \xi_{ij}^\circ$. (Symbols are explained in the Appendix of this chapter.) Note that a substantial deviation must occur before any change in synaptic strength occurs, and that the change saturates with increasing deviation. In computer simulations we typically let the change saturate at a value of 20% of the current p_{ij}°. **B:** Permanent modification of synaptic strength. Hypothetical graph (*upper*) of the sum of $D_{ij}(t)$ over i, the deviation from set level of the synaptic strength over presynaptic terminals of the jth cell. If this sum exceeds a threshold value for a sufficient time (denoted by stippled box), a modification of all synaptic strengths of the jth cell ensues. Hypothetical graph (*lower*) of the transmitter concentration set level p_{ij}° versus the same time scale as in the upper graph. Modification of synaptic strength occurs by restting p_{ij}°, shown here to occur with the same sign as D_{ij} and with zero time delay after threshold is achieved.

$$\xi_{ij}^\circ = \left[\frac{1}{c_{ij}^\circ} + \frac{1}{p_{ij}^\circ} + \frac{1}{R_{ij}^\circ} \right]^{-1} \tag{5}$$

The amount of local semipermanent change depends on the deviation in synaptic strength $D_{ij}(t) = \xi_{ij}(t) - \xi_{ij}^\circ$ in the terminal, with the sign of the change determined by the sign of $D_{ij}(t)$.

Permanent total-cell synaptic modification depends on the deviations in synaptic strength D_{ij} of all of the cells' synapses. Figure 11B shows a hypothetical example of the sum of $D_{ij}(t)$ over all presynaptic terminals $[\sum_i D_{ij}(t)]$ belonging to cell j versus time. If, within a given time period, the area under this curve exceeds some threshold, as shown by the stippled area, all transmitter levels p_{ij}° for all i are reset by a small fixed amount in a direction determined by the sign of D_{ij}. R_{ij}° can be similarly reset. Note that this change in permanent synaptic strength, as well as that in the local semipermanent case, could have either the same sign as D_{ij} or the opposite sign. However, the choice is probably fixed for a given cell and a given transmitter type. Opposite sign assignments reflect a negative feedback system in which the permanent changes are such as to make the transient fluctuations smaller. Same sign assignments reflect a positive feedback resetting of the cell to match the ambient level of activity, but do not necessarily lead to instability, due to the plasticity property discussed below. In fact, the major properties of the model are independent of this choice of sign assignation; it could be that examples of both types of cells exist. We also note that not all cortical cells need be plastic, and that the above model may only apply to a subpopulation of neurons.

The two permanent changes in p_{ij}° can take place after varying delays. We usually choose the delay for the local semipermanent change to be shorter than that for the permanent total-cell change. We have tested this model in a preliminary computer simulation; the results suggest that it is fairly robust with respect to choice of parameter values, and can reproduce both the transient and the longer-term effects.

The "significant activation" referred to in the text is that level of activation necessary to induce a permanent change in synaptic strength. Clearly this is determined by the particular choice of parameters for each cell and by the current state of its synapses. Whether the synapse is strengthened or weakened depends on which of the two substances, calcium or transmitter, first returns to its rest level after activation. This in turn depends on the spatiotemporal pattern of stimulation. We might, in general, expect that strong coactivated stimulation to a group would cause its cells to have large deviations of both calcium and transmitter. Uncorrelated input would lead to smaller deviations due to the intermittent chances for recovery of calcium and transmitter to their resting levels. Although the rate constants must be taken into account, the saturable nature of the calcium pump implies that large deviations in calcium should return to normal levels relatively more slowly than large deviations in transmitter. For example, we might expect transmitter to normalize before calcium after strong coactivated stimulation, and calcium to normalize before transmitter after uncorrelated input. In the first case, if calcium remains elevated after transmitter levels have normalized, $\xi_{ij}(t)$ exceeds ξ_{ij}° so D_{ij} is positive and synaptic strength will be strengthened (provided the choice of sign for the change in synaptic strength is the same as the sign of D_{ij}). If, as in the second case, transmitter levels remain depressed after calcium has returned to normal, $\xi_{ij}(t)$ remains less than ξ_{ij}°, so D_{ij} is negative and the synapse will be weakened (with the same choice of sign). If the cell is quiescent, $\xi_{ij}(t)$ remains close to ξ_{ij}°, D_{ij} is near zero, and no change in synaptic strength occurs. (Note that if the sign of the synaptic modification was opposite to the sign of D_{ij} then synaptic strength would be weakened in the first case, strengthened in the second case, and unchanged in the last case.)

This system has an interesting plasticity property. As p_{ij} gets larger, its relative effect on ξ_{ij} decreases. As the synapse gets stronger with p_{ij}° increasing, it becomes more difficult to change the set level of synaptic strength. Therefore strong synapses are less plastic and weak synapses are more plastic. This keeps the strong synapses from growing without bound. It also maintains the strong synapses while giving the weak ones, which can be considered less important, more chance to change in response to input. Note, however, that these strong synapses will have increased sensitivities to fluctuations of the calcium level. Note also that while both the transient and the small, local, semipermanent changes can accentuate the differences in strength among the different synapses of a cell, the total-cell permanent modifications change all synaptic strengths together, making them all either stronger or weaker.

In contrast to these properties, a Hebb synapse (in which strengthening of a synapse occurs if the postsynaptic cell often fires together with the presynaptic cell) tends to increase its capacity to strengthen as it grows stronger, leading to unbounded increase. Moreover, the Hebb rule poses difficulties for the rapid strengthening of weak synapses: If the postsynaptic cell cannot be presently fired, strengthening the synapse depends mainly on chance correlations with stimulation by other terminals. The present model has the advantage that weakened synapses are highly dependent on stimulation and can be more quickly strengthened.

It is important to stress that the workings of this model nevertheless achieve a similar result to that of the Hebb rule, but within the context of neuronal groups. This is the case because large coactivated stimuli lead to strengthening of a group's connections, whereas uncorrelated stimuli lead to weakening of these connections. Instead of "informational" changes occurring at individual synapses, such changes occur *a posteriori* by means of group competition and selection.

Acknowledgments

We are grateful to Dr. Michael Merzenich for making his data available to us before publication. Drs. Vernon Mountcastle and George Reeke gave critical comments on this chapter, but are obviously not responsible for any remaining errors. Dr. Merzenich and Dr. Pierre Landry kindly gave permission for the reproduction of illustrations.

References

Bertolotti, R., U. Rutishauser, and G. M. Edelman (1980) A cell surface molecule involved in aggregation of embryonic liver cells. *Proc. Natl. Acad. Sci. USA* 77:4831–4835.

Bindman, L., and O. Lippold (1981) *The Neurophysiology of Cerebral Cortex,* University of Texas Press, Austin.

Buskirk, D. R., J. Thiery, U. Rutishauser, and G. M. Edelman (1980) Antibodies to a neural cell adhesion molecule disrupt histogenesis in cultured chick retinae. *Nature* **285**:488–489.

Chan-Palay, V., G. Nilaver, S. L. Palay, M. C. Beinfeld, E. A. Zimmerman, J.-Y. Wu, and T. L. O'Donohue (1981) Chemical heterogeneity in cerebellar Purkinje cells: existence and coexistence of glutamic acid decarboxylase-like and motilin-like immunoreactivities. *Proc. Natl. Acad. Sci. USA* **78**:7787–7791.

Chan-Palay, V., S. L. Palay, and J.-Y. Wu (1982) Sagittal cerebellar microbands of taurine neurons: immunocytochemical demonstration by using antibodies against the taurine-synthesizing enzyme cysteine sulfinic acid decarboxylase. *Proc. Natl. Acad. Sci. USA* **79**:4221–4225.

Chomsky, N. (1980) *Rules and Representations,* Columbia University Press, New York.

Constantine-Paton, M. (1981) Induced ocular-dominance zones in tectal cortex. In *The Organization of the Cerebral Cortex,* F. O. Schmitt, F. G. Worden, G. Adelman, and S. G. Dennis, eds., pp. 47–67, MIT Press, Cambridge, Massachusetts.

Cowan, W. M. (1978) Aspects of neural development. In *International Review of Physiology and Neurobiology IV,* Vol. 17, R. Porter, ed., pp. 150–191, University Park Press, Baltimore.

Cronholm, B. (1951) Phantom limb in amputees: study of changes in integration of centripetal impulses with special reference to referred sensations. *Acta Psychiatr. Neurol. [Suppl.]* **72**:7–31.

de Lacoste-Utamsing, C., and R. L. Holloway (1982) Sexual dimorphism in the human corpus callosum. *Science* **216**:431–432.

Devor, M., and P. D. Wall (1981) Effects of peripheral nerve injury on receptive fields of cells in the cat spinal cord. *J. Comp. Neurol.* **199**:227–291.

Dow, B. M., A. Z. Snyder, R. G. Vautin, and R. Bauer (1981) Magnification factor and receptive field size in foveal striate cortex of the monkey. *Exp. Brain Res.* **44**:213–228.

Edelman, G. M. (1976) Surface modulation in cell recognition and cell growth. *Science* **192**:21,8–226.

Edelman, G. M. (1978) Group selection and phasic reentrant signaling: a theory of higher brain function. In *The Mindful Brain: Cortical Organization and the Group-Selective Theory of Higher Brain Function,* G. M. Edelman and V. B. Mountcastle, eds., pp. 55–100, MIT Press, Cambridge, Massachusetts.

Edelman, G. M. (1981) Group selection as the basis for higher brain function. In *Organization of the Cerebral Cortex,* F. O. Schmitt, F. G. Worden, G. Adelman, and S. G. Dennis, eds., pp. 51–100, MIT Press, Cambridge, Massachusetts.

Edelman, G. M. (1983) Cell adhesion molecules. *Science* **219**:450–457.

Edelman, G. M., and C.-M. Chuong (1982) Embryonic to adult conversion of neural cell adhesion molecules in normal and *staggerer* mice. *Proc. Natl. Acad. Sci. USA* **79**:7036–7040.

Edelman, G. M., and G. N. Reeke, Jr. (1982) Selective networks capable of representative transformations, limited generalizations, and associative memory. *Proc. Natl. Acad. Sci. USA* **79**:2091–2095.

Finkel, L. H., and G. M. Edelman (1984) Neuronal homeostasis and channel coupling: a basis for selection in synaptic populations. (in preparation.)

Friedman, D. P., and E. G. Jones (1980) Focal projection of electrophysiologically defined groupings of thalamic cells on the monkey somatic sensory cortex. *Brain Res.* **191**:249–252.

Fujisawa, H., N. Tani, K. Watanabe, and Y. Ibata (1982) Branching of regenerating retinal axons and preferential selection of appropriate branches for specific neuronal connection in the newt. *Dev. Biol.* **90**:43–57.

Gallin, W. J., G. M. Edelman, and B. A. Cunningham (1983) Characterization of L-CAM, a major cell adhesion molecule from embryonic liver cells. *Proc. Natl. Acad. Sci. USA* **80**:1038–1042.

Gardner, E. P., and R. M. Costanzo (1980a) Spatial integration of multiple-point stimuli in primary somatosensory cortical receptive fields of alert monkeys. *J. Neurophysiol.* **43**:420–443.

Gardner, E. P., and R. M. Costanzo (1980b) Temporal integration of multiple-point stimuli in primary somatosensory cortical receptive fields of alert monkeys. *J. Neurophysiol.* **43**:444–468.

Gilbert, C. D., and T. N. Wiesel (1979) Morphology and intracortical projections of functionally characterised neurones in the cat visual cortex. *Nature* **280**:120–125.

Grumet, M., U. Rutishauser, and G. M. Edelman (1982) Neural cell adhesion molecule is on embryonic muscle cells and mediates adhesion to nerve cells *in vitro. Nature* **295**:693–695.

Hand, P. J., and T. Van Winkle (1977) The efferent connections of the feline nucleus cuneatus. *J. Comp. Neurol.* **171**:83–109.

Hawkins, R. D., T. W. Abrams, T. J. Carew, and E. R. Kandel (1983) A cellular mechanism of classical conditioning in *Aplysia:* activity dependent amplification of presynaptic facilitation. *Science* **219**:400–405.

Hoeltzell, P. B., and R. W. Dykes (1979) Conductivity in the somatosensory cortex of the cat—evidence for cortical anisotropy. *Brain Res.* **177**:61–82.

Hoffman, S., B. C. Sorkin, R. Brackenbury, R. Mailhammer, U. Rutishauser, B. A. Cunningham, and G. M. Edelman (1982) Chemical characterization of a neural cell adhesion molecule purified from embryonic brain membranes. *J. Biol. Chem.* **257**:7720–7729.

Hubel, D. H., and T. N. Wiesel (1977) Functional architecture of macaque monkey visual cortex. *Proc. R. Soc. Lond. [Biol.]* **198**:1–59.

Jones, E. G. (1975) Varieties and distribution of non-pyramidal cells in the somatic sensory cortex of the squirrel monkey. *J. Comp. Neurol.* **160**:205–268.

Jones, E. G. (1981) Anatomy of cerebral cortex: columnar input–output organization. In *The Organization of the Cerebral Cortex,* F. O. Schmitt, F. G. Worden, G. Adelman, and S. G. Dennis, eds., pp. 199–235, MIT Press, Cambridge, Massachusetts.

Jones, E. G., and T. P. S. Powell (1970) An electron microscopic study of the laminar pattern and mode of termination of afferent fibre pathways in the somatic sensory cortex of the cat. *Philos. Trans. R. Soc. Lond. [Biol.]* **257**:45–62.

Jones, E. G., and S. P. Wise (1977) Size, laminar, and columnar distribution of efferent cells in the sensory motor cortex of monkeys. *J. Comp. Neurol.* **175**:391–438.

Jones, E. G., H. Burton, and R. Porter (1975) Commissural and corticocortical "columns" in the somatic sensory cortex of primates. *Science* **190**:572–574.

Jones, E. G., J. D. Coulter, and S. H. C. Hendry (1978) Intracortical connectivity of architectonic fields in the somatic, motor, and parietal cortex of monkeys. *J. Comp. Neurol.* **181**:291–348.

Kaas, J. H., R. J. Nelson, M. Sur, and M. M. Merzenich (1981) Organization of somatosensory cortex in primates. In *The Organization of the Cerebral Cortex,* F. O. Schmitt, F. G. Worden, G. Adelman, and S. G. Dennis, eds., pp. 237–261, MIT Press, Cambridge, Massachusetts.

Kosar, E., and P. J. Hand (1981) First somatosensory cortical columns and associated neuronal clusters of nucleus ventralis posterolateralis of the cat: an anatomical demonstration. *J. Comp. Neurol.* **198**:515–539.

Kubovy, M., and J. R. Pomerantz, eds. (1981) *Perceptual Organization,* Lawrence Erlbaum Associates, Hillsdale, New Jersey.

Landry, P., and M. Deschênes (1981) Intracortical arborizations and receptive fields of identified ventrobasal thalamocortical afferents to the primary somatic sensory cortex in the cat. *J. Comp. Neurol.* **199**:345–371.

Landry, P., J. Villemure, and M. Deschênes (1982) Geometry and orientation of thalamocortical arborizations in the cat somatosensory cortex as revealed by computer reconstruction. *Brain Res.* **237**:222–226.

Laskin, S. E., and W. A. Spencer (1979) Cutaneous masking. II. Geometry of excitatory and inhibitory receptive fields of single units in somatosensory cortex of the cat. *J. Neurophysiol.* **42**:1061–1082.

Lee, K. J., and T. A. Woolsey (1975) A proportional relationship between peripheral innervation density and cortical neuron number in the somatosensory system of the mouse. *Brain Res.* **99**:349–353.

Llinás, R. (1979) The role of calcium in neuronal function. In *The Neurosciences: Fourth Study Program,* F. O. Schmitt and F. G. Worden, eds., pp. 555–571, MIT Press, Cambridge, Massachusetts.

Lorente de Nó, R. (1938) Cerebral cortex: architecture, intracortical connections, motor projections. In *Physiology of the Nervous System,* J. F. Fulton, ed., pp. 291–339, Oxford University Press, New York.

May, R. M., and R. H. MacArthur (1972) Niche overlap as a function of environmental variability. *Proc. Natl. Acad. Sci. USA* **69**:1109–1113.

Mayr, E. (1982) *The Growth of Biological Thought: Diversity, Evolution, and Inheritance,* Harvard University Press, Cambridge, Massachusetts.

Merzenich, M. M., J. H. Kaas, M. Sur, and C.-S. Lin (1978) Double representation of the body surface within cytoarchitectonic areas 3b and 1 "SI" in the owl monkey (*Aotus trivirgatus*). *J. Comp. Neurol.* **181**:41–74.

Merzenich, M. M., J. H. Kaas, J. T. Wall, R. J. Nelson, M. Sur, and D. J. Felleman (1983a) Topographic reorganization of somatosensory cortical areas 3b and 1 in adult monkeys following restricted deafferentation. *Neuroscience* **8**:33–55.

Merzenich, M. M., J. H. Kaas, J. T. Wall, M. Sur, R. J. Nelson, and D. J. Felleman (1983b) Progression of change following median nerve section in the cortical representation of the hand in areas 3b and 1 in adult owl and squirrel monkeys. *Neuroscience* **10**:639–665.

Merzenich, M. M., G. M. Edelman, M. Sur, and J. H. Kaas (1984a) Origins of topographic order in cortical fields: some observations and hypotheses on the selectional dynamics of functional maps. *J. Neurosci.* (submitted).

Merzenich, M. M., R. J. Nelson, M. P. Stryker, M. Cynader, A. Schoppmann, and J. M. Zook (1984b) Somatosensory cortical map changes following digit amputation in adult monkeys. *J. Comp. Neurol.* **224**:591–604.

Meyer, R. L. (1980) Mapping the normal and regenerating retinotectal projection of goldfish with autoradiographic methods. *J. Comp. Neurol.* **189**:273–289.

Mountcastle, V. B. (1978) An organizing principle for cerebral function: the unit module and the distributed system. In *The Mindful Brain: Cortical Organization and the Group-Selective Theory of Higher Brain Function,* G. M. Edelman and V. B. Mountcastle, eds., pp. 7–50, MIT Press, Cambridge, Massachusetts.

Parnas, H., and L. A. Segel (1980) A theoretical explanation for some effects of calcium on the facilitation of neurotransmitter release. *J. Theor. Biol.* **84**:3–29.

Pasternak, J. F., and T. A. Woolsey (1975) The number, size, and spatial distribution of neurons in lamina IV of the mouse SmI neocortex. *J. Comp. Neurol.* **160**:291–306.

Peters, A., and A. Fairen (1978) Smooth and sparsely-spined stellate cells in the visual cortex of the rat: a study using a combined Golgi-electron microscope technique. *J. Comp. Neurol.* **181**:129–172.

Poggio, G. F., and V. B. Mountcastle (1963) The functional properties of ventrobasal thalamic neurons studied in unanesthetized monkeys. *J. Neurophysiol.* **26**:755–806.

Pons, T., M. Sur, and J. H. Kaas (1982) Axonal arborizations in area 3b of somatosensory cortex in the owl monkey, *Aotus trivirgatus. Anat. Rec.* **202**:151A.

Quilliam, T. A. (1975) Neuro-cutaneous relationships in fingerprint skin. In *The Somatosensory System,* H. H. Kornhuber, ed., pp. 193–199, Thieme-Edition/Publishing Sciences Group, Stuttgart.

Rakic, P. (1977) Prenatal development of the visual system in rhesus monkey. *Philos. Trans. R. Soc. Lond. [Biol.]* **278**:245–260.

Rockel, A. J., R. W. Hiorns, and T. P. S. Powell (1980) The basic uniformity in structure of the neocortex. *Brain* **103**:221–244.

Rockland, K. S., and J. S. Lund (1982) Widespread periodic intrinsic connections in the tree shrew visual cortex. *Science* **215**:1532–1534.

Rothbard, J. B., R. Brackenbury, B. A. Cunningham, and G. M. Edelman (1982) Differences in the carbohydrate structure of neural cell-adhesion molecules from adult and embryonic chicken brains. *J. Biol. Chem.* **257**:11064–11069.

Rowe, M. H., and J. Stone (1977) Naming of neurons. *Brain. Behav. Evol.* **14**:185–216.

Rutishauser, U., W. E. Gall, and G. M. Edelman (1978) Adhesion among neural cells of the chick embryo. IV. Role of the cell surface molecule CAM in the formation of neurite bundles in cultures of spinal ganglia. *J. Cell Biol.* **79**:382–393.

Schmidt, J. T. (1982) The formation of retinotectal projections. *Trends Neurosci.* **46**:111–115.

Shepherd, G. M. (1979) *The Synaptic Organization of the Brain,* 2nd edn., Oxford University Press, New York.

Shinoda, Y., J. Yokota, and T. Futami (1981) Divergent projection of individual corticospinal axons to motoneurons of multiple muscles in the monkey. *Neurosci. Lett.* **23**:7–12.

Shinoda, Y., J. Yokata, and T. Futami (1982) Morphology of physiologically identified rubrospinal axons in the spinal cord. *Brain Res.* **242**:321–325.

Sinclair, J. D. (1981) *The Rest Principle: A Neurophysiological Theory of Behavior,* Lawrence Erlbaum Associates, Hillsdale, New Jersey.

Somogyi, P., T. F. Freund, N. Halasz, and Z. F. Kisvarday (1981) Selectivity of neuronal [^{3}H]GABA accumulation in the visual cortex as revealed by Golgi staining of the labeled neurons. *Brain Res.* **225**:431–436.

Sur, M. and S. M. Sherman (1982) Retinogeniculate terminations in cats—morphological differences between X-cell and Y-cell axons. *Science* **218**:338–391.

Sur, M., M. M. Merzenich, and J. H. Kaas (1980) Magnification, receptive field area, and "hypercolumn" size in areas 3b and 1 of somatosensory cortex in owl monkeys. *J. Neurophysiol.* **44**:295–311.

Sur, M., J. T. Wall, and J. H. Kaas (1981) Modular segregation of functional cell classes within the postcentral somatosensory cortex of monkeys. *Science* **212**:1059–1061.

Szentágothai, J. (1975) The module-concept in cerebral cortex architecture. *Brain Res.* **95**:475–496.

Talbot, W. H., I. Darian-Smith, H. H. Kornhuber, and V. B. Mountcastle (1968) The sense of flutter-vibration: comparison of the human capacity with response patterns of mechanoreceptive afferents from the monkey hand. *J. Neurophysiol.* **31**:301–334.

Thiery, J.-P., J.-L. Duband, U. Rutishauser, and G. M. Edelman (1982) Cell adhesion molecules in early chick embryogenesis. *Proc. Natl. Acad. Sci. USA* **79**:6737–6741.

Vernon, M. D. (1970) *A Further Study of Visual Perception,* Hafner, Darien, Connecticut.

von der Malsburg, C., and J. D. Cowan (1982) Outline of a theory for the ontogenesis of iso-orientation domains in visual cortex. *Biol. Cybern.* **45**:49–56.

White, E. L. (1978) Identified neurons in mouse SmI cortex which are postsynaptic to thalamocortical axon terminals: a combined Golgi electron microscopic and degeneration study. *J. Comp. Neurol.* **181**:627–662.

White, E. L., and S. M. Hersch (1982) A quantitative study of thalamocortical and other synapses involving the apical dendrites of corticothalamic projection cells in mouse SmI cortex. *J. Neurocytol.* **11**:137–157.

Whitelaw, V. A., and J. D. Cowan (1981) Specificity and plasticity of retinotectal connections: a computational model. *J. Neurosci.* **1**:1369–1387.

Winfield, D. A., R. N. L. Brooke, J. J. Sloper, and T. P. S. Powell (1981) A combined Golgi electron microscopic study of the synapses made by the proximal axon and recurrent collaterals of a pyramidal cell in the somatic sensory cortex of the monkey. *Neuroscience* **6**:1217–1230.

(1987)

John C. Pearson, Leif H. Finkel, and Gerald M. Edelman

Plasticity in the organization of adult cerebral cortical maps: a computer simulation based on neuronal group selection

The Journal of Neuroscience 7: 4209–4223

Recent experimental evidence from the somatosensory, auditory, and visual systems documents the existence of functional plasticity in topographic map organization in adult animals. This evidence suggests that an ongoing competitive organizing process controls the locations of map borders and the receptive field properties of neurons. A computer model based on the process of neuronal group selection has been constructed that accounts for reported results on map plasticity in somatosensory cortex.

The simulations construct a network of locally connected excitatory and inhibitory cells that receives topographic projections from 2 receptor sheets corresponding to the glabrous and dorsal surfaces of the hand (a typical simulation involves approximately 1500 cells, 70,000 intrinsic and 100,000 extrinsic connections). Both intrinsic and extrinsic connections undergo activity-dependent modifications according to a synaptic rule based on heterosynaptic interactions.

Repeated stimulation of the receptor sheet resulted in the formation of neuronal groups—local sets of strongly interconnected neurons in the network. Cells in most groups were found to have similar receptive fields: they were exclusively glabrous or dorsal despite equal numbers of anatomical connections from both surfaces. The sharpness of map borders was due to the sharpness of the underlying group structure; shifts in the locations of these borders resulted from competition between groups.

Following perturbations of the input, the network underwent changes similar to those observed experimentally in monkey somatosensory cortex. Repeated local tapping on the receptor sheet resulted in a large increase in the magnification factor of the stimulated region. Transection of the connections from a glabrous region resulted in the organization of a new representation of corresponding dorsal region. The detailed simulations provide several insights into the mechanisms of such changes, as well as a series of predictions about cortical behavior for further experimental test.

One of the long-standing problems in neuroscience has been to determine the principles underlying the formation and maintenance of ordered topographic maps. The prevailing view has been that these maps, once developmentally established, remain fixed for the duration of an animal's lifetime. Early observations suggested the possibility, however, that certain cortical maps may be labile (Leyton and Sherrington, 1917). More recently, evidence has emerged that maps in the somatosensory cortex continually reorganize, even in adult animals (Kaas et al., 1983). This evidence suggests that the functional or physiologically recorded map may be related to the underlying anatomical map through complex dynamic processes. Such processes are likely to be involved inasmuch as the presence of divergent and overlapping arborizations in the underlying cortical anatomy allow for a large degree of possible variability in the receptive field map. Given the anatomical constraints, it is difficult to understand how single cortical cells acting independently could generate somatotopic maps with sharp but movable borders. The observed plasticity of such maps can be accounted for by the presence of local groups of functionally interactive cells that act cooperatively to yield map organization. Competition between such neuronal groups could give rise to continuous map borders that could shift dynamically upon changes in input.

In an effort toward understanding these complex processes, we present here a detailed model of the dynamic control of map organization. This model, which is based on the theory of neuronal group selection (Edelman, 1978), is chiefly concerned with the functional properties of synaptic populations undergoing modifications within a fixed network anatomy during various forms of sensory stimulation. In developing this model for computer simulation, we deliberately restricted ourselves to the simplest network that would yield insights into synaptic selection in maps. This minimal model, while explicitly detailed, does not incorporate features such as multiple ascending synaptic levels, interconnected cortical areas, and multiple cell types, and therefore does not strictly simulate real cortex. The structure chosen was nonetheless based on realistic anatomical and physiological assumptions and allowed us to investigate (1) factors determining the receptive field of a cell, (2) principles controlling the magnification factor of a representation, (3) determinants of the locations of map borders, and (4) relative contributions to map plasticity of changes in synaptic strengths of extrinsic versus intrinsic connections.

Although several of the results have general application, our empirical reference in this paper is specifically to the somatosensory cortex of adult monkeys (Mountcastle, 1957) and the plasticity of cortical somatotopic maps (Kaas et al., 1983). Map changes quite similar to those with which we will be concerned have also been observed in adult animals of a number of species and in several sensory modalities at both cortical and subcortical levels (see Mountcastle, 1984, for review).

Areas 3b and 1 of owl and squirrel monkey cortex each contain

This work was supported by grants from the International Business Machines Corporation, Johnson and Johnson, and Senator Jacob Javits Center for Excellence in Neuroscience Award NS-22789. We thank Dr. George N. Reeke, Jr. for advice and extensive help in implementation of the simulations.

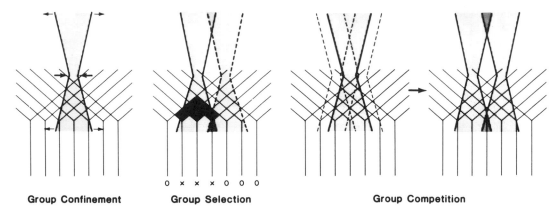

Group Confinement   **Group Selection**   **Group Competition**

Figure 1. Schematic representation of neuronal group processes in a qualitative model of map organization. Hourglass figures represent outlines of neuronal groups extending through all cortical laminae (waist of hourglass is layer IV); ascending Y-shaped figures represent outlines of divergent, overlapping thalamocortical afferents. *Group confinement* is a property of the intrinsic cortical connectivity which restricts activity to local domains, allowing groups to form. *Group selection* requires coactive extrinsic inputs, which strengthen the intrinsic connections of a group through synaptic modifications following a particular synaptic rule. The ×'s denote coactive afferents, the ○'s denote uncorrelated afferents. The *blackened region* receives maximum coactive and minimum uncorrelated input. This leads, through a synaptic modification mechanism dependent on coactive inputs, to selection of the *leftmost* of the 2 groups. *Group competition* controls which cells belong to which groups and also regulates the overlap of the receptive fields of adjacent groups. In the hypothetical case shown here, competition between 3 groups leads to the complete dissolution of the central one. Such competition is effected through the synaptic rule and depends upon the balance of stimulation received by the various groups (from Edelman and Finkel, 1984).

a complete somatotopic representation of the body surface; cells in these areas respond to light touch (Merzenich et al., 1978; Dykes, 1983; Whitsel and Kelly, 1986). Detailed microelectrode penetrations (Merzenich et al., 1983a) reveal that these maps are dynamic: under normal circumstances there are marked shifts over time in map borders between body parts. More dramatic changes are seen after perturbation of the input. For example, if one or more fingers are amputated, if a cutaneous nerve is transected, or if a region is repeatedly stimulated for prolonged periods, map borders can move hundreds of microns, and entirely new representations can emerge (Merzenich et al., 1983a, b; Jenkins et al., 1984).

To account for these results, we have previously described a qualitative model (Edelman and Finkel, 1984) of cortical map organization based on the theory of neuronal group selection (Edelman, 1978, 1981). This theory proposes that the nervous system operates as a selective system, similar in some respects to the operation of natural selection on organisms. In the nervous system, however, the selection takes place by specific neural mechanisms involved in the development of connectivity and experience-dependent synaptic modifications. The population proposed to be undergoing selection consists of variant neuronal groups—local sets of approximately 500–1500 strongly interconnected neurons. The cells in a group act collectively in determining their receptive field properties, and thus groups serve as the basic units of map organization.

Neuronal groups are not built-in anatomical structures, but functional units whose membership is determined by synaptic strengths. A set of 3 heuristic processes that function in parallel to govern group behavior has been proposed (Fig. 1; Edelman and Finkel, 1984). Groups are assumed to arise through a process of group confinement, an intrinsic cortical process that depends upon the patterns of activity flow in the cortex, the balance of excitation and inhibition in different laminae, and local variabilities in connectivity. The second process of group selection involves differential changes in the strengths of syn-

aptic connections based on correlated inputs. Only the presumptive groups that are most strongly activated strengthen and refine their receptive fields. Once selected, a process of competition between groups over cell membership and receptive field properties is responsible for the reorganizations seen in adult maps.

This model, depicted in Figure 1, provides only a general qualitative scheme for understanding maps in terms of population variables. In order to establish that such variables could account in mechanistic detail for the experimentally observed properties of map plasticity, we have instantiated them in the present study, which employs detailed computer simulations. Using this synthetic approach to neural modeling, we show explicitly that neuronal groups can be formed in an initially unorganized network and that a network organized into such groups exhibits an ordered topographic map with many of the observed properties of cortical maps. This model was subjected to stringent computer tests, providing the opportunity to determine in detail the effect of various perturbations upon map reorganization.

Materials and Methods

Anatomical connectivity. The computer model simulates a 2-dimensional network of interconnected excitatory (e-cells) and inhibitory (i-cells) neurons and an input array of sensory receptors. The cells are uniformly spread over a rectangular grid. All simulations reported here used a 32 × 16 grid with a total of 1024 e-cells and 512 i-cells, i.e., 2 e-cells and 1 i-cell at each of 512 (=32×16) grid points. The e-cell to i-cell ratio is not a critical factor in network behavior and was chosen for convenience since receptive field measurements are primarily made on e-cells.

Two identical sensory receptor arrays, corresponding to the glabrous and dorsal surfaces of the hand, are topographically mapped onto the network (Fig. 2). Regions corresponding to 4 fingers and a subjacent palm are present, and the 2 arrays are joined along the border of digit 1. Each array contains 512 receptors with 96 (=8×12) glabrous and 96 dorsal receptors on each finger, and 128 (=32×4) receptors in the glabrous and dorsal subphalangeal regions. Instructions in the program's input can create and move a 2-dimensional stimulus about the receptor

Table 1. Number of connections received by a cell as a function of distance

Ring	Number of connections/cell					
	$e \to e$	$i \to e$	$r \to e$	$e \to i$	$i \to i$	$r \to i$
0	1	1	2	1	0	0
1	8	8	16	4	0	0
2	8	8	32	8	0	0
3	0	0	48	24	0	0
4	0	0	0	32	0	0

The excitatory (e) cells and inhibitory (i) cells in the network receive connections from each other and from receptors (r) in an input array (e.g., e → i means an input to an inhibitory cell from an excitatory cell). The number of connections each cell receives from each cell type and from receptors is specified as a function of distance or "ring" (see Fig. 3). The number of r → e connections listed are from both glabrous and dorsal receptor arrays, each array contributes an equal number of connections per cell.

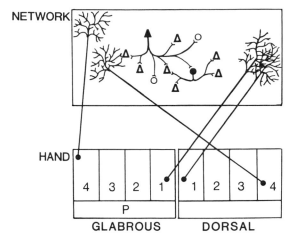

Figure 2. Schematic diagram of the basic elements and architecture of the model. The network consists of a 2-dimensional array of both excitatory cells (*triangles*) and inhibitory cells (*circles*). The intrinsic connections are characterized by local excitation and lateral inhibition. Excitatory cells receive connections from nearby excitatory and inhibitory cells, whereas inhibitory cells receive connections from relatively more distant excitatory cells. Excitatory cells also receive excitatory connections from 2 external arrays of receptors, corresponding to the glabrous and dorsal regions of the hand. The arrays contain regions corresponding to digits 1–4 and the palm (*P*), and they are joined along the border of digit 1. These regions are defined by convention only; there are no anatomical boundaries on the arrays. Arborizations from nearby receptors overlap extensively in the network, and each array projects topographically onto the network in such a fashion that corresponding glabrous and dorsal regions project to the same network location.

sheet, activating those receptors it covers (the stimulus can be any size or shape; we typically use a 3 × 3 solid square). The effect of the receptors on the cells of the network is exclusively excitatory.

Parameters of the receptor–cell connection scheme detailed in Figure 3 are given in Table 1: Each e-cell receives connections of equal density from the 7 × 7 region centered around the topographically corresponding receptor in both the glabrous and dorsal receptor arrays; i-cells do not receive any extrinsic input. Each e-cell receives 49 glabrous and 49 dorsal inputs, for a total of 100,352 r → e connections. Arborizations of fibers from nearby receptors overlap extensively in the network; the regions of external input for adjacent cells overlap by 86% on average.

There are 4 classes of intrinsic connections within the network, denoted by e → e, i → e, e → i, and i → i, where e and i represent e-cells and i-cells, respectively. All excitatory synapses are assumed to be within one length constant on the distal dendritic tree; all inhibitory inputs are assumed to be on the proximal dendrite and act to shunt the potentials produced more distally. The number of connections of each class received by a cell is specified according to the distance between the pre- and postsynaptic elements (see Table 1, Fig. 3). The choice of which particular cells are connected is decided randomly; multiple connections are allowed but self-connections are not.

All cells in the network receive the same number of synapses, but near the edges, those connections that would have extended outside the network border are made instead to the cell located inside the network at the mirror image of the original target cell. Thus, the density of connections is higher near the borders of the network. As discussed below, these boundary conditions affect the population dynamics of the network.

The scheme of connections was constrained by considerations of scale and was arrived at empirically through a series of tests checking for network stability under a range of input conditions. The scheme of intrinsic connections is essentially one of local excitation and lateral inhibition (Fig. 3B): e-cells excite nearby e-cells and slightly more distant i-cells; i-cells inhibit nearby e-cells. The effect of activating a local population of e-cells is a build-up of activity in that area followed by inhibition of a larger concentric region.

Neuronal properties. Each neuron in the network is characterized by a number of parameters (Table 2) that control the response of the cell to input stimulation. At each time step, the voltage of each cell is determined based upon the voltage of the cell during the previous time step and upon the excitatory and inhibitory inputs received by the cell during that time step. The output, s, of each is cell is then determined as a sigmoidal function of the voltage, v, as defined in equation (1):

$$ s_i = \sigma(v_i, \theta_s, \epsilon_s) = [\exp - (v_i - \theta_s)/\epsilon_s + 1]^{-1} \qquad (1) $$

where θ_s and ϵ_s are parameters determining the inflection point and the nonlinearity, respectively, of the sigmoidal function, σ. For small voltages ($v_i < 0.2\,\theta_s$) s_i is set to zero. The output is a continuous function, corresponding to the firing rate of a single neuron or the instantaneous averaged firing of a local ensemble of neurons. The voltage, v, undergoes exponential decay (rate δ_v) and is increased by the sum of the input from e-cells and receptors multiplied by 2 dynamic shunting functions, σ_I and σ_v:

$$ v_i(t + 1) = (1 - \delta_v)v_i(t) + \sigma_I\sigma_v[\kappa_E \sum_{j \epsilon E} \eta_{ij}(t)s_j(t) $$
$$ + \kappa_R \sum_{j \epsilon R} \eta_{ij}(t)r_j(t + 1)] \qquad (2) $$

where

$$ \sigma_I = \sigma\left(\sum_{j \epsilon I} s_j(t), \theta_I, - \epsilon_I\right), \qquad \sigma_v = \sigma[v_i(t), \theta_v, - \epsilon_v] $$

σ_I simulates shunting inhibition and σ_v simulates synaptic saturation—the decrease in transmembrane ionic driving force with increase in v. η is the postsynaptic strength, which for e-cells is plastic as defined below. r_j is the activity of receptor j, and is 0 or 1, signaling the absence (0) or presence (1) of a stimulus at that point on the hand. The definitions and values of the parameters in this paper are listed in Table 2. Equation (2) is schematically illustrated in Figure 4.

Shunting inhibition, in the form of a nonnegative multiplicative term, was used instead of hyperpolarizing inhibition, a subtractive term, because of the greater dynamic stability it conferred on the network. The excitatory input potentials to a cell are reduced to zero when a sufficiently large number of inhibitory cells fires. This kind of inhibition can always balance the excitatory processes and thus return the network to equilibrium after periods of intense activation. As discussed below, this is especially important in networks with synaptic plasticity properties that tend to strengthen excitatory synapses.

Synaptic plasticity rules. The rule for synaptic plasticity used here is based on known properties of hippocampal (Wigstrom and Gustafsson, 1983; Kelso et al., 1986; Malinow and Miller, 1986), cerebellar (Ito et al., 1982), and a variety of invertebrate synapses (Hawkins et al., 1983; Huganir et al., 1986), and is adapted from the dual rules model (Finkel, 1985; Finkel and Edelman, 1985, 1987). In this model, local biochemical modifications of the channels or receptors at a synapse are governed by the spatial and temporal pattern of heterosynaptic inputs to the neuron. The main assumption, which is supported by a growing body of experimental evidence (reviewed in Finkel and Edelman, 1987), is

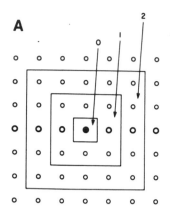

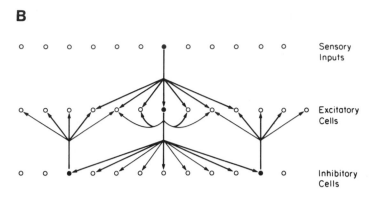

Figure 3. Cell–cell connection scheme. *A,* Depiction of the square "rings" (0th, 1st, and 2nd) used to assign connections (only a small part of the network is shown) as a function of distance between cells (small circles). The rings shown here are those of the cell marked with the *solid circle.* Each cell in the network has a similar set of rings constructed about it for the purpose of assigning connections. Every cell within a given ring is considered to be the same distance from the cell in the center (0th ring). An identical construction is used to assign the extrinsic connections from the receptor array to the network. The line of *thicker circles* corresponds to the row of cells whose connections are depicted in *B. B,* Schematic of a 1-dimensional section through the network showing the spatial distribution of excitatory and inhibitory connections. The output connections of the cells marked with *solid circles* are drawn. The *thick* and *thin lines* represent high- and low-density connections, respectively (Table 1). Corresponding to each of the 1024 grid points there is 1 glabrous receptor, 2 e-cells, and 1 i-cell. Only 1 e-cell per grid point is drawn.

that the modifiability of a channel or receptor depends upon its functional state (e.g., open, closed, inactivated).

In the present model, a simplified version of this postsynaptic rule is used and only the e → e and r → e connections are plastic. Each plastic postsynaptic terminal contains an equal number of channels, each of which is assumed to have 4 conducting states, O, P, O*, and P* (Fig. 5A). The O (open) and P (plastic) states have ionic conductance, g; the corresponding modified states, O* and P*, have conductance, g^* (where $g^* > g$). Only channels in the P states are modifiable. The net synaptic strength, η, defined as the conversion factor between presynaptic activity and postsynaptic potential, depends upon the fraction of the channels in each conducting state, as defined in equation (3), where o, p, o^*, and p^* are the fraction of channels in each respective state (i.e., $o + p + o^* + p^* = 1$).

$$\eta = g(o + p) + g^*(o^* + p^*) \tag{3}$$

The postsynaptic rule can, in general, be applied to multiple channel states—open, closed, or inactivated (Finkel and Edelman, 1985). In this simplified version, we have subsumed the closed channel states into the closed receptor state ($r_j = s_j = 0$ in equation 2).

The channels undergo state transitions as illustrated in Figure 5A, and these transitions are the basis for synaptic plasticity. The transition rate from O → P is an increasing sigmoidal function of voltage, while the backward transition from P → O is an exponential decay. Thus, the larger the voltage in the postsynaptic cell, the larger the P/O ratio. The transitions between the modified channels are the same except for different parameter values. Note that such transitions do not change the synaptic strength.

On the other hand, transitions from P → P* strengthen the synapse and transitions from P* → P weaken it. The forward transition rate from P → P* is controlled by the amount of modifying substance, m_{ij}, present at the postsynaptic terminal:

$$m_{ij}(t + 1) = \kappa_m s_j - \delta_m m_{ij}(t) \quad (0 \leq m \leq 1) \tag{4}$$

As shown in equation (4) $m(t)$ grows at a rate (κ_m) proportional to the activity of the presynaptic cell, s_j, and exponentially decays (rate δ_m) with time (see Table 2 for parameter values). The backward transition from P* → P is a P* independent decay.

The net result of these transitions is expressed in equations 5–8, with parameters defined in Table 2 and $\sigma_{op} = \sigma[v(t), \theta_{op}, \epsilon_{op}], \sigma_{op}^* = \sigma[v(t), \theta_{op}^*, \epsilon_{op}^*]$:

$$o(t + 1) = o(t)(1 - \kappa_{op}\sigma_{op}) + \delta_{po}p(t) \tag{5}$$

$$o^*(t + 1) = o^*(t)(1 - \kappa_{op}^*\sigma_{op}^*) + \delta_{po}^*p^*(t) \tag{6}$$

$$p(t + 1) = p(t)[1 - \delta_{po} - \kappa_m m(t)^4] + \kappa_{op}\sigma_{op}o(t) \tag{7}$$
$$+ \min(\delta_p, p^*)$$

$$p^*(t + 1) = p^*(t)[1 - \delta_{po}^* - \min(\delta_p, p^*)] \tag{8}$$
$$+ \kappa_m m(t)^4 p(t) + \kappa_{op}^* \sigma_{op}^* o^*(t)$$

To strengthen a synapse with this rule requires the conjunction of 2 events: First, the postsynaptic voltage must have risen high enough, relative to θ_{op}, that a significant fraction of the unmodified channels have made the transition to the P state; second, the modifying substance, m, must have grown to near its maximum value of 1 (since the modification is proportional to m^4). To weaken a synapse with this rule requires the conjunction of low m and high voltage (relative to θ_{op}^*). The time window for the conjunction of these 2 events is determined by the growth and decay rates of the state transitions and the production of modifying substance (Finkel and Edelman, 1985). These synaptic relationships are demonstrated in the simple simulation shown in Figure 5B.

Program operation. The simulations were performed on IBM 4331 and 3090 computers. Programs were written in FORTRAN with extensive use of assembler utility routines (Reeke, 1984). Large simulations required ~3.5 megabytes of memory and ~80 min of CPU time on the 3090.

The receptive fields of all cells in the network could be determined simultaneously. This was accomplished by stimulating each point of the input array (in sequence) with a stimulus of a given size (typically 3 × 3) and recording the average response of each cell in the network during the stimulation of each such point (the stimulus was typically "on" for 3 steps and "off" for 7 steps). Note that the receptive fields were measured and not simply computed according to some rule.

Analysis of receptive fields and connection strengths was performed with a separate program and displayed on an IBM 5080 graphics terminal. This program can display many different features of the data, such as anatomical connections, connection strengths, individual receptive fields or receptive field maps, receptive field overlaps, etc., and was an essential tool in discovering the interactions between different levels of the system. The graphics program could also create movies of the cellular variables and could make graphs of any variable over time.

Results

Formation of neuronal groups

Although the synaptic efficacies of anatomical connections are difficult to determine in experimental preparations, they are straightforward to examine in this model network. Figure 6A represents the e → e connection strengths of a representative 12 × 6 region of the network containing 144 excitatory cells and 2448 connections as they were initially assigned, prior to

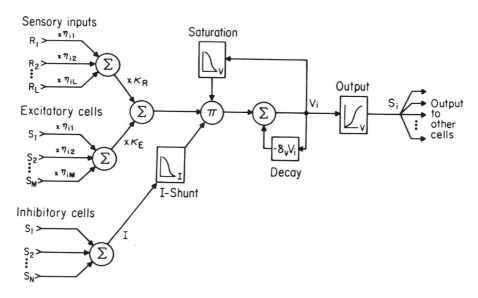

Figure 4. Schematic of the algorithm used to calculate the voltage, v, and the output, s, of a cell in the simulation (equations 1 and 2). The excitatory inputs from receptors (R_i) and excitatory cells (S_i) are multiplied by synaptic strength terms (η_{ij}), summed separately, and are then multiplied by scaling factors (κ_E, κ_R) and added together. This sum is multiplied by 2 fractions, one representing the shunting effect of the inhibitory input (I) and the other the reduction in synaptic current due to synaptic saturation (reduction of the transmembrane driving potential with increasing transmembrane potential). This product represents the net input to the cell. This input is then combined with a fraction $(1 - \delta_v)$ of the voltage remaining from the previous time step. This yields the net voltage of the cell, which is then used to compute the output, S, of the cell by means of the sigmoidal function shown. The output is transmitted to other cells.

stimulation. The initial distribution was Gaussian (mean = 0.5, SD = 0.17, range = 0.1–1). The initial r → e connection strengths followed the same distribution. Note that, on average, the connection strengths appear similar across the network.

Figure 6B shows neuronal groups that formed after stimulation of the hand; these groups are clusters of cells that have generally strengthened their mutual connections and weakened all others. The receptor sheet was stimulated in a random sequence of positions that eventually covered the entire hand. The stimulus was a 3 × 3 solid square that simultaneously activated a 3 × 3 square region of receptors, which in turn projected to a 9 × 9 region of the network. Each position on the hand was stimulated with this stimulus for 3 cycles of 6 steps on, 4 steps off. The stimulation was repeated until the entire hand had been covered 4 times. Within a given pass, the individual stimuli did not overlap, but stimuli in each pass overlapped those from other passes with varying offsets, and they were applied in a different random order. The stimuli were applied without regard to the glabrous/dorsal border or to the individual finger and palm borders. Thus, stimuli straddled these borders to perhaps a greater degree than occurs naturally in the monkey.

During the first pass of stimulation, each stimulus excited an approximately 12 × 12 region of the network (due to the divergence of the input projection and the intrinsic connections). At the end of the first pass, there were relatively large clusterings of slightly strengthened connection strengths. With subsequent passes, the regions of activation shrank and became more intense as the groups became stronger, smaller, and more tightly packed. The group structure became relatively stable after about 3 passes, but the borders between groups continued to shift as the groups competed with each other for cells. During this com-

Table 2. Values of model parameters used in the simulation

	E	I	
A. Neuronal			
θ_s	20	20	output threshold
ϵ_s	6	6	output nonlinearity
θ_I	4	—	shunt threshold
ϵ_I	0.4	—	shunt nonlinearity
θ_v	80	80	saturation threshold
ϵ_v	10	10	saturation nonlinearity
δ_v	0.5	0.4	voltage decay rate
κ_E	4.5	1	e-cell input scale factor
κ_R	1	—	receptor input scale factor
B. Synaptic			
g	0.1		unmodified channel conductance
g^*	1		modified channel conductance
κ_{op}	0.4		max. O → P transition rate
κ_{op}^*	0.4		max. O* → P* transition rate
δ_{po}	0.05		P → O decay rate
δ_{po}^*	0.05		P* → O* decay rate
κ_p	0.4		max. P → P* modification rate
δ_p	0.01		P* → P demodification rate
κ_m	0.3		mod. substance growth rate
δ_m	0.05		mod. substance decay rate
θ_{op}	20		O → P transition threshold
ϵ_{op}	2		O → P transition nonlinearity
θ_{op}^*	30		O* → P* transition threshold
ϵ_{op}^*	3		O* → P* transition nonlinearity

Values of both the neuronal and synaptic parameters used in the equations of the simulations. The E and I columns (A) are the e- and i-cell parameters, respectively; the dashes in the I column refer to parameters which are irrelevant because of the particular connectivity used, i.e., there were no i → i (θ_I, ϵ_I) or r → i (κ_R) connections. The various θ's and ϵ's are parameters that determine the inflection point and the slope at the inflection point, respectively, of the sigmoidal functions (see equation 1) used to simulate the nonlinear kinetics of state transitions.

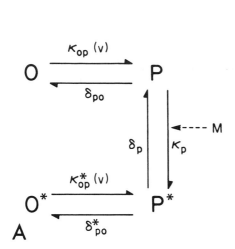

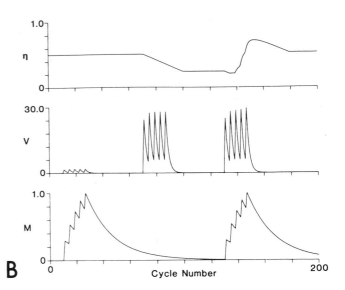

Figure 5. The synaptic modification rule. *A,* Transition scheme governing postsynaptic plasticity in the model. O, P, O*, and P* represent the fraction of channels at a given synapse that are in each of the 4 conducting channel states. $\kappa(v)$ and $\kappa^*(v)$ are the state transition rates and are increasing sigmoidal functions of cell voltage, v; M is the amount of modifying substance, and the remaining Greek letters are constants given in Table 2B. The modified states O* and P* have a larger conductance than the unmodified states O and P. Thus, synaptic strength is increased in the M-dependent P $\rightarrow$ P* transition, and weakened by decay from P* $\rightarrow$ P. The ratio of P channels to O channels is determined by the voltage history of the postsynaptic cell. *B,* Illustrative simulation of the postsynaptic rule in a simple network. The network consists of one postsynaptic cell receiving multiple inputs; changes in the strength (η) of a single given synapse are related to the modifying substance (M) present at the synapse and the voltage (V) of the postsynaptic cell. At the start, $\eta = 0.5$, with 4/9 of the channels in state O* and 5/9 in state O. During the first set of 30 cycles, only the given synapse was stimulated with 5 short bursts. The V produced was insufficient to induce channel transitions into the P or P* states, and η therefore remained unchanged despite the fact that the stimulation produced significant amounts of M. During the second set of 30 cycles, a large number of other synapses were stimulated and the large heterosynaptically generated V drove the O and O* channels into the P and P* states, respectively. Because the given synapse was not stimulated, M was low, and the predominant transition was the P* $\rightarrow$ P decay that reduced η. The third set of 30 cycles was the same as the second, but the given synapse was also stimulated, producing high concentrations of M. In this case, the predominant transition was P · P* and the synapse was strengthened.

petition, the sizes and shapes of the groups changed, but in accord with the notion of group confinement (Edelman and Finkel, 1984), there was a minimum and maximum allowable size.

Group formation was fairly robust with respect to the stimulation protocol. Protocols employing different random sequences of stimulation, or using stimuli that varied over a several-fold range of sizes, intensities, or durations all led to generically similar group structures. Neither the sizes nor the locations of the groups were determined solely by the character of such input stimulation. Each receptor projects to a 7 × 7 region of the network, and each group occupies a small arbitrary

(roughly 3 × 3) domain within the 12 × 12 region initially excited by the stimulus. Furthermore, all network areas were stimulated equally. Thus, the locations of the groups were not prespecified by the anatomy or the input but depended upon local inhomogeneities in the patterns of connections, their initial strengths, and the historical sequence of stimulation.

Figure 6C is a magnified (× 2.5) view of the 12 × 6 region in Figure 6B that contains the groups marked "*" and "†". It is evident that most cells belong to only one group, although a few cells have strong connections to 2 groups (see the green connections of group *). With further stimulation, these cells are usually captured exclusively by one group. As a result of group

Please note: Figure 6 appears opposite page 348.

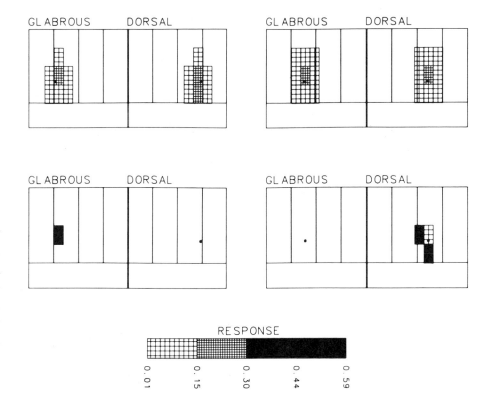

Figure 7. Receptive field plots of representative cells from the adjacent groups labeled * and † in Figure 6*B.* The receptive fields of group * are shown on the *left* and those of group † on the *right,* both before (*top*) and after (*bottom*) the groups had formed. The average response of the cell to stimulation at each point of the hand is represented by a block, the shade of which codes the strength of the response (as indicated by the scale at the bottom of the fig.) and the size of which is equal to the size of the stimulus used. Each finger contains 8 receptors widthwise and 12 receptors lengthwise, thus the rectangular receptive field in the *bottom-left panel* covers an area of 3 × 3 receptors. *Small dots* mark the locations of the centers of the glabrous and dorsal regions of the hand that project to the cell. The X dimension of the hand shown here is compressed by a factor of 2 in order to facilitate display. (This accounts for the rectilinear appearance of the actually square-shaped receptive fields). There are 3 important changes in the receptive fields as a result of group formation: (1) The peak response has increased and shifted; (2) the size of the receptive field has decreased; and (3) the receptive fields have become exclusively glabrous or dorsal.

formation, the distribution of connection strengths changes from a Gaussian with a mean of 0.5 to a bimodal distribution with widely separated peaks. This bimodal distribution is stable once the groups have formed, even though the groups continue to shift, grow, and shrink as they compete with each other.

Formation of an ordered topographic map

The formation of groups organized the receptive fields of cells in the network. This can be seen by considering the 2 adjacent groups labeled * and † in Figure 6, *B* and *C.* Figure 7 shows the receptive fields (see Materials and Methods) of a typical cell in each of these 2 regions before and after the groups had formed. The receptive fields of cells in the initial network were large, occupying the major part of one finger, they were relatively weak, and all cells had receptive fields on both the glabrous and the dorsal surfaces of the hand. This is as would be expected given the anatomy: each cell receives an equal number of inputs from the glabrous and dorsal surfaces. With the formation of neuronal groups, however, 4 dramatic changes are seen in the receptive fields of the component cells: (1) the sizes of the receptive fields decrease dramatically, (2) the overlap of the fields of cells within a group increases, (3) the strengths of the responses increase, and (4) the receptive fields of cells become either exclusively glabrous or exclusively dorsal, but not mixed. The case of cells with receptive fields centered on the lateral or medial surfaces of the fingers or palm is, of course, an exception inasmuch as these fields can extend onto both surfaces of the hand. Some receptive fields straddle the borders between digits as a result of the stimulation protocol which did not respect these borders (see Materials and Methods). Such receptive fields are,

however, occasionally observed in the monkey (Merzenich et al., 1983a).

The local topography of the mapping is shown in Figure 8, which is a display of the centers of the receptive fields of cells encountered in 2 linear tracks across the network (corresponding to 2 tangential electrode penetrations in cortex). One track was made horizontally across the network (at a midvertical position) and encountered 64 cells from left to right. The receptive field centers of these cells are marked with rectangles. The second track was made vertically from the top to the bottom of the network, and the receptive field centers of the 32 cells encountered are marked with circles. The receptive field centers were determined by weighting the contribution of each receptor in the receptive field by its response—thus these are not strictly the geometrical centers, but the centers of activity of the receptive fields. Figure 8 (top) shows the receptive field centers before group formation (corresponding to the network in Fig. 6.4). The initial topography is such that the receptive field centers move in a generally smooth progression across the surface of the receptor sheets. The small degree of scatter arises from the random component in the underlying anatomical connectivity (see Materials and Methods). Note that all cells initially have both glabrous and dorsal components to their receptive fields. Figure 8 (bottom) shows the receptive fields of the same cells determined after the formation of neuronal groups (corresponding to Fig. 6*B*). The receptive field centers are numbered according to the order in which cells were encountered in the 2 tracks. (Primed numbers refer to the vertical track; unprimed numbers refer to the horizontal track.) The receptive field centers have shifted into a number of clusters separated by gaps. The clusters cor-

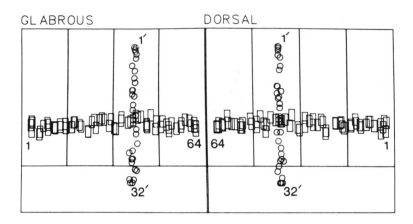

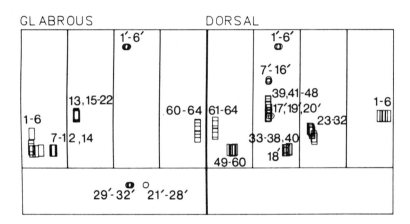

Figure 8. Local topography of the mapping. *Top,* Before group formation. *Rectangles* mark the centers of the receptive fields of 64 cells encountered as the network was traversed from left to right along a horizontal line (located midway between top and bottom of the network in the vertical dimension). *Circles* mark receptive field centers of 32 cells found along a second track running vertically from top to bottom of the network. The first and last receptive field centers in each track are numbered (those in the vertical track are primed, e.g., 1′ and 32′). Prior to group formation, each cell has both glabrous and dorsal receptive field components, and the receptive field centers move in a generally smooth linear progression across the receptor surface. Note that the rectangles correspond to the size of a single receptor. *Bottom,* After group formation. Receptive field centers of the same cells as in *Top,* labeled in the order of encounter along the same horizontal (*rectangles*) and vertical (*circles*) tracks. Each track passes through several neuronal groups (see Fig. 6*B*). Cells in the same group have superposed or highly overlapped receptive field centers. But the receptive field center shifts considerably between adjacent cells belonging to 2 different groups (e.g., cells 48 and 49). The transition between cells belonging to glabrous and dorsal groups is also seen (e.g., cells 22 and 23, or cells 20′ and 21′). Note that the horizontal and vertical tracks intersect, accounting for the superposition of some receptive field centers in the 2 tracks.

respond to the receptive fields of cells in the same group; as different groups are encountered along the track, the receptive fields locations shift. Thus, in the horizontal track, cells 1–6 were at the network edge and had mixed receptive fields, cells 7–12 and 14 were in a glabrous group, cells 13 and 15–22 were in another glabrous group, cells 23–32 were in a dorsal group, 33–38 and 40 in another dorsal group, and so on. Cells in the same group share highly overlapped receptive fields, and as one passes from one group to the next, the receptive field location suddenly shifts, even between adjacent cells. Note that the appearance that large regions of the receptor sheet are not covered follows from the fact that only the centers of the receptive fields are displayed, and again only those from a single vertical or horizontal row of cells.

Receptive field changes following group formation are seen best in the receptive field map. This map (Fig. 9) displays 2 types of receptive field information: for each excitatory cell in the network, the map indicates (1) the digit or palm on which the center of the receptive field is located and (2) whether the receptive field is on the glabrous surface, dorsal surface, or both. The map is coded such that receptive field locations on adjacent digits or palmar regions are distinguished by alternate light-gray and dark-gray solid fill background. In addition, cells with receptive fields on the glabrous surface are individually marked with a small black rectangle, those with receptive fields on the dorsal surface are marked with a small white rectangle, and cells

with mixed glabrous and dorsal responses are unmarked. A cell is labeled "glabrous" if 80% or more of its summed response to all stimuli is to glabrous stimuli; conversely, it is labeled "dorsal" if more than 80% of its summed response to all stimuli is to dorsal stimuli. If a cell meets neither of these conditions, it is labeled "mixed." The initial receptive field map (Fig. 9*A*) shows that topographic organization is present before groups have formed; this follows from the topography inherent in the anatomical projection from the hand to the network. Initially, all cells respond to both dorsal and glabrous inputs (i.e., have "mixed" receptive fields). Although the exact balance varies, the initial difference between dorsal and glabrous influences was equal to within 20% for all cells.

After groups had formed, a well-ordered topographic representation of the fingers and palm was observed, with segregated zones of representation of the dorsal and glabrous surfaces (Fig. 9*B*). Although different stimulation schemes yielded different receptive field maps, all schemes employing locally correlated stimuli on the hand resulted in ordered maps with compact regions of dorsal and glabrous representation. Within each group, the nonlinear and highly cooperative interactions between voltage and synaptic strengths lead to similar changes in all cells of the group in response to glabrous versus dorsal stimulation. The receptive field choice depends upon the early balance of glabrous versus dorsal stimulation received by the group and by nearby groups. Early biases are amplified into the resulting organiza-

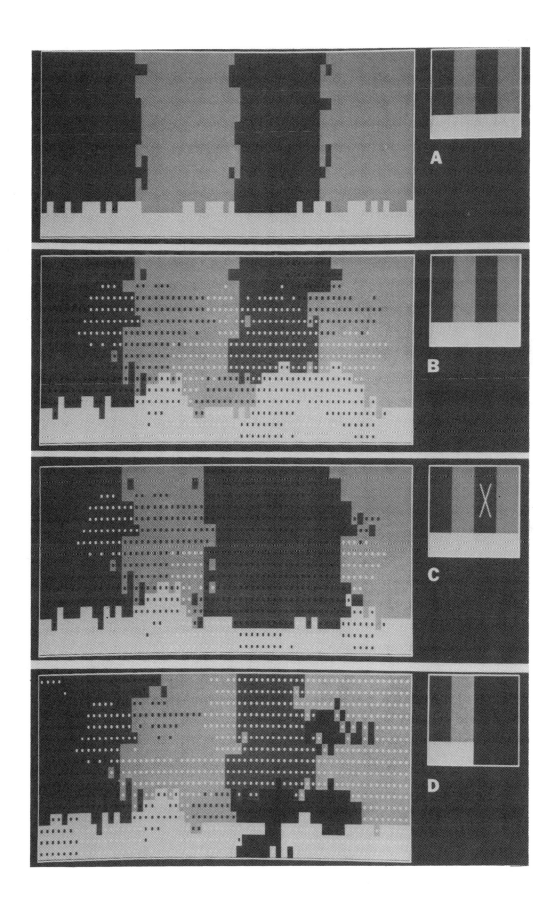

tion. The ratio of groups responding to glabrous versus those responding to dorsal stimulation depended rather sharply (see Discussion) upon the relative balance of stimulation to the 2 surfaces of the hand. In the example shown here, the glabrous and dorsal surfaces were stimulated equally, and of the 19 non-mixed groups present, 12 are glabrous and 7 are dorsal (the dorsal groups contain slightly more cells on the average; thus, 59% of the nonmixed cells are glabrous and 41% are dorsal). Although this distribution appears skewed in favor of glabrous groups, the asymmetry is not statistically significant and follows from the small total number of groups. Nonetheless, the apparent tendency of the glabrous and dorsal groups to form in domains exclusive of the other (see Fig. 9B) suggests that whether a group becomes a glabrous or dorsal responder may depend to some degree upon the nature of nearby groups.

In this simulation, 32.3% of the e-cells remained mixed, i.e., their responses to dorsal or glabrous stimulation were equal to within a factor of 4. Most of these cells were found at the borders of the network; 95% of the cells within 3 boxes of the right-hand border were mixed, 51.2% of the cells within 3 boxes of the other borders were mixed, while only 6.3% of the nonborder cells (located within the central 26 × 10 region of the network) were mixed. The high proportion of mixed cells near the borders is due to the higher connection density at these sites (see Materials and Methods). Higher local connection densities generate higher cellular voltages in response to local stimuli, and so can be more easily strengthened from a weakened state, thus preventing either the dorsal or glabrous stimuli from gaining domination of the group.

The very high percentage of mixed cells at the right-hand border is due to the fact that the glabrous/dorsal surfaces are continuous along the middle of the input array (which projects to the right-hand edge of the network). Thus, during group formation, stimuli straddle this midline and glabrous and dorsal receptors are coactivated. This naturally occurs at the edges of the monkey hand (Merzenich et al., 1978).

The mixed receptive fields of cells in the central region of the network are due to groups competing for cells. An examination of the intrinsic connection strengths of the network revealed that most (88%) of these mixed cells were located between groups with opposite receptive field types and that they shared strong connections with both groups. As the network receives additional stimulation, these mixed cells are generally captured by one group or the other and then exhibit the receptive field type of that group. Because group competition is an ongoing process in the network, we expect that there will always be a small percentage of mixed cells in the central region, located predominantly between groups of opposite receptive field type.

Simulations of reported experiments

We used the network with the group structure shown in Figure 6B and the receptive field map shown in Figure 9B to simulate a number of reported experiments (Merzenich et al., 1983a, b, 1984; Jenkins et al., 1984). We will discuss 2 such simulations that yielded results qualitatively similar to those observed experimentally.

Results of simulated repetitive tapping of digit 2

The first simulation involved increased stimulation of a local region of the hand and was designed to investigate factors that control the magnification factor (the ratio of the area of a cortical representation to the area of the corresponding body region represented). We applied repeated stimulation to the glabrous surface of digit 2; the same protocol was employed as in group formation, but the individual stimuli were 4 times as intense ($\kappa_R = 4$). Digit 2 was stimulated exclusively, and its entire surface was covered several times. This stimulation was applied to the network that already had the mature group structure shown in Figure 6, B and C.

The stimulation produced the new receptive field map shown in Figure 9C. The area of representation of the glabrous surface of digit 2 expanded greatly (here by a factor of 13.7) to nearly the anatomical limit of the underlying projection. The total area of representation of digit 2 (both glabrous and dorsal surfaces) increased by a factor of 2.3. The borders of the representation of this digit expanded in all directions, increasing the magnification factor of the digit at the expense of that of neighboring regions. The representations of digits 3 and 4 were relatively unchanged.

The extent to which map borders shift depends upon the intensity of the stimulation, provided that the intensity exceeds certain minimal levels. However, in general, the more intense the stimulation, the greater is the change in group structure. In the example shown here, the group structure was radically affected with many groups merging due to the intense, locally correlated nature of the stimuli. Less intense stimulation leaves

←

Figure 9. Receptive field maps after normal stimulation and perturbations. The position of each excitatory cell in the network (the 2 excitatory cells at the same network grid point are displayed in adjacent positions) is marked with a block colored according to the location of the center of the cell's receptive field on the hand, as indicated by the diagram of the hand (which is compressed along the X dimension by a factor of 2 to facilitate display). Cells that responded primarily to stimulation of the glabrous or dorsal surface are marked with a *small black* or *white rectangle*, respectively, while cells with mixed glabrous/dorsal responses are not marked. A, Prior to group formation, topographic order is present (inasmuch as the projection from the hand is topographic by design), but the receptive fields of all the cells are mixed, reflecting the fact that initially the inputs from both surfaces are roughly equal. *B,* After group formation, the map borders representing hand regions have shifted because of the establishment of group borders, and most of the cells are exclusively glabrous or dorsal responders. A significant fraction of the cells retain mixed receptive fields, but these lie primarily on the edges of the network (see text). C, Starting with a network with well-formed groups (Figs. 6B, 9B), glabrous digit 2 was repetitively stimulated (as indicated by the X on this digit in the hand diagram). Note that the representation of glabrous digit 2 has expanded greatly (here by a factor of 13.7) at the expense of the representations of adjacent digits and of its own dorsal representation. This expansion is due to the growth of the groups representing glabrous digit 2, as well as to other groups having switched their receptive fields. Further stimulation does not produce more expansion because of the anatomical limits of the projection. D, Starting with the same network with well-formed groups (Figs. 6B, 9B), the inputs from glabrous digits 1 and 2 and subjacent palm (as indicated by the *black regions* in the hand diagram) were interrupted, corresponding to a transection of the median nerve in monkeys. All other extrinsic connections remain intact, including all connections from the dorsal surface. Cells unresponsive to all stimulation are colored *black*. There is a new representation of the dorsum of digits 1 and 2 and subjacent palm in the network region, which, before the transection, contained a representation of the glabrous surfaces of these regions. The new representation is not complete, and there remain silent, unresponsive regions. These regions remain silent unless very intense stimulation is used. This results from the fact that their connections with the dorsum are so weak that normal stimulation does not produce voltages high enough to enable synaptic strengthening.

the group structure unchanged, but such stimulation gives rise at maximum to only a 2-fold increase in the magnification factor. Even after intense stimulation, the original group structure can be largely recovered by applying several passes of normal stimulation to the hand, and this additional stimulation leaves the increased magnification factor of digit 2 intact.

The results of this simulation correspond reasonably closely to the experimental result found after repeated tapping on the glabrous surface of a single digit in the owl monkey (Jenkins et al., 1984). The experimentally reported observation was made after hundreds of thousands of repeated stimuli; those in the simulation occurred after only hundreds. There is no reported evidence on experimental changes after shorter stimulation protocols, but it is likely that the simulated connections are relatively more "plastic" than those in the real nervous system—a compromise that is necessary for compressing the simulation into a manageable number of iterations.

Results of simulated nerve transection

The second simulated experiment involved decreasing the net stimulation to a region. This was accomplished by transecting the connections from half of the glabrous surface of the hand (digits 1 and 2 and subjacent palm), corresponding roughly to transection of the median nerve in the monkey. Once cut, there was absolutely no activation from the median half of the glabrous hand to the network. The receptors from the rest of the hand remained intact, and the entire hand (both affected and unaffected regions) was lightly stimulated (3 steps on, 7 steps off) in a random sequence with a 3×3 stimulus. This background stimulation was to simulate the light touches that an animal would unavoidably encounter.

We examined the receptive field maps at various times after the transection. Immediately after the cut, i.e., before any stimulation of the hand, the cells that formerly had receptive fields in the denervated region were no longer responsive. These "silenced cells" received weak connections from the dorsal surface of the transected region, and small postsynaptic potentials were observable. This population of weak inputs, acting together, produced sufficient postsynaptic voltage to strengthen their connections over time due to the voltage-dependent properties of the synaptic rule. This ability to strengthen such weakened connections is a property that distinguishes voltage-dependent (Finkel and Edelman, 1987) from output-dependent synaptic rules such as the Hebb rule (Hebb, 1949).

Shortly after the simulated transection (i.e., after 2 passes of stimulation), the former area of representation of the median half of the glabrous surface is occupied by a representation of the corresponding dorsal surface of the hand (Fig. 9D). This new representation is topographic, but the borders between the fingers and with the palm are different than before. There is a large silent region (the blackened cells) in which cells are still not responsive. Note that the representation of the unaffected glabrous half of the hand is relatively unchanged from that seen before the transection. Note also that the locations of the borders and the magnification factors of digits 1 and 2 and the palm differ from the original glabrous representation, yet the map shows continuity and compactness. The group structure corresponding to this map (not shown) was almost identical to the pretransection structure.

With normal stimulation, the silent regions remain essentially constant despite extended periods of stimulation (12 passes). With repeated stimulation, the silent areas eventually become

responsive to dorsal stimuli, providing that the intensity of the stimulation is increased. As discussed above, such an increase also changes the group structure. These results are very similar to those found experimentally with the recovery from transection of the median nerve in owl monkeys (for comparison, see Figure 2 in Merzenich et al., 1983b).

Discussion

The major results of the computer simulations reported here concern the dynamic control of topographic map organization as a result of the formation of neuronal groups. We have shown that a network with locally connected excitatory and inhibitory cells, divergent overlapping extrinsic connections similar to those of the thalamocortical projection (Gilbert and Wiesel, 1979; Landry and Deschenes, 1981), and realistic synaptic plasticity rules will spontaneously organize into neuronal groups when activated by locally correlated stimulation of the input array. After group formation, the receptive fields of cells in the network become smaller, stronger, and exclusively restricted to either the glabrous or dorsal surface of the hand, despite the fact that all cells of the network still receive equal numbers of anatomical connections from both surfaces of the hand. Groups act collectively to segregate the network into exclusively glabrous or dorsal domains in which all cells have similar receptive fields. After repetitive tapping of a local region, or transection of extrinsic fibers, there are en masse shifts in the receptive fields of cells in the affected groups, leading to dramatic changes in the receptive field map of the network. The results of these simulations correspond closely to results seen in monkey cortex after similar perturbations.

Group formation depends upon the positive feedback between changes in connection strength and cellular potential. The properties of the synaptic rule are such that the same conditions that strengthen the active synapses onto a cell weaken the inactive ones. In general, this prevents a cell from belonging to more than one group and ensures that the borders between groups remain sharp even though their locations may shift. Groups form under a variety of stimulation protocols; however, all such protocols lead to a point of stability after which further stimulation does not significantly change the group structure.

The segregation of the map into neuronal groups is similar to the tendency of all systems with short-range excitation and long-range inhibition to organize into domains (Turing, 1952; Meinhardt, 1982). The critical difference is that neuronal groups, once formed from the fixed anatomy, act as independent competitive organizers of a functional map out of that divergent and overlapping anatomical substrate. The receptive field of each group is restricted to either the glabrous or dorsal surface depending upon historical events: whether the group received greater stimulation from one side or the other and whether one side initially dominated the stimulation to the group and established a slight advantage. Such competitive advantages tend to become amplified during selection, leading to the dramatic strengthening of one class of inputs and the weakening of others.

It is important to note that group formation involves synaptic modifications in both intrinsic and extrinsic connections. It is not known in vivo, whether these changes are independent or whether one necessarily follows upon the other. However, our experience with various trial simulations suggests that group formation is most robust if intrinsic connections are plastic concurrently with extrinsic connections. The scheme yielding the best defined and most densely packed groups was one in which the synaptic plasticity parameters for extrinsic and intrinsic connections were identical (Table 2), and in which the voltage necessary to weaken connections was higher than that required to strengthen them ($\theta_{op}^* > \theta_{op}$). In this scheme, the voltage required to weaken extrinsic connections can be achieved only in a well-formed group (due to the stronger intragroup intrinsic connections and therefore larger voltages within a group); thus, *only the cells in a group* can refine their receptive fields by weakening some subset of the extrinsic connections they receive. All subsequent results were found to depend on the quality of the groups formed. In networks with poor group structure, the cells had large receptive fields that retained components on both surfaces of the hand.

One of the most critical features of the present computer model is the robustness of the results with respect to changes in the parameters. Of the 23 neuronal and synaptic parameters in the model (Tables 1 and 2), we found the most critical relationships to be (1) the number of inhibitory inputs to a cell relative to the threshold of the inhibitory shunt (θ_I); (2) the scale factors of the excitatory inputs (κ_E, κ_R) relative to the firing threshold (θ_s); (3) the voltage threshold for channel transitions (θ_{op}, θ_{op}^*) with respect to firing threshold (θ_s); and (4) the ratio of the rates for modification and demodification (κ_p, δ_p, respectively).

Although the results were largely independent of the values of the neuronal parameters chosen, they obviously required self-consistency (e.g., synaptic saturation must occur at a voltage greater than the firing threshold). Of somewhat greater sensitivity were the parameters involved in the synaptic plasticity rules. By adjusting the synaptic plasticity parameters (Table 2), we could create groups of different sizes or different packing densities, groups surrounded by regions of weakened connections of various widths, and groups with wider or narrower receptive fields.

The critical feature of the postsynaptic rule in group formation and map organization is the ability to strengthen or weaken subsets of connections in a context-dependent fashion (i.e., based on heterosynaptic input voltages). Although channel- and receptor-based modification schemes seem ideally suited to such heterosynaptic mechanisms, a variety of other synaptic mechanisms might subserve similar roles (Finkel and Edelman, 1987). We have not considered presynaptic modifications in the present simulations; however, previous studies (Finkel and Edelman, 1985) have shown that pre- and postsynaptic mechanisms operating in parallel lead to a wide class of properties that can, for example, couple short- and long-term modifications.

The model tested here was deliberately constructed to be a minimal one, and it is not surprising that its performance left a number of problems to be solved. The most serious shortcoming is that the model does not follow the inverse rule (Edelman and Finkel, 1984), namely, that receptive field size is inversely related to magnification factor (Daniel and Whitteridge, 1961; Sur et al., 1980). In particular, the large increase in magnification factor in the "repetitive tap" simulation was not accompanied by receptive field decreases on glabrous digit 2. One reason for this failure is that, after group formation, many receptive fields are as small as possible, and are unable to shrink further. Another possible reason is that, due to limitations on network size, each peripheral region (e.g., each finger) is represented by just a few groups, too few presumably to generate the intergroup interactions responsible for the inverse rule.

There are also several remaining difficulties related to the

properties of the mapping. In the simulations shown here, 7% of the surface of the hand was not represented in the network. These nonrepresented receptors mapped to cells located at the extreme borders of the network. It is not clear from reported maps (Merzenich et al., 1978) whether the complete surface of the hand is actually represented in areas 3b or 1, and it might be of particular interest to examine the completeness of representations located near cytoarchitectonic borders. Another residual problem is that biasing the ratio of glabrous to dorsal stimulation by a factor of 2 results in a map in which all but a few groups primarily respond to the more frequently stimulated surface. This appears to be an unusually sharp dependence on the stimulation ratio of glabrous to dorsal inputs. The cause of this problem is related to the relatively small number of groups in the network, the rate of group formation, and the stereotyped nature of our stimulation. Finally, it was observed that under certain relatively rare circumstances, bursts of activation of moderate intensity were not self-extinguishing. This problem could have been eliminated by introducing synaptic depression or long-lasting hyperpolarizing inhibition, but because the pathology was rare, we decided to simply set the voltages of all cells to zero between successive stimulations.

The functional somatosensory mapping problem we have considered contrasts in some respects to that confronting the primary visual cortex. The mechanisms underlying the segregation may be analogous in both cases, and may result from a large degree of local coactivation; however, the functional properties of the mappings appear to differ. In the visual system, corresponding points on the 2 retinae are frequently, if not usually, costimulated. In the somatosensory cortex, corresponding points on the 2 surfaces of the hand are rarely, if ever, costimulated. Visual cortex displays postcritical period ocular dominance stripes and the functional property of stereopsis. Somatosensory cortex displays segregated domains of dorsal and glabrous representation that remain plastic into adult life but whose functional relevance is currently unknown.

This comparison sharpens the question of the functional importance of plastic changes in cortical maps. From the viewpoint of a selective theory, the divergent and overlapped nature of the anatomy is an unavoidable result of development which involves dynamic processes of cell adhesion, movement, and death, rather than prespecified molecular markers (Edelman, 1986). Given these developmental constraints, a dynamic selective process is required to create precise functional maps. The observed map plasticity is then an ongoing manifestation of the existence of somatic neural selection. Over evolutionary time scales, this somatic selection could generate well-adapted functional maps despite the changing anatomical substrates (such as the growth of existing areas or the addition of new areas). During the lifetime of an animal, plasticity in functional maps ensures that magnification factors reflect recent usage, ensuring the devotion of finer discriminitive abilities (as reflected by smaller receptive fields) to more frequently used peripheral sites. Competitive plasticity also maximizes the use of cortical representation space, ensuring that large areas are not devoted to nonadaptive representations. A final possibility has to do with what Mountcastle (1984) has termed "parallel and serial processing" in somesthesis: The reentrant linking of representations in other cortical and subcortical areas may be facilitated by the ability of each individual representation to undergo plastic changes in location or modality.

Although the present model does not address the developmental aspects of the formation of topographic projections, it may, nevertheless, be of some relevance to the organization of such projections, particularly in cases where there is dynamic, activity-dependent reorganization such as in the retinotectal projection (Schmidt, 1985; Fraser and Hunt, 1986). In contrast, the model may not apply strictly to certain specialized areas in which map borders are fixed by the anatomy itself. This occurs in the rodent whisker barrel fields (Woolsey and Van der Loos, 1970; Killackey, 1973), and possibly in the somatosensory cortex of the raccoon (Warren and Pubols, 1984; Rasmusson and Nance, 1986). Even in these cases, however, the assumptions of the model may apply to map changes at the level of the thalamus, dorsal column nuclei, or spinal cord. There is substantial evidence for such subcortical map changes (Wall and Eggers, 1971; Dostrovsky et al., 1976; Devor and Wall, 1981), and we would expect that they play an important role in the overall mapping changes observed at the cortical level. Due to the convergence and divergence of fibers, local shifts at the dorsal column or thalamic level could give rise to much larger shifts at the cortical level. In addition, the reentrant (Edelman, 1981) nature of these projections (the presence of substantial reciprocal projections which send phasically coordinated signals back to earlier levels) implies that map changes at the different levels will closely correspond. The network considerations addressed here could be extended to the modeling of these situations.

It is useful, finally, to present a number of predictions prompted by the results of the simulations:

1. Neuronal groups as defined in this study will be found in the cortex.

2. Abolition of shunting inhibition (through chloride channel blockers such as Zn^{2+}) should generally lead to greater network instabilities than abolition of hyperpolarizing inhibition. The effects of the actions of barbiturates, benzodiazepines, and specific toxins such as bicuculline and picrotoxin on GABA-receptor-associated chloride channels (Olsen, 1987) may be related to the network instabilities observed here.

3. The minimum extent for segregated zones of like modality in a map is one group diameter. Statistical analyses of the size distribution of segregated areas in cortical maps might reveal the presence of a discrete subunit size. There should be 2 distinct classes of map border shifts: large shifts that occur over distances representing an integral number of groups and much smaller local shifts due to the exchange of individual cells between groups. Besides the results reported here, other reported experiments such as digit amputations, or local cortical ablations, will be accounted for in further tests of the model.

4. If 2 adjacent digits are independently stimulated for prolonged periods of time, the representation of each would expand in all directions except along their common border.

5. Cells with mixed glabrous and dorsal receptive fields may be found at the borders of neuronal groups, particularly between dorsal and glabrous groups, and in higher density at the edges of a cytoarchitectonic region.

6. Concurrent stimulation of a glabrous and a corresponding dorsal region should lead to a group with a mixed receptive field. If repeated for a prolonged time, the previously segregated representations may be subsumed into a new conjoint representation. It would then be of interest whether in a psychophysical experiment, stimulation of just the glabrous or just the dorsal surface of the region could be subjectively localized in an appropriate manner. In other words, does the perception of

the location of a stimulus depend upon unique cortical loci for the representation of that location, or can it be independently identified, for example, from the firing properties of different modalities or comparisons between multiple representations?

The network simulations presented here are based on a general synthetic approach to neural modeling in which experimental phenomena observed at several different structural and physiological levels are simulated together in sufficiently powerful computers using simplified but realistic assumptions. Given an understanding of such minimal models, we suggest that this approach may be valuable in understanding other dynamic processes of selection and mapping in complex nervous systems. It will be of particular interest, for example, to determine the effects of adding additional synaptic stages between the receptor sheet and the "cortex" and also to incorporate a laminated cortex with layer-specific inputs and outputs.

References

Daniel, P. M., and D. Whitteridge (1961) The representation of the visual field in the cerebral cortex in monkeys. J. Physiol. (Lond.) *159:* 302–321.

Devor, M., and P. D. Wall (1981) Effects of peripheral nerve injury on receptive fields of cells in the cat spinal cord. J. Comp. Neurol. *199:* 227–291.

Dostrovsky, J. O., J. Millar, and P. D. Wall (1976) The immediate shift of afferent drive of dorsal column nucleus cells following deafferentation: A comparison of acute and chronic deafferentation in gracile nucleus and spinal cord. Exp. Neurol. *52:* 480–495.

Dykes, R. W. (1983) Parallel processing of somatosensory information: A theory. Br. Res. Rev. *6:* 47–115.

Edelman, G. M. (1978) Group selection and phasic reentrant signalling: A theory of higher brain function. In *The Mindful Brain,* G. M. Edelman and V. B. Mountcastle, eds., pp. 51–100, MIT Press, Cambridge, MA.

Edelman, G. M. (1981) Group selection as the basis for higher brain function. In *Organization of the Cerebral Cortex,* F. O. Schmitt, F. G. Worden, G. Adelman, and S. G. Dennis, eds., pp. 535–563, MIT Press, Cambridge, MA.

Edelman, G. M., and L. H. Finkel (1984) Neuronal group selection in the cerebral cortex. In *Dynamic Aspects of Neocortical Function,* G. M. Edelman, W. E. Gall, and W. M. Cowan, eds., pp. 653–695, Wiley, New York.

Finkel, L. H. (1985) Selection in synaptic regulation and neural mapping. In *Molecular Basis of Animal Form* (Proc. of UCLA Symposium), G. M. Edelman, ed., pp. 571–618, Alan R. Liss, New York.

Finkel, L. H., and G. M. Edelman (1985) Interaction of synaptic modification rules within populations of neurons. Proc. Natl. Acad. Sci. USA *82:* 1291–1295.

Finkel, L. H., and G. M. Edelman (1987) Population rules for synapses in networks. In *Synaptic Function,* G. M. Edelman, W. E. Gall, and W. M. Cowan, eds., pp. 711–757, Wiley, New York.

Fraser, S. E., and R. K. Hunt (1986) A physiological measure of shifting connections in the *Rana-pipiens* retinotectal system. J. Embryol. Exp. Morphol. *94:* 149–161.

Gilbert, C. D., and T. N. Wiesel (1979) Morphology and intracortical projections of functionally characterized neurons in the cat visual cortex. Nature *280:* 120–125.

Hawkins, R. D., T. W. Abrams, T. J. Carew, and E. R. Kandel (1983) A cellular mechanism of classical conditioning in Aplysia—Activity dependent amplification of pre-synaptic facilitation. Science *219:* 400–405.

Hebb, D. O. (1949) *The Organization of Behavior,* Wiley, New York.

Huganir, R. L., A. H. Delacour, P. Greengard, and G. P. Hess (1986) Phosphorylation of the nicotinic acetylcholine receptor regulates its rate of desensitization. Nature *321:* 774–776.

Ito, M., M. Sakurai, and P. Tongroach (1982) Climbing fiber-induced depression of both mossy fiber responsiveness and glutamate sensitivity of cerebellar Purkinje cells. J. Physiol. (Lond.) *324:* 113–134.

Jenkins, W. M., M. M. Merzenich, and M. T. Ochs (1984) Behaviorally controlled differential use of restricted hand surfaces induce changes in the cortical representation of the hand in area 3b of adult owl monkeys. Soc. Neurosci. Abstr. *10:* 665.

Kaas, J. H., M. M. Merzenich, and H. P. Killackey (1983) The reorganization of somatosensory cortex following peripheral-nerve damage in adult and developing mammals. Annu. Rev. Neurosci. *6:* 325–356.

Kelso, S. R., A. H. Ganong, and T. H. Brown (1986) Hebbian synapses in hippocampus. Proc. Natl. Acad. Sci. USA *83:* 5326–5330.

Killackey, H. P. (1973) Anatomical evidence for cortical subdivisions based on vertically discrete thalamic projections from the ventral posterior nucleus to cortical barrels in the rat. Brain Res. *51:* 326–331.

Landry, P., and M. Deschenes (1981) Intracortical arborizations and receptive fields of identified ventrobasal thalamocortical afferents to the primary somatic sensory cortex in the cat. J. Comp. Neurol. *199:* 345–371.

Leyton, A. S. F., and C. S. Sherrington (1917) Observations on the excitable cortex of the chimpanzee, orangutan, and gorilla. Q. J. Exp. Physiol. *11:* 137–222.

Malinow, R., and J. P. Miller (1986) Postsynaptic hyperpolarization during conditioning reversibly blocks induction of long-term potentiation. Nature *320:* 529–530.

Meinhardt, H. (1982) *Models of Biological Pattern Formation,* Academic, New York.

Merzenich, M. M., J. H. Kaas, M. Sur, and C. S. Lin (1978) Double representation of the body surface within cytoarchitectonic Areas 3b and 1 in "S-I" in the owl monkey *Aotus trivirgatus.* J. Comp. Neurol. *181:* 41–74.

Merzenich, M. M., J. H. Kaas, J. T. Wall, R. J. Nelson, M. Sur, and D. J. Felleman (1983a) Topographic reorganization of somatosensory cortical areas 3b and 1 in adult monkeys following restricted deafferentation. Neuroscience *8:* 33–55.

Merzenich, M. M., J. H. Kaas, J. T. Wall, R. J. Nelson, M. Sur, and D. J. Felleman (1983b) Progression of change following median nerve section in the cortical representation of the hand in areas 3b and 1 in adult owl and squirrel monkeys. Neuroscience *10:* 639–665.

Merzenich, M. M., R. J. Nelson, M. P. Stryker, M. Cynader, A. Schoppman, and J. M. Zook (1984) Somatosensory cortical map changes following digit amputation in adult monkeys. J. Comp. Neurol. *224:* 591–605.

Mountcastle, V. B. (1957) Modality and topographic properties of single neurons of cat's somatic sensory cortex. J. Neurophysiol. *20:* 408–434.

Mountcastle, V. B. (1984) Central nervous mechanisms in mechanoreceptive sensibility. In *Handbook of Physiology, Sect. 1: The Nervous System,* Vol. 3, pp. 789–878, American Physiological Society, Bethesda, MD.

Olsen, R. W. (1987) The γ-aminobutyric acid/benzodiazepine/barbituate receptor-chloride ion channel complex of mammalian brain. In *Synaptic Function,* G. M. Edelman, W. E. Gall, and W. M. Cowan, eds., pp. 257–271, Wiley, New York.

Rasmusson, D. D., and D. M. Nance (1986) Non-overlapping thalamocortical projections for separate forepaw digits before and after cortical reorganization in the racoon. Brain Res. Bull. *16:* 399–406.

Reeke, G. N., Jr. (1984) The ROCKS System of computer programs for macromolecular crystallography. J. Appl. Crystallogr. *17:* 125–130.

Schmidt, J. T. (1985) Formation of retinotopic connections—selective stabilization by an activity-dependent mechanism. Cell. Mol. Neurobiol. *5:* 65–84.

Sur, M., M. M. Merzenich, and J. H. Kaas (1980) Magnification, receptive field area and 'hypercolumn' size in areas 3b and 1 of somatosensory cortex in owl monkeys. J. Neurophysiol. *44:* 295–311.

Turing, A. (1952) The chemical basis of morphogenesis. Phil. Trans. R. Soc. B *237:* 37–72.

Wall, P. D., and M. D. Eggers (1971) Formation of new connections in adult rat brains after partial deafferentation. Nature *232:* 542–544.

Warren, S., and B. H. Pubols (1984) Somatosensory thalamocortical connections in the racoon: An HRP study. J. Comp. Neurol. *227:* 597–606.

Whitsel, B. L., and D. G. Kelly (1986) Knowledge acquisition ("learning") by the somatosensory cortex. In *Brain Structure and Function,* E. G. Wegman, J. Davis, and R. Newburgh, eds., AAAS Neuroscience Symposium.

Wigstrom, H., and B. Gustafsson (1983) Heterosynaptic modulation of homosynaptic long-lasting potentiation in the hippocampal slice. Acta Physiol. Scand. *119:* 455–458.

Woolsey, T. A., and H. Van der Loos (1970) The structural organization of layer IV in the somatosensory region (SI) of mouse cerebral cortex. The description of a cortical field composed of discrete cytoarchitectonic units. Brain Res. *27:* 205–242.

→

Figure 6. The formation of neuronal groups. *A.* Initial e · e connection strengths (η) before stimulation of a small (12 × 6) region of the network chosen for illustration and containing 144 excitatory cells and 2448 connections. A straight line has been drawn between all pairs of connected cells (the lines do not indicate the directionality of the connections), and the locations of the cells are marked with *circles.* The color of each line represents the strength of that connection, as indicated by the scale at the bottom. To reduce superposition of lines, the inputs and outputs are drawn to points slightly above and below the cells, respectively. About 16% of the connections are between the same pairs of cells and are represented by single lines. *B.* The e · e connection strengths of the network following external stimulation of the entire surface of the hand with small locally correlated stimuli in a random sequence of positions. Neuronal groups have formed due to clusters of nearby cells strengthening their mutual connections while weakening most others. These groups collectively determine the receptive field properties of their component cells and organize the receptive field map via group competition. The 2 adjacent groups marked "*" and "†" are located within the region shown in *A* and *C. C.* Magnified (×2.5) view of the 12 × 6 region of *B* containing the groups marked "*" and "†" (same region as in *A* but after group formation). Note the clear blue borders (composed of many weakened connections) separating the groups. The border of weakened connections around a group forms a "moat," which protects it from encroachment by other groups and is a stabilizing force in the network. Borders between groups shift as cells are captured by competing groups. The properties of these group borders are responsible for the dynamics of functional boundaries between hand regions as seen in the global receptive field maps (see Fig. 9). In the particular case shown here, the group */† structural border corresponds to a glabrous/dorsal functional boundary (see Fig. 9B).

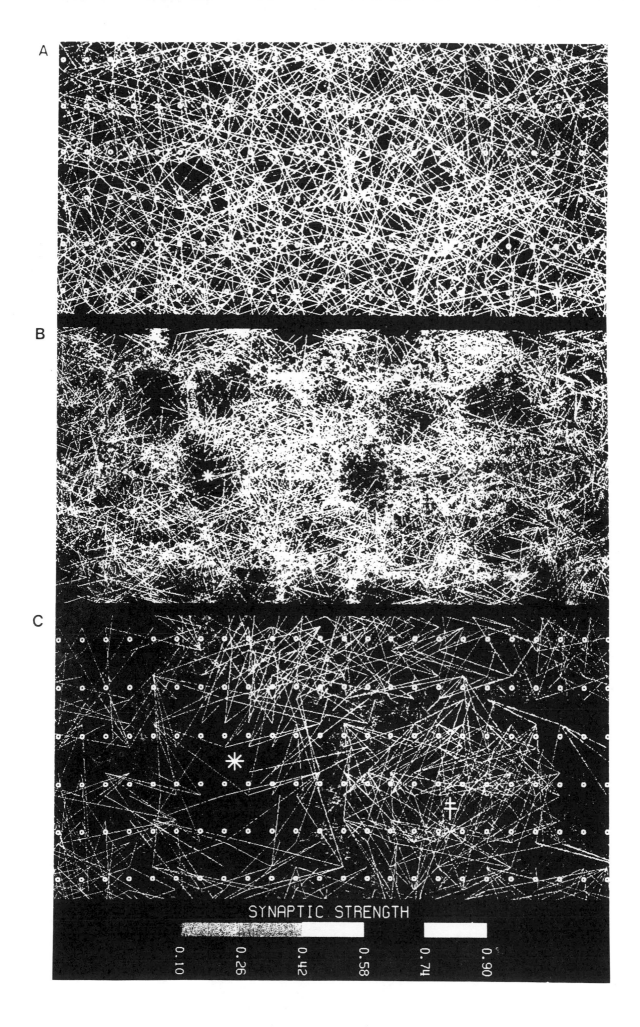

SYNAPTIC STRENGTH

0.10   0.26   0.42   0.58   0.74   0.90

The Function of Cerebellar Networks and their Genesis & Modification

A Genesis

Principal Axes of Tensor Ellipsoid Established by Generating Corticonuclear Dyads of Eigenvectors, Found by Proprioception Execution Reverberation

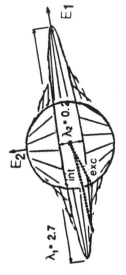

$$c = E_j$$

$$\tilde{g}^{nk} = \sum_j D_j = \sum_j E_j \times E_j$$

B Modification

Curvature of Tensor Ellipsoid Modified. Based on Goal-Performance Error, via Eigenvalue-Correction by CF Dyad

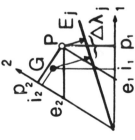

$$c = \sum_j (\Delta\lambda_j)^{1/2} \cdot E_j = \sum_j \left(\frac{E_j \cdot e}{E_j \cdot p} - \frac{E_j \cdot e}{E_j \cdot i} \right)^{1/2} \cdot E_j$$

$$\Delta g^{nk} = \sum_j \Delta\lambda_j \cdot (E_j \times E_j)$$

C Function

Covariant Intention –
Contravariant Execution
via Essential Network

D Network

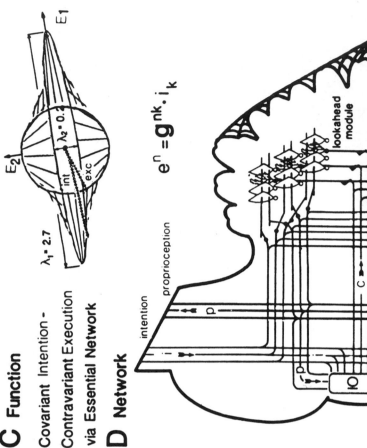

$$e^n = g^{nk} \cdot i_k$$

$$g^{nk}$$

Fig. 5. *Co-ordination by the cerebellar networks, and their genesis and modification by metaorganization.* (A) Metaorganization-algorithm for the genesis of network-matrix that approximates the metric g^{nk} by the dyads of its eigenvectors; D_m, via climbing fiber vector, carrying the eigenvector; $c = E_m$. Such algorithm sets up a tensor-ellipsoid with principal axes of the eigenvectors (cf. Fig. 5C). (B) Metaorganization-algorithm for the modification of the network matrix, in order to correct the eigenvalues of the tensor-ellipsoid. Geometrical inset-diagram illustrates, by means of a simplified two-dimensional frame, that a goal (G), given by intention-components (i_{1-2}) is improperly executed if the existing eigenvalue is incorrect. Thus, the execution-components (e^{1-2}) add to an erroneous performance-point (P), that is covariantly relayed back by perception (p_{1-2}). Graph demonstrates, that by the projections of points G and P to the established eigenvectors (E_m) the difference of the existing and the desirable eigenvalues can be measured. Thus, a correction-vector (c) is established by the olive, so that climbing fibers imprint a dyad of correction (Δg_{nk}). (C) Geometrical representation of the function of the essential cerebellar network as a covariant intention to contravariant execution transformer. A circle of execution-vectors (exc), when expressed in the form of intentions (int), would be distorted into an ellipse. This tensor ellipsoid is determined by its eigenvectors (E_{1-2}) and eigenvalues (λ). Thus the function of the cerebellum is symbolized as a geometrical "mirror-like" transformation of distortion-prone intentions into proper execution. (D) Composite diagram of circuits necessary for the essential function, plus its genesis and modification. Proprioceptive signals are shown in green, intention in blue, execution in red and correction in yellow. The essential function is implemented by the blue-to-red spacetime metric circuit (g^{nk}), the genesis is implemented by the green-to-red reverberation and imprinting (via the yellow circuit) of the corticonuclear network. The olivary system (IO; yellow) subserves modification by relying on the green proprioceptive, blue intention and red execution signals. Temporal "lookahead-module" of stacks of Purkinje cells symbolize that the metric transformation is not restricted to the space domain, but applies to a unified spacetime manifold.

20

Introduction

(1985)
A. Pellionisz and R. Llinás

Tensor network theory of the metaorganization
of functional geometries in the central nervous system
Neuroscience 16: 245–273

(Comments by Anderson) This is a difficult paper about geometry. Rodolfo Llinás is a neurophysiologist, well known for over two decades of productive work on the cerebellum. Andras Pellionisz has done well-known work on theoretical neurobiology for about the same period. This paper is the product of one of a relatively small number of close collaborations between a theoretician and an experimentalist, where each contributed extensively to the final result.

Neural network models nearly always represent information as collections of values of neural activity shown by many model neurons: formally, state vectors. A state vector is a point in a high-dimensional space. Spaces have geometries, and this paper suggests that we should not take this geometry for granted. Network models make use of geometry to some extent already because they depend heavily on concepts of "nearness" in the sense of distance or angle between points in a state space. As only one example, models to explain the development of topographic maps in the brain (see von der Malsburg, paper 8; Amari, paper 9; Kohonen, paper 37) develop so that units physically near to one another in an array of units become more correlated in their response properties. Neural networks in essence put a state vector into the system as input and get as output another state vector and make use of the structure of the real world through correlations represented in the input state vectors.

It is a neural network truism that networks develop so as to pick up the statistical structure of their environment. However, there is another aspect of the environment that most network models have not made much use of up to this time. Animals move about in the world, touch it, and are touched by it. The ultimate output of *any* biological neural computation must be a motor act. Motor acts have sensory consequences; there is a sensory-motor, motor-sensory loop closed by the environment. (One of the most intellectually exciting things about the rapidly developing field of robotics is that it is not possible to avoid these biological problems when constructing artificial systems.)

Organisms do not exist in a world of random, high-dimensional vectors. Their world is a three-dimensional geometrical structure that is accurately described by Euclidean geometry. Animals like us, with internal skeletons, interact with that three-dimensional geometry by contracting muscles to pull bones around. A crucial point made in this paper is that the intrinsic geometry of motor action is not necessarily simple and three-dimensional, just because its actions operate in a three-dimensional world. There are hundreds of muscles, most of which have different effects on the position of the parts of the body. The complexity of the motor system suggests that interacting with nature is not simple. A particular body motion almost always involves the coordinated contraction of many muscles. Worse, muscles do not act independently. Two different muscles may produce components of force in the same direction or can oppose each other. The motor output is usually underdetermined, so that many different patterns of motor neuron output can give rise to the same overall force.

Consider the simple situation of a limb held in a position in space, which is diagrammed in the paper's figure 1. Forces designed to move a limb in a particular direction in space are the result of a high-dimensional output vector driving the muscles. Each muscle provides a force on the limb, and the overall force is the resultant of all the muscle forces together, which add by simple physics.

At the same time each muscle contains an elaborate set of proprioceptive sensors that tell the brain which muscles are contracting and how strongly. This is the primary information the sensorimotor system is using to close the loop.

Now the mathematizing can start. We are performing a set of coordinate transformations, involving sensory input, motor proprioception, and motor output. When faced with a problem, the wise theoretician starts by looking at the techniques others have already developed for similar problems. Most of us are already familiar with the geometry of simple coordinate transformations from linear algebra or physics. But there is a highly developed area of mathematics called *tensor theory* that handles the truly general problems involved in the conversion of one geometrical representation into another. Tensor theory, however, has a legendary reputation for difficulty and complexity, partially deserved. Part of the blame for this situation lies in extremely abstract mathematical treatments and the arcane and idiosyncratic notation commonly used. Books on tensor theory written by mathematicians are generally useless for anyone else, but there are reasonable (usually older) books that try to develop some degree of geometrical intuition for engineers and physicists (see Bickley and Gibson 1962, Hay 1953, Kay 1988).

Suppose we have two coordinate systems. Every description of a point in one system by a set of coordinates corresponds to another set of numbers in the other system; there are functions relating the descriptions of points in the two coordinate systems. There are three key concepts that are required to understand the ideas that Pellionisz and Llinás are trying to convey: covariance, contravariance, and the metric tensor. These concepts are firmly established in mathematics, but it is usually easy to avoid using them because in our familiar orthogonal coordinate system, the need for them disappears.

Suppose we have a set of coordinate axes and we want to describe a point. (Like calculus the argument can hold in general for curved coordinate axes if we move "very small" distances.) To describe a point in space, we need a set of vector components to do the description. There are two distinct types of vector components we could use:

The first way is diagrammed in Figure 1 and is described as *covariant* vector components. Operationally we might describe the point by the movements of a ship looking for an island. It sails along one axis until it detects the island off to one side. It then moves perpendicular to its original course to get to the island. Note that this description really depends only on the direction of one coordinate axis. The covariant representation picks out the component of the point along one or another coordinate axis.

The second way is diagrammed in Figure 2 and is described mathematically as *contravariant* vector components. Operationally the contravariant operation works more like a car on a highway, which cannot freely change direction, but can move only along the directions of the coordinate axes: Therefore the point is so many units along on one coordinate axis and

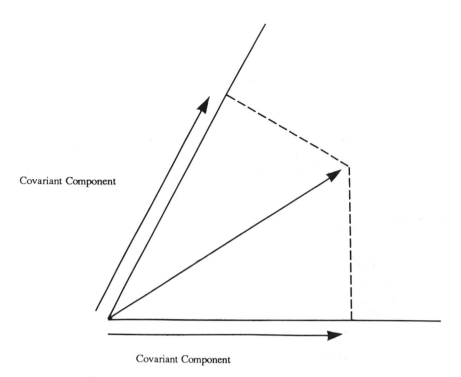

Covariant Component

Covariant Component

Figure 1 Covariant representation

so many units along another coordinate axis. Contravariance is very familiar to most scientists because it describes the way forces add in the familiar *parallelogram of forces.*

Notice that in the case of our familiar Euclidean coordinate system, the covariant and contravariant representations are the same, so this distinction is not needed.

With this distinction clear, Pellionisz and Llinás start to think about what it might mean. The contravariant description fits very well with the intuitive notion of the addition of forces produced by muscles, if each coordinate axis is identified with muscle motor activity. Because these individual forces add up like physical forces to produce a resultant, they are contravariant in nature.

The proprioceptive sensors act much more like the covariant vector representation. The covariant description would pick up the component of a force along the given coordinate axes. If we assume that the coordinate axes are identified with proprioceptors in a given muscle, then these sensors will respond only to force components along the muscle axis, that is, a muscle does not in general know what is going on in other muscles except through their components along the first muscle.

So the problem of sensorimotor transformation in these terms becomes one of relating a covariant sensory representation to a contravariant motor representation. But the whole system is connected together through the world — they are both looking at different aspects of the same thing: muscle forces and actions.

Pellionisz and Llinás suggest that the cerebellum might be the brain structure that closes the internal loop in the nervous system: That is, it transforms the sensory representation into the motor representation, mathematically, by transforming a covariant representation into a contravariant representation. Is there a standard mathematical way to describe this transformation that would give us insight into what the cerebellum might be doing?

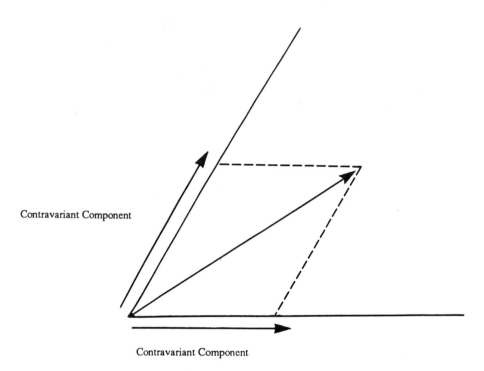

Contravariant Component

Contravariant Component

Figure 2 Contravariant Representation

In tensor theory the covariant and contravariant representations are related by what is called the *metric tensor*. The name metric tensor is appropriate geometrically because it is concerned with computation of distance and angle. Clearly the distance between two points must not change, no matter what the coordinate axes used to describe them look like, because distance is something real. Similarly the angle between two vectors must not change with different axes. The metric tensor can be constructed by simple rules from the covariant and contravariant representations.

Once the metric tensor is assumed to be realized in a neural structure, we have access to the full power of the neural network connection matrix mechanism. For example, every matrix has eigenvectors and in this case there is a physical feedback loop between input and output. Therefore we can predict oscillations or resonances in the resulting dynamical systems with frequencies and amplitudes related to the large positive eigenvalues of the connection matrix. These eigenvectors would be particularly important in learning and one might make corrections in the functioning of the system by manipulating the magnitudes of the eigenvalues. Because we are working on the metric tensor, all these changes will amount to changing the geometry of the internal representation in response to the interaction of internal (neural) geometry with external (physical) geometry. These two geometries are different, but they can interact to organize each other. The term *metaorganization* is used to describe this process.

The bulk of the paper is devoted to suggestions about what the neural structures might be doing, based on the tensor interpretation of the function of sensorimotor cerebellar pathway function and the known neurophysiology and neuroanatomy.

For novice readers there are two notational pitfalls to watch for in this paper. Tensor mathematics makes frequent of the Einstein convention (yes, *that* Einstein), also called the summation convention. Because summations are so frequent, the convention holds that when the same index appears twice in an expression, there is an implied summation over that index, so, for example, $\sum a_i x_i$ is written as $a_i x_i$. This convention is used in equations 1 and 2 of the paper. There is also lavish use of superscripts and subscripts to represent vector components. Superscripts *do not* mean powers, but particular vectors or vector component. A general rule is that covariant vectors use subscripts and contravariant vectors use superscripts, but this is unfortunately not invariable notation.

Many neural modelers have a somewhat static and deliberately simple input-output view of the nervous system, where input data are processed like raw materials in a factory, with the output appearing at the shipping dock. In nature, however, when the input-output loop is closed through the environment, some unusual and powerful techniques become applicable, and the nature of the computation changes.

To say that an approach is radical means that it represents a fundamental change in orientation. In this collection there are two radical approaches to the nervous system that are at variance with ideas that are taken for granted by both neural scientists and network modelers. The ideas presented in this paper form one set, and the paper by Skarda and Freeman (paper 21) is the other. These two papers should be read carefully. They are important.

References

W.G. Bickley and R.E. Gibson (1962), *Via Vector to Tensor*. New York: Wiley.

G.E. Hay (1953), *Vector and Tensor Analysis*. New York: Dover.

D.C. Kay (1988), *Tensor Calculus*. New York: Schaum's Outlines, McGraw-Hill.

(1985)
A. Pellionisz and R. Llinás

Tensor network theory of the metaorganization
of functional geometries in the central nervous system
Neuroscience 16: 245–273

Abstract—Here we present an elaboration and a quantitative example for a hypothetical neuronal process, implementing what we refer to as the metaorganization principle. This process allows the internalization of external (body) geometries into the central nervous system (CNS) and a reciprocal and equally important action of the CNS geometry on the external (body) geometry. The hypothesis is based on the distinction, within the CNS, between covariant sensory and contravariant motor vectorial expressions of the extrinsic geometry. These sensory and motor expressions, given in natural co-ordinate systems, are transformed from one to the other by a neuronal network which acts as a metric tensor. The metric tensor determines the relationship of these two expressions and thus comprises the functional geometry of the system.

The emergence through metaorganization of networks that implement such metric function is viewed as the result of interactions between the covariant motor execution which generates a physical action on the external world (via the musculoskeletal system) and the covariant sensory proprioception which measures the effect of such motor output. In this transformation of contravariants to covariants by the physical geometry of the motor system, a covariant metric tensor is expressed implicitly. However, co-ordinated motor action requires its dual tensor (the contravariant metric) which is assembled in the CNS based on the metaorganization principle, i.e. the ability of CNS and external geometries to mold one another. The two metric transformations acting on each other detect error signals whenever the match of the physical and functional geometries is imperfect. Such error signals are utilized by the metaorganization process to improve the match between the two metrics, so that with use the internal representation becomes increasingly homeometric with the geometry of the external world.

The proposed physical process by which the metaorganization principle is implemented is based on oscillatory reverberation. If covariant proprioception is used as a recurrent signal to the motor apparatus, as if it were a contravariant motor expression, then reverberations at their steady-state yield the eigenvectors and eigenvalues of the system. The stored eigenvectors and eigenvalues can serve, respectively, (1) as a means for the genesis of a metric (in the form of its spectral representation) with the given eigenvectors and (2) as a means of comparing the eigenvalues that are implicit in the external body geometry and those of the internal metric. The difference between these eigenvalues is then used to modify the metric so that it "evolves" to perform a more accurate covariant–contravariant transformation.

The metric can be represented by the dyadic outer products of its eigenvectors where each dyad is weighted by the corresponding eigenvalue. Such a spectral representation yields in a uniform manner (a) the contravariant metric (in the case of complete CNS hyperspaces) and (b) the Moore–Penrose generalized inverse of the covariant metric tensor (in the case of non-Riemannian overcomplete CNS hyperspaces).

The metaorganization of metric networks, together with the sensorimotor covariant embedding network, provides an explanation of the emergence of a whole sensorimotor apparatus leading to the feasibility of constructing truly brain-like robotic systems.

1. INTRODUCTION

1.1 Geometries and brain function

The evolvement of the CNS through natural selection is the fundamental means by which multicellular organisms develop optimal interactions with the world. In terms of abstract geometry this can be expressed by stating that the function of the brain is to match the system of relations among objects in the external world, with a multidimensional inner functional geometry, in a manner such that these geometries approach homeomorphism if not isomorphism.[50,80] While general considerations as such may be of significance in brain theory, the nature of the interaction between the inner and outer geometries must be defined in a concrete manner.

Sensorimotor operations are the appropriate paradigms of brain function to consider first for such elaboration. Here, the relation between the external world and its internal representation in the brain can be directly observed and quantitatively treated as it is expressed by the precision of goal-oriented movements.

Sensorimotor transformations, most particularly those involving the cerebellum, have already been investigated from the point of view of how they adapt to an alteration of geometries, either of the external physical arrangement or its inner representation. As an example of the former, modification of the vestibulo-ocular reflex, as in the case of vision inverted by reversing prisms, has been amply studied.[23] For the latter the compensation for unilateral vestibular ablation has also been analysed in detail.[58] The issue in this paper is to define the mechanism by which the relationship between inner brain geometry and the external world are matched in accordance with the modified conditions. This point has been raised in preliminary communications.[75,82,85]

1.2. The essentials for a geometrical approach to brain function

The general hypothesis of the geometrical interpretation of brain function hinges on the assumption that the relation between the brain and the external world is determined by the ability of the CNS to construct an internal model of the external world using an interactive relationship between sensory and motor expressions. This relation is evident, for instance, in the orienting-response of an animal in a new environment. Indeed the process of sensory detection involves a significant amount of motor activity.[32] Such observations strongly indicate that the sensorimotor transformations are the gauging tool by which the CNS relates to the external world. It has been demonstrated in detail in human and animal experimentation that a convergence of sensory and motor information is necessary to form internal models of novel objects.[23,63]

At the level of mathematical analysis, the basis for formalizing the above in terms of a geometrical representation appears to be the dual expression of extrinsic physical objects by intrinsic "CNS vectors". These vectorial expressions, with respect to reference frames intrinsic to the organism, are covariant for sensory analysis and contravariant for motor synthesis. The geometrical relationship between these two vectorial components is comprised in a neuronal network acting as a metric tensor.[81]

1.2.1. Fundamental mathematical concepts inherent in covariant and contravariant neuronal representations.
The covariant–contravariant distinction is of cardinal importance, as their relationship determines the metric, which comprises the functional geometry of the system. Indeed these two ways in which the CNS relates to the external world are profoundly different. The primary expression derives from an external object a multitude of covariant vector components, which constitutes a sensory input to the CNS. Such a vector arises from the firing frequencies of a set of sensory neurons which collectively represent an extrinsic physical state. The secondary expression is the implementation of a physical reality from a multitude of contravariant components; e.g. generating a displacement of the arm through the activation of individual motor units. This dual relationship between CNS expressions and physical invariants via the sensory and motor systems is fundamental. The question is not whether such different expressions exist but, rather, whether it is possible to construct a precisely formulated general concept which encompasses the functional essence of (a) the above sensory and motor properties and (b) the transformations which convert one into the other. The most fundamental difference between these two expressions appears to be their causality; i.e. that in the former the components arise from the physical reality, while in the latter the physical reality arises from the components.

Sensory reception is therefore an analysis (i.e. a differentiation) while motor execution is a synthesis (i.e. an integration). The covariant expression is based on a process of comparing the features of the external physical reality (which is co-ordinate-system-invariant) with a set of internal physical states (which serve as the measuring standard within the CNS). Each of these relationships yields a quantity which is then used as an inner measure of one aspect of the external reality. An example of this procedure in the CNS is the inertial force generated by the endolymphatic mass in each semicircular canal, each yielding one individual measure (a cosine component) of the head-acceleration. Note that as defined in calculus, establishing the relation of the rates of change is a differentiation. Given two invariants their infinitesimal relationship yields the derivative. It is also well known that, following the chain-rule of differentiation, such derivative components of x change with the alteration of the frame a in a manner obeying the following rule of covariant transformation:[14,94,101]

$$x_i = (\partial a^j / \partial a^i) \times x_j. \qquad (1)$$

The biological significance of these known mathematical properties was expressed in the proposal that these projection-type covariant components correspond to sensory processes.[81]

Motor actions, on the other hand, are integrative-type operations. In a motor process such as displacement of the eye by the co-contraction of the extraocular muscles, the physical summation of the components is of the essence and not the differential-type sensory relationship of one physical invariant to another. Infinitesimally, the summation is implemented by the parallelogram components that obey the contravariant transformation.[14,101]

$$x^i = (\partial a^i / \partial a^j) \times x^j. \qquad (2)$$

Reference frames are invoked by both the sensory and motor processes. These are instruments, intrinsic to the structure of the organism, through which extrinsic points of physical spaces are related to arithmetical manifolds within the CNS.

Note that so far the only requirement in the interpretation of sensory covariants and motor contravariants is that the derivatives of the manifold should exist, i.e. that the manifold which arises from the use of reference frames be smooth. This is the necessary and sufficient prerequisite for the existence of covariant sensory and contravariant motor expressions.

Transformation of co- and contravariants through the metric is a different problem from the simple distinction between these two types of representation. The central question is whether a concise expression can be given for the transformation between these co- and contravariant vectoral forms. As is well-known, such expressions can be obtained since any geometry can be most concisely characterized by its metric tensor (also called fundamental tensor,)[19,46] which expresses the relationship between covariants and contravariants. Indeed, a study of any geometry may well start with the definition of its metric. It has been stressed,[84] however, that the geometry of the CNS hyperspaces cannot be *a priori* characterized by a known metric; e.g. by an Euclidean metric (as in Cartesian tensor analysis that is used in engineering)[98] or by a Riemannian metric (as in the tensor analysis of four-dimensional manifolds used in relativity theory).[19] The features of the metric in a mathematical CNS hyperspace cannot be taken for granted; in fact the metric is the unknown in brain research. Indeed if a CNS hyperspace is amorphous, a metric in the strict sense may not even exist; sensory covariants and motor contravariants may be unrelated (which would manifest itself in a dysmetric motor action). The existence of any metric in the CNS poses the question to the experimenter "how to find it" and to the theorist, "how such metric is developed in complex organisms".

1.2.2. Fundamental differences in biological interpretation of the contravariant motor activation and covariant proprioception, commensurate with tensions. The metaorganization principle will be elaborated in this paper by means of a quantitative illustration. The model diagram shown in Fig. 1 has been used in a preliminary form in preceding publications on tensor network theory.[75,76] First it will be shown, by means of a specific quantitative example, that the active forces that are exerted by the muscles upon innervation are proportional to the contravariant physical components of the impressed load G. In contrast, the passive forces that are measurable by proprioceptive peripheral sensory system, can be determined proportionally to covariant orthogonal projection components of G.

The motor execution mechanism, shown schematically in Fig. 1(A), assumes that the three-joint arm moves in the two-dimensional plane of the paper, meaning that the motor system is overcomplete. A flexor and an extensor muscle at each of the three joints are depicted in Fig. 1(A): the shoulder, elbow and wrist. The pectoralis muscle (1) acts as a flexor, and the deltoideus (2) acts as an extensor of the upper arm at the shoulder joint. Thus the difference between the forces exerted by them would be the force acting at the index finger in direction alpha (Fig. 1B). Likewise, the triceps muscle (3) extends while the brachialis (4) flexes the lower arm and thus the resultant force is along direction beta. In turn the extensor carpi ulnaris (5) generates a force along direction gamma, working against the force of the flexor carpi radialis (6).

The α, β and γ directions shown in Fig. 1(B) determine a local non-orthogonal frame of reference. The general considerations in 1.2.1. are demonstrated in detail, in Figs 1(C) and (D), namely in such non-orthogonal frames of reference two vectorial expressions are possible, each with different characteristics. If a load force (G) is attached to the index finger (Fig. 1C), and it is assumed that the arm holds this load in a stationary position, both the active and passive forces are expressed in the (position-dependent) local system of co-ordinates as introduced in Fig. 1(B). However, the active motor actions rotate the arm-segments by means of the forces exerted by the muscles (Fig. 1C), whereas peripheral proprioceptive organs detect different, passive forces (Fig. 1D).

The contravariant character of the forces exerted by the muscles follows directly from the fact that in a steady-state the active forces must balance; the muscle components must yield a resultant force that is equal but opposite in direction to the load (G, see Fig. 1C). These physical components of the load (G) are, by definition, the contravariant components that add according to the parallelogram rule. The forces of the muscles have always been regarded to be the physical components that balance the load (G). Tensor theory simply re-phrases this by stating that the vectorial expression of an object in any system of co-ordinates by means of physical components is of the contravariant type. It has been discussed previously,[8,76] and is obvious from Fig. 1(C), that such a contravariant expression of a given load (G) in an overcomplete frame of reference is not unique. Indeed, an infinite number of configurations of the components along α, β and γ can result in the same load (G). In fact it is this mathematical indeterminacy that raises the question of how does the CNS arrive, in a co-ordinated act, at a particular choice from an infinite number of possible solutions. The most obvious demonstration of such overcompleteness can be shown by remembering that any constant can be added to the forces exerted by both an agonist (flexor) and antagonist (extensor) muscle-pair, without changing the resultant, since the two forces act along a common co-ordinate axis and thus the additions cancel one another. While such addition to both components of a pair of muscles is mathematically redundant, its physiological significance is obvious. The same stationary position of the arm can be held with the muscles contracting minimally, or in an overexerted stiff manner; consequently, the holding position may be delicate or robust. The understanding that additions of cancelling force-pairs will not modify position makes it possible to consider in the rest of the paper only the differences of forces in reciprocally innervated muscle pairs acting along common axes. Such "pairing", however, is only for simplifying convenience; the scheme to be presented in this paper also applies to the separate treatment of muscles acting along different axes.

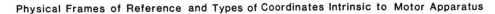

Physical Frames of Reference and Types of Coordinates Intrinsic to Motor Apparatus

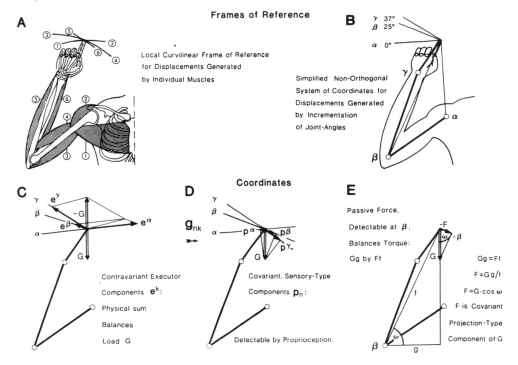

Contravariant Execution e^k ➤ Covariant Proprioception p_n Implies Covariant Metric g_{nk} of Physical Geometry

Fig. 1. *Schematic representation of the physical geometry of an exemplary motor executor apparatus, which is to be matched by a functional geometry (implemented by the cerebellum), their match enabling the co-ordinated control of the multiarticulate limb.* (A) and (B) show the frame of reference of limb-displacements, that is intrinsic to the motor apparatus. (C)–(E) demonstrate the two different kinds of co-ordinates (contravariant and covariant) that express the physical invariant of a displacement by active muscle components and passive proprioceptive components, respectively—the two vectorial expressions implying the covariant metric inherent in the physical geometry of the motor apparatus. (A) Individual muscles determine a local curvilinear frame of reference for displacements of the limb by six major muscles. 1, pectoralis; 2, deltoideus; 3, triceps; 4, brachialis; 5, extensor carpi ulnaris; 6, flexor carpi radialis. (B) Simplified, non-orthogonal rectilinear frame of reference of limb-movements. The α, β and γ local displacement-directions belong to individual incrementation of the joint-angles. (C) Physical (contravariant, parallelogram-type) vectorial expression of an invariant G in the intrinsic frame of reference. (D) Proprioceptive (covariant, projection-type) expression of the same G; with unique components even in an overcomplete frame. (E) Contravariant components physically execute motor acts, covariant components are in turn detectable by proprioception. Thus a contravariant metric tensor is implied in the physical geometry of a motor apparatus.

It must be emphasized that in the non-orthogonal system of co-ordinates shown in Fig. 1, in addition to the contravariant active physical muscle forces, a different covariant-type vectorial expression of the load (G) is also possible (Fig. 1D). The covariants are the passive force-components, measured as the orthogonal projections of the load-vector (G) onto the co-ordinate axes. The nature and the functional role of the passive forces, detectable by peripheral proprioceptive systems such as the tendon organs, have not been conclusively defined in motor physiology, despite thorough analysis.[59,97] The prevalent ideas are that this system monitors the load on the motor apparatus or provides an overload-preventing warning signal. The role of proprioception is therefore particularly intriguing in oculomotor actions, where the load of the system is constant.[29] In contrast, it has been suggested in tensor theory of the CNS that proprioception serves to supply the components of the dual complementer motor vector, the covariant counterpart of the contravariant motor action.[75] It is well known that peripheral receptor organs are capable of measuring passive stretch. Such a passive force may significantly differ from the active force exerted by the given muscle. For instance, while the active force generated by a muscle is proportional to its own motoneuron-activation, a stretch in the tendon of the given muscle arises from an interaction of the activity of many muscles as well as from external load factors. Since the tendons utilize the same α, β and γ local system of co-ordinates as the motor actuators, and they express the physical object of the load in a sensory manner, they yield the covariant components of the load. This proposal is substantiated below with the help of Fig. 1(E).

Muscles exert force on the skeletal system (even if the action arises from a variety of active and passive factors) through their tendons. Thus, if a load (G) is balanced in a stationary position, the passive force (F), proportionally detectable at the elbow-joint denoted by β, would be the difference of the tendon-forces of the extensor and flexor carpi. This passive force F, measurable by a strain-gauge in the tendon at β, must balance the torque $(G g)$, exerted by the load, by $(F f)$ (cf. Fig. 1E). From the similarity of the GF and fg triangles, it follows that $F = G.\cos (\omega)$, which is the definition of the covariant, orthogonal projection-type component. Note that the set of covariant proprioception components of G, measured as the tensions in the tendons, is unique, in contrast to the non-uniqueness of the contravariant components.

The scheme in Fig. 1 presents a motor effector mechanism in which the dual sets of co- and contra-variant components are available. This poses the following challenge to the CNS: given a contravariant motor execution vector the proprioceptive system must provide the corresponding covariant vector. Such contravariant-to-covariant relation is implied in the physical geometry of the effector mechanism. Thus when an internal functional geometry is developed by the CNS the physical geometry must be matched by this homeometric internal representation. It is suggested that the matching of the physical geometry with its functional counterpart is furnished by the cerebellum. Below, a concise account is given of how the cerebellar circuit may perform as a co-ordinator once the circuit is available (point 1.2.3) and how such explanation leads to the question of how such networks may emerge (point 1.3).

1.2.3. Utilization of dual vectorial representations to explain CNS functions: the tensor model of cerebellum. Tensor network theory of the CNS evolved as a mathematical formulation, with the use of the above basic terms of covariants and contravariants, of the geometrical concept of brain function, especially that of the cerebellum.[74–78,80–83] The tensor model can concisely explain in the above terms the function of the cerebellar circuit, once that circuit is available through the development of a sensorimotor system.

A general tensorial interpretation of the CNS is based on the notion that the intrinsic natural frames of reference, in which neurons attribute ordered sets of activity-values (co- and contravariant vectors) to physical invariants of the external world, invoke multidimensional arithmetic manifolds. The functional geometry of such a CNS hyperspace is comprised by its metric tensor, which can be implemented by a matrix—perhaps the most natural abstract representation of a neuronal network. Sensorimotor systems could therefore be functionally explained in

a three-stage scheme.[81] This consists of (1) a sensory metric (an internal representation of the geometry of the external world) which could be the optic tectum (see the scheme in Ref. 74), (2) a cerebellar motor metric network that endows the executor mechanism with a functional spacetime geometry (see the scheme in Ref. 83), and (3) a sensorimotor transformation that relates the two CNS geometries to one another; e.g. by embedding one space, such as the sensory, into another, such as the motor (see the scheme in Ref. 76).

A tensorial interpretation of a particular sensorimotor system yields a functional scheme (e.g. Fig. 1, in Ref. 76). Such network schemes provide a mathematical interpretation of sensory processes, as yielding covariant vectorial expressions, and motor processes, as executing invariants with contravariant components. Moreover, tensorial schemes can formally describe the nature of sensorimotor integration as transforming a covariant vector, assigned to an invariant expressed in the sensory frame, into a contravariant expression in the motor frame. In turn, the problem of co-ordination (the uniqueness of a motor expression in an overcomplete executor-mechanism) can be resolved as a covariant embedding followed by a cerebellar motor transformation from covariant intention to contravariant execution, even in the case when the covariant metric is singular.[74–76]

A tensorial interpretation of the cerebellum, which is suggested to be the crucial final step of the sensorimotor system, is shown in Fig. 2. The cerebellum is featured as an "add-on" unit;[75–77] the scheme in Fig. 2 demonstrates that a direct spinal cord pathway could carry a motor intention-vector to represent the motor output directly. Such approximative sensorimotor transduction may have been an early evolutionary "solution", where the directly obtainable but incorrect motor vectors were used for motor execution. According to the "add-on" scheme, cerebellectomy results in the direct execution of covariant motor intention, through the down-going spinal pathway shown schematically in Fig. 2. This feature of the model corresponds to classical knowledge[33] that ablation of the cerebellum does not break the sensorimotor transduction (and thus the cerebellum cannot be considered as the organ implementing this function); the ablation does result, however, in a "dysmetric" motor activity decomposed both in space and time.

The detailed operation of the essential cerebellar circuit is described as follows. The covariant components of the motor intention-vector, belonging to a co-ordinate-system-invariant displacement (inv), are shown in the upper left circle of Fig. 2. These components are the orthogonal projections from the invariant to each motor axis. Taking the motor apparatus shown in Fig. 1 as a symbolic example, these axes are 0, 25 and 37° with respect to each other. Thus, a 5° physical invariant displacement,

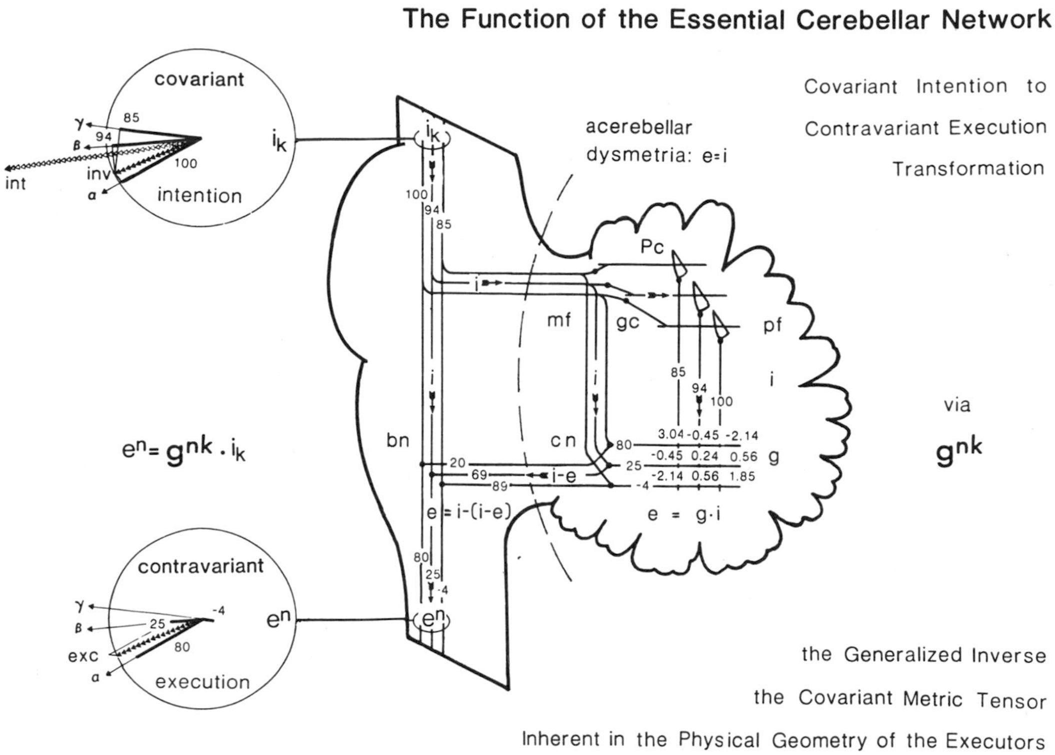

The Function of the Essential Cerebellar Network

covariant

85
γ
94
β
100
int inv
α
i_k
intention

Covariant Intention to
Contravariant Execution
Transformation

acerebellar
dysmetria: e≈i

Pc

$e^n = g^{nk} \cdot i_k$

mf gc pf

bn cn

85
94
100

$$\begin{pmatrix} 3.04 & -0.45 & -2.14 \\ -0.45 & 0.24 & 0.56 \\ -2.14 & 0.56 & 1.85 \end{pmatrix} g$$

80
25
-4

20
69
89

i−e

via

g^{nk}

$e = i-(i-e)$

$e = g \cdot i$

contravariant

-4
γ
25
β 80
exc
α
e^n

execution

the Generalized Inverse
the Covariant Metric Tensor
Inherent in the Physical Geometry of the Executors

Fig. 2. *Functional scheme of the essential cerebellar network: co-ordination by acting as a metric tensor, transforming covariant intention into contravariant execution.* Sensorimotor transformation, by means of covariant-embedding procedure, yields independently and uniquely established projection-type intention components (even in case of overcompleteness) of an invariant (inv; upper left circle). This i_k vector, if it directly descends (through the brain stem nuclei, bn) on the motor apparatus, would physically add to an incorrect execution (int; e.g. in acerebellar dysmetria). The role of the essential cerebellar network is to transform, by the "add-on" circuitry in the cerebellar cortex and nuclei, this intention to contravariant execution e^n (exc; lower left circle). The metric-transformation is accomplished by the cerebellar corticonuclear network g^{nk}, by which the intention (i), carried by mossy fibers (mf) to parallel fibers (pf) and to Purkinje cells (PC) is connected to cerebellar nuclear cells (cn). The inhibitory execution vector (e), together with the mossy fiber collaterals to the nuclei, forms a corticofugal output (i − e). This signal gives rise in the brain stem nuclei (bn) to the $e = i - (i - e)$ execution-vector output. Note that the olivary-climbing fiber system is not required for the essential cerebellar coordinative function.

with an arbitrary magnitude of 100, will yield a covariant vector $i_k = (100\ 94\ 85)^T$ where superscript T denoted the transpose of the row-vector into column-vector. While these components do represent the displacement, their physical summation would yield a different displacement (int) with a different amplitude and direction (Fig. 2, upper left).

In contrast, the metric-type transformation through the cerebellar neuronal network yields contravariants that physically add to exactly yield the required invariant exc (Fig. 2, lower left inset). The three-segment limb with the α, β and γ system of co-ordinates therefore requires a contravariant metric-type transformer. This can be expressed numerically as g^{nk}, shown by a quantitative 3×3 matrix in Fig. 2. The system of connectivities, which implements such a matrix is the network between Purkinje and cerebellar nuclear cells (Fig. 2). This

scheme conforms with the known cerebellar anatomy.[36,48,52,69,70] Any i_k covariant motor intention vector that enters the cerebellar cortex by mossy fiber activity will generate, through g^{nk}, the contravariant execution vector e^n via cerebellar Purkinje cells (Pc) in the cerebellar nuclei (cn). This vector $e^n = (80\ 25\ -4)^T$ impinges on the cerebellar nuclear cells in an inhibitory form.[38] Together with the excitatory mossy fiber collaterals into the nuclei, the cerebellar nucleo-fugal output will be $i_k - e^n = (20\ 69\ 89)^T$. In the brain stem nuclei (bn) this output will transform the intention vector into the required execution vector. This vector leaves the spinal relay nuclei as $e = i - (i - e) = (85\ 25\ -4)^T$.

Note that the network essential to this covariant–contravariant transformation contains only mossy fibers, granule cells, Purkinje cells, cerebellar nuclear neurons and brain stem nuclear neurons. Strictly speaking therefore, neither the climbing fiber system (and the inferior olive) nor the proprioceptive sensory mechanism is required for the explanation of the co-ordinative function of the cerebellum (the covariant–contravariant transformation) implemented by the "essential cerebellar network" (Fig. 2).[76,77] As elaborated elsewhere,[85] however, the climbing fiber system is essential in answering the question "how might such a network emerge?"

1.3 Problem: the genesis and modification of neuronal networks serving as covariant–contravariant metric-type transformers

The above exposition (point 1.2.3) of how the CNS could function by tensor-transformations assumes that the required matrices are in place, implemented by neuronal networks. A more profound question, however may be[82] "how are neuronal networks organized such that they can embody and functionally support the necessary geometrical transformations?" While it is crucial to emphasize (as discussed in detail in Ref. 51) that the development of motor co-ordination is not the function of the cerebellum (since the function is co-ordination), after identifying the function that cerebellar neuronal networks perform, answering the underlying developmental question may be very revealing from the point of view of emergence of neuronal networks in the CNS in general.

This major theoretical problem of network-organization can be readily illustrated by the cerebellum. Indeed the geometry of the motor apparatus is physically explicit and it is known that the matching functional geometry (implemented by the cerebellar neuronal network) develops from specific genetic and epigenetic arrangements which are expressed in the embriogenesis of the cerebellum.[64,69,92] Once the basic co-ordination-function is performed by the emerged cerebellar networks, it is also known that a misalignment between the geometry of the execution system and a pre-existing functional motor geometry can result in a functional error. If this mismatch is minor, it may·be absorbed by the overcompleteness of the functional transformaton.[83] For misalignments of the geometries that follow a certain trend (e.g. when motor co-ordination has to keep up with the increase in body size during growth) the cerebellar system must respond with a degree of adaptability, just as in every subsystem of the CNS.[51] It is also known that major discrepancies may trigger realignment of the internal and external geometries—an important function that allows the organism to resume an optimal interaction with the surrounding world (cf. the reversal of the vestibulo-ocular reflex by prisms and the ensuing compensation).[23] As suggested in the three-step scheme of sensorimotor transformation,[76,83] the neuronal networks implementing a sensory metric tensor and a motor metric are the means of incorporation of such functional geometries. Therefore the adaptability of the whole

sensorimotor operation raises the question how a limited degree of adaptibility of each of these metrics may contribute to a maintained match of the external physical and internal functional geometries. As for the cerebellum, the assumed position-dependent motor metric-function implies, for example, that the neuronal network must undergo constant phasic updating by the climbing fiber system in order to perform the required non-Euclidean (non-constant) metric function.

While the question of emergence of neuronal networks, acting as metric tensors, can be conveniently approached at the level of motor co-ordination, this question is more profound than a limited study of sensorimotor operations implies. Indeed one of the fundamental challenges in neuroscience is that of providing a formal account of the ability of geometries, intrinsic and extrinsic to CNS, to organize one another so that a set of optimally interactive geometries can evolve.

2. METAORGANIZATION OF CNS GEOMETRIES

2.1. The principle of metaorganization

In search of the principles by which neuronal networks could be organized, one needs to rely on the power of both the mathematical formalism and of the biological insights derived from direct experimental aquaintance with the problem.

2.1.1. Optimal mathematical characteristics of the procedure of establishing metric networks: iterative algorithm for eigenvector-expansion. A general principle in all biological systems appears to be that their structure is parallelly organized and distributed and their function develops by iterative procedural means. An example is the acquisition of cerebellar temporal lookahead by the implementation of a type of Taylor series expansion.[80] Thus, when addressing the questions of the distributed implementations of neuronal metrics, one may consider the manner in which matrices, acting as metric tensors, can be established by iterative reverberative procedures in a form of matrix-expansion.

Another lead is provided by the fact that the primary entities in CNS function are the covariant sensory and contravariant motor expressions, and not the metrics that may or may not connect them. The co- and contravariant inter-relations evoked by external physical reality can manifest themselves in case of a lack of an explicit realization or even in case of a total absence of an ordinary metric: both sensory and motor processes are possible without an intermediate co-ordinated transfer. Any metric expression is therefore secondary, as it derives from a process by which given co- or contravariants may be converted into one another.

As for a matrix acting as a metric, such matrix is symmetrical and determined by those co- and contravariant vectors which constitute eigenvectors. The metric is indeed fully characterized by these special input–output vectors that are identical in their normalized form.[91]

The above two mathematical considerations provided the impetus for pointing to the steady-state covariant–contravariant reverberation as the key for a formal geometrical characterization of the function and emergence of neuronal networks. An eventual identity of covariant sensory information and contravariant motor output (where the input can directly determine the output in the form of an eigenvector without the necessity of an interconnected metric transformation) provides the basis of metaorganization.

2.1.2. Optimal characteristics for the biological procedure for establishing metric networks: tensorial interpretation of tremor. The formative aspects of oscillatory behavior are most conspicuous during embryogenesis.[49] It is known, for example, that embryos evolve through characteristic tremor and oscillatory twitching.[8,30] Reverberative resonance is therefore a dominant characteristic which may reveal fundamental properties of the movement effector and the functional properties of related neuronal networks. Oscillations have also been analysed in detail by numerous workers both from biological and mathematical points of view (see Refs 4, 5, 12, 22, 24, 28, 60, 68 and 100).

The most significant feature of tremor may be expressed formally by assuming that the proprioception system provides a covariant measure of the contravariant motor execution. Indeed it has been suggested[75] that musculoskeletal systems endowed with proprioceptive feedback, where the frame of reference both for motor execution and sensory reception is common, can base their function on the following fact. The contravariant motor action and the covariant proprioception, belonging to the same physical invariant, represent together the covariant metric tensor. That is, for any given contravariant execution vector the proprioception yields the covariant counterpart. Thus for a motor system the contravariant motor action and its covariant proprioception together define the covariant metric tensor inherent in the physical geometry of the motor apparatus. However, in motor co-ordination the contravariant metric is required to implement the proper transformation of covariant motor intention vectors into their contravariant executable form.

The above considerations lead to the metaorganization principle, summarized in the following. (1) The eigenvectors of the covariant metric of a motor system can be established by reverberations, resulting from the return of covariant proprioception to motor effectors as if they were contravariants. (2) This oscillation will reach a steady-state of covariant–contravariant eigenvectors. (3) These eigenvectors and eigenvalues (or the generalized inverses of the latter) can be used to generate either a duplicate or a complementer of the covariant metric tensor. (4)

The resulting metric-type networks (e.g. that of the cerebellum) can be used as an internal function representation of an external geometry (e.g. used for motor co-ordination).

It is important to emphasize that co-ordination established by metaorganization may not be necessary for some stereotyped movements (especially those in lower vertebrates). Operations such as basic locomotory or grooming actions do not represent the class of co-ordinated goal-oriented movements that are the focus of this study. Rather they seem to be 'preprogrammed'' activities based on fixed-pattern generators at spinal cord level, for which a higher cortical involvement of the intention, or a cerebellar co-ordination of the execution, is not necessary.

2.1.3. Reverberation of proprioceptive covariants as contravariants, in order to establish the eigenvectors implicit in the physical geometry of the motor apparatus. The interpretation (in section 1.2) of the proprioception signals and motor signals as covariants versus contravariants provides a concrete example of the physical implementation of the metaorganization of CNS. The proposed procedure will be shown to yield a co-ordinated control of an overcomplete muscular system. The implementation is based on the reverberation of the covariant proprioception-afferent as if it were a contravariant-executor motoneuron efferent. This proprioception-execution reverberation will set up an oscillation of the motor apparatus that reaches a steady-state when the input and output signals are identical, i.e. when they both constitute an eigenvector of the system.

The procedure shown in Fig. 3, utilizes the motor system of Fig. 1 and the cerebellar neuronal network in Fig. 2 with an arbitrary vector descending the motor executor system. It is emphasized that this initial vector could be arbitrary and may arise from internal "noise" of the circuits. Let the motoneurons innervating the pectoralis muscle produce a burst of spikes of unitary strength which results in a movement of the hand along the α direction. This arbitrary motor signal can be described as a contravariant vector $\mathbf{e} = (1 \quad 0 \quad 0)^T$, where superscript T denotes the transpose of the row-vector into column-vector.

According to section 1.2.2, the peripheral sensors, which measure the tensions in the tendons, are capable of yielding the covariant sensory components of the generated invariant. These components arise geometrically by establishing the orthogonal projection components of the unitary motor vector $\mathbf{e}$ (along direction α, to the β and γ axes). These covariant components can be calculated from the contravariant vector by multiplying it with the covariant metric tensor of the motor system, which is simply the table of cosines among the axes.[77] The local system of coordinates for the movements of the index finger is shown in Fig. 1, by axes at 185, 160 and 148° angles, in the two-dimensional physical plane, where the angles are measured from the customary right-horizontal 0° direction. Thus the covariant metric of the physical motor apparatus is:

$$\mathbf{g}_{nk} = \cos(\phi_{nk})$$

$$= \begin{vmatrix} \cos(185\text{-}185) & \cos(185\text{-}160) & \cos(185.148) \\ \cos(160\text{-}185) & \cos(160\text{-}160) & \cos(160\text{-}148) \\ \cos(148\text{-}185) & \cos(148\text{-}160) & \cos(148\text{-}148) \end{vmatrix}$$

$$= \begin{vmatrix} 1.000 & 0.906 & 0.799 \\ 0.906 & 1.000 & 0.978 \\ 0.799 & 0.978 & 1.000 \end{vmatrix} \quad (3)$$

Given that such a covariant metric of the motor execution is represented by a matrix where the components are the cosines of the angles among the axes, two properties of the matrix are given: (1) the matrix is symmetrical, since $\phi_{nk} = \phi_{kn}$ and (2) its components are real values since $\cos(\phi_{nk})$ is a real number for any angle. Symmetrical real-valued matrices constitute a special subclass of Hermitian matrices[87] and thus are characterized by having a set of orthogonal eigenvectors with eigenvalues that are real numbers.[11] Thus an actual physical procedure to generate such metric matrices is possible; these are implemented by reverberation, as shown in the remaining part of this section.

The numerical example, shown in Fig. 3, starts with the initial arbitrary contravariant motor execution vector $_0\mathbf{e} = (1\ 0\ 0)^T$. The corresponding first covariant expression, detected by proprioception, will therefore be $_1\mathbf{p} = (1.000\ 0.960\ 0.799)^T$. One can establish these values either geometrically, by taking the orthogonal projection to the other axes of the nonzero component of $_0\mathbf{e}$, or by computing its components through the covariant metric according to $\mathbf{p} = \mathbf{g} \times \mathbf{e}$. It is assumed that $\mathbf{p}$ is normalized before it is reverberated as if it were contravariant (normalized vectors are denoted by barred symbols). This vector will descend on the motor system as $_1\bar{\mathbf{e}} = (0.638\ 0.578\ 0.509)^T$. This contravariant output will then produce an arm position that will be measured covariantly in the second reverberation by the proprioceptors, which detect tension in the tendons ($_2\mathbf{p}$). Application of the covariant metric reveals that $_2\mathbf{p} = (1.568\ 1.654\ 1.584)^T$. If this proprioceptive vector is reverberated for the second time in normalized form as $\bar{\mathbf{p}}$, it will be executed as $_2\bar{\mathbf{e}} = (0.565\ 0.596\ 0.571)^T$. This vector will then be covariantly measured as $_3\mathbf{p} = (1.561\ 1.666\ 1.605)^T$ and reverberated in the third cycle in a normalized form as $_3\bar{\mathbf{e}} = (0.559, 0.597\ 0.575)^T$. As verified through the application of this vector to the covariant metric, the third sensory proprioception will yield $_3\mathbf{p} = (1.560\ 1.666\ 1.606)^T$. Repeating the cycle, the fourth contravariant return will be $_4\bar{\mathbf{e}} = (0.559\ 0.597\ 0.575)^T$. Note that the above reverberation stabilizes with a vector that is identical in its proprioceptive and execution forms. The reverberated signals are identical after the third cycle: $_3\bar{\mathbf{e}} = _3\mathbf{p} = _4\mathbf{p} = (0.559\ 0.597\ 0.575)^T$.

The example of reverberation shown in Fig. 3 demonstrates that after a rapid convergence the

oscillation of the system reaches a steady-state of the eigenvectors. Without such normalization, during the reverberation each component of the nth covariant sensory vector would be $\lambda = 2.791$-times greater than the corresponding nth contravariant motor vector component:

$$_n\mathbf{p} = \lambda \times {}_n\mathbf{e} = 2.791 \times {}_n\mathbf{e}$$
$$= 2.791 \times (0.559\ 0.597\ 0.575)^T. \quad (4)$$

The factor λ is known as the eigenvalue.[87] It can be measured by the same operation as the normalization since λ is the necessary degree of change of the magnitude (normalization) of the vector before its reverberation.

Such a covariant–contravariant pair, given above in normalized form as $_3\mathbf{e} = _4\mathbf{p} = \mathbf{E}_1 = (0.559\ 0.597\ 0.575)^T$, where the covariant and contravariant forms differ by only a constant coefficient for each component, is called an eigenvector of the covariant metric in the given frame of reference and the $\lambda_1 = 2.791$ constant is the first eigenvalue belonging to the first eigenvector $\mathbf{E}_1$.

The above iterative mathematical method of finding an eigenvalue and the belonging eigenvector is widely used in computer science in the case of large symmetrical real-value matrices as in Hermitian matrices (cf. 7.27 in Ref. 11). Although the eigenvector-decomposition of matrices was not applied to the metric tensor and the co- and contravariant tensorial aspects had not been recognized, the neurobiological significance of such decomposition has been greatly exploited (see, for example, Ref. 5).

The utilization of the eigenvectors found by reverberation for the genesis of a metric-type network is illustrated in Fig. 4. The most crucial step of the metaorganization-process is the relaying of the found eigenvector to a cortico-nuclear array of neurons, both directly (e.g. via climbing fiber collaterals to the cerebellar nuclei) and indirectly (e.g. via climbing fibers to the Purkinje cells which in turn project to the nuclei). Such convergence of the same (climbing fiber) vector may imprint an array of neurons by the dyadic (outer) product of the vector with itself. Such a dyad $\mathbf{D}_1 = \mathbf{E}_1 > < \mathbf{E}_1$ (symbol $> <$ denotes the outer product of vectors) can be seen both in the connectivity diagram and also numerically (Fig. 4). The dyadic product of an eigenvector with itself will be called an "eigendyad". As shown, $\mathbf{D}_1$ will serve as the first approximation of $\mathbf{g}^{nk}$, denoted by $\tilde{\mathbf{g}}^{nk}$.

Once the first eigenvector and corresponding eigenvalue is established, the remaining eigenvectors of the system can be found by reverberating a vector whose direction is orthogonal to that of the previously found eigenvectors. Reverberation can therefore proceed by filtering out from $\mathbf{p}$, before every reverberation, the already found eigenvector-component $\mathbf{p}_F = (\mathbf{E}_1 > < \mathbf{E}_1) \times \mathbf{p}$, (see Fig. 4 in Ref. 11):

$$\mathbf{p} - \mathbf{p}_F = \mathbf{p} - \sum_m (\mathbf{E}_m > < \mathbf{E}_m) \times \mathbf{p}. \quad (5)$$

The Function of the Proprioception–Motor Execution Spinal Circuit

Establish Eigenvectors via Subcortical Reverberation

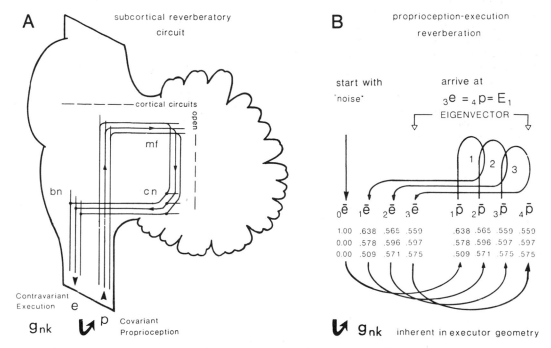

Fig. 3. *Oscillatory reverberation of motor execution-proprioception, establishing the eigenvectors of the motor apparatus.* (A) Subcortical reverberatory circuits. Ascending spinocerebellar pathways carry covariant proprioception (p) of any execution (e), via mossy fiber (mf) collaterals into the cerebellar nuclei (cn). The reverberation-loop closes on the brain stem nuclei (bn), with descending motoneuron pathways, carrying execution components that will be physically assembled as contravariants (e). The covariant metric $\mathbf{g}_{nk}$, inherent in the physical geometry of the motor apparatus, will provide for any contravariant executor vector its proprioceptive covariant counterpart. (B) A quantitative example for the stabilization of the execution (e)-proprioception (p) reverberation in the eigenvector ($\mathbf{E}_1$). Barred vectorial symbols denote normalized vectors. Starting with an arbitrary $_0\mathbf{e} = (1 \quad 0 \quad 0)$ execution, already after the second reverberation the execution and proprioception vectors are identical, meaning that an eigenvector is established.

Without this filtering the reverberation would again converge to the same eigenvector; while the filtering forces the reverberation to be confined to the direction orthogonal to the previously found eigenvectors. The above iterative computation technique of the eigenvectors and eigenvalues is possible since in real-valued symmetrical matrices the eigenvectors are mutually orthogonal and the eigenvalues are real (7.27 in Ref. 11 and theorem 4-4 in Ref. 87).

Similarly it can be calculated that the above mathematical but physically implementable method of filtered reverberations leads to the second normalized eigenvector and the corresponding eigenvalue:

$$\mathbf{E}_2 = (-0.783 \quad 0.153 \quad 0.603)^T; \quad \lambda_2 = 0.209.$$

The end of the reverberative iterative search, indicating that all the eigenvectors and eigenvalues have been found, can be determined as follows. In a physical process it can be monitored when the rever-

berating vector, filtered for all previously found eigenvectors, becomes zero. At that point no more eigenvectors can be found and thus the search stops. In a mathematical process, when the covariant metric can be made explicitly available by numerical calculation, the end-point of the reverberative search can also be determined by comparing the sum of found eigenvalues to the trace (tr) of the matrix of the covariant metric, which is defined as the sum of the diagonal elements.[87] Since

$$\mathrm{tr}(\mathbf{g}_{nk}) = \mathrm{tr}(\mathbf{g}^{nk}) = \sum_m \lambda_m; \qquad (6)$$

in the above case

$$\mathrm{tr}(\mathbf{g}_{nk}) = \mathrm{tr}(\mathbf{g}^{nk}) = 1 + 1 + 1 = 2.791 + 0.209. \qquad (7)$$

In our example this means that only two non-zero eigenvalues can be found and therefore the search can end. The existence of only two non-zero eigenvectors in a three-matrix reflects the fact that the three-axis frame of reference is overcomplete compared to the two-dimensional space. Since the eigenvectors of a symmetrical real-valued matrix are mutually orthogonal, when the motor apparatus shown in Figs 1–3 is confined into a two-dimensional plane, only a second orthogonal vector can be found in addition to the first direction determined by the eigenvector.

2.1.4. Spectral representation of the covariant metric tensor and its proper inverse (or Moore–Penrose generalized inverse) as expressed by their eigendyads; the outer products of eigenvectors weighed by the corresponding eigenvalues. The covariant metric tensor was established in (3) by calculation as a matrix composed of the cosines among co-ordinate axes. In the physical motor mechanism this metric is only implicitly available in the sense that for every particular contravariant motor execution vector the physical effector system provides its covariantly measured

proprioceptive vectorial counterpart. However, with the use of the eigenvectors and eigenvalues found by the above physical oscillation the metric tensor can be made explicit either in its co- or contravariant form. Accordingly a neuronal network can be constructed that implements the matrix which establishes functional geometries, e.g. the transformation from covariant motor intention into contravariant motor execution which was proposed as the basis for motor co-ordination.[81]

The method of constructing the metric is based on the spectral representation of the covariant metric[76] (cf. p. 132, theorem 7.3 in Ref. 11, or theorem 8.8 in Ref. 91):

$$\mathbf{g}_{nk} = \sum_m \lambda_m \times (\tilde{\mathbf{E}}_m > \ < \tilde{\mathbf{E}}_m) \qquad (8)$$

where $\tilde{\mathbf{E}}_m$ is the mth normalized eigenvector and $\tilde{\mathbf{E}}_m > \ < \tilde{\mathbf{E}}_m$ is the outer (dyadic) matrix product of the mth eigenvector.

The Function of the Olivo–Cerebellar Climbing Fiber System
Metaorganization (Genesis & Modification) of Functional Geometry

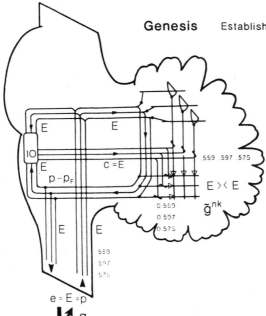

Genesis   Establish the Principal Axes of CB Tensor Ellipsoid, via

1) Implementation of the Eigenvectors in the Olive

2) Genesis of Corticonuclear Eigendyad Networks

  a) Reverberation Stabilizes in First Eigenvector: E_1 cfs Imprint First Eigendyad D_1

$$\tilde{g}^{nk} = D_1 = E_1 > < E_1 =$$

$$= \begin{bmatrix} .559 \\ .597 \\ .575 \end{bmatrix} \begin{bmatrix} .559 & .597 & .575 \end{bmatrix} = \begin{bmatrix} .312 & .334 & .321 \\ .334 & .356 & .343 \\ .321 & .344 & .331 \end{bmatrix}$$

  b) Imprinted Eigendyad Filters Further Reverberation

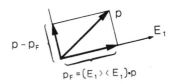

$$p_F = (E_1 > < E_1) \cdot p$$

Fig. 4. *Genesis of the cerebellar corticonuclear metric via metaorganization, by means of imprinting the dyads of eigenvectors found by reverberation. The reverberatory scheme shown in Fig. 3 is supplemented by the olivary system (IO), which compares the ascending proprioception (p) and descending execution-vector (e). (1) Having detected an identity, an eigenvector (E) is found, that is implemented in the olive. (2) The eigenvector is utilized to generate the corticonuclear network, by being transmitted, via climbing fiber vector (c = **E**) to both the Purkinje cells and the cerebellar nuclear cells. (a) The dyad of the eigenvector (eigendyad) **D₁** is shown numerically, yielding the first approximation of the metric g̃ⁿᵏ; in effect determining the principal axes of the cerebellar tensor ellipsoid (cf. Fig. 5C). (b) The filtering of the reverberation. After having found the first eigenvector, the already established **D₁** dyad serves as a filter that removes the **p_F = (E₁ > < E₁)**. **p** components from the proprioception vector **p**, forcing the reverberation-vector **p − p_F** to be orthogonal to the already established eigenvector.*

In the given example the above formula yields the spectral representation of $\mathbf{g}_{nk}$ as follows:

$$\mathbf{g}_{nk} = 2.791 \begin{vmatrix} 0.559 \\ 0.597 \\ 0.575 \end{vmatrix} \begin{matrix} 0.559 & 0.597 & 0.575 \end{matrix}$$

$$+ 0.209 \begin{vmatrix} -0.783 \\ 0.153 \\ 0.603 \end{vmatrix} \begin{matrix} -0.783 & 0.153 & 0.603 \end{matrix} \quad (9)$$

$$= 2.791 \begin{vmatrix} 0.312 & 0.334 & 0.321 \\ 0.334 & 0.356 & 0.343 \\ 0.321 & 0.344 & 0.331 \end{vmatrix}$$

$$+ 0.209 \begin{vmatrix} 0.613 & -0.120 & -0.472 \\ -0.120 & 0.023 & 0.092 \\ -0.472 & 0.092 & 0.364 \end{vmatrix}$$

$$= \begin{vmatrix} 0.999 & 0.907 & 0.800 \\ 0.907 & 0.999 & 0.976 \\ 0.800 & 0.976 & 1.000 \end{vmatrix}. \quad (10)$$

The resulting covariant metric is, with practical precision, identical to the one computed directly from the cosines. The computation was actually performed for 7 decimal digits; however, as shown here, results come within ± 0.002 precision even if the calculation is rounded to the biologically relevant 3 digits.

The two most important aspects of metaorganization are that the above iterative procedure which yields the spectral representation of the covariant metric (a) is established by a physically executable oscillation which is set up simply by a recurrent reverberation and (b) will yield not just the covariant metric tensor itself, but also either its proper inverse (if it exists) or its Moore–Penrose generalized inverse (in case of overcompleteness). The former applies if the space is complete (e.g. it is Riemannian) and thus the inverse of the covariant metric tensor exists. The latter applies if the covariant metric is singular and thus the space is non-Riemannian. The unified expression of the proper, or generalized metric, is:

$$(\mathbf{g}_{nk})^+ = \sum_m \lambda_m^+ \times (\mathbf{\hat{E}}_m > < \mathbf{\hat{E}}_m) \quad (11)$$

where λ_m^+ is the generalized inverse of the mth eigenvalue (3.6.2. in Ref. 1).

$$\lambda_m^+ = \begin{cases} 1/\lambda_m & \text{if } \lambda_m \neq 0 \\ 0 & \text{if } \lambda_m = 0. \end{cases} \quad (12)$$

For further details of the mathematics of generalized inverses and the Moore–Penrose pseudoinverse see Refs 1 and 9. For its introduction into tensor network theory of the CNS see Refs 74–78. For non-tensorial neurobiological applications of the generalized inverse see Ref. 41 and for robotics see Ref. 40. It is emphasized that in the metaorganization algorithm (a) the spectral decomposition is applied not to any matrix, but specifically to the covariant metric tensor, and (b) the eigenvector, established via

an oscillation, is used to generate a generalized inverse of the covariant metric, expressed not in Cartesian but in non-orthogonal co-ordinates.

In the given numerical example, the above formula of Moore–Penrose-generalized inverse of the covariant metric yields:

$$(\mathbf{g}_{nk})^+ = 1/2.791 \begin{vmatrix} 0.559 \\ 0.597 \\ 0.575 \end{vmatrix} \begin{matrix} 0.559 & 0.597 & 0.575 \end{matrix}$$

$$+ 1/0.209 \begin{vmatrix} -0.783 \\ 0.153 \\ 0.603 \end{vmatrix} \begin{matrix} -0.783 & 0.153 & 0.603 \end{matrix} \quad (13)$$

and, if the dyads of eigenvectors ("eigendyads"), weighed by the eigenvalue are explicitly calculated, is equal to

$$(\mathbf{g}_{nk})^+ = \begin{vmatrix} 0.112 & 0.120 & 0.115 \\ 0.120 & 0.127 & 0.123 \\ 0.115 & 0.123 & 0.118 \end{vmatrix} +$$

$$+ \begin{vmatrix} 2.933 & -0.574 & -2.259 \\ -0.574 & 0.110 & 0.440 \\ -2.259 & 0.440 & 1.742 \end{vmatrix} =$$

$$= \begin{vmatrix} 3.045 & -0.454 & -2.114 \\ -0.454 & 0.237 & 0.563 \\ -2.144 & 0.563 & 1.860 \end{vmatrix}. \quad (14)$$

The verbal expression of the above is the following. The Moore–Penrose-generalized inverse of a matrix, that conserves the eigenvectors of the original matrix, is constructed as the sum of dyadic outer product of each eigenvector with itself; i.e. of the dyads weighted by the (generalized) inverse of the corresponding eigenvalue.

Note that the Moore–Penrose-generalized inverse of the covariant metric tensor has already been numerically calculated by applying the meta-organization principle and algorithm as proposed earlier.[74-78] The numerical example of Fig. 2, using the metric-type neuronal network, has also been shown with the Moore–Penrose-generalized inverse components of the contravariant metric. Nevertheless, an exposition of the reverberative procedure has not hitherto been offered. The metaorganization principle is elaborated here as an oscillatory procedure in accordance with the classic notions on recurrent reverberating circuits; the theory of closed "self re-exciting" chains of neurons,[60] the control-theoretical emphasis on "feedback and oscillation" in Chap IV of Ref. 100, the emphasis on reverberation in Ref. 12 and the recent analysis of the central role of motor oscillations at the neuronal level in motor development.[49]

2.2 Conceptual interpretation of the principle of meta-organization of neuronal networks

A basic interpretation of the principle of meta-organization relies on the fact that the orthogonal spectral decomposition of the matrix of the covariant metric is conceptually equivalent to viewing the motor-transformation through the metric not as a wholly integrated operation, but as composed of transformations through separable eigendyads. As shown each eigendyad is the outer product of a normalized eigenvector with itself, the eigenvalue serving as a coefficient. It can easily be verified that an eigendyad transforms an eigenvector into itself, which will only be stretched or shortened by the eigenvalue coefficient. Since the eigenvectors are mutually orthogonal, each eigendyad operates only on that vector component which lies in its own direction; it is "intransparent" (producing zero output) to components that are diagonal to it. In the metric transformation of contravariants into covariants the magnification coefficient is the eigenvalue of the covariant metric. This explanation that the reverse contravariant metric-type transformation (via the generalized inverse of the covariant metric) must be performed through the same set of eigendyads (serving as the eigenvector-transformers), while the coefficient of each dyad must be the generalized inverse of the eigenvalue.[77, 78]

It must be emphasized, however, that this decomposition into independent "channels" of amplification (for biological correlates of such channels, see Ref. 47) is only possible along the mutually orthogonal eigenvectors of the system. Therefore, a customary interpretation of a horizontal eye movement, for example, as a separable direction from vertical and torsional eye movements may be improper. The eigenvectors of the oculomotor-covariant metric (a) have not even been established at the time of such customary interpretation and (b) when they have recently been calculated, they turned out to be greatly different from the horizontal direction (by about 45°, cf. Ref. 77). Thus some of the most immediate experimental paradigms, derived from the proposed metaorganization principle are (a) to establish experimentally the eigenvectors in biological systems and (b) to determine if the amplification of co- to contravariant vector-components can be independently altered along the mutually orthogonal eigenvectors and interdependently along all other directions, as suggested here by this theory.

A more abstract conceptual interpretation of the metaorganization principle is possible by a graphic depiction of the function of the cerebellum, as a geometrical distortion which is implemented by the covariant metric and its generalized inverse. Such is possible in the form of a tensor-ellipsoid (see Fig. 5C, after Ref. 78). The covariant–contravariant transformation (and vice versa) is visualized in Fig. 5(C) as a geometrical distortion of an ellipsoid of the cerebellar input intention vectors i_k into a circle of execution vectors e^n. Such transformation is determined by the principal direction-axes of the ellipsoid (given by the eigenvectors) and by the magnitude-distortion (where the lengths of the principal axes

along each eigenvector correspond to the eigenvalue).

This geometrical definition of the primary cerebellar function leads one to the secondary question of the development of the function through the emergence of the neuronal network that implements this transformation.[51] While the geometrical symbolism in Fig. 5(C) provides a concise interpretation of the function itself in the first place, secondarily it also suggests that its development may be determined by the double procedure[78, 79] of (1) establishing and storing of the eigenvectors of the tensor-ellipsoid and (2) trimming the eigenvalues (i.e. adjusting the principal axes to their proper lengths). The steps by which these tasks are accomplished are reviewed next.

2.3 Elaboration of the metaorganization principle, explaining the genesis and modification of cerebellar metric-type neuronal networks

In section 1.2.3. it was summarized and quantitatively demonstrated how a covariant–contravariant transformer-matrix can serve as a cerebellar motor coordinator. In section 2.3.1 below, a concrete numerical example is given for how the metaorganization principle can be implemented by a process in the CNS to generate such cerebellar networks.

2.3.1. The genesis of functional geometries as implemented by neuronal networks. The summary diagram in Fig. 5 (after Refs 75–78) illustrates a general scheme of the function, genesis and modification of the cerebellar networks. By including Fig. 2, it shows that the function of the essential cerebellar network can be interpreted as performing a covariant–contravariant transformation. However, Fig. 5 also indicates that this network converts the motor intention-signals into motor signals, taking in account not only space co-ordinates as shown in Fig. 2, but also spacetime co-ordinates as shown in Ref. 83. The "stacks" of Purkinje cells, which serve as "temporal lookahead-modules",[80,83] each model requiring about two hundred cells, are illustrated by a schematic triad of Purkinje neurons (Fig. 5D).

The illustration shown in Fig. 5, also encompasses the circuitry necessary for the establishment of the eigenvectors by reverberation and the network-approximation of the metric by its eigendyads (see Figs 3 and 4). The covariant proprioception vectors, **p**, enter to the cerebellum via mossy fibers that give collaterals to the cerebellar nuclei. Because the Purkinje cell–cerebellar nuclear cell synaptic connectivity is established late in embryogenesis,[92] we propose that reverberation specifies this connectivity in an epigenetic manner. Thus, initially for any proprioceptive input, the mossy fiber input to the cerebellar cortex will yield a zero vector through the Purkinje cells at the cerebellar nuclei before the metaorganization process is implemented. As a result the nucleofugal output will carry the same information as the mossy fiber input itself. This output is then introduced in the

Please note: Figure 5 appears opposite page 349.

motor system as if it were a contravariant effector vector, with only a signal-reversal at the brain stem nuclei, thus leading to stabilizing oscillations.

The imprinting of the eigendyads into the cerebellar corticonuclear circuitry is illustrated in Figs 4 and 5(A). In the scheme shown in Fig. 5 small additional circuits are necessary for normalizing the amplitude of the reverberation and for identity detection to monitor the eigenvalue stabilization when $\bar{\mathbf{e}} = \bar{\mathbf{p}}$. Both operations can easily be accomplished by taking their inner product. This can be accomplished by introducing an interneuron (see below). Indeed, in order to normalize the amplitude, the inner product is initially obtained by multiplying $\mathbf{p}$ with itself. With this factor the local inhibitory interneuron can reduce the magnitude of the vector. This operation corresponds to the amplitude-stabilization by Golgi cells proposed earlier.[86] Here the effect of the Golgi inhibition is normalization, with the firing rate of the Golgi cell being the measue of the eigenvalue. In order to monitor the degree of eigenvector-stabilization, for the inner product of $\bar{\mathbf{p}}$ and $\bar{\mathbf{e}}$ the interneuron is organized such that it will only reach a unitary firing rate when $\bar{\mathbf{p}}$ and $\bar{\mathbf{e}}$ are eigenvectors. Such a simple interneuron circuit can determine whether the convergence of the inner product of the two normalized vectors is close enough to (1.00 in absolute value) to indicate that an eigenvector has been found. At that point both the eigenvalue, automatically provided by the normalizer, and the corresponding eigenvector (taken either from the ascending or descending pathway) are available for constructing the eigendyads as shown in section 2.1.4. Such imprinting requires (a) a convergence of the identical eigenvector on both the row and column elements of a matrix in order to establish their product and (b) that ionic mechanisms are capable of triggering chemical changes at the postsynaptic element[52] which may modify intrinsic electro-responsiveness in a manner proportional to this product. The mossy fiber–parallel fiber–Purkinje cell system and the climbing fiber–Purkinje cell system could in principle be capable of generating such modification, since both these pathways carry the eigenvectors at such steady-state of the oscillation. Still, several considerations support the argument that such an adaptive modification may occur through the corticonuclear synaptic network. First the inferior olive signal is received directly from olivocerebellar collaterals arriving at the nuclei[16] and indirectly via the climbing fiber activation of Purkinje cells,[38] so that a convergence capable of evoking the required integration[54] can occur. Second, modification of the cerebellar nuclei is consistent with the finding that vestibular adaptation is retained after ablation of most of the cerebellar cortex.[15,58] Third, as will be seen in section 2.3.2, in pathological conditions where a modification of the corticonuclear circuitry after its initial genesis may be required, the direct and indirect climbing fiber vectors facilitate an adaptive change at the site of their convergence, presumably in the cerebellar nuclei.

During the process of imprinting the eigendyads into the corticonuclear cytoarchitecture, as proposed recently,[78] the inferior olive would store the eigenvectors and eigenvalues found by reverberation. Such storage will be required for the conformation of the genesis; the ongoing modification of the network. The suggestion that the olive has storage properties is particularly apt in view of the intrinsic capacity of olivary and related neurons for rebound oscillation.[49] Long-term ionic conductance-change mechanisms, consistent with the proposed storage, have been demonstrated experimentally.[55-57] According to this view, following the storage of the mth eigenvector $\mathbf{g}3$ the olive would signal a climbing fiber vectorial correction $\mathbf{c} = \bar{\mathbf{E}}_m$, which would modify the corticonuclear integrative properties by an additive

$$\mathbf{g}'_{nk} = \mathbf{g}_{nk} + \Delta \mathbf{g} = \mathbf{g}_{nk} + (\mathbf{c} > \ < \mathbf{c})$$
$$= \mathbf{g}_{nk} + (\bar{\mathbf{E}}_m > \ < \bar{\mathbf{E}}_m) \quad (15)$$

thereby imprinting the actual eigendyad. Using the first eigenvector–eigenvalue, it can be easily verified that such corticonuclear convergence of climbing fiber vectors will yield the first eigendyad shown in 2.1.4. The result of this procedure will be an approximation of the metric by its eigendyads:

$$\tilde{\mathbf{g}}^{nk} = \sum_m \mathbf{D}_m$$

(cf. Fig. 5A), a matrix which has the correct eigendirections (principal axes of the tensor-ellipsoid), while the eigenvalues may be uncalibrated (incorrect).

A remarkable feature of the scheme proposed in Figs 4 and 5 is that in the reverberative search for the subsequent second and third eigenvectors, the filtering-out of the already imprinted eigenvectors can be automatically provided by the eigendyads which have already been generated. For example, after having imprinted the first eigendyad, the reverberative search for the second eigenvector requires the $\mathbf{p} - \mathbf{p}_F = \mathbf{p} - (\mathbf{E}_1 \times \mathbf{p})$ motor output; the vector which contains only that component of the reverberated vector which is orthogonal to the established eigenvector. The mossy fiber input to the cerebellar cortex would transform, through the corticonuclear network, into its eigenvector projection, since the network is "intransparent" to (yields zero product with) vectors orthogonal to the eigenvector. Thus the nucleofugal output will be exactly the required filtered vector. With the use of such filtering via the already generated eigendyads, the reverberation can proceed to find all the subsequent eigenvectors in one continuous series of stabilizing oscillations, as shown by a computer simulation.[77] When all eigenvectors are found and the respective eigendyads are imprinted into the corticonuclear circuitry, the proprioceptive reverberation automatically becomes superfluous, since following the normalization of the reverberated vector, each corticonuclear eigendyad filters out its own eigenvector-projection. The removal of all eigenvector components leaves a zero resultant of the proprioceptive vector in the nucleofugal output. On one hand this prediction of the metaorganization principle is congruent with experimental data which indicate that the proprioception system is not essential for general motor performance of an already established system.[96] On the other hand the above proposal can in fact be tested experimentally by determining whether proprioception is a vital element of the genesis of neuronal networks subserving motor co-ordination, as the metaorganization principle predicts.

2.3.2. Modification of the functional geometries implemented by neuronal networks. This section shows that the same procedure that is suitable for generating the neuronal network (in the form of spectral representation by eigendyads) is capable of carrying out modifications in order to adapt the metric to possible changes in overall motor status.[51] The errors in the performance (produced by a network established with incorrectly calibrated eigenvalues) can be used for its iterative perfection.

The procedure is based on the two-stage character of the metaorganization: (1) the establishing, by a reverberative "revolution", the eigenvectors of the physical apparatus and thus imprinting the eigendyads (determining the principal axes) into a network and then (2) calibrating by a gradual "evolution" the eigenvalues of the functional geometry in order to match the exact values along the principal directions to those of the physical system.

The modification procedure of calibrating the eigenvalues, introduced in Ref. 78, is elaborated here by using a concise summary diagram in Fig. 5B. This diagram is shown for two dimensions (since the motor apparatus of Fig. 1 is confined to a plane) and demonstrates the adjustment of only one eigenvalue. Nevertheless, since the eigenvectors are mutually orthogonal, all eigenvalues (even if more than two) can be altered by a single operation in a parallel manner and since it contains no restriction for dimensionality the procedure is valid for any dimensional motor system.

Assume that a given eigenvector, $\mathbf{E}_m$, of the physical system has been properly established, but it was imprinted into an eigendyad with an incorrect eigenvalue-coefficient. In such a case, as shown in the diagram of Fig. 5(B), the components of an intended vector $\mathbf{i}$ (that covariantly represents the goal G) will result, through the erroneous metric, in a contravariant execution vector $\mathbf{e}$ that results in a performance, P, deviating from the goal, G. The physical state of affairs represented by P will then be covariantly measured by the sensory mechanism yielding the covariant components of the proprioception (performance) vector $\mathbf{p}$. Note that the three vectors $\mathbf{i}$, $\mathbf{e}$ and $\mathbf{p}$, together with an eigenvector $\mathbf{E}_m$ (assumed to be stored in the olive),[78] contain all the information necessary for correcting the erroneous metric that

was imprinted earlier. Since the metric can be constructed, in this spectral representation, as the sum of eigendyads with the eigenvalue-coefficients, the difference betwen the existing and desired eigenvalues can serve to correct the eigenvalues of the existing metric by adding the dyad formed by the climbing fiber vector, $\mathbf{c}$.

The modification is based on the fact that the inner product, $\mathbf{E}_m \times \mathbf{e}$, represents the orthogonal projection component of the output vector $\mathbf{e}$ of the network-metric to the eigenvector, $\mathbf{E}_m$. Similarly, $\mathbf{E}_m \times \mathbf{i}$, represents the projection to the eigenvector $\mathbf{E}_m$ of the input vector $\mathbf{i}$. Thus the eigenvalue inherent in the existing erroneous contravarant metric network is $_n\lambda_m = (\mathbf{E}_m \times \mathbf{e}_m)/(\mathbf{E}_m \times \mathbf{i})$. Likewise the eigenvalue that is implicit in the contravariant metric of the physical effector mechanism is $_p\lambda_m = (\mathbf{E}_m \times \mathbf{e})/(\mathbf{E}_m \times \mathbf{p})$. If the task is to correct the $_n\lambda_m$ in order to become $_p\lambda_m$, then the correction of the eigenvalue should be:

$$\lambda_m = {_p\lambda_m} - {_n\lambda_m} = (\mathbf{E}_m \times \mathbf{e})/(\mathbf{E}_m \times \mathbf{p})$$
$$- (\mathbf{E}_m \times \mathbf{e})/(\mathbf{E}_m \times \mathbf{i}) \quad (16)$$

This can be accomplished, by adding a modification-matrix $\Delta \mathbf{g}$, that is the dyadic product of the climbing fiber correction-vector, $\mathbf{c}$ to the existing network-matrix:[77]

where

$$\mathbf{g}^{nk} = \mathbf{c} > < \mathbf{c}$$

$$\mathbf{c} = \sum_m \left[(\mathbf{E}_m \times \mathbf{e})/(\mathbf{E}_m \times \mathbf{p}) \right.$$
$$\left. - (\mathbf{E}_m \times \mathbf{e})/(\mathbf{E}_m \times \mathbf{i}) \right]^{1/2} \cdot \mathbf{E}_m. \quad (17)$$

The process of calibrating the eigenvalues of the metric (by the above modification algorithm) is illustrated below by a numerical example that uses the cerebellar scheme (Figs 2–5).

Suppose that both eigenvectors shown in section 2.3.1 have been properly established but that the second eigenvalue was erroneously set. Instead of using the correct $\lambda_2 = 0.209$, assume that an incorrect $\lambda_2 = 0.300$ exists in the imprinted corticonuclear eigendyad. The erroneous coefficient of the second eigendyad results in a matrix-component:

$$1/0.3 \begin{vmatrix} 0.613 & -0.120 & -0.472 \\ -0.120 & 0.023 & 0.092 \\ -0.472 & 0.092 & 0.364 \end{vmatrix}$$

$$= \begin{vmatrix} 2.043 & -0.400 & -1.573 \\ -0.400 & 0.077 & 0.307 \\ -1.573 & 0.307 & 1.213 \end{vmatrix} \quad (18)$$

and thus, together with the (properly established) first eigendyad, the erroneous metric is

$$\mathbf{g}' = \begin{vmatrix} 2.155 & -0.280 & -1.458 \\ -0.280 & 0.204 & 0.430 \\ -1.458 & 0.430 & 1.331 \end{vmatrix}. \quad (19)$$

Let an arbitrary intention vector be $\mathbf{i} = (-100 \ 100 \ 100)^T$. Thus, through the error-laden $\mathbf{g}'$, this covariant vector will be transformed into a contravariant execution vector $\mathbf{e} = (-389.3 \; 91.7 \; 321.9)^T$. This execution vector will result in the physical output of P instead of G. Through the covariant metric, implicit in the physical geometry as expressed in section 2.1.4, the invariant P will be measured by the performance vector as

$$\mathbf{p}_i = \begin{vmatrix} 1.000 & 0.906 & 0.799 \\ 0.906 & 1.000 & 0.978 \\ 0.799 & 0.978 & 1.000 \end{vmatrix} \begin{vmatrix} -389.3 \\ 91.7 \\ 321.9 \end{vmatrix}$$

$$= \begin{vmatrix} -49.0 \\ 53.8 \\ 100.5 \end{vmatrix}. \qquad (20)$$

Since $\mathbf{E}_2 = (-0.783 \; 0.153 \; 0.603)^T$, the inner products required for establishing the climbing fiber vector $\mathbf{c}$ are:

$$\mathbf{E}_2 \times \mathbf{e} = 512.9 \qquad (21)$$

$$\mathbf{E}_2 \times \mathbf{i} = 153.9 \qquad (22)$$

$$\mathbf{E}_2 \times \mathbf{p} = 107.2 \qquad (23)$$

The ratio, representing the eigenvalue inherent in the physical geometry, therefore, is

$$512.9/107.2 = 4.785 \qquad (24)$$

and the ratio, representing the eigenvalue erroneously implemented in the network is

$$513.0/153.9 = 3.333. \qquad (25)$$

From the above, the required correction is $\lambda = 4.785 - 3.333 = 1.452$, and thus the modification-dyad, to be imprinted into the corticonuclear network is

$$1.452 \begin{vmatrix} 0.613 & -0.120 & -0.472 \\ -0.120 & 0.023 & 0.092 \\ -0.472 & 0.092 & 0.364 \end{vmatrix}$$

$$= \begin{vmatrix} 0.890 & -0.174 & -0.685 \\ -0.174 & 0.033 & 0.134 \\ -0.685 & 0.134 & 0.529 \end{vmatrix}. \qquad (26)$$

This modification-dyad added to the erroneous second dyad of (18) results in the proper second dyad as shown in section 2.1.4.

The dyadic product of the climbing fiber correction vector, $\mathbf{c}$, can be impressed on the corticonuclear network as a whole, via CFs that project both to the PCs and the CB nuclear cells. The emerging corticonuclear matrix will then act as an appropriate metric producing a zero error in the next performance. In this trial-and-error process the internal geometry becomes increasingly homeometric with the external one. Thus through the CF system the physical geometry is matched with its proper internal representation.

In the example it was assumed that the first eigendyad was imprinted with the correct eigenvalue.

However, since the eigenvectors are mutually orthogonal the modification procedure is independent along each eigenvector and thus the modification of all eigenvalues may be implemented simultaneously in a single reverberation.

The means of implementation of the proposed metric-modification at a single neuron level (either at the PCs or at NCs or at their conjunction) has not yet been conclusively established. Such a task is all the more difficult, since one component of the correction-matrix may either be positive, negative or zero.[78] Therefore the required perturbation at a single-neuron level should be expected as a bimodal effect, including at times an indetectable zero action.[10,17,37] Moreover, the correction in any matrix component is a function of all vector elements. Thus if only a single dimension is controlled by the experimental paradigm, as in conventional analyses, the prediction of a single component of the matrix may prove to be a very complex matter. Finally any alteration is expected to be much more pronounced at the site of the dyadic convergence (at NC), as opposed to the site of the intensive search, the CB cortex. These factors, plus a lack of a conceptual framework accounting for what is defined in Ref. 78 as the "CB functional triad; co-ordination, timing and adaptation", may explain the meager experimental results, despite dedicated efforts through one and a half decades, in an attempt to conclusively demonstrate an adaptive feature of the CB at the PC level.[34,46,37]

Some additional comments are warranted regarding the operations of the inferior olive. It is assumed that the inferior olive expresses the difference between the eigenvalues in the external physical geometry and those in the functional geometry implemented by the corticonuclear cerebellar network. The equation yielding the climbing fiber vector $\mathbf{c}$ [introduced in Ref. 78 and elaborated in (17)], is one of several possible implementations for the task. The advantage of the proposal above is that it measures the eigenvector of the physical geometry and the eigenvalue inherent in the already generated network. The disadvantage of this solution is that it requires nontrivial vectoral calculations in the olive, although it is known that the olive does receive of all the ascending and descending signals necessary for such a "comparator function".[7,65]

It is therefore noteworthy, that a simplified operation could also be utilized by the olive, one not based on measuring the eigenvalue of the cerebellar neuronal network. Rather, it could utilize the stored eigenvalue that can be imprinted into the olive at the same time as the eigendyads are imprinted into the corticonuclear network. Relying on the stored eigenvalue, its comparison with the error signal can be used to determine the required modification of the existing eigenvalue. The error $\mathbf{d} = \mathbf{i} - \mathbf{p}$ may arise as a difference between intention and proprioception or between intention and performance, as detected through the total sensorimotor loop. Thus, the new eigenvalue should be:

$$_{new}\lambda_m = {}_{old}\lambda_m \times (\mathbf{E}_m \times \mathbf{d})/(\mathbf{E}_m \times \mathbf{p}) \qquad (27)$$

This formula, that interprets the climbing fiber vector as based on the error vector, corresponds well to the experimental evidence showing that climbing fibers express functional errors in intrinsic frames of reference.[61,90] This requires a "computation" in the olive that is simpler than the full formula given in equation (17). The disadvantage of the simple computation is that it may accumulate errors, since instead of measuring the actual eigenvalue of the network the process relies on a stored, and possibly imperfect, eigenvalue by which the network was generated.

A final, but most important comment is that the process of calibrating the eigenvalues by iteration can perfect the metric if the eigenvectors have been precisely established and only the eigenvalues are incorrect. However, if the eigenvectors themselves are improper, the above modification-process may continue indefinitely without ever converging to the proper metric. If the intrinsic system of co-ordinates is experimentally altered and the old eigenvectors are entirely improper, the system needs to regress to a revolution (a drastic re-assessment of the principal directions and values) by re-doing the entire oscillatory reverberative process. This prediction of the theory corresponds to the findings that after major disturbance to the cerebellar coordination-apparatus (e.g. vestibular nerve ablation),[58] one of the earliest and most dramatic phases of the compensation process is marked by violent shaking and oscillatory behavior, observable in the animal and at the olivary level.[58]

3. GENESIS AND MODIFICATION OF THE THREE-STEP NETWORK OF THE TENSORIAL SENSORIMOTOR SCHEME

3.1. The three-stage tensorial scheme of sensorimotor systems

In section 2, the mathematical principle and the physical process of the metaorganization was elaborated. It was applied to the metric-type motor network that organizes the functional geometry of a neuronal system through the generalized inverse of the covariant metric of a motor apparatus. With this background the three basic transformation matrices used in the tensorial sensorimotor scheme may be developed in principle as well as in physical reality. The building-blocks of the system are (a) a matrix which serves as a contravariant sensory metric, (b) a matrix which expresses the covariant embedding involved in sensorimotor transformation and (c) a matrix which serves as a motor metric. The entire procedure will be demonstrated in the model scheme shown in Fig. 6.

The function of these transformations, once the matrices are available, has been quantitatively dem-onstrated elsewhere.[78] The system shown in Fig. 6 has been simplified and the diagram serves only as a model by showing how the above three matrices may be generated.

3.2 Metaorganization of motor geometry: cerebellar metric-type networks

The first step must be to generate, via the metaorganization process, the neuronal networks comprising the functional geometry of the executor mechanism. In the case shown in Fig. 6(A), this means generating the cerebellar network g^{nk}. The motor geometry must be established first since the metaorganization process applies as soon as a motor system and the proprioceptive system are available and connected to the external physical reality. At this stage the process does not require the sensorimotor transformation matrix or the sensory metric. This is in contrast to the generation of the sensory metric which, as will be shown in section 3.4, presumes the availability of the motor metric. Indeed, as pointed out recently[49] such order in the developing of the particular networks is consistent with the classical morphological studies.[88] In particular, in the case of the cerebellum, the first part to be developed is the cerebellar nuclei and then the Purkinje cell nuclear pathways, followed by the development of the input to Purkinje cells. After this the connectivity is refined.[44,88] Accordingly, the metaorganization of motor geometry, as the first stage of development, may start as soon as the muscles and proprioception peripheral organs begin to function. This agrees with the observations of embryonic twitches[8,30] and the fact that in some species cerebellar neuronal networks are reasonably well developed at the neonatal stage.[2]

The development of the motor-metric-type cerebellar network is shown by Fig. 6(A), according to the steps described in section 2. There are two additional points to be considered.

The calibration of the proprioceptive vector components can be accomplished by using the ratio of the spike-frequency bursts from the motoneurons which innervate each muscle (shown schematically in Fig. 6B) and the registered response returning via the proprioceptive reverberation. This is possible since the "base vector" represented by a single-motor impulse has only one non-zero component and thus it is therefore both co- and contravariant. For the same reason the calibration is independent of whether the calibrator signal is transmitted through a developed cerebellar metric or entirely bypasses this circuit without undergoing a cerebellar covariant–contravariant transformation.

A second point follows from the fact that tensor analysis deals with general co-ordinates. Thus, while in order to keep the complexity of the presentation minimal, only two-dimensional spatial co-ordinates are shown here, the principles apply to any multi-dimensional system such as one with space- or torque-time etc. co-ordinates. Thus the generation and modification of metrics involved not only setting or altering the connections, i.e. the electroresponsiveness of the components in the metric network, such as required for altering the spatial metric, but also involves a modification of the dynamic temporal characteristics of neurons. One manner in which this can be accomplished refers to changing the zero-first-second order time-derivative properties of single neurons,[53,72,73] in effect changing the characteristic oscillation frequencies of the neurons or of small assemblies.[48] If findings on ongoing modulation of the electroresponsiveness at the PC level[10,17,37] are made unambiguous, they could be interpreted as means for such subtle modulation of the Taylor-coefficients of the Purkinje cells in the temporal

lookahead-module but not the means of the setting of the eigenvalue-coefficients of the corticonuclear eigendyads.

3.3. Development of the sensorimotor network, implementing the covariant embedding transformation

Although the sensory system shown in Figs 6(B) and (C) is diagrammatic (being composed of two non-orthogonal axes at 150 and 270°) the basic features relevant to tensor theory are well represented; (a) the sensory frame covariantly measures the action generated by the muscles and (b) it utilizes a non-orthogonal system that is different from that for the motor execution both in its direction and number of axes. In the analysis of sensory mechan-

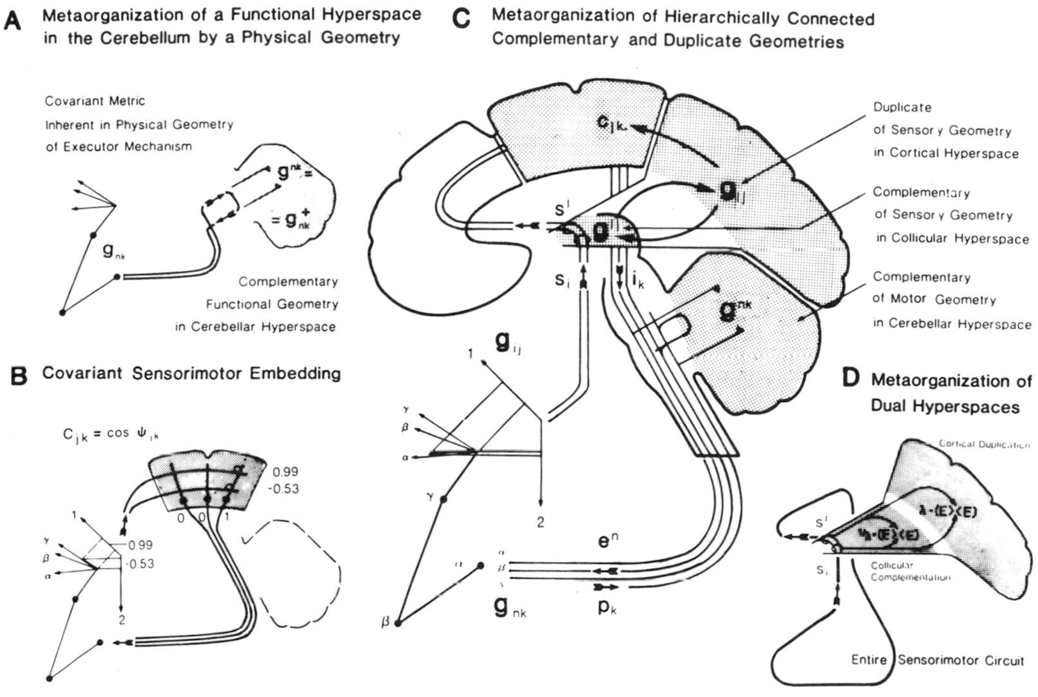

Fig. 6. *Schematic illustration of the metaorganization of functional CNS geometries.* (A) Interaction of a physical geometry inherent in the motor apparatus with a functional geometry of the cerebellar neuronal network. Reverberation of contravariant execution to covariant motor proprioception yields the eigenvectors of the covariant metric inherent in the motor geometry g_{nk}. Thus its inverse (g^{nk}) or Moore–Penrose-generalized inverse $(g_{nk})^+$ may be obtained in spectral representation. (B) Covariant embedding of the sensory geometry into the motor hyperspace. The jth unit-vector of the motor apparatus $(0\ \ 0\ \ 1)$ generate unitary displacement along the jth motor axis. Its projection to the kth sensory axis (cos ψ_{jk}, cf. numerical example in the text) will provide the c_{jm} matrix-component of the sensorimotor transformation matrix (C) Metaorganization of the three basic sensorimotor matrices, and the generation of a hierarchically connected metageometry that represents the whole sensorimotor system. Once the cerebellar g^{nk} and sensorimotor c_{jk} matrices are available, metaorganization may be used to organize a sensory metric tensor, replacing the set of direct connections (Kronecker-delta) from the sensory receptors (s_i) to sensory perceptors (s^j). For every s^j the entire sensorimotor circuit yields the corresponding s_i; implying the covariant sensory metric. Thus the eigenvectors can be established by reverberation and the inverse (or generalized inverse) metric tensor g^{ij} may be generated, corresponding to the collicular neuronal network. (D) Metaorganization of dual hyperspaces is possible, if both the complementer and the dual metric tensor is generated, one by using the generalized inverses of the eigenvalues as coefficients of the eigendyads, the other by using the found eigenvalues themselves. As shown in (C) such a process may be used to generate, together with the collicular contravariant sensory metric tensor (g^{ij}) a cortical duplicate of the covariant sensory metric (g_{ij}). These dual geometries may then be reverberated to mold one another and the duplicate geometry of the sensorimotor system (its internal model) may be used for initiation of motor acts without external sensory input [big arrows in part (C) symbolize such interactions].

isms such as the six semicircular canals of the vestibular apparatus,[78-80] both the anatomical realism and the ensuing quantitative complexity is significantly greater. In both the realistic and simplified cases, however, attention must be focused on the transformation matrix that changes the sensory vector into the motor vector (Fig. 6B). The function of the sensorimotor covariant embedding matrix is discussed in detail in Ref. 78. In the case of the vestibulo-ocular reflex model (see Fig. 5 in Ref. 79), the process of establishing such a covariant-embedding matrix was qualitatively elaborated to show that each unit-vector of the motor system should be covariantly measured along the sensory axes, yielding a matrix of the cosines among the sensory and motor axes.

Mathematically, this is a trivial operation both in the simple model presented in this paper and in the more complex vestibulo-ocular reflex.[79,89] The matrix elements are the cosine-projections of each motor unit-vector onto the sensory axes. Thus, in the case shown, the motor axes with 185, 160 and 148° have to be projected onto each of the sensory axes with 270 and 150° angles:

$$
\mathbf{c}_{jk} = \cos(\phi_{jk})
$$
$$
= \begin{vmatrix} \cos(185° - 270°) & \cos(185° - 150°) \\ \cos(160° - 270°) & \cos(160° - 150°) \\ \cos(148° - 270°) & \cos(148° - 150°) \end{vmatrix}
$$
$$
= \begin{vmatrix} 0.087 & 0.819 \\ -0.342 & 0.985 \\ -0.530 & 0.999 \end{vmatrix}. \quad (28)
$$

In order to establish these components of the sensorimotor transformation matrix in the CNS, it is necessary to assume that each "base vector" of the motor system is generated by a spike burst of a premotor (Pyramidal-type) neuron, such as are schematically represented by Fig. 1 in Refs 75, 76 and 78 and by Fig. 6(B) in this paper. These cells are designated here as "premotor neurons" because they use the motor frame of reference and are capable of generating a movement. However, since they will be connected to the sensory mechanism by the covariant-embedding matrix, they express the displacement in a covariant manner. Therefore a direct execution of such signals without a cerebellar-type covariant–contravariant transformation would result in a dysmetric movement. The firing of each large Pyramidal-type premotor neuron can be evoked by a strong burst of activity in a small cortical cell (e.g. layer IV), while Golgi-type inhibitory neurons ensure that other large Pyramidal cells are silenced during this operation (cf. Fig. 1 in Ref. 76). Thus during this special sensorimotor "imprinting"stage only one vertical column of a Pyramidal cell may produce an excitation at one time, producing a "base vector" signal that descends to the motor mechanism and generates a movement. It is noteworthy that these

"base vectors", as in the calibration process proposed in section 3.2, are both co- and contravariants. Thus in establishing the sensorimotor matrix, the cerebellum is again "transparent" as a covariant–contravariant transformer; it is not necessary for the cerebellum to partake in this procedure.

Second, the elementary movements will be measured covariantly by the sensory system. Since the sensorimotor transformation is a pre-requisite to the establishing of the sensory metric, it follows that the sensorimotor transformation must precede the development of the sensory metric. However, direct connections between the input and output elements of the sensory system are necessary and thus it is assumed that in an initial state the matrix of the sensory metric is a Kronecker-delta, i.e. a set of such direct connections. This permits the covariantly measured sensory components of the motor base vector to be transferred directly to the Pyramidal cells. This covariant vector will produce a synaptic activation that yields the exact coefficients to be imprinted into the premotor neuron and thus result in the required components of the sensorimotor matrix (cf. Fig. 6B).

Note that the two procedures of proprioceptive calibration and sensorimotor imprinting can be combined into a single process, since both rely on the "straddling" of the motor system by the unitary firings of individual actuators. However, while the motor-metric network may be organized during embryogenesis (since it only requires motor effectors and proprioceptive reverberation), the development of certain sensory mechanisms (for instance, vision) must commence postnatally.

3.4. Metaorganization of the sensory geometry: tectal metric-type networks

The final stage of the emergence of sensorimotor networks is the development of a sensory metric (Figs 6C and D). This requires not only the availability, but the active participation of the developed sensorimotor embedding transformation and the cerebellar motor metric networks. The development of a sensory metric by means of a motor metric as proposed here is consistent with (a) the presence of a separate, explicit CNS sensory metric that expresses invariants both covariantly and contravariantly in the same frame of reference, the inner product enabling geometrical judgements on the invariant[83] and (b) the fact that sensory functions such as vision cannot emerge without the active participation of motor mechanisms, such as eye movements.[32]

The process is based on a generalization of the metaorganization principle. Metaorganization could develop a network that implements a secondary geometry when the primary geometry was inherent in the motor executor mechanism (see section 2). The physical geometry of the musculoskeletal system provides a proprioceptive covariant vector which is a counterpart for every contravariant motor action.

The generalization of the metaorganization principle is based on the recognition of the fact that any system, not only a physical apparatus, that is capable of providing the dual counterpart to any particular input vector can serve as the primary geometry and thus be duplicated or complemented by the process of metaorganization.

Note that the sensory metric network on one hand and the rest of the sensorimotor scheme on the other constitute two halves of a circle, which are joined through an external invariant. After completion of the development of the sensorimotor embedding and the motor metric networks, however, the undeveloped "sensory metric network" is still only a set of input and output neurons which have the presumed direct system of connections (a Kronecker-delta) from the sensory receptors to the sensory perceptors. Looking at the input and output neurons of this "sensory metric network" reveals, however, that while the input neurons may be improperly connected to the sensory output neurons within the sensory metric network: the output neurons are properly connected to the sensory input neurons through the periphery via the sensorimotor metric networks: the external motor machinery and the sensory apparatus. That is, while one half-circle is still unorganized, the other is perfectly functional. Thus any arbitrary vector, s^j, over the set of sensory perceptor neurons (even one generated by internal "noise" of the system) can be transformed through the sensorimotor embedding network, c_{jk}, into motor intention vector i_k, then through the cerebellar motor metric into motor execution vector, e^n. The physical invariant, emerging from the contravariant motor execution will then be covariantly measured by the sensory mechanism to yield a sensory reception vector, s_i. Therefore, as shown schematically in Fig. 6(D), to any contravariant s^j the total pathway that includes the external physical motor and sensory mechanisms will yield the appropriate covariant counterpart, s_i. This is the necessary and sufficient condition for the applicability of the metaorganization process, which then can serve to modify the geometry of the contravariant sensory metric from the Kronecker-delta to the actual functional representation of the remaining circuit.

Given simplified sensory and motor frames, the reverberation process of s_i (as if it were s^j) through the entire motor and sensory systems, will yield the normalized eigenvectors $E_1 = (2^{-1/2} \ 2^{-1/2})^T$ and $E_2 = (2^{-1/2} \ -2^{-1/2})^T$ with the corresponding eigenvalues of $\lambda_1 = 0.5$ and $\lambda_2 = 1.5$. Therefore, the contravariant sensory metric can be generated in its eigendyad-expansion:

$$\mathbf{g}^{ij} = 1/0.5 \begin{vmatrix} 0.500 & 0.500 \\ 0.500 & 0.500 \end{vmatrix} + 1/1.5 \begin{vmatrix} 0.500 & -0.500 \\ -0.500 & 0.500 \end{vmatrix}$$

$$= \begin{vmatrix} 1.333 & 0.666 \\ 0.666 & 1.333 \end{vmatrix}. \quad (29)$$

This sensory metric, shown in Fig. 6 as $\mathbf{g}^{ij}$ (elaborated in Fig. 1 in Ref. 76), can be implemented (using a scaling factor of 4/3) as a simple neuronal network with twice as many direct connections between sensory receptors and sensory perceptor neurons as the number of cross connections.

Since the metaorganization procedure applied here is conceptually identical to that described in section 2, only two general comments will be made here, in order to illustrate how the proposal of establishing the sensory metric fits into the hierarchy of the top-down and bottom-up approaches used in brain theory. At the top level, the process of finding the eigenvectors of the sensory metric by reverberations, would look like a rhythmic oscillatory exercise of the motor mechanism, accompanied by an intense introspective use of the sensory apparatus—similar to the behavior observed during embryogenesis.[48] At the bottom level of the neuronal circuits subserving sensory information processing, the primary covariant–contravariant sensory transformation may take place in the neuronal network such as the optic tectum (cf. elaboration in Ref. 74).

The suggestion that such a network could be generated by generalized metaorganization raises a novel functional interpretation of the actual neuronal circuits that are known to be involved in sensory preprocessing. The process of metaorganization requires that the eigenvectors, found by reverberation, be stored. The implementation of this function can be accomplished by neuronal networks of small nuclei such as the inferior olive rather than cortical networks where the spectral expansion of the metric by its eigendyads is implemented. However, in order to serve as the "imprinter" and continuous "corrector" of the cortical network, as explained by the metaorganization process, such a nucleus must be intimately connected to a cortex. A possibility exists that the nucleus isthmi, known to be endowed by the above-described properties,[25] could play a similar role in generating the tectal circuits.

4. DISCUSSION

It seems quite clear that an analysis of basic sensorimotor transformations requires the use of general hypotheses regarding how the brain might implement functional geometries. The principle of metaorganization is capable of embodying such a concept since it is general enough to encompass many features of related geometries, yet can be elaborated (as in this paper) in specific network models.

A basic assumption of the metaorganization process is that the set of relations among the elements and among elements of another system may exhibit certain common basic features, since one may be embedded into the other. Identity of the two geometries, however, is not required; in the analyzed case the points of one space represent physical locations in a Euclidean space, while the internal functional motor hyperspace is of higher dimensionality and non-Elucidean (not even Riemannian).

A most practical feature of the metaorganization process is that it enables an explicit study of how an existing and well-defined primary geometry (such as the physical geometry of the motor apparatus), organizes a much less explicit and often ill-defined functional geometry which is implemented by a neuronal network.

The emergence of highly organized structuro-functional features of neuronal assemblies is often labeled as "adaptation", "self-organization", or "learning" in the CNS. While the principle of meta-organization and its algorithm is closely related to these notions (which have no precise and generally accepted definition), it differs from them in several fundamental respects. First, the geometrical re-definition of the emergence of networks in meta-organization is based on an identification of two entities: (a) one that governs the process of organization and (b) another that is being formed. For example, the first geometry is defined as that arising from the physical structure of the effector system, while the latter is defined as an abstract geometry over a multi-dimensional manifold. The well-defined nature of these two entities, which mold one another, tempts one to compare them with the notion of "self-organization", which has generated much interest without, however, defining the entity that is responsible for the organizing the "self". Second, since the metaorganization principle is elaborate using formal geometrical analysis, tensor network theory of the CNS and the process of metaorganization can be demonstrated quantitatively by using specific neuronal networks.

4.1. Metaorganization of CNS hyperspaces: a geometrical re-definition of the notions of "adaptation", "self-organization" and "learning"

Adaptation, self-organization and learning have been conceptualized and elaborated using many different approaches.

Viewing the CNS as an adaptive control system[26,27,34,35] represents two aspects of the CNS. "Control" insures that a system conforms to the internal order defined by the neuronal networks. "Adaptation", in turn, enables the CNS to conform with the external conditions. One limitation of an approach that separates, rather than unifies, control and adaptation may be that it assumes the concepts and formalisms of control-system theory. Borrowing from engineering, neuroscientists almost invariably chose its most limited form, the feedback-gain control of a single variable. That description did not lead to a network theory of existing neuronal circuits. Formally, the unselective borrowing from control engineering, even in the form of modern multi-variable control theory[11,21,45,68] may lead to major distortions. For example, since engineers express vectors in convenient Cartesian orthogonal co-

ordinates for man-made systems, some neuro-scientists may be led to believe that a vectorial notation that does not distinguish covariant and contravariant expressions may still be adequate to describe biological vector transformations. Admitting to the possibility that nature may have selected other than Cartesian co-ordinate systems and that most natural frames of reference are demonstrably non-orthogonal (cf. vestibulo-collic reflex)[67] leads to the inevitability of using a conceptual and mathematical apparatus that can express physical invariants in general non-orthogonal coordinate systems (such as tensor analysis, or other mathematical apparatus as listed in Ref. 75).

In order to compare the metaorganization principle with the hypothesis that the CNS is a self-organizing system, it is necessary to briefly assess the development of the latter concept. The view of the CNS as a self-organizing system originates from automata theory.[99] Basic considerations on the functional organization of the brain immediately elevated self-organization to one of the most intriguing chapters of Cybernetics.[100] Postulating a synaptic mechanism which may underlie the organization of behavior[31] provided a link between the abstract theory of the emergence of neuronal systems and experimental neuroscience. However, research at that time did not provide either a formal definition or a rigorous elaboration of the general notion.

A second major increase in interest in self-organization occurred in the 1960s,[12,20,102] when self-organization was tied to concepts of "learning", "optimization", "adaptation" and "approaching a steady-state in relating to external systems".[6] It was explicitly stated,[6] however, that a precise definition was still lacking at that time.

Finally, self-organization has attracted intensive theoretical interest again in the last decade.[3,18,26,42,62] Although the mathematical sophistication inherent in these new models is unsurpassed, a generally accepted definition of self-organization, both in a philosophical or mathematical sense, remains elusive. Therefore the term is used in neurobiology in a largely intuitive sense.[95] It may be applied to a specific phenomenon such as the emergence of temporally stable neuronal patterns, or to such abstract phenomena as human learning. Philosophically, however, the usage of the term "self" to an organizing principle or a process appears contradictory, since the organization of the "self" must surely be separable from the steps which generated it. Indeed, the question may not be, how does the CNS organize itself, but rather, how is the "self" organized in the CNS by the rest of the body and by the external world.

A geometrical redefinition may become helpful in alleviating some of the problems. For example, by providing separate definition for the two interacting geometries that is the geometry of physical features of motor systems and the functional geometry of neuronal networks that co-ordinate their actions, the causative relationship between these two becomes explicit and quantifiable.

4.2. Oscillations and tremor

One aim of tensor network theory is to serve as a help with a general interpretation of experimental data relating to brain function. It is therefore significant to determine if some basic experimental observations may be formally related to general principles of CNS organization. Indeed, neuroscientists have long wondered if phenomenology as basic as biological oscillation and resonance may provide a key to the mechanism which determines the organization of the neuronal networks of the CNS. This possibility is supported by the argument that oscillations and resonance are observed during development at several levels of the neuraxis. Such processes may thus be the means of development of electrical properties of the neuronal elements that constitute the neuronal nets.[49] In fact, neuronal oscillation and resonance determine much of the developing limbs and thus must provide, by recurrent afferent activity, crucial information about the dynamics of body-reference frames during early neurogenesis. Moreover, it is quite possible that such an internal searching mechanism may be operant in the adult form and may become quite explicit in pathological conditions. For example, it has long been known that in patients with Parkinson's disease, mechanical oscillatory stimulation of a finger may induce tremor which irradiates upwards along the limb,[39] in a manner similar to the Jacksonian "march" of motor seizures following localized lesion of the motor cortex. This "tremor–march" phenomenon indicates that the several segmental levels of the CNS which control limb movement are coupled to each other such that they may phase-lock and resonate when tremor occurs in only one segment. Such dissipative functional structures are of the essence when considering that the entire limb may be used as a single element or as a set of separate compartments.[43] The importance of the interaction of sensory feedback and motor output becomes clearer when considering that this interaction begins to occur very early in development even prior to the generation of co-ordinated movement and could thus serve as an epigenetic organization influence in determining the selective stabilization of neuronal networks.[13]

4.3. Generalization of the metaorganization principle: tensorial interpretation of the hierarchy of dual (complementer and duplicate) geometries in the CNS

The principle of metaorganization was elaborated in section 2 for a motor system where the primary geometry was directly identifiable. Active muscular forces are thought to represent contravariants, while passive tendon-forces represent covariant expressions of motor action. This primary physical contravariant–covariant transformation was complemented by establishing a secondary functional geometry which implemented a covariant–contravariant operator. This was accomplished by finding the eigenvectors and eigenvalues of the existing motor mechanism. Several generalizations[75] of the metaorganization principle lead to its application to systems that are beyond such primary geometries as those inherent in motor mechanisms.

The first generalization of this principle was made possible by the realization that the primary geometry does not have to be represented by a single physical metric transformation, but could be an entire sensorimotor chain which becomes a completed circle through its interaction with an external physical invariant. This was the case when constructing the sensory metric (Fig. 6D), where the entire sensorimotor chain provided for any contravariant sensory perception vector, s^j, the corresponding covariant perception-vector, s_i. This was attained through (a) a sensorimotor neuronal network, (b) a motor metric operator and (c) a physical invariant generated by the motor system where this invariant was physically measured by the sensory apparatus.

Beyond the above, the metaorganization principle may be applied to any metric tensor (e.g. one that is manifested only in an abstract functional geometry). For instance, once the network of the sensory metric is developed as a geometry which is secondary to the primary geometry inherent in the external world, the sensory metric itself may then be used as a primary geometry for metaorganizing its own secondary geometry in a hierarchically coupled neuronal network. For instance, the optic tectum itself may generate a secondary space in the cerebral cortex (that is "empty", i.e. "amphorous" in its pristine state), by serving as the organizer of the higher-order mold in this cortex of the tectal primary functional geometry.

The third generalization follows from the simple fact that the metaorganization process builds the secondary geometry from the eigenvectors and eigenvalues of the primary geometry. In generating the eigendyads, metaorganization could utilize either the eigenvalues of the initial system themselves of the initial system or their generalized inverses (or both). Metaorganization can thus result either in a secondary geometry which is a duplicate or a complement of the primary geometry, or both. This generalization leads to a study of hierarchically connected hyperspaces where the primary spaces (comprising sensorimotor metrics) are directly connected to physical geometries external to the CNS but where the secondary hyperspaces are built upon these sensorimotor metrics. Each geometry may in turn breed higher order duplicate or complement geometries in connected hyperspaces. As pointed out,[75] the intelligence implemented by such a hierarchy of metageometries may depend on (a) the number of levels of connected hyperspaces or (b) the precision with which one metageometry is molded by another.

4.3.1. Biological generalization of metaorganization: nucleocortical structures as metagenerators. While the theoretical implications of the above proposals may be far-reaching, the immediate task is to systematically close the gap between experimental data and theory. This must be accomplished at the system, network, cellular and subcellular levels. Techniques of modeling neurons and neuronal networks[71,73] may be used to determine if network and system-level proposals are compatible with our knowledge of the physiology and biophysics of single elements. Initial checks of general theories as described above should actually be suggested by the proponents of such theories. First, the relation of nucleocortical CNS systems can be studied to determine whether the nuclear structures serve to embody the functional eigenvectors and eigenvalues of primary geometries or whether the cerebral cortical structures embody eigendyadic expansions implementing the secondary functional geometry as determined by the eigenvectors and eigenvalues. A particularly relevant possibility is that the thalamoneocortical and other similarly arranged neuronal networks could in fact be dynamically organized as proposed here for the olivocerebellar neuronal apparatus.

Second, because of its possible use in system-level research the limitations of the metaorganization principle also need to be pointed out by the proponents. As shown in section 3, the three neuronal networks of a sensorimotor mechanism could be established if the system was organized in a closed loop with regards to one physical invariant (in the example in section 3 the invariant was a physical displacement). This is, however, not the case for systems such as the vestibulo-ocular reflex.[79] There, although the motor metric can be organized by the metaorganization process, the sensorimotor transformation network and the last step, the sensory metric, cannot be similarly generated. Indeed while the oculomotor metric could in principle be generated by metaorganization,[78] since the extraocular muscle activity and its derived proprioception do represent the same invariant eye movement,[66] the CNS cannot use metaorganization to generate the full vestibulo-ocular reflex network, because eye movements cannot be detected by the vestibular apparatus. However, systems such as the vestibulo-ocular reflex can emerge from a hierarchy of primary sensorimotor systems, such as the vestibulo-collic reflex and retino-extraocular reflx.[79] Finally metaorganization can be used, as will be shown elsewhere, to generate the three sensorimotor networks in each primary system and a seventh network to tie the two closed reverberative primary mechanisms into a hierarchical sensorimotor architecture of the vestibulo-ocular reflex. Thus while the metaorganization principle and algorithm is applicable to quantitatively feature the development and function of some specific neuronal networks such

as the cerebellum, its ultimate use at other levels of CNS function remains largely unexplored at present.

Acknowledgements—This work was supported by grant NS 13742 from NINCDS. We thank Dr J. I. Simpson for his valuable discussions and reading of the manuscript. The authors also express their gratitude for all their colleagues (far too numerous to list here) who offered constructive criticism to tensor network theory.

Note added in proof:

After this work was accepted for publication, a paper appeared offering some remarks on the uses of tensor network theory [Arbib M. and Amari S. I. (1985) *J. theor. Biol.* **112**, 123–155]. While generally supportive and appreciative of the tensor approach and advocating its further use, the paper also raised five specific points of concern. These can be readily dealt with here as they are off the mark regarding the basic principles of tensor network theory and probably originate from a misunderstanding of our approach.

(1) "Modern mathematics has developed many techniques for coordinate-free analysis of structure. PL [Pellionisz and Llinás] write as if the use of tensor analysis were the only such technique". This remark is incorrect. The tensor approach was explicitly compared to other mathematical techniques, see chapter in Ref. 75 entitled "Comparison of tensor approach with other geometric theories: Representation, modeling, mapping, differential geometry, lie algebra".

(2) "PL speak of a CNS hyperspace F but never prove that F is a Riemannian manifold." This remark is based on a fundamental misunderstanding of tensor network theory. Indeed, engineering typically uses Cartesian tensors of Euclidean space; relativity uses tensors in Riemannian space. What we face, however, is not a duty to conform with previous scientific approaches but a challenge to create methods that conform with CNS function and thus we have proposed tensor analysis of brain hyperspaces. The important point to be understood here is that CNS hyperspaces need not be confined either to Euclidean or Riemannian geometry. The remark is also incomplete. The non-Euclidean character of the geometry has been demonstrated by a quantitative computer model; see section entitled "Position-dependent metric" of Fig. 5 in Ref. 81.

(3) In tensor network theory "every array of numbers must be the co-ordinates of either a covariant or contravariant vector . . . ." This is not so; for instance, the cerebellar nucleofugal vector [(i–e) in Fig. 2. of the above "Metaorganization" paper, or in Ref. 76] is neither co- nor contravariant. More to the point, we wrote in Ref. 84: the " . . . task is to establish whether the way of assigning the components to the invariant is a covariant or contravariant procedure". Once mathematical vectors have been assigned by a co- or contravariant method to an invariant, such arrays of numbers can, of course, be manipulated, e.g. by subtraction, so that the primary character of the original arrays is no longer evident.

(4) Tensor network theory "makes no use of tensor theory beyond the metaphorical use of the terms 'covariant', 'contravariant' and 'metric tensor' . . . ." This remark is incorrect. We have used multidimensional tensorial analyses of spacetime manifolds, tensor transformations by covariant embedding, quantitative exposition of the curved character of CNS hyperspaces, covariant–contravariant transformations by the Moore–Penrose-generalized inverse, contraction of tensors and network elaborations. Readers acquainted with some of our other twenty or so papers published on this subject (not cited by these authors) will be aware of these uses and developments.

(5) "The tensor theory is grounded in *no* data on cerebellar anatomy, physiology or function." This is clearly an oversight by our colleagues.

Naturally tensor network theory requires further elaboration, such as offered in the above "Metaorganization"

paper. The fact remains, however, that the introduction of non-orthogonal natural co-ordinates to describe sensorimotor transformations does seem to result in advancements in interpreting the anatomy, physiology and function of the CNS.

REFERENCES

1. Albert A. (1972) *Regression and the Moore–Penrose Pseudoinverse.* Academic Press, New York.
2. Altman J. (1972) Postnatal development of the cerebellar cortex in the rat. I–III. *J. comp. Neurol.* **145**, 353–514.
3. Amari S. I. (1983) Field theory of self-organizing neuronal nets. *IEEE Trans. Systems, Man Cybernetics*, SMC-13, Vol. **5**, 741–748.
4. Anderson J. A. and Mozer M. C. (1981) Categorization and selective neurons. In *Parallel Models of Associative Memory* (eds Hinton G. E. and Anderson J. A.). Lawrence Erlbaum Associates, New Jersey.
5. Anderson J. A., Silverstein J. W., Ritz S. A. and Randall S. J. (1977) Distinctive features, categorical perception and probability learning: some applications of a neuronal model. *Psychol. Rev.* **84**, 413–451.
6. Andrew A. M. P. (1969) Statistical theory and self-organization. In *Progress of Cybernetics*, Vol. 1. (ed. Rose J.), pp. 359–381. Gordon and Breach, London.
7. Amstrong D. M. (1974) Functional significance of connections of the inferior olive. *Physiol. Rev.* **54**, 358–417.
8. Beckoff A., Stein P. S. G. and Hamburger V. (1975) Coordinated motor output in the hindlimb of the 7-day chick embryo. *Proc. natn. Acad. Sci. U.S.A.* **72**, 1245–1248.
9. Ben-Israel A. and Greville T. N. E. (1980) *Generalized Inverses: Theory and Applications.* Robert E. Krieger Publ., New York.
10. Bloedel J. R., Dichgans J. and Precht W. (1984) *Cerebellar Functions.* Springer, Berlin.
11. Brogan W. L. (1974) *Modern Control Theory.* Quantum, New York.
12. Caianiello E. R. (1961) Outline of a theory of thought-processes and thinking machines. *J. theor. Biol.* **2**, 204–235.
13. Changeux J. P. and Danchin A. (1976) Selective stabilization of developing synapses as a mechanism for the specification of neuronal networks. *Nature* **264**, 705–712.
14. Coburn N. (1970) *Vector and Tensor Analysis.* Dover, New York.
15. Demer J. L. and Robinson D. A. (1982) Effects of reversible lesions and stimulation of olivocerebellar system on vestibuloocular reflex plasticity. *J. Neurophysiol.* **47**, 1084–1107.
16. Desclin J. C. (1974) Histological evidence supporting the inferior olive as the major source of cerebellar climbing fibers in rat. *Brain Res.* **77**, 365–384.
17. Ebner T. J., Qi-Xiang Yu and Bloedel J. R. (1983) Increases in Purkinje cell gain associated with naturally activated climbing fiber input. *J. Neurophysiol.* **50**, 205–219.
18. Eigen M. and Schuster P. (1978) The hypercycle: a principle of natural self-organization. B. The abstract hypercycle. *Naturwissenchaften* **65**, 7–41.
19. Einstein A. (1916) The foundation of the general theory of relativity. In *The Principle of Relativity* (ed. Sommerfeld A.), pp. 111–164. Dover, New York.
20. Foerster H., von and Zopf G. W. (1982) (eds) *Principles of Self-Organization.* Pergamon Press, Oxford.
21. Fossard A. and Guegueu C. (1977) *Multivariable System Control.* North-Holland, Amsterdam.
22. Goodman D. and Kelso J. A. S. (1983) Exploring the functional significance of physiological tremor: a bio-spectroscopic approach. *Expl Brain Res.* **49**, 419–431.
23. Gonshor A. and Melvill-Jones G. (1973) Changes of human vestibulo-ocular response induced by vision-reversal during head rotation. *J. Physiol., Lond.* **234**, 102–103.
24. Grissell R., Hodgson J. P. E. and Yanowich M. (eds) (1983) *Oscillations in Mathematical Biology, Lecture Notes in Biomathematics.* Springer, New York.
25. Grobstein P. and Comer C. (1983) The nucleus isthmi as an intertectal relay for the ipsilateral oculotectal projection in the frog *Rana pipiens. J. comp. Neurol.* **217**, 54–74.
26. Grossberg S. (1978) A theory of human memory: self-organization and performance of sensory-motor codes, maps and plans. In *Progress in Theoretical Biology*, Vol. 5 (eds Rosen R. and Snell F.), pp. 233–374. Academic Press, New York.
27. Grossberg S. (1979) Biological competition: decision rules, pattern formation, and oscillation. *Proc. natn. Acad. Sci., U.S.A.* **77**, 2338–2342.
28. Grossberg S. (1981) Adaptive resonance in development, perception and cognition. In *Mathematical Psychology and Psychophysiology* (ed. Grossberg S.), pp. 107–156. American Mathematics Society, Erlbaum Press, New Jersey.
29. Guthrie B. L., Porter J. D. and Sparks D. L. (1982) Role of extraocular muscular proprioception in eye movements studied by chronic deafferentation of intra-orbital structures. *Soc. Neurosci. Abstr.* **8**, 156.
30. Hamburger V. and Balaban M. (1963) Observations and experiments on spontaneous rhythmical behavior in the chick embryo. *Devl. Biol.* **7**, 533–545.
31. Hebb D. O. (1949) *The Organization of Behaviour.* John Wiley, New York.
32. Held R. (1968) Action contingent development in neonatal animals. In *Experience and Capacity* (ed. Kimble D. B.). New York Academy of Sciences, New York.
33. Holmes G. (1939) The cerebellum in man. *Brain* **63**, 1.
34. Ito M. (1970) Neurophysiological aspects of the cerebellar motor control system. *Int. J. Neurol.* **7**, 162–176.
35. Ito M. (1974) The control mechanism of cerebellar motor systems. In *The Neurosciences, IIIrd study program* (eds Schmitt F. O. and Worden F. G.), pp. 293–303. M.I.T. Press, Cambridge, MA.
36. Ito M. (1984) *The Cerebellum and Neural Control.* Raven Press, New York.
37. Ito M., Sakurai M., Tongroach P. (1982) Climbing fibre induced depression of both mossy fibre responsiveness and glutamate sensitivity of cerebellar Purkinje cells. *J. Physiol., Lond.* **324**, 113–134.
38. Ito M., Yoshida M., Obata K., Kawai N., Udo M. (1970) Inhibitory control of intracerebellar nuclei by the Purkinje cell axons. *Exp. Brain Res.* **10**, 64–80.

39. Jung R (1941) Physiologische Untersuchungen über den Parkinsontremor und andere Zitterformen beim Menschen. *Z. ges. Neurol. Psychiat.* **173**, 263–330.

40. Klein C. and Huang C. H. (1983) Review of pseudoinverse control for use with kinematically redundant manipulators *IEEE Trans. Systems, Man Cybernetics.* SMC-13, Vol. **3**, 245–250.

41. Kohonen T. (1972) Correlation matrix memories. *IEEE Trans. Comp.* Vol. C-21, 353–359.

42. Kohonen T. (1982) A simple paradigm for the self-organized formation of structured feature maps. In *Competition and Co-operation in Neural Nets.* Proceedings of the US–Japan joint seminar held at Kyoto, Japan, February 1982. Lecture Notes No. 45 (Managing ed. Levin S.; Amari S. and Arbib M. A.), Chap. 17, pp. 248–266. Springer, Berlin.

43. Kugler P. N., Scott Kelso J. A. and Turvey M. T. (1980) On the concept of coordinative structures and dissipative structures: I. Theoretical lines of convergence. In *Tutorials in Motor Behavior* (eds Stelmach G. E. and Requin J.), pp. 3–47. North-Holland, Amsterdam.

44. Larramendi L. M. H. (1969) Analysis of synaptogenesis in the cerebellum of the mouse. In *Neurobiology of Cerebellar Evolution and Development* (ed. Llinás R.), pp. 803–843. American Medical Association, Chicago.

45. Layton J. M. (1976) *Multivariable Control Theory.* P. Peregrinus, Stevenage.

46. Levi-Civita T. (1926) *The Absolute Differential Calculus (Calculus of Tensors)* (ed. Persico E.). Dover, New York.

47. Lisberger S. G. and Fuchs A. F. (1978) Role of primate flocculus during rapid behavioral modification of vestibuloocular reflex. I. Purkinje cell acting during visually guided horizontal smooth-pursuit eye movements and passive head rotation. *J. Neurophysiol.* **41**, 733–763.

48. Llinás R. (ed) (1969) *Neurobiology of Cerebellar Evolution and Development.* American Medical Association, Chicago, IL.

49. Llinás R. (1985) Possible role of tremor in the organization of the nervous system. In *Movement Disorders: Tremor,* (eds Findlay L. J. and Capildeo R.), pp. 473–478. Macmillan, London.

50. Llinás R. and Pellionisz A. (1984) La mente in quanto proprietà tensoriale dei circuiti cerebrali. In *Livelli di Realtà* (ed. Palmarini M. P.), pp. 191–198. Feltrinelli, Italy.

51. Llinás R. and Pellionisz A. (1985) Cerebellar function and the adaptive feature of the central nervous system. In *Reviews of Oculomotor Research* (eds Berthoz A. and Melvill-Jones G.), pp. 223–232. Elsevier, Amsterdam.

52. Llinás R. and Simpson J. I. (1981) Cerebellar control of movement. In *Handbook of Behavioral Neurobiology* (eds Towe A. L. and Luschei E. S.), Vol. V. *Motor Co-ordination,* pp. 231–302. Plenum Press, New York.

53. Llinás R. and Sugimori M. (1980) Electrophysiological properties of *in vitro* Purkinje cell somata in mammalian cerebellar slices. *J. Physiol., Lond.* **305**, 171–195.

54. Llinás R. and Volkind R. (1973) The olivo-cerebellar system: functional properties as revealed by harmaline-induced tremor. *Expl Brain Res.* **18**, 69–87.

55. Llinás R. and Yarom Y. (1981) Electrophysiology of mammalian inferior olivary neurones *in vitro.* Different types of voltage-dependent ionic conductances. *J. Physiol., Lond.* **315**, 549–567.

56. Llinás R. and Yarom Y. (1981) Properties and distribution of ionic conductances generating electroresponsiveness of mammalian inferior olivary neurones *in vitro. J. Physiol., Lond.* **315**, 569–584.

57. Llinás R., Yarom Y. and Sugimori M. (1981) The isolated mammalian brain *in vitro:* a new technique for the analysis of the electrical activity of neuronal circuit function. *Fedn Proc. Fedn Am. Socs exp. Biol.* **40**, 2240–2245.

58. Llinás R., Walton K., Hillman D. E. and Sotelo C. (1975) Inferior olive: its role in motor learning. *Science, N.Y.* **190**, 1230–1231.

59. Loeb G. E. and Hoffer J. A. (1981) Muscle spindle function during normal and perturbed locomotion in cats. In *Muscle Receptors and Movement* (eds Taylor A. and Prochatzka A.), pp. 219–228. Macmillan, London.

60. Lorente de Nó R. (1933) Vestibulo-ocular reflex arc. *Archs Neurol. Psychiat, Chicago* **30**, 245–291.

61. Maekawa K. and Simpson J. I. (1973) Climbing fiber responses evoked in vestibulo-cerebellum of rabbit from visual system. *J. Neurophysiol.* **36**, 649–666.

62. Malsburg C., von der (1973) Self-organization of orientation sensitive cells in the striate cortex. *Kybernetik* **14**, 85–100.

63. Melvill-Jones G. and Davies P. R. T. (1976) Adaptation of cat vestibulo-oclar reflex to 200 days of optically reversed vision. *Brain Res.* **103**, 551–554.

64. Mugnaini E. (1969) Ultrastructural studies on the cerebellar histogenesis. II. Maturation of nerve cell populations and establishment of synaptic connections in the cerebellar cortex of the chick. In *Neurobiology of Cerebellar Evolution and Development* (ed. Llinás R.), pp. 749–782. American Medical Association, Chicago, IL.

65. Oscarsson O. (1969) The saggital organization of the cerebellar anterior lobe as revealed by the projection patterns of the climbing fiber system. In *Neurobiology of Cerebellar Evolution and Development* (ed. Llinás R.), pp. 525–537. American Medical Association, Chicago, IL.

66. Ostriker G., Pellionisz A. and Llinás R. (1984) Tensorial computer movie display of the metaorganization of oculomotor metric network. *Soc. Neurosci. Abstr.* **10**, 162.

67. Ostriker G., Pellionisz A. and Llinás R. (1985) Tensorial computer model of gaze. I. Oculomotor activity is expressed with natural, non-orthogonal coordinates. *Neuroscience* **4**, 483–500.

68. Owens D. H. (1978) *Feedback and Multivariable Systems.* P. Peregrinus, Stevenage.

69. Palay S. L. and Chan-Palay V. (1974) *Cerebellar Cortex: Cytology and Organization.* Springer, Berlin.

70. Palay S. L. and Chan-Palay V. (eds) (1982) *The Cerebellum: New Vistas.* Springer, New York.

71. Pellionisz A. (1970) Computer simulation of the pattern transfer of large cerebellar neuronal fields. *Acta biochim. biophys. hung.* **5**, 71–79.

72. Pellionisz A. (1976) Proposal for shaping the dynamism of Purkinje cells by climbing fiber activation. *Brain Theory Newslett.* **2**, 2–6.

73. Pellionisz A. (1979) Modeling of neurons and neuronal networks. In *The Neurosciences, IV. Study Program* (eds Schmitt F. O. and Worden F. G.), pp. 525–550. M.I.T. Press, Cambridge, MA.

74. Pellionisz A. (1983) Sensorimotor transformations of natural coordinates via neuronal networks: Conceptual and formal unification of cerebellar and tectal models. In II. *Workshop on Visuomotor Co-ordination in Frog and Toad,* Mexico City, November 1982 (eds Lara R. and Arbib M. A.). COINS Technical Report, Amherst, MA.

75. Pellionisz A. (1983) Brain theory: connecting neurobiology to robotics. Tensor analysis: utilizing intrinsic coordinates to describe, understand and engineer functional geometries of intelligent organisms. *J. theor. Neurobiol.* **2**, 185–213.

76. Pellionisz A. (1984) Co-ordination: a vector-matrix description of transformations of overcomplete CNS coordinates and a tensorial solution using the Moore–Penrose generalized inverse. *J. theor. Biol.* **110**, 353–375.
77. Pellionisz A. (1984) Tensorial computer movie of the genesis and modification of cerebellar networks as dyadic expansions of the eigenvectors stored in the inferior olive. *Soc. Neurosci. Abstr.* **10**, 909.
78. Pellionisz A. (1985) Tensorial brain theory in cerebellar modelling. In *Cerebellar Functions* (eds Bloedel J. R., Dichgans J. and Precht W.), pp. 201–229. Springer, Berlin.
79. Pellionisz A. (1985) Tensorial aspects of the multidimensional approach to the vestibulo-oculomotor reflex and gaze. In *Reviews of Oculomotor Research—I. Adaptive Mechanisms in Gaze Control* (eds Berthoz A. and Melvill-Jones G.), pp. 281–296. Elsevier, Amsterdam.
80. Pellionisz A. and Llinás R. (1979) Brain modeling by tensor network theory and computer simulation. The cerebellum: distributed processor for predictive coordination. *Neuroscience* **4**, 323–348.
81. Pellionisz A. and Llinás R (1980) Tensorial approach to the geometry of brain function: cerebellar co-ordination via metric tensor. *Neuroscience* **5**, 1125–1136.
82. Pellionisz A. and Llinás R. (1981) Genesis and modification of the geometry of CNS hyperspace. Cerebellar space-time metric tensor and "motor learning". *Soc. Neurosci. Abstr.* **7**, 641.
83. Pellionisz A. and Llinás R. (1982) Space-time representation in the brain. The cerebellum as a predictive space-time metric tensor. *Neuroscience* **7**, 2949–2970.
84. Pellionisz A. and Llinás R. (1982) Tensor theory of brain function. The cerebellum as a space-time metric. In *Competition and Co-operation in Neural Nets*. Proceedings of the US–Japan joint seminar held at Kyoto, Japan, February 1982. Lecture Notes No. 45 (managing ed. Levin S.; eds Amari S. and Arbib M. A.), Chap. 23, pp. 394–417. Springer, Berlin.
85. Pellionisz A. and Szentàgothai J. (1973) Dynamic single unit simulation of a realistic cerebellar network model. *Brain Res.* **49**, 83–99.
86. Pellionisz A., Ostriker G. and Llinás R. (1983) Generation and modification of neuronal networks acting as metric tensors: a computer demonstration of the process of organizing sensorimotor transformations. *Soc. Neurosci. Abstr.* **9**, 310.
87. Pettofrezzo A. J. (1966) *Matrices and Transformations*. Dover, New York.
88. Ramón y Cajal S. (1971) *Histologie du Systeme Nerveux de l'Homme et des Vertebres*, Vol. II. Maloine, Paris.
89. Simpson J. I. and Pellionisz A. (1984) The vestibulo-ocular reflex in rabbit as interpreted using the Moore–Penrose generalized inverse transformation of intrinsic coordinates. *Soc. Neurosci. Abstr.* **10**, 909.
90. Simpson J. I., Graf W. and Leonard C. (1981) The coordinate system of visual climbing fibers to the flocculus. in *Progress in Oculomotor Research* (eds Fuchs A. and Becker W.), pp. 475–484. Elsevier North-Holland, Amsterdam.
91. Sneider D. M., Steeg M. and Young F. H. (1982) *Linear Algebra*. Macmillan, New York.
92. Sotelo C. (1975) Anatomical, physiological and biochemical studies of the cerebellum from mutant mice. II. Morphological study of cerebellar cortical neurons and circuits in the weaver mouse. *Brain Res.* **94**, 19–44.
93. Sotelo C., Llinás R. and Baker R (1974) Structural study of inferior olivary nucleus of the morphological correlates of electronic coupling. *J. Neurophysiol.* **37**, 541–559.
94. Synge J. L. and Schild A. (1949) *Tensor Calculus*. Dover, New York.
95. Szentàgothai J. (1984) Downward causation? *A. Rev. Neurosci.* **7**, 1–11.
96. Taub E. (1977) Movement in nonhuman primates deprived of somatosensory feedback. In *Exercise and Sports Sciences Review* (ed. Keegh J. F.), Vol. 4, pp. 335–374. Journal Publishing Affiliates, Santa Barbara.
97. Taylor A. and Prochazka A. (1981) (eds) *Muscle Receptors and Movement*. Macmillan, London.
98. Temple G. (1960) *Cartesian Tensors*. John Wiley, New York.
99. Turing A. M. (1948) Intelligent machinery. *Rep. natn. phys. Lab., Teddington*.
100. Wiener N. (1948) *Cybernetics or Control and Communication in the Animal and in the Machine*. M.I.T. Press, Cambridge, MA.
101. Wrede R. C. (1972) *Introduction to Vector and Tensor Analysis*. Dover, New York.
102. Yovits M. C., Jacobi E. T. and Goldstein G. D. (eds) (1962) *Self-Organizing Systems*. Spartan Books, Washington, D.C.

(*Accepted* 3 *May* 1985)

21
Introduction

(1987)
Christine A. Skarda and Walter J. Freeman

How brains make chaos in order to make sense of the world
Behavioral and Brain Sciences 10: 161–195

Walter Freeman and his collaborators have worked on understanding the operation of olfactory bulb and prepyriform cortex for nearly 30 years. During that time he pioneered the application of systems analysis to neurobiology, proposed a series of biologically based network models, and, in this paper, he and Christine Skarda discuss and review an important and original model for olfactory function based on the theory of chaos.

The journal in which the paper appeared deserves comment. Scientific journals primarily publish papers for the archives. However the editor of *Behavioral and Brain Sciences*, Stevan Harnad, founded the journal to provoke discussion about important ideas in cognitive science and neuroscience. The mechanism Harnad uses is to invite interested parties to provide short comments on a manuscript. The paper, the comments on it, and the response of the author to the commentators are published simultaneously in the journal. *Behavioral and Brain Sciences* can be exciting reading, and the exchanges between the authors of the paper and the commentators are often more illuminating than the original paper would be by itself. At its best, this journal can provide a unique snapshot of current thinking on the subject.

The approach described by Freeman and Skarda has a number of unusual features. Most of the physiology and analysis involves the dynamics of gross electrical potentials such as the EEG (electroencephalograph), and not the behavior of single units. In neuroscience EEG recordings have been viewed with suspicion for decades because in many cases it is hard to determine their origin, they are extremely noisy, and the connection between single-unit information processing and the EEG is unclear. However, the sophisticated experimental work using gross potentials reviewed in this paper may indicate an imminent return of the EEG to respectability.

Freeman and his collaborators use the olfactory system of the rabbit as their preparation. They present an animal with odors, associate particular odors with conditioned responses, and study the electrical responses of the nervous system. The olfactory bulb and prepyriform cortex form a structure with a simple and regular anatomy, and many of the details of the connections between cells have been determined. The olfactory receptors project in parallel to the bulb, where they are believed to generate different spatial patterns of activation for different odors; odor is a paradigm for a distributed sensory system.

Gross potentials in the range between about 10 and 160 Hz are recorded by an array of 64 electrodes, which covers a fair fraction of the animal's olfactory bulb. Single units are *not* recorded. The connection between single units and the observed gross potentials comes from previous experimental work that determined that the EEG can be related to the postsynaptic potentials of various cell types. Looking at many locations simultaneously shifted emphasis to the study of the spatial aspects of information processing by many cells and away from what has been called "microelectrode myopia" where there is a detailed study of the behavior of a single cell at a time.

Information processing by the olfactory bulb generates as output neural activity patterns where "every neuron in the bulb participated in every olfactory discriminative response." The "odorant specific information was found to exist in the spatial patterns of the amplitude of the waveform of an oscillation of EEG potential that was common to all 64 channels."

Although the idea that a spatially distributed activity pattern is both the input and the processed output of a neural network should cause little disturbance to those familiar with current neural network research, it should be appreciated that the theory sketched in this paper is both radical and unfamiliar to many neuroscientists. However the authors also go considerably beyond what is by now traditional in neural net research. Freeman has been concerned with the temporal dynamics of the nervous system since early in his career. The circuitry of the bulb and prepyriform cortex form a complex feedback network with massive amounts of excitation and inhibition. There are many possibilities for instability. The olfactory system, like other parts of cortex, is biased off by inhibition. In the absence of inputs and arousal, there is little activity. However, when the olfactory system functions to make discriminations, large oscillations in the EEG are seen.

Skarda and Freeman suggest that the oscillatory behavior is due to the operation of a complex dynamical system, generated by the neural interconnections, that is controlling odor discriminations. There are a number of neural network models that form simple dynamical systems. Although nonlinear dynamical systems can be very complex in detail, they can often be *qualitatively* described more simply. For example, most energy-minimizing models contain *point attractors*, and the final state of the system is one of a number of stable points. This kind of one-shot computation is easy to analyze, but the whole system must be reset to perform another operation. The real nervous system must operate in continuous time, and the dynamics must, of necessity, be much more complex. A more complex qualitative behavior is a *limit cycle*, where the state of the system oscillates in a fixed pattern. If the limit cycle is an attractor, starting points outside the limit cycle are attracted into it as the system evolves in time.

Skarda and Freeman suggest that the dynamics of the olfactory computation are *chaotic*. There has been a great deal of interest in chaos recently, including a good popular book (Gleick 1987) that became a surprise best-seller. Chaotic behavior is *not* random, but it is not predictable either, and many of the statistics of a chaotic system look statistically like noise. Often the behavior of a dynamical system can be controlled by a small number of control parameters, for example, gains in a neural system. When the known (and some inferred) connections in the olfactory system are put in place in a simplified block diagram of the major structures, the resulting dynamical system can show behavior ranging from silence to chaotic limit cycle oscillation (that is, quasi-periodic oscillation) to "epileptic seizures," depending on just a few parameters. The activity of the simulated system looks, qualitatively, like the different modes recorded in the real olfactory system.

Skarda and Freeman suggest that inhalation causes these control parameters to change the qualitative behavior of the dynamical system from off to a state where there are a number of potential limit cycle attractors and then back again to off. Each attractor corresponds to a learned odor. The inhaled odor drives the state of the system into one of the attractors. The odor analysis cycle is linked to inhalation, so when the inhalation is over, the control parameters change so as to erase the potential attractors and prepare the system for the next inhalation-classification cycle.

Limit cycle attractors can be learned by a Hebbian synaptic modification rule, forming what Skarda and Freeman call a *nerve cell assembly* (NCA), named after Hebb's cell assemblies, a mutually reinforcing group of connected cells that tends to act as a whole in retrieval. In one of the more vivid scientific images in our memory, Skarda and Freeman refer to the nerve cell assembly as "a filamentous network in the bulb resembling mold growing on a piece of bread." When part of the nerve cell assembly is activated, it tends to activate the rest and thereby determines which attractor characterizes the final system state. (As some of the commentators point out, this could be viewed as an example of the pattern completion properties of associative neural networks of many kinds, though Skarda and Freeman might disagree.)

Many, though not all, aspects of the model and its behavior have been tested. As Skarda and Freeman put it, the experimental data are merely a "small clearing in a large forest." The underlying network theory, though remarkably well developed, is still early in its history. But the authors make extensive use of ideas that surely will characterize the future of biologically based neural network research: first, great emphasis on spatial and system-wide interactions and, second, use of the qualitative mathematics of complex temporally evolving dynamical systems.

We will forgo the opportunity to comment on the *BBS* comments except to observe that, like criticism in general, some is constructive, some is destructive, some is informative, some misses the point entirely, and some is self-serving. Assignment of commentaries to categories is left to the readers.

Reference

J. Gleick (1987), *Chaos: Making a New Science*. New York: Viking.

(1987)
Christine A. Skarda and Walter J. Freeman

How brains make chaos in order to make sense of the world
Behavioral and Brain Sciences 10: 161–195

Abstract: Recent "connectionist" models provide a new explanatory alternative to the digital computer as a model for brain function. Evidence from our EEG research on the olfactory bulb suggests that the brain may indeed use computational mechanisms like those found in connectionist models. In the present paper we discuss our data and develop a model to describe the neural dynamics responsible for odor recognition and discrimination. The results indicate the existence of sensory- and motor-specific information in the spatial dimension of EEG activity and call for new physiological metaphors and techniques of analysis. Special emphasis is placed in our model on chaotic neural activity. We hypothesize that chaotic behavior serves as the essential ground state for the neural perceptual apparatus, and we propose a mechanism for acquiring new forms of patterned activity corresponding to new learned odors. Finally, some of the implications of our neural model for behavioral theories are briefly discussed. Our research, in concert with the connectionist work, encourages a reevaluation of explanatory models that are based only on the digital computer metaphor.

Keywords: brain theory; chaos; cognitivism; connectionism; EEG; nonlinear dynamics; olfaction; perception; sensation

1. Introduction

To understand brain function we need to know how the sensory systems process their information. Recent connectionist models provide an interesting explanatory alternative to earlier information-processing models based on the digital computer that viewed neurons as two-state logical decision elements organized into networks to compute simple Boolean functions. In the present article we outline the results of experiments in our laboratory that demonstrate the existence of sensory- and motor-specific information in the spatial dimension of EEG activity in the central nervous system. On the basis of our data we develop an explanatory model of the neural states responsible for sensory encoding; this model departs significantly from alternatives patterned after digital computers and it converges with recent connectionist models in the computational principles it uses. We suggest, however, that brains rely on mechanisms not found in other models; we propose four such mechanisms that may be necessary to solve problems critical to the efficient functioning and survival of any system that has to behave adaptively in an environment subject to unpredictable and often violent fluctuations.

Special emphasis is placed in our model on "chaotic" brain activity.[1] We propose that the brain relies on chaotic as opposed to steady or random activity for several purposes: Chaos constitutes the basic form of collective neural activity for all perceptual processes and functions as a controlled source of noise, as a means to ensure continual access to previously learned sensory patterns, and as the means for learning new sensory patterns.

2. Methodological considerations

How does a sensory system process information? Models based on the digital computer define computation as a physical operation governed by the substates of the parts of the system as defined by rules operating on symbol tokens in virtue of their formal syntactic structure corresponding to real physical differences in the system. The formal elements or symbols are required to be discrete – that is, context independent; each distinct semantic property must be associated with a distinct physical property (Pylyshyn 1984, pp. 50, 74).

For many years physiologists have applied the computational model when interpreting their data. Thus, they found that the "code" of peripheral sensory systems is based on "labeled lines" (Bullock & Horridge 1965, p. 274); the quality of a stimulus is conveyed by the selection of one or more axons from the immense number available, and the intensity is conveyed by the number of action potentials per unit time on each axon. This model worked for peripheral motor systems and for some parts of central nervous systems, to the extent that "feature detector" and "command" neurons could be identified. However, the search for this kind of information-processing scheme in the case of central associative functions has not been successful (Barlow 1972: Perkel & Bullock 1968).

Our attempt to understand information processing in olfaction was based on three premises. (1) When an animal that is conditioned to discriminate between two odorant stimuli inhales one of them (a conditioned stimulus [CS]) and then responds correctly (with a conditioned response [CR]), there will exist, somewhere and for some time during the interval between the onsets of the CS and CR, some odor-specific information in the olfactory bulb to serve as the basis for the correct CR. (2) This information will be encoded in the form of a space–time pattern of neural activity for each odorant CR. (3) These patterns will be manifested, however indirectly, in the electroencephalographic (EEG) potentials recorded from the bulbar surface. After 12 years of search we at last identified some of the postulated patterns (Freeman & Viana Di Prisco 1986a). The results were beyond surprising; they took us so far outside the range of our previous expectations that we had no physiological metaphors with which to pin them down, and we had to draw on some new and fascinating fields of mathematics and physics in order to understand their implications.

In principle the experiments were simple. Thirsty rabbits were conditioned (Viana Di Prisco & Freeman 1985) to lick (CR+) in response to an odorant (CS+) followed after 2 seconds by delivery of water, and merely to sniff (CR−) in response to an unreinforced odorant (CS−). Each rabbit had an array of 64 electrodes implanted permanently onto the lateral surface of the left olfactory bulb. The 64 EEG traces were amplified, filtered, and measured in brief time epochs within each trial; when made with adequate safeguards (Freeman 1987b) these measurements from collections of trials served to classify EEG epochs into groups both with respect to CSs and with respect to CRs. The odorant-specific information was found to exist in the spatial patterns of the amplitude of the waveform of an oscillation of EEG potential that was common to all 64 channels and, by inference, to the entire bulb. We concluded that every neuron in the bulb participated in every olfactory discriminative response because they all participated in the oscillation. All that distinguished one odorant EEG pattern from another was the spatial configuration of the average intensity over an event time window at the common frequency, in the manner that patterns of monochromatic light are distinguished from each other by shades of gray. Local variations in phase, amplitude modulation, frequency modulation, and other aspects of the 64 traces were not found to contain odorant-specific information.

With regard to our first premise (that odor-specific information must exist in the bulb), we chose to study the olfactory system because it is the simplest and phylogenetically the most stable and representative of sensory systems, is the best understood in its structure and function, and can be studied in its earlier stages without directly involving the brain stem and thalamus. We selected the rabbit because its head is sufficiently large to support the electrical connectors needed for chronic implantation and recording from 64 channels, yet the bulb is sufficiently small so that the electrode array forms a window covering a substantial portion of its surface area (20% in the rabbit, as opposed to 6% in the cat; Freeman 1978). We used appetitive conditioning so as to have distinguishable behavioral responses from each animal: licking with or without sniffing to the CS+ (CR+) and sniffing alone to the CS− (CR−). We found that high relative frequencies of occurrence for these autoshaped CRs (naturally occurring motor activity patterns) emerged within a very few trials in the first session, that they were stably maintained for numerous sessions, and that they were subject to quantitative assay with ease and reliability (Freeman 1981; Viana Di Prisco & Freeman 1985).

3. Neurophysiological results

3.1. Spatial analysis of neural activity. With regard to our second premise (that the odor-specific information is encoded as space–time patterns of activity), the set of chemoreceptor neurons in the nose and the set of mitral cells in the bulb to which they send their axons (Figure 1) both exist in the form of a sheet. Evidence from measurements of receptor unit activity, the electro-olfactogram, and odorant absorption to the mucosa upon stimulation with odorants show that receptor cells sensitive to a particular odorant are clustered nonuniformly in density in the mucosa, and that their spatial patterns of activation differ for differing odorants (reviewed in Moulton 1976:

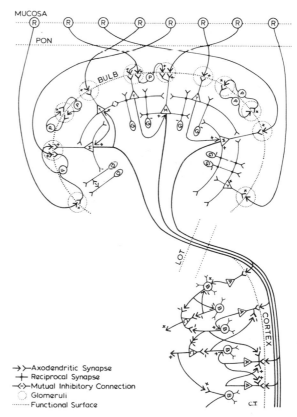

Figure 1.   Schematic diagram of the main cell types and their interconnections in the olfactory bulb and prepyriform cortex: R, receptor; PON, primary olfactory nerve; LOT, lateral olfactory tract; M, mitral cell; G, granule cell; P, periglomerular cell; A, superficial pyramidal cell; B, granule cell; C, deep pyramidal cell. From Freeman (1972).

Freeman & Skarda 1985). The projection of the primary olfactory nerve (PON) onto the bulb has a degree of topographic order. Studies with 2-deoxyglucose (2-DOG) accumulation in the bulb after 45 minutes of exposure to an odorant show uneven clustering of dense patches in the outer (glomerular) layer of the bulb, indicating that a spatial pattern of receptor activity may result in a spatial pattern of neural activity in the bulb, which might in turn transmit odor-specific information to the olfactory cortex. However, metabolic studies cannot reveal the dynamic form of that neural activity in time periods on the order of 0.1 sec.

With regard to our third premise (that the odor-specific information is manifested in the EEG), single neurons in the receptor layer, bulb, and cortex respond selectively to test arrays of odorants at various concentrations. The variability and overlap of response profiles involving multiple odorants are high at all steps of the olfactory system, there being no indication that more centrally located neurons are more "narrowly tuned" to odorants than are receptors. The number and even the existence of "primary odors" analogous to colors or tastes are unknown.

Our early attempts to demonstrate spatial patterns of bulbar unit activity in responses to odorants were based on simultaneous multi-unit extracellular recording from 10 microelectrodes; the spatial sample was too small, and the time required to collect a sample (several minutes) was much too long. We turned to EEG recording from the bulbar surface because we had found a close statistical relationship in time and space between the amplitude of the EEG potential at selected points on the bulbar surface and the firing rates of mitral and tufted cells located at depths of several hundred microns below those points. That is, the surface EEG (Figure 2), consisting largely of extracellular compound postsynaptic potentials of granule cells, the dominant inhibitory interneurons deep within the bulb (Figure 1), provided indirect access to a spatial image of the locally averaged mitral cell activity patterns that constituted the bulbar output to the olfactory cortex. The theory and experimental evidence for this inference, including volume conductor theory and studies of the dynamics of bulbar neurons, have been compiled in a monograph (Freeman 1975) to which the interested reader is referred.

Measurements of the spatial spectrum of the bulbar EEG (Freeman 1980; Freeman & Baird, in press) were used to fix the optimal intervals between electrodes in arrays (the spatial digitizing increment) at 0.5 mm, corresponding to a Nyquist frequency of 1.0 c/mm. An 8 × 8 array gave a "window" onto the bulb of about 3.5 × 3.5 mm, given the restriction to 64 channels. Measurements of the temporal spectrum of the rabbit EEG indicated that the range of greatest interest was 20–90 Hz. Filters were set at 10 and 160 Hz; the temporal digitizing increment at 2 msec gave a Nyquist frequency of 250 Hz. A fixed duration of 76 msec was adopted as the minimum for the bulbar response on single inhalations, so that measurement of a single unaveraged event upon inhalation of an odorant or the background air for control consisted of 64 × 38 time values, digitized at 12 bits with retention of the 8 most significant bits. Each trial yielded 3 control events and 3 test odor events. Each session yielded 10 CS+ and 10 CS− trials, constituting 120

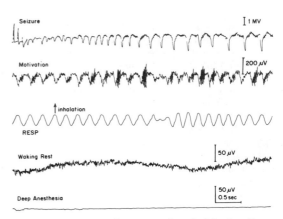

Figure 2. Four classes of states are identified for the olfactory system from EEG traces. Fluctuations are suppressed under deep anesthesia (lowest trace). In waking but unmotivated animals the amplitude is low and the trace is irregular and unpredictable. Under motivation the irregular activity is interrupted by brief oscillatory bursts following activation of the olfactory bulb by receptors on inhalation. Under several seconds of intense electrical stimulation of the LOT (top trace) an epileptic seizure is released. It is initiated after the failure of excitatory input transmission as shown by the decreasing responses at left to the last 5 pulses of the stimulus train. The seizure spike train then progressively emerges from a relatively quiet post-stimulus state. From Freeman (1987a).

events. The data base for the study comprised 18 sessions with each of 5 rabbits after a familiarization period.

Acquisition of these data required 64 preamplifiers, a high-speed multiplexer and ADC, and a dedicated computer (Perkin Elmer 3220) and disc. The limiting factor on data acquisition proved to be the core-to-disc data transfer rate with double buffering during the 6-second trial periods. Procedures were devised for off-line editing and artifact rejection (Freeman & Schneider 1982), temporal filtering and decomposition (Freeman & Viana Di Prisco 1986b), spatial filtering and deconvolution (Freeman 1980; Freeman & Baird, in press), and multivariate statistical analysis of the results of measurement (Freeman & Grajski, in press; Grajski, Breiman, Viana Di Prisco & Freeman, in press). The procedures are reviewed elsewhere in detail (Freeman 1987b).

The measurement process consisted of curve-fitting of the 64 traces in each event. A set of 5 elementary waveforms or basis functions was identified as common to all 64 traces in varying degree. The sum of these 5 basis functions was fitted by regression to each trace, yielding 5 matrices of 64 amplitude values that incorporated 80% of the total variance of the event, as well as the matrix of residuals and the two matrices of the residues of high- and low-pass digital filtering, all expressed as root mean square amplitudes. Evaluation consisted of determining which of these 8 matrices best served (or served at all) to classify events correctly with respect to CSs and CRs. No data were discarded until they were tested in this way. Moreover, the coefficients of the basis functions were examined to determine whether they contained odorant-specific information.

The end results were unequivocal. The matrices of amplitude of the dominant basis function (the one containing the largest fraction of total power), and only these, sufficed to classify events correctly. They did so at far above chance levels with respect to the two odorants in 4 of the 5 rabbits, who discriminated them behaviorally, but not the events recorded from the fifth rabbit, who failed to discriminate them (Freeman & Grajski, in press; Freeman & Viana Di Prisco 1986b; Grajski et al., in press).

An example of an event (unaveraged traces) is shown in Figure 3. The key property is that every trace had the same temporal waveform. Exceptions were due either to artifacts or to electrodes not placed on the bulb. The amplitude differed between channels so as to form a spatial pattern that (on the average) was relatively constant and easily identified with each animal. These amplitude patterns after familiarization remained constant unless and until odorant conditioning was undertaken. New patterns emerged only in association with reinforced odorants, not visual or auditory CSs or UCSs alone. They remained stable within sessions and across sessions provided the S-R contingencies were unchanged.

Multiple patterns emerged under discriminative conditioning. When a new odorant CS+ was introduced or when a previous CS+ was changed to a CS−, the entire set of spatial patterns appeared to change. The amount of change between stages that involved an altered S-R contingency, when measured as a fraction of the total between-session, within-stage variance, was relatively small (7%). The information in these stable spatial patterns that served to classify events correctly with respect to CSs and CRs was not localizable to subsets of channels. That is, the information density (as distinct from content) was spatially homogeneous, much as a letter-space on a printed page is of equal value whether it contains a letter, a punctuation mark, or no character at all.

3.2. The appearance of background activity. It is our belief that this is the first demonstration of the existence of sensory- and motor-specific information in the spatial dimensions of the EEG activity in any part of the cerebral cortex. The reason this has not been shown before is that

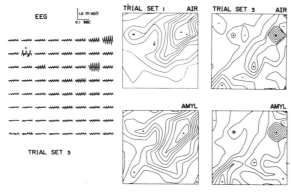

Figure 3. Left: A display of single unaveraged EEG traces is shown comprising a single odor burst among 10 bursts in a file from one trial set. The (x) marks an example of a bad channel record that was replaced during editing by an average of two adjacent records. Right: The root mean square amplitudes are compared for bursts without odor (above, "air") and with an odor (below, "amyl" acetate). There is a significant difference between the two patterns on the left but not the two on the right. From Freeman and Schneider (1982).

problems had to be solved at all levels of the project. These included practical problems such as array design and manufacture, surgical implantation, control and measurement of rabbit behavior, management of data flows on the order of 1.2 million bits per trial and several billion bits in each series of experiments, and basic theoretical problems in diverse fields including volume conductor analysis, statistical mechanics, nonequilibrium thermodynamics, nonlinear dynamics, and multivariate statistics applied to neural activity. The manufacture of arrays of electrodes, magnetic pick-ups, or optical probes and their preamplifiers merely opens the floodgates for the data. The difficult problems begin with the adaptation of recording to the conditions of normal, learned behavior, and with the rational design of algorithms for data reduction and refinement. Our methods happen to be the first that succeeded; there being no precedents, we have no other data with which to compare our results. Just as we have pioneered in their acquisition, we must now break new ground in attempting to understand what they tell us about brain function.

The elemental phenomenon that must be dealt with in olfaction, as in all of brain physiology, is the background activity manifested in the "spontaneous" EEG (Figure 2) and unit activity of neurons throughout the CNS. How does it arise, and what roles does it play? This activity is exceedingly robust; it survives all but the most drastic insults to cerebral tissue, such as near-lethal anesthesia, ischemia, or hypoxia. Perhaps the only reliable way to suppress it without killing the tissue is to isolate surgically small slabs of cortex (Burns 1958) by cutting neural connections while preserving the blood supply (and even then it may not be completely abolished). This procedure works for both the bulb and the prepyriform cortex (Freeman 1986), provided they are isolated from each other as well as from receptors and the rest of the brain. Under complete surgical transection of neural connections but with sufficient circulation for viability, each structure goes "silent" except when it is electrically or chemically stimulated. When perturbed and then left alone each structure generates a response and again falls silent. The responses to electrical impulse stimuli are observed through averaged evoked potentials (AEPs) and post-stimulus time histograms (PSTHs) of action potentials.

The state of a dynamic structure is said to be stable if the system returns to that state after perturbation. If the basal state is steady and nonoscillating, the system is said to be at an equilibrium. When the values of amplitude or energy are plotted on a graph, one against another, a response has the appearance of a curve or trajectory that ends at a point as the system goes to equilibrium. The same point is reached from many starting conditions under perturbation. Hence the point is said to represent an "attractor," and the set of starting conditions defines a "basin" for the attractor (Figure 4). When the system is placed by control of its input into the basin of an attractor, the system dynamics is said to be governed by the attractor.

When the stable equilibrium state of the bulb (Figure 2, bottom trace) or cortex is induced by deep anesthesia (Freeman 1986) or by cryogenic blockade of the axonal connections between the bulb and prepyriform cortex (Gray 1986) it is reversible. As recovery takes place the

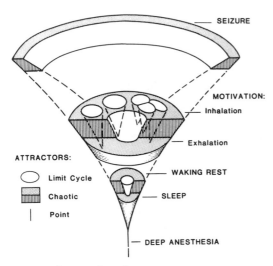

Figure 4. This vase-shaped structure is an attempt to portray a state space diagram for olfactory dynamics. The two horizontal dimensions constitute the axes for the amplitudes of activity of an excitatory subset and an inhibitory subset. The vertical axis serves to represent a bifurcation parameter, in this case the average level of driving input to the two subsets, consisting of input from centripetal activation of receptors and the input from centrifugal projection relating to arousal and motivation. The lowermost line represents an equilibrium or point attractor. Shaded areas represent a chaotic attractor, and the open circles represent limit cycle attractors. The activity for each stage is shown in Figure 2. A phase portrait derived from this diagram is shown in Figure 11. From Freeman (1987a).

background activity reappears; the system can be said to "bifurcate" or change to a new state, such that the point attractor is replaced by a point "repellor" (Figure 4). A repellor is manifested when attempts to quash or inhibit activity fail or succeed only transiently. The interconnected structures, the bulb and prepyriform cortex, cannot stay at equilibrium and must enter ceaseless activity, even if they are only connected to each other and not to the rest of the brain (Freeman 1987a). A bifurcation takes place when the system undergoes a major transition in its dynamics, equivalent to, for example, the transition from sleep to waking, or from normal to seizure activity. The governing equations are the same, but the solutions change radically. We say that the control of the system dynamics is shifted from a point attractor to a chaotic attractor. This simply means that the system falls into a condition of restless, but bounded, activity. It is stationary in the statistical sense, but its mathematical properties differ from those of "noise" (Grassberger & Procaccia 1983).

This background activity is statistically indistinguishable from what we call band-limited noise – that is, white noise passed through a band pass filter. We had known for years that the interval histograms of spike trains from single neurons conform to a Poisson process with a refractory period, so we had inferred that the background EEG was a local average of the dendritic potentials reflecting or governing the spike trains, a kind of "Brownian motion." In seeming confirmation of this view the correlation coefficient between pairs of traces fell with increasing

distance between their recording sites. From our recent studies we now know that this view was incorrect. The instantaneous frequency of bulbar EEG activity is always and everywhere the same, no matter how "noisy" the waveform may seem. The inverse relation of correlation with distance is due to small but systematic phase gradients extending over the entire bulb (Freeman & Baird, in press) and not to statistical independence of the samples. The commonality of waveform does not extend outside the bulb, but does extend over distances of several mm within it, much too far to be accounted for by volume conduction. The bulbar EEG is a global property that arises from dense feedback interactions within the bulb and yet is conditioned or made possible by extra-bulbar feedback interactions.

3.3. Evidence for chaos. An explanation of the neural mechanism of the background activity stemmed from our use of an assay, the Grassberger–Procaccia (1983) algorithm, to measure the degrees of freedom (the Hausdorff dimension) of a prolonged sample of the EEG from our animals at rest. Preliminary estimates ranged between 4 and 7 (Freeman 1987b), indicating that the activity reflected not "noise" but chaos (see note 1). This crucial distinction is analogous to the difference between the noise of a crowd at a ball game and the noise of a family dispute. Chaos is indistinguishable from random noise in appearance and in statistical properties, but it is deterministic and not stochastic (Garfinkel 1983; Rössler 1983). It has relatively small degrees of freedom; it can be turned on and off virtually instantaneously, as with a switch, through bifurcation (see sect. 3.2), unlike thermal noise, for example, which requires relatively slow heating and cooling. Chaos is controlled noise with precisely defined properties. Any system that needs random activity can get it more cheaply and reliably from a chaotic generator than from a noise source. Even the random number generators of digital computers are algorithms for chaos; given the same seed, sequences of random numbers are precisely replicated.

In order to replicate the EEGs of the olfactory system,

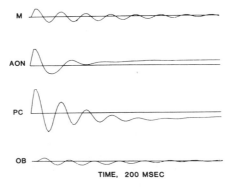

Figure 5. Impulse responses of the neural sets simulated for M (mitral unit activity), A of the AON (EEG), E of the PC (EEG), and G of the OB (EEG activity). The internal gains, k_{ee}, k_{ei}, and k_{ii}, are: OB (0.25, 1.50, 1.50, 1.80); AON (1.50, 1.50, 1.50, 1.80); PC (0.25, 1.40, 1.40, 1.80). The nonzero equilibria are not detectable with AEPs; the negative value for the PC is consistent with the silence of the PC after section of the LOT through the AON. From Freeman (1986).

we used sets of nonlinear ordinary differential equations that had already been used separately to model the bulb, anterior olfactory nucleus (AON), and prepyriform cortex (PC) with respect to their averaged evoked potentials (Figure 5). We coupled them into an interactive network (Figure 6). With proper settings of the feedback gains and distributed delays in accordance with our understanding of the anatomy and physiology of the larger system, the model yielded sustained chaotic activity that was statistically indistinguishable from the background EEG of resting animals (Figure 7). Under conditions of simulated receptor input the model generated "bursts" of oscillation that closely resembled those events seen in olfactory EEGs (Figure 8) during inhalation.

With some minor changes in gains between the bulb and AON the model system entered a degenerate state

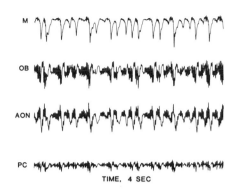

Figure 7. Examples of chaotic background activity generated by the model, simulating bulbar unit activity (M) and the EEGs of the OB, AON, and PC. Q_m = 5.0, k_{ME} = 1.5, k_{EG} = 0.67. k_{EP} = 1.0, k_{PM} = 0.1, k_{MA} = 1.0, k_{EA} = 1.5, k_{AI} = 1.0, k_{AP} = 1.0

with a Hausdorff dimension near 2, manifesting a repetitive spike (Figure 2) that very closely resembled an epileptiform spike train that accompanied an electrically induced olfactory seizure (Figure 9). This phenomenon offered one means of studying the transition from a stable point attractor to a chaotic attractor (Babloyantz & Destexhe 1986) (Figure 4). We did this by increasing an excitatory gain connection in the model (k_{PM} in Figure 10, between sets P and M in Figure 6). This yielded the Ruelle-Takens-Newhouse route to chaos (Schuster 1984). The chaotic attractor of the "seizure" state of the model was a 2-torus; the chaotic attractor of a normal hyperchaotic background activity was much higher in dimension, and its geometric structure remained unknown. These results, which represent the first successful simulation of normal and abnormal EEG activity, and the experimental evidence supporting the mathematical model (Freeman 1987a) are reviewed elsewhere (Freeman 1986).

Given this broad picture of the dynamics of this neural system (Figures 2, 3, and 4) we can sketch a metaphorical picture of its multiple stable states in terms of a phase portrait. Each state is represented (Figure 11) by a surface in the two dimensions of the activity level of a representative local subset of excitatory neurons (left–

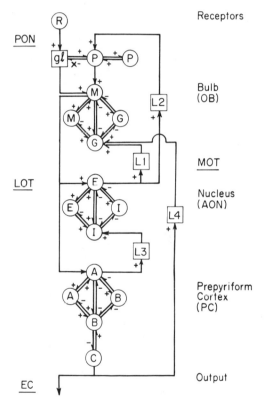

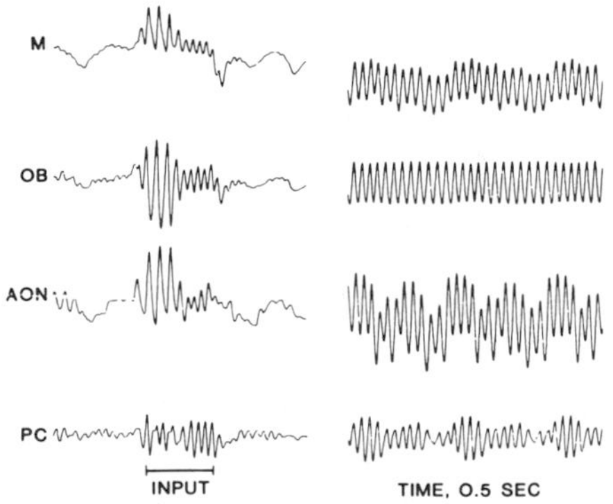

Figure 6. Flow diagram for the equation of the olfactory system. Each circle (except R) represents a second-order nonlinear differential equation (Freeman 1987a). Input from receptors (R) by the primary olfactory nerve (PON) is to periglomerular (P) and mitral (M) cells through the glomeruli (gl) subject to attenuation (x-), with connections to granule cells (G). Output by the lateral olfactory tract (LOT) is to the superficial pyramidal cells of the AON (E) and PC (A), each with inhibitory neurons respectively (I) and (B). Output of the PC is by deep pyramidal cells (C) into the external capsule (EC) and centrifugally to the AON and OB in the medial olfactory tract (MOT). The AON also feeds back to the granule cells (G) and the glomerular layer (P). Excitation is (+); inhibition is (−). Latencies (L1 to L4) are calculated from measurements of the conduction velocities and distances between structures. Each part is treated as a lumped system in this first approximation. Each path is assigned a gain – for example, $k_{MG} = k_{ee}$ in the OB, k_{ME} from the OB to the AON, and k_{EG} from the AON to the OB. From Freeman (1986).

Figure 8. Left: A simulated burst induced by giving a surge of input at R similar to receptor input density during inhalation and exhalation lasting 0.2 sec. Right: Sustained input onto preexisting chaotic activity. From Freeman (1986).

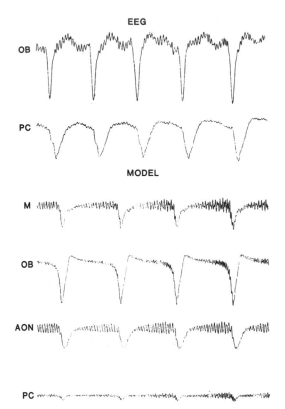

Figure 9. Examples of 2-second time segments of EEGs recorded from a rat during a seizure, comparing these with the outputs of the model (see Figure 7). From Freeman (1987a).

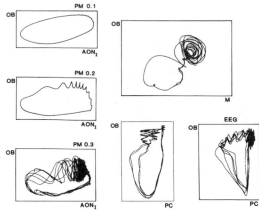

Figure 10. The traces at left show the spike train output (1.0 sec) of the model for 3 values of K_{PM}, showing a low-dimension limit cycle (above), a high-dimension limit cycle, and a chaotic attractor. (In one sense the limit cycle has only one dimension, that along its trajectory, but in another sense it exists in multiple dimensions, so that it never crosses itself.) Reconstruction of the chaotic attractor in 3 dimensions shows that it is a 2-torus without detectable orifices or folds. The upper-right frame shows a short segment (0.25 sec) from a different perspective. The lower-right frames compare the accessible OB and PC EEG traces during a seizure in a rat with the comparable output variables of the model. Although related, they are not identical. From Freeman (1987a).

right axis) and another of inhibitory neurons (axis in-out of the page). Vertical height in each place indicates the amount of energy in the active state of a point. An evoked potential would appear as a counterclockwise spiral trajectory; background activity would appear as a roughly circular squiggle around the base of the central projection. The equilibrium state of deep anesthesia is represented in the lowest plate at the bottom of a well. Its lowest point is the point attractor. The shift upward from one plate to the next depends on the degree of interaction within the system (the bifurcation parameter), which is subject to numerous parameters in the model and to various conditions in the brain relating to input and arousal. The sequence of bifurcation to the waking but unmotivated state is shown by the emergence of the central uplift, a point repellor, and the formation of a surrounding well that contains at its base the chaotic attractor. The state changes by which the central uplift occurs results in transfer of governance from a point attractor to a chaotic attractor (Figure 4).

Figure 11 indicates that the olfactory system and its corresponding model have a hierarchy of states. The basic neural dynamics and the equations are the same in all states but, depending on various neural conditions and model parameters, the systems behave differently (e.g., during waking, sleeping, bursts, interburst intervals, seizures, and so on). Both systems display the capacity for abrupt, dramatic, global jumps from one state to another. These are the bifurcations. These are analogous to phase

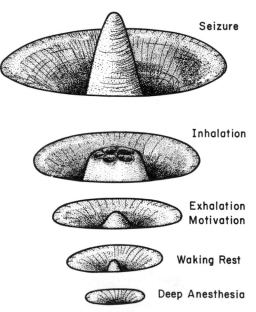

Figure 11. A set of hypothetical phase portraits is constructed from the bifurcation diagram shown in Figure 4. Inhalation results in the emergence of the collection of learned limit cycle attractors, one of which may be selected by odorant input placing the system in its basin. Alternatively, the response may fall into the chaotic well. This appears to occur on about 10% of control inhalations and about 40% of the test odor inhalations after completion of training, as well as reliably with novel odorants (Freeman & Viana Di Prisco 1986). On exhalation the learned attractors vanish, so the system is freed to accept new input. At the top is the chaotic attractor of seizure; at the bottom is the point attractor of deep anesthesia. From Freeman (1987a).

transitions in physical systems: ice to water to steam, for example. The bifurcations occur in many forms and varieties, so a formal definition is difficult if not impossible to provide.

3.4. Roles of chaos in odor recognition.

This configuration is retained under increasing motivation (as by food or water deprivation), resulting in higher amplitudes of background activity, but only during late exhalation. During late inhalation and early exhalation a surge of receptor input reaches the bulb, depolarizes the mitral cells, sensitizes the bulb, and induces an oscillatory burst. This is a bifurcation from a low-energy chaotic state to a high-energy state with a narrow temporal spectral distribution of its energy, suggesting that it is governed by a limit cycle attractor. Order emerges from chaos in two respects. First, a narrow spectral peak emerges, indicating high temporal coherence. Second, the local amplitudes of oscillation take on values that are reproducibly related to particular odorants serving as CSs. The values differ for different odors, indicating that multiple limit cycle attractors exist, one for each odorant an animal has learned to discriminate behaviorally, and each one leading to regular oscillation in a burst.

As hypothesized in Figure 11, these attractors are latent during late exhalation and in the absence of motivation. They reappear, all of them, with each inhalation under motivation and then vanish with exhalation. We postulate that the selection of an attractor upon inhalation is made by the presence of a CS odorant in the inhaled air or by the absence of an odorant, leading to the selection of an attractor corresponding to the background odor, the behavioral status quo. That is, the chemical stimulation of a particular set of receptors places the mechanism into a particular basin when the attractors emerge under bifurcation. The system is released into its basal state with exhalation, setting the stage for the processing of a new sample of information about an odor in the inhaled air.

The dominance of a chaotic attractor, perhaps in some sense closely related at all levels, is seen to extend from the low-level state of rest to the high-energy state of seizure. We conjecture that chaotic activity provides a way of exercising neurons that is guaranteed not to lead to cyclic entrainment or to spatially structured activity (Conrad 1986). It also allows rapid and unbiased access to every limit cycle attractor on every inhalation, so that the entire repertoire of learned discriminanda is available to the animal at all times for instantaneous access. There is no search through a memory store. Moreover, the chaotic well during inhalation provides a catch-basin for failure of the mechanism to converge to a known attractor, either because the sample is inadequate or because a novel or unfamiliar odor is present in the inhaled air. In either case a "disorderly" or chaotic burst results that is characterized by a relatively low peak frequency and a broad temporal spectrum reflecting excessive frequency modulation. Despite the spatial commonality of waveform, these bursts do not converge to a consistent spatial pattern of amplitude modulation, unless by repeated presentation under reinforcement a new CS and a new CR are formed, in which case a new limit cycle attractor emerges. In other words, the chaotic well provides an escape from all established attractors, so that an animal can classify an odorant as "novel" with no greater delay

than for the classification of any known sample, and it gains the freedom to maintain unstructured activity while building a new attractor.

In our view, then, chaos plays several crucial roles; the system is designed and built so as to ensure its own steady and controlled source of "noise" (i.e., chaos). Most remarkably, "signals" are not detected "in" the chaos because the mechanism turns the chaos "off" when it turns a signal "on." The immunity of EEGs to trauma shows that the mechanism is extremely stable, but not absolutely so. Petit mal type seizures (Figure 2) occur when the feedback control system is driven outside its normal range by excessive electrical stimulation and develops a dynamic asymmetry. This imbalance results in a pathological instability that carries the system temporarily into a degenerate and low- dimensional basin of chaotic activity; its pattern resembles the EEG spike activity seen during the early stage of recovery from "silence" under deep anesthesia. We believe that this common form of epilepsy manifests an "Achilles heel" of a common and widespread neural mechanism for the genesis and maintenance of various forms of chaos as the essential ground states of the perceptual apparatuses of the brain.

3.5. Learning and nerve cell assemblies.

The neural mechanisms that underlie changes leading to the formation of a new limit cycle attractor have been described and discussed elsewhere in detail (Freeman 1975; 1979a–c; 1981; 1983b). Our model is based on studies of changes in the waveforms of averaged evoked potentials in the olfactory system when the electrical stimulus is used as a CS+ or CS−, and on replication of these waveforms by the impulse response solutions to differential equations simulating the dynamics of the bulb or cortex. Briefly, the excitatory neurons in each of these structures are synaptically linked by axon collaterals ending mainly on the cell bodies in bidirectional synapses (Willey 1973). When these neurons are co-activated pair-wise by a CS+ their joint synapses are strengthened in accordance with the Hebb rule (Viana Di Prisco 1984). The required reinforcement is mediated by norepinephrine, which is released into the bulb and cortex (and elsewhere) by the locus coeruleus (Gray 1986; Gray, Freeman & Skinner, 1986). Our models indicate that a modest increase of 25–40% in synaptic strength can increase the sensitivity of the bulb to a CS+ by 40,000-fold (Freeman 1979a; 1979b).

The linking together of a selected subset of neurons comprising perhaps 1–5% of the total by strengthened excitatory synapses constitutes the formation of a nerve cell assembly (NCA). Thereafter, excitation of any portion of it tends to disseminate into activating the whole of it. We imagine that each NCA exists as a filamentous network in the bulb resembling mold growing on a piece of bread. We hypothesize that the activation of some of the neurons of a specified NCA selects the basin of the attractor into which the bulbar mechanism converges on inhalation.

The key to understanding this switching device lies in an appreciation of the static nonlinearity that governs the behavior of neurons in an interactive mass. When left without input, neurons tend to fall below threshold and remain silent. Under maintained excitation they give steady output. Owing to the ionic mechanism of the action potential there is a dynamic range near threshold in which the tendency to form an action potential increases exponentially with depolarization. Restorative forces released by an action potential serve to limit the rate of firing, but only after the fact, so to speak.

During exhalation, when receptor input is low, the bulbar neurons tend to fall to a low level of activity and sensitivity. During inhalation the surge of receptor input not only excites bulbar neurons, it augments exponentially their tendency to fire in response to input from receptors and from each other. Their strength of interaction increases dramatically over the entire bulb. At some point a threshold is reached in which the entire bulbar mechanism bifurcates from a low-energy chaotic state to a high-energy state. The NCA operates at the moment of choice when the surge of receptor input strongly forces the bulb far away from its rest state to some new activity pattern.

We view the bulb as operating in two modes. During late exhalation and early inhalation it is in a receiving or diastolic mode (Figures 2, 3, and 11). Intrinsic interaction strength is low. The activity of afferent axons is imposed on bulbar neurons, which are free to accept it and to adopt corresponding levels of firing. Both the temporal and spatial transfer functions are broadly tuned so as to accept information and maintain it by local firing (Freeman & Ahn 1976). This is the low-level chaotic state. On bifurcation the mechanism converts to the transmitting, or systolic, mode. Internal interaction goes to a high level. The temporal transfer function of the model changes to a sharp peak at the burst frequency, and the spatial transfer function changes to give a rapid fall-off in energy above zero c/mm. The bulbar neurons no longer respond to receptor input but instead to each other. The information carried by each neuron is disseminated over the entire bulb and is integrated by every neuron in the bulb. It is also sent out of the bulb to the cortex, where it undergoes further temporal and spatial integration. The integration is facilitated by the high temporal coherence of the oscillatory burst and by the occurrence of the burst center frequency in the optimal pass band of the prepyriform cortex viewed as a passive filter (Freeman 1975; Bressler 1987a,b). Feedback from the prepyriform cortex and AON to the bulb has the form of modulatory biases, because the conducting pathways have strongly dispersive delays that act as low pass filters and smooth the feedback activity. Upon reduction in receptor input during exhalation the system collapses back into low-level chaos and the diastolic mode.

3.6. Strong and weak points of our model. This view of olfactory discrimination arises from insights gained by inspection of the activity patterns revealed by these new data. It is consistent with most of what is known or believed about olfactory function from conventional electrophysiology, including the specificities of neuronal firing in response to odorant stimulation in anesthetized animals and the spatial patterns of selective 2-DOG (2-deoxyglucose) uptake in the glomerular layer (Lancet, Greer, Kauer & Shepherd 1982) on prolonged exposure of waking animals to odorants. It is also compatible with findings in olfactory psychophysics, particularly those relating to the relatively small number of odorants subject to absolute identification in the absence of prolonged

training or (in man) the use of verbal labels (Cain 1980). It also solves the problem of neuroanatomical interfacing by the bulb between the receptors and the primary olfactory cortex as follows.

The input path to the bulb, the primary olfactory nerve (PON), has a certain spatial organization that is imposed by ontogenetic development and by functional needs to be met in getting receptor input into the glomeruli in the face of lifelong replacement of the primary receptors (every 120 days, on the average). The output path, the lateral olfactory tract (LOT), has its own constraints in its ontogeny and in the need to service an array of targets ranging from the AON and tubercle to the amygdaloid nucleus and hippocampal rudiments. By our hypothesis, within a few msec following bifurcation all information that is fed into the bulb during its "diastole" (the inter-burst period) is spread and mixed uniformly through the bulb during its "systole" (the burst). Each fraction of the bulbar output, perhaps on the order of 20%, irrespective of which part of the bulb it comes from, suffices to convey with adequate resolution all that the bulb has to say. Hence there need be no coordination or sharing of constraints in the developmental construction of the input and output paths, particularly with respect to their topographic organizations.

Several challenges and uncertainties exist for the physiology of our model. One of the key features by which it must stand or fall is its requirement that the interneurons in the outer layer of the bulb (Figures 1 and 6), the periglomerular cells, must be excitatory to each other and to mitral cells (Freeman 1987a). Substantial but indirect experimental evidence has been adduced in support of this requirement (Martinez & Freeman 1984) as well as against it (Shepherd 1972). The cells in question are mixed populations of cells secreting GABA, dopamine, and one or more neuropeptides. Conventional wisdom has it that small GABA-ergic neurons are inhibitory. This appears to be valid for the deep-lying granule cells. Recent studies in the hippocampus have shown that GABA is hyperpolarizing when applied to the basal dendrites of pyramidal cells but depolarizing when applied to the apical dendrites (Misgeld, Deisz, Dodt & Lux 1986), suggesting that a chloride gradient along the apical dendritic shafts might reverse the sign of action of GABA between the two parts of the pyramidal cells (Newberry & Nicoll 1985). Were this or an equivalent mechanism to hold for the mitral cells in the bulb, an important prediction by our model would be confirmed.

Another key property of our model is the requirement of mutually inhibitory feedback among inhibitory interneurons in the bulb, AON, and cortex. No direct demonstration that this does or does not exist has yet been devised. Evidence for chemical and electrical synapses between granule cells has been sought but not found. The possibility exists that the stellate cells of Golgi, Cajal, and Blanes, which are thought to be GABA-ergic, inhibit granule cells through their widely distributed axons, and might receive inhibitory input from them.

A third weakness concerns the requirement for mutually excitatory connections among mitral cells in the bulb and among superficial pyramidal cells in the prepyriform cortex, which are modified under learning. The evidence that these requirements hold comes largely from recordings of field potentials and is therefore indirect. Studies of the predicted synaptic changes and their kinetics under modulatory neurochemical agents may be crucial for the support of our model. However, we emphasize that the jury is still out on these questions, that an answer of a particular kind is required for each by our model, and that some other answers can falsify it. We therefore have a brain theory that can be tested, elaborated, or negated by physiological experiments; it is not merely computational.

In its mathematical structure our model is still in its infancy. We have some experience with a distributed system of coupled equations in bifurcation between equilibrium and limit cycle states (Freeman 1979c), but our chaotic generator is a lumped model using ordinary differential equations. In its psychological dimension our model is extremely limited, being competent to simulate only preattentive cognition (Freeman 1983a; Julesz 1984) and the instantaneous apperception of a stimulus, and not attentive inspection or sequential analysis. The feasibility of extending these ideas and experimental methods to neocortical systems is under exploration; evidence has been found that the visual cortex in a rhesus monkey operates according to the same basic neural dynamics as the olfactory bulb (Freeman & van Dijk, submitted). Most important, no claim for firm and substantial understanding of large-scale neural circuitry can be advanced until the mathematical theorists of distributed dissipative systems have caught up with experimentalists, or until engineers have built hardware models based on our equations and determined whether they behave the way parts of brains do. We are pleased to present something new to think about.

4. Philosophical aspects

4.1. Neural dynamics and the digital computer.
Our present hypothesis is that odor discrimination and recognition depend on self-organizing neural processes in the olfactory bulb. The process that we label the "expectation" of an odor is realized in the formation of strengthened connections in a network of neurons constituting the NCA. This assembly, whose role is to amplify and stereotype the small input received on any given inhalation, produces a disseminated but low-density activity pattern in response to the stimulus, and then provides the crucial mechanism for mediating the emergence of an odor-specific activity pattern in a process of bifurcation. With this state change the entire olfactory bulb, rather than the limited number of nerve cells comprising the NCA, is engaged by a process of global integration to produce a stereotypic activity pattern mediated by the NCA but going far beyond it. Thus, when placed in a learned input domain, the neural system has a tendency to generate a qualitatively distinctive form of ordered behavior that emerges from the chaotic background state.

Several important lessons concerning recent explanatory models in cognitive science can be drawn from our research. First, our model, based on self-organizing neural dynamics, makes it desirable to reevaluate the adequacy of the explanatory models based on digital and analog computers that have until recently provided the most influential metaphor in cognitive science. According to this metaphor, the behavior of a system is caused by the formal manipulation of bits of data (symbols) according to rules and operations specified by programs designed for a given task or tasks. The metaphor involves a distinction between system hardware and software, the functioning of a central processor that operates on the data and drives the system, and a memory housed in a separate space. Several factors have contributed to the decline of this metaphor, among them the evidence that implementations of it fail to produce behaviors in which animals and humans excel (Dreyfus & Dreyfus 1986) and the emergence of alternatives in the form of "connectionist" models.

Our data indicate that what takes place in the olfactory system does not resemble the processes responsible for generating behavior in the classical computer paradigm. In the olfactory bulb, learning consists in the selective strengthening of excitatory connections among the neurons leading to the constitution of an NCA and to the possibility of bifurcation to a global activity state manifesting an attractor. Learning takes place during the first 2 seconds following odor CS+ and UCS presentation with the release of norepinephrine in the bulb and elsewhere. Memory for an odor consists in the set of strengthened excitatory connections of the NCA, which, when activated under stimulus input, possesses the tendency to produce a global activity pattern characteristic of a given odor. These are not the types of mechanisms used by digital or analog computers. No program-specified rule or operation is brought to bear on input to the olfactory system. The component neurons generate their own ordered response to stimuli; they are self-organizing. There is no central processor, and learning and memory are functions distributed throughout the neural network.

The process of odor recognition and discrimination can be conceived in terms of dynamic interactions at the level of the neural mass without appeal to symbols. There is preliminary evidence from anatomical and EEG studies indicating that this distributed model can be generalized for neural dynamics throughout the cortex (Freeman & Skarda 1985; Freeman & van Dijk, submitted). This means that the classical computer analogy may be unsuitable to explain the neural bases of behavior. This does not mean that digital computer models are to be discarded. Von Neuman machines have successfully produced some interesting classes of behavior, and to date psychological models seem to lend themselves more simply to formulations stated in terms of symbols and their formal manipulation by rules. What we wish to point out here is that brains do not use the same principles as the digital computer to produce behavior. This information may help neurophysiologists in framing hypotheses for further research. Rather than viewing brain function along the lines suggested by the classical computer paradigm – as a rule-driven and controlled system solving problems, completing patterns, and forming hypotheses by manipulating symbols – neural dynamics suggest that the brain should be viewed as a self-organized process of adaptive interaction with the environment.

4.2. Neural dynamics and connectionist models.
Our model supports the line of research pursued by proponents of connectionist or parallel distributed processing (PDP) models in cognitive science (Baird, in press; Feldman & Ballard 1982; Hinton 1985; Hinton & Anderson

1981; Hopfield 1982; Kohonen 1984; Rumelhart, Mc-Clelland & PDP Research Group 1986). Although the models that fall under the rubric of connectionism are not identical, they do share a number of basic characteristics (Feldman & Ballard 1982). Each involves a processing system consisting of a densely interconnected network of units that interact with one another by sending and receiving signals modulated by the weights associated with the connections between the units. Processing is distributed throughout the system. The units may be organized into layers, and each layer sends to and receives signals from other layers composed of densely interconnected units. The state of each layer results from a synthesis of the states of other layers from which it receives input.

What takes place in the brain may resemble the dynamic processes of self-organization used by these models. Our neural model and the connectionist models converge in several respects. Both rely on parallel, distributed processes among highly interconnected units in interacting networks to produce behavior; both emphasize a self-organized or bottom-up, rather than a rule-driven or top-down, explanatory approach; and both rely heavily on organized feedback among components within the system.

The convergence of our model with connectionist models is instructive. Equally striking are the dissimilarities (Baird, in press). Comparing the models shows that the study of brain dynamics provides essential information about the physical processes responsible for behavior that is not available from current engineering research alone. Our data show that neural dynamics exhibit features not found in connectionist models, features that we hypothesize are essential for odor recognition and discrimination. Modifying the connectionist models along these lines could yield more flexible systems capable of operating successfully in a more realistic environment.

4.3. Feedback of multiple kinds. The first point of difference between our model and connectionism concerns the process of feedback. Neural masses possess (and their collective dynamic behavior is determined by) dense local feedback among the neural units comprising the bulb and within it the multiple existing NCAs. This property is essential for the complicated dynamical processes of neural interaction needed for state changes and for the chaotic and limit cycle behaviors discussed above. Without locally dense feedback formed by the dendritic plexus that provides for a continuum of local interactions in a spatially distributed manner, the dynamic processes responsible for odor recognition and discrimination could not take place.

There are two points to make regarding feedback in connectionist models. First, approaches of the perceptron class (Hinton 1985; Rosenblatt 1962; Rumelhart et al. 1986) do not realize this kind of feedback in their models, even to the extent circumscribed by limitations on the hardware. Some models of this class do involve feedback from one layer of units to another layer (Hinton 1985; Rumelhart et al. 1986). In these models the activity of one layer (B) is fed back to a previous layer (A), thereby modifying the weights of the units in layer A. In contrast to these models the process of "backward propagation" in the brain imposes long delays, temporal dispersions, and

spatial divergences that do not hold for local feedback (Figure 5, L1–L4). Feedback between layers (e.g., between bulb and prepyriform cortex) is not equivalent to the short-latency, focused feedback taking place in the neuropil. There each node has surrounding plexuses of connections which concurrently excite and inhibit by recursive actions. Second, most connectionist models (e.g., Anderson, Silverstein, Ritz & Jones 1977; Hopfield 1982; Kohonen 1984) have excitatory feedback dominantly or exclusively; the role of inhibition has received scant attention. Models based on symmetric matrices of connection weights cannot simulate neural functions because of the existence in the nervous system of the mix of positive and negative feedback. There are exceptions in the connectionist literature; the models developed by Grossberg (1980) feature the local inhibitory feedback found in the neural mass. But the types of dynamics and of connectivity in those models still do not approach those occurring in the bulb and its NCAs, and we doubt that they can produce the global behaviors that characterize its neural dynamics.

4.4. Roles of chaos. A second, related point of difference between neural dynamics and connectionism involves the nature of dynamic behavior exhibited, on the one hand, by neural masses, and on the other hand, by connectionist networks. Our data support the hypothesis that neural dynamics are heavily dependent on chaotic activity. We have suggested that without chaotic behavior the neural system cannot add a new odor to its repertoire of learned odors. Chaos provides the system with a deterministic "I don't know" state within which new activity patterns can be generated, as shown by what happens when the system encounters a previously unknown odor. If the odor occurs without reinforcement, habituation takes place; thereafter, the neural system exhibits patterned activity that we have identified as the control state for the status quo. With reinforcement, however, a completely different process occurs. If the odor is novel and the system does not already have a global activity pattern corresponding to the odor, then instead of producing one of its previously learned activity patterns, the system falls into a high-level chaotic state rather than into the basin for the background odor. This "chaotic well" enables the system to avoid all of its previously learned activity patterns and to produce a new one.

In the neural system, we postulate that the process of state change leading to the unstructured chaotic domain is essential for preventing convergence to previously learned patterns, and hence for the emergence of new patterned activity in the bulb and the corresponding ability of the animal to recognize new odors. In the olfactory system the chaotic background state provides the system with continued open-endedness and readiness to respond to completely novel as well as to familiar input, without the requirement for an exhaustive memory search.

Connectionist models can certainly be modified to produce chaotic and oscillatory behavior, but current theorists have not included these behaviors in their models, nor have they adequately explored the potential benefits of doing so. One reason for this may be that we all lack the appropriate mathematical tools to implement these behaviors at the spatial computational level. Another is that engineers have traditionally viewed oscillatory and chaotic behaviors as undesirable and something to be eliminated (Garfinkel 1983).

The connectionist model reviewed by Hopfield and Tank (1986) is instructive in this regard. This model captures the dynamics of a system at a point in time after the bifurcation included in our model from diastole to systole has taken place. It is pictured in their phase portrait by a set of point attractors. Input places the system into the basin of one or another of these point attractors, to which the system then converges. There are two problems with this model from our perspective. First, the neural system does not exhibit behavior that can be modeled with point attractors, except under deep anesthesia or death. Convergence to a point attractor amounts to "death" for the system. In the Hopfield and Tank model, after the system converges to a point attractor there is no intrinsic mechanism by which the system can escape from it. An obvious solution is to turn the system off and then to reset it so that it is free to converge again to another point attractor. This is like using a muzzle-loader instead of a machine gun. Second, their connectionist model lacks an intrinsic mechanism like the chaotic well in our model that enables the neural system to add new odors to its repertoire. Without such a mechanism the system cannot avoid reproducing previously learned activity patterns and can only converge to behavior it has already learned. The neural system does not have this problem; chaotic mechanisms enable the neural network to learn new behaviors.

4.5. Pattern completion versus destabilization. A third difference between neural dynamics and connectionism concerns the general conceptual framework in which the two models are explained. Connectionist models are sometimes understood as pattern completion devices, in which, for example, when the receptor units are given part of a pattern as input, the complete pattern can be reconstructed by interactions among appropriately weighted units comprising the network.

The neural system we have described is not best thought of as a pattern completion device, although it may do that (Freeman 1983b). The problem is epistemological; we do not know what a completed pattern is (so convergence to it cannot be ascertained as in an error correction device), nor, we suspect, does the brain. We postulate that an NCA is activated wholly by input to any of its neural members, but we have no measure or observation of what the NCA looks like or how completely it is activated. The output of the system does not consist of the "completed" pattern of the NCA but of the entire bulb governed by an attractor. This global state tends to recur within certain "clusters" of spatial patterns, possibly expressed as vectors in some high-dimensional space, but no two are identical, and there is no expression for a boundary, such as the outline of a letter that is to be filled in. Most generally, these neural activity patterns are generated from within. Whatever "meaning" they have is embedded in the self-organized matrix of the entire brain. We have no way of knowing what constitutes a "completed" pattern or how to distinguish it from an "incomplete" one, either in terms of neural activity patterns or the mental life of an animal, presuming it

exists. The pattern-completion concept is realizable only in terms of ideographs or conventional signs and symbols, and if we reject these, as we have for neurophysiology, then the concept too must go.

We also think that the term "pattern" in the expressions "pattern completion" and "neural activity pattern" has very different connotations and different implications for our understanding of system dynamics. The term "pattern completion" describes a process in which a circumscribed structure can be generated as output from input that provides information about only part of the structure. Generally, the process depends on a prior "optimal" presentation of the pattern to adjust the weights among units comprising the network. The neural system works differently. It cannot depend on optimal input in its first (or, in fact, any) encounter with an object against which to compare or judge subsequent input. In the neural system, chaos is the rule, and the patterned activity to which the system converges following each state change is never twice the same, so again the notion of pattern completion loses its meaning.

We think that the notion of "destabilization" provides a better description of the essentials of neural functioning than the concept of pattern completion. In an alert, motivated animal, input destabilizes the system, leading to further destabilization and a bifurcation to a new form of patterned activity. We hypothesize that convergence to an attractor in one system (e.g., the olfactory bulb) in turn destabilizes other systems (e.g., the motor system), leading to further state changes and ultimately to manipulation of and action within the environment. Our research leads us to postulate that behavior can best be modeled as a sequence of ordered, stable states in an evolutionary trajectory (Freeman & Skarda 1985). Input to the system continually destabilizes the present stable state and necessitates convergence to a new form of behavior.

4.6. The sensory/motor loop. This raises a fourth issue. The fundamental character of behavior is adaptive interaction in the world (Churchland 1986; Skarda 1986). Feedback from the consequences of behavior modifies the system and projects it into a higher order of stability. In the nervous system, each change in the dynamic structure of the system, which in our mathematical model requires a new solution with its own trajectory, occurs in a sequence of state changes. The convergence to a patterned activity state, which marks the end state of this process, is externally manifested in some physical state (e.g., chewing) or in some anatomical structure (Ermentrout, Campbell & Oster 1986). What is important here is that this state has a musculoskeletal pattern that constitutes both input to and output from the nervous system. The global activity pattern we record is the result of the destabilizing effects of receptor input to the system, but it is likewise the cause of motor output (e.g., licking) that causes further sensory input and manipulation of the environment, as well as being the result of previous motor activity (e.g., sniffing). These global patterns of the nervous system are at all times locked into both sensory and motor patterns of input and output.

We know that the neural system accomplishes this, but our model clearly does not contain a description of the mechanism by which this interaction is achieved. There are existing prototypes that can be drawn upon by theorists in the work of Walter (1953), Ashby (1952), and Grossberg (1980) of systems with perceptual processes that interact with the environment via motor functions. Further interdisciplinary research along these lines is required before the mechanisms responsible for adaptive interaction will be understood.

Our data lead us to the view that the neural processes of self-organization in the olfactory bulb are quite selective. The olfactory system does not respond to each odor presented to it by producing a corresponding activity pattern. Neural dynamics and the formation of patterned activity that can be correlated with a specific odor are a function of "motivation." What we have labeled motivation can also be characterized as a complex process whereby the organism predictively controls and maintains itself in the optimal condition given the circumstances in which it exists and acts. These global objectives constrain neural dynamics in two ways: They limit the possible range of patterned neural behaviors and they mediate interaction among various neural subsystems, such as that between the brain stem including reticular formation, the locus coeruleus, and the olfactory system relating to arousal, attention motivation, learning, and so on.

Nonbiological self-organizing systems are different. Their behavior is not constrained by either of the global constraints operating in the neural system (Ashby 1952). Storms, for example, are self-organized phenomena that can be mathematically modeled using the same principles we use to model neural dynamics. A storm takes in and gives out energy, moves across a random path buffeted by external forces, and finally dissipates when it has depleted its energy sources. Storms, however, do not exhibit adaptive responses: The system dynamics of a vortex are not constrained by a global demand for preservation of the system, and the system does not incorporate information about its environment. The storm may, for example, move toward land, but it does not do so under the constraint to survive as a unity.

The distinction we have drawn between brains and nonbiological forms of self-organization does not guarantee that brain dynamics will always exhibit the self-promoting constraint just outlined. Sometimes brains produce behaviors that resemble the system dynamics characteristic of weather patterns; we identify some "neural storms" as seizures (Freeman 1986). The presence, however, of a self-organized neural process that is not self-promoting disrupts normal functioning at all levels. These otherwise common and efficient nonbiological forms of self-organization take on a pathological character when they occur in the brain. We propose that they are identified as pathological because they violate the global constraints for self-promotion and adaptive control characteristic of normal brain functioning. Thus, a difference between biological and nonbiological forms of self-organization shows up at the level of the neural assembly long before there is any reason to refer to "consciousness" or "beliefs." Self-preservation plays a central role in biological self-organized systems, and processes that do not possess this feature may be selected against during evolution.

The constraints on self-organization operative in the nervous system are not present in all biological systems.

For example, plants exhibit adaptive behavior indicating that their systems are governed by the constraint for self-promotion over time. Eucalyptus trees influence (modify) their environment by inhibiting the growth of other tree species and shrubs in their vicinity, and they promote their own rainfall from coastal fog. These are clear examples of self-promoting control of the environment, a feature that sets apart biological self-organized systems from nonbiological ones. But brains introduce a further constraint, not found in other biological forms. The key property of brain dynamics, we suggest, is control of body movement in space for the self-promoting purposes of search, attack, ingestion, escape, and reproduction. Plants have no brains. This is why we claim that there can be no adequate explanation of brain function without consideration of sensation in conjunction with movement. Nervous system dynamics is a self-organized process constrained by the requirement that the system anticipate and incorporate the immediate consequences of its own output within the larger constraints of regulating its well-being and the long-term optimization of its chances for survival. This is subsumed in J. J. Gibson's (1979) theory of "affordances." We are a long way yet from understanding how brains accomplish this.

ACKNOWLEDGMENT
Supported by grant MH06686 from the National Institute of Mental Health.

NOTE
1. "Chaos" in the oldest sense means the formless void from which order springs. The term is now commonly applied to disorderly, unpredictable happenings that give an observer no sense of regularity. In the technical sense used here it describes a kind of activity that appears to be random or stochastic by every standard statistical test, but is not. It is deterministic, in the sense that it can be reliably simulated by solving sets of coupled nonlinear ordinary differential equations or generated by building a system to certain specifications and putting energy into it. It is pseudorandom noise that can be reproduced with high precision if the initial conditions are identical on repeated runs, but which is unpredictable if new initial conditions are used. In contrast to noise, chaos has fewer degrees of freedom and is said to be low-dimensional. Chaos exists in many forms and degrees; Rössler (1983) has formulated an instructive hierarchy of equations to exemplify types of chaotic activity that will be of great interest for neural theorists. Introductory texts are by Schuster (1984) and Abraham and Shaw (1985).

Open Peer Commentary

Commentaries submitted by the qualified professional readership of this journal will be considered for publication in a later issue as Continuing Commentary on this article. Integrative overviews and syntheses are especially encouraged.

Chaotic dynamics in brain activity

A. Babloyantz
Faculté des Sciences, Université Libre de Bruxelles, Campus Plaine CP 231, 1050 Brussels, Belgium

Skarda & Freeman (S&F) attempt to extend the recent advances in the analyses of nonlinear dynamical systems to the study of the olfactory bulb.

The suggestion that brain activity has chaotic deterministic dynamics is not new and has already been proposed by several authors (Kaczmarek & Babloyantz 1977; Nicolis 1985a; Roschke & Basar, in press). The degree of chaos in various stages of sleep and wakefulness has been evaluated from human EEG recordings (Babloyantz & Destexhe, in press; Babloyantz, Nicolis & Salazar 1985; Layne, Mayer-Kress & Holzfuss 1986; Rapp, Zimmerman, Albano, Deguzman & Greenbaun 1985). A low-dimensional deterministic chaos was found in an episode of petit mal seizure (Babloyantz & Destexhe 1986).

Reference to the above-cited material might have strengthened the main point of S&F's target article, namely, that brain activity in animals as well as in man conforms to deterministic dynamics of a chaotic nature.

In order to describe the various concepts of nonlinear dynamics without the help of mathematics, several misleading statements are introduced by S&F. "Chaos is controlled noise with precisely defined properties" (Sect. 3.3, para. 1) is an example. To understand S&F's paper, the reader must refer to more technical publications.

In spite of these remarks, S&F's combination of multiple electrode recordings and dimensional analyses is a very promising method for analyzing brain activity. Such an approach sheds light on some aspects of cerebral dynamics not accessible by other methods.

Chaos, symbols, and connectionism

John A. Barnden
Computer Science Department, Indiana University, Bloomington, Ind. 47405

As I have no doubt that the study of chaotic behavior in neural networks is an interesting and fruitful line of research, I shall confine my comments largely to some philosophical claims Skarda & Freeman (S&F) make and to the relationship of their model to connectionism.

Governing metaphors should be kept constantly under review as a matter of principle. But I am not convinced that S&F's findings and arguments constitute a serious threat to the "digital computer metaphor," or, more precisely, to views of the brain as a symbol-manipulation device. There is, first, the danger of extrapolating from findings and theories about low-level sensory mechanisms to high-level cognition. S&F are sensitive to the danger and freely admit that their model is extremely limited psychologically (see end of Sect. 3.6), but they would nevertheless like us to allow the extrapolation. More important, however, S&F do not give us any *new* reason to be worried about viewing higher-level cognitive processes as based on symbol manipulation. As far as I know, the "symbol manipulationists" have in any case always presumed that low levels of perception are at least largely based on specialized mechanisms that are probably not to be regarded profitably as manipulating symbols in any conventional sense. [The fact that AI (artificial intelligence) researchers and others simulate such mechanisms on digital computers is of course only weakly relevant here.] To show, therefore, that the olfactory bulb is best described as operating in a way foreign to symbol manipulation is not to push the backs of the symbol manipulationists any nearer to the wall.

The question of what the rest of the brain does with the output of the olfactory bulb (and directly connected brain centers) is significant. S&F themselves come near to suggesting that the bulb produces symbols when they say the inhalation of a learned odor pushes the bulb into a qualitatively distinctive, stereotypic state of activity. What is to stop us regarding these patterns as symbols? In what way is the idea that the rest of the brain uses these patterns in a symbol-manipulation style rendered implausible? I am not arguing that the rest of the brain does so use them, but only wondering what light is thrown on the issue by the S&F model.

S&F might reply that the activity pattern resulting from a specific learned odor varies somewhat in response to environmental context and preexisting internal state, and therefore cannot be regarded as a symbol. This point has some force, but there appears to be nothing to stop me from retreating slightly and saying that the rest of the brain proceeds to *extract* a symbol – corresponding to some invariant part or aspect of the pattern. (That such a part or aspect exists is surely at the basis of S&F's model.) Also, no retreat at all might be necessary if we allowed symbols to embody a certain amount of "fuzz." This would depart from the conventional view of symbols in artificial intelligence and cognitive science, but it is not clear that the unfuzziness of symbols is crucial to those fields, even if most researchers in those fields think it is. The most crucial aspect of the symbol-manipulation view seems to me to be the ability to form complex structures out of basic symbols, to analyze such structures, to compare symbols, and to associate symbols with symbols and other entities. None of these abilities requires unfuzziness of symbols in principle [Nelson Goodman's (1968) views on notational systems notwithstanding].

S&F would do well to be more careful about nomenclature when making their philosophical claims. The metaphor that their attack is directed at is surely the symbol-manipulation metaphor, not a metaphor of the brain as a digital computer as such, since it is clear that the brain is not like a computer at a low level of description. Now, at the electronic level of description a computer does not operate by symbol manipulation any more than a neural net does at the neurophysiological level of description, so that any terminology that confuses levels is likely to be misleading. When, for instance, S&F say in Sect. 4.1 that the process of odor recognition and discrimination can be conceived in terms of dynamic interactions at the level of the neural mass without appeal to symbols, we might well respond that the behavior of a program running on a computer can be conceived in terms of dynamic interactions at the level of the electronic mass without appeal to symbols. That this response would not (I take it) get at the heart of what the authors are saying would be their own fault, to put it abruptly.

While we are on the subject of levels, I dispute the implication in Sect. 4.2 that "self-organized" is correlated with "bottom-up" or that "rule-driven" is antithetical to "self-organized." A rule-driven system can be self-organized at the level of rules (since rules can modify themselves and other rules), and a top-down decomposition of a system can involve elements of self-organization at any level. Actually, it is not clear that either connectionists or S&F are adopting a bottom-up approach. To be sure, they are suggesting particular low-level mechanisms to explain particular high-level behaviors, but that does not make the approaches bottom-up. It is more that they are adopting a top-down approach different from those taken by certain other researchers.

I am a little puzzled at the claimed divergence from connectionism with respect to types of feedback (Sect. 4.3). There seems to be nothing in the spirit of connectionism that disallows "locally dense feedback." Also, inhibitory feedback, which is claimed by S&F to have been given scant attention in connectionism, has played a very significant role in connectionist thinking for some time. One need only look, for instance, at the model of McClelland and Rumelhart (1981) and at the importance given to lateral inhibition in the Kohonen (1984) book cited by S&F. On the other hand, I do agree that connectionists would do well to look more closely at the transmission delays and temporal dispersion effects on connections (whether or not they are feedback connections). I think it is really best to regard S&F's reliance on chaos and certain feedback effects as constituting a (most intriguing) extension of present-day connectionism rather than as diverging from it.

Finally, I would be interested to know what happens in the olfactory bulb and in S&F's model when several individually learned odors are presented simultaneously. Can a spurious output result, by virtue of the combined odors pushing the system into an activity state corresponding to another learned odor? Does this, if it happens, have any correlation to observed behavior? What new light is thrown on whether the output patterns can be usefully viewed as taking part in symbol manipulation?

Spatial analysis of brain function: Not the first

Robert M. Boynton

Department of Psychology, University of California at San Diego, La Jolla, Calif. 92093

Skarda & Freeman (S&F) believe that their work is "the first demonstration of the existence of sensory- and motor-specific information in the spatial dimensions of the EEG activity in any part of the cortex" (Sect. 3.2, para. 1). Not so: Their attention should be directed to *Toposcopic Studies of Learning*, a book by Donald W. DeMott (1970). In addition to reporting his own work on toposcopy (study of the cortex in two dimensions of space), DeMott reviews the history of the subject, stating that two earlier reviews had been published previously, one by A. Rémond in 1955, the other by Livanov and Anan'yev in 1961 (which I will not cite directly, because I have not seen them). He states that the first toposcopic experiments that produced useful data were published by Lilly and Cherry (1951; 1954) using a 25-channel apparatus.

DeMott studied a variety of learning problems in the monkey while trying to record simultaneously from as many as 400 electrode positions in the brain. He describes both AC and DC changes in the recorded potentials and relates his results to such phenomena as dominant focus, contingent negative variation, hemispheric dominance, and localization of function. For example, in his "one tone, one-string problem," a monkey received a grape reward for pulling the string, contingent upon the presence of the tone. Five Cebus and four Saimiri were studied over several sessions. On some trials, toposcopic patterns, in the form of an array of lights whose intensities were proportional to brain potentials, were recorded with a high-speed camera of original design at 250 frames per second. DeMott discerned a distinctive pattern of electrical activity associated with the first behavioral signs of learning, one that straddled the parieto-occipital sulcus. Such activity was never otherwise observed, even during analogous visual learning studies. He refers to this activity as an apparent "lateral movement of activity in the region of the focus . . . sharply limited, as if by an invisible fence around the critical area" (p. 93).

DeMott's book also includes detailed discussion of the design and manufacture of electrode arrays and of the problems encountered with respect to surgical implantation as well as the formidable problems of data analysis in what was, for him – given his limited resources – the precomputer era.

S&F also state, "there being no precedents, we have no other data with which to compare our results. Just as we have pioneered in their acquisition, we must now break new ground in attempting to understand what they tell us about brain function" (Sect. 3.2, para. 1). As I hope the foregoing will attest, these matters are what DeMott's monograph is largely about. Otherwise, it is a personal history (I find it a sad one) of what can happen to those who arrive before their time and choose to go it alone. With uncommon frankness, he tells of his long struggle with journal editors and grant reviewers, who eventually put an end to his research career on August 31, 1968, ten years after the toposcopic project had begun. His efforts deserve to be remembered.

Such carping out of the way, I will conclude by saying that I otherwise enjoyed the paper by S&F. Better than most of us, they have utterly banished the homunculus, or "green man," from their thinking and have called attention to the fundamental weaknesses of the simple-minded brain-computer analogies. Yet I find S&F's records difficult to interpret, just as reviewers found DeMott's. Only time will tell whether chaos is in fact the route to making sense of the world.

Can brains make psychological sense of neurological data?

Robert Brown

Department of Psychology, University of Exeter, Exeter EX4 4QG, England

Churchland (1980) distinguishes two varieties of scepticism concerning the usefulness of brain research for our understanding of how the mind-brain works: "boggled" and "principled" scepticism. Presumably this distinction is only a makeshift one, and scepticism merely an imprecise "folk-psychological" notion, but since the terms have not yet been eliminated from our psychological vocabulary I will assume that they are still meaningful. Skarda & Freeman's (S&F's) target article, for all its good intentions, increases my scepticism (of both kinds).

Being blinded by science could well be a function of one's own intellectual eyesight. No one expects the general theory of relativity to be easily assimilable in comic-book format, but an argument is still expected to meet the criteria of clarity and intelligibility. In their account of the collection, analysis, and interpretation of data S&F mystify and intimidate, albeit unwittingly. It must be a small and specialised community indeed that can follow each of the technical and mathematical steps with a truly critical eye. This is not a trivial criticism. It is claimed that the model can be tested, elaborated, negated, or falsified. We know that falsification (or potential falsification) is not the cut-and-dried procedure it was once thought; given such sheer complexity, what would it really take to falsify this model? There could be many an inferential slip 'twixt sniff and sip, and how many would honestly be the wiser?

However, boggled scepticism is not a serious complaint; it can be cured in this case (in principle) by getting down to the hard work of understanding volume conductor analysis and the Ruelle-Takens-Newhouse route to chaos (Schuster 1984). Clashes of principle are clearly more serious, occasionally terminal, disorders. S&F's main metatheoretical thrust is that in view of certain complex neurological findings (in conjunction with certain relatively simple behavioural manipulations) the computational metaphor, although not to be scrapped outright, needs a serious overhaul. An alternative view is that the computational metaphor, although not immune to attack, cannot seriously be threatened by this *kind* of attack, for the following reasons:

Clarity and chaos. It is difficult to appreciate S&F's argument clearly because of a marked tendency to switch chaotically between different levels of discourse. On the one hand they appear to support naïve materialism at the *neural* level; the "theory can be tested . . . by physiological experiments; it is not *merely* computational" (Sect. 3.6, para. 5; italics added). Of course, computational theorists are not constrained by the merely physiological, but that is beside the point. On the other hand we are told that we will not understand "large-scale neural circuitry . . . until the mathematical theorists . . . have caught up with experimentalists, or until engineers have built hardware models . . . and determined whether they behave the way parts of brains do" (Sect. 3.6, para. 6). What does this imply for the bedrock status of the neural/physiological? Are hardware models somehow more convincing simulations than "mere" computer simulations (hardware *and* software)? Perhaps, because there is a subsequent favourable reference to the simple mechanical models of the early cyberneticists. And if we change a few substantives in the quotation, it sounds suspiciously like what computationists are doing for cognition anyway – that is, *they* will never understand complex cognitive processes until appropriate formal languages have been developed for their description and they have been successfully simulated on computers. Finally, what is one to make of "the *brain* should be viewed as a self-organized *process*" (Sect. 4.1, para. 4; italics added); this is symptomatic of the general confusion over structure and function, description and explanation, computers and computation.

Metaphor and simile. Part of this confusion arises from the assumption that the *computational* metaphor is just the *computer* metaphor. S&F's characterisation of the former is essentially a description of a rather basic computer; I doubt whether many computational theorists would wish to defend such a description as adequately capturing the features of a complex organism. The computational metaphor is usually seen as much more abstract; indeed, it has often been said that, since any process can be construed as a computational process, the metaphor is tainted with overgenerality, tautology, irrefutability, or emptiness. [See Pylyshyn: "Computation and Cognition" *BBS* 3(1) 1980.]

The main problem with metaphorical assertions is that they can be taken as literally false (it doesn't rain "cats and dogs"). Why, then, can't they be taken as literally true, as saying something about "reality" ("information is held in short-term memory and transferred to a long-term store")? Now, whereas metaphor misleadingly implies a kind of identity, simile makes the weaker implication of resemblance. If the rain is "*like* lead shot" we can at least ask, "In what respect?" There has been much needless debate because relations of simple resemblance have been stated or understood as something stronger. How can a model of discrimination be explanatory if it contains a primitive element that discriminates? If we say that a suitably programmed computer "understands questions," does it *really* understand? How can we have visual images when there cannot *really* be pictures in our heads? There are many such examples. On the other hand, when simile is seen for what it is, such problems do not arise; hydraulic ethological models were never seriously criticised because there seem to be no pipes and valves in the nervous system, and Freudian hypotheses are not falsified by pointing to the absence of three interacting figurines in the skull. [See also Hoyle: "The Scope of Neuroethology" *BBS* 7(3) 1984.]

The computational metaphor has strength, flexibility, and appeal because it is not really a metaphor, it is just a simile; and if the functional resemblance between two systems is sufficiently convincing, that is all that matters. But S&F are not convinced. Why? They look into the nervous system (albeit very indirectly) and find no symbols, only dynamic neural patterns. Is this surprising? Symbols are in the eye of the beholder. One can look at this page and find no symbols, only patterns of grey. The popular dogma that brains and computers deal in symbols is misleading; their currency is electricity. By saying that a device manipulates symbols we are attributing intentionality to it – how else would it know what things were or were not "symbols"? But if dynamic neural patterns are to be *discriminated*, then surely they can be named, formalised, *computed*? Otherwise we would only see chaos, in its everyday sense.

It would be foolish to suggest that neural dynamics or statics are completely irrelevant for an understanding of mind and

behaviour, and equally foolish to suggest that the computational metaphor is impregnable. If S&F are simply claiming that their data require different kinds of computations, then this is unexceptionable, but they seem to be simultaneously attacking a straw man and trying to throw the baby out with the bath water (not literally, of course). Principled attacks on the computational approach are likely to be top-down in terms of intentional and experiential arguments (Dreyfus 1972; Gauld & Shotter 1977; Searle 1980). And since computational theorists handle intentionality at worst trivially and at best controversially, I fail to see how neuroscientists could even begin to tackle the issues.

When the "chaos" is too chaotic and the "limit cycles" too limited, the mind boggles and the brain (model) flounders

Michael A. Corner and Andre J. Noest
Netherlands Institute for Brain Research, 1105 AZ Amsterdam, The Netherlands

Let's start from the beginning. To begin with, the olfactory bulb must respond to each odor the mucosa is capable of discriminating with some sort of specific pattern of excitation, presumably derived from the ontogenetically determined distribution of osmochemical receptor specificities. If each class of receptor cells is spread out over a large enough area of the olfactory mucosa, a widespread projection of odor-specific sensory volleys can be guaranteed even if, as in other sensory systems, nearest neighbor relations are largely preserved in the central projections. In this sense Skarda & Freeman's (S&F's) tantalizingly brief statement in Sect. 3.6 about the absence of a requirement for ontogenetic constraints on afferent topography is true enough, as far as it goes (provided, of course, that each receptor's terminal field does not encroach too much upon the territory of its neighbors). The next step in olfactory discrimination would be the evocation of a diffuse polyneuronal oscillation in the bulb during the inhalation phase of each sniff in a motivated animal. This "something is out there" carrier waveform is manifested as a "chaotic" broad-band EEG signal within the gamma range of frequencies (ca. 40–80 cps). The dual effect of a smell – to provide sensory information together with a nonspecific signal preparing the brain for dealing with it – thus resembles, in general terms, the classical picture of a "reticular arousal system" linked to sensory projections to the neocortex. In the latter case, however, rather than high-frequency waves being triggered, low-frequency waves (EEG alpha and delta bands) become suppressed during arousal. Alerting responses in the septohippocampal system in turn consist of a synchronized neuronal oscillation, but one which is much slower (in the EEG theta band) than the one found in the olfactory system. Why these differences?

S&F's suggestive attempt to generalize their paleocortical model by postulating the existence of similar waves (i.e., in the EEG "gamma" range) in the neocortex (that have gone undetected owing to cytoarchitectonic differences between the two structures) fails to reach our plausibility threshold. The laminar organization of neocortical tissues would appear to be eminently suitable, despite its relative complexity, for detecting even weakly synchronized fluctuations of neuronal activity. An important task facing any theory which aspires, albeit implicitly, to providing a general explanation of the biological significance of "brain waves" must surely be to explain the appearance of prominent cortical oscillations – alpha rhythms, "spindling," delta waves – precisely at those times (ranging from drowsiness to deep sleep) when sensory processes appear to be at a minimum even with respect to internal sources – as in dreaming. On the other hand, the basic notion of widely synchronized neuronal carrier waves that become "destabilized" by afferent input (see Sect. 4.5), in a spatially distinctive manner for each discriminable stimulus, is by no means excluded by differences among brain regions displaying the precise characteristics of these (chaotic) waves. Perhaps the major challenge for S&F's model, therefore, will be to account for the olfactory system displaying the very EEG waveform and amplitude-pattern that have actually been observed. By the same token, light needs to be shed on the possible significance of the low-amplitude, highly chaotic, "background" EEG present between sniffs (as well as continuously in a nonmotivated animal). This is the activity, after all, which the authors believe (see Sect. 3.2) constitutes "the elemental phenomenon . . . in all of brain physiology"(!). Disappointingly, it is almost totally neglected thereafter, although this omission became apparent to us only after our realization that the broad-band EEG gamma waves seen during (motivated) inhalation in a naïve animal were *not*, in fact, what was meant by the term "background" activity as used in the target article!

Odor-specific differences are reported to become overtly manifest in the multichannel olfactory EEG only after proper reinforcement has taken place. Spatially distinctive amplitude patterns are then detectable, taking the form of extensive limit-cycle activity in the bulb, contained within a relatively narrow band of EEG gamma frequencies. These patterns presumably reflect the magnification of preexisting differences in the spatial distribution of afferent signals and evoked synaptic activities in the bulb, without which no distinction among various inhaled (unconditioned) odors could have been made in the first place. What, then, needs to be "learned" about such signals or (as S&F would put it) to be added to the animal's smell repertoire? Nothing else, surely, than that the odor in question has acquired a particular behavioral significance: *eat* it, *jump* it, *avoid* it, and so on. This being the case, isn't it possible – even likely – that each recognizable new EEG pattern carries information not about the input but, rather, about the *output* side of the olfactory loop (i.e., the motor response system to which the stimulus has become linked by virtue of conditioning)? We're very much interested in knowing, therefore, exactly how many of these distinctive spatial patterns have in fact been identified, and whether two odors with more or less the same "meaning" for the organism would stand much chance of being discriminated on the basis of EEG analysis.

Finally, serious semantic ambiguities have arisen in the course of our attempt to understand the more strictly mathematical aspects of S&F's paper. After satisfactorily dispensing with the straw man of digital computers as useful for modeling any kind of brain, the authors proceed to find fault with "connectionist" models because of their current shortcomings in the light of recent neurophysiological findings. But in what sense is the Freeman model – not the lumped (i.e., spatially averaged) version described here, which, by definition, is incapable of even beginning to deal with the spatial EEG patterns on which the whole theory rests, but the promised but still preliminary distributed model – itself not a connectionist model? In the absence of any definition of a qualitatively new class of models incorporating features that are inherently absent in a connectionist approach, S&F's scheme must be considered as constituting simply a possible improvement *within* that category. If we then try to pinpoint what their precise suggestions for the incorporation of new features are, we are unable to find any satisfactory starting point for carrying out the proposed improvements. Several of the deficiencies attributed to existing models, such as failure to incorporate inhibition, asymmetric synapses, or endogenous noise in the system, fail to do justice to the state of the art in this field. Even if the next step were to entail the introduction of coupled limit-cycle oscillators, distributed models involving sheets of interacting circuits (each resembling the basic one in the lumped model presented by Freeman & Skarda) have in fact already been studied extensively.[1]

Even in structurally homogeneous variants of such models, oscillating activity can (among many other possibilities) become ordered in spatially inhomogeneous, nonperiodic patterns. These can usually be characterized by topologically conserved phase patterns involving "vortex" – or "string" – singularities embedded in a smooth phase-field. It can be predicted that in case of spatial smoothing over a scale larger than the size of the vortices, such *phase* patterns would appear instead as spatially nonuniform *amplitude* patterns associated with a smooth phase-field. If the present data turn out not to be explicable along these lines, then it seems logical to assume some form of "pinning" of the oscillatory patterns by structural disorder. It is plausible to suppose that each of the many possible distinct patterns could then be "nucleated" by the appropriate set of incoming stimuli. Developing such conjectures into testable theories will probably require that investigators start delving into the complexities of structurally inhomogeneous models. In view of the many possible ways of generalizing the existing ones, it would be extremely helpful if experimentalists attempted to specify, as precisely as possible, the lessons to be learned (for example, from olfactory cortex physiology) that would allow such improved models to be developed.

It is wonderful for psycho(physio)logists to master the mathematics of cooperative networks, and to try to apply this knowledge to the unraveling of the deepest (or even the superficial) mysteries of the brain, but the required conceptual underpinnings for such flights into higher spheres must not be neglected. In our opinion, much more attention needs to be devoted to such fundamental things as clarity of definitions, explication of assumptions, rigor in logical structure, and completeness in the consideration of relevant theoretical and empirical material.

NOTE
1. There exists a considerable body of literature on spatially distributed, coupled limit-cycle oscillations. Good lists of core references are cited by Oono and Kohmoto (1985) and Winfree (1980).

On the differences between cognitive and noncognitive systems

D. C. Earle
Department of Psychology, Washington Singer Laboratories, University of Exeter, Exeter EX4 4QG, England

Skarda & Freeman (S&F) interpret their findings as supporting the proposal that brain function is a self-organized process of adaptive interaction with the environment, a process to be conceived in connectionist terms and involving parallel distributed processing. These views are set in opposition to the proposal that the brain is a rule-driven and controlled system solving problems, completing patterns, and forming hypotheses by manipulating symbols.

Two separate issues are conflated here. The first concerns the question whether the appropriate model for the brain is the connectionist model, with distributed parallel processing, or that taken from the digital computer, with a limited-capacity central processor and a sequential organization. This question is separate from whether the brain is a symbol-manipulating and rule-driven problem-solving device. The former is a question about the functional architecture of the brain, whereas the latter is the question whether or not the brain is an information-processing device. A distributed information-processing system may implement rules, complete patterns, manipulate symbols, and, if need be, formulate hypotheses. Consider, for example, a distributed information-processing system that takes as its input a symbolic representation, performs a transformation, and then outputs a different symbolic representation. Such a system is exemplified by certain implementations of the cooperative stereo-matching algorithm proposed by

Marr and Poggio (1976). An information-processing system may be described at the highest level in terms of its computational theory; however, the computational theory may be realised in devices using different functional architectures – that is, devices with distributed parallel processing or sequential processing.

To adopt the proposal that the brain is an information-processing and symbol-manipulating system is a methodological decision of its proponents, and as such constitutes adherence to a particular research programme. An information process may be realised in a neural system or a computer, whether it is sequentially organized or performs distributed parallel processing, but on the higher level of analysis it remains an information-processing system. As such, it should be described using informational terms – that is, rules, symbols, representations, and the language of information-processing operations (e.g., detection and discrimination). Information processes are not to be conceived directly in neurophysiological terms or in the terminology of electronics. If, for example, one says of a certain cell in the visual cortex that it is a bar detector or that it makes a measurement on the image, then one describes that cell in information-processing terms (insofar as detection and measurement are information-processing operations). At this level of description the output of such a cell and its interactions with any neighbouring cells are symbolic in that they represent a detection or its absence, or a measurement.

If the information-processing paradigm is not adopted, then the appropriate terminology is not that of symbols, rules, and so on, but a description in terms of whatever are now judged to be the intrinsic properties of the system being described. In the case of a neural system, these may be synaptic connections, inhibition, fatigue, electrical impulses, and perhaps chaos, attractors, and repellors. Thus, an account of the visual tilt aftereffect can be given in terms of differential fatigue of cortical cells with oriented receptive fields without recourse to the language of information-processing systems; it can be given in terms of the intrinsic properties of the neural substrate. In such a case there may be no basis for adopting the information-processing paradigm and giving an account using the notion of bar detectors – although, in principle, the account could be phrased in these terms were that paradigm to be adopted. It may not be necessary to use the language and concepts of information processing to give an account of the tilt aftereffect, but when considering the correspondence problem in stereopsis (Marr 1982) there may be considerable advantages in using such a language. The connectionist movement offers two fundamental challenges: First, a different functional architecture for information-processing systems is proposed. Second, and separately, the connectionists claim to provide a way of describing the behavior of aggregates of processors without the assumption that the processing is an informational one.

The problem of distinguishing between cognitive and noncognitive self-organising and distributed processing systems may now be viewed differently from the position adopted by S&F. I propose that the critical property distinguishing cognitive from noncognitve systems is not adaptivity, but information processing. One would not want to say of a weather system that it is an information-processing system, and one would explain its behaviour in terms of the intrinsic properties of the system – that is, the pressure and temperature of air masses, humidity levels, turbulence, and so on. A variety of homeostatic and adaptive devices (e.g., thermostats and eucalyptus trees) can also be described in terms of their intrinsic properties without appeal to informational concepts. Perhaps the major challenge of the connectionist movement in relation to psychology is that, although not necessitating a noncognitivist stance, it nevertheless promises to provide a noncognitive account of complex behaviour.

Finally, it is to be noted that S&F have given a connectionist account only of neural activity in the olfactory bulb. Their claim, however, is to have given such an account of odour recognition and discrimination, and this is a different matter. As they are at pains to emphasize, the connectionist processing that they describe for the olfactory bulb must be linked to the motor system to enable interaction with the environment – that is, discriminative behaviour. To this end, a particular pattern of neural activity in the bulb must serve as the condition for a condition-action link. One difficulty here is that a distributed parallel processing module may be embedded in a more complex hybrid and controlled system with a sequential organization. Furthermore, a condition-action link can be interpreted as a rule in an information system or as a direct neural pathway in a noncognitive system. Skarda & Freeman attempt to draw conclusions concerning the brain as a whole on the basis of the study of only a small part of the neural substrate of a discriminative interaction with the environment.

The virtues of chaos

Alan Garfinkel

Department of Kinesiology, University of California at Los Angeles, Los Angeles, Calif. 90024

Only recently (Lorenz 1963) was it realized that deterministic systems can display behavior that appears random. This phenomenon, called "chaos," offers a new approach to modeling erratic processes. It should be stressed that the chaos that arises in deterministic systems is not total chaos, but rather is controlled and bounded, and has definite qualitative form. It also differs from ordinary random behavior in that it is low-dimensional, whereas traditional "noise" arises from the central limit theorem, which predicts a normal distribution from the addition of a large number of independent contributions.

Skarda & Freeman (S&F) propose that the background EEG in the olfactory bulb is chaotic. The principal evidence for this claim is their report of calculations of the "dimension" as lying between 4 and 7. Such calculations of apparent dimension are one way of distinguishing chaos from noise, although there are difficulties and pitfalls in this approach (see especially Grassberger, 1986, for a discussion of fallacious calculations).

But the calculation of dimension is only one way of distinguishing chaos from noise, and it suffers from being just a number. Methods like attractor reconstruction and Poincaré sections (Froehling, Crutchfield, Farmer, Packard & Shaw 1981) have the additional advantage that they give qualitative pictures of the behavior and of the form of its underlying mechanisms. Such information is much deeper; the dictum here is that "quantitative is just poor qualitative." See Roux, McCormick, and Swinney (1981) and Farmer, Hart, and Weidman (1982) for applications of these methods to chemical chaos and fluid turbulence.

Once one has established the fact that a given phenomenon is a chaotic process, the next question is: What is chaos doing there? S&F suggest that it is playing a functional role, an idea that is something of an about-face for chaos. Most writers on the subject tend to assume that chaos is something bad; the proposed examples of chaos in physiology, such as cardiac and respiratory arrhythmias (Glass & Mackey 1979), would support this view. But chaotic behavior can also be functional and adaptive. Consider the chaos of fluid turbulence. Turbulent fluids have useful properties that are not found in nonturbulent states. For example, the mixing properties of turbulence greatly increase the fluid's ability to take imposed heat or movement and equipartition it out.

A striking example of the functional role of chaos can be found in a study of population dynamics by Auslander, Guchenheimer, and Oster (1978). They study a model of a coevolving host/parasite system and find that, for certain ranges of key parameters, the host species displays chaotic variations in population level over time. They interpret this by suggesting that "for a host population being pursued by a coevolving predator, it is surely adaptive to maintain a demographic and genetic pattern as 'untrackable' to the parasite as possible" (p. 290).

It may well be that in physiology, chaotic behavior can be quite useful, serving to randomize a system in cases where regular behavior would be damaging. A case in point might be the normal cortical EEG. It is interesting that many writers have suggested that epileptic seizures might be examples of chaos. In fact, the opposite seems to be true: In seizures, the EEG becomes regular and periodic, and it is the normal ("desynchronized") EEG that is irregular. Given the undesirability of periodic cortical behavior, it is reasonable to suppose that the nervous system has evolved a reliable mechanism to desynchronize the EEG. As an example of the utility of such "active desynchronization," consider the behavior of a platoon of soldiers crossing a bridge. Since periodic behavior (marching in ranks) might set the bridge into destructive resonant oscillation, the soliders "break ranks." It is likely that the nervous system can effect a similar active desynchronization, in situations where randomness is too important to be left to chance. In the case of the soldiers, there is a commanding officer who gives the order to desynchronize. Here the difference between high-dimensional noise and low-dimensional chaos becomes crucial. If one wanted to desynchronize a process, the availability of a chaotic attractor would offer an opportunity to do it by a low-dimensional control: Only a few parameters need be altered to move the system into and out of chaos.

A similar phenomenon may occur in muscle activation. If individual motor units were to fire periodically, they might tend to synchronize, producing undesirable tremor. Hence, there may well be an active desynchronization mechanism in sustained contraction that "spreads out" the motor unit timings to fill the time interval of the activity.

In general, it may be that for all oscillatory processes in physiology, a perfectly periodic oscillation is undesirable. Chaos could here play the role of introducing a useful wobble into the period or amplitude, while retaining the overall form of the process.

Stable self-organization of sensory recognition codes: Is chaos necessary?

Stephen Grossberg

Center for Adaptive Systems, Boston University, Boston, Mass. 02215

Freeman and his colleagues have developed one of the classical experimental and modeling paradigms of neurobiology through a remarkable synthesis of technical virtuosity, physical intuition, and intellectual courage. Their systematic approach has led them to articulate a number of fundamental problems concerning the self-organization of sensory codes and to propose possible approaches to the solutions of these problems. Due to these characteristics, data and modeling ideas from the Freeman school provide one of the best vertebrate sources of quantitative results about interactions between cortical sensory representations and their appetitive modulation, and have therefore played a valuable role in testing the principles and mechanisms of adaptive resonance theory (Grossberg 1982a).

Even in such a systematically explored neural paradigm, definitive data are more the exception than the rule. In the absence of data that afford a unique specification of generative neural mechanisms, a number of theoretical tools can be invoked to impose additional constraints. Two such tools are mathematical and simulation analyses of the emergent properties of those model neural systems that are consistent with basic neural organizational principles and the data at hand.

Such results are briefly reviewed here to help weigh the key hypotheses of Skarda & Freeman (S&F).

After reviewing fundamental facts about spatial pattern coding by temporally entrained waveforms and the role of associative learning and expectancies, S&F focus on their central "conjecture that chaotic activity provides a way of exercising neurons that is guaranteed not to lead to cyclic entrainment or to spatially structured activity. It also allows rapid and unbiased access to every limit cycle attractor on every inhalation, so that the entire repertoire of learned discriminanda is available to the animal at all times for instantaneous access" (Sect. 3.4, para. 3). They propose this hypothesis in an unusually strong form, going on to claim that "without chaotic behavior the neural system cannot add a new odor to its repertoire of learned odors" (Sect. 4.4, para. 1).

S&F's hypothesis raises the difficult issue that a data phenomenon, despite its *correlation* with a particular functional property, may not be *necessary* to achieve that functional property. When this is true, it is not possible to assert that the system has been *designed* to generate the property for that functional purpose. One can defeat the claim that the property in question is necessary by providing a mathematical counterexample of its necessity.

Gail Carpenter and I (Carpenter & Grossberg 1987) have done just that. We have completely analyzed an explicit example of an adaptive resonance theory architecture, called ART 1, which shares many features with those of the Freeman data, and we have mathematically proved that this architecture has the following properties. ART 1 can self-organize, self-stabilize, and self-scale a sensory recognition code in response to an arbitrary, possibly infinite, list of binary input patterns. During code learning, it carries out an efficient self-adjusting memory search; after learning self-stabilizes, recognition occurs without search by direct access to the optimal learned recognition code. The course of learning is, moreover, remarkably stable; all adaptive weights, or long-term memory traces, oscillate at most once through time due to their dynamic buffering by system interactions.

Such ART architectures have been explicitly designed to provide "the system with continued open-endedness and readiness to respond to completely novel as well as to familiar input, without the requirement for an exhaustive memory search" (S&F, Sect. 4.4., para. 2). To discover systems capable of coping with this "stability-plasticity dilemma," all the operations of ART systems have been developed to explain and predict difficult parametric data from a number of behavioral and neural paradigms: for example, Cohen and Grossberg (1986), Grossberg (1987a,b), Grossberg and Stone (1986).

The key point for present purposes is that chaos plays no role in the extremely flexible and powerful learning and recognition performance of such a system. Hence chaos is not *necessary* to achieve the type of competence that has been uniquely ascribed to it by S&F.

This argument does not deny that chaos has been measured in S&F's experiments. In fact, one of the important mathematical issues in neural network theory concerns the manner in which parameter changes within a single neural model can cause bifurcations between point attractors, limit cycle attractors, and bursting or chaotic attractors. In a book to which Freeman and I both contributed, I reviewed results concerning how suitable parameter changes could cause a cooperative-competitive feedback network to bifurcate from one with point attractors into one with limit cycle attractors of a type (standing waves) that could support an olfactory code (Grossberg 1981). It was there suggested how a parameter called the quenching threshold (QT) could modulate the olfactory bulb's excitability in phase with the breath cycle; and it had been known for some time (Ellias & Grossberg 1975) how such gain changes could cause a Hopf bifurcation from a point attractor into a limit cycle. The bifurcation described by S&F from a low-energy state to a high-energy state with a narrow temporal spectral distribution is clarified by such results. So too is their observation that during early inhalation, intrinsic interaction strength is low, since one way to alter the QT is by altering the gain of system interactions, as occurs in ART 1 through its *attentional gain control* channel (Carpenter & Grossberg, 1987). When attentional gain control is low, cell populations can become decoupled.

These relationships between point attractors and limit cycle attractors delineate a family of models, all of which can support similar functional coding properties, with or without chaos. A formal model with such functional properties can also possess a tonically active point equilibrium or chaotic attractor in its rest state. Such a state of tonic activation can support one or more basic functional properties [e.g., maintaining a baseline activity that can be excited or inhibited without a loss of sensitivity, feeding signals into habituating chemical transmitters that can compensate for spatial fluctuations in the basal activation level and therefore keep the tissue in a spatially unbiased state (Grossberg 1983), or driving antagonistic rebounds in response to sudden offsets of sensory inputs (Grossberg 1980)]. All these functions can be carried out equally well by point or chaotic attractors. On the other hand, in a state of tonic activity but low attentional gain control, a physically realized network of cells can exhibit small but complex, even chaotic, fluctuations.

In summary, just as one can conceive of slime mold aggregations that proceed continuously or in a pulsatile fashion through time as parametric variations of a single model, so too can one envisage a sensory coding model in which point or chaotic attractors support similar functional characteristics. Thus, although the issues raised by S&F are important ones for understanding cortical design, further argument is needed to support their strong claim for the *necessity* of chaos to achieve key functional coding properties.

S&F have also raised the legitimate challenge that "no claim for firm and substantial understanding of large-scale neural circuitry can be advanced until the mathematical theorists of distributed dissipative systems have caught up with experimentalists, or until engineers have built hardware models" (Sect. 3.6, para. 6). The Carpenter-Grossberg (1987) theorems have, in fact, provided such mathematical guarantees about the ART 1 architecture, and these guarantees have encouraged engineers to start building an ART 1 chip in hardware. The kind of functional competence Skarda & Freeman have seen in their data is thus already helping to define the technological products of a biologically derived artificial intelligence.

ACKNOWLEDGMENT
Supported in part by the Air Force Office of Scientific Research (AFOSR 85-0149) and the National Science Foundation (NSF IRI-84-17756).

Is chaos the only alternative to rigidity?

Daniel S. Levine

Department of Mathematics, University of Texas at Arlington, Arlington, Tex. 76019

The Freeman laboratory continues to do exciting work in the neural representations of olfactory stimuli, as it has for almost 20 years. As always, the Skarda & Freeman (S&F) work is pioneering, both technically and philosophically. The changes in EEG patterns from a neutral to a reinforcing odorant stimulus are particularly significant. From the modeler's perspective, however, I retain some skepticism about the philosophical role of chaos that S&F propound.

S&F write that "the process of state change leading to the unstructured chaotic domain is essential for preventing convergence to previously learned patterns, and hence for the emergence of new patterned activity" (Sect. 4.4, para. 2). Although the authors state this most strongly for the olfactory

bulb, they clearly hope to apply the same principle to other sensory modalities, and have adduced some evidence for it in the visual system.

In neural models of the "connectionist" variety, based on nonlinear differential equations, the capacity to respond to both novel and familiar inputs can exist even in the absence of chaos. In fact, learning often transforms novel inputs to familiar ones, with the consequent change in response properties. A series of articles by Grossberg (in particular, 1975; 1980; 1982b) discusses a striving for balance between an attentional system (which biases the network's responses toward previously learned inputs) and an arousal system (which enables the network to overcome the attention system's rigidity when important new events occur). One mechanism for responding to novel events in these networks is the activity of populations of "mismatch detectors," which are actively inhibited by *correspondence* between the activity patterns in two separate on-center off-surround fields of cell populations (such as one field representing an actual "bottom-up" stimulus event and another representing a "top-down" expectation of an event). This correspondence causes the total energy from the summation of the two fields to be sufficiently large to shut off the mismatch detector activity, which plays a role analogous to S&F's chaos. Like the chaotic EEG pattern, mismatch activity ensues if an unfamiliar pattern occurs, because the mismatch is not inhibited by correspondence. Hence, in Grossberg's model as in S&F's work, "an animal can classify an odorant as 'novel' with no greater delay than for the classification of any known sample" (S&F, Sect. 3.4, para. 3).

There is obviously no complete isomorphism between model network "minimal anatomies" (Grossberg 1975) and real neuroanatomies. S&F's point about the limitations of the connectionist model of Hopfield and Tank (1986) is well taken (Sect. 4.4, para. 4). Both in that model and in the more general model of Cohen and Grossberg (1983), theorems show that the network always converges to an equilibrium state representing a "decision" about short-term pattern storage. As S&F rightly point out, such behavior is too circumscribed for the actual nervous system. In fact, in real-time simulations of behavioral data, networks of that variety typically model only the short-time dynamics of a part of an entire network that includes both associative and competitive parts. An example of such real-time simulation occurs in the Pavlovian conditioning model of Grossberg and Levine (submitted) [also summarized by Levine (1986)].

Hence there is room for many years of research on how established neural network theories of specific processes concatenate into large-scale systems that actually reproduce significant data, in the olfactory cortex and elsewhere. Obviously, the chaotic EEG patterns in the resting olfactory bulb are important to the theory of that area. Whether the chaos is essential to the purpose of the bulb's function or epiphenomenal to other things that are essential, I cannot hazard a guess. The answer will be related to that of the larger unanswered question concerning what the EEG measures in general!

Chaos in brains: Fad or insight?

Donald H. Perkel

Theoretical Neurobiology Facility, Department of Psychobiology and Department of Physiology and Biophysics, University of California, Irvine, Calif. 92717

The brain sciences, in their more reflective phases, are notorious for their immersion in analogy and metaphor (e.g., Arbib 1972). Traditional brain metaphors arise from technology. The nineteenth-century analogy between neuronal processes and undersea cables survives as modern cable theory. Subsequent technological metaphors have been based on telegraphic networks, telephone exchanges, control systems (Ashby 1952), digital computers (von Neumann 1958), holograms, and nonlinear networks (Hopfield & Tank 1986; Rosenblatt 1962; Rumelhart, Hinton & Williams 1986). Each of these metaphors has contributed valuable insights, some more than others; none provides a global theory of brain function.

Mathematical structures have also served as neural metaphors. Probabilistic examples include random-walk models for impulse-interval distributions (Fienberg 1974: Gerstein & Mandelbrot 1964; Sampath & Srinivasan 1977), stochastic point-process models of nerve-impulse sequences (Moore, Perkel & Segundo 1966; Perkel, Gerstein & Moore 1967a; 1967b), and the binomial model for quantal release of neurotransmitter (del Castillo & Katz 1954; Zucker 1973). Other primarily mathematical theories include the formal neuron model of McCulloch and Pitts (1943), interacting oscillator theories of the EEG, thermodynamically inspired theories of interacting populations of nerve cells (Cowan 1968), information theory as a paradigm for brain function, tensors as the basis of cerebellar function (Pellionisz & Llinás 1979), and the "trion" theory of cortical cell assemblies (Shaw, Silverman & Pearson 1985), essentially a probabilistic cellular automaton (Wolfram 1984).

Not all of these mathematical metaphors have fared well in the neuroscientific community. Random-walk models for impulse-interval distributions make nonunique predictions. The strict binomial model for neurotransmitter release yields misleading interpretations of experimental data (Brown, Perkel & Feldman 1976). Other mathematical models have been criticized on the grounds that the mathematical structure has dictated the biological assumptions or that the theory was leading the data.

Recently, much attention has been paid to the modern treatment of nonlinear differential equations, including catastrophe theory, bifurcation theory, Poincaré maps, strange attractors, "chaos," and fractals. Biological applications have abounded, sparked by May's (1976) demonstration of chaotic behavior in population dynamics. Bifurcation theory has been applied to excitable cells (Chay & Rinzel 1985). Skarda & Freeman (S&F) make broad claims about the explanatory role of bifurcations and the emergence of "chaos" in the functioning of the olfactory bulb. Similar claims have been advanced for activity in invertebrate ganglia (Mpitsos & Cohan 1986) and in cardiac arrhythmias (Mandell 1986), among others.

The question that immediately arises is whether the biological phenomena themselves dictate or justify the theory's mathematical structures. The alternative is that the beauty, versatility, and power of the mathematical approach may have led its aficionado to find areas of application in the spirit of the proverbial small boy with a hammer, who discovers an entire world in need of pounding. Is bifurcation theory merely a trendy framework for a Procrustean approach to nervous-system function? Does it make any more sense to say that the olfactory bulb makes chaos to make sense of the world of smell than it does to say that the cerebellum is a tensor, or that the hippocampus is a map, or that the visual system is a Fourier transformer, or that cognitive processes are executions of computer programs? Is the theory of familiar and strange attractors a natural way of looking at neurobiological phenomena – at the olfactory bulb in particular – or is it a method in search of a roosting place?

At the cellular level, the use of bifurcation theory by Chay and Rinzel (1985) clarifies the behavior of their system in a plausible and rewarding way; it enriches our insight. However, the bulb is immeasurably more complex, far less perfectly characterized, and harder to measure than the single cell; bifurcation analysis of the bulb is necessarily more risky, less readily quantifiable, and more subject to distortion.

Assuming that surface EEG measurements sufficiently well represent mitral-cell firing rates, what S&F have sketched is not a theory of odor recognition and learning, or of olfactory bulb

function, but rather an outline of a research program to produce and refine such theories. Their experimental findings, although far from conclusive, in fact make their argument plausible, in the context of the behavior of other nonlinear dynamic systems.

S&F correctly point out that connectionist models can generate chaotic behavior if artificial constraints on connectivity are lifted. A serious problem, however, remains: How does the system read out the information – that is, the identity of a familiar odorant – when its "representation" is so dynamic and volatile? The answer must lie in the anatomy and physiology of the bulb and more central structures, but the working principles of specific odorant identification remain to be elucidated.

Do the operating principles of the olfactory system hold for other sensory systems that have highly topographic anatomical representations? It may be that widespread chaos and self-organization are peculiar to the olfactory system or the brain stem, and that topographic systems "use" chaos in a much more restricted fashion.

Inhibition, as S&F point out, is essential to the operation of the system. Unaccountably, they mention the strengthening of excitatory synapses but not inhibitory synapses, although Wilson, Sullivan, and Leon (1985) describe increased inhibition in mitral cells after olfactory learning. It seems prudent to impute plasticity to inhibitory synapses as well.

S&F lament the weakness of the purely mathematical methods. The inescapable remedy is to mount a series of increasingly realistic, large-scale simulations of the system. The chief contribution of digital computers to theoretical neurobiology may be as tools for analysis and synthesis, rather than as marginally appropriate metaphors.

Finally, what is most attractive about S&F's theoretical approach is the biological flavor of its predictions. The picture of a spontaneously active bulb, goaded by sensory input into chaotic-appearing nonrecurring spatiotemporal patterns of activity, was sketched almost half a century ago: "millions of flashing shuttles weave a dissolving pattern, though never an abiding one; a shifting harmony of subpatterns" – the "enchanted loom" of Sherrington (1940; rev. ed. 1953, p. 178). When the skeletal theory has been fleshed out with more fine-grained experimental evidence and correspondingly realistic simulation studies, it may well be that bifurcation theory and chaos, arising out of "connectionist" models, may provide a cohesive, unifying, and apt theory for widespread aspects of brain functioning.

Connectionist models as neural abstractions

Ronald Rosenfeld, David S. Touretzky, and the Boltzmann Group
Computer Science Department, Carnegie Mellon University, Pittsburgh, Pa. 15213

Skarda & Freeman's (S&F's) findings and interpretations provide strong support for the connectionist paradigm. They clearly illustrate the importance of distributed representations and dynamic system theory for understanding computation in the brain. The paper concludes by criticizing various aspects of current connectionist models. It is this criticism that we wish to address.

Connectionist models are chiefly concerned with computational aspects of cognitive phenomena. At the current stage of this research, simplicity is often preferable to biological fidelity. We realize that the brain is likely to employ mechanisms beyond our present computational taxonomy, let alone our understanding or mathematical tools, but we nonetheless believe that current models, crude though they may be, advance the understanding of cognitive systems and contribute to the emergence of a new taxonomy. One should not confuse claims about the accuracy of certain connectionist models vis-à-vis real nervous systems with claims about their computational adequacy or scientific utility. S&F appear to have made this mistake.

S&F's target article repeatedly emphasizes the superiority of dynamic attractors over static ones, holding that connectionist models are inadequate since they do not have the former. But this is not so; a Boltzmann machine (Ackley et al. 1985) annealed down to a temperature slightly above its freezing point is manifesting a dynamic attractor state very similar to the one advocated by S&F. More important, the target article fails to demonstrate any computational advantage of dynamic models. Connectionist models are abstractions. Stationary patterns of activity in these models need not correspond to stationary patterns in the brain, just as connectionist units and their weighted connections need not correspond one-for-one with real neurons and synapses. Connectionists are perfectly happy to stipulate that the stable states of a Hopfield net (Hopfield 1982) or a Boltzmann machine are abstractions of dynamic attractors in the brain. We will abandon models with simple point attractors only if dynamic models can be shown to have useful computational properties that static ones lack. We have not yet seen the evidence that could support such a claim.

S&F maintain that chaotic behavior is essential for learning, but they do not make clear what role chaos is supposed to play in the learning that takes place in the rabbit olfactory bulb. The target article claims that a chaotic well – a "don't-know" state – is a prerequisite for the system to learn to recognize new odor categories. But which of the characteristics of chaos are necessary to the role it plays in generating new attractors, and which are irrelevant? S&F's article does not answer this key question.

S&F further criticize connectionist models because of their need to be externally reset after reaching a stable state. But the olfactory bulb does in fact settle into a single (albeit dynamic) state that is computationally equivalent to a corner of a hypercube; and it does not spontaneously escape from one dynamic attractor to other interesting ones. The return to the chaotic well (cf. the center of the hypercube) that takes place at exhalation in the rabbit appears to be precisely a forced reset action.

S&F next advise connectionists to give up the view of neural networks as pattern completion devices. They maintain that no pattern completion activity takes place in the olfactory bulb, since its output is a coherent global state generated from within, not merely a completed pattern within one nerve cell assembly (NCA). But to say that no pattern completion takes place in the olfactory bulb is to mix levels of description. Receptor cells send their pulses to the olfactory bulb, which in turn settles into a dynamically stable state – one of several preexisting possibilities. This is precisely what pattern completion is about! Stationary pattern completion activity in connectionist models is an abstraction. It need not correspond to stationary pattern completion in the brain. On the other hand, the "destabilization" paradigm advocated by S&F is merely a metaphor, and will remain so until it is supported by a concrete computational model.

The target article rightly points out that feedback mechanisms in the brain are far richer than those used in many connectionist models. But it also maintains that the "long delays, temporal dispersions, and spatial divergences" (Sect. 4.3, para. 2) present in the brain are *necessary* for the production of global behavior. In order to extend connectionist models to include these features, one must first have some idea of their essential role. There is no (computational) point in blindly simulating neural circuitry without first having an analytical handle on the role of the elements involved. By starting our analysis and simulation with minimal assumptions, we make sure that only essential features of the system will be admitted into our models.

Finally, we would like to point out some technical difficulties in the use of nerve cell assemblies to explain the formation of stable states. It is postulated that the NCAs are responsible for the selection of the basin to which the system bifurcates. According to this hypothesis, each NCA corresponds to a specif-

ic basin, and therefore to a specific known odor. The neurons in each NCA are supportive of one another, so that activating only some of them will cause the whole assembly to become active. How, then, is similarity between odors accounted for in this model? Do NCAs of two similar odors share neurons? If so, the presence of the first odor will activate its associated NCA. The latter will in turn activate the other NCA, irrespective of whether the odor it stands for is present. Moreover, what happens when a combination of two or more familiar odors is presented to the receptor cells? Are several NCAs activated simultaneously? What kind of basin is created, and how is it related to the basins of the component odors? What state does the system settle into eventually? The target article does not address these issues.

Chaos can be overplayed

René Thom
Institut des Hautes Études Scientifiques, 91440 Bures-sur-Yvette, France

More than a century ago the German mathematician B. Riemann, in his little-known philosophical writings, addressed the mind-body problem as follows: "When we think a given thought, then the meaning of this thought is expressed in the shape of the corresponding neurophysiological process." It is comforting to see this old idea unearthed after hard experimental work, and put forward by Skarda & Freeman (S&F) as a major discovery. (Here, of course, "meaning" has to be understood as a nonverbal conceptualization of smells in the rabbit's psyche.) First, it seems to me, there is a gap to be filled in the findings of S&F: To what extent does the shape of the EEG amplitude on the bulb depend on the experimental procedure – in particular, on the nature of the conditioning stimulus? Would the pattern observed for a given odorant when the subject is conditioned, say, by subsequent electric shocks, be the same as the one observed when reinforcement is obtained by giving water to the thirsty subject? The rather rough model offered for the underlying general dynamics is very suggestive (S&F's Figure 11), but the idea that for each of these attractors (or rabbits' pseudoconcepts) there should exist a specific triggering NCA (nerve cell assembly) seems to me another instance of what A. N. Whitehead (1960) called the "fallacy of misplaced concreteness" (p. 11). For if, as S&F claim, there exists in principle a virtual infinity of such attractors (due to the infinite fecundity of "chaos"), then this would require an infinite number of distinct NCAs, something difficult to accept.

Here one sees clearly the limits of neurophysiological research. When one tries to describe the anatomical constraints imposed by some specific functional behavior on the physiological level, "connectionist models" ultimately mean very little – namely, that a neural mass exhibits internal symmetry of a geometric type (translation, rotation, etc.) and that this symmetry may lead to corresponding "first integrals" of the associated neural dynamics. S&F give for the word "chaos" the definition once proposed by Ruelle-Takens (1971): differential systems which display the property of sensitivity to initial data. In this they follow the present fashion, to which I do not personally subscribe. "Chaos" and "chaotic" should be reserved for systems that cannot be explicitly described either quantitatively or qualitatively (there are plenty of them). Hence, such chaotic systems have no equations. Systems defined by equations have attractors (the precise mathematical definition of which may in fact be very difficult). It is to be expected that after the present initial period of word play, people will realize that the term "chaos" has in itself very little explanatory power, as the invariants associated with the present theory – Lyapunov exponents, Hausdorff dimension, Kolmogoroff-Sinai entropy (Guckenheimer & Holmes 1983) – show little robustness in the presence of noise.

The same misuse of terminology may be seen in S&F's systematic use of "self-organizing process." By that, I suppose, they mean a process that, starting from a given set Ω of initial data, will follow a specific trajectory (Γ) to a very good approximation, at least for a given time span [or, more generally, a process exhibiting spatially invariant configurations, as for Rayleigh (1916)–Bénard (1900) convective patterns]. In such a case, the old concept of "chreod," once proposed by C. H. Waddington (1957), would do the same job, and could be given under the notion of "morphogenetic field" a very precise mathematical formulation.

All in all, I would say that the main interest of the target article lies in the physiological description of the effects of Pavlovian conditioning on a given sensory input: formation of a high-frequency peak, spatially modulated in amplitude according to a specific pattern on the bulbar surface. This dynamical finding suggests that the propagative character of Pavlovian conditioning – the "*prégnance*"[1] of the stimulus – could be explained as a purely dynamical effect of resonance.

NOTE
1. The French word "prégnance" was proposed by this commentator as a property of an externally perceived form that is the opposite of "saillance" (saliency).

Cognition as self-organizing process

Gerhard Werner

Department of Psychiatry, University of Pittsburgh, Pittsburgh, Pa. 15213

Cognitivists of the representation-computation persuasion could, with some justification, support their case by pointing to the absence of neurobiologically viable and conceptually consistent alternative theories. The experimental findings and the elegant interpretations presented in the target article weaken this argument substantially. Although admittedly limited to "preattentive cognition" and not incorporating aspects of attentive stimulus exploration, Skarda & Freeman's (S&F's) model contains elements of potentially more general relevance, which are awaiting further elaboration of mathematical theories of distributive, dissipative systems, and more extended validation of the correspondence between brain electrical events and stimulations according to the operational principles proposed; nor is there anywhere else in the brain evidence for the occurrence of stimulus-related high-amplitude bursts of oscillatory activity comparable to the olfactory EEG on which the interpretation of the experimental data is based. Moreover, within its own domain, the model presupposes a number of modulatory neurochemical processes and synaptic connections that await empirical confirmation before conclusive validation is possible.

Notwithstanding this current restriction in generality and conclusiveness, the concepts developed in the target article raise tantalizing issues by sketching the outlines of an internally consistent and coherent model of perception and cognition that eliminates some of the solipsistic implications of representational cognitivism.

The evidence assembled by S&F attributes a primary role to cooperative, self-organizing activity in neural structures, which can individuate situation-specific, spatiotemporal profiles of neural activity, contingent on past stimulus exposure and behavior-regulating expectancies. The conceptual implications of this position merit underscoring: History is not represented as a stored image of the past; nor is the present a mirror of the environment. Instead, environmental events are specified by states of neural activity that are the result of the neuronal system's internal organization and dynamics. In this sense, the neural structure *uses* information to *create* its own internal states, which acquire meaning: The internal states are the

neuronal system's *own symbols*, as these states stand in a regular relation to events in the world and signify potentials for action. This distinction highlights the departure from current cognitivism, for which meaning is assigned to symbols by an observer. It seems that Dretske (1986) drew a similar distinction in another context.

Once symbols are viewed as the system's own creations, any reference to representations becomes superfluous; Occam's razor can unburden us of the Trojan horse that was smuggled from the land of Artificial Intelligence into Neuroscience. Perhaps the protestations that representations exist only in the mind of the observer who jointly beholds an environment and an observed organism (brain) will at last be heard (Maturana & Varela 1980).

The overriding importance of the work reviewed by S&F lies, in my view, in the fact that it sketches the outlines of a neurologically based approach to cognition as an alternative to the tenets of current cognitivism. This in itself represents an important contribution in proposing a viable alternative to representational-computational cognitivism, and in suggesting modifications of current connectionist models. The target article sets the stage for a "pluralistic methodology," which P. Feyerabend (1975) considers a vital element in support of competitive argumentation among theories, forcing each into greater articulation, and all of them contributing to greater clarity.

Authors' Response

Physiology: Is there any other game in town?

Christine A. Skarda[a] and Walter J. Freeman[b]

[a]CREA, Ecole Polytechnique, 75005 Paris, France and [b]Department of Physiology-Anatomy, University of California, Berkeley, Calif. 94720

We thank the commentators for taking the time to read, think about, and critically respond to our target article. The material we presented is diverse and difficult, despite (or perhaps in part because of) our effort to simplify it and make it accessible to researchers in other disciplines. Our exposition and our hypotheses extend from basic physiology through behavioral and cognitive theory, relying on mathematical techniques for quantitative description and prediction. The commentaries touch on all these levels and we have grouped our responses accordingly. Our overall conclusion is that our proposed view of the brain and the dynamics by which it generates behavior emerge intact from this scrutiny. However, we think that there is a problem of miscommunication that stems from failure of physiologists, psychologists, and modelers alike to follow through with careful consideration of the logical consequences of both new and long-standing findings on brain function.

Meetings, symposia, and workshops on neural networks and connectionism deriving from brain studies have now become commonplace. Yet we believe that physicists, engineers, and mathematicians have little understanding of the functional architecture of networks of real neurons, and that neural networking is just the newly derived technical capability to handle large arrays of interconnected elements with dynamic properties that, although simple for the element, are endlessly complex for the array. Underlying this work is a weak description of a nervous system that bypasses the basic questions about the essential character and organization of brains. Physiologists and anatomists, however, are equally deficient in failing to face the epistemological and philosophical consequences of their findings and conclusions and in interpreting them in terms other than those they have inherited from reflexologists.

Our main point lies beyond level confusion, misuse of terminology, and misconstrual of the tenets of cognitive science; it is that brains don't work at all in the way everyone, including ourselves, expected them to. We asked a simple question: What is the physical form in which sensory information is registered in the olfactory bulb? The answer we found – namely, a spatial pattern of chaotic activity covering the entire olfactory bulb, involving equally all the neurons in it, and existing as a carrier wave or wave packet for a few tens of milliseconds – is orthogonal to the axes of virtually every explanatory system we are aware of. It is therefore not surprising that some of our descriptions were misunderstood, and that some of the comments should be tangential to what we wrote. The full implications take time to sink in, as do the lessons to be learned for a new technology.

What emerges from our work, as recognized most clearly by **Werner**, is the conclusion that the concept of "representation" (e.g., symbols, schemata, codes, maps) is unnecessary as the keystone for explaining the brain and behavior. This is because the dynamics of basins and attractors can suffice to account for behavior without recourse to mechanisms for symbol storage and invariant retrieval, "teachers" in learning devices, error-correcting feedback, comparators, correlators, associators, and the fine-grain point-to-point topographic connectionism that is required for their effectuation. The nervous system tolerates (indeed thrives on) an enormous degree of what can only be called sloppiness in its design, construction, and maintenance. This is difficult for engineers and logicians to come to terms with, even when it is dressed up as chaos; but as **Garfinkel** (1983), Holden (1986), Rössler (1983), Shaw (1984), and others who write about chaos have pointed out, it is a quality that makes the difference in survival between a creature with a brain in the real world and a robot that cannot function outside a controlled environment.

In sum, cognitivists have written repeatedly for some years that rule-driven, symbol-manipulating devices are the only realistic hope for mimicking and explaining behavior. We submit that the brain can do better.

Psychology: Insight or level confusion? Several commentators have raised the issue of levels of description. Have we confused different levels of description? Is our view hopelessly muddled? We think not. **Barnden**'s comments are especially instructive in this regard.

Barnden does not contest our model of olfactory functioning as a distributed, self-organized process whose functional architecture resembles current connectionist models, but he raises two important points. First, he points out that our model of relatively low-level sensory neural mechanisms cannot be generalized without further data and argument to higher-level cognitive processes. We agree, but Barnden goes on to claim that

because "'symbol manipulationists' have in any case always presumed that low levels of perception are at least largely based on specialized mechanisms that are probably not to be regarded profitably as manipulating symbols in any conventional sense," we consequently have nothing new to offer to the debate. It is not clear which symbol manipulationists Barnden is referring to here, but we believe that he is mistaken. First, the neural processes captured by our model (after the first synapse) cannot be equated with simple transducer processes or with reflexes, both of which have traditionally been viewed as nonsymbolic. Second, it is not true that symbol manipulationists hold that input analysis, even at a relatively low level, does not involve symbolic manipulation. On the contrary, input analyses taking place after the transducer level have been considered paradigmatic examples of symbolic processing, whereas more central or higher cognitive processes have eluded analysis in similar terms. As one prominent proponent of the symbol-manipulation view says, "Input systems are computationally elaborated. Their typical function is to perform inference-like operations on representations [i.e., symbols] of impinging stimuli" [Fodor 1983, p. 83; see also multiple book review in *BBS* 8(1) 1985]. This is precisely the view that our model challenges.

Barnden also raises a more fundamental issue: Even if the lower-level sensory mechanisms could, as we claim, be explained in terms of nonsymbolic processing, what is to stop him and others from viewing the patterned output to higher cortical areas or the processes taking place in those areas in terms of symbol manipulation? Can the dynamic patterns of output from the olfactory bulb be the symbols Barnden feels compelled to look for in the brain? It is significant that Barnden is persuaded by our model to depart from the conventional view of symbols as strings of discrete bits of information that encode distinct physical properties, and to introduce what he refers to as "a certain amount of 'fuzz.'" The patterns he wants to equate with symbols are context-dependent; at best they are roughly correlated with events in the world, as he admits. As a result, crucial aspects of symbolic processing (e.g., decompositionality and inference) are jeopardized. We do have a good understanding of logical operations on conventional symbols, but we have no model for logical operations on context-dependent ones. Of course, one could still refer to these patterns as symbols, but what does the use of this term now buy us? Without the ability to perform conventional logical operations of the sort used by traditional symbolic processing, the use of the term "symbol" for the kinds of patterns we find in the olfactory system is not doing the work it did in models developed by the symbol manipulationists, and in the end it is misleading, because researchers are led to view the functional architecture of the system in a way that is not compatible with the distributed processing carried on by neural networks.

Earle grasped an important point missed by some of our commentators (**Barnden** and **Brown**): What we proposed on the basis of our data and the ensuing model is that the functional architecture of brains resembles the distributed, self-organized processes of connectionist models rather than the rule-driven symbol-manipulating processes characteristic of digital computers. Contrary to an apparently popular assumption, physiologists are not so naïve as to conclude, because they don't find symbols floating around in the neural tissue, that the brain is not a symbol-manipulation system. We agree with Barnden and Brown that a machine-level claim would be ineffectual against this position. But our model is pitched at the level of the functional architecture of the system: Our point is that brains use the functional architecture of distributed networks similar in many ways to present-day connectionist models. Connectionist models are not plausibly conceived of as symbol-manipulating, rule-driven systems; so why, if brains use a similar form of information processing, are the latter so construed?

We disagree, however, with **Earle**'s further claims that connectionist models promise a "noncognitive" account of behavior, and that information processing requires symbols and rules. Connectionist models are not attempts to provide a noncognitive account of behavior, if by "noncognitive" is meant not having to do with cognitive processes. Connectionist models are explicitly cognitive: Such models deal with mental processes (e.g., pattern recognition and completion, generalization, discrimination, associative memory) and the mechanisms responsible for cognition. Admittedly, our model and connectionist models in general do not appeal to rules or symbols, but this is not equivalent to the claim that they are noncognitive. As has been pointed out, connectionist models, although exhibiting regularities in processing information, do not apply rules; nor is the "currency" of such systems symbols (Rumelhart, McClelland & PDP Research Group 1986). But it is incorrect to equate information processing with rule-driven symbol manipulation. The point of connectionism is that a distributed system of interacting elements is able to produce behavior that was previously thought to require rules and symbols. Surely the appropriate response is to ask what makes Earle and others think that rule-driven symbolic processing is more cognitive than connectionist models. The connectionist challenge is not to cognitive models per se, but to a specific class of cognitive models based on the digital computer.

We accept **Brown**'s concession that we did not wittingly seek to mystify or intimidate our readers. We suggest that our argument is not so confused as his quotations out of context might imply, and although we do not think we are "naïve materialists," we do take brain functioning and the constraints it places on our model seriously. Unlike Brown, we don't view our model as "merely physiological." We suspect that there is a lot packed into Brown's use of the word "merely" here – specifically, a commitment to the functionalist view that what neuroscience tells us about is irrelevant to the concerns of cognitive psychology. The underlying assumption is that physiology is irrelevant to computational issues because it is concerned only with the specifics of structural implementation (neurons, membrane constants, neurotransmitters, and so on). But this is not true. We feel that our research demonstrates that physiologists need not be (and, in fact, are not) saddled with a function-structure distinction that once and for all limits their research project to structural minutiae: Admittedly we investigated the structural properties of neural nets, but we did so in the context of viewing these networks as functional units whose input–output dynamics are captured by our model. And contrary to the functionalist

assumption, our research at the physiological level led us to produce a theory of its functional organization. We suggest that the fashionable dismissal of neuroscience popularized by a functionalism tied to the symbolic form of information processing is too simplistic in its understanding of neuroscience as practiced by researchers. (Parenthetically, our experience has been that, contrary to Brown's assertion, substantial numbers of theorists believe that the functional architecture of neural activity is identical to that of digital computers; but perhaps our dismal experience is attributable to cultural lag, and fewer people still think this way than we have inferred. Perhaps.)

What about the role of modeling, an issue raised by **Brown**? As a theory of whole brain function that purports to explain the changes in mass action of neurons that accompany learning new patterns of behavior, our theory spans three levels. As such it must provide the conceptual framework for the display and verification of neurophysiological correlates of behavior. And as a model of "the integrative action of the nervous system" (Sherrington 1906), it must describe or simulate the dynamic functional properties of the nervous system. Finally, because the theory attempts to explain behavior as well as brain function, it has failed if it does not yield neurobehavioral correlates or lead to methods for simulating animal and human behavior.

In previous discussions (Freeman 1981) we have adopted the tenet advanced by Craik (1952) that the essence of explanation lies in simulation. To understand some event or process, according to this view, is to generate or operate a model of it. To answer **Brown,** we think this can be done for our theory by using differential equations that replicate the electrophysiological patterns to make models that perform the computational operations we attribute to the brain regions we have studied. We suppose that it makes little difference a priori whether the models are made with hardware or software, although as experimentalists (naïve materialists?) we prefer to work with the former. Brown is surely as aware as we are of the pitfalls in complex programming and numerical integration; in this respect there is no advantage over hardware. In this use the computer serves as an analog, and therefore as a simile, not a metaphor. But we view the software as a helpful approach in the design of a device, just as a blueprint is a stage in the design of a tool.

We accept **Barnden**'s criticism of our use of top-down and bottom-up; the point we wished to make is that our model resembles connectionist models in being a system that exhibits regularities and processes information without being rule-driven and manipulating symbols. Barnden also raises a physiological issue: He asks why we have not performed experiments involving the simultaneous presentation of several odors. We have not done this because it is inappropriate in our system. In olfactory physiology we have the problem of chemical reactions upon mixing odors, of new odors arising (e.g., butter and vanilla give "cake"), of optimizing the ratio of concentrations, of solubility coefficients, and so on. These factors prohibit the kind of experimentation Barnden proposes for olfaction in animals. Our theory of functional architecture should first be tested in vision or audition; if it is found to be valid, his proposed experiments can be done with relative ease.

The last word in our dialogue with psychologists we give to **Werner.** We feel that he has done a major service by expressing in clear and concise language the major theoretical implications of our target article for cognitive science. Although we originally undertook our work in order to find experimental support for the symbol-manipulationist view of information processing (Freeman 1983a), the relationship we established between measurements of behavior and electrochemical events in the nervous system forced us to adopt an alternative model (Freeman & Skarda 1985). This led us to the view that brains have a capacity to learn using cooperative activity in neural networks without anything like what the computational model based on digital computers had thought necessary. In our neural model, as in connectionist models, there is no discrete semantic interpretation given to activity in a neural net or to elements of the net; this activity varies not only with the presence and absence of particular environmental events, but also with the context. We did not come to this view without spending several frustrating years of inspecting EEG records and unit activity.

As **Werner** points out, the concepts of "representation" and "symbol" are deeply rooted in the minds of cognitive scientists; they will be eliminated or replaced only by the acquisition of a substantial body of data showing that they are unnecessary to explain behavior. Unlike Werner, however, we don't think that referring to these neural patterns as the "neuronal system's *own symbols*" is helpful. The distinction we wish to emphasize is not that between the first-person and third-person points of view. Our point is that the system can produce adaptive, ordered, cognitive behavior without using functional architecture based on rules and symbol manipulation. The neural patterns of our model are not symbols for the system because a distributed network doesn't require symbols to produce behavior.

Physiology: What's in a brain? The commentaries from physiologists raised several issues: the relationship of our theory to other theories, questions about the physiological role and scope of chaotic activity in the brain, and specific questions about the physiology of the system. We respond to each of these in turn.

First a word or two about the relationship of our theory to other theories: What is really new about our work? We thank **Boynton** for mentioning the pioneering work of Demott (1970). We have cited it in previous reports and could add to the list of pioneers in this field Walter (1953), Lilly and Cherry (1955), and Livanov (1977). Although these projects were able – using ingenious and imaginative devices to analyze huge quantities of data – to show that spatiotemporal patterns exist in brain activity, technical limitations prevented them from reliably reproducing or understanding the significance of the observed patterns.

Our claim to priority is not for the detection and display of patterns, nor for the technologies required for transduction, processing, and display. The electrode array is a journeyman device when seen in company with the exotic apparatus for optical, magnetic, and biochemical transduction, and our use of the digital computer is minor league in comparison with uses by meteorologists and geologists. Our primary accomplishment is the systematic measurement of repeated blocks of data, decomposition of the data into sections, the systematic testing of each of those sections for information relating to behavior, and the statistical validation of the results. By following our prescription we believe that others can find the same or similar patterns. Our priority, then, is more like that of Columbus than the Vikings: Although not the first to discover the New World, he was the first to show others how to get there and back reliably. It is this reliability of the technology to the multivariate system, and in particular the demonstration of behaviorally significant regularities in the spatial dimensions of the data, that forms the substance of our claim to priority.

Access to the digital computer is not the only basis for the difference between "seeing" that spatial patterns exist in the brain and comprehending their significance. What is crucial is the development of the necessary software. Early on we presented cinematic displays of the space–time patterns of olfactory EEG waves from electrode arrays (Freeman 1972), but the ability to demonstrate odorant specificity required that we devise the tools for measurement, a task that took 12 years to complete. Unfortunately the available theory of neural action in perception was not merely unhelpful, it was misleading. We made repeated attempts without success to locate "hot spots" of the kind purportedly revealed by 2-deoxyglucose, or to find information in phase or frequency patterns. Eventually, the key to the problem was found not in the display techniques or in the theory of nonlinear dynamics; it lay in the development of adequate techniques of measurement, including use of a behavioral assay to validate those techniques (Freeman 1987b).

We wish to point out in this connection that three technical aspects of our procedures are crucial. One is the use of spectral analyses in the temporal and spatial domains of EEG recordings as the basis for determining digitizing intervals and interelectrode distances for array recording. This, combined with theoretical analyses of the biophysical properties of the neurons generating the EEGs, provided the basis for the separation of "signal" from "noise" by filtering. A second is the use of a behavioral assay and the repetition of analytic procedures while optimizing the filter parameter for the extraction of the desired information. The third is the detailed analysis of the variance that led to our realization that the significant spatial patterns of EEG potentials were best seen after normalization of the amplitudes by channel.

Several commentators, including **Corner & Noest,** raise the issue of the relationship of our model to connectionist models. At the risk of repeating our target article, we concur with those commentators who pointed out that our approach is inherently "connectionist" and indeed "must be considered as constituting simply a possible improvement *within* that category" (Corner & Noest); our criticisms of other species within the genus should not be construed as a denial of our membership. As **Barnden** points out, our model is an "extension of present-day connectionism." We recognize that in this rapidly evolving field, some of the criticisms we directed against other connectionist models are already out of date. Nevertheless, we find that too many connectionists are preoccupied with the structural properties of their models (e.g., relationships between the numbers of nodes and the memory capacity of a net) to the exclusion of the description and analysis of the dynamics. The tested models that we are at present acquainted with and that can be described in terms of basins and attractors are endowed with equilibrium attractors. Our results require that these be replaced with limit-cycle and chaotic attractors if they are to be relevant to the brain and the behavior it controls. In one sense this is a small step, but in many ways it is very difficult. Corner & Noest note that an extensive literature already exists on the properties of spatially distributed coupled oscillators; they sketch briefly an exciting possible route for further description and understanding of this baffling but vital system. We believe that their particular example (concerning the expression of phase patterns into spatially nonuniform amplitude patterns owing to spatial smoothing) may be directly relevant to bulbar EEG analysis, but not in the manner they suggest. As we have reported (Freeman & Baird, in press; Freeman & Viana Di Prisco 1986b), the phase pattern appears as a conic gradient in spherical coordinates, and the local differences in EEG amplitude are closely related to local differences in subsurface neural firing rates that are not subject to spatial smoothing by the volume conductor. We hope that Corner & Noest will "start delving into the complexities of structurally inhomogeneous models," and we ask them what information they need to have "specified more precisely" in order to "allow such improved models" to be developed.

In a more general vein, **Perkel** asks whether our use of nonlinear dynamics and bifurcation theory is metaphorical [the brain is (like) a . . .] or operational [the dynamics of the bulb is described by the equation $f(x) = . . .$]. We believe that it is operational, because our equations are constructed in accordance with the anatomy and known biophysical properties of component neurons and their interconnections, and are solved with boundary and initial conditions that conform to the gross anatomy and the neural input. We adjusted the parameters until the solutions to the equations conformed to the observed and measured patterns of neural activity, and we did not accept solutions for which the required parameter values were anatomically or physiologically unrealistic. In this respect our "theory" is no more or less metaphorical than any other use of descriptive equations properly selected. Superficially, at least, experimentalists can afford to be both skeptical and cavalier about theories: If a tool seems promising, we learn to use it; if it works, we continue to use it; if not, we find another. In the olfactory system we find that the language of basins and attractors helps us to assemble and simulate many aspects of patterned neural activity. The methods provide insights for further research, evidence that other parts of the cerebrum may operate in closely related ways (Freeman & van Dijk, submitted), and ways to test this hypothesis. What more can one ask of theory?

Babloyantz points out that ours isn't the first physiological account to postulate chaotic activity based on EEG recordings. She provides a useful list of references to recent work on the dimensional analysis of putative chaos in human scalp EEG recordings, to which we add work by Nicolis (1985b) and Nicolis and Tsuda (1985) on chaotic dynamics of information processing by the brain. (**Perkel**, by the way, asked whether chaos is unique to olfaction. Babloyantz and others have clearly demonstrated that it is

not.) These and related studies have established that low dimensions appear in analyses of records from subjects in deep sleep and in certain forms of epilepsy. But in these studies the estimated dimensions of waking EEGs are so high that the distinction between chaos and noise or a mix of the two becomes blurred (see commentary by **Thom**). A further difficulty with these studies is that the single channel of the scalp EEG is undefined with respect to the numbers of functional entities (and therefore of dimensions) that contribute to the record (as distinct from our deliberate restriction to activity from a single entity); and the scalp EEG is subject to much stronger spatial and temporal smoothing than pial recordings, leading to artifactual reduction in the apparent dimension. So, although our research is not the first to postulate chaotic activity based on EEG recordings, we do believe our work makes important new contributions by eliminating some of these difficulties.

Contrary to **Babloyantz**'s assertion, our main point is not that brain activity conforms to the dynamics of chaos, but that the brain organizes its own space–time patterns of function and thereby its own structure. We postulate that it generates chaotic activity as an essential precursor to the emergence of ordered states. Far from being misleading, we think that our statement that "chaos is a controlled noise" is appropriate. The patterns of activity we observe in the bulb have commonality of waveform over cortical regions comprising hundreds of millions of neurons, with phase gradients and spectral distributions (both temporal and spatial) that are held within narrow limits; amplitudes (root mean square) that are regulated precisely in accordance with motivational state; and, above all, the maintenance of sustained basal activity without recurring spatial patterns. The generator of this activity is exceedingly robust, a neural mechanism that we can readily believe has been present in vertebrates for over four hundred million years. The activity looks like "noise," serves (we believe) purposes met by unstructured or pseudorandom activity, and is turned on and off rapidly and reliably with respiration in a controlled manner. We agree with Babloyantz that to understand our target article properly readers will have to seek out and study "more technical publications" as cited here and elsewhere, and we hope that the paper will motivate some of them to do so.

As to our view of the underlying physiology, **Perkel** questions why we propose that strengthening of excitatory synapses, but not inhibitory ones, occurs with learning. We base our hypothesis on measurements of changes in the waveform of averaged evoked potentials when animals are trained to respond to electrical stimuli (Emery & Freeman 1969), and on determinations of the parameter changes that are necessary and sufficient to replicate these pattern changes in the solutions of differential equations that model the neural dynamics (Freeman 1979b). Interestingly, several theoretical advantages accrue from the experimental result that only the excitatory synapses change. One is the exquisite sensitivity of the olfactory system, arising from the form of the sigmoid curve under recurrent excitation. Another is the pattern stabilization and figure completion that results from strengthened excitatory connections (Babloyantz & Kaczmarek 1981). Yet another is the exploitation of the Hebb (1949) rule, which is the basis for learning under reinforcement in our model; it is difficult to see how this rule might be implemented toward formation of a nerve-cell assembly if the synapses to be strengthened were inhibitory. The findings of Wilson, Sullivan, and Leon (1985) are fully consistent with our model; we have shown elsewhere (Gonzalez-Estrada & Freeman 1980) that observed suppression of mitral cell discharge can be the manifestation of profound excitatory action onto those same cells, given the proper system parameters. Here, indeed, is an opportunity for theory to come forward and explain the paradoxical and counterintuitive.

Perkel also raises what he refers to as the "serious problem" of how the system can read out the identity of a familiar odorant when static and invariant representations'do not exist in the bulb or elsewhere in the olfactory system as the basis for osmic memory. We have proposed elsewhere (Freeman & Skarda 1985) that the coherent, phase-locked activity generated by mitral cells, falling onto the prepyriform cortex after spatial and temporal reorganization in the olfactory tract, causes further bifurcation in that structure, initiating the process of response selection. But Perkel's question is important, because we do not yet know how that is done. For us, the really serious issue is not that the event is a transitory bundle of energy rather than a fixed state; it is that of developing a model based on distributed dynamic networks that can explain how a dynamic state (which need not have gone to completion) can lead to state changes in the rest of the nervous system leading to a response. One advantage of a connectionist model is that it doesn't require the fixed states that symbolic processing requires, and it allows us to conceive of new forms of interaction among subsystems like those found in the brain.

Corner & Noest's chief challenge to our target article concerns the issue of projection of afferent activity from the receptors to the bulb. As they see it, each odorant stimulus activates a set of receptors that in turn activates its odorant-specific pattern in the bulb, with "magnification of preexisting differences in the spatial distribution of afferent signals. . . . What, then, needs to be 'learned' about such signals? . . . Nothing else, surely, than . . . behavioral significance." Corner & Noest fail to grasp that the major task for learning to identify an odor is the formation of a nerve-cell assembly by the pair-wise strengthening of synapses between co-activated mitral cells (Hebb 1949). This task reflects the necessity for establishing an equivalence over all receptors (and the mitral cells to which they transmit) that are sensitive to a particular odor in an invariant manner. This is the key problem that Lashley (1942) posed in terms of stimulus equivalence. The formation of the nerve-cell assembly, in accordance with the postulate proposed by Hebb, takes place only under reinforcement and involves the release of norepinephrine into the bulb (Gray, Freeman & Skinner 1986). As we discussed in our target article, the EEG spatial patterns are as closely related statistically to the CR (conditional response) as to the CS (conditional stimulus). In answer to Corner & Noest's specific query, there were nine distinctive patterns for each of the four subjects that learned the discriminations, including discriminable spatial patterns that had the same odorant as CS but with different "meaning" (that is, that elicited a different CR) at different stages in the training program.

Finally, **Corner & Noest** mention several issues that, although not relevant to the main points raised in our target article, are of special interest to physiologists, so we'll address them here. First, we think that the resemblance Corner & Noest point out between the classical brainstem mechanisms for cortical arousal, on the one hand, and the energizing effect of receptor input to the olfactory bulb, on the other, is not to be taken seriously. The nonspecific arousal process is mediated by ascending reticular axons operating on and through the thalamic reticular nuclei, whereas specific sensory activity is carried by distinctive sensory pathways through modality-specific thalamic nuclei. The "dual" input to the bulb is carried by one and the same pathway; receptor axons carry action potentials that bear specific information by depolarizing the apical dendrites of selected mitral cells. Massive depolarization of the whole system brings about a bifurcation that leads to response selection. This is not the "preparation" of the bulb by the prior action of a parallel ascending pathway; it is a result of the concomitant induction of an instability of the system receiving the input. Moreover, the time and distance scales of these phenomena are significantly different. Reticular activation is broadcast to all parts of the nervous system by ascending and descending projections, irrespective of the modality of the arousing stimulus, and the aroused state tends to last for seconds to minutes with gradual abatement. The transition in the olfactory system is localized to the bulb and cortex, and it terminates during exhalation in a fraction of a second. Finally, the arousal response is centrifugally induced in the olfactory system as well as in other sensory cortices, whereas the formation of the burst is dependent on the centripetal sensory input and requires that the bulb already be in the aroused state.

Second, we are in fact unable to explain alpha suppression in arousal or the enhancement of hippocampal theta in certain states involving orienting, but these phenomena lie outside the scope of our data and models. Our models do not generate activity in the alpha and high theta ranges (roughly 5 to 15 Hz) without impermissible parameter settings, but neither does the olfactory system.

Third, it is not the case, as stated by **Corner & Noest,** that gamma EEG waves "have gone undetected" in the neocortex. Systematic studies as well as anecdotal reports abound attesting to the presence of "40 Hz" activity, as it is commonly called, in many areas of the neocortex (e.g., Chatrian, Bickford & Uihlein 1960; Sheer 1976). In our opinion Corner & Noest underestimate the strength of the signal degradation imposed on neocortical EEG potentials by the spatial dispersion of the generating cells in directions perpendicular to the pia. The three cortical structures with the most striking alignment of their generating cells in this respect are the bulb, the prepyriform cortex, and the hippocampus, and these three have EEG amplitudes that easily exceed the amplitudes of neocortical EEGs by 10- to 20-fold. Moreover, the relatively low amplitudes of that activity, especially at the scalp, are confounded by electromyographic (EMG) potentials that badly obscure gamma activity (40 to 90 Hz). Hence the gamma activity is known to exist, but it is poorly documented and has largely been ignored.

Fourth, we agree with **Corner & Noest** that "the basic

notion of widely synchronized neuronal carrier waves . . . is by no means excluded by differences among brain regions displaying the precise [frequency] characteristics of these (chaotic) waves," but we do not consider as "major" the challenge to account for the observed frequencies and amplitudes of olfactory EEG activity or to show their theoretical advantages. We have demonstrated repeatedly that the gamma range is the characteristic frequency band for neurons with passive membrane time constants on the order of 5 msec, and that the amplitudes are the result of the cytoarchitecture of the laminar structures. These are as they are because of the properties of the neurons that comprise the areas and generate the waves, not because these properties critically influence olfactory information processing. We suspect that neocortical cell assemblies tend much more strongly to chaotic activity, which renders them all the less accessible to our present understanding; but we do not consider it incumbent on us at this time to explain why this is so, or to show what advantages might accrue to vision or audition thereby. We have attempted to understand and explain paleocortical dynamics and to speculate a bit about the neocortex, not to propose a general theory of the EEG.

Mathematics: The uses and abuses of chaos. Chaos and its possible role in pattern recognition figured prominently in our target article. We suggested that in the brain chaos is necessary for learning new odors. Not all the commentators agreed with this, but as **Garfinkel** noted, the view that chaos plays a functional role is "something of an about face" for a phenomenon that has traditionally been viewed as highly undesirable. We are especially encouraged by the examples he cites that indicate chaos is not merely tolerated but essential for optimal performance of systems in search of their own goals or states of minimal energy. These uses for chaos translate readily into the maintenance of background activity while avoiding hypersynchrony, as in epilepsy; the flexibility and adaptiveness of behavior in the face of unpredictable environments; and the speed of operation of brains in entering and leaving states sequentially. We suggested that flexibility in responding to the changing olfactory environment is provided by the chaotic basal state, and that chaos doesn't merely provide noise in the manner of a Boltzmann machine to avoid local minima in a convergence process, but that it allows a relatively high energy state to be maintained between signal episodes, so that the neural system does not have to be dragged out of or dropped into a deep energy well with each bifurcation. It can flip lightly and quickly with each sample and flip back again. Furthermore, because the same mechanism generates both chaos and carrier, the "noise" is shut off when the "signal" goes on and vice versa. The signal is detected between the noise periods and not in them, so that the "signal/noise ratio" concept is not applicable here.

Most of the objections to our use of chaos were based on proposed alternative models that don't require chaotic activity. The commentaries of **Grossberg, Levine,** and **Rosenfeld, Touretzky & the Boltzmann Group** belong to this category. By way of preface, however, we want to make our general position on chaos clear. We are the first

to admit that we have no proof that chaos is essential to pattern recognition, whether biological or artificial, or that nonzero equilibria under noise might not serve as well. We believe, however, that we have shown that chaos exists in the olfactory system, and that our suggestions as to its roles are plausible and useful; certainly chaos should not be averaged out, discarded, or ignored. Although our understanding of chaos is rudimentary in comparison with our needs, the most effective way to proceed is by close cooperation between theorists and experimentalists, as exemplified by our exchanges with **Garfinkel,** especially in the analysis of spatially distributed systems of coupled oscillators. Now, on to some of the objections.

In the past two decades **Grossberg** and his associates have consistently produced imaginative, detailed, yet comprehensive models expressing the formal bases of learned behavior generated by nervous systems. We note, however, that Grossberg's *"Gedanken"* experiments have been designed primarily to explain phenomena deriving from psychophysics; the relationship to neurophysiology occurs through his use of neural "metaphors," such as the cellular dipole representing local inhibitory feedback, the first-order decay process representing passive membrane, shunting inhibition, and the modifiable synapse. We view these terms as metaphorical because, in using them, Grossberg normalizes his state variables to dimensionlessness in time and space. In principle, of course, he could retain the conversion factors and return to the metric of the relevant nervous system, but in practice he does not because his avowed interest lies in general principles and not in specific examples. It is accordingly necessary for experimentalists to supply the conversion factors in order to test his theories, to the extent that they are intended to explain the brain.

Grossberg's claim, based on his work on olfactory coding and its explanation by his adaptive resonance model (1976; 1981) and recently incorporated in his ART 1, is that chaos is unnecessary in his model. What are we to make of this claim in relation to our data? A comparison of ART 1 with our KII model shows that both consist of excitatory and inhibitory neurons formed into three or more serial layers with massively parallel axonal connections between them. The initial layer in both models is comprised of the sensory transducer neurons; Grossberg's layer S1 purports to embody our olfactory bulb, and his layer S2 the prepyriform cortex. His element for arousal from mismatch or attentional biasing may correspond topologically to the anterior olfactory nucleus, because this is a key site for centrifugal brainstem control of the bulb. Within each layer there is local negative (inhibitory) feedback, and there is extensive feedback between layers S1 and S2. Both systems have the ability to modify synaptic weights under reinforcement during learning. Both invoke the sigmoid curve as the static nonlinearity that dominates the dynamics.

However, despite these superficial resemblances the differences between the two systems are so great that direct comparisons tend to be nonproductive and misleading. In ART 1 the most important modifiable synapses are at the input from layer S1 to layer S2, equivalent to that between the lateral olfactory tract and the prepyriform pyramidal cell, and from S2 to S1 equivalent to that between the medial olfactory tract and the granule cell (not the mitral cell, as **Grossberg**'s model states). In ART 1 the input pattern is sustained and maintained for matching purposes at the input synapse to S1, equivalent to the primary olfactory nerve synapsing on mitral cells. In our KIII set the input is ignored after bifurcation. Moreover, this synapse is the site of dynamic range compression and signal normalization (presynaptic inhibition); none of these synapses change in relation to associative learning in KIII, though they are subject to posttetanic and long-term potentiation. Shunting inhibition in ART 1 is multiplicative; recurrent inhibition in KIII is additive. In ART 1 local inhibitory feedback serves primarily for contrast enhancement. In the KIII set it serves primarily for generating the carrier frequency of bulbar output. In Grossberg dynamics, the state variables tend to fixed values (equilibrium attractors). Long-range excitatory connections are not prominent in ART 1; the distance of excitatory transmission is kept below that of inhibitory transmission. In the KIII set long-range excitatory connections in both the bulb and cortex are crucial for the formation of Hebb-type nerve-cell assemblies, because it is here that the synapses are modified in associative learning. In ART 1 the Hebb rule is applied to modification at the input level by virtue of feedback of spatially detailed and precisely timed information from S2 to S1. This cannot occur in the KIII set, because it models the feedback from the prepyriform cortex to the bulb, and this has such marked spatial divergence and temporal dispersion in both forward and feedback directions that no such transmission of detailed information is feasible. The pathways act as strong low-pass filters and remove it.

From these and related anatomical and physiological measurements we conclude that function in the olfactory system cannot depend on precise timing and precise topographic mapping. Its algorithms must be reliable in the face of continual smoothing of activity by temporal dispersion under axonal transmission and by spatiotemporal integration in dendrites. This is one of several reasons that we insist repeatedly that behaviorally relevant neural information is to be found in the average activity of ensembles (as manifested in the EEG) and not in the activity of single neurons, once the first stage of carriage by sensory neurons has been passed.

In addition, although **Grossberg** has often stated that his models hold good for both the single neuron and for the ensemble, we maintain that this cannot be so, because the static sigmoid nonlinearity that dominates the dynamics of both ART 1 and the KIII model holds only for the ensemble and not for the single neuron. He has also claimed that his results hold for both steady-state and oscillatory solutions (equilibrium and limit-cycle attractors). In our view he has not adequately demonstrated the pattern-recognition dynamics of the oscillatory standing-wave type of system to substantiate this claim.

From these considerations it should be apparent that although we and **Grossberg** appear to be thinking and writing about the same nervous system, in actuality we are skew, almost entirely disjunct, because of the differences between our methods, values, and data bases. Of course, Grossberg's assertion would be valid if we had claimed that chaos was required for all pattern-recogni-

tion devices. Such a claim, however, would be foolish. We readily acknowledge the validity of his claims about equilibrium solutions for ART 1, but we want to point out that his dynamics have not yet been developed sufficiently to simulate the actual performance of our KIII model. Until he is able to expand his "minimal anatomies" to include and fully exploit modifiable excitatory crosscoupling within S1 and within S2, and to establish the proofs of performance of this system with periodic attractors, as he has for the fixed points of ART 1, we cannot concede that he has a counterexample. His model is not in the same domain. We conclude that Grossberg's cautionary note that chaos is inessential in ART 1 is important to consider, but that we must await further development of his ART models that explicitly exhibit the anatomy and dynamics we observe in the brain before we can be bound by his logic. And should his models prove to be less flexible than he might desire, we recommend a small dose of chaos.

In a related vein, we accept **Levine**'s point that some connectionist models have the capacity to respond to novel as well as to familiar input, so that input can be rapidly identified as novel and the learning process can begin. Such a process is embodied in **Grossberg**'s ART 1 model and in work cited by Levine. Our difficulty, as discussed in our response to Grossberg above, is that our analysis indicates the olfactory system is not capable of performing the operations required for match and mismatch detection, at least in the manner carried out by ART 1. This is because the feedback pathway from the putative layer S2 (the prepyriform cortex) to layer S1 (the olfactory bulb) is incapable of sustaining transmission of information with the requisite specificity of timing and spatial resolution. That is, we see no realistic way that fibers in the medial olfactory tract can return an organized pattern from the prepyriform cortex to the bulb and "match," "correlate," or "compare" it with a pattern in the bulb that is sustained by input from the receptors. Furthermore, our recordings tell us that after bifurcation the bulbar activity pattern reflects the generalization to a stereotypic form affected by a class of inputs based on experience rather than current individual inputs. We therefore contend that although Levine and Grossberg are on the track of devices that may far outperform the simpler connectionist models currently in vogue, these do not help to explain the dynamics of those parts of the nervous system with which we are familiar. If their models can be made to do what brains can do, or even to outperform them, then they need not trouble with chaos. If they cannot, then, like theorists of the past several decades, they might consider returning to the nervous system for some more insights and ideas. This is what von Neumann (1958) did in his quest for mastery of the newly conceived programmable digital computer.

The other large-scale assault on our target article from connectionists came from **Rosenfeld et al.** who presented clear-cut arguments strongly defending their views and practices without effectively, we think, eroding our claims or responding to our findings or our speculations concerning the significance of their models for cognitive science. We recognize and have repeatedly stated that all models are abstractions, that the value of each model depends on how well the selection of detail to be included or excluded helps the modeler to attain a stated goal, and that judicious selection is more to be valued than mere fidelity to some "view" of how an aspect of the brain being modeled actually works. That "view" in itself being a hypothesis and therefore a model of sorts, we think that Rosenfeld et al. have invited us into a cul-de-sac with their allegation that we are confused. Furthermore, we believe that they have short-changed themselves in their efforts to "contribute to the emergence of a new taxonomy" of connectionist models by their apparent refusal to add some more cages to their zoo for models with dynamic attractors. To be sure, we have no evidence for the computational superiority of dynamic attractors in mathematical form, nor do we have bench-mark studies comparing the speed, accuracy, capacity, stability, and so on of two or more models having point versus chaotic attractors that perform some common task. We are not aware that benchmark studies exist as yet for comparative evaluation of different species of point models. But it is not true that we have no "evidence that could support [our] claim" for the value of dynamic attractors. The bulk of our target article presents evidence that the olfactory system works with dynamic attractors; we cited additional evidence that suggests the rest of the cerebrum may do so as well. This type of evidence is considered by some connectionists to be relevant to artificial intelligence (AI), considering that the performance of the brain still outclasses those of AI models.

Rosenfeld et al. ask us, "Which of the characteristics of chaos are necessary to the role it plays in generating new attractors, and which are irrelevant?" Our answer is that the following characteristics are necessary. We have stated that in order for the Hebb rule to operate, the neurons involved in the learning process must be active during the CS-induced activity under reinforcement of the UCS (unconditional stimulus), but that the activity must not conform to the attractor of a known odor. Hence, if the intensity of the activity must be high and its pattern should not conform to any previous spatial pattern of activity, then the pattern must appear to be random – i.e., chaotic – and must cover the entire bulb. On the other hand, the following aspects are irrelevant. The time series looks random. We find that its spectrum is broad in comparison to the spectrum of bursts with known odorants, and there is more low temporal frequency energy.

Rosenfeld et al. write of a "forced reset action" existing in the dynamics of the bulb during exhalation, that is analogous to the action of turning their devices "off." This is a significant mischaracterization of the dynamics of our model. During inhalation there is a forced choice leading to capture of the system at a "single (albeit dynamic) state that is computationally equivalent to the corner of a hypercube" (hypertorus?), which in our model is due to an obligatory side effect of the input surge; but during exhalation there is *relaxation* to the basal state, not forced reset. Furthermore, there is no reset to the "center of the hypercube," even if the center could be computed within a reasonable time; instead, in our model *the entire hypercube vanishes*. It is re-created with each new inhalation causing bifurcation; this is the essence of self-organization.

Rosenfeld et al. have likewise failed to grasp the significance of our remarks on "pattern completion." There is a simple sense of "pattern completion" that can

be said to take place: the conjectured extensive spread of activity through a nerve cell assembly (NCA) when any subset of its neurons is excited. There is another sense that is untenable: This is to suppose that the NCA is like the form of the letter "A" that is filled in by mutual excitation within the NCA following excitation of some fraction of its parts. The NCA is formed by repeated presentations of an odorant at sufficiently dilute concentration to prevent adaptation, and we suppose that the entirety is never activated on any one presentation, nor would that presentation be in any sense necessary, crucial, or identifiable even if it did occur. Furthermore, the successful convergence into the basin of a correct attractor, according to our model, depends on activating an NCA but does not specify that the activation need be complete, or even need asymptotically approach completion. The outcome may be a behavioral pattern, so that a stimulus–response configuration may be said to go to completion, but this does not require that an internal dynamic activity pattern go to "completion" in some kind of exemplary archetypal or normative state. The regularities in spatial pattern we have observed do represent possible outcomes, but cannot be shown, we believe, to be "completed" in the sense commonly used. We agree that our notion of "destabilization" is a metaphor until realized in software or hardware, and we intend to pursue it further; but we deny that generalization over equivalent stimuli, which is done by a basin and its attractor, is the same as pattern completion.

Moreover, in response to **Rosenfeld et al.** we wish to point out that we cannot deal with the concept of "similarity" in our model for the same reason that we cannot handle "concentration." Both of these require serial processing of successive images or samples with comparison over time. We emphasize again that our model deals only with preattentive [or what Julesz (1984) terms "pop-out"] cognition. We do not have anything useful to say about attentive cognition, except that in our opinion it must involve proprioceptive and reafferent information so that successive sensory information samples can be combined with the information about what is done to get them. We also think it unlikely that each modality will be found to have such neural machinery separately, so that it should be sought after the combination of sensory input from all modalities into gestalts. From neurological considerations the most likely site of convergence is the entorhinal cortex (Lorente de Nó 1934), for which the hippocampus may serve as a stack register for temporal integration of serial gestalts. Much work needs to be done on multiple coexisting NCAs, but not in the context chosen by Rosenfeld et al. or at least not in neurobiological studies. As a postscript, we share their aversion to blind simulation of neural circuitry in the absence of any analytic handle on it, which is our reason for having made such a heavy investment in linear analysis of neural dynamics (Freeman 1972; 1975; 1987b). We would also like to agree on "minimal assumptions" and "essential features," if only we knew them in advance.

Finally, while we have been occupied with adding some neural-based variations to the kinds of models contained in the connectionist zoo, and the connectionists were busy questioning our reasons for doing so, **Thom** was taking a shot at us all. We understand Thom's suspicion that at present "'connectionist models' ultimately mean very little," especially those deriving from the spinglass analogy. However, we do not understand what he means when he says that "a neural mass exhibits internal symmetry of a geometric type (translation, rotation, etc.)." We assume that the collection of local elements comprising a mutually excitatory set is interconnected by feedback connections between each pair of elements, and that the gain coefficients representing synaptic weights can take the form of a matrix. In the naïve state we assume that the weights are uniform or nearly so. With learning under the Hebb rule, in which the connections between pairs of neurons are more strongly weighted by co-activity, the symmetry of the matrix in our model is preserved, because each pair of neurons is reciprocally connected. The weights in both directions depend on the correlation of activity by the same pair. Symmetry does not hold for the negative feedback connections between excitatory and inhibitory cells, but in our model these weights are fixed and can be partialed out. Recent advances have shown that symmetry in this sense need not be maintained in connectionist models, and that with sufficient asymmetry limit-cycle attractors appear. Surely this is not surprising, but these more complicated systems are more difficult to comprehend.

We are also puzzled by **Thom**'s statement that "such chaotic systems have no equations." If by this he means that the EEG cannot be simulated or fitted by a closed function such as cosine or Bessel, we surely agree. But we have shown that high-dimensional sets of coupled ordinary differential equations (ODEs) generate activity that is statistically indistinguishable from the EEG. Why is it permissible to call it chaos before we find the ODEs, but not after? We suspect that Thom's criticisms of terminology are directed more toward his fellow mathematicians than toward us. Certainly there are degrees of unpredictability and sensitivity to initial conditions, ranging from a barely detectable wobble about a point or limit-cycle trajectory to the sort of wildness that "cannot be explicitly described." Our ODEs simulate all of these gradations.

We are willing to adopt whatever convention mathematicians eventually agree upon. **Thom** offers the choice between an oxymoron and a neologism (between "self-organizing process" and "chreod") to label the process of the emergence of order in a system without prior specification from the outside. What is important to us is not the name, which explains little, but the concept by which we conceive of a very large number of neurons that are coupled into a coherent mass, which, when highly interactive, has degrees of freedom far lower than the number of neurons, perhaps so few as can be counted on the fingers of one hand or two. The finding that ODEs modeled after the olfactory system can be made to generate olfactory seizure patterns as unpredictable as one finds in nature is for us a liberation from the tyranny of Fourier decomposition. We recognize the weakness of the measures of the invariants of chaos that mathematicians have thus far made available to us (see our reply to **Babloyantz**), but that problem is not germane to questions of terminology. It is obvious that the whole field of dynamical systems is uncomfortable with terminology in transition. Perhaps it is a measure of our immersion in reflex determinism that we have such difficulty finding

words and concepts for these common phenomena. Thom compounds our discomfort by his final comment that "Pavlovian conditioning . . . could be explained as a purely dynamical effect" (if only he had stopped here) "of resonance"! The bulk of our target article, and for that matter of most of connectionism, is devoted to explaining the energy-consuming dynamical character of brain function, but the term "resonance" – as in sympathetic vibrations or a Helmholtz resonator, the passive transfer or accumulation of energy at specific temporal frequencies, the ringing of tuned oscillators – is empty at best and misleading and obfuscating at worst. We urge that the language of basins and attractors be used; perhaps this will also have to be discarded at some future time when it has also been debased by the verbal inflation that comes with overuse, but surely by then we will have a new vocabulary to debate with and about.

A final point needs to be made before we conclude. **Thom** is too generous in characterizing our experimental data as having "gaps"; at best, they constitute a small clearing in a large forest. The particular experiment he describes, in which one odorant serves as a CS for an appetitive UCS at another stage, has shown that the two EEG patterns differ. More to the point, when a rabbit is conditioned aversively to respond seriatim to odorant A, then B, C, and D, and is again conditioned to A, the spatial pattern changes with each new odorant, but it does not revert with reintroduction of odorant A to pattern A on the first conditioning. It changes to a new pattern on the repeat conditioning (Freeman & Schneider 1982). This result is contrary to expectations based on analogy with digital computer memory. It says something profound not so much about brains as about our preconceptions about the static nature of memory and our need to believe in mnemonic invariants. One might ask, how could the rabbit know that it was the same odorant in both stages of conditioning if there was a different spatial pattern in the second stage? The answer is that we have no sure way of knowing whether the animal can retain such information and make such judgments over the weeks required to do the experiment, and even if it could, which seems highly unlikely, the background and context are changed, and these are influential in shaping the forms of associative memories.

We do not commit Whitehead's (1960) "fallacy of misplaced concreteness." We do not claim an infinite storage capacity in the bulb for osmic memories; on the contrary, the psychophysical studies referred to in our target article show that the retentive capacity of the olfactory analyzer, if language is not used, is limited to about 16 odors at any given time. But the learning ability allows the repertoire to be modified and updated without increasing the total content. We have not yet attempted to address the questions of how new NCAs are overlaid or intertwined with preexisting ones, or what happens to the old ones, how they are deselected, and so forth. This is fertile ground for further studies in physiology, theory, and hardware modeling.

References

Abraham, R. H. & Shaw, C. D. (1985) *Dynamics, the geometry of behavior*, vol. 2. Ariel Press. [aCAS]

Ackley, D. H., Hinton, G. E., & Sejnowski, T. J. (1985). A learning algorithm for Boltzmann machines. *Cognitive Science* 9:147–69. [RR]

Anderson, J. A., Silverstein, J. W., Ritz, S. A. & Jones, R. S. (1977) Distinctive features, categorical perception, and probability learning: Some applications of a neural model. *Psychological Review* 84:413–51. [aCAS]

Arbib, M. A. (1972) *The metaphorical brain.* Wiley-Interscience. [DHP]

Ashby, W. R. (1952) *Design for a brain.* Chapman & Hall. [aCAS, DHP]

Auslander, D., Guckenheimer, J. & Oster, G. (1978) Random evolutionarily stable strategies. *Theoretical Population Biology* 13:276–93. [AG]

Babloyantz, A. & Destexhe, A. (1986) Low-dimensional chaos in an instance of epilepsy. *Proceedings of the National Academy of Sciences of the United States of America* 83:3513–17. [a CAS, AB]

  (in press) Strange attractors in the human cortex. In: *Temporal disorder and human oscillatory systems,* ed. L. Rensing, U. an der Heiden & M. C. Mackey. Springer. [AB]

Babloyantz, A. & Kaczmàrek, L. K. (1981) Self-organization in biological systems with multiple cellular contacts. *Bulletin of Mathematical Biology* 41:193–201. [rCAS]

Babloyantz, A., Nicolis, C. & Salazar, M. (1985) Evidence of chaotic dynamics of brain activity during the sleep cycle. *Physics Letters* 111A:152. [AB]

Baird, B. (in press) Nonlinear dynamics of pattern formation and pattern recognition in the rabbit olfactory bulb. *Physica D.* [aCAS]

Barlow, H. B. (1972) Single units and sensation: A neuron doctrine for perceptual psychology? *Perception* 1:371–94. [aCAS]

Bénard, H. (1900) Les tourbillons cellulaires dans une nappe liquide. *Revue Générale des Sciences Pures et Appliquées* 12:1309–28. [RT]

Bressler, S. (1987a) Relation of olfactory bulb and cortex I: Spatial variation of bulbo-cortical interdependence. *Brain Research.* 409:285–93. [aCAS]

  (1987b) Relation of olfactory bulb and cortex II: Model for driving of cortex by bulb. *Brain Research.* 409:294–301. [aCAS]

Brown, T. H., Perkel, D. H. & Feldman, M. W. (1976) Evoked neurotransmitter release: Statistical effects of nonuniformity and nonstationarity. *Proceedings of the National Academy of Sciences of the United States of America* 73:2913–17. [DHP]

Bullock, T. H. & Horridge, G. A. (1965) *Structure and function in the nervous systems of invertebrates,* vol. 1. W. H. Freeman. [aCAS]

Burns, B. D. (1958) *The mammalian cerebral cortex.* Edward Arnold. [aCAS]

Cain, W. S. (1980) Chemosensation and cognition. In: *Olfaction and taste VII,* ed. H. van der Starre. IRL Press. [aCAS]

Carpenter, G. A. & Grossberg, S. (1987) A massively parallel architecture for a self-organizing neural pattern recognition machine. *Computer Vision, Graphics, and Image Processing* 37:54–115. [SG]

Chatrian, G. E., Bickford, R. G. & Uihlein, A. (1960) Depth electrographic study of a fast rhythm evoked from human calcarine region by steady illumination. *Electroencephalography and Clinical Neurophysiology* 12:167–76. [rCAS]

Chay, T. R. & Rinzel, J. (1985) Bursting, beating, and chaos in an excitable membrane model. *Biophysical Journal* 47:357–66. [DHP]

Churchland, P. S. (1980) A perspective on mind-brain research. *Journal of Philosophy* 77:185–207. [RB]

  (1986) *Neurophilosophy: Toward a unified understanding of the mindbrain.* MIT/Bradford. [aCAS]

Cohen, M. A. & Grossberg, S. (1983) Absolute stability of global pattern formation and parallel memory storage by competitive neural networks. *IEEE Transactions on Systems, Man, and Cybernetics* 13:815–26. [DSL]

  (1986) Neural dynamics of speech and language coding: Developmental programs, perceptual grouping, and competition for short term memory. *Human Neurobiology* 5:1–22. [SG]

Conrad, M. (1986) What is the use of chaos? In: *Chaos,* ed. A. V. Holden. Manchester University Press. [aCAS]

Cowan, J. D. (1968) Statistical mechanics of nerve nets. In: *Neural networks,* ed. E. R. Caianiello. Springer-Verlag. [DHP]

Craik, K. (1952) *The nature of explanation.* Cambridge University Press. [rCAS]

del Castillo, J. & Katz, B. (1954) Quantal components of the end-plate potential. *Journal of Physiology (London)* 124:560–73. [DHP]

DeMott, D. W. (1970) *Toposcopic studies of learning.* Charles C. Thomas. [rCAS, RMB]

Dretske, F. (1986) *Boston studies in the philosophy of science.* Vol. 90: *Minds, machines and meaning, philosophy and technology II,* ed. C. Mitcham & H. Hunning. Reidel. [GW]

Dreyfus, H. L. (1972) *What computers can't do.* Harper & Row. [RB]

Dreyfus, H. & Dreyfus, S. (1986) *Mind over machine.* Free Press. [aCAS]

Ellias, S. A. & Grossberg, S. (1975) Pattern formation, contrast control, and oscillations in the short term memory of shunting on-center off-surround networks. *Biological Cybernetics* 20:69–98. [SG]

Emery, J. D. & Freeman, W. J. (1969) Pattern analysis of cortical evoked potential parameters during attention changes. *Physiology and Behavior* 4:60–77. [rCAS]

Ermentrout, B., Campbell, J. & Oster, G. (1986) A model for shell patterns based on neural activity. *Veliger* 28(4):369–88. [aCAS]

Farmer, D., Hart, J. & Weidman, P. (1982) A phase space analysis of baroclinic flow. *Physics Letters* 91A:22–24. [AG]

Feldman, J. A. & Ballard, D. H. (1982) Connectionist models and their properties. *Cognitive Science* 6:205–54. [aCAS]

Feyerabend, P. (1978) *Against method.* Verso. [GW]

Fienberg, S. E. (1974) Stochastic models for single neurone firing trains: A survey. *Biometrics* 30:399–427. [DHP]

Fodor, J. A. (1983) *The modularity of mind: An essay on faculty psychology.* Bradford/MIT Press. [rCAS]

Freeman, W. J. (1972) Waves, pulses and the theory of neural masses. *Progress in Theoretical Biology* 2:87–165. [arCAS]

  (1975) *Mass action in the nervous system.* Academic Press. [arCAS]

  (1978) Spatial properties of an EEG event in the olfactory bulb and cortex. *Electroencephalography and Clinical Neurophysiology-EEG Journal* 44:586–605. [aCAS]

  (1979a) Nonlinear gain mediating cortical stimulus-response relations. *Biological Cybernetics* 33:237–47. [aCAS]

  (1979b) Nonlinear dynamics of pleocortex manifested in the olfactory EEG. *Biological Cybernetics* 35:21–34. [arCAS]

  (1979c) EEG analysis gives model of neuronal template-matching mechanism for sensory search with olfactory bulb. *Biological Cybernetics* 35:221–34. [aCAS]

  (1980) Use of spatial deconvolution to compensate for distortion of EEG by volume conduction. *IEEE Transactions on Biomedical Engineering* 27:421–29. [aCAS]

  (1981) A physiological hypothesis of perception. *Perspectives in Biology and Medicine* 24:561–92. [arCAS]

  (1983a) Physiological basis of mental images. *Biological Psychiatry* 18:1107–25. [arCAS]

  (1983b) Dynamics of image formation by nerve cell assemblies. In: *Synergetics of the brain,* ed. E. Basar. H. Flohr & A. Mandell. Springer-Verlag. [aCAS]

  (1986) Petit mal seizure spikes in olfactory bulb and cortex caused by runaway inhibition after exhaustion of excitation. *Brain Research Reviews* 11:259–84. [aCAS]

  (1987a) Simulation of chaotic EEG patterns with a dynamic model of the olfactory system. *Biological Cybernetics* 56:139–50. [aCAS]

  (1987b) Techniques used in the search for the physiological basis of the EEG. In: *Handbook of electroencephalography and clinical neurophysiology,* vol. 3A, part 2, ch. 18, ed. A. Gevins & A. Remond. Elsevier. [arCAS]

Freeman, W. J. & Ahn, S. M. (1976) Spatial and temporal characteristic frequencies of interactive neural masses. *Proceedings, Institute of Electronics and Electrical Engineering, International Conference on Proc. IEEE. Intern. Conf. Cybernetics and Society* 1–3:279–84 [aCAS]

Freeman, W. J. & Baird, B. (in press) Correlation of olfactory EEG with behavior: Spatial analysis. *Behavioral Neuroscience.* [aCAS]

Freeman, W. J. & Grajski, K. A. (in press) Correlation of olfactory EEG with behavior: Factor analysis. *Behavioral Neuroscience.* [aCAS]

Freeman, W. J. & Schneider, W. S. (1982) Changes in spatial patterns of rabbit olfactory EEG with conditioning to odors. *Psychophysiology* 19:44–56. [arCAS]

Freeman, W. J. & Skarda. C. A. (1985) Spatial EEG patterns, nonlinear dynamics and perception: The neo-Sherringtonian view. *Brain Research Reviews* 10:147–75. [arCAS]

Freeman, W. J. & van Dijk, B. (submitted) Spatial patterns of visual cortical fast EEG during conditioned reflex in a rhesus monkey. [aCAS]

Freeman, W. J. & Viana Di Prisco, G. (1986a) EEG spatial pattern differences with discriminated odors manifest chaotic and limit cycle attractors in olfactory bulb of rabbits. In: *Brain theory,* ed. G. Palm. Springer-Verlag. [aCAS]

  (1986b) Correlation of olfactory EEG with behavior: Time series analysis. *Behavioral Neuroscience* 100:753–63. [arCAS]

Froehling, H., Crutchfield, J., Farmer. D., Packard, N. & Shaw, R. (1981) On determining the dimension of chaotic flows. *Physica* 3D:605–17. [AG]

Garfinkel, A. (1983) A mathematics for physiology. *American Journal of Physiology* 245: (Regulatory, Integrative and Comparative Physiology) 14:R455–66. [arCAS]

Gauld, A. & Shotter, J. (1977) *Human action and its psychological investigation.* Routledge & Kegan Paul. [RB]

Gerstein, G. L. & Mandelbrot B. (1964) Random walk models for the spike activity of a single neuron. *Biophysical Journal* 4:41–68. [DHP]

Gibson, J. J. (1979) *The ecological approach to visual perception.* Houghton Mifflin. [aCAS]

Glass. L. & Mackey, M. (1979) Pathological conditions resulting from instabilities in physiological control systems. *Annals of New York Academy of Sciences* 316:214–35. [AG]

Gonzalez-Estrada, M. T. & Freeman, W. J. (1980) Effects of carnosine on olfactory bulb EEG, evoked potential and DC potentials. *Brain Research* 202:373–86. [rCAS]

Goodman, N. (1968) *Languages of art: An approach to a theory of symbols.* Bobbs-Merrill. [JAB]

Grajski, K., Breiman, L., Viana Di Prisco, G. & Freeman, W. J. (in press) Classification of EEG spatial patterns with a tree-structured methodology: CART [Classification and regressive trees]. *IEEE Transactions in Biomedical Engineering.* [aCAS]

Grassberger, P. (1986) Do climatic attractors exist? *Nature* 323:609–12. [AG]

Grassberger, P. & Procaccia, I. (1983) Measuring the strangeness of strange attractors. *Physica* 9D:189–208. [aCAS]

Gray, C. M. (1986) Centrifugal regulation of olfactory coding and response plasticity in the olfactory bulb of the conscious rabbit. Ph.D. thesis, Baylor University. [aCAS]

Gray, C. M., Freeman, W. J. & Skinner, J. E. (1986) Chemical dependencies of learning in the rabbit olfactory bulb: Acquisition of the transient spatial-pattern change depends on norepinephrine. *Behavioral Neuroscience* 100:585–96. [arCAS]

Grossberg, S. (1975) A neural model of attention, reinforcement, and discrimination learning. *International Review of Neurobiology* 18:263–327. [DSL]

(1976) Adaptive pattern classification and universal recoding. II: Feedback, expectation, olfaction, and illusions. *Biological Cybernetics* 23:187–202. [rCAS]

(1980) How does the brain build a cognitive code? *Psychological Review* 87:1–51. [aCAS, DSL]

(1981) Adaptive resonance in development, perception, and cognition. In: *Mathematical psychology and psychophysiology,* ed. S. Grossberg. American Mathematical Society. [rCAS, SG]

(1982a) *Studies of mind and brain: Neural principles of learning, perception, development, cognition, and motor control.* Reidel. [SG]

(1982b) Processing of expected and unexpected events during conditioning and attention: A psychophysiological theory. *Psychological Review* 89:529–72. [DSL]

(1983) Neural substrates of binocular form perception: Filtering, matching, diffusion, and resonance. In: *Synergetics of the brain,* ed. E. Basar, H. Flohr, H. Haken & A. J. Mandell. Springer-Verlag. [SG]

(1987a) *The adaptive brain. I: Cognition, learning, reinforcement, and rhythm.* Elsevier/North-Holland. [SG]

(1987b) *The adaptive brain, II: Vision, speech, language, and motor control.* Elsevier/North-Holland. [SG]

Grossberg, S. & Levine, D. S. (submitted) Neural dynamics of attentionally modulated Pavlovian conditioning: Blocking, interstimulus interval, and secondary reinforcement. [DSL]

Grossberg, S. & Stone, G. O. (1986) Neural dynamics of word recognition and recall: Attentional priming, learning, and resonance. *Psychological Review* 93:46–74. [SG]

Guckenheimer, J. & Holmes, P. (1983). *Dynamical systems and bifurcations of vector fields.* Springer. [RT]

Hebb, D. D. (1949) *The organization of behavior.* Wiley. [arCAS]

Hinton, G. (1985) Learning in parallel networks. *Byte* 10:265. [aCAS]

Hinton, G. & Anderson, J. A. (1981) *Parallel models of associative memory.* Erlbaum. [aCAS]

Holden, A. V. ed. (1986) *Chaos.* Manchester University Press. [rCAS]

Hopfield, J. J. (1982) Neural networks and physical systems with emergent collective computational abilities. *Proceedings of the National Academy of Sciences of the United States of America* [arCAS, RR]

Hopfield, J. J. & Tank, D. W. (1986) Computing with neural circuits: A model. *Science* 233:625–33. [aCAS, DSL, DHP]

Julesz, B. (1984) A brief outline in the texton theory of human vision. *Trends in Neuroscience* 7:41–45. [aCAS]

Kaczmarek, L. K. & Babloyantz, A. (1977) Spatiotemporal patterns in epileptic seizures. *Biological Cybernetics* 26:199. [AB]

Kohonen, T. (1984) *Self-organization and associative memory.* Springer-Verlag. [aCAS, JAB]

Lancet, D., Greer, C. A., Kauer, J. S. & Shepherd, G. M. (1982) Mapping of odor-related neuronal activity in the olfactory bulb by high-resolution 2-deoxyglucose autoradiography. *Proceedings of the National Academy of Sciences of the United States of America* 79:670–74. [aCAS]

Lashley, K. S. (1942) The problem of cerebral organization in vision. In: *Biological symposia VII,* ed. J. Cattel. J. Cattel Press. [rCAS]

Layne, S. P., Mayer-Kress, G. & Holzfuss, J. (1986) Problems associated with dimensional analysis of EEG data. In: *Dimensions and entropies in chaotic systems,* ed. G. Mayer-Kress. Springer. [AB]

Levine, D. S. (1986) A neural network model of temporal order effects in classical conditioning. In: *Modelling of biomedical systems,* ed. J. Eisenfeld & M. Witten. Elsevier. [DSL]

Lilly, J. C. & Cherry, R. B. (1951) Traveling waves of action and of recovery during responses and spontaneous activity in the cerebral cortex. *American Journal of Physiology* 167:806. [RMB]

(1954) Surface movements of click responses from acoustical cerebral cortex of cat: Leading and trailing edges of a response figure. *Journal of Neurophysiology* 17:521–32. [RMB]

(1955) Surface movements of figures in spontaneous activity of anesthetized cortex: Leading and trailing edges. *Journal of Neurophysiology* 18:18–32. [rCAS]

Livanov, M. N. (1977) *Spatial organization of cerebral processes.* Wiley. [rCAS]

Lorente de Nó, R. (1934) Studies in the structure of the cerebral cortex. I: The area entorhinalis. *Journal von Psychologie und Neurologie* 45:381–438. [rCAS]

Lorenz, E. (1963) Deterministic nonperiodic flow. *Journal of Atmospheric Sciences* 20:130–41. [AG]

Mandell, A. J. (1986) Complexity versus disorder in the cardiac monitoring problem: A four-minute warning. Technical report, Mathematics Institute, University of Warwick. Coventry, England. [DHP]

Marr, D. (1982) *Vision.* Freeman. [DCE]

Marr, D. & Poggio, T. (1976) Cooperative computation of stereo disparity. *Science* 194:283–87. [DCE]

Martinez, D. M. & Freeman, W. J. (1984) Periglomerular cell action on mitral cell in olfactory bulb shown by current source density analysis. *Brain Research* 308:223–33. [aCAS]

Maturana, H. R. & Varela, F. J. (1980) *Boston studies in the philosophy of science.* Vol. 42: *Autopoiesis and cognition,* ed. R. S. Cohen & M. W. Wartofsky. Reidel. [GW]

May, R. M. (1976) Simple mathematical models with very complicated dynamics. *Nature* 261:459–67. [DHP]

McClelland, J. L. & Rumelhart, D. E. (1981) An interactive activation model of context effects in letter perception: Part 1. *Psychological Review* 88:375–407. [JAB]

McCulloch, W. S. & Pitts, W. H. (1943) A logical calculus of the ideas immanent in nervous activity. *Bulletin of Mathematical Biophysics* 5:115–33. [DHP]

Misgeld, U., Deisz, R., Dodt, H. & Lux, H. (1986) The role of chloride transport in postsynaptic inhibition of hippocampal neurons. *Science* 232:1413–15. [aCAS]

Moore, G. P., Perkel, D. H. & Segundo, J. P. (1966) Statistical analysis and functional interpretation of neuronal spike data. *Annual Review of Physiology* 28:493–522. [DHP]

Moulton, D. C. (1976) Spatial patterning of response to odors in the peripheral olfactory system. *Physiological Reviews* 56:578–93. [aCAS]

Mpitsos, G. J. & Cohan. C. S. (1986) Convergence in a distributed nervous system: Parallel processing and self-organization. *Journal of Neurobiology* 17:517–45. [DHP]

Newberry, N. & Nicoll, R. (1985) Comparison of the action of baclofen with γ-aminobutyric acid on rat hippocampal pyramidal cells in vitro. *Journal of Physiology* 360:161–85. [aCAS]

Nicolis, J. S. (1985a) *Hierarchical systems.* Springer. [AB]

(1985b) *Chaotic dynamics of information processing with relevance to cognitive brain functions.* Kybernetes 14:167–73. [rCAS]

Nicolis, J. S. & Tsuda, I. (1985) Chaotic dynamics of information processing: The "magic number seven plus-minus two" revisited. *Bulletin of Mathematical Biology* 47:343–65. [rCAS]

Oono, Y. & Kohmoto, M. (1985) Discrete model of chemical turbulence. *Physical Review Letters* 55:2927–31. See especially the references to the work of Kuramoto, Yamada et al., most of which has been published in the journal *Progress in Theoretical Physics* over the past decade. [MAC]

Pellionisz, A. & Llinás, R. (1979) Brain modeling by tensor network theory and computer simulation. The cerebellum: Distributed processor for predictive coordination. *Neuroscience* 4:323–48. [DHP]

Perkel, D. H. & Bullock, T. H. (1968) Neural coding. *Neurosciences Research Program Bulletin* 6:221–348. [aCAS]

Perkel, D. H., Gerstein, G. L. & Moore, G. P. (1967a) Neuronal spike trains and stochastic point processes. I. The single spike train. *Biophysical Journal* 7:391–418. [DHP]

(1967b) Neuronal spike trains and stochastic point processes. II. Simultaneous spike trains. *Biophysical Journal* 7:419–40. [DHP]

Pylyshyn, Z. W. (1984) *Computation and cognition: Toward a foundation for cognitive science.* Bradford Books/MIT Press. [aCAS]

Rapp, P. E., Zimmerman, I. D., Albano, A. M., Deguzman, G. C. & Greenbaun, N. N. (1985) Dynamics of spontaneous neural activity in the simian motor cortex. *Physics Letters* 110A:335. [AB]

Rayleigh, Lord (John William Strutt) (1916) *Philosophical Magazine* 32:529–46. [RT]

Riemann, B. (1902) *Gesammelte Werke, Nachträge.* Teubner. [RT]

Roschke, J. & Basar, E. (in press) EEG is not a simple noise. Strange attractors in intercranial structures. In: *Dynamics of sensory and cognitive signal processing in the brain,* ed. E. Basar. Springer. [AB]

Rosenblatt, F. (1962) *Principles of neurodynamics, perceptrons and the theory of brain mechanisms.* Spartan. [aCAS, DHP]

Rössler, O. E. (1983) The chaotic hierarchy. *Zeitschrift für Naturforschung.* 38A:788–802. [arCAS]

Ruelle, D. & Takens, F. (1971) On the nature of turbulence. *Communications in Mathematical Physics* 20:167 [RT]

Rumelhart, D. E., Hinton, G. E. & Williams. R. J. (1986) Learning representations by back-propagating errors. *Nature* 323:533–36. [DHP]

Rumelhart, D., McClelland, J. L. & PDP Research Group (1986) *Parallel distributed processing: Explorations in the microstructures of cognition,* vol. I: *Foundations.* MIT/Bradford. [arCAS]

Sampath, G. & Srinivasan, S. K. (1977) *Stochastic models for spike trains of single neurons.* Springer-Verlag. [DHP]

Schuster, H. (1984) *Deterministic chaos: An introduction.* Physik-Verlag. [aCAŜ, RB]

Searle, J. R. (1980) Minds, brains, and programs. *Behavioral and Brain Sciences* 3:417–57. [RB]

Shaw, G. L., Silverman. D. J. & Pearson, J. C. (1985) Model of cortical organization embodying a basis for a theory of information processing and memory recall. *Proceedings of the National Academy of Sciences of the United States of America* 82:2364–68. [DHP]

Shaw, R. (1984) *The Dripping Faucet as a Model Chaotic System.* Ariel Press. [rCAS]

Sheer, D. (1976) Focused arousal and 40 Hz EEG. In: *The neuropsychology of learning disorders: Theoretical approaches,* ed. R. M. Knights & D. J. Baker, University Park Press. [rCAS]

Shepherd, G. M. (1972) Synaptic organization of the mammalian olfactory bulb. *Physiological Review* 52:864–917. [aCAS]

Sherrington, C. (1906) *The integrative action of the nervous system.* Yale University Press. [rCAS]
(1940) *Man on his nature* (rev. ed. 1953). Cambridge University Press. [DHP]

Skarda, C. A. (1986) Explaining behavior: Bringing the brain back in. *Inquiry* 29:187–202. [aCAS]

Thom, R. (1981) Morphologie du sémiotique, recherches sémiotiques. *Semiotic Inquiry* 1:301–10. [RT]

Turner, J. S., Roux, J. C., McCormick, W. D. & Swinney, H. L. (1981) Alternating periodic and chaotic regimes in a chemical reaction – experiment and theory. *Physics Letters* 85A:9–14 [AG]

Viana Di Prisco, G. (1984) Hebb synaptic plasticity. *Progress in Neurobiology* 22:89–102. [aCAS]

Viana Di Prisco, G. & Freeman, W. J. (1985) Odor-related bulbar EEG spatial pattern analysis during appetitive conditioning in rabbits. *Behavioral Neuroscience* 99:964–78. [aCAS]

von Neumann, J. (1958) *The computer and the brain.* Yale University Press. [rCAS, DHP]

Waddington, C. H. (1957) *The strategy of the genes.* Allen and Unwin. [RT]

Walter, W. G. (1953) *The living brain.* Norton. [arCAS]

Whitehead, A. N. (1960) *Process and reality.* Harper & Row. [rCAS, RT]

Willey, T. J. (1973) The untrastructure of the cat olfactory bulb. *Journal of Comparative Neurology* 152:211–32. [aCAS]

Wilson, D. A., Sullivan, R. M. & Leon, M. (1985) Odor familiarity alters mitral cell response in the olfactory bulb of neonatal rats. *Developmental Brain Research* 22:314–17. [rCAS, DHP]

Winfree, A. T. (1980) *The geometry of biological time* (section 8D). Springer-Verlag. [MAC]

Wolfram, S. (1984) Cellular automata as models of complexity. *Nature* 311:419–24. [DHP]

Zucker, R. S. (1973) Changes in the statistics of transmitter release during facilitation. *Journal of Physiology (London)* 241:69–89. [DHP]

22
Introduction

(1987)
Eric I. Knudsen, Sascha du Lac, and Steven D. Esterly

Computational maps in the brain
Annual Review of Neuroscience 10: 41–65

When one sees an information processing technique used almost everywhere in the nervous system, there must be a reason. And, more practically, it might be a good idea to use the same idea as a basis for computation and representation in artificial neural networks as well.

Topographic maps of a sensory or computational parameter are such a technique. Virtually every sensory system has associated with it a map of one or more parameters of the input. There are spatially organized maps in vision, maps of frequency in audition, and maps of the body surface for touch. There are also a great many maps that are not based on such obvious aspects of the input signal, but may have to be derived from it by a complex computation: maps of range to target in the bat sonar system (see paper 16), spatial maps of "interest" in the superior colliculus (see paper 15), and maps of the spatial location of a noise source in the environment, as described in more detail in this paper.

This review paper is a discussion of some of the mapping relations found in the nervous system. Because of the research interests of the authors, it describes in considerable detail the remarkable maps of auditory space found in the barn owl, but it also mentions numerous other systems.

The barn owl hunts in the dark, and its ability to catch prey without visual guidance depends on its ability to localize small animals by the noises they make. An elaborate neural processing mechanism is devoted to generating a map of auditory space in the superior colliculus. The biological computation for localizing sound sources requires data on differences in intensity and time delay between the two ears, as well as some subtle cues involving direction-dependent shaping of the spectrum caused by the anatomy of the head and ears. Deriving a map of auditory space involves the accurate merging of several different streams of processing, each with its own specific modality maps, to form an overall map, as described in the section entitled, "Constructing a Map from Maps." Clearly a good deal of effort has been devoted to forming the map, and the map must aid in the computation of target distance and direction. It may not be so startling to the readers of this collection, but the presence of "computational" in the title of the review, as well as its frequent use in the first few pages, clearly implies that the authors think a major function of the maps is to enhance computation, and the owl spatial map is one good example of such a system. Most neural network modelers would agree with this, though many (notoriously conservative) neuroscientists would not be so bold.

The basic idea is that if a map is formed, then units responding to similar aspects of an input are physically close together. One result is that the maps "transform their input almost instantaneously into a place-coded probability distribution that represents values of the mapped parameter as locations of peaks in activity within the map." A simple organization at a higher level can then make effective use of such codes.

Although maps are relatively easy to form (see papers 8 and 9) and easy to work with, a price must also be paid. In general very many computing units are required to form a map. The economics of the nervous system are different from the economics of artificial systems. Units, especially units that can be wired with relatively simple local connection rules, are cheap. However, with artificial systems, there is often a temptation to use "efficient" coding schemes. For example, in the superior colliculus sensorimotor system described by McIlwain (paper 15), all that is really required at the output of the system are two numbers: the coordinates of the point in visual space where the eyes should be directed. Instead thousands of neurons devote their entire efforts to generating a distributed representation of the same thing. The advantages of maps for computation must be such as to make up for a lot of seeming wastefulness. Although maps require very large numbers of elements, they have been used in a number of artificial systems. They are almost always effective and reliable, at least partially due to the large numbers of units involved, producing systems that are very good at low noise "consensus" computations.

Knudsen, du Lac, and Esterly make some generalizations about biological maps that are worth noting. Biological maps are prewired. That is, the animal is born with them. Although they can be modified to some extent, the basic structure is present from birth. One often finds, for example, in visual cortex, potent developmental effects. Exposing an immature animal to a warped environment early in development will make detectable effects on the organization of cortex and its units. Such changes are usually for the worse, but probably reflect the operation of mechanisms that serve, in more normal environments, to tune an animal to its particular surroundings. Although for many years it was thought that plastic changes in cortical maps were restricted to very young organisms, recent work (see the review section of paper 18) indicates that adults also show limited plasticity, and clear but localized changes can be formed in cortical maps in adults by changing the environment. The maximum degree of modifiability seems to be limited by genetically determined underlying wiring.

Tuning of responses of single units is relatively broad. Therefore activity in response to a pertinent input can take up a sizable region of the map. Modelers call such a response a distributed representation because many active units are required to describe an input. Units usually are sensitive to a range of several parameters. Cells in visual cortex may be *most* sensitive to moving lines of a particular orientation and velocity, but will respond with some activation over as much as a factor of two in velocity and as much as 90° in orientation. This leads to a standard conceptual "problem" with distributed systems. Humans (or animals) can often behaviorally estimate a parameter — say, orientation or pitch — with great precision, but the individual cells in their nervous system that respond to that parameter often are more broadly tuned. This sometimes leads to a search for extremely sharply tuned cells, but in a distributed system, of course, what is presumably used in discrimination is a function of the separation between entire activity patterns, and not to single active units.

Again we have come across the fine balance the nervous system must strike between having cells that are correlated in their activity, hence redundant, and cells that are highly decorrelated, hence efficient encoders (see Barlow, paper 14, and Linsker, paper 31).

One way of using maps and decorrelating at the same time is the simultaneous use of several maps. In visual cortex, perhaps the best-studied example, there is a map of orientation preference, but also maps of eye dominance, location in the visual field, and perhaps other parameters. A cell is under the influence of several maps and can develop an individualistic response pattern. Cells also may respond to several mapped parameters (say, orientation and location in the visual field) and some parameters that may not be as strongly mapped (perhaps sensitivity, width of receptive field, and so on), again causing a particular cell to have a response pattern all its own.

Maps seemed to be used to develop cells with commonalities of response, but not necessarily with highly correlated responses to particular stimuli. Although most neural network mapping models are based on formation of local correlations, in fact the nervous system seems to try to avoid them to some extent. Hubel and Wiesel (1977) have proposed the intriguing notion of the cortical *hypercolumn*, which seems to capture some of this flavor. In the visual cortex a hypercolumn is a group of cells about one square millimeter in area. Because units respond to a region of the visual field, all the units in the hypercolumn respond to roughly the same area of visual space. But the hypercolumn contains all orientations, all degrees of response to the two eyes, and so on. So all the cells in a hypercolumn see the same region in space, but all respond to different aspects of the pattern in that region. Commonality of response does not necessarily mean high correlation of response over all patterns.

A map seems to be an effective parallel computing strategy when (1) computing units are cheap, (2) there are some clear organizing parameters required for the computation, (3) the requirements of the task are known in some detail, (4) highly precise wiring is not possible, but a largely prewired system is required, and (5) relatively inflexible representation of information is acceptable.

Reference

D. H. Hubel and T. N. Wiesel (1977), Functional architecture of macaque monkey visual cortex. *Proceedings of the Royal Society of London, Series B* 198: 1–59.

(1987)
Eric I. Knudsen, Sascha du Lac, and Steven D. Esterly

Computational maps in the brain
Annual Review of Neuroscience 10: 41–65

Introduction

Computation is the essence of brain function. Through computation, the nervous system sorts and evaluates sensory information that is of biological importance. Based on the results, decisions are made and executive commands for behavioral responses are issued; these commands in turn require further computation to produce the spatial and temporal patterns of motor neuron activity that mediate behavior. The "computational map" is a key building block in the infrastructure of information processing by the nervous system. For the purposes of this chapter, we define "computation" as any transformation in the representation of information. In a computational map, there is a systematic variation in the value of the computed parameter across at least one dimension of the neural structure. The neurons that make up such a map represent an array of preset processors or filters, each tuned slightly differently, that operate in parallel on the afferent signal. Consequently, they transform their input almost instantaneously into a place-coded probability distribution that represents values of the mapped parameter as locations of peaks in activity within the map. Sorted in this fashion, the derived information can be accessed readily by higher order processors (which themselves may be computational maps) using relatively simple schemes of connectivity.

Many computational processes in the nervous system are not mapped. For example, neurons selective for a particular parameter value or set of parameter values often are clustered to form functional modules in the brain, but there is no systematic variation in their tuning, i.e. there is no map. Conversely, some neural maps are not computational, such as maps of sensory epithelia, which simply reproduce the peripheral representation of the sensory information. In this chapter, we restrict our discussion to maps that are derived through computation.

Most of the computational maps discovered so far are involved in processing sensory information. As is discussed in ensuing sections, they map parameters of the sensory world that are crucially important to the animal. Computational maps in the visual system include those of line orientation preference and ocular dominance in the primary visual cortex (Hubel & Wiesel 1963, 1977) and a map of movement direction in cortical middle temporal visual area MT[1] (Albright et al 1984). A map of color in cortical area V4 has been suggested, but its topography has not been demonstrated (Zeki 1974, 1980). Computational auditory maps include maps of interaural delay, interaural intensity difference, and sound source location in the brainstem (Knudsen & Konishi 1978, Knudsen 1982, King & Palmer 1983, Middlebrooks & Knudsen 1984, Wenstrup et al 1986, Sullivan & Konishi 1986, Konishi et al 1986) and maps of amplitude spectrum and time interval in the auditory cortex (Suga 1977, O'Neill & Suga 1982). In all cases, these maps are most precisely elaborated and occupy the greatest portions of the brain in species that have highly developed sensory capacities, such as monkeys (vision) and owls and bats (audition). However, similar visual and auditory maps have been found to exist in more generalized species such as the cat, ferret, and guinea pig.

Computational maps are also involved in motor programming. The best known is the map of motor space, or gaze direction, in the superior colliculus (optic tectum in nonmammals) of the midbrain (e.g. Roucoux et al 1980, Wurtz & Albano 1981). In computational motor maps, systematic variations of a movement are represented topographically across the neural structure. These maps are computational in that the topographically organized command must be transformed into spatio-temporal patterns of motor neuron activity, and it is the site of peak activity in the map that dictates the transformation that is to be made. Thus, computational motor maps demonstrate the principles of computational sensory maps operating in reverse: instead of representing the results of systematically varying computations (as do sensory maps), they represent the source code that commands systematically varying computations.

The realization that the nervous system makes use of computational maps leads to such questions as, under what conditions does the nervous system map a computational

[1] Abbreviations used: FM, frequency modulation; ICc, central nucleus of the inferior colliculus; IID, interaural intensity difference; ICx, external nucleus of the inferior colliculus; LSO, lateral superior olive; MSO, medial superior olive; MT, middle temporal visual area; n. Lam, nucleus laminaris; VI, primary visual cortex; VLVp, posterior division of the ventral nucleus of the lateral lemniscus.

process, and what advantages are derived from such maps? In this chapter, we discuss properties common to known computational maps and consider the implications of neural activity that is topographically organized. The need for brevity requires that many details of specific maps be omitted, and the reader is directed to original papers and reviews for such information. As our focus of discussion, we use the synthesis of the auditory map of space in the brainstem. The auditory space map is a high order map that is itself dependent upon lower order mapped and nonmapped computations. As such, its synthesis demonstrates fundamental properties of computational maps as well as interactions of parallel and serial maps in a hierarchy of information processing.

Examples of Computational Maps

The most familiar computational maps were discovered in the primary visual cortex (VI) of cats and monkeys by Hubel & Wiesel (1963, 1968). They found that VI contains two kinds of repeating computational maps: maps of preferred line orientation, which represent the angle of tilt of a line stimulus, and maps of ocular dominance, which represent the relative strengths of excitatory influence of each eye (Figure 1). (Ocular dominance only becomes a computational map with the creation of binocular cells. In primates, this occurs in layers outside of layer 4C.) Orientation and ocular dominance are mapped across the cortical surface along independent, though often not perpendicular, axes. Arrays of neurons which together represent all values of ocular dominanance or line orientations have been termed *hypercolumns*. Each hypercolumn processes information from a small region of visual space; neighboring hypercolumns process information from overlapping but systematically shifted portions of visual space. Thus, hypercolumns are examples of computational maps that are repeated within a larger, noncomputational (retinotopic) map.

Cortical area MT, or V5, in the macaque monkey is a higher order visual area that contains repeating maps of movement direction, again organized within the context of retinotopy (Albright et al 1984). The tuning of individual neurons for direction of motion is broad, but changes systematically across the cortical surface such that 180° of movement directions are represented across a 0.5 mm slab of cortex. Adjacent slabs represent motion in opposite directions.

A greater number of computational maps have been discovered in the auditory system. Three of these, the maps of interaural delay, interaural intensity difference, and space, contribute to the spatial analysis of sound and are described in detail in the next section. Two others have been

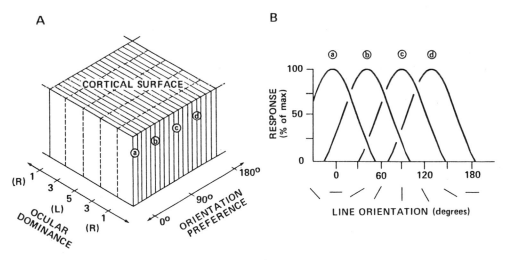

Figure 1 Computational maps in the primary visual cortex (V1) of monkeys. *A.* A schematic diagram of hypercolumns for ocular dominance and line orientation in V1. The axes of these maps are independent, but often are not perpendicular. The ocular dominance map represents systematically the relative strengths of the excitatory influence of each eye. The numerical scale refers to the ocular dominance groups defined by Hubel & Wiesel. Here, units excited exclusively by the right eye are assigned a value of 1, and units excited exclusively by the left eye are assigned a value of 5. In the map of orientation preference, neurons are tuned to the angle of tilt of a line stimulus; the tuning of neurons varies systematically across the map over a 180° range of orientations. Adapted from Hubel & Wiesel (1977).

B. Representative tuning curves of neurons in V1 for line orientation. Response is plotted as a function of stimulus orientation. The circled letters identify tuning curves with the positions indicated in the map in *A*. Neuronal tuning in the orientation map, as in other computational maps, can be quite broad: While each neuron responds maximally to a narrow range of orientations, a substantial response can be elicited by stimuli over a 50° range of orientations. Based on data from Schiller et al (1976).

found in the auditory cortex of the mustache bat. In a portion of the bat's primary auditory cortex, neurons are tuned for the amplitude as well as for the frequency of sound (Suga 1977, Suga & Manabe 1982). The best amplitude for exciting neurons varies systematically across the cortical surface along a dimension that is perpendicular to the tonotopic (receptotopic) axis. Thus, the map represents the amplitude spectrum of an acoustic stimulus topographically.

A high order area of the bat's auditory cortex maps the time interval between acoustic events (Suga & O'Neill 1979, Suga et al 1983). Neurons in this area (the "frequency modulation processing area") are tuned to the interval between two frequency modulated (FM) sounds, and the best time interval for exciting neurons varies systematically across the cortical surface. In this map, tonotopy is absent, and instead neurons are grouped in modules according to the ranges of frequencies contained in the FM component of the sonar pulses. This is a case of computational maps occurring within functional clusters. The bat uses time interval information to determine the delay of echoes relative to emitted sonar pulses and, therefore, the distance of objects (the same type of information could be used by other species to categorize and identify vocalizations; Liberman et al 1954, Margoliash 1983).

The superior colliculus (optic tectum) in all species tested contains a computational motor map that directs orienting movements of the eyes, head, and/or ears (Robinson 1972, Stryker & Schiller 1975, Roucoux et al 1980, Stein & Clamann 1981). For example, in primates, neurons in the intermediate and deep collicular layers discharge prior to saccadic eye movements, and the magnitude and direction of the eye movement associated with the discharge of neurons varies topographically with location in the colliculus (Sparks et al 1976). Moreover, focal electrical simulation of the colliculus elicits saccadic eye movements, the magnitude and direction of which also vary systematically with the site of stimulation (Robinson 1972, Stryker & Schiller 1975). The data indicate that the output of the superior colliculus (optic tectum) initiates specific motor programs that depend on the location of maximum activity in the motor map.

Computational Maps in Auditory Space Analysis

Cues for the Analysis of Auditory Space
The map of auditory space represents the apex of a hierarchy of sensory information processing (Figure 2). In the auditory system, "space" must be computed from a variety of cues that are only indirectly related to the location of a sound source. These include binaural differences in the

timing and intensity of spectral components of sound, and monaural cues that result from direction-dependent spectral shaping by the head and external ears. The computational process involves two steps: *(a)* the determination of cue values, and *(b)* the association of particular sets of cue values with appropriate locations in space. Both steps are handled in computational maps.

The values of the cues and their relationships to sound source location depend upon the size and shape of the external ears, the position of the external ears on the head, and the mode of operation of the eardrum, i.e. whether it operates as a pressure or a pressure-gradient receiver (Searle et al 1976, Colburn & Durlach 1978, Coles et al 1980, Knudsen 1980). These physical properties vary across the animal kingdom, and consequently different species use different cues and ranges of cue values to generate maps of auditory space. However, the basic task

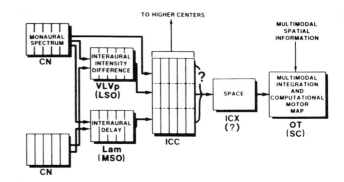

Figure 2 Steps in the synthesis of a map of auditory space in the barn owl; note that not all connections of the auditory pathway are shown. The names of analogous structures in mammals are shown in parentheses. Monaural intensity and phase spectra of acoustic stimuli are represented in the firing rate and time of firing of neurons in the tonotopically organized cochlear nuclei (CN) (tonotopic organization is indicated throughout the figure by *vertical stripes*). The CN project to both the nucleus laminaris (Lam) and the posterior division of the ventral nucleus of the lateral lemniscus (VLVp). Neurons in the VLVp in birds and in the lateral superior olive (LSO) in mammals compute frequency-specific interaural intensity differences by combining inhibitory input from one CN with frequency-matched excitatory input from the other CN. Neurons in the n. Lam in birds and in the medial superior olive (MSO) in mammals compute frequency-specific interaural delays by cross-correlating signals from each CN. The VLVp (LSO) and Lam (MSO) project in parallel to the central nucleus of the inferior colliculus (ICc). The ICc also receives direct input from the cochlear nucleus. Neurons in the external nucleus of the inferior colliculus (ICx) receive convergent projections from the ICc. Sharp frequency tuning and tonotopic organization disappears in the ICx. Instead, neurons are tuned for source location and, in the barn owl, they form a map of auditory space. This spatial information is sent to the optic tectum (OT) in birds and to the superior colliculus (SC) in mammals. The OT (SC) also receives topographically ordered somatosensory and visual input and contains a computational motor map as described in the text.

of evaluating binaural and monaural cues is the same for all animals.

The cues for sound localization are frequency-specific. For example, an interaural intensity difference (IID) of 6 dB at 2 kHz signifies locations in space different from those signified by the same interaural intensity difference at 8 kHz (Shaw 1974, Knudsen 1980). Even interaural delay exhibits some frequency dependence (Kuhn 1977, Roth et al 1980). For this reason, localization cues must be evaluated in a frequency-specific manner (for a review see Knudsen 1983a). Conveniently, the cochlea breaks down the signal into its frequency components even before the signal is transduced.

Information about the timing and intensity of each frequency component is conveyed to the cochlear nuclei by frequency-tuned fibers in the auditory nerve. There, timing and intensity information is processed by neurons that project in parallel pathways to pontine nuclei specialized for comparing signals from the two ears (Figure 2; Sullivan & Konishi 1984, Cant & Morest 1984). Although major transformations in the representations of the afferent signal occur by the level of the cochlear nuclei, none of the computational processes appear to be mapped. Only a map of frequency tuning, which is a topographic representation of the sensory epithelium, is apparent.

The Computation of Interaural Delay

The first computational map appears at the initial site of binaural convergence. Neurons in the medial superior olive (MSO) in mammals and in the nucleus laminaris (n. Lam) in birds compute the interaural delay of frequency-specific signals from each ear. They receive information about the timing of individual frequency components at each ear from neurons in the cochlear nuclei that discharge in phase with frequency components of the stimulus. When sounds are presented binaurally, the response rate of MSO (n. Lam) neurons varies dramatically as a function of interaural delay (Goldberg & Brown 1969, Moushegian et al 1975, Moiseff & Konishi 1983). The most and least favorable interaural delays (i.e. those eliciting maximum and minimum responses, respectively) can be predicted from the difference in the latencies of a neuron's responses to stimulation of each ear alone. The optimal interaural delays are those that cause the phase-locked excitatory input from each ear to arrive simultaneously, while the least favorable delays are those that cause the excitatory inputs to arrive 180° out of phase with each other.

That these neurons compute interaural delay on the basis of the relative timing of phase-locked afferent signals has an important consequence for higher order neurons that must interpret their outputs: Different interaural delays that give rise to the same interaural phase cannot be distin-

guished (Rose et al 1966, Kuwada et al 1984, Takahashi & Konishi 1986). Thus, the responses of these neurons are said to be phase-ambiguous. In the derivation of sound source location, phase ambiguity can equate with spatial ambiguity (Knudsen 1984a, Esterly 1984). As we discuss, the resolution of phase ambiguity to yield an unambiguous measure of interaural delay is a computational problem that is solved by higher order neurons.

Maps of Interaural Delay

Maps of Interaural Delay in the Nucleus Laminaris and Medial Superior Olive

Although it is clear that different units in the MSO (n. Lam) are tuned for different values of interaural delay, a map of interaural delay has yet to be demonstrated at the single unit level. However, the evidence that such a map exists is strong; it is based on the structured morphology of afferent and postsynaptic elements in the MSO (n. Lam), and on the systematic variation in the interaural delay tuning of field potentials in this nucleus (Figure 3).

The pattern of the afferent projections from the cochlear nuclei to the MSO (n. Lam) suggests a systematically varying delay-line (Scheibel & Scheibel 1974, Young & Rubel 1983, Konishi et al 1986). The MSO (n. Lam) is a slab shaped nucleus containing bipolar neurons with dendrites oriented oppositely and perpendicularly to the plane of the nucleus. Afferent axons from the cochlear nucleus bifurcate, with one branch of each axon projecting to the ipsilateral and the other to the contralateral MSO (n. Lam). Frequency-matched afferents from each cochlear nucleus converge systematically on opposing dendrites of MSO (n. Lam) neurons, establishing a tonotopic organization along one axis of the nucleus. The afferent axons enter at opposite edges of the nucleus and run in a straight line along an iso-frequency plane (Figure 3A). Presynaptic arbors peel off from the stem axons as they pass through the nucleus (in chickens, the contralateral afferents are as described, but the ipsilateral afferents form multiple arbors of equal length; Young & Rubel 1983). The progressive increase in axonal length to successive portions of an afferent's terminal field is ideally suited to act as a delay-line. The axonal geometry predicts that afferent action potentials sweep systematically through the MSO from one edge to the other, the waves of excitation from opposite ears traversing the nucleus in opposite directions.

Electrophysiological evidence supports this prediction. An electrode placed in n. Lam (MSO) records a field potential that is a spectrally filtered analog of the acoustic stimulus (Wernick & Starr 1968, Sullivan & Konishi 1986, Konishi et al 1986). The field potential can be elicited by stimulation of either ear. In the owl, as the electrode pene-

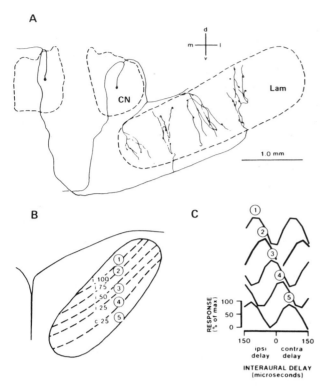

Figure 3 Evidence for a map of interaural delay in the n. laminaris of the barn owl. *A.* Camera lucida drawings of cochlear nucleus (CN) axons filled with horseradish peroxidase. The axons project from each CN to an isofrequency lamina in n. laminaris (Lam). Axons from each cochlear nucleus enter Lam from opposite sides of the nucleus and form presynaptic arbors as they penetrate the nucleus. This geometry suggests that the axons are acting as oppositely oriented delay-lines; this predicts that the positions of neurons receiving simultaneous input from the two ears vary as a function of interaural delay. Courtesy of Dr. Catherine E. Carr.

B. Systematic variation in the tuning of the field potential for interaural delay within an isofrequency (5 kHz) lamina of Lam. *Dashed lines* indicate recording locations exhibiting the same interaural delay tuning, indicated as microseconds of ipsilateral (*i*) or contralateral (*c*) delay. *Circled numbers* indicate locations where responses in *C* were recorded.

C. Tuning of field potentials in Lam for interaural delay. Each *curve* indicates the normalized response magnitude as a function of interaural delay for the recording sites indicated in *B*. The optimal delay shifts systematically as a function of position in the nucleus. *Double peaks* reflect delays that differ by one period of the stimulus frequency (5 kHz). These data are from Sullivan & Konishi (1986).

trates the nucleus along an axis that is parallel to the afferent projection, the phase of the field potential (relative to the monaural stimulus) changes systematically, the sign of the change depending on which ear is stimulated (Sullivan & Konishi 1986). If the phase of the potential evoked by ipsilateral ear stimulation retards as the electrode progresses, then the phase of the potential evoked by contralateral ear stimulation advances—just as the opposing orientations of the axonal delay-lines predict.

As with single units in the n. Lam (MSO), the field potential at any given site is tuned for the interaural delay of a binaural stimulus (Figure 3C), and the interaural delay that elicits the maximum response can be predicted from the relative latencies of monaural responses: the optimal delay is the one that causes the signals from each ear to arrive simultaneously, or in phase (Wernick & Starr 1968, Konishi et al 1986). A change in interaural delay from this value causes the response amplitude to diminish, and when the binaural signals arrive 180° out of phase, the field potential virtually disappears (Figure 3C).

The systematic mapping of interaural delay that is suggested by the anatomy of the afferent projection is observed in the field potential (Sullivan & Konishi 1986). As an electrode passes through the n. Lam along an iso-frequency plane, optimal interaural delays change gradually from large ipsilateral delays to large contralateral delays (Figure 3). In the barn owl, each n. Lam contains a complete representation of interaural delays corresponding to contralateral source locations (delay at the ipsilateral ear), and a more limited representation of delays corresponding to sources in the frontal half of the ipsilateral hemifield (delay at the contralateral ear). Delays corresponding to frontal locations are thus represented in the nuclei on both sides of the brain. This range conforms to the range of spatial representation in the maps of space in the midbrain (see below).

To reiterate, a map of interaural delay has yet to be demonstrated with single unit recordings. The evidence that it exists is *(a)* neurons in the MSO (n. Lam) are tuned for interaural delay by their selectivity for a coincidence of phase-locked excitation from the two sides of the brain; *(b)* the geometry of the afferent projection from each cochlear nucleus creates delay-lines that are oriented in opposing directions; *(c)* the timing of field potentials elicited by monaural stimulation varies systematically with electrode position, just as predicted by the anatomy of the afferent fibers; and *(d)* the tuning of the field potential for interaural delay, which mimics that of single units, varies topographically across the nucleus and represents precisely the physiological range of interaural delays.

Maps of Interaural Delay in the Inferior Colliculus

Neurons in the MSO (n. Lam) project to a restricted zone of another tonotopically organized nucleus, the central nucleus of the inferior colliculus (ICc) (Figure 2; Roth et al 1978, Semple & Aitkin 1979, Takahashi & Konishi 1985). Studies in the barn owl and in the cat demonstrate that neurons in this zone also are tuned for interaural delay, and that interaural delay tuning is mapped within iso-frequency planes (Yin et al 1983, Aitkin et al 1985, Wagner et al 1986), an organization that mimics that of the MSO (n.

Lam). The data from barn owls indicate further that *(a)* neuronal selectivity for interaural delay has been sharpened considerably, probably by lateral inhibitory interactions within the delay map, and *(b)* the maps of interaural delay are aligned across iso-frequency planes (Wagner et al 1986). For example, a neuron in the ICc tuned to a delay of 100 μsec at 3 kHz is aligned with neurons tuned to the same delay at other frequencies. Although this organization reflects an organization that exists already in the MSO (n. Lam), that it exists in the ICc greatly simplifies the next step in the computational process: the integration of interaural delays across frequency. Before discussing this next step, we review the processing of the other binaural cue for sound localization: frequency-specific interaural intensity difference.

Maps of Interaural Intensity Difference

The frequency-by-frequency analysis of interaural intensity differences begins in the lateral superior olive (LSO) in mammals and in the posterior division of the ventral nucleus of the lateral lemniscus (VLVp) in birds (Figure 2; Boudreau & Tsuchitani 1970, Guinan et al 1972, Moiseff & Konishi 1983). In the LSO, excitatory input comes directly from the ipsilateral cochlear nucleus. Frequency-matched inhibitory input comes from the contralateral cochlear nucleus by way of the medial nucleus of the trapezoid body. The antagonistic influences of these binaural inputs vary in parallel over a wide range of sound levels, so that the response rate of an LSO (VLVp) neuron indicates the binaural difference in sound intensity, independent of the overall intensity. This simple subraction causes neurons to be sensitive to interaural intensity difference, but not tuned for interaural intensity difference: The neurons respond ever more strongly, up to a saturating level, as the interaural intensity difference increases beyond some threshold value. The important parameter that varies within the population is the interaural intensity difference threshold. Some neurons begin to respond even when the sound in the excitatory ear is weaker than sound in the inhibitory ear, while others require the sound in the excitatory ear to be much stronger than sound in the inhibitory ear before they respond. Preliminary data indicate that interaural intensity difference thresholds vary systematically across VLVp in the barn owl (J. A. Manley and M. Konishi, personal communication). Based on the highly regular cellular anatomy in the LSO (Scheibel & Scheibel 1974), it is possible that a similar map of thresholds exists there as well.

The earliest stage for which there is documentation of a map of interaural intensity difference is in the ICc, the next nucleus in the ascending pathway (Figure 2). Neurons in the LSO (VLVp) project to a zone in the ICc that adjoins the MSO (n. Lam) projection zone (Roth et al 1978, Semple & Aitkin 1979, Takahashi & Konishi 1985). Neurons in the LSO projection zone, like those in the LSO itself, are sharply tuned for frequency and are sensitive, but not tuned, for interaural intensity difference. (The interaural intensity difference sensitivity is opposite to that found in the LSO on the same side: ICc neurons are excited by stimulation of the contralateral ear and are inhibited by stimulation of the ipsilateral ear.) In the bat, neurons in this zone of the ICc are organized according to their sensitivity to interaural intensity difference, in addition to being tonotopically organized (Wenstrup et al 1986). At one edge of the zone, ipsilateral inhibition is weak and neurons respond even when the interaural intensity difference favors the ipsilateral ear. As an electrode moves across the zone, the efficacy of ipsilateral inhibition increases and the interaural intensity difference required to drive neurons shifts until, at the opposite edge of the zone, only large interaural intensity difference's favoring the contralateral ear are sufficient to drive the neurons. Thus, this computational map represents the interaural intensity difference of a given frequency topographically by the extent of maximally activated neurons across the LSO projection zone in the ICc.

Synthesis of a Map of Auditory Space

At the level of the ICc, the stage is set for the computation of sound source location. Frequency-specific interaural delays and intensity differences have been measured and mapped, and the peripherally filtered spectrum of the stimulus is represented along the tonotopic axis of the nucleus (Figure 2). Auditory space is computed by combining these cues. In the classical auditory pathway, this computation does not take place until sometime after the information passes through the primary auditory cortex (Middlebrooks & Pettigrew 1981, Jenkins & Merzenich 1984). However, in a secondary auditory pathway in the midbrain, the computation is performed immediately. In owls, this pathway leads from the ICc to the external nucleus of the inferior colliculus (ICx), then on to the optic tectum. (The analogous pathway has not been found in other species.)

To construct a map in which neurons are tuned to sounds from specific regions in space, auditory cue values must be associated with appropriate source locations. Although each of the cue values mapped in the ICc varies with source location, any single value can correspond with many possible locations (Knudsen 1980, Calford et al 1986). The spatial ambiguity associated with frequency-specific cue values can be eliminated by combining cues across frequencies. In barn owls, this integrative step occurs as the space map is synthesized in the ICx (Knudsen 1983a,b, 1984a). In cats, neurons broadly tuned for frequency and sharply tuned for space are concentrated in the rostral portion of the ICx (Aitkin et al 1984), but the first documented appearance of an auditory space map is in the superior colliculus (Middlebrooks & Knudsen 1984).

Constructing a Map from Maps

The maps of localization cues in the ICc simplify the circuitry for computing space. The systematic relationship between interaural delay and sound source azimuth enables a map of azimuth to be created in the barn owl by a topographic projection to the ICx from the delay sensitive zone of each iso-frequency planes. In addition, since these maps of interaural delay are aligned across iso-frequency planes, delay tuning that is independent of frequency would result if the outputs of aligned neurons (from different iso-frequency planes) simply converged on a neuron in the space map. This systematic convergent projection occurs from the ICc to the ICx in the barn owl (Knudsen 1983b, Wagner et al 1986).

A map of space would also result from a roughly topographic projection from each frequency-specific interaural intensity difference map. This is because, in general, interaural intensity differences tend to increase with angular distance from the midline, i.e. as a function of source azimuth (in owls with asymmetrical ears, interaural intensity differences increase with azimuth for low frequencies and with elevation for high frequencies; Knudsen 1980). Due to this relationship, the iso-frequency maps of interaural intensity difference in the ICc each represent the azimuth (or elevation in barn owls) of the source in a roughly topographic fashion. In cats, the map of auditory space in the superior colliculus is based, in large part, on such a topographic variation in interaural intensity difference sensitivity (Wise & Irvine 1985).

Finally, a systematic projection from along the tonotopic axis of the ICc contributes to the construction of the space map. This projection reflects the systematic relationship between the spectral shaping of the signal by the external ears and source location: High frequency components of sound (wavelengths shorter than the dimensions of the external ears) are differentially enhanced when the source is in front of the external ear, and are increasingly attenuated as the source moves away from the axis of the external ear (Harrison & Downey 1970, Knudsen 1980, Phillips et al 1982). Accordingly, although frequency tuning is broad, neurons tuned to locations in front of the pinnae tend to respond to higher frequencies, while neurons tuned to locations away from the axis of the pinnae respond preferentially to lower frequencies (Knudsen 1984b, Middlebrooks 1986).

The Auditory Map of Space

The properties of the space map in the optic tectum (superior colliculus) are remarkably similar over a variety of species (Knudsen 1982, King & Palmer 1983, Middlebrooks & Knudsen 1984, Wong 1984). The map consists of neurons that respond strongly only when the source is in a particular region of space, called the neuron's "best area" (Figure 4B).

The location of a best area is independent of the spectral properties or the intensity of the sound source. As a stimulus moves away from a neuron's best area, the response of the neuron decreases and most neurons possess a receptive field beyond which stimuli are completely ineffective. The map of space is based on a systematic ordering of neurons according to the locations of their best areas. The map is primarily of contralateral space, and, at least in cats and owls, the map is two-dimensional, representing both the horizontal (azimuth) and vertical (elevation) location of the

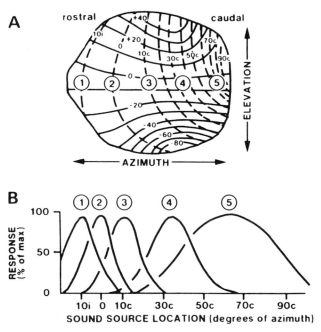

Figure 4 The representation of auditory space in the owl's optic tectum. *A.* The auditory map of space. In this flattened two-dimensional projection of the tectal surface, each *contour line* indicates the locations of units tuned to the same azimuth (*dashed lines*) or the same elevation (*solid lines*). The spatial tuning of units varies systematically across the tectum. Space is expressed in double pole coordinates, with 0° azimuth, 0° elevation directly in front of the animal; *i* signifies ipsilateral space, *c* signifies contralateral space. *Circled numerals* indicate the positions of units whose responses are shown in *B.*

B. Tuning of tectal units for sound source location. Each *curve* indicates the normalized response of a unit as a function of stimulus azimuth. Tuning is sharpest in the expanded representation of frontal space and broader in the representation of peripheral space. These data are from Knudsen (1982).

sound source (Knudsen 1982, Middlebrooks & Knudsen 1984).

Neurons in the auditory map of space respond best to broad-band stimuli (sounds containing multiple frequencies); their spatial tuning is a consequence of the convergence of multiple cue values across frequency. This convergence enables facilitatory and inhibitory interactions to sharpen spatial tuning and eliminate ambiguities (Wise & Irvine 1984, Hirsch et al 1985, Esterley 1984, Takahashi & Konishi 1986).

The sharpness of spatial tuning varies across species. In barn owls, the azimuthal dimension of best areas (defined as the area from which a stimulus elicits greater than 50% of the maximum response) ranges from 3 to 50° (Knudsen 1982). In cats, it ranges from 10 to more than 90° (Middlebrooks & Knudsen 1984), and in guinea pigs it is rarely less than 20° and is usually much larger (King & Palmer 1983). These species' differences reflect differences in the spatial resolution of the cues available to each species and differences in the precision of the auditory system in processing the cues.

Properties of Computational Maps

A number of fundamental properties shared by the auditory maps of interaural delay, interaural intensity difference, and sound source location are found in other computational maps as well. Regardless of the parameter being analyzed, neurons are typically quite broadly tuned for the mapped parameter, and the map's algorithm can operate independently of conscious guidance. Although details of tonography vary, all maps represent ranges of parameter values that are biologically relevant, and they often magnify the representation of certain ranges of values that are of particular importance to the animal. In the following sections, we use examples from the auditory and visual systems to discuss the implications of these shared properties of computational maps.

Tuning for the Mapped Parameter Is Broad

In computational maps, neurons tend to respond to a broad range of parameter values. As a result, a stimulus will activate neurons across a large portion of a computational map. For example, in the maps of orientation preference found in the visual cortex, although any given neuron responds maximally to line stimuli over a small range of orientations, it may respond at least weakly to almost any orientation (Figure 1). In primates, the range of orientations to which the average neuron will respond at least half maximally is about 50–60° (Schiller et al 1976, Albright 1984). Since the entire range of orientations is 180°, neurons throughout almost one third of the map are activated

strongly by any given stimulus orientation. Similarly, neurons in the visual map of movement direction in area MT of the macaque respond at least half maximally to moving stimuli over 90° of a 360° range of directions, and for any given stimulus, neurons throughout almost the entire map will be active at some level (Maunsell & Van Essen 1983a, Albright et al 1984).

Despite the fact that neurons in computational maps are broadly tuned, precise information about the values of parameters is contained in the output of these maps. Although the neurons respond to wide ranges of parameter values, their tuning curves are peaked (Figures 1, 3, and 4). Moreover, the tuning curves of neurons shift systematically across the map. These systematic differences in tuning curves give rise to systematic differences in response rates across the map for any given stimulus. Thus, high resolution information about the value of the mapped parameter is contained in the relative responses of neurons. To access this detailed information, a subsequent processor must be sensitive to relative levels of activity within a large population of neurons and must detect locations of peak activity within the map.

Computations Are Preset

The neurons that make up computational maps perform preset computations in parallel on the afferent signal. "Preset" does not mean that the computations cannot be modulated by descending influences, as indeed they must be in certain cases such as in the interpretation of interaural intensity difference cues by animals that can turn their ears (Middlebrooks & Knudsen 1986). Rather, it means that the neurons do not *need* input from higher centers in order to carry out their computations. The basic computations rely entirely on patterns of connectivity that are intrinsic to the processing circuit. Neither does "preset" imply genetically hardwired. Although the basic patterns of connectivity that underlie the maps are undoubtedly genetically determined, the details can be influenced extensively by experience, as in the auditory map of space and the visual map of line orientations (Knudsen 1985, Stryker et al 1978), or by patterns of correlated neuronal activity, as in the visual map of eye dominance (LeVay et al 1980, Stryker & Harris 1986). An important consequence of the computations being preset and executed in parallel is that information is processed rapidly in maps.

Factors Influencing Topography

A computational map is not necessarily an end-point, but usually an intermediate step in processing information. The generation of a map indicates that the parameter is being evaluated at that particular site in the nervous system, and that the value of the parameter is crucial for subsequent processing. The topography of a map may reflect the mechanism by which the computation is carried out (as in the map of interaural delay in n. Lam; Figure 3), economy of axonal and dendritic circuitry, developmental constraints, and/or the needs of subsequent processors. An example of map topography that seems to be regulated by a subsequent processor is the auditory space map in the owl's ICx (Knudsen & Konishi 1978). The magnification properties and the extent of spatial representation are not predicted by the properties of localization cues. Instead, they conform to the topography of the visual map of space in the optic tectum (Knudsen 1982). The topographical match of the auditory and visual maps in the optic tectum enables space-specific bimodal integration to occur throughout the tectum, and provides spatially consistent, modality-independent information to the computational motor map (Figure 2). The hypothesis that map topography conforms to the requirements of subsequent processors suggests that computational maps of the same parameter that feed into different processors may exhibit different topographies. For example, a cortical map of auditory space that subserves cognitive functions may exhibit different topographical properties from those of the tectal map.

The range of parameter values represented in a computational map corresponds with the needs of the animal. When all possible values of a parameter are important, as is the case for line orientation and movement direction, the entire range of values is represented in the map (e.g. Figure 1). However, when only a limited range of parameter values is biologically relevant, as is the case for parameters such as interaural delay and amplitude spectrum, the range of the map is restricted to those values (Figure 3; Suga 1977). For example, the maximum interaural delay that the barn owl experiences is approximately 170 µsec, which corresponds to the range of delays mapped in the owl's nucleus laminaris (Moiseff & Konishi 1981, Sullivan & Konishi 1986).

The relative magnification of the representation of parameter values can vary within a map. Where such anisotropies occur, they correlate with behavioral performance. Thus, the greatly expanded representation of frontal space in the owl's auditory space map (Figure 4) corresponds to a region of exceptionally high localization accuracy and precision (Knudsen et al 1979). Similarly, a disproportionately large representation of horizontal and vertical line orientations in the foveal region of V1 of the macaque monkey is reflected in an enhanced ability to discriminate stimuli at these angles (Mansfield 1974). These anisotropies do not arise as a result of variations in receptor densities (as do analogous anisotropies in maps of the sensory epithelium), but instead must be created

through a differential scaling of the algorithms that generate the map.

Limits to the Number of Simultaneously Mapped Parameters

In theory, the number of parameters that can be mapped independently and continuously in one area is limited to the number of dimensions in the neural structure. In the cortex, where columnar organization uses one dimension for functional specialization, serial processing, and ordering the distribution of information (Maunsell & Van Essen 1983b, Bolz & Gilbert 1986), only two dimensions are left for mapping. The nervous system overcomes this limitation by organizing fine-grain maps within coarse-grain maps. For example, numbers and letters can be mapped simultaneously along a single dimension in the following way:

1A 1B 1C 2A 2B 2C 3A 3B 3C

The letters form a fine-grain map within a coarse-grain map of numbers. On the local scale, the relative activity of neurons is determined by their tuning for the parameter mapped in fine grain, while on a broader scale relative activity is determined by the neurons' tuning for the parameter mapped in coarse grain. This is, in essence, how the primary visual cortex simultaneously maps two dimensions of space, orientation preference, ocular dominance, and possibly other parameters across only two dimensions of the cortex (Hubel & Wiesel 1977).

Notice, however, that nesting one map within another erodes some of the advantages of mapping. Map-dependent neural interactions, described in the next section, operate optimally only for the parameter mapped in fine grain. Moreover, the circuitry necessary for processing and accessing specific information becomes more complicated. For example, separate regions of the map must be sampled to compare sequential values of the coarse-grain parameter having the same fine-grain parameter value (e.g. 1A, 2A, 3A). Only by merging, and thereby losing, the information contained in the fine-grain map, can the information in the coarse-grain map be accessed in a simple topographic manner. Thus, nesting maps within maps deteriorates to a complex, though systematic, representation requiring intricate connections to process and access the information. Perhaps this is one reason that different parameters are mapped in separate, functionally specialized areas of the brain.

Advantages of Mapping

Efficient Information Processing

The nervous system must continuously analyze complex events in a dynamic environment. This requires strategies of processing that are capable of handling large amounts of information rapidly. Computational maps, with their parallel arrays of preset processors, are ideally suited for such a task: They rapidly sort and process components of complex stimuli, and represent the results in a simple, systematic form.

Information that is represented in this manner is simple to access. When parameter values are presorted in a map, further processing of the information can be based on relatively straightforward schemes of connectivity. Recall, for example, that by mapping interaural delays and interaural intensity differences, the nervous system is able to derive sound source location by using simple patterns of convergence and gradients of projections. Similarly, the map of auditory space that results from these schemes of connectivity can itself be readily integrated with other topographic maps of sensory space from other modalities.

By encoding various kinds of stimulus parameters in a common, mapped code, the nervous system can employ a single strategy for reading the information. Whether the desired information is the orientation or the direction of motion of a visual stimulus, the time interval between two particular sounds, or the location of a sound source in space, the answer is always represented as the location of a peak of activity within a population of neurons.

Maps Enable Additional Interactions

When a parameter is represented in topographic form, a variety of neuronal mechanisms can operate to further sharpen tuning in ways not possible if the information is in a non-topographic code. One class of mechanisms is regional interactions such as local facilitation and lateral inhibition, which can only work on mapped information. A second class is nonspiking synaptic interactions which operate only over relatively short distances (e.g. Watanabe & Bullock 1960, Pearson 1979). Finally, there are nonsynaptic interactions that result from changes in the electrical and chemical environment caused by synchronously active neurons in the immediate vicinity (e.g. Haas & Jeffreys 1984).

Detecting Maps

Not all computations are mapped. However, concluding that a computational map does not exist in a given area of the nervous system or for a given parameter is difficult for several reasons. First, neurons are commonly tuned for a multitude of parameters (known and unknown), the vast majority of which will not be mapped. Discovering which of the parameters may be mapped becomes increasingly difficult as the response properties of neurons become more complex. Second, the size of the map may be small. A hypercolumn in the primate visual cortex occupies less than one square millimeter of cortical surface (Hubel & Wiesel 1977), and there is no reason that maps might not be even smaller. Theoretically, a single line of neurons could function as a map; such a map would be difficult to demonstrate. Third, complicated topography can make detection of the map difficult. The axes may be irregular, convoluted, or curved (as in the auditory amplitude map; Suga 1977, Suga & Manabe 1982). In addition, a map can be obscured by embedded fine-grain maps and functional clusters.

What About High Order Computational Maps?

The nervous system has been shown to use computational maps to derive and represent both basic sensory parameters, such as line orientation in vision and interaural delay in audition, and more abstracted parameters, such as sound source location, which depend on the interactions of multiple parameters. However, the computational maps discovered so far are of relatively low order: They map fundamental sensory or motor parameters. This does not mean that higher order maps are scarce. Rather, it reflects the experimental conditions under which most animals are studied. Low order maps can operate independently of attention, behavioral significance, or levels of consciousness, and they have been revealed in untrained, anesthetized animals. Only when cortical areas are explored under conditions that require animals to perform sophisticated analyses or behavioral responses (i.e. to use their brains) can high order computational maps, if present, be revealed. Another difficulty with uncovering high order maps is anticipating the organizational parameters of the maps. In general, however, high order maps might be be expected in areas of the brain that process aspects of perception or behavior for which the value of a parameter is the essence of the analysis, such as binocular disparity for visual depth (Poggio 1984), rise time or direction and rate of frequency modulation in vocalization analysis (Liberman et al 1967, Kuhl 1981), or the absolute positions of objects in personal and extrapersonal space (Anderson et al 1985).

Summary

The nervous system performs computations to process information that is biologically important. Some of these computations occur in maps—arrays of neurons in which the tuning of neighboring neurons for a particular parameter value varies systematically. Computational maps transform the representation of information into a place-coded probability distribution that represents the computed values of parameters by sites of maximum relative activity. Numerous computational maps have been discovered, including visual maps of line orientation and direction of motion, auditory maps of amplitude spectrum and time interval, and motor maps of orienting movements. The construction of the auditory map of space is the most thoroughly understood: information about interaural delays and interaural intensity differences is processed in parallel by separate computational maps, and the outputs of these maps feed into a higher order processor that integrates sets of cues corresponding to sound source locations and creates a map of auditory space.

Computational maps represent ranges of parameter values that are relevant to the animal, and may differentially magnify the representation of values that are of particular importance. The tuning of individual neurons for values of a mapped parameter is broad relative to the range of the map. Consequently, neurons throughout a large portion of a computational map are activated by any given stimulus, and precise information about the mapped parameter is coded by the locations of peak activity.

There are a number of advantages of performing computations in maps. First, information is processed rapidly because the computations are preset and are executed in parallel. Second, maps simplify the schemes of connectivity required for processing and utilizing the information. Third, a common, mapped representation of the results of different kinds of computations allows the nervous system to employ a single strategy for reading the information. Finally, maps enable several classes of neuronal mechanisms to sharpen tuning in a manner not possible for information that is represented in a non-topographic code.

Acknowledgments

We thank Drs. Masakazu Konishi, John Middlebrooks, Carla Shatz, David Van Essen, and Herman Wagner for reviewing the manuscript, and Ms. Brenda Robertson for typing the manuscript. Preparation of the manuscript was supported by grants from the March of Dimes (1-863), the National Institutes of Health (ROl NS 16099-06 and 5T32 NS 0715807), the National Institute of Mental Health (5T32 MH 17047-04), and a Neuroscience Development award from the McKnight Foundation.

Literature Cited

Aitkin, L. M., Gates, G. R., Phillips, S. C. 1984. Responses of neurons in inferior colliculus to variations in sound-source azimuth. *J. Neurophysiol.* 52: 1–17

Aitkin, L. M., Pettigrew, J. D., Calford, M. B., Phillips, S. C., Wise, L. Z. 1985. Representation of stimulus azimuth by low frequency neurons in inferior colliculus of the cat. *J. Neurophysiol.* 53: 43–59

Albright, T. D. 1984. Direction and orientation selectivity of neurons in visual area MT of the macaque. *J. Neurophysiol.* 52: 1106–30

Albright, T. D., Desimone, R., Gross, C. G. 1984. Columnar organization of directionally selective cells in visual area MT of the macaque. *J. Neurophysiol.* 51: 16–31

Anderson, R. A., Essick, G. K., Siegel, R. M. 1985. Encoding of spatial location by posterior parietal neurons. *Science* 230: 456–58

Bolz, J., Gilbert, C. D. 1986. Generation of end-inhibition in the visual cortex via interlaminar connections. *Nature* 320: 362–65

Boudreau, J. C., Tsuchitani, C. 1970. Cat superior olive S-segment cell discharge to tonal stimulation. *Contrib. Sensory Physiol.* 4: 143–213

Calford, M. B., Moore, D. R., Hutchings, M. E. 1986. Central and peripheral contributions to coding of acoustic space by neurons in inferior colliculus of cat. *J. Neurophysiol.* 55: 587–603

Cant, N. B., Morest, D. K. 1984. The structural basis for stimulus coding in the cochlear nucleus. In *Hearing Sciences: Recent Advances,* ed. C. Berlin, pp. 371–421. San Diego: College-Hill Press

Colburn, H. S., Durlach, N. I. 1978. Models of binaural interaction. *Hundb. Percept.* 4: 467–518

Coles, R. B., Lewis, D. B., Hill, K. G., Hutchings, M. E., Gower, D. M. 1980. Directional hearing in the Japanese quail *Coturnix coturnix japonica).* II. Cochlear physiology. *J. Exp. Biol.* 86: 153–70

Esterly, S. D. 1984. Responses of spacespecific neurons in the optic tectum of the owl to narrow-band sounds. *Soc. Neurosci.* 10: 1149 (Abstr.)

Goldberg, J. M., Brown, P. B. 1969. The response of binaural neurons of dog superior olivary complex to dichotic tonal stinauli: Some physiological mechanisms of sound localization. *J. Neurophysiol.* 32: 613–36

Guinan, J. J. Jr., Norris, B. E., Guinan, S. S. 1972. Single auditory units in the superior olivary complex. II: Locations of unit categories and tonotopic organization. *Intern. J. Neurosci.* 4: 147–66

Haas, H. L., Jeffreys, J. G. R. 1984. Low calcium field burst discharge of CA1 pyramidal neurons in rat hippocampal slices. *J. Physiol.* 354: 185–201

Harrison, J. M., Downey, P. 1970. Intensity changes at the ear as a function of the azimuth of a tone source: A comparative study. *J. Acoust. Soc. Am.* 47: 1509–18

Hirsch, J. A., Chan, J.C. K., Yin, T. C. T. 1985. Responses of neurons in the cat's superior colliculus to acoustic stimuli. I. Monaural and binaural response properties. *J. Neurophysiol.* 53: 726–45

Hubel, D. H., Wiesel, T. N. 1963. Shape and arrangements of columns in cat's striate cortex. *J. Physiol. London* 165: 559–68

Hubel, D. H., Wiesel, T. N. 1968. Receptive fields and functional architecture of monkey striate cortex. *J. Physiol.* 195: 215–43

Hubel, D. H., Wiesel, T. N. 1977. Functional architecture of macaque monkey visual cortex. *Proc. R. Soc. London Ser. B* 198: 1–59

Jenkins, W. M., Merzenich, M. M. 1984. Role of cat primary auditory cortex for sound-localization behavior. *J. Neuro- physiol.* 52: 819–47

King, A. J., Palmer, A. R. 1983. Cells responsive to free-field auditory stimuli in guinea-pig superior colliculus: Distribution and response properties. *J. Physiol. London* 342: 361–81

Knudsen, E. I. 1980. Sound localization in birds. In *Comparative Studies of Hearing in Vertebrates,* ed. A. N. Popper, R. R. Fay, pp. 287–322. Berlin/Heidelberg/New York: Springer

Knudsen, E. I. 1982. Auditory and visual maps of space in the optic tectum of the owl. *J. Neurosci.* 2: 1177–94

Knudsen, E. I. 1983a. Space coding in the vertebrate auditory system. In *Bioacoustics,* ed. B. Lewis, pp. 311–44. London: Academic

Knudsen, E. I. 1983b. Subdivisions of the inferior colliculus in the barn owl *(Tyto alba). J. Comp. Neurol.* 218: 174–86

Knudsen, E. I. 1984a. Synthesis of a neural map of auditory space in the owl. In *Dynamic Aspects of Neocortical Function,* ed. G. M. Edelman, W. M Cowan, W. E. Gall, pp. 375–96. New York: Wiley

Knudsen, E. I. 1984b. Auditory properties of space-tuned units in owl's optic tectum. *J. Neurophysiol.* 52: 709–23

Knudsen, E. I. 1985. Experience alters the spatial tuning of auditory units in the optic tectum during a sensitive period in the barn owl. *J. Neurosci.* 5: 3094–3109

Knudsen, E. I., Konishi, M. 1978. A neural map of auditory space in the owl. *Science* 200: 795–97

Knudsen, E. I., Blasdel, G. G., Konishi, M. 1979. Sound localization by the barn owl measured with the search coil technique. *J. Comp. Physiol.* 133: 1–11

Konishi, M., Takahashi, T. T., Wagner, H., Sullivan, W. E., Carr, C. E. 1986. Neurophysiological and anatomical substrates of sound localization in the owl. In *Functions of the Auditory System,* ed. G. M. Edelman, W. E. Gall. New York: Wiley. In press

Kuhl, P. K. 1981. Discrimination of speech by nonhuman animals: Basic auditory sensitivities conducive to the perception of speech-sound categories. *J. Acoust. Soc. Am.* 70: 340–49

Kuhn, G. F. 1977. Model for the interaural time differences in the azimuthal plane. *J. Acoust. Soc. Am.* 62: 157–67

Kuwada, S., Yin, T. C. T., Syka, J., Buunen, T. J. F., Wickesberg, R. E. 1984. Binaural interaction in low-frequency neurons in inferior colliculus of the cat. IV. Comparison of monaural and binaural response properties. *J. Neurophysiol.* 51: 1306–25

LeVay, S., Wiesel, T. N., Hubel, D. H. 1980. The development of ocular dominance columns in normal and visually deprived monkeys. *J. Comp. Neurol.* 191: 1–51

Liberman, A. M., Delattre, P. C., Cooper, F. S. 1954. The role of selected stimulus-variables in the perception of the unvoiced stop consonants. *Am. J. Psychol.* 65: 497–516

Liberman, A. M., Cooper, F. S., Shankweiler, D. P., Studdart-Kennedy, M. 1967. Perception of the speech code. *Psychol. Rev.* 74: 431–61

Mansfield, R. J. W. 1974. Neural basis of orientation perception in primate vision. *Science* 186: 1133–35

Margoliash, D. 1983. Acoustic parameters underlying the responses of song-specific neurons in the white-crowned sparrow. *J. Neurosci.* 3: 1039–57

Maunsell, J. H. R., Van Essen, D. C. 1983a Functional properties of neurons in middle temporal visual area (MT) of macaque monkey. I. Selectivity for stimulus direction, velocity and orientation. *J. Neurophysiol.* 49: 1127–47

Maunsell, J. H. R., Van Essen, D C. 1983b. The connections of the middle temporal visual area (MT) and their relationship to a cortical hierarchy in the macaque monkey. *J. Neurosci.* 3: 2563–86

Middlebrooks, J. C. 1986. Binaural mechanisms of spatial tuning in the cat's superior colliculus distinguished using monoaural occlusion. *J. Neurophysiol.* In Press

Middlebrooks, J. C., Knudsen, E. I. 1984. A neural code for auditory space in the cat's superior colliculus. *J. Neurosci.* 4: 2621–34

Middlebrooks, J. C., Knudsen, E. I. 1986. Changes in external ear position modify the spatial tuning of auditory units in the cat's superior colliculus. *J. Neurophysiol.* In press

Middlebrooks, J. C., Pettigrew, J. D. 1981. Functional classes of neurons in primary auditory cortex of the cat distinguished by sensitivity to sound location. *J. Neurosci.* 1: 107–20

Moiseff, A., Konishi, M. 1981. Neuronal and behavioral sensitivity to binaural time differences in the owl. *J. Neurosci.* 1: 40–48

Moiseff, A., Konishi, M. 1983. Binaural characteristics of units in the owl's brainstem auditory pathway: Precursors of restricted spatial receptive fields. *J. Neurosci.* 3: 2553–62

Moushegian, G., Rupert, A. L., Gidda, J. 1975. Functional characteristics of superior olivary neurons to binaural stimuli. *J. Neurophysiol.* 38: 1037–48

O'Neill, W. E., Suga, N. 1982. Encoding of target-range information and its representation in the auditory cortex of the mustached bat. *J. Neurosci.* 2: 17–24

Pearson, K. G. 1979. Local neurons and local interactions in the nervous system of invertebrates. In *The Neurosciences Fourth Study Program,* ed. F. O. Schmitt, F. G. Worden. Cambridge: MIT Press

Phillips, D. P., Calford, M B., Pettigrew, J. D., Aitkin, L. M., Semple, M. N. 1982. Directionality of sound pressure transformation at the cat's pinna. *Hearing Res.* 8: 13–28

Poggio, G. F. 1984. Processing of stereoscopic information in primate visual cortex See Knudsen 1984a, pp. 613–35

Robinson, D. A. 1972. Eye movements evoked by collicular stimulation in the alert monkey. *Vision Res.* 12: 1795–1808

Rose, J. E., Gross, N. B., Geisler, C. D., Hind, J. E. 1966. Some neural mechanisms in the inferior colliculus of the cat which may be relevant to localization of a sound source. *J. Neurophysiol.* 29: 288–314

Roth, G. L., Aitkin, L. M., Anderson, R. A., Merzenich, M. M. 1978. Some features of the spatial organization of the central nucleus of the inferior colliculus of the cat. *J. Comp. Neurol.* 182: 661–80

Roth, G. L., Kochhar, R. K., Hind, J. E. 1980. Interaural time differences: Implications regarding the neurophysiology of sound localization. *J. Acoust. Soc. Am..* 68: 1643–51

Roucoux, A., Guitton, D., Crommelinck, M. 1980. Stimulation of the superior colliculus in the alert cat. II. Eye and head movements evoked when the head is unrestricted. *Exp. Brain Res.* 39: 75–85

Scheibel, M. E., Scheibel, A. B. 1974. Neuropil organization in the superior olive of the cat. *Exp. Neurol.* 43: 339–48

Schiller, P. H., Finlay, B. L., Volman, S. F. 1976. Quantitative studies of single-cell properties in monkey striate cortex. II. Orientation specificity and ocular dominance. *J. Neurophysiol.* 39: 1320–33

Searle, C. L., Braida, L. D., Davis, M. F., Colburn, H. S. 1976. Model for auditory localization. *J. Acoust. Soc. Am.* 60: 1164–75

Semple, M. N., Aitkin, L. M. 1979. Representation of sound frequency and laterality by units in central nucleus of cat inferior colliculus. *J. Neurophysiol.* 42: 1626–39

Shaw, E. A. G. 1974. Transformation of sound pressure level from the free field to the eardrum in the horizontal plane. *J. Acoust. Soc. Am.* 56: 1848–61

Sparks, D. L., Holland, R., Guthrie, B. L. 1976. Size and distribution of movement fields in the monkey superior colliculus. *Brain Res.* 113: 21–34

Stein, B. E., Clamann, H. P. 1981. Control of pinna movements and sensorimotor register in cat superior colliculus. *Brain Behav. Evol.* 19: 180–92

Stryker, M. P., Harris, W. A. 1986. Binocular impulse blockade prevents the formation of ocular dominance columns in cat visual cortex. *J. Neurosci.* 6: 2117–33

Stryker, M. P., Schiller, P. M. 1975. Eye and head movements evoked by electrical stimulation of monkey superior colliculus. *Exp. Brain Res.* 23: 103–12

Stryker, M. P., Sherk, H., Leventhal, A. G., Hirsch, H.V.B. 1978. Physiological consequences for the cat's visual cortex of effectively restricting early visual experience with oriented contours. *J. Neurophysiol.* 41: 896–909

Suga, N. 1977. Amplitude spectrum representation in the doppler-shifter-CF processing area of the auditory cortex of the mustache bat. *Science* 196: 64–67

Suga, N., Manabe, T. 1982. Neural basis of amplitude-spectrum representation in auditory cortex of the mustached bat. *J. Neurophysiol.* 47: 225–55

Suga, N., O'Neill, W. E. 1979. Neural axis representing target range in the auditory cortex of the mustache bat. *Science* 206: 351–53

Suga, N., O'Neill, W. E., Kujirai, K., Manabe, T. 1983. Specificity of combination-sensitive neurons for processing of complex biosonar signals in auditory cortex of the mustached bat. *J. Neurophysiol.* 49: 1573–1626

Sullivan, W. E., Konishi, M. 1984. Segregation of stimulus phase and intensity coding in the cochlear nucleus of the barn owl. *J. Neurosci.* 4: 1787–99

Sullivan, W. E., Konishi, M. 1986. A neural map of interaural phase difference in the owl's brainstem. *Proc. Natl. Acad. Sci.* In press

Takahashi, T. T., Konishi, M. 1985. Parallel pathways in the owl's brainstem auditory system. *Anat. Res.* 211: 191A

Takahashi, T. T., Konishi, M. 1986. Selectivity for interaural time difference in the owl's midbrain. *J. Neurosci.* In press

Wagner, H., Takahashi, T. T., Konishi, M. 1986. The central nucleus of the inferior colliculus as an input stage to the map of auditory space in the barn owl. *Abstr. Assoc. Res. Otolaryng.*, pp. 44–45

Watanabe, A., Bullock, T. H. 1960. Modulation of activity of one neuron by sub-threshold slow potential in another in lobster cardiac ganglion. *J. Gen Physiol.* 43:1031–45

Wenstrup, J. J., Ross, L. S., Pollack, G. D. 1986. Binaural response organization within a frequency-band representation of the inferior colliculus: Implications for sound localization. *J. Neurosci.* 6: 962–73

Wernick, J. S., Starr, A. 1968. Binaural interaction in the superior olivary complex of the cat: An analysis of field potentials evoked by binaural-beat stimuli. *J. Neurophysiol.* 31: 428–41

Wise, L. Z., Irvine, D. R. F. 1984. Interaural intensity difference sensitivity based on facilitatory binaural interaction in cat superior colliculus. *Hearing Res.* 16: 181–87

Wise, L. Z., Irvine, D. R. F. 1985. Topographic organization of interaural intensity difference sensitivity in deep layers of cat superior colliculus: Implications for auditory spatial representation. *J. Neurophysiol.* 54: 185–211

Wong, D. 1984. Spatial tuning of auditory neurons in the superior colliculus of the echolocating bat, *Myotis lucifugus. Hearing Res.* 16: 261–70

Wurtz, R. H., Albano, J. E. 1981. Visual motor function of the primate superior colliculus. *Ann. Rev. Neurosci.* 3: 189–226

Yin, T. C. T., Chan, J. C. K., Kuwada, S. 1983. Characteristics, delays, and their topographical distribution in the inferior colliculus of the cat. In *Mechanisms of Hearing,* ed. W. R. Webster, L. M. Aitkins, pp. 94–99. Melbourne: Monash Univ. Press

Young, S. R., Rubel, E.W. 1983. Frequency-specific projections of individual neurons in chick brainstem auditory nuclei. *J. Neurosci.* 3: 1373–78

Zeki, S. M. 1974. Functional organization of a visual area in the posterior bank of the superior temporal sulcus of the rhesus monkey. *J. Physiol.* 236: 549–73

Zeki, S. M. 1980. The representation of colours in the cerebral cortex. *Nature* 284: 412–18

23

Introduction

(1988)
David Zipser and Richard A. Andersen

A back-propagation programmed network that simulates response properties of a subset of posterior parietal neurons
Nature 331: 679–684

Back propagation is by far the most popular neural network learning algorithm at this time (see papers 41 and 42, *Neurocomputing: Foundations of Research*). It is a supervised, error correction algorithm and assumes a multilayered, feed-forward architecture. In its simplest form an error vector is formed at the output layer, that is, the difference between what the output should have been and what it actually was. This error vector is then propagated backward through the connections in the network, which are assumed to have the same connection strengths in both the forward and backward directions. The algorithm gives a local rule for computing the change in connection strengths between units in the network. Back propagation is an extremely useful algorithm because it is simple and robust and does well in practice on a wide range of problems. In some cases units in the middle layers (the *hidden units*) develop interesting response properties, that is, they have become feature detectors for different important aspects of the input. The most common forms of back propagation do gradient descent learning and can be shown to be minimizing least-mean-square error across the training set.

Although neural networks were originally inspired by brain architecture, there are some serious difficulties with back propagation as a biological learning rule. The most important problem is that real neurons transmit information in only one direction, and the error signal would have to return by a different pathway, causing obvious problems in synchronizing weight changes in the forward and backward direction. Also, back propagation sometimes takes a very long time to learn.

However, back propagation does seem to be able to find statistically optimal solutions to many problems. For example, the features computed by the middle layers often seem to be the best way to represent input information so it can be used best by higher layers. One nice thing about optimal solutions is that they are the same however they were obtained. One can go from Boston to New York City by land, sea, or air, by walking, running, or driving. However, the end location is always the same. Seeing someone in New York does not reveal what means of transportation was used to get there. For example, the middle layer representations found by back propagation and by the Boltzmann machine (see paper 38 in *Neurocomputing: Foundations of Research*) are often similar, even though the learning algorithms are very different.

McIlwain (paper 15) discusses a simple sensorimotor computation in the superior colliculus that moves the eyes to the most "interesting" portion of the visual field. Zipser and Andersen discuss a slightly more complex version of visual spatial computation than that shown in the superior colliculus.

An image falls on the retina. The image contains information about stationary objects in the environment. The eyes can change position, thereby moving the retinal image. But the object in the environment has not moved. Somehow the world must be kept stationary. This problem, in its generality, involves a very complex computation that is not understood. But evidence suggests a small piece of it seems to be done by area 7a of the posterior parietal cortex, an area that seems to bring together eye position and retinal position to form a spatial location representation.

It is possible to record from cells in this area to find out what they are responding to when the eyes change location. The majority of the cells respond to *both* position of the eyes and to visual stimulation of the retina. The cells respond to light over about 15°, and to eye position over a very wide area, showing again (as we also saw in the colliculus) that cells respond over a wider and wider spatial area as processing continues, rather than becoming more spatially localized.

It is hard to do experiments to study the interaction between stimulation of a particular retinal location and the position of the eyes, but it can be done. Suppose a particular constant location on the retina is stimulated as the eyes move to different positions. The visual receptors always see the same pattern, and the output of the retina will be the same, but the parietal cortex cells will respond differently, depending on where the eyes are positioned. The interaction between eye position and retinal response is nonlinear. The amplitude of the response of the cell to light, the *gain*, is multiplied by a quantity that is related to eye position. To a first approximation the gain is linearly related to different eye position in the x and y directions, suggesting that there is a planar spatial gain field.

It is unlikely that this multiplicative nonlinear interaction between a planar eye position gain field and a retinal location-dependent visual response would have been predicted a priori. But almost all neuroscientists have the naive faith that such an interaction will be optimal, when properly understood.

So Zipser and Andersen set out to see what kind of solutions back propagation would produce, when a similar problem was posed to an artificial network. Unfortunately exact anatomical connections in this area are not known. So Zipser and Andersen posed the problem in a quite general way. They assumed a three-layer, fully connected feed-forward network, where every cell is connected to every cell in lower and higher layers. The input representation contained two parts. The first was a two-dimensional topographic representation of the retina, so a spot of "light" falling on the retina excited a small group of cells. Second, the eye position was coded as a set of one-dimensional topographic maps, with a particular eye position represented as areas of activity on separate x and y coordinate axes.

In the absence of data two reasonable output — that is, head centered — representations of the "real" spatial location were used. One output representation used separate one-dimensional maps for the x and y axes, with regions of activity corresponding to the x and y spatial locations, the same type of coding used in the eye position map. In the other output representation, a two-dimensional topographic map of head-centered space was used, where an active region represents where the point of light is located, the same coding as the retinal input map. There were 96 input units, from 9 to 36 middle-layer units, and 64 output units for the two-dimensional topographic map, and 32 output units for the set of monotonic "bar graph" output units. Varying numbers of middle-layer units made little difference in the results.

Given a point of light in space, there is a simple relation between where the light falls on the retina and where the eyes are pointed. The network was taught, using back propagation, a set of input activities and the desired output patterns corresponding to different illuminated points. The network did not seem to find the problem difficult and learned the transformation quickly. The interest in this simulation was not in the correct answer, but in the responses of units in the middle layer: How are they responding to the input patterns and do those responses look like those seen in parietal cortex region 7a?

There appears to be a striking similarity between the responses of middle-layer units in the simulation and those observed in actual parietal units. The middle units tended to develop multiplicative interactions between the simulated retinal activity and eye position. Also the gain fields tended to be planar. The different output representations behaved somewhat differently in detail, but both gave the same general pattern of middle-layer responses. It is difficult to do quantitative matches between the physiological data and the simulation, but to most observers there is a strong degree of resemblance between the simulated and real cell responses when the data are plotted in the same way.

This simulation provides support for the ideas, first, that computation of spatial location from the interaction of eye position and retinal activation is what the cells in the parietal area are actually doing and, second, that the cells are doing it in an optimal way. It does *not* demonstrate that the cortex uses back propagation, merely that an optimal solution to the problem, however obtained, looks like what the brain uses. It would be extraordinarily inefficient to use a slow learning algorithm to organize cortex from a tabula rasa in each individual for such a low-level perceptual transformation. It would be much more efficient to transmit the approximately correct solution by way of genetically determined connection patterns for a cortical region and then use learning for final adjustment.

This paper demonstrates the power of back propagation as a valuable tool for the experimental study of representations, both for artificial systems and as an aid to understanding what is seen experimentally by neuroscientists.

(1988)

David Zipser and Richard A. Andersen

A back-propagation programmed network that simulates response properties of a subset of posterior parietal neurons

Nature 331: 679–684

Neurons in area 7a of the posterior parietal cortex of monkeys respond to both the retinal location of a visual stimulus and the position of the eyes and by combining these signals represent the spatial location of external objects. A neural network model, programmed using back-propagation learning, can decode this spatial information from area 7a neurons and accounts for their observed response properties.

THIS article addresses the question of how the brain carries out computations such as coordinate transformations which translate sensory inputs to motor outputs. Visual inputs are collected in the coordinate frame of the retina on which the visual environment is imaged, but motor movements such as reaching are made to locations in external space. Changes in eye position will alter the retinal locations of targets while their spatial locations remain constant. As a result, visual inputs must be transformed from retinal coordinates to coordinates that specify the location of visual objects with respect to the body to perform accurately directed movements.

Lesions to the posterior parietal cortex in monkeys and humans produce profound spatial deficits in both motor behaviour and perception[1-5]. Humans with lesions to this area can still see but they appear to be unable to integrate the position of their bodies with respect to visual inputs. The lesion data further suggest that it is the inferior parietal lobule, which comprises the posterior half of the posterior parietal cortex,

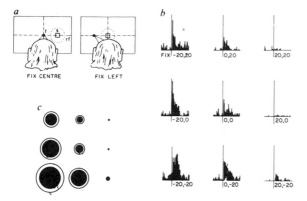

Fig. 1 *a*, Experimental protocol for determining spatial gain fields, with the projection screen viewed from behind the monkey's head. These experiments were carried out several years before the start of the modelling described here[10], but some of the data are being presented for the first time. To determine the effect of eye position, the monkey with head fixed, fixates on a point, *f*, at one of 9 symmetrically placed locations on the projection screen. The stimulus, S, is always presented at the same retinal location, chosen as the maximum-response zone of the retinal-receptive field. The stimulus consists of 1- or 6-degree diameter spots flashed for 500 ms. Each measurement is repeated 8 times. *b*, Peri-stimulus histograms of a typical gain field determination. The nine histograms are located in the same relative positions as the fixations that produced them. The vertical line indicates the time of visual stimulus onset. *c*, A graphic method for illustrating these data in which the diameter of the darkened inner circle, representing the visually evoked gain fields is calculated by subtracting the background activity recorded 500 ms before the stimulus onset from the total activity during the stimulus. The outer circle diameter, representing the total response gain fields, corresponds to the total activity during the stimulus. The annulus diameter corresponds to the background activity that is due to an eye-position signal alone, recorded during the 500 ms before the stimulus presentation.

which is involved in spatial processes.

Anatomical and physiological experiments in macaque monkeys indicate that the inferior parietal lobule contains at least four separate cortical fields. Area 7a contains visual and eye-position neurons[6-10]; area 7b contains somatosensory and reach-related cells[9,11]; area MST contains visual motion and smooth pursuit eye movement activity (refs 12–14; R. H H. Wurtz and W. T. Newsome, personal communication); and area LIP contains visual and saccade-related activity[15,16]. It has been proposed[10,17,18] that the area most likely to perform spatial transformations is area 7a. Most of the cells in this region were found to receive a convergence of both eye-position and retinal signals. The interaction between eye-position and visual responses was non-linear, and in most cases the visual rsponse could be modelled as a gain that was a function of eye position multiplied by the response profile of the retinal receptive field. Thus the visual receptive field remained retinotopic, but the magnitude of the response was modulated by eye position. This modulation can be shown to produce a tuning for the location of targets in head-centred coordinates that is eye-position-dependent; the cells will fire most for a particular location in craniotopic space, but only when the eyes are at the appropriate positions in the orbits. No cells were found that coded target location over all eye positions (eye-position-independent coding), indicating that this information can only be contained in the pattern of activity of a population of neurons. Here we describe a neural network model that shows how eye-position-independent location can be extracted from a population of area 7a neurons. The model also reproduces the non-linear interactions of eye position and retinal position information seen in actual area 7a neurons, and

demonstrates response properties, such as large receptive fields, which are strikingly similar to those observed in single-unit recording studies.

The neural modelling technique we use differs significantly from most previous approaches, which first found an algorithm to accomplish the computation, and then specified neural models to implement the algorithm. Our approach is based on the use of a neural network training procedure, called 'back propagation', which can programme artificial neural networks to compute arbitrary functions (refs 19–23; S. R. Lehky and T. J. Sejnowski, personal communication). Unlike computer programming, programming by training uses only examples of input and output. This means that it is not necessary to know in advance the algorithm that the network will use; the learning process will discover an appropriate algorithm. Back propagation networks have internal or hidden units that are free to take on the response properties to best accomplish the computational task being learned. It is the properties of these hidden units that we find resemble those of cortical neurons. The back-propagation procedure accomplishes learning by adjusting the strengths of the synapses within the network.

Experimental results from area 7a

The experimental data that must be accounted for by any model of area 7a were collected previously in an extensive series of studies with awake, unanaesthetized monkeys[10]. Here we describe new analyses of these data that facilitate a comparison of area 7a cells with the units generated by training the network model.

Three of the major classes of area 7a neurons are of interest here: the eye-position cells responding to eye-position only (15% of all cells sampled from area 7a), the visual cells responding to visual stimulation only (21%), and the spatially tuned cells responding to both eye position and visual stimulation (57%). Neurons in the first two classes presumably represent the eye position and retinal locaton information available to area 7a as input. The interaction of eye position and visual information found in the third class of cells produces a representation for the head-centred location of visual targets that is eye-position-dependent.

The experimental protocol involved recording neuronal activity extra-cellularly from awake, unanaesthetized monkeys trained in various visuospatial tasks[10] (see Fig. 1). The eye-position sensitivity was tested by having the animal fixate on a small point at different eye positions, with the head fixed in otherwise total darkness. The eye-position cells typically showed a linear increase in activity for a range of horizontal or vertical eye positions, although some cells showed more complex eye-position coding. An ensemble of 30 eye-position unit responses is shown in Fig. 4c. The receptive fields of the visual cells were tested by flashing a spot stimulus at different locations in the visual field while the animal fixated on a target at a single eye position. Surfaces were fit to these data points using a gaussian interpolation. These cells typically had large receptive fields equally distributed across the visual field for the population of neurons with a single peak of activity. The shape of the receptive fields approximated a symmetrical gaussian with a $1/e$ width of 15 degrees (see legend to Fig. 4).

The spatially tuned neurons were the largest group and showed a convergence of eye position and retinal position information. The receptive fields are very large (often over 80 degrees in diameter) and have one or more peaks that form a smoothly changing, hilly landscape. A set of 12 retinal receptive fields from spatially tuned cells, arranged according to peak eccentricity and complexity, is shown in Fig. 2.

As mentioned above, the evoked visual response of spatially tuned neurons varies as a function of eye position. This effect was examined by collecting data under the condition in which the visual stimulus always appears at the peak location in the retinal receptive field, but with the animal fixating at nine

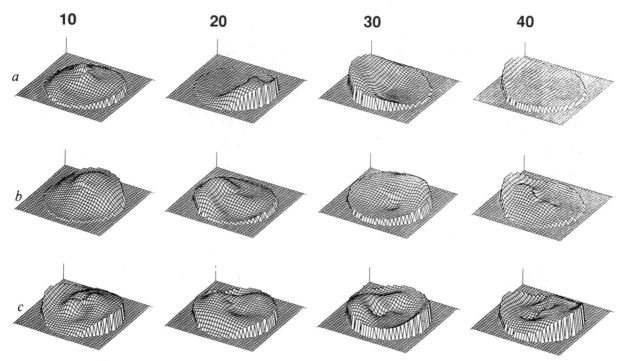

Fig. 2 The receptive fields of spatially tuned neurons from area 7a, arranged in rows with the eccentricity of the field maxima increasing to the right, and in columns with the complexity of the fields increasing downwards. Receptive fields were sampled at 17 radially spaced points, with one sample taken at the centre of the field, and four samples taken on each of four circles of radius 10, 20, 30 and 40 degrees. All the fields in row *a* have single peaks. Those in row *b* have a single large peak but some complexities in the field. The fields in row *c* are the most complex with multiple peaks. The data have been normalized so that the highest peak in each field is the same height.

different eye positions[10]. These plots are referred to as spatial gain fields. Figure 1 demonstrates the experimental protocol for mapping spatial gain fields.

The majority of the spatial gain fields are roughly planar. This planar behaviour is evident in Fig. 1c, where the darkened inner circles are proportional to the magnitude of the visual evoked response, the outer circle diameter to the total activity during the flashed stimulus, and the annulus diameter the background activity due to the eye position alone. The data for the visually evoked response in Fig. 1c can be fitted by a plane tilted up for eye positions to the left and also tilted up for downward eye positions. Analysis using linear regressions in the two dimensions of eye position indicated that the gain fields for the visually evoked activity (represented by the dark inner circles) were planar, or had a large planar component, for 55% of the neurons. Interestingly, 80% of the total response gain fields (represented by the outer circles) were planar or largely planar.

A useful way to further characterize the nonlinear combinations of eye and retinal information is to compare the contributions of each to the total response of the cells. This can be done simply by comparing the dark inner circles, which represent the visual contribution to the response, with the white annuli, which represent the eye position contribution to the response. This comparison shows three basic types of gain fields. For 28% the background and evoked activities change in a parallel fashion (Fig. 3b, e, f). In most of the cells (43%), the evoked activity changes with eye position while the background activity, if any, remained constant (Fig. 3a, c, d); three-quarters of these cells had very low or undetectable background activity. The remaining 28% of the neurons showed the interesting property that the background and evoked activities changed in different directions, so that the activity of either alone was grossly non-planar, but the overall activity was planar (Fig. 3g, h, i).

The neural network model

We used a three-layer network (illustrated in Fig. 4) that was trained to map visual targets to head-centred coordinates, given any arbitrary pair of eye and retinal positions. The first, or input, layer has two sections, an array of units on which the visual stimulus is represented, and a set of units representing eye position. The second layer consists of the hidden units, which map the input to the output. Each hidden unit receives input

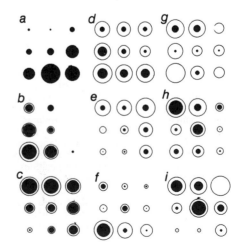

Fig. 3 The spatial gain fields of 9 neurons (*a–i*) from area 7a in the format of Fig. 1c.

Fig. 4 *a*, Back-propagation network used to model area 7a. The visual input consists of 64 units with gaussian receptive fields with $1/e$ widths of 15 degrees. The centre of each receptive field occupies a position in an 8 by 8 array with 10 degree spacings. The shading represents the level of activity for a single-spot stimulus, with darker shading representing higher rates of activity. The units have been arrayed topographically for illustrative purposes only; this pattern is not an aspect of the model as each hidden unit receives input from every one of the 64 retinal input units. The eye position input consists of 4 sets of 8 units each with two sets coding horizontal position (one for negative slope and one for positive slope) and two sets coding vertical position. Shading represents the level of activity. The intercepts have been ordered for illustrative purposes only and do not represent information available to the hidden layer. Each eye position cell projects to every unit in the hidden layer. Two output representations were used; the gaussian output format is shown on the right and the monotonic format on the left. The gaussian format units have gaussian shaded receptive fields plotted in head-centred coordinates. They have $1/e$ widths of 15 degrees and are centred on an 8 by 8 array in head coordinate space with 10 degree spacings. The monotonic format units have firing rates that are a linear function of position of the stimulus in head-centred coordinates. There are four sets of 8 units with two sets of opposite slope for vertical position and two sets for horizontal position in head-centred coordinates. Again, shading represents the degree of activity and the topographic ordering is for illustrate purposes only. The small boxes containing W indicate the location of the synapses whose weights are trained by back propagation. Each hidden unit projects to every cell in the output layer. The output activity of the hidden and output layer units is calculated by the logistic function: $\text{output} = 1/(1 + e^{-\text{net}})$, where $\text{net} = (\text{weighted sum of inputs}) + \text{bias}$. The arrow for the connections represents the direction of activity propagation; error was propagated back in the opposite direction. The back-propagation procedure guarantees that the synaptic weight changes will always move the network towards lower error by implementing a gradient descent in error in the multi-dimensional synaptic weight space.

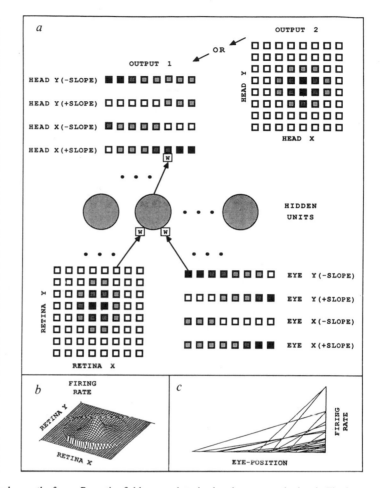

b, Area 7a visual neuron receptive field with a single peak near the fovea. Receptive fields were plotted using the same method as in Fig. 3. Visual cells that had no eye-position-related activity or modulation of their responses by eye position were used to model the retinal input to the network. *c*, A composite of 30 area 7a-eye-position units, whose firing rates are plotted as a function of horizontal or vertical eye deviation. The slopes and intercepts are experimental values for eye-position neurons.

from every input unit and projects to every unit in the third output layer. The output of each unit of the hidden and output layers is computed as an S-shaped (logistic) function of the synaptic strength weighted sum of its inputs, plus a bias term. The training paradigm uses back propagation learning, which consists of choosing an input and desired output, applying the input to the first layer of the network and propagating the activity it generates through the network to the output units. The actual output is then subtracted from the desired output to generate an error. This error is used to adjust the weights of synapses on the output layer units and hidden layer units in a manner prescribed by the back propagation procedure[19]. Training begins with all weights randomized, resulting in large errors, and the training cycle is repeated until the error is reduced to desired levels.

The retinal position and eye position inputs to the network are modelled using characteristics of the cells in the posterior parietal cortex that respond to visual stimuli only and eye position only. The visual input consisted of 64 gaussian-shaped receptive fields, with $1/e$ widths of 15 degrees and with each peak separated by 10 degrees in an 8 by 8 array. The eye position input consisted of four sets of 8 units with single sets for positive and negative slopes for horizontal and vertical eye position.

We used two representations of location in head-centred coordinates at the output layer. One (output 2 in Fig. 4*a*) was

a gaussian format in which each unit had a gaussian receptive field similar to the representation of the retinal input, but coding location in head-centred rather than retinal coordinates. The other (output 1 in Fig. 4*a*) was a monotonic format, in which the activity of each neuron is a linear function of the location of the stimulus in head-centred coordinates. For the gaussian format, a 64-unit array similar to the retinal input array was used and for the monotonic format, a 32-unit array similar to the eye position input array was used. The gaussian and monotonic formats were chosen because they represent the most common types of coding formats found for brain cells. Also the monotonic format has the interesting feature that it has the same representation as the eye-position code at the input. Thus, if the animal foveates the visual stimulus, the resulting eye-position signal could be used as the teacher to indicate the correct location of the stimulus in head-centred coordinates.

The model network was trained using randomly selected pairs of input eye positions and retinal positions. The teacher signal (desired output) used to train the output units was the true spatial location in head-centred coordinates implied by the inputs, and was represented in either the monotonic or gaussian format. The network trained quickly: after $\sim$1,000 trials, accuracies equivalent to the distance between retinal unit centres were reached. When training was continued, error continued to decrease, but at a lower rate.

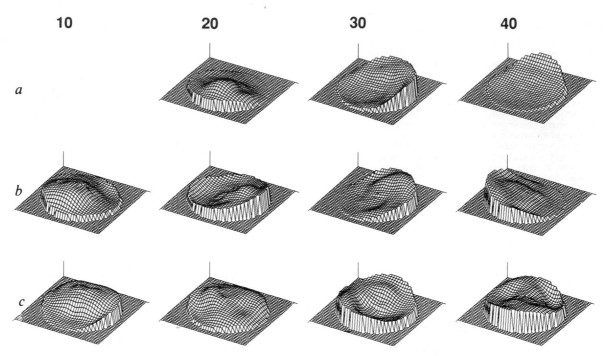

Fig. 5 Hidden unit retinal receptive fields generated by the back propagation model. These plots were generated by holding the eye-position input to the network constant and simulating visual stimulation at the same 17 retinal positions used in the experiments on area 7a. The hidden unit activities were normalized and plotted in the same way as the experimental data shown in Fig. 3. The data shown here are from a series of 4 training sessions using networks with 25 hidden units and the monotonic format output. Similar results were obtained for the gaussian format output. All the fields, except for C-10, C-20 and C-30, are from networks that have received 1,000 learning trials. The remaining three are from untrained networks, resulting only from the random synaptic weights assigned at the start of a training run. Very complex fields are only rarely found in trained networks. No hidden unit with a single peak at 10 degrees appeared in this data set and such units are very rare in trained networks. No spatially tuned neurons with central receptive fields were found in area 7a, and no such fields appeared in the trained model. But central receptive fields are found among the visual neurons in 7a, and this kind of unit was among those used as input to the model network.

Agreement of model with experiment

To evaluate the model, we first compare the experimental and model retinal receptive fields. The model receptive fields were categorized according to their complexity, and the eccentricity of their activity maxima (Fig. 5), as had been done previously

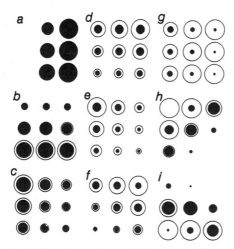

Fig. 6 Hidden unit spatial gain fields generated by the model network. Fields *a–f* were generated using the monotonic format output; the rest used the gaussian format output.

for the experimental receptive fields (Fig. 2). Comparison of the top lines in Figs 2 and 5 shows that the trained models generate single-peak receptive fields resembling those observed experimentally at all eccentricities except 10 degrees. The fully trained model also produces moderately complex fields like those found in line 2, but rarely produces receptive fields as complex as those in the bottom line of Fig. 2. This kind of highly complex field is not distinguishable from the untrained model receptive fields shown in the bottom of Fig. 5. The comparison process contains an element of subjectivity, but it demonstrates that the trained model generates retinal receptive fields remarkably similar to the experimentally observed fields. The gain fields generated by the model are shown in Fig. 6. All the total-response gain fields, whether generated by the monotonic or the gaussian output format, were planar in shape. This result compares with 80% of the experimental fields in this planar class. When the model gain fields are examined in more detail, taking into account the non-linearities of the visual response fields, there are significant differences between the eye position and retinal output formats. For example, when trained with the monotonic output format, 67% of the visual response gain fields were planar, but when trained with the gaussian output format only 13% fall in this class. These figures compare with 55% in this class for the experimental data. The irregular visual response gain fields generated by the gaussian output format are more radically irregular than those generated by the monotonic output format. Thus it appears that to account for the details of the visual response gain fields, it may be necessary to use both types of output representation. It should be pointed out, however, that whereas the visual receptive fields and the total gain fields were virtually unaffected by changing parameters of the model, the visual response gain fields were very sensitive to parameters such as threshold value and output representation. The number of hidden units had little effect, giving similar results for simulations ranging from 9 to 36 hidden units.

The striking similarity between model and experimental data certainly supports the conjecture that the cortex and the network generated by back propagation compute in similar ways. As back propagation generates optimal solutions which produce the least error, these results also suggest that the brain chooses optimal solutions with respect to error. The similarity of the model and test results raises the question of what physiological mechanisms could subserve this equivalence. Presently the back-propagation paradigm is structured at a level higher than implementation, and obviously cannot be applied literally to the brain, because information does not travel backwards rapidly through axons. That the back-propagation method appears to discover the same algorithm that is used by the brain in no way implies that back propagation is actually used by the brain. One approach to understanding the physiological significance of these results is to generate models incorporating features found in the brain, such as Hebbian-like learning at synapses and reciprocal back-projection pathways for propagating error, and determine whether these models generate similar results. In this regard it is interesting to note that all cortico-cortical and thalamocortical connections have reciprocal feedback pathways.

An important consideration in interpreting the results is how closely does the model response actually resemble the cortical data? This is a complex issue because there is error in the experimental data, and additional errors introduced by the interpolation process used to produce the full-field views of the receptive fields. Examination of the magnitudes of these errors indicates that they could not account for the various receptive field types, or eye-position gain fields observed experimentally and in the model. The methods of comparison between model and experiment that we have used are to some degree subjective. Perhaps a more objective comparison procedure will eventually be developed, but it is unlikely that, given the complex nature of the data to be compared, any such technique will substantially alter our conclusions concerning the degree of similarity between model and experimental data.

From the physiological perspective these experiments raise the possibility that the posterior parietal cortex learns to associate body position with visual position to localize accurately the position of objects with respect to the body. This idea about the importance of learning is reasonable considering that it would not be practical for spatial representations to be hard-wired because the body dimensions change during development. Furthermore, adaptation experiments show that distortion of space with prisms leads to rapid recalibration, suggesting that these representations are still plastic in adults. As the model, by definition, does not have a topographic organization to localize in space, it shows that the brain does not need a topographic organization to localize in space. The organization of the network is not a product of the spatial position of the cell bodies, but rather is contained in the pattern of the weights of the synaptic connections.

Finally, there is the question of where the output units of the model could exist in the brain. One possible location would be areas that receive projection from area 7a. Although eye position effects on visual responses have been described at several locations in the brain (refs 24–26; S. Funahashi, C. J. Bruce, P. S. Goldman-Rakic; and R. Lal, M. J. Friedlander, personal communication), an eye-position-independent coding has yet to be unequivocally demonstrated. But it is also possible that the final spatial output could only exist in the behaviour of the animal. For example, the muscles innervating the eye or limb are broadly tuned, and the position of the eye or limb is coded in a distributed fashion over the activity of several muscles. Thus the final spatial output may not exist in any single cell in the brain, but rather might be found only in the pointing of the eye or finger accurately to a location in space.

We thank David Rumelhart, Francis Crick and Emilio Bizzi for stimulating discussion during the development of this model and Carol Andersen for editorial assistance. D.Z. was supported by grants from the System Development Foundation, the AFOSR and the Office of Naval Research. R.A.A. was supported by the NIH, the Sloan Foundation and Whitaker Health Sciences Foundation.

Received 19 October 1987; accepted 19 January 1988.

1. Critchley, M. The Parietal Lobes (Hafner, New York, 1953).
2. Lynch, J. C. Behav. Brain Sci. 3, 484–534 (1980).
3. Andersen, R. A. in Spatial Cognition: Brain Bases and Development (eds Stiles-Davis, J., Kritchevsky, M. & Bellugi, U.) (University of Chicago Presss, in the press).
4. Bock, O., Eckmiller, R. & Andersen, R. A. Brain Res. (in the press).
5. Andersen, R. A. in Handbook of Physiology: The Nervous System V 483–518 (eds Mountcastle, V. B., Plum, F. & Geiger, S. R. (1987).
6. Mountcastle, V. B., Lynch, J. C., Georgopoulos, A., Sakata, H. & Acuna, C. J. Neurophysiology 38, 871–908 (1975).
7. Lynch, J. C., Mountcastle, V. B., Talbot, W. H. & Yin, T. C. T. J. Neurophysiol. 40, 362–389 (1977).
8. Andersen, R. A. & Mountcastle, V. B. J. Neurosci. 3, 532–548 (1983).
9. Andersen, R. A., Siegel, R. M. & Essick, G. K. Expl Brain Res. 67, 316–322 (1987).
10. Andersen, R. A., Essick, G. K. & Siegel, R. M. Science 230, 456–458 (1985).
11. Robinson, C. J. & Burton, H. J. comp. Neurol. 192, 69–92 (1980).
12. Tanaka, K. et al. J. Neurosci. 6, 134–144 (1986).
13. Saito, H. et al. J. Neurosci. 6, 145–157 (1986).
14. Sakata, H., Shibutani, H., Ito, Y. & Tsurugai, K. Expl Brain Res. 61, 658–663 (1986).
15. Gnadt, J. W. & Andersen, R. A. Expl Brain Res. (in the press).
16. Andersen, R. A. & Gnadt, J. W. in Reviews in Occulomotor Research Vol. 3 (eds Wurtz, R. & Goldberg, M.) (Elsevier, Amsterdam, in the press).
17. Andersen, R. A. in Neurobiology of Neocortex. Dahlem Koferenzen (eds Rackic, P. & Singer., W.) (Wiley, Chichester, in the press).
18. Andersen, R. A. & Zipser, D. Can. J. Physiol. Pharmac. (in the press).
19. Rumelhart, D. E., Hinton, G. E. & Williams, R. J. in Parallel Distributed Processing: Explorations in the Microstructure of Cognition Vol. 1 (eds Rumelhart, D. E. & McClelland, J. L.) 318–362 (MIT, Cambridge, 1986).
20. Zipser, G. Institute for Cognitive Science, Report 8608 (UCSD, La Jolla, 1986).
21. Zipser, D. & Rabin, D. E. in Parallel Distributed Processing: Explorations in the Microstructure of Cognition Vol. 1 (eds Rumelhart, D. E. & McClelland, J. L.) 488–506 (MIT, Cambridge, 1986).
22. Ackley, D. H., Hinton, G. E. & Sejmowski, T. J. Cognitive Sci. 9, 147–169 (1985).
23. Sejnowski, T. J., Kienker, P. K. & Hinton, G. E. Physica 22D, 260–275 (1986).
24. Schlag, J., Schlag-Rey, M., Peck, C. K. & Joseph, J. Expl Brain Res. 40, 170–184 (1980).
25. Peck, C. K., Schlag-Rey, M. & Schlag, J. J. comp Neurol. 194, 97–116 (1980).
26. Aicardi, G., Battaglini, P. P. & Galletti, G. J. Physiol., Lond. 390, 271 (1987).

24
Introduction

(1988)
Thomas H. Brown, Paul F. Chapman,
Edward W. Kairiss, and Claude L. Keenan

Long-term synaptic potentiation
Science 242: 724–728

Neural networks are fun and give rise to interesting engineering and computing, but there is also a real brain to understand. The connection strengths in neural networks are usually described as oversimplified versions of the synapses that connect neurons together. In the past few years a great deal has been learned about the real synapses that seem to be involved in some kinds of human learning. This brief review paper from *Science*, though technical, gives an idea of the biology of the leading candidate for a synapse showing Hebbian modification. More details can be obtained from the extensive list of references or from Brown, Kairiss, and Keenan (1990).

Every connectionist model assumes that changing the strength of connections between computing units stores memory. However, the physiological basis of learning and memory is not so clear. There are lots of plausible alternate candidates. For example, we could store information as sequences of base pairs or amino acids in macromolecules. This is an attractive idea because we already have the genetic machinery present in the cell nucleus for reading macromolecules. So memory might be stored in the form of tiny "tapes," read by a tiny "tape deck." This idea was seriously considered in the 1960s, but simply does not seem to be used by the brain.

Another technique would be to store information in the form of reverberating loops of activity. Once a loop is established, activity circulates until it is deliberately stopped. Norbert Wiener (paper 2) thought highly of this idea. However, as we all know, when the power goes off, memory in computers is lost. Occasionally deep coma, freezing, or other mishaps to humans or animals causes brain electrical activity to be apparently lost, yet there may be no damage to memory. This result suggests a permanent, physical change as the essential part of the long-term storage process, though activity in loops might be an important part of short-term memory.

So for over 100 years neuroscientists have considered it almost an article of faith that changes in synaptic strength are what store memory. Until the last decade, however, there was surprisingly little direct evidence for this important assumption. This was largely because of the extreme difficulty of the experiments needed to study synaptic change due to learning. Changes in very small structures must be reliably detected and measured. The changes must be associated with what look like significant behavioral changes. And there are many processes that produce short-term changes in synaptic strength, so changes associated with memory must be long.

In the 1970s evidence started to accumulate that changes in synaptic strength were indeed associated with events that looked very much like significant learning. For example, in the gastropod mollusc *Aplysia*, Eric Kandel had demonstrated that synaptic modification was clearly responsible for the habituation of a simple withdrawal response (see Kandel 1976).

However, what Kandel demonstrated was a purely *presynaptic* effect. The change in synaptic strength underlying habituation had no component due to what was happening postsynaptically, that is, on the output-cell side. This was disturbing because the most common assumption about learning in neural networks involves the use of some variant or other of the Hebb rule. The Hebb rule and its many variants all require that modification is due to a *conjunction* between presynaptic and postsynaptic activity.

The neural phenomenon in mammals most often mentioned in conjunction with associative learning is called *long-term potentiation*, or LTP, which is a rapidly produced, long-lasting increase in synaptic strength produced by certain patterns of stimulation. It is found in a cortical structure called the *hippocampus*, which is known from a number of lines of evidence to be involved in memory. Intense interest has centered on a synaptic complex in the hippocampus that uses the amino acid neurotransmitter glutamate. Part of the complex is responsive to a glutamate analog called NMDA, and part of it is a more traditional synapse with receptors sensitive to another glutamate analog, quisqualate. (Differential sensitivity to transmitter analogs is often used by physiologists to investigate the details of synaptic structure. Very different receptors may use the same neurotransmitter.)

Neurons work by modulation of ionic flow through the neuron membrane. Ions pass through the membrane through *channels*, holes through the cell membrane that are formed by protein molecules. The action potential, the basic information-transmission act of a neuron, reflects an enormous increase in the conductance to sodium ions of a *sodium channel*. The resulting electrochemical interactions make a large change in voltage inside the cell. Synaptic interactions, the basis for all the connectionist connection strengths, also involve flows of ions through channels, which have the end result of changing the membrane potential of the cell.

The sodium channels are *voltage dependent*. As the membrane potential inside the cell becomes more positive, the sodium channels become more and more conductive, raising the membrane potential still more, creating a positive-feedback system, which terminates when the channels are fully open. They quickly close to reestablish the original state.

Most channels associated with synaptic strength are not voltage dependent. One theoretical implication of this is that a single synaptic strength can be assumed to have a constant value in the generic connectionist neuron; that is, the strength of one synapse does not depend on activity caused by other synapses. Conductivity of these channels is controlled only by the presence or absence of particular molecules.

The NMDA synapse has aspects of *both* systems. Conductivity to ion flow is a function of both the presence of certain molecules *and* the membrane potential. The reason for this seems to be a site located *in* the channel that binds magnesium ions. Even if the channel is opened by a neurotransmitter, conductance can be blocked by the presence of magnesium ions, just like a cork in a pipe. But the blockage is voltage dependent. Therefore if the postsynaptic cell becomes excited, the magnesium block is removed, and the channel can now conduct. Channel conductance is highest for calcium ions, which then flow into the postsynaptic cell.

The NMDA channel has a very long time constant compared with the traditional quisqualate channel. A large amount of pre- and postsynaptic activity occurring over many hundreds of milliseconds will tend to keep the channel open, as well as uncorking it. This corresponds to short-term Hebbian modification, with time constants of hundreds of milli-seconds, or even seconds. NMDA receptors are found in many parts of the brain and may play a role in short-term variations in strengths of many synapses, an effect that may complicate the behavior of real neural networks.

In the hippocampus, however, an *additional* effect occurs. For reasons not yet fully understood, the significant calcium currents due to the active NMDA channel activates enzymes that produce *permanent* changes in the synaptic strength. Many modifiable synapses on hippocampal cells are located on structures called *dendritic spines*, which are thin processes, a couple of microns long, with synaptic complexes at their end. Evidence accu-mulated over decades strongly suggests that dendritic spines are implicated in learning; for example, their shape changes in response to some kinds of environmental manipulation. By changes in spine geometry, it is possible to make changes in the influence of one cell on another, without changing the strengths of other connections. This kind of independent change in synaptic strength is usually assumed by modelers, but may in fact not be that easy to accomplish physically in a very small, highly interconnected system. The isolated synapse at the end of the spine also controls its own ionic environment to a large degree. For example, the calcium ion concentration may become very high in the spine because of the difficulty of diffusion and ion exchange with the rest of the cell through the narrow spine neck.

One might speculate about how the observed conjunctional rule modification agrees with what is usually assumed theoretically. One major difference seems to be the suggestion that there is a *modification threshold*, so that there is no long-term change unless activity exceeds some critical value, that is, small correlations between pre- and postsynaptic activity are not learned. This actually would make little difference to most networks because many simula-tions suggest that it is the large weights that do the computation. One rule of thumb is that the largest 25 percent of the weights contain most of the information processing power of the system.

Another point of interest is the cooccurrence of a short-duration and long-duration effect. Both the early current passed through the NMDA channel and the long-term change seem to be in the same direction. This suggests that, as far as neural information representation is concerned, short- and long-term memory may be organized similarly. A very short-term Hebbian modification has been suggested as an information processing technique by some modelers (von der Malsburg and Bienenstock 1986).

Most theoretical realizations of the Hebb rule assume more than simple excitatory con-junction. There are three other quadrants of correlated activity as well. For example, suppose the presynaptic cell is consistently excited when the postsynaptic cell is not firing or inhibited, that is, anticorrelation. Does this weaken the synapse? There is some early evidence that anticorrelation can produce synaptic weakening, *long-term depression* (Stanton and Sejnowski 1989), by a mechanism other than the NMDA synapse.

Properties of the NMDA synapse and of LTP are currently one of the hottest areas in neuroscience. The reasons for this are obvious. The synaptic structure itself has complex and fascinating physiology and biophysics. But, more important, we now have *direct experimen-tal evidence* of the kind of modification based on a conjunction between pre- and postsynaptic activity that has been *assumed* to exist by modelers for decades. The exact quantitative details of the modification produced will surely be worked out in the next few years and, for the first time, we can start using *real* learning rules in our neural networks.

Acknowledgment

Some of the organization of ideas presented in this introduction owes a debt to a lecture by Charles F. Stevens at Brown University in October 1989.

References

T.H. Brown, E.W. Kairiss, and C.L. Keenan (1990), Hebbian synapses: biophysical mechanisms and algorithms. *Annual Review of Neuroscience* 13: 475–511.

E.R Kandel (1976), *Cellular Basis of Behavior*. San Francisco: W. H. Freeman.

P.K. Stanton and T.J. Sejnowski (1989), Associative long term depression in the hippocampus induced by Hebbian covariance. *Nature* 339: 215–218.

C. von der Malsburg and E. Bienenstock (1986), Statistical coding and short term synaptic plasticity: a scheme for knowledge representation in the brain. In E. Bienenstock, F. Fogelman-Soulie, and G. Weisbuch (Eds.), *Disordered Systems and Biological Organization*. Berlin: Springer.

(1988)
Thomas H. Brown, Paul F. Chapman,
Edward W. Kairiss, and Claude L. Keenan

Long-term synaptic potentiation
Science 242: 724–728

Long-term synaptic potentiation (LTP) is a leading candidate for a synaptic mechanism of rapid learning in mammals. LTP is a persistent increase in synaptic efficacy that can be quickly induced. The biophysical process that controls one type of LTP is formally similar to a synaptic memory mechanism postulated decades ago by the psychologist Donald Hebb. A key aspect of the modification process involves the *N*-methyl-D-aspartate (NMDA) receptor–ionophore complex. This ionophore allows calcium influx only if the endogenous ligand glutamate binds to the NMDA receptor and if the voltage across the associated channel is also sufficiently depolarized to relieve a magnesium block. According to one popular hypothesis, the resulting increase in the intracellular calcium concentration activates protein kinases that enhance the postsynaptic conductance. Further biophysical and molecular understanding of the modification process should facilitate detailed explorations of the mnemonic functions of LTP.

D ISCOVERING THE PHYSICAL BASIS OF LEARNING IN HU-mans and other mammals is among the greatest remaining challenges facing the neurosciences. One of the oldest and most popular ideas holds that learning involves use-dependent modifications in the strengths of preexisting synaptic connections among neurons [for review, see (1)]. Theoretical studies have shown that networks of processing elements with modifiable interconnections can indeed display powerful associative learning and self-organizational capabilities (2). Neurobiological studies of learning in higher invertebrates have convincingly demonstrated that certain forms of Pavlovian conditioning do in fact result from activity-dependent changes in synaptic efficacy (3). These studies have motivated the search for analogous synaptic mechanisms for information storage in mammals. The phenomenon of LTP is a leading candidate for this function.

The LTP hypothesis for learning has captured the attention of neuroscientists working at several different levels of organization—molecular, cellular, systems, and behavioral. This review (i) explains what LTP is and why there has been such an explosion of interest in this phenomenon; (ii) summarizes several hypotheses regarding the biophysical and molecular mechanisms underlying LTP; (iii) identifies some of the technical developments that are driving the current growth in our understanding of this extraordinary form of synaptic plasticity; and (iv) poses a challenge to researchers in this field. This challenge is to provide a convincing linkage between LTP and learning and to elucidate how endogenously generated LTP mediates its mnemonic functions.

The authors are in the Department of Psychology, Yale University, New Haven, CT 06520.

Properties of LTP

LTP was first described in the rabbit hippocampal formation by Bliss and colleagues (4). The essence of LTP is a rapid and persistent synaptic enhancement (4–6). By rapid we mean that the modification can be induced by brief (tens of milliseconds) stimulation of an afferent input (usually at 100 to 400 Hz). By persistent we mean that it outlasts previously discovered forms of synaptic enhancement such as facilitation, augmentation, and posttetanic potentiation (PTP) [see table 1 of (7)]. Of the latter, PTP is the most persistent, typically lasting a few (1 to 10) minutes after a brief stimulation. LTP is not unique to the hippocampal formation (6, 8), but it has only been reported at excitatory synapses (5, 7).

In neurophysiological studies that utilize intracellular recording techniques, the synaptic enhancement is measured as the increase in the amplitude of the excitatory postsynaptic potential (EPSP) or the excitatory postsynaptic current (EPSC) produced by a single-pulse stimulation of an afferent input. Almost all intracellular recordings of LTP have been performed on the brain slice preparation [reviewed in (7)]. In studies that employ extracellular recording techniques, enhancement is measured as an increase in the amplitude or the slope of some component of the field potential produced by stimulating the afferent input. Extracellular (field potential) recordings suggest that LTP can remain stable in vivo for weeks or possibly months (9). The maximum duration of LTP in vitro is uncertain. Usually the posttetanic synaptic enhancement is only monitored for 15 to 60 min in brain slices. In such experiments LTP is commonly defined as any use-dependent synaptic enhancement that clearly outlasts PTP.

Varieties of LTP. There are several different types of LTP. Racine and co-workers have examined the time course of the enhancement in vivo and suggested that different forms of LTP can be classified based on decay time constants (9). In studies of brain slices a discrimination is sometimes made between "decremental" LTP (which decays over the course of tens of minutes) and "nondecremental" LTP (which shows little or no detectable decay over this time period) (10). Comparative studies have suggested that it might be reasonable to separate associative types of LTP from other types (6–8, 10–14). Another way to categorize varieties of LTP is based on whether the induction of the modification is dependent on the activation of particular types of receptors (7, 10, 11). One must therefore recognize that several different mechanisms may be included within the class of synaptic modifications that are called LTP (11). The following discussion is mainly concerned with an NMDA receptor–dependent form of associative LTP.

Associative LTP. High-frequency (tetanic) stimulation is not always sufficient to induce LTP. In some synaptic systems, the intensity of the electrical shocks delivered in the tetanic stimulation is important (4, 5, 15). Low-intensity stimulation fails to induce LTP in these systems. There are several possible interpretations of this intensity effect (5, 7, 10, 11, 15). One interpretation is that LTP induction depends on the strength of the postsynaptic response during the tetanic stimulation. The postsynaptic response amplitude depends on the number of stimulated afferents, which in turn depends on the stimulus intensity. According to this interpretation, tetanic stimulation of a small number of afferent inputs fails to induce LTP because these inputs collectively produce a weak (**W**) postsynaptic response. Tetanic stimulation of a larger number of afferent inputs succeeds in inducing LTP because these inputs produce a strong (**S**) postsynaptic response. This intensity effect, which has been demonstrated at two of the three most commonly studied synaptic systems of the hippocampus, is relevant to the phenomenon of associative LTP (*11–13, 16*).

Associative LTP refers to a particular type of interaction between separately and independently stimulated **W** and **S** synaptic inputs to a neuron (*12, 13, 16*). The nature of the interaction that defines associative LTP is taken from the perspective of the **W** input. It is a synaptic enhancement that can be induced in the **W** input if both the **W** and the **S** input are stimulated together at about the same time, but not if each is stimulated separately at very different times or if only one of them is stimulated (*1, 11–13, 16*). Activity in the **S** input enables enhancement to occur in just those **W** inputs that are eligible for change by virtue of being active at about the same time (*11, 16*).

The synaptic activity–enhancement relations that govern associative LTP are pertinent to its possible role as a synaptic substrate for learning. These relations include the following (*11–13, 16*): (i) The induction of the modification is rapid; (ii) the enhancement of synaptic strength is persistent; (iii) the modification in one synaptic input can be conditionally controlled by temporal contiguity with activity in another input to the same region; and (iv) the associative enhancement appears to be specific to just those synapses that are active at the proper time. These are also features of the synaptic mechanisms that underlie simple forms of associative memory in the marine mollusk *Aplysia* (*3*).

Hebbian form of LTP. The spatiotemporal features of associative LTP (*11, 16*) can be accounted for by the type of learning mechanism postulated several decades ago by the psychologist Donald Hebb (*17*). The following passage has come to be known as Hebb's postulate for learning (*17*):

> When an axon of cell A is near enough to excite a cell B and repeatedly or persistently takes part in firing it, some growth process or metabolic change takes place in one or both cells such that A's efficiency, as one of the cells firing B, is increased.

The evolution of the contemporary concept of a Hebbian synaptic modification is reviewed elsewhere (*1*). The core idea is a use-dependent synaptic enhancement based on an interaction between concurrent pre- and postsynaptic activity (*1, 18*). A Hebbian mechanism explains associative LTP as follows: The EPSC generated by the **S** input allows the required co-occurrence between presynaptic activity in the **W** input and some critical level of postsynaptic depolarization in the target cell. Because the essential interaction between pre- and postsynaptic activity only occurs if the **W** and **S** inputs are stimulated at about the same time, this mechanism confers a high degree of spatiotemporal specificity.

The Hebbian interpretation was tested directly in the hippocampus (*19*) by substituting for the usual **S** input a combination of current- and voltage-clamp procedures that either prevented or forced simultaneous pre- and postsynaptic spiking activity (Fig. 1). A synaptic input was repetitively stimulated under either of two extreme conditions—while applying a voltage clamp to the soma of the postsynaptic neuron to prevent postsynaptic action potentials and somatic depolarization (Fig. 1A, left traces) or while applying a simultaneous depolarizing current step to force action potential firing in the postsynaptic neuron (Fig. 1A, right traces). The microelectrode-injected current was similar in magnitude and dura-

tion to the current normally produced by the **S** input during a tetanic stimulation.

Neither postsynaptic activity alone nor synaptic stimulation conducted while applying a voltage clamp to the postsynaptic cell soma produced LTP (Fig. 1C). However, LTP was induced when presynaptic stimulation was paired with simultaneous postsynaptic depolarization (Fig. 1C). The interactive mechanism also had the required spatiotemporal specificity to account for what was known about associative LTP (*11–13, 16*). The Hebbian nature of this type of hippocampal LTP is one of the best documented and least controversial findings in this field. In 1986, four independent groups reported similar findings (*19, 20*).

Mechanisms of LTP

The problem of understanding LTP mechanisms can be divided into three parts (*5–8, 11*). The initial sequence of events that triggers or sets into motion the modification process is termed "induction." The set of mechanisms that constitute the proximal cause of the synaptic enhancement is called "expression." The factors that govern the duration of the enhancement are referred to as "maintenance." A complete understanding of LTP requires investigation of each of these aspects and the way in which they interact (Fig. 2).

Induction of LTP. The experiments of Kelso *et al.* (*19*) demonstrated that some consequence of postsynaptic depolarization enables LTP induction at just those synapses that are eligible to change by virtue of being concurrently active. By injecting the postsynaptic cells with a local anesthetic, they further showed that the postsynap-

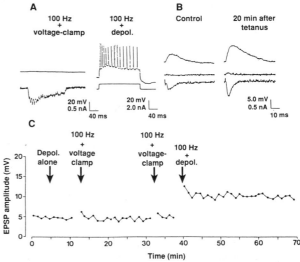

Fig. 1. Direct demonstration of the interactive mechanism. All recordings are of Schaffer collateral synaptic responses in hippocampal neurons of region CA1. (**A**) (Left) Voltage-clamp record of inward synaptic currents (lower trace) and membrane potential (upper trace) during the synaptic stimulation train. (Right) Current-clamp recording of postsynaptic action potentials (upper trace) produced by an outward current step (lower trace) that is paired with the synaptic stimulation train. (**B**) Current-clamp (top traces) and voltage-clamp (bottom traces) records before and 20 min after pairing synaptic stimulation with the outward current step. Middle trace is the membrane potential during voltage clamp. (**C**) EPSP amplitudes as a function of the time of occurrence (arrows) of three manipulations: an outward current step alone (Depol. alone) or synaptic stimulation trains delivered while applying either a voltage clamp (100 Hz + voltage clamp) or an outward current step (100 Hz + depol.). Each point is the average of five consecutive EPSP amplitudes. Modified from (*19*).

Fig. 2. Summary of some key events suspected to participate in various aspects of LTP. The conjunction of transmitter binding and postsynaptic depolarization causes the opening of Ca^{2+}-permeable channels and a resulting increase in the intracellular Ca^{2+} concentration ($[Ca^{2+}]_i$). The neurotransmitter binding step can be blocked by AP5. Activation of protein kinases is mediated by elevated $[Ca^{2+}]_i$ plus binding of particular ligands to the enzyme. The kinase activation step can be blocked by SPH. The kinase can become activator-independent, at which point SPH does not block the catalytic activity. Either form of the kinase can phosphorylate a substrate that ultimately causes synaptic enhancement. Substrate phosphorylation can be reversibly blocked by H-7.

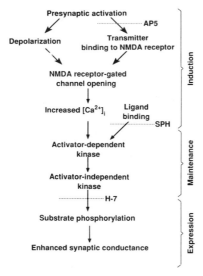

tic contribution to this interactive mechanism does not require the elicitation of Na^+-dependent action potentials. The induction step appears instead to be controlled by the NMDA subtype of receptor for glutamate (21, 22), which is thought to be a neurotransmitter in these synapses. The key observation was that antagonists for the NMDA receptor, such as DL-2-amino-5-phosphonopentanoate (AP5), block LTP induction but neither prevent the expression of LTP that has already been induced nor impair ordinary synaptic transmission (21, 22). The voltage- and neurotransmitter-dependent gating of Ca^{2+} influx through the NMDA receptor–associated channels (23, 24) suggests an attractive explanation for the Hebbian interactive mechanism (Fig. 2).

The NMDA receptor–ionophore complex must receive two signals simultaneously to become highly permeable to Ca^{2+}: glutamate must be bound to the NMDA receptor and the membrane must be sufficiently depolarized to relieve a Mg^{2+} block of the channel that occurs at voltages close to the normal resting potential (23, 24). The Mg^{2+} block is relieved when the membrane is depolarized to levels achieved by tetanic stimulation of the **S** input. When the Mg^{2+} block is removed, glutamate binding to the NMDA receptor causes the associated channel to open to a 50-pS conductance state that is permeable to Ca^{2+} (23, 24).

It is easy to see how the properties of the NMDA receptor–ionophore complex can account for aspects of associative LTP if we assume that an increase in the Ca^{2+} concentration in some postsynaptic compartment of the cell is necessary for LTP induction (25). Tetanic stimulation of a **W** input causes presynaptic glutamate release but fails to depolarize the membrane enough to relieve the Mg^{2+} block. Stimulating a **W** input therefore fails to induce LTP unless the stimulation is accompanied by strong postsynaptic depolarization produced by either a microelectrode or by an **S** input (16, 19, 20). To explain the input specificity requires further consideration of the spatial distribution of the postsynaptic Ca^{2+} signal. If we assume that the critically involved NMDA receptors are on the heads of the dendritic spines, then the peak transient increase in the Ca^{2+} concentration will be restricted to the immediate region of the stimulated synapses (7, 11, 26).

The working hypothesis shared by many laboratories is that Ca^{2+} serves as a second messenger or cofactor to trigger enzyme transloca-

tion or activation (25, 27, 28). A popular extension of this idea is that a Ca^{2+}-dependent protein kinase plays an essential role in the mechanisms of LTP (27–29). Activation of certain protein kinases, including Ca^{2+}-calmodulin–dependent protein kinase (CamKII) and Ca^{2+}-phospholipid–dependent protein kinase (PKC), requires both a critical Ca^{2+} concentration and binding of a ligand (calmodulin or lipids) to the enzyme (27, 28, 30) (Fig. 2). These kinases can act as switches (30) in that they can be converted to an activator-independent form, requiring neither Ca^{2+} nor ligand for catalytic activity (31, 32). For this reason the duration of the catalytic activity can greatly exceed the duration of the activators.

Maintenance of LTP. Some recent pharmacological discoveries are furnishing intriguing clues into enzymatic events that may control the maintenance of LTP (27, 28). One notion is that the maintenance of LTP depends on conversion of a protein kinase to an activator-independent form (see Fig. 2). Supporting evidence comes from studies of the effects on LTP of sphingosine (SPH), which blocks PKC and CamKII activation by preventing ligand binding (28, 31). When present prior to tetanic stimulation, SPH prevents LTP (28). However, SPH does not suppress LTP when added after tetanic stimulation (28). One interpretation is that LTP is maintained by an activator-independent protein kinase (28, 32).

Expression of LTP. If LTP is in fact maintained by the continued activity of a protein kinase (28, 29) [as opposed to the presence of a long-lived phosphorylated substrate (27)], then blocking the catalytic activity of the kinase should suppress the expression of LTP. The catalytic activity of two enzymes that have been suggested to participate in LTP—CamKII and PKC—can be reversibly blocked by H-7 (32). When added after a tetanic stimulation, H-7 reversibly suppresses the expression of LTP (28).

The expression of LTP ultimately involves an increase in the measured postsynaptic conductance (7, 11, 33). There is no evidence that LTP is accompanied by generalized changes in the excitability or the passive membrane properties of the postsynaptic neurons (12, 33). Elsewhere we consider at length three plausible explanations for the increase in the measured synaptic conductance (7, 11): an increase in transmitter release (5); an increase in the sensitivity of the postsynaptic membrane to released transmitter (29); and a decrease in the series resistance of dendritic spines (34).

There is compelling evidence that some forms of LTP involve a presynaptic modification that increases transmitter release (5, 6, 8), but in most synapses there is no basis for ruling out other possibilities. Hebbian synapses in particular would seem to be logical candidates for a postsynaptic modification. However it is theoretically possible that the induction of the modification occurs on the postsynaptic side of the cleft and that the expression of the enhancement involves a presynaptic change (5, 7, 11, 35).

Significance of LTP

LTP has attracted so much interest for three reasons. First, it is the type of modification that connectionist theories of learning have long envisioned. Second, recent technical advances make it possible to understand in great detail the molecular and biophysical mechanisms responsible for this type of use-dependent modification in synapses from the mammalian brain. Third, the knowledge generated by these technical advances will enable explorations of the role of particular synaptic modifications in the development and organization of behavior in mammals.

Psychology, computation, and physiology. The idea of a Hebb-like physiological mechanism for learning can be traced back at least to the end of the 19th century (1). The psychologist William James (36), writing in 1890 about the physiological basis of associative memory, proposed a "law of neural habit" that can be seen as an antecedent to Hebb's (17) postulate for learning. Hebb's theory has become refined and quantified by the rapidly expanding field of computational neuroscience (1, 37, 38). Theoretical studies have shown that useful and potentially powerful forms of learning and self-organization can emerge in networks of elements that are interconnected by various formal representations of a Hebbian modification (38). This theoretical work thus amplified the significance of the subsequent neurophysiological discovery (19, 20) of a Hebbian synaptic mechanism in the hippocampus.

The growth of in vitro technology. The spectacular technical progress that has been made in the past decade has created great optimism that we shall soon be able to understand in considerable depth the mechanisms that control the induction, maintenance, and expression of LTP. A large part of this new technology involves in vitro methods that enable detailed study of identifiable classes of synapses of the adult mammalian brain. Three such methods are being combined to study LTP: the acute brain slice preparation (14, 39), the single microelectrode current- and voltage-clamp technique (7, 10, 11, 14, 19, 33), and improved visualization procedures for imaging cellular and subcellular neuronal structures in living brain slices (7, 11, 40). This combination of methods enables experiments on synapses of the adult mammalian brain that previously could only be done in the vertebrate peripheral nervous system, certain invertebrate ganglia, or in cell cultures. Further developments in optical techniques combined with a new generation of molecular probes promise to open up additional experimental opportunities (41).

Linking LTP to learning. The significance of LTP ultimately rests on its functional role. The challenge to researchers in this field is to demonstrate that LTP is endogenously generated and to elucidate the nature of its involvement in the development and organization of behavior. The goal of exploring linkages to learning is becoming more attainable as we discover the molecular and biophysical mechanisms that control the induction, maintenance, and expression of LTP. Such knowledge provides experimental tools that can be used to explore the possibility that endogenously generated LTP participates in some aspect of learning or memory.

If LTP does in fact serve a mnemonic function, then pharmacological agents that specifically block the induction step might be expected to interfere with the acquisition of new associations but not the retention of old associations. One study that was designed to explore this possibility (42) demonstrated that intraventricular administration of AP5 prevents learning a new spatial memory task without affecting retention of previously learned behaviors. Conversely, drugs that specifically impair the maintenance or expression of LTP might be expected to affect retention but not initial acquisition. The effects of agents such as SPH and H-7 on acquisition and retention have not yet been explored.

Pharmacological manipulations are not the only avenue available for exploring linkages to learning. Another approach has been to determine whether LTP induction affects subsequent learning. Two studies have shown that learning is in fact influenced by electrical stimulation procedures that induce LTP in the hippocampus (43).

We must admit that the evidence linking LTP to learning is not yet convincing (44). However the explosion of new experimental technologies available for studying mammalian synapses will surely generate knowledge about LTP mechanisms that can be used to probe the functional role of this intriguing form of neuroplasticity (45).

REFERENCES AND NOTES

1. T. H. Brown, A. H. Ganong, E. W. Kairiss, C. L. Keenan, *Annu. Rev. Neurosci.*, in press.

2. J. A. Anderson and G. Hinton, in *Parallel Models of Associative Memory*, G. Hinton and J. A. Anderson, Eds. (Erlbaum, Hillsdale, NJ, 1981), p. 9; M. A. Arbib, *Brains, Machines, and Mathematics* (Springer-Verlag, New York, ed. 2, 1987); N. H. Donegan, M. A. Gluck, R. F. Thompson, in *Computational Models of Learning in Simple Neural Systems* (vol. 22 of *Psychology of Learning and Motivation*), R. D. Hawkins and G. H. Bower, Eds. (Academic Press, New York, in press); G. M. Edelman, *Neural Darwinism* (Basic Books, New York, 1987); R. S. Sutton and A. G. Barto, *Psychol. Rev.* **88**, 135 (1981); T. Kohonen, *Content-Addressable Memories* (Springer-Verlag, New York, ed. 2, 1987); L. N. Cooper, P. Munro, C. Schofield, in *Synaptic Modification, Neuron Selectivity, and Nervous System Organization*, W. B. Levy, J. A. Anderson, S. Lehmkuhle, Eds. (Erlbaum, Hillsdale, NJ, 1985), p. 5; D. L. McClelland, D. E. Rumelhart, G. E. Hinton, in *Parallel Distributed Processing: Explorations in the Microstructure of Cognition*, D. L. McClelland and D. E. Rumelhart, Eds. (MIT Press, Cambridge, 1986), p. 3.
3. J. H. Byrne, *Physiol. Rev.* **67**, 329 (1987); T. J. Carew and C. L. Sahley, *Annu. Rev. Neurosci.* **9**, 1217 (1986); E. R. Kandel, M. Klein, B. Hochner, M. Schuster, S. A. Siegelbaum, in *Synaptic Function*, G. M. Edelman, W. E. Gall, W. M. Cowan, Eds. (Wiley, New York, 1987), p. 471.
4. T. V. P. Bliss and T. Lomo, *J. Physiol. (London)* **232**, 331 (1973); T. V. P. Bliss and A. R. Gardner-Medwin, *ibid.*, p. 357.
5. T. V. P. Bliss and M. A. Lynch, in *Long-Term Potentiation: From Biophysics to Behavior*, P. W. Landfield and S. A. Deadwyler, Eds. (Liss, New York, 1988), p. 3.
6. D. A. Baxter, G. D. Bittner, T. H. Brown, *Proc. Natl. Acad. Sci. U.S.A.* **82**, 5978 (1985).
7. T. H. Brown, V. C. Chang, A. H. Ganong, C. L. Keenan, S. R. Kelso, in *Long-Term Potentiation: From Biophysics to Behavior*, P. W. Landfield and S. A. Deadwyler, Eds. (Liss, New York, 1988), p. 197.
8. C. A. Briggs, T. H. Brown, D. A. McAfee, *J. Physiol. (London)* **359**, 503 (1985).
9. R. J. Racine and M. deJonge, in *Long-Term Potentiation: From Biophysics to Behavior*, P. W. Landfield and S. A. Deadwyler, Eds. (Liss, New York, 1988), p. 167; R. J. Racine, N. W. Milgram, S. Hafner, *Brain Res.* **260**, 217 (1983).
10. D. Johnston, W. F. Hopkins, R. Gray, in *Long-Term Potentiation: From Biophysics to Behavior*, P. W. Landfield and S. A. Deadwyler, Eds. (Liss, New York, 1988), p. 355.
11. T. H. Brown, A. H. Ganong, E. W. Kairiss, C. L. Keenan, S. R. Kelso, in *Neural Models of Plasticity*, J. H. Byrne and W. O. Berry, Eds. (Academic Press, New York, in press).
12. G. Barrionuevo and T. H. Brown, *Proc. Natl. Acad. Sci. U.S.A.* **80**, 7347 (1983).
13. W. B. Levy and O. Steward, *Brain Res.* **175**, 233 (1979).
14. D. Johnston and T. H. Brown, in *Brain Slices*, R. Dingledine, Ed. (Plenum, New York, 1984), p. 51.
15. T. V. P. Bliss and A. R. Gardner-Medwin, *J. Physiol. (London)* **232**, 357 (1973); B. L. McNaughton, R. M. Douglas, G. V. Goddard, *Brain Res.* **157**, 277 (1978).
16. S. R. Kelso and T. H. Brown, *Science* **232**, 85 (1986).
17. D. O. Hebb, *The Organization of Behavior* (Wiley, New York, 1949), p. 62.
18. For reasons developed and discussed elsewhere (1) we interpret synaptic "activity" quite broadly. It need not refer to the elicitation of action potentials.
19. S. R. Kelso, A. H. Ganong, T. H. Brown, *Proc. Natl. Acad. Sci. U.S.A.* **83**, 5326 (1986).
20. R. Malinow and J. P. Miller, *Nature* **320**, 529 (1986); B. R. Sastry, J. W. Goh, A. Auyeung, *Science* **232**, 988 (1986); H. Wigstrom, B. Gustafsson, Y.-Y. Huang, W. C. Abraham, *Acta Physiol. Scand.* **126**, 317 (1986).
21. G. L. Collingridge and T. V. P. Bliss, *Trends Neurosci.* **10**, 288 (1987); C. W. Cotman, D. T. Monoghan, A. H. Ganong, *Annu. Rev. Neurosci.* **11**, 61 (1988).
22. D. T. Monoghan and C. W. Cotman, *J. Neurosci.* **5**, 2909 (1985); E. W. Harris and C. W. Cotman, *Neurosci. Lett.* **70**, 132 (1986).
23. C. E. Jahr and C. F. Stevens, *Nature* **325**, 522 (1987); R. Gray and D. Johnston, *ibid.* **327**, 620 (1987).
24. M. L. Mayer, G. L. Westbrook, P. B. Guthrie, *ibid.* **309**, 261 (1984); L. Nowak, P. Bregestovski, P. Ascher, A. Herbet, A. Prochiantz, *ibid.* **307**, 462 (1984).
25. T. V. Dunwiddie and G. Lynch, *Brain Res.* **169**, 103 (1979); G. Lynch, J. Larsen, S. Kelso, G. Barrionuevo, F. Schottler, *Nature* **305**, 719 (1983).
26. E. Gamble and C. Koch, *Science* **236**, 1311 (1987).
27. R. F. Akers, D. Lovinger, P. Colley, D. Linden, A. Routtenberg, *ibid.* **231**, 587 (1986); R. F. Akers and A. Routtenberg, *Brain Res.* **334**, 147 (1985); G.-Y. Hu *et al.*, *Nature* **328**, 462 (1987); D. M. Lovinger, K. L. Wong, K. Murakami, A. Routtenberg, *Brain Res.* **436**, 177 (1987); M. A. Lynch, M. P. Clements, M. L. Errington, T. V. P. Bliss, *Neurosci. Lett.* **84**, 291 (1988); J. H. Schwartz and S. M. Greenberg, *Annu. Rev. Neurosci.* **10**, 459 (1987).
28. D. B. Madison, R. Malinow, R. W. Tsien, *J. Physiol. (London)* **398**, 18P (1988); *Soc. Neurosci. Abstr.* **14**, 18 (1988); R. Malinow, D. B. Madison, R. W. Tsien, *ibid.*, p. 18; *Biophys. J.* **53**, 429a (1988); *Nature*, in press.
29. An alternative idea is that LTP is mediated by a Ca^{2+}-dependent protease. M. Baudry, J. Larson, G. Lynch, in *Long-Term Potentiation: From Biophysics to Behavior*, P. W. Landfield and S. A. Deadwyler, Eds. (Liss, New York, 1988), p. 109.
30. J. E. Lisman, *Proc. Natl. Acad. Sci. U.S.A.* **82**, 3055 (1985); S. G. Miller and B. Kennedy, *Cell* **44**, 861 (1986); J. H. Schwartz and S. M. Greenberg, *Annu. Rev. Neurosci.* **10**, 459 (1987); F. Crick, *Nature* **312**, 101 (1984).
31. Y. A. Hannun, C. R. Loomis, A. H. Merrill, R. M. Bell, *J. Biol. Chem.* **261**, 12604 (1986).
32. H. Hidaka, M. Inagaki, S. Kawamoto, Y. Sasaki, *Biochemistry* **23**, 5036 (1984); P. J. Parker *et al.*, *Science* **233**, 853 (1986); Y. Lai, A. C. Nairn, P. Greengard, *Proc. Natl. Acad. Sci. U.S.A.* **83**, 5253 (1986), M. Wolf, H. Levine III, W. S. May, Jr., P. Cuatrecasas, N. Sahyoun, *Nature* **317**, 546 (1985); W. S. May, Jr., N. Sahyoun, M. Wolf, P. Cuatrecasas, *ibid.*, p. 549; G.-Y. Hu *et al.*, *ibid.* **328**, 426 (1987); Y. Nishizuka, *Science* **225**, 1365 (1984); *Nature* **334**, 661 (1988).
33. G. Barrionuevo, S. Kelso, D. Johnston, T. H. Brown, *J. Neurophysiol.* **55**, 540 (1986).

34. E. Fifkova, *Cell. Mol. Neurobiol.* **5**, 47 (1985).
35. D. Piomelli, E. Shapiro, J. Feinmark, J. H. Schwartz, *J. Neurosci.* **7**, 3675 (1987); S. Bevan and J. N. Wood, *Nature* **328**, 20 (1987); G. Collingridge, *ibid.* **330**, 604 (1987).
36. W. James, *Psychology: Briefer Course* (Harvard Univ. Press, Cambridge, 1984).
37. T. J. Sejnowski, C. Koch, P. S. Churchland, *Science* **241**, 1299 (1988).
38. T. J. Sejnowski and G. Tesauro, in *Neural Models of Plasticity*, J. H. Byrne and W. O. Berry, Eds. (Academic Press, New York, in press); G. Tesauro, *Biol. Cybern.* **55**, 187 (1986); J. A. Anderson, in *Synaptic Modification, Neuron Selectivity, and Nervous System Organization*, W. B. Levy, J. A. Anderson, S. Lehmkuhle, Eds. (Erlbaum, Hillsdale, NJ, 1985), p. 153; M. F. Bear, L. N. Cooper, F. F. Ebner, *Science* **237**, 42 (1987); J. J. Hopfield and D. W. Tank, *ibid.* **233**, 625 (1986); R. Linsker, *Proc. Natl. Acad. Sci. U.S.A.* **83**, 8390 (1986); T. Kohonen, *Self-Organization and Associative Memory* (Springer-Verlag, Berlin, 1984); A. H. Klopf, *Psychobiology* **16**, 85 (1988); R. Linsker, *Proc. Natl. Acad. Sci. U.S.A.* **83**, 7508 (1986); G. Palm, *Neural Assemblies: An Alternative Approach* (Springer-Verlag, New York, 1982); J. C. Pearson, L. H. Finkel, G. M. Edelman, *J. Neurosci.* **7**, 4209 (1987); W. B. Levy and B. Burger, *IEEE 1st Int. Conf. Neural Networks, San Diego* **4**, 11 (1987).
39. P. Schwartzkroin and K. Wester, *Brain Res.* **89**, 107 (1975); P. Andersen, S. H. Sundberg, O. Sveen, H. Wigstrom, *Nature* **266**, 736 (1977).
40. C. L. Keenan, P. F. Chapman, V. C. Chang, T. H. Brown, *Brain Res. Bull.*, in press.
41. Probes that have been found useful to studies of dynamics of living cells are already having a tremendous impact on cell biology. Examples of such probes include a variety of voltage- and Ca^{2+}-sensitive dyes and fluorescently labeled monoclonal antibodies [L. B. Cohen and S. Lesher, *Soc. Gen. Physiol. Ser.* **40**, 71 (1986); P. Saggau, M. Galvan, G. Ten Bruggengate, *Neurosci. Lett.* **69**, 53 (1986); C. G. Blasdel and G. Salama, *Nature* **321**, 579 (1986); R. Y. Tsien, *Soc. Gen. Physiol. Ser.* **40**, 327 (1986); J. A. Connor, *Proc. Natl. Acad. Sci. U.S.A.* **83**, 6179 (1986); A. B. MacDermott, M. L. Mayer, G. L. Westbrook, S. J. Smith, J. L. Barker, *Nature* **321**, 519 (1986); J. A. Connor, W. J. Wadman, P. E. Hockberger, R. K. S. Wong, *Science* **240**, 649 (1988); M. S. Schindler and L. W. Jiang, *J. Cell Biol.* **102**, 859 (1986)].
42. R. G. M. Morris, E. Anderson, G. S. Lynch, M. Baudry, *Nature* **319**, 774 (1986).
43. Two studies showed an effect on acquisition rate: One reported that prior induction of LTP facilitated acquisition of a classically conditioned discrimination task [T. W. Berger, *Science* **224**, 627 (1984)], while the other demonstrated that prior induction of LTP prevented acquisition of a complex spatial task [B. L. McNaughton, C. A. Barnes, G. Rao, J. Baldwin, M. Rasmussen, *J. Neurosci.* **6**, 563 (1986)].
44. C. A. Barnes, *Trends Neurosci.* **11**, 163 (1988); T. W. Berger and R. J. Sclabassi, in *Long-Term Potentiation: From Biophysics to Behavior*, P. W. Landfield and S. A. Deadwyler, Eds. (Liss, New York, 1988), p. 467; D. J. Weisz, G. A. Clark, R. F. Thompson, *Behav. Brain Res.* **12**, 145 (1984); R. W. Skelton, A. S. Scarth, D. M. Wilkie, J. J. Miller, A. G. Phillips, *J. Neurosci.* **7**, 3081 (1987).
45. Supported by the Air Force Office of Scientific Research and the Office of Naval Research. We thank T. J. Carew and L. K. Kaczmarek for useful discussion.

III
Statistics and Pattern Classification

25, 26, 27
Introduction

(1965)
Nils Nilsson

Learning Machines, New York, NY: McGraw-Hill,
Chapter 1, "Trainable pattern classifiers," pp. 1–13; and Chapter 2, "Some important discriminant
functions: their properties and their implementations," pp. 15–42

(1967)
T. M. Cover and P. E. Hart

Nearest neighbor pattern classification
IEEE Transactions on Information Theory, IT–13: 21–27

(1974)
Bruce G. Batchelor

Methods of pattern classification
Practical Approach to Pattern Classification, London: Plenum, pp. 35–51

At present a large majority of the applications, both scientific and engineering, of neural networks are as static pattern classifiers. This has been true of neural network research since the beginning. It is clearly the model present even in the early perceptron research. We present here three papers that discuss some aspects of pattern classification that are particularly relevant to neural networks.

Pattern classification is an active field of statistics and engineering and is of great practical importance. Duda and Hart 1973 is a classic reference. A recent book by Pao (1989) makes the connection between neural networks and pattern recognition quite explicit, as does much of the work of Kohonen (see Kohonen 1984, for example). It is important to know that many neural network classification algorithms have already been analyzed in the pattern recognition literature.

Adaptive pattern classification is a natural way to use a neural network. We have an input, which is data of some kind. And we have an output category, which could be the name of a character, one of ten digits, whether a product is acceptable or defective, or whether a mortgage application should be approved or rejected. The virtue of a neural network for pattern classification, it is claimed, is that by presenting the network examples of the category, the weights in the network will change automatically so as to allow the network to correctly classify *new* examples of the category; that is, the network *generalizes* in a good way by seeing a limited set of examples.

Practical pattern classification almost always makes a critical assumption about the statistical structure of the world. Suppose we describe an input pattern as a point in state space—as a set of input element activities—and we know or are told the classification of this point. Then it is often unconsciously assumed that nearby patterns are likely to be given the same categorization. This assumption is surely conditioned on our experiences as humans with a world that usually acts this way; that is, similar things tend to have the same name. ("If it looks like a duck, walks like a duck, and quacks like a duck . . . ") Such an assumption about similarity allows a natural generalization mechanism: Points close in state space are very probably going to be given the same classification. The underlying model of pattern classification that this represents is one where there are *regions* of some size in state space, and each region is given a particular classification. It is always assumed that the representation, the way information is coded in the state vectors, allows the clustering to occur.

Cases where this representation assumption *does not* apply are likely to be difficult for neural networks. For example, a notoriously hard problem for neural networks is parity, a generalization of Exclusive-OR (X-OR); that is, classification is based on whether the number of ones in a binary vector is even or odd. One reason the problem is hard is because a change of only one component *always* causes change of category, therefore adjacent binary vectors are not classified the same. The infatuation of many neural network researchers with X-OR and parity is perverse.

Given the belief—based on experiment, not theory!—that nearby points are more likely to be given the same classification than distant ones, *nearest neighbor* algorithms and their numerous variants become obvious. Suppose we have a set of points in state space that have been given classifications. Suppose a new pattern is to be classified. The *distance* from the new pattern to all the old ones is computed. The new pattern is given the classification of the previously classified point that is closest to it, that is, its *nearest neighbor* .

The chapter excerpted from Batchelor (paper 27) gives a brief and exceptionally lucid review of a number of simple pattern classification algorithms. The linear classifier, as Nilsson (paper 25) points out, is essentially the computing unit used by a perceptron, a threshold logic unit, and the perceptron learning theorem lets us set the weights of this classifer by exposure to a training set. One point that Batchelor makes is that often techniques that seem different—for example, nearest neighbor algorithms and the linear classifier—are in fact similar. The connection to neural networks is sometimes immediate.

A more technical discussion of the nearest neighbor model can be found in paper 26, a review by Cover and Hart. One of the most important results to be derived from this paper is a derivation of the accuracy of nearest neighbor techniques, when many examples are stored. It can be extremely good for such a simple technique. The best possible classifier in a probabilistic system is called the *Bayes classifier*. A Bayes classifier assumes that *everything* is known about the distribution of the possible inputs, that is, how probable it is that a particular point belongs to any given classifiction. Cover and Hart prove that, in the limit of many stored points, the nearest neighbor technique will never do more than a factor of two worse than the Bayes classifier. In practice they usually do better than this.

Let us make one quick digression, necessitated by several unfortunate recent experiences at neural network meetings. On an alarmingly large number of occasions, the results of a neural network classifier will be compared with a Bayes classifier, and the neural network will seem to do better. All this means is that the researcher has neglected to implement a proper Bayes classifier; for example, he *assumed* that the underlying distributions for the inputs were one thing (usually Gaussian), which they were not. Naturally the Bayes classifier did not work well. Neural net enthusiasts will have to be satisified with merely matching, not surpassing, results obtained with perfect information.

The excerpt from Nilsson's classic book, *Learning Machines* , shows one way to construct nearest neighbor categorizers from model neurons. Let us assume we have as our basic computing unit something like the generic neural net neuron. This is a two-stage device, with a first stage that takes an inner product between the input pattern and the synaptic weights and a second stage that performs a nonlinear compression of this inner product, using a sigmoidal function or clipping.

Let us consider the inner product. Mathematically, the inner product between vectors *a* and *b* is given by the length of *a* times the length of *b* times the cosine of the angle between them. Let us assume *a* and *b* are kept the same length. Then the *maximum* inner product will be given when *a* and *b* are pointing in the same direction. In terms of neural network computing elements, this means that if the input pattern is the same shape as the synaptic weights, the response of the unit will be at its maximum if the lengths of the vectors are not changed. Each elementary computing unit behaves like a filter that responds most strongly when it is excited by the same pattern as its weights. This is the basic pattern matching operation that gives selectivity to neural networks. In more complex neural net neurons, the nonlinearity applied to the inner product is almost always assumed to be monotonic and therefore does not affect the maxima of the single-unit pattern matching operation, though the nonlinearity has powerful effects on the dynamics of the system.

Suppose we have an input pattern and a set of model neurons with different patterns of weights. To take the simplest case, suppose all the vectors representing the input patterns and the sets of weights have the same length. Then the unit with the weights that are *most* like the input pattern will show the most activity. As Nilsson shows by simple algebra, this activity will be proportional to the distance between the input pattern and the weight vector. Suppose each time an example is seen, a model neuron has its weights set equal to the pattern of that example. If a classification is attached to each model neuron, the classification of the most active unit will be the classification given by a nearest neighbor classifier.

Given networks composed of many units, each of which will respond most strongly to particular patterns, many nearest neighbor pattern classification algorithms become easy to implement in a neural network. The computational speed of a network is a direct function of the fact that many inner product operations can be done simultaneously and in parallel. For example, if each unit represents a stored example, a nearest neighbor classification takes one time step, and the most active unit gives the classification.

Although the simplicity and power of nearest neighbor classifiers has been known for many years, they have not been used very often for practical reasons. Many classified examples must be stored, and a new input requires computation of distances from all of them. Because of this, a good deal of effort has been devoted to making more efficient versions of the technique.

As one example, suppose all the points in a sizable region of state space have the same classification. Therefore we may have very many nearby examples with the same classification. Then we could *approximate* regions where all the points have the same classification by storing a *single* point—often called a *prototype* or in Batchelor's term a *locate*—somewhere in the middle of this region. We need only store enough prototypes to approximate the regions accurately. How well this trick works depends on the shapes of the classification regions and how well separated they are. Different measures of distance (that is, Euclidean, city block, or other) can give different region boundary shapes.

Constructing the most useful and accurate prototypes for a given task is the subject of much pattern recognition and neural network literature. One approach, especially useful when the regions of state space associated with a classification have odd shapes, is to store a large number of prototype patterns or locates, each associated with its own radius. All points within the radius are given the same classification, and a single classification may be represented by multiple points. This is the technique used by Reilly, Cooper, and Elbaum (see paper 28). Other examples of the effective construction and use of prototype patterns in this collection are the LVQ algorithms of Kohonen (paper 37), as well as Steinbuch's learning matrix network (paper 4).

Prototype techniques are used under other names. In some speech recognition systems, patterns representing different speech sounds are stored in a "codebook." The initial classification of the speech sound takes the input pattern and measures its distance from the classified patterns in the codebook, the nearest giving the identification of the speech sound.

An interesting class of related but less well-known techniques that can also be implemented with a neural network are *potential function classifiers*, described during the 1960s by several Russian workers (see Batchelor for references). They assumed that each stored example acted like an electric charge, giving rise to an electric potential at every point in state space. Just like physical electric potentials, all the potentials due to a particular classification summed. The classification of a point becomes the classification with the highest potential value, not just the geometric distance to an example.

Potential function classifiers were placed in a neural network context by Bachmann, Cooper, Dembo, and Zeitouni (paper 29). The attractiveness of the potential function classifiers to network applications lies in their well-behaved formation of an *energy landscape*, which can be used by an energy-minimizing network, for example, Hopfield nets (papers 27 and 35, *Neurocomputing: Foundations of Research*) to perform computation.

Potential function classifiers take an example and "blur" it over a region of state space. The sum of many blurred examples of a category can give an estimate of the probability of a classification at a point in space. The related technique of *Parzen windows* is used in an early version of Bell Laboratories' VLSI-based digit recognition system (paper 36, see also Slansky and Wassel 1981).

Explicit reasoning "by past example" has been suggested as a robust paradigm for artifical intelligence by Stanfill and Waltz (1987). The idea of parallel computation of similarity and subsequent choice of the most active responder as the classification is also described in Selfridge's Pandemonium model (paper 9, *Neurocomputing: Foundations of Research*) from the late 1950s. One conclusion of this discussion is that much of the functionality of neural networks can be obtained from closely related but simpler techniques, for example, nearest neighbor algorithms, without needing complex network structure and dynamics at all.

References

R.O. Duda and P.E. Hart (1973), *Pattern Classification and Scene Analysis*. New York, NY: Wiley.

T. Kohonen (1984), *Self organization and associative memory*. Berlin: Springer.

Y.-H. Pao (1989), *Adaptive Pattern Recognition and Neural Networks*. Reading, MA: Addison-Wesley.

J. Slansky and G.N. Wassel (1981), *Pattern Classifiers and Trainable Machines*. New York: Springer.

C. Stanfill and D.L. Waltz (1987), The memory based reasoning paradigm. Technical Report 87-2, Thinking Machines Corporation, Cambridge, MA.

(1965)
Nils Nilsson

Learning Machines, New York, NY: McGraw-Hill,
Chapter 1, "Trainable pattern classifiers," pp. 1–13; and Chapter 2, "Some important discriminant
functions: their properties and their implementations," pp. 15–42

1.1 Machine classification of data

At the forefront of research supporting the current technological revolution lies the challenging prospect of mechanizing a wide variety of intellectual tasks which heretofore have been perfomed only by humans. Already, for example, there have been some moderately successful attempts to endow machines with the ability to play chess, predict the weather, prove theorems, recognize speech sounds, diagnose diseases, sort photographs, and read handwriting.

Many of these tasks involve the ability to classify or sort data. One example of a sorting task is weather prediction. A forecast must be based on certain weather measurements, for example, the present values of atmospheric pressure and atmospheric pressure changes at a number of stations. Suppose that today the forecaster wishes to predict whether or not it will rain tomorrow at a certain station. In effect he must be able to sort or place a given set of measured weather data into one of two categories: *(a)* those data that indicate rain tommorow, and *(b)* those data that do not. To be successful the classification must be performed in such a way that the resulting forecast and the actual outcome are, on the average, in close agreement.

Other data-sorting tasks include speech and character recognition, medical diagnosis, and speaker identification. The mechanization of any of these jobs requires a device which accepts input data and responds with an output indicating the classification of this data. Table 1.1 shows several sorting tasks and the appropriate inputs and responses of the classifier.

Table 1.1 A list of sorting tasks

Task	Input data	Response
Weather prediction	Weather measurements	Forecast
Handwritten-character recognition	Optical signal	Name of character
Medical diagnosis	Symptoms	Name of disease
Speech recognition	Acoustic waveform	Name of word
Speaker recognition	Acoustic waveform	Name of speaker
Photographic sorting	Optical signal	Category of photograph

The purpose of this book is to present a unified treatment of the mathematical theory underlying the design of data-classifying machines. Some aspects of this general theory derive from a branch of statistics dealing with the classification of measurements. More recent contributions stem from research on perceptrons and other "adaptive" decision networks.

1.2 The basic model

We shall assume that each set of data to be classified is a set of d real numbers, $^*x_1, x_2, \ldots, x_d$. Such a set we shall call a *pattern,* and we shall call the individual numbers *components* of the pattern. Any device for sorting patterns into categories will be called a *pattern classifier.* In the weather-prediction example discussed previously, we might have $d = 4$ and

$$x_1 = 1023$$
$$x_2 = 1013$$
$$x_3 = 4$$
$$x_4 = -7$$

These four numbers might be the current atmospheric pressures (in millibars) at stations 1 and 2 and the pressure changes at these stations, respectively.

Suppose that there are R categories into which the patterns must be sorted. We shall label these categories by the integers $1, 2, \ldots, R$. One of these integers, perhaps R, might correspond to a "reject" or "null" category. Thus, in our weather-forecasting example we might have $R = 3$ and the following:

Category	Prediction
1	Rain tomorrow
2	No rain tomorrow
3	Undecided

*In most of what follows, we shall make no restrictions on the values of the real numbers $x_1, x_2, \ldots, x_d$. The few instances in which we assume that they are binary numbers will be explicitly noted.

We shall adopt as our basic model of a pattern classifier a device with d input lines and one output line (see Fig. 1.1). The d input lines are activated simultaneously by the pattern, and the output line responds[*] with a signal i_0 which may have one of R distinct values. Each value of the response represents a category into which a pattern may be placed, and we shall accordingly label the response values by the integers $1, \ldots, R$.

It is the purpose of this chapter to develop further this basic model and to introduce two philosophies for the design of pattern classifiers. First, however, a few words are in order about a key assumption underlying the model, namely that the data to be classified consist of a finite set of real numbers.

1.3 The problem of what to measure

In assuming that the data to be classified consist of d real numbers, we are obliged to mention, at least briefly, the difficulties that attend selecting these numbers from any given physical situation. Before operating a pattern classifier to forecast the weather, we must first decide which d measurements to use as the input pattern. If d can be very large, we might not need to exercise much care in the selection of measurements because it is likely that most of the important ones can be included. But in the more usual and practical cases, in which (for economic reasons) d is smaller than we might like it to be, the problem of measurement selection is a pressing one.

Unfortunately, there is very little theory to guide our selection of measurements. At worst this selection process is guided solely by the designer's intuitive ideas about which measurements play an important role in the classification to be performed. At best the process can make use of known information about some measurements that are certain to be important. A weather forecaster in the northern hemisphere might know, for example, that he must look to the west to gather the most important measurements on which to base a forecast.

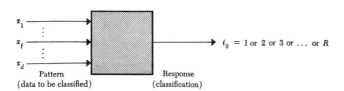

Figure 1.1 A pattern classifier

It is beyond the scope of this book to discuss the problems of measurement selection in greater detail. Most of the measurement-selection techniques that have been developed are specific to a particular application and thus would not be appropriate topics in a general treatment such as this. We shall henceforth assume that the d measurements yielding the pattern to be classified have been selected as wisely as possible while remembering that the pattern classifier cannot itself compensate for a careless selection of measurements.

1.4 Decision surfaces in pattern space

Let us return now to the development of our pattern-classifier model. Some of the interesting properties of this model can be conveniently discussed in geometric terms. Any pattern can be represented by a point in a d-dimensional Euclidean space E^d called the *pattern space*. The rectangular coordinates of the point are the real numbers $x_1, x_2, \ldots,$ and x_d. The vector $\mathbf{X}$ extending from the origin to the point $(x_1, x_2, \ldots, x_d)$ can also be used to represent the pattern. The components of $\mathbf{X}$ are the same numbers $x_1, x_2, \ldots, x_d$. We shall denote both the pattern point and the pattern vector by the symbol $\mathbf{X}$.

A pattern classifier is thus a device which maps the points of E^d into the category numbers, $1, \ldots, R$. Let the symbol $\mathcal{R}_i$ denote the set of points in E^d which are mapped into the number i. Then, for each category number, we have a set of points in E^d denoted by one of the symbols $\mathcal{R}_1$, $\mathcal{R}_2, \ldots, \mathcal{R}_R$. As an example, consider the sets shown in Fig. 1.2 where $d = 2$ and $R = 3$. A point in the plane is mapped into the numbers 1, 2, or 3 according to its membership in $\mathcal{R}_1$, $\mathcal{R}_2$ or $\mathcal{R}_3$ respectively. For example, the pattern $(5, -3)$ would be placed in category 2.

Note that the point sets of Fig. 1.2 are separated from each other by surfaces (curves in E^2) called *decision surfaces*. We shall not consider in this book any mappings requiring an infinite number of decision surfaces or any mappings that cannot be described by such surfaces.[**] In general, the decision surfaces divide E^d into R regions which we shall call *decision regions*. The ith region $\mathcal{R}_i$ is the set of points which map into the ith category number. For convenience, we shall arbitrarily assume that patterns which lie *on* decision surfaces do not belong to any of the

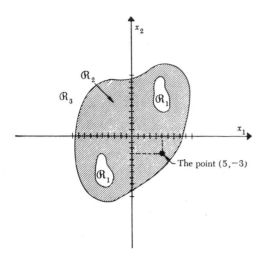

Figure 1.2 Point sets in E^2 which map into category numbers

decision regions; the response of the pattern classifier to such patterns shall be undefined.

1.5 Discriminant functions

The decision surfaces of any pattern classifier can be implicitly defined by a set of functions containing R members. Let $g_1(\mathbf{X})$, $g_2(\mathbf{X})$, . . ., $g_R(\mathbf{X})$ be scalar and single-valued functions of the pattern $\mathbf{X}$. These functions, which we call *discriminant functions,* are chosen such that for all $\mathbf{X}$ in $\mathscr{R}_i$, $g_i(\mathbf{X}) > g_j(\mathbf{X})$ for $i, j = 1, \ldots, R, j \neq i$. That is, in $\mathscr{R}_i$, the ith discriminant function has the largest value. We also assume that discriminant functions are continuous across the decision surfaces; then the decision surface separating contiguous regions $\mathscr{R}_i$ and $\mathscr{R}_j$ is given by

$$g_i(\mathbf{X}) - g_j(\mathbf{X}) = 0 \qquad (1.1)$$

Figure 1.3 illustrates three discriminant functions and the decision regions that they imply in the x_1, x_2 plane. Note that the decision surfaces in the x_1, x_2 plane are given by the projections of the intersections of the discriminant functions. Of course, the location and form of the decision surfaces do not uniquely specify the discriminant functions. For one thing, the same arbitrary constant can be added to each discriminant function without altering the implied decision surfaces. In general, any monotonic nondecreasing function (e.g., logarithmic) can be used to convert a set of given discriminant functions into an equivalent set.

The notion of discriminant functions is a useful one primarily because it suggest a convenient and familiar, if not unique, method by which decision surfaces can be implemented. The following exposition of this method will produce a more detailed functional block diagram of the

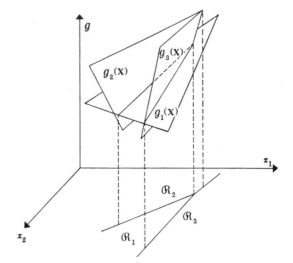

Figure 1.3 Examples of discriminant functions for two-dimensional patterns

basic model for a pattern classifier discussed in Sec. 1.2. Our discriminant-function pattern classifier, illustrated in Fig. 1.4 would employ R *disriminators,* each of which computes the value of a discriminant function. The outputs of the discriminators will be called *discriminants.* In classifying a pattern $\mathbf{X}$, the R discriminants are compared by a maximum selector which indicates the largest discriminant.

An interesting form results when there are only two categories, $R = 2$. Here, the maximum selector must decide which is the larger, $g_1(\mathbf{X})$ or $g_2(\mathbf{X})$. It turns out that this decision can be implemented by evaluating the *sign* of a single discriminant function $g(\mathbf{X}) \triangleq g_1(\mathbf{X}) - g_2(\mathbf{X})$. If $g(\mathbf{X})$ is positive, $\mathbf{X}$ is placed in category 1; if $g(\mathbf{X})$ is negative, $\mathbf{X}$ is placed in category 2.[*] The equation $g(\mathbf{X}) = 0$ gives the decision surface separating the regions $\mathscr{R}_1$ and $\mathscr{R}_2$. The sign of $g(\mathbf{X})$ can be evaluated by a threshold element whose threshold value is equal to zero. For this reason the threshold element assumes an important role in pattern-classifying machines. We shall use the block diagram of Fig. 1.5 as a basic model of a two-category pattern classifier, which we call a *pattern dichotomizer.*

Using the basic models of Figs. 1.4 and 1.5 we can state that the central problem in the design of pattern classifiers is the specification of the discriminant functions $g_1, g_2, \ldots, g_R(R > 2)$ or of the discriminant function g (R

---

[*] Even in the case $R > 2$ the number of discriminant functions can be reduced from R to $R - 1$ by selecting one of them, say $g_1(\mathbf{X})$, and then subtracting $g_1(\mathbf{X})$ from all of the others. Then the pattern classifier will place $\mathbf{X}$ in category 1 if the largest of the resulting discriminants is negative: otherwise it will place $\mathbf{X}$ into the category corresponding to the largest discriminant. For simplicity of exposition we shall always assume that there are actually R discriminant functions (unless $R = 2$)

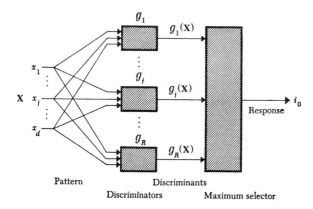

Figure 1.4   Basic model for a pattern classifier

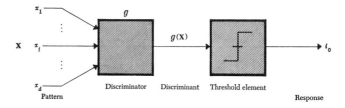

Figure 1.5   Basic model for a pattern dichotomizer

= 2). In the following sections we shall discuss a class of methods by which this selection might be made.

1.6   The selection of discriminant functions

Discriminant functions can be selected in a variety of ways. Sometimes they are calculated with precision on the basis of complete a priori knowledge about the patterns to be classified. At other times reasonable guesses are made on the basis of qualitative knowledge about the patterns. In each of these cases, especially in the second, it may be necessary to "touch up" or adjust the discriminators to achieve acceptable performance on actual patterns. This adjustment process is usually performed by using a set of patterns which are representative of the actual patterns which the machine must classify.* Making a few final adjustments is always an important phase in the design of any equipment. In this book we are interested in those cases in which it is the *major* phase.

We shall assume here that little if any a priori knowledge exists about the patterns to be classified. We might make guesses at discriminant functions, but usually these are very poor indeed. The performance level which the pattern classifier is eventually to achieve must be achieved largely by an adjustment process, which has become known as *training.*

The training process proceeds as follows: a large number of patterns are chosen as typical of those which the machine must ultimately classify. This set of patterns is called the *training set.* The desired classifications of these patterns are assumed to be known. Discriminant functions are then chosen, by methods to be discussed in general below and more specifically later, which perform adequately on the training set. We shall say that these discriminant functions

are obtained by *training.* A pattern classifier whose discriminant functions can be obtained by training is called a *trainable pattern classifier.*

1.7   Training methods

In this book we shall discuss examples of two types of training methods, *parametric* and *nonparametric.* The parametric methods are appropriate for classification tasks where each pattern category $i, i = 1, \ldots, R$, is known a priori to be characterized by a set of *parameters,* some of whose values are unknown. If the values of these parameters were known, adequate discriminant functions based on them could be directly specified. In the parametric training methods the training set is used for the purpose of obtaining estimates of the parameter values, and the discriminant functions are then determined by these estimates.

Let us discuss a particular example of the parametric method. Suppose we have two classes of patterns and we wish to design a pattern dichotomizer. It is known a priori that the pattern points in category 1 tend to cluster close to some central cluster point $\mathbf{X}_1$, and that the pattern points in category 2 tend to cluster close to another cluster point $\mathbf{X}_2$. The coordinates of the points $\mathbf{X}_1$ and $\mathbf{X}_2$ constitute the parameters of the pattern sets. The exact values of the coordinates of the points $\mathbf{X}_1$ and $\mathbf{X}_2$ are not known, however. If they were known, it might be reasonable for the pattern classifier to divide the pattern space into two regions $\mathscr{R}_1$ and $\mathscr{R}_2$ by some simple decision surface such as a hyperplane. A useful hyperplane might be one which bisects and is normal to the line joining $\mathbf{X}_1$ and $\mathbf{X}_2$. A discriminant function which would implement this kind of separation is

$$g(\mathbf{X}) = (\mathbf{X}_1 - \mathbf{X}_2) \cdot \mathbf{X} + \tfrac{1}{2}|\mathbf{X}_2|^2 - \tfrac{1}{2}|\mathbf{X}_1|^2 \qquad (1.2)$$

where $\mathbf{A} \cdot \mathbf{B}$ is the dot or scalar product of the vectors $\mathbf{A}$ and $\mathbf{B}$, and $|\mathbf{A}|^2 = \mathbf{A} \cdot \mathbf{A}$ is the squared magnitude of the vector $\mathbf{A}$. The hyperplane decision surface $g(\mathbf{X}) = 0$ is illustrated in Fig. 1.6 for the case $d = 2$.

The parametric training method in this case would use the training set to derive estimates of $\mathbf{X}_1$ and $\mathbf{X}_2$. Suppose the training set consisted of N_1 patterns belonging to cate-

---

* The adjustments can occur after the machine is constructed by making changes in the organization, structure, or parameter values of the parts of the machine, or it can occur before hardware construction by making these changes on a simulated machine using, for example, a digital computer.

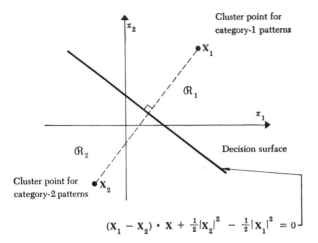

Figure 1.6 A linear decision surface based on parameters of the pattern sets

gory 1 and N_2 patterns belonging to category 2. Reasonable estimates for $\mathbf{X}_1$ and $\mathbf{X}_2$ might then be the respective sample means (centers of gravity) of the patterns in each category. Once these sample means were estimated, Eq. (1.2) could be used for the specification of $g(\mathbf{X})$, and the parametric training process would be completed.

The nonparametric training methods are most appropriately applied when no assumptions can be made about characterizing parameters. In the usual applications of these methods, functional *forms* are assumed for the discriminant functions such as linear, quadric, or piecewise linear (to be discussed later). These forms have unspecified coefficients which are adjusted or set in such a way that the discriminant functions perform adequately on the training set. For example, we might decide to use a linear discriminant function of the form

$$g(\mathbf{X}) = w_1 x_1 + w_2 x_2 + \ldots + w_d x_d + w_{d+1}$$

in a two-category pattern classifier. The equation $g(\mathbf{X}) = 0$ gives a hyperplane which is the decision surface. The training process is then one of adjusting the coefficients $(w_1, w_2, \ldots, w_d, w_{d+1})$ so that the decision surface implements an acceptable separation of the two classes of patterns in the training set.

1.8 Summary of book by chapters

In the next chapter we discuss several families of discriminant functions as possible candidates for use in a pattern-classifying machine. We examine the properties of some in detail, and present block diagrams to suggest the manner in which they might be employed.

Chapter 3 will investigate decision-theoretic parametric training methods. The mathematical foundation underly-

ing these training methods seems to be more extensive than the theory supporting the nonparametric training methods. On the other hand, employment of decision-theoretic methods presently requires restrictive assumptions about the nature of the pattern classes. These assumptions are not necessary for the use of some of the nonparametric methods.

In Chapter 4 we begin our discussion of examples of some of the nonparametric training methods. There we shall introduce some of the more important training algorithms currently in use. The presentation will be accompanied by geometrical representations which can enhance understanding of the concepts underlying these algorithms.

Theorems about the convergence properties of the nonparametric training algorithms are stated and proved in Chapter 5. These theorems apply to a large class of discriminant functions and are therefore of fundamental importance.

The concept of a layered machine is introduced in Chapter 6. Most of the pattern classifiers containing threshold elements that have been proposed are layered machines. While there is only a scanty mathematical understanding of these machines, two complementary viewpoints are discussed which aid formulation of meaningful questions. Unfortunately, the discriminant functions employed by layered machines do not belong to the class of functions for which the theorems of Chapter 5 apply; nevertheless, there do exist some useful training procceures for layered machines which shall be discussed.

Chapter 7 treats machines with piecewise linear decision surfaces. Some of the training methods suggested for these machines appear to avoid certain disadvantages inherent in the training methods introduced in Chapters 4 and 6.

1.9 Bibliographical and historical remarks

A comprehensive survey of early work on trainable pattern-classifying machines has been written by Hawkins.[1] Sebestyen[2] identifies the task of finding "clustering" transformations as central to the design of pattern classifiers. A paper by Kanal et al.[3] contains an excellent formulation of the pattern-classification problem and also points out that many schemes currently attracting the attention of engineers have antecedents in the statistical literature.

The problem of data classification has indeed received much attention by statisticians. A report by Harley et al.[4] contains an excellent summary (by Kanal) of statistical methods for pattern classification. Of the many sources referenced in that summary we might mention the books of Fisher[5] and Rao.[6] Anderson[7] also deals with the application of statistical techniques to classification problems.

The problem of selection of measurements has also received some attention by both statisticians and engineers. Bahadur,[8] Lewis,[9] and Marill and Green[10] propose and discuss tests for the "effectiveness" of measurements. Miller[11] illustrates a method for selecting a small number of "good" measurements from a larger pool of measurements. Block, Nilsson, and Duda[12] describe a method for determining *features* of patterns. Some specific examples of measurement devices for optical character recognition are discussed in a book edited by Fischer et al.[13] Reports by Brain et al.[14] discuss the development of "optical preprocessors" for visual data.

References

1 Hawkins, J.: Self-organizing Systems: A Review and Commentary, *Proc. IRE,* vol. 49 no. 1, pp. 31-48, January, 1961.

2 Sebestyen, G.: "Decision-making Processes in Pattern Recognition," The Macmillan Company, New York, 1962.

3 Kanal, L., et al.: Basic Principles of Some Pattern Recognition Systems, *Proc. National Electronics Conference,* vol. 18, pp. 279–295, October, 1962.

4 Harley, T., et al.: Semi-automatic Imagery Screening Research Study and Experimental Investigation, *Philco Reports* VO43-2 and VO43-3, vol. I, sec. 6, and Appendix H, prepared for U.S. Army Electronics Research and Development Laboratory under Contract DA-36-039-SC-90742, March 29, 1963.

5 Fisher, R. A.: "Contributions to Mathematical Statistics," John Wiley & Sons, Inc., New York, 1952.

6 Rao, C. R.: "Advanced Statistical Methods in Biometric Research," John Wiley & Sons, Inc., New York, 1952.

7 Anderson, T. W.: "Introduction to Multivariate Statistical Analysis," chap. 6, John Wiley & Sons, Inc., New York, 1958.

8 Bahadur, R. R.: On Classification Based on Responses to *n* Dichotomous Items, in H. Solomon (ed.), "Studies in Item Analysis and Prediction" Stanford University Press, Stanford, California, 1961.

9 Lewis, P. M.: The Characteristic Selection Problem in Recognition Systems, *Trans. IRE on Info. Theory,* vol. IT-8, no. 2, pp. 171–178, February, 1962.

10 Marill, T., and D. M. Green: On the Effectiveness of Receptors in Recognition Systems, *Trans. IEEE on Info. Theory,* vol. IT-9, no. 1, pp. 11–17, January, 1963.

11 Miller, R. G.: "Statistical Prediction by Discriminant Analysis," *Meteorological Monographs,* vol. 4, no. 25, American Meteorological Society, Boston, Massachusetts, October, 1962.

12 Block, H. D., N. J. Nilsson and R. O. Duda: Determination and Detection of Features in Patterns, in J. Tou and R. Wilcox (eds.), "Computer and Information Sciences," Spartan Books, Washington, D.C., 1964.

13 Fischer, G. L., Jr., et al.: "Optical Character Recognition," Spartan Books, Washington, D.C., 1962.

14 Brain, A. E., et al.: Graphical Data Processing Research Study and Experimental Investigation, *Reports* 7, 8, 9, and 13, prepared for U.S. Army Signal Research and Development Laboratory under Contract DA 36-039- SC-78343 and continuation, 1962 and 1963.

Chapter 2 Some Important Discrimination Functions: Their Properties and Their Implementations

2.1 Families of discriminant functions

The task of selecting a discriminant function for use in a pattern-classifying machine is simplified by first limiting the class of functions from which the selection is to be made. For this reason we consider *families* of discriminant functions. A discriminant function family can be defined through the use of *parameters* whose values determine the members of the family. For example, suppose a discriminant function $g(\mathbf{X})$ depends also on the values of M real parameters. We make this dependence explicit by writing $g(\mathbf{X})$ in the form

$$g(\mathbf{X}) = g(\mathbf{X}; w_1, w_2, \ldots, w_M) \tag{2.1}$$

The set of functions that can be obtained by varying the values of the parameters, throughout their ranges, is called a *family* of functions. A particular function belonging to this family can be selected by choosing the appropriate values of the parameters. The training of a machine restricted to employ discriminant functions belonging to a particular family can then be accomplished by adjusting the values of the parameters. We shall often call these parameters *weights*. In this book we shall be interested in only those pattern-classifying machines whose discriminant functions are obtained by selecting or adjusting the values of weights.

Here we shall define several families of discriminant functions and study their properties, leaving the subject of training to later chapters. One of the simplest is the family of linear functions to which we now turn.

2.2 Linear discriminant functions

Let us consider first the family of discriminant functions of the form

$$g(\mathbf{X}) = w_1 x_1 + w_2 x_2 + \ldots + w_d x_d + w_{d+1} \tag{2.2}$$

This function is a linear function of the components of $\mathbf{X}$; we shall denote discriminant functions of this form by the term *linear discriminant function*. A complete specification of any linear discriminant function is achieved by specifying the values of the weights or parameters of the function family.

A pattern classifier employing linear discriminant functions can be simply implemented using weighting and summing devices as discriminators. Such a machine, termed a *linear machine,* is depicted in Fig. 2.1. In Fig. 2.1

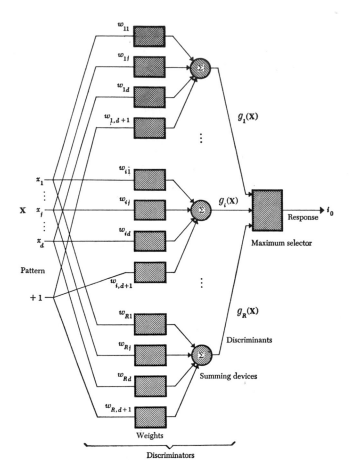

Figure 2.1 A linear machine

we employ the notation w_{ij} to represent the coefficient of x_j in the ith linear discriminant function. An important special case of a linear machine is a minimum-distance classifier with respect to points. We shall consider this special case first before discussing the properties of linear machines in general.

2.3 Minimum-distance classifiers

Suppose we are given the R points $\mathbf{P}_1, \mathbf{P}_2, \ldots, \mathbf{P}_R$ in E^d. The Euclidean distance between an arbitrary point $\mathbf{X}$ and $\mathbf{P}_i$ is given by

$$|\mathbf{X} - \mathbf{P}_i| = \sqrt{(\mathbf{X} - \mathbf{P}_i) \cdot (\mathbf{X} - \mathbf{P}_i)} \qquad (2.3)$$

Associated with each point $\mathbf{P}_i$ is a category number i, $i = 1$, $\ldots, R$. A *minimum-distance classifier,* with respect to the points $\mathbf{P}_1, \mathbf{P}_2, \ldots, \mathbf{P}_R$, places each point $\mathbf{X}$ into that category i_0 which is associated with the nearest point $\mathbf{P}_{i_0}$ of the points $\mathbf{P}_1, \mathbf{P}_2, \ldots, \mathbf{P}_R$. That is, for any $\mathbf{X}$, the quantities $|\mathbf{X} - \mathbf{P}_i| = 1, \ldots, R$ are calculated, and $\mathbf{X}$ is placed into the

category associated with the smallest. The points $\mathbf{P}_1, \mathbf{P}_2, \ldots, \mathbf{P}_R$ are called *prototype points*.

An equivalent classification is obtained by comparing the squared distances $|\mathbf{X} - \mathbf{P}_i|^2$, $i = 1, \ldots, R$. Squaring both sides of Eq. (2.3) we obtain

$$|\mathbf{X} - \mathbf{P}_i|^2 = (\mathbf{X} - \mathbf{P}_i) \cdot (\mathbf{X} - \mathbf{P}_i)$$
$$= \mathbf{X} \cdot \mathbf{X} - 2\mathbf{X} \cdot \mathbf{P}_i + \mathbf{P}_i \cdot \mathbf{P}_i \} \qquad (2.4)$$

The minimum-distance classification can be effected by comparing the expressions $\mathbf{X} \cdot \mathbf{P}_i - \frac{1}{2}\mathbf{P}_i \cdot \mathbf{P}_i$ for $i = 1, \ldots, R$ and selecting the largest. It is clear that the discriminant functions in this case can be given by

$$g_i(\mathbf{X}) = \mathbf{X} \cdot \mathbf{P}_i - \frac{1}{2}\mathbf{P}_i \cdot \mathbf{P}_i \quad \text{for } i = 1, \ldots, R \qquad (2.5)$$

We conclude that a minimum-distance classifier is a linear machine. Suppose that the components of $\mathbf{P}_i$ are $p_{i1}, p_{i2}, \ldots, p_{id}$. Then the linear machine of Fig. 2.1 is a minimum-distance classifier with respect to the points $\mathbf{P}_1, \mathbf{P}_2, \ldots, \mathbf{P}_R$ if the weights are given the values

$$w_{ij} = p_{ij} \quad \begin{aligned} i &= 1, \ldots, R \\ j &= 1, \ldots, d \end{aligned}$$

and

$$w_{i,d+1} = -\frac{1}{2}\mathbf{P}_i \cdot \mathbf{P}_i \quad i = 1, \ldots, R \qquad (2.6)$$

Minimum-distance classifiers would be appropriate in situations where each category is represented by a single prototype pattern $\mathbf{P}_i$, $i = 1, \ldots, R$, around which all other patterns in the category tend to cluster.[*]

2.4 The decision surfaces of linear machines

Suppose that two decision regions $\mathscr{R}_i$ and $\mathscr{R}_j$ of a linear machine share a common boundary. The decision surface separating these two regions is then a segment of the surface S_{ij} having the equation

$$g_i(\mathbf{X}) - g_j(\mathbf{X}) = 0 \qquad (2.7)$$

For linear machines, the surfaces S_{ij}, $i,j = 1, \ldots, R$, $i \neq j$, are linear surfaces given by the equations

$$(w_{i1} - w_{j1})x_1 + (w_{i2} - w_{j2})x_2 + \ldots + (w_{id} - w_{jd})x_d$$
$$+ (w_{i,d+1} - w_{j,d+1}) = 0 \quad \text{for } i, j = 1, \ldots, R, i \neq j \qquad (2.8)$$

There are $R(R-1)/2$ such equations and thus the same number of surfaces S_{ij}. For $d = 2$, a linear surface is called a line; for $d = 3$, a plane; and for $d > 3$, a hyperplane. Thus, the decision surfaces of a linear machine are segments of at most $R(R-1)/2$ hyperplanes.

---

[*] The dot product operation of Eq. (2.5), performed by a minimum-distance classifier, is sometimes called *template matching*. This usage derives from optical methods for image classification. The terms *correlation detection* and *matched filtering* are also used to describe this operation.

In many cases some of the hyperplanes defined by Eq. (2.8) are not actually used as decision surfaces. The hyperplane S_{ij} is not used if $\mathcal{R}_i$ and $\mathcal{R}_j$ are not contiguous. Such hyperplanes are called *redundant*. Figure 2.2 is an example showing some linear-machine decision regions and surfaces for a case in which $d = 2$ and $R = 4$. Note that the decision surfaces are segments of hyperplanes (lines for $d = 2$), and that S_{12} is redundant. In the special case in which the linear machine is a minimum-distance classifier, the surface S_{ij} is the hyperplane which is the perpendicular bisector of the line segment joining the points. Figure 2.3 shows the decision regions and surfaces for the minimum-distance classifier with respect to the two-dimensional points $\mathbf{P}_1, \mathbf{P}_2$, and $\mathbf{P}_3$.

We note in the examples of Figs. 2.2 and 2.3 that the decision regions are *convex* (a region is convex if and only if the straight-line segment connecting two arbitrary points in the region lies entirely within the region). It will be left as an exercise for the reader to verify that the decision regions of a linear machine are always convex.

2.5 Linear classifications of patterns

Suppose we have a finite set χ of distinct patterns $\{\mathbf{X}_1, \mathbf{X}_2, \ldots, \mathbf{X}_N\}$, N in number. Let the patterns of χ be classified in such a way that each pattern in χ belongs to only one of R categories. This classification divides χ into the subsets $\chi_1, \chi_2, \ldots, \chi_R$ such that each pattern in χ_i belongs to category i for $i = 1, \ldots, R$.

If a linear machine can place each of the patterns in χ into the proper categories we say that the classification of χ is a *linear* classification and that the subsets $\chi_1, \chi_2, \ldots, \chi_R$ are *linearly separable*. Stated another way, a classification of χ is linear and the subsets $\chi_1, \chi_2, \ldots, \chi_R$ are linearly separable if and only if linear discriminant functions $g_1, g_2, \ldots, g_R$ exist such that

$$g_i(\mathbf{X}) > g_j(\mathbf{X}) \quad \text{for all } \mathbf{X} \text{ in } \chi_i$$
$$j = 1, \ldots, R, j \neq i \quad \text{for all } i = 1, \ldots, R \quad (2.9)$$

As a special case of the above definition let $R = 2$. We say that a dichotomy of χ into two subsets χ_1 and χ_2 is a linear dichotomy if and only if a linear discriminant function g exists such that

$$g(\mathbf{X}) > 0 \quad \text{for all } \mathbf{X} \text{ in } \chi_1$$
$$g(\mathbf{X}) < 0 \quad \text{for all } \mathbf{X} \text{ in } \chi_2 \quad (2.10)$$

Clearly χ_1 and χ_2 are linearly separable if and only if a hyperplane exists which has each member of χ_1 on one side and each member of χ_2 on the other side.

Because the decision regions of a linear machine are convex, it is easy to show that if the subsets $\chi_1, \chi_2, \ldots, \chi_R$ are linearly separable, then each *pair* of subsets $\chi_i, \chi_{ij}, i, j = 1, \ldots, R, i \neq j$, is also linearly separable. That is, if $\chi_1, \chi_2, \ldots, \chi_R$ are linearly separable, then $\chi_1, \chi_2, \ldots, \chi_R$ are also *pairwise linearly separable*.

2.6 The threshold logic unit (TLU)

If $R = 2$, a linear machine employs a single linear discriminant function $g(\mathbf{X})$ defined by

$$g(\mathbf{X}) = w_1 x_1 + w_2 x_2 + \ldots + w_d x_d + w_{d+1}$$

If $g(\mathbf{X}) > 0$, $i_0 = 1$; if $g(\mathbf{X}) < 0$, $i_0 = 2$. The decision regions $\mathcal{R}_1$ and $\mathcal{R}_2$ are separated by a hyperplane decision surface defined by $g(\mathbf{X}) = 0$.

The pattern dichotomizer with linear $g(\mathbf{X})$ can be implemented according to the block diagram in Fig. 2.4. Such a structure, consisting of weights, summing device, and threshold element, is called a *threshold logic unit* (TLU). We shall ordinarily assume that the threshold element is a

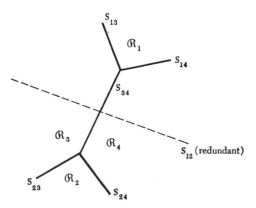

Figure 2.2 Examples of decision regions and surfaces resulting from linear discriminant functions

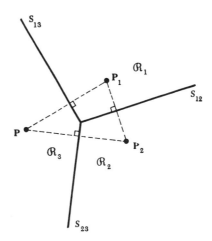

Figure 2.3 Decision regions for a minimum-distance classifier with respect to the points $\mathbf{P}_1, \mathbf{P}_2, \mathbf{P}_3$

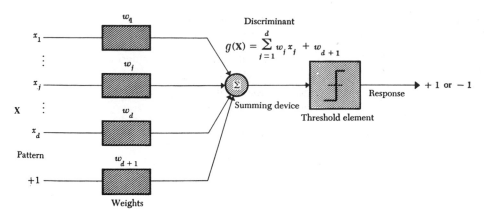

Figure 2.4 The threshold logic unit (TLU)

device which responds with a +1 signal if $g(\mathbf{X}) > 0$ and a −1 signal if $g(\mathbf{X}) < 0$. We must then associate a TLU output of +1 with pattern category 1 and a TLU output of −1 with pattern category 2. The last term in $g(\mathbf{X})$, w_{d+1}, can be provided by a weight whose value w_{d+1} is energized by a signal of +1. Usually this +1 signal is associated with the pattern as a $(d + 1)$st input x_{d+1}, whose value is always equal to +1.

Because the TLU implements a hyperplane decision surface, it is important to list some facts about hyperplane boundaries in order to understand some of the properties of a TLU. Let us define the d-dimensional vector $\mathbf{w}$, with components $w_1, w_2, \ldots, w_d$. The hyperplane equation can then be written as

$$\mathbf{X} \cdot \mathbf{w} = -w_{d+1} \tag{2.12}$$

Let $\mathbf{n}$ be a unit vector normal to the hyperplane at some point $\mathbf{P}$ on the hyperplane and directed into the half-space for which $\mathbf{X} \cdot \mathbf{w} > -w_{d+1}$ (see Fig. 2.5). This half-space is called the positive side of the hyperplane.

From Fig. 2.5 we have an alternative equation for the hyperplane

$$(\mathbf{X} - \mathbf{P}) \cdot \mathbf{n} = 0$$

or

$$\mathbf{X} \cdot \mathbf{n} = \mathbf{P} \cdot \mathbf{n} \tag{2.13}$$

Dividing Eq. (2.12) by $|\mathbf{w}|$ and then comparing with Eq. (2.13) yields the relations

$$\mathbf{n} = \frac{\mathbf{w}}{|\mathbf{w}|}$$

and

$$\mathbf{n} \cdot \mathbf{P} = -\frac{w_{d+1}}{|\mathbf{w}|} \tag{2.14}$$

where

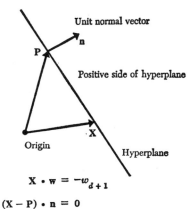

$$\mathbf{X} \cdot \mathbf{w} = -w_{d+1}$$

$$(\mathbf{X} - \mathbf{P}) \cdot \mathbf{n} = 0$$

Figure 2.5 Hyperplane geometry

$$|\mathbf{w}| = \sqrt{\sum_{i=1}^{d} w_i^2}$$

Note from Fig. 2.5 that the absolute value of $\mathbf{n} \cdot \mathbf{P}$ is the normal Euclidean distance from the origin to the hyperplane. We shall denote this distance by the symbol Δ_w, which we set equal to $w_{d+1}/|\mathbf{w}|$. (If $\Delta_w > 0$, the origin is on the positive side of the hyperplane.)

The equation

$$\mathbf{X} \cdot \mathbf{n} + \Delta_w = 0 \tag{2.15}$$

is said to be the *normal form* equation of a hyperplane. The direction $\mathbf{n}$ is called the *orientation* of the hyperplane, and the distance Δ_w, is called the *position* of the hyperplane.

It is also easy to show that the normal Euclidean distance from the hyperplane to an arbitrary point $\mathbf{X}$ is expressed by

$$\frac{1}{\sqrt{\sum_{i=1}^{d} w_i^2}} (w_1 x_1 + w_2 x_2 + \ldots + w_d x_d + w_{d+1})$$

From our expressions for $\mathbf{n}$ and Δ_w we note the following special cases of interest:

1. If $w_{d+1} = 0$, the hyperplane passes through the origin.

2. If $w_i = 0$ for any $i = 1, \ldots, d$, the hyperplane is parallel to the ith coordinate axis.

At this point, we can conveniently summarize some of the properties of a TLU:

1. A TLU dichotomizes patterns by a hyperplane decision surface in E^d.

2. The hyperplane has an orientation given by the weight values $w_1, w_2 \ldots, w_d$.

3. The hyperplane has a position proportional to w_{d+1}.

4. The distance from the hyperplane to an arbitrary pattern $\mathbf{X}$ is proportional to the value of $g(\mathbf{X})$.

The TLU has been used as the elemental building block of many pattern-classifying machines. Some of these will be considered in detail in Chapter 6.

2.7 Piecewise linear discriminant functions

As a special case of discriminant functions which we shall call *piecewise linear*, we shall first consider those of a minimum-distance classifier with respect to point sets.

Suppose we are given R finite point sets $\wp_1, \wp_2, \ldots, \wp_R$. For each $i = 1, \ldots, R$, let the ith point set consist of the L_i points $\mathbf{P}_i^{(1)}, \mathbf{P}_i^{(2)}, \ldots, \mathbf{P}_i^{(L_i)}$. Let us define the Euclidean distance $d(\mathbf{X}, \wp_i)$ from an arbitrary point X to the point set $\wp_i$ by

$$d(\mathbf{X}, \wp_i) = \min_{j = 1, \ldots, L_i} |\mathbf{X} - \mathbf{P}_i^{(j)}| \qquad (2.16)$$

That is, the distance between X and $\wp_i$ is the smallest of the distances between X and each point in $\wp_i$. Let us associate with each set $\wp_i$ a category number i for $i = 1, \ldots, R$. We define a *minimum-distance classifier* with respect to the point sets $\wp_1, \wp_2, \ldots, \wp_R$ as one which places each pattern $\mathbf{X}$ into the category associated with the closest point set.

For each $i = 1, \ldots, R,$ we define the functions

$$g_i(\mathbf{X}) = \max_{j = 1, \ldots, L_i} \left\{ \mathbf{P}_i^{(j)} \cdot \mathbf{X} - \tfrac{1}{2} \mathbf{P}_i^{(j)} \cdot \mathbf{P}_i^{(j)} \right\} \qquad (2.17)$$

Note that $\left\{ \mathbf{P}_i^{(j)} \cdot \mathbf{X} - \tfrac{1}{2} \mathbf{P}_i^{(j)} \cdot \mathbf{P}_i^{(j)} \right\}$ will be a maximum for that $\mathbf{P}_i^{(j)}$ in $\wp_i$ which is closest to $\mathbf{X}$. Therefore, for any $\mathbf{X}$, the largest of the R discriminants $g_1(\mathbf{X}), \ldots, g_R(\mathbf{X})$ will be the one whose index i_0 is associated with the point set $\wp_{i_0}$ closest to $\mathbf{X}$. Thus the $g_i(\mathbf{X})$ given by Eq. (2.17) can be

used as discriminant functions in a minimum-distance classifier with respect to point sets. Such a classifier would be appropriate if each pattern category were represented by a finite number of prototype patterns around one or the other of which each of the patterns in the category clustered.

Minimum-distance classifiers with respect to point sets prompt us to consider the general family of discriminant functions of the form

$$g_i(\mathbf{X}) = \max_{j = 1, \ldots, L_i} \left\{ g_i^{(j)}(\mathbf{X}) \right\} \quad i = 1, \ldots, R \qquad (2.18)$$

where each $g_i^{(j)}(\mathbf{X})$, called a *subsidiary discriminant function*, is given by an expression of the form

$$g_i^{(j)}(\mathbf{X}) = w_{i1}^{(j)} x_1 + w_{i2}^{(j)} x_2 + \ldots + w_{id}^{(j)} x_d + w_{i,d+1}^{(j)} \qquad (2.19)$$

where the weights $w_{ik}^{(j)}$, $i = 1, \ldots, R$, $j = 1, \ldots, L_i$, $k = 1, \ldots, d+1$, are the parameters of the family. Since each of these discriminant functions $g_i(\mathbf{X})$ is a piecewise linear function of the components of $\mathbf{X}$ we shall call them *piecewise linear* discriminant functions.[*]

Any machine employing piecewise linear discriminant functions will be called a piecewise linear machine, of which a minimum-distance classifier with respect to point sets is a special case.

The structure of Fig. 2.6 is an implementation for piecewise linear machines. The subsidiary discriminators are organized into R banks. If, for any pattern $\mathbf{X}$, the ith bank contains the largest subsidiary discriminant, then $\mathbf{X}$ is placed in category i.

The minimum-distance classifier with respect to point sets can be implemented by the block diagram of Fig. 2.6 by an appropriate selection of the weights. If the components of the points $\mathbf{P}_i^{(j)}$ are given by the numbers $p_{i1}^{(j)}, p_{i2}^{(j)}, \ldots, p_{id}^{(j)}$ for $i = 1, \ldots, R$ and $j = 1, \ldots, L_i$ then the weights shown in Fig. 2.6 can have the values

$$w_{ik}^{(j)} = p_{ik}^{(j)} \quad \begin{aligned} &\text{for } i = 1, \ldots, R \\ &\qquad j = 1, \ldots, L_i \\ &\qquad k = 1, \ldots, d \end{aligned}$$

and

$$w_{i,d+1}^{(j)} = -\tfrac{1}{2} \mathbf{P}_i^{(j)} \cdot \mathbf{P}_i^{(j)} \quad \begin{aligned} &\text{for } i = 1, \ldots, R \\ &\qquad j = 1, \ldots, L_i \end{aligned} \qquad (2.20)$$

The decision surfaces for piecewise linear machines consist of sections of hyperplanes, just as do those for linear machines. In the piecewise linear case, the decision regions $\mathscr{R}_1, \ldots, \mathscr{R}_R$ are not, in general, convex regions.

---

[*]These are not completely general piecewise linear functions since Eq. (2.18) constrains them to be convex.

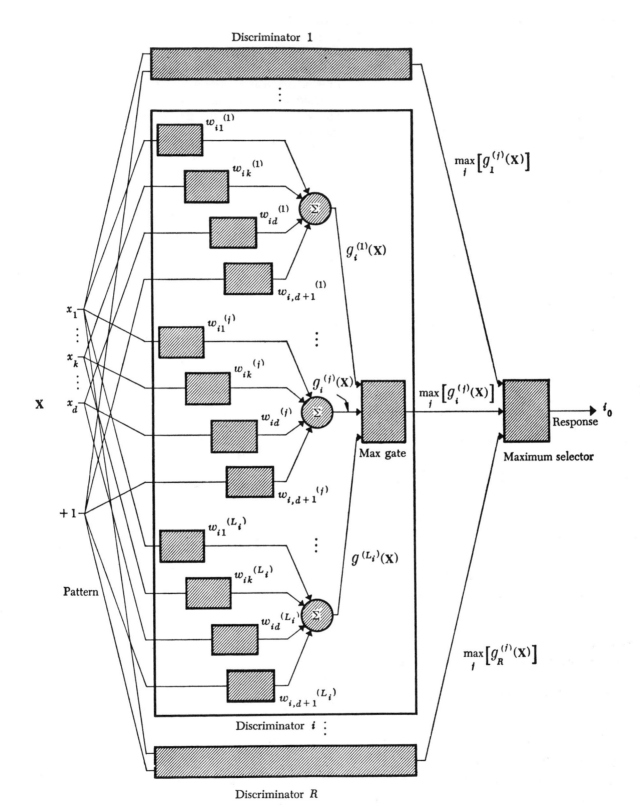

Figure 2.6 A piecewise linear machine

An example of decision surfaces and regions for $R = 2$ and $d = 2$ is shown in Fig. 2.7 for a minimum-distance classifier with respect to the point sets $\wp_1$ and $\wp_2$.

2.8 Quadric discriminant functions

A *quadric discriminant* function has the form

$$g_i(\mathbf{X}) = \sum_{j=1}^{d} w_{jj}x_j^2 + \sum_{j=1}^{d-1} \sum_{k=j+1}^{d} w_{jk} x_j x_k + \sum_{j=1}^{d} w_j x_j + w_{d+1} \quad (2.21)$$

Any machine which employs quadric discriminant functions will be called a *quadric machine*. A quadric discriminant function has $(d + 1)(d +2)/2$ parameters or weights consisting of

d weights as coefficients of x_j^2 terms $\qquad\qquad w_{jj}$

d weights as coefficients of x_j terms $\qquad\qquad w_j$

$d(d-1)/2$ weights as coefficients of $x_j x_k$ terms, $k \neq j$ $\quad w_{jk}$

1 weight which is not a coefficient $\qquad\qquad w_{d+1}$

Equation (2.21) can be put into matrix form after making the following definitions. Let the matrix $\mathbf{A} = [a_{jk}]$ have components given by

$$\begin{aligned} a_{jj} &= w_{jj} & j = 1, \ldots, d \\ a_{jk} &= \tfrac{1}{2}w_{jk} & j, k = 1, \ldots, d, j \neq k \end{aligned} \quad (2.22)$$

Let the (column) vector $\mathbf{B} = \begin{pmatrix} b_1 \\ \ldots \\ b_d \end{pmatrix}$ have components given by

$$b_j = w_j \quad j = 1, \ldots, d \quad (2.23)$$

Let the scalar $C = w_{d+1}$. Then

$$g(\mathbf{X}) = \mathbf{X}^t \mathbf{A}\mathbf{X} + \mathbf{X}^t \mathbf{B} + C$$

where $\mathbf{X}$ is considered to be a column vector and $\mathbf{X}^t$ denotes the transpose of $\mathbf{X}$ (a row vector).

The term $\mathbf{X}^t \mathbf{A}\mathbf{X}$ is called a *quadratic form*. If all the eigenvalues of $\mathbf{A}$ are positive, the quadratic form is never negative for any vector $\mathbf{X}$ and equal to zero only for

$$\mathbf{X} = \begin{pmatrix} 0 \\ 0 \\ \ldots \\ 0 \end{pmatrix}$$

When these conditions are met, both the matrix $\mathbf{A}$ and the quadratic form are called *positive definite*. If $\mathbf{A}$ has one or more of its eigenvalues equal to zero and all the others positive, then the quadratic form will never be negative, and it and $\mathbf{A}$ are called *positive semidefinite*.

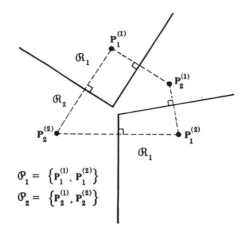

$$\wp_1 = \left\{ \mathbf{P}_1^{(1)}, \mathbf{P}_1^{(2)} \right\}$$
$$\wp_2 = \left\{ \mathbf{P}_2^{(1)}, \mathbf{P}_2^{(2)} \right\}$$

Figure 2.7 Decision regions for a minimum-distance classifier with respect to the point sets $\wp_1$, $\wp_2$

2.9 Quadric decision surfaces

The decision surfaces of quadric machines are sections of second-degree surfaces which we shall call *quadric surfaces*. Specifically, if $\mathcal{R}_i$ and $\mathcal{R}_j$ share a common boundary, it is a section of the surface S_{ij} given by an equation of the form

$$\mathbf{X}^t[\mathbf{A}^{(i)} - \mathbf{A}^{(j)}]\mathbf{X} + \mathbf{X}^t[\mathbf{B}^{(i)} - \mathbf{B}^{(j)}] + [C^{(i)} - C^{(j)}] = 0 \quad (2.25)$$

It is of interest to consider the varieties of quadric surfaces defined by

$$\mathbf{X}^t \mathbf{A}\mathbf{X} + \mathbf{X}^t \mathbf{B} + C = 0 \quad (2.26)$$

If $\mathbf{A}$ is positive definite, the surface of Eq. (2.26) is called a *hyperellipsoid*. The axes of the hyperellipsoid are in the directions of the eigenvectors of $\mathbf{A}$. In the special case in which $\mathbf{A}$ is an identity (or any scalar) matrix, the surface is called a *hypersphere*.

If $\mathbf{A}$ is not positive definite but is positive semidefinite, the surface is called a *hyperellipsoidal cylinder*. Cross sections of this cylinder are lower-dimensional hyperellipsoids whose axes are in the directions of the eigenvectors of $\mathbf{A}$ having nonzero eigenvalues.

If none of the above conditions is fulfilled by $\mathbf{A}$ (or its negative), the surface is called a *hyperhyperboloid*.

We shall see in Chapter 3 an important application of quadric surfaces.

2.10 Implementation of quadric discriminant functions

There are two important methods of implementing quadric discriminant functions. One is suggested by Eq. (2.21) and will be of importance when we study training procedures. The other implementation can be derived by studying the properties of the matrix **A**. This implementation is of somewhat lesser importance and is discussed in detail in the Appendix.

To explain the more important implementation we first define the M-dimensional vector **F** whose components f_1, $f_2, \ldots, f_M$ are functions of the x_i, $i = 1, \ldots, d$. The first d components of **F** are $x_1^2, x_2^2, \ldots, x_d^2$; the next $d(d-1)/2$ components are all the pairs $x_1 x_2$, $x_1 x_3, \ldots, x_{d-1} x_d$; the last d components are $x_1, x_2, \ldots, x_d$. The total number of these components is $M = [d(d + 3)]/2$. We shall write this correspondence as

$$\mathbf{F} = \mathbf{F}(\mathbf{X}) \qquad (2.27)$$

where $\mathbf{F}(\mathbf{X})$ is a one-to-one transformation. For every **X** in E^d there is a unique **F** in E^M. This one-to-one correspondence allows us to write $g(\mathbf{X})$ as a *linear* function of the components of **F** with the result that for every quadric discriminant function of **X** there corresponds a linear discriminant function of **F**. Equation (2.21) can therefore be written as

$$g(X) = w_1 f_1 + w_2 f_2 + \ldots + w_M f_M + w_{M+1} \qquad (2.28)$$

The implementation of a quadric discriminator, suggested by Eq. (2.28), is shown in Fig. 2.8. It consists of a *quadric processor*, for converting **X** into **F**, followed by weights and a summing device. All variations within the family of quadric discriminant functions can be achieved by varying the weights. A quadric machine can therefore be implemented by a quadric processor followed by a linear machine.

2.11 Φ functions

We noted in Sec. 2.10 that a quadric discriminant function can be considered to be a linear function of the components of a vector **F**. If we examine Eq. (2.28), which defines the quadric discriminant function, we see that the weights w_1, $w_2, \ldots, w_M, w_{M+1}$ appear linearly. That is, the parameters which determine a specific quadric function from among a whole family of quadric functions appear linearly in the function. There is an important class of function families whose parameters have this property. We shall call the members of these function families Φ functions.

A Φ function, with parameters (weights) $w_1, w_2, \ldots,$ w_{M+1} is a function $\Phi(\mathbf{X}; w_1, w_2, \ldots, w_{M+1})$ which depends linearly on the parameters. A Φ function can be written in the form

$$\Phi(\mathbf{X}) = w_1 f_1(\mathbf{X}) + w_2 f_2(\mathbf{X}) + \ldots + w_M f_M(\mathbf{X}) + w_{M+1} \quad (2.29)$$

where the $f_i(\mathbf{X})$, $i = 1, \ldots, M$, are linearly independent, real, single-valued functions independent of the weights. Since there are $M + 1$ weights we shall say that the number of *degrees of freedom* is equal to $M + 1$. Specific examples of Φ function families are

1. Linear functions: $f_i(\mathbf{X}) = x_i$ for $i = 1, \ldots, d$

2. Quadric functions $f_i(\mathbf{X})$ is of the form $x_k^n x_l^m$ for $k, l = 1, \ldots, d$, and $n, m = 0$ and 1

3. rth-order polynominal functions: $f_i(\mathbf{X})$ is of the form

$$x_{k_1}^{n_1} x_{k_2}^{n_2} \ldots x_{k_r}^{n_r} \text{ for}$$

$$k_1, k_2 \ldots, k_r = 1, \ldots, d$$

and

$$n_1, n_2, \ldots, n_r = 0 \text{ and } 1$$

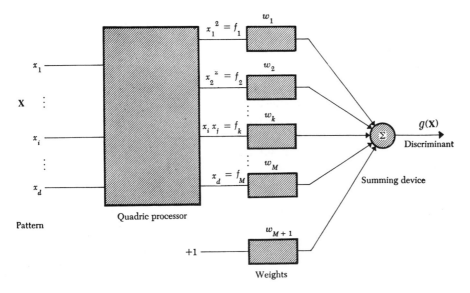

Figure 2.8 A quadric discriminator

In later discussions of the properties of Φ functions we use the notation

$$\mathbf{F}(\mathbf{X}) = \{f_1(\mathbf{X}), f_2(\mathbf{X}), \ldots, f_M(\mathbf{X})\} \qquad (2.30)$$

We shall assume that $\mathbf{F}(\mathbf{X})$ is a mapping of $\mathbf{X}$ into a vector $\mathbf{F}$ in an M-dimensional space which we call Φ space. The decision surfaces separating $\mathfrak{R}_i$ and $\mathfrak{R}_j$ will be called Φ surfaces, if the discriminant functions $g_i(\mathbf{X})$ and $g_j(\mathbf{X})$ are Φ functions. A Φ surface in the pattern space has corresponding to it a hyperplane in the Φ space. Therefore any linear function of $\mathbf{F}$ is a Φ function of $\mathbf{X}$. Many of the results to be presented in this book are developed for linear discriminant functions, but by the above considerations we can extend the application of these results to the whole class of Φ functions. We shall call any pattern-classifying machine employing Φ functions a Φ *machine*. A Φ machine consists of a Φ *processor* (which computes $\mathbf{F}$ from $\mathbf{X}$) followed by a linear machine. Note that piecewise linear machines are not Φ machines since piecewise linear discriminant functions are not linear in their parameters.

2.12 The utility of Φ functions for classifying patterns

Having described some important families of discriminant functions, we now compare the relative utilities of these families. The ultimate test of a discriminant function family is the question: How efficient are the members of this family for use in classifying patterns? In this section we shall formulate and answer a specific question of this nature for the entire class of Φ functions (including linear, quadric, rth-degree polynomial, etc.). We shall restrict our attention to the case $R = 2$.

Suppose we have N patterns represented as points in E^d. Clearly, there exist a total of 2^N distinct classifications of these patterns into two categories (dichotomies); each pattern may independently be assigned to category 1 or category 2. For example, there are eight classifications of the three patterns $\mathbf{X}_1$, $\mathbf{X}_2$, and $\mathbf{X}_3$. These are listed in Table 2.1.

Table 2.1 The eight classifications of three patterns

Classification	Pattern Categories		
	$\mathbf{X}_1$	$\mathbf{X}_2$	$\mathbf{X}_3$
1	1	1	1
2	1	1	2
3	1	2	1
4	1	2	2
5	2	1	1
6	2	1	2
7	2	2	1
8	2	2	2

One measure of the effectiveness of a discriminant function family would be the total number of dichotomies of N patterns that its members could effect. We shall show that if the positions of the N pattern points satisfy some quite mild conditions, the number of dichotomies that can be implemented by a Φ *function will depend only on the number of patterns N and the number of parameters M + 1 of the Φ function*, not on the configuration of the patterns or on the form of the Φ function.

2.13 The number of linear dichotomies of N points of d dimensions

We shall begin by calculating the number of dichotomies of N patterns achievable by a linear discriminant function (i.e., a TLU). Recall that each of these dichotomies is called a *linear dichotomy*. For N d-dimensional patterns, let $L(N,d)$ be the number of linear dichotomies. $L(N,d)$ is equal to twice the number of ways in which N points can be partitioned by a $(d-1)$-dimensional hyperplane. (For each distinct partition, there are two different classifications).

Before obtaining a general expression for $L(N,d)$ consider the case $N = 4$, $d = 2$ as an example. Figure 2.9a shows four points in a two-dimensional space. The lines l_i, $i = 1, \ldots, 7$ effect all possible *linear partitions* of these four points. Consider l_3 in particular. It could be the decision surface implementing either of the following: (1) $\mathbf{X}_1$ and $\mathbf{X}_2$ in category 1, and $\mathbf{X}_3$ and $\mathbf{X}_4$ in category 2; or (2) $\mathbf{X}_3$ and $\mathbf{X}_4$ in category 1, and $\mathbf{X}_1$ and $\mathbf{X}_2$ in category 2.

Note that the exact configuration of the points does not influence the *number*, seven, of linear partitions unless three of the points are collinear (Fig. 2.9b). In the latter case, there are only six linear partitions. For $N > d$, we say that a set of N points is in *general position* in a d-dimensional space if and only if no subset of $d + 1$ points lies on a $(d-1)$-dimensional hyperplane. When $N \leq d$, a set of N points is in general position if no $(N-2)$-dimensional hyperplane contains the set. Thus the four points in Fig. 2.9a are in general position, whereas the four points of Fig. 2.9b are not. Unless otherwise noted, we shall always assume that the N points for which we are calculating $L(N,d)$ are in general position.*

Thus, depending only on the condition of general position of the points, and otherwise independent of the configuration of the points, we observe from Fig. 2.9a

* In some special cases, important in practice, the pattern points may not be in general position. For example, if the pattern components are binary, the pattern points are the vertices of a hypercube; in this case general position implies that no subset of $d + 1$ vertices may lie on the same $(d-1)$-dimensional face. Even when the pattern points are not in general position, the derivation to follow yelds a useful upper bound on $L(N,d)$.

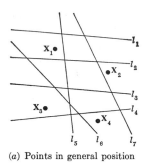

(a) Points in general position

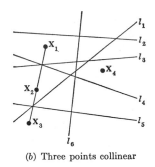

(b) Three points collinear

Figure 2.9 Linear partitions of four points in E2

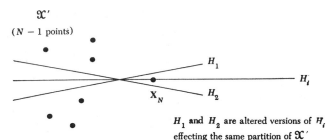

H_1 and H_2 are altered versions of H_i effecting the same partition of $\mathfrak{X}'$

Figure 2.10 Two separations of χ in E^2

that $L(4,2) = 2 \cdot 7 = 14$. This number is to be compared with the $2^4 = 16$ total possible dichotomies of four pattern points.

We shall now derive a general expression for $L(N,d)$ by developing a recursion relation which it must satisfy.[*] Assume that we have a set χ' of $N - 1$ points $\mathbf{X}_1, \mathbf{X}_2, \ldots,$ $\mathbf{X}_{N-1}$ in general position in E^d. There are $L(N - 1, d)$ linear dichotomies of χ'. We wish to find out by how much this number of linear dichotomies is increased if the set χ' is enlarged to include one more point $\mathbf{X}_N$. Let the enlarged set of N points $\mathbf{X}_1, \mathbf{X}_2, \ldots, \mathbf{X}_N$ be denoted by the symbol χ. The additional point $\mathbf{X}_N$ is chosen so that the points in χ are in general position in E^d.

Clearly, some of the dichotomies of the smaller set χ' can be achieved by hyperplanes which pass through the additional point $\mathbf{X}_N$. Let us say that exactly $L_{\mathbf{X}_N}(N - 1, d)$ of the $L(N - 1, d)$ linear dichotomies of the $N - 1$ points in χ' can be achieved by hyperplanes passing through $\mathbf{X}_N$. Then $L(N - 1, d) - L_{\mathbf{X}_N}(N - 1, d)$ of the linear dichotomies of χ' cannot be achieved by these constrained hyperplanes. Each of these linear dichotomies of χ' not achievable by a hyperplane passing through $\mathbf{X}_N$ determines *one* dichotomy of the larger set χ. For each of the linear dichotomies of χ' that *can* be achieved by a hyperplane passing through $\mathbf{X}_N$, there are *two* possible dichotomies of χ: one for which $\mathbf{X}_N$ is placed in category 1, and one for which $\mathbf{X}_N$ is placed in category 2. (That is, for these dichotmoies, $\mathbf{X}_N$ can be arbitrarily classified by a slight motion of the hyperplane.)[**] Clearly, then, the total number of linear dichotomies of the complete set χ is given by

---

[*] In some of the derivations to follow in this and subsequent sections, we shall use some facts from geometry which, while obvious for two- and three-dimensional spaces, happen to be valid in any finite-dimensional space. Of course, each of these derivations could also be given in algebraic form, but with the disadvantage of a more cumbersome presentation.

[**] To illustrate, let H_i be a hyperplane which partitions χ' and suppose that H_i can be made to pass through $\mathbf{X}_N$ without altering the partition of χ'. The hyperplane H_i can now be moved to one of two positions with respect to $\mathbf{X}_N$, still without altering the partition of χ'. These positions are illustrated in Fig. 2.10 for the case $d = 2$.

$$L(N, d) = L(N - 1, d) - L_{\mathbf{X}_N}(N - 1, d) + 2L_{\mathbf{X}_N}(N - 1, d)$$

$$= L(N - 1, d) + L_{\mathbf{X}_N}(N - 1, d) \qquad (2.31)$$

where $L_{\mathbf{X}_N}(N - 1, d) = $ the number of linear dichotomies of $N - 1$ points achievable by a hyperplane passing through $\mathbf{X}_N$.

We must now calculate $L_{\mathbf{X}_N}(N - 1, d)$. We shall show that

$$L_{\mathbf{X}_N}(N - 1, d) = L(N - 1, d - 1) \qquad (2.32)$$

The argument used in verifying the above equation is as follows: First construct a line (one-dimensional hyperplane) through $\mathbf{X}_N$ and each point in χ'. We now have a set of $N - 1$ lines. Because the members of χ are in general position, each of these lines is distinct (i.e., no three points of χ are on the same line). Select some hyperplane H having an intersection with each of these lines and let these intersections be given by the $N - 1$ points in the set $\wp = \{\mathbf{P}_1, \ldots, \mathbf{P}_{N-1}\}$ Clearly, the number of separations of χ by a $(d - 1)$-dimensional hyperplane passing through $\mathbf{X}_N$ is equal to the number of separations of $\wp$ by a $(d - 2)$-dimensional hyperplane in H. But H is a $(d - 1)$-dimensional space, and therefore the number of linear separations of $\wp$ is equal to $L(N - 1, d - 1)$ thus verifying Eq. (2.32). The set $\wp$ is in general position in a $(d - 1)$-dimensional space as a consequence of the general position of χ. Therefore, we can use the recursion relation

$$L(N, d) = L(N - 1, d) + L(N - 1, d - 1) \qquad (2.33)$$

to solve for $L(N,d)$. Using the obvious boundary conditions

$$L(1, d) = 2 \quad \text{and} \quad L(N, 1) = 2N \qquad (2.34)$$

it is easy to verify the $L(N,d)$ is given by

$$L(N, d) = 2 \sum_{i=0}^{d} \binom{N - 1}{i} \quad \text{for } N > d$$

$$= 2^N \qquad \text{for } N \leq d \qquad (2.35)$$

where $\binom{N - 1}{i}$ is the binomial coefficient $(N - 1)!/(N - 1 - i)!i!\cdot$

The values of $L(N,d)$, for $N = 1$ through 8 and $d = 1$ through 5, are given in Table 2.2. The table can easily be extended to higher values of N and d by using the recursion equation (2.33).

2.14   The effects of constraints

In the derivation of $L(N,d)$ we saw that the number of linear dichotomies of a set χ' of $N - 1$ points, achievable by a hyperplane constrained to pass through a point X_N, was equal to $L(N - 1, d - 1)$. That is, the effect of the single constraint on the separating hyperplane was to reduce the dimension of the space by one. We shall generalize on this result in this section.

Suppose that we have a set χ of N points and a set of $\mathscr{Z}$ of K points ($K < d$) in E^d. We desire to know the number $L_{\mathscr{Z}}(N, d)$ of linear dichotomies of χ achievable by a hyperplane constrained to contain all the points of $\mathscr{Z}$. We shall assume that the points of $\mathscr{Z}$ are in general position, meaning, in this case, that no $(K - 2)$-dimensional hyperplane contains all of them.

We now construct a set of N distinct K-dimensional hyperplanes, each containing $\mathscr{Z}$ and one of the points in χ. Figure 2.11 illustrates this construction. Let H be a $(d - K)$-dimensional hyperplane intersecting each of the N K-dimensional hyperplanes in a point. Let $\wp$ be the set of N intersection points. Clearly, the number of linear dichotomies of χ by $(d - 1)$-dimensional hyperplanes passing through $\mathscr{Z}$ is equal to the number of linear dichotomies of $\wp$ by $(d - K - 1)$-dimensional hyperplanes in H. We have an expression for this number if the points in $\wp$ are in general position on H. That is, no $(d - K + 1)$ or more of the points in $\wp$ can lie on the same $(d - K - 1)$-dimensional hyperplane. This condition is met if the points in χ satisfy the following (mild) conditions:

Table 2.2   A partial table of $L(N,d)$

Number of Patterns, N	Dimension, d				
	1	2	3	4	5
1	2	2	2	2	2
2	4	4	4	4	4
3	6	8	8	8	8
4	8	14	16	16	16
5	10	22	30	32	32
6	12	32	52	62	64
7	14	44	84	114	126
8	16	58	128	198	240

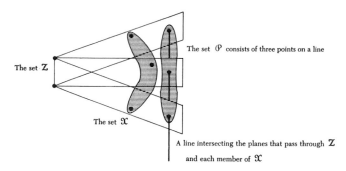

Figure 2.11   An illustration of the construction used in the text for K = 2, N = 3, d = 3

1.   No $(d - K + 1)$ or more points of χ may lie on the same $(d - K - 1)$-dimensional hyperplane.

2.   No $(d - K + 1)$ or more points of χ may lie on the same $(d - 1)$-dimensional hyperplane containing $\mathscr{Z}$.

We see then that the effect of the K constraints imposed by $\mathscr{Z}$ is to reduce the dimensionality of the space by K. We then have

$$L_Z(N, d) = L(N, d - K) \qquad (2.36)$$

2.15   The number of Φ function dichotomies

Suppose our discriminant function family is of the form

$$g(\mathbf{X}) = w_1 f_1(\mathbf{X}) + \ldots + w_M f_M(\mathbf{X}) = w_{M+1} \qquad (2.37)$$

that is, a Φ function family. We shall assume that the functions, $f_i(\mathbf{X})$, $i = 1, \ldots, M$, are such that the loci of points in the pattern space satisfying the equations $g(\mathbf{X}) = 0$ are families of surfaces. The separations that these surfaces (called Φ surfaces) effect on a set χ of N points are called Φ *dichotomies*. If there is no Φ surface in the pattern space containing $M + 1$ or more members of χ, then we say that the members of χ are in Φ *general position*.

For any Φ function family, we desire to know the number $\Phi(N,d)$ of Φ dichotomies of a set χ of N points in the pattern space. Corresponding to each point $\mathbf{X}$ in the pattern space there is a point $\mathbf{F} = \{f_1(\mathbf{X}), \ldots, f_M(\mathbf{X})\}$ in Φ space; therefore, corresponding to the set χ of N points in Φ general position in the pattern space, there is a set $\mathscr{F}$ of N points in general position in the Φ space. Since any linear dichotomy of $\mathscr{F}$ in Φ space corresponds to a Φ dichotomy of χ in the pattern space, $\Phi(N,d)$ is equal to $L(N, M)$, which is the number of linear dichotomies of the set $\mathscr{F}$ of N points in Φ space.

For the members of χ in Φ general position we thus express the number of dichotomies of χ implementable by *any* Φ function family as

$$\Phi(N, d) = L(N, M) = 2 \sum_{i=0}^{M} \binom{N-1}{i} \qquad \text{for} > M$$

$$= 2^N \qquad \text{for } N \leq M$$

(2.38)

The following special cases of Φ functions will illustrate the use of the above expression:

1. $\Phi(\mathbf{X})$ is a special quadric function of the form

$$\Phi(\mathbf{X}) = |\mathbf{X} - \mathbf{W}|^2 - a^2 \qquad (2.39)$$

Here, $\Phi(\mathbf{X}) = 0$ defines a hypersphere, where $\mathbf{W}$ is the center of the hypersphere and a is its radius. Expanding the above equation yields

$$\Phi(\mathbf{X}) = \mathbf{X} \cdot \mathbf{X} - 2\mathbf{X} \cdot \mathbf{W} + \mathbf{W} \cdot \mathbf{W} - a^2 \qquad (2.40)$$

Therefore $\mathbf{F}$ is $(d + 1)$-dimensional; i.e., $M = d + 1$. The first d components of $\mathbf{F}$ can be taken to be the d components of $\mathbf{X}$, and the $(d + 1)$th component of $\mathbf{F}$ is $|\mathbf{X}|^2$. Therefore, for a hypersphere

$$\Phi(N, d) = L(N, d + 1) \qquad (2.41)$$

The above expression assumes, of course, that the points in χ are in Φ general position; that is, no $d + 2$ points in χ lie on the same hypersphere. We conclude that a hypersphere decision surface is slightly more powerful than a hyperplane decision surface, since $L(N, {}^{\wedge}d + 1) > L(N,d)$ (see Table 2.2).

2. $\Phi(\mathbf{X})$ is an rth-order polynomial function. The function $f_i(\mathbf{X})$ is of the form $X_{k_1}^{n_1} x_{k_2}^{n_2} \dots x_{k_r}^{n_r}, k_1, k_2, \dots, k_r = 1, \dots, d;$ and $n_1, n_2, \dots, n_r = 0$ and 1. In this case M is given by

$$M = \sum_{i=1}^{r} \binom{d+i-1}{i}$$

$$= \binom{d+r}{r} - 1 \qquad (2.42)$$

If $r = 2$ we have a general quadric function for which $M = d(d + 3)/2$, as derived in Sec. 2.10. For general quadric functions

$$\Phi(N, d) = L[N, \frac{d(d + 3)}{2}] \qquad (2.43)$$

Note that the general quadric surface is a much more powerful decision surface than is the hyperplane or the hypersphere.

2.16 Machine capacity

Suppose that we are given a Φ machine with $M + 1$ adjustable weights and a set χ of N patterns in Φ general position

in the pattern space. There are 2^N possible dichotomies of these patterns; if one of these dichotomies is selected at random (with probability 2^{-N}, what is the probability $P_{N,M}$ that it can be implemented (for some setting of the weights) by the given Φ machine? The answer is obtained by dividing the number of Φ dichotomies by $2N$. That is,

$$P_{N, M} = 2^{1-N} \sum_{i=0}^{M} \binom{N-1}{i} \qquad \text{for } N > M$$

$$= 1 \qquad \text{for } N \leq M$$

(2.44)

The probability $P_{N,M}$ has a number of interesting characteristics. These can best be seen if we normalize by setting $N = \lambda(M + 1)$. A plot of the function $P_{\lambda(M + 1), M}$ versus λ for various values of M appears in Fig. 2.12.

Note the pronounced threshold effect, for large $M + 1$, around $\lambda = 2$. Also note that for each value of M

$$P_{2(M + 1), M} = \frac{1}{2} \qquad (2.45)$$

The threshold effect around $2(M + 1)$ can be expressed quantitively by

$$\lim_{M \to \infty} P_{(2 + \varepsilon)(M + 1), M} = 0 \quad \text{for all } \varepsilon > 0$$

and

$$\lim_{M \to \infty} P_{(2 - \varepsilon)(M + 1), M} = 1 \quad \text{for all } \varepsilon > 0 \qquad (2.46)$$

These characteristics of $P_{N,M}$ lead us naturally to define the capacity C of a Φ machine as

$$C = 2(M + 1) \qquad (2.47)$$

That is, the capacity is twice the number of degrees of freedom or twice the number of weights in the Φ machine. For large M we can be almost certain of being able to achieve any specific dichotomy of fewer than C patterns with a given Φ machine. On the other hand, we are almost

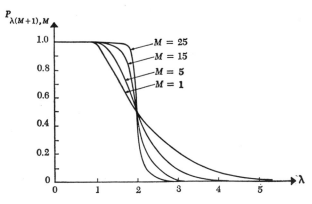

Figure 2.12 $P_{\lambda(M + 1),M}$ versus λ for various values of M

certain to fail to achieve any specific dichotomy of more than C patterns.

The capacity of a Φ machine is, then, a quite useful measure of its ability to dichotomize patterns.[*] To compare the various Φ machines that we have discussed in this chapter, we tabulate their capacities in Table 2.3.

2.17 Bibliographical and historical remarks

A detailed treatment of the properties of hyperplane decision surfaces is contained in reports hy Highleyman.[1,2] The *Learning Matrix* of Steinbuch[3] is an example of a trainable pattern-classifying machine with linear discriminant functions. The TLU and the subject of pairwise linear separability have been well studied by switching theorists; a paper by Winder[4] contains an excellent survey of the switching theory literature on the TLU. Tests for linear separability have been developed by Singleton[5] and others.

The implementation of a quadric machine (Fig. 2.8) was proposed by Koford.[6] The material on Φ functions is based on the work of Cover.[7,8]

Papers by Joseph,[9] Winder,[10] and Cameron[11] all contain calculations of the number of linear dichotomies of N d-dimensional points. The derivation of this number given in Sec. 2.13 is a version of one given by Cover.[7,8] The effects of constraints on the number of linear dichotomies and the extension of these results to Φ surfaces are also due to Cover.[7] Based on experimental and theoretical results on the number of linear dichotomies, both Koford[12] and Brown[13] suggested that the capacity of a TLU was equal to twice the number of variable weights. Winder[14] has also supported this conclusion. Further theoretical work by Cover and Efron[15] and later by Cover[7,8] provided the basis for the material on machine capacity in Sec. 2.16.

Table 2.3 The capacities of some ϕ machines

Decision boundary in pattern space implemented by ϕ machine	Capacity
Hyperplane	$2(d + 1)$
Hypersphere	$2(d + 2)$
General quadric surface	$(d + 1) + (d + 2)$
rth-order polynomial surface	$2 \begin{pmatrix} d + r \\ r \end{pmatrix}$

[*] Our expression for the capacity of a Φ machine is based on the number of dichotomies it can implement. Generalization of this treatment for $R > 2$ leads to the question: How many of the R^N classifications of N patterns in d dimensions can a given Φ machine implement? We have seen that for $R = 2$ the answer to this question is independent of the position of the pattern points (provided that they are in general position). The answer for $R > 2$ has not yet been obtained and may not be independent of the position of the pattern points.

References

1 Highleyman, W. H.: "Linear Decision Functions, with Applications to Pattern Recognition," Ph.D. Dissertation, Elect. Eng. Dept., Polytechnic Institute of Brooklyn, New York, June, 1961.

2 —: Linear Decision Functions with Application to Pattern Recognition, *Proc. IRE*, vol. 50, no. 6, pp. 1501–1514, June, 1962.

3 Steinbuch, K., and V.A.W. Piske: Learning Matrices and Their Applications, *Trans. IEEE on Elect. Computers*, vol. EC-12, no. 5, pp. 846–862, December, 1963.

4 Winder, R. O.: Threshold Logic in Artifical Intelligence, *IEEE Publication S-142, Artifical Intelligence* (a combined preprint of papers presented at the winter general meeting, 1963), pp. 107–128, New York, 1963.

5 Singleton, R. C.: A Test for Linear Separability as Applied to Self-organizing Machines, in Yovits, Jacobi, and Goldstein (eds.), "Self-organizing Systems—1962," pp. 503–524, Spartan Books, Washington, D.C., 1962.

6 Koford, J.: Adaptive Network Organization, *Stanford Electronics Laboratory Quarterly Research Review No.* 3, III-6, 1962.

7 Cover, T. M.: Classification and Generalization Capabilities of Linear Threshold Units, *Rome Air Development Center Technical Documentary Report RADC-TDR-64-32*, February, 1964.

8 —: Geometrical and Statistical Properties of Linear Threshold Devices, *Stanford Electronics Laboratories Technical Report* 6107-1, May 1964.

9 Joseph, R. D.: The Number of Orthants in n-Space Intersected by an s-Dimensional Subspace, *Tech. Memorandum* 8, Project PARA, Cornell Aeronautical Laboratory, Buffalo, New York, 1960.

10 Winder, R. O.: "Threshold Logic," Ph.D. dissertation, Princeton University, Princeton, New Jersey, 1962.

11 Cameron, S. H.: An Estimate of the Complexity Requisite in a Universal Decision Network, "Proceedings of 1960 Bionics Symposium," *Wright Air Development Division Technical Report* 60-600, pp. 197–211, December, 1960.

12 Widrow, B.: Generalization and Information Storage in Networks of Adaline "Neurons," in Yovits, Jacobi, and Goldstein (eds.), "Self-organizing Systems—1962," p. 442, Spartan Books, Washington, D.C., 1962.

13 Brown, R.: Logical Properties of Adaptive Networks, *Stanford Electronics Laboratory Quarterly Research Review No.* 4, III-6–III-9, 1963.

14 Winder, R. O.: Bounds on Threshold Gate Realizability, *Trans. IEEE on Elect. Computers*, vol. EC-12, no. 5, pp. 561–564, October, 1963.

15 Cover, T. M., and B. Efron: paper in preparation.

(1967)
T. M. Cover and P. E. Hart

Nearest neighbor pattern classification
IEEE Transactions on Information Theory
IT–13: 21–27

Abstract—The nearest neighbor decision rule assigns to an un-classified sample point the classification of the nearest of a set of previously classified points. This rule is independent of the under-lying joint distribution on the sample points and their classifications, and hence the probability of error R of such a rule must be at least as great as the Bayes probability of error R^*—the minimum prob-ability of error over all decision rules taking underlying probability structure into account. However, in a large sample analysis, we will show in the M-category case that $R^* \leq R \leq R^*(2 - MR^*/(M-1))$, where these bounds are the tightest possible, for all suitably smooth underlying distributions.. Thus for any number of categories, the probability of error of the nearest neighbor rule is bounded above by twice the Bayes probability of error. In this sense, it may be said that half the classification information in an infinite sample set is contained in the nearest neighbor.

I. Introduction

IN THE CLASSIFICATION problem there are two extremes of knowledge which the statistician may possess. Either he may have complete statistical knowledge of the underlying joint distribution of the observation x and the true category θ, or he may have no knowledge of the underlying distribution except that which can be inferred from samples. In the first extreme, a standard Bayes analysis will yield an optimal decision procedure and the corresponding minimum (Bayes) prob-ability of error of classification R^*. In the other extreme, a decision to classify x into category θ is allowed to depend only on a collection of n correctly classified samples $(x_1, \theta_1), (x_2, \theta_2), \cdots, (x_n, \theta_n)$, and the decision procedure is by no means clear. This problem is in the domain of nonparametric statistics and no optimal classification procedure exists with respect to all underlying statistics.

If it is assumed that the classified samples (x_i, θ_i) are independently identically distributed according to the dis-tribution of (x, θ), certain heuristic arguments may be made about good decision procedures. For example, it is reasonable to assume that observations which are close together (in some appropriate metric) will have the same classification, or at least will have almost the same posterior probability distributions on their respective classifications. Thus to classify the unknown sample x we may wish to weight the evidence of the nearby x_i's most heavily. Perhaps the simplest nonparametric decision procedure of this form is the *nearest neighbor* (NN) rule, which classifies x in the category of its nearest neighbor. Surprisingly, it will be shown that, in the large sample case, this simple rule has a probability of error which

Manuscript received February 23, 1966; revised April 29, 1966. This work has been supported at Stanford University by U. S. Army Electronics Command under Contract DA28-043-AMC-01764(E) and by USAF under Contract AF49(638)1517; and at the Stanford Research Institute, Menlo Park, Calif., by RADC under Contract AF30(602)-3945.

T. M. Cover is with the Department of Electrical Engineering, Stanford University, Stanford, Calif.

P. E. Hart is with the Stanford Research Institute, Menlo Park, Calif.

is less than twice the Bayes probability of error, and hence is less than twice the probability of error of any other decision rule, nonparametric or otherwise, based on the infinite sample set.

The first formulation of a rule of the nearest neighbor type and primary previous contribution to the analysis of its properties, appears to have been made by Fix and Hodges [1] and [2]. They investigated a rule which might be called the k_n-nearest neighbor rule. It assigns to an unclassified point the class most heavily represented among its k_n nearest neighbors. Fix and Hodges established the consistency of this rule for sequences $k_n \to \infty$ such that $k_n/n \to 0$. In reference [2], they investigate numerically the small sample performance of the k_n-NN rule under the assumption of normal statistics.

The NN rule has been used by Johns [3] as an example of an empirical Bayes rule. Kanal [4], Sebestyen [5] (who calls it the proximity algorithm), and Nilsson [6] have mentioned the intuitive appeal of the NN rule and suggested its use in the pattern recognition problem. Loftsgaarden and Quesenberry [7] have shown that a simple modification of the k_n-NN rule gives a consistent estimate of a probability density function. In the above mentioned papers, no analytical results in the nonparametric case were obtained either for the finite sample size problem or for the finite number of nearest neighbors problem.

In this paper we shall show that, for any number n of samples, the single-NN rule has strictly lower probability of error than any other k_n-NN rule against certain classes of distributions, and hence is admissible among the k_n-NN rules. We will then establish the extent to which "samples which are close together have categories which are close together" and use this to compare in Section VI the probability of error of the NN-rule with the minimum possible probability of error.

II. THE NEAREST NEIGHBOR RULE

A set of n pairs $(x_1, \theta_2), \cdots, (x_n, \theta_n)$ is given, where the x_i's take values in a metric space X upon which is defined a metric d, and the θ_i's take values in the set $\{1, 2, \cdots, M\}$. Each θ_i is considered to be the index of the category to which the ith individual belongs, and each x_i is the outcome of the set of measurements made upon that individual. For brevity, we shall frequently say "x_i belongs to θ_i" when we mean precisely that the ith individual, upon which measurements x_i have been observed, belongs to category θ_i.

A new pair (x, θ) is given, where only the measurement x is observable by the statistician, and it is desired to estimate θ by utilizing the information contained in the set of correctly classified points. We shall call

$$x'_n \; \varepsilon \; \{x_1, x_2, \cdots, x_n\}$$

a nearest neighbor to x if

$$\min d(x_i, x) = d(x'_n, x) \quad i = 1, 2, \cdots, n. \quad (1)$$

The nearest neighbor rule decides x belongs to the category θ'_n of its nearest[1] neighbor x'_n. A mistake is made if $\theta'_n \neq \theta$. Notice that the NN rule utilizes only the classification of the nearest neighbor. The $n - 1$ remaining classifications θ_i are ignored.

III. ADMISSIBILITY OF NEAREST NEIGHBOR RULE

If the number of samples is large it makes good sense to use, instead of the single nearest neighbor, the majority vote of the nearest k neighbors. We wish k to be large in order to minimize the probability of a non-Bayes decision for the unclassified point x, but we wish k to be small (in proportion to the number of samples) in order that the points be close enough to x to give an accurate estimate of the posterior probabilities of the true class of x.

The purpose of this section is to show that, among the class of k-NN rules, the single nearest neighbor rule (1-NN) is admissible. That is, for the n-sample problem, there exists no k-NN rule, $k \neq 1$, which has lower probability of error against all distributions. We shall show that the single NN rule is undominated by exhibiting a simple distribution for which it has strictly lower probability of error P_e. The example to be given comes from the family of distributions for which simple decision boundaries provide complete separation of the samples into their respective categories. Fortunately, one example will serve for all n.

Consider the two category problem in which the prior probabilities $\eta_1 = \eta_2 = \frac{1}{2}$, and the conditional density f_1 is uniform on the unit disk D_1 centered at $(-3, 0)$, and the conditional density f_2 is uniform on the unit disk D_2 centered at $(3, 0)$ as shown in Fig. 1. In the n-sample problem, the probability that j individuals come from category 1, and hence have measurements lying in D_1, is $(\frac{1}{2})^n \binom{n}{j}$. Without loss of generality, assume that the unclassified x lies in category 1. Then the NN rule will make a classification error only if the nearest neighbor x'_n belongs to category 2, and thus, necessarily, lies in D_2. But, from inspection of the distance relationships, if the nearest neighbor to x is in D_2, then each of the x_i must lie in D_2. Thus the probability $P_e(1; n)$ of error of the NN rule in this case is precisely $(\frac{1}{2})^n$—the probability that $x_1, x_2, \cdots, x_n$ all lie in D_2. Let $k = 2k_0 + 1$. Then the k-NN rule makes an error if k_0 or fewer points lie in D_1. This occurs with probability

$$P_e(k; n) = (\tfrac{1}{2})^n \sum_{i=0}^{k_0} \binom{n}{j}. \quad (2)$$

Thus in this example, the 1-NN rule has strictly lower P_e than does any k-NN rule, $k \neq 1$, and hence is admissible in that class. Indeed

---

[1] In case of ties for the nearest neighbor, the rule may be modified to decide the most popular category among the ties. However, in those cases in which ties occur with nonzero probability, our results are trivially true.

$$P_e(k; n) \uparrow \tfrac{1}{2} \quad \text{in} \quad k, \quad \text{for any} \quad n,$$

$$P_e(k; n) \downarrow 0 \quad \text{in} \quad n, \quad \text{for any} \quad k > 0, \qquad (3)$$

and

$$P_e(k_n; n) \to 0, \quad \text{if} \quad 0 < \frac{k_n}{n} \leq \alpha < 1, \quad \text{for all} \quad n.$$

In general, then, the 1-NN rule is strictly better than the $k \neq$ 1-NN rule in those cases where the supports of the densities $f_1, f_2, \cdots, f_M$ are such that each in-class distance is greater than any between-class distance.

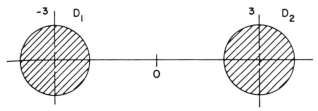

Fig. 1. Admissibility of nearest neighbor rule.

IV. BAYES PROCEDURE

In this section we shall present the simplest version of the Bayes decision procedure for minimizing the probability of error in classifying a given observation x into one of M categories. All the statistics will be assumed known. Bear in mind, however, that the NN rule is nonparametric, or distribution free, in the sense that it does not depend on any assumptions about the underlying statistics for its application. The Bayes risk serves merely as a reference—the limit of excellence beyond which it is not possible to go.

Let x denote the measurements on an individual and X the sample space of possible values of x. We shall refer to x as the observation. On the basis of x a decision must be made about the membership of the individual in one of M specified categories.

For the purposes of defining the Bayes risk, we assume $f_1(x)$, $f_2(x)$, $\cdots$, $f_M(x)$, probability densities at x with respect to a σ-finite measure ν, such that an individual in category i gives rise to an observation x according to density f_i. Let $L(i, j)$ be the loss incurred by assigning an individual from category i to category j.

Let $\eta_1, \eta_2, \cdots, \eta_M, \eta_i \geq 0, \sum \eta_i = 1$, be the *prior* probabilities of the M categories. The conditional probability $\hat{\eta}_i(x)$ of an individual with measurements x belonging to category i is, by the Bayes theorem,

$$\hat{\eta}_i = \frac{\eta_i f_i}{\sum \eta_i f_i}, \qquad i = 1, 2, \cdots, M. \qquad (4)$$

Thus the random variable x transforms the prior probability vector η into the *posterior* probability vector $\hat{\eta}(x)$. If the statistician decides to place an individual with measurements x into category j, the conditional loss is

$$r_j(x) = \sum_{i=1}^{M} \hat{\eta}_i(x) L(i, j). \qquad (5)$$

For a given x the conditional loss is minimum when the individual is assigned to the category j for which $r_j(x)$ is lowest. Minimizing the conditional expected loss obviously minimizes the unconditional expected loss. Thus the minimizing decision rule δ^*, called the Bayes decision rule with respect to η, is given by deciding the category j for which r_j is lowest. Using δ^*, the conditional Bayes risk $r^*(x)$ is

$$r^*(x) = \min_j \left\{ \sum_{i=1}^{M} \hat{\eta}_i(x) L(i, j) \right\}, \qquad (6)$$

and the resulting overall minimum expected risk R^*, called the Bayes risk, is given by

$$R^* = Er^*(x), \qquad (7)$$

where the expectation is with respect to the compound density

$$f(x) = \sum_{i=1}^{M} \eta_i f_i(x). \qquad (8)$$

V. CONVERGENCE OF NEAREST NEIGHBORS

Most of the properties of the NN rules hinge on the assumption that the conditional distributions of θ_n' and θ approach one another when $x_n' \to x$. In order to put bounds on the NN risk for as wide a class of underlying statistics as possible, it will be necessary to determine the weakest possible conditions on the statistics which guarantee the above convergence.

Lemma (Convergence of the Nearest Neighbor)

Let x and $x_1, x_2, \cdots$ be independent identically distributed random variables taking values in a separable metric space X. Let x_n' denote the nearest neighbor to x from the set $\{x_1, x_2, \cdots, x_n\}$. Then $x_n' \to x$ with probability one.

Remark: In particular, $x_n' \to x$ with probability one for any probability measure in Euclidean n-space. We prove the lemma in this generality in order to include in its coverage such standard pathological candidates for counterexamples as the Cantor ternary distribution function defined on X the real line.

Since the convergence of the nearest neighbor to x is independent of the metric, the bounds on the risks of the NN rule will be independent of the metric on X.

Proof: Let $S_x(r)$ be the sphere $\{\bar{x} \, \varepsilon \, X : d(x, \bar{x}) \leq r\}$ of radius r centered at x, where d is the metric defined on X.

Consider first a point $x \, \varepsilon \, X$ having the property that every sphere $S_x(r), r > 0$, has nonzero probability measure. Then, for any $\delta > 0$,

$$P\{ \min_{k=1,2,\cdots,n} d(x_k, x) \geq \delta \} = (1 - P(S_x(\delta))^n \to 0 \qquad (9)$$

and therefore, since $d(x_k, x)$ is monotonically decreasing in k, the nearest neighbor to x converges to x with probability one.

It remains to argue that the random variable x has this property with probability one. We shall do so by proving that the set N of points failing to have this property has probability measure zero. Accordingly, let N be the set of all x for which there exists some r_x sufficiently small that $P(S_x(r_x)) = 0$.

By the definition of the separability of X, there exists a countable dense subset A of X. For each $x \, \varepsilon \, N$ there exists, by the denseness of A, a_x in A for which $a_x \, \varepsilon \, S_x(r_x/3)$. Thus, there exists a small sphere $S_{a_x}(r_x/2)$ which is strictly contained in the original sphere $S_x(r_x)$ and which contains x. Thus $P(S_{a_x}(r_x/2)) = 0$. Then the possibly uncountable set N is contained in the countable union (by the countability of A) of spheres $\bigcup_{x \varepsilon N} S_{a_x}(r_x)$. Since N is contained in the countable union of sets of measure zero, $P(N) = 0$, as was to be shown.

VI. Nearest Neighbor Probability of Error

Let $x_n' \, \varepsilon \, \{x_1, x_2, \cdots, x_n\}$ be the nearest neighbor to x and let θ_n' be the category to which the individual having measurement x_n' belongs. If θ is indeed the category of x, the NN rule incurs loss $L(\theta, \theta_n')$. If $(x, \theta), (x_1, \theta_1), \cdots, (x_n, \theta_n)$ are random variables, we define the n-sample NN risk $R(n)$ by the expectation

$$R(n) = E[L(\theta, \theta_n')] \qquad (10)$$

and the (large sample) NN risk R by

$$R = \lim_{n \to \infty} R(n). \qquad (11)$$

Throughout this discussion we shall assume that the pairs $(x, \theta), (x_1, \theta_1), \cdots, (x_n, \theta_n)$ are independent identically distributed random variables in $X \times \Theta$. Of course, except in trivial cases, there will be some dependence between the elements x_i, θ_i of each pair.

We shall first consider the $M = 2$ category problem with probability of error criterion given by the $0 - 1$ loss matrix

$$L = \begin{bmatrix} 0 & 1 \\ 1 & 0 \end{bmatrix}, \qquad (12)$$

where L counts an error whenever a mistake in classification is made. The following theorem is the principal result of this discussion.

Theorem

Let X be a separable metric space. Let f_1 and f_2 be such that, with probability one, x is either 1) a continuity point of f_1 and f_2, or 2) a point of nonzero probability measure. Then the NN risk R (probability of error) has the bounds

$$R^* \leq R \leq 2R^*(1 - R^*). \qquad (13)$$

These bounds are as tight as possible.

Remarks: In particular, the hypotheses of the theorem are satisfied for probability densities which consist of any mixture of δ-functions and piecewise continuous density functions on Euclidean d-space. Observe that $0 \leq R^* \leq R \leq 2R^*(1 - R^*) \leq \frac{1}{2}$; so $R^* = 0$ if and only if $R = 0$, and $R^* = \frac{1}{2}$ if and only if $R = \frac{1}{2}$. Thus in the extreme cases of complete certainty and complete uncertainty the NN probability of error equals the Bayes probability of error. Conditions for equality of R and R^* for other values of R^* will be developed in the proof.

Proof: Let us condition on the random variables x and x_n' in the n-sample NN problem. The conditional NN risk $r(x, x_n')$ is then given, upon using the conditional independence of θ and θ_n', by

$$r(x, x_n') = E[L(\theta, \theta_n') \mid x, x_n'] = P_r\{\theta \neq \theta_n' \mid x, x_n'\}$$
$$= P_r\{\theta = 1 \mid x\}P_r\{\theta_n' = 2 \mid x_n'\}$$
$$+ P_r\{\theta = 2 \mid x\}P_r\{\theta_n' = 1 \mid x_n'\} \qquad (14)$$

where the expectation is taken over θ and θ_n'. By the development of (4) the above may be written as

$$r(x, x_n') = \hat{\eta}_1(x)\hat{\eta}_2(x_n') + \hat{\eta}_2(x)\hat{\eta}_1(x_n'). \qquad (15)$$

We wish first to show that $r(x, x_n')$ converges to the random variable $2\hat{\eta}_1(x)\hat{\eta}_2(x)$ with probability one.

We have not required that f_1, f_2 be continuous at the points x of nonzero probability measure $\nu(x)$, because these points may be trivially taken into account as follows. Let $\nu(x_0) > 0$; then

$$P_r\{x_0 \neq x_n'\} = (1 - \nu(x_0))^n \to 0. \qquad (16)$$

Since x_n', once equalling x_0, equals x_0 thereafter,

$$r(x, x_n') \to 2\hat{\eta}_1(x_0)\hat{\eta}_2(x_0) \qquad (17)$$

with probability one.

For the remaining points, the hypothesized continuity of f_1 and f_2 is needed. Here x is a continuity point of f_1 and f_2 with conditional probability one (conditioned on x such that $\nu(x) = 0$). Then, since $\hat{\eta}$ is continuous in f_1 and f_2, x is a continuity point of $\hat{\eta}$ with probability one. By the lemma, x_n' converges to the random variable x with probability one. Hence, with probability one,

$$\hat{\eta}(x_n') \to \hat{\eta}(x) \qquad (18)$$

and, from (15), with probability one,

$$r(x, x_n') \to r(x) = 2\hat{\eta}_1(x)\hat{\eta}_2(x), \qquad (19)$$

where $r(x)$ is the limit of the n-sample conditional NN risk.

As shown in (6) the conditional Bayes risk is

$$r^*(x) = \min\{\hat{\eta}_1(x), \hat{\eta}_2(x)\}$$
$$= \min\{\hat{\eta}_1(x), 1 - \hat{\eta}_1(x)\}. \qquad (20)$$

Now, by the symmetry of r^* in $\hat{\eta}_1$, we may write

$$r(x) = 2\hat{\eta}_1(x)\hat{\eta}_2(x) = 2\hat{\eta}_1(x)(1 - \hat{\eta}_1(x))$$
$$= 2r^*(x)(1 - r^*(x)). \qquad (21)$$

Thus as a by-product of the proof, we have shown in the large sample case, that with probability one a randomly chosen x will be correctly classified with probability $2r^*(x)(1 - r^*(x))$. For the overall NN risk R, we have, by definition,

$$R = \lim_n E[r(x, x_n')] \tag{22}$$

where the expectation is taken over x and x_n'. Now L, and hence r, is bounded by one; so applying the dominated convergence theorem,

$$R = E[\lim_n r(x, x_n')]. \tag{23}$$

The limit, from (19) and (21), yields

$$\begin{aligned} R &= E[r(x)] \\ &= E[2\hat{\eta}_1(x)\hat{\eta}_2(x)] \\ &= E[2r^*(x)(1 - r^*(x))]. \end{aligned} \tag{24}$$

Since the Bayes risk R^* is the expectation of r^*, we have

$$R = 2R^*(1 - R^*) - 2 \operatorname{Var} r^*(x). \tag{25}$$

Hence

$$R \le 2R^*(1 - R^*), \tag{26}$$

with equality iff $\operatorname{Var} r^* = 0$, which holds iff $r^* = R^*$ with probability one. Investigating this condition we find that for $R = 2R^*(1 - R^*)$ it is necessary and sufficient that

$$\frac{\eta_1 f_1(x)}{\eta_2 f_2(x)} = R^*/(1 - R^*) \quad \text{or} \quad (1 - R^*)/R^* \tag{27}$$

for almost every x (with respect to the probability measure ν).

Rewriting (24), we have

$$\begin{aligned} R &= E[r^*(x) + r^*(x)(1 - 2r^*(x))] \\ &= R^* + E[r^*(x)(1 - 2r^*(x))] \\ &\ge R^* \end{aligned} \tag{28}$$

with equality if and only if $r^*(x)(1 - 2r^*(x)) = 0$ almost everywhere (with respect to ν). Thus the lower bound $R = R^*$ is achieved if and only if r^* equals 0 or $\frac{1}{2}$ almost everywhere and $Er^* = R^*$. Examples of probability distributions achieving the upper and lower bounds will be given at the end of this section following the extension to M categories.

Consider now the M-category problem with the probability of error criterion given by the loss function $L(i, j) = 0$, for $i = j$, and $L(i, j) = 1$, for $i \ne j$. The substitution trick of (21) can no longer be used when $M \ne 2$.

Theorem (Extension of Theorem 1 to $M \ne 2$)

Let X be a separable metric space. Let $f_1, f_2, \cdots, f_M$ be probability densities with respect to some probability measure ν such that, with probability one, x is either 1) a continuity point of $f_1, f_2, \cdots, f_M$, or 2) a point of nonzero probability measure. Then the NN probability of error R has the bounds

$$R^* \le R \le R^*\left(2 - \frac{M}{M - 1} R^*\right). \tag{29}$$

These bounds are as tight as possible.

Proof: Since $x_n' \to x$ with probability one, the posterior probability vector $\hat{\eta}(x_n') \to \hat{\eta}(x)$ with probability one. The conditional n-sample NN risk $r(x, x_n')$ is

$$r(x, x_n') = E[L(\theta, \theta_n') \mid x, x_n'] = \sum_{i \ne j}^M \hat{\eta}_i(x)\hat{\eta}_j(x_n') \tag{30}$$

which converges with probability one to the large sample conditional risk $r(x)$ defined by

$$r(x) = \sum_{i \ne j} \hat{\eta}_i(x)\hat{\eta}_j(x) = 1 - \sum_{j=1}^M \hat{\eta}_j^2(x). \tag{31}$$

The conditional Bayes risk $r^*(x)$, obtained by selecting, for a given x, the maximum $\hat{\eta}_i(x)$, say $\hat{\eta}_k(x)$, is given by

$$r^*(x) = 1 - \max_i \{\hat{\eta}_i(x)\} = 1 - \hat{\eta}_k(x). \tag{32}$$

By the Cauchy-Schwarz inequality

$$\begin{aligned} (M - 1) \sum_{i \ne k}^M \hat{\eta}_i^2(x) &\ge \left[\sum_{i \ne k}^M \hat{\eta}_i(x)\right]^2 \\ &= [1 - \hat{\eta}_k(x)]^2 = (r^*(x))^2. \end{aligned} \tag{33}$$

Adding $(M - 1)\hat{\eta}_k^2(x)$ to each side,

$$\begin{aligned} (M - 1) \sum_{i=1}^M \hat{\eta}_i^2(x) &\ge (r^*(x))^2 + (M - 1)\hat{\eta}_k^2(x) \\ &= (r^*(x))^2 + (M - 1)(1 - r^*(x))^2 \end{aligned} \tag{34}$$

or

$$\sum_{i=1}^M \hat{\eta}_i^2(x) \ge \frac{(r^*(x))^2}{M - 1} + (1 - r^*(x))^2 \tag{35}$$

Substituting (35) into (31),

$$r(x) \le 2r^*(x) - \frac{M}{M - 1}(r^*(x))^2. \tag{36}$$

Taking expectations, and using the dominated convergence theorem as before,

$$R = 2R^* - \frac{M}{M - 1}(R^*)^2 - \frac{M}{M - 1} \operatorname{Var} r^*(x). \tag{37}$$

Hence

$$R \le R^*\left(2 - \frac{M}{M - 1} R^*\right) \tag{38}$$

with equality if and only if $\operatorname{Var} r^*(x) = 0$. Of course, $\operatorname{Var} r^* = 0$ implies $r^*(x) = R^*$ with probability one.

The upper bound is attained for the no-information experiment $f_1 = f_2 = \cdots = f_M$, with $\eta_1 = 1 - R^*$, and $\eta_i = R^*/(M - 1); i = 2, \cdots, M$. The lower bound $R = R^*$ is attained, for example, when $\eta_i = 1/M, i = 1, 2, \cdots, M$, and

$$f_i(x) = \begin{cases} 1, & 0 \leq x \leq \dfrac{MR^*}{M - 1} \text{ or } i \leq x \leq i + 1 - \dfrac{MR^*}{M - 1} \\ 0, & \text{elsewhere.} \end{cases} \quad (39)$$

VII. EXAMPLE

Let the real valued random variable x have triangular densities f_1 and f_2 with prior probabilities $\eta_1 = \eta_2 = \frac{1}{2}$, as shown in Fig. 2. The density $f = \eta_1 f_1 + \eta_2 f_2$ on x is uniform on $[0, 1]$, thus facilitating calculation of the distribution of the nearest neighbor x'_n.

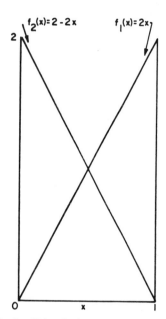

Fig. 2. Triangle densities for example.

The probability of error for this example in the n-sample single NN case is

$$R(n) = E[\eta_1 \eta_2 f_1(x) f_2(x'_n) + \eta_1 \eta_2 f_2(x) f_1(x'_n)]$$
$$= E[x(1 - x'_n) + (1 - x)x'_n]. \quad (40)$$

Upon performing a lengthy but straightforward calculation, we obtain

$$R(n) = \frac{1}{3} + \frac{1}{(n + 1)(n + 2)}. \quad (41)$$

Thus

$$R = \lim_{n \to \infty} R(n) = \frac{1}{3}. \quad (42)$$

The NN risk R is to be compared to the Bayes risk

$$R^* = \int \min \{\eta_1 f_1, \eta_2 f_2\} \, d\nu$$
$$= \int_0^1 \min\{x, 1 - x\} \, dx = \frac{1}{4}. \quad (43)$$

Exhibiting corresponding terms we have

$$R^* \leq R \leq 2R^*(1 - R^*)$$
or
$$\frac{1}{4} \leq \frac{1}{3} \leq \frac{3}{8}. \quad (44)$$

In this example we have found an exact expression for the NN risk $R(n)$ for any finite sample size. Observe that $R(1) = \frac{1}{2}$, in agreement with simpler considerations, and that $R(n)$ converges to its limit approximately as $1/n^2$.

VIII. THE k-NN RULE

From Section V it is also possible to conclude that the kth nearest neighbor to x converges to x with probability one as the sample size n increases with k fixed. Since each of the nearest neighbors casts conditionally independent votes as to the category of x, we may conclude, in the 2-category case for odd k, that the conditional k-NN risk $r_k(x)$ is given in the limit (with probability one) as n increases, by

$$r_k(x) = \hat{\eta}_1(x) \sum_{j=0}^{(k-1)/2} \binom{k}{j} \hat{\eta}_1^j(x)(1 - \hat{\eta}_1(x))^{k-i}$$
$$+ (1 - \hat{\eta}_1(x)) \sum_{j=(k+1)/2}^{k} \binom{k}{j} \hat{\eta}_1^j(x)(1 - \hat{\eta}_1(x))^{k-i}. \quad (45)$$

Note that the conditional NN risks $r_k(x)$ are monotonically decreasing in k (to $\min \{\hat{\eta}_1(x), 1 - \hat{\eta}_1(x)\}$), as we might suspect. Thus the least upper bounds on the unconditional NN risks R_k will also be monotonically decreasing in k (to R^*).

Observe that in (45) r_k is symmetric in $\hat{\eta}_1$ and $1 - \hat{\eta}_1$. Thus r_k may be expressed solely in terms of $r^* = \min \{\hat{\eta}_1, 1 - \hat{\eta}_1\}$ in the form

$$r_k = \rho_k(r^*)$$
$$= r^* \sum_{j=0}^{(k-1)/2} \binom{k}{j}(r^*)^j(1 - r^*)^{k-i}$$
$$+ (1 - r^*) \sum_{j=(k+1)/2}^{k} \binom{k}{j}(r^*)^j(1 - r^*)^{k-i}. \quad (46)$$

Now let $\bar{\rho}_k(r^*)$ be defined to be the least concave function greater than $\rho_k(r^*)$. Then

$$r_k = \rho_k(r^*) \leq \bar{\rho}_k(r^*), \quad (47)$$

and, by Jensen's inequality,

$$R_k = Er_k = E\rho_k(r^*) \leq E\bar{\rho}_k(r^*) \leq \bar{\rho}_k(Er^*) = \bar{\rho}_k(R^*). \quad (48)$$

So $\bar{\rho}_k(R^*)$ is an upper bound on the large sample k-NN risk R_k. It may further be shown, for any R^*, that $\bar{\rho}_k(R^*)$ is the least upper bound on R_k by demonstrating simple statistics which achieve it. Hence we have the bounds

$$R^* \leq R_k \leq \bar{\rho}_k(R^*) \leq \bar{\rho}_{k-1}(R^*) \leq \cdots$$

$$\leq \bar{\rho}_1(R^*) = 2R^*(1 - R^*) \qquad (49)$$

where the upper and lower bounds on R_k are as tight as possible.

IX. Conclusions

The single NN rule has been shown to be admissible among the class of k_n-NN rules for the n-sample case for any n. It has been shown that the NN probability of error R, in the M-category classification problem, is bounded below by the Bayes probability of error R^* and above by $R^*(2 - MR^*/(M - 1))$. Thus *any* other decision rule based on the infinite data set can cut the probability of error by at most one half. In this sense, half of the available information in an infinite collection of classified samples is contained in the nearest neighbor.

References

[1] E. Fix and J. L. Hodges, Jr., "Discriminatory analysis, non-parametric discrimination," USAF School of Aviation Medicine, Randolph Field, Tex., Project 21-49-004, Rept. 4, Contract AF41(128)-31, February 1951.

[2] ——, "Discriminatory analysis: small sample performance," USAF School of Aviation Medicine, Randolph Field, Tex., Project 21-49-004, Rept. 11, August 1952.

[3] M. V. Johns, "An empirical Bayes approach to non-parametric two-way classification," in *Studies in Item Analysis and Prediction*, H. Solomon, Ed. Stanford, Calif.: Stanford University Press, 1961.

[4] L. N. Kanal, "Statistical methods for pattern classification," Philco Rept., 1963; originally appeared in T. Harley et al., "Semi-automatic imagery screening research study and experimental investigation," *Philco Reports*, V043-2 and V043-3, Vol. I, sec. 6, and Appendix H, prepared for U. S. Army Electronics Research and Development Lab. under Contract DA-36-039-SC-90742, March 29, 1963.

[5] G. Sebestyen, *Decision Making Processes in Pattern Recognition*. New York: Macmillan, 1962, pp. 90–92.

[6] Nils Nilsson, *Learning Machines*. New York: McGraw-Hill, 1965, pp. 120–121.

[7] D. O. Loftsgaarden and C. P. Quesenberry, "A nonparametric estimate of a multivariate density function," *Annals Math Stat.*, vol. 36, pp. 1049–1051, June 1965.

(1974)
Bruce G. Batchelor

Methods of pattern classification
Practical Approach to Pattern Classification, London: Plenum, pp. 35–51

3.1 Introduction

One of the most bewildering aspects of our subject is the large number of schemes that have been suggested for classification. At first sight, it seems that there have been as many suggestions as authors. When we look closer we see that there are four or five basic techniques for classification, and that the remainder are merely refinements of these. So far, there has been little attempt to compare the various methods of classification. This is probably due to their obvious differences, which have, for a long time, hidden their similarities. In the following chapter, we shall attempt to show that most of the classifiers described in the literature are simply variations upon the same basic theme. Once this is appreciated it will become easier to decide which classifiers are best. This chapter is a catalogue of the most significant classifiers, and prepares us for this comparison.

3.2 Linear Classifier

The linear classifier [1, 2, 3] is one of the simplest pattern classifiers, yet it is still frequently encountered in the literature, despite the recent discovery of other, more powerful techniques. The major reasons for this continuing popularity are that it is well understood, it can readily be implemented in electronic hardware, and training methods exist which have been proved to converge. It should also be added that many problems can be solved quite adequately using a linear classifier. (In such a situation it would generally be unjustified to use a more complex technique.)

In a 2-dimensional space the decision surface of a linear classifier is a straight line, while in 3 dimensions we obtain a plane, and in q dimensions a hyperplane. The orientation of this hyperplane can be determined by q parameters, which we shall call weights, and shall denote by $W_1, ..., W_q$. One further parameter is required, which will be represented by V. The decision (M) of a two-class linear classifier is calculated as follows:

$$M = \mathrm{sgn}\left(V + \sum_{i=1}^{q} W_i X_i\right)$$

(3.1)

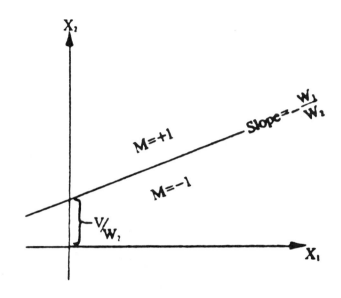

Figure 3.1 Decision surface of a linear classifier in a 2-dimensional space.

$M = +1$ on one side of the hyperplane, and -1 on the other (Figures 3.1 and 3.2). By varying V we shift the hyperplane to a new position parallel to the old one. If V is zero the hyperplane intersects the origin. In later chapters, we shall find that it is more convenient to use the following homogenous form for the linear classifier:

$$M = \mathrm{sgn}\left(\sum_{i=1}^{q+1} W_i X_i\right)$$

(3.2)

where

$$\left.\begin{aligned} W_{q+1} &\equiv V \\ X_{q+1} &\equiv 1 \end{aligned}\right\}$$

3.3 ϕ-Machine

To achieve a more flexible decision surface we could add a descriptor transformation network to the linear classifier (Figure 3.3). If the transformation network calculates polynomial terms the resulting classifier is called a ϕ-machine [3].

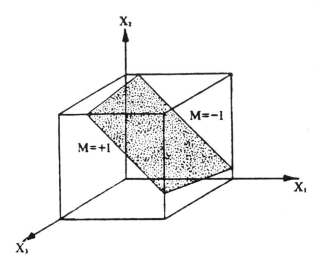

Figure 3.2 Decision surface of a linear classifier in a 3-dimensional space.

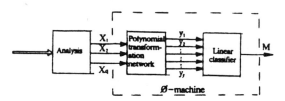

Figure 3.3 Structure of a φ-machine.

A simple φ-machine might calculate the following:

$$
\left.
\begin{aligned}
Y_1 &= X_1 \\
Y_2 &= X_2 \\
Y_3 &= X_1^2 \\
Y_4 &= X_1^3 \\
Y_5 &= 1 \\
M &= \text{sgn}\left(\sum_{i=1}^{5} W_i Y_i\right)
\end{aligned}
\right\} \qquad (3.4)
$$

A typical decision surface from a φ-machine is shown in Figure 3.4. Notice, however, that the decision surface of a φ-machine need not be continuous.

It should be also noted that the W_i are contained in a linear equation. (This allows us to use the same learning rules for a φ-machine and linear classifier.)

3.4 Piece-wise Linear Classifier

The piece-wise linear classifiers (PWLC) are capable of realising complex decision surfaces without using the expensive polynomial transformation network required by a φ-machine. Many forms of PWLC have been suggested,

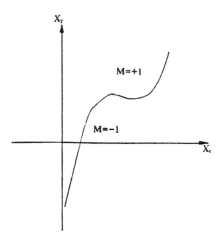

Figure 3.4 Typical decision surface produced by a φ-machine in a 2-dimensional space.

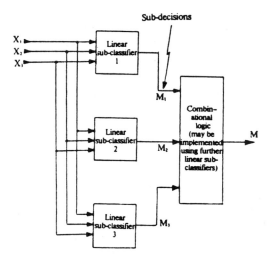

Figure 3.5 Structure of a piece-wise linear classifier.

but they all consist of at least two layers of units.[*] The bottom layer contains a number (N_1) of linear sub-classifiers. The higher layers combine the decisions from the bottom layer (Figure 3.5). The combinational logic may be implemented using conventional digital logic, or a layered network of linear subclassifiers. The latter alternative has the advantage that its logical function may be modified by varying the weights in the second and higher layers.

Figures 3.6 and 3.7 show decision surfaces produced by a PWLC in 2 and 3-dimensional spaces. Any surface that can be represented by a finite number of hyperplanar segments can be realised by a PWLC.

*To avoid ambiguity, we shall use the term subclassifier to indicate a classifier-like device which forms part of a larger system, for which we shall reserve the name classifier.

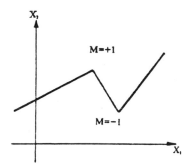

Figure 3.6 Decision surface of a piece-wise linear classifier in a 2-dimensional space.

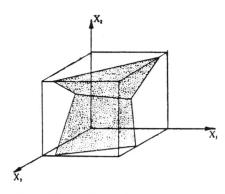

Figure 3.7 Decision surface of a piece-wise linear classifier in a 3-dimensional space.

3.5 Nearest Neighbour Classifier

The three classification techniques described so far are all based on the linear classifier. We are now going to depart from this approach. Superficially there is little resemblance between the Nearest Neighbour Classifier (NNC) and the remaining schemes to be discussed in this chapter. However, it will soon become apparent that they store information in the same way. We begin by describing the NNC which is possibly the simplest scheme using this storage organisation.

The NNC makes use of the correspondence between similarity and distance, discussed in the previous chapter. Imagine a machine which stores a number of representative **X**-vectors from each class. Each new pattern is then assigned to the class of the most similar stored representative. If we assume that there is an inverse relationship between similarity and distance in the descriptor space, we must minimise the distance between the **X**-vector and the stored representatives. This machine is the NNC.

The storage in an NNC is divided into areas in which we can store one q-dimensional vector, called a *locate*. Let there be:

1. N_{-1} locates, denoted by $\mathbf{B}_{-1,1}, \ldots, \mathbf{B}_{-1,N_{-1}}$. These locates will be associated with the NNC decision, $M = -1$.

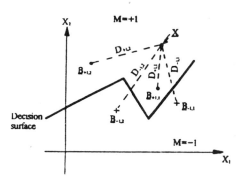

Figure 3.8 Decision surface of a Nearest Neighbour Classifier in a 2-dimensional space. Notice that this surface is identical to that shown in Figure 3.6. To find the classification of the point **X,** we calculate the distances $D_{+1,1}$ $D_{+1,2}$ and find the minimum (in this case $D_{+1,1}$). The classifications for this point is $+1$.

2. N_1 locates, denoted by $\mathbf{B}_{+1,1}, \ldots, B_{+1,N_{+1}}$. These locates will be associated with the NNC decision, $M = +1$.

In addition we shall let:

$$\mathbf{B}_{i,j} = (B_i, j, 1, \ldots, B_i, j, q) \tag{3.5}$$

As usual, q is the dimensionality of the space.

Let $D_{i,j}$ be the Euclidean distance between the locate $\mathbf{B}_{i,j}$ and the **X**-vector. Then

$$D_{i,j} = \sqrt{\sum_{k=1}^{q} (B_{i,j,k} - X_k)^2} \tag{3.6}$$

The decision of the NNC is given by M where

$$M = \operatorname{sgn}\left(\min_{j=1,\ldots,N_{-1}} (D_{-1,j}) - \min_{j=1,\ldots,N_{+1}} (D_{+1,j}) \right) \tag{3.7}$$

In the simple example shown in Figure 3.8 we find that

$$D_{+1,1} < D_{-1,1} < D_{+1,2} < D_{-1,2}$$

The decision surface of a NNC is piece-wise linear. In fact it can realise any such surface, if there are enough locates. To emphasise this point, we have deliberately made the decision surfaces in Figures 3.6 and 3.8 identical.

We do not wish to give the impression that the locates are necessarily representatives of the pattern classes. As far as we are concerned, the locates are simply points in X-space which help us to draw the decision surface. They will be particularly useful in later chapters when we consider the way the decision surface changes during learning.

3.6 Variations of the NNC

3.6.1 Alternative Distance Measures
In the preceding section, we defined the NNC in terms of the Euclidean distance. Since this is relatively difficult to

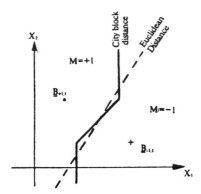

Figure 3.9 Comparison of the decision surfaces of two simple NNCs which use the same two locates, but different distance measures (Euclidean and city block distances).

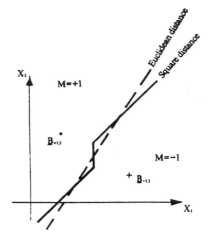

Figure 3.10 Comparison of the decision surfaces of two NNCs using the Euclidean and square distances. The same two locates are used.

calculate in analogue hardware, various other distances [4] have been proposed:

1. The city block distance (sometimes called Manhattan distance):

$$\sum_{K=1}^{q} \left| B_{I,J,K} - X_K \right| \tag{3.8}$$

2. The square distance:

$$\max_{K=1,\dots,q} \left| B_{I,J,K} - X_K \right| \tag{3.9}$$

3. An octagonal distance [5], equal to a weighted sum of the city block and square distances:

$$\sum_{K=1}^{q} \left| B_{I,J,K} - X_K \right| + \sqrt{q} \max_{K=1,\dots,q} \left| B_{I,J,K} - X_K \right| \tag{3.10}$$

The advantage of these distances lies in their computational simplicity, but as we shall see later they introduce some strange effects. It has been proposed that any of these might be used in lieu of the Euclidean distance in the NNC. Figures 3.9–3.11 compare a simple NNC using the Euclidean distance to others which use the same (two) locates but other distances.

3.6.2 Adding Weights to the NNC

Our last modification to the NNC is the introduction of weights. We shall denote these by $W_{-1,1}, \ldots, W_{-1,N_{-1}}$ and $W_{+1,1}, \ldots, W_{+1,N_{+1}}$.

The decision of the modified NNC is then given by:

$$M = \text{sgn} \left(\min_{j=1,\dots,N_{-1}} (W_{-1,j} D_{-1,j}) \, \min_{j=,\dots,N_{+1}} (W_{+1,j} D_{+1,j}) \right) \tag{3.11}$$

Of course the $D_{i,j}$ could be calculated using any of the distances defined in expressions (3.6, 3.8, 3.9 or 3.10). If the Euclidean distance is used, the decision surface consists of fragments of hyperspheres, and is thus said to be piecewise hyperspherical (Figure 3.12). The classifier defined by equation (3.11) will be called the *modified NNC* to distinguish it from the normal form (equation (3.7)).

3.7 Potential Function Classifier

Potential Function Classifier (PFC) is a term applied to a large number of pattern classifiers, which can be defined by the same form of equation. Like the modified NNC, the PFCs employ both locates and weights. We shall therefore continue to use the notation developed in the two previous sections.

A typical PFC might calculate a decision M using the following rule:

$$M = \text{sgn} \left(\sum_{j=1}^{N_{+1}} \left(\frac{W_{+1,j}}{D_{+1,j}} \right) - \sum_{j=1}^{N_{-1}} \left(\frac{W_{-1,j}}{D_{-1,j}} \right) \right) \tag{3.12}$$

where $D_{i,j}$ is given by equation (3.6). This is just one example from a range of classifiers, which can all be defined by the following form of equation:

$$M = \text{sgn} \left(\sum_{j=1}^{N_{+1}} P(D_{+1,j}) W_{+1,j} - \sum_{j=1}^{N_{-1}} P(D_{-1,j}) W_{-1,j} + T \right) \tag{3.13}$$

where T is a scalar quantity which can be zero, positive or negative, and $P(D)$ is a monotonically decreasing function of D. Equation (3.13) defines the general two-class PFC.

The name Potential Function Classifier was suggested by the Russian workers, who first proposed this method of classification [6, 7]. They imagined that the q-dimensional descriptor space contained negative electrical charges of magnitude $W_{-1,1}, \ldots, W_{-1,N_{-1}}$ placed at $\mathbf{B}_{-1,1}, \ldots,$

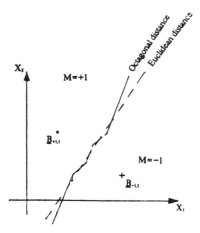

Figure 3.11 Comparison of the decision surfaces of two NNCs using the Euclidean and octagonal distances. The same two locates are used.

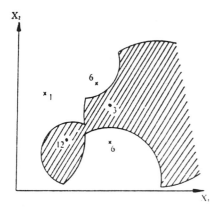

Figure 3.12 Decision surface of a modified NNC in a 2-dimensional space Numbers denote values of the weights, W_i.

$B_{-1,N_{-1}}$; similarly for positive charges $W_{+1,1}, \ldots, W_{+1,N_{+1}}$ at $B_{+1,1}, \ldots, B_{+1,N_{+1}}$ They then considered the electro-static potential, and noted that the sign of the potential at a point $\mathbf{X}$ is given by (3.12). The zero-potential surface in the electrostatic model is identical with the decision surface of the classifier defined by equation (3.12).

3.8 Variations of the PFC

The PFC was first envisaged through the use of the electro-static analogue, which is now of little more than historic interest. Other forms of potential decay function ($P(D)$ in (3.13)) have been proposed [8 10], often to avoid the infinite values which can occur in (3.12) (when the $\mathbf{X}$-vector is coincident with any of the locates). Another suggestion makes use of the following potential decay function

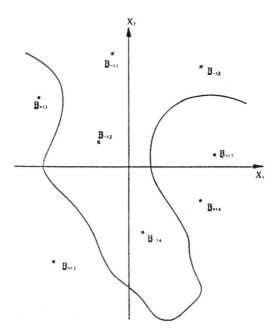

Figure 3.13 Decision surface of a heterpolar Potential Function Classifier in a 2-dimensional space.

$$P(D) = 1/D^2 \tag{3.14}$$

This would allow us to eliminate the square-root operation required by (3.6). Many other possibilities exist. For example, we could use any of the distances defined in (3.8) to (3.10), rather than the Euclidean distance.

There are even more variations that we must consider. One of the most significant is the unipolar PFC [8], which has an equation of the form:

$$M = \operatorname{sgn}\left(T - \sum_{j=1}^{N_{-1}} P(D_{-1,j})W_{-1,j}\right) \tag{3.15}$$

This type of classifier stores locates for only one class. Equation (3.15) is a special case of (3.13), with $N_{+1} = 0$. The author prefers the term *homopolar* rather than *unipolar*. We can then use the term *heteropolar* for those PFCs which store locates for each class. (Equation (3.12) defines a typical heteropolar PFC.)

With such an enormous range of possibilities, it is difficult to choose typical decision surfaces to illustrate the power of the PFCs. We have attempted to do this in Figures 3.13 and 3.14 for both the heteropolar and homopolar PFCs.

3.9 Classifier Described by G. S. Sebestyen

In 1962 G. S. Sebestyen published his book [1] which has now become a standard text for pattern recognition workers. In this book he describes a technique for classification

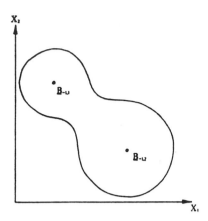

Figure 3.14 Decision surface of a homopolar Potential Function Classifier in a 2-dimensional space.

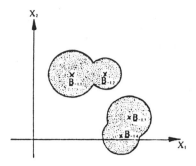

Figure 3.15 Decision surface of a Compound Classifier in a 2-dimensional space.

which closely resembles the PFCs although it preceded them by about 3 years. Like the heteropolar PFC, the Sebestyen classifier (SC) calculates its decision using equation (3.13) in which:

$$\left. \begin{array}{l} T = 0 \\ P(D) = \exp\left(-\alpha D^2\right) \quad \text{where } \alpha \text{ is a positive scalar} \end{array} \right\} \quad (3.16)$$

3.10 Compound Classifier

Imagine a handful of coins have been dropped on to a table. The "shadow" they cast is a typical decision surface produced by a Compound Classifier (figure 3.15). In a 3-dimensional space the decision surface consists of a number of spheres which may, or may not, overlap. In multi-dimensional spaces the decision surface is piecewise hyperspherical.

The Compound Classifier (CC) was first conceived [12, 13] as a layered device (Figure 3.16):

1. the bottom layer contains a number of subclassifiers. Each of these decides whether the input point **X** lies inside a hypersphere. Such a device will be termed a hypersphere subclassifier.

2. the top layer combines the sub-decisions from the bottom layer by forming their logical union.

Each subclassifier requires the storage of one q-dimensional locate to define the position of the hypersphere. Its size can be fixed by one further parameter. It will be convenient in the next chapter to have a description of the CC in terms of the double suffix notation already developed for the NNC and PFC. We shall assume then that there are N_{-1}, locates: $\mathbf{B}_{-1,1}, \ldots, \mathbf{B}_{-1,N_{-1}}$. The size parameters will be represented by $F_1, \ldots, F_{N_{-1}}$. The jth sub-decision U_j is calculated as follows:

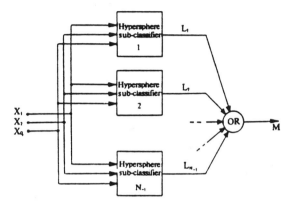

Figure 3.16 Structure of a Compound Classifier.

$$U_j = \text{sgn}\left(F_j - D_{-1,j}\right) \quad (3.17)$$

where $D_{-1,j}$ is defined by equation (3.6). The overall decision of the CC *(M)* is then calculated as follows:

$$M = \begin{cases} +1, & \bigcup_{J=1}^{N_{-1}} (U_j = +1) \\ -1, & \text{otherwise} \end{cases} \quad (3.18)$$

Equations (3.17) and (3.18) are the original form of definition of the CC. In order to cornpare the CC to the other classifiers we shall find it more convenient to rewrite the definition in terms of the minimum selector function:

$$M = \text{sgn}\left(1 - \min_{j=1,\ldots,N_{-1}} (D_{-1,j}/F_j)\right) \quad (3.19)$$

It is quite easy to verify that equations (3.18) and (3.19) give identical values for *M*. Equation (3.18) reflects the two-layer structure shown in Figure 3.15, while (3.19) will allow us to compare the CC with the other classifiers.

By now the reader will not be surprised that the CC can use the alternative distances defined in (3.8)–(3.10). The decision surfaces then consist of elements like those shown in Figures 3.17 and 3.18.

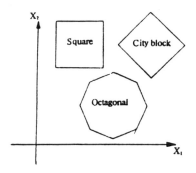

Figure 3.17 Alternatives to the circle obtained by using the non-Euclidean distances.

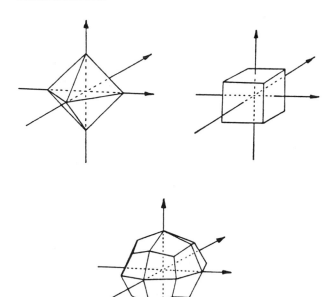

Figure 3.18 Alternatives to the sphere, obtained by using the non-Euclidean distances:
(A) city block distance
(B) square distance
(C) octangle distance.

(Reproduced by permission of the Institution of Electrical Engineers)

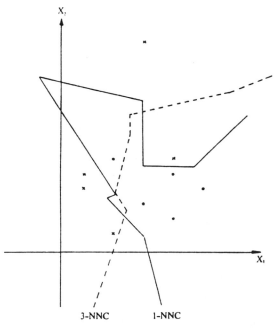

3-NNC   1-NNC

Figure 3.19 Comparison of the decision surfaces of the NNC (ordinary NNC, or 1-NNC) and the k-NNC. These classifiers use the same locates. Notice that the 3-NNC (and, in general, the k-NNC) produces less complicated surfaces, having fewer "corners". Hence the 1-NNC is capable of greater efficiency, although its locates must be carefully selected, since the effect of a single locate is more pronounced. In this example the surface due to the 3-NNC could be realised by a 1-NNC with only 7 locates

3.11 The k-Nearest Neighbour Classifier

The description of the k-Nearest Neighbour Classifier is only included here for completeness. The author feels that it is not particularly useful[*] since its decision surface can be duplicated by other simpler classifiers.

The first point that should be made is that the ordinary NNC (section 3.5) is a special case of the k-NNC with k equal to one. The k-NNC uses locates, but not weights.[†] Let the locates again be denoted by $\mathbf{B}_{i,j}(i = \pm 1, j = 1, ..., N_i)$. Let the distances[‡] from the locate $\mathbf{B}_{i,j}$ to the input pattern

* It does have an intuitive appeal for many pattern recognition workers, which accounts for its continuing popularity [2]. Our approach assumes that it is impossible to store more than a few locates (perhaps 20). Other workers are prepared to accept a general-purpose digital computer as a solution to the pattern recognition problem (we are not), and are therefore prepared to store either the complete training set, or most of it. They make little or no attempt to eliminate atypical locates, and would find that an ordinary NNC produces many small "islands" of errors in the measurement space. These "islands" may be eliminated by employing the k-NNC, which forms a "consensus opinion" from the k closest locates, thereby achieving a rather smoother decision surface than the ordinary NNC using the same locates (Figure 3.19).
† Of course, it is possible to suggest a complicated version of the k-NNC which does use weights. There is little merit apparent.
‡ Again we have the option of using the Euclidean, city block, square or octagonal distances. The k-NNC has a piece-wise linear decision surface when using the Euclidean distance.

$\mathbf{X}$ be $D_{i,j}$ The k-NNC selects those locates whose rank-distances from $\mathbf{X}$ are less than or equal to k. The decision of the k-NNC is then found by choosing the more frequently occurring class, among this group of k closest locates.

The decision surface of the k-NNC ‡ is piece-wise linear and can therefore be exactly modelled by the ordinary NNC or the PWLC. For this reason, we feel that there is little point in continuing to discuss the k-NNC in any great detail. The reader with a particular interest in this topic will find a more complete description in [2].

3.12 Summary

This chapter has listed over 20 classifiers ranging from the simple linear classifier to the more complex machines, such as the PFC. No doubt the newcomer to the subject is wondering why we have so many different schemes. The reason is that nobody has yet simplified the subject by indicating which classifiers are worth studying further, and which should be discarded as useless. To summarise this chapter, we have listed the most significant classifiers in Table 3.1. The properties of the four alternative distances are summarised in Table 3.2.

Table 3.1 Summary of the principal methods of pattern classification (it is assumed that Euclidean distances are used)

Classifier	Equation	Decision surface
Linear	3.2	Hyperplane
φ-machine	—	Polynomial
Piece-wise linear (PWLC)	—	Fragments of hyperplanes
Nearest Neighbour (NNC)	3.7	Piece-wise linear
Modified NNC	3.11	General piece-wise hypershpere
Potential Function (PFC)	3.13	Not simply described
Homopolar PFC	3.15	Not simply described
Sebestyen's Classifier	3.16	Variant of PFC
Compound Classifier (CC)	3.17–18 or 3.19	Union of hyperspheres
k-NCC	—	Piece-wise linear

Table 3.2 Summary of the four distance functions.

Distance	Equation	Equivalent of circle	Values compared to Euclidean distance	
			Minimum	Maximum
Euclidean	3.6	Circle	1.00	1.00
Square	3.8	Square (sides parallel to axes)	$\dfrac{1}{\sqrt{q}}$	1.00
City block	3.9	Square (sides 40° to axes)	1.00	$\sqrt{q}$
Octagonal	3.10	Regular octagon	$\dfrac{2+\sqrt{q}}{\sqrt{2}}$	$\sqrt{(\sqrt{q}+q)^2}$

References

1. H. C. Andrews, Introduction to Mathematical Techniques in Pattern Recognittion (Wiley, New York, 1972).

2. E. A. Patrick, Fundamentals of Pattern Recognition (Prentice-Hall, Englewood Cliffs, N.J., 1972).

3. N. J. Nilsson, Learning Machines (McGraw-Hill, New York, 1965).

4. A. Rosenfeld and J. L. Pfaltz, Distance Functions on Digital Pictures, *Pattern* Recognition, **1**, 33–61, 1968.

5. B. G. Batchelor, Improved Distance Measure for Pattern Recognition, *Electronics* Letters, **7**, 18, 521–4, 1971.

6. M. A. Aiserman, E. M. Braverman and L. I. Rozonoer, Potential Functions Technique and Extrapolation in Learning System Theory, *Proc. Congr., I.F.A.C.,* 3rd June, London, 1966.

7. A. G. Arkadev and E. M. Braverman, Teaching Computers to Recognise Patterns, (Academic Press, London, 1967).

8. C. J. W. Mason and C. H. McFall, Some Experiences with the Method of Potential Functions, in *Pattern Recogntion, I.E.E. Conf. Publication,* **42**, 69–76, 1968.

9. B. G. Batchelor, N. L. Ford and B. R. Wilkins, Family of Pattern Classifiers, *Electronics Letters,* **6**, 12, 386–9, 1970.

10. B. G. Batchelor, N. L. Ford and B. R. Wilkins, Learning in a Potential Function Classifier, *Electronics Letters,* **6**, 25, 826–8, 1970.

11. G. S. Sebestyen, Decision-making Processes in Pattern Recognition (Macmillan, New York, 1962).

12. B. G. Batchelor, Learning Machines for Patten Recognition, *Ph. D. Thesis* Southampton, 1969.

13. B. G. Batchelor and B. R. Wilkins, Adaptive Discriminant Functions, in *Pattern Recognition, I.E.E. Conf. Publication,* **42**, 168–178, 1968.

28
Introduction

(1982)
Douglas L. Reilly, Leon N. Cooper, and Charles Elbaum

A neural model for category learning
Biological Cybernetics 45: 35–41

There has been considerable interest in practical applications of neural networks in the past few years. The three authors of this paper are founders of a corporation, Nestor, Inc., which is one of the most prominent start-up companies in neural networks. Leon Cooper is a relative old-timer to neural networks (see paper 25 in *Neurocomputing: Foundations of Research*), and Nestor was founded in the mid-1970s to exploit what Cooper and Charles Elbaum thought were the commercial possibilities of a simple and powerful pattern recognition and classification algorithm. This paper, which is largely based on Douglas Reilly's Ph.D. thesis, describes a simple neural network classification algorithm. Classification tasks are a natural mode of operation for neural networks, and most applications, even at present, are based on classification: that is, the task of deciding which of several classes an output pattern belongs to.

The classification technique described in this paper was the basis for early Nestor products, including what became the *NestorWriter*, an ingenious system that recognizes characters handprinted on a special graphical input device. After a little training with the handwritten printing of a particular user, *NestorWriter* is quite accurate. Although the requirements for a special input device limit the general applicability of this product—mostly to such things as filling in forms on a computer where the special hardware and related data handling are not hard to provide—it is a pioneering practical neural network application.

The basic algorithm described in this paper turns out to be at heart a variant of a nearest neighbor classifier (see papers 25, 26, and 27). This is because the elementary computing units in almost all neural networks take an inner product between the synaptic strengths of a model neuron and its input activities. If the input activities form the same pattern as the synaptic weight, all the terms in the inner product are positive, so a model neuron is, in some sense, "tuned" to the pattern of its weights. If a set of patterns has to be classified, a good way to start might be to have a set of neurons and a set of best examples of the patterns to be classified. That is, each neuron has connection strengths with the same pattern as the best examples. When a new pattern has to be classified, it is not hard to arrange things so that the unit that responds most strongly will be the one with the pattern of weights that most closely matches the input pattern (see the discussion in the excerpt from Nilsson's *Learning Machines*, paper 25). Although the basic idea is simple and can be done in parallel—an input pattern can be matched at the same time to a "template" of connection strengths in many cells at once—there are a number of important details to be worked out before a practical system is possible. Reilly, Cooper, and Elbaum propose a three-layer network to implement their algorithm, calling the layers the F (input) bank, G (prototype) bank, and the H (output) bank. *Bank* is their idiosyncratic word for what is most often called a *layer* of model neurons.

Although multilayer nets are often hard to teach, the output (H) layer implements a simple, preprogrammed algorithm that ensures that the network will function as a classification algorithm. In correct operation one and only one element in the output layer will be active, which gives the classification. This is sometimes called a grandmother cell representation.

The output (H) layer is connected to the middle layer by connections that are arranged so as to ensure that (1) only one output cell is active at a time and (2) several prototype- (G-) layer cells may be connected to a single output layer cell; that is, several different prototype-layer cells may be given the same output classification. The selectivity and information processing power of the system comes from the connections between the F (input) and the G (prototype) layers. The authors make one unusual assumption for a neural net. They assume that the number of cells in the G (prototype) layer is not fixed but can increase with time.

In operation, data from some input devices are presented to the first layer of cells. Units are standard neural network neurons: An inner product is taken between the input pattern and the weights. The results of the inner product are compared with a threshold, and if the inner product exceeds threshold, the output is the inner product, with a possible additive scaling constant, otherwise it is zero. It is important to note that *all input vectors are normalized*, that is, of length one, so all possible inputs lie on the unit hypersphere.

At first there may be no units at all in the prototype (G) layer, or perhaps there are preset starting weights corresponding to a set of units for letters, or digits, or some other initial set of classifications. As in any pattern recognition task, the initial representation of the input data is of critical importance, and the performance of the algorithm in practice is due largely to the careful design of the way raw information is used to construct the initial state vectors of activity fed to the input (F) layer.

Given an input pattern, every prototype-layer cell computes (in parallel, with the right hardware) the inner product between its weights and the input pattern. The authors observe that every set of weights defines what they call a "prototype." When a pattern is input, many prototype cells may show output activity. Suppose that the cell that responds best has weights corresponding to an *A*. Then the input pattern is classified as an *A*. If the classification is correct the weights are not changed. If the pattern is *not* an *A* something is done.

First, suppose that no unit responded to the pattern. Then a *new* prototype cell is added to the prototype (G) layer. The weights of the new cell are set equal to a constant, λ, times the unrecognized input pattern. The cell is assumed to be responsive to that pattern, and the pattern is present at the input, so the weights are changed proportional to the conjunction between input and output. Therefore learning in the system follows a version of the Hebb rule. The new prototype cell is given the appropriate connection to the output layer. If the input pattern were to recur, then it would cause the new prototype cell to respond, and the output layer would give the correct classification.

Second, suppose the input pattern is recognized, but incorrectly. The incorrectly responding cell has its weights reduced by being multiplied by some constant less than one, so that future presentation of the input pattern will give no response at the misresponding cell.

Geometrically this is a very simple system. Input vectors can only lie on the unit hypersphere. Each prototype cell has a region of the hypersphere where it gives the largest response of all the prototype cells: This is a region on the surface of the hypersphere centered on the prototype and with a certain radius. The radius is determined by how strong the weights are. All input patterns falling within this radius will be given the classification of that prototype. If the weights are multiplied by a constant, λ, less than one, the region will shrink; if λ is greater than one, it will expand. A misclassification shrinks the radius of the region until the offending point is no longer within the region. A new prototype cell, formed in response to a new pattern, forms a new region with some initial radius.

In the data there may be very complicated boundaries that separate the regions that belong to different classifications. The power of the system described in this paper is that, by making enough prototype cells, it can approximate decision regions of any shape. As the system gains more and more experience, and more and more prototype cells, it approximates complicated decision regions more and more closely.

A weakness of the system arises from the same source. Strangely shaped decision regions may require very many prototype cells to classify inputs, especially near the boundaries of the regions. Even worse are noisy systems where boundaries can overlap, that is, the same point may be first given one classification and then another. Situations like this often arise in practice. Overall, however, the system is robust and simple and is effective for many practical applications.

(1982)

Douglas L. Reilly, Leon N. Cooper, and Charles Elbaum

A neural model for category learning
Biological Cybernetics 45: 35–41

Abstract. We present a general neural model for supervised learning of pattern categories which can resolve pattern classes separated by nonlinear, essentially arbitrary boundaries. The concept of a pattern class develops from storing in memory a limited number of class elements (prototypes). Associated with each prototype is a modifiable scalar weighting factor (λ) which effectively defines the threshold for categorization of an input with the class of the given prototype. Learning involves (1) commitment of prototypes to memory and (2) adjustment of the various λ factors to eliminate classification errors. In tests, the model ably defined classification boundaries that largely separated complicated pattern regions. We discuss the role which divisive inhibition might play in a possible implementation of the model by a network of neurons.

I. Introduction

A common concern of neural models has been the problem of relating the function of complex systems of neurons to what is known of individual neurons and their interconnections. In this paper we discuss a neural model that displays a form of learning manifested in human behavior: supervised learning of pattern categories. The terms pattern and event are used here synonymously to refer to a state of the environment that is characterized by a set of measurements. A category of patterns is a set of patterns in the same class. Their members may yield "roughly" the same value for some measurement (or collection of measurements) made on them (e.g. with reference to some feature set). However, one can imagine a category resulting from an association between a collection of

very unlike events and a particular system response (e.g., calling "a" and "A" by the sound of the first letter in the alphabet). In this case, the criterion defining the category is the association itself.

There are several difficulties in the problem of pattern classification that we address here. A given pattern class appears in the primary sensory neurons in a vast variety of manifestations. Consider all of the recognizable distortions of the Arabic numeral "three". All of these must be classified as "three" and at the same time be distinguished from other classes (1, 2, 4, etc.) and all of their distortions. Therefore, the problem of classification involves a separation of "different" classes as well as a grouping together of all distorted members of the same class. Our model is capable of making the separation as well as the grouping with a simple instruction procedure that seems at least roughly comparable to that employed in human learning.

There is a growing body of research dealing with the general problem of learning in an adaptive system composed of neuron like elements. Early work in this field introduced the notion of correlation matrix memories, showing how it was possible for a system to learn associations between pairs of input and output vectors (x^i, y^i) (Kohonen, 1972). Category learning has frequently been viewed as learning an association between y^i and a set of noisy versions of x^i. Models for such concept formation have been proposed which make use of varying amounts of interaction with an external "teacher" (e.g., Amari, 1977; Grossberg, 1978; Barto et al., 1981; Bobrowski, 1982). Among the various approaches in such systems, learning rules incrementally adjust elements of some weight vector w whose inner product with the input x is an important contributing factor to the output of the system.

In our approach pattern classification is accomplished through prototype formation. Evidence from psychological experiments suggests that learning of pattern classes might involve abstraction of a pro-

* This work was supported in part by the Alfred P. Sloan Foundation and the Ittleson Foundation, Inc.

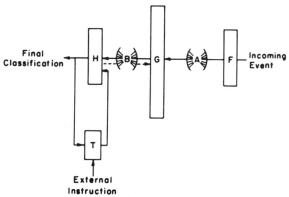

Fig. 1. Architecture of the model. Shown are coding neurons (*F*), prototype cells (*G*), classification cells (*H*), mapping (*A*) from *F* to *G*, mapping (*B*) from *G* to *H*, and the external instructor (*T*). Arrows mark information flow

Table 1. Classification of system responses for various values of α and Q as defined by (2)

Classification	α	Q	$\mathbf{h}$
Correct	1	0	$\mathbf{h}^c$
Unidentified	0	0	0
Incorrect	0	1	$\mathbf{h}^r, r \neq c$
Confusion	0	≥ 2	$\sum\limits_{r \neq c}^{Q} \mathbf{h}^r$
	1	≥ 1	$\mathbf{h}^c + \sum\limits_{r \neq c}^{Q} \mathbf{h}^r$

totype to represent a category of stimuli (e.g., Posner and Keele, 1968, 1970; Franks and Bransford, 1971). Some knowledge of class variance must also be learned. A closely related argument holds that categories are learned by retaining in memory examples of each class (e.g., Brooks, 1978; Medin and Schaffer, 1978). In pattern recognition theory, the technique of nearest neighbor classification is effectively an exemplar learning scheme (Cover and Hart, 1967; Duda and Hart, 1973). The focus of algorithms for such training has been to find and store the example set of minimal size which can guarantee performance within some acceptable error rate.

Here no distinction is made between the single (prototype) and multiple exemplar theory. Any class member stored in memory will be referred to as a prototype for that class. We will discuss learning in a system of neurons and, in particular, a model for prototype formation and development in a class of distributed memory neural networks.

II. Overview

In the architecture we consider, afferents from coding neurons, *F*, project onto prototype cells, *G*, which in turn synapse with classification neurons, *H* (see Fig. 1). Each class of events will be represented by the activity of a unique *H* neuron. An input event is coded by a vector of firing rates (**f**) in the *F* bank. If it causes activity in an *H* cell, it is classified as belonging to the category associated with that cell.

We define four possible network responses to an input pattern. Let $\mathbf{f}(c)$ represent an incoming pattern belonging to the cth class of events, and let **h** be the vector of output firing rates of the *H* neurons. Further, let $\mathbf{h}^x$ be defined as a vector with components

$$(\mathbf{h}^x)_j = \delta_{xj}. \tag{1}$$

The response **h** can be written, in general, as

$$\mathbf{h} = \alpha \mathbf{h}^c + \sum_{r \neq c}^{Q} \mathbf{h}^r. \tag{2}$$

If $\alpha = 1$ and $Q = 0$, then the system has correctly classified the input pattern. A response characterized by $\alpha = 1$ and $Q \geq 1$, or $\alpha = 0$ and $Q \geq 2$, we refer to as confusion, since the system is unable to decide upon any of several pattern classifications. The case where $\alpha = 0$ and $Q = 1$ is an outright incorrect response. When $\alpha = 0$ and $Q = 0$, no categorization has been made and the pattern is unidentified. Table 1 summarizes the responses.

The synaptic connections between *G* and *F* are represented in the mapping *A*. In our learning models, a prototype for a class is "imprinted" on the synapses between a *G* cell and the *F* set, thus becoming the most effective stimulus for that cell. For any given class, there may be more than one prototype; each will correspond to a different G_i. The mapping *B*, between cell groups *G* and *H*, develops so that the subset of *G* cells which can cause a given *H* cell to fire consists of prototypes representing the same class. A sufficient stimulus for an *H* cell to fire will be supraliminal activity in any member of its corresponding *G* cell subset.

The *H* set of neurons (and indirectly, *G*) has an additional source of input, that diagrammed by the block *T* in Fig. 1. Through *T*, an external supervisor can correct the network classification responses. The specific form of the mapping *B*, along with some aspects of *A*, will develop as a result of interaction with input patterns and with *T*. Essentially, *T* can cause the commitment of a *G* cell to a prototype and the strengthening of the association between this *G* cell and the proper classification cell. We assume synaptic modification as the vehicle for these network changes. One can imagine a variety of ways in which synaptic changes can result in cell coupling between the *G* and *H* sets. For example, simple Hebbian modification can produce the desired association if the particular *H* cell was receiving concurrent stimulation from *T*. The only requirement of this procedure is that cell commitment never involve a previously committed cell. For simplicity, we further assume that

(1) cell commitment is rapid (i.e., occurring within the duration of event presentation)

(2) only one cell is committed to any one prototype.

In the mapping A, an element A_{ij} represents the logical synapse between G_i and F_j; i.e., it summarizes the total effectiveness of neuron F_j in firing G_i. In accordance with a distributed memory model studied by Anderson and by Cooper, among others (e.g., Anderson, 1970, 1972; Kohonen, 1972, 1977; Cooper, 1973; Nass and Cooper, 1975; Anderson and Cooper, 1978), we take the firing rate of G_i (call it g_i) to be a weighted sum of the firing rates of the F neurons (f_j), gated by some threshold function

$$g_i = \Theta\left(\sum_j A_{ij} f_j\right), \tag{3}$$

where

$$\Theta(x) = 0 \qquad \text{if} \quad x \leq \theta$$
$$= x - b \quad \text{if} \quad x > \theta. \tag{4}$$

Given a prototype $\mathbf{P}(c)$ representing a class c of inputs, the equality

$$A_{ij} = P_j(c), \quad \text{all } j \tag{5}$$

establishes a correspondence between the ith G cell and a particular class of patterns c. The synapse vector of G_i takes on the value of the prototype.

Each prototype cell has a "region of influence" in the input space of events. It is defined as the set of input patterns that satisfies the threshold condition for cell firing. For convenience, assume input events to be normalized ($\mathbf{f} \cdot \mathbf{f} = 1$). The region of influence defined by cell G_i with threshold θ is the intersection of the surface of a unit hypersphere with a cone of angular width γ,

$$\gamma = \cos^{-1}\theta, \tag{6}$$

where γ is the angle between $\mathbf{P}(c)$ and an input $\mathbf{f}$ at threshold.

A class of patterns defines a region or set of regions in the pattern space of input events. Class regions corresponding to different pattern categories are assumed to be strictly disjoint. A priori, we choose not to restrict the complexity that the shape of class boundaries may display. To identify the class of an input event, the neural network must characterize and learn the arrangement of class regions. Our model develops by itself a set of prototypes whose influence regions map out the areas belonging to different categories in the pattern space without prior information of what these areas are. One approach to such prototype organization will be discussed. Several others, differing

in their methods of cell modification and in their assumptions about interaction between G cells, or equivalently, between prototypes stored in memory will be discussed elsewhere.

III. Prototype Formation and Development

For the present, we continue the assumption of normalized input patterns ($\mathbf{f} \cdot \mathbf{f} = 1$). Each committed prototype cell has a synapse vector of the form (for the ith cell),

$$\mathbf{A}^i = \lambda_i \mathbf{p}^i, \tag{7}$$

where $\mathbf{p}^i$ is a normalized ($\mathbf{p}^i \cdot \mathbf{p}^i = 1$) prototype vector and $\lambda_i > 1$. The vector $\mathbf{p}^i$ corresponds to some previously seen input pattern whose presentation failed to excite the H cell of the appropriate class. Modification to prototype cell synapses is governed by the following conditions.

1. New Classification

If $\mathbf{f}(c)$ is presented and

$$\mathbf{h} \cdot \mathbf{h}^c = 0 \tag{8}$$

i.e., the H cell for the cth class does not fire, then a new G cell (call it G_k) is committed to $\mathbf{f}(c)$ and the synapse between G_k and H_c is assigned strength 1. The synapses of G_k with F are modified according to

$$A_{kj} \to P_{kj} = \lambda_0 f_j, \tag{9}$$

where $\lambda_0 > 1$.

2. Confusion

If presentation of $\mathbf{f}(c)$ causes firing rate activity in some H_w where $w \neq c$, then this results in a signal from the T channel to reduce the λ factors of each currently active G cell associated with H_w. The quantity λ is diminished until the response of the cell to $\mathbf{f}(c)$ lies at threshold. If G_r is such a unit, then

$$\lambda_r \to \lambda_r'$$

such that

$$\lambda_r' \mathbf{p}^r \cdot \mathbf{f}(c) = 1. \tag{10}$$

For convenience, we have taken $\theta = 1$.

These two rules for prototype acquisition and modification will enable the network to learn the geography of the pattern classes.

In an untrained network, all G cells are uncommitted. The strengths of the synapses between G and H are all zero or some arbitrarily small number. When a pattern $\mathbf{f}(c)$ is presented to this system, no H cell responds above threshold. Information from the T element enters the system, identifying the correct class of the input. A single G cell is committed to $\mathbf{f}(c)$ as a prototype for that class and, simultaneously, the synapse between this G cell and H_c is set equal to 1. Since this input represents the first example of any pattern class, we can let $c = 1$. If the same pattern were to be presented again to the system, the response of the G cell would be

$$\lambda_0 \mathbf{p}^1(c) \cdot \mathbf{f}(c) = \lambda_0 > 1. \tag{11}$$

The output signal, λ_0, from this G cell would cause H_c to fire.

Suppose a second pattern $\mathbf{f}^2(c')$ is presented to the system. Assume $c' = c$. If

$$\lambda_0 \mathbf{p}^1(c) \cdot \mathbf{f}^2(c) > 1 \tag{12}$$

then H_c will fire and the pattern will be correctly classified. Thus no change occurs. If

$$\lambda_0 \mathbf{p}^1(c) \cdot \mathbf{f}^2(c) < 1 \tag{13}$$

then $\mathbf{f}^2(c)$ will be committed to a new G cell [prototype $\mathbf{P}^2(c)$] and the synapse between this G cell and H_c will be set equal to 1. In this way, a class can be characterized by more than one prototype.

Consider the situation in which $c' \neq c$. Whether or not the existing prototype cell fires past threshold, there will be no active H cells of the class of $\mathbf{f}^2$. The subsequent T signal causes a new prototype cell to be committed to $\mathbf{f}^2$, along with the setting of the synaptic connection between this G cell and a new H cell. If, in addition,

$$\lambda_0 \mathbf{p}^1(c) \cdot \mathbf{f}^2(c') > 1 \tag{14}$$

then λ_0 is reduced to λ_1 such that

$$\lambda_1 \mathbf{p}^1(c) \cdot \mathbf{f}^2(c') = 1. \tag{15}$$

As the system learns, the λ factors associated with any active incorrect class prototypes will be reduced, leaving only the correct H cell to respond to the pattern.

The strategy of this network learning scheme is made clearer by considering the problem geometrically. The size of the influence region of a prototype cell is directly proportional to the magnitude, λ, of the prototype. Class territories in the space of events are defined by covering them with the overlapping influence fields of a set of prototypes drawn from class samples. Should the influence region of a given prototype extend into the territory of some differing class to the point of incorrectly classifying or confusing a member of that class, the λ factor of the prototype is reduced until its region of influence just excludes the disputed pattern. Prototype modification only decreases λ factors. Influence fields of existing prototype

cells are never enlarged in an effort to include (classify) an event, since for many of these elements, even slightly larger regions of influence have previously resulted in incorrect identifications. Consequently, a pattern that is excluded from the influence regions of all existing prototypes for its class is an occasion for commitment of a new G cell, with the pattern assuming the role of the new prototype.

Note that the prototype cells in memory are completely decoupled in that there are no mutual inhibitory or excitatory interactions among them. In the network's classification response, there is no vote counting among prototypes. The activity of a single prototype cell counts as heavily as the possibly concerted activity of a set of prototype cells, all specific to some other class.

This model was tested in computer simulations using a design set of input patterns. The patterns were vectors randomly generated in a normalized three dimensional pattern space. Samples were constrained to lie on the top half of a unit sphere ($z > 0$) and represented two classes of patterns labelled A and B. In one arrangement the A region was chosen as a spherical cap centered on the z axis and ringed by the B region, a surrounding band on the sphere's surface. The projection of this design is a pair of concentric circles on the $x - y$ plane. A second geometry pictured the A and B regions as separated by a sinusoidal boundary on the sphere's surface.

Patterns arrived in cycles (trials). A trial consisted in presentation of 200 novel A vectors and 200 novel B vectors, randomly distributed with respect to class. After some number of trials, the distribution of prototypes was graphed together with the effective boundaries between the A and B classes. In this space these boundaries are paths along a spherical surface. They are displayed by graphing projections on the $x - y$ plane.

The graphs in Figs. 2–4 illustrate the performance of the model in resolving class boundaries for the two different geometries. In Fig. 2, the class regions were separated by a gap, i.e., an area of pattern space containing no input patterns. When the angular width of this gap is less than $(\lambda_0)^{-1}$, there can develop prototypes for each class which have influence regions extending right up to the boundary with the other class. Consequently the gap is claimed for both pattern categories. Should a pattern from this region be selected as an input, its contested status (response confusion by the model) would cause the influence region of one or the other class to withdraw from a portion of the gap.

Note that in practice, the model need not develop a single decision surface separating pattern classes. In Figs. 3 and 4, there is no gap between the hypothetical

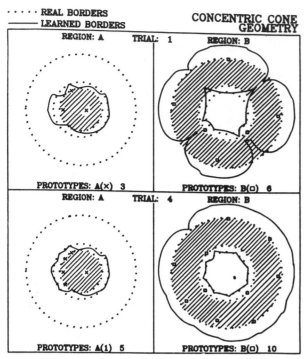

Fig. 2. Prototype regions for the concentric cone geometry with a gap. Region A: shaded area within innermost (first) dotted circle. Region B: shaded annulus defined by second and third dotted circles. Projections of prototype vectors on sphere's surface are plotted as crosses (A) and squares (B). Pictured are graphs of prototype boundaries (solid lines) as they appear after the first and fourth trials. Total numbers of prototypes are given below each graph

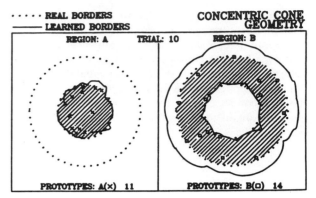

Fig. 3. Prototype regions for concentric cone geometry with no gap. Region A: shaded area within innermost (first) dotted circle. Region B: shaded annulus bounded by first ans second dotted circles. Prototype boundaries (solid lines) pictured after 10 trials

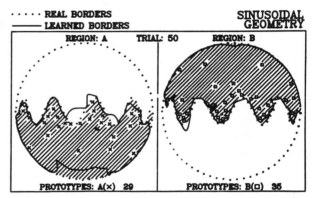

Fig. 4. Prototype regions for sinusoidally separated pattern zones. Region A: bottom scalloped semicircle (shaded area within dotted lines). Region B: upper scalloped semicircle (shaded area within dotted lines). Prototype boundaries (solid lines) pictured after 50 trials

category regions. A single border separates them, yet in the model, this border is approximated by a double line. If either the prototype or the classification cells were coupled by some mutual interaction (e.g., inhibition), this double border could, in places, be replaced by a single boundary. The nature of such a line would be a function of the specific form of the interaction. Excepting such coupling, it is only in the limit of studying a very large number of design samples that the double line category borders could be expected to merge into a single curve lying along the actual class boundary. The response to any input located in an area where the double lines extend beyond each other will be confusion. Patterns falling in regions from which both prototype generated boundaries have retreated will be identified with neither pattern class.

In the case of prototypes committed to inputs near a class border, the initially large influence regions can result in many incorrect or confused responses until the magnitude of the prototype is appropriately scaled. This creates a somewhat unstable learning process which does not converge smoothly to the final pattern

region mapping[1]. Nonetheless, it is clear that this model can resolve pattern classes of arbitrary complexity.

IV. Possible Neural Realization

It is likely that category learning is conducted in different areas of the brain by a variety of.cell assemblies. Indeed, one can imagine a number of specific networks of neurons that could implement the important features of our model. We consider a possible

---

1 There are a variety of means of improving this. For example, the magnitude of the initial λ_0 may decrease in time so that prototypes committed late in the process leave smaller initial regions of influence. Alternatively, each new prototype may be automatically tested against each existing prototype (treated as an incoming pattern)

neural substrate whose function could relate to one aspect of prototype development in the model.

It has been calculated that under certain conditions, activity in inhibitory fibers whose synapses are located on or near the cell body can have a divisive effect on the somatic membrane potential (Blomfield, 1974). Inhibitory current across these synapses is postulated to increase membrane conductance, thus shunting off a fraction of the summed post-synaptic potential arriving at the cell from its dendrites. The result is to scale the cell output by some multiplicative factor. Inhibitory synapses occurring amidst the excitatory ones further out along the dendritic spines and shafts would have their normal subtractive effect on cell firing rate. Divisive or shunting inhibition has also been considered elsewhere (Poggio, 1981; Kogh et al., 1982).

Cells have been found in different areas of the brain with significant numbers of synapses on or near the perikaryon that are predominantly characterized by flat vesicles and/or symmetric membrane differentiation (e.g., Davis et al., 1979; White et al., 1980). Such morphology is widely considered to be indicative of inhibitory function. By contrast, synapses located on the dendritic shafts and spines of such cells are both excitatory and inhibitory. This anatomy is consistent with that assumed for divisive inhibition. Indeed, other investigators have observed scaling of cell response as a function of inhibitory transmitter released into the soma (Rose, 1977) and under certain conditions of visual stimulus presentation (Dean et al., 1980).

Divisive inhibition is a candidate mechanism for implementing the λ factor scaling of prototype cell response assumed in the prototype learning model. There its principal effect is to provide for a modifiable cell threshold. The distinction which the model makes between prototype commitment and changes in λ is in the same spirit as the functional distinction which Blomfield's model suggests for synapses. The initial commitment of a prototype might involve changes in the spiny synapses and those in general distal to the soma. Such modification could occur according to any of a number of schemes previously suggested (e.g., correlation learning). Cell tuning, on the other hand, would be controlled largely by adjustments to inhibitory synapses proximal to the soma. Long term changes in somatic membrane conductance might even result from very different inhibitory effects (e.g., chemical deposition within the cell body due to active inhibitory afferents).

The processes of modification to sites distal and proximal to the soma might be mutually interactive in a number of ways. For example, one can imagine the somatic membrane conductance of a cell increased to such a point that the cell rarely fires. (In the model,

such was the case for a cell committed to a prototype near a class boundary). Lack of post-synaptic response in conjunction with pre-synaptic activity might cause, as some have suggested (Cooper et al., 1979), the distal synapses of such a cell to lose the information of the stored prototype. This could free the cell to become committed to a new preferred pattern. At the same time, distal modification could be an ongoing process which performs some type of averaging over those inputs able to cause cell firing (the Hebbian requirement). If the environment presented a sequence of smoothly varying events of sufficient duration, the distal modification might cause the cell to "follow" the inputs. In this way, the preferred pattern of the cell could change with only a minimum of change in the degree of cell tuning.

V. Conclusion

Category learning plays an important role in a broad range of mental activity, from learning sequences of task oriented sensori-motor controls to very complex problems in conceptualization. As such it is probably implemented in different ways by different cell assemblies throughout the brain. A successful model for category learning should be consistent with the general features of this host of sub-networks and with their perhaps locally unique architectures. We have presented one such model with properties thought to be characteristic of the neural system as a whole. Among these are: coding of information by neuron firing rates, synaptic transmission of information from cell to cell, excitatory and inhibitory interactions among cells, distributed memory stored over the entire set of synaptic junctions and initially unspecified cell interconnections that are modified by the history of the system's experiences. This model suggests that it is possible to construct plausible neuron networks that incorporate these features and that can display a powerful ability to learn to identify and distinguish categories of events. In a separate publication we will report on the application of this and a related model to a practical problem in categorization (Reilly et al., 1982). The model learning systems were trained to classify examples of unconstrained handwritten numerals. By detecting only very simple information about patterns, the system achieved a high degree of accuracy (approximately 98%) in tests against patterns not viewed during training.

Acknowledgements. We would like to express our appreciation to our colleagues at the Brown University Center for Neural Science for their interest and helpful advice. In particular, we thank Messrs. Paul Munro, Michael Paradiso and Christopher Scofield for several useful discussions.

References

Amari, S.I.: Neural theory of association and concept-formation. Biol. Cybern. **26**, 175–185 (1977)

Anderson, J.A.: Two models for memory organization using interacting traces. Math. Biosci. **8**, 137–160 (1970)

Anderson, J.A.: A simple neural network generating an interactive memory. Math. Biosci. **14**, 197–220 (1972)

Anderson, J.A., Cooper, L.N.: Les modeles mathematiques de l'organization biologique de la memoire. Pluriscience 168–175. Encyclopaedia Universalis, Paris (1978)

Barto, A.G., Sutton, R.S., Brouwer, P.S.: Associative search network: a reinforcement learning associative memory. Biol. Cybern. **40**, 201–211 (1981)

Blomfield, S.: Arithmetical operations performed by nerve cells. Brain Res. **69**, 115–124 (1974)

Bobrowski, L.: Rules for forming receptive fields of formal neurons during unsupervised learning processes. Biol. Cybern. **43**, 23–28 (1982)

Brooks, L.: Non-analytical concept formation and memory for instances. In: Cognition and categorization, pp. 169–211, Rosch, E., Lloyd, B. (eds.). Hillsdale, N.J.: Lawrence Erlbaum Associates 1978

Cooper, L.N.: A possible organization of animal memory and learning. In: Proceedings of the nobel Symposium on collective properties of physical systems, Vol. 24, pp. 252–264, Lundquist, B., Lundquist, S. (eds.). London, New York: Academic Press 1973

Cooper, L.N., Liberman, F., Oja, E.: A theory for the acquisition and loss of neuron specificity in visual cortex. Biol. Cybern. **33**, 9–28 (1979)

Cover, T.M., Hart, P.E.: Nearest neighbor pattern classification. IEEE Trans. Inform. Theor. **13**, 21–27 (1967)

Davis, T.L., Sterling, P.: Microcircuitry of cat visual cortex: classification of neurons in layer IV of area 17, and identification of the patterns of lateral geniculate input. J. Comp. Neur. **188**, 599–628 (1979)

Dean, A.F., Hess, R.F., Tolhurst, D.J.: Divisive inhibition involved in directional selectivity. J. Physiol. **308**, 84p–85p (1980)

Duda, R.O., Hart, P.E.: Pattern classification and scene analysis. New York: Wiley 1973

Franks, J.J., Bransford, J.D.: Abstraction of visual patterns. J. Exp. Psychol. **90**, 65–74 (1971)

Grossberg, S.: Adaptive pattern classification and universal recoding. II. Feedback, expectation, olfaction, illusions. Biol. Cybern. **23**, 187–202 (1976)

Kogh, C., Poggio, T., Torre, V.: Retino-ganglion cells: a functional interpretation of dendritic morphology. Philos. Trans. R. Soc. (to be published)

Kohonen, T.: Correlation matrix memories. IEEE Trans. Comput. **21**, 353–359 (1972)

Kohonen, T.: Associative memory – a system-theoretical approach. Berlin, Heidelberg, New York: Springer 1977

Medin, D.L., Schaffer, M.M.: Context theory of classification learning. Psychol. Rev. **85**, 207–238 (1978)

Nass, M.M., Cooper, L.N.: A theory for the development of feature detecting cells in visual cortex. Biol. Cybern. **19**, 1–18 (1975)

Poggio, T.: A theory of synaptic interactions. In: Theoretical approaches in neurobiology, pp. 28–38, Reichardt, W., Poggio, T. (eds.). London: MIT Press 1981

Posner, M.I., Keele, S.W.: On the genesis of abstract ideas. J. Exp. Psychol. **77**, 353–363 (1968)

Posner, M.I., Keele, S.W.: Retention of abstract ideas. J. Exp. Psychol. **83**, 304–308 (1970)

Reilly, D.L., Cooper, L.N., Elbaum, C.: An application of two learning systems to pattern recognition: handwritten characters (to be published)

Rose, D.: On the arithmetical operation performed by inhibitory synapses onto the neuronal soma. Exp. Brain Res. **28**, 221–223 (1977)

White, E.L., Rock, M.P.: Three-dimensional aspects and synaptic relationships of a Golgi-impregnated spiny stellate cell reconstructed from serial thin sections. J. Neurocytol. **9**, 615–636 (1980)

Received: March 12, 1982

Dr. D.L. Reilly
Center for Neural Science and
Department of Physics
Brown University
Providence, RI 02912
USA

29
Introduction

(1987)
Charles M. Bachmann, Leon N. Cooper, Amir Dembo, and Ofer Zeitouni

A relaxation model for memory with high storage density
Proceedings of the National Academy of Sciences 84: 7529–7531

This short paper contains an ingenious combination of two major streams of neural network research. A large class of neural network models contains a system *energy* function, and the dynamics of the network can be shown to minimize system energy. The state of the system evolves with time, and the system state vector eventually stabilizes in a local minimum that contains the results of the system computation.

Leon Cooper was one of the coauthors of the previous paper in this volume which proposed a way of using a simple neural network as a pattern classifier by letting neurons adaptively "tune" themselves to learned inputs, producing a model closely related to a nearest neighbor classifier (paper 28). Such a system is a pattern classifier that simply produces a classification at the output. Sometimes it is valuable to be able to use an energy-minimizing system with internal dynamics to do other kinds of computations that are beyond the scope of a pattern classifier, such as association or the reconstruction of missing information.

To use an energy-minimizing system, it is necessary to construct an energy surface that has minima in the right places. In many models this is done with a learning procedure, usually Hebbian in some form, so that local energy minima will fall on or near learned system states. However, such systems almost always have as well a number of other local minima that were not explicitly learned. One can either view these additional, unlearned states as spurious or as creative, depending on whether the aim of the system is literal reconstruction of an input or a more complex kind of inferential process. (Those with interests in cognitive science usually prefer the latter; engineering applications often require the former—part of the continuing conflict between literalness and flights of fancy.)

The authors of this paper suggest a way of deliberately constructing an energy surface that has a controllable number of minima that can be placed exactly where desired. The model they use is that of electric charges of varying strength placed at various locations in state space. Energy minima can be shown to occur only at the locations of the charges, thereby controlling the possible output states of the system. Charges can also be placed close together, producing a high storage capacity in terms of discrete output states. Determination of the shapes of the basins of attraction of each local minimum can be quite complex, however, and if there are many minima, the basins are liable to be correspondingly small.

This storage process is very similar to a pattern recognition technique called a *potential function classifier*. Potential function classifiers were studied at length by Russian workers in the 1960s (see references in Batchelor, paper 27). Their idea also was to place charges in state space. If multiple examples of a category are stored, there is a complex summed electric potential corresponding to a particular classification. If the classification of a particular point is requested, then the potentials for each category are determined, and the largest potential gives the classification.

Because these are not physical charges, a number of variant potential functions have been investigated, often with advantages for particular problems. One problem with storage of simple electric charges, for example, is that there is an infinitely deep energy minimum exactly at the charge location, which can sometimes cause computational difficulties. There also exists a series of closely related pattern recognition techniques that basically store blurry representations of particular examples. Addition of effects from various learned examples allows estimation of the underlying probability distributions of the data, for example, in Parzen windows (Sklansky and Wassel 1981).

The authors of this short paper have combined the idea of a potential function classifier with the notion of energy minimization, allowing the system dynamics to reconstruct previously stored information.

Reference

J. Sklansky and G.N. Wassel (1981), *Pattern Classifiers and Trainable Machines*. New York: Springer.

(1987)

Charles M. Bachmann, Leon N. Cooper, Amir Dembo, and Ofer Zeitouni

A relaxation model for memory with high storage density
Proceedings of the National Academy of Sciences 84: 7529–7531

ABSTRACT   We present a relaxation model for memory based on a generalized coulomb potential. The model has arbitrarily large storage capacity and, in addition, well-defined basins of attraction about stored memory states. The model is compared with the Hopfield relaxation model.

Equilibrium associative and distributed memories that are content addressable and can recall stored memories more or less imperfectly have been known and studied for years (1–5). Concomitantly, relaxation models have been the subject of much exploration (6). In 1982, Hopfield (7) introduced a relaxation model of memory storage and retrieval that incorporates simultaneously a distributed memory correlation matrix and a relaxation process from a given input to an equilibrium state. Although learning procedures can be included, the model has not emphasized these. Among the problems of this model are poor recall of stored memories when the number of stored items exceeds some percentage of the number of involved neurons.

The correlation matrix originally employed by Hopfield has relatively weak recall properties when employed as an equilibrium distributed memory; it gives perfect recall only when the inputs are orthogonal. When the inputs are not orthogonal, one can still achieve perfect recall by some orthogonal modification procedure such as Widrow–Hoff (8), or what Kohonen calls an *optimal associative mapping* (9). Such procedures work if the number of stored memories is equal to or smaller than the dimension of the system (the number of input synapses on each neuron). A procedure for storing as many memories as desired for a given dimension has also been discussed (10). In this procedure items can be stored at arbitrary points with variable regions of influence on a hypersphere.

In this paper we present a general method for the construction of a relaxation memory in which an arbitrary number of items can be stored. The essence of the problem is to define a function whose minima lie at designated points, corresponding to the items to be stored, and to show that these are the only minima of the function. Then an appropriate relaxation procedure is defined, so that any entering pattern relaxes to one of the stored items.

Hopfield's Model and Some Improvements

In the Hopfield model (7), neurons are binary-valued threshold units and are completely interconnected, with the strength of the connections given by a correlation matrix formed from the memory states to be stored in the system:

$$w_{ij} = \sum_{s=1}^{m} \mu_i^s \mu_j^s, \qquad [1]$$

where $\mu_i = \pm 1$ and w_{ij} represents the connection strength between μ_i and μ_j. Input states are relaxed to local minima of a Liapunov function,

$$\xi = -\frac{1}{2} \sum_{i,j} w_{ij} \mu_i \mu_j \qquad [2]$$

by random, asynchronous updating of the neurons in the layer according to:

$$\mu_i \rightarrow 2\theta \left(\sum_{j=1}^{N} w_{ij} \mu_j \right) - 1. \qquad [3]$$

In its original form, the Hopfield model functions poorly as a categorizer when $(m/N) \lesssim 0.1$, where m = the number of stored states and N = the number of neurons. Given the limitations of the original model, improvements have been sought. "Unlearning," an approach first tried by Hopfield *et al.* (11), employs the relaxation of random states to a stable state (often spurious attractors); a correlation matrix is formed from the relaxed state, and then an amount proportional to this is subtracted from the original matrix:

$$w_{ij} \rightarrow w_{ij} - \alpha\mu_i^{\text{relaxed}}\, \mu_j^{\text{relaxed}} \qquad [4]$$

With "unlearning," the number of stored states that can be correctly recalled approaches N and error correction is improved, but falls to zero as $m \rightarrow N$ (12).

Recently, an interesting variation of Hopfield's unlearning has been studied by Potter (12). The algorithm is a hybrid combining elements of Hopfield's unlearning with a modification reminiscent of the Widrow–Hoff algorithm (8):

$$w_{ij} \rightarrow w_{ij} - \alpha(\mu_i^{\text{target}} - \mu_i^{\text{relaxed}})\mu_j^{\text{input}}(\mu_j^{\text{input}} + 1). \qquad [5]$$

The symmetry of the synaptic matrix is preserved by making the same modification to w_{ji} each time a modification is performed on the element w_{ij}. In simulations for which all of the input states at a radius of one Hamming unit from each stored state were used for the modification procedure, a radius of attraction of one Hamming unit was observed for m just below N. Above N, the radius of attraction and the percentage of stable stored states decreases. In ref. 13, it has been shown that Potter's algorithm may be viewed as an "*effective orthogonalization*" of the input with respect to the nonlinear relaxation process; a more complete discussion of Potter's algorithm is given there.

High-Density Storage Model

In what follows we present a general method for the construction of a high storage-density neural memory. We define a function with an arbitrary number of minima that lie at preassigned points and define an appropriate relaxation procedure.

Let $\vec{x}^1, \ldots, \vec{x}^m$ be a set of m arbitrary distinct memories in R^N. The "energy" function we will use is:

$$\xi = -\frac{1}{L} \sum_{i=1}^{m} Q_i |\vec{\mu} - \vec{x}^i|^{-L} \qquad [6]$$

where we assume throughout that $N \geq 3$, $L \geq (N - 2)$, and $Q_i > 0$ and use $| \cdots |$ to denote the Euclidean distance. Note that for $L = 1$, $N = 3$, ξ is the electrostatic potential induced by fixed particles with charges $-Q_i$. If $Q_i > 0$, this energy function possesses global minima at $\vec{x}^1, \ldots, \vec{x}^m$ (where $\xi(\vec{x}^i) = -\infty$) and has no local minima except at these points. A rigorous proof is presented in Dembo and Zeitouni (14) together with the complete characterization of functions having this property.

As a relaxation procedure, we can choose any dynamical system for which ξ is strictly decreasing. In this instance, the theory of dynamical systems guarantees that for almost any initial data, the trajectory of the system converges to one of the desired points $\vec{x}^1, \ldots, \vec{x}^m$. However, to give concrete results and to further exploit the resemblance to electrostatics, consider the relaxation:

$$\dot{\vec{\mu}} = \vec{E}_{\vec{\mu}} \triangleq -\sum_{i=1}^m Q_i |\vec{\mu} - \vec{x}^i|^{-(L+2)} (\vec{\mu} - \vec{x}^i) \qquad [7]$$

where for $N = 3$, $L = 1$, Eq. 7 describes the motion of a positive test particle in the electrostatic field $\vec{E}_{\vec{\mu}}$ generated by the negative fixed charges $-Q_1, \ldots, -Q_m$ at $\vec{x}^1, \ldots, \vec{x}^m$.

Because the field $\vec{E}_{\vec{\mu}}$ is just minus the gradient of ξ, it is clear that along trajectories of Eq. 7, $d\xi/dt \leq 0$, with equality only at the fixed points of Eq. 7, which are exactly the stationary points of ξ.

Therefore, using Eq. 7 as the relaxation procedure, we can conclude that entering at any $\vec{\mu}(0)$, the system converges to a stationary point of ξ. The space of inputs is partitioned into m domains of attraction, each one corresponding to a different memory, and the boundaries (a set of measure zero), on which $\vec{\mu}(0)$ will converge to a saddle point of ξ.

We can now explain why $\xi_{\vec{\mu}}$ has no spurious local minima, at least for $L = 1$, $N = 3$, using elementary physical arguments. Suppose ξ has a spurious local minimum at $\vec{y} \neq \vec{x}^1, \ldots, \vec{x}^m$, then in a small neighborhood of $\vec{y}$ that does not include any of the $\vec{x}^i$, the field $\vec{E}_{\vec{\mu}}$ points towards $\vec{y}$. Thus, on any closed surface in that neighborhood, the integral of the normal inward component of $\vec{E}_{\vec{\mu}}$ is positive. However, this integral is just the total charge included inside the surface, *which is zero*. Thus we arrive at a contradiction, so $\vec{y}$ cannot be a local minimum.

We now have a relaxation procedure, such that almost any $\vec{\mu}(0)$ is attracted by one of the $\vec{x}^i$, but we have not yet specified the shapes of the basins of attraction. By varying the charges Q_i, we can enlarge one basin of attraction at the expense of the others (and vice versa).

Even when all of the Q_i are equal, the position of the $\vec{x}^i$ might cause $\vec{\mu}(0)$ not to converge to the closest memory, as emphasized in the example in Fig. 1. However, let $r = \min_{1 \leq i \neq j \leq m} |\vec{x}^i - \vec{x}^j|$ be the minimal distance between any two memories; then, if $|\vec{\mu}(0) - \vec{x}^i| \leq r/(1 + 3^{1/k})$, it can be shown that $\vec{\mu}(0)$ will converge to $\vec{x}^i$, provided that $k \triangleq (L + 1)/(N + 1) \geq 1$. Thus, if the memories are densely packed in a hypersphere, by choosing k large enough (i.e., enlarging the parameter L), convergence to the closest memory for any "interesting" input, that is an input $\vec{\mu}(0)$ with a distinctive closest memory, is guaranteed.

The detailed proof of the above property is given in ref. 14. It is based on bounding the number of $\vec{x}^j$, $j \neq i$, in a hypersphere of radius R ($R \geq r$) around $\vec{x}^i$, by $[2(R/r) + 1]^N$, then bounding the magnitude of the field induced by any $\vec{x}^j$, $j \neq i$, on the boundary of such a hypersphere by $(R - |\vec{\mu}(0) - \vec{x}^i|)^{-(L+1)}$, and finally integrating to show that for $|\vec{\mu}(0) - \vec{x}^i| \leq \theta r/(1 + 3^{1/k})$, with $\theta < 1$, the convergence of $\vec{\mu}(0)$ to $\vec{x}^i$ is within finite time T, which behaves like θ^{L+2} for $L >> 1$ and $\theta < 1$ (fixed). Intuitively the reason for this behavior is the short-range nature of the fields used in Eq. 7. Because of this, we also expect extremely low convergence rate for inputs $\vec{\mu}(0)$ far away from *all* of the $\vec{x}^i$.

The radial nature of these fields suggests a way to overcome this difficulty, that is to increase the convergence rate

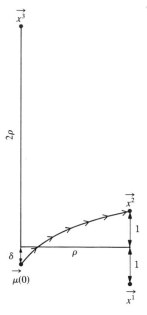

FIG. 1. Model of memory convergence when $\vec{\mu}(0)$ is closer to $\vec{x}^1$ but converges to $\vec{x}^2$, due to the existence of $\vec{x}^3$ (assuming arbitrary distance $\rho >> 1$ and arbitrary distance $\delta << 1$). $\vec{\mu}(0)$ is the input state; $\vec{x}^1$, $\vec{x}^2$, and $\vec{x}^3$ are stored memories.

from points very far away without disturbing all of the aforementioned desirable properties of the model. Assume that we know in advance that all of the $\vec{x}^i$ lie inside some large hypersphere S around the origin. Then, at any point $\vec{\mu}$ outside S, the field $\vec{E}_{\vec{\mu}}$ has a positive projection radially into S. By adding a long-range force to $\vec{E}_{\vec{\mu}}$, effective only outside of S, we can hasten the movement towards S, from points far away, without creating additional minima inside of S. As an example the force ($-\vec{\mu}$ for $\vec{\mu} \notin S$; 0 for $\vec{\mu} \in S$) will pull any test input $\vec{\mu}(0)$ to the boundary of S within the small finite time $T \approx 1/|S|$, and from then on the system will behave inside S according to the original field $\vec{E}_{\vec{\mu}}$.

Up to this point, our derivations have been for a continuous system, but from it, we can deduce a discrete system. We shall do this mainly for a clearer comparison between our high-density memory model and the discrete version of Hopfield's model. Before continuing in that direction, note that our continuous system has *unlimited storage capacity* unlike Hopfield's continuous system (15), which, like his discrete model, has limited capacity.

For the discrete system, assume that the $\vec{x}^i$ are composed of elements ± 1 and replace the Euclidean distance in Eq. 6 with the normalized Hamming distance $|\vec{\mu}^1 - \vec{\mu}^2| \triangleq (1/N)\sum_{j=1}^N |\mu_j^1 - \mu_j^2|$. This places the vectors $\vec{x}^i$ on the unit hypersphere.

The relaxation process for the discrete system will be of the type defined in Hopfield's model in Eq. 3. Choose at random a component to be updated (that is, a neighbor $\vec{\mu}'$ of $\vec{\mu}$ such that $|\vec{\mu}' - \vec{\mu}| = 2/N$), calculate the "energy" difference, $\delta\xi = \xi(\vec{\mu}') - \xi(\vec{\mu})$, and only if $\delta\xi < 0$, change this component, that is:

$$\mu_i \rightarrow \mu_i \cdot \theta[\xi(\vec{\mu}') - \xi(\vec{\mu})], \qquad [8]$$

where $\xi(\vec{\mu})$ is the potential energy in Eq. 6 and i is the component to be updated. Because there is a finite number of possible $\vec{\mu}$ vectors (2^N), convergence in finite time is guaranteed.

This relaxation procedure is rigid because the movement is limited to points with components ± 1. Therefore, although the local minima of $\xi(\vec{\mu})$ defined in Eq. **6** are only at the desired points $\vec{x}^i$, the relaxation may get stuck at some $\vec{\mu}$ which is not a stationary point of $\xi(\vec{\mu})$. However, the short-range behavior of the potential $\xi(\vec{\mu})$, unlike the long-range behavior of the quadratic potential used by Hopfield (Eq. **2**), gives rise to results similar to those we have quoted for the continuous model (Eq. **7**).

Specifically, let the stored memories $\vec{x}^1, \ldots, \vec{x}^m$ be separated from one another by having at least ρN different components ($0 < \rho \leq 1/2$ and ρ fixed), and let $\vec{\mu}(0)$ agree with at least one $\vec{x}^i$ with at most $\theta \rho N$ errors between them ($0 \leq \theta < 1/2$, with θ fixed), then $\vec{\mu}(0)$ converges monotonically to that $\vec{x}^i$ by the relaxation procedure given in Eq. **8**.

This result holds independently of m, provided that N is large enough (typically, $N \rho \ln[(1 - \theta)/\theta] \geq 1$) and L is chosen so that $N/L \leq \ln[(1 - \theta)/\theta]$. The proof is constructed by bounding the cumulative effect of terms $|\vec{\mu} - \vec{x}^j|^{-L}, j \neq i$, to the energy difference $\delta \xi$ and showing that it is dominated by $|\vec{\mu} - \vec{x}^i|^{-L}$. For details, we refer the reader again to ref. 14.

Note the importance of this property: unlike the Hopfield model that is limited to $m \leq N$, the suggested system is optimal in the sense of information theory, because for every set of memories $\vec{x}^1, \ldots, \vec{x}^m$ separated from each other by a Hamming distance ρN, up to $(1/2)\rho N$ errors in the input can be corrected, provided that N is large and L properly chosen.

As for the complexity of the system, we note that the nonlinear operation a^{-L}, for $a > 0$ and L integer (which is at the heart of our system computationally) is equivalent to $e^{-L\ln(a)}$ and can be implemented, therefore, by a simple electrical circuit composed of diodes, which have exponential input–output characteristics, and resistors, which can carry out the necessary multiplications.

Further, since both $|\vec{x}^i|$ and $|\vec{\mu}|$ are held fixed in the discrete system, where all states are on the unit hypersphere, $|\vec{\mu} - \vec{x}^i|^2$ is equivalent to the inner product of $\vec{\mu}$ and $\vec{x}^i$, up to a constant. A detailed implementation can be found in ref. 14.

To conclude, the suggested model involves about $m \cdot N$ multiplications followed by m nonlinear operations and then $m \cdot N$ additions. The original model of Hopfield involves N^2 multiplications and additions and then N nonlinear operations *but is limited to* $m \leq N$. Therefore, whenever the Hopfield model is applicable, the complexity of both models is comparable.

This work was supported by Office of Navy Research Contracts N00014-86-K0041 and N00014-85-K-0607, Army Research Office Contracts DAAG-29-84-K-0262 and DAAG29-84-K-0082, and the Weizmann Postdoctoral Fellowship (A.D. and O.Z.).

1. Anderson, J. A. (1970) *Math. Biosci.* **8**, 137–160.
2. Anderson, J. A. (1972) *Math. Biosci.* **4**, 197–220.
3. Cooper, L. N. (1974) in *Proceedings of the Nobel Symposium on Collective Properties of Physical Systems*, eds. Lindquist, B. & Lindquist, S. (Academic, New York), pp. 252–264.
4. Kohonen, T. (1972) *IEEE Trans. Comput.* C **21**, 353–359.
5. Kohonen, T. (1977) *Associative Memory: A System Theoretic Approach* (Springer, Berlin).
6. Metropolis, N., Rosenbluth, A. W., Rosenbluth, M. N., Teller, A. H. & Teller, E. (1953) *J. Chem. Phys.* **21**, 1087–1092.
7. Hopfield, J. J. (1982) *Proc. Natl. Acad. Sci. USA* **79**, 2554–2558.
8. Widrow, G. & Hoff, M. E. (1960) in *Institute of Radio Engineers, Western Electronic Show and Convention, Wescon Convention Record* (Institute of Radio Engineers, New York), Vol. 4, Part 4, pp. 96–104.
9. Kohonen, T. (1984) *Self-Organization and Associative Memory* (Springer, Berlin), pp. 172–174.
10. Reilly, D. E., Cooper, L. N. & Elbaum, C. (1982) *Biol. Cybern.* **45**, 35–41.
11. Hopfield, J. J., Feinstein, D. I. & Palmer, R. G. (1983) *Nature (London)* **304**, 158–159.
12. Potter, T. W. (1987) Dissertation (State University of New York, Binghamton).
13. Bachmann, C. M. (1986) *ARO Technical Report* (Brown University Center for Neural Science, Providence, RI).
14. Dembo, A. & Zeitouni, O. (1987) *ARO Technical Report* (Brown University Center for Neural Science, Providence, RI).
15. Hopfield, J. J. (1984) *Proc. Natl. Acad. Sci. USA* **81**, 3088–3092.

Correction. In the article "A relaxation model for memory with high storage density" by Charles M. Bachmann, Leon N Cooper, Amir Dembo, and Ofer Zeitouni, which appeared in number 21, November 1987, of *Proc. Natl. Acad. Sci. USA* (**84**, 7529–7531), the authors request that the following correction be noted. The acknowledgments should read as follows: This work was supported by Office of Naval Research Contracts N00014-86-K0041 and N00014-85-K-0607, Army Research Contracts DAAG29-84-K-0202 and DAAG-29-84-K-0082, and the Weizmann Postdoctoral Fellowship (A.D. and O.Z.).

(1988)
Teuvo Kohonen, György Barna, and Ronald Chrisley

Statistical pattern recognition with neural networks: benchmarking studies
Proceedings of the IEEE International Conference on Neural Networks, San Diego, 1988,
pp. I-61 – I-68

When someone buys a new car or a new computer, or develops a new algorithm, the first thing the proud owner wants to do is to see how well it works and compare it with the (inferior) equipment owned by friends. Informal benchmarks are a way of life.

However, meaningful comparison studies of neural network algorithm performance are uncommon. This paper by Kohonen, Barna, and Chrisley is careful in the way it compares several popular algorithms. Although Kohonen and his coworkers are neural network pioneers, they also have extensive experience with traditional pattern recognition and statistics.

Let us assume we are testing classification algorithms, where we want to know in which of several categories input data belong. Pattern classification is the most common application of neural networks at this time. If the different categories are well separated, and if there is relatively little noise, then many algorithms will work well and performance criteria such as learning speed, reliability, and convenience may become critical.

Suppose, however, there is a large amount of noise present, enough noise so that the distributions of possible examples can actually overlap. That is, a particular input pattern could belong to *either* one category *or* to another category. This situation often occurs in practice. What is usually done is to try to estimate in which category a particular example is most *likely* to be. That is, if the chance that a particular example is a member of category *A* is 99 percent and of category *B* is 1 percent, then it is almost certainly a member of category *A*.

However, to apply these statistical techniques, it is necessary to know the underlying probability distribution of the categories. If we knew *everything* about the category probabilities, we could make the best decisions, and such a system would be an *ideal Bayes classifier*. Unfortunately we almost never have this knowledge, and we must estimate probabilities based on what we observe, which will always contain errors when estimating the category probabilities. One of the practical strengths of neural networks seems to be that for many problems they can make useful estimates of category structure based on relatively few observations.

Along with the benchmarks, this paper also briefly describes a pair of nearest neighbor algorithms, developed by Kohonen, that have received attention because of their good performance, their simplicity, and their firm theoretical basis. They are called LVQ and LVQ2, standing for the first and second version of the *learning vector quantizer.*

Nearest neighbor algorithms (see papers 25, 26, and 27) classify patterns by referring to previously classified examples. The classification of a new example is determined by giving it the classification of the nearest stored example. A major practical problem with nearest neighbor algorithms is the necessity to store a large number of examples. Many techniques have been developed to store only a small number of especially useful classified examples.

For example, in this collection Reilly, Elbaum, and Cooper (paper 28), stores examples with a radius around the example, so that new examples within the radius are not stored unless the system makes a mistake.

This paper's new classification models, LVQ and LVQ2, start with a fixed number of processing units, each of which stores a classified pattern. Several different units may store patterns with the same classification, which is important because that allows better approximation of odd distributions and multimodal categories. Initialization requires a "reasonable" set of initial categorizations, but this can be done in several ways. The strategy followed by both LVQ techniques will be to move this classified point around, that is, in a neural network context, to change the weights of the unit responding to this pattern, so that it can do the best statistical job of classifying new examples.

Let us consider LVQ, the first model. During training suppose an example, with a known classification, is to be learned. If the nearest neighbor to the example is classified the same way as the example, then the stored pattern will shifted slightly *toward* the example. If the nearest neighbor has the wrong classification, then the stored pattern is modified and shifted *away* from the incorrect example. The patterns stored in the units minimize the number of incorrect categorizations (because they moved away from them) and maximize the number of correct categorizations (because they moved toward them). Units will develop stored patterns that are good representatives of their categories because they are surrounded by points with the same classification, as well as being moved away from regions with other classifications.

The first benchmark test done by the authors was to set up a situation in which the categories overlapped. In one (easy) case the two categories had different means, so that the centers of the categories were separated in state space, though there was overlapping of examples at the edges. In the other (hard) case the two categories had exactly the same mean, but different variances. Individual examples of both categories are most likely to occur at the mean value. However, the categories can still be separated to some extent, because one category (with the small variance) is more likely to occur at the mean value than the other (with large variance), whereas the large variance case is more likely to occur far away from the category mean. This category structure is exceptionally hard for many algorithms to learn.

The most accurate algorithm in both hard and easy cases was the Boltzmann machine (paper 38 in *Neurocomputing: Foundations of Research*). Theoretically the Boltzmann machine, properly used, will find the true lowest-error solution for the system. However, the LVQ algorithm did significantly better overall than back propagation, the most popular neural network classification algorithm, for both the hard and easy cases (paper 41 in *Neurocomputing: Foundations of Research*). Also LVQ learning uses only a fraction of computer time used by back propagation or the Boltzmann machine.

LVQ2 is an ingenious modification of LVQ, based on the definition of an ideal Bayes classifier. Suppose we have two stored patterns, each with a different classification. Suppose an example falls on the line between the two stored patterns. The point on the line halfway between the examples will be the decision boundary between the two classifications: That is, on one side of the line, a point will have one classification, and on the other, it will have the other classification. We would like this decision boundary—where the two stored patterns are equally distant—to coincide with the point of equal probability of the two categories.

This geometry would mean that the classification given on each side of the decision boundary would be to the *most probable* classification.

We can accomplish this by moving both of the patterns in tandem *only* if a misclassification is made, instead of just modifying the nearest pattern as in LVQ. The most important misclassifications will be made in a region around the decision boundary. If a misclassification is made in this window—if the new pattern was closest to a wrong classification—we will modify *two* stored patterns—the nearest pattern with the correct pattern *and* the nearest pattern that was responsible for the incorrect classification. The modification to the patterns is made so that the stored pattern with the correct classification will be moved toward the example and the incorrect pattern will be moved away from the example. If one pattern is *more* probable than the other in the window, the most probable pattern will be misclassified most often, and the boundary will shift to the stable situation where the patterns are equally probable. If the two categories become equally probable in the window, the desired goal, then on the average the stored patterns will not move because they will move in one direction as often as in the other.

When tested with speech data, LVQ2 is very effective, slightly better than LVQ, and learns at about the same rate. Both algorithms are potentially very fast, and as the authors point out, LVQ has been implemented on an IBM PC/AT for a speech recognition system. These simple algorithms are much faster and simpler than back propagation. The authors also point out that LVQ is more stable than back propagation, in which undesirable behavior sometimes develops when the dimensionality of the system increases. The LVQ algorithms have been applied to several sets of speech data by others, with success, essentially duplicating the results of this paper (see McDermott and Katagiri 1989).

Other papers in this collection point out the direct connection between a nearest neighbor classifier and neural networks. Although the more powerful neural network algorithms, such as back propagation and the Boltzmann machine, have real virtues, for many practical classification problems there seems to be little doubt that simple models using nearest neighbor techniques may make good engineering sense. They are reliable, fast, and understandable—all substantial virtues—and can be realized in parallel with the same kinds of elementary computing units used by many more complex neural networks.

Reference

E. McDermott and S. Katagiri (1989), LVQ-based shift tolerant phoneme recognition. *ATR Technical Report TR-A-0059*, ATR Auditory and Visual Research Laboratories, Kyoto.

(1988)

Teuvo Kohonen, György Barna, and Ronald Chrisley

Statistical pattern recognition with neural networks: benchmarking studies
Proceedings of the IEEE International Conference on Neural Networks, San Diego, 1988,
pp. I-61 – I-68

Abstract

Successful recognition of natural signals, e.g., speech recognition, requires substantial statistical pattern recognition capabilities. This is at odds with the fact that the bulk of work on applying neural networks to pattern recognition has concentrated on non-statistical problems. Three basic types of neural-like networks (Backpropagation network, Boltzmann machine, and Learning Vector Quantization), were applied in this work to two representative artificial statistical pattern recognition tasks, each with varying dimensionality. The performance of each network's different approach to solving the tasks was evaluated and compared, both to the performance of the other two networks, and to the theoretical limit. The Learning Vector Quantization was further benchmarked against the parametric Bayes classifier and the k-nearest-neighbor classifier using natural speech data. A novel Learning Vector Quantization classifier (LVQ2) is introduced the first time in this work.

1. Introduction. – The "Bayes Machine"

Some of our colleagues have claimed that the biological neural networks, due to their inherent nonlinearities, mostly implement decision processes (cf., e.g., Hopfield, in press). Whatever the truth about their purpose, if we concentrate on this aspect with artificial neural networks, then evaluation of their decision-making accuracy ought to be based on standard **decision-theoretic analyses**. At least one might speculate that the simple least-square error criteria that are often used would perhaps be unsatisfactory with real statistical problems.

By and large the only generally valid statistical decision theory is based on the average cost or loss in misclassification, formulated in terms of the Bayes expressions for conditional probabilities (briefly called "Bayes classifier") (cf., e.g., Devijver and Kittler 1982, Kohonen 1988a, Patrick 1972). In standard pattern recognition theory, and obviously with most of the problems that occur in neural computing, too, it is reasonably accurate to assume the unit misclassification cost the same for all classes. Assume then that $x \in \mathbf{R}^n$ is the vector of input observables (pattern elements, set of attribute values, etc.), and $\{C_i, i=1,2,...,K\}$ is the set of classes (identities) to which x may belong. Let $p(x|C_i)$ be the probability density function of x in class C_i, and $P(C_i)$ the a priori probability of occurrence of samples from class C_i; in other words, $d_i(x) = p(x|C_i)P(C_i)$ corresponds to the "class distribution" of those samples of x which belong to class C_i. Here the $d_i(x)$, or any monotonically increasing functions of them like the logarithms, are also called **discriminant functions** (cf. section 7.1). The average rate of misclassifications is minimized if x is conclusively classified according to the following rule:

x is assigned to C_i iff $d_i(x) > d_j(x)$ for all $j \neq i$.

(See the one-dimensional case in Fig. 1.) The main problem, of course, is to obtain analytic expressions for the $d_i(x)$. Notice that even a large number of samples of x, as such, does not define any analytical probability density function. One has to use either *parametric methods*, e.g. by fitting the samples to parametrized Gaussian functions, or *nonparametric methods* whereby some fixed kernel function that is everywhere continuous must be defined around every available sample of x. For general distributions, none of these methods is satisfactory. Either the accuracy may remain low (like in parametric methods), or the computations become heavy (nonparametric methods). The dream about an ideal "Bayes machine" has therefore been around for a while.

The "Boltzmann machine" and "Backpropagation network" are based on a least-square error criterium. If enough training samples and internal parameters are available, it might seem that their input-output transformations can be defined to an arbitrary accuracy. However, since their design is not based on decision-theoretic arguments, it is not obvious how well they perform in **conflicting** cases, i.e., when the "class distributions" intersect. We found this problem of such a fundamental importance in practical applications with stochastic data, that we decided to "benchmark" these models, together with a few others, on certain typical-looking statistical data. In this work we have concentrated on statistical accuracy, although comparison of certain other figures like computing speed would also have been interesting. It seems, however, that it is not so easy to define comparison criteria for the latter, because, for instance, the "sigmoid function" in Boltzmann machines and Backpropagation networks can be computed in many different ways. In the concluding section we are trying to report our general experiences about typical computing times. Roughly speaking, of the methods studied, the LVQ is the fastest, then the Backpropagation network, and finally the Boltzmann machines. The statistically best Boltzmann machine, however, contains circuit elements (plenty of precision level detectors for all input signals) which are very difficult to realize in massive circuits and may thus not be practicable with real problems.

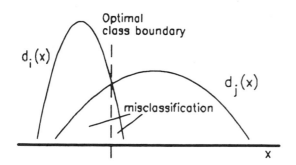

Fig. 1. Minimization of misclassification rate.

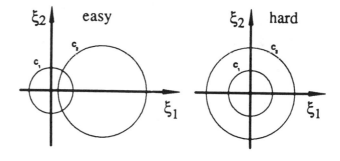

Fig. 2. Illustration of the two tasks. (Square roots of the variances are indicated by circles.)

2. Selection of the tasks

Numerous neural network studies have been performed with discrete, class-separable data. Some benchmarking studies have earlier also been performed on low-dimensional statistical data (Huang and Lippmann, 1987). Based on practical experiences, however, we felt that the nature of the statistical problems might change with higher dimensionality of input vectors. Therefore we introduced a model of artificial data with **dimensionality ranging from 2 to 8.**

Intentionally, we thus defined our benchmarking data to represent statistically difficult cases, where we wanted to have: 1. Heavy intersection of the class distributions. 2. High degree of nonlinearity of the class boundaries. 3. High dimensionality of the input vectors. - To this end we defined two artificial data sets and had two natural data sets available.

As far as the above three properties are taken into account, it is not desirable to load the artificial datum model by any further unnecessary details or complexities. For **benchmarking purposes** we thus decided to use for the artificial data symmetric, heavily overlapping Gaussian distributions (with different variances for the classes) because it is then easy, for reference, to compute the theoretical accuracy limits of the Bayes classifier. With artificial data, we also restricted to a two-class problem, since we believed it yields answers to the most essential questions. Let us denote $x=(\xi_1,\xi_2,...,\xi_n)$. Class C_1 was represented by a multivariate normal distribution with zero mean and square root of variance equal to 1 in all the dimensions, class C_2 by a normal distribution with mean $\bar{x}_1=(\bar{\xi}_1,0,0,...,0)$ and square root of variance equal to 2 in all dimensions, respectively. In one task the relative offset between classes was $\xi_1=2.32$ ("easy task"), in the other $\xi_1=0$ ("hard task"), respectively (cf. Fig. 2).

We also wanted to make experiments with **natural data**.To that end we had available manually segmented real speech spectra (computed over 30 millisecond intervals) with which it was possible to test the Learning Vector Quantization methods against theoretical limits. These tests were carried out for 18 phonemic classes simultaneously. The different classes had different statistics. We have not yet been able to carry out the corresponding tests for the Backpropagation network and Boltzmann machines, because these experiments are very time-consuming indeed, whereas for LVQ, computing time is no problem.

3. Backpropagation

Backpropagation (BP) is a learning algorithm for multi-layer feedforward networks, as introduced in Werbos (1974) and Parker (1982).

3.1. Particular configuration

A standard, two-layer backpropagation network as described in Rumelhart, Hinton, and Williams (1986) was used. Two, as opposed to three, layers were used since the optimal decision regions for all tasks were known to be convex, and it has been shown in Lippmann (1987) that a two-layer network is sufficient to form convex decision regions. The advantage in convergence time that a three-layer network sometimes has over two-layer networks was irrelevant, since asymptotic error rates were the only basis of comparison. The learning rate was 0.01 and the momentum coefficient was 0.9. There were 8 nodes in the hidden layer, with a number of inputs equal to the dimensionality of the input vectors and the number of output nodes equaling the number of classes, which was 2 in all tasks. This, combined with a bias weight for each node, provided for a total of $8 \cdot d + 26$ weights, where d is the dimensionality of input. Although it is possible that increasing the BP resources per dimension at a faster rate could allow BP to better track the theoretical limit in the higher dimensions, it has also been noted that adding units to a BP network does not always result in improved performance.

During training, it was stipulated that the correct output for a sample of a given class should be 1 for the node corresponding to the sample's class, and 0 for the other node. For recognition and testing purposes, the network was considered to have correctly classified the sample if the output node with the greatest activation from that sample was associated with the sample's class.

3.2. Experimental results

Table 1 gives the assymptotic error rates for BP's performance on both tasks. Notice that for a constant amount of computational resources (weights), and as dimensionality increased, BP's performance improved at a rate significantly less than the rate improvement of the theoretical limit. Lowering the learning parameter frequently caused the network to get stuck in local minima, while raising the rate often prevented convergence.

4. Boltzmann machines

The Boltzmann machine (BM) is a parallel computing network, consisting of simple processing units which are connected by bidirectional links. The links are represented by real numbers while the units can be in the states 'on' or 'off'. For details, further references and applications see Ackley, Hinton and Sejnowski (1985), Prager, Harrison and Fallside (1986).

4.1. Particular configurations

Although the BM was originally designed for binary units, the tasks described in Section 2 require continuous inputs. Two types of input units were therefore used (as in Prager et al., 1986):
a) continuous input units, allowed by the generalization of the learning rule;
b) groups of binary input units, used with a binary coding scheme.
In case a) the input values were shifted to the positive range. In case b) in each dimension the input range was divided into 20 subranges. Thus, 20 input units must be used for each dimension. All of them were set 'off' except the one which is associated with the subrange containing the input value of the dimension, which is set 'on'. We call this scheme "BM2".

In addition, there were always 2 hidden and 2 output units. This corresponds to the numbers of weights equal to $80 \cdot d + 3$ in case a) and $4 \cdot d + 3$ in case b). When the output units are clamped, the clamping patterns are {on,off} and {off,on} for class C_1 and C_2, respectively. The probabilities for two units being simultaneously 'on' in the unclamped and clamped modes, respectively, were estimated over 10,000 samples.

For updating the w_{ij} weights, only the sign of Δw_{ij} was determined by the gradient descent learning algorithm detailed in Ackley et al. (1985). The absolute value of Δw_{ij} was constant (Δw) for each update and slowly decreased over time.

4.2. Experiments

The experimental results for the above configurations are shown in Table 2. Increasing the number of input or hidden units did not decrease the error significantly. The value of Δw was initially about two times the average of the absolute values of w_{ij} and slowly decreased (to 1/5th of the initial value at about the 500,000th sample). Reaching the minimal error level required about 4-500,000 samples.

5. Learning Vector Quantization

Learning Vector Quantization (LVQ) is a nearest-neighbor method operating explicitly in the input domain (Kohonen 1988a, 1988b). It consists of a **predetermined number** of processing units, each unit having a d-element **reference vector**, and each unit being associated with one of the classes of the input samples. Let c be the processing unit that is the closest to x, in some appropriate metric; this is then also the classification of x . During learning, unit c is updated. Here t is the discrete-time index (integer). The exact form of this change is:

$$m_c(t+1) = m_c(t) + \alpha(t)(x(t) - m_c(t))$$
$$\text{if x and the closest unit belong to the same class ,}$$

$$m_c(t+1) = m_c(t) - \alpha(t)(x(t) - m_c(t))$$
$$\text{if x and the closest unit belong to different class ,}$$

$$m_i(t+1) = m_i(t) \quad \text{for } i \neq c , \tag{2}$$

where $0 < \alpha(t) < 1$, and α is decreasing monotonically with time.

5.1. Particular configuration

The number of processing units was chosen to be $5 \cdot d$, thus resulting in $5 \cdot d^2$ weights. For calculating the closest unit the Euclidian metric was used.

Since the LVQ learning algorithm assumes a good initial state, the traditional k-means clustering (cf. Makhoul et al., 1985), was used to initialize the processing units. Then each of the processing units was associated with one of the classes, by running the system without learning and collecting statistics on how frequently each of the processing units was the closest to the samples from each class.

During learning, α decreased from 0.01 to 0 over 100,000 samples.

5.2. Experimental results

The experimental results are in Table 1. We have found that if the number of processing units in LVQ can be increased without limits, we might reach the theoretical limit. Here the number of units was kept comparable to that used in the other methods.

Table 1   **Error percentages for artificial data. All figures in the last four columns are given with 0.1% accuracy.**

	dim.	theoretical limit	BP	BM (continuous)	BM2 (binary)	LVQ
$\bar{\xi}_1=2.32$	2	16.4	16.4	29.2	16.5	17.0
	3	13.7	14.0	26.2	14.0	14.6
	4	11.6	12.5	24.5	11.7	13.1
	5	9.8	11.0	23.9	10.2	12.2
	6	8.4	10.8	23.4	8.7	10.7
	7	7.2	9.72	22.9	8.2	10.1
	8	6.2	11.3	22.7	6.7	10.0
$\bar{\xi}_1=0$	2	26.4	26.3	*	26.5	26.5
	3	21.4	21.5	*	21.6	21.8
	4	17.6	19.4	*	18.0	18.8
	5	14.8	19.5	*	15.2	16.9
	6	12.4	20.7	*	12.7	15.3
	7	10.6	16.7	*	11.0	14.5
	8	9.0	18.9	*	9.4	13.4

* no convergence was observed.

6. Another Learning Vector Quantization (LVQ2)

The method discussed in this section is being introduced the first time here.

The basic LVQ can easily be modified to better comply with Bayes' philosophy. Consider Fig. 3 which represents a one-dimensional two-class case. Assume that the neighboring reference values m_i and m_j are initially in a wrong position. The (incorrect) discrimination surface, however, is always defined as the midpoint ("midplane") of m_i and m_j. Let us define a symmetric *window* with nonzero width around the midpoint and stipulate that *corrections to m_i and m_j shall only be made if x falls into the window, on the wrong side of the midpoint.* If the corrections are made according to Eq. (3), it will be easy to see that for vectors falling into the window, the corrections of both m_i and m_j, on the average, have such a direction that the midplane moves towards the crossing point of the class distributions (cf. Fig. 1), and thus asymptotically coincides with the Bayes decision border.

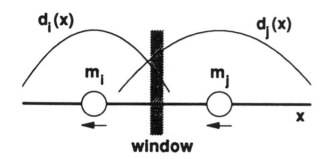

$$m_i(t+1) = m_i(t) - \alpha(t)(x(t)-m_i(t)) \quad ,$$

$$m_j(t+1) = m_j(t) + \alpha(t)(x(t)-m_j(t)) \quad ,$$

if C_i is the nearest class, but x belongs to $C_j \neq C_i$ where C_j is the next-to-nearest class; furthermore x must fall into the "window". In all the other cases,

Fig. 3.

$$m_k(t+1) = m_k(t) . \tag{3}$$

7. Experiments with speech data

Benchmarking studies for LVQ and LVQ2 were also made on real 15-channel speech spectra which were manually picked up from stationary regions of (Finnish) speech waveforms. We applied two independent data sets, each consisting of 1550 phonemic samples, using one data set for training, and the other for testing, respectively. All results of this section have been collected to Table 2.

7.1. Parametric Bayes classifier

For a reference we used the familiar parametric Bayes classifier, in which each class is described by a multivariate normal distribution (in reality, two times the logarithm of the class distribution, from which a constant term has been dropped)

$$d_i(x) = 2 \log P(C_i) - \log |\psi_i| - (x-\bar{x}_i)^T \psi_i^{-1} (x-\bar{x}_i) \tag{4}$$

where ψ_i is the covariance matrix of those x values that belong to class C_i, and $|\psi_i|$ its determinant, respectively; $\bar{x}_i$ the class mean of $x \in C_i$. In the case that ψ_i^{-1} does not exist for the set of samples from which ψ_i is computed, it may be replaced by the **pseudoinverse** ψ_i^+ (cf. Albert 1972, Kohonen 1988a).

After the ψ_i and $\bar{x}_i$ were computed from the training data set, classification was performed on the test data set like in Eq. (1).

7.2. kNN (k-nearest-neighbor) classifier

In this classification algorithm, a large number of training or reference data is collected for each class, and each of the test vectors x is compared against all of them. A majority voting over k nearest reference vectors is performed in order to decide to which class x belongs. This method is computationally heavy, and it approximates the Bayes classifier only if the number of reference vectors is large.

In our tests we compared all the 1550 test vectors against all the 1550 training vectors, using k=5 or k=6 in voting (this seemed to be the optimum in the present case).

7.3. LVQ and LVQ2

The same training and test data sets as above were used in this method. Because LVQ and LVQ2 need an appreciable number of training cycles for asymptotic convergence, the training data were applied reiteratively. It turned out that half a dozen iterations over the training data were sufficient for final accuracy. There were 117 nodes in the network.

7.4. The results

Table 2 represents the results of Secs. 7.1 through 7.3. On the first row, data set 1 was used for training and data set 2 for testing; on the second row, the roles of the data sets were switched.

Table 2   **Speech recognition experiments; error percentages for independent test data**

	Parametric Bayes	kNN	LVQ	LVQ2
Test 1	12.1	12.0	10.2	9.8
Test 2	13.8	12.1	13.2	12.0

8. Discussion

Notice that for both tasks with artificial data, the relative offset of the two class distributions was constant, whereby it is a natural phenomenon that the theoretically minimal error rate decreases with increasing dimensionality, since the relative value of the "probability mass" of the intersection is then a decreasing function of dimensionality.

It is interesting to note that one of the methods, the BM2 with the dynamic range of each of its inputs divided into 20 subranges, almost followed the theoretical accuracy limit. This method, however, is a brute-force approach, and it is questionable how the precision input discrimination levels can be implemented in massive networks. It also needs a much higher number of units and weights than the other methods. A typical learning time for the BM models, even in this simple two-class problem, was five hours of CPU time on our Masscomp MC 5600 computer, although it had the fast (3000-Whetstone) "Lightning" floating point processor!

The BP network, while being reasonably accurate at low dimensionality (e.g., 2) was significantly inferior with higher dimensionalities, especially in the "hard task" ($\xi_1=0$). Typical learning time for this particular BP network would be somewhat less than an hour on Masscomp. The BP results seem to be much more unstable than those obtained by the other methods.

With regard to accuracy, the Learning Vector Quantization models fell between these extremes. Typical learning time was a couple of tens of minutes on the Masscomp. On the other hand, LVQ has previously been programmed for microprocessors, and in speech recognition experiments, re-learning all the phonemic classes then only required about 10 minutes on an IBM PC/AT! Notice that the "sigmoid function" in BMs and BP networks is computationally much heavier than the distance computations in Learning Vector Quantization methods; the latter can even be based on integer arithmetic. On the other hand, it seems that comparable accuracy needs roughly similar amounts of nodes and interconnects in any of the models studied.

As we were not yet able to make comparative studies on speech data using Boltzmann machines or BP networks, we do not dare to speculate anything about their relative merits in this task. The very good accuracies yielded by the LVQ methods for speech may be explained by the fact that vector quantization of the pattern space is very advantageous, if the class regions are "piled up" such that there are neighboring classes on all sides of most classes. This was not the case for the artificial two-class problem, where the reference vectors of class C_2 in particular had to surround those of class C_1 on all sides, which is difficult if the dimensionality is high.

In any event, these results show that in statistical pattern recognition, the Learning Vector Quantization is a very viable alternative to the comparatively older BM and BP, and is statistically superior to those BM and BP approaches which are realistic in practice.

Acknowledgement. The work of one of the authors, Ronald Chrisley, was made possible via a Fulbright Graduate Study Grant under the Fulbright-Hayes Exchange Program.

References

Ackley, D.H., Hinton, G.E., and Sejnowski, T.J. (1985): A learning algorithm for Boltzmann machines. Cognitive Science **9**, 147-69.

Albert, A. (1972): *Regression and the Moore-Penrose Pseudoinverse.* Academic, New York.

Devijver, P.A. and Kittler, J. (1982): *Pattern recognition: A statistical approach.* Prentice Hall, London.

Hopfield, J.J. (in press): Neural computations and neural systems. *Proc. of Conference on Computer Simulation in Brain Science, Copenhagen, Denmark, Aug. 20-22, 1986.* Cambridge University Press.

Huang, W.Y. and Lippmann, R.P. (1987): Comparisons between neural net and conventional classifiers. *Proceedings of the 1st IEEE International Conference on Neural Networks,* Vol. IV, 485-94.

Kohonen, T. (1988a): *Self-organization and associative memory.* (2nd ed.) Springer, Berlin-Heidelberg-New York-Tokyo.

Kohonen, T. (1988b): An introduction to neural computing. Neural Networks **1**, 3-16.

Lippmann, R. (1987): An introduction to computing with neural nets. IEEE ASSP Mag. **4**, 4-22.

Makhoul, J., Roucos, S., and Gish, H. (1985): Vector quantization in speech coding. Proc. IEEE **73**, No. 11, 1551-88.

Parker D.P. (1982): Learning logic. Invention Report, S81-64, File 1, Office of Technology Licensing, Stanford University.

Patrick, E.A. (1972): *Fundamentals of Pattern Recognition.* Prentice-Hall, Englewood Cliffs, NJ.

Prager, R.W., Harrison, T.D., and Fallside, F. (1986): Boltzmann machines for speech recognition. Computer Speech and Language **1**, 3-27.

Rumelhart, D.E., Hinton, G.E., and Williams, R.J. (1986): Learning internal representations by error propagation. in *Parallel Distributed Processing: Explorations in the Microstructure of Cognition, Volume 1: Foundations.* MIT Press, Cambridge. pp. 318-62.

Werbos, P.J. (1974): Beyond regression: New tools for prediction and analysis in the behavioral sciences. Thesis in applied mathematics, Harvard University, Aug. 1974.

31
Introduction

(1988)
Ralph Linsker

Self-organization in a perceptual network
Computer Magazine 21: 105–117

Animals are very good at seeing what needs to be seen. The mammalian visual system takes varying patterns of light intensity—images—cast on the retina and turns them into neural discharge patterns, which are then processed by additional layers of the nervous system. Somehow this process leads to recognition and appropriate response to visual events.

Learning how the nervous system and the sensory receptors accomplish this transduction and information processing is one of the most popular and exciting areas of neurobiology and psychology. Sensory systems are full of marvelous engineering. And one thing that seems to be true about the process is that, *given the totality of behavioral, physical, and developmental constraints faced by the sensory systems*, it would not be possible to do better than the biological system.

For example, visual receptors respond to single absorbed quanta, the sensitivity of auditory receptors is just above thermal noise, the sensitivity of the olfactory system to some biologically significant compounds (say, pheromones in some insects) is a single molecule, and so on. When we are close to the receptors, often the limits of behavior are obvious to us: single quanta, single molecules, thermal noise. However, as sensory information processing continues, the optimal information processing strategy is no longer so clear.

In the vertebrate visual system neurons respond to particular aspects of the environment. To a first approximation the visual system is organized as a series of layers of cells. Layers tend to look at successively more complex *features* of the environment. In the simplified picture of the visual system discussed by Linsker, an early layer of cells shows *center-surround* organization; that is, a cell responds with excitation to light falling on a small circular region of space. Surrounding the excitatory region is a larger annulus of inhibition. The opposite arrangement, inhibitory center–excitatory surround, is also found. At higher layers, further removed from the retina, cells are found that respond to oriented line segments; that is, receptive fields are no longer symmetric, but respond to extended patterns of light, displaying orientation. In mammals cells in visual cortex with similar orientations tend to be close to each other, another example of the kind of topographic relations that find their fullest expression in the mapping relations found in the biological systems described in papers 16 and 22. Modeling the development of visual cortex has given rise to a number of important network ideas about self-organization (see, for example, papers 9 and 10). Although much structure is built-in from birth, there is also strong evidence of adaptive processes at work during visual system development.

This paper, by Ralph Linsker, looks at the problem of optimal sensory processing from an abstract point of view. This paper also uses principal component analysis as a way of understanding the kind of optimal processing being developed.

The main claim of this paper is that the observed responses of cells in the visual system are consequences of assuming (1) some simple learning and connection rules in a layered structure and (2) that the resulting organization maximizes information preservation, if certain kinds of resources are limited.

Linsker assumes a feed-forward, hierarchical layered structure, with each layer composed of a large number of simple neural elements of the traditional kind. In fact for much of the paper, the simplest linear neuron is used, that is, a model neuron that only takes the inner product between weights and input activities. Linsker assumes two important constraints in setting up the network. First, a cell is locally connected, that is, a cell receives inputs from a limited region of the layer below it. Linsker suggests, as an example, a Gaussian falloff of connection density with distance. Second, what Linsker calls a *saturation constraint* is assumed, that is, the magnitude of the individual connection strengths cannot exceed some maximum value.

The model neurons are assumed to follow a simple Hebb learning rule, where synapses change strength based on an interaction between both presynaptic and postsynaptic activation. The actual rule that Linsker uses contains the product of both pre- and postsynaptic activity, a traditional outer-product rule, as well as additive terms corresponding to pure presynaptic and pure postsynaptic activity. Linsker then shows that this form of Hebbian learning gives an expression for rate of change of the weights that contains the covariance matrix for the inputs to the cells. (Hebb synapses are sometimes known as *correlational synapses* for reasons related to this observation.)

Once the link to the covariance matrix is established, Linsker then points out that the cell, after learning, is maximizing the variance of the cell, that is, the ". . . cell's output value exhibits the largest possible spread." Here the connection to principal component analysis becomes clear: when a single cell maximizes its variance, it is responding to the first principal component in the set of inputs. Because the cell is responding to the first principal component over a restricted local region in its input layer, it is responding to important local features. (For further discussion of principal component analysis in the context of neural networks see the next two papers, papers 32 and 33.)

When Linsker simulates this system, a remarkable self-organization occurs in successively higher layers. Suppose the input is white noise. First, a kind of local average is taken by the first layer above the input. In the second layer center-surround organization develops. And in higher layers regions that look like orientation-selective receptive fields develop. Moreover, with proper adjustment of parameters, there is often local structure in the higher layer, so nearby cells may show similar orientations. This is not unexpected because nearby cells are receiving similar, but not identical, inputs. Linsker has some remarkable figures showing the kind of noisy regularity shown by his simulations—regions of similar orientation preference, say—and the actual organization of orientation-selective cells in primary visual cortex.

Linsker uses these results to suggest that the nervous system is coding information so as to preserve maximum information about the input activities, subject to constraints on connectivity, synapse dynamic range, and so forth. This implies that cells tend to develop efficient codings of information. This suggestion has been made independently by several vision researchers, who point out that lateral inhibition is not only a way of enhancing edges, but also of preserving information that must be transmitted through a channel with limited capacity (see the introduction to the paper by Barlow, paper 14).

Linsker's results also show the remarkable self-organizing properties of simple Hebbian synapses. The strong suggestion is that the receptive fields seen in the mammalian visual system are statistically optimal for information preservation. One nice aspect of the kinds of organization seen in the simulations is that they are easy to realize biologically. It is easy to build such receptive fields *if the topography of the input layer corresponds roughly to the sensory topography*, that is, if the input layer is organized as a topographic map. A center-surround organization can be constructed easily from a small region of visual space. Different points in the region would be near one another on the map. More orientation-selective units could be produced by simply connecting a few center-surround cells. Even a little randomness in the input map would lead to an oriented receptive field. So this line of thought leads to the attractive possibility that statistically optimal cell responses are also very easy to construct with the kinds of mapping known to exist in the visual system.

Although the approach suggested by Linsker gives an intriguing interpretation to data from higher mammals, for the lower vertebrates the situation is not so simple. For example, the frog's eye (see paper 13) sees buglike patterns with one class of retinal receptors. Whatever optimality is being shown here is optimized using a different and more complex set of constraints relevant to the behavioral task. There must be a constant contest between genetic prewiring of responses to specific important patterns, and more general statistical optimality applicable to very large classes of patterns.

(1988)
Ralph Linsker

Self-organization in a perceptual network
Computer Magazine 21: 105–117

A young animal or child perceives and identifies features in its environment in an apparently effortless way. No presently known algorithms even approach this flexible, general-purpose perceptual capability. Discovering the principles that may underlie perceptual processing is important both for neuroscience and for the development of synthetic perceptual systems.

Two important aspects of the mystery of perception are

(1) What processing functions does the neural "machinery" perform on perceptual input, and what is the circuitry that implements these functions?

(2) How does this "machinery" come to be?

Unlike conventional computer hardware, neural circuitry is not hard-wired or specified as an explicit set of point-to-point connections. Instead it develops under the influence of a genetic specification and epigenetic factors, such as electrical activity, both before and after birth. How this happens is in large part unknown.

Biological development processes are far too complex to hope that a relatively complete understanding of how a perceptual system develops and functions will soon emerge. But we are familiar with complex synthetic systems, such as computers, whose principles of organization can be understood without one's knowing

How can a perceptual system develop to recognize specific features of its environment, without being told which features it should analyze, or even whether its identifications are correct?

in detail how the components work. Furthermore, the same principles can be used to build computers in any of several different technologies. Might there be organizing principles

(1) that explain some essential aspects of how a perceptual system develops and functions;

(2) that we can attempt to infer without waiting for far more detailed experimental information; and

(3) that can lead to profitable experimental programs, testable predictions, and applications to synthetic perception as well as neuroscientific understanding?

I believe the answer is yes, and that the use of theoretical neural networks that embody biologically-motivated rules and constraints is a powerful tool in this study.

This optimism is encouraged by recent work[1] in which I have found that a multilayered network, developing according to simple yet biologically plausible "Hebb-type" rules,[2] self-organizes to produce feature-analyzing "cells." These "cells" have response properties that are qualitatively similar to those cells of the first few processing stages of the mammalian visual system.[3] These properties include sensitivity to light-dark contrast and sensitivity to the orientation of an edge or bar. These properties develop before birth in certain animals, hence before structured visual experience, and in the theoretical network the corresponding properties develop even in the absence of structured input, using only random signaling activity in the input layer of the network.

Why does a feature-analyzing function emerge from these development rules? Is it a mere accident or curiosity? Or are the development rules perhaps acting to optimize some quantity that is important to the information processing function of a perceptual system?

In this article, I briefly summarize the network ideas from an earlier publication[1] and review some of the main results. This sets the stage for exploring why a feature-analyzing function emerges. I then show that even a single developing cell of a layered network exhibits a remarkable set of optimization properties. These properties are closely related to issues in statistics, theoretical physics, adaptive signal processing, the formation of knowledge representations in artificial intelligence, and information theory.

Next, I use these results to infer an information-theoretic principle that can be applied to the network as a whole, rather than a single cell. The organizing principle I propose is that the network connections develop in such a way as to maximize the amount of information that is preserved when signals are transformed at each processing stage, subject to certain constraints.

I illustrate how this principle works for some very simple cases. Much more work will be needed to apply the principle to practical computations of biologically important cases, but the approach appears very promising. I conclude with some speculative comments on why this principle, or some variant of it, may be important for the emergence of perceptual function in biological and synthetic systems.

A layered self-adaptive network

The visual system is the best studied perceptual system in mammals. Visual information is processed in stages. Simple aspects of form, such as contrast and edge orientation, are analyzed in the earlier stages; more complex features are analyzed later. Other aspects of visual processing, such as color and motion analysis, proceed in parallel with the analysis of form.

Both the retina and cortex are organized into layers of cells with interconnections within and between layers. Within an anatomical layer, at least for the early processing stages, there is a population of cells each of which performs approximately the same processing function on its inputs. This population of cells can be thought of as an array of filters. Each cell processes input from a limited region of visual space, called the "receptive field" of that cell. More than one population of cells can share an anatomical layer.

Many cells respond to input activity by firing an electrical pulse, or *action potential*, that travels down the output fiber, or axon. These pulses cause a chemical neurotransmitter substance to be released at synapses, or regions of near-contact with other cells. The latter cells receive and process these chemical input signals. Some cells, for example in the retina, do not produce action potentials, but instead exhibit more graded electrochemical phenomena that can be used for signaling.

Although a cell's response function is in general nonlinear, visual neurophysiologists have found that for many cells, a linear summation approximation is appropriate. In this approximation, the cell's output response varies monotonically with some linear combination of the cell's input signal values. For cells that produce action potentials, the output response can be defined as the firing rate at which the cell generates action potential pulses in response to its input signals.

Specification of the network. Will a simple self-adaptive network develop feature-analyzing cells without our specifying which features are to be analyzed? If it does, are these cell types related to those observed in biological systems? To address these questions, we first study a network that embodies some of the important biological properties described above, but omits many complicating factors. This approach is useful both because many of the details are unknown, and because our goal is to understand what principles are most important for the development of perceptual functions. For example, if we want to know how nonlinearity of response may be important for development, it is valuable to see first whether a linear response system exhibits the main feature-analyzing properties that are biologically observed. Also, feedback connections from later to earlier processing stages are known to exist, but it is not known how these connections might relate to the development of feature-analyzing functions. (There are many other functions that feedback may serve, such as control of dynamic range, attentional mechanisms, and so on.) We choose to analyze networks without feedback, to understand their developmental properties first.

The interconnections within the retina are known to be more complicated than a simple feedforward arrangement. Also, mechanisms that are not dependent on neural activity appear to be involved in the development of some feature-analyzing

properties. The main purpose of our simulations is to explore what types of simple yet biologically plausible development rules *suffice* to generate feature-analyzing cell assemblies, rather than to rule out other ways of generating them. From the results of our simple model, we will infer a potential organizing principle that can encompass nonlinear cell response, more complex connectivity, and a variety of ways of forming and modifying connections.

Our network is shown in Figure 1. The cells are organized into two-dimensional layers A, B, C, and so on, with feedforward connections to each cell from an overlying neighborhood of cells of the previous layer. Layer A receives input from the visual world (if there is any such input). We focus especially on the case in which there is no input, but instead only random activity of the cells of layer A, with no correlation of activity from one cell to the next. This activity resembles random noise or snow on a TV screen. We consider this case in order to understand how certain feature-analyzing cells may emerge even before birth, as has been observed in certain primates.

The positions of the connections to each cell need not be regular as in Figure 1, but can be chosen randomly according to a density distribution, such as a Gaussian, that favors connections from nearby cells of the previous layer. For simplicity, these positions are fixed for the duration of the development process. Each cell, at each time, has some signaling activity which we denote by a real number. Each cell exhibits a simple linear response, that is, the output is a linear combination of the inputs, with each input being weighted by a *connection strength* that will develop in a certain way. Each model cell thus acts as a linear filter.

Two points should be noted:

(1) Defining the output response as a nonlinear, for example sigmoid, function of the weighted sum of the inputs would more closely approximate some properties of the firing rates of biological neurons. These are always nonnegative and saturate at some maximum rate. However, we will see that even a linear response rule can lead to the formation of feature-analyzing cells, and we will explore what properties of linear adaptive filters are responsible for this formation. Some of the insights gained will be applicable to the nonlinear response case as well.

(2) Any transformation implemented by a feedforward sequence of layers of lin-

ear filters is a linear transformation, and hence could be implemented by a single layer of connections with properly chosen, or in this case hardwired, connection strengths. However, our purpose is not to implement a particular transformation, but rather to study what transformations are learned by a network without supervision. This multistage learning process depends upon the presence of multiple network layers.

A Hebb rule. For the development process, we use a version of an idea proposed by the neuropsychologist Donald Hebb in 1949. This idea has been central to much work on synthetic neural networks over the years, as well as to the thinking of neuroscientists about how the development of synaptic connections may relate to memory and learning phenomena. Hebb's idea was that if cell 1 is one of the cells providing input to cell 2, and if cell 1's activity tends to be "high" whenever cell 2's activity is "high", then the future contribution that the firing of cell 1 makes to the firing of cell 2 should increase.

In the language of neural networks, the connection strength is increased, or made more positive. A mathematical formulation needs to be more precise than this, and state under what conditions the strength may decrease. We use a form in which the change in strength contains a term proportional to the product of input and output activities at that connection. The Hebbian idea of modifying connection strengths according to the degree of correlated activity between input and output is central to what follows.

For an analogy to a Hebbian rule, consider a group of people whose collective opinion on a question is by definition the weighted average of the opinions of its members. If, over time, a member's opinion tends to agree with the group's opinion, then the analog of the Hebb rule states that the individual member's vote on future issues is to be weighted more strongly. The member's vote is given less weight, or even negative weight, if he consistently disagrees with the group's opinion. This type of positive-feedback control of weighting factors tends to lead to consensus within the group. As we shall see, it has other surprising consequences for the properties of the group, or output cell, response.

Mathematical formulation. This subsection and the next summarize simulations that are described in detail in my

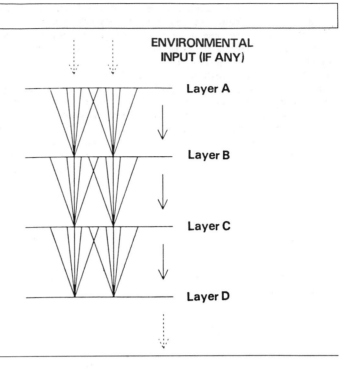

Figure 1. **A layered self-adaptive network with local feedforward connections. Each two-dimensional layer contains many cells. Five input connections to each of two cells in layers B, C, and D are shown. Several hundred inputs to each cell are used in simulations. Each cell also provides input to many cells of the following layer. Lateral connections within a layer, as discussed in the text, are not indicated here.**

previous work.[1]

Consider a cell M and the cells L_1, L_2, . . . , L_N that provide input to M. For simplicity, we avoid treating effects that depend upon the time sequence of signal activity values. Instead, we think of the activity history of a layer as a set of "snapshots," in which the ordering of the snapshots plays no role. That is, a set of activity values, denoted by $(L_1^\pi, L_2^\pi, . . . , L_N^\pi)$, is presented as input to the M cell, the M cell generates an output activity value M^π, and a new set of input activities is then presented. The superscript π indexes the presentation of inputs, that is, the particular snapshot, and the corresponding output. Then the linear response rule is

$$M^\pi = a_1 + \Sigma_j L_j^\pi c_j \qquad (1)$$

where c_j is the strength of the jth input connection to the M cell. Our Hebb-type rule is

$$(\Delta c_i)^\pi = a_2 L_i^\pi M^\pi + a_3 L_i^\pi + a_4 M^\pi + a_5 \qquad (2)$$

where the a's are arbitrary constants ($a_2 > 0$). We assume that the c values change slowly from one presentation to the next. Then we can average Equation 2 over an ensemble of many presentations, and use Equation 1 to express M^π in terms of the $\{L_j^\pi\}$ to obtain the rate of change of each c value. Some algebraic manipulation[1] gives

$$\dot{c}_i = \Sigma_j Q_{ij} c_j + [k_1 + (k_2/N)\Sigma c_j] \qquad (3)$$

where $k_{1,2}$ are particular combinations of the constants $a_{1\text{-}5}$. Apart from the determined values of $k_{1,2}$, the constants $a_{1\text{-}5}$ play no further role in what follows. Here

$$Q_{ij} \equiv <(L_i^\pi - \overline{L}) \times (L_j^\pi - \overline{L})> \qquad (4)$$

is the covariance of the activities of input cells i and j, where $< . . . >$ and the overbar both denote the ensemble average. (For our purposes, $\overline{L}$, the ensemble average of the input activity at a synapse, can

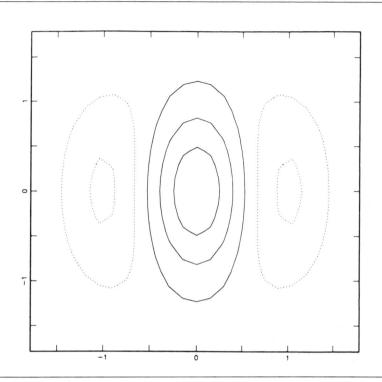

Figure 2. Receptive field map of a computed orientation-selective cell. A point of illumination at any position in the plane evokes an output response from the model cell that is proportional to the contour value at that position. Positive contour values (solid curves) denote an excitatory output response; negative values (dotted curves) denote an inhibitory response. Contour values range from − 0.45 to + 0.75 in steps of 0.30. The peak response (at the receptive field center) is normalized to unity. The parameter values that generated this particular orientation-selective cell, and the units (r_G) of distance along the axes, are given in reference 1. (See Figure 1a, p. 8780). Axes denote distance of illumination point from receptive field center.

Simulation results. A few parameters for each layer of cells determine the mature c values of the cells in that layer. These parameters include k_1 and k_2 and the breadth of the region in the previous layer that provides input to a cell of the developing layer. (See Figure 1.) As we shall see, the choice of the $k_{1,2}$ values determines the mature value of the total connection strength Σc_j of the inputs to the M cell.

When we explore the parameter space, we find that there are a limited number of ways each layer can develop. Briefly, we find that a sequence of feature-analyzing cell types emerges as one layer after another matures.

The first cell type emerges in layer B. There is a parameter regime in which each c value reaches its excitatory limit c_+. In this case, each B cell, once it has matured, computes the local average of the activity in the overlying region of layer A from which it receives input.

Once the B cells have matured in this way, nearby B cells have correlated activity. Each activity pattern in layer B is a blurred image of random snow. If one B cell's activity happens to be "high" at a given time, its neighbors' activities are likely to be "high" also. As a result of this activity correlation, a new cell type emerges in layer C. This *center-surround* cell type[1] acts as a contrast-sensitive filter—it responds maximally to a bright circular spot centered on the cell's receptive field, against a dark background. Center-surround cells having the reverse property—they respond maximally to a dark spot on a bright background—also emerge.

The Q function for pairs of center-surround cells in layer C determines the developmental possibilities for the C-to-D connections, and so on. We find that the next new type of feature-analyzing cell to emerge as we pass to succeeding layers is an *orientation-selective* cell. This cell responds maximally to a bright edge or bar against a dark background, or the reverse, when the edge or bar has a particular orientation. The receptive field map for such a computed cell is shown in Figure 2. This map is a contour plot showing the response of the cell to point illumination, as a function of the position of the illumination in visual space.

Each orientation-selective cell will develop to favor an arbitrary orientation if the network contains only feedforward connections as in Figure 1. However, if lateral connections between nearby cells of the orientation-selective cell layer are

be taken to be the same for all synapses i, j.) The appearance of the input covariance matrix Q does not mean that there is any direct interaction between synapses i and j. Q appears simply because the Hebb rule causes $\dot{c}_i$ to depend upon the product $<L_i^n M^n>$, and M^n in turn depends upon all the $\{L_j^n\}$ values (via Equation 1). The Q matrix will play an important role in what follows.

To prevent c values from becoming infinite during the development process, a saturation constraint is imposed. Each c value is constrained to lie between two values c_- and c_+. In a more biologically realistic case, there are excitatory synapses that have $0 \leq c \leq c_+$ and inhibitory synapses that have $c_- \leq c \leq 0$. The analysis of this case gives the same result.

First the connections from layer A to B mature, or develop to their final values. That is, the initial c values are chosen at random, the set of differential equations given by Equation 3 (for $i = 1, 2, \ldots, N$) is solved, using the Q_{ij} function that applies to layer A activity. (For random snow activity in layer A, Q_{ij} is 1 when i and j are the same A cell, and 0 otherwise.) Knowing the mature c values for the A-to-B connections, as well as the Q_{ij} function for layer A, then allows us to compute the Q_{ij} function for the mature layer B. Then the development of the B-to-C connections is computed, using the Q_{ij} function appropriate to layer B. By repeating the process, we compute in turn the connection strengths for successive layers of connections.

included in the simulation, then the orientation preferences of the cells in the layer can become organized in certain arrangements. Cells having similar orientation preferences develop to occupy irregular band-shaped regions. (See reference 1 and the front cover, right side, of this issue.)

Discussion of the simulations. Center-surround cells are a prominent feature of mammalian retina. Orientation-selective cells emerge in cat and monkey visual cortex.[3,4] Irregular band-shaped regions of cells of similar orientation—called *orientation columns*—are a prominent feature in the orientation-selective cell layers.[3,4] (Once again, see the front cover, left side.) The role that lateral connections in cortex play in the formation of orientation selectivity is at present experimentally unsettled. As we noted, certain primates exhibit well-formed orientation selectivity at birth, in the absence of any structured visual experience.

Our point is not to suggest that feature-analyzing cells—particularly the center-surround cells—arise in animals in the same way they do in this synthetic network. As noted previously, the anatomy of inter-layer connections in the retina is more complex than a simple feedforward arrangement. Furthermore, center-surround cells can be constructed by a simple non-adaptive model in which excitatory inputs from some narrow region, and inhibitory inputs from a broader region, both converge on a cell. In our simulations we assumed that the breadth of the input region to a cell was the same for excitatory and inhibitory synapses, in order to avoid biasing the solution toward the formation of a center-surround cell type.

Our point is rather that a set of progressively more complex feature-analyzing cell types develops in the layered network, and that these cell types, and their organization, qualitatively exhibit some of the most salient features found in the first few stages of mammalian visual processing. The results suggest that some properties whose origin has been mysterious—such as orientation selectivity — may have a natural explanation in terms of the functioning of a Hebb-type development process in a layered network.

Two simple examples of how *structured* input to layer A would affect the simulation results are worth noting:

(1) If nearby pixels have correlated intensity values, and this is the only important input correlation present, then Q in layer A would resemble the Gaussian Q

that we found in layer B. The subsequent development of the model would proceed in a way similar to that which we described, except that the appearance of each feature-analyzing cell type could be advanced one layer.

(2) If layer A is shown an ensemble of patterns, each consisting of sinusoidal stripes with arbitrary phase and orientation, then orientation selectivity can develop as early as layer B.[1]

We have assumed, for simplicity, that the statistical properties of the ensemble of presentations, that is, the covariances Q_{ij}, are unchanged or stationary during development. If the ensemble statistics change, cells that had reached their apparently final mature c values may change these c values in accordance with the new ensemble characteristics. Thus, although we always speak of cell *development*, the present approach is equally applicable to studying questions of cell *plasticity* during the life of the animal.

Hebb rules and optimization properties

We have seen that even a simple layered network with local feedforward connections obeying a Hebb-type rule develops a sequence of progressively more sophisticated feature-analyzing properties as we pass from one layer to the next. We will now examine some remarkable optimization properties of a Hebb-type rule.

Maximization of output activity variance. Consider a cell M that receives input from cells $L_1, L_2, \ldots, L_N$. Here and later, "input" means local input to cell M, not the environmental input to the network as a whole. Similarly, "output" refers to the M cell's activity value, not the output from the network as a whole. Let the M cell's development be described as in Equations 1-4, with a saturation constraint on the range of each c value. We assume that the ensemble statistical properties of the L-cell activities, that is, the Q_{ij} function for the L cells as in Equation 4, are unaffected by the choice of c values. This is true if there is no feedback from M, or the cells it influences, to the L cells. It should be a satisfactory approximation if the feedback is present but is sufficiently weak, although this has not been studied quantitatively.

Define the function

$$E \equiv E_Q + E_k \tag{5}$$

where

$$E_Q \equiv -(1/2)<(M^n - \overline{M})^2> \\ = -(1/2)\Sigma_i\Sigma_j Q_{ij}c_ic_j \tag{6}$$

and

$$E_k \equiv -k_1\Sigma c_j - (k_2/2N)(\Sigma c_j)^2 \tag{7}$$

I have constructed the function E to have the property that $-\partial E/\partial c_i = \dot{c}_i$ for each i. This means that, as the Hebb rule causes each of the c values to change with time, the value of E, as a function of the c's, decreases along a path of locally steepest, or gradient, descent. (If $\dot{c}_i > 0$, then $\partial E/\partial c_i < 0$, so c_i increases and E decreases with time. If $\dot{c}_i < 0$, then $\partial E/\partial c_i > 0$, so c_i decreases and E again decreases with time.)

The value of E thus achieves a local minimum at cell maturity. Moreover, for the cases of interest here—including those that lead to the center-surround and orientation-selective cell types—this minimum is a *global* near-minimum as well.[1] We therefore will focus on the case in which the development process does not get stuck in high-lying local minima. This appears to be the typical case for a perceptual network exposed to a large ensemble of presentations, although it is an empirical finding and I have not established the limits of its validity.

What is the meaning of E achieving a global, or absolute, minimum value? For any given value of total connection strength Σc_j, E is minimized when $<(M^n - \overline{M})^2>$—the statistical variance of M—is maximized. Changing the values of the parameters $k_{1,2}$ adjusts, or tunes, the mature value of Σc_j. The E_k term, which is a function of Σc_j and $k_{1,2}$ only, plays a role similar to a Lagrange multiplier term, although E_k is parabolic rather than linear in Σc_j.

Therefore, the development rule of Equation 3 causes a cell to develop so as to maximize the variance of its output activity, subject to the constraint that the total connection strength have a given, parameter-determined, value and subject to the saturation bounds for each c value. Let us see intuitively what variance maximization means to a perceptual system.

Consider first a hypothetical M cell whose c values are such that the cell's output variance is zero. That is, regardless of the input values $(L_1^n, L_2^n, \ldots, L_N^n)$ chosen from the ensemble of presentations,

533

Linsker 1988

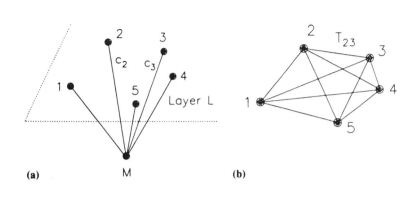

Figure 3. Relationship between networks: (a) a single M cell (with N inputs) of a layered self-adaptive network; (b) a Hopfield network with N cells and $N(N-1)/2$ connections, where $N = 5$.

the output is always the same. This cell would be useless for conveying any information about the environment to later parts of the perceptual system.

On the other hand, if the c values are chosen in a different and special way, then the M cell's output value exhibits the largest possible spread or variance, consistent with the constraints on the c's, as the set of input values ranges over its ensemble. We have shown that a Hebb-type rule tends to generate c values satisfying this special condition. In an informal sense, provided certain conditions are met, the Hebb rule acting on our described M cell tends to produce an M cell whose output activity optimally preserves the information contained in the set of input activities. Later, we will make this statement more precise, by applying some concepts from information theory, and we will modify it to accommodate the situation in which multiple M cells interact with one another.

Optimization in another type of neural network. Hopfield[5] emphasized that the dynamics of a neural network can be described in some cases by the local minimization of a function. An interesting mathematical relationship exists between the E function defined in Equations 5-7 and Hopfield's energy function— although the network structure and behavior that each describes are very different.

Once again, our E function is $E \equiv E_Q + E_k$ where E_Q is shown in Equation 6. The development rule causes E_Q to be minimized subject to the constraint that Σc_j have a specified value and subject to the saturation constraints on each c value. The arrangement described by Equation 6 consists of one M cell with N inputs from cells $L_1, L_2, \ldots, L_N$ and is shown in Figure 3a. The $N \times N$ matrix of elements Q_{ij} is the covariance matrix of the input cell activities. The c's are the connection strengths from each input cell to the output cell. The minimization of E describes the development of the c's under the influence of the ensemble of inputs characterized by the covariance matrix Q.

In Hopfield's case,[5] as illustrated in Figure 3b, there are N cells and the activity state of the ith cell is called V_i. Each pair of cells is connected with fixed connection strength T_{ij}, so the number of connections is of order $N^2/2$, and the energy function is

$$E' \equiv -(1/2)\Sigma_i\Sigma_j T_{ij}V_iV_j \qquad (8)$$

The activities V_i change with time according to a linear summation rule with a threshold: V_i increases, unless it is already at its upper limit, if $\Sigma T_{ij}V_j > 0$, and decreases if $\Sigma T_{ij}V_j < 0$. If the T_{ij} matrix is symmetric, then the V_i's change so as to decrease the value of E' to a local minimum. Connection strengths are fixed;

there is no learning or network development. The dynamical process described by Equation 8 is the change in the activities $\{V_i\}$ from some initial state to a final state of locally minimum E'. If we want to use the network for memory retrieval, a suitable choice of T_{ij} is given by an expression that is essentially the covariance of V_i^k and V_j^k over the ensemble of memories, indexed by k, to be stored.

Note that E' has the identical structure as our E_Q, if we identify V_i with c_i and T_{ij} with Q_{ij}. When T is a covariance matrix, Hopfield's network computes a local minimum of E' using N cells and order $N^2/2$ connections, explicitly embodying the T values. The state for which E' is minimal is the set of final activities $(V_1, V_2, \ldots, V_N)$.

One cell of our network computes a local minimum of the same function, our E_Q, using N connections. The Q function, which corresponds to T, is nowhere explicitly represented in the network. The Hebb rule implicitly responds to the covariance matrix, Q, as the ensemble of input patterns is presented to the M cell. The state for which E_Q is minimal is not a set of activities, but a set of mature connection strengths $(c_1, c_2, \ldots, c_N)$.

Thus, for T matrices that are covariance matrices, one cell of our network can locally optimize the same function as a fully connected Hopfield-type network. In our network, this optimization process consists of developing a final set of c values, starting with some initial set of values, under the influence of a statistically stationary ensemble of input patterns having covariance matrix T. In the Hopfield-type network case, the process consists of seeking a final set of cell activity values starting with some initial set of values, in a network whose connection strengths are fixed and prespecified to be the T values themselves.

These considerations lead to an interesting connection, only briefly outlined here, between memory retrieval and perception in a network model.

Memory retrieval and perception in a network model. If there are sufficiently few memory patterns to be stored, relative to N, then E' or E_Q will tend to have minima at the $\{V_i\}$ or $\{c_i\}$ values, respectively, corresponding to those memories. Depending upon the initial choice of the V's or c's, one or another of these memory states will be activated or selected. In the case of Hopfield's network, "activated" means that the final activity state will match one of the stored memories. In the case of a cell in a layered self-adaptive network, "selected" means that the final set of c values will cause the M cell to be a matched filter for one of these memories. That is, the mature M cell will respond most strongly when presented with the set of input activities corresponding to that memory.

If the number of patterns in the ensemble is large, then the E_Q function will no longer capture details of any one of the patterns. The structure of the E_Q function may become simpler. The global minimum of E_Q will lie at the $(c_1, c_2, \ldots)$ value for which the M cell's variance is maximized. The mature M cell will function as a feature-analyzing cell, rather than as a matched filter to a particular memory. The particular feature or pattern element to which the mature cell will optimally respond, such as an oriented edge, need not even appear in any of the presented patterns.

Principal component analysis. There is a special case in which variance maximization corresponds to an important, and widely-used, statistical method for feature extraction. This is the case in which the output variance is maximized subject to the constraint that $\Sigma c_i^2 = 1$. Oja[6] showed that this maximization can be achieved by using a particular form of the Hebb rule, equivalent to

$$\dot{c}_i \propto \langle M^\pi (L_i^\pi - M^\pi c_i) \rangle \qquad (9)$$

For this expression, we put $M^\pi \equiv \Sigma L_i^\pi c_i$ and define the activities, subtracting nonzero mean values if necessary, so that $\langle L_i^\pi \rangle = 0$ for all i. The additional term in the Hebb-type rule, proportional to c_i, causes Σc_i^2 to be close to 1, and no explicit constraint needs to be imposed.

In statistics, principal component analysis, or PCA, is a standard method, reviewed in Huber,[7] for identifying "interesting" but unanticipated structure, such as clustering, in high-dimensional data sets. For example, an economist confronted with 1000 dimensions of data, such as the prices of different commodities, may want to know which several features of the data, for example, which several linear combinations of the 1000 quantities, are most salient.

PCA works as follows. Consider a set of data points indexed by π, each point $\mathbf{L}^\pi$ having coordinates $(L_1^\pi, L_2^\pi, \ldots, L_N^\pi)$. For PCA, we compute a vector $\mathbf{c}$ for which the projection of the set of data points

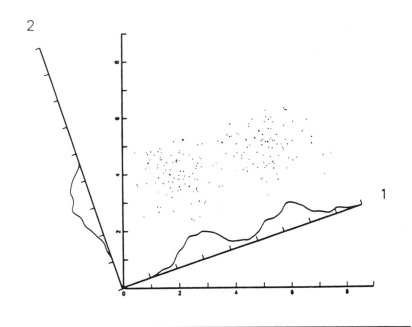

Figure 4. Illustration of principal component analysis. A cloud of data points is shown in two dimensions, and the density plots formed by projecting this cloud onto each of two axes 1 and 2 are indicated. The projection onto axis 1 has maximum variance, and clearly shows the bimodal, or clustered, character of the data.

onto the axis parallel to $\mathbf{c}$ has maximum variance. The projection of $\mathbf{L}^\pi$ onto $\mathbf{c}$, when $\Sigma c_i^2 = 1$, is just $M^\pi = \Sigma_i L_i^\pi c_i$, and the variance of the projected distribution is identical to the variance of M^π.

An example of PCA is illustrated in Figure 4. Projecting the cloud of data points onto line 1 captures the salient feature of the data—that there are two clusters. The variance, or spread, of the data points along this axis is greater than for any other projection axis. Projecting the cloud onto line 2 would obscure the cluster structure. While the cluster structure is evident in the raw data of the two-dimensional plot shown here, such structure is often totally concealed in high-dimensional data sets, until an analysis method such as PCA is applied.

Since the PCA method corresponds to choosing $\mathbf{c}$ so as to maximize the variance of M^π subject to $\Sigma c_i^2 = 1$, it follows that the mature M cell generated by Oja's version of the Hebb rule performs PCA on its set of inputs.[6]

Optimal inference. Consider an arbitrary M cell characterized by a set of c values and having the linear response rule $M^\pi = \Sigma_i L_i^\pi c_i$ with $\langle L_i^\pi \rangle = 0$ for all i. Suppose we know the c values, and are told a particular value of the output, M^π. We are asked to estimate the input activities $(L_1^\pi, L_2^\pi, \ldots, L_N^\pi)$ for that presentation. Let us score any such estimate by

(1) computing the difference between the estimate L_i^π(est) and the true value of L_i^π
(2) squaring this difference, and
(3) summing this squared error over i.

Averaging this score over an ensemble of presentations gives the mean square error

$$\text{MSE} \equiv \Sigma_i \langle [L_i^\pi - L_i^\pi(\text{est})]^2 \rangle \qquad (10)$$

What estimation rule will give the best, meaning the minimum, MSE? For a linear estimation rule of the form $L_i^\pi(\text{est}) = g_i M^\pi$, where we want to know what g values to use, the answer is found by minimizing MSE with respect to each of the g_i's. This is easily done by differentiating MSE. It is also a simple case of the Gauss-Markoff theorem,[8] which applies more generally to the optimal estimation of a set of inputs given a set of outputs, rather than just one output. The result is

$$L_i^{\pi}(\text{opt est}) =$$
$$M^{\pi} \times (\Sigma_j Q_{ij} c_j)/(\Sigma_i \Sigma_j c_i Q_{ij} c_j) \qquad (11)$$

The MSE corresponding to this optimal estimate is then

$$\text{MSE(opt)} = \Sigma_i < [L_i^{\pi} - L_i^{\pi}(\text{opt est})]^2 >$$
$$= \Sigma_i < (L_i^{\pi})^2 > - H \qquad (12)$$

where

$$H = [\Sigma_i (\Sigma_j Q_{ij} c_j)^2]/(\Sigma_i \Sigma_j c_i Q_{ij} c_j) \qquad (13)$$

Expressed in matrix form, with $\mathbf{c}$ denoting the column vector $(c_1, c_2, \ldots)$ and $\mathbf{Q}$ denoting the matrix (Q_{ij}), we have $H = (\mathbf{c}^{\mathbf{T}} \mathbf{Q} \mathbf{Q} \mathbf{c})/(\mathbf{c}^{\mathbf{T}} \mathbf{Q} \mathbf{c})$, where the superscript $\mathbf{T}$ denotes the matrix transpose.

The calculation so far involves a standard use of optimal estimation theory.[8] The linear filter, represented here by the set of c values, is specified. The result of a measurement using the filter—that is, the output value—is given. The task is to reconstruct the input values with minimum error, using a simple mean squared error criterion.

We now go beyond this simple framework to ask[9]: For what linear filter—what set of c values—is this minimum-error reconstruction the most accurate? That is, what choice of c's minimizes MSE(opt) of Equation 12?

Since the first term on the right-hand side of Equation 12 is independent of the c's, minimizing MSE(opt) is accomplished by maximizing H. The mathematical condition for this to occur is that the vector $\mathbf{c}$ be an eigenvector of $\mathbf{Q}$ having maximal eigenvalue. This is identical to the condition that $\mathbf{c}$ needs to satisfy in order for the M cell to perform PCA on its input values. Therefore the PCA condition and the principle of optimal inference—namely, that MSE(opt) be minimized, or H be maximized—lead to the same set of c values. A Hebb rule of the form of Equation 9 generates an M cell that satisfies both conditions. In the presence of other constraints, or additional cost terms, there is no guarantee that PCA and H-maximization are equivalent, since the PCA principle maximizes the quantity

$(\mathbf{c}^{\mathbf{T}} \mathbf{Q} \mathbf{c})/(\mathbf{c}^{\mathbf{T}} \mathbf{c})$ which is not identical to the expression for H in Equation 13.

Optimization in the presence of processing noise and constraints on output variance. We have identified several optimization properties related to the cell's output variance. Suppose, however, that for some reason the variance is itself constrained. For example, the output activity may be confined to lie within some operating range. This is a biologically plausible situation. In this case, what is optimized by a suitable Hebb-type rule? We will discuss this case for a particular processing model, giving only the main results and omitting the details.

Suppose the signal L_j^{π} on the jth input line or connection is corrupted by noise, v_j^{π}, where v_j^{π} has a mean of zero and a variance B, and is uncorrelated both with the noise on other input lines and with any of the input signals L_j^{π}. The cell computes the weighted sum $x = \Sigma_j (L_j^{\pi} + v_j^{\pi}) c_j$. The variance of x is the sum of two terms: the variance due to the signal in the absence of noise, $\Sigma_{ij} Q_{ij} c_i c_j$; and the variance due to the noise, $B \Sigma c_j^2$. Consider a suitable synaptic modification rule in which $\dot{c}_i$ contains a term of the form $< L_i x >$. This rule causes the model cell to develop such that the variance of x due to the signal is maximized relative to the variance due to the noise. This type of signal-to-noise optimization property can also emerge when the cell's output M is a monotonic nonlinear function of x, such as a sigmoid function, if the synaptic modification rule is of the form described.

Adaptive signal processing. Returning to the case of a linear-response model neuron, suppose we wish to train a linear cell to respond to each of a set of prescribed input vectors by generating an output that best matches a prescribed desired output. An input vector is denoted $\mathbf{L}^{\pi} = (L_1^{\pi}, L_2^{\pi}, \ldots , L_N^{\pi})$ and each desired output is a scalar number M_{des}^{π}. The actual output is $M^{\pi} = \Sigma_j L_j^{\pi} c_j$ where each $<L_i^{\pi}> = 0$ and the optimal c values are to be determined by a learning process. A mean square measure of error is used:

$$\text{MSE}' = < (M^{\pi} - M_{\text{des}}^{\pi})^2 > \qquad (14)$$

where $< \ldots >$ again indicates the ensemble average. MSE' is a minimum when the c values are chosen to satisfy $<M_{\text{des}}^{\pi} L_i^{\pi}> = \Sigma_j Q_{ij} c_j$ for all i. (Recall that $Q_{ij} = <L_i^{\pi} L_j^{\pi}>$.) The least mean square, or LMS, algorithm of Widrow and

Hoff[10] uses an estimate of the gradient of MSE' and in effect performs gradient descent to compute the optimal c values. An ensemble-averaged form of the algorithm can be written as

$$\dot{c}_i \propto < L_i (M_{\text{des}}^{\pi} - \Sigma_j L_j^{\pi} c_j) > \qquad (15)$$

Equations 14 and 15 give an objective function to be minimized and an algorithm for a *supervised* learning process. Both the inputs and the desired outputs are presented to the cell, and the error term $(M_{\text{des}}^{\pi} - M^{\pi})$—the amount by which the actual output differs from the desired output—is fed back to change the c values until the mean square error is minimized.

Our optimal inference criterion, namely, the minimization of the objective function of Equation 12, and a Hebb-type rule that implements it (Equation 9) are formally similar to Equations 14 and 15. But the optimal inference criterion provides a method for *unsupervised* learning. The criterion does not make any use of a desired output; it simply states that the M cell should have the property that knowing its output activity value allows one to infer the input activities with greatest possible accuracy.

Information theory and the principle of maximum information preservation

For a single M cell receiving inputs from a given set of L cells, we have seen that, for a particular Hebb rule given in Equation 9, knowledge of the output activity value allows inference of the input values with greatest accuracy, in the sense of minimum mean squared error. For more general Hebb-type rules, we found that the variance of the output activity was maximized subject to various constraints. This result led us to suggest that, at least in an intuitive sense, a Hebb rule may act to generate an M cell whose output activity *preserves maximum information* about the input activities, subject to constraints.

We will now make this notion of maximum information preservation more precise, and will extend it to the case of an entire layer of M cells, by introducing some concepts from information theory. The goal is to see what this principle implies for the development of each layer of a perceptual system. That is, given the statistical properties of the ensemble of input patterns at layer L, and certain constraints, what particular processing functions do the connections from layer L to layer M, and within layer M, develop to implement?

Shannon information. We will regard each presentation of real-valued inputs $\mathbf{L} = (L_1, L_2, \ldots, L_N)$ as a message, where L_i denotes the activity of the ith L cell in the layer. We omit the π superscripts for clarity. Strictly speaking, even one real number carries an infinite amount of information. To avoid encountering expressions of the form, $\infty - \infty$, and because infinite precision is physically and biologically meaningless, we will think of the N-dimensional space of the L vectors as being divided into small boxes. Each box is labeled by its location $\mathbf{L}$. Two messages are regarded as identical if they lie in the same box. In the end, we will pass to the continuum limit, and the sums will become integrals.

Given an ensemble of messages, let $P(\mathbf{L})$ be the probability that a randomly chosen message lies in box $\mathbf{L}$. Shannon[11] showed, in a classic paper, that the information conveyed by sending a message that lies in box $\mathbf{L}$ is $I(\mathbf{L}) = [-\ln P(\mathbf{L})]$. The average information conveyed per message is $< [-\ln P(\mathbf{L})] > = -\Sigma_\mathbf{L} P(\mathbf{L}) \ln P(\mathbf{L})$, where $< \ldots >$ is the usual ensemble average. If the base-2, rather than natural, logarithm were used here, the information would be measured in bits.

Now suppose each input presentation $\mathbf{L}$ generates a set of output values, denoted by the vector $\mathbf{M}$, via some known computation. Suppose that we are told the value of $\mathbf{M}$—or, more strictly, which discrete box $\mathbf{M}$ lies in. (In general, $\mathbf{M}$ will not be uniquely determined by $\mathbf{L}$ because noise may be introduced in the computation of $\mathbf{M}$.) How much additional information would we need to reconstruct the input message $\mathbf{L}$ that gave rise to $\mathbf{M}$? (Shannon calls the ensemble average of this amount of additional information the equivocation.)

The answer is $I_\mathbf{M}(\mathbf{L}) = [-\ln P(\mathbf{L}|\mathbf{M})]$, where $P(\mathbf{L}|\mathbf{M})$ is the conditional probability of the input message lying in box $\mathbf{L}$ given that the output lies in box $\mathbf{M}$. Therefore the amount of information that knowing $\mathbf{M}$ conveys about $\mathbf{L}$ is the difference, $I(\mathbf{L}) - I_\mathbf{M}(\mathbf{L}) = \ln[P(\mathbf{L}|\mathbf{M})/P(\mathbf{L})]$. The ensemble average of this quantity is the rate R, per message, of transmission of information from the cell's inputs to its output. This is the average amount of information that knowing $\mathbf{M}$ conveys

about $\mathbf{L}$. We have

$$R = <\ln[P(\mathbf{L}|\mathbf{M})/P(\mathbf{L})]> \quad (16)$$

We have a standard identity $P(\mathbf{L}|\mathbf{M}) P(\mathbf{M}) = P(\mathbf{L},\mathbf{M}) = P(\mathbf{M}|\mathbf{L}) P(\mathbf{L})$, where $P(\mathbf{L},\mathbf{M})$ is the joint probability that the input lies in box $\mathbf{L}$ and the output lies in box $\mathbf{M}$. Using this gives

$$\begin{aligned} R &= <\ln[P(\mathbf{M}|\mathbf{L})/P(\mathbf{M})]> \\ &= - <\ln P(\mathbf{M})> + <\ln P(\mathbf{M}|\mathbf{L})> \\ &\equiv <I(\mathbf{M})> - <I_\mathbf{L}(\mathbf{M})> \end{aligned} \quad (17)$$

The right-hand side is the ensemble average of the total information conveyed by $\mathbf{M}$, minus the information that $\mathbf{M}$ conveys to one who already knows $\mathbf{L}$. This second term is the "information" that $\mathbf{M}$ conveys about the processing noise, rather than about the signal $\mathbf{L}$.

Maximum information preservation. Let us now state the proposed principle of maximum information preservation for each layer, or processing stage, of a perceptual network: Given a layer L of cells, and the stationary ensemble statistical properties of the signal activity values in the layer, and given that layer L is to provide input to another cell layer M, the transformation of activity values from L to M is to be chosen such that the rate R of information transmission from L to M is maximized, subject to constraints and/or additional cost terms. These constraints or costs may reflect, for example, biochemical and anatomical limitations on the formation of connections, or on the character of the allowed transformations.

The formulation of this principle arose from studying Hebb-type rules and recognizing certain optimization properties to which they lead for single M cells. Once formulated, however, the principle is independent of any particular local algorithm, whether Hebb-related or otherwise, that may be found to implement it. Let us explore

(1) the consequences of the principle for some simple cases;

(2) how the principle might be implemented; and

(3) how it may fit within a broader view of neural development.

A single M cell. Under certain conditions, maximizing the output activity variance of the M cell maximizes the Shannon information rate R. We illustrate this for a particularly simple but instructive case. The argument can be made somewhat

more general than this, but it is not true that maximum information rate and maximum activity variance coincide when the probability distribution of signal values is arbitrary.

Suppose the M cell receives inputs from a set of L cells $L_1, L_2, \ldots, L_N$, and that the M cell's output in the presence of processing noise has the form

$$M^\pi = (\Sigma_i L_i^\pi c_i) + v^\pi \quad (18)$$

Here π indexes the particular set of input and output values, so that if $\mathbf{L}$ is repeated but the output M is different, owing to noise, this counts as a different set of input-output values. The quantity v^π is the noise, a random variable differing from one presentation to the next. Suppose that

(1) M has a Gaussian distribution, with variance denoted by V;

(2) v has a Gaussian distribution with a mean of zero and variance denoted by B; and

(3) v is uncorrelated with any of the input components; that is, $<vL_i> = 0$ for all i.

Then, omitting the details, we find that the information rate is

$$R = (1/2)\ \ln(V/B) \quad (19)$$

For a given noise variance, B, this rate is maximized by maximizing the output variance V of the M cell. Note that V/B is essentially a signal-to-noise ratio.

Suppose that the noise model consists instead of independent Gaussian noise, v_i, being introduced on each input line i, where each v_i has variance B. Then $M^\pi = \Sigma_i(L_i^\pi + v_i^\pi)c_i$, and the information rate is found to be $R = (1/2)\ \ln[V/(B\Sigma c_i^2)]$. In this case, R is maximized for fixed B when $(V/\Sigma c_i^2)$ is maximized—that is, when the connection strengths are chosen so as to perform principal component analysis on the cell's inputs.

Redundancy and diversity. Suppose there is an arbitrary number of L cells but just two coupled linear M cells. Each M cell's output is some linear combination of the L cell's activities:

$$M_1^\pi = (\Sigma_i t_{1i} L_i^\pi) + v_1^\pi \quad (20)$$

$$M_2^\pi = (\Sigma_i t_{2i} L_i^\pi) + v_2^\pi \quad (21)$$

Each noise term is Gaussian and of variance B, the noise terms for the two M cells are uncorrelated with each other, and each noise term is uncorrelated with any of the

L cell activities. We treat the case in which M_1 and M_2 have Gaussian distributions, with $<M_1^\pi> = <M_2^\pi> = 0$. Our task is to determine what values of the t_{ni}'s lead to the maximum information being preserved during the processing of L-cell activities to give M-cell output activities.

Note that the t_{ni}'s do not in general stand for the strengths of particular connections. There may be both feedforward and lateral (M-to-M) connections whose joint effect, possibly over several time steps, is to produce the M-cell outputs of Equations 20 and 21. Our concern here is not with the particular connection strengths, nor with the development rule that may implement them, such as a Hebb-type rule, but rather with understanding what cell response properties—what t_{ni} values—are induced by the principle of maximum information preservation.

Omitting details of the proof, the resulting information rate for this case is

$$R = (1/2) \ln(\text{Det } Q^M) - \ln B \qquad (22)$$

where the elements of the 2×2 covariance matrix Q^M are $Q_{nm}^M \equiv <M_n^\pi M_m^\pi>$ and "Det" denotes the determinant. We find

$$\text{Det } Q^M = B^2 + B(W_1 + W_2) \\ + W_1 W_2 (1 - \varrho_{12}^2) \qquad (23)$$

where W_n is the output variance of cell M_n in the absence of noise, and ϱ_{12} is the correlation coefficient of the activities of M cells 1 and 2, also in the absence of noise.

To maximize R, given B, we must maximize Det Q^M. When B is large, the third term on the right-hand side of Equation 23, which is independent of B, is small compared with the second term, which is of order B. In that case, maximizing Det Q^M means maximizing $(W_1 + W_2)$. If no constraint prevents us, we can achieve this maximization by maximizing W_1 and W_2 separately. But this means constructing each M cell so that its output variance, which is W_n in the absence of noise, or $W_n + B$ in the presence of noise, is maximized. This is exactly what we found to be the optimum solution when there is only one M cell. (See Equation 19.)

If the noise B is smaller, then the third term becomes relatively more important. The rate R is then maximized by making an optimal tradeoff between keeping W_1 and W_2 large, and making the responses of the two M cells uncorrelated.

We have thus found that, depending upon the noise level, there is competition between the value of having redundant M cell responses, which mitigate the information-destroying effects of noise, and the informational value of having different cells extract different linear combinations of the input. A high noise level favors redundancy. In this case, both M cells compute the same linear combination of inputs, if there is only one such combination that yields maximum output activity variance. A lower noise level favors diversity of response. In this case, the M cells compute different linear combinations of the L cell activities, even though each M cell's output variance may be reduced as a result of this choice.

To make this more concrete, consider a simple example. There are two L cells, and the Q matrix for L cell activity has $Q_{11} = Q_{22} = 1$ and $Q_{12} = Q_{21} = q$ with $0 < q < 1$. We arbitrarily impose the constraint that $t_{n1}^2 + t_{n2}^2 = 1$ for each M cell ($n = 1, 2$).

The solution that maximizes the preservation of information then has $t_{11} = t_{22}$ and $t_{12} = t_{21}$, and the values of t_{11} and t_{12} are given in Figure 5 as a function of B and q. For large B, both M cells receive the same linear combination of inputs: $(L_1 + L_2)/\sqrt{2}$. For smaller B, the cells measure different linear combinations of L_1 and L_2. In the limit as B approaches zero, one M cell receives input only from cell L_1 and the other only from L_2.

A layer of M cells with nonlinearity and lateral connections. What does the principle of maximum information preservation, which we shall call the *infomax principle*, imply qualitatively in this more general case? Maximizing R means that we attempt to (1) maximize the total information conveyed by the output message **M**, and (2) minimize the information that **M** conveys to one who already knows the input message **L**. These criteria are related, but not equivalent, to the property of encoding signals so as to reduce redundancies present among the inputs to the perceptual system. The general idea that information theory can be useful for understanding perception is an old one. Significant contributions were made by Attneave in 1954, Barlow in the 1950s and 1960s, and Marr in 1970. Much of this work has focused on the role of redundancy reduction. This property is one, but only one, aspect of the infomax principle. For example, we have seen that infomax also leads to the introduction of redundancy when this is useful in countering the effects of noise.

I have analyzed the qualitative conse-quences of the infomax principle in some very simple models.[12] The results show that the principle can, under certain conditions, lead to L-to-M transformations with the following properties:

- Topographic mapping from layer L to layer M, when the spatial extent of lateral connections within layer M is assumed to be limited. That is, near-neighbors in L tend to map to near-neighbors in M.
- Map distortions, in which a greater number of M cells tend to represent the types of layer-L excitation patterns that occur more often.
- The infomax principle selects which features of the input signals are represented in layer M. Features having relatively high signal-to-noise ratios are favored. This is the extension of our previous redundancy-diversity result to the full-layer case.
- Orientation-selective cells, and the arrangement of such cells in orientation columns, can emerge for some very simple types of model input.
- When time-delayed information is made available to the layer, the infomax principle can cause M cells to extract and encode temporal correlations, in a manner similar to the extraction of spatial correlations.

I must emphasize that much work is required to determine the consequences of the infomax principle for cases involving more biologically realistic patterns of activity.

Discussion

From a simplified set of assumptions—a linear summation response, a simple Hebb-type rule having a covariance form, and feedforward connections only—we derived an optimization principle for the development of a single cell. This principle states that the mature M cell is such that its output activity variance is maximized subject to constraints. More generally, we can have cost terms instead of, or in addition to, constraints. Then the function maximized involves both the variance and the additional cost function.

This led us to infer a proposed principle of maximum information preservation, subject to constraints. It is equivalent to variance maximization in some simple cases, but it has a much broader scope. For example, it can be applied to cases in which a layer of L cells provides input to an entire layer of M cells, with lateral as well as feed-forward connections. It can likewise apply to cases in which the response function is not necessarily linear.

The consequences of this proposed principle are only beginning to be explored. One set of issues that needs clarification is the choice of biologically appropriate constraints and cost terms. A second, related, issue involves the choice of algorithms, whether of Hebb type or otherwise, that control the development of feedforward and lateral connections so as to implement the optimization principle. While much work needs to be done, I suggest that this principle, or something like it, may play an important role in determining the character of perceptual processing at least in its early stages, where there is a chance that feedback influences may not affect the development of feature-analyzing function in an essential way. Possibly the principle may play some role even in the presence of significant feedback, but it is not clear at this time how best to analyze this case.

What might we expect to be the character of a layer of cells developing according to the principle of maximum information preservation, for cases of biological interest? Although the necessary calculations for sufficiently realistic cases have not yet been carried out, we can speculate on the outcome.

Suppose there is a constraint on the distance within layer M over which the activity of one M cell can affect another. There might be, for example, a constraint on the length of lateral connections. Suppose also that each region of layer M "sees", or receives input from, only a limited region of layer L,.and that nearby regions of M "see" nearby regions of L. Then, if the noise variance B is large, and there are not many M cells that "see" the same set of L cells, we might find that each M cell develops so as to maximize its activity variance, and performs processing that is redundant with that of many of its neighbors.

On the other hand, if B is smaller, or there are a large number of M cells that "see" the same L region, we may expect that the M cells in a region do not all perform the same processing function on the inputs from the L layer. Instead, they might span a range of feature-analyzing properties, each of which has a moderately high variance.

In the visual system of cats and monkeys, there are multiple layers of center-surround cells, followed by layers of

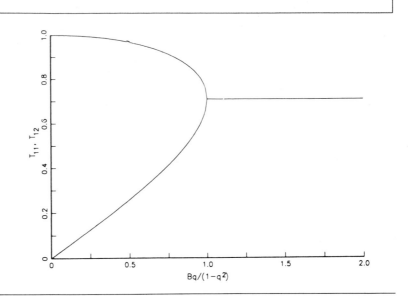

Figure 5. Values of the coefficients t_{ni} that maximize the preservation of information from layer L to M, for a simple case with two L and two M cells. Each M cell output (see Equations 20 and 21) includes random noise having variance B, and q is the correlation, or covariance, of the activities of the two L cells. For $x \equiv Bq/(1 - q^2) \geq 1$, both M cells redundantly compute the same linear combination of the L cell activities (all $t_{ni} = 1/\sqrt{2}$). For $x < 1$, the optimal t values satisfy $t_{11} = t_{22}$ and $t_{12} = t_{21}$, where the upper curve gives t_{11} and the lower curve gives t_{12}, or the reverse. The curves for $x < 1$ are given by $y = (1/2)[(1 + x)^{1/2} \pm (1 - x)^{1/2}]$; this is derived by maximizing Det Q^M. (See Equation 23.)

orientation-selective cells. The orientation-selective cells begin at a different layer in cats than in monkeys. It is possible that, in response to the ensemble of inputs seen by a particular layer, the layer can develop either center-surround or orientation-selective cells, as occurred in our previous model simulations.[1] Perhaps a parameter such as the noise level B "tunes" for redundancy or diversity of response. Redundancy could favor center-surround cell formation, with many cells performing substantially the same processing function. Diversity could favor the formation of orientation-selective cells spanning the entire range of orientation preferences within each region of the layer. (Of a group of cells comprising all orientation preferences, only a small fraction will fire when presented with an oriented edge of illumination.) Hubel and Wiesel discovered[3,4] that orientation-selective cells are arranged, within a cortical layer, so that each small region of cortex ($\approx 1 \times 1$ mil-

limeter) contains the "machinery" for analyzing substantially all edge orientations seen by either eye within a small region of visual space. Perhaps the principle of maximum information preservation, combined with limits on lateral interaction distance, can account for this efficient organization.

Local algorithms. The infomax principle is stated in terms of maximizing a complicated expression (see Equation 16). Is there an algorithm or process that deals with much simpler quantities and computations—local to each cell or pair of connected cells in a network—and yet implements the infomax principle, at least approximately?

I have found[12] that, for some simple cases, a Hebb-related algorithm developed by Kohonen[13] implements some of the qualitative features required by the infomax principle. This algorithm was developed to show how lateral connections can induce topographic order in a simple model, and makes no reference to noise or information content. These results suggest that it may be possible to devise a local algorithm that more fully embodies the requirements of the infomax principle.

The relationship between the principle and such an algorithm would be complementary. The principle would suggest what the function of the algorithm, and the lateral connections it describes, might be—that is, what role the processes and connections might serve in the construction of a perceptual system. The algorithm would show how a complex optimization principle could be implemented by a network of cells that individually have little computational power.

Although I have focused on algorithms that perform activity-dependent modification of connections, other types of mechanisms may be used to implement a given optimization principle. Biochemical cell-cell adhesion markers, chemical or other gradients that may help to establish topographic maps, particular cell types that implement complex types of connectivity (as in the retina), and other mechanisms may all play a role. An organizing principle by itself does not determine the many design details that a particular system—biological or synthetic—may use to implement it.

Infomax and perceptual data. Why might it be important for a perceptual system to maximize the amount of information preserved from one layer to the next?

Presumably, one goal of a perceptual system is to provide the brain with the means of discriminating different environmental situations that may demand different responses by the animal.

For a very simple network with only a couple of layers of processing from environmental input to motor output, we could imagine using some sort of supervised learning mechanism. The mechanism would pair inputs with the desired output responses and adjust the connection strengths accordingly. Such a process involving more than a few layers, however, appears biologically implausible, and its performance may scale poorly as the number of layers is increased.

In a complex network, or in an animal's brain, it is totally unclear how a component layer is to "decide" what transformation its connections should perform—*if* we assume that the layer needs to "know" what environmental features are important for the animal to respond to. This is

the classic artificial intelligence credit assignment problem: if the final output from a complex system is correct, which connections should be rewarded or strengthened?

The approach we propose avoids this problem. Instead of requiring that a connection or layer "know about" the ultimate goals of the animal, we use only local information. The information that reaches a layer is processed so that the maximum amount of information is preserved. We have seen that this does not in general lead to a trivial one-to-one identity mapping, in which each M cell receives input from only one L cell. In general, the identity mapping is not a solution that maximally preserves information, owing to the role of noise in our model. Instead, each M cell tends to respond to features that are statistically and information-theoretically most significant, in a sense similar to that of principal component analysis. Applying the principle of maximum information preservation to each layer of processing in turn, results in the emergence of a sequence of feature-analyzing functions.

The following analogy may help you to see intuitively how the process works. Imagine a person in an organization, whose job is to make the most informative possible summary of the data that he receives each week. The type of data he receives depends upon the environment external to the organization, the structure of the organization (what "layer" he is part of), and various constraints. Over time, he finds that a particular representation of information—for example, graphical plots involving various variables—serves him best in preparing his summary. If he is allowed to interact with others in his "layer", the criterion can be broadened (as we did for the cells) to state that the composite output of his layer should be as informative as possible.

Note that some set of processing functions will end up being provided by this person's "layer", without the workers needing to know either what the goals of the entire organization are, or what information is deemed most important by their superiors in later "layers".

In both the organizational analogy and the real network, there is no need for any higher layer to attempt to reconstruct the raw data from the summary. The point is rather to enable the higher layers to use environmental information to discriminate the relative value of different actions. If the needed information has been lost at intermediate stages, it cannot

be used. If a local optimization principle is to be used—one that does not attempt to take account of remote high-level goals—then we do not know what particular information is going to be needed at high levels. Since we don't know what information we can afford to discard, it is reasonable to preserve as much information as possible within the imposed constraints. The principle of maximum information preservation thus appears to be an extremely natural and attractive one to use in the construction of a layered perceptual system.

Evolution and infomax. The infomax principle may determine what transformation each layer of a given network will implement. However, it does not specify the "gross architecture" of the network; that is, which layers provide input to which other layers. Nor does it specify the various parameters that may affect layer development, such as noise level, the allowed range of lateral connections, and so on. These aspects of the design may be determined by biological evolution, or by other principles not yet identified.

For an analogy, think of an electronic circuit designer who is not free to modify the properties of the components he or she uses, but who can connect them to form a variety of circuits. In the case of our proposed principle, each "component" is an entire cell layer, and the infomax principle determines that layer's behavior given a particular gross architecture or "circuit design". Thus evolution can "close the loop" on the design process, favoring the survival of organisms whose perceptual systems are well-adapted to their environment.

There is a separate and important evolutionary function that a *generic* principle for the development of a perceptual network layer—whether it be infomax or some other principle—can serve. Suppose that an evolutionary mutation produces a modified eye, or merges auditory signals into the visual pathway at some new point. If there were no generic principle for layer development, we might imagine that mutations would have to occur simultaneously in the processing function of several layers, for those layers to be able to use the novel input properly. But if there is such a generic principle—one that applies to each layer regardless of what type of input reaches it—then the novel input will automatically be processed in accordance with that principle. This suggests that the existence of a generic principle may greatly increase the likelihood of a mutation being adaptive.

A broader context. Other complex systems, besides neural networks, pose challenges similar to those we have discussed. How might complex structures and behaviors that may appear goal-oriented emerge from relatively simple local rules? We have seen that a local dynamical rule of Hebb type, acting at synapses, leads to an optimization principle—variance maximization—at the level of the whole cell. This suggested an optimization principle—maximum information preservation—that may apply at the level of an entire layer. From the standpoint of information theory, we may find that the immune response system and biological evolution, among other complex systems, have certain abstract similarities to the process of neural development and plasticity, although the dynamical rules and the substrates upon which they act are quite different.

A great deal of work remains to be done, if we are to take this or some other proposed organizing principle, extract testable predictions from it, and determine its scope and limitations. We need to identify and test such principles, in order to complement and help to focus the enormous amount of detail being revealed by progress in experimental neuroscience. The study of such principles may also provide the understanding needed to develop synthetic perceptual systems that require no explicit programming. □

References

1. R. Linsker, "From Basic Network Principles to Neural Architecture" (series), *Proc. Nat'l Academy of Sciences USA*, Vol. 83, Oct.-Nov. 1986, pp. 7508-7512, 8390-8394, 8779-8783.

2. D.O. Hebb, *The Organization of Behavior*, Wiley, New York, 1949.

3. D.H. Hubel and T.N. Wiesel, "Brain Mechanisms of Vision," *Scientific American*, Vol. 241, Sept. 1979, pp. 150-162.

4. D.H. Hubel and T.N. Wiesel, "Functional Architecture of Macaque Monkey Visual Cortex" (Ferrier lecture), *Proc. Royal Society London*, Vol. B198, 1977, pp. 1-59.

5. J.J. Hopfield, "Neural Networks and Physical Systems with Emergent Collective Computational Abilities," *Proc. Nat'l. Acad. Sci. USA*, Vol. 79, April 1982, pp. 2554-2558.

6. E. Oja, "A Simplified Neuron Model as a Principal Component Analyzer," *J. Math. Biology*, Vol. 15, 1982, pp. 267-273.

7. P. Huber, "Projection Pursuit," *Ann. Statistics*, Vol. 13, No. 2, June 1985, pp. 435-475.

8. P.B. Liebelt, *An Introduction to Optimal Estimation*, Addison-Wesley, Reading, Mass., 1967.

9. R. Linsker, "Development of Feature-Analyzing Cells and their Columnar Organization in a Layered Self-Adaptive Network," in R. Cotterill, ed., *Computer Simulation in Brain Science*, Cambridge Univ. Press, pp. 416-431, in press.

10. B. Widrow and S.D. Stearns, *Adaptive Signal Processing*, Prentice-Hall, Englewood Cliffs, N.J., 1985.

11. C.E. Shannon, "A Mathematical Theory of Communication," *Bell Systems Tech. J.*, Vol. 27, 1948, pp. 623-656.

12. R. Linsker, "Towards an Organizing Principle for a Layered Perceptual Network," in D. Anderson, ed., *Neural Information Processing Systems—Natural and Synthetic*, Amer. Inst. of Physics (NY), to appear.

13. T. Kohonen, *Self-Organization and Associative Memory*, Springer-Verlag, 1984.

Ralph Linsker is on the research staff of the IBM T.J. Watson Research Center. His chief research interests are in the fields of neuroscience and machine perception and learning. Since coming to IBM in 1981 his interests have also included computer design and design automation and medical laser applications. He holds five patents and received IBM's Outstanding Innovation Award for a printed-circuit interconnection design system that has been in production use at IBM since 1983. In the field of medical lasers, he and his colleagues found that pulsed far-ultraviolet radiation can ablate blood-vessel lesions without thermal damage.

Linsker received the BA (summa cum laude) and PhD (in 1972) in theoretical physics from Columbia University, and the MD (in 1976) from Cornell University Medical College. He has done work in theoretical physics at the Princeton Plasma Physics Laboratory, and medical work at New York Hospital.

Introduction

(1988)
Garrison W. Cottrell, Paul Munro, and David Zipser

Image compression by back propagation: an example of extensional programming,
Advances in Cognitive Science, Volume 3, N. E. Sharkey, (Ed.), Norwood, NJ: Ablex

(1989)
Pierre Baldi and Kurt Hornik

Neural networks and principal component analysis: learning from examples without local minima
Neural Networks 2: 53–58

Neural networks are statistics for amateurs. A properly designed network, when learning and responding, performs good statistical inference, based on what it saw when it learned and what it sees when it responds. Most networks conceal the statistics from the user, who is often unaware and uninterested in what is going on internally in the network. The user does not care, for example, what the exact values of the weights are and how the weights reflect environmental structure.

Most technically trained individuals have some usually minimal and sometimes unpleasant exposure to statistics. Fundamentally, however, statistics is a way of extracting meaning from an environment. Statistics forms the basis of signal processing, communication theory, and neural networks. The deep connections between neural network algorithms and statistics have been obvious from the modern beginnings of the field. However, with the easy availability of powerful computers, there is sometimes a tendency to simulate a complex system before it is understood, because it is so easy to simulate and so hard to think.

A good deal of recent evidence suggests that many neural networks are doing something like, what is called in statistics, *principal component analysis*. It is worth describing principal component analysis briefly because the connection to the simpler neural net algorithms is powerful and obvious. The previous paper, by Ralph Linsker (paper 31), explicitly uses principal component analysis, and the close connection between Hebbian learning and principal components is also pointed out by Anderson and colleagues (paper 22, *Neurocomputing: Foundations of Research*). Principal component analysis is discussed in many books on statistics. A good introduction can be found in *Principal Component Analysis* (Jolliffe 1986). The expansion used to find principal components is sometimes referred to as a *Karhunen-Loeve expansion* and arises in engineering discussions of the best way to represent a set of data with the least number of descriptors (Young and Calvert 1974).

The pair of papers we present here show the discovery, and theoretical confirmation, of the presence of something like principal component analysis in a simple, multilayer neural network applied to image compression.

There are some more general issues that arise here as well. One of the important claims for multilayer networks, the most common architecture, is that units in the middle layers "discover" effective ways of representing the input information. In fact the most frequently cited paper on back propagation is entitled, "Learning Internal Representations by Error Propagation" (paper 41 in *Neurocomputing: Foundations of Research*).

Effective internal representation of input data is also the motivation for what is called *feature analysis* in psychology and pattern recognition. One major motivation of feature analysis is dimensionality reduction. Another is a desire to take a complex problem and describe it understandably, in a way that captures the essence of the discriminations that must be made. Suppose we take a square, represented as an array of pixels. There are many different possible squares, in different locations, orientations, and sizes. All these pixel arrays are different in detail, though they represent the same thing. Asking a system to recognize a square, based strictly on learning the different pixel arrays, is difficult and would consume an immense amount of memory; more important, it would not generalize well to squares that were not in the training set. (It is surprising that, even now, one sometimes sees papers in the literature using this unpromising approach.) But suppose we were able to process the pixel array and extract some more general "features" intermediate between the raw pixel data and the final classification and make distinctions based on these features. An example of one possible set of features of a square (there are many different possibilities) might be four equal-length lines (first feature), four right-angle corners (second feature), no isolated ends (third feature), and all corners formed from only two line segments (fourth feature). This description is economical and applies to all squares, even ones never seen before, so it generalizes well.

The obvious architecture for a multilayer network is to have early layers extract features that are then used as input to higher levels. This is an oversimplified version of the way the mammalian visual system works, in which a spatially arranged array of retinal receptors, roughly a pixel array, becomes successively more and more transformed. For example, in primary visual cortex, units respond selectively to orientation, presumably a usefully abstract and general featurelike entity. (As Linsker suggests, it may also be statistically optimal. See the previous paper, paper 31.)

Once the desirability of feature analysis is clear, the practical problem becomes deciding what the intermediate-level features should be. One important claim made for back propagation is that, as part of its operation, it will develop good representations in the hidden layer. And there are several astonishing examples of the development of such representations known; for example, the hidden layer units developed in a genealogical simulation (see paper 42 in *Neurocomputing: Foundations of Research*) which pick up such features as "nationality," "generation," and so on.

Are the features developed in the hidden layer in a multilayer neural network related at all to traditional ideas about pattern analysis known from statistics and pattern recognition? The connection between neural networks and principal component analysis is obvious in some simple situations: The detailed mathematical development can be picked up from the references. Suppose we have a set of examples of data that we wish to work with, examples from a training set, for instance. They form a cloud of points in a very high dimensional state space. To describe the location of a particular point takes a great many numbers. Suppose we want to describe a point in a more compact way, so that we can make the *best* description of a data item, so as to differentiate it from the other members of the training set with the *smallest* number of descriptors.

543
Introduction

Suppose we want to find the particular set of vectors that do the best job of describing the data set as the sum of a small number of components. We are going to *throw away* information, but we would like to throw away as little important information as possible. The principal components are the vectors that minimize the *mean square error* between the actual points in the data set and the points that can be described with a given smaller number of components. Therefore, given some fixed number of descriptors, that number of principal components will give the most accurate description of the data set, in terms of least mean square error. Sometimes the principal components are described as the best set of linear features. In statistics this process is explained by saying that the principal components do the best job of accounting for the variance in the data set.

Principal components are easy to find. (We will ignore normalizing constants for this discussion.) Mathematically, suppose we have a set of data vectors, $\{x_1, x_2 \ldots, x_n\}$, and we want to describe them. The first thing we do is form an outer product matrix, A, where

$$A = \sum_{i=1}^{n} (x_i x_i^T)$$

In statistics, when points of experimental data are used and with appropriate normalization, this is sometimes called the *sample covariance matrix*.

The principal components are the *eigenvectors* of this matrix. Because the matrix is symmetric, the eigenvectors are orthogonal to each other. The *eigenvalues* are a measure of how much variance of the data set that eigenvector accounts for. The larger the eigenvalue, the better job it does describing the members of the data set.

The relation with simple neural networks is now obvious. The outer product matrix is exactly what the connection matrix looks like with a Hebbian learning rule in an autoassociative system. Because the outer product form of Hebb synapse is essentially a measure of covariation between pre- and postsynaptic activity, it is not surprising to find this connection (see also Oja 1982).

Principal components are, however, part of a linear technique. Many interesting features are nonlinear, for example, the previous descriptors of the square. The representations in the hidden layer in back propagation are derived from the operation of a nonlinear system. And, in a general nonlinear system, where an arbitrary set of inputs is to be associated with arbitrary outputs, the connection to the covariance matrix is not clear. But, one might argue, the nonlinear systems used in neural networks are often not *that* nonlinear. Indeed the strange term *semilinear* is sometimes used to describe the nonlinear sigmoid that compresses the output of the inner product box in the generic connectionist neuron. And the hidden layer is doing something much like efficient feature extraction with dimensionality reduction, because it must represent the input information in, usually, a smaller number of hidden units than input units. (Interestingly, if there are a very large number of hidden units, a fully connected back propagation network will often develop hidden units that have learned specific examples from the training set. As long as there are not too many members in the training set, this is the guaranteed zero-error solution.)

The task that the first paper, by Cottrell, Munro, and Zipser, describes is image compression. The network they use is sometimes called an *encoder* network. It is a three-layer network, but the input and output are constrained to be the same pattern, that is, given an input the network must reproduce that input. But there are fewer hidden units than input units;

in the case of this paper, there are 64 input and output units and 16 hidden units. The input pattern must pass through a bottleneck because it must be described by a small number of hidden units, and the reconstruction at the output layer is based on the activity of the hidden units. The practical importance of the problem is that it can be used to save expensive time on a communications channel, where time is literally money. If you can describe a pattern on 64 units of the input layer satisfactorily with 16 activities, why not just send the 16 hidden-layer activities and speed up transmission by a factor of four?

The data used by Cottrell, Munro, and Zipser were raw pixel image data from several photographs of natural scenes. Back propagation was used to develop the best data representation at the hidden layer. The best (mean square) solution to this problem in the linear case is known: the 16 principal components with the largest eigenvalues. What representation at the hidden layer would the nonlinear network develop?

The computational result is that the result of processing by the hidden units was very close to what would have been obtained by principal component analysis, though nothing so simple as a one hidden unit–one principal component identity occurred. The space spanned by the activation of the 16 hidden units was roughly the same as the space generated by the first 16 principal components. That is, the hidden units and the principal components were describing the same region of state space. The major difference was that the activities of the hidden units were such as to equalize the information transmitted across the hidden units—that is, each hidden unit was roughly of the same importance in the information it transmitted about the image. The amount of variance accounted for by the principal components is a function of the eigenvalue and can differ a great deal between principal components.

The second paper, by Baldi and Hornik, puts this experimental result on a firmer theoretical foundation. *If we assume that the hidden units are linear*, then Baldi and Hornik show that the solution that the network will find is indeed to have the hidden units span the principal component space; and the hidden units, as found by Cottrell, Munro, and Zipser, will have roughly equal importance to information transmission. Baldi and Hornik make another interesting observation: It is known that back propagation, which adjusts weights to minimize error by using gradient descent, is very slow. Baldi and Hornik suggest that one reason for this is that the error surface that the network is descending has many plateaus on it, though only a single global minimum. The gradient is very small on a plateau, and the network changes weights very slowly there. For this network it might be more practical to simply compute the principal components directly than to use back propagation to come up with the same solution. Also, as suggested by the simulations, for working with real-world data such as natural images, the nonlinear system seems to behave much like the straightforward and easily computed linear solution.

The conclusion of this short pair of papers is significant. Traditional statistics and pattern recognition often offer important insights into why a network works as it does. There is also a suggestion that for work with real-world data as opposed to extremely nonlinear problems like exclusive-OR or parity, one might start with simple and well understood statistical techniques.

References

I.T. Jolliffe (1986), *Principal Component Analysis*. New York, NY: Springer.

E. Oja (1982), A simplified neuron model as a principal component analyzer. *Journal of Mathematical Biology* 15: 267–273.

T.Z. Young and T.W. Calvert (1974), *Classification, Estimation and Pattern Recognition*. New York, NY: Elsevier.

(1988)
Garrison W. Cottrell, Paul Munro, and David Zipser

Image compression by back propagation: an example of extensional programming
Advances in Cognitive Science, Volume 3, N. E. Sharkey, (Ed.), Norwood, NJ: Ablex

INTRODUCTION

The recent discovery of powerful learning algorithms for parallel distributed networks has made it possible to program computation in a new way. These new techniques allow us to program massively parallel networks by example rather than by algorithm. This kind of *extensional programming* is especially useful when there are no known techniques for solving a problem. This is often the case with the computations associated with basic cognitive processes such as vision and audition. In this paper we compare extensional programming to the traditional approach using a well-understood problem in image analysis, i.e., bandwidth compression. Our results demonstrate that a very simple learning method is able to program networks to do image compression about as well as the best known techniques.

The technique we employ is known as *back propagation*, developed by Rumelhart, Hinton, and Williams (1986a). It can be considered a generalization of the perceptron learning procedure for multilayer nonlinear networks of neuronlike computing elements and answers the basic objections of Minsky and Papert (1969) to such learning mechanisms. Training the network consists of repeated presentations of input-output pairs representing the function to be learned. The learning algorithm operates by adjusting the weights between the elements of the network in such a way as to reduce the overall error in the output. In many cases, the network finds a solution to the problem that was unknown in advance to the user. In doing so, it develops its own *internal representation* of the input that is useful for solving the problem. It is often difficult to analyze this representation because many units are involved and the representations are highly *distributed* over the set of internal units. A subgoal of the present research is to make a first step towards unraveling the nature of these representations by applying the learning mechanism to a domain where the types of useful representations have been well studied.

Another aspect of this work is that the representation of images in an efficient format by neuronlike computing elements may give us clues to the way such information is represented in actual neural tissue. The learning procedure itself is not particularly biologically plausible (Zipser, in press), but the mechanisms it discovers for solving problems are. Whether or not there is anything like back propagation in the brain, we learn something about how the brain *could* solve problems from the solutions it discovers. Such information could be useful in guiding neurobiologists in their observations of cell firings during cognitive tasks.

The rest of the paper is organized as follows. First we provide an intuitive introduction to the back-propagation algorithm, its application to *encoder problems*, of which image compression is an example, and an abbreviated look at current techniques in image compression. Details of back propagation and its derivation can be found in Rumelhart, Hinton, and Williams (1986b). Some important mathematical properties of the image compression technique we consider are provided in the Appendix. Readers who are familiar with these areas are encouraged to pass on to the results section. It should be noted that we knew none of the techniques for image compression until after we completed the main part of the project. They are presented for comparison purposes and because they are useful in analyzing the solution discovered by the network. Following the background we present the results of our simulations. Several simple network architectures are shown to demonstrate near state-of-the-art compression of image information, and the nature of the internal representation developed by the networks is explored. This is followed by a discussion of the significance of the results. Finally, we suggest problems left unsolved.

BACKGROUND

The Back-Propagation Algorithm for PDP Networks

Parallel distributed processing (PDP) models[1] consist of networks of simple neuronlike processing units connected by weighted links. The units communicate by passing real-valued activation across the links. In the kind of PDP networks we will be considering, the networks are arranged in layers, with the outer layers corresponding to input and output (see Figure 1), and activation only passing one way through the network. A model of a particular function is built by picking a representation of the domain and range of the function as patterns of activation across input and output units. Units in the internal layers are referred to as *hidden units*, and correspond to an *internal representation* of the input environment that is useful in producing the desired output. *Supervised learning schemes* are ones in which the network is given repeated examples of the desired input-output mapping, and the network adjusts the weights between units to produce the desired function. The network thus *programs itself* to solve the task.

Output Patterns

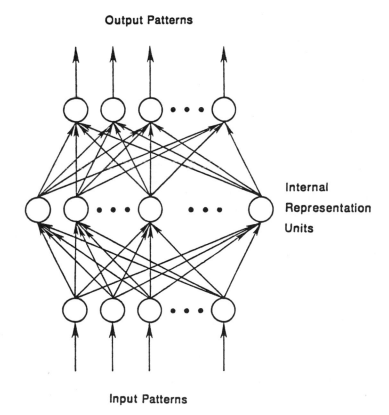

Internal
Representation
Units

Input Patterns

FIGURE 1. A feed-forward PDP network.

---

[1] These are also known as *connectionist* models (Feldman & Ballard, 1982).

Back propagation is a supervised learning scheme for PDP networks that is currently accepted in the PDP community as the best known technique. The basic idea is to change the weights between the units in such as a way as to reduce the error in the output. An input pattern is presented to the network, and activation is propagated forward through the network to the output units. The correct output pattern is provided to the output units in the form of a *teaching signal*. It is clear how output units should change their weights to reduce the error. If their value is too low, they should raise the weights on active input lines. If their value is too high, they should lower the weights. This will tend to make them attain the proper value in the same situation in the future. What is difficult to determine is how the hidden units should change their weights—there is no explicit teacher for them. Back propagation provides a rule for propagating an error signal back through the network from the output units, which tells the hidden units which way to change their weights. The surprising thing is that the rule for changing the weights is a purely *local* one, in the sense that every unit can find out its error through the connections that already exist in the network.

The weight-changing rule is derived by defining an error measure—the mean square error of the output—and taking the partial derivative of this with respect to the weights. Intuitively, we can think of the error as a surface over the space of possible weights. Taking the partial derivative tells us which way to move in weight space in order to go downhill fastest. Because this is a gradient descent algorithm for reducing the error, it is subject to the major problem associated with gradient descent procedures, i.e. *local minima* in the error surface. However, experience has shown that we very rarely run into the problem of local minima in networks with many weights.

The Encoder Problem

Image compression is a type of *encoder problem*.[2] That is, a network is given the problem of performing an identity mapping over some set of inputs. The network is constrained to perform this mapping through a narrow channel of the network, forcing it to develop an efficient encoding in that channel. There are two interesting aspects to this: (a) the network is developing a compact representation of its "environment"; and (b) although the algorithms used were developed as supervised learning schemes, this problem can be regarded as unsupervised since the output is the same as the input— the system self-organizes to encode the environment.

An example is shown in Figure 2, from Rumelhart et al. (1986). The network shown here is an *N-K-N* encoder—a three layer network in which the input and output layers have N units each, and an intermediate layer with K units ($K < N$) that is the "channel" between the other two. The problem presented to the network is to associate one unit being on in the input layer with a corresponding one being on in the output layer, with no a priori mapping existing between the two. In their simulations, they found that with $K = \log_2(N)$, the network could learn the binary encoding of the environment.

Image Compression Techniques

Introduction

The efficient encoding of the information contained in a digitized image is of considerable practical interest due to the sheer number of bits in a typical image. Applications include reducing storage and transmission requirements, and using the encoding as a feature analysis of the image. The idea is to take a section of the image and *transform* it into a domain where the information can be encoded more efficiently. If we are willing to allow some degradation of the image, it is possible to take an image which is represented by eight bits per picture element (or *pixel*) and transmit it using less than 1 bit/pixel.

---

[2] Ackley, Hinton, and Sejnowski (1985) were the first to demonstrate a learning algorithm for PDP networks that could solve the encoder problem.

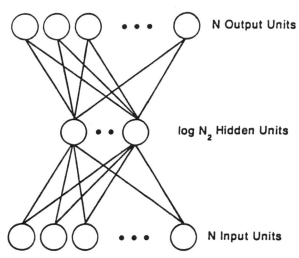

FIGURE 2. An *N-K-N* encoder (from Rumelhart et al. 1986). One unit at a time in the input vector is "on." The network learns the binary encoding of the position of the "on" unit in order to turn on the same unit in the output.

Basic Concepts

For our purposes, we define an *image* as a discretized $M \times N$ light intensity function $f(x,y)$, where x and y correspond to the spatial coordinates within the image, and $f(x,y)$ is a light intensity value from 0 to $2^K - 1$, where K will typically be 8 for us. One element of $f(x,y)$ is often referred to as a *pixel*, for *picture element*. *Image compression* then refers to the process of converting these $M \times N \times K$ bits to another representation where fewer bits can be used, and a new version of the image, $g(x,y)$ can be constructed which is a "reasonable" reconstruction of the original. By reasonable, we mean within some *fidelity criterion* of the original image.

The choice of a fidelity criterion is problematic, since most analytic measures that have been used do not correspond in a neat way to people's subjective ratings of images. However, for objective comparison, usually some form of mean-square error measure is used. If $g(x,y)$ is the reproduced image, then the error is given by

$$e(x,y) = g(x,y) - f(x,y),$$

the mean-square error is given by

$$MSE = \frac{1}{M \times N} \sum_{x=0}^{M-1} \sum_{y=0}^{N-1} e^2(x,y),$$

and the normalized MSE with respect to the average squared intensity of the image is given by

$$NMSE = \frac{MSE}{\frac{1}{M \times N} \sum_{x=0}^{M-1} \sum_{y=0}^{N-1} f^2(x,y)}.$$

This is what we will use, expressed in percent.

Image compression is measured in terms of the bits per pixel of the output image actually transmitted over the channel. Although one might think it should be the ratio of bits in the original image to bits in the encoded image, this can be a misleading measure. If the original image uses 15 bits/pixel, the final image could use significantly less without any apparent degradation, due to limitations in the resolving power of the human eye. Hence the number of bits used in the encoding per pixel of the restored image is a typical measure used. This is independent of the number of bits used for the original pixels. This is then plotted relative to some fidelity criterion, for example, the NMSE defined above.

Current Techniques

The following discussion has been adapted from Gonzales and Wintz (1977). Depending on the requirements of the application, techniques for image compression fall into two classes: error-free encoding and encoding relative to a fidelity criterion. We will be concerned with the second class, since we wish to find something comparable to our networks' behavior. In particular, we will consider *transform encoding* techniques.

A typical encoding system consists of three processes, as shown in Figure 3. The first stage maps the input data from the pixel domain to another domain that is useful for reducing the number bits that must be used to encode the data. The quantizer rounds off the the output of the mapper, and the coder assigns a code word (such as a Huffman code) to the quantizer output. In our work, we have simply used the output of the quantizer as the final result to be "transmitted," so we will not consider the coder further.

The Mapper

The kinds of mapping we will be considering are *linear transformations*.[3] First the $M \times N$ image is divided into $n \times n$ subimages and the subimages are encoded separately. In *nonadaptive* transform encoding, the same coder is used for all subimages. In *adaptive* transform encoding, the subimage is classified in some way first by a pattern-matching algorithm, and the best available encoder is used for each type of subimage. Some researchers advocate a different type of adaptive coding in which the

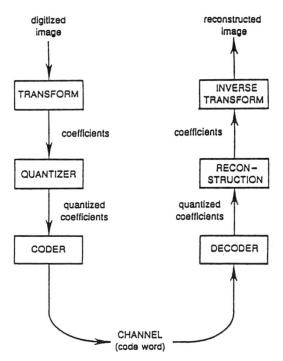

FIGURE 3. A typical image compression system.

---

[3] Other types of mappings are also used, such as run-length and DPCM encoding, but are not comparable to the network model, so we will not consider them further.

same transform is used for each, but the quantizer is adaptive for each subimage's coefficients (Tescher, 1979). We will consider this possibility later.

Considering each $n \times n$ subimage as a vector x, a linear transformation is of the form

$$y = Ax,$$

where A is an $n^2 \times n^2$ array, giving a new n^2-vector y. If A is invertible, then so is the encoding. The reconstructed image is the inverse transform

$$\hat{x} = By$$

where B is usually A^{-1}. The point of the transformation is to take the pixels, which are usually highly correlated, and produce numbers, which are less correlated. These can often be encoded more efficiently than the original pixels.

The idea is illustrated in Figure 4. This is a scatter-plot of height vs. weight for some hypothetical set of people. Notice that height and weight are highly correlated and thus, to some degree, redundant information. If we rotate the axes of the coordinate system along the direction of maximum variance, with the restriction that the axes be orthogonal, we get a new set of axes as shown. We now have two sets of numbers that are less correlated than the original pair of coordinates—the distance along the y_1 axis, which might be called "size," and the distance from that axis, y_2. Notice that the magnitude of the y_1 coordinate is about the same as either of the orginal x coordinates, and the y_2 coordinate is considerably smaller. Thus we should be able to use a smaller number of bits to encode them. Also, if we were willing to tolerate some error in the reproduction, we could simply transmit the y_1 coordinate and get most of the information, since the y_1 coordinate captures most of the variance of the plot. This scatter-plot could just as well be a plot of neighboring pixel values, which are typically highly correlated.

The same procedure can be used for an $n \times n$ array of pixels. If each pixel is represented by an intensity level between 0 and $2^K - 1$, then we can represent any such image in a n^2-dimensional coordinate system with each axis labeled $0, \ldots, 2^K - 1$. Each image corresponds to a point in this space. In this case, the desired rotation of the coordinate system involves n^2 axes.

There is a procedure that finds just this set of axes, called the *Hotelling* or *principal components* transform. Its derivation and the computational properties discussed below are given in more detail in the Appendix. Briefly, the rows of the transform matrix A are formed from the eigenvectors of the covariance matrix of the x-vectors. This could be done for each patch independently (adaptive encoding) but typically the patches to be reconstructed (the x-vectors) are treated as multiple instances of the same vector variable, and the same transform is used for each patch. For example, the axes shown in Figure 4 are the eigenvectors of the covariance matrix of x_1 and x_2. They are arranged in A in order of amount of variance accounted for.

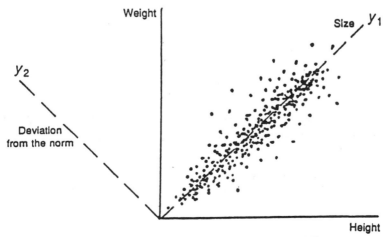

FIGURE 4. Height vs. weight scatter plot for a large population. (Adapted from Mozer, 1983.)

There are several things that are of note. First, it can be shown that the coefficients *y* are *uncorrelated*, as desired. Second, if one uses the first *K* rows of the matrix A formed in this way, rather than the whole thing, and thus send only *K* coefficients to the quantizer, then this is provably optimal in the mean-square error sense for *K* coefficients (see the Appendix). The problem with the Hotelling transform is the computational expense involved in computing the eigenvectors anew for each image. There are deterministic transforms (that is, that don't depend on the image), such as the discrete cosine/Fourier and Walsh-Hadamard transforms, which approach the Hotelling transform in variance accounted for in the first *K* coefficients. Hence the Hotelling transform is more a standard for comparison than a useful algorithm. However, we considered it because it will be a useful solution to compare and contrast to the solution discovered by back propagation.

Basis Images

Each pixel of the reconstructed image patch is a linear combination of the transmitted y_i coefficients. But taken as a whole, the image patch can be regarded as a linear combination of *basis images*, one for each coefficient.[4] The set of basis images for the Hotelling and Hadamard transforms of a picture of a cameraman (from Gonzales and Wintz, 1977) are shown in Figure 5. The Hadamard transform is a deterministic one, so these basis images are the same for all images it is applied to. The Hotelling basis images depend on the transformation matrix A, which in turn depends on the statistics of the particular image. The ones shown here are for a 256×256 image, with 16×16 subimages. For image compression, only a subset of the coefficients are actually transmitted—those that account for most of the variance. These correspond to some square of basis images in the upper left-hand corner of the total array of basis images. Typically, at least half of the coefficients can be discarded this way without visible degradation of the image.

The Quantizer

The number of possible values of the coefficients transmitted, the y_i's, can be considered infinite. Hence we have to have a strategy for assigning them to some finite number of values if we wish to

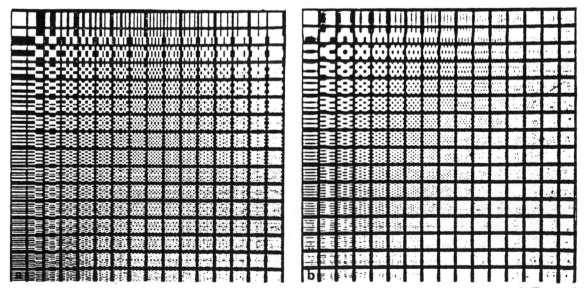

FIGURE 5. The set of basis images from two types of transforms. *A*: The set of Walsh-Hadamard basis images. *B*: The set of Hotelling basis images for a particular image. (From Gonzales & Wintz, 1977. Reprinted by permission.)

[4] This really requires viewing the transform as a two-dimensional one, but the idea is clear enough without getting into a jumble of subscripts. For each coefficient, the basis image is the corresponding column of the reconstruction matrix B.

achieve true data compression. This is called *quantization*. There are two aspects to quantization. First, for a particular range of values, one could use a *uniform* quantizer, i.e., equally spaced values, or, depending on where the coefficients "spend the most time," one could use a *nonuniform* quantizer, with more values in the "busy" regions (Max, 1960).

Second, there is the issue of whether to use the same quantizer across all coefficients or not. Since the variance of the coefficients can be considerably different from one to the other, this is usually unwise. One strategy, then, is to normalize the coefficients by their standard deviation, resulting in unit variance for all the coefficients, so that one quantizer (and hence the same number of values) may be used for all.

However, the coefficients with the largest variance contribute the most information, thus it is better to assign them more quantization levels. This is called *block quantization*. Huang and Schultheiss (1963) found that the number of bits used to code a particular coefficient should be proportional to the log of the variance of the coefficient. This minimizes the mean square error in quantized coefficients. In a completely linear system, this also minimizes the mean square error in the output due to quantization.

RESULTS

The problem to be solved is the compression of the information in a single image. The network used here does this by learning an identity mapping through a narrow channel. The result is that the image can be represented with very little loss of information with 1 bit/pixel, representing an eight-fold compression of the information in the image. The network also does a good job of compressing several images it was not trained on.

We have conducted several trials with three-layer networks, generally training them on a single image. The network we have used most often consists of 16 hidden units each of which receive input from an 8×8 patch of the image. These then are completely connected to an 8×8 unit output patch. This is diagrammed in Figure 6.

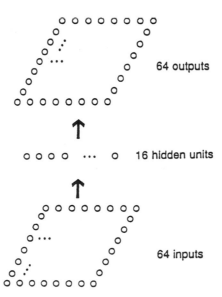

FIGURE 6. The network used in most of our examples.

The function computed by the units is the *logistic* function:

$$output = \frac{2}{1 + e^{-x}} - 1$$

where the x is the weighted sum of the inputs and a bias term. This is an S-shaped function that ranges from −1 to 1 (see Figure 7). It is sometimes referred to as the *squashing function* because it takes the linear input and "squashes" it into a small range.

In order to have a representation of the gray levels of the image that could be produced by this function, the gray levels of the image were converted linearly from the 0 to 255 range to the range 0 to 1, or 0 to .85. Although the latter representation appears to work the best, the results presented here derive from the former for historical reasons. Other conversions, such as to the range −1 to 1, didn't work as well because they force the output units into ranges hard to get at by the logistic function.

The training regime consisted of randomly sampling patches of the image, allowing activation to propagate through the network, and then back-propagating the error on each trial, adjusting the weights. It was found that a learning rate of .25 worked well initially, and better results were obtained by then lowering the learning rate to .01. This was a hard problem, and typically we would let the network run for 100,000 iterations at .25 and another 50,000 at .01. The use of momentum (see Rumelhart et al., 1986a) did not seem to help.

After training, the resulting "patch compressor" was tested by using it to compress and reconstruct the whole image by dividing the image into nonoverlapping patches and reconstructing one at a time. In order to achieve true compression, the outputs of the hidden units must be quantized. Two things made this easy for us. First, the squashing function forces all outputs into the range −1 to 1, so no scaling is necessary. Second, back propagation tended to distribute the error relatively evenly over the hidden units in this situation. Thus the hidden unit output variances were about equal, so block quantization was not used. We simply used a uniformly spaced quantizer that retained the endpoints (−1 and 1) of the output values (see Figure 8). Quantization then consists of linearly transforming the outputs of the hidden units (which were in the interval [−1,1]) to some integer range corresponding to the number of bits required, and then back again, effectively restricting their information to the number of bits used. Better results could be obtained by taking into account the output values most often used and using nonuniform bucket spacing. It turns out that in this problem, the hidden units rarely reach the outer limits of the squashing function, so the endpoints of the quantizer were wasted.

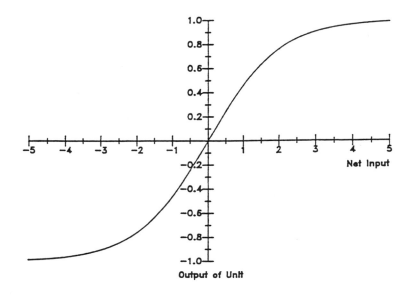

FIGURE 7. The logistic activation function.

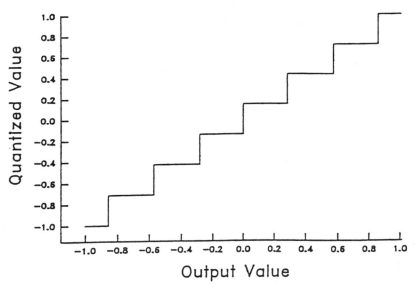

FIGURE 8. The quantization buckets used in reconstructing the image with three bits of output values (four or five bits are usually necessary).

Compression Results

The original image and the reconstructed image are shown in Figure 9. In this reconstruction, the outputs of the hidden units were restricted to eight bits (or 256 quantized values). This corresponds to a compression rate of 2 bits/pixel, with a corresponding error of 0.413%. It turns out that this is as good as this network does without any quantization.[5] One thing to notice here is that the network has done a good job of avoiding edge effects around the patches from the reconstruction process. Most of the errors are at the edges of objects in the image and in the stripes on the seated man's shirt.

By reducing the quantization of the hidden unit outputs, better compression results can be obtained without sacrificing much in mean square error. Figure 10 shows the effects of quantization. Notice that apparently most of the information is captured by restricting the hidden units to 32 output values (Figure 10A), with minor mean square error cost. This corresponds to an encoding rate of 1.25 bits/pixel. When quantization is reduced to four bits, the effects become pronounced.

Another approach to getting better compression results is to enlarge the input patch or reduce the number of hidden units. Figures 11 and 12 show the results of two experiments along these lines. Figure 11 shows the result of using a 16×16 input patch with 16 hidden units, and five bits of quantization on the hidden unit outputs—a pretty lousy picture, but it is based on only .312 bits/pixel. Figure 12 is more successful. This is the result of using the original 8×8 input patch, but only eight hidden units, with 32 quantization levels. Here we have a relatively decent picture with a compression rate of .625 bits/pixel.

There is a possible trade-off between the number of hidden units and the number of bits used in quantization. It seems reasonable to expect that if there are more hidden units, we can get away with fewer output values. This is partially true. The image in Figure 13 was obtained using an 8×8 input patch through 32 hidden units and four bits of output. This is the only network we have trained that reproduces the shirt stripes, so in that sense it is a "good" image. However, the NMSE is comparable to the case of using four bits with 16 hidden units, and there is a patchiness effect—the patches used to reconstruct the image become visible. Also, due the increase in the number of hidden units, this is an unimpressive compression rate of 2 bits/pixel, and reducing the number of quantization levels any more makes the picture unacceptable. (On the other hand, raising the rate to 3 bits/pixel produces a

---

[5] As expected, throwing away half the coefficients (i.e., using 32 hidden units) results in no visible degradation. With six bits of quantized values, this corresponds to 3 bits/pixel.

FIGURE 9. *A*: The original image of the Intelligent Systems Group (ISG) at UCSD. *B*: The reconstructed image using eight bits (or 256 quantization values), representing 2 bits/pixel, resulting in NMSE of 0.413%.

FIGURE 10.

FIGURE 10. Quantization effects. *A*: 5 bits, 1.25 bits/pixel, NMSE 0.474%. *B*: 4 bits, 1 bit/pixel, NMSE 0.676%. *C*: 3 bits, .75 bits/pixel, NMSE 1.796%.

near-perfect image). The reason is that we are not working the network very hard. Taken to its extreme, suppose we had 64 hidden units. Then each hidden unit would just have to duplicate the output of the corresponding input unit. They would require most of the output range to be faithful, and no compression would be attained because restricting the bits of the hidden units would incur too much error. Thus it is important to force the network through a bottleneck or no efficient encoding is achieved.

Another possible way to achieve better performance at 1 bit/pixel is to increase the patch size along with the number of hidden units. In Figure 14, we show the result of using a network with a 16×16 input patch and 64 hidden units. This is the same ratio of units as in the 64×16 case, hence the same quantization level results in the same bit rate. Using four bits of quantization levels results in only marginally less mean square error cost than in the 64×16 case, but the image is qualitatively better than the one in Figure 10B using 1 bit/pixel. This beneficial effect is due to using a larger input patch. Figure 15 is a graph relating normalized mean-square error (NMSE) to the ratio of patch size to bit rate for two different patch sizes. It shows that the bigger patch attains a lower NMSE for the same bit rate.

At the outset of this research, we expected that perhaps a network could be trained that would work well for all images, justifying the expense of the initial training. This is a somewhat misplaced dream, given that our network learns, in some sense, the statistics of the image it is trained on, and different images have different statistics. However, we thought, perhaps it will work well for a class of images. It turns out that it does a creditable job of reproducing some images that it wasn't trained on. Two of the images we tested it on and their reproductions are shown in Figure 16.

An interesting aside here is that a linear version of the network without quantization[6] does a much better job of generalizing to other images, in some cases resulting in less NMSE than on the training

---

[6] In this case, all of the units in the network are linear, and back propagation is the same—the derivative of the activation function is simply a constant, and so can be ignored. This is a generalization of the Widrow-Hoff delta rule to layered networks.

FIGURE 11. A reproduction using a 16×16 input patch and 16 hidden units. Compression rate is .312 bits/pixel, NMSE 2.670%.

FIGURE 12. The reproduced image using eight hidden units, 32 quantizer levels, resulting in .625 bits/pixel, NMSE 1.182%.

FIGURE 13. The reproduced image using 32 hidden units, four bits of quantized levels, 2 bits/pixel, NMSE 0.625%.

FIGURE 14. The reproduced image using a 16×16 input patch, 64 hidden units, and four bits of quantization levels. This is a compression rate of 1 bit/pixel, NMSE 0.590%.

Cottrell, Munro, and Zipser 1988

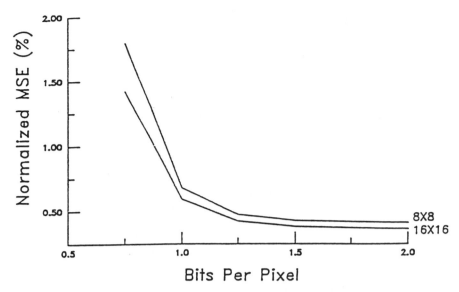

FIGURE 15. Graph showing effects of larger input patch.

image. However, this does not necessarily mean compression because in the linear reconstructions the outputs of the hidden units were not quantized. Since the units are linear, their activation is not restricted to a particular range, and quantization of the hidden unit outputs requires knowledge of their statistics to be done properly. Preliminary study shows that the linear version is comparable to the nonlinear version when quantized, but we have not looked at its generalization behavior under these circumstances. It is likely that the range of hidden unit values will vary more widely with images of different energy. The linear network seems a perfect candidate for adaptive quantization as proposed by Tescher (1979). This approach could make the linear version quite attractive by allowing use of the dynamic range of the linear version, which is probably how it achieves such better generalization results.

The Network's Solution

Now the question is: What is the nature of the solution the network has discovered? What is the internal representation at the hidden unit layer? We don't have an analytic answer to this question. However, we can compare the network's solution to the principal components transform to get an idea of what it does.

First we set up some correspondences between our network and the usual image compression system. Recall that the first step in transform encoding is to multiply the patch vector by a matrix to obtain less correlated coefficients:

$$y = Ax.$$

The analog in our network is that A is the weight matrix between the input and hidden unit layers, with each row of A corresponding to the input weights on one hidden unit, and each hidden unit output a semilinear version of y_i.

Both back propagation and principal components analysis (PCA) minimize mean square error, but probably in different ways since there are many ways to accomplish this. Principal components does it by having each row of A be the projection of the image onto axes corresponding to decreasing amounts of the variance. The first hidden unit responds to the direction of maximum variance, the next to an orthogonal axis that accounts for the next highest amount of variance, etc. Each hidden unit then has variance equal to the eigenvalues of the corresponding eigenvectors, which start large and quickly diminish. Thus all hidden units, or rows of the matrix A, are not equal in accounting for the error of the output.

The variance of the coefficients is strongly correlated with the amount of image variance along the axis the hidden unit reflects. We ran an experiment where during the reconstruction process, we recorded the mean square error of the resulting image if each hidden unit's output was set to 0.[7] The results of this experiment are given in Table 1. We can see from the table that while the hidden units don't account for equal amounts of error, they are not spread out in the way that a principal component analysis would be. The variance of each unit is also shown in Table 1. The variances are about equal and are highly correlated with the output error without the corresponding hidden unit. If the network were doing a principal components analysis, the hidden units would be individually responding to the eigenvectors of the covariance matrix, then their variances would be equal to the eigenvalues of those eigenvectors, which typically differ by orders of magnitude from the first to the last. The network, on the other hand, finds axes where the variances are much closer together. The tendency of the network to produce variances within a similar range is probably due to the constraint that the hidden units operate in a fixed range. Figure 17 is a histogram of the outputs of all of the hidden units collapsed together during reconstruction of the training image. It is handy that the squashing function has this "built-in" range constraint, essentially solving some aspects of the quantization problem for us as part of its solution. This explains why it was easy to obtain good results with a simple-minded quantizer. On the other hand, the histogram shows that there are much better quantizers for this network—one that takes into account where the outputs are spending most of their time would have given better results.

Figure 18A shows the weight matrix for each of eight hidden units thresholded at various levels, one hidden unit per row. This shows what pattern in the input excites each hidden unit most. Figure 18B shows the output patch driven by each hidden unit alone. Again, each row corresponds to one hidden unit, and the columns correspond to different levels of activation from the hidden unit. The left-hand column corresponds to the hidden unit outputting a −1, the right-hand column a +1. One obvious thing to note here is that the hidden units try to reproduce what they "see." Figure 18C shows the same information as 18B, but on a color monitor to show the gray scale. (18B is a thresholded version of 18C.) These are the basis images for the network. An interesting point here is that they look more alike than different in their level of complexity. That is, there is not a clear ordering as there is for the basis images of the Hotelling transform.

TABLE 1

HIDDEN UNIT STATISTICS

Unit	Average	Variance	MSE Without the Unit
0	0.342	0.10347	286.828
1	0.344	0.11533	397.380
2	-0.364	0.12112	355.864
3	0.349	0.11144	347.517
4	-0.346	0.12042	434.365
5	-0.348	0.10504	319.268
6	0.355	0.11542	391.452
7	-0.346	0.12734	459.412
8	-0.341	0.11305	358.808
9	-0.361	0.11763	428.412
10	0.320	0.09896	295.973
11	-0.343	0.12459	414.386
12	-0.343	0.11999	414.046
13	-0.332	0.10390	312.565
14	-0.351	0.11661	417.271
15	0.359	0.10821	359.726

[7] This is analogous to pulling the plug wires on an engine one at a time and watching the RPM to see how much each cylinder is contributing to the engine speed.

A

B

FIGURE 16.

FIGURE 16. Two images reproduced by the network trained on the image in Figure 9A. *A*: The Symbolics Graphics group. *B*: Reproduced image, using six bits of quantized values, 1.5 bits/pixel, NMSE 1.267%. *C*: Cadillac. *D*: Reproduced Cadillac, 1.5 bits/pixel, NMSE 0.764%.

DISCUSSION

This study has produced results that have implications for both connectionist networks and image compression. These are discussed and summarized below.

Implications for Connectionist Networks

Extensional Programming

The major result of this study is that a relatively straightforward application of the back-propagation learning procedure to a problem that has been studied for many years results in near state-of-the-art performance. This performance was obtained not by programming a connectionist solution to the problem, but by the process of *extensional programming*. In this procedure, many examples of the desired behavior are presented and the network must program itself to achieve the behavior. This suggests that other problems for which solutions are not known in advance may be solved by back propagation.

A major problem with this technique is determining post hoc how the network solved the problem. In our case, we have some pieces of the answer, mainly because image compression is a well-studied problem. Hence we have some idea what to look for, if not an analytical solution. By comparison of our network to the techniques of image compression, we can gain insight into the solution found. However, this will not be the case in general. The importance of back propagation is that whether or not we

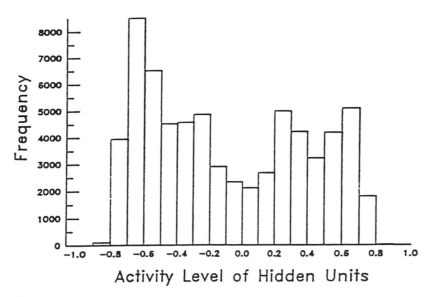

FIGURE 17. Histogram of output values of hidden units during reconstruction of the ISG picture.

know of an algorithm for the solution of a problem, back propagation will in many cases find a solution to the mapping simply from examples of the input-output patterns.

Linear Networks

There is currently a bias in the connectionist community, shared by the authors of this article, against linear networks. This is partly due to the assumption that "interesting" problems must require nonlinearity for their solution. While the results were only alluded to, we found that a linear version of the network produced results compatible with the nonlinear version. Since identity mapping is a linear problem this is not too surprising. However, it is useful to check whether nonlinearity is necessary for a particular problem. If not, the elimination of evaluating the logistic function can lead to more efficient solutions and a more tractable analysis of the solution discovered. If both approaches appear viable, comparison of the two can lead to a better understanding of nonlinear solutions. This approach needs to be carried further in future work. The linear network lends itself to analysis much more readily than the nonlinear one. Williams (1985) gives an empirical test that would give us an idea of how well the principal components are reflected by the linear network.

Internal Representations

One of the typical ways to speak of the solutions discovered by back-propagation learning is to say that the network discovers regularities in the input. This report adds at least a new vocabulary for discussing the kinds of regularities discovered in the case of autocoding. We can look at the *variance* of the hidden units as indicative of their usefulness in the resulting solution. It may not be the case that hidden units span the principal subspace of the covariance matrix, that is, the space spanned by a PCA solution, but it is possible that the hidden units are finding the best approximation to this within the constraint that the logistic function imposes of a limited range on the coefficients. If this turns out to be true, then we may speak of the hidden units as finding at least an analog of the principal subspace and as discovering useful *axes of covariance* of the input.

(a) (b)

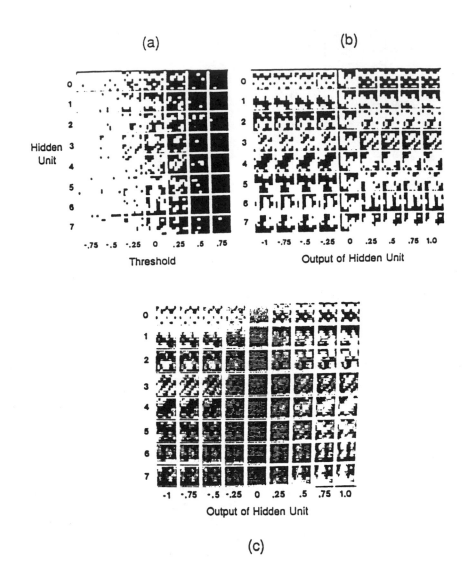

(c)

FIGURE 18. The internal representation. A: The weight matrices from the input patch to eight hidden units, thresholded from −.75 to +.75. The middle column (zero threshold) shows the "canonical" feature responded to by that hidden unit. B: The output patch driven by each hidden unit at different output values from −1 to 1. C: The same picture as B on a color monitor.

Implications for Image Compression

A major result of this work is the application of a new way of minimizing mean square error to a real-world problem that shows it is competitive with PCA. This new technique has several possible advantages over PCA and other current techniques. Some of these need confirmation by further investigation.

One major advantage of the nonlinear version is the relatively equal distribution of error among all of the coefficients. This should lead to a reduction in the effects of channel errors. In PCA and other techniques that approximate it, channel errors that affect the coefficients with high variance can result in a patch that is dominated by the corresponding basis image. The relatively equal contributions of each basis image in the network solution should mitigate these effects. In particular, we know in advance what range the value should be in, and if a coefficient is suspected of being in error, an acceptable restoration of the patch can probably be effected by simply eliminating that coefficient or replacing it with its average value.

Second, because of the fixed range of the coefficients, problems with "tracking" the coefficients by an adaptive quantizer are mitigated. Adaptive quantizers try to follow coefficients as they change, changing the quantization as the coefficients shift. They can "lose track." In our system, we know in advance the range of the coefficients, which should make this less of a problem.

Third, the ability of our network to generalize to novel images is striking. The performance of the linear network is especially encouraging in this regard. This requires some qualification. First, it is likely that this generalization does not apply to images with very different statistics, such as text. Second, investigation is needed to compare this network to the results of current techniques on the same images. We do not know the results in this area, and we are not aware of the existence of a testbed of images for this purpose, although one probably exists.

OPEN QUESTIONS

There are more possibilites suggested by this work for future research than we could possibly pursue. We discuss a few of them here.

First, the parameter space of training image types, patch sizes, number of layers, and sizes of those layers is large. It is certain that there are better ones than the ones we considered. Some interesting possibilities suggest themselves. One is to use larger input patches than output patches to give the hidden units some context for their target. This should lead to faster elimination during the training of edge effects. Another possibility, suggested by Geoff Hinton (personal communication, 1986) is to use larger output patches than the input patches. This forces the hidden units to learn to predict the context. This should also work to eliminate edge effects of reconstruction patches. Finally, it is possible that several hidden layers may be able to do what one cannot. Not enough is known about the ability of back propagation to scale up to many layers to make a sound judgement on this.

Another research direction is to try to improve the performance of the nonlinear network on novel images. One of the sources of error in the reconstructions of novel images is that the average intensity of these images differs from that of the training image. The average intensity of the training image appears to be reflected in the biases of the output units. It is a simple matter to estimate the average intensity of the novel image from a few samples. The question is whether appropriately modifying the biases of the output units will give a better result.

An alternative approach suggested earlier is to apply Tescher's adaptive quantizer to the linear network. If the linear network is capturing most of the useful information of the image, but the quantization based on the training image defeats it, this should give considerable improvement.

Initially we had planned to compare the operation of the hidden units to what is known about neurons found in the visual system. Time constraints have made this another avenue for future investigation.

A final project is to use the outputs of the hidden units as inputs to a pattern classification device. The beauty of back propagation is that it can be used to train the pattern classifier as well, giving the procedure an elegance not obtained by heterogeneous techniques.

CONCLUSIONS

The major result of this work is in demonstrating the efficacy of current connnectionist techniques for programming by example rather than algorithm. We have termed this *extensional programming*. The results here suggest that this technique is a powerful one. Its naive application to a problem of current interest among engineers resulted in respectable performance compared to current techniques.

However, back propagation is not a panacea—it brings new problems of its own. Designing a connectionist representation of the input (and output for nonautocoding problems) is itself an art. The representation must contain enough information to license solution of the problem, without providing so much that the solution is trivial. This is not always hard. Hinton (1986) has shown that at least in some domains, back propagation can even design the input representation simply from the occurrence of a token in context.

The results of this study suggest that one useful approach to problems for which no algorithm is known, or for which no parallel algorithm is known, is to use connectionist representations of the problem and allow the network to discover the program itself. Analysis of the the programs thus discovered may aid in our understanding of the problem and lead to methods for doing the programming ourselves. A variety of problems that cognitive science is concerned with are of this character—the input-output behavior is known, but the algorithm is not. With extensional programming we can begin to investigate algorithms that we did not invent ourselves.

REFERENCES

Ackley, D. H., Hinton, G. E., & Sejnowski, T. J. (1985). A learning algorithm for Boltzmann machines. *Cognitive Science, 9,* 147-169.

Feldman, J. A., & Ballard, D. H. (1982). Connectionist models and their properties. *Cognitive Science, 6,* 205-254.

Gonzales, R. C., & Wintz, P. (1977). *Digital image processing,* Reading, MA: Addison-Wesley.

Hinton, G. E. (1986). Learning distributed representations of concepts. In *Proceedings of the Eighth Annual Conference of the Cognitive Science Society.* Hillsdale, NJ: Lawrence Erlbaum Associates.

Huang, J. J. Y., & Schultheiss, P. M. (1963). *IEEE Transactions on Communications Systems, 11,* 289-296.

Max, J. (1960). *IRE Transactions on Information Theory, 6,* 7-12.

Mozer, M. C. (1983). *Principal component analysis using parallel computation* (ICS Progress Report, First Quarter). La Jolla: University of California, San Diego, Institute for Cognitive Science.

Rumelhart, D. E., Hinton, G. E., and Williams, R. J. (1986a). Learning internal representations by error propagation. In D. E. Rumelhart, J. L. McClelland, & the PDP Research Group, *Parallel distributed processing: Explorations in the microstructure of cognition. Vol. 1. Foundations.* Cambridge: MIT Press/Bradford Books.

Rumelhart, D. E., Hinton, G. E., and Williams, R. J. (1986b). Learning representations by back-propagating errors. *Nature, 323,* 533-536.

Tescher, A. G. (1979). Transform image coding. In W. K. Pratt (Ed.), *Image transmission techniques.* New York: Academic Press.

Williams, R. J. (1985). *Feature discovery through error correction learning* (Tech. Rep. 8501). La Jolla: University of California at San Diego, Institute for Cognitive Science.

Zipser, D. (in press). Programming neural nets to do spatial computations. In N. E. Sharkey (Ed.), *Advances in cognitive science* (Vol. 2). Norwood, NJ: Ablex.

APPENDIX: SOME DETAILS OF PRINCIPAL COMPONENT ANALYSIS

The transformation matrix for the Hotelling transform is formed by first computing (or estimating) the covariance matrix of the **x** (image) vectors

$$\mathbf{C_x} = E\{(\mathbf{x}-\mathbf{m})(\mathbf{x}-\mathbf{m})'\}$$

where

$$\mathbf{m_x} = E\{\mathbf{x}\}$$

is the mean vector, E is the expected value operation, and prime ($'$) indicates transposition. Note $\mathbf{C_x}$ is an $n^2 \times n^2$ matrix if **x** is of length n^2. Then the eigenvectors of this matrix are computed.

Let e_i and $\lambda_i, i=1,2,...,n^2$ be the eigenvectors and eigenvalues of $\mathbf{C_x}$, such that $\lambda_i \geq \lambda_j$, for all $i < j$. Then the transform matrix **A** is formed by taking these eigenvectors in order as the rows. Then the Hotelling transform is

$$\mathbf{y} = \mathbf{A}(\mathbf{x}-\mathbf{m}).$$

The eigenvectors that form **A** correspond to the axes of Figure 4, and the y_i's to the coordinate along each axis.

It can be shown that the covariance matrix of the **y** vectors is a diagonal matrix consisting of the eigenvalues of $\mathbf{C_x}$, i.e., the elements of **y** are *uncorrelated*. Also, the variance of each y_i is λ_i.

To reconstruct **x** from **y**, we need to invert the mapping. Since $\mathbf{C_x}$ is a real, symmetric matrix, it is always possible to find a set of orthonormal eigenvectors, hence $\mathbf{A}^{-1} = \mathbf{A}'$ and

$$\mathbf{x} = \mathbf{A}'\mathbf{y} + \mathbf{m_x}.$$

For image compression purposes, an important property of this mapping is that we can use the first K eigenvectors that account for the most variance. Then we will have K coefficients in **y**, corresponding to K hidden units in the network. Now the reconstruction is an approximation, but it is an optimal one. Let

$$\hat{\mathbf{x}} = \mathbf{A}'_K \mathbf{y} + \mathbf{m_x}$$

represent the approximation to **x** obtained in this way. It can be shown that the mean square error between **x** and $\hat{\mathbf{x}}$ is given by

$$MSE = \sum_{j=1}^{N^2} \lambda_j - \sum_{j=1}^{K} \lambda_j$$

$$= \sum_{j=K+1}^{N^2} \lambda_j.$$

Since the λ_j decrease monotonically, the error is minimized by taking the eigenvectors associated with the largest eigenvalues. Hence the Hotelling transform is optimal with respect to mean square error for a given number of coefficients retained.

(1989)

Pierre Baldi and Kurt Hornik

Neural networks and principal component analysis:
learning from examples without local minima
Neural Networks 2: 53–58

Abstract—*We consider the problem of learning from examples in layered linear feed-forward neural networks using optimization methods, such as back propagation, with respect to the usual quadratic error function* E *of the connection weights. Our main result is a complete description of the landscape attached to* E *in terms of principal component analysis. We show that* E *has a unique minimum corresponding to the projection onto the subspace generated by the first principal vectors of a covariance matrix associated with the training patterns. All the additional critical points of* E *are saddle points (corresponding to projections onto subspaces generated by higher order vectors). The auto-associative case is examined in detail. Extensions and implications for the learning algorithms are discussed.*

Keywords—Neural networks, Principal component analysis, Learning, Back propagation.

1. INTRODUCTION

Neural networks can be viewed as circuits of highly interconnected units with modifiable interconnection weights. They can be classified, for instance, according to their architecture, algorithm for adjusting the weights, and the type of units used in the circuit. We shall assume that the reader is familiar with the basic concepts of the field; general reviews, complements, and references can be found in Rumelhart, McClelland, and the PDP Research Group (1986a), Lippman (1987), and Grossberg (1988).

The network architecture considered here is of the type often described in Rumelhart Hinton, and Williams (1986b), namely layered feed-forward networks with one layer of input units, one layer of output units, and one or several layers of hidden units. We assume that there are T input patterns x_t $(1 \leq t \leq T)$ and T corresponding target output patterns y_t which are used to train the network. For this purpose, a quadratic error function is defined as usual to be: $E = \Sigma_t \|y_t - F(x_t)\|^2$ where F is the current function implemented by the network. During the training phase, the weights (and hence F) are successively modified, according to one of several possible algorithms, in order to reduce E. Back propagation, the best known of such algorithms, is just a way of implementing a gradient descent method for E. The main thrust of this paper is not the study of a specific algorithm but rather a precise description of the salient features of the surface attached to E when the units are linear.

Linear units are the simplest one can use in these circuits. They are often considered as uninteresting for: (a) only linear functions can be computed in linear networks (and most "interesting" functions are nonlinear); and (b) a network with several layers of linear units can always be collapsed into a linear network without any hidden layer by multiplying the weights in the proper fashion.

As a result, nonlinear units are most commonly used: linear threshold gates or, when continuity or differentiability is required, units with a sigmoid input–output function. In this setting, the results of numerous simulations have led several people to believe that descent methods, such as back propagation, applied to the error function E are not seriously plagued by the problem of local minima (either because global minima are found, either because the local minima encountered are "good enough" for practical purposes) and that, for instance, the solu-

*Permanent address: Institut für Statistik and Wahrscheinlichkeitstheorie, Technische Universität Wien, Wiedner Haupstr. 8-10/107, A-1040 Wien, Austria.

The final stages of this work were supported by NSF grant DMS-8800323 to P. B.

tions obtained have remarkable generalization properties. The complete absence, to this date, of any analytical result supporting these claims would alone by itself justify a careful investigation of the simpler linear case.

In addition, recent work of Linsker (1986a, 1986b, 1986c) and Cottrell, Munro, and Zipser (in press) seems to indicate that, for some tasks, linear units can still be of interest, not as much for the global map they implement but for the internal representation of the input data and the transformations that occur in the different layers during the learning period.

Linsker, for instance, has shown that in a layered feed-forward network of linear units with random inputs and a Hebb type of algorithm for adjusting the synaptic weights, spatial opponent and orientation selective units spontaneously emerge in successive hidden layers, in a way which does not contradict what is observed in the early visual system of higher animals. Cottrell *et al.* (in press) have used linear units together with the technique of auto-association to realize image compression. Auto-association, which is also called auto-encoding or identity mapping (see Ackley, Hinton, & Sejnowski; 1985; Ellman & Zipser, 1988) is a simple trick intended to avoid the need for having a teacher, that is, for knowing the target values y_t, by setting $x_t = y_t$. In this mode, the network will tend to learn the identity map which in itself is not too exciting. However, if this is done using one narrow layer of hidden units, one expects the network to find efficient ways of compressing the information contained in the input patterns. An analysis of linear auto-association has been provided by Bourlard and Kamp (1988) based on singular value decomposition of matrices. However, their results for the linear case, which are comprised by ours, do not give a description of the landscape of E.

Our notation will be as follows. All vectors are column vectors and prime superscripts denote transposition. To begin with, we shall assume that both x_t and y_t are n-dimensional vectors and that the network consists of one input layer with n inputs, one hidden layer with $p (p \leq n)$ units, and one output layer with n units (see Figure 1). The weights con-

necting the inputs to the hidden layer are described by a $p \times n$ real matrix B and those from the hidden layer to the output by an $n \times p$ real matrix A. With these assumptions, the error function can be written:

$$E(A, B) = \sum_{1 \leq t \leq T} \|y_t - ABx_t\|^2. \quad (1)$$

We define the usual sample covariance matrices $\Sigma_{XX} = \Sigma_t x_t x_t'$, $\Sigma_{XY} = \Sigma_t x_t y_t'$, $\Sigma_{YY} = \Sigma_t y_t y_t'$, and $\Sigma_{YX} = \Sigma_t y_t s_t'$. We consider the problem of finding the matrices A and B so as to minimize E. In Section 2, we use spectral analysis to describe the properties of the landscape attached to E in the general situation. The auto-associative case and its relations to principal component analysis follow immediately as a special case. In Section 3, we briefly examine some consequences for the optimization algorithms. All mathematical proofs are deferred to the Appendix.

It is important to notice from the onset that if C is any $p \times p$ invertible matrix, then $AB = ACC^{-1}$ $B = (AC)(C^{-1}B)$. Therefore the matrices A and B are never unique since they can always be multiplied by appropriate invertible matrices. Whenever uniqueness occurs it is in terms of the global map $W = AB$ (equivalently, one could partition the matrices into equivalence classes). Notice also that W has rank at most p and recall that if Σ_{XX} is invertible the solution to the problem of minimizing $E(L) = \Sigma_t \|y_t - Lx_t\|^2$, where L is an $n \times n$ matrix without any rank restrictions, is unique and given by $L = \Sigma_{YX}\Sigma_{XX}^{-1}$ which is the usual slope matrix for the ordinary least squares regression of Y on X. Finally, if M is an $n \times p(p \leq n)$ matrix we shall denote by P_M the matrix of the orthogonal projection onto the subspace spanned by the columns of M. It is well known that $P_M^2 = P_M$ and $P_M' = P_M$. If in addition M is of full rank p, then $P_M = M(M'M)^{-1}M'$.

2. MAIN RESULTS: THE LANDSCAPE OF E

Our main result is that:
E has, up to equivalence, a unique local and global minimum corresponding to an orthogonal projection onto the subspace spanned by the first principal eigenvectors of a covariance matrix associated with the training patterns. All other critical points of E are saddle points.

More precisely, one has the following four facts.
Fact 1: For any fixed $n \times p$ matrix A the function $E(A, B)$ is convex in the coefficients of B and attains its minimum for any B satisfying the equation

$$A'AB\Sigma_{XX} = A'\Sigma_{YX}. \quad (1)$$

If Σ_{XX} is invertible and A is full rank p, then E is strictly convex and has a unique minimum reached when

$$B = \hat{B}(A) = (A'A)^{-1}A'\Sigma_{YX}\Sigma_{XX}^{-1}. \quad (3)$$

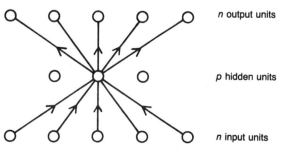

FIGURE 1. The network.

n output units

p hidden units

n input units

In the auto-associative case, (3) becomes

$$B = \hat{B}(A) = (A'A)^{-1}A'. \qquad (3')$$

Fact 2: For any fixed $p \times n$ matrix B the function $E(A, B)$ is convex in the coefficients of A and attains its minimum for any A satisfying the equation

$$AB\Sigma_{XX}B' = \Sigma_{YX}B'. \qquad (4)$$

If Σ_{XX} is invertible and B is of full rank p, then E is strictly convex and has a unique minimum reached when

$$A = \hat{A}(B) = \Sigma_{YX}B'(B\Sigma_{XX}B')^{-1}. \qquad (5)$$

In the auto-associative case, (5) becomes

$$A = \hat{A}(B) = \Sigma_{XX}B'(B\Sigma_{XX}B')^{-1}. \qquad (5')$$

Fact 3: Assume that Σ_{XX} is invertible. If two matrices A and B define a critical point of E (i.e., a point where $\partial E/\partial a_{ij} = \partial E/\partial b_{ij} = 0$) then the global map $W = AB$ is of the form

$$W = P_A\Sigma_{YX}\Sigma_{XX}^{-1} \qquad (6)$$

with A satisfying

$$P_A\Sigma = P_A\Sigma P_A = \Sigma P_A \qquad (7)$$

where $\Sigma = \Sigma_{YX}\Sigma_{XX}^{-1}\Sigma_{XY}$. In the auto-associative case, $\Sigma = \Sigma_{XX}$ and (6) and (7) become

$$W = AB = P_A \qquad (6')$$

$$P_A\Sigma_{XX} = P_A\Sigma_{XX}P_A = \Sigma_{XX}P_A. \qquad (7')$$

If A is of full rank p, then A and B define a critical point of E if and only if A satisfies (7) and $B = \hat{B}(A)$, or equivalently if and only if A and W satisfy (6) and (7).

Notice that in (4), the matrix $\Sigma_{YX}\Sigma_{XX}^{-1}$ is the slope matrix for the ordinary least squares regression of Y on X. It is easily seen that Σ is the sample covariance matrix of the best unconstrained linear approximation $\hat{y}_t = \Sigma_{YX}\Sigma_{XX}^{-1}x_t$ of Y based on X.

Fact 4: Assume that Σ is full rank with n distinct eigenvalues $\lambda_1 > \ldots > \lambda_n$. If $\mathscr{I} = \{i_1, \ldots, i_p\}$ ($1 \leq i_1 < \ldots < i_p \leq n$) is any ordered p-index set, let $U_{\mathscr{I}} = [u_{i_1}, \ldots, u_{i_p}]$ denote the matrix formed by the orthonormal eigenvectors of Σ associated with the eigenvalues $\lambda_{i_1}, \ldots, \lambda_{i_p}$. Then two full rank matrices A and B define a critical point of E if and only if there exist an ordered p-index set $\mathscr{I}$ and an invertible $p \times p$ C matrix such that

$$A = U_{\mathscr{I}}C \qquad (8)$$

$$B = C^{-1}U'_{\mathscr{I}}\Sigma_{YX}\Sigma_{XX}^{-1}. \qquad (9)$$

For such a critical point we have

$$W = P_{U_{\mathscr{I}}}\Sigma_{YX}\Sigma_{XX}^{-1} \qquad (10)$$

$$E(A, B) = tr\Sigma_{YY} - \sum_{i \in \mathscr{I}} \lambda_i. \qquad (11)$$

Therefore a critical W of rank p is always the product of the ordinary least squares regression matrix followed by an orthogonal projection onto the subspace spanned by p eigenvectors of Σ. The critical map W associated with the index set $\{1, 2, \ldots, p\}$ is the unique local and global minimum of E. The remaining $\binom{n}{p} - 1$ p-index sets correspond to saddle points. All additional critical points defined by matrices A and B which are not of full rank are also saddle points and can be characterized in terms of orthogonal projections onto subspaces spanned by q eigenvectors, with $q < p$ (see Figure 2). In the auto-associative case, (8) (9) and (10) become

$$A = U_{\mathscr{I}}C \qquad (8')$$

$$B = C^{-1}U'_{\mathscr{I}} \qquad (9')$$

$$W = P_{U_{\mathscr{I}}} \qquad (10')$$

and therefore the unique locally and globally optimal map W is the orthogonal projection onto the space spanned by the first p eigenvectors of Σ_{XX}.

Remark: At the global minimum, if C is the identity I_p then the activities of the units in the hidden layer are given by $u'_1\hat{y}_t, \ldots, u'_p\hat{y}_t$ the so-called *principal components* of the $\hat{y}_t$'s (see for instance Kshirsagar, 1972). In the auto-associative case, these activities are given by $u'_1 x_t, \ldots, u'_p x_t$. They are the coordinates of the vector x_t along the first p eigenvectors of Σ_{XX}.

The assumptions on the rank or eigenvalues of the matrices appearing in the statements of the facts are by no means restrictive. They are satisfied in most practical situations and also in the case of random matrices with probability one. For instance a non-invertible Σ_{XX} corresponds to a poor choice of the training patterns with linear dependencies and a rank deficient matrix A (or B) to a very poor utilization of the units in the network. For back propagation, the initial weights are usually set at random which yields, with probability one, matrices A and B of full rank. Σ is a covariance matrix and therefore its eigenvalues are always non-negative. To assume that they are all strictly positive is equivalent to assuming

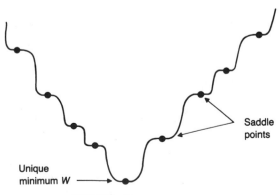

FIGURE 2. The landscape of E.

that both Σ_{XX} and Σ_{YX} are of full rank. Full rank matrices are dense and in a realistic environment with noise and finite precision, we can always slightly perturb the conditions so as to make Σ invertible and with distinct eigenvalues. Furthermore, in the proofs in Appendix B, we describe the structure of the critical points with deficient rank and what happens in the case where some of the eigenvalues of Σ are equal.

We have also restricted our analysis to the case of linear units without bias and to networks containing a single hidden layer. The generalization of our result to the affine case is straightforward either by pre-subtracting the mean from the input and target data, or by adding a unit which is kept at a fixed value. A rigorous extension to the nonlinear sigmoid case or the case involving linear threshold units seems more difficult. However, our results, and in particular the main features of the landscape of E, hold true in the case of linear networks with several hidden layers.

One of the central issues in learning from examples is the problem of generalization, that is, how does the network perform when exposed to a pattern never seen previously? In our setting, a precise quantitative answer can be given to this question. For instance, in the auto-associative case, the distortion on a new pattern is exactly given by its distance to the subspace generated by the first p eigenvectors of Σ_{XX}.

It is reasonable to think that for most solutions found by running a gradient descent algorithm on the function E, the final matrix C will not be the identity I_p. In fact, we even expect C to be rather "random" looking. This is the main reason why the relation of auto-association to principal component analysis was not apparent in earlier simulations described in the literature and why, in the solutions found by back propagation, the work load seems to be evenly distributed among the units of the hidden layer. If in (9') we take $C = I_p$, then $B = U'_y$. Therefore the synaptic vector corresponding to the "first" hidden unit is exactly equal to the dominant eigenvector of the input correlation matrix. This is in fact exactly the same result as the one obtained by Oja (1982) in a different setting, using differential equations to approximate a constrained form of Hebbian learning on a single linear unit with n stochastic inputs. In other words, up to equivalence, the solution sought by a back propagation type of algorithm in the auto-associative case and by Hebbian learning are identical on one single linear "neuron." It remains to be checked whether simultaneous Hebbian learning on p units, probably with some appropriate form of lateral inhibition, leads to the same results as those encountered here for the auto-association.

3. CONCLUDING REMARKS ON THE ALGORITHMS

One of the nice features of the landscape of E is the existence, up to equivalence, of a unique local and global minimum which, in addition, can be described in terms of principal component analysis and least squares regression. Consequently, this optimum could also be obtained from several well-known algorithms for computing the eigenvalues and eigenvectors of symmetric positive definite matrices (see for instance Atkinson, 1978). By numerical analysis standards, these algorithms are superior to gradient methods for the class of problems considered here. However, though efficiency considerations are of importance, one should not disregard back propagation on this sole basis, for its introduction in the design of neural networks was guided by several other considerations. In particular, in addition to its simplicity, error back-propagation can be applied to nonlinear networks and to a variety of problems without having any detailed a priori knowledge of their structure or of the mathematical properties of the optimal solutions.

A second nice feature of the landscape of E is that if we fix A (resp. B) with full rank, then E is a strictly convex quadratic form and there exists a unique minimum reached for $B = \hat{B}(A)$ (resp. $A = \hat{A}(B)$). In this case, gradient descent with appropriate step width (or "learning rate") leads to a convergence with a residual error decaying exponentially fast. Of course, $\hat{B}(A)$ (resp. $\hat{A}(B)$) can also be obtained directly by solving the linear system in (2). This also suggests another optimization strategy which consists of successively computing, starting for instance from a random A, $\hat{B}(A)$, $\hat{A}(\hat{B}(A))$, . . . and so forth, which in fact is a Newton's type of method. In any case, from a theoretical standpoint, one should notice that, although E has no local minima, both gradient descent and Newton's type of methods could get stuck in a saddle point. However, as exemplified by simulations (Cottrell et al., in press), this seems unlikely to happen, especially with the way error back-propagaton is usually implemented, with a descent direction computed by differentiating E after presentation of one or just a few training patterns. Such a direction is clearly distinct from a true gradient.

REFERENCES

Ackley, D. H., Hinton, G. E., & Sejnowski, T. J. (1985). A learning algorithm for Boltzmann machines. *Cognitive Science*, **9**, 147–169.

Atkinson, K. E. (1978). *An introduction to numerical analysis.* New York: John Wiley & Sons.

Bourlard, H., & Kamp, Y. (1988). Auto-association by multilayer perceptrons and singular value decomposition. *Biological Cybernetics*, **59**, 291–294.

Cottrell, G. W., Munro, P. W., & Zipser, D. (in press). Image compression by back propagation: A demonstration of extensional programming. In N. E. Sharkey (Ed.), *Advances in cognitive science* (Vol. 2). Norwood, NJ: Abbex.

Ellman, J. L., & Zipser, D. (1987). *Learning the hidden structure of speech.* (Tech. Rep. No. 8701). San Diego: Institute for Cognitive Science, University of California.

Grossberg, S. (1988). Nonlinear neural networks: Principles, mechanisms and architectures. *Neural Networks,* **1,** 17–61.

Kshirsagar, A. N. (1972). *Multivariate analysis.* New York: Marcel Dekker, Inc.

Linsker, R. (1986a). From basic network principles to neural architecture: Emergence of spatial opponent cells. *Proceedings of the National Academy of Sciences USA,* **83,** 7508–7512.

Linsker, R. (1986b). From basic network principles to neural architecture: Emergence of orientation selective cells. *Proceedings of the National Academy of Sciences USA,* **83,** 8390–8394.

Linsker, R. (1986c). From basic network principle to neural architecture: Emergence of orientation columns. *Proceedings of the National Academy of Sciences USA,* **83,** 8779–8783.

Lippman, R. P. (1987). An introduction to computing with neural nets. *IEEE Transactions on Acoustics, Speech, and Signal Processing Magazine,* 4–22.

Magnus, J. R., & Neudecker, H. (1986). Symmetry, 0-1 matrices and Jacobians. *Econometric Theory,* **2,** 157–190.

Oja, E. (1982). A simplified neuron model as a principal component analyzer. *Journal of Mathematical Biology,* **15,** 267–273.

Pollock, D. S. G. (1979). The algebra of econometrics. New York: John Wiley & Sons.

Rumelhart, D. E., McClelland, J. L., & the PDP Research Group (1986a). *Parallel distributed processing: Explorations in the microstructure of cognition* (Vols. 1 & 2). Cambridge, MA: MIT Press.

Rumelhart, D. E., Hinton, G. E., & Williams, R. J. (1986b). Learning internal representation by error propagaton. In *Parallel distributed processing: Explorations in the microstructure of cognition* (pp. 318–362). Cambridge, MA: MIT Press.

APPENDIX A: MATHEMATICAL PROOFS

We have tried to write proofs which are self-contained up to very basic results of linear algebra. Slightly less elementary results which are often used in the proofs (sometimes without explicit mentioning) are listed below as a reminder for the reader. For any matrices P, Q, R we have $tr(PQR) = tr(RPQ) = tr(QRP)$, provided that these quantities are defined. Thus in particular if P is idempotent, that is, $P^2 = P$, then

$$tr(PQP) = tr(P^2Q) = tr(PQ). \qquad (a)$$

If U is orthogonal, that is $U'U = I$, then

$$tr(UQU') = tr(U'UQ) = tr(Q). \qquad (b)$$

The Kronecker product $P \otimes Q$ of any two matrices P and Q is the matrix obtained from the matrix P by replacing each entry p_{ij} of P with the matrix $p_{ij}Q$. If P is any $m \times n$ matrix and p_j its jth column, then vec P is the $mn \times 1$ vector vec $P = [p'_1, \ldots, p'_n]'$. Thus the vec operation transforms a matrix into a column vector by stacking the columns of the matrix one underneath the other. We then have (see for instance Magnus & Neudecker, 1986) for any matrices P, Q, R

$$tr(PQ') = (\text{vec } P)' \text{ vec } Q \qquad (c)$$

$$\text{vec}(PQR') = (R \otimes P) \text{ vec } Q \qquad (d)$$

$$(P \otimes Q)(R \otimes S) = PR \otimes QS \qquad (e)$$

$$(P \otimes Q)^{-1} = P^{-1} \otimes Q^{-1} \qquad (f)$$

$$(P \otimes Q)' = P' \otimes Q' \qquad (g)$$

whenever these quantities are defined. Also:
if P and Q are symmetric and positive semidefinite (resp. positive definite) then $P \otimes Q$ is symmetric and positive semidefinite (resp. positive definite). $\qquad (h)$

Finally, let us introduce the input data matrix $X = [x_1, \ldots, x_T]$ and the output data matrix $Y = [y_1, \ldots, y_T]$. It is easily seen that $XX' = \Sigma_{XX}$, $XY' = \Sigma_{XY}$, $YY' = \Sigma_{YY}$, $YX' = \Sigma_{YX}$ and $E(A, B) = \|\text{vec}(Y - ABX)\|^2$. In the proofs of facts 1 and 2, we shall use the following well known lemma.

Lemma: The quadratic function

$$F(z) = \|c - Mz\|^2 = c'c - 2c'Mz + z'M'Mz$$

is convex. A point z corresponds to a global minimum of F if and only if it satisfies the equation $\nabla F = 0$, or equivalently $M'Mz = M'c$. If in addition $M'M$ is positive definite, then F is strictly convex and the unique minimum of F is attained for $z = (M'M)^{-1}M'c$.

Proof of fact 1: For fixed A, use (d) to write $\text{vec}(Y - ABX) = \text{vec } Y - \text{vec}(ABX) = \text{vec } Y - (X' \otimes A) \text{ vec } B$ and thus $E(A, B) = \|\text{vec } Y - (X' \otimes A) \text{ vec } B\|^2$. By the above lemma, E is convex in the coefficients of B and B corresponds to a global minimum if and only if $(X' \otimes A)'(X' \otimes A) \text{ vec } B = (X' \otimes A)' \text{ vec } Y$. Now on one hand $(X' \otimes A)'(X' \otimes A) \text{ vec } B = (X' \otimes A) \text{ vec } B = (XX' \otimes A'A) \text{ vec } B = (\Sigma_{XX} \otimes A'A) \text{ vec } B = \text{vec}(A'AB\Sigma_{XX})$. On the other hand $(X' \otimes A)' \text{ vec } Y = (X \otimes A') \text{ vec } Y = \text{vec}(A'YX') = \text{vec}(A'\Sigma_{YX})$. Therefore

$$A'AB\Sigma_{XX} = A'\Sigma_{YX},$$

which is (2). If A is full rank, $A'A$ is symmetric and positive definite. As a covariance matrix, Σ_{XX} is symmetric and positive semidefinite; if, in addition, Σ_{XX} is invertible, then Σ_{XX} is also positive definite. Because of (h), $(X' \otimes A)'(X' \otimes A) = \Sigma_{XX} \otimes A'A$ is also symmetric and positive definite. Applying the above lemma, we conclude that if Σ_{XX} is invertible and A is a fixed full rank matrix, then E is strictly convex in the coefficients of B and attains its unique minimum at the unique solution $B = \hat{B}(A) = (A'A)^{-1}A'\Sigma_{YX}\Sigma_{XX}^{-1}$ of (2), which is (3). In the auto-associative case, $x_t = y_t$. Therefore $\Sigma_{XX} = \Sigma_{YY} = \Sigma_{XY} = \Sigma_{YX}$ and the above expression simplifies to (3').

Proof of Fact 2: For fixed B, use (d) to write $\text{vec}(Y - ABX) = \text{vec } Y - \text{vec}(ABX) = \text{vec } Y - (X'B' \otimes I) \text{ vec } A$ and so $E(A, B) = \|\text{vec } Y - (X'B' \otimes I) \text{ vec } A\|^2$. By the above lemma, E is convex in the coefficients of A and A corresponds to a global minimum if and only if $(X'B' \otimes I)'(X'B' \otimes I) \text{ vec } A = (X'B' \otimes I)' \text{ vec } Y$. Since $(X'B' \otimes I)'(X'B' \otimes I) \text{ vec } A = (BXX'B' pr \otimes I) \text{ vec } A = (B\Sigma_{XX}B' \otimes I) \text{ vec } A = \text{vec}(AB\Sigma_{XX}B')$ and $(X'B' \otimes I)' \text{ vec } Y = (BX \otimes I) \text{ vec } Y = \text{vec}(YX'B') = \text{vec}(\Sigma_{YX}B')$ we have

$$AB\Sigma_{XX}B' = \Sigma_{YX}B',$$

which is (4). If B and Σ_{XX} are full rank, then the symmetric and positive semi-definite matrix $B\Sigma_{XX}B'$ becomes full rank and therefore positive definite. Because of (h), $(X'B' \otimes I)'(X'B' \otimes I) = (B\Sigma_{XX}B' \otimes I)$ is also positive definite and (5) and (5') are easily derived as in the end of the proof of fact 1.

Notice that from facts 1 and 2, two full rank matrices A and B define a critical point for E if and only if (2) and (4) are simultaneously satisfied. In all cases of practical interest where Σ_{YX} is full rank both $\hat{A}(B)$ and $\hat{B}(A)$ are full rank. In what follows, we shall assume that A is of full rank p. The case *rank* $(A) < p$ is, although intuitively of no practical interest, slightly more technical and its treatment will be postponed to Appendix B.

Proof of Fact 3: Assume first that A and B define a critical point of E, with A full rank. Then from fact 1 we get $B = \hat{B}(A)$ and thus

$$W = AB = A(A'A)^{-1}A'\Sigma_{YX}\Sigma_{XX}^{-1} = P_A\Sigma_{YX}\Sigma_{XX}^{-1}$$

which is (6). Multiplication of (4) by A' on the right yields

$$W\Sigma_{XX}W' = AB\Sigma_{XX}B'A' = \Sigma_{YX}B'A' = \Sigma_{YX}W'$$

or

$$P_A\Sigma_{YX}\Sigma_{XX}^{-1}\Sigma_{XX}\Sigma_{XX}^{-1}\Sigma_{XY}P_A = \Sigma_{YX}\Sigma_{XX}^{-1}\Sigma_{XY}P_A$$

or equivalently $P_A\Sigma P_A = \Sigma P_A$. Since both Σ and P_A are symmetric, $P_A\Sigma P_A = \Sigma P_A$ is also symmetric and therefore $\Sigma P_A = (\Sigma P_A)' = P_A'\Sigma' = P_A\Sigma$. So $P_A\Sigma = P_A\Sigma P_A = \Sigma P_A$, which is (7). Hence if A and B correspond to a critical point and A is full rank then (6) and (7) must hold and $B = \hat{B}(A)$.

Conversely, assume that A and W satisfy (6) and (7), with A full rank. Multiplying (6) by $(A'A)^{-1}A'$ on the left yields $B = (A'A)^{-1}A'\Sigma_{YX}\Sigma_{XX}^{-1} = \hat{B}(A)$ and (2) is satisfied. From $P_A\Sigma P_A = \Sigma P_A$ and using (6) we immediately get $AB\Sigma_{XX}B'A' = \Sigma_{YX}B'A'$ and multiplication of both sides by $A(A'A)^{-1}$ on the right yields $AB\Sigma_{XX}B' = \Sigma_{YX}B'$, which is (4). Thus A and B satisfy (2) and (4) and therefore they define a critical point of E.

Proof of Fact 4: First notice that since Σ is a real symmetric covariance matrix, it can always be written as $\Sigma = U\Lambda U'$ where U is an orthogonal column matrix of eigenvectors of Σ and Λ is the diagonal matrix with non-increasing eigenvalues on its diagonal. Also if Σ is full rank, then Σ_{XX}, Σ_{YX} and Σ_{XY} are full rank too.

Now clearly if A and B satisfy (8) and (9) for some C and some $\mathscr{I}$ then A and B are full rank p and satisfy (3) and (5). Therefore they define a critical point of E.

For the converse, we have

$$P_{U'A} = U'A(A'UU'A)^{-1}A'U = U'A(A'A)^{-1}A'U = U'P_A U$$

or, equivalently, $P_A = UP_{U'A}U'$. Hence (7) yields

$$UP_{U'A}U'U\Lambda U' = P_A\Sigma = \Sigma P_A = U\Lambda U'UP_{U'A}U'$$

and so $P_{U'A}\Lambda = \Lambda P_{U'A}$. Since $\lambda_1 > \ldots > \lambda_n > 0$, it is readily seen that $P_{U'A}$ is diagonal. $P_{U'A}$ is an orthogonal projector of rank p and its eigenvalues are 1 (p times) and 0 ($n - p$ times). Therefore there exists a unique index set $\mathscr{I} = \{i_1, \ldots, i_p\}$ with $1 \le i_1 < \ldots < i_p \le n$ such that $P_{U'A} = I_{\mathscr{I}}$ where $I_{\mathscr{I}}$ is the diagonal matrix with entry $i = 1$ if $i \in \mathscr{I}$ and 0 otherwise. It follows that

$$P_A = UP_{U'A}U' = UI_{\mathscr{I}}U' = U_{\mathscr{I}}U_{\mathscr{I}}'$$

where $U_{\mathscr{I}} = [u_{i_1}, \ldots, u_{i_p}]$. Thus P_A is the orthogonal projection onto the subspace spanned by the columns of $U_{\mathscr{I}}$. Since the column space of A coincides with the column space of $U_{\mathscr{I}}$, there exists an invertible $p \times p$ matrix C such that $A = U_{\mathscr{I}}C$. Moreover, $B = \hat{B}(A) = C^{-1}U_{\mathscr{I}}'\Sigma_{YX}\Sigma_{XX}^{-1}$ and (8) and (9) are satisfied. There are $\binom{n}{p}$ possible choices for $\mathscr{I}$ and therefore, up to equivalence, $\binom{n}{p}$ critical points with full rank.

From (8) and (9), (10) results immediately.

Remark: In the most general case with n-dimensional inputs x_i and m-dimensional outputs y_i, Σ has $r(r \le m)$ distinct eigenvalues $\lambda_1 \ge \ldots \ge \lambda_r \ge 0$ with multiplicities $m_1, \ldots, m_r$. Using the above arguments, it is easily seen that $P_{U'A}$ will now be block-diagonal $[P_1, \ldots, P_r]$ where $P_1, \ldots, P_r$ are orthogonal projectors of dimension $m_1, \ldots, m_r$ and thus A is of the form $A = (UV)_{\mathscr{I}}C$ where V is block-diagonal $[V_1, \ldots, V_r]$, $V_1, \ldots, V_r$ being orthogonal matrices of dimension $m_1, \ldots, m_r$. For all such choices of V, UV is a matrix of normalized eigenvectors of Σ corresponding to ordered eigenvalues of Σ. The geometric situation, as expected, does not really change but the parameterization becomes more involved as U is no longer unique.

To prove (11), use (c) to write $E(A, B) = (\text{vec}(Y - ABX))' \text{vec}(Y - ABX) = (\text{vec } Y)' \text{vec } Y - 2(\text{vec}(ABX))' \text{vec } Y + (\text{vec } ABX)' \text{vec } ABX = trYY' - 2trABXY' + trABXX'B'A' = tr\Sigma_{YY} - 2tr\Sigma_{XY} + trW\Sigma_{XX}W'$. If A is full rank and $B = \hat{B}(A)$, then $W = A\hat{B}(A) = P_A\Sigma_{YX}\Sigma_{XX}^{-1}$ and therefore $tr(W\Sigma_{XX}W') = tr(P_A\Sigma P_A) = tr(P_A\Sigma) = tr(UP_{U'A}U'U\Lambda U') = tr(P_{U'A}U'U\Lambda) = tr(P_{U'A}\Lambda)$ and $tr(W\Sigma_{YX}) = tr(P_A\Sigma) = tr(P_{U'A}\Lambda)$. So for an arbitrary A of rank p,

$$E(A, \hat{B}(A)) = tr\Sigma_{YY} - trP_{U'A}\Lambda.$$

If A is of the form $U_{\mathscr{I}}C$, then $P_{U'A} = I_{\mathscr{I}}$. Therefore

$$E(A, \hat{B}(A)) = tr\Sigma_{YY} - trI_{\mathscr{I}}\Lambda = tr\Sigma_{YY} - \sum_{i \in \mathscr{I}} \lambda_i$$

which is (11).

We shall now establish that whenever A and B satisfy (8) and (9) with $\mathscr{I} \ne \{1, 2, \ldots, p\}$ there exist matrices $\bar{A}$, $\bar{B}$ arbitrarily close to A, B such that $E(\bar{A}, \bar{B}) < E(A, B)$. For this purpose it is enough to slightly perturb the column space of A in the direction of an eigenvector associated with one of the first p eigenvalues of Σ which is not contained in $\{\lambda_i, i \in \mathscr{I}\}$. More precisely, fix two indices j and k with $j \in \mathscr{I}$, $k \notin \mathscr{I}$. For any ϵ, put $\bar{u}_j = (1 + \epsilon^2)^{-1/2}(u_j + \epsilon u_k)$ and construct $\bar{U}_{\mathscr{I}}$ from $U_{\mathscr{I}}$ by replacing u_j with

$\bar{u}_j$. Since $k \notin \mathscr{I}$, we still have $\bar{U}_{\mathscr{I}}'\bar{U}_{\mathscr{I}} = I_p$. Now let $\bar{A} = \bar{U}_{\mathscr{I}}C$ and $\bar{B} = \hat{B}(\bar{A}) = C^{-1}\bar{U}_{\mathscr{I}}'\Sigma_{YX}\Sigma_{XX}^{-1}$. A simple calculation shows that the diagonal elements $\bar{\delta}_i$ of $P_{U'\bar{A}}$ are

$$\bar{\delta}_i = \begin{cases} 0 & \text{if } i \notin \mathscr{I} \cup \{k\} \\ 1 & \text{if } i \in \mathscr{I} \text{ and } i \ne j \text{ and } i \ne k \\ 1/(1 + \epsilon^2) & \text{if } i = j \\ \epsilon^2/(1 + \epsilon^2) & \text{if } i = k. \end{cases}$$

Therefore $E(\bar{A}, \bar{B}) = tr\Sigma_{YY} - trP_{U'\bar{A}}\Lambda = tr\Sigma_{YY} - [\Sigma_{i \in \mathscr{I} - \{j\}}\lambda_i + \lambda_j/(1 + \epsilon^2) + \epsilon^2\lambda_k/(1 + \epsilon^2)] = tr\Sigma_{YY} - \Sigma_{i \in \mathscr{I}}\lambda_i - \epsilon^2(\lambda_k - \lambda_j)/(1 + \epsilon^2) = E(A, B) - \epsilon^2(\lambda_k - \lambda_j)/(1 + \epsilon^2)$. By taking values of ϵ arbitrarily small, we see that any neighborhood of A, B contains points of the form $\bar{A}$, $\bar{B}$ with a strictly smaller error function. Thus if $\mathscr{I} \ne \{1, 2, \ldots, p\}$, then (8) and (9) define a saddle point and not a local minimum. Notice that, in any case, it could not be a local maximum because of the strict convexity of E, with fixed full rank A, in fact 1.

APPENDIX B: THE RANK DEFICIENT CASE

We now complete the proof of fact 3 (equations (6) and (7)) and fact 4, in the case where A is not of full rank. Using the Moore-Penrose inverse A^+ of the matrix A (see for instance Pollock, 1979), the general solution to equation (2) can be written as

$$B = A^+\Sigma_{YX}\Sigma_{XX}^{-1} + (I - A^+A)L,$$

where L is an arbitrary $p \times n$ matrix. We have $P_A = AA^+$ and $AA^+A = A$ and so $W = AB = AA^+\Sigma_{YX}\Sigma_{XX}^{-1} + A(I - A^+A)L = P_A\Sigma_{YX}\Sigma_{XX}^{-1} + (A - AA^+A)L = P_A\Sigma_{YX}\Sigma_{XX}^{-1}$, which is (6). Multiplication of (4) by A' on the right yields $W\Sigma_{XX}W' = \Sigma_{YX}W'$ and (7) follows as usual. Observe that in order for A and B to determine a critical point of E, L must in general be constrained by (4); $L = 0$ is always a solution.

In any case, as in the proof of fact 4 for full rank A, if *rank* $A = r$ we conclude that $P_{U'A}$ is an orthogonal projector of rank r commuting with Λ, so that $P_{U'A} = I_{\mathscr{I}}$ for an index set $\mathscr{I} = \{i_1, \ldots, i_r\}$ with $1 \le i_1 < \ldots < i_r \le n$ and $P_A = UP_{U'A}U' = U_{\mathscr{I}}U_{\mathscr{I}}'$. Again as the column space of A is identical to the column space of $U_{\mathscr{I}}$, we can write A in the form

$$A = [U_{\mathscr{I}}, O]C,$$

where O denotes a matrix of dimension $n \times (p - r)$ with all entries 0. At any critical point A, B of E, A will be of the above form and, from (2), B will be of the form

$$B = A^+\Sigma_{YX}\Sigma_{XX}^{-1} + (I - A^+A)L,$$

where L is constrained by (4). No matter what L actually is, using

$$A^+ = C^{-1}\begin{bmatrix} U_{\mathscr{I}}' \\ O \end{bmatrix}$$

we obtain that

$$B = C^{-1}\begin{bmatrix} U_{\mathscr{I}}' \\ O \end{bmatrix}\Sigma_{YX}\Sigma_{XX}^{-1} + \left(I - C^{-1}\begin{bmatrix} U_{\mathscr{I}}' \\ O \end{bmatrix}[U_{\mathscr{I}}, O]C\right)L$$

$$= C^{-1}\begin{bmatrix} U_{\mathscr{I}}'\Sigma_{YX}\Sigma_{XX}^{-1} \\ O \end{bmatrix} + C^{-1}\left(I_p - \begin{bmatrix} I_r \\ O \end{bmatrix}\right)CL$$

$$= C^{-1}\begin{bmatrix} U_{\mathscr{I}}'\Sigma_{YX}\Sigma_{XX}^{-1} \\ P \end{bmatrix} + C^{-1}\begin{bmatrix} O \\ I_{p-r} \end{bmatrix}CL$$

$$= C^{-1}\begin{bmatrix} U_{\mathscr{I}}'\Sigma_{YX}\Sigma_{XX}^{-1} \\ \text{last } p - r \text{ rows of } CL \end{bmatrix}.$$

Now, by assumption, Σ has full rank n, and so $U_{\mathscr{I}}'\Sigma_{YX}\Sigma_{XX}^{-1}$ has full rank r. Upon slightly perturbing the last $p - r$ rows of CB (which are also the last $p - r$ rows of CL), we can always obtain $\bar{B}$ arbitrarily close to B such that $\bar{B}$ has maximal rank and $W = A\bar{B} = AB$ and thus $E(A, B) = E(A, \bar{B})$. Now $\bar{B}$ has full rank and so E is strictly convex in the elements of A. Putting $\bar{A} = (1 - \epsilon)A + \epsilon\hat{A}(\bar{B})$ with $0 < \epsilon < 1$, we have $E(\bar{A}, \bar{B}) < E(A, \bar{B}) = E(A, B)$. If $\epsilon \to 0$, $\bar{A} \to A$ and therefore (A, B) is a saddle point for E.

IV
Current Applications and Future Problems

Introduction

(1988)
Marvin L. Minsky and Seymour A. Papert

Epilog: the new connectionism
Perceptrons, third edition, Cambridge, MA: MIT Press, pp. 247–280

This paper and the next one (Fodor and Pylyshyn, paper 35) have a common theme: Both are well-thought-out criticisms of the abilities of neural networks to do computation. One (Minsky and Papert) makes a number of pointed comments about the limited powers of simple neural networks, and the other (Fodor and Pylyshyn) suggests some important problems in human cognition that neural networks, in their present incarnation, may fundamentally be unable to solve. Both argue that neural networks, as currently implemented, show inadequate computational flexibility for many purposes, in particular for explaining human cognition.

The recent resurgence of research in neural networks, after a long period of neglect, has been exhilarating to many long-term participants. It is always a gratifying experience to be noticed after being ignored for many years, especially when there is the perception of unjustified persecution endured and overcome.

However, neural networks are part of science and engineering. A feeling of moral superiority, of truth crushed to earth, and rising again, has nothing to do with whether the models actually work and accomplish what it is claimed they can.

Neural net folklore has it that the first edition in 1969 of the book *Perceptrons* by Marvin Minsky and Seymour Papert was the cause of the death of neural networks in the beginning of the 1970s. This widespread belief led to a dramatic moment at the 1988 International Conference on Neural Networks in San Diego. Marvin Minsky had been invited to give a plenary talk to the conference and announced to the audience that "I am not the devil," suggesting that he had received a bum rap for forcing early neural network research into undeserved and unfunded neglect. Whatever the reasons for the collapse of neural net research at that time—and, realistically, the publication of *Perceptrons* was only one of many reasons—it was a matter of considerable interest when a third edition of *Perceptrons* was released in 1988. The epilog, reprinted here, was appended to the new edition and gives a few of Minsky and Papert's thoughts on the renaissance of neural net research.

Perceptrons was a brilliant analysis of what a simple neural network could and, more important could not compute. (The introduction to *Perceptrons* was reprinted as paper 13 in *Neurocomputing: Foundations of Research*.) We strongly recommend that anyone interested in neural networks read *Perceptrons* in any edition. The book showed that there were severe limitations on the computational power of simple perceptrons, sufficiently severe to make them unable to solve a number of significant problems. Many of the limitations of the perceptron as a device arose from its structure. The version analyzed by Minsky and Papert contained a single layer of modifiable connections and was linear in its fundamental synaptic inner product operation. It was capable of correctly classifying only *linearly separable* regions of state space. But many real problems are not linearly separable, for example, the simplest representations of some logic functions, such as exclusive-OR (X-OR).

In the current epilog Minsky and Papert devote most of their attention to discussing the *PDP* books, that is, the two-volume *Parallel Distributed Processing* set that has become a classic and an essential reference in neural net research (McClelland and Rumelhart 1986, Rumelhart and McClelland 1986). Supporters of neural networks have often claimed that systems with multiple layers of modifiable connections are immune from the processing power limitations of single-layer networks, an opinion strongly stated in the *PDP* books in several places. There is also a widely-held belief that Minsky and Papert stopped research on complex, multilayer systems with their influential conjecture that extension of the perceptron architecture to multilayer systems would be "sterile." There is the impression throughout the epilog that Minsky and Papert are offended by this kind of simplistic dismissal of their criticisms. Minsky and Papert reiterate that their aim was *not* to destroy perceptrons but to *understand* their limitations, so that the strengths of perceptrons could be used appropriately, and so they would not be applied to problems for which they were unsuited.

Minsky and Papert are interested in very simple questions, such as, What can (and can not) a perceptron learn? How long does it take to learn it? and Does it get harder or easier to learn as the number of elements increase? In the epilog Minsky and Papert point out, quite reasonably, that these are the kinds of questions you would ask of any kind of computer and that their criticisms have not been properly answered, even now, by neural network enthusiasts.

In the most common learning architectures—for example, back propagation, associative networks, the perceptron—the object of learning is to produce a correct set of weights connecting computing elements together. These algorithms are supervised, that is, the correct answers are known and the answer given by the network can be compared with the correct answers. The learning procedure involves repeated presentations of a training set, and the network tries to adjust its weights so as to reduce as much as possible the error in the response of the network to the training set. The best set of weights are those that give the most accurate input-output relationships of the network, by some definition.

Perhaps the most telling technical argument made by Minsky and Papert is the observation that the learning rules, even in complex, multilayer systems such as back propagation, are still doing gradient descent as they adjust the network weights: That is, they try to reduce the system error at each learning step. The problems and limitations of gradient descent are well known, even though back propagation does a better job overcoming them than simpler models. The major problem involves getting stuck in local minima, where every small change in weights increases the system error, but somewhere else there exists a set of weights that give even lower error than the minimum the system is in.

Minsky and Papert mention with a little glee, one suspects, the casual dismissal of this difficulty in the *PDP* volumes, where it is observed that getting stuck in local minima is rarely a practical problem. Minsky and Papert say that the entire history of pattern recognition shows otherwise. They comment that "In the early years of cybernetics, everyone understood that hill-climbing was always available for working easy problems, but that it almost always became impractical for problems of larger sizes and complexity." They go on to comment, with perhaps just a trace of sarcasm, that "... we applaud those who bravely and romantically are empirically applying hill-climbing methods to many new domains . . . ."

It should be pointed out that there are a few neural network learning algorithms that are theoretically capable of overcoming the problems of gradient descent. An example would be the Boltzmann machine (paper 38 in *Neurocomputing: Foundations of Research*), based on the technique of simulated annealing (see papers 33 and 37 in *Neurocomputing: Foundations of Research*). Such techniques involve, effectively, adding noise to the system so there then becomes a finite probability of *increasing* the error at a given step. Such a system can climb out of local minima to discover the true lowest-error solution. The "genetic algorithm" of John Holland (Holland 1975) provides a different way of avoiding the difficulties of simple gradient descent by "recombining" good solutions in the hope of finding even better ones, in analogy with the operation of the biological genetic apparatus. Although the genetic algorithm is not a neural network there has been recent interest in combining neural networks with genetic algorithms.

Perhaps the distinction between local and global minima and the problems with algorithms that only reduce a quantity might become clear with a simple behavioral example. Suppose there is an animal that has to get food that is visible through a fence. Suppose the fence has a distant opening in it. The animal's ultimate aim is to reduce the distance between it and the food to zero.

Animals with even small amounts of the kind of behavioral flexibility that we call intelligence soon discover that the way to get to the goal requires it to go deliberately (not randomly!) away from the goal. This greatly increases immediately perceived error but it is the best way to find a way *through* the fence. Simple error minimization seems to miss something important about the process of learning or performing a complex cognitive task. This point is made even more strongly by Fodor and Pylyshyn (paper 35).

There are other important points made by Minsky and Papert: gradient descent learning algorithms such as back propagation have long convergence times and scale badly to larger systems. As Minsky and Papert point out, it is simply unacceptable for a network to require tens or hundreds of thousands of learning trials if there is going to be any attempt to maintain "biological plausibility." As is well known to psychologists, a good deal of very complex learning can take place in a single trial. For example, during early childhood children are learning several words a day and experiments suggest that often a single presentation is adequate to learn a new word.

Returning to our animal faced with the food seen through a fence, in the real world this problem must be solved quickly or abandoned as not worth the effort. When faced with this problem, a human, and some other mammals, can solve it rapidly or quit, based on past learning that almost certainly did not include this particular fence, this particular opening, and that particular goal. It seems unlikely that building a network that learned all possible fences with all possible openings would be the right way to attack this problem.

Minsky and Papert devote the last parts of the epilog to discussing ways of connecting simple systems together to generate the kinds of flexibility required by even the simplest problems arising in the real world. The approach taken by Minsky and Papert is to combine simple networks together in what Minsky (1986) calls "The Society of Mind," an idea developed at length in a book of that name.

References

J. Holland (1975), *Adaptation in Natural and Artificial Systems*. Ann Arbor, MI: University of Michigan Press.

J. McClelland and D. Rumelhart (1986), *Parallel Distributed Processing, Volume II*. Cambridge, MA: MIT Press.

M. Minsky (1986), *The Society of Mind*. New York: Simon and Schuster.

D. Rumelhart and J. McClelland (1986), *Parallel Distributed Processing, Volume I*. Cambridge, MA: MIT Press.

Epilog: the new connectionism

Perceptrons, third edition Cambridge, MA: MIT Press, pp. 247–280

When perceptron-like machines came on the scene, we found that in order to understand their capabilities we needed some new ideas. It was not enough simply to examine the machines themselves or the procedures used to make them learn. Instead, we had to find new ways to understand the problems they would be asked to solve. This is why our book turned out to be concerned less with perceptrons per se than with concepts that could help us see the relation between patterns and the types of parallel-machine architectures that might or might not be able to recognize them.

Why was it so important to develop theories about parallel machines? One reason was that the emergence of serial computers quickly led to a very respectable body of useful ideas about algorithms and algorithmic languages, many of them based on a half-century's previous theories about logic and effective computability. But similarly powerful ideas about parallel computation did not develop nearly so rapidly—partly because massively parallel hardware did not become available until much later and partly because much less knowledge that might be relevant had been accumulated in the mathematical past. Today, however, it is feasible either to simulate or to actually assemble huge and complex arrangements of interacting elements. Consequently, theories about parallel computation have now become of immediate and intense concern to workers in physics, engineering, management, and many other disciplines—and especially to workers involved with brain science, psychology, and artificial intelligence.

Perhaps this is why the past few years have seen new and heated discussions of network machines as part of an intellectually aggressive movement to establish a paradigm for artificial intelligence and cognitive modeling. Indeed, this growth of activity and interest has been so swift that people talk about a "connectionist revolution." The purpose of this epilogue, added in 1988, is to help present-day students to use the ideas presented in *Perceptrons* to put the new results into perspective and to formulate more clearly the research questions suggested by them. To do this succinctly, we adopt the strategy of focusing on one particular example of modern connectionist writing. Recently, David Rumelhart, James McClelland, and fourteen collaborators published a two-volume work that has become something of a connectionist manifesto: *Parallel Distributed Processing* (MIT Press, 1986). We shall take this work (henceforth referred to as *PDP*) as our connectionist text. What we say about this particular text will not, of course, apply literally to other writings on this subject, but thoughtful readers will seize the general point through the particular case. In most of this epilogue we shall discuss the examples in *PDP* from inside the connectionist perspective, in order to flag certain problems that we do not expect to be solvable within the framework of any single, homogeneous machine. At the end, however, we shall consider the same problems from the perspective of the overview we call "society of mind," a conceptual framework that makes it much more feasible to exploit collections of specialized accomplishments.

PDP describes *Perceptrons* as pessimistic about the prospects for connectionist machinery:

"... even though multilayer linear threshold networks are potentially much more powerful ... it was the limitations on what perceptrons could possibly learn that led to Minsky and Papert's (1969) pessimistic evaluation of the perceptron. Unfortunately, that evaluation has incorrectly tainted more interesting and powerful networks of linear threshold and other nonlinear units. As we shall see, the limitations of the one-step perceptrons in no way apply to the more complex networks." (vol. 1, p. 65)

We scarcely recognize ourselves in this description, and we recommend rereading the remarks in section 0.3 about romanticism and rigor. We reiterate our belief that the romantic claims have been less wrong than the pompous criticisms. But we also reiterate that the discipline can grow only when it makes a parallel effort to critically evaluate its apparent accomplishments. Our own work in *Perceptrons* is based on the interaction between an enthusiastic pursuit of models of new phenomena and a rigorous search for ways to understand the limitations of these models.

In any case, such citations have given our book the reputation of being mainly concerned with what perceptrons cannot do, and of having concluded with a qualitative evaluation that the subject was not important. Certainly, some chapters prove that various important predicates have perceptron coefficients that grow unmanageably large. But many chapters show that other predicates can be surprisingly tractable. It is no more apt to describe our mathematical theorems as pessimistic than it

584

Chapter 34

would be to say the same about deducing the conservation of momentum from the laws of mechanics. Theorems are theorems, and the history of science amply demonstrates how discovering limiting principles can lead to deeper understanding. But this happens only when those principles are taken seriously, so we exhort contemporary connectionist researchers to consider our results seriously as sources of research questions instead of maintaining that they "in no way apply."

What Perceptrons Can't Do

To put our results into perspective, let us recall the situation in the early 1960s: Many people were impressed by the fact that initially unstructured networks composed of very simple devices could be made to perform many interesting tasks—by processes that could be seen as remarkably like some forms of learning.

A different fact seemed to have impressed only a few people: While those networks did well on certain tasks and failed on certain other tasks, there was no theory to explain what made the difference—particularly when they seemed to work well on small ("toy") problems but broke down with larger problems of the same kind.

Our goal was to develop analytic tools to give us better ideas about what made the difference. But finding a comprehensive theory of parallel computation seemed infeasible, because the subject was simply too general. What we had to do was sharpen our ideas by working with some subclass of parallel machines that would be sufficiently powerful to perform significant computations, that would also share at least some of the features that made such networks attractive to those who sought a deeper understanding of the brain, and that would also be mathematically simple enough to permit theoretical analysis. This is why we used the abstract definition of *perceptron* given in this book. The perceptron seemed powerful enough in function, suggestive enough in architecture, and simple enough in its mathematical definition, yet understanding the range and character of its capabilities presented challenging puzzles.

Our prime example of such a puzzle was the recognition of connectedness. It took us many months of work to capture in a formal proof our strong intuition that perceptrons were unable to represent that predicate. Perhaps the most instructive aspect of that whole process was that we were guided by a flawed intuition to the proof that perceptrons cannot recognize the connectivity in any general or practical sense. We had assumed that perceptrons could not even detect the connectivity of hole-free blobs—because, as we supposed, no local forms of evidence like those in figure 5.7 could correlate with the correct decision.

Yet, as we saw in subsection 5.8.1, if a figure is known to have no holes, then a low-order perceptron can decide on its connectivity; this we had not initially believed to be possible. It is hard to imagine better evidence to show how artificial it is to separate "negative" from "positive" results in this kind of investigation. To explain how this experience affected us, we must abstract what we learned from it.

First we learned to reformulate questions like "Can perceptrons perform a certain task?" Strictly speaking, it is misleading to say that perceptrons cannot recognize connectedness, since for any particular size of retina we can make a perceptron that will recognize any predicate by providing it with enough φs of sufficiently high order. What we did show was that the general predicate requires perceptrons of unbounded order. More generally, we learned to replace globally qualitative questions about what perceptrons cannot do with questions in the spirit of what is now called computational complexity. Many of our results are of the form $M = f(R)$, where R is a measure of the size of the problem and M is the magnitude of some parameter of a perceptron (such as the order of its predicates, how many of them might be required, the information content of the coefficients, or the number of cycles needed for learning to converge). The study of such relationships gave us a better sense of what is likely to go wrong when one tries to enlarge the scale of a perceptron-like computation. In serial computing it was already well known that certain algorithms depending on search processes would require numbers of steps of computation that increased exponentially with the size of the problem. Much less was known about such matters in the case of parallel machines.

The second lesson was that in order to understand what perceptrons can do we would have to develop some theories of "problem domains" and not simply a "theory of perceptrons." In previous work on networks, from McCulloch and Pitts to Rosenblatt, even the best theorists had tried to formulate general-purpose theories about the kinds of networks they were interested in. Rosenblatt's convergence theorem is an example of how such investigations can lead to powerful results. But something qualitatively different was needed to explain why perceptrons could recognize the connectedness of hole-free figures yet be unable to recognize connectedness in general. For this we needed a bridge between a theory about the computing device and a theory about the content of the computation. The reason why our group-invariance theorem was so useful here was that it had one foot on the geometric side and one on the computational side.

Our study of the perceptron was an attempt to understand general principles through the study of a special case. Even today, we still know very little, in general, about how the costs of parallel computation are affected by increases in the scale of problems. Only the cases we understand can serve as bases for conjectures about what will happen in other situations. Thus, until there is evidence to the contrary, we are inclined to project the significance of our results to other networks related to perceptrons. In the past few years, many experiments have demonstrated that various new types of learning machines, composed of multiple layers of perceptron-like elements, can be made to solve many kinds of small-scale problems. Some of those experimenters believe that these performances can be economically extended to larger problems without encountering the limitations we have shown to apply to single-layer perceptrons. Shortly, we shall take a closer look at some of those results and see that much of what we learned about simple perceptrons will still remain quite pertinent. It certainly is true that most of the theorems in this book are explicitly about machines with a single layer of adjustable connection weights. But this does not imply (as many modern connectionists assume) that our conclusions don't apply to multilayered machines. To be sure, those proofs no longer apply unchanged, because their antecedent conditions have changed. But the phenomena they describe will often still persist. One must examine them, case by case. For example, all our conclusions about order-limited predicates (see section 0.7) continue to apply to networks with multiple layers, because the order of any unit in a given layer is bounded by the *product* of the orders of the units in earlier layers. Since many of our arguments about order constrain the representations of group-invariant predicates, we suspect that many of those conclusions, too, will apply to multilayer nets. For example, multilayer networks will be no more able to recognize connectedness than are perceptrons. (This is not to say that multilayer networks do not have advantages. For example, the product rule can yield logarithmic reductions in the orders and numbers of units required to compute certain high-order predicates. Furthermore, units that are arranged in loops can be of effectively unbounded order; hence, some such networks *will* be able to recognize connectedness by using internal serial processing.)

Thus, in some cases our conclusions will remain provably true and in some cases they will be clearly false. In the middle there are many results that we still think may hold, but we do not know any formal proofs. In the next section we shall show how some of the experiments reported in *PDP* lend credence to some such conjectures.

Recognizing Symmetry

In this section we contrast two different networks, both of which recognize symmetrical patterns defined on a six-point linear retina. To be precise, we would like to recognize the predicate *X is symmetric about the midpoint of R*. Figure 1 shows a simple way to represent this is as a perceptron that uses R φ units, each of order 2. Each one of them will locally detect a deviation from symmetry at two particular retinal points. Figure 2 shows the results of an experiment from *PDP*. It depicts a network that represents $\psi SYMMETRY$ in quite a different way. Amazingly, this network uses only two φ functions—albeit ones of order R.

The weights displayed in figure 2 were produced by a learning procedure that we shall describe shortly. For the moment, we want to focus not on the learning problem but on the character of the coefficients. We share the sense of excitement the *PDP* experimenters must have experienced as their machine converged to this strange solution, in which this predicate seems to be portrayed as having a more holistic character than would be suggested by its conjunctively local representation. However, one must ask certain questions before celebrating this as a significant discovery. In *PDP* it is recognized that the lower-level coefficients appear to be growing exponentially, yet no alarm is expressed about this. In fact, anyone who reads section 7.3 should recognize such a network as employing precisely the type of computational structure that we called stratification. Also, in the case of network 2, the learning procedure required 1,208 cycles through each of the 64 possible examples—a total of 77,312 trials (enough to make us wonder if the time for this procedure to determine suitable coefficients increases exponentially with the size of the retina). *PDP* does not address this question. What happens when the retina has 100 elements? If such a network required on the order of 2^{200} trials to learn, most observers would lose interest.

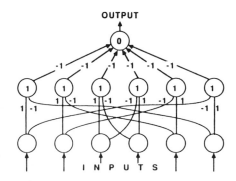

Figure 1 Symmetry using order-2 disjunction.

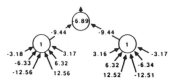

Actual coefficients from PDP experiment

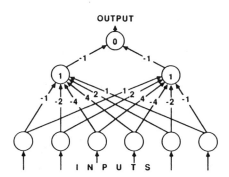

Figure 2 Symmetry using order-R Stratification.

This observation shows most starkly how we and the authors of *PDP* differ in interpreting the implications of our theory. Our "pessimistic evaluation of the perceptron" was the assertion that, although certain problems can easily by solved by perceptrons on small scales, the computational costs become prohibitive when the problem is scaled up. The authors of *PDP* seem not to recognize that the coefficients of this symmetry machine confirm that thesis, and celebrate this performance on a toy problem as a success rather than asking whether it could become a profoundly "bad" form of behavior when scaled up to problems of larger size.

Both of these networks are in the class of what we called Gamba perceptrons in section 13.1—that is, ordinary perceptrons whose φ functions are themselves perceptrons of order 1. Accordingly, we are uncomfortable about the remark in *PDP* that "multilayer linear threshold networks are potentially much more powerful than single-layer perceptrons." Of course they are, in various ways—and chapter 8 of *PDP* describes several studies of multilayer perceptron-like devices. However, most of them—like figure 2 above—still belong to the class of networks discussed in *Perceptrons*.

Also in chapter 8 of *PDP*, similar methods are applied to the problem of recognizing parity—and the very construction described in our section 13.1, through which a Gamba perceptron can recognize parity, is rediscovered. Figure 3 here shows the results. To learn these coefficients, the procedure described in *PDP* required 2,825 cycles through the 16 possible input patterns, thus consuming 45,200 trials for the network to learn to compute the parity predicate for only four inputs. Is this a good result or a bad result?

We cannot tell without more knowledge about why the procedure requires so many trials. Until one has some theory of that, there is no way to assess the significance of any such experimental result; all one can say is that 45,200 = 45,200. In section 10.1 we saw that if a perceptron's φ functions include only masks, the parity predicate requires doubly exponential coefficients. If we were sure that *that* was happening, this would suggest to us that we should represent 45,200 (approximately) as 2^{2^4} rather than, say, as 2^{16}. However, here we suspect that this would be wrong, because the input units aren't masks but predicates—apparently provided from the start—that already know how to "count." These make the problem much easier. In any case, the lesson of *Perceptrons* is that one cannot interpret the meaning of such an experimental report without first making further probes.

Learning

We haven't yet said how those networks learned. The authors of *PDP* describe a learning procedure called the "Generalized Delta Rule"—we'll call it GD—as a new breakthrough in connectionist research. To explain its importance, they depict as follows the theoretical situation they inherited:

"A further argument advanced by Minsky and Papert against perceptron-like models with hidden units is that there was no indication how such multilayer networks were to be trained. One of the appealing features of the one-layer perceptron is the existence of a powerful learning procedure, the perceptron convergence procedure of Rosenblatt. In Minsky and Papert's day, there was no such powerful learning procedure for the more complex multilayer systems. This is no longer true . . . . The GD procedure provides a direct generalization of the perceptron learning procedure which can be applied to arbitrary networks with multiple layers and feed-back among layers. This procedure can, in principle, learn arbitrary functions including, of course, parity and connectedness." (vol. 1, p. 113)

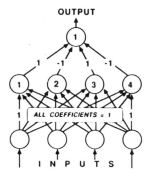

Figure 3 Parity using gamba masks.

In Minsky and Papert's day, indeed! In this section we shall explain why, although the GD learning procedure embodies some useful ideas, it does not justify such sweeping claims. But in order to explain why, and to see how the approach in the current wave of connectionism differs from that in *Perceptrons*, we must first examine with some care the relationship between two branches of perceptron theory which could be called "theory of learning" and "theory of representation." To begin with, one might paraphrase the above quotation as saying that, until recently, connectionism had been paralyzed by the following dilemma:

Perceptrons could learn anything that they could represent, but they were too limited in what they could represent.

Multilayered networks were less limited in what they could represent, but they had no reliable learning procedure.

According to the classical theory of perceptrons, those limitations on representability depend on such issues as whether a given predicate P can be represented as a perceptron defined by a given set Φ on a given retina, whether P is of finite order, whether P can be realized with coefficients of bounded size, whether properties of several representable predicates are inherited by combinations of those predicates, and so forth. All the results in the first half of our book are involved with these sorts of representational issues. Now, when one speaks about "powerful learning procedures," the situation is complicated by the fact that, given enough input units of sufficiently high order, even simple perceptrons can represent—and therefore learn—arbitrary functions. Consequently, it makes no sense to speak about "power" in absolute terms. Such statements must refer to relative measures of sizes and scales.

As for learning, the dependability of Rosenblatt's Perceptron Convergence theorem of section 11.1—let's call it PC for short—is very impressive: If it is possible at all to represent a predicate P as a linear threshold function of a given set of predicates Φ, then the PC procedure will eventually discover some particular set of coefficients that actually represents P. However, this is not, in itself, a sufficient reason to consider PC interesting and important, because that theorem says nothing about the crucial issue of efficiency. PC is not interesting merely because it provides a systematic way to find suitable coefficients. One could always take recourse, instead, to simple, brute-force search—because, given that some solution exists, one could simply search through all possible integer coefficient vectors, in order of increasing magnitude, until no further "errors" occurred. But no one would consider such an exhaustive process to be an interesting foundation for a learning theory.

What, then, makes PC seem significant? That it discovers those coefficients in ways that are intriguing in several

other important respects. The PC procedure seems to satisfy many of the intuitive requirements of those who are concerned with modeling what really happens in a biological nervous system. It also appeals to both our engineering aesthetic and our psychological aesthetic by serving simultaneously as both a form of guidance by error correction and a form of hill-climbing. In terms of computational efficiency, PC seems much more efficient than brute-force procedures (although we have no rigorous and general theory of the conditions under which that will be true). Finally, PC is so simple mathematically as to make one wish to believe that it reflects something real.

Hill-Climbing and the Generalized Delta Procedure

Suppose we want to find the maximum value of a given function $F(x,y,z,\ldots)$ of n variables. The extreme brute-force solution is to calculate the function for all sets of values for the variables and then select the point for which F had the largest value. The approach we called hill-climbing in section 11.3 is a local procedure designed to attempt to find that global maximum. To make this subject more concrete, it is useful to think of the two-dimensional case in which the $x - y$ plane is the ground and $z = F(x,y)$ is the elevation of the point (x,y,z) on the surface of a real physical hill. Now, imagine standing on the hill in a fog so dense that only the immediate vicinity is visible. Then the only resort is to use some diameter-limited local process. The best-known method is the method known as "steepest ascent," discussed in section 11.6: First determine the slope of the surface in various directions from the point where you are standing, then choose the direction that most rapidly increases your altitude and take a step of a certain size in that direction. The hope is that, by thus climbing the slope, you will eventually reach the highest point.

It is both well known and obvious that hill-climbing does not always work. The simplest way to fail is to get stuck on a local maximum—an isolated peak whose altitude is relatively insignificant. There simply is no local way for a hill-climbing procedure to be sure that it has reached a global maximum rather than some local feature of topography (such as a peak, a ridge, or a plain) on which it may get trapped. We showed in section 11.6 that PC is equivalent (in a peculiar sense) to a hill-climbing procedure that works its way to the top of a hill whose geometry can actually be proved not to have any such troublesome local features—provided that there actually exists some perceptron-weight vector solution A^* to the problem. Thus, one could argue that perceptrons "work" on those problems not because of any particular virtue of the perceptrons or of their hill-climbing procedures but because the hills for those soluble problems have clean topographies. What are the prospects of finding a learning procedure that works equally well on all problems, and not merely on those that have linearly separable decision functions? The authors of *PDP* maintain that they have indeed discovered one:

"Although our learning results do not guarantee that we can find a solution for all solvable problems, our analyses and results have shown that, as a practical matter, the error propagation scheme leads to solutions in virtually every case. In short, we believe that we have answered Minsky and Papert's challenge and have found a learning result sufficiently powerful to demonstrate that their pessimism about learning in multilayer machines was misplaced." (vol. 1, p. 361)

But the experiments in *PDP,* though interesting and ingenious, do not actually demonstrate any such thing. In fact, the "powerful new learning result" is nothing other than a straightforward hill-climbing algorithm, with all the problems that entails. To see how GD works, assume we are given a network of units interconnected by weighted, unidirectional links. Certain of these units are connected to input terminals, and certain others are regarded as output units. We want to teach this network to respond to each (vector) input pattern $\mathbf{X}_p$ with a specified output vector $\mathbf{Y}_p$. How can we find a set of weights $w = \{w_{ij}\}$ that will accomplish this? We could try to do it by hill-climbing on the space of $\mathbf{W}s$, provided that we could define a suitable measure of relative altitude or "success." One problem is that there cannot be any standard, universal way to measure errors, because each type of error has different costs in different situations. But let us set that issue aside and do what scientists often do when they can't think of anything better: sum the squares of the differences. So, if $\mathbf{X}(\mathbf{W},\mathbf{X})$ is the network's out-put vector for internal weights $\mathbf{W}$ and inputs $\mathbf{X}$, define the altitude function $E(\mathbf{W})$ to be this sum:

$$E(\mathbf{W}) = -\sum_{\substack{\text{all input} \\ \text{patterns } p}} [\mathbf{Y}_p - \mathbf{Y}(\mathbf{W}, \mathbf{X}_p)]^2.$$

In other words, we compute our measure of success by presenting successively each stimulus $\mathbf{X}_p$ to the network. Then we compute the (vector) difference between the actual output and the desired output. Finally, we add up the squares of the magnitudes of those differences. (The minus sign is simply for thinking of climbing up instead of down.) The error function E will then have a maximum possible value of zero, which will be achieved if and only if the machine performs perfectly. Otherwise there will be at least one error and $E(\mathbf{W})$ will be negative. Then all we have to do is climb the hill $E(\mathbf{W})$ defined over the (high-dimensional) space of weight vectors $\mathbf{W}$. If our paths reaches a $\mathbf{W}$ for which $E(\mathbf{W})$ is zero, our problem will be solved and we will be able to say that our machine has "learned from its experience."

We'll use a process that climbs this hill by the method of steepest ascent. We can do this by estimating, at every step, the partial derivatives $\partial E/\partial w_{ij}$ of the total error with respect to each component of the weight vector. This tells us the direction of the gradient vector $dE/d\mathbf{W}$, and we then proceed to move a certain distance in that direction. This is the mathematical character of the Generalized Delta procedure, and it differs in no significant way from older forms of diameter-limited gradient followers.

Before such a procedure can be employed, there is an obstacle to overcome. One cannot directly apply the method of gradient ascent to networks that contain threshold units. This is because the derivative of a step-function is zero, whenever it exists, and hence no gradient is defined. To get around this, *PDP* applies a smoothing function to make those threshold functions differentiable. The trick is to replace the threshold function for each unit with a monotonic and differentiable function of the sum of that unit's inputs. This permits the output of each unit to encode information about the sum of its inputs while still retaining an approximation to the perceptron's decision-making ability. Then gradient ascent becomes more feasible. However, we suspect that this smoothing trick may entail a large (and avoidable) cost when the predicate to be learned is actually a composition of linear threshold functions. There ought to be a more efficient alternative based on how much each weight must be changed, for each stimulus, to make the local input sum cross the threshold

In what sense is the particular hill-climbing procedure GD more powerful than the perceptron's PC? Certainly GD can be applied to more networks than PC can, because PC can operate only on the connections between one layer of φ units and a single output unit. GD, however, can modify the weights in an arbitrary multilayered network, including nets containing loops. Thus, in contrast to the perceptron (which is equipped with some fixed set of φs that can never be changed), GP can be regarded as able to change the weights inside the φs. Thus GD promises, in effect, to be able discover useful *new* φ functions—and many of the experiments reported in *PDP* demonstrate that this often works.

A natural way to estimate the gradient of $E(W)$ is to estimate $\partial E/\partial w_{ij}$ by running through the entire set of inputs for each weight. However, for large networks and large problems that could be a horrendous computation. Fortunately, in a highly connected network, all those many components of the gradient are not independent of one another, but are constrained by the algebraic "chain rule" for the derivatives of composite functions. One can exploit those constraints to reduce the amount of computation by applying the chain-rule formula, recursively, to the mathematical description of the network. This recursive computation is called "back-propagation" in *PDP*. It can substantially reduce the amount of calculation for each hill-climbing step in networks with many connections. We have the impression that many people in the connectionist community do not understand that this is merely a particular way to compute a gradient and have assumed instead that back-propagation is a new learning scheme that somehow gets around the basic limitations of hill-climbing.

Clearly GD would be far more valuable than PC if it could be made to be both efficient and dependable. But virtually nothing has been proved about the range of problems upon which GD works both efficiently and dependably. Indeed, GD can fail to find a solution when one exists, so in that narrow sense it could be considered *less* powerful than PC.

In the early years of cybernetics, everyone understood that hill-climbing was always available for working easy problems, but that it almost always became impractical for problems of larger sizes and complexities. We were very pleased to discover (see section 11.6) that PC could be represented as hill-climbing; however, that very fact led us to wonder whether such procedures could *dependably* be generalized, even to the limited class of multilayer machines that we named Gamba perceptrons. The situation seems not to have changed much—we have seen no contemporary connectionist publication that casts much new theoretical light on the situation. Then why has GD become so popular in recent years? In part this is because it is so widely applicable, and because it does indeed yield new results (at least on problems of rather small scale). Its reputation also gains, we think, from its being presented in forms that share, albeit to a lesser degree, the biological plausibility of PC. But we fear that its reputation also stems from unfamiliarity with the manner in which hill-climbing methods deteriorate when confronted with larger-scale problems.

In any case, little good can come from statements like "as a practical matter, GD leads to solutions in virtually every case" or "GD can, in principle, learn arbitrary functions." Such pronouncements are not merely technically wrong; more significantly, the pretense that problems do not exist can deflect us from valuable insights that could come from examining things more carefully. As the field of connectionism becomes more mature, the quest for a general solution to all learning problems will evolve into an understanding of which types of learning processes are likely to work on which classes of problems. And this means that, past a certain point, we won't be able to get by with vacuous generalities about hill-climbing. We will really need to know a great deal more about the nature of those surfaces for each specific realm of problems that we want to solve.

On the positive side, we applaud those who bravely and romantically are empirically applying hill-climbing methods to many new domains for the first time, and we expect such work to result in important advances. Certainly these researchers are exploring networks with architectures far more complex than those of perceptrons, and some of their experiments already have shown indications of new phenomena that are well worth trying to understand.

Scaling Problems Up in Size

Experiments with toy-scale problems have proved as fruitful in artificial intelligence as in other areas of science and engineering. Many techniques and principles that ultimately found real applications were discovered and honed in microworlds small enough to comprehend yet rich enough to challenge our thinking. But not every phenomenon encountered in dealing with small models can be usefully scaled up. Looking at the relative thickness of the legs of an ant and an elephant reminds us that physical structures do not always scale linearly: an ant magnified a thousand times would collapse under its own weight. Much of the theory of computational complexity is concerned with questions of scale. If it takes 100 steps to solve a certain kind of equation with four terms, how many steps will it take to solve the same kind of equation with eight terms? Only 200, if the problem scales linearly. But for other problems it will take not twice 100 but 100 squared.

For example, the Gamba perceptron of figure 2 needs only two φ functions rather than the six required in figure 1. In neither of these two toy-sized networks does the number seem alarmingly large. One network has fewer units; the other has smaller coefficients. But when we examine how those numbers grow with retinas of increasing size, we discover that whereas the coefficients of figure 1 remain constant, those of figure 2 grow exponentially. And, presumably, a similar price must be paid again in the number of repetitions required in order to learn.

In the examination of theories of learning and problem solving, the study of such growths in cost is not merely one more aspect to be taken into account; in a sense, it is the only aspect worth considering. This is because so many problems can be solved "in principle" by exhaustive search through a suitable space of states. Of course, the trouble with that in practice is that there is usually an exponential increase in the number of steps required for an exhaustive search when the scale of the problem is enlarged. Consequently, solving toy problems by methods related to exhaustive search rarely leads to practical solutions to larger problems. For example, though it is easy to make an exhaustive-search machine that never loses a game of noughts and crosses, it is infeasible to do the same for chess.

We do not know if this fact is significant, but many of the small examples described in *PDP* could have been solved as quickly by means of exhaustive search—that is, by systematically assigning and testing all combinations of small integer weights.

When we started our research on perceptrons, we had seen many interesting demonstrations of perceptrons solving problems of very small scale but not doing so well when those problems were scaled up. We wondered what was going wrong. Our first "handle" on how to think about scaling came with the concept of the order of a predicate. If a problem is of order *N,* then the number of φs for the corresponding perceptron need not increase any faster than as the *N*th power of *R*. Then, whenever we could show that a given problem was of low order, we usually could demonstrate that perceptron-like networks could do surprisingly well on that problem. On the other hand, once we developed the more difficult techniques for showing that certain other problems have unbounded order, this raised alarming warning flags about extending *their* solutions to larger domains.

Unbounded order was not the only source of scaling failures. Another source—one we had not anticipated until the later stages of our work—involved the size, or rather the information content, of the coefficients. The information stored in connectionist systems is embodied in the strengths of weights of the connections between units. The idea that learning can take place by changing such strengths has a ring of biological plausibility, but that plausibility fades away if those strengths are to be represented by numbers that must be accurate to ten or twenty decimal orders of significance.

The Problem of Sampling Variance

Our description of the Generalized Delta Rule assumes that it is feasible to compute the new value of $E(\mathbf{W})$ at every step of the climb. The processes discussed in chapter 8 of *PDP* typically require only on the order of 100,000 iterations, a range that is easily accessible to computers (but that might in some cases strain our sense of biological plausibility). However, it will not be practical, with larger problems, to cycle through all possible input patterns. This means that when precise measures of $E(\mathbf{W})$ are unavailable, we will be forced to act, instead, on the basis of incomplete samples—for example, by making a small hill-climbing step after each reaction to a stimulus. (See the discussion of complete versus incremental methods in subsection 12.1.1.) When we can no longer compute $dE/d\mathbf{W}$ precisely but can only estimate its components, then the actual derivative will be masked by a certain amount of sampling noise. The text of *PDP* argues that using sufficiently small steps can force the resulting trajectory to come arbitrarily close to that which would result from knowing $dE/d\mathbf{W}$ precisely. When we tried to prove this, we were led to suspect that the choice of step size may depend so much on the higher derivatives of the smoothing functions that large-scale problems could require too many steps for such methods to be practical.

So far as we could tell, every experiment described in chapter 8 of *PDP* involved making a complete cycle through all possible input situations before making any change in weights. Whenever this is feasible, it completely eliminates sampling noise—and then even the most minute correlations can become reliably detectable, because the variance is zero. But no person or animal ever faces situations that are so simple and arranged in so orderly a manner as to provide such cycles of teaching examples. Moving from small to large problems will often demand this transition from exhaustive to statistical sampling, and we suspect that in many realistic situations the resulting sampling noise would mask the signal completely. We suspect that many who read the connectionist literature are not aware of this phenomenon, which dims some of the prospects of successfully applying certain learning procedures to large-scale problems.

Problems of Scaling

In principle, connectionist networks offer all the potential of universal computing devices. However, our examples of order and coefficient size suggest that various kinds of scaling problems are likely to become obstacles to attempts to exploit that potential. Fortunately, our analysis of perceptrons does not suggest that connectionist networks need always encounter these obstacles. Indeed, our book is rich in surprising examples of tasks that simple perceptrons can perform using relatively low-order units and small coefficients. However, our analysis does show that parallel networks are, in general, subject to serious scaling phenomena. Consequently, researchers who propose such models must show that, in their context, those phenomena do not occur.

The authors of *PDP* seem disinclined to face such problems. They seem content to argue that, although we showed that single-layer networks cannot solve certain problems, we did not know that there could exist a powerful learning procedure for multilayer networks—to which our theorems no longer apply. However, strictly speaking, it is wrong to formulate our findings in terms of what perceptrons can and cannot do. As we pointed out above, perceptrons of sufficiently large order can represent *any* finite predicate. A better description of what we did is that, in certain cases, we established the computational costs of what perceptrons can do as a function of increasing problem size. The authors of *PDP* show little concern for such issues, and usually seem content with experiments in which small multilayer networks solve particular instances of small problems.

What should one conclude from such examples? A person who thinks in terms of *can* versus *can't* will be tempted to suppose that if toy machines can do something, then larger machines may well do it better. One must always probe into the practicality of a proposed learning algorithm. It is no use to say that "procedure *P* is capable of learning to recognize pattern *X*" unless one can show that this can be done in less time and at less cost than with exhaustive search. Thus, as we noted, in the case of symmetry, the authors of *PDP* actually recognized that the coefficients were growing as powers of 2, yet they did not seem to regard this as suggesting that the experiment worked only because of its very small size. But scientists who exploit the insights gained from studying the single-layer case might draw quite different conclusions.

The authors of *PDP* recognize that GD is a form of hill-climber, but they speak as though becoming trapped on local maxima were rarely a serious problem. In reporting their experiments with learning the XOR predicate, they remark that this occurred "in only two cases . . . in hundreds of times." However, that experiment involved only the toy problem of learning to compute the XOR of two arguments. We conjecture that learning XOR for larger numbers of variables will become increasingly intractable as we increase the numbers of input variables, because by its nature the underlying parity function is absolutely un-correlated with any function of fewer variables. Therefore, there can exist no useful correlations among the outputs of the lower-order units involved in computing it, and that leads us to suspect that there is little to gain from following whatever paths are indicated by the artificial introduction of smoothing functions that cause partial derivatives to exist.

The *PDP* experimenters encountered a more serious local-maximum problem when trying to make a network learn to add two binary numbers—a problem that contains an embedded XOR problem. When working with certain small networks, the system got stuck reliably. However, the experimenters discovered an interesting way to get around this difficulty by introducing longer chains of intermediate units. We encourage the reader to study the discussion starting on page 341 of *PDP* and try to make a more complete theoretical analysis of this problem. We suspect that further study of this case will show that hill-climbing procedures can indeed get multilayer networks to learn to do multidigit addition. However, such a study should be carried out not to show that "networks are good" but to see which network architectures are most suitable for enabling the information required for "carrying" to flow easily from

the smaller to the larger digits. In the *PDP* experiment, the network appears to us to have started on the road toward inventing the technique known to computer engineers as "carry jumping."

To what extent can hill-climbing systems be made to solve hard problems? One might object that this is a wrong question because "hard" is so ill defined. The lesson of *Perceptrons* is that we must find ways to make such questions meaningful. In the case of hill-climbing, we need to find ways to characterize the types of problems that lead to the various obstacles to climbing hills, instead of ignoring those difficulties or trying to find universal ways to get around them.

The Society of Mind

The preceding section was written as though it ought to be the principal goal of research on network models to determine in which situations it will be feasible to scale their operations up to deal with increasingly complicated problems. But now we propose a somewhat shocking alternative: Perhaps the scale of the toy problem is that on which, in physiological actuality, much of the functioning of intelligence operates. Accepting this thesis leads into a way of thinking very different from that of the connectionist movement. We have used the phrase "society of mind" to refer to the idea that mind is made up of a large number of components, or "agents," each of which would operate on the scale of what, if taken in isolation, would be little more than a toy problem. [See Marvin Minsky, *The Society of Mind* (Simon and Schuster, 1987) and Seymour Papert, *Mindstorms* (Basic Books, 1982).]

To illustrate this idea, let's try to compare the performance of the symmetry perceptron in *PDP* with human behavior. An adult human can usually recognize and appreciate the symmetries of a kaleidoscope, and that sort of example leads one to imagine that people do very much better than simple perceptrons. But how much can people actually do? Most people would be hard put to be certain about the symmetry of a large pattern. For example, how long does it take you to decide whether or not the following pattern is symmetrical?

DB4HWUK85HCNZEWJKRKJWEZNCH58KUWH4BD

In many situations, humans clearly show abilities far in excess of what could be learned by simple, uniform networks. But when we take those skills apart, or try to find out how they were learned, we expect to find that they were made by processes that somehow combined the work (already done in the past) of many smaller agencies, none of which, separately, need to work on scales much larger than do those in *PDP*. Is this hypothesis consistent with the *PDP* style of connectionism? Yes, insofar as the computations of the nervous system can be represented as the operation of societies of networks. But no, insofar as the mode of operation of those societies of networks (as we imagine them) raises theoretical issues of a different kind. We do not expect procedures such as GD to be able to produce such societies. Something else is needed.

What that something must be depends on how we try to extend the range of small connectionist models. We see two principal alternatives. We could extend them either by scaling up small connectionist models or by combining small-scale networks into some larger organization. In the first case, we would expect to encounter theoretical obstacles to maintaining GD's effectiveness on larger, deeper nets. And despite the reputed efficacy of other alleged remedies for the deficiencies of hill-climbing, such as "annealing," we stay with our research conjecture that no such procedures will work very well on large-scale nets, except in the case of problems that turn out to be of low order in some appropriate sense. The second alternative is to employ a variety of smaller networks rather than try to scale up a single one. And if we choose (as we do) to move in that direction, then our focus of concern as theoretical psychologists must turn toward the organizing of small nets into effective large systems. The idea that the lowest levels of thinking and learning may operate on toy-like scales fits many of our common-sense impressions of psychology. For example, in the realm of language, any normal person can parse a great many kinds of sentences, but none of them past a certain bound of involuted complexity. We all fall down on expressions like "the cheese that the rat that the cat that the dog bit chased ate." In the realm of vision, no one can count great numbers of things, in parallel, at a single glance. Instead, we learn to "estimate." Indeed, the visual joke in figure 0.1 shows clearly how humans share perceptrons' inability to easily count and match, and a similar example is embodied in the twin spirals of figure 5.1. The spiral example was intended to emphasize not only that low-order perceptrons cannot perceive connectedness but also that humans have similar limitations. However, a determined person can solve the problem, given enough time, by switching to the use of certain sorts of serial mental processes.

Beyond Perceptrons

No single-method learning scheme can operate efficiently for every possible task; we cannot expect any one type of machine to account for any large portion of human psychology. for example, in certain situations it is best to carefully accumulate experience; however, when time is limited, it is necessary to make hasty generalizations and act accordingly. No single scheme can do all things. Our

human semblance of intelligence emerged from how the brain evolved a multiplicity of ways to deal with different problem realms. We see this as a principle that underlies the mind's reality, and we interpret the need for many kinds of mechanisms not as a pessimistic and scientifically constraining limitation but as the fundamental source of many of the phenomena that artificial intelligence and psychology have always sought to understand. The power of the brain stems not from any single, fixed, universal principle. Instead it comes from the evolution (in both the individual sense and the Darwinian sense) of a variety of ways to develop new mechanisms and to adapt older ones to perform new functions. Instead of seeking a way to get around that need for diversity, we have come to try to develop "society of mind" theories that will recognize and exploit the idea that brains are based on many different kinds of interacting mechanisms.

Several kinds of evidence impel us toward this view. One is the great variety of different and specific functions embodied in the brain's biology. Another is the similarly great variety of phenomena in the psychology of intelligence. And from a much more abstract viewpoint, we cannot help but be impressed with the practical limitations of each "general" scheme that has been proposed—and with the theoretical opacity of questions about how they behave when we try to scale their applications past the toy problems for which they were first conceived.

Our research on perceptrons and on other computational schemes has left us with a pervasive bias against seeking a general, domain-independent theory of "how neural networks work." Instead, we ought to look for ways in which particular types of network models can support the development of models of particular domains of mental function—and vice versa. Thus, our understanding of the perceptron's ability to perform geometric tasks was actually based on theories that were more concerned with geometry than with networks. And this example is supported by a broad body of experience in other areas of artificial intelligence. Perhaps this is why the current preoccupation of connectionist theorists with the search for general learning algorithms evokes for us two aspects of the early history of computation.

First, we are reminded of the long line of theoretical work that culminated in the "pessimistic" theories of Gödel and Turing about the limitations on effective computability. Yet the realization that there can be no general-purpose decision procedure for mathematics had not the slightest dampening effect on research in mathematics or in computer science. On the contrary, awareness of those limiting discoveries helped motivate the growth of rich cultures involved with classifying and understanding more specialized algorithmic methods. In other words, it was the realization that seeking overgeneral solution methods would be as fruitless as—and equivalent to—trying to solve the unsolvable halting problem for Turing machines. Abandoning this then led to seeking progress in more productive directions.

Our second thought is about how the early research in artificial intelligence tended to focus on general-purpose algorithms for reasoning and problem solving. Those general methods will always play their roles, but the most successful applications of AI research gained much of their practical power from applying specific knowledge to specific domains. Perhaps that work has now moved too far toward ignoring general theoretical considerations, but by now we have learned to be skeptical about the practical power of unrestrained generality.

Interaction and Insulation

Evolution seems to have anticipated these discoveries. Although the nervous system appears to be a network, it is very far from being a single, uniform, highly interconnected assembly of units that each have similar relationships to the others. Nor are all brain cells similarly affected by the same processes. It would be better to think of the brain not as a single network whose elements operate in accord with a uniform set of principles but as a network whose components are themselves networks having a large variety of different architectures and control systems. This "society of mind" idea has led our research perspective away from the search for algorithms, such as GD, that were hoped to work across many domains. Instead, we were led into trying to understand what specific kinds of processing would serve specific domains.

We recognize that the idea of distributed, cooperative processing has a powerful appeal to common sense as well to computational and biological science. Our research instincts tell us to discover as much as we can about distributed processes. But there is another concept, complementary to distribution, that is no less strongly supported by the same sources of intuition. We'll call it *insulation*.

Certain parallel computations are by their nature synergistic and cooperative: each part makes the others easier. But the And/Or of theorem 4.0 shows that under other circumstances, attempting to make the same network perform two simple tasks at the same time leads to a task that has a far greater order of difficulty. In those sorts of circumstances, there will be a clear advantage to having mechanisms, not to connect things together, but to keep such tasks apart. How can this be done in a connectionist net? Some recent work hints that even simple multilayer perceptron-like nets can learn to segregate themselves into quasi-separate components—and that suggests (at least in principle) research on uniform learning procedures. But it

also raises the question of how to relate those almost separate parts. In fact, research on networks in which different parts do different things and learn those things in different ways has become our principal concern. And that leads us to ask how such systems could develop *managers* for deciding, in different circumstances, which of those diverse procedures to use.

For example, consider all the specialized agencies that the human brain employs to deal with the visual perception of spatial scenes. Although we still know little about how all those different agencies work, the end result is surely even more complex than what we described in section 13.4. Beyond that, human scene analysis also engages our memories and goals. Furthermore, in addition to all the systems we humans use to dissect two-dimensional scenes into objects and relationships, we also possess machinery for exploiting stereoscopic vision. Indeed, there appear to be many such agencies—distinct ones that employ, for example, motion cues, disparities, central correlations of the Julesz type, and memory-based frame-array-like systems that enable us to imagine and virtually "see" the occluded sides of familiar objects. Beyond those, we seem also to have been supplied with many other visual agencies—for example, ones that are destined to learn to recognize faces and expressions, visual cliffs, threatening movements, sexual attractants, and who knows how many others that have not been discovered yet. What mechanisms manage and control the use of all those diverse agencies? And from where do those managers come?

Stages of Development

In *Mindstorms* and in *The Society of Mind,* we explained how the idea of intermediate, hidden processes might well account for some phenomena discovered by Piaget in his experiments on how children develop their concepts about the "conservation of quantity." We introduced a theory of mental growth based on inserting, at various times, new inner layers of "management" into already existing networks. In particular, we argued that, to learn to make certain types of comparisons, a child's mind must construct a multilayer structure that we call a "society-of-more." The lower levels of that net contain agents specialized to make a variety of spatial and temporal observations. Then the higher-level agents learn to classify, and then control, the activities of the lower ones. We certainly would like to see a demonstration of a learning process that could spontaneously produce the several levels of agents needed to embody a concept as complex as that. Chapter 17 of *The Society of Mind* offers several different reasons why this might be very difficult to do except in systems under systematic controls, both temporal and architectural. We suspect that it would require far too long, in comparison with an infant's months of life, to create sophisticated agencies entirely by undirected, spontaneous learning. Each specialized network must begin with promising ingredients that come either from prior stages of development or from some structural endowment that emerged in the course of organic evolution.

When should new layers of control be introduce? If managers are empowered too soon, when their workers still are too immature, they won't be able to accomplish enough. (If every agent could learn from birth, they would all be overwhelmed by infantile ideas.) But if the managers arrive too late, that will retard all further growth. Ideally, every agency's development would be controlled by yet another agency equipped to introduce new agents just when they are needed—that is, when enough has been learned to justify the start of another stage. However, that would require a good deal of expertise on the controlling agency's part. Another way—much easier to evolve—would simply enable various agencies to establish new connections at genetically predetermined times (perhaps while also causing lower-level parts to slow further growth). Such a scheme could benefit a human population on the whole, although it might handicap individuals who, for one reason or another, happen to move ahead of or behind that inborn "schedule." In any case, there are many reasons to suspect that the parts of any system as complex as a human mind must grow through sequences of stage-like episodes.

Architecture and Specialization

The tradition of connectionism has always tried to establish two claims: that connectionist networks can accomplish interesting tasks and that they can learn to do so with no explicit programming. But a closer look reveals that rarely are those two virtues present in the same device. It is true that networks, taken as a class, can do virtually anything. However, each particular type of network can best learn only certain types of things. Each particular network we have seen seems relatively limited. Yet our wondrous brains are themselves composed of connected networks of cells.

We think that the difference in abilities comes from the fact that a brain is not a single, uniformly structured network. Instead, each brain contains hundreds of different types of machines, interconnected in specific ways which predestine that brain to become a large, diverse society of partially specialized agencies. We are born with specific parts of our brains to serve every sense and muscle group, and with perhaps separate sections for physical and social matters (e.g., natural sounds versus social speech, inanimate scenes versus facial expressions, mechanical contacts versus social caresses). Our brains also embody proto-

specialists involved with hunger, laughter, anger, fear, and perhaps hundreds of other functions that scientists have not yet isolated. Many thousands of genes must be involved in constructing specific internal architectures for each of those highly evolved brain centers and in laying out the nerve bundles that interconnect them. And although each such system is embodied in the form of a network-based learning system, each almost surely also learns in accord with somewhat different principles.

Why did our brains evolve so as to contain so many specialized parts? Could not a single, uniform network learn to structure itself into divisions with appropriate architectures and processes? We think that this would be impractical because of the problem of representing knowledge. In order for a machine to learn to recognize or perform X, be it a pattern or a process, that machine must in one sense or another learn to represent or embody X. Doing that efficiently must exploit some happy triadic relationship between the structure of X, the learning procedure, and the initial architecture of the network. It makes no sense to seek the "best" network architecture or learning procedure because it makes no sense to say that any network is efficient by itself: that makes sense only in the context of some class of problems to be solved. Different kinds of networks lend themselves best to different kinds of representations and to different sorts of generalizations. This means that the study of networks in general must include attempts, like those in this book, to classify problems and learning processes; but it must also include attempts to classify the network architectures. This is why we maintain that the scientific future of connectionism is tied not to the search for some single, universal scheme to solve all problems at once but to the evolution of a many-faceted technology of "brain design" that encompasses good technical theories about the analysis of learning procedures, of useful architectures, and of organizational principles to use when assembling those components into larger systems.

Symbolic versus Distributed

Let us now return to the conflict posed in our prologue: the war between the connectionists and the symbolists. We hope to make peace by exploiting both sides.

There are important virtues in the use of parallel distributed networks. They certainly often offer advantages in simplicity and in speed. And above all else they offer us ways to learn new skills without the pain and suffering that might come from comprehending how. On the darker side, they can limit large-scale growth because what any distributed network learns is likely to be quite opaque to other networks connected to it.

Symbolic systems yield gains of their own, in versatility and unlimited growth. Above all else they offer us the prospect that computers share: of not being bound by the small details of the parts of which they are composed. But that, too, has its darker side: symbolic processes can evolve worlds of their own, utterly divorced from their origins. Perceptrons can never go insane—but the same cannot be said of a brain.

Now, what are symbols, anyway? We usually conceive of them as compact things that represent more complex things. But what, then, do we mean by *represent?* It simply makes no sense, by itself, to say that "*S* represents *T*," because the significance of a symbol depends on at least three participants: on *S*, on *T*, and on the context of some process or user *U*. What, for example, connects the word *table* to any actual, physical table? Since the words people use are the words people learn, clearly the answer must be that there is no direct relationship between *S* and *T*, but that there is a more complex triadic relationship that connects a symbol, a thing, and a process that is active in some person's mind. Furthermore, when the term *symbol* is used in the context of network psychology, it usually refers to something that is reassignable so that it can be made to represent different things and so that the symbol-using processes can learn to deal with different symbols.

What do we mean by *distributed?* This usually refers to a system in which each end-effect comes not from any single, localized element-part, but from the interactions of many contributors, all working at the same time. Accordingly, in order to make a desired change in the output of a distributed system, one must usually alter a great many components. And changing the output of any particular component will rarely have a large effect in any particular circumstance; instead, such changes will tend to have small effects in many different circumstances.

Symbols are tokens or handles with which one specialist can manipulate representations within another specialist. But now, suppose that we want one agency to be able to exploit the knowledge in another agency. So long as we stay inside a particular agency, it may be feasible to use representations that involve great hosts of internal interactions and dependencies. But the fine details of such a representation would be meaningless to any outside agency that lacks access to, or the capacity to deal with, all that fine detail: Indeed, if each representation in the first agency involves activities that are uniformly distributed over a very large network, then direct communication to the other agency would require so many connection paths that both agencies would end up enmeshed together into a single, uniform net—and then all the units of both would interact.

How, then, could networks support symbolic forms of activities? We conjecture that, inside the brain, agencies with different jobs are usually constrained to communicate with one another only through neurological bottlenecks (i.e., connections between relatively small numbers of units that are specialized to serve as symbolic recognizers and memorizers). The recognizers learn to encode significant features of the representation active in the first network, and the memorizers learn to evoke an activity that can serve a corresponding function in the receiving network. But in order to prevent those features from interfering too much with one another, there must be an adequate degree of insulation between the units that serve these purposes. And that need for insulation can lead to genuine conflicts between the use of symbolic and distributed representations. This is because distributed representations make it hard to combine (in arbitrary, learnable ways) the different fragments of knowledge embodied in different representations. The difficulty arises because the more distributed is the representation of each fragment, the fewer fragments can be simultaneously active without interfering with one another. Sometimes those interactions can be useful, but in general they will be destructive. This is discussed briefly in section 8.2 of *The Society of Mind:*

"The advantages of distributed systems are not alternatives to the advantages of insulated systems: the two are complementary. To say that the brain may be composed of distributed systems is not the same as saying that it *is* a distributed system—that is, a single network in which all functions are uniformly distributed. We do not believe that any brain of that sort could work, because the interactions would be uncontrollable. To be sure, we have to explain how different ideas can become connected to one another—but we must also explain what keeps our separate memories intact. For example, we praised the power of metaphors that allow us to mix the ideas we have in different realms—but all that power would be lost if all our metaphors got mixed! Similarly, the architecture of a mind-society must encourage the formation and maintenance of distinct levels of management by preventing the formation of connections between agencies whose messages have no mutual significance. Some theorists have assumed that distributed systems are inherently both robust and versatile but, actually, those attributes are more likely to conflict. Systems with too many interactions of different types will tend to be fragile, while systems with too many interactions of similar types will tend to be too redundant to adapt to novel situations and requirements."

A larger-scale problem is that the use of widely distributed representations will tend to oppose the formulation of knowledge about knowledge. This is because information embodied in distributed form will tend to be relatively inaccessible for use as a subject upon which other knowledge-based processes can operate. Consequently (we conjecture), systems that use highly distributed representations will tend to become conceptual dead ends as a result of their putting performance so far ahead of comprehension as to retard the growth of reflective thought. Too much diffusing of information can make it virtually impossible (for other portions of the brain) to find out how results, however useful, are obtained. This would make it very difficult to dissect out the components that might otherwise be used to construct meaningful variations and generalizations. Of course such problems won't become evident in experiments with systems that do only simple things, but we can expect to see such problems grow when systems try to learn to do more complex things. With highly distributed systems, we should anticipate that the accumulation of internal interactions may eventually lead to intractable credit-assignment problems. Perhaps the only ultimate escape from the limitations of internal interactions is to evolve toward organizations in which each network affects others primarily through the use of *serial* operations and specialized short-term-memory systems, for although seriality is relatively slow, its uses makes it possible to produce and control interactions between activities that occur at different and separate places and times.

The Parallel Paradox

It is often argued that the use of distributed representations enables a system to exploit the advantages of parallel processing. But what *are* the advantages of parallel processing? Suppose that a certain task involves two unrelated parts. To deal with both concurrently, we would have to maintain their representations in two decoupled agencies, both active at the same time. Then, should either of those agencies become involved with two or more subtasks, we would have to deal with each of them with no more than a quarter of the available resources. If that proceeded on and on, the system would become so fragmented that each job would end up with virtually no resources assigned to it. In this regard, distribution may oppose parallelism: the more distributed a system is—that is, the more intimately its parts interact—the fewer *different* things it can do at the same time. On the other side, the more we do *separately* in parallel, the less machinery can be assigned to each element of what we do, and that ultimately leads to increasing fragmentation and incompetence.

This is not to say that distributed representations and parallel processing are always incompatible. When we simultaneously activate two distributed representations in the same network, they will be forced to interact. In favorable circumstances, those interactions can lead to useful parallel computations, such as the satisfaction of simultaneous constraints. But that will not happen in general; it will occur only when the representations happen to mesh in suitably fortunate ways. Such problems will be especially serious when we try to train distributed systems to deal with problems that require any sort of structural analysis in which the system must represent relationships be-

tween substructures of related types—that is, problems that are likely to compete for the same limited resources.

On the positive side, there are potential virtues to embodying knowledge in the form of networks of units with weighted interconnections. For example, distributed representations can sometimes be used to gain the robustness of redundancy, to make machines that continue to work despite having injured, damaged, or unreliable components. They can embody extremely simple learning algorithms, which operate in parallel with great speed.

Representations and Generalizations

It is often said that distributed representations are inherently possessed of useful holistic qualities; for example, that they have innate tendencies to recognize wholes from partial cues—even for patterns they have not encountered before. Phenomena of that sort are often described with such words as *generalization, induction,* or *gestalt.* Such phenomena certainly *can* emerge from connectionist assemblies. The problem is that, for any body of experience, there are always *many* kinds of generalizations that can be made. The ones made by any particular network are likely to be inappropriate unless there happens to be an appropriate relationship between the network's architecture and the manner in which the problem is represented. What makes architectures and representations appropriate? One way to answer that is to study how they affect which signals will be treated as similar.

Consider the problem of comparing an arbitrary input pattern with a collection of patterns in memory, to find which memory is most similar to that stimulus. In section 12.7 we conjectured that solving best-match problems will always be very tedious when serial hardware is used. *PDP* suggests another view in regard to parallel, distributed machines: "This is precisely the kind of problem that is readily implemented using highly parallel algorithms of the kind we consider." This is, in some ways, plausible, since a sufficiently parallel machine could simultaneously match an input pattern against every pattern in its memory. And yet the assertion is quaintly naive, since *best match* means different things in different circumstances. Which answers should be accepted as best always depends on the domain of application. The very same stimulus may signify food to one animal, companionship to another, and a dangerous predator to a third. Thus, there can be no single, universal measure of how well two descriptions match; every context requires appropriate schemes. Because of this, distributed networks do not magically provide solutions to such best-match problems. Instead, the functional architecture of each particular network imposes its own particular sort of metrical structure on the space of stimuli. Such structures may often be useful. Yet, that can give us no assurance that the outcome will correspond to what an expert observer would consider to be the very best match, given that observer's view of what would be the most appropriate response in the current context or problem realm.

We certainly do not mean to suggest that networks cannot perform useful matching functions. We merely mean to emphasize that different problems entail different matching criteria, and that hence no particular type of network can induce a topology of similarity or nearness that is appropriate for every realm. Instead, we must assume that, over the course of time, each specialized portion of the brain has evolved a particular type of architecture that is reasonably likely to induce similarity relationships that are useful in performing the functions to which that organ is likely (or destined) to be assigned. Perhaps an important activity of future connectionist research will be to develop networks that can *learn* to embody wide ranges of different, context-dependent types of matching functions.

We have also often heard the view that machines that employ localized or symbolic representations must be inherently less capable than are distributed machines of insight, consciousness, or sense of self. We think this stands things on their heads. It is *because* our brains primarily exploit connectionist schemes that we possess such *small* degrees of consciousness, in the sense that we have so little insight into the nature of our own conceptual machinery. We agree that distributed representations probably are used in virtually every part of the brain. Consequently, each agency must learn to exploit the abilities of the others without having direct access to compact representations of what happens inside those other agencies. This makes direct insight infeasible; the best such agencies can do is attempt to construct their own models of the others on the basis of approximate, pragmatic models based on presuppositions and concepts already embodied in the observing agency. Because of this, what appear to us to be direct insights into ourselves must be rarely genuine and usually conjectural. Accordingly, we expect distributed representations to tend to produce systems with only limited abilities to reflect accurately on how they do what they do. Thinking about thinking, we maintain, requires the use of representations that are localized enough that they can be dissected and rearranged. Besides, distributed representations spread out the information that goes into them. The result of this is to mix and obscure the effects of their separate elements. Thus their use must entail a heavy price; surely, many of them must become "conceptual dead ends" because the performances that they produce emerge from processes that other agencies cannot comprehend. In other words, when the representations of concepts are distrib-

uted, this will tend to frustrate attempts of other agencies to adapt and transfer those concepts to other contexts.

How much, then, can we expect from connectionist systems? Much more than the above remarks might suggest, since reflective thought is the lesser part of what our minds do. Most probably, we think, the human brain is, in the main, composed of large numbers of relatively small distributed systems, arranged by embryology into a complex society that is controlled in part (but only in part) by serial, symbolic systems that are added later. But the sub-symbolic systems that do most of the work from underneath must, by their very character, block all the other parts of the brain from knowing much about how they work. And this, itself, could help explain how people do so many things yet have such incomplete ideas of how those things are actually done.

35
Introduction

(1988)
Jerry A. Fodor and Zenon W. Pylyshyn

Connectionism and cognitive architecture: a critical analysis
Cognition 28: 3–72

This paper and the preceding one by Minsky and Papert are important criticisms of the ability of neural networks to perform computation. Jerry Fodor and Zenon Pylyshyn discuss aspects of human cognition that neural networks, in their present incarnation, may be unable to explain because their architecture is fundamentally inadequate. Fodor and Pylyshyn see the current debate about connectionism and cognition as a continuation of a longstanding argument in psychology about the adequacy of association as a model for cognition. The lack of computational *flexibility* shown by simple neural networks is also discussed in this long paper, which was originally a journal article in a special issue of the journal *Cognition*. The entire issue was reprinted as a book, *Connections and Symbols* (Cambridge, MA: MIT Press, 1988).

It is interesting to compare the writing styles of the two papers. Minsky and Papert are terse and direct. Fodor and Pylyshyn are verbose, and their discursive paper contains a forest of footnotes, philosophical and psychological references, and convoluted sentences, and is overall much harder to follow and requires a much broader background for understanding. It views computation in neural networks from a wide historical and philosophical perspective.

Neural networks, as they currently exist, are used for a number of different things. For many practical applications networks are useful parallel algorithms, capable of learning, and with some other desirable properties as well, such as noise resistance and good generalization. However, much of the excitement about neural networks arises from the widely held belief that networks are brainlike and that their ultimate development will lead to truly intelligent machines based on the architecture of the brain. Most neural network research until recently was done by academic cognitive scientists and psychologists who believed that neural networks were a good model for the human mind. (See, for example, the affiliations of the authors of the chapters in the *Parallel Distributed Processing* (*PDP*) books, McClelland and Rumelhart 1986 and Rumelhart and McClelland 1986.) There is a strong claim, often stated throughout the two-volume *PDP* collection, that use of neural networks for cognitive modeling is the right direction to go to understand the architecture of the human mind. Connectionists are aiming for much larger game than merely producing a network to process waveforms or evaluate credit histories: They want to know how we *really* work, inside our heads.

The essential criticism made by Fodor and Pylyshyn is, surprisingly, one that an engineer would be happy to make: Connectionism is such an inefficient way to compute that it would be foolish to build a brain like that. Part of the reason that the article is so long is that there are a great many qualifications that have to be placed on almost every assertion. Fodor and Pylyshyn are perfectly prepared to admit that the hardware of the brain is based on neurons and is in some sense physically "connectionist." But, they would claim, the kinds of computations actually done, however they are carried out in practice, reflect a very different, higher-level, and much more flexible computational strategy, one based on the manipulation of symbols. Their hedges should not obscure, however, the fact that the arguments being made are simple and telling.

Essentially all simple neural networks form part of an "associationist" tradition prominent in the history of psychology and going back at least to Aristotle (see paper 1). Associationists view mental life as being composed of often arbitrary associations between different events that happened to occur at the same time, or in quick succession, and the more often the events occur together, the stronger the association between them will be. Variations of this approach have been studied for centuries, and, at some time in their academic career, college students are exposed to the associative notion that a "stimulus" coupled with a "response" is the essence of learning. Neural networks are part of this tradition; the point of weight modification rules in networks is to make sure that the right responses are produced by the appropriate stimuli.

The problem with associationism, as has also been clear for several hundred years, is that there are severe limitations on the kinds of behavior that can be explained like this. *Some* important aspects of human psychology clearly work this way. Proportionally *more* aspects of animal behavior can be explained this way. The defects in associationism are clearest for human language, a recently evolved, species-specific behavior. Whether something qualitatively new is present in human cognitive organization is an open question. In any case connectionists have now generated a number of enthusiastic and often uncritical applications of neural networks to language specifically and cognition in general. Therefore the Fodor and Pylyshyn paper should be viewed not just as a criticism of neural networks but as a new volley in an old battle that has been going on for centuries. As Fodor and Pylyshyn comment, ". . . it's an instructive paradox that the current attempt to be thoroughly modern and 'take the brain seriously' should lead to a psychology not readily distinguishable from the worst of Hume and Berkeley. . . ."

Fodor and Pylyshyn first discuss what they call the *classical* view of mental operation. In essence (subject to many caveats) this view postulates "a language of thought," that is, "mental representations have *a combinatorial syntax and semantics* ." The classical view is held by almost all linguists and is dominant in virtually all branches of artificial intelligence. Unexpectedly the beauty of this highly abstract approach is in its practicality. Syntax allows extreme flexibility and generality in mental operations. The great power of the traditional digital computer arises in part from the fact that it is deliberately designed to be an extreme example of this organization: a programming language operating on data is the paradigm of the classical view.

Fodor and Pylyshyn use a linguistic example to demonstrate the computational flexibility of the classical architecture. Suppose we have a sentence of the form *A and B* that we hold is true. An example they use is *John went to the store and Mary went to the store.* The truth of this sentence logically entails the truth of *Mary went to the store.* This arises from the rules of logic and of grammar. However, it is not easy for a neural network to handle this problem. A simple net could easily learn that *John went to the store and Mary went to the store* is associated with *Mary went to the store.* But the power of the classical approach arises from the fact that *every* sentence of this form gives rise to the same result: The truth of the assertion

The moon is high and the night is beautiful implies *The moon is high*. There is *no need* to learn many examples. The rule alone is adequate to make the inference and all that needs to be learned is the rule. Given *any* sentence of the appropriate form, the correct conclusion can be drawn.

Given the appallingly slow learning of most complex neural networks, and the combinatorial number of possible sentences that can be combined, *it makes practical sense* to assume that a logical syntax exists to handle this class of problems. In fact it would be hard to figure out how language could function without some global rulelike operations, of which this is a particularly simple example. At the same time, as has been extensively discussed (see Rumelhart and McClelland 1986), language rules have many exceptions and come in varying degrees of "softness." For example, we have used the combinatorial power of conjunction in the example, but Fodor and Pylyshyn give some other sentences with a different twist: *John and Mary went to the store* implies *John went to the store* but *The flag is red, white, and blue* does not necessarily imply *The flag is blue*.

However, peculiarities like this do not show that grammar is not rule-based, and therefore connectionist. It may show instead that the language implementation we are stuck with just may not be very good, perhaps because language is lately evolved and full of bugs. Language rarely provides absolutely clear cut examples of combinatorial grammars in operation. It seems as if the real world is too imprecise and sloppy to be entirely pinned down by symbolic grammars, providing a strong argument for the presence of neural networks somewhere in the system.

In language some areas clearly lend themselves to neural networks: Fodor, in talks, has often mentioned that language up to the lexicon could be handled effectively by neural networks. In fact the lexicon — our detailed knowledge of what words mean — is an almost ideal candidate for the virtues of neural networks because an appropriate word can be produced in response to an immense number of novel situations that differ in detail.

One of the strengths of neural networks has always been claimed to be good generalization. But when words are combined, sentences are formed. Understanding even pairs of words in novel combinations is hard. The ability to understand immediately sentences or phrases that are new to the listener is difficult to explain on the basis of simple association. Fodor, in talks, uses as an example of a novel phrase easily produced by a symbol-based syntax, *antimissile missile*, which has the clear meaning to most listeners of "a missile that shoots down missiles." One more application of the same symbol-based operation leads to the next phrase, an *anti-antimissile missile,* "a missile that shoots down missiles that shoot down missiles," and so on. And a moment's thought comes up with new and understandable combinations like *antithief thief*, which might mean roughly what is meant by the proverb, "Set a thief to catch a thief." Examples like this are numerous, in fact combinatorially numerous. And that demonstrates exactly the point Fodor and Pylyshyn are making. These examples are both novel and immediately understandable. This is ability to generalize with a vengeance, generalization beyond the power of any simple network that learns specific examples.

There have been attempts to build neural networks that realize parts of the classical account, for example, networks to do certain kind of Lisp-like operations (Touretsky, 1989). However, even charitable observers, sometimes even including the creators of the models, have noted that the resulting networks are a bit unreasonable and that the operations they are performing seem unnatural. One might speculate that if there is a qualitative difference between human and animal cognition it lies right here. Somehow, perhaps not very well or very efficiently, the human brain has developed a way of handling a few kinds of simple rulelike operations corresponding to the rudiments of a mental syntax based on symbol-like entities. And this limited ability has led to what amounts to a breakthrough in the practicality and flexibility of biological computation. Considering that this facility evolved less than a million years ago, even a little symbol processing may go a long way.

Both this paper and the preceding one are making valid points, though Fodor and Pylyshyn are sometimes a little polemical. Fodor and Pylyshyn in particular have presented in clear form what may be the major technical problem confronted by neural networks: Is it possible to build a simple and reliable network that can reproduce the kinds of rule-governed behavior that does in fact seem to be part of human cognition? The advantages of a neural network with this ability are immensely practical, for it would allow for far greater computational flexibility and generalization than the current, simple networks can give by themselves.

References

J.L. McClelland and D.E. Rumelhart (1986), *Parallel Distributed Processing, Volume 2*. Cambridge, MA: MIT Press.

D.E. Rumelhart and J.L. McClelland (1986), On learning the past tenses of English verbs. In J.L. McClelland and D.E. Rumelhart (Eds.), *Parallel Distributed Processing, Volume 2*. Cambridge, MA: MIT Press.

D.E. Rumelhart and J.L. McClelland (Eds.), (1986), *Parallel Distributed Processing, Volume 1*. Cambridge, MA: MIT Press.

D.S. Touretsky (1989), BoltzCONS: Dynamic symbol structures in a connectionist network. Technical Report CMU-CS-889-182, from School of Computer Science, Carnegie-Mellon University, Pittsburgh, PA. To appear in *Artificial Intelligence*, 1990.

(1988)
Jerry A. Fodor and Zenon W. Pylyshyn

Connectionism and cognitive architecture: a critical analysis*
Cognition 28: 3–72

Abstract

This paper explores differences between Connectionist proposals for cognitive architecture and the sorts of models that have traditionally been assumed in cognitive science. We claim that the major distinction is that, while both Connectionist and Classical architectures postulate representational mental states, the latter but not the former are committed to a symbol-level of representation, or to a 'language of thought': i.e., to representational states that have combinatorial syntactic and semantic structure. Several arguments for combinatorial structure in mental representations are then reviewed. These include arguments based on the 'systematicity' of mental representation: i.e, on the fact that cognitive capacities always exhibit certain symmetries, so that the ability to entertain a given thought implies the ability to entertain thoughts with semantically related contents. We claim that such arguments make a powerful case that mind/brain architecture is not Connectionist at the cognitive level. We then consider the possibility that Connectionism may provide an account of the neural (or 'abstract neurological') structures in which Classical cognitive architecture is implemented. We survey a number of the standard arguments that have been offered in favor of Connectionism, and conclude that they are coherent only on this interpretation.

1. Introduction

Connectionist or *PDP* models are catching on. There are conferences and new books nearly every day, and the popular science press hails this new wave of theorizing as a breakthrough in understanding the mind (a typical example is the article in the May issue of *Science 86,* called "How we think: A new theory"). There are also, inevitably, descriptions of the emergence of Connectionism as a Kuhnian

*This paper is based on a chapter from a forthcoming book. Authors' names are listed alphabetically. We wish to thank the Alfred P. Sloan Foundation for their generous support of this research. The preparation of this paper was also aided by a Killam Research Fellowship and a Senior Fellowship from the Canadian Institute for Advanced Research to ZWP. We also gratefully acknowledge comments and criticisms of earlier drafts by: Professors Noam Chomsky, William Demopoulos, Lila Gleitman, Russ Greiner, Norbert Hornstein, Keith Humphrey, Sandy Pentland, Steven Pinker, David Rosenthal, and Edward Stabler. Reprints may be obtained by writing to either author: Jerry Fodor, CUNY Graduate Center, 33 West 42 Street, New York, NY 10036, U.S.A.; Zenon Pylyshyn, Centre for Cognitive Science, University of Western Ontario, London, Ontario, Canada N6A 5C2.

"paradigm shift". (See Schneider, 1987, for an example of this and for further evidence of the tendency to view Connectionism as the "new wave" of Cognitive Science.)

The fan club includes the most unlikely collection of people. Connectionism gives solace both to philosophers who think that relying on the pseudoscientific intentional or semantic notions of folk psychology (like goals and beliefs) misleads psychologists into taking the computational approach (e.g., P.M. Churchland, 1981; P.S. Churchland, 1986; Dennett, 1986); and to those with nearly the opposite perspective, who think that computational psychology is bankrupt because it doesn't address issues of intentionality or meaning (e.g., Dreyfus & Dreyfus, in press). On the computer science side, Connectionism appeals to theorists who think that serial machines are too weak and must be replaced by radically new parallel machines (Fahlman & Hinton, 1986), while on the biological side it appeals to those who believe that cognition can only be understood if we study it as neuroscience (e.g., Arbib, 1975; Sejnowski, 1981). It is also attractive to psychologists who think that much of the mind (including the part involved in using imagery) is not discrete (e.g., Kosslyn & Hatfield, 1984), or who think that cognitive science has not paid enough attention to stochastic mechanisms or to "holistic" mechanisms (e.g., Lakoff, 1986), and so on and on. It also appeals to many young cognitive scientists who view the approach as not only anti-establishment (and therefore desirable) but also rigorous and mathematical (see, however, footnote 2). Almost everyone who is discontented with contemporary cognitive psychology and current "information processing" models of the mind has rushed to embrace "the Connectionist alternative".

When taken as a way of modeling *cognitive architecture,* Connectionism really does represent an approach that is quite different from that of the Classical cognitive science that it seeks to replace. Classical models of the mind were derived from the structure of Turing and von Neumann machines. They are not, of course, committed to the details of these machines as exemplified in Turing's original formulation or in typical commercial computers; only to the basic idea that the kind of computing that is relevant to understanding cognition involves operations on symbols (see Fodor 1976, 1987; Newell, 1980, 1982; Pylyshyn, 1980, 1984a, b). In contrast, Connectionists propose to design systems that can exhibit intelligent behavior without storing, retrieving, or otherwise operating on structured symbolic expressions. The style of processing carried out in such models is thus strikingly unlike what goes on when conventional machines are computing some function.

Connectionist systems are networks consisting of very large numbers of simple but highly interconnected "units". Certain assumptions are generally made both about the units and the connections: Each unit is assumed to receive real-valued activity (either excitatory or inhibitory or both) along its input lines. Typically the units do little more than sum this activity and change their state as a function (usually a threshold function) of this sum. Each connection is allowed to modulate the activity it transmits as a function of an intrinsic (but modifiable) property called its "weight". Hence the activity on an input line is typically some non-linear function of the state of activity of its sources. The behavior of the network as a whole is a function of the initial state of activation of the units and of the weights on its connections, which serve as its only form of memory.

Numerous elaborations of this basic Connectionist architecture are possible. For example, Connectionist models often have stochastic mechanisms for determining the level of activity or the state of a unit. Moreover, units may be connected to outside environments. In this case the units are sometimes assumed to respond to a narrow range of combinations of parameter values and are said to have a certain "receptive field" in parameter-space. These are called "value units" (Ballard, 1986). In some versions of Connectionist architecture, environmental properties are encoded by the pattern of states of entire populations of units. Such "coarse coding" techniques are among the ways of achieving what Connectionists call "distributed representation".[1] The term 'Connectionist model' (like 'Turing machine' or 'von Neumann machine') is thus applied to a family of mechanisms that differ in details but share a galaxy of architectural commitments. We shall return to the characterization of these commitments below.

Connectionist networks have been analysed extensively—in some cases using advanced mathematical techniques.[2] They have also been simulated on computers and shown to exhibit interesting aggregate properties. For example, they can be "wired" to recognize patterns, to exhibit rule-like behavioral regularities, and to realize virtually any mapping from patterns of (input) parameters to patterns of (output) parameters—though in most cases multi-parameter, multi-valued mappings require very large numbers of units. Of even greater interest is the fact that such networks can be made to learn; this is achieved by modifying the weights on the connections as a function of certain kinds of feedback (the exact way in which this is done constitutes a preoccupation of Connectionist research and has led to the development of such important techniques as "back propagation").

In short, the study of Connectionist machines has led to a number of striking and unanticipated findings; it's surprising how much computing can be done with a uniform network of simple interconnected elements. Moreover, these models have an appearance of neural plausibility that Classical architectures are sometimes said to lack. Perhaps, then, a new Cognitive Science based on Connectionist networks should replace the old Cognitive Science based on Classical computers. Surely this is a proposal that ought to be taken seriously: if it is warranted, it implies a major redirection of research.

Unfortunately, however, discussions of the relative merits of the two architectures have thus far been marked by a variety of confusions and irrelevances. It's our view that when you clear away these misconceptions what's left is a real disagreement about the nature of mental processes and mental representations. But it seems to us that it is a matter that was substantially put to rest about thirty years ago; and the arguments that then appeared to militate decisively in favor of the Classical view appear to us to do so still.

In the present paper we will proceed as follows. First, we discuss some methodological questions about levels of explanation that have become enmeshed in the substantive controversy over Connectionism. Second, we try to say

---

[1] The difference between Connectionist networks in which the state of a single unit encodes properties of the world (i.e., the so-called 'localist' networks) and ones in which the pattern of states of an entire population of units does the encoding (the so-called 'distributed' representation networks) is considered to be important by many people working on Connectionist models. Although Connectionists debate the relative merits of localist (or 'compact') versus distributed representations (e.g., Feldman, 1986), the distinction will usually be of little consequence for our purposes, for reasons that we give later. For simplicity, when we wish to refer indifferently to either single unit codes or aggregate distributed codes, we shall refer to the 'nodes' in a network. When the distinction is relevant to our discussion, however, we shall explicitly mark the difference by referring either to units or to aggregates of units.

[2] One of the attractions of Connectionism for many people is that it does employ some heavy mathematical machinery, as can be seen from a glance at many of the chapters of the two volume collection by Rumelhart, McClelland and the PDP Research Group (1986). But in contrast to many other mathematically sophisticated areas of cognitive science, such as automata theory or parts of Artificial Intelligence (particularly the study of search, or of reasoning and knowledge representation), the mathematics has not been used to map out the limits of what the proposed class of mechanisms can do. Like a great dael of Artificial Intelligence research, the Connectionist approach remains almost entirely experimental; mechanisms that look interesting are proposed and explored by implementing them on computers and subjecting them to empirical trials to see what they will do. As a consequence, although there is a great deal of mathematical work within the tradition, one has very little idea what various Connectionist networks and mechanisms are good for in general.

what it is that makes Connectionist and Classical theories of mental structure incompatible. Third, we review and extend some of the traditional arguments for the Classical architecture. Though these arguments have been somewhat recast, very little that we'll have to say here is entirely new. But we hope to make it clear how various aspects of the Classical doctrine cohere and why rejecting the Classical picture of reasoning leads Connectionists to say the very implausible things they do about logic and semantics. In part four, we return to the question what makes the Connectionist approach appear attractive to so many people. In doing so we'll consider some arguments that have been offered in favor of Connectionist networks as general models of cognitive processing.

Levels of explanation

There are two major traditions in modern theorizing about the mind, one that we'll call 'Representationalist' and one that we'll call 'Eliminativist'. Representationalists hold that postulating representational (or 'intentional' or 'semantic') states is essential to a theory of cognition; according to Representationalists, there are states of the mind which function to encode states of the world. Eliminativists, by contrast, think that psychological theories can dispense with such semantic notions as representation. According to Eliminativists the appropriate vocabulary for psychological theorizing is neurological, or perhaps behavioral, or perhaps syntactic; in any event, not a vocabulary that characterizes mental states in terms of what they represent. (For a neurological version of eliminativism, see P.S. Churchland, 1986; for a behavioral version, see Watson, 1930; for a syntactic version, see Stich, 1983.)

Connectionists are on the Representationalist side of this issue. As Rumelhart and McClelland (1986a, p. 121) say, PDPs "are explicitly concerned with the problem of internal representation". Correspondingly, the specification of what the states of a network *represent* is an essential part of a Connectionist model. Consider, for example, the well-known Connectionist account of the bistability of the Necker cube (Feldman & Ballard, 1982). "Simple units representing the visual features of the two alternatives are arranged in competing coalitions, with inhibitory ... links between rival features and positive links within each coalition .... The result is a network that has two dominant stable states" (see Figure 1). Notice that, in this as in all other such Connectionist models, the commitment to mental representation is explicit: the label of a node is taken to express the representational content of the state that the device is

in when the node is excited, and there are nodes corresponding to monadic and to relational properties of the reversible cube when it is seen in one way or the other.

There are, to be sure, times when Connectionists appear to vacillate between Representationalism and the claim that the "cognitive level" is dispensable in favor of a more precise and biologically-motivated level of theory. In particular, there is a lot of talk in the Connectionist literature about processes that are "sub-symbolic"—and therefore presumably *not* representational. But this is misleading: Connectionist modeling is consistently Representationalist in practice, and Representationalism is generally endorsed by the very theorists who also like the idea of cognition 'emerging from the subsymbolic'. Thus, Rumelhart and McClelland (1986a, p. 121) insist that PDP models are "... strongly committed to the study of representation and process". Similarly, though Smolensky (1988, p. 2) takes Connectionism to articulate regularities at the "sub-symbolic level" of analysis, it turns out that sub-symbolic states do have a semantics, though it's not the semantics of representations at the "conceptual level". According to Smolensky, the semantical distinction between symbolic and sub-symbolic theories is just that "entities that are typically represented in the symbolic paradigm by [single] symbols are typically represented in the sub-symbolic paradigm by a large number of sub-symbols".[3] Both the conceptual and the sub-symbolic levels thus postulate representational states, but sub-symbolic theories slice them thinner.

We are stressing the Representationalist character of Connectionist theorizing because much Connectionist methodological writing has been preoccupied with the question, 'What level of explanation is appropriate for theories of cognitive architecture?' (see, for example, the exchange between Broadbent, 1985, and Rumelhart & McClelland, 1985). And, as we're about to see, what one says about the levels question depends a lot on what stand one takes about whether there are representational states.

It seems certain that the world has causal structure at very many different levels of analysis, with the individuals recognized at the lowest levels being, in general, very small and the individuals recognized at the highest levels being,

---

[3] Smolensky seems to think that the idea of postulating a level of representations with a semantics of subconceptual features is unique to network theories. This is an extraordinary view considering the extent to which *Classical* theorists have been concerned with feature analyses in every area of psychology from phonetics to visual perception to lexicography. In fact, the question whether there are 'sub-conceptual' features is *neutral* with respect to the question whether cognitive architecture is Classical or Connectionist.

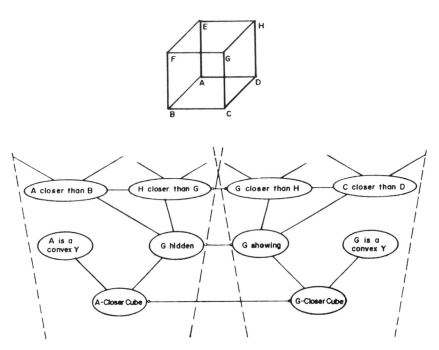

Figure 1 A Connectionist network model illustrating the two stable representations of the Necker cube. (Reproduced from Feldman and Ballard, 1982, p. 221, with permission of the publisher, Ablex Publishing Corporation.)

in general, very large. Thus there is a scientific story to be told about quarks; and a scientific story to be told about atoms; and a scientific story to be told about molecules ... ditto rocks and stones and rivers ... ditto galaxies. And the story that scientists tell about the causal structure that the world has at any one of these levels may be quite different from the story that they tell about its causal structure at the next level up or down. The methodological implication for psychology is this: If you want to have an argument about *cognitive* architecture, you have to specify the level of analysis that's supposed to be at issue.

If you're *not* a Representationalist, this is quite tricky since it is then not obvious what makes a phenomenon cognitive. But specifying the level of analysis relevant for theories of cognitive architecture is no problem for either Classicists or Connectionists. Since Classicists and Connectionists are both Representationalists, for them any level at which states of the system are taken to encode properties of the world counts as a *cognitive* level; and no other levels do. (Representations of "the world" include of course, representations of symbols; for example, the concept WORD is a construct at the cognitive level because it represents something, namely words.) Correspondingly, it's the architecture of representational states and processes that discussions of *cognitive architecture* are about. Put differently, the architecture of the cognitive system consists of the set of basic operations, resources, functions, principles, etc. (generally the sorts of properties that would

be described in a "user's manual" for that architecture if it were available on a computer), whose domain and range are the *representational states* of the organism.[4]

It follows, that, if you want to make good the Connectionist theory *as a theory of cognitive architecture*, you have to show that the processes which operate on *the representational states* of an organism are those which are specified by a Connectionist architecture. It is, for example, *no use at all,* from the cognitive psychologist's point of view, to show that the *non*representational (e.g., neurological, or molecular, or quantum mechanical) states of an organism constitute a Connectionist network, because that would *leave open* the question whether the mind is a such a network *at the psychological level*. It is, in particular, perfectly possible that nonrepresentational neurological states are interconnected in the ways described by Connectionist models *but that the representational states them-*

[4]Sometimes, however, even Representationalists fail to appreciate that it is *representation* that distinguishes cognitive from noncognitive levels. Thus, for example, although Smolensky (1988) is clearly a Representationalist, his official answer to the question "What distinguishes those dynamical systems that are cognitive from those that are not?" makes the mistake of appealing to complexity rather than intentionality: "A river ... fails to be a cognitive dynamical system only because it cannot satisfy a *large* range of goals under a *large* range of conditions." But, of course, that depends on how you individuate goals and conditions; the river that wants to get to the sea wants first to get half way to the sea, and then to get half way more, ..., and so on; quite a lot of goals all told. The real point, of course, is that states that represent goals play a role in the etiology of the behaviors of people but not in the etiology of the 'behavior' of rivers.

selves are not. This is because, just as it is possible to implement a *Connectionist* cognitive architecture in a network of causally interacting nonrepresentational elements, so too it is perfectly possible to implement a *Classical* cognitive architecture in such a network.[5] In fact, the question whether Connectionist networks should be treated as models at some level of implementation is moot, and will be discussed at some length in Section 4.

It is important to be clear about this matter of levels on pain of simply trivializing the issues about cognitive architecture. Consider, for example, the following remark of Rumelhart's: "It has seemed to me for some years now that there must be a unified account in which the so-called rule-governed and [the] exceptional cases were dealt with by a unified underlying process—a process which produces rule-like and rule-exception behavior through the application of a single process ... [In this process] ... both the rule-like and non-rule-like behavior is a product of the interaction of a very large number of 'sub-symbolic' processes." (Rumelhart, 1984, p. 60.) It's clear from the context that Rumelhart takes this idea to be very tendentious; one of the Connectionist claims that Classical theories are required to deny.

But in fact it's not. For, *of course* there are 'sub-symbolic' interactions that implement both rule-like and rule-violating behavior: for example, quantum mechanical processes do. *That's* not what Classical theorists deny; indeed, it's not denied by anybody who is even vaguely a materialist. Nor does a Classical theorist deny that rule-following and rule-violating behaviors are both implemented by the very same neurological machinery. For a Classical theorist, neurons implement *all* cognitive processes in precisely the same way: viz., by supporting the basic operations that are required for symbol-processing.

What *would* be an interesting and tendentious claim is that there's no distinction between rule-following and rule-violating mentation *at the cognitive or representational or symbolic level;* specifically, that it is not the case that the etiology of rule-following behavior is mediated by the representation of explicit rules.[6] We will consider this idea in Section 4, where we will argue that it too is *not* what divides Classical from Connectionist architecture; Classi-

cal models *permit* a principled distinction between the etiologies of mental processes that are explicitly rule-governed and mental processes that aren't; but they don't demand one.

In short, the issue between Classical and Connectionist architecture is not about the explicitness of rules; as we'll presently see, Classical architecture is not, per se, committed to the idea that explicit rules mediate the etiology of behavior. And it is not about the reality of representational states; Classicists and Connectionists are all Representational Realists. And it is not about nonrepresentational architecture; a Connectionist neural network can perfectly well implement a Classical architecture at the cognitive level.

So, then, what *is* the disagreement between Classical and Connectionist architecture about?

2. The nature of the dispute

Classicists and Connectionists all assign semantic content to *something.* Roughly, Connectionists assign semantic content to 'nodes' (that is, to units or aggregates of units; see footnote 1)—i.e., to the sorts of things that are typically labeled in Connectionist diagrams; whereas Classicists assign semantic content to *expressions*—i.e., to the sorts of things that get written on the tapes of Turing machines and stored at addresses in von Neumann machines.[7] But Classical theories disagree with Connectionist theories about what primitive relations hold among these content-bearing entities. Connectionist theories acknowledge *only causal connectedness* as a primitive relation among nodes; when you know how activation and inhibition flow among them, you know everything there is to know about how the nodes in a network are related. By contrast, Classical theories acknowledge not only causal relations among the semantically evaluable objects that they posit, but also a range of structural relations, of which constituency is paradigmatic.

This difference has far reaching consequences for the ways that the two kinds of theories treat a variety of cognitive phenomena, some of which we will presently examine at length. But, underlying the disagreements about details are two architectural differences between the theories:

---

[5]That Classical architectures can be implemented in networks is not disputed by Connectionists; see for example Rumelhart and McClelland (1986a, p. 118): "... one can make an arbitrary computational machine out of linear threshold units, including, for example, a machine that can carry out all the operations necessary for implementing a Turing machine; the one limitation is that real biological systems cannot be Turing machines because they have finite hardware."

[6]There is a different idea, frequently encountered in the Connectionist literature, that this one is easily confused with: viz., that the distinction between regularities and exceptions is merely stochastic (what makes 'went' an irregular past tense is just that the *more frequent* construction is the one exhibited by 'walked'). It seems obvious that if this claim is correct it can be readily assimilated to Classical architecture (see Section 4).

[7]This way of putting it will do for present purposes. But a subtler reading of Connectionist theories might take it to be total machine *states* that have content, e.g., the state of *having such and such a node excited.* Postulating connections among labelled nodes would then be equivalent to postulating causal relations among the corresponding content bearing machine states: To say that the excitation of the node labelled 'dog' is caused by the excitation of nodes labelled [d], [o], [g] is to say that the machine's representing its input as consisting of the phonetic sequence [dog] causes it to represent its input as consisting of the word 'dog'. And so forth. Most of the time the distinction between these two days of talking does not matter for our purposes, so we shall adopt one or the other as convenient.

1. *Combinatorial syntax and semantics for mental representations.* Classical theories—but not Connectionist theories—postulate a 'language of thought' (see, for example, Fodor, 1975); they take mental representations to have *a combinatorial syntax and semantics,* in which (a) there is a distinction between structurally atomic and structurally molecular representations; (b) structurally molecular representations have syntactic constituents that are themselves either structurally molecular or structurally atomic; and (c) the semantic content of a (molecular) representation is a function of the semantic contents of its syntactic parts, together with its constituent structure. For purposes of convenience, we'll sometime abbreviate (a)–(c) by speaking of Classical theories as committed to "complex" mental representations or to "symbol structures".[8]

2. *Structure sensitivity of processes.* In Classical models, the principles by which mental states are transformed, or by which an input selects the corresponding output, are defined over structural properties of mental representations. Because Classical mental *representations* have combinatorial structure, it is possible for Classical mental *operations* to apply to them by reference to their form. The result is that a paradigmatic Classical mental process operates upon any mental representation that satisfies a given structural description, and transforms it into a mental representation that satisfies another structural description. (So, for example, in a model of inference one might recognize an operation that applies to any representation of the form *P&Q* and transforms it into a representation of the form *P.*) Notice that since formal properties can be defined at a variety of levels of abstraction, such an operation can apply equally to representations that differ widely in their structural complexity. The operation that applies to representations of the form *P&Q* to produce *P* is satisfied by, for example, an expression like "(AvBvC) & (DvEvF)", from which it derives the expression "(AvBvC)".

We take (1) and (2) as the claims that define Classical models, and we take these claims quite literally; they constrain the physical realizations of symbol structures. In particular, the symbol structures in a Classical model are assumed to correspond to real physical structures in the brain and the *combinatorial structure* of a representation is supposed to have a counterpart in structural relations among physical properties of the brain. For example, the relation

'part of', which holds between a relatively simple symbol and a more complex one, is assumed to correspond to some physical relation among brain states.[9] This is why Newell (1980) speaks of computational systems such as brains and Classical computers as *"physical* symbols systems".

This bears emphasis because the Classical theory is committed not only to there being a system of physically instantiated symbols, but also to the claim that the physical properties onto which the structure of the symbols is mapped *are the very properties that cause the system to behave as it does.* In other words the physical counterparts of the symbols, and their structural properties, *cause* the system's behavior. A system which has symbolic expressions, but whose operation does not depend upon the structure of these expressions, does not qualify as a Classical machine since it fails to satisfy condition (2). In this respect, a Classical model is very different from one in which

[9]Perhaps the notion that relations among physical properties of the brain instantiate (or encode) the *combinatorial structure* of an expression bears some elaboration. One way to understand what is involved is to consider the conditions that must hold on a mapping (which we refer to as the 'physical instantiation mapping') from expressions to brain states if the causal relations among brain states are to depend on the combinatorial structure of the encoded expressions. In defining this mapping it is not enough merely to specify a physical encoding for each symbol; in order for the *structures* of expressions to have causal roles, structural relations must be encoded by physical properties of brain states (or by sets of functionally equivalent physical properties of brain states).

Because, in general, Classical models assume that the expressions that get physically instantiated in brains have a generative syntax, the definition of an appropriate physical instantiation mapping has to be built up in terms of (a) the definition of a primitive mapping from atomic symbols to relatively elementary physical states, and (b) a specification of how the structure of complex expressions maps onto the structure of relatively complex or composite physical states. Such a structure-preserving mapping is typically given recursively, making use of the combinatorial syntax by which complex expressions are built up out of simpler ones. For example, the physical instantiation mapping **F** for complex expressions would be defined by recursion, given the definition of **F** for *atomic* symbols and given the *structure* of the complex expression, the latter being specified in terms of the 'structure building' rules which constitute the generative syntax for complex expressions. Take, for example, the expression '(A&B)&C'. A suitable definition for a mapping in this case might contain the statement that for any expressions *P* and *Q*, **F**[*P&Q*] = B(**F**[*P*],**F**[*Q*]), where the function B specifies the physical relation that holds between physical states **F**[*P*] and **F**[*Q*]. Here the property B serves to physically encode (or 'instantiate') the relation that holds between the expressions *P* and *Q*, on the one hand, and the expressions *P&Q*, on the other.

In using this rule for the example above *P* and *Q* would have the values 'A&B' and 'C' respectively, so that the mapping rule would have to be applied twice to pick the relevant physical structures. In defining the mapping recursively in this way we ensure that the relation between the expressions 'A' and 'B', and the composite expression 'A&B', is encoded in terms of a physical relation between constituent states that is identical (or functionally equivalent) to the physical relation used to encode the relation between expressions 'A&B' and 'C', and their composite expression '(A&B)&C'. This type of mapping is well known because of its use in Tarski's definition of an interpretation of a language in a model. The idea of a mapping from symbolic expressions to a structure of physical states is discussed in Pylyshyn (1984a, pp. 54–69), where it is referred to as an 'instantiation function' and in Stabler (1985), where it is called a 'realization mapping'.

[8]Sometimes the difference between simply postulating representational states and postulating representations with a combinatorial syntax and semantics is marked by distinguishing theories that postulate *symbols* from theories that postulate *symbol systems.* The latter theories, but not the former, are committed to a "language of thought". For this usage, see Kosslyn and Hatfield (1984) who take the refusal to postulate symbol systems to be the characteristic respect in which Connectionist architectures differ from Classical architectures. We agree with this diagnosis.

behavior is caused by mechanisms, such as energy minimization, that are not responsive to the physical encoding of the structure of representations.

From now on, when we speak of 'Classical' models, we will have in mind *any* model that has complex mental representations, as characterized in (1) and structure-sensitive mental processes, as characterized in (2). Our account of Classical architecture is therefore neutral with respect to such issues is whether or not there is a separate executive. For example, Classical machines can have an "object-oriented" architecture, like that of the computer language *Smalltalk,* or a "message passing" architecture, like that of Hewett's (1977) *Actors*—so long as the objects or the messages have a combinatorial structure which is causally implicated in the processing. Classical architecture is also neutral on the question whether the operations on the symbols are constrained to occur one at a time or whether many operations can occur it the same time.

Here, then, is the plan for what follows. In the rest of this section, we will sketch the Connectionist proposal for a computational architecture that does away with complex mental representations and structure sensitive operations. (Although our purpose here is merely expository, it turns out that describing exactly what Connectionists are committed to requires substantial reconstruction of their remarks and practices. Since there is a great variety of points of view within the Connectionist community, we are prepared to find that some Connectionists in good standing may not fully endorse the program when it is laid out in what we take to be its bare essentials.) Following this general expository (or reconstructive) discussion, Section 3 provides a series of arguments favoring the Classical story. Then the remainder of the paper considers some of the reasons why Connectionism appears attractive to many people and offers further general comments on the relation between the Classical and the Connectionist enterprise.

2.1 Complex mental representations

To begin with, consider a case of the most trivial sort; two machines, one Classical in spirit and one Connectionist.[10] Here is how the Connectionist machine might reason. There is a network of labelled nodes as in Figure 2. Paths between the nodes indicate the routes along which activation can spread (that is, they indicate the consequences that exciting one of the nodes has for determining the level of

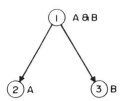

Figure 2 A possible Connectionist network for drawing inferences from A&B to A or to B.

excitation of others). Drawing an inference from A&B to A thus corresponds to an excitation of node 2 being caused by an excitation of node 1 (alternatively, if the system is in a state in which node 1 is excited, it eventually settles into a state in which node 2 is excited; see footnote 7).

Now consider a Classical machine. This machine has a tape on which it writes expressions. Among the expressions that can appear on this tape are: 'A', 'B', 'A&B', 'C', 'D', 'C&D', 'A&C&D'... etc. The machine's causal constitution is as follows: whenever a token of the form P&Q appears on the tape, the machine writes a token of the form P. An inference from A&B to A thus corresponds to a tokening of type 'A&B' on the tape causing a tokening of type 'A'.

So then, what does the architectural difference between the machines consist in? In the Classical machine, the objects to which the content A&B is ascribed (viz., tokens of the expression 'A&B') literally contain, as proper parts, objects to which the content A is ascribed (viz., tokens of the expression 'A'). Moreover, the semantics (e.g., the satisfaction conditions) of the expression 'A&B' is determined in a uniform way by the semantics of its constituents.[11] By contrast, in the Connectionist machine none of this is true; the object to which the content A&B is ascribed (viz., node 1) is causally connected to the object to which the content A is ascribed (viz., node 2); but there is no structural (e.g., no part/whole) relation that holds between them. In short, it is characteristic of Classical systems, but not of Connectionist systems, to exploit arrays of symbols some of which are atomic (e.g., expressions like 'A') but indefinitely many of which have other symbols as syntactic and semantic parts (e.g., expressions like 'A&B').

It is easy to overlook this difference between Classical and Connectionist architectures when reading the Connectionist polemical literature or examining a Connectionist model. There are at least four ways in which one might be led to do so: (1) by failing to understand the difference between what arrays of symbols do in Classical machines

---

[10]This illustration has not any particular Connectionist model in mind, though the caricature presented is, in fact, a simplified version of the Ballard (1987) Connectionist theorem proving system (which actually uses a more restricted proof procedure based on the *unification* of Horn clauses). To simplify the exposition, we assume a 'localist' approach, in which each semantically interpreted node corresponds to a single Connectionist unit; but nothing relevant to this discussion is changed if these nodes actually consist of patterns over a cluster of units.

[11]This makes the "compositionality" of data structures a defining property of Classical architecture. But, of course, it leaves open the question of the degree to which *natural* languages (like English) are also compositional.

and what node labels do in Connectionist machines; (2) by confusing the question whether the nodes in Connectionist networks have *constituent* structure with the question whether they are *neurologically distributed;* (3) by failing to distinguish between a representation having semantic and syntactic constituents and a concept being encoded in terms of microfeatures, and (4) by assuming that since representations of Connectionist networks have a graph structure, it follows that the nodes in the networks have a corresponding constituent structure. We shall now need rather a long digression to clear up these misunderstandings.

2.1.1.   The role of labels in Connectionist theories

In the course of setting out a Connectionist model, intentional content will be assigned to machine states, and the expressions of some language or other will, of course, be used to express this assignment; for example, nodes may be labelled to indicate their representational content. Such labels often have a combinatorial syntax and semantics; in this respect, they can look a lot like Classical mental representations. The point to emphasize, however, is that it doesn't follow (and it isn't true) that the nodes to which these labels are assigned have a combinatorial syntax and semantics. 'A&B', for example, can be tokened on the tape of the Classical machine *and can also appear as a label in a Connectionist machine* as it does in diagram 2 above. And, of course, the expression 'A&B' is syntactically and semantically complex: it has a token of 'A' as one of its syntactic constituents, and the semantics of the expression 'A&B' is a function of the semantics of the expression 'A'. But it isn't part of the intended reading of the diagram that node 1 itself has constituents; the node—unlike its label— has no semantically interpreted parts.

It is, in short, important to understand the difference between Connectionist labels and the symbols over which Classical computations are defined. The difference is this: Strictly speaking, the labels play *no role at all* in determining the operation of a Connectionist machine; in particular, the operation of the machine is unaffected by the syntactic and semantic relations that hold among the expressions that are used as labels. To put this another way, the node labels in a Connectionist machine are not part of the causal structure of the machine. Thus, the machine depicted in Figure 2 will continue to make the same state transitions regardless of what labels we assign to the nodes. Whereas, by contrast, the state transitions of Classical machines are causally determined *by the structure—including the constituent structure—of the symbol arrays that the machines transform:* change the symbols and the system behaves quite differently. (In fact, since the behavior of a Classical machine is sensitive to the syntax of the representations it

computes on, even interchanging *synonymous*—semantically equivalent—representations affects the course of computation.) So, although the Connectionist's labels and the Classicist's data structures both constitute languages, only the latter language constitutes a medium of computation.[12]

2.1.2   Connectionist networks and graph structures

The *second* reason that the lack of syntactic and semantic structure in Connectionist representations has largely been ignored may be that Connectionist networks look like general graphs; and it is, of course, perfectly possible to use graphs to describe the internal structure of a complex symbol. That's precisely what linguists do when they use 'trees' to exhibit the constituent structure of sentences. Correspondingly, one could imagine a graph notation that expresses the internal structure of mental representations by using arcs and labelled nodes. So, for example, you might express the syntax of the mental representation that corresponds to the thought that John loves the girl like this:

John $\rightarrow$ loves $\rightarrow$ the girl

Under the intended interpretation, this would be the structural description of a mental representation whose content is that John loves the girl, and whose constituents are: a mental representation that refers to *John,* a mental representation that refers to *the girl,* and a mental representation that expresses the two-place relation represented by $\rightarrow$ loves $\rightarrow$.

But although graphs can sustain an interpretation as specifying the logical syntax of a complex mental representation, this interpretation is inappropriate for graphs of Connectionist networks. Connectionist graphs are not structural descriptions of mental representations; they're specifications of causal relations. All that a Connectionist can mean by a graph of the form $\mathbf{X} \rightarrow \mathbf{Y}$ is: *states of node X causally affect states of node Y.* In particular, the graph can't mean *X is a constituent of Y* or *X is grammatically related to Y* etc., since these sorts of relations are, in general,

---

[12]Labels aren't part of the *causal structure* of a Connectionist machine, but they may play an essential role in its *causal history* insofar as designers wire their machines to respect the semantical relations that the labels express. For example, in Ballard's (1987) Connectionist model of theorem proving, there is a mechanical procedure for wiring a network which will carry out proofs by unification. This procedure is a function from a set of node labels to a wired-up machine. There is thus an interesting and revealing respect in which node labels are relevant to the operations that get performed when the function is executed. But, of course, the machine on which the labels have the effect is not the machine whose states they are labels of; and the effect of the labels occurs at the time that the theorem-proving machine is constructed, not at the time its reasoning process is carried out. *This* sort of case of labels 'having effects' is thus quite different from the way that symbol tokens (e.g., tokened data structures) can affect the causal processes of a Classical machine.

not defined for the kinds of mental representations that Connectionists recognize.

Another way to put this is that the links in Connectionist diagrams are not generalized pointers that can be made to take on different functional significance *by an independent interpreter,* but are confined to meaning something like "sends activation to". The intended interpretation of the links as causal connections is intrinsic to the theory. If you ignore this point, you are likely to take Connectionism to offer a much richer notion of mental representation than it actually does.

2.1.3. Distributed representations

The *third* mistake that can lead to a failure to notice that the mental representations in Connectionist models lack combinatorial syntactic and semantic structure is the fact that many Connectionists view representations as being *neurologically distributed;* and, presumably, whatever is distributed must have parts. It doesn't follow, however, that whatever is distributed must have *constituents;* being neurologically distributed is very different from having semantic or syntactic constituent structure.

You have constituent structure when (and only when) the parts of semantically evaluable entities are themselves semantically evaluable. Constituency relations thus hold among objects all of which are at the representational level; they are, in that sense, *within* level relations.[13] By contrast, neural distributedness—the sort of relation that is assumed to hold between 'nodes' and the 'units' by which they are realized—is a *between* level relation: The nodes, but not the units, count as representations. To claim that a node is neurally distributed is presumably to claim that its states of activation correspond to patterns of neural activity—to aggregates of neural 'units'—rather than to activations of single neurons. The important point is that nodes that are distributed in this sense can perfectly well be syntactically and semantically atomic: Complex spatially-distributed implementation in no way implies constituent structure.

There is, however, a different sense in which the representational states in a network might be distributed, and this sort of distribution also raises questions relevant to the constituency issue.

[13] Any relation specified as holding among representational states is, by definition, within the 'cognitive level'. It goes without saying that relations that are 'within-level' by this criterion can count as 'between-level' when we use criteria of finer grain. There is, for example, nothing to prevent hierarchies of levels of representational states.

2.1.4. Representations as 'distributed' over microfeatures

Many Connectionists hold that the mental representations that correspond to commonsense concepts (CHAIR, JOHN, CUP, etc.) are 'distributed' over galaxies of lower level units which themselves have representational content. To use common Connectionist terminology (see Smolensky, 1988), the higher or "conceptual level" units correspond to vectors in a "sub-conceptual" space of microfeatures. The model here is something like the relation between a defined expression and its defining feature analysis: thus, the concept BACHELOR might be thought to correspond to a vector in a space of features that includes ADULT, HUMAN, MALE, and MARRIED; i.e., as an assignment of the value + to the first two features and − to the last. Notice that distribution over microfeatures (unlike distribution over neural units) is a relation among representations, hence a relation at the cognitive level.

Since microfeatures are frequently assumed to be derived automatically (i.e., via learning procedures) from the statistical properties of samples of stimuli, we can think of them as expressing the sorts of propertics that are revealed by multivariate analysis of sets of stimuli (e.g., by multidimensional scaling of similarity judgments). In particular, they need not correspond to English words; they can be finer-grained than, or otherwise atypical of, the terms for which a non-specialist needs to have a word. Other than that, however, they are perfectly ordinary semantic features, much like those that lexicographers have traditionally used to represent the meanings of words.

On the most frequent Connectionist accounts, theories articulated in terms of microfeature vectors are supposed to show how concepts are *actually* encoded, hence the feature vectors are intended to *replace* "less precise" specifications of macrolevel concepts. For example, where a Classical theorist might recognize a psychological state of entertaining the concept CUP, a Connectionist may acknowledge only a *roughly analogous* state of tokening the corresponding feature vector. (One reason that the analogy is only rough is that which feature vector 'corresponds' to a given concept may be viewed as heavily context dependent.) The generalizations that 'concept level' theories frame are thus taken to be only approximately true, the exact truth being stateable only in the vocabulary of the microfeatures. Smolensky, for example (p. 11), is explicit in endorsing this picture: "Precise, formal descriptions of the intuitive processor are generally tractable not at the conceptual level, but only at the subconceptual level."[14] This treatment of the relation between commonsense concepts and microfeatures is exactly analogous to the standard Connectionist treatment of rules; in both cases, macrolevel theory is said to provide a vocabulary adequate for formulating generalizations that roughly approximate the facts about behavioral regularities. But the constructs of the macrotheory do *not* correspond to the causal mechanisms that generate these regularities. If you want a theory of these mechanisms, you need to replace talk about rules and concepts with talk about nodes, connections, microfeatures, vectors and the like.[15]

Now, it is among the major misfortunes of the Connectionist literature that the issue about whether commonsense concepts should be represented by sets of microfeatures has gotten thoroughly mixed up with the issue about combinatorial structure in mental representations. The crux of the mix-up is the fact that sets of microfeatures can overlap, so that, for example, if a microfecture corresponding to '+ has-a-handle' is part of the array of nodes over which the commonsense concept CUP is distributed, then you might think of the theory as representing '+ has-a-handle' as a *constituent* of the concept CUP; from which you might conclude that Con-

nectionists have a notion of constituency after all, contrary to the claim that Connectionism is not a language-of-thought architecture (see Smolensky, 1988).

A moment's consideration will make it clear, however, that even on the assumption that concepts are distributed over microfeatures, '+ has-a-handle' is not a constituent of CUP in anything like the sense that 'Mary' (the word) is a constituent of (the sentence) 'John loves Mary'. In the former case, "constituency" is being (mis)used to refer to a semantic relation between predicates; roughly, the idea is that macrolevel predicates like CUP are defined by sets of microfeatures like 'has-a-handle', so that it's some sort of semantic truth that CUP applies to a subset of what 'has-a-handle' applies to. Notice that while the extensions of these predicates are in a set/subset relation, the predicates themselves are not in any sort of part-to-whole relation. The expression 'has-a-handle' isn't *part of* the expression CUP any more than the English phrase 'is an unmarried man' is part of the English phrase 'is a bachelor'.

Real constituency does have to do with parts and wholes; the symbol 'Mary' is literally a part of the symbol 'John loves Mary'. It is because their symbols enter into real-constituency relations that natural languages have both atomic symbols and complex ones. By contrast, the definition relation can hold in a language where *all* the symbols are syntactically atomic; e.g., a language which contains both 'cup' and 'has-a-handle' as atomic predicates. This point is worth stressing. The question whether a representational system has real-constituency is independent of the question of microfeature analysis; it arises both for systems in which you have CUP as semantically primitive, and for systems in which the semantic primitives are things like '+ has-a-handle' and CUP and the like are defined in terms of these primitives. It really is very important not to confuse the semantic distinction between primitive expressions and defined expressions with the syntactic distinction between atomic symbols and complex symbols.

So far as we know, there are no worked out attempts in the Connectionist literature to deal with the syntactic and semantical issues raised by relations of real-constituency. There is, however, a proposal that comes up from time to time: viz., that what are traditionally treated as complex symbols should actually be viewed as just sets of units, with the role relations that traditionally get coded by constituent structure represented by units belonging to these sets. So, for example, the mental representation corresponding to the belief that John loves Mary might be the feature vector { *+John-subject; +loves; +Mary-object* }. Here 'John-subject' 'Mary-object' and the like are the labels of units; that is, they are atomic (i.e., micro-) features, whose status is analogous to 'has-a-handle'. In particular, they have no internal syntactic analysis, and there is no structural rela-

---

[14]Smolensky (1988, p. 14) remarks that "unlike symbolic tokens, these vectors lie in a topological space, in which some are close together and others are far apart." However, this seems to radically conflate claims about the Connectionist model and claims about its implementation (a conflation that is not unusual in the Connectionist literature as we'll see in Section 4). If the space at issue is *physical*, then Smolensky is committed to extremely strong claims about adjacency relations in the brain; claims which there is, in fact, no reason at all to believe. But if, as seems more plausible, the space at issue is *semantical* then what Smolensky says isn't true. Practically any cognitive theory will imply distance measures between mental representations. In Classical theories, for example, the distance between two representations is plausibly related to the number of computational steps it takes to derive one representation from the other. In Connectionist theories, it is plausibly related to the number of intervening nodes (or to the degree of overlap between vectors, depending on the version of Connectionism one has in mind). The interesting claim is not that an architecture offers *a* distance measure but that it offers the *right* distance measure—one that is empirically certifiable.

[15]The primary use that Connectionists make of microfeatures is in their accounts of generalization and abstraction (see, for example, Hinton, McClelland, & Rumelhart, 1986). Roughly, you get generalization by using overlap of microfeatures to define a similarity space, and you get abstraction by making the vectors that correspond to *types* be subvectors of the ones that correspond to their *tokens*. Similar proposals have quite a long history in traditional Empiricist analysis, and have been roundly criticized over the centuries. (For a discussion of abstractionism see Geach, 1957; that similarity is a primitive relation—hence not reducible to partial identity of feature sets—was, of course, a main tenet of Gestalt psychology, as well as more recent approaches based on "prototypes".) The treatment of microfeatures in the Connectionist literature would appear to be very close to early proposals by Katz and Fodor (1963) and Katz and Postal (1964), where both the idea of a feature analysis of concepts and the idea that relations of semantic containment among concepts should be identified with set-theoretic relations among feature arrays are explicitly endorsed.

tion (except the orthographic one) between the feature 'Mary-object' that occurs in the set {John-subject; loves; Mary-object} and the feature 'Mary-subject' that occurs in the set {Mary-subject; loves; John-object}. (See, for example, the discussion in Hinton, 1987 of "role-specific descriptors that represent the conjunction of an identity and a role [by the use of which] we can implement part-whole hierarchies using set intersection as the composition rule." See also, McClelland, Rumelhart & Hinton, 1986, p. 82–85, where what appears to be the same treatment is proposed in somewhat different terms.)

Since, as we remarked, these sorts of ideas aren't elaborated in the Connectionist literature, detailed discussion is probably not warranted here. But it's worth a word to make clear what sort of trouble you would get into if you were to take them seriously.

As we understand it, the proposal really has two parts: On the one hand, it's suggested that although Connectionist representations cannot exhibit real-constituency, nevertheless the Classical distinction between complex symbols and their constituents can be replaced by the distinction between feature sets and their subsets; and, on the other hand, it's suggested that role relations can be captured by features. We'll consider these ideas in turn.

1. Instead of having complex symbols like "John loves Mary" in the representational system, you have feature sets like {+*John-subject; +loves; +Mary-object*}. Since this set has {+*John-subject*}, {+*loves; +Mary-object*} and so forth as sub-sets, it may be supposed that the force of the constituency relation has been captured by employing the subset relation.

However, it's clear that this idea won't work since not all subsets of features correspond to genuine constituents. For example, among the subsets of {+*John-subject; +loves; +Mary-object*} are the sets {+*John-subject; +Mary-object*} and the set {+*John-subject; +loves*} which do not, of course, correspond to constituents of the complex symbol "John loves Mary".

2. Instead of defining roles in terms of relations among constituents, as one does in Classical architecture, introduce them as microfeatures.

Consider a system in which the mental representation that is entertained when one believes that John loves Mary is the feature set {+*John-subject; +loves; +Mary-object*}. What representation corresponds to the belief that John loves Mary and Bill hates Sally? Suppose, pursuant to the present proposal, that it's the set {+*John-subject; +loves; +Mary-object; +Bill-subject; +hates; +Sally-object*}. We now have the problem of distinguishing that belief from the belief that John loves Sally and Bill hates Mary; and from the belief that John

hates Mary and Bill loves Sally; and from the belief that John hates Mary and Sally and Bill loves Mary; etc., since these other beliefs will all correspond to precisely the same set of features. The problem is, of course, that nothing in the representation of Mary as +*Mary-object* specifies whether it's the loving or the hating that she is the object of; similarly, mutatis mutandis, for the representation of John as +*John-subject*.

What has gone wrong isn't disastrous (yet). All that's required is to enrich the system of representations by recognizing features that correspond not to (for example) just being a subject, but rather to being the subject of a loving of Mary (the property that John has when John loves Mary) and being the subject of a hating of Sally (the property that Bill has when Bill hates Sally). So, the representation of John that's entertained when one believes that John loves Mary and Bill hates Sally might be something like +*John-subject-hates-Mary-object*.

The disadvantage of this proposal is that it requires rather a lot of microfeatures.[16] How many? Well, a number of the order of magnitude of the *sentences* of a natural language (whereas one might have hoped to get by with a vocabulary of basic expressions that is not vastly larger than the *lexicon* of a natural language; after all, natural languages do). We leave it to the reader to estimate the number of microfeatures you would need, assuming that there is a distinct belief corresponding to every grammatical sentence of English of up to, say, fifteen words of length, and assuming that there is an average of, say, five roles associated with each belief. (Hint: George Miller once estimated that the number of well-formed 20-word sentences of English is of the order of magnitude of the number of seconds in the history of the universe.)

The alternative to this grotesque explosion of atomic symbols would be to have *a combinatorial syntax and semantics for the features*. But, of course, this is just to give up the game since the syntactic and semantic relations that hold among the parts of the complex feature +*((John subject) loves (Mary object))* are the very same ones that Classically hold among the constituents of the complex symbol "John loves Mary"; these include the role relations which Connectionists had proposed to reconstruct using just sets of atomic features. It is, of course, no accident that the Connectionist proposal for dealing with role relations runs into these sorts of problems. Subject, object and the rest are Classically defined *with respect to the geometry of*

---

[16] Another disadvantage is that, strictly speaking it doesn't work; although it allows us to distinguish the belief that John loves Mary and Bill hates Sally from the belief that John loves Sally and Bill hates Mary, we don't yet have a way to distinguish believing that (John loves Mary because Bill hates Sally) from believing that (Bill hates Sally because John loves Mary). Presumably nobody would want to have microfeatures corresponding to these.

constituent structure trees. And Connectionist representations don't have constituents.

The idea that we should capture role relations by allowing features like *John-subject* thus turns out to be bankrupt; and there doesn't seem to be any other way to get the force of structured symbols in a Connectionist architecture. Or, if there is, nobody has given any indication of how to do it. This becomes clear once the crucial issue about structure in mental representations is disentangled from the relatively secondary (and orthogonal) issue about whether the representation of commonsense concepts is 'distributed' (i.e., from questions like whether it's CUP or 'has-a-handle' or both that is semantically primitive in the language of thought).

It's worth adding that these problems about expressing the role relations are actually just a symptom of a more pervasive difficulty: A consequence of restricting the vehicles of mental representation to sets of atomic symbols is a notation that fails quite generally to express the way that concepts group into propositions. To see this, let's continue to suppose that we have a network in which the nodes represent concepts rather than propositions (so that what corresponds to the thought that John loves Mary is a distribution of activation over the set of nodes {JOHN; LOVES; MARY} rather than the activation of a single node labelled JOHN LOVES MARY). Notice that it cannot plausibly be assumed that all the nodes that happen to be active at a given time will correspond to concepts that are constituents of the *same* proposition; least of all if the architecture is "massively parallel" so that many things are allowed to go on—many concepts are allowed to be entertained—simultaneously in a given mind. Imagine, then, the following situation: at time t, a man is looking at the sky (so the nodes corresponding to SKY and BLUE are active) and thinking that John loves Fido (so the nodes corresponding to JOHN, LOVES, and FIDO are active), and the node FIDO is connected to the node DOG (which is in turn connected to the node ANIMAL) in such fashion that DOG and ANIMAL are active too. We can, if you like, throw it in that the man has got an itch, so ITCH is also on.

According to the current theory of mental representation, this man's mind at t is specified by the vector {+JOHN, +LOVES, +FIDO, +DOG, +SKY, +BLUE, +ITCH, +ANIMAL}. And the question is: *which subvectors of this vector correspond to thoughts that the man is thinking?* Specifically, what is it about the man's representational state that determines that the simultaneous activation of the nodes, {JOHN, LOVES, FIDO} constitutes his thinking that John loves Fido, but the simultaneous activation of FIDO, ANIMAL and BLUE does *not* constitute his thinking that Fido is a blue animal? It seems that we made it too easy for ourselves when we identified the

thought that John loves Mary with the vector {+JOHN, +LOVES, +MARY}; at best that works only on the assumption that JOHN, LOVES and MARY are the only nodes active when someone has that thought. And that's an assumption to which no theory of mental representation is entitled.

It's important to see that this problem arises precisely because the theory is trying to use sets of atomic representations to do a job that you really need complex representations for. Thus, the question we're wanting to answer is: Given the total set of nodes active at a time, what distinguishes the subvectors that correspond to propositions from the subvectors that don't? This question has a straightforward answer if, contrary to the present proposal, complex representations are assumed: When representations express concepts that belong to the same proposition, they are not merely simultaneously active, but also *in construction with each other.* By contrast, representations that express concepts that don't belong to the same proposition may be simultaneously active; but, they are ipso facto *not* in construction with each other.

In short, you need two degrees of freedom to specify the thoughts that an intentional system is entertaining at a time: one parameter (active vs inactive) picks out the nodes that express concepts that the system has in mind; the other (in construction vs not) determines how the concepts that the system has in mind are distributed in the propositions that it entertains. For symbols to be "in construction" in this sense is just for them to be constituents of a complex symbol. Representations that are in construction form parts of a geometrical whole, *where the geometrical relations are themselves semantically significant.* Thus the representation that corresponds to the thought that John loves Fido is not a *set* of concepts but something like a *tree* of concepts, and it's the geometrical relations in this tree that mark (for example) the difference between the thought that John loves Fido and the thought that Fido loves John.

We've occasionally heard it suggested that you could solve the present problem consonant with the restriction against complex representations if you allow networks like this:

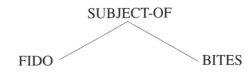

The intended interpretation is that the thought that Fido bites corresponds to the simultaneous activation of these nodes; that is, to the vector {+FIDO, +SUBJECT OF, +BITES}—with similar though longer vectors for more complex role relations.

But, on second thought, this proposal merely begs the question that it set out to solve. For, if there's a problem about what justifies assigning the proposition John loves Fido as the content of the set {JOHN, LOVES, FIDO}, there is surely the same problem about what justifies assigning the proposition Fido is the subject of bites to the set {FIDO, SUBJECT-OF, BITES}. If this is not immediately clear, consider the case where the simultaneously active nodes are {FIDO, SUBJECT-OF, BITES, JOHN}. Is the propositional content that Fido bites or that John does?[17]

Strikingly enough, the point that we've been making in the past several paragraphs is very close to one that Kant made against the Associationists of his day. In "Transcendental Deduction (B)" of The First Critique, Kant remarks that:

... if I investigate ... the relation of the given modes of knowledge in any judgement; and distinguish it, as belonging to the understanding, from the relation according to laws of the reproductive imagination [e.g., according to the principles of association], which has only subjective validity, I find that a judgement is nothing but the manner in which given modes of knowledge are brought to the objective unity of apperception. This is what is intended by the copula "is". It is employed to distinguish the objective unity of given representations from the subjective.... Only in this way does there arise from the relation a *judgement*, that is a relation which is *objectively valid*, and so can be adequately distinguished from a relation of the same representations that would have only subjective validity—as when they are connected according to laws of association. In the latter case, all that I could say would be 'If I support a body, I feel an impression of weight'; I could not say, 'It, the body, is heavy'. Thus to say 'The body is heavy' is not merely to state that the two representations have always been conjoined in my perception, ... what we are asserting is that they are combined in the object ... (CPR, p. 159; emphasis Kant's)

A modern paraphrase might be: A theory of mental representation must distinguish the case when two concepts (e.g., THIS BODY, HEAVY) are merely *simultaneously entertained* from the case where, to put it roughly,

the property that one of the concepts expresses is predicated of the thing that the other concept denotes (as in the thought: THIS BODY IS HEAVY). The relevant distinction is that while both concepts are "active" in both cases, in the latter case but *not* in the former the active concepts are in construction. Kant thinks that "this is what is intended by the copula 'is' ". But of course there are other notational devices that can serve to specify that concepts are in construction; notably the bracketing structure of constituency trees.

There are, to reiterate, two questions that you need to answer to specify the content of a mental state: "Which concepts are 'active' " and "Which of the active concepts are in construction with which others?" Identifying mental states with sets of active nodes provides resources to answer the first of these questions but not the second. That's why the version of network theory that acknowledges sets of atomic representations but no complex representations fails, in indefinitely many cases, to distinguish mental states that are in fact distinct.

But we are *not* claiming that you can't reconcile a Connectionist architecture with an adequate theory of mental representation (specifically with a combinatorial syntax and semantics for mental representations). On the contrary, of course you can: All that's required is that you use your network to implement a Turing machine, and specify a combinatorial structure for its computational language. What it appears that you can't do, however, is have both a combinatorial representational system and a Connectionist architecture *at the cognitive level*.

So much, then, for our long digression. We have now reviewed one of the major respects in which Connectionist and Classical theories differ; viz., their accounts of mental *representations*. We turn to the second major difference, which concerns their accounts of mental *processes*.

2.2 Structure sensitive operations

Classicists and Connectionists both offer accounts of mental processes; but their theories differ sharply. In particular, the Classical theory relies heavily on the notion of the logico/syntactic form of mental representations to define the ranges and domains of mental operations. This notion is, however, unavailable to orthodox Connectionists since it presupposes that there are nonatomic mental representations.

The Classical treatment of mental processes rests on two ideas, each of which corresponds to an aspect of the Classical theory of computation. Together they explain why the Classical view postulates at least three distinct levels of organization in computational systems: not just a physical level and a semantic (or "knowledge") level, but a syntactic level as well.

---

[17] It's especially important at this point not to make the mistake of confusing diagrams of Connectionist networks with constituent structure diagrams (see section 2.1.2 above). Connecting SUBJECT-OF with FIDO and BITES does not mean that when all three are active FIDO is the subject of BITES. A network diagram is not a specification of the internal structure of a complex mental representation. Rather, it's a specification of a pattern of causal dependencies among the states of activation of nodes. Connectivity in a network determines which sets of simultaneously active nodes are possible; but it has no *semantical* significance.

The difference between the paths between nodes that network diagrams exhibit and the paths between nodes that constituent structure diagrams exhibit is precisely that the latter but not the former specify parameters of mental representations. (In particular, they specify part/whole relations among the constituents of complex symbols.) Whereas network theories define semantic interpretations over sets of (causally interconnected) representations of concepts, theories that acknowledge complex symbols define semantic interpretations over sets of representations of concepts *together with specifications of the constituency relations that hold among these representations*.

The first idea is that it is possible to construct languages in which certain features of the syntactic structures of formulas correspond systematically to certain of their semantic features. Intuitively, the idea is that in such languages the syntax of a formula encodes its meaning; most especially, those aspects of its meaning that determine its role in inference. All the artificial languages that are used for logic have this property and English has it more or less. Classicists believe that it is a crucial property of the Language of Thought.

A simple example of how a language can use syntactic structure to encode inferential roles and relations among meanings may help to illustrate this point. Thus, consider the relation between the following two sentences:

1. John went to the store and Mary went to the store.

2. Mary went to the store.

On the one hand, from the semantic point of view, (1) entails (2) (so, of course, inferences from (1) to (2) are truth preserving). On the other hand, from the syntactic point of view, (2) is a constituent of (1). These two facts can be brought into phase by exploiting the principle that sentences with the *syntactic* structure '(S1 and S2)$_s$' entail their sentential constituents. Notice that this principle connects the syntax of these sentences with their inferential roles. Notice too that the trick relies on facts about the grammar of English; it wouldn't work in a language where the formula that expresses the conjunctive content *John went to the store and Mary went to the store* is *syntactically* atomic.[18]

Here is another example. We can reconstruct such truth preserving inferences as *if Rover bites then something bites* on the assumption that (a) the sentence 'Rover bites' is of the syntactic type **Fa**, (b) the sentence 'something bites' is of the syntactic type $\exists x$ (**Fx**) and (c) every formula of the first type entails a corresponding formula of the second type (where the notion 'corresponding formula' is cashed syntactically; roughly the two formulas must differ only in that the one has an existentially bound variable at the syntactic position that is occupied by a constant in the other). Once again the point to notice is the blending of syntactical and semantical notions: The rule of existential generalization applies to formulas in virtue of their syntactic form. But the salient property that's preserved under applications of the rule is semantical: What's claimed for the transformation that the rule performs is that it is *truth* preserving.[19]

There are, as it turns out, examples that are quite a lot more complicated than these. The whole of the branch of logic known as proof theory is devoted to exploring them.[20] It would not be unreasonable to describe Classical Cognitive Science as an extended attempt to apply the methods of proof theory to the modeling of thought (and similarly, of whatever other mental processes are plausibly viewed as involving inferences; preeminently learning and perception). Classical theory construction rests on the hope that syntactic analogues can be constructed for non-demonstrative inferences (or informal, commonsense reasoning) in something like the way that proof theory has provided syntactic analogues for validity.

The second main idea underlying the Classical treatment of mental processes is that it is possible to devise machines whose function is the transformation of symbols, and whose operations are sensitive to the syntactical structure of the symbols that they operate upon. This is the Classical conception of a computer: it's what the various architectures that derive from Turing and von Neumann machines all have in common.

Perhaps it's obvious how the two 'main ideas' fit together. If, in principle, syntactic relations can be made to

---

[18] And it doesn't work uniformly for English conjunction. Compare: *John and Mary are friends* → **John are friends*; or *The flag is red, white and blue* → *The flag is blue*. Such cases show either that English is not the language of thought, or that, if it is, the relation between syntax and semantics is a good deal subtler for the language of thought than it is for the standard logical languages.

[19] It needn't, however, be strict truth-preservation that makes the syntactic approach relevant to cognition. Other semantic properties might be preserved under syntactic transformation in the course of mental processing—e.g., warrant, plausibility, heuristic value, or simply *semantic non-arbitrariness*. The point of Classical modeling isn't to characterize human thought as supremely logical; rather, it's to show how a family of types of semantically coherent (or knowledge-dependent) reasoning are mechanically possible. Valid inference is the paradigm only in that it is the best understood member of this family; the one for which syntactical analogues for semantic relations have been most systematically elaborated.

[20] It is not uncommon for Connectionists to make disparaging remarks about the relevance of logic to psychology, even thought they accept the idea that inference is involved in reasoning. Sometimes the suggestions seems to be that it's all right if Connectionism can't reconstruct the theory of inference that formal deductive logic provides since it has something even better on offer. For example, in their report to the U.S. National Science Foundation. McClelland, Feldman, Adelson, Bower & McDermott (1986) state that "... connectionist models realize an evidential logic *in contrast to* the symbolic logic of conventional computing (p. 6; our emphasis)" and that "evidential logics are becoming increasingly important in cognitive science and have a natural map to connectionist modeling" (p. 7). It is, however, hard to understand the implied contrast since, on the one hand, evidential logic must surely be a fairly conservative extension of "the symbolic logic of conventional computing" (i.e., most of the theorems of the latter have to come out true in the former) and, on the other, there is not the slightest reason to doubt that an evidential logic would 'run' on a Classical machine. Prima facie, the problem about evidential logic isn't that we've got one that we don't know how to implement; it's that we haven't got one.

parallel semantic relations, and if, in principle, you can have a mechanism whose operations on formulas are sensitive to their syntax, then it may be possible to construct a *syntactically* driven machine whose state transitions satisfy *semantical* criteria of coherence. Such a machine would be just what's required for a mechanical model of the semantical coherence of thought; correspondingly, the idea that the brain *is* such a machine is the foundational hypothesis of Classical cognitive science.

So much for the Classical story about mental processes. The Connectionist story must, of course, be quite different: Since Connectionists eschew postulating mental representations with combinatorial syntactic/semantic structure, they are precluded from postulating mental processes that operate on mental representations in a way that is sensitive to their structure. The sorts of operations that Connectionist models do have are of two sorts, depending on whether the process under examination is learning or reasoning.

2.2.1. Learning If a Connectionist model is intended to learn, there will be processes that determine the weights of the connections among its units as a function of the character of its training. Typically in a Connectionist machine (such as a 'Boltzman Machine') the weights among connections are adjusted until the system's behavior comes to model the statistical properties of its inputs. In the limit, the stochastic relations among machine states recapitulates the stochastic relations among the environmental events that they represent.

This should bring to mind the old Associationist principle that the strength of association between 'Ideas' is a function of the frequency with which they are paired 'in experience' and the Learning Theoretic principle that the strength of a stimulus-response connection is a function of the frequency with which the response is rewarded in the presence of the stimulus. But though Connectionists, like other Associationists, are committed to learning processes that model statistical properties of inputs and outputs, the simple mechanisms based on co-occurrence statistics that were the hallmarks of old-fashioned Associationism have been augmented in Connectionist models by a number of technical devices. (Hence the 'new' in 'New Connectionism'.) For example, some of the earlier limitations of associative mechanisms are overcome by allowing the network to contain 'hidden' units (or aggregates) that are not directly connected to the environment and whose purpose is, in effect, to detect statistical patterns in the activity of the 'visible' units including, perhaps, patterns that are more abstract or more 'global' than the ones that could be detected by old-fashioned perceptrons.[21]

---

[21]Compare the "little s's" and "little r's" of neo-Hullean "mediational" Associationists like Charles Osgood.

In short, sophisticated versions of the associative principles for weight-setting are on offer in the Connectionist literature. The point of present concern, however, is what all versions of these principles have in common with one another and with older kinds of Associationism: viz., these processes are all *frequency*-sensitive. To return to the example discussed above: if a Connectionist learning machine converges on a state where it is prepared to infer A from A&B (i.e., to a state in which when the 'A&B' node is excited it tends to settle into a state in which the 'X' node is excited) the convergence will typically be caused by statistical properties of the machine's training experience: e.g., by correlation between firing of the 'A&B' node and firing of the 'A' node, or by correlations of the firing of both with some feedback signal. Like traditional Associationism, Connectionism treats learning as basically a sort of statistical modeling.

2.2.2. Reasoning Association operates to alter the structure of a network *diachronically* as a function of its training. Connectionist models also contain a variety of types of 'relaxation' processes which determine the *synchronic* behavior of a network; specifically, they determine what output the device provides for a given pattern of inputs. In this respect, one can think of a Connectionist model as a species of analog machine constructed to realize a certain function. The inputs to the function are (i) a specification of the connectedness of the machine (of which nodes are connected to which); (ii) a specification of the weights along the connections; (iii) a specification of the values of a variety of idiosyncratic parameters of the nodes (e.g., intrinsic thresholds; time since last firing, etc.); (iv) a specification of a pattern of excitation over the input nodes. The output of the function is a specification of a pattern of excitation over the output nodes; intuitively, the machine chooses the output pattern that is most highly associated to its input.

Much of the mathematical sophistication of Connectionist theorizing has been devoted to devising analog solutions to this problem of finding a 'most highly associated' output corresponding to an arbitrary input; but, once again, the details needn't concern us. What is important, for our purposes, is another property that Connectionist theories share with other forms of Associationism. In traditional Associationism, the probability that one Idea will elicit another is sensitive to the strength of the association between them (including 'mediating' associations, if any). And the strength of this association is in turn sensitive to the extent to which the Ideas have previously been correlated. Associative strength was not, however, presumed to be sensitive to features of the content or the structure of representations per se. Similarly, in Connectionist models, the selection of an output corresponding to a given input is a function of properties of the paths that connect them (including the weights, the states of intermediate units, etc.). And the weights, in turn, are a function of the statistical properties of events in the environment (or of relations between patterns of events in the environment and implicit 'predictions' made by the network, etc.). But the syntactic/semantic structure of the representation of an input is *not* presumed to be a factor in determining the selection of a corresponding output since, as we have seen, syntactic/semantic structure is not defined for the sorts of representations that Connectionist models acknowledge.

To summarize: Classical and Connectionist theories disagree about the nature of mental representation; for the former, but not for the latter, mental representations characteristically exhibit a combinatorial constituent structure and a combinatorial semantics. Classical and Connectionist theories also disagree about the nature of mental processes; for the former, but not for the latter, mental processes are characteristically sensitive to the combinatorial structure of the representations on which they operate.

We take it that these two issues define the present dispute about the nature of cognitive architecture. We now propose to argue that the Connectionists are on the wrong side of both.

3   The need for symbol systems: Productivity, systematicity, compositionality and inferential coherence

Classical psychological theories appeal to the constituent structure of mental representations to explain three closely related features of cognition: its productivity, its compositionality and its inferential coherence. The traditional argument has been that these features of cognition are, on the one hand, pervasive and, on the other hand, explicable only on the assumption that mental representations have internal structure. This argument—familiar in more or less explicit versions for the last thirty years or so—is still intact, so far as we can tell. It appears to offer something close to a demonstration that an empirically adequate cognitive theory must recognize not just causal relations among representational states but also relations of syntactic and semantic constituency: hence that the mind cannot be, in its general structure, a Connectionist network.

3.1   Productivity of thought

There is a classical productivity argument for the existence of combinatorial structure in any rich representational system (including natural languages and the language of thought). The representational capacities of such a system are, by assumption, unbounded under appropriate idealiza-

tion: in particular, there are indefinitely many propositions which the system can encode.[22] However, this unbounded expressive power must presumably be achieved by finite means. The way to do this is to treat the system of representations as consisting of expressions belonging to a generated set. More precisely, the correspondence between a representation and the proposition it expresses is, in arbitrarily many cases, built up recursively out of correspondences between parts of the expression and parts of the proposition. But, of course, this strategy can operate only when an unbounded number of the expressions are nonatomic. So linguistic (and mental) representations must constitute *symbol systems* (in the sense of footnote 8). So the mind cannot be a PDP.

Very often, when people reject this sort of reasoning, it is because they doubt that human cognitive capacities are correctly viewed as productive. In the long run there can be no a priori arguments for (or against) idealizing to productive capacities; whether you accept the idealization depends on whether you believe that the inference from finite performance to finite capacity is justified, or whether you think that finite performance is typically a result of the interaction of an unbounded competence with resource constraints; Classicists have traditionally offered a mixture of methodological and empirical considerations in favor of the latter view.

From a methodological perspective, the least that can be said for assuming productivity is that it precludes solutions that rest on inappropriate tricks (such as storing all the pairs that define a function); tricks that would be unreasonable in practical terms even for solving finite tasks that place sufficiently large demands on memory. The idealization to unbounded productive capacity forces the theorist to separate the finite specification of a method for solving a computational problem from such factors as the resources that the system (or person) brings to bear on the problem at any given moment.

The empirical arguments for productivity have been made most frequently in connection with linguistic competence. They are familiar from the work of Chomsky (1968) who has claimed (convincingly, in our view) that the knowledge underlying linguistic competence is generative—i.e., that it allows us *in principle* to generate (/understand) an unbounded number of sentences. It goes without saying that no one does, or could, *in fact* utter or

---

[22]This way of putting the productivity argument is most closely identified with Chomsky (e.g., Chomsky, 1965; 1968). However, one does not have to rest the argument upon a basic assumption of infinite generative capacity. Infinite generative capacity can be viewed, instead, as a consequence or a corollary of theories formulated so as to capture the greatest number of generalizations with the fewest independent principles. This more neutral approach is, in fact, very much in the spirit of what we shall propose below. We are putting it in the present form for expository and historical reasons.

understand tokens of more than a finite number of sentence types; this is a trivial consequence of the fact that nobody can utter or understand more than a finite number of sentence tokens. But there are a number of considerations which suggest that, despite de facto constraints on performance, one's knowledge of one's language supports an unbounded productive capacity in much the same way that one's knowledge of addition supports an unbounded number of sums. Among these considerations are, for example, the fact that a speaker/ hearer's performance can often be improved by relaxing time constraints, increasing motivation, or supplying pencil and paper. It seems very natural to treat such manipulations as affecting the transient state of the speaker's memory and attention rather than what he knows about—or how he represents—his language. But this treatment is available only on the assumption that the character of the subject's performance is determined by interactions between the available knowledge base and the available computational resources.

Classical theories are able to accommodate these sorts of considerations because they assume architectures in which there is a functional distinction between memory and program. In a system such as a Turing machine, where the length of the tape is not fixed in advance, changes in the amount of available memory *can be affected without changing the computational structure of the machine;* viz., by making more tape available. By contrast, in a finite state automaton or a Connectionist machine, adding to the memory (e.g., by adding units to a network) alters the connectivity relations among nodes and thus does affect the machine's computational structure. Connectionist cognitive architectures cannot, by their very nature, support an expandable memory, so they cannot support productive cognitive capacities. The long and short is that if productivity arguments are sound, then they show that the architecture of the mind can't be Connectionist. Connectionists have, by and large, acknowledged this; so they are forced to reject productivity arguments.

The test of a good scientific idealization is simply and solely whether it produces successful science in the long term. It seems to us that the productivity idealization has more than earned its keep, especially in linguistics and in theories of reasoning. Connectionists, however, have not been persuaded. For example, Rumelhart and McClelland (1986a, p. 119) say that they "... do not agree that [productive] capabilities are of the essence of human computation. As anyone who has ever attempted to process sentences like 'The man the boy the girl hit kissed moved' can attest, our ability to process even moderate degrees of center-embedded structure is grossly impaired relative to an ATN [Augmented Transition Network] parser .... What is needed, then, is not a mechanism for flawless and effortless

processing of embedded constructions ... The challenge is to explain how those processes that others have chosen to explain in terms of recursive mechanisms can be better explained by the kinds of processes natural for PDP networks."

These remarks suggest that Rumelhart and McClelland think that the fact that center-embedding sentences are hard is somehow an *embarrassment* for theories that view linguistic capacities as productive. But of course it's not since, according to such theories, performance is an effect of interactions between a productive competence and restricted resources. There are, in fact, quite plausible Classical accounts of why center-embeddings ought to impose especially heavy demands on resources, and there is a reasonable amount of experimental support for these models (see, for example, Wanner & Maratsos, 1978).

In any event, it should be obvious that the difficulty of parsing center-embeddings can't be a consequence of their recursiveness per se since there are many recursive structures that are strikingly easy to understand. Consider: 'this is the dog that chased the cat that ate the rat that lived in the house that Jack built.' The Classicist's case for productive capacities in parsing rests on the transparency of sentences like these.[23] In short, the fact that center-embedded sentences are hard perhaps shows that there are some recursive structures that we can't parse. But what Rumelhart and McClelland need if they are to deny the productivity of linguistic capacities is the much stronger claim that there are no recursive structures that we can parse; and this stronger claim would appear to be simply false.

Rumelhart and McClelland's discussion of recursion (pp. 119–120) nevertheless repays close attention. They are apparently prepared to concede that PDPs can model recursive capacities only indirectly—viz., by implementing Classical architectures like ATNs; so that *if* human cognition exhibited recursive capacities, that would suffice to show that minds have Classical rather than Connectionist architecture at the psychological level. "We have not dwelt

---

[23]McClelland and Kawamoto (1986) discuss this sort of recursion briefly. Their suggestion seems to be that parsing such sentences doesn't really require recovering their recursive structure: "... the job of the parser [with respect to right-recursive sentences] is to spit out phrases in a way that captures their *local* context. Such a representation may prove sufficient to allow us to reconstruct the correct bindings of noun phrases to verbs and prepositional phrases to *nearby* nouns and verbs" (p. 324; emphasis ours). It is, however, by no means the case that all of the semantically relevant grammatical relations in readily intelligible embedded sentences are local in surface structure. Consider: '*Where* did the man who owns the cat that chased the rat that frightened the girl say that he was going to move to (X)?' or '*What* did the girl that the children loved to listen to promise your friends that she would read (X) to them?' Notice that, in such examples, a binding element (italicized) can be arbitrarily displaced from the position whose interpretation it controls (marked 'X') without making the sentence particularly difficult to understand. Notice too that the 'semantics' doesn't determine the binding relations in either example.

on PDP implementations of Turing machines and recursive processing engines *because we do not agree with those who would argue that such capacities are of the essence of human computation*" (p. 119, our emphasis). Their argument that recursive capacities *aren't* "of the essence of human computation" is, however, just the unconvincing stuff about center-embedding quoted above.

So the Rumelhart and McClelland view is apparently that if you take it to be independently obvious that some cognitive capacities are productive, then you should take the existence of such capacities to argue for Classical cognitive architecture and hence for treating Connectionism as at best an implementation theory. We think that this is quite a plausible understanding of the bearing that the issues about productivity and recursion have on the issues about cognitive architecture; in Section 4 we will return to the suggestion that Connectionist models can plausibly be construed as models of the implementation of a Classical architecture.

In the meantime, however, we propose to view the status of productivity arguments for Classical architectures as moot; we're about to present a different sort of argument for the claim that mental representations need an articulated internal structure. It is closely related to the productivity argument, but it doesn't require the idealization to unbounded competence. Its assumptions should thus be acceptable even to theorists who—like Connectionists—hold that the finitistic character of cognitive capacities is intrinsic to their architecture.

3.2 Systematicity of cognitive representation

The form of the argument is this: Whether or not cognitive capacities are really *productive,* it seems indubitable that they are what we shall call 'systematic'. And we'll see that the systematicity of cognition provides as good a reason for postulating combinatorial structure in mental representation as the productivity of cognition does: You get, in effect, the same conclusion, but from a weaker premise.

The easiest way to understand what the systematicity of cognitive capacities amounts to is to focus on the systematicity of language comprehension and production. In fact, the systematicity argument for combinatorial structure in *thought* exactly recapitulates the traditional Structuralist argument for constituent structure in sentences. But we pause to remark upon a point that we'll re-emphasize later; linguistic capacity is a paradigm of systematic cognition, but it's wildly unlikely that it's the only example. On the contrary, there's every reason to believe that systematicity is a thoroughly pervasive feature of human and infrahuman mentation.

What we mean when we say that linguistic capacities are *systematic* is that the ability to produce/understand some sentences is *intrinsically* connected to the ability to produce/understand certain others. You can see the force of this if you compare learning languages the way we really do learn them with learning a language by memorizing an enormous phrase book. The point isn't that phrase books are finite and can therefore exhaustively specify only *non-*productive languages; that's true, but we've agreed not to rely on productivity arguments for our present purposes. Our point is rather that you can learn *any part of a phrase book without learning the rest.* Hence, on the phrase book model, it would be perfectly possible to learn that uttering the form of words 'Granny's cat is on Uncle Arthur's mat' is the way to say (in English) that Granny's cat is on Uncle Arthur's mat, and yet have no idea at all how to say that it's raining (or, for that matter, how to say that Uncle Arthur's cat is on Granny's mat). Perhaps it's self-evident that the phrase book story must be wrong about language acquisition because a speaker's knowledge of his native language is never like that. You don't, for example, find native speakers who know how to say in English that John loves the girl but don't know how to say in English that the girl loves John.

Notice, in passing, that systematicity is a property of the mastery of the syntax of a language, not of its lexicon. The phrase book model really does fit what it's like to learn the *vocabulary* of English since when you learn English vocabulary you acquire a lot of basically *independent* capacities. So you might perfectly well learn that using the expression 'cat' is the way to refer to cats and yet have no idea that using the expression 'deciduous conifer' is the way to refer to deciduous conifers. Systematicity, like productivity, is the sort of property of cognitive capacities that you're likely to miss if you concentrate on the psychology of learning and searching lists.

There is, as we remarked, a straightforward (and quite traditional) argument from the systematicity of language capacity to the conclusion that sentences must have syntactic and semantic structure: If you assume that sentences are constructed out of words and phrases, and that many different sequences of words can be phrases of the same type, the very fact that one formula is a sentence of the language will often imply that other formulas must be too: in effect, systematicity follows from the postulation of constituent structure.

Suppose, for example, that it's a fact about English that formulas with the constituent analysis 'NP Vt NP' are well formed; and suppose that 'John' and 'the girl' are NPs and 'loves' is a Vt. It follows from these assumptions that 'John loves the girl,' 'John loves John,' 'the girl loves the girl,' and 'the girl loves John' must all be sentences. It follows too that anybody who has mastered the grammar of English must have linguistic capacities that are systematic in respect of these sentences; he *can't but* assume that all of them are sentences if he assumes that any of them are. Compare the situation on the view that the sentences of English are all atomic. There is then no structural analogy between 'John loves the girl' and 'the girl loves John' and hence no reason why understanding one sentence should imply understanding the other; no more than understanding 'rabbit' implies understanding 'tree'.[24]

On the view that the sentences are atomic, the systematicity of linguistic capacities is a mystery; on the view that they have constituent structure, the systematicity of linguistic capacities is what you would predict. So we should prefer the latter view to the former.

Notice that you can make this argument for constituent structure in sentences without idealizing to astronomical computational capacities. There are productivity arguments for constituent structure, but they're concerned with our ability—in principle—to understand sentences that are arbitrarily long. Systematicity, by contrast, appeals to premises that are much nearer home; such considerations as the ones mentioned above, that no speaker understands the form of words 'John loves the girl' except as he also understands the form of words 'the girl loves John'. The assumption that linguistic capacities are productive "in principle" is one that a Connectionist might refuse to grant. But that they are systematic *in fact* no one can plausibly deny.

We can now, finally, come to the point: the argument from the systematicity of linguistic capacities to constituent structure in sentences is quite clear. *But thought is systematic too,* so there is a precisely parallel argument from the systematicity of thought to syntactic and semantic structure in mental representations.

What does it mean to say that thought is systematic? Well, just as you don't find people who can understand the sentence 'John loves the girl' but not the sentence 'the girl loves John,' so too you don't find people who can *think the thought* that John loves the girl but can't think the thought that the girl loves John. Indeed, in the case of verbal organisms the systematicity of thought *follows from* the systematicity of language if you assume—as most psychologists do—that understanding a sentence involves entertaining the thought that it expresses; on that assumption, nobody *could* understand both the sentences about John and the girl unless he were able to think both the thoughts about John and the girl.

But now if the ability to think that John loves the girl is intrinsically connected to the ability to think that the girl loves John, that fact will somehow have to be explained. For a Representationalist (which, as we have seen, Connectionists are), the explanation is obvious: Entertaining thoughts requires being in representational states (i.e., it requires tokening mental representations). And, just as the systematicity of language shows that there must be structural relations between the sentence 'John loves the girl' and the sentence 'the girl loves John,' so the systematicity of thought shows that there must be structural relations between the mental representation that corresponds to the thought that John loves the girl and the mental representation that corresponds to the thought that the girl loves John;[25] namely, the two mental representations, like the two sentences, *must be made of the same parts.* But if this explanation is right (and there don't seem to be any others on offer), then mental representations have internal structure and there is a language of thought. So the architecture of the mind is not a Connectionist network.[26]

To summarize the discussion so far: Productivity arguments infer the internal structure of mental representations from the presumed fact that nobody has a *finite* intellectual competence. By contrast, systematicity arguments infer the internal structure of mental representations from the patent fact that nobody has a *punctate* intellectual competence. Just as you don't find linguistic capacities that consist of the ability to understand sixty-seven unrelated sentences, so too you don't find cognitive capacities that consist of the

---

[24] See Pinker (1984, Chapter 4) for evidence that children never go through a stage in which they distinguish between the internal structures of NPs depending on whether they are in subject or object position; i.e., the dialects that children speak are always systematic with respect to the syntactic structures that can appear in these positions.

[25] It may be worth emphasizing that the structural complexity of a mental representation is not the same thing as, and does *not* follow from, the structural complexity of its propositional content (i.e., of what we're calling "the thought that one has"). Thus, Connectionists and Classicists can agree to agree that *the thought that P&Q* is complex (and has the thought that *P* among its parts) while agreeing to disagree about whether mental representations have internal syntactic structure.

[26] These considerations throw further light on a proposal we discussed in Section 2. Suppose that the mental representation corresponding to the thought that John loves the girl is the feature vector {+*John-subject; +loves; +the-girl-object*} where '*John-subject*' and '*the-girl-object*' are atomic features; as such, they bear no more structural relation to '*John-object*' and '*the-girl-subject*' than they do to one another or to, say, '*has-a-handle*'. Since this theory recognizes no structural relation between '*John-subject*' and '*John-object*', it offers no reason why a representational system that provides the means to express one of these concepts should also provide the means to express the other. This treatment of role relations thus makes a mystery of the (presumed) fact that anybody who can entertain the thought that John loves the girl can also entertain the thought that the girl loves John (and, mutatis mutandis, that any natural language that can express the proposition that John loves the girl can also express the proposition that the girl loves John). This consequence of the proposal that role relations be handled by "role specific descriptors that represent the conjunction of an identity and a role" (Hinton, 1987) offers a particularly clear example of how failure to postulate internal structure in representations leads to failure to capture the systematicity of representation systems.

ability to think seventy-four unrelated thoughts. Our claim is that this isn't, in either case, an accident: A linguistic theory that allowed for the possibility of punctate languages would have gone not just wrong, but *very profoundly* wrong. And similarly for a cognitive theory that allowed for the possibility of punctate minds.

But perhaps not being punctate is a property only of the minds of language users; perhaps the representational capacities of infraverbal organisms do have just the kind of gaps that Connectionist models permit? A Connectionist might then claim that he can do everything "up to language" on the assumption that mental representations lack combinatorial syntactic and semantic structure. Everything up to language may not be everything, but it's a lot. (On the other hand, a lot may be a lot, but it isn't everything. Infraverbal cognitive architecture mustn't be so represented as to make the eventual acquisition of language in phylogeny and in ontogeny require a miracle.)

It is not, however, plausible that only the minds of verbal organisms are systematic. Think what it would mean for this to be the case. It would have to be quite usual to find, for example, animals capable of representing the state of affairs *a***R***b,* but incapable of representing the state of affairs *b***R***a.* Such animals would be, as it were, *a***R***b* sighted but *b***R***a* blind since, presumably, the representational capacities of its mind affect not just what an organism can think, but also what it can perceive. In consequence, such animals would be able to learn to respond selectively to *a***R***b* situations but quite *un*able to learn to respond selectively to *b***R***a* situations. (So that, though you could teach the creature to choose the picture with the square larger than the triangle, you couldn't for the life of you teach it to choose the picture with the triangle larger than the square.)

It is, to be sure, an empirical question whether the cognitive capacities of infraverbal organisms are often structured that way, but we're prepared to bet that they are not. Ethological cases are the exceptions that prove the rule. There *are* examples where salient environmental configurations act as 'gestalten'; and in such cases it's reasonable to doubt that the mental representation of the stimulus is complex. But the point is precisely that these cases are *exceptional;* they're exactly the ones where you expect that there will be some special story to tell about the ecological significance of the stimulus: that it's the shape of a predator, or the song of a conspecific ... etc. Conversely, when there is no such story to tell you expect structurally similar stimuli to elicit correspondingly similar cognitive capacities. That, surely, is the least that a respectable principle of stimulus generalization has got to require.

That infraverbal cognition is pretty generally systematic seems, in short, to be about as secure as any empirical premise in this area can be. And, as we've just seen, it's a

premise from which the inadequacy of Connectionist models as cognitive theories follows quite straightforwardly: as straightforwardly, in any event, as it would from the assumption that such capacities are generally productive.

3.3 Compositionality of representations
Compositionality is closely related to systematicity; perhaps they're best viewed as aspects of a single phenomenon. We will therefore follow much the same course here as in the preceding discussion: first we introduce the concept by recalling the standard arguments for the compositionality of natural languages. We then suggest that parallel arguments secure the compositionality of mental representations. Since compositionality requires combinatorial syntactic and semantic structure, the compositionality of thought is evidence that the mind is not a Connectionist network.

We said that the systematicity of linguistic competence consists in the fact that "the ability to produce/understand some of the sentences is intrinsically connected to the ability to produce/understand certain of the others". We now add that which sentences are systematically related is not arbitrary from a semantic point of view. For example, being able to understand 'John loves the girl' goes along with being able to understand 'the girl loves John', and there are correspondingly close semantic relations between these sentences: in order for the first to be true, John must bear to the girl the very same relation that the truth of the second requires the girl to bear to John. By contrast, there is no intrinsic connection between understanding either of the John/girl sentences and understanding semantically unrelated formulas like 'quarks are made of gluons' or 'the cat is on the mat' or '$2 + 2 = 4$'; it looks as though semantical relatedness and systematicity keep quite close company.

You might suppose that this covariance is covered by the same explanation that accounts for systematicity per se; roughly, that sentences that are systematically related are composed from the same syntactic constituents. But, in fact, you need a further assumption, which we'll call the 'principle of compositionality': insofar as a language is systematic, a lexical item must make approximately the same semantic contribution to each expression in which it occurs. It is, for example, only insofar as 'the', 'girl', 'loves' and 'John' make the same semantic contribution to 'John loves the girl' that they make to 'the girl loves John' that understanding the one sentence implies understanding the other. Similarity of constituent structure accounts for the semantic relatedness between systematically related sentences only to the extent that the semantical properties of the shared constituents are context-independent.

Here it's idioms that prove the rule; being able to understand 'the', 'man', 'kicked' and 'bucket' isn't much help with understanding 'the man kicked the bucket', since 'kicked' and 'bucket' don't bear their standard meanings in this context. And, just as you'd expect, 'the man kicked the bucket' is *not* systematic even with respect to syntactically closely related sentences like 'the man kicked over the bucket' (for that matter, it's not systematic with respect to the 'the man kicked the bucket' read literally).

It's uncertain exactly how compositional natural languages actually are (just as it's uncertain exactly how systematic they are). We suspect that the amount of context induced variation of lexical meaning is often overestimated because other sorts of context sensitivity are misconstrued as violations of compositionality. For example, the difference between 'feed the chicken' and 'chicken to eat' must involve an *animal/food* ambiguity in 'chicken' rather than a violation of compositionality since if the context 'feed the...' could *induce* (rather than select) the meaning *animal,* you would expect 'feed the veal', 'feed the pork' and the like.[27] Similarly, the difference between 'good book', 'good rest' and 'good fight' is probably not meaning shift but syncategorematicity. 'Good *NP*' means something like *NP that answers to the relevant interest in NPs:* a good book is one that answers to our interest in books (viz., it's good to read); a good rest is one that answers to our interest in rests (viz., it leaves one refreshed); a good fight is one that answers to our interest in fights (viz., it's fun to watch or to be in, or it clears the air); and so on. It's because the meaning of 'good' is syncategorematic and has a variable in it for relevant interests, that you can know that a good flurg is a flurg that answers to the relevant interest in flurgs without knowing what flurgs are or what the relevant interest in flurgs is (see Ziff, 1960).

In any event, the main argument stands: systematicity depends on compositionality, so to the extent that a natural language is systematic it must be compositional too. This illustrates another respect in which systematicity arguments can do the work for which productivity arguments have previously been employed. The traditional argument for compositionality is that it is required to explain how a finitely representable language can contain infinitely many nonsynonymous expressions.

Considerations about systematicity offer one argument for compositionality; considerations about entailment offer another. Consider predicates like '... is a brown cow'. This expression bears a straightforward semantical 'relation to the predicates '... is a cow' and '... is brown'; viz., that the first predicate is true of a thing if and only if both of the others are. That is, '... is a brown cow' severally entails '... is brown' and '... is a cow' and is entailed by their conjunction. Moreover—and this is important—this se-

---

[27] We are indebted to Steve Pinker for this point.

mantical pattern is not peculiar to the cases cited. On the contrary, it holds for a very large range of predicates (see '... is a red square,' '... is a funny old German soldier,' '... is a child prodigy;' and so forth).

How are we to account for these sorts of regularities? The answer seems clear enough; '... is a brown cow' entails '... is brown' because (a) the second expression is a constituent of the first; (b) the syntactical form '(adjective noun)$_N$' has (in many cases) the semantic force of a conjunction, and (c) 'brown' retains its semantical value under simplification of conjunction. Notice that you need (c) to rule out the possibility that 'brown' means *brown* when in it modifies a noun but (as it might be) *dead* when it's a predicate adjective; in which case '... is a brown cow' wouldn't entail '... is brown' after all. Notice too that (c) is just an application of the principle of composition.

So, here's the argument so far: you need to assume some degree of compositionality of English sentences to account for the fact that systematically related sentences are always semantically related; and to account for certain regular parallelisms between the syntactical structure of sentences and their entailments. So, beyond any serious doubt, the sentences of English must be compositional to some serious extent. But the principle of compositionality governs the semantic relations between words *and the expressions of which they are constituents.* So compositionality implies that (some) expressions *have* constituents. So compositionality argues for (specifically, presupposes) syntactic/semantic structure in sentences.

Now what about the compositionality of mental representations? There is, as you'd expect, a bridging argument based on the usual psycholinguistic premise that one uses language to express ones thoughts: Sentences are used to express thoughts; so if the ability to use some sentences is connected with the ability to use certain other, semantically related sentences, then the ability to think some thoughts must be correspondingly connected with the ability to think certain other, semantically related thoughts. But you can only think the thoughts that your mental representations can express. So, if the ability to think certain thoughts is interconnected, then the corresponding representational capacities must be interconnected too; specifically, the ability to be in some representational states must imply the ability to be in certain other, semantically related representational states.

But then the question arises: *how could* the mind be so arranged that the ability to be in one representational state is connected with the ability to be in others that are semantically nearby? What account of mental representation would have this consequence? The answer is just what you'd expect from the discussion of the linguistic material. Mental representations must have internal structure, just the way that sentences do. In particular, it must be that the mental representation that corresponds to the thought that John loves the girl contains, as its parts, the same constituents as the mental representation that corresponds to the thought that the girl loves John. That would explain why these thoughts are *systematically* related; *and, to the extent that the semantic value of these parts is context-independent, that would explain why these systematically related thoughts are also semantically related.* So, by this chain of argument, evidence for the compositionality of sentences is evidence for the compositionality of the representational states of speaker/hearers.

Finally, what about the compositionality of infraverbal thought? The argument isn't much different from the one that we've just run through. We assume that animal thought is largely systematic: the organism that can perceive (hence learn) that *a**R**b* can generally perceive (/learn) that *b**R**a*. But, systematically related thoughts (just like systematically related sentences) are generally semantically related too. It's no surprise that being able to learn that the triangle is above the square implies being able to learn that the square is above the triangle; whereas it would be *very* surprising if being able to learn the square/triangle facts implied being able to learn that quarks are made of gluons or that Washington was the first President of America.

So, then, what explains the correlation between systematic relations and semantic relations in infraverbal thought? Clearly, Connectionist models don't address this question; the fact that a network contains a node labelled X has, so far as the constraints imposed by Connectionist architecture are concerned, *no implications at all* for the labels of the other nodes in the network; in particular, it doesn't imply that there will be nodes that represent thoughts that are semantically close to X. This is just the semantical side of the fact that network architectures permit arbitrarily punctate mental lives.

But if, on the other hand, we make the usual Classicist assumptions (viz., that systematically related thoughts share constituents and that the semantic values of these shared constituents are context independent) the correlation between systematicity and semantic relatedness follows immediately. For a Classicist, this correlation is an 'architectural' property of minds; it couldn't but hold if mental representations have the general properties that Classical models suppose them to.

What have Connectionists to say about these matters? There is some textual evidence that they are tempted to deny the facts of compositionality wholesale. For example, Smolensky (1988) claims that: "Surely ... we would get quite a different representation of 'coffee' if we examined the difference between 'can with coffee' and 'can without coffee' or 'tree with coffee' and 'tree without coffee'; or

'man with coffee' and 'man without coffee' ... context insensitivity is not something we expect to be reflected in Connectionist representations ....".

It's certainly true that compositionality is not generally a feature of Connectionist representations. Connectionists can't acknowledge the facts of compositionality because they are committed to mental representations that don't have combinatorial structure. But to give up on compositionality is to take 'kick the bucket' as a model for the relation between syntax and semantics; and the consequence is, as we've seen, that you make the systematicity of language (and of thought) a mystery. On the other hand, to say that 'kick the bucket' is aberrant, and that the right model for the syntax/semantics relation is (e.g.) 'brown cow', is to start down a trail which leads, pretty inevitably, to acknowledging combinatorial structure in mental representation, hence to the rejection of Connectionist networks as cognitive models.

We don't think there's any way out of the need to acknowledge the compositionality of natural languages and of mental representations. However, it's been suggested (see Smolensky, op cit.) that while the principle of compositionality is false (because content isn't context invariant) there is nevertheless a "family resemblance" between the various meanings that a symbol has in the various contexts in which it occurs. Since such proposals generally aren't elaborated, it's unclear how they're supposed to handle the salient facts about systematicity and inference. But surely there are going to be serious problems. Consider, for example, such inferences as

(i) Turtles are slower than rabbits.

(ii) Rabbits are slower than Ferraris.

. . .

(iii) Turtles are slower than Ferraris.

The soundness of this inference appears to depend upon (a) the fact that the same relation (viz., *slower than*) holds between turtles and rabbits on the one hand, and rabbits and Ferraris on the other; and (b) the fact that that relation is transitive. If, however, it's assumed (contrary to the principle of compositionality) that 'slower than' means something different in premises (i) and (ii) (and presumably in (iii) as well)—so that, strictly speaking, the relation that holds between turtles and rabbits is *not* the same one that holds between rabbits and Ferraris—then it's hard to see why the inference should be valid.

Talk about the relations being 'similar' only papers over the difficulty since the problem is then to provide a notion of similarity that will guaranty that if (i) and (ii) are true, so too is (iii). And, so far at least, no such notion of similarity has been forthcoming. Notice that it won't do to require just that the relations all be similar in respect of their *transitivity,* i.e., that they all be transitive. On that account, the argument from 'turtles are slower than rabbits' and 'rabbits are furrier than Ferraris' to 'turtles are slower than Ferraris' would be valid since 'furrier than' is transitive too.

Until these sorts of issues are attended to, the proposal to replace the compositional principle of context invariance with a notion of "approximate equivalence ... across contexts" (Smolensky, 1988) doesn't seem to be much more than hand waving.

3.4 The systematicity of inference

In Section 2 we saw that, according to Classical theories, the syntax of mental representations mediates between their semantic properties and their causal role in mental processes. Take a simple case: It's a 'logical' principle that conjunctions entail their constituents (so the argument from $P\&Q$ to P and to Q is valid); Correspondingly, it's a psychological law that thoughts that $P\&Q$ tend to cause thoughts that P and thoughts that Q all else being equal. Classical theory exploits the constituent structure of mental representations to account for both these facts, the first by assuming that the combinatorial semantics of mental representations is sensitive to their syntax and the second by assuming that mental processes apply to mental representations in virtue of their constituent structure.

A consequence of these assumptions is that Classical theories are committed to the following striking prediction: inferences that are of similar logical type ought, pretty generally,[28] to elicit correspondingly similar cognitive capacities. You shouldn't, for example, find a kind of mental life in which you get inferences from $P\&Q\&R$ to P but you don't get inferences from $P\&Q$ to P. This is because, according to the Classical account, this logically homogeneous class of inferences is carried out by a correspondingly homogeneous class of psychological mechanisms: The premises of both inferences are expressed by mental representations that satisfy the same syntactic analysis (viz., $S_1\&S_2\&S_3\& \ldots S_n$); and the process of drawing the inference corresponds, in both cases, to the same formal operation of detaching the constituent that expresses the conclusion.

The idea that organisms should exhibit similar cognitive capacities in respect of logically similar inferences is so natural that it may seem unavoidable. But, on the contrary: there's nothing in principle to preclude a kind of cognitive

model in which inferences that are quite similar from the logician's point of view are nevertheless computed by quite different mechanisms; or in which some inferences of a given logical type are computed and other inferences of the same logical type are not. Consider, in particular, the Connectionist account. A Connectionist can certainly model a mental life in which, if you can reason from $P\&Q\&R$ to P, then you can also reason from $P\&Q$ to P. For example, the network in (Figure 3) would do:

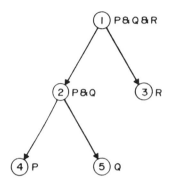

Figure 3 A possible Connectionist network which draws inferences from $P\&Q\&R$ to P and also draws inferences from $P\&Q$ to P.

But notice that *a Connectionist can equally model a mental life in which you get one of these inferences and not the other.* In the present case, since there is no structural relation between the $P\&Q\&R$ node and the $P\&Q$ node (remember, all nodes are atomic; don't be misled by the node *labels*) there's no reason why a mind that contains the first should also contain the second, or vice versa. Analogously, there's no reason why you shouldn't get minds that simplify the premise *John loves Mary and Bill hates Mary* but no others; or minds that simplify premises with 1, 3, or 5 conjuncts, but don't simplify premises with 2, 4, or 6 conjuncts; or, for that matter, minds that simplify only premises that were acquired on Tuesdays . . . etc.

In fact, the Connectionist architecture is *utterly indifferent* as among these possibilities. That's because it recognizes no notion of syntax according to which thoughts that are alike in inferential role (e.g., thoughts that are all subject to simplification of conjunction) are expressed by mental representations of correspondingly similar syntactic form (e.g., by mental representations that are all syntactically conjunctive). So, the Connectionist architecture tolerates gaps in cognitive capacities; it has no mechanism to enforce the requirement that logically homogeneous inferences should be executed by correspondingly homogeneous computational processes.

But, we claim, you don't find cognitive capacities that have these sorts of gaps. You don't, for example, get minds that are prepared to infer *John went to the store* from *John*

---

[28]The hedge is meant to exclude cases where inferences of the same logical type nevertheless differ in complexity in virtue of, for example, the length of their premises. The inference from $(A\lor B\lor C\lor D\lor E)$ and $(-B \& -C \& -D \& -E)$ to A is of the same logical type as the inference from $A\lor B$ and $-B$ to A. But it wouldn't be very surprising, or very interesting, if there were minds that could handle the second inference but not the first.

and Mary and Susan and Sally went to the store and from *John and Mary went to the store* but not from *John and Mary and Susan went to the store*. Given a notion of logical syntax—the very notion that the Classical theory of mentation requires to get its account of mental processes off the ground—it is a *truism* that you don't get such minds. Lacking a notion of logical syntax, it is a *mystery* that you don't.

3.5 Summary

It is perhaps obvious by now that all the arguments that we've been reviewing—the argument from systematicity, the argument from compositionality, and the argument from influential coherence—are really much the same: If you hold the kind of theory that acknowledges structured representations, it must perforce acknowledge representations with *similar* or *identical* structures. In the linguistic cases, constituent analysis implies a taxonomy of sentences by their syntactic form, and in the inferential cases, it implies a taxonomy of arguments by their logical form. So, if your theory also acknowledges mental processes that are structure sensitive, then it will predict that similarly structured representations will generally play similar roles in thought. A theory that says that the sentence 'John loves the girl' is made out of the same parts as the sentence 'the girl loves John', and made by applications of the same rules of composition, will have to go out of its way to explain a linguistic competence which embraces one sentence but not the other. And similarly, if a theory says that the mental representation that corresponds to the thought that *P&Q&R* has the same (conjunctive) syntax as the mental representation that corresponds to the thought that *P&Q* and that mental processes of drawing inferences subsume mental representations in virtue of their syntax, it will have to go out of its way to explain inferential capacities which embrace the one thought but not the other. Such a competence would be, at best, an embarrassment for the theory, and at worst a refutation.

By contrast, since the Connectionist architecture recognizes no combinatorial structure in mental representations, gaps in cognitive competence should proliferate arbitrarily. It's not just that you'd expect to get them from time to time; it's that, on the 'no-structure' story, *gaps are the unmarked case*. It's the *systematic* competence that the theory is required to treat as an embarrassment. But, as a matter of fact, inferential competences are *blatantly* systematic. So there must be something deeply wrong with Connectionist architecture.

What's deeply wrong with Connectionist architecture is this: Because it acknowledges neither syntactic nor semantic structure in mental representations, it perforce treats them not as a generated set but as a list. But lists, qua lists,

have no structure; any collection of items is a possible list. And, correspondingly, on Connectionist principles, any collection of (causally connected) representational states is a possible mind. So, as far as Connectionist architecture is concerned, there is nothing to prevent minds that are arbitrarily unsystematic. But that result is *preposterous*. Cognitive capacities come in structurally related clusters; their systematicity is pervasive. All the evidence suggests that *punctate minds can't happen*. This argument seemed conclusive against the Connectionism of Hebb, Osgood and Hull twenty or thirty years ago. So far as we can tell, nothing of any importance has happened to change the situation in the meantime.[29]

A final comment to round off this part of the discussion. It's possible to imagine a Connectionist being prepared to admit that while systematicity doesn't *follow from*—and hence is not explained by—Connectionist architecture, it is nonetheless *compatible* with that architecture. It is, after all, perfectly possible to follow a policy of building networks that have *a**R**b* nodes only if they have *b**R**a* nodes ... etc. There is therefore nothing to stop a Connectionist from stipulating—as an independent postulate of his theory of mind—that all biologically instantiated networks are, de facto, systematic.

But this misses a crucial point: It's not enough just to stipulate systematicity; one is also required to specify a mechanism that is able to enforce the stipulation. To put it another way, it's not enough for a Connectionist to agree that all minds are systematic; he must also explain *how nature contrives to produce only systematic minds*. Presumably there would have to be some sort of mechanism, over and above the ones that Connectionism per se posits,

---

[29]Historical footnote: Connectionists are Associationists, but not every Associationist holds that mental representations must be unstructured. Hume didn't, for example. Hume thought that mental representations are rather like pictures, and pictures typically have a compositional semantics: the parts of a picture of a horse are generally pictures of horse parts.

On the other hand, allowing a compositional semantics for mental representations doesn't do an Associationist much good so long as he is true to this spirit of his Associationism. The virtue of having mental representations with structure is that it allows for structure sensitive operations to be defined over them; specifically, it allows for the sort of operations that eventuate in productivity and systematicity. Association is not, however, such an operation; all *it* can do is build an internal model of redundancies in experience by altering the probabilities of transitions among mental states. So far as the problems of productivity and systematicity are concerned, an Associationist who acknowledges structured representations is in the position of having the can but not the opener.

Hume, in fact, cheated; he allowed himself not just Association but also "Imagination", which he takes to be an 'active' faculty that can produce new concepts out of old parts by a process of analysis and recombination. (The idea of a unicorn is pieced together out of the idea of a horse and the idea of a horn, for example.) Qua associationist Hume had, of course, no right to active mental faculties. But allowing imagination in gave Hume precisely what modern Connectionists don't have: an answer to the question how mental processes can be productive. The moral is that if you've got structured representations, the temptation to postulate structure sensitive operations and an executive to apply them is practically irresistible.

the functioning of which insures the systematicity of biologically instantiated networks; a mechanism such that, in virtue of its operation, every network that has an *a***R***b* node also has a *b***R***a* node ... and so forth. There are, however, no proposals for such a mechanism. Or, rather, there is just one: The only mechanism that is known to be able to produce pervasive systematicity is Classical architecture. And, as we have seen, Classical architecture is not compatible with Connectionism since it requires internally structured representations.

4 The lure of Connectionism

The current popularity of the Connectionist approach among psychologists and philosophers is puzzling in view of the sorts of problems raised above; problems which were largely responsible for the development of a syntax-based (proof theoretic) notion of computation and a Turing-style, symbol-processing notion of cognitive architecture in the first place. There are, however, a number of apparently plausible arguments, repeatedly encountered in the literature, that stress certain limitations of conventional computers as models of brains. These may be seen as favoring the Connectionist alternative. We will sketch a number of these before discussing the general problems which they appear to raise.

• *Rapidity of cognitive processes in relation to neural speeds: the "hundred step" constraint.* It has been observed (e.g., Feldman & Ballard, 1982) that the time required to execute computer instructions is in the order of nanoseconds, whereas neurons take tens of milliseconds to fire. Consequently, in the time it takes people to carry out many of the tasks at which they are fluent (like recognizing a word or a picture, either of which may require considerably less than a second) a *serial* neurally-instantiated program would only be able to carry out about 100 instructions. Yet such tasks might typically require many thousands—or even millions—of instructions in present-day computers (if they can be done at all). Thus, it is argued, the brain must operate quite differently from computers. In fact, the argument goes, the brain must be organized in a highly parallel manner ("massively parallel" is the preferred term of art).

• *Difficulty of achieving large-capacity pattern recognition and content-based retrieval in conventional architectures.* Closely related to the issues about time constraints is the fact that humans can store and make use of an enormous amount of information—apparently without effort (Fahlman & Hinton, 1987). One particularly dramatic skill that people exhibit is the ability to recognize patterns from among tens or even hundreds of thousands of alternatives (e.g., word or face recognition). In fact, there is reason to

believe that many expert skills may be based on large, fast recognition memories (see Simon & Chase, 1973). If one had to search through one's memory serially, the way conventional computers do, the complexity would overwhelm any machine. Thus, the knowledge that people have must be stored and retrieved differently from the way conventional computers do it.

• *Conventional computer models are committed to a different etiology for "rule-governed" behavior and "exceptional" behavior.* Classical psychological theories, which are based on conventional computer ideas, typically distinguish between mechanisms that cause regular and divergent behavior by postulating systems of explicit unconscious rules to explain the former, and then attributing departures from these rules to secondary (performance) factors. Since the divergent behaviors occur very frequently, a better strategy would be to try to account for both types of behavior in terms of the same mechanism.

• *Lack of progress in dealing with processes that are nonverbal or intuitive.* Most of our fluent cognitive skills do not consist in accessing verbal knowledge or carrying out deliberate conscious reasoning (Fahlman & Hinton, 1987; Smolensky, 1988). We appear to know many things that we would have great difficulty in describing verbally, including how to ride a bicycle, what our close friends look like, and how to recall the name of the President, etc. Such knowledge, it is argued, must not be stored in linguistic form, but in some other "implicit" form. The fact that conventional computers typically operate in a "linguistic mode", inasmuch as they process information by operating on syntactically structured expressions, may explain why there has been relatively little success in modeling implicit knowledge.

• *Acute sensitivity of conventional architectures to damage and noise.* Unlike digital circuits, brain circuits must tolerate noise arising from spontaneous neural activity. Moreover, they must tolerate a moderate degree of damage without failing completely. With a few notable exceptions, if a part of the brain is damaged, the degradation in performance is usually not catastrophic but varies more or less gradually with the extent of the damage. This is especially true of memory. Damage to the temporal cortex (usually thought to house memory traces) does not result in selective loss of particular facts and memories. This and similar facts about brain damaged patients suggests that human memory representations, and perhaps many other cognitive skills as well, are *distributed* spatially, rather than being neurally localized. This appears to contrast with conventional computers, where hierarchical-style control keeps the crucial decisions highly localized and where memory storage consists of an array of location-addressable registers.

• *Storage in conventional architectures is passive.* Conventional computers have a passive memory store which is accessed in what has been called a "fetch and execute cycle". This appears to be quite unlike human memory. For example, according to Kosslyn and Hatfield (1984, pp. 1022, 1029):

In computers the memory is static: once an entry is put in a given location, it just sits there until it is operated upon by the CPU.... But consider a very simple experiment: Imagine a letter *A* over and over again ... then switch to the letter *B*. In a model employing a von Neumann architecture the 'fatigue' that inhibited imaging the *A* would be due to some quirk in the way the CPU executes a given instruction .... Such fatigue should generalize to all objects imaged because the routine responsible for imaging was less effective. But experiments have demonstrated that this is not true: specific objects become more difficult to image, not all objects. This finding is more easily explained by an analogy to the way invisible ink fades of its own accord ... with invisible ink, the representation itself is doing something—there is no separate processor working over it... .

• *Conventional rule-based systems depict cognition as "all-or-none"*. But cognitive skills appear to be characterized by various kinds of continuities. For example:

• *Continuous variation in degree of applicability of different principles,* or in the degree of relevance of different constraints, "rules", or procedures. There are frequent cases (especially in perception and memory retrieval), in which it appears that a variety of different constraints are brought to bear on a problem simultaneously and the outcome is a combined effect of all the different factors (see, for example, the informal discussion by McClelland, Rumelhart & Hinton, 1986, pp. 3–9). That's why "constraint propagation" techniques are receiving a great deal of attention in artificial intelligence (see Mackworth, 1987).

• *Nondeterminism of human behavior:* Cognitive processes are never rigidly determined or precisely replicable. Rather, they appear to have a significant random or stochastic component. Perhaps that's because there is randomness at a microscopic level, caused by irrelevant biochemical or electrical activity or perhaps even by quantum mechanical events. To model this activity by rigid deterministic rules can only lead to poor predictions because it ignores the fundamentally stochastic nature of the underlying mechanisms. Moreover, deterministic, all-or-none models will be unable to account for the gradual aspect of learning and skill acquisition.

• *Failure to display graceful degradation.* When humans are unable to do a task perfectly, they nonetheless do something reasonable. If the particular task does not fit exactly into some known pattern, or if it is only partly understood, a person will not give up or produce nonsensical behavior. By contrast, if a Classical rule-based computer program fails to recognize the task, or fails to match a pattern to its stored representations or rules, it usually will be unable to do anything at all. This suggests that in order to display graceful degradation, we must be able to represent prototypes, match patterns, recognize problems, etc., in various *degrees*.

• *Conventional models are dictated by current technical features of computers and take little or no account of the facts of neuroscience.* Classical symbol processing systems provide no indication of how the kinds of processes that they postulate could be realized by a brain. The fact that this gap between high-level systems and brain architecture is so large might be an indication that these models are on the wrong track. Whereas the architecture of the mind has evolved under the pressures of natural selection, some of the Classical assumptions about the mind may derive from features that computers have only because they are explicitly designed for the convenience of programmers. Perhaps this includes even the assumption that the description of mental processes at the cognitive level can be divorced from the description of their physical realization. At a minimum, by building our models to take account of what is known about neural structures we may reduce the risk of being misled by metaphors based on contemporary computer architectures.

Replies: Why the usual reasons given for preferring a Connectionist architecture are invalid

It seems to us that, as arguments against Classical cognitive architecture, all these points suffer from one or other of the following two defects.

1. The objections depend on properties that are not in fact intrinsic to Classical architectures, since there can be perfectly natural Classical models that don't exhibit the objectionable features. (We believe this to be true, for example, of the arguments that Classical rules are explicit and Classical operations are 'all or none'.)

2. The objections are true of Classical architectures insofar as they are implemented on current computers, but need not be true of such architectures when differently (e.g., neurally) implemented. They are, in other words, directed at the implementation level rather than the cognitive level, as these were distinguished in our earlier discussion. (We believe that this is true, for example, of the arguments about speed, resistance to damage and noise, and the passivity of memory.)

In the remainder of this section we will expand on these two points and relate them to some of the arguments presented above. Following this analysis, we will present what we believe may be the most tenable view of Connectionism; namely that it is a theory of how (Classical) cognitive systems might be implemented, either in real brains or in some 'abstract neurology'.

Parallel computation and the issue of speed

Consider the argument that cognitive processes must involve large scale parallel computation. In the form that it takes in typical Connectionist discussions, this issue is irrelevant to the adequacy of Classical *cognitive* architecture. The "hundred step constraint", for example, is clearly directed at the implementation level. All it rules out is the (absurd) hypothesis that cognitive architectures are implemented in the brain in the same way as they are implemented on electronic computers.

If you ever have doubts about whether a proposal pertains to the implementation level or the symbolic level, a useful heuristic is to ask yourself whether what is being claimed is true of a conventional computer—such as the DEC VAX—at *its* implementation level. Thus although most algorithms that run on the VAX are serial,[30] at the implementation level such computers are 'massively parallel'; they quite literally involve simultaneous electrical activity throughout almost the entire device. For example, every memory access cycle involves pulsing every bit in a significant fraction of the system's memory registers— since memory access is essentially a destructive read and rewrite process, the system clock regularly pulses and activates most of the central processing unit, and so on.

The moral is that the absolute speed of a process is a property *par excellence* of its implementation. (By contrast, the *relative* speed with which a system responds to different inputs is often diagnostic of distinct processes; but this has always been a prime empirical basis for deciding among alternative algorithms in information processing psychology). Thus, the fact that individual neurons require tens of milliseconds to fire can have no bearing on the predicted speed at which an algorithm will run *unless there is at least a partial, independently motivated, theory of how the operations of the functional architecture are implemented in neurons*. Since, in the case of the brain, it is not even certain that the firing[31] of neurons is invariably the relevant implementation property (at least for higher level

cognitive processes like learning and memory) the 100 step "constraint" excludes nothing.

Finally, absolute constraints on the number of serial steps that a mental process can require, or on the time that can be required to execute them, provide weak arguments against Classical architecture because Classical architecture in no way excludes parallel execution of multiple symbolic processes. Indeed, it seems extremely likely that many Classical symbolic processes are going on in parallel in cognition, and that these processes interact with one another (e.g., they may be involved in some sort of symbolic constraint propagation). Operating on symbols can even involve "massively parallel" organizations; that might indeed imply new architectures, but they are all *Classical* in our sense, since they all share the Classical conception of computation as symbol-processing. (For examples of serious and interesting proposals on organizing Classical processors into large parallel networks, see Hewett's, 1977, *Actor* system, Hillis', 1985, "Connection Machine", as well as any of a number of recent commercial multi-processor machines.) The point here is that an argument for a network of parallel computers is not in and of itself either an argument against a Classical architecture or an argument for a Connectionist architecture.

Resistance to noise and physical damage (and the argument for distributed representation)

Some of the other advantages claimed for Connectionist architectures over Classical ones are just as clearly aimed at the implementation level. For example, the "resistance to physical damage" criterion is so obviously a matter of implementation that it should hardly arise in discussions of cognitive-level theories.

It is true that a certain kind of damage-resistance appears to be incompatible with localization, and it is also true that representations in PDP's are distributed over groups of units (at least when "coarse coding" is used). But distribution over units achieves damage-resistance only if it entails that representations are also *neurally* distributed.[32] However, neural distribution of representations is just as com-

---

[30] Even in the case of a conventional computer, whether it should be viewed as executing a serial or a parallel algorithm depends on what 'virtual machine' is being considered in the case in question. After all, a VAX *can* be used to simulate (i.e., to implement) a virtual machine with a parallel architecture. In that case the relevant algorithm would be a parallel one.

[31] There are, in fact, a number of different mechanisms of neural interaction (e.g., the "local interactions" described by Rakic, 1975). Moreover, a large number of chemical processes take place at the dendrites, covering a wide range of time scales, so even if dendritic transmission were the only relevant mechanism, we still wouldn't know what time scale to use as our estimate of neural action in general (see, for example, Black, 1986).

[32] Unless the 'units' in a Connectionist network really are assumed to have different spatially-focused loci in the brain, talk about distributed representation is likely to be extremely misleading. In particular, if units are merely *functionally* individuated, any amount of distribution or functional entities is compatible with any amount of spatial compactness of their neural representations. But it is not clear that units do, in fact, correspond to any anatomically identifiable locations in the brain. In the light of the way Connectionist mechanisms are designed, it may be appropriate to view units and links as functional/mathematical entities (what psychologists would call "hypothetical constructs") whose neurological interpretation remains entirely open. (This is, in fact, the view that some Connectionists take; see Smolensky, 1988.) The point is that distribution over mathematical constructs does not buy you damage resistance; only *neural* distribution does!

patible with Classical architectures as it is with Connectionist networks. In the Classical case all you need are memory registers that distribute their contents over physical space. You can get that with fancy storage systems like optical ones, or chemical ones, or even with registers made of Connectionist nets. Come to think of it, we already had it in the old style "ferrite core" memories!

The physical requirements of a Classical symbol-processing system are easily misunderstood. (Confounding of physical and functional properties is widespread in psychological theorizing in general; for a discussion of this confusion in relation to metrical properties in models of mental imagery, see Pylyshyn 1981.) For example, conventional architecture requires that there be distinct symbolic expressions for each state of affairs that it can represent. Since such expressions often have a structure consisting of concatenated parts, the adjacency relation must be instantiated by *some* physical relation when the architecture is implemented (see the discussion in footnote 9). However, since the relation to be physically realized is *functional* adjacency, there is no necessity that physical instantiations of adjacent symbols be *spatially* adjacent. Similarly, although complex expressions are made out of atomic elements, and the distinction between atomic and complex symbols must somehow be physically instantiated, there is no necessity that a token of an atomic symbol be assigned a smaller region in space than a token of a complex symbol; even a token of a complex symbol of which it is a constituent. In Classical architectures, as in Connectionist networks, functional elements can be physically distributed or localized to any extent whatever. In a VAX (to use our heuristic again) pairs of symbols may certainly be functionally adjacent, but the symbol tokens are nonetheless spatially spread through many locations in physical memory.

In short, the fact that a property (like the position of a symbol within an expression) is functionally local has no implications one way or the other for damage-resistance or noise tolerance unless the functional-neighborhood metric corresponds to some appropriate *physical* dimension. When that is the case, we may be able to predict adverse consequences that varying the physical property has on objects localized in functional space (e.g., varying the voltage or line frequency might damage the left part of an expression). But, of course, the situation is exactly the same for Connectionist systems: even when they are resistant to spatially-local damage, they may not be resistant to damage that is local along some other physical dimensions. Since spatially-local damage is particularly frequent in real world traumas, this may have important practical consequences. But so long as our knowledge of how cognitive processes might be mapped onto brain tissue remains very

nearly nonexistent, its message for cognitive science remains moot.

"Soft" constraints, continuous magnitudes, stochastic mechanisms, and active symbols

The notion that "soft" constraints which can vary continuously (as degree of activation does), are incompatible with Classical rule-based symbolic systems is another example of the failure to keep the psychological (or symbol-processing) and the implementation levels separate. One can have a Classical rule system in which the decision concerning which rule will fire resides in the functional architecture and depends on continuously varying magnitudes. Indeed, this is typically how it is done in practical "expert systems" which, for example, use a Bayesian mechanism in their production-system rule-interpreter. The soft or stochastic nature or rule-based processes arises from the interaction of deterministic rules with real-valued properties of the implementation, or with noisy inputs or noisy information transmission.

It should also be noted that rule applications need not issue in "all or none" behaviors since several rules may be activated at once and can have interactive effects on the outcome. Or, alternatively, each of the activated rules can generate independent parallel effects, which might get sorted out later—depending say, on which of the parallel streams reaches a goal first. An important, though sometimes neglected point about such aggregate properties of overt behavior as continuity, "fuzziness", randomness, etc., is that they need not arise from underlying mechanisms that are themselves fuzzy, continuous or random. It is not only possible in principle, but often quite reasonable in practice, to assume that apparently variable or non-deterministic behavior arises from the interaction of multiple deterministic sources.

A similar point can be made about the issue of "graceful degradation". Classical architecture does not require that when the conditions for applying the available rules aren't precisely met, the process should simply fail to do anything at all. As noted above, rules could be activated in some measure depending upon how close their conditions are to holding. Exactly what happens in these cases may depend on how the rule-system is implemented. On the other hand, it could be that the failure to display "graceful degradation" really is an intrinsic limit of the current class of models or even of current approaches to designing intelligent systems. It seems clear that the psychological models now available are inadequate over a broad spectrum of measures, so their problems with graceful degradation may be a special case of their general unintelligence: They may simply not be smart enough to know what to do when a limited stock of methods fails to apply. But this needn't be a principled limitation of Classical architectures: There is, to our knowledge, no reason to believe that something like Newell's (1969) "hierarchy of weak methods" or Laird, Rosenberg and Newell's (1986) "universal subgoaling", is in principle incapable of dealing with the problem of graceful degradation. (Nor, to our knowledge, has any argument yet been offered that Connectionist architectures are in principle capable of dealing with it. In fact current Connectionist models are every bit as graceless in their modes of failure as ones based on Classical architectures. For example, contrary to some claims, models such as that of McClelland and Kawamoto, 1986, fail quite unnaturally when given incomplete information.)

In short, the Classical theorist can view stochastic properties of behavior as emerging from interactions between the model and the intrinsic properties of the physical medium in which it is realized. It is essential to remember that, from the Classical point of view, overt behavior is par excellence an interaction effect, and symbol manipulations are supposed to be only one of the interacting causes.

These same considerations apply to Kosslyn and Hatfield's remarks (quoted earlier) about the commitment of Classical models to 'passive' versus 'active' representations. It is true, as Kosslyn and Hatfield say, that the representations that von Neumann machines manipulate 'don't *do* anything' until a CPU operates upon them (they don't decay, for example). But, even on the absurd assumption that the mind has *exactly* the architecture of some contemporary (Von Neumann) computer, it is obvious that its behavior, and hence the behavior of an organism, is determined not just by the logical machine that the mind instantiates, but also by the protoplasmic machine in which the logic is realized. Instantiated representations *are* therefore bound to be active, even according to Classical models; the question is whether the kind of activity they exhibit should be accounted for by the cognitive model or by the theory of its implementation. This question is empirical and must not be begged on behalf of the Connectionist view. (As it is, for example, in such passages as "The brain itself does not manipulate symbols; the brain is the medium in which the symbols are floating and in which they trigger each other. There is no central manipulator, no central program. There is simply a vast collection of 'teams'—patterns of neural firings that, like teams of ants, trigger other patterns of neural firings .... We feel those symbols churning within ourselves in somewhat the same way we feel our stomach churning." (Hofstadter, 1983, p. 279). This appears to be a serious case of *Formicidae in machina*: ants in the stomach of the ghost in the machine.)

Explicitness of rules

According to McClelland, Feldman, Adelson, Bower, and McDermott (1986, p. 6), ". . . Connectionist models are leading to a reconceptualization of key psychological issues, such as the nature of the representation of knowledge ... . One traditional approach to such issues treats knowledge as a body of rules that are consulted by processing mechanisms in the course of processing; in Connectionist models, such knowledge is represented, often in widely distributed form, in the connections among the processing units."

As we remarked in the Introduction, we think that the claim that most psychological processes are rule-implicit, and the corresponding claim that divergent and compliant behaviors result from the same cognitive mechanisms, are both interesting and tendentious. We regard these matters as entirely empirical and, in many cases, open. In any case, however, one should not confuse the rule-implicit/rule-explicit distinction with the distinction between Classical and Connectionist architecture.[33]

This confusion is just ubiquitous in the Connectionist literature: it is universally assumed by Connectionists that Classical models are committed to claiming that regular behaviors must arise from explicitly encoded rules. But this is simply untrue. Not only is there no reason why Classical models are required to be rule-explicit but—as a matter of fact—arguments over which, if any, rules are explicitly mentally represented have raged for decades *within* the Classicist camp. (See, for relatively recent examples, the discussion of the explicitness of grammatical rules in Stabler, 1985, and replies; for a philosophical discussion, see Cummins, 1983.) The one thing that Classical theorists do agree about is that it *can't* be that *all* behavioral regularities are determined by explicit rules; at least some of the causal determinants of compliant behavior *must* be *im*plicit. (The

---

[33] An especially flagrant example of how issues about architecture get confused with issues about the explicitness of rules in the Connectionist literature occurs in PDP, Chapter 4, where Rumelhart and McClelland argue that PDP models provide "... a rather plausible account of how we can come to have innate 'knowledge'. To the extent that stored knowledge is assumed to be in the form of explicit, inaccessible rules ... it is hard to see how it could 'get into the head' of the newborn. It seems to us implausible that the newborn possesses elaborate symbol systems and the systems for interpreting them required to put these explicit, inaccessible rules to use in guiding behavior. On our account, we do not need to attribute such complex machinery. If the innate knowledge is simply the prewired connections, it is encoded from the start in just the right way to be of use by the processing mechanisms." (p. 42). A priorizing about what it does and doesn't seem likely that newborns possess strikes us as a bad way to do developmental cognitive psychology. But Rumelhart and McClelland's argument is doubly beside the point since a Classicist who shares their prejudices can perfectly well avail himself of the same solution that they endorse. Classical architecture does *not* require "complex machinery" for "interpreting" explicit rules since classical machines do not *require* explicit rules at all. Classical architecture is therefore *neutral* on the Empiricism/Nativism issue (and so is Connectionism, as Rumelhart and McClelland elsewhere correctly remark).

arguments for this parallel Lewis Carroll's observations in "What the Tortoise Said to Achilles"; see Carroll 1956.) All other questions of the explicitness of rules are viewed by Classicists as moot; and every shade of opinion on the issue can be found in the Classicist camp.

The basic point is this: not all the functions of a Classical computer can be encoded in the form of an explicit program; some of them must be wired in. In fact, the entire program can be hard-wired in cases where it does not need to modify or otherwise examine itself. In such cases, Classical machines can be *rule implicit* with respect to their programs, and the mechanism of their state transitions is entirely subcomputational (i.e., subsymbolic).

What *does* need to be explicit in a Classical machine is not its program but the symbols that it writes on its tapes (or stores in its registers). These, however, correspond not to the machine's rules of state transition but to its data structures. Data structures are *the objects that the machine transforms, not the rules of transformation*. In the case of programs that parse natural language, for example, Classical architecture requires the explicit representation of the structural descriptions of sentences, but is entirely neutral on the explicitness of grammars, contrary to what many Connectionists believe.

One of the important inventions in the history of computers—the stored-program computer—makes it *possible* for programs to take on the role of data structures. But nothing in the architecture *requires* that they always do so. Similarly, Turing demonstrated that there exists an abstract machine (the so-called Universal Turing Machine) which can simulate the behavior of any target (Turing) machine. A Universal machine is "rule-explicit" about the machine it is simulating (in the sense that it has an explicit representation of that machine which is sufficient to specify its behavior uniquely). Yet the target machine can perfectly well be "rule-implicit" with respect to the rules that govern *its* behavior.

So, then, you can't attack Classical theories of cognitive architecture by showing that a cognitive process is rule-implicit; Classical architecture *permits* rule-explicit processes but does *not* require them. However, you *can* attack Connectionist architectures by showing that a cognitive process is rule *explicit* since, by definition, Connectionist architecture precludes the sorts of logico-syntactic capacities that are required to encode rules and the sorts of executive mechanisms that are required to apply them.[34]

[34]Of course, it *is* possible to simulate a "rule explicit process" in a Connectionist network by first implementing a Classical architecture in the network. The slippage between networks as architectures and as implementations is ubiquitous in Connectionist writings, as we remarked above.

If, therefore, there should prove to be persuasive arguments for rule explicit cognitive processes, that would be very embarrassing for Connectionists. A natural place to look for such arguments would be in the theory of the acquisition of cognitive competences. For example, much traditional work in linguistics (see Prince & Pinker, 1988) and all recent work in mathematical learning theory (see Osherson, Stov, & Weinstein, 1984), assumes that the characteristic output of a cognitive acquisition device is a recursive rule system (a grammar, in the linguistic case). Suppose such theories prove to be well-founded; then that would be incompatible with the assumption that the cognitive architecture of the capacities acquired is Connectionist.

On "Brain style" modeling

The relation of Connectionist models to neuroscience is open to many interpretations. On the one hand, people like Ballard (1986), and Sejnowski (1981), are explicitly attempting to build models based on properties of neurons and neural organizations, even though the neuronal units in question are idealized (some would say more than a little idealized: see, for example the commentaries following the Ballard, 1986, paper). On the other hand, Smolensky (1988) views Connectionist units as mathematical objects which can be given an interpretation in either neural or psychological terms. Most Connectionists find themselves somewhere in between, frequently referring to their approach as "brain-style" theorizing.[35]

Understanding both psychological principles *and* the way that they are neurophysiologically implemented is much better (and, indeed, more empirically secure) than only understanding one or the other. That is not at issue. The question is whether there is anything to be gained by designing "brain style" models that are uncommitted about how the models map onto brains.

Presumably the point of "brain style" modeling is that theories of cognitive processing should be influenced by the facts of biology (especially neuroscience). The biological facts that influence Connectionist models appear to include the following: neuronal connections are important to the patterns of brain activity; the memory "engram" does not appear to be spatially local; to a first approximation, neurons appear to be threshold elements which sum the activity arriving at their dendrites; many of the neurons in

[35]The PDP Research Group views its goal as being "to replace the 'computer metaphor' as a model of the mind with the 'brain metaphor' ..." (Rumelhart & McClelland, 1986a, Ch. 6, p.75). But the issue is not at all which metaphor we should adopt; metaphors (whether 'computer' or 'brain') tend to be a license to take one's claims as something less than serious hypotheses. As Pylyshyn (1984a) points out, the claim that the mind has the architecture of a Classical computer is not a metaphor but a literal empirical hypothesis.

the cortex have multidimension "receptive fields" that are sensitive to a narrow range of values of a number of parameters; the tendency for activity at a synapse to cause a neuron to "fire" is modulated by the frequency and recency of past firings.

Let us suppose that these and similar claims are both true and relevant to the way the brain functions—an assumption that is by no means unproblematic. The question we might then ask is: What follows from such facts that is relevant to inferring the nature of the cognitive architecture? The unavoidable answer appears to be, very little. That's not an a priori claim. The degree of relationship between facts at different levels of organization of a system is an empirical matter. However, there is reason to be skeptical about whether the sorts of properties listed above are reflected in any more-or-less direct way in the structure of the system that carries out reasoning.

Consider, for example, one of the most salient properties of neural systems: they are networks which transmit activation culminating in state changes of some quasi-threshold elements. Surely it is not warranted to conclude that reasoning consists of the spread of excitation among representations, or even among semantic components of representations. After all, a VAX is also correctly characterized as consisting of a network over which excitation is transmitted culminating in state changes of quasi-threshold elements. Yet at the level at which it processes representations, a VAX is *literally* organized as a von Neumann architecture.

The point is that the structure of "higher levels" of a system are rarely isomorphic, or even similar, to the structure of "lower levels" of a system. No one expects the theory of protons to look very much like the theory of rocks and rivers, even though, to be sure, it is protons and the like that rocks and rivers are 'implemented in'. Lucretius got into trouble precisely by assuming that there must be a simple correspondence between the structure of macrolevel and microlevel theories. He thought, for example, that hooks and eyes hold the atoms together. He was wrong, as it turns out.

There are, no doubt, cases where special empirical considerations suggest detailed structure/function correspondences or other analogies between different levels of a system's organization. For example, the input to the most peripheral stages of vision and motor control *must* be specified in terms of anatomically projected patterns (of light, in one case, and of muscular activity in the other); and independence of structure and function is perhaps less likely in a system whose input or output must be specified somatotopically. Thus, at these stages it is reasonable to expect an anatomically distributed structure to be reflected by a distributed functional architecture. When, however,

the cognitive process under investigation is as abstract as reasoning, there is simply no reason to expect isomorphisms between structure and function; as, indeed, the computer case proves.

Perhaps this is all too obvious to be worth saying. Yet it seems that the commitment to "brain style" modeling leads to many of the characteristic Connectionist claims about psychology, and that it does so via the implicit—and unwarranted—assumption that there ought to be similarity of structure among the different levels of organization of a computational system. This is distressing since much of the psychology that this search for structural analogies has produced is strikingly recidivist. Thus the idea that the brain is a neural network motivates the revival of a largely discredited Associationist psychology. Similarly, the idea that brain activity is anatomically distributed leads to functionally distributed representations for concepts which in turn leads to the postulation of microfeatures; yet the inadequacies of feature-based theories of concepts are well-known and, to our knowledge, micro-feature theory has done nothing to address them (see Bolinger, 1965; J.D. Fodor, 1977). Or again, the idea that the strength of a connection between neurons is affected by the frequency of their co-activation gets projected onto the cognitive level. The consequence is a resurgence of statistical models of learning that had been widely acknowledged (both in Psychology and in AI) to be extremely limited in their applicability (e.g., Minsky & Papert, 1972, Chomsky, 1957).

So although, *in principle,* knowledge of how the brain works could direct cognitive modeling in a beneficial manner, *in fact* a research strategy has to be judged by its fruits. The main fruit of "brain style modeling" has been to revive psychological theories whose limitations had previously been pretty widely appreciated. It has done so largely because assumptions about the structure of the brain have been adopted in an all-too-direct manner as hypotheses about cognitive architecture; it's an instructive paradox that the current attempt to be thoroughly modern and 'take the brain seriously' should lead to a psychology not readily distinguishable from the worst of Hume and Berkeley. The moral seems to be that one should be deeply suspicious of the heroic sort of brain modeling that purports to address the problems of cognition. We sympathize with the craving for biologically respectable theories that many psychologists seem to feel. But, given a choice, truth is more important than respectability.

Concluding comments: Connectionism as a theory of implementation

A recurring theme in the previous discussion is that many of the arguments for Connectionism are best construed as claiming that cognitive architecture is *implemented* in a certain kind of network (of abstract "units"). Understood this way, these arguments are neutral on the question of what the cognitive architecture is.[36] In these concluding remarks we'll briefly consider Connectionism from this point of view.

Almost every student who enters a course on computational or information-processing models of cognition must be disabused of a very general misunderstanding concerning the role of the physical computer in such models. Students are almost always skeptical about "the computer as a model of cognition" on such grounds as that "computers don't forget or make mistakes", "computers function by exhaustive search," "computers are too logical and unmotivated," "computers can't learn by themselves; they can only do what they're told," or "computers are too fast (or too slow)," or "computers never get tired or bored," and so on. If we add to this list such relatively more sophisticated complaints as that "computers don't exhibit graceful degradation" or "computers are too sensitive to physical damage" this list will begin to look much like the arguments put forward by Connectionists.

The answer to all these complaints has always been that the *implementation,* and all properties associated with the particular realization of the algorithm that the theorist happens to use in a particular case, is irrelevant to the psychological theory; only the algorithm and the representations on which it operates are intended as a psychological hypothesis. Students are taught the notion of a "virtual machine" and shown that *some* virtual machines *can* learn, forget, get bored, make mistakes and whatever else one likes, providing one has a theory of the origins of each of the empirical phenomena in question.

Given this principled distinction between a model and its implementation, a theorist who is impressed by the virtues of Connectionism has the option of proposing PDP's as theories of implementation. But then, far from providing a revolutionary new basis for cognitive science,

these models are in principle neutral about the nature of cognitive processes. In fact, they might be viewed as advancing the goals of Classical information processing psychology by attempting to explain how the brain (or perhaps some idealized brain-like network) might realize the types of processes that conventional cognitive science has hypothesized.

Connectionists do sometimes explicitly take their models to be theories of implementation. Ballard (1986) even refers to Connectionism as "the implementational approach". Touretzky (1986) clearly views his BoltzCONS model this way; he uses Connectionist techniques to implement conventional symbol processing mechanisms such as pushdown stacks and other LISP facilities.[37] Rumelhart and McClelland (1986a, p. 117), who are convinced that Connectionism signals a radical departure from the conventional symbol processing approach, nonetheless refer to "PDP implementations" of various mechanisms such as attention. Later in the same essay, they make their position explicit: Unlike "reductionists," they believe " ... that new and useful concepts emerge at different levels of organization". Although they then defend the claim that one should understand the higher levels "... through the study of the interactions among lower level units", the basic idea that there *are* autonomous levels seems implicit everywhere in the essay.

But once one admits that there really are cognitive-level principles distinct from the (putative) architectural principles that Connectionism articulates, there seems to be little left to argue about. Clearly it is pointless to ask whether one should or shouldn't do cognitive science by studying "the interaction of lower levels" as opposed to studying processes at the cognitive level since we surely have to do *both*. Some scientists study geological principles, others study "the interaction of lower level units" like molecules. But since the fact that there are genuine, autonomously-stateable principles of geology is never in dispute, people who build molecular level models do not claim to have invented a "new theory of geology" that will dispense with all that old fashioned "folk geological" talk about rocks, rivers and mountains!

---

[36]Rumelhart and McClelland maintain that PDP models are more than *just* theories of implementation because (1) they add to our understanding of the problem (p. 116), (2) studying PDPs can lead to the postulation of different macrolevel processes (p. 126). Both these points deal with the heuristic value of "brain style" theorizing. Hence, though correct in principle, they are irrelevant to the crucial question whether Connectionism is best understood as an attempt to model neural implementation, or whether it really does promise a "*new* theory of the mind" incompatible with Classical information-processing approaches. It is an empirical question whether the heuristic value of this approach will turn out to be positive or negative. We have already commented on our view of the recent history of this attempt.

[37]Even in this case, where the model is specifically designed to implement Lisp-like features, some of the rhetoric fails to keep the implementation-algorithm levels distinct. This leads to talk about "emergent properties" and to the claim that even when they implement Lisp-like mechanisms, Connectionist systems "can compute things in ways in which Turing machines and von Neumann computers can't." (Touretzky, 1986). Such a claim suggests that Touretzky distinguishes different "ways of computing" not in terms of different algorithms, but in terms of different ways of implementing the same algorithm. While nobody has proprietary rights to terms like "ways of computing", this is a misleading way of putting it; it means that a DEC machine has a "different way of computing" from an IBM machine even when executing the identical program.

We have, in short, no objection at all to networks as potential implementation models, nor do we suppose that any of the arguments we've given are incompatible with this proposal. The trouble is, however, that if Connectionists do want their models to be construed this way, then they will have to radically alter their practice. For, it seems utterly clear that most of the Connectionist models that have actually been proposed must be construed as theories of cognition, not as theories of implementation. This follows from the fact that it is intrinsic to these theories to ascribe representational content to the units (and/or aggregates) that they postulate. And, as we remarked at the beginning, a theory of the relations among representational states is ipso facto a theory at the level of cognition, not at the level of implementation. It has been the burden of our argument that when construed as a cognitive theory, rather than as an implementation theory, Connectionism appears to have fatal limitations. The problem with Connectionist models is that all the reasons for thinking that they might be true are reasons for thinking that they couldn't be *psychology*.

Conclusion

What, in light of all of this, are the options for the further development of Connectionist theories? As far as we can see, there are four routes that they could follow:

1. Hold out for unstructured mental representations as against the Classical view that mental representations have a combinatorial syntax and semantics. Productivity and systematicity arguments make this option appear not attractive.

2. Abandon network architecture to the extent of opting for structured mental *representations* but continue to insist upon an Associationistic account of the nature of mental *processes*. This is, in effect, a retreat to Hume's picture of the mind (see footnote 29), and it has a problem that we don't believe can be solved: Although mental representations are, on the present assumption, structured objects, *association is not a structure sensitive relation*. The problem is thus how to reconstruct the semantical coherence of thought without postulating psychological processes that are sensitive to the structure of mental representations. (Equivalently, in more modern terms, it's how to get the causal relations among mental representations to mirror their semantical relations without assuming a proof-theoretic treatment of inference and—more generally—a treatment of semantic coherence that is syntactically expressed, in the spirit of proof-theory.) This is the problem on which traditional Associationism foundered, and the prospects for solving it now strike us as not appreciably better than they were a couple of hundred years ago. To put it a little differently: if you need structure in mental representations anyway to account for the productivity and systematicity of minds, why not postulate mental processes that are structure sensitive to account for the coherence of mental processes? Why not be a Classicist, in short.

In any event, notice that the present option gives the Classical picture a lot of what it wants: viz., the identification of semantic states with relations to structured arrays of symbols and the identification of mental processes with transformations of such arrays. Notice too that, as things now stand, this proposal is Utopian since there are no serious proposals for incorporating syntactic structure in Connectionist architectures.

3. Treat Connectionism as an implementation theory. We have no principled objection to this view (though there are, as Connectionists are discovering, technical reasons why networks are often an awkward way to implement Classical machines). This option would entail rewriting quite a lot of the polemical material in the Connectionist literature, as well as redescribing what the networks are doing as operating on symbol structures, rather than spreading activation among semantically interpreted nodes.

Moreover, this revision of policy is sure to lose the movement a lot of fans. As we have pointed out, many people have been attracted to the Connectionist approach because of its promise to (a) do away with the symbol level of analysis, and (b) elevate neuroscience to the position of providing evidence that bears directly on issues of cognition. If Connectionism is considered simply as a theory of how cognition is neurally implemented, it may constrain cognitive models no more than theories in biophysics, biochemistry, or, for that matter, quantum mechanics do. All of these theories are also concerned with processes that *implement* cognition, and all of them are likely to postulate structures that are quite different from cognitive architecture. The point is that 'implements' is transitive, and it goes all the way down.

4. Give up on the idea that networks offer (to quote Rumelhart & McClelland, 1986a, p. 110) "... a reasonable basis for modeling cognitive processes in general". It could still be held that networks sustain *some* cognitive processes. A good bet might be that they sustain such processes as can be analyzed as the drawing of statistical inferences; as far as we can tell, what network models really are is just analog machines for computing such inferences. Since we doubt that much of cognitive processing does consist of analyzing statistical relations, this would be quite a modest estimate of the prospects for network theory compared to what the Connectionists themselves have been offering.

This is, for example, one way of understanding what's going on in the argument between Rumelhart and McClelland (1986b) and Prince and Pinker (1988), though neither paper puts it in quite these terms. In effect, Rumelhart and McClelland postulate a mechanism which, given a corpus of pairings that a 'teacher' provides as data, computes the statistical correlation between the phonological form of the ending of a verb and the phonological form of its past tense inflection. (The magnitude of the correlations so computed is analogically represented by the weights that the network exhibits at asymptote.) Given the problem of inflecting a new verb stem ending in a specified phonological sequence, the machine chooses the form of the past tense that was most highly correlated with that sequence in the training set. By contrast, Prince and Pinker argue (in effect) that more must be going on in learning past tense morphology than merely estimating correlations since the statistical hypothesis provides neither a close fit to the ontogenetic data nor a plausible account of the adult competence on which the ontogenetic processes converge. It seems to us that Pinker and Prince have, by quite a lot, the best of this argument.

There is an alternative to the Empiricist idea that all learning consists of a kind of statistical inference, realized by adjusting parameters; it's the Rationalist idea that some learning is a kind of theory construction, effected by framing hypotheses and evaluating them against evidence. We seem to remember having been through this argument before. We find ourselves with a gnawing sense of deja vu.

References

Arbib, M. (1975). Artificial intelligence and brain theory: Unities and diversities. *Biomedical Engineering, 3,* 238–274.

Ballard, D.H. (1986). Cortical connections and parallel processing: Structure and function. *The Behavioral and Brain Sciences, 9,* 67–120.

Ballard, D.H. (1987). Parallel Logical Inference and Energy Minimization. Report TR142, Computer Science Department, University of Rochester.

Black, I.B. (1986). Molecular memory mechanisms. In Lynch, G. (Ed.), *Synapses, circuits, and the beginnings of memory.* Cambridge, MA: M.I.T. Press, A Bradford Book.

Bolinger, D. (1965). The atomization of meaning. *Language, 41,* 555–573.

Broadbent, D. (1985). A question of levels: Comments on McClelland and Rumelhart. *Journal of Experimental Psychology: General, 114,* 189–192.

Carroll, L. (1956). What the tortoise said to Achilles and other riddles. In Newman, J.R. (Ed.), *The world of mathematics; Volume Four.* New York: Simon and Schuster.

Chomsky, N. (1957). *Syntactic structures.* The Hague: Mouton.

Chomsky, N. (1965). *Aspects of the theory of syntax.* Cambridge: MA: M.I.T. Press.

Chomsky, N. (1968). *Language and mind.* New York: Harcourt, Brace and World.

Churchland, P.M. (1981). Eliminative materialism and the propositional attitudes. *Journal of Philosophy, 78,* 67–90.

Churchland, P.S. (1986). *Neurophilosophy.* Cambridge, MA: M.I.T. Press.

Cummins, R. (1983). *The nature of psychological explanation.* Cambridge, MA: M.I.T. Press.

Dennett, D. (1986). The logical geography of computational approaches: A view from the east pole. In Brand, M. & Harnish, M. (Eds.), *The representation of knowledge.* Tuscon, AZ: The University of Arizona Press.

Dreyfus, H., & Dreyfus, S. (in press). Making a mind vs modelling the brain: A.I. back at a branch point. *Daedalus.*

Fahlman, S.E., & Hinton, G.E. (1987). Connectionist architectures for artificial intelligence. *Computer, 20,* 100 109.

Feldman, J.A. (1986). Neural representation of conceptual knowledge. Report TR189. Department of Computer Science, University of Rochester.

Feldman, J.A., & Ballard, D.H. (1982). Connectionist models and their properties, *Cognitive Science, 6,* 205–254.

Fodor, J. (1976). *The language of thought,* Harvester Press, Sussex. (Harvard University Press paperback).

Fodor, J.D. (1977). *Semantics: Theories of meaning in generative grammar.* New York: Thomas Y. Crowell.

Fodor, J. (1987). *Psychosemantics.* Cambridge, MA: M.I.T. Press.

Frohn, H., Geiger, H., & Singer, W. (1987). A self-organizing neural network sharing features of the mammalian visual system. *Biological Cybernetics, 55,* 333–343.

Geach, P. (1957). *Mental acts.* London: Routledge and Kegan Paul.

Hewett, C. (1977). Viewing control structures as patterns of passing messages. *The Artificial Intelligence Journal, 8,* 232–364.

Hillis, D. (1985). *The connection machine.* Cambridge, MA: M.I.T. Press.

Hinton, G. (1987). Representing part-whole hierarchies in connectionist networks. Unpublished manuscript.

Hinton, G.E., McClelland, J.L., & Rumelhart, D.E. (1986). Distributed representations. In Rumelhart, D.E., McClelland, J.L. and the PDP Research Group. *Parallel distributed processing: Explorations in the microstructure of cognition. Volume 1:* Foundations. Cambridge, MA: M.I.T. Press/Bradford Books.

Hofstadter, D.R. (1983). Artificial intelligence: Sub-cognition as computation. In F. Machlup & U. Mansfield (Eds.), *The study of information: Interdisciplinary messages.* New York: John Wiley & Sons.

Kant, I. (1929). *The critique of pure reason.* New York: St. Martins Press.

Katz, J.J. (1972). *Semantic theory.* New York: Harper & Row.

Katz, J.J., & Fodor, J.A. (1963). The structure of a semantic theory, *Language, 39,* 170 210.

Katz, J., & Postal, P. (1964). *An integrated theory of linguistic descriptions.* Cambridge, MA: M.I.T. Press.

Kosslyn, S.M., & Hatfield, G. (1984). Representation without symbol systems. *Social Research, 51,* 1019–1054.

Laird, J., Rosenbloom, P., & Newell, A. (1986). *Universal subgoaling and chunking: The automatic generation and learning of goal hierarchies.* Boston, MA: Kluwer Academic Publishers.

Lakoff, G. (1986). Connectionism and cognitive linguistics. Seminar delivered at Princeton University, December 8, 1986.

Mackworth, A. (1987). Constraint propagation. In Shapiro, S.C. (Ed.). *The encyclopedia of artificial intelligence, Volume 1*. New York: John Wiley & Sons.

McClelland, J.L., Feldman, J., Adelson, 5., Bower, G., & McDermott, D. (1986). *Connectionist models and cognitive science: Goals, directions and implications*. Report to the National Science Foundation, June, 1986.

McClelland, J.L., & Kawamoto, A.H. (1986). Mechanisms of sentence processing: Assigning roles to constituents. In McClelland, Rumelhart and the PDP Research Group (Eds.), *Parallel distributed processing: volume 2*. Cambridge, MA: M.I.T. Press, Bradford Books.

McClelland, J.L., Rumelhart, D.E., & Hinton, G.E. (1986). The appeal of parallel distributed processing. In Rumelhart, McClelland and the PDP Research Group, (Eds.), *Parallel distributed processing: volume 1*. Cambridge, MA: M.I.T. Press/Bradford Books.

Minsky, M., & Papert, F. (1972). *Artificial Intelligence Progress Report*, AI Memo 252, Massachusetts Institute of Technology.

Newell, A. (1969). Heuristic programming: Ill-structured problems. In Aronofsky, J. (Ed.), *Progress in operations research, III*. New York: John Wiley & Sons.

Newell, A. (1980). Physical symbol systems. *Cognitive Science, 4*, 135–183.

Newell, A. (1982). The knowledge level. *Artificial Intelligence, 18*, 87–127.

Osherson, D., Stov, M., & Weinstein, S. (1984). Learning theory and natural language. *Cognition, 17*, 1–28.

Pinker, S. (1984). *Language, learnability and language development*. Cambridge: Harvard University Press.

Prince, A., & Pinker, S. (1988). On language and connectionism: Analysis of a parallel distributed processing model of language acquisition. *Cognition, 28*, this issue.

Pylyshyn, Z.W. (1980). Cognition and computation: Issues in the foundations of cognitive science. *Behavioral and Brain Sciences, 3:1*, 154–169.

Pylyshyn, Z.W. (1981). The imagery debate: Analogue media versus tacit knowledge. *Psychological Review, 88*, 16–45.

Pylyshyn, Z.W.(1984a). *Computation and cognition: Toward a foundation for cognitive science*. Cambridge, MA: M.I.T. Press, A Bradford Book.

Pylyshyn, Z.W.(1984b). Why computation requires symbols. *Proceedings of the Sixth Annual Conference of the Cognitive Science Society, Boulder, Colorado, August, 1984*. Hillsdale, NJ: Erlbaum.

Rakic, P. (1975). Local circuit neurons. *Neurosciences Research Program Bulletin, 13*, 299–313.

Rumelhart, D.E. (1984). The emergence of cognitive phenomena from sub-symbolic processes. In *Proceedings of the Sixth Annual Conference of the Cognitive Science Society, Boulder, Colorado, August, 1984*. Hillsdale, NJ: Erlbaum.

Rumelhart, D.E., & McClelland, J.L. (1985). Level's indeed! A response to Broadbent. *Journal of Experimental Psychology: General, 114*, 193–197.

Rumelhart, D.E., & McClelland, J.L. (1986a). PDP Models and general issues in cognitive science: In Rumelhart, McClelland and the PDP Research Group (Eds.), *Parallel distributed processing, volume 1*. Cambridge, MA: M.I.T. Press, A Bradford Book.

Rumelhart, D.E., & McClelland, J.L. (1986b). On learning the past tense of English verbs. In Rumelhart, McClelland and the PDP Research Group (Eds.), *Parallel distributed processing, volume 1*. Cambridge, MA: M.I.T. Press, A Bradford Book.

Schneider, W. (1987). Connectionism: Is it a paradigm shift for psychology? *Behavior Research Methods, Instruments, & Computers, 19*, 73–83.

Sejnowski, T.J. (1981). Skeleton filters in the brain. In Hinton, G.E., & Anderson, A.J. (Eds.), *Parallel models of associative memory*. Hillsdale, NJ: Erlbaum.

Simon, H.A., & Chase, W.G. (1973). Skill in chess. *American Scientist, 621*, 394–403.

Smolensky, P. (1988). On the proper treatment of connectionism. *The Behavioral and Brain Sciences, 11*, forthcoming.

Stabler, E. (1985). How are grammars represented? *Behavioral and Brain Sciences, 6*, 391–420.

Stich, S. (1983). *From folk psychology to cognitive science*. Cambridge, MA: M.I.T. Press.

Touretzky, D. S. (1986). BoltzCONS: Reconciling connectionism with the recursive nature of stacks and trees. *Proceedings of the Eighth Annual Conference of the Cognitive Science Society*. Amherst, MA, August, 1986. Hillsdale, NJ: Erlbaum.

Wanner, E., & Maratsos, M. (1978). An ATN approach to comprehension. In Halle, M., Bresnan, J., & Miller, G.A. (Eds.), *Linguistic theory and psychological reality*. Cambridge, MA: M.I.T. Press.

Watson, J. (1930). *Behaviorism*, Chicago: University of Chicago Press.

Woods, W.A. (1975). What's in a link? in Bobrow, D., & Collins, A. (Eds.), *Representation and understanding*. New York: Academic Press.

Ziff, P. (1960). *Semantic analysis*. Ithaca, NY: Cornell University Press.

Introduction

(1988)
L. D. Jackel, H. P. Graf, W. Hubbard, J. S. Denker, D. Henderson, and Isabelle Guyon

An application of neural net chips: handwritten digit recognition
Proceedings of the IEEE International Conference on Neural Networks,
San Diego, 1988, pp. II-107 – II-115

(1990)
Y. LeCun, B. Boser, J. S. Denker, D. Henderson, R. E. Howard, W. Hubbard, and L. D. Jackel

Backpropagation applied to handwritten zip code recognition
Neural Computation 1: 541–551

We discuss these two papers together because they are from the same group at AT&T Bell Laboratories discussing the same problem, digit recognition with a neural network. It is interesting to see the evolution of the data sets, models, and techniques used over the course of the project.

For those of us who teach courses about neural networks, the following incident occurs at least twice a semester: (1) A student enthusiastically expresses great interest in neural networks. (2) The student wants to do a programming project, usually on his personal computer, to test his new knowledge with a specific problem. (3) The student decides to use his personal computer to recognize printed characters. (4) After digits and letters are recognized, the student assumes he can go on to do something hard.

Unfortunately, as we point out to the student when it is our turn to speak, recognizing characters is one of those problems that seems simple but in fact is extremely difficult to do well. Letters and digits have become the nearly universal first pattern set that a novice neural network is trained on. The pattern set is usually some low-resolution pixel array, corresponding vaguely to letters. The neural net literature is full of cartoonlike character shapes, with jagged edges, presented as figures designed to test the powers of association, reconstruction, invariance, and generalization of the neural network under development.

A group at AT&T Bell Laboratories has been working on neural networks for many years and was the earliest group in a major corporation to devote a significant amount of time, money, and staff effort to neural networks. Among other accomplishments they developed a series of neural network VLSI chips, one of which is used for the set of experiments on digit recognition described in the first paper.

The task they set themselves was to use neural network techniques to recognize hand-printed digits. We reprint here two papers—progress reports in an ongoing investigation—that describe their efforts and their degree of success. The data set used in the first paper consisted of two sets of digits produced by their own group, one carefully printed and one done more hastily. The second paper used a more challenging data set: the U.S. Post Office's

"Zip Code Data Base," which consists of over 9,000 handprinted digits taken from envelopes. The source of this data set also suggests one of the many potential practical applications of digit recognition. Another obvious application would be the recognition of the amounts on bank checks.

One psychological problem with neural networks is that they work "pretty well" almost immediately. With a little effort and persistence, and with even an indifferent representation of the input data, it is possible to obtain results on simple problems—for example, recognition of a few characters—that are "reasonable." (Reasonable is sometimes defined as impressing visitors.) But doing things right is always hard, and the payoff for doing things right sometimes seems small by comparison. To get 75 percent correct on a character classification task may take a week, and can be done with a commercial simulator package right out of the box, working on nearly unprocessed data. To get 90 percent correct on the same task may take months, and to get over 95 percent may take years of work by many talented people. The Bell Labs group makes a sarcastic comment along these lines early in the first paper, obviously speaking from unhappy experience.

Segmenting a number with many digits, that is, picking out single digits from a zip code or an amount on a check, is a remarkably difficult problem. In fact many errors in operating digit recognition systems are due to segmentation errors. But let us suppose we can start with an isolated digit. The digit is first scaled so all examples become roughly the same size on a 16×16–pixel block. This can involve expansions, contractions, and shearing transformations of the image.

One clear conclusion of both papers is that simply applying a powerful learning algorithm to the raw pixel array and expecting the system to learn to correctly classify digits does not work. This is referred to in the first paper as the "no brains required" strategy.

The major differences between the first paper (from 1988) and the second (from 1990) falls in the way they handle the early stages of analysis of the pixel array. The traditional approach to pattern recognition—used everywhere from linguistics to computational vision—takes the pixel array and looks for "features" in the pattern of activity. Features describe a complex data set (say, spoken speech or a pixel array) in terms of some exceptionally useful and salient descriptors. For example, the image of a triangle could be described as coordinates of a large set of pixels. Different triangles might be described by very different sets of pixels. We could describe a geometrical triangle as connected (one feature), containing three straight lines (another feature), three corners (another feature), and with each corner formed from only two lines (yet another feature). All triangles will have the same feature description, although there are huge numbers of different pixel arrays that can represent triangles. It would be an unwise neural net engineer who, given the choice of recognizing triangles with the feature description or the pixel description, chooses the pixel array.

The problem is choosing the right features. The first paper used a set of features that were chosen by the experimenters, using their intuition and experience. The features were spatially localized, that is, only involved patterns on a small contiguous neighborhood of pixels, 5×5 pixels or 7×7 pixels. The features at a particular location were detected by templates that were constructed to respond strongly to oriented line segments, the ends of lines, and arcs. (Template feature matching is the same as convolution with a kernel. The kernel is the template.) This particular set of features chosen was suggested by the kind of processing known to exist in the mammalian visual system. The feature vectors were then concatenated to make up a 180-dimensional vector, which was the input data actually used for the recognition computation.

Once the large vector representing the digit was constructed, the network went to work. In the first paper the most successful recognition algorithms used were very simple: successful ones were basically nearest neighbor classifiers, that is, an input was compared with stored examples and the classification of the nearest stored examples was used. The overall best performance in the first paper, by a small margin, was found with a technique called *Parzen windows,* a classic pattern recognition technique that consists of storing "blurred" representations of the training set. During classification all the blurred representations of a single category are added up to form an estimate of the underlying probability distribution for the categories. The most probable category is the output classification (see Sklansky and Wassel 1981).

The special VLSI chip that was developed and used by the Bell Labs group for the computations in the first paper used 54 elements. By suitable programming, almost all of the operations in the recognition process were performed by the chip. The basic chip operation was template matching, with the template loaded onto the connections. Most of the computation that was done was related to the skeletonization and the feature extraction: the actual recognition step was done as another template match. The first paper found that the traditional high-powered neural network learning algorithms did not perform as well as the simple nearest neighbor or Parzen window methods.

The second paper, from 1990, involves personnel from the same group at AT&T Bell Laboratories and the same problem, but now the group had considerably more experience applying a neural network to the problem of digit recognition. The data set used in the second paper was the zip code data base. (See also Denker et al. 1989 for an early try at the zip code data base, intermediate in development between the two papers presented here.)

What are the best features to use for the early stages of analysis of the image? If one knew how to do it, the best strategy would be for the network to learn to choose its own features, based on the data it must classify. The second paper uses the powerful backpropagation network algorithm (papers 41 and 42 in *Neurocomputing: Foundations of Research*) combined with a modified and constrained architecture designed largely to allow discovery and use of a good set of low-level features by the network.

The backpropagation network used had three hidden layers. Instead of everything connecting to everything—the traditional fully connected backpropagation architecture— the first two hidden layers are severely constrained in their connectivity and number of free parameters. The first layer was designed to pick up local features, so that only a small number of pixels in a local region projected to a single unit in the first hidden layer. More, the first hidden layer was assumed to be composed of a number of modules. Each module was formed from a group of units, each unit looking at different local regions on the pixel array. During learning each unit in a module was forced to have *identical* weights (with the exception of the bias or threshold weight). Therefore every unit in a module looked for the same feature, but in different locations in the array. There were twelve such independent *feature maps* in the first hidden layer. The features that were developed during learning by the first layer turned out, in some cases, to be similar to the intuitively chosen feature set and to biologically observed visual features. The second hidden layer looked at "features" of the "feature maps": The same technique was used as in the first layer, but the units in the second layer could pick up higher-order correlations in the input, over larger spatial extents.

Instead of the special purpose neural net VLSI that was used in the first paper, the Bell group used off-the-shelf digital signal processing (DSP) chips in conjunction with a personal computer. Several commercially available neural network accelerators have made the same design decision, probably because there is already an enormous commercial market for DSP chips. DSP chips are easily available, highly developed, reliable, relatively cheap, and designed to do the kinds of computations (multiply-accumulates, that is, inner products) that neural networks require.

There are a number of important lessons to be learned from these two papers. Prominent among them are that there is no magical neural network substitute for hard work and engineering insight and that effective early processing and data representation are keys to making a network that does the job.

References

J.S. Denker, W.R. Gardner, H.P. Graf, D. Henderson, R.E. Howard, W. Hubbard, L.D. Jackel, H.S. Baird, and I. Guyon (1989), Neural network recognizer for handwritten zip code digits. In D.S. Touretsky (Ed.), *Advances in Neural Information Processing Systems, I*. San Mateo: Morgan-Kaufman.

J. Sklansky and G.N. Wassel (1981), *Pattern Classifiers and Trainable Machines*. New York, NY: Springer.

(1988)

L. D. Jackel, H. P. Graf, W. Hubbard, J. S. Denker, D. Henderson, and Isabelle Guyon

An application of neural net chips: handwritten digit recognition
Proceedings of the IEEE International Conference on Neural Networks,
San Diego, 1988, pp. II-107 – II-115

Abstract

A general purpose, fully-interconnected neural-net chip has been used to perform computationally intensive tasks for handwritten digit recognition. The chip has nearly 3000 programmable connections which can be set for template matching. The templates can be reprogrammed as needed during the recognition sequence.

The recognition process proceeds in four major steps. First, the image is *captured* using a TV camera and a digital framegrab. This image is converted, using a digital computer, to either black or white pixels and scaled to fill a 16x16 pixel frame. Next, using the neural-net chip, the image is *skeletonized* i.e. the image is thinned to a backbone one pixel wide. Then, the chip is reprogrammed, and a *feature map* is created by template matching stored primative patterns on the chip with regions on the skeletonized image. Finally, *recognition,* based on the feature map, is achieved using any one of a variety of statistical and heuristic techniques on a digital computer. Best scores range between 90% and 99% correct classification, depending on the quality of the original handwritten digits.

I. Introduction

This paper reports on our ongoing experiments in handwritten digit recognition using a neural net chip. This particular application was chosen because digit recognition maps nicely onto our chip and because it represents a problem of considerable practical value.

Early results are encouraging and our recognition accuracy is improving rapidly as we tune the system.

II. Recognition Strategy

Several groups have attempted neural-net digit recognition using automatic learning algorithms or associative-memory techniques [1,2], in most cases using bit-maps of the images for input into the net. In such experiments it is hoped that the network will develop a reasonable "representation" of the the image features that will then lead to high-accuracy classification. This son of "no-brains-required" approach has obvious appeal: raw data is fed into a black-box algorithm (such as back-propagation), and one just turns the crank. One need not be expert in machine vision or statistical analysis. Although credible results can be obtained with such methods, high-accuracy classification is difficult.

In our experiments we have not used the currently popular automatic learning algorithms, but have appealed to the neurobiology for hints on how to do feature extraction. The most characteristically "neural" aspect of our approach is our use of parallel, analog computation on the chip to evaluate many component, low-resolution, vector dot products. The chip is thus a fast template-matching engine.

Our recognition process is adapted to map onto our chip. We are constrained by the number of connections, the number of neurons, the analog accuracy of the circuit, the analog depth of the synapses, and the digital I/O from the chip. The chip was designed to demonstrate the feasibility of analog neural-net processing and was not specifically designed for image processing.

Our general strategy is to extract features from the image and then do classification based on the resultant feature maps. The chip and the four major operations (image capture and scaling, skeletonization, feature extraction, and digit classification) are described in detail in following sections.

III. The Chip

The 54 neuron chip we use has been extensively described elsewhere [3–4]. The connection strengths are stored digitally on the chip in a bank of static RAM cells. The data input and output to the chip is through a 4-bit wide bus.

For our application, the connections on the chip are set to store a number of parallel templates. A schematic representation of this circuit is shown in Figure 1. The chip compares an input vector to this list of template vectors. The input vector is a binary string, with one bit per pixel. The components of the stored vectors have one of three values, +1 (excitation), 0 (don't care), or −4 (inhibition). All the templates are compared in parallel to the input vector by taking the dot product of the input with each template. If the dot product for a comparison is greater than a threshold value, a "1"(match) is reported by the circuit.

Input vector

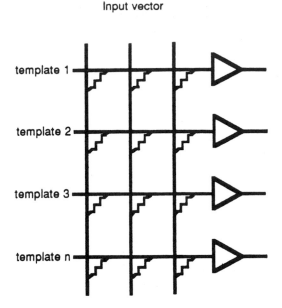

Figure 1 Schematic of circuit configuration for template matching. An input vector is compared in parallel to all the templates, which are determined by the resistor values. On the chip, active circuits replace the resistors and allow inhibition as well as excitation.

a)   b)

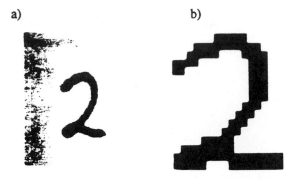

Figure 2 An example of a gray-scale image a) captured by the framegrab, and b) the binarized, scaled image used for further processing.

a captured gray-scale image and the resultant 16 x 16 image is shown in Figure 2.

Otherwise, a "0" (no match) is reported. The threshold can be set individually for each template.

For the low accuracy dot products required in template matching, analog electronic circuits on our chip have advantages over digital circuits: the analog circuits can be more compact and faster. This is because the summation in the dot product is computed "for free" just by adding the component currents in a summing wire.

IV. Image Capture

As the first step in the recognition process, a digital computer, equipped with frame-grab hardware, captures a video image of a hand-written character. The computer adaptively thresholds the gray-level image into black or white pixel. This image is scaled both horizontally and vertically to fill a 16 x 16 pixel block. (The horizontal scaling left justifies the image and is constrained to be no greater than 120% of the vertical scaling. Thus, "1"s become fat, vertical bars on the left side of the field, and not squares, as would be the case if the horizontal scaling were not bounded.) The 16 x 16 field size was chosen because our largest templates were limited by the 54 neuron chip to 7 x 7 pixels and we wanted these templates to cover a large fraction of the whole image. The 16 x 16 format appears adequate for digits, but it is probably too small to deal with the more complex alphabetical characters. An example of

V. Skeletonization

The width of written line strokes for characters varies both with character size, writing implement, and writing style. To compensate for this variation, our 16 x 16 image is processed by a "skeletonization" or line-thinning step. Although features can be extracted reliably for any particular width of lines, the width does not carry much information and a smaller number of features suffices to analyze the skeletonized images. The objective for a skeletonizer is to eat away pixels of the image until only a backbone of the character remains. Thus broad strokes are reduced to skinny lines. This process is traditionally done by scanning a 3 x 3 window across the image, and then using table look up to determine whether or not the middle pixel in the window ought to be deleted. [5–6] The table is designed so that pixels that are crucial to maintaining connectivity are not deleted. With larger windows, such as 5 x 5, table look up becomes impractical. But larger windows offer the possibility of more clever skeletonization which can be less noise sensitive and can preserve straight edges. In our experiment we used such 5 x 5 windows to illustrate the potential of neural-net hardware.

Skeletonization with our chip proceeds in the following way. A 5 x 5 pixel window is raster scanned across the image. The 25 bits representing the pixels in each window are compared to 20 25-bit templates stored on the chip. Each template tests for a particular condition that allows the deletion of the middle pixel in the window. If the match of the image data to any of the templates exceeds a preset threshold, the center pixel is deleted. Examples of some of the templates used for skeletonization are shown in Figure 3. These templates were chosen in a systematic, but ad hoc manner. "Learning" was done by trial and error.

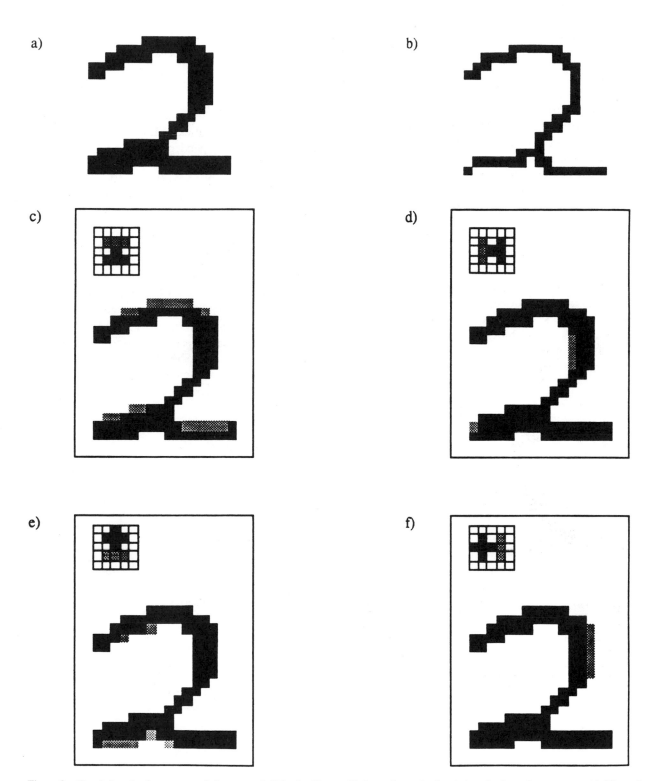

Figure 3   The skeletonization process: a) shows a scaled binarized image, b) shows the result after skeletonization using one pass with 20 templates, c) -f) show typical templates used for thinning in the upper left of each box. Black is excitation, gray is inhibition, and white is don't care. The pixels deleted by each template are shown in gray on the large image in each box.

VI. Feature Extraction

In the feature extraction process, the skeletonized image is raster scanned with a 7 x 7 pixel window. Currently, for feature extraction, the input window is compared to only 25 templates in parallel, but the chip can support up to 49 templates. The templates for feature extraction, which are loaded on the chip after skeletonization is complete, were chosen by hand, and were inspired by results from experimental neurobiology. The templates check for the presence of oriented lines, oriented line end-stops, and arcs. Examples of some of the templates are shown in Figure 4. Whenever a feature template match exceeds the preset threshold, a 1 is set in the map for that corresponding feature. Thus, there is a feature map for every template. Some of the templates search for the same feature, but on a different size scale. The maps for such features are "OR"ed together after the scan is completed.

The feature extraction process maps a 16 x 16 image into 20 16 x 16 images. To reduce the amount of data, each feature map is coarse-blocked into a 3 x 3 array. The 20 3 x 3 feature maps make up a 180 bit vector which is used for digit classification. The coarse blocking also has the effect of building a fair amount of translation and rotation invariance into the processing.

VII. Classification

Several classification schemes were used. They include a k-nearest neighbor classifier, a Bayesian classifier that assumes statistical independence of the vector components, and a Parzen window classifier [7]. The Parzen window classifier gave the lowest error rates.

Results depended on the quality of the data being tested. The first database of 150 digits was taken by asking members of our research community to write the digits 0-9 on a piece of paper. Some carefully drew the digits. Many scrawled out the digits as fast a possible and dared our machine to recognize them. On this data set classification accuracy ranged from about 95% (k-nearest neighbor) to 96% (Parzen windows). Many of these digits were hard to identify by humans (such as open 9's and open 4's). As a next step, we gave local researchers a form with examples of model digits drawn on the bottom. They were instructed to write 10 examples of each digit following the model.

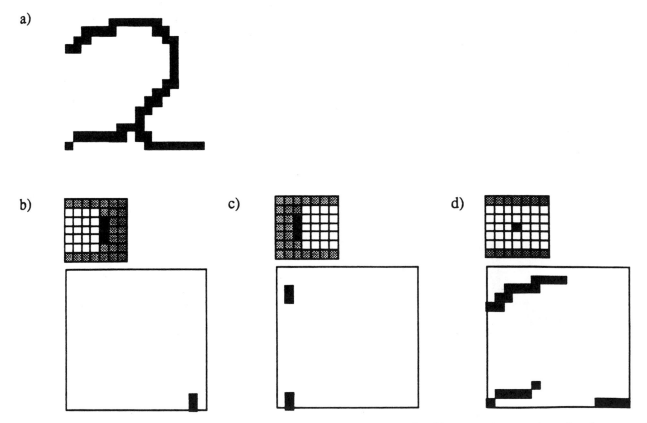

Figure 4 The feature extraction process: a) shows a skeletonized image, b)–d) show examples of feature templates, and the resultant feature maps for the image shown in a). In the templates, black is excitation and gray is inhibition. b) and c) check for line endstops, d) checks for horizontal lines.

There were to be no "hats" on "1"s, or slashes through "7"s or "0"s. Writers were asked to imagine they were filling out a form for a tax refund. Not surprisingly, our recognizer achieved 99% recognition with the Parzen windows, and 98% with the other methods on this database of 1200 digits. Work is now in progress to test Zipcode data taken from mail pieces. Results should be available at the time of this meeting.

VIII. Discussion

To illustrate the effectiveness of feature extraction, we used our classification schemes on 256-bit vectors made up of bit maps of the images with no skeletonization and no feature extraction. For each classification scheme, we found the error at least doubled, thus clearly demonstrating the utility of feature extraction. We also ran back-propagation on the 180-bit feature vectors from the first database of "sloppy" digits. Results were slightly worse than those of the two other weaker methods.

The chip has enough computing power to evaluate all the templates at one window location in one microsecond. Thus, less than a millisecond should be required for the skeletonization and feature extraction across the whole 16 x 16 image. Actual processing times were about three orders of magnitude slower. This is because the current system has a severe I/O bottle neck between the chip and the host computer. The host is also slow at formatting the pixel window data to be sent to the chip. The bottleneck and the formatting problem should be eliminated when the chip is incorporated into a special-purpose image-processing system.

IX. Conclusion

We have used a neural net chip to do fast skeletonization and feature extraction for a task in handwritten digit recognition. Results, so far, are promising and indicate that our approach may be an attractive alternative to conventional methods.

References

[1] See, for example, E. Gullichsen and E. Chang, "Pattern Classification by Neural Network: An experimental System for Icon Recognition", Proc. IEEE First Int. Conf. on Neural Networks, San Diego, p. IV-725 (1987).

[2] or, G. A. Carpenter and S. Grossberg, "The ART of Adaptive Pattern Recognition by a Self-Organizing Neural Network", Computer, 21, 77 (1988).

[3] H. P. Graf, W. Hubbard, L. D. Jackel, P.G.N. deVegvar, "A CMOS Associative Memory Chips",Proc. IEEE First Int. Conf. on Neural Networks, San Diego, p. III-461 (1987).

[4] H.P Graf and P. deVegvar, "A CMOS Implementation of a Neural Network Model", Proc. 1987 Stanford Conf. Advanced Res. VLSI, P. Losleben (ed.) MIT Press p. 351 (1987).

[5] N. J. Naccache and R. Shinghal, "SPTA: A Proposed Algorithm for Thinning Binary Patterns" IEEE Trans. Systems, Man, and Cybernetics, SMC-14, 409 (1984).

[6] T. Pavlidis, "Algorithms for Graphics and Image Processing", Computer Science Press (1982).

[7] R. O. Duda and P. E. Hart, "Pattern Classification and Scene Analysis", John Wiley and Sons (1973).

(1990)

Y. LeCun, B. Boser, J. S. Denker, D. Henderson, R. E. Howard, W. Hubbard, and L. D. Jackel

Backpropagation applied to handwritten zip code recognition
Neural Computation 1: 541–551

The ability of learning networks to generalize can be greatly enhanced by providing constraints from the task domain. This paper demonstrates how such constraints can be integrated into a backpropagation through the architecture of the network. This approach has been successfully applied to the recognition of handwritten zip code digits provided by the U.S. Postal Service. A single network learns the entire recognition operation, going from the normalized image of the character to the final classification.

1 Introduction

Previous work performed on recognizing simple digit images (LeCun 1989) showed that good generalization on complex tasks can be obtained by designing a network architecture that contains a certain amount of a priori knowledge about the task. The basic design principle is to reduce the number of free parameters in the network as much as possible without overly reducing its computational power. Application of this principle increases the probability of correct generalization because it results in a specialized network architecture that has a reduced entropy (Denker *et al.* 1987; Patarnello and Carnevali 1987; Tishby *et al.* 1989; LeCun 1989), and a reduced Vapnik–Chervonenkis dimensionality (Baumand Haussler 1989).

In this paper, we apply the backpropagation algorithm (Rumelhart *et al.* 1986) to a real-world problem in recognizing handwritten digits taken from the U.S. Mail. Unlike previous results reported by our group on this problem (Denker *et al.* 1989), the learning network is directly fed with images, rather than feature vectors, thus demonstrating the ability of backpropagation networks to deal with large amounts of low-level information.

2 Zip Codes

2.1 Data Base

The data base used to train and test the network consists of 9298 segmented numerals digitized from handwritten zip codes that appeared on U.S. mail passing through the Buffalo, NY post office. Examples of such images are shown in Figure 1. The digits were written by many different people, using a great variety of sizes, writing styles, and instruments, with widely varying amounts of care; 7291 examples are used for training the network and 2007 are used for testing the generalization performance. One important feature of this data base is that both the training set and the testing set contain numerous examples that are ambiguous, unclassifiable, or even misclassified.

2.2 Preprocessing

Locating the zip code on the envelope and separating each digit from its neighbors, a very hard task in itself, was performed by Postal Service contractors (Wang and Srihari 1988). At this point, the size of a digit image varies but is typically around 40 by 60 pixels. A linear transformation is then applied to make the image fit in a 16 by 16 pixel image. This transformation preserves the aspect ratio of the character, and is performed after extraneous marks in the image have been removed. Because of the linear transformation, the resulting image is not binary but has multiple gray levels, since a variable number of pixels in the original image can fall into a given pixel in the target image. The gray levels of each image are scaled and translated to fall within the range −1 to 1.

3 Network Design

3.1 Input and Output

The remainder of the recognition is entirely performed by a multilayer network. All of the connections in the network are adaptive, although heavily constrained, and are trained using backpropagation. This is in contrast with earlier work (Denker *et al.* 1989) where the first few layers of connections were hand-chosen constants implemented on a neural-network chip. The input of the network is a 16 by 16 normalized image. The output is composed of 10 units (one per class) and uses place coding.

3.2 Feature Maps and Weight Sharing

Classical work in visual pattern recognition has demonstrated the advantage of extracting local features and combining them to form higher order features. Such knowledge

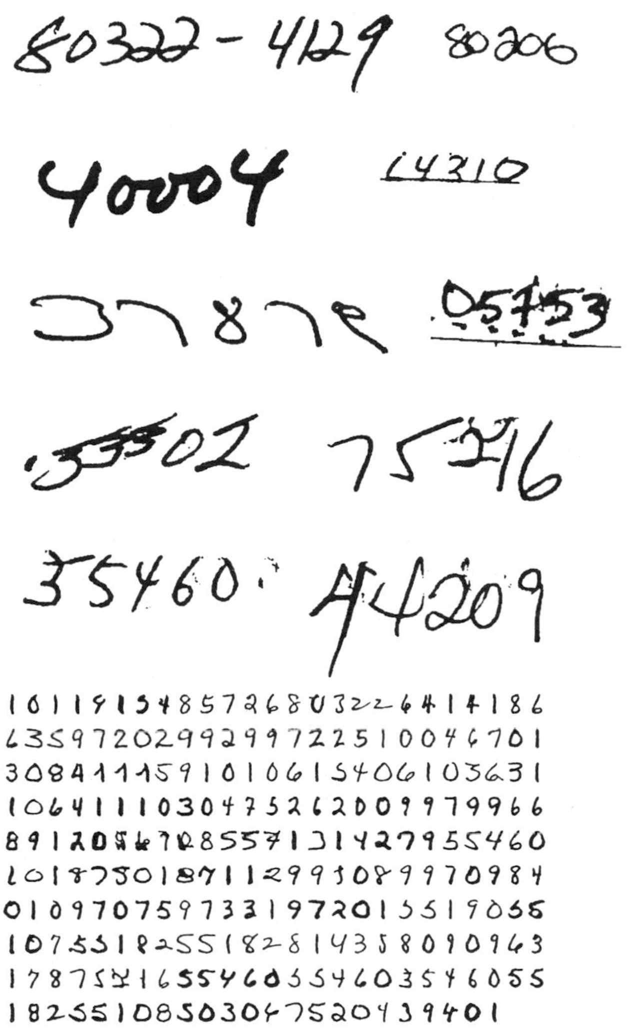

Figure 1 Examples of original zip codes (top) and normalized digits from the testing set (bottom).

can be easily built into the network by forcing the hidden units to combine only local sources of information. Distinctive features of an object can appear at various locations on the input image. Therefore it seems judicious to have a set of feature detectors that can detect a particular instance of a feature anywhere on the input plane. Since the *precise* location of a feature is not relevant to the classification, we can afford to lose some position information in the process. Nevertheless, *approximate* position information must be preserved, to allow the next levels to detect higher order, more complex features (Fukushima 1980; Mozer 1987).

The detection of a particular feature at any location on the input can be easily done using the "weight sharing" technique. Weight sharing was described in Rumelhart *et al.* (1986) for the so-called T-C problem and consists in having several connections (links) controlled by a single

parameter (weight). It can be interpreted as imposing equality constraints among the connection strengths. This technique can be implemented with very little computational overhead.

Weight sharing not only greatly reduces the number of free parameters in the network but also can express information about the geometry and topology of the task. In our case, the first hidden layer is composed of several planes that we call *feature maps*. All units in a plane share the same set of weights, thereby detecting the same feature at different locations. Since the exact position of the feature is not important, the feature maps need not have as many units as the input.

3.3 Network Architecture

The network is represented in Figure 2. Its architecture is a direct extension of the one proposed in LeCun (1989). The network has three hidden layers named H1, H2, and H3, respectively. Connections entering H1 and H2 are local and are heavily constrained.

H1 is composed of 12 groups of 64 units arranged as 12 independent 8 by 8 feature maps. These 12 feature maps will be designated by H1.1, H1.2, ..., H1.12. Each unit in a feature map takes input on a 5 by 5 neighborhood on the input plane. For units in layer H1 that are one unit apart, their receptive fields (in the input layer) are two pixels apart. Thus, the input image is *undersampled* and some position information is eliminated. A similar two-to-one undersampling occurs going from layer H1 to H2. The motivation is that high resolution may be needed to detect the presence of a feature, while its exact position need not be determined with equally high precision.

It is also known that the kinds of features that are important at one place in the image are likely to be important in other places. Therefore, corresponding connections on each unit in a given feature map are constrained to have the same weights. In other words, each of the 64 units in H1.1 uses the same set of 25 weights. Each unit performs the same operation on corresponding parts of the image. The function performed by a feature map can thus be interpreted as a nonlinear subsampled convolution with a 5 by 5 kernel.

Of course, units in another map (say H1.4) share *another* set of 25 weights. Units do not share their biases (thresholds). Each unit thus has 25 input lines plus a bias. Connections extending past the boundaries of the input plane take their input from a virtual background plane whose state is equal to a constant, predetermined background level, in our case −1. Thus, layer H1 comprises 768 units (8 by 8 times 12), 19,968 connections (768 times 26), but only 1068 free parameters (768 biases plus 25 times 12 feature kernels) since many connections share the same weight.

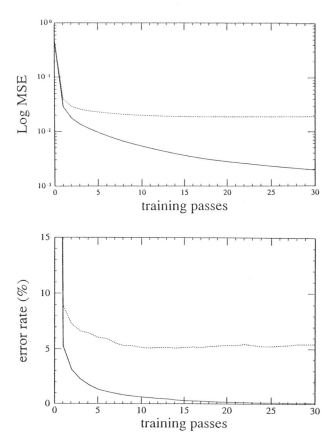

Figure 2 Network architecture.

Layer H2 is also composed of 12 feature maps. Each feature map contains 16 units arranged in a 4 by 4 plane. As before, these feature maps will be designated as H2.1, H2.2, . . ., H2.12. The connection scheme between H1 and H2 is quite similar to the one between the input and H1, but slightly more complicated because H1 has multiple two-dimensional maps. Each unit in H2 combines local information coming from 8 of the 12 different feature maps in H1. Its receptive field is composed of eight 5 by 5 neighborhoods centered around units that are at identical positions within each of the eight maps. Thus, a unit in H2 has 200 inputs, 200 weights, and a bias. Once again, all units in a given map are constrained to have identical weight vectors. The eight maps in H1 on which a map in H2 takes its inputs are chosen according to a scheme that will not be described here. Connections falling off the boundaries are treated as in H1. To summarize, layer H2 contains 192 units (12 times 4 by 4)and there is a total of 38,592 connections between layers H1 and H2 (192 units times 201 input lines). All these connections are controlled by only 2592 free parameters (12 feature maps times 200 weights plus 192 biases).

Layer H3 has 30 units, and is fully connected to H2. The number of connections between H2 and H3 is thus 5790

(30 times 192 plus 30 biases). The output layer has 10 units and is also fully connected to H3, adding another 310 weights. In summary, the network has 1256 units, 64,660 connections, and 9760 independent parameters.

4 Experimental Environment

All simulations were performed using the backpropagation simulator SN (Bottou and LeCun 1988) running on a SUN-4/260.

The nonlinear function used at each node was a scaled hyperbolic tangent. Symmetric functions of that kind are believed to yield faster convergence, although the learning can be extremely slow if some weights are too small (LeCun 1987). The target values for the output units were chosen within the quasilinear range of the sigmoid. This prevents the weights from growing indefinitely and prevents the output units from operating in the flat spot of the sigmoid. The output cost function was the mean squared error.

Before training, the weights were initialized with random values using a uniform distribution between $-2.4/F_i$ and $2.4/F_i$ where $2.4/F_i$ is the number of inputs (fan-in) of the unit to which the connection belongs. This technique tends to keep the total inputs within the operating range of the sigmoid.

During each learning experiment, the patterns were repeatedly presented in a constant order. The weights were updated according to the so-called stochastic gradient or "on-line" procedure (updating after each presentation of a single pattern) as opposed to the "true" gradient procedure (averaging over the whole training set before updating the weights). From empirical study (supported by theoretical arguments), the stochastic gradient was found to converge much faster than the true gradient, especially on large, redundant data bases. It also finds solutions that are more robust.

All experiments were done using a special version of Newton's algorithm that uses a positive, diagonal approximation of the Hessian matrix (LeCun 1987; Becker and LeCun 1988). This algorithm is not believed to bring a tremendous increase in learning speed but it converges reliably without requiring extensive adjustments of the parameters.

5 Results

After each pass through the training set, the performance was measured both on the training and on the test set. The network was trained for 23 passes through the training set (167,693 pattern presentations).

After these 23 passes, the MSE averaged over the patterns and over the output units was 2.5×10^{-3} on the training set and 1.8×10^{-2} on the test set. The percentage of misclassified patterns was 0.14% on the training set (10 mistakes) and 5.0% on the test set (102 mistakes). As can be seen in Figure 3, the convergence is extremely quick, and shows that backpropagation *can* be used on fairly large tasks with reasonable training times. This is due in part to the high redundancy of real data.

In a realistic application, the user usually is interested in the number of rejections necessary to reach a given level of accuracy rather than inthe raw error rate. We measured the percentage of test patterns that must be rejected in order to get 1% error rate on the *remaining* test patterns. Our main rejection criterion was that the difference between the activity levels of the two most active units should exceed a given threshold. The percentage of rejections was then 12.1% for 1% classification error on the remaining (non-rejected) test patterns. It should be emphasized that the rejection thresholds were obtained using performance measures on the *test set*.

Some kernels synthesized by the network can be interpreted as feature detectors remarkably similar to those found to exist in biological vision systems (Hubel and Wiesel 1962) and/or designed into previous artificial character recognizers, such as spatial derivative estimators or off-center/on-surround type feature detectors.

Most misclassifications are due to erroneous segmentation of the image into individual characters. Segmentation is a very difficult problem, especially when the characters overlap extensively. Other mistakes are due to ambiguous patterns, low-resolution effects, or writing styles not present in the training set.

Other networks with fewer feature maps were tried, but produced worse results. Various fully connected, unconstrained networks were also tried, but generalization performances were quite bad. For example, a fully connected network with one hidden layer of 40 units (10,690 connections total) gave the following results: 1.6% misclassification on the training set, 8.1% misclassifications on the test set, and 19.4% rejections for 1% error rate on the remaining test patterns. A full comparative study will be described in another paper.

5.1 Comparison with Other Work

The first several stages of processing in our previous system (described in Denker *et al.* 1989) involved convolutions in which the coefficients had been laboriously hand designed. In the present system, the first two layers of the network are constrained to be convolutional, but the system automatically learns the coefficients that make up the kernels. This "constrained backpropagation" is the key to success of the present system: it not only builds in shift-invariance, but vastly reduces the entropy, the Vapnik-Chervonenkis dimensionality, and the number of free parameters, thereby proportionately reducing the amount of training data required to achieve a given level of generalization performance (Denker *et al.* 1987; Baum and Haussler 1989). The present system performs slightly better than the previous system. This is remarkable considering that much less specific information about the problem was built into the network. Furthermore, the new approach seems to have more potential for improvement by designing more specialized architectures with more connections and fewer free parameters.[1]

Waibel (1989) describes a large network (but still small compared to ours) with about 18,000 connections and 1800 free parameters, trained on a speech recognition task. Because training time was prohibitive (18 days on an Alliant mini-supercomputer), he suggested building the network from smaller, separately trained networks. We did not need such a modular construction procedure since our training times were "only" 3 days on a Sun workstation, and in any case it is not clear how to partition our problem into separately trainable subproblems.

5.2 DSP Implementation

During the recognition process, almost all the computation time is spent performing multiply accumulate operations, a task that digital signal processors (DSP) are specifically

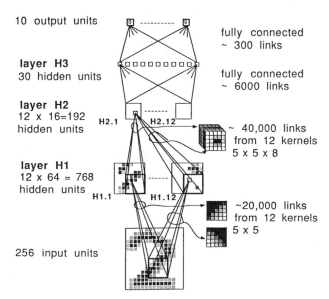

10 output units

layer H3
30 hidden units

fully connected
~ 300 links

fully connected
~ 6000 links

layer H2
12 x 16=192
hidden units

H2.1   H2.12

~ 40,000 links
from 12 kernels
5 x 5 x 8

layer H1
12 x 64 = 768
hidden units

H1.1   H1.12

~20,000 links
from 12 kernels
5 x 5

256 input units

Figure 3 Log mean squared error (MSE) (top) and raw error rate (bottom) versus number of training passes.

[1]A network similar to the one described here with 100,000 connections and 2600 free parameters recently achieved 9% rejection for 1% error rate. That is about 30% better than the best of the hand-coded-kernel networks.

designed for. We used an off-the-shelf board that contains 256 kbytes of local memory and an AT&T DSP-32C general purpose DSP with a peak performance of 12.5 million multiply add operations per second on 32 bit floating point numbers (25 MFLOPS). The DSP operates as a coprocessor; the host is a personal computer (PC), which also contains a video acquisition board connected to a camera.

The personal computer digitizes an image and binarizes it using an adaptive thresholding technique. The thresholded image is then scanned and each connected component (or segment) is isolated. Components that are too small or too large are discarded; remaining components are sent to the DSP for normalization and recognition. The PC gives a variable sized pixel map representation of a single digit to the DSP, which performs the normalization and the classification.

The overall throughput of the digit recognizer including image acquisition is 10 to 12 classifications per second and is limited mainly by the normalization step. On normalized digits, the DSP performs more than 30 classifications per second.

6   Conclusion

We have successfully applied backpropagation learning to a large, real-world task. Our results appear to be at the state of the art in digit recognition. Our network was trained on a low-level representation of data that had minimal preprocessing (as opposed to elaborate feature extraction). The network had many connections but relatively few free parameters. The network architecture and the constraints on the weights were designed to incorporate geometric knowledge about the task into the system. Because of the redundant nature of the data and because of the constraints imposed on the network, the learning time was relatively short considering the size of the training set. Scaling properties were far better than one would expect just from extrapolating results of backpropagation on smaller, artificial problems.

The final network of connections and weights obtained by backpropagation learning was readily implementable on commercial digital signal processing hardware. Throughput rates, from camera to classified image, of more than 10 digits per second were obtained.

This work points out the necessity of having flexible "network design" software tools that ease the design of complex, specialized network architectures.

Acknowledgments

We thank the U.S. Postal Service and its contractors for providing us with the data base. The Neural Network simulator SN is the result of a collaboration between Léon-Yves Bottou and Yann LeCun.

References

Baum, E. B., and Haussler, D. 1989 What size net gives valid generalization? *Neural Comp.* **1**, 151–160.

Becker, S., and LeCun, Y. 1988. *Improving the Convergence of Back-Propagation Learning with Second-Order Methods.* Tech. Rep. CRG-TR-88-5, University of Toronto Connectionist Research Group.

Bottou, L.-Y., and LeCun, Y. 1988. Sn: A simulator for connectionist models. In *Proceedings of NeuroNimes 88,* Nimes, France.

Denker, J., Schwartz, D., Wittner, B., Solla, S. A., Howard, R., Jackel, L., and Hopfield, J. 1987. Large automatic learning, rule extraction and generalization. *Complex Syst.* **1**, 877–922.

Denker, J. S., Gardner, W. R., Graf, H. P., Henderson, D., Howard, R. E., Hubbard, W., Jackel, L. D., Baird, H. S., and Guyon, I. 1989. Neural network recognizer for handwritten zip code digits. In D. Touretzky, ed. *Advances in Neural Information Processing Systems,* pp. 323–331. Morgan Kaufmann, San Mateo, CA.

Fukushima, K. 1980. Neocognitron: A self-organizing neural network model for a mechanism of pattern recognition unaffected by shift in position. *Biol. Cybernet.* **36**, 193–202.

Hubel, D. H., and Wiesel, T. N. 1962. Receptive fields, binocular interaction and functional architecture in the cat's visual cortex. *J. of Physiol.* **160**, 106–154.

LeCun, Y. 1987. Modèles connexionnistes de l'apprentissage. Ph.D. thesis, Université Pierre et Marie Curie, Paris, France.

LeCun, Y. 1989. Generalization and network design strategies. In *Connectionism in Perspective,* R. Pfeifer, Z. Schreter, F. Fogelman, and L. Steels, eds. North-Holland, Amsterdam.

Mozer, M.C. 1987. Early parallel processing in reading: A connectionist approach. In *Attention and Performance, XII: The Psychology of Reading,* M. Coltheart, ed., Vol. XII pp. 83–104. Erlbaum, Hillsdale, NY.

Patarnello, S., and Carnevali, P. 1987. Learning networks of neurons with boolean logic. *Europhys. Lett.* **4**(4), 503–508.

Rumelhart, D. E., Hinton, G. E., and Williams, R. J. 1986. Learning internal representations by error propagation. In *Parallel Distributed Processing: Explorations in the Microstructure of Cognition,* D. E. Rumelhart and J. L. McClelland, eds., Vol. I, pp. 318–362. Bradford Books, Cambridge, MA.

Tishby, N., Levin, E., and Solla, S. A. 1989. Consistent inference of probabilities in layered networks: Predictions and generalization. In *Proceedings of the International Joint Conference on Neural Networks,* Washington, DC.

Waibel, A. 1989. Consonant recognition by modular construction of large phonemic time-delay neural networks. In *Advances in Neural Information Processing Systems,* D. Touretzky, ed., pp. 215–223. Morgan Kaufmann, San Mateo, CA.

Wang, C. H., and Srihari, S. N. 1988. A framework for object recognition in a visually complex environment and its application to locating address blocks on mail pieces. *Int. J. Computer Vision* **2**, 125.

38
Introduction

(1988)
Teuvo Kohonen

The "neural" phonetic typewriter
Computer 21: 11–22

Computer magazine, published by the Computer Society of the Institute of Electrical and Electronics Engineers (IEEE), devoted its March 1988 issue to "Artificial Neural Systems." This paper, by Teuvo Kohonen, who has done distinguished work in neural network research for two decades, is taken from that issue, as is paper 31 in this volume. Kohonen's paper describes the application of a map-forming network to a difficult pattern recognition problem, speech recognition.

Recognition of speech by machines, like other perceptual tasks that humans do well, seems easy and yet in reality is very hard. As Kohonen points out, there is currently no successful speaker-independent general-purpose speech recognition system on the commercial market, though there are a number of useful systems that require training for individual speakers or that have limitations on vocabulary or grammar. Because of the widely accepted belief that neural network architecture has some, albeit tenuous, relationship to the brain, speech recognition seems like a natural problem for neural networks. There are now several neural net speech recognition systems that have been studied in some detail (see the review by Lippman (1989)). All show promise. The system described by Kohonen has probably progessed furthest toward development as a practical system. The model is also of more general interest because of its design, which uses a self-organizing topographic network, described in more detail by Kohonen (Paper 30 in *Neurocomputing: Foundations of Research*).

The model starts from the observation that sensory systems in the mammalian brain are organized topographically. For example, in the early stages of visual processing in cortex, units that are physically close to each other tend to respond to about the same region of the visual field. (See papers 15, 16, and 22 for more details about the biology of topographic maps.) Kohonen's model is designed to produce topographic maps that reflect the intrinsic organization of the inputs that drive them.

Map formation is accomplished by having the learning process encourage the development of neighborhoods, so that cells that are nearby will respond similarly to the input stimuli. Map-forming algorithms with a similar structure to Kohonen's are analyzed in the papers in this collection by Willshaw and von der Malsburg (paper 8) and by Amari (paper 9).

Kohonen assumes that there is a set of simple neural network neurons, arranged in a two-dimensional array. Neurons in the array are laterally interconnected, so that nearby units mutually excite each other and units farther apart inhibit each other. An important assumption is that all neurons receive the same input activity pattern: The system is fully connected. Local excitation surrounded by inhibition at greater distances is sometimes called a *Mexican hat* function, from its shape, and something like it is common in the visual system. The argument is that network dynamics arising from this interconnection pattern when an input pattern is applied to the network tend to form a local region of high activity—a "bubble"—surrounded by no activity. The bubble will be centered on the region of highest activity.

Although bubble formation is based on network dynamics, it is not actually necessary for the formal learning algorithm: The essential effect is formation of a neighborhood of activity, with a certain radius, centered on the most responsive units. The next step is to have all the units in the area of activity modify their synaptic weights using a Hebbian rule so that the weights become *more* like the input vector. The units in the neighborhood will then tend to become more like each other in their response because they are more likely to respond to the same pattern.

A simple network with this learning rule will self-organize. Suppose we have input patterns taken randomly from points on a two-dimensional input array, and we have a two-dimensional set of units. After training the units will reproduce the two-dimensional distribution from which the input patterns were drawn, so that units with the best response to similar spatial coordinates in the input distribution will be physically close to each other.

But the network will also generate topographic maps based on "closeness" when the inputs have a much more complex and higher-dimensional structure. For example, in speech it is not at all clear what the dimensions of the speech signal are. This has been a matter for debate among linguists for a generation. However, there is no doubt that there is *some* structure in the speech signals.

Suppose we train the network on data derived from speech. Kohonen actually uses a straightforward spectral representation, derived from a fast Fourier transform, of a segment of the speech waveform a few milliseconds long; fifteen numbers characterize the spectrum during that interval. This representation is sometimes modified slightly by adding a component representing amplitude or by incorporating two spectra taken from different times, 30 milliseconds apart.

A phoneme is roughly defined as an elementary sound in speech, say, a /t/ or an /o/. One reason speech recognition is hard is that there is a great deal of variation between different examples of the same phoneme from the same speaker, and much more between the same phoneme spoken by different speakers. In addition, a phoneme is strongly influenced by its neighbors so the same phoneme from the same speaker in different contexts may vary considerably.

Kohonen arranges the neural elements in the system in a two-dimensional array of about 100 units. The training process produces a "striking result." Even though phonemes were never explicitly taught to the system, different examples of the same phoneme tend to occur nearby each other on the map. The closeness process, whatever structure it is finding, seems to make contiguous regions on the array of units correspond to the same phoneme.

Once the map displays this behavior, and learning in this network is quite rapid, the speech problem becomes finding which region on the map corresponds to which phoneme. A word containing several phonemes corresponds to a trajectory on the map (see Kohonen's figure 8). If the map regions are connected to the appropriate letters on a typewriter, we have constructed a "phonetic typewriter." Because the correspondence between phonemes and written letters is so regular in Finnish, spelling produced this way is often correct. (This simple technique would not work well in English, which has notoriously irregular spelling.)

The learning process used to form maps depends on the formation of regions where cells are similar in responses, that is, an input tends to excite a region of cells. Is this true for the biological maps found in the brain? For some organizing parameters this seems true at first glance: In visual cortex, nearby cells respond to nearby regions in the visual field. However, cells in cortex respond to many other stimulus parameters as well: For example, they respond best to stimuli moving with a certain velocity, or to bars with a preferred orientation, or to input from just one eye or to input from both eyes, and to several other independent parameters as well. Often there are multiple superimposed maps; for example, the visual field map is laid on top of cells responding to one or the other eye or to favored orientations. Are nearby cells really correlated in their discharges? Often they are not. It does not make sense, from an information theoretic point of view, to use highly correlated units. If two units are highly correlated in their responses to possible input patterns, they are conveying less information than two uncorrelated units would. Suppose two cells are perfectly correlated, over the set of possible input patterns. Then one cell is redundant and can be removed with no loss of information capacity. If the cells are uncorrelated, both are necessary because the behavior of one cannot be predicted from the other.

It has been conjectured that one of the functions of lateral inhibition is to make cells behave *less* like each other, to become less correlated, thereby making more efficient use of the cells and transmission pathways in the visual system (see Linsker, paper 31, and Barlow, paper 14). Although the idea of mapping based on similarity is important, other processes are going on in the real nervous system as well.

Reference

R. Lippman (1989), Review of neural networks for speech recognition. *Neural Computation* 1: 1–38.

(1988)
Teuvo Kohonen

The "neural" phonetic typewriter
Computer 21: 11–22

In 1930 a Hungarian scientist, Tihamér Nemes, filed a patent application in Germany for the principle of making an optoelectrical system automatically transcribe speech. His idea was to use the optical sound track on a movie film as a grating to produce diffraction patterns (corresponding to speech spectra), which then could be identified and typed out. The application was turned down as "unrealistic." Since then the problem of automatic speech recognition has occupied the minds of scientists and engineers, both amateur and professional.

Research on speech recognition principles has been pursued in many laboratories around the world, academic as well as industrial, with various objectives in mind.[1] One ambitious goal is to implement automated query systems that could be accessed through public telephone lines, because some telephone companies have observed that telephone operators spend most of their time answering queries. An even more ambitious plan, adopted in 1986 by the Japanese national ATR (Advanced Telecommunication Research) project, is to receive speech in one language and to synthesize it in another, on line. The dream of a phonetic typewriter that can produce text from arbitrary dictation is an old one; it was envisioned by Nemes and is still being pursued today. Several dozen devices, even special microcircuits, that can recognize isolated

---

Based on a neural network processor for the recognition of phonetic units of speech, this speaker-adaptive system transcribes dictation using an unlimited vocabulary.

---

words from limited vocabularies with varying accuracy are now on the market. These devices have important applications, such as the operation of machines by voice, various dispatching services that employ voice-activated devices, and aids for seriously handicapped people. But in spite of big investments and the work of experts, the original goals have not been reached. High-level speech recognition has existed so far only in science fiction.

Recently, researchers have placed great hopes on artificial neural networks to perform such "natural" tasks as speech recognition. This was indeed one motivation for us to start research in this area many years ago at Helsinki University of Technology. This article describes the result of that research—a complete "neural" speech recognition system, which recognizes phonetic units, called *phonemes*, from a continuous speech signal. Although motivated by neural network principles, the choices in its design must be regarded as a compromise of many technical aspects of those principles. As our system is a genuine "phonetic typewriter" intended to transcribe orthographically edited text from an unlimited vocabulary, it cannot be directly compared with any more conventional, word-based system that applies classical concepts such as dynamic time warping[1] and hidden Markov models.[2]

Why is speech recognition difficult?

Automatic recognition of speech belongs to the broader category of pattern recognition tasks,[3] for which, during the past 30 years or so, many heuristic and even sophisticated methods have been tried. It may seem strange that while progress in many other fields of technology has been astoundingly rapid, research invest-ments in these "natural" tasks have not yet yielded adequate dividends. After ini-tial optimism, the researchers in this area have gradually become aware of the many difficulties to be surmounted.

Human beings' recognition of speech consists of many tasks, ranging from the detection of phonemes from speech wave-forms to the high-level understanding of messages. We do not actually hear all speech elements; we realize this easily when we try to decipher foreign or uncom-mon utterances. Instead, we continuously relate fragmentary sensory stimuli to con-texts familiar from various experiences, and we unconsciously test and reiterate our perceptions at different levels of abstrac-tion. In other words, what we believe we *hear*, we in fact *reconstruct* in our minds from pieces of received information.

Even in clear speech from the same speaker, distributions of the spectral sam-ples of different phonemes overlap. Their statistical density functions are not Gaus-sian, so they cannot be approximated ana-lytically. The same phonemes spoken by different persons can be confused too; for example, the /ɛ/ of one speaker might sound like the /n/ of another. For this rea-son, absolutely speaker-independent detection of phonemes is possible only with relatively low accuracy.

Some phonemes are spectrally clearer and stabler than others. For speech recog-nition purposes, we distinguish three acoustically different categories:

(1) Vocal (voiced, nonturbulent) pho-nemes, including the vowels, semivowels (/j/, /v/), nasals (/m/, /n/, /ŋ/), and liquids (/l/, /r/)

(2) Fricatives (/s/, / š /, /z/, etc.)

(3) Plosives (/k/, /p/, /t/, /b/, /d/,/g/, etc.)

The phonemes of the first two categories have rather well-defined, stationary spec-tra, whereas the plosives are identifiable only on the basis of their transient proper-ties. For instance, for /k,p,t/ there is a silence followed by a short, faint burst of voice characteristic of each plosive, depending on its point of articulation (lips, tongue, palate). The transition of the speech signal to the next phoneme also varies among the plosives.

A high-level automatic speech recogni-tion system also should interpret the semantic content of utterances so that it can maintain selective attention to partic-ular portions of speech. This ability would call for higher thinking processes, not only

> **Machine interpretation of complete sentences has been accomplished only with artificially limited syntax.**

imitation of the operation of the preatten-tive sensory system. The first large exper-imental speech-understanding systems followed this line of thought (see the report of the ARPA project,[4] which was com-pleted around 1976), but for commercial application such solutions were too expen-sive. Machine interpretation of the mean-ing of complete sentences is a very difficult task; it has been accomplished only when the syntax has been artificially limited. Such "party tricks" may have led the pub-lic to believe that practical speech recog-nition has reached a more advanced level than it has. Despite decades of intensive research, no machine has yet been able to recognize general, continuous speech produced by an arbitrary speaker, when no speech samples have been supplied.

Recognition of the speech of arbitrary speakers is much more difficult than generally believed. Existing commercial speaker-independent systems are restricted to isolated words from vocabularies not exceeding 40 words. Reddy and Zue esti-mated in 1983 that for speaker-independent recognition of connected speech, based on a 20,000-word vocabu-lary, a computing power of 100,000 MIPS, corresponding to 100 supercomputers, would be necessary.[5] Moreover, the detailed programs to perform these oper-ations have not been devised. The difficul-ties would be even greater if the vocabularies were unlimited, if the utter-ances were loaded with emotions, or if speech were produced under noisy or stressful conditions.

We must, of course, be aware of these difficulties. On the other hand, we would never complete any practical speech recog-nizer if we had to attack all the problems simultaneously. Engineering solutions are

therefore often restricted to particular tasks. For instance, we might wish to recognize isolated commands from a limited vocabulary, or to type text from dictation automatically. Many satisfactory techniques for speaker-specific, isolated-word recognition have already been devel-oped. Systems that type English text from clear dictation with short pauses between the words have been demonstrated.[6] Typing unlimited dictation in English is another intriguing objective. Systems designed for English recognize words as complete units, and various grammatical forms such as plural, possessive, and so forth can be stored in the vocabulary as separate word tokens. This is not possible in many other languages—Finnish and Japanese, for example—in which the grammar is implemented by inflections and there may be dozens of different forms of the same root word. For inflec-tional languages the system must construct the text from recognized phonetic units, taking into account the transformations of these units due to coarticulation effects (i.e., a phoneme's acoustic spectrum varies in the context of different phonemes).

Especially in image analysis, but in speech recognition too, many newer methods concentrate on structural and syntactic relationships between the pattern elements, and special grammars for their analysis have been developed. It seems, however, that the first step, preanalysis and detection of primary features such as acoustic spectra, is still often based on rather coarse principles, without careful consideration of the very special statistical properties of the natural signals and their clustering. Therefore, when new, highly parallel and adaptive methods such as arti-ficial neural networks are introduced, we assume that their capacities can best be uti-lized if the networks are made to adapt to the real data, finding relevant features in the signals. This was in fact one of the cen-tral assumptions in our research.

To recapitulate, speech is a very difficult stochastic process, and its elements are not unique at all. The distributions of the different phonemic classes overlap seri-ously, and to minimize misclassification errors, careful statistical as well as struc-tural analyses are needed.

The promise of neural computers

Because the brain has already imple-mented the speech recognition function (and many others), some researchers have reached the straightforward conclusion that artificial neural networks should be able to do the same, regarding these networks as a panacea for such "natural" problems. Many of these people believe that the only bottleneck is computing power, and some even expect that all the remaining problems will be solved when, say, optical neural computers, with a vast computing capacity, become feasible. What these people fail to realize is that *we may not yet have discovered what biological neurons and neural systems are like.* Maybe the machines we call neural networks and neural computers are too simple. Before we can utilize such computing capacities, we must know *what* and *how* to compute.

It is true that intriguing simulations of new information-processing functions, based on artificial neural networks, have been made, but most of these demonstrations have been performed with artificial data that are separable into disjoint classes. Difficulties multiply when natural, stochastic data are applied. In my own experience the quality of a neural network must be tested in an on-line connection with a natural environment. One of the most difficult problems is dealing with input data whose statistical density functions overlap, have awkward forms in high-dimensional signal spaces, and are not even stationary. Furthermore, in practical applications the number of samples of input data used for training cannot be large; for instance, we cannot expect that every user has the patience to dictate a sufficient number of speech samples to guarantee ultimate accuracy.

On the other hand, since digital computing principles are already in existence, they should be used wherever they are superior to biological circuits, as in the syntactic analysis of symbolic expressions and even in the spectral analysis of speech waveforms. The discrete Fourier transform has very effective digital implementations.

Our choice was to try neural networks in a task in which the most demanding statistical analyses are performed—namely, in the optimal detection of the phonemes. In this task we could test some new learning methods that had been shown to yield a recognition accuracy comparable to the decision-theoretic maximum, while at the same time performing the computations by simple elements, using a minimal amount of sample data for training.

In practical neural-network applications, the number of input samples used for training cannot be large.

Acoustic preprocessing

Physiological research on hearing has revealed many details that may or may not be significant to artificial speech recognition. The main operation carried out in human hearing is a frequency analysis based on the resonances of the basilar membrane of the inner ear. The spectral decomposition of the speech signal is transmitted to the brain through the auditory nerves. Especially at lower frequencies, however, each peak of the pressure wave gives rise to separate bursts of neural impulses; thus, some kind of time-domain information also is transmitted by the ear. On the other hand, a certain degree of synchronization of neural impulses to the acoustic signals seems to occur at all frequencies, thus conveying phase information. One therefore might stipulate that the artificial ear contain detectors that mimic the operation of the sensory receptors as fully as possible.

Biological neural networks are able to enhance signal transients in a nonlinear fashion. This property has been simulated in physical models that describe the mechanical properties of the inner ear and chemical transmission in its neural cells.[7,8] Nonetheless, we decided to apply conventional frequency analysis techniques, as such, to the preprocessing of speech. The main motivations for this approach were that the digital Fourier analysis is both accurate and fast and the fundamentals of digital filtering are well understood. Standard digital signal processing has been considered sufficient in acoustic engineering and telecommunication. Our decision was thus a typical engineering choice. We also believed the self-organizing neural

network described here would accept many alternative kinds of preprocessing and compensate for modest imperfections, as long as they occur consistently. Our final results confirmed this belief; at least there were no large differences in recognition accuracies between stationary and transient phonemes.

Briefly, the complete acoustic preprocessor of our system consists of the following stages:

(1) Noise-canceling microphone

(2) Preamplifier with a switched-capacitor, 5.3-kHz low-pass filter

(3) 12-bit analog-to-digital converter with 13.02-kHz sampling rate

(4) 256-point fast Fourier transform, computed every 9.83 ms using a 256-point Hamming window

(5) Logarithmization and filtering of spectral powers by fourth-order elliptic low-pass filters

(6) Grouping of spectral channels into a 15-component real-pattern vector

(7) Subtraction of the average from all components

(8) Normalization of the resulting vector into constant length

Operations 3 through 8 are computed by the signal processor chip TMS 32010 (our design is four years old; much faster processors are now available).

In many speech recognition systems acoustic preprocessing encodes the speech signal into so-called LPC (linear predictive coding) coefficients,[1] which contain approximately the same information as the spectral decomposition. We preferred the FFT because, as will be shown, one of the main operations of the neural network that recognizes the phonemes is to perform metric clustering of the phonemic samples. The FFT, a transform of the signal, reflects its clustering properties better than a parametric code.

We had the option of applying the overall root-mean-square value of the speech signal as the extra sixteenth component in the pattern vector; in this way we expected to obtain more information on the transient signals. The recognition accuracy remained the same, however, within one percent. We believe that the acoustic processor can analyze many other speech features in addition to the spectral ones. Another trick that improved accuracy on the order of two percent was to make the true pattern vector out of two spectra 30 ms apart in the time scale. Since the two samples represent two different states of the signal, dynamic information is added

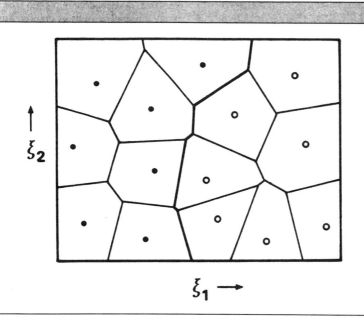

Figure 1. Voronoi tessellation partitions a two-dimensional (ξ_1, ξ_2) "pattern space" into regions around reference vectors, shown as points in this coordinate system. All vectors (ξ_1, ξ_2) in the same partition have the same reference vector as their nearest neighbor and are classified according to it. The solid and open circles, respectively, represent reference vectors of two classes, and the discrimination "surface" between them is drawn in bold.

to the preanalysis.

Because the plosives must be distinguished on the basis of the fast, transient parts of the speech waveform, we selected the spectral samples of the plosives from the transient regions of the signal, on the basis of the constancy of the waveform. On the other hand, there is evidence that the biological auditory system is sensitive not only to the spectral representations of speech but to their particular transient features too, and apparently it uses the nonlinear adaptive properties of the inner ear, especially its hair cells, the different transmission delays in the neural fibers, and many kinds of neural gating in the auditory nuclei (processing stations between the ear and the brain). For the time being, these nonlinear, dynamic neural functions are not understood well enough to warrant the design of standard electronic analogies for them.

Vector quantization

The instantaneous spectral power values on the 15 channels formed from the FFT can be regarded as a 15-dimensional real vector in a Euclidean space. We might think that the spectra of the different phonemes of speech occupy different regions of this space, so that they could be detected by some kind of multidimensional discrimination method. In reality, several problems arise. One of them, as already stated, is that the distributions of the spectra of different phonemic classes overlap, so that it is not possible to distinguish the phonemes by any discrimination method with 100 percent certainty. The best we can do is to divide the space with optimal discrimination borders, relative to which, on the average, the rate of misclassifications is minimized. It turns out that analytical definition of such (nonlinear) borders is far from trivial, whereas neural networks can define them very effectively. Another problem is presented by the coarticulation effects discussed later.

A concept useful for the illustration of these so-called vector space methods for pattern recognition and neural networks is called *Voronoi tessellation*. For simplicity, consider that the dissimilarity of two or more spectra can be expressed in terms of their vectorial difference (actually the norm of this difference) in an *n*-dimensional Euclidean space. Figure 1 exemplifies a two-dimensional space in which a finite number of *reference vectors* are shown as points, corresponding to their coordinates. This space is partitioned into regions, bordered by lines (in general, hyperplanes) such that each partition contains a reference vector that is the nearest neighbor to any vector within the same partition. These lines, or the midplanes of the neighboring reference vectors, constitute the Voronoi tessellation, which defines a set of *discrimination* or *decision surfaces*. This tessellation represents one kind of *vector quantization*, which generally means quantization of the vector space into discrete regions.

One or more neighboring reference vectors can be made to define a category in the vector space as the union of their respective partitions. Determination of such reference vectors was the main problem on which we concentrated in our neural network research. There are, of course, many classical mathematical approaches to this problem.[3] In very simple and straightforward pattern recognition, samples, or prototypes, of earlier observed vectors are used as such for the reference vectors. For the new or unknown vector, a small number of its nearest prototypes are sought; then majority voting is applied to them to determine classification. A drawback of this method is that for good statistical accuracy an appreciable number of reference vectors are needed. Consequently, the comparison computations during classification, expecially if they are made serially, become time-consuming; the unknown vector must be compared with all the reference vectors. Therefore, our aim was to describe the samples by a much smaller representative set of reference vectors without loss of accuracy.

Imagine now that a fixed number of discrete neurons is in parallel, looking at the speech spectrum, or the set of input signals. Imagine that each neuron has a template, a reference spectrum with respect to which the degree of matching with the input spectrum can be defined. Imagine further that the different neurons compete, the neuron with the highest matching score being regarded as the "winner." The input spectrum would then be assigned to the winner in the same way that an arbitrary vector is assigned to the closest reference vector and classified according to it in the above Voronoi tessellation.

660
Chapter 38

There are neural networks in which such templates are formed adaptively, and which perform this comparison in parallel, so that the neuron whose template matches best with the input automatically gives an active response to it. Indeed, the self-organizing process described below defines reference vectors for the neurons such that their Voronoi tessellation sets near-optimal decision borders between the classes—i.e., the fraction of input vectors falling on the wrong side of the borders is minimized. In classical decision theory, theoretical minimization of the probability for misclassification is a standard procedure, and the mathematical setting for it is the Bayes theory of probability. In what follows, we shall thus point out that the vector quantization and nearest neighbor classification resulting in the neural network defines the reference vectors in such a way that their Voronoi tessellation very closely approximates the theoretical Bayesian decision surfaces.

The neural network

Detailed biophysical analysis of the phenomena taking place at the cell membrane of biological neurons leads to systems of nonlinear differential equations with dozens of state variables for each neuron; this would be untenable in a computational application. Obviously it is necessary to simplify the mathematics, while retaining some essentials of the real dynamic behavior. The approximations made here, while reasonably simple, are still rather "neural" and have been influential in many intriguing applications.

Figure 2 depicts one model neuron and defines its signal and state variables. The input signals are connected to the neuron with different, variable "transmittances" corresponding to the coupling strengths of the neural junctions called *synapses*. The latter are denoted by μ_{ij} (here i is the index of the neuron and j that of its input). Correspondingly, ξ_{ij} is the signal value (signal activity, actually the frequency of the neural impulses) at the jth input of the ith neuron.

Each neuron is thought to act as a pulse-frequency modulator, producing an output activity η_i (actually a train of neural impulses with this repetition frequency), which is obtained by integrating the input signals according to the following differential equation. (The biological neurons have an active membrane with a

capacitance that integrates input currents and triggers a volley of impulses when a critical level of depolarization is achieved.)

$$d\eta_i/dt = \sum_{j=1}^{n} \mu_{ij}\xi_{ij} - \gamma(\eta_i) \quad (1)$$

The first term on the right corresponds to the coupling of input signals to the neuron through the different transmittances; a linear, superpositive effect was assumed for simplicity. The last term, $-\gamma(\eta_i)$, stands for a nonlinear leakage effect that describes all nonideal properties, such as saturation, leakage, and shunting effects of the neuron, in a simple way. It is assumed to be a stronger than linear function of η_i. It is further assumed that the inverse function γ^{-1} exists. Then if the ξ_{ij} are held stationary, or they are changing slowly, we can consider the case $d\eta_i/dt \sim 0$, whereby the output will follow the integrated input as in a nonlinear, saturating amplifier according to

$$\eta_i = \sigma[\sum_{j=1}^{n} \mu_{ij}\xi_{ij}] \quad (2)$$

Here $\sigma[.]$ is the inverse function of γ, and it usually has a typical sigmoidal form, with low and high saturation limits and a proportionality range between.

The settling of activity according to Equation 1 proceeds very quickly; in biological circuits it occurs in tens of milliseconds. Next we consider an adaptive process in which the transmittances μ_{ij} are assumed to change too. This is the effect regarded as "learning" in neural circuits, and its time constants are much longer. In biological circuits this process corresponds to changes in proteins and neural structures that typically take weeks. A simple, natural adaptation law that already has suggested many applications is the following: First, we must stipulate that parametric changes occur very selectively; thus dependence on the signals must be nonlinear. The classical choice made by most modelers is to assume that changes are proportional to the *product* of input and output activities (the so-called law of Hebb). However, this choice, as such, would be unnatural because the parameters would change in one direction only (notice that the signals are positive). Therefore it is necessary to modify this law—for example, by including some kind of nonlinear "forgetting" term. Thus we can write

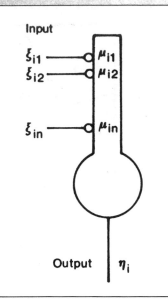

Figure 2. Symbol of a theoretical neuron and the signal and system variables relating to it. The small circles correspond to the input connections, the synapses.

$$d\mu_{ij}/dt = \alpha\eta_i\xi_{ij} - \beta(\eta_i)\mu_{ij} \quad (3)$$

where α is a positive constant, the first term is the "Hebbian" term, and the last term represents the nonlinear "forgetting" effect, which depends on the activity η_i; forgetting is thus "active." As will be pointed out later, the first term defines changes in the μ_{ij} in such a direction that the neuron tends to become more and more sensitive and selective to the particular combination of signals ξ_{ij} presented at the input. This is the basic adaptive effect.

On the other hand, to stabilize the output activity to a proper range, it seems very profitable for $\beta(\eta_i)$ to be a scalar function with a Taylor expansion in which the constant term is zero. Careful analyses have shown that this kind of neuron becomes selective to the so-called *largest principal component* of input.[9] For many choices of the functional form, it can further be shown that the μ_{ij} will automatically become normalized such that the vector formed from the μ_{ij} during the process tends to a constant length (norm) indepen-

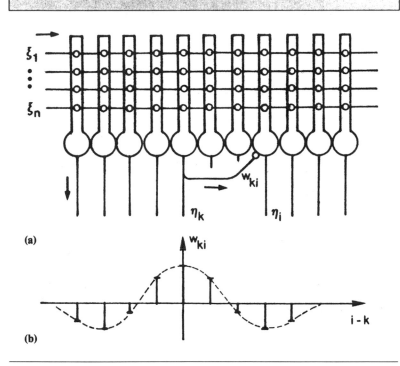

Figure 3. (a) Neural network underlying the formation of the phonotopic maps used in speech recognition. (b) The strengths of lateral interaction as a function of distance (the "Mexican hat" function).

dent of the signal values that occur in the process.[9] We shall employ this effect a bit later in a further simplification of the model.

One cannot understand the essentials of neural circuits unless one considers their behavior as a *collective* system. An example occurs in the "self-organizing feature maps" in our speech recognition application. Consider Figure 3a, where a set of neurons forms a layer, and each neuron is connected to its neighbors in the lateral direction. We have drawn the network one-dimensionally for clarity, although in all practical applications it has been two-dimensional. The external inputs, in the simplest model used for pattern recognition, are connected in parallel to all the neurons of this network so that each neuron can simultaneously "look" at the same input. (Certain interesting but much more complex effects result if the input connections are made to different portions of the network and the activation is propagated through it in a sequence.)

The feedback connections are coupled to the neurons in the same way as the external inputs. However, for simplicity, only the latter are assumed to have adaptive synapses. If the feedbacks were adaptive, too, this network would exhibit other more complex effects.[9] It should also be emphasized that the biological synaptic circuits of the feedbacks are different from those of the external inputs. The time-invariant coupling coefficient of the feedback connections, as a function of distance, has roughly the "Mexican hat" form depicted in Figure 3b, as in real neural networks. For negative coupling, signal-inverting elements are necessary; in biological circuits inversion is made by a special kind of inhibitory interneuron. If the external input is denoted

$$I_i = \sum_{j=1}^{n} \mu_{ij}\xi_{ij} \qquad (4)$$

then the system equation for the network

activities η_i, denoting the feedback coupling from neuron k to neuron i by w_{ki}, can be written

$$d\eta_i/dt = I_i + \sum_{k \in S_i} w_{ki}\eta_k - \gamma(\eta_i) \qquad (5)$$

where k runs over the subset S_i of those neurons that have connections with neuron i. A characteristic phenomenon, due to the lateral feedback interconnections, will be observed first: The initial activity distribution in the network may be more or less random, but over time the activity develops into clusters or "bubbles" of a certain dimension, as shown in Figures 4 and 5. If the interaction range is not much less than the diameter of the network, the network activity seems to develop into a single bubble, located around the maximum of the (smoothed) initial activity.

Consider now that there is no external source of activation other than that provided by the input signal connections, which extend in parallel over the whole network. According to Equations 1 and 2, the strength of the initial activation of a neuron is proportional to the dot product $m_i^T x$ where m_i is the vector of the μ_{ij}, x is the vector of the ξ_{ij}, and T is the transpose of a vector. (We use here concepts of matrix algebra whereby m_i and x are column vectors.) Therefore, the bubble is formed around those units at which $m_i^T x$ is maximum.

The saturation limits of $o[.]$ defined by Equation 2 stabilize the activities η_i to either a low or a high value. Similarly, $\beta(\eta_i)$ takes on either of two values. Without loss of generality, it is possible to re-scale the variables ξ_{ij} and μ_{ij} to make $\eta_i \in \{0,1\}$, $\beta(\eta_i) \in \{0,\alpha\}$, whereby Equation 3 will be further simplified and split in two equations:

$$d\mu_{ij}/dt = \alpha(\xi_{ij} - \mu_{ij}) \qquad (6a)$$
if $\eta_i = 1$ and $\beta = \alpha$ (inside the bubble)

$$d\mu_{ij}/dt = 0 \qquad (6b)$$
for $\eta_i = \beta = 0$ (outside the bubble)

It is evident from Equation 6 that the transmittances μ_{ij} then adaptively tend to follow up the input signals ξ_{ij}. In other words, these neurons start to become selectively sensitized to the prevailing input pattern. But this occurs only when the bubble lies over the particular neuron. For another input, the bubble lies over other neurons, which then become sensitized to that input. In this way different parts of the network are automatically "tuned" to different inputs.

The network will indeed be tuned to different inputs in an ordered fashion, as if a continuous map of the signal space were formed over the network. The continuity of this mapping follows from the simple fact that the vectors m_i of contiguous units (within the bubbles) are modified in the same direction, so that during the course of the process the neighboring values become smoothed. The ordering of these values, however, is a very subtle phenomenon, the proof or complete explanation of which is mathematically very sophisticated[9] and cannot be given here. The effect is difficult to visualize without, say, an animation film. A concrete example of this kind of ordering is the phonotopic map described later in this article.

Shortcut learning algorithm

In the time-continuous process just described, the weight vectors attain asymptotic values, which then define a vector quantization of the input signal space, and thus a classification of all its vectors. In practice, the same vector quantization can be computed much more quickly from a numerically simpler algorithm. The bubble is equivalent to a neighborhood set N_c of all those network units that lie within a certain radius from a certain unit c. It can be shown that the size of the bubble depends on the interaction parameters, and so we can reason that the radius of the bubble is controllable, eventually being definable as some function of time. For good self-organizing results, it has been found empirically that the radius indeed should decrease in time monotonically. Similarly $\alpha = \alpha(t)$ ought to be a monotonically decreasing function of time. Simple but effective choices for these functions have been determined in a series of practical experiments.[9]

As stated earlier, the process defined by Equation 1 normalizes the weight vectors m_i to the same length. Since the bubble is formed around those units at which $m_i^T x$ is maximum, its center also coincides with that unit for which the norm of the vectorial difference $x - m_i$ is minimum.

Combining all the above results, we obtain the following shortcut algorithm. Let us start with random initial values $m_i = m_i(0)$. For $t = 0, 1, 2, \ldots$, compute:

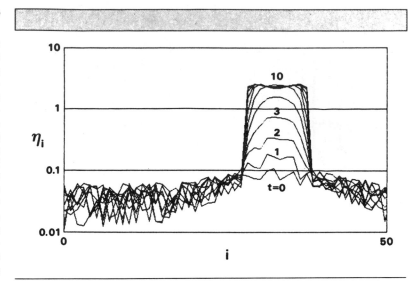

Figure 4. Development of the distribution of activity over time (t) into a stable "bubble" in a laterally interconnected neural network (cf. Figure 3). The activities of the individual neurons (η_i) are shown in the logarithmic scale.

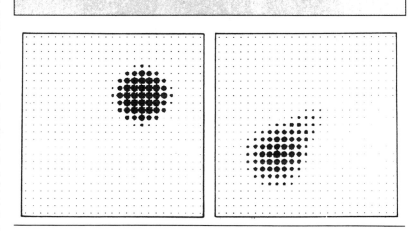

Figure 5. "Bubbles" formed in a two-dimensional network viewed from the top. The dots correspond to neurons, and their sizes correspond to their activity. In the picture on the right, the input was changing slowly, and the motion of the bubble is indicated by its "tail."

(1) *Center of the bubble (c)*:

$$\|x(t) - m_c(t)\| = \min_i \{\|x(t) - m_i(t)\|\} \quad (7a)$$

(2) *Updated weight vectors*:

$m_i(t + 1) = m_i(t) + \alpha(t) (x(t) - m_i(t))$
for $i \in N_c$

$m_i(t + 1) = m_i(t)$
for all other indices i (7b)

As stated above, $\alpha = \alpha(t)$ and $N_c = N_c(t)$ are empirical functions of time. The asymptotic values of the m_i define the vector quantization. Notice, too, that Equation 7a defines the classification of input according to the closest weight vector to x.

We must point out that if N_c contained the index i only, Equations 7a and 7b

stochastic input vector x, a function of time, to the network. The self-organizing process has been used to create a "topographic," two-dimensional map of speech elements onto the network.

Superficially this network seems to have only one layer of neurons; due to the lateral interactions in the network, however, its topology is in effect even more complicated than that of the famous multilayered Boltzmann machines or backpropagation networks.[11] Any neuron in our network is also able to create an internal representation of input information in the same way as the "hidden units" in the backpropagation networks eventually do. Several projects have recently been launched to apply Boltzmann machines to speech recognition. We should learn in the near future how they compete with the design described here.

The input vectors x, representing short-time spectra of the speech waveform, are computed in our system every 9.83 milliseconds. These samples are applied in Equations 7a and 7b as input data in their natural order, and the self-organizing process then defines the m_i, or the weight vectors of the neurons. One striking result is that the various neurons of the network become sensitized to spectra of different phonemes and their variations in a two-dimensional order, although teaching was not done by the phonemes; only spectral samples of input were applied. The reason is that the input spectra are clustered around phonemes, and the process finds these clusters. The maps can be calibrated using spectra of known phonemes. If then a new or unknown spectrum is presented at the inputs, the neuron with the closest transmittance vector m_i gives the response, and so the classification occurs in accordance with the Voronoi tessellation in which the m_i act as reference vectors. The values of these vectors very closely reflect the actual speech signal statistics.[11] Figure 6 shows the calibration result for different phonemic samples as a gray-level histogram of such responses, and Figure 7 shows the map when its neurons are labeled according to the majority voting for a number of different responses.

The speech signal is a continuous waveform that makes transitions between various states, corresponding to the phonemes. On the other hand, as stated earlier, the plosives are detectable only as transient states of the speech waveform. For that reason their labeling in Figure 7 is not reliable. Recently we solved the

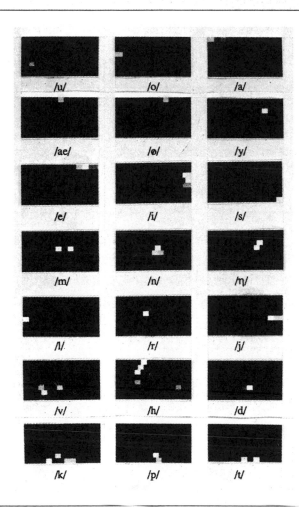

Figure 6. The signal of natural speech is preanalyzed and represented on 15 spectral channels ranging from 200 Hz to 5 kHz. The spectral powers of the different channel outputs are presented as input to an artificial neural network. The neurons are tuned automatically, without any supervision or extra information, to the acoustic units of speech identifiable as phonemes. In this set of pictures the neurons correspond to the small rectangular subareas. Calibration of the map was made with 50 samples of each test phoneme. The shaded areas correspond to histograms of responses from the map to certain phonemes (white: maximum).

would superficially resemble the classical vector quantization method called *k-means clustering*.[10] The present method, however, is more general because the corrections are made over a wider, dynamically defined neighborhood set, or bubble N_c, so that an *ordered* mapping is obtained. Together with some fine adjustments of the m_i vectors,[9] spectral recognition accuracy is improved significantly.

Phonotopic maps

For this discussion we assume that a lattice of hexagonally arranged neurons forms a two-dimensional neural network of the type depicted in Figure 3. As already described, the microphone signal is first converted into a spectral representation, grouped into 15 channels. These channels together constitute the 15-component

problem of more accurate detection of plosives and certain other phonemic categories by using special, auxiliary maps in which only a certain category of phonemes was represented, and which were trained by a subset of samples. For this purpose we first detect the presence of such phonemes (as a group) from the waveform, and then we use this information to activate the corresponding map. For instance, the occurrence of /k,p,t/ is indicated by low signal energy, and the corresponding spectral samples are picked from the transient regions following silence. The nasals as a group are detectable by responses obtained from the middle area of the main map.

Another problem is *segmentation* of the responses from the map into a standard phonemic transcription. Consider that the spectral samples are taken at regular intervals every 9.83 milliseconds, and they are first labeled in accordance with the corresponding phonemic spectra. These labeled samples are called *quasiphonemes*; in contrast, the duration of a true phoneme is variable, say, from 40 to 400 milliseconds. We have used several alternative rules for the segmentation of quasiphoneme sequences into true phonemes. One of them is based on the degree of stability of the waveform; most phonemes, let alone plosives, have a unique stationary state. Another, more heuristic method is to decide that if m out of n successive quasiphonemes are the same, they correspond to a single phoneme; e.g., $m = 4$ and $n = 7$ are typical values.

The sequences of quasiphonemes can also be visualized as trajectories over the main map, as shown in Figure 8. Each arrowhead represents one spectral sample. For clarity, the sequence of coordinates shown by arrows has been slightly smoothed to make the curves more continuous. It is clearly discernible that convergence points of the speech waveform seem to correspond to certain (stationary) phonemes.

This kind of graph provides a new means, in addition to some earlier ones, for the visualization of the phonemes of speech, which may be useful for speech training and therapy. Profoundly deaf people may find it advantageous to have an immediate visual feedback from their speech.

It may be necessary to point out that the phonotopic map is not the same thing as the so-called formant maps used in phonetics. The latter display the speech signal in coordinates that correspond to the two lowest formants, or resonant frequencies

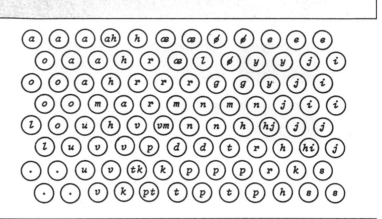

Figure 7. The neurons, shown as circles, are labeled with the symbols of the phonemes to which they "learned" to give best responses. Most neurons give a unique answer; the double labels here show neurons that respond to two phonemes. Distinction of /k,p,t/ from this map is not reliable and needs the analysis of the transient spectra of these phonemes by an auxiliary map. In the Japanese version there are auxiliary maps for /k,p,t/, /b,d,g/, and /m,n,η/ for more accurate analysis.

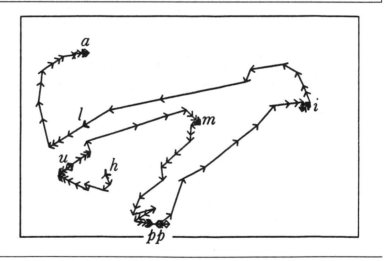

Figure 8. Sequence of the responses obtained from the phonotopic map when the Finnish word *humppila* was uttered. The arrows correspond to intervals of 9.83 milliseconds, at which the speech waveform was analyzed spectrally.

of the vocal tract. Neither is this map any kind of principal component graph for phonemes. The phonotopic map displays the images of the complete spectra as points on a plane, the distances of which

approximately correspond to the *vectorial differences* between the original spectra; so this map should rather be regarded as a *similarity graph*, the coordinates of which have no explicit interpretation.

Actually, the phoneme recognition accuracy can still be improved by three or four percent if the templates m_i are fine-tuned: small corrections to the responding neurons can be made automatically by turning their template vectors toward x if a tentative classification was correct, and away from x if the result was wrong.

Postprocessing in symbolic form

Even if the classification of speech spectra were error-free, the phonemes would not be identifiable from them with 100-percent reliability. This is because there are *coarticulation effects* in speech: the phonemes are influenced by neighboring phonemes. One might imagine it possible to list and take into account all such variations. But there may be many hundreds of different *frames* or *contexts* of neighboring phonemes in which a particular phoneme may occur. Even this, however, is an optimistic figure since the neighbors too may be transformed by other coarticulation effects and errors. Thus, the correction of such transformed phonemes should be made by reference to some kind of *context-sensitive stochastic grammar*, the rules of which are derived from real examples. I have developed a program code that automatically constructs the grammatical transformation rules on the basis of speech samples and their correct reference transcriptions.[12] A typical error grammar may contain 15,000 to 20,000 rules (productions), and these rules can be encoded as a data structure or stored in an associative memory. The optimal amount of context is determined automatically for each rule separately. No special hardware is needed; the search of the matching rules and their application can be made in real time by efficient and fast software methods, based on so-called hash coding, without slowing down the recognition operation.

The two-stage speech recognition system described in this article is a genuine phonetic typewriter, since it outputs orthographic transcriptions for unrestricted utterances, the forms of which only approximately obey certain morphological rules or regularities of a particular language. We have implemented this system for both Finnish and (romanized) Japanese. Both of these languages, like Latin, are characterized by the fact that their orthography is almost identical to their phonemic transcription.

Figure 9. The coprocessor board for the neural network and the postprocessing functions.

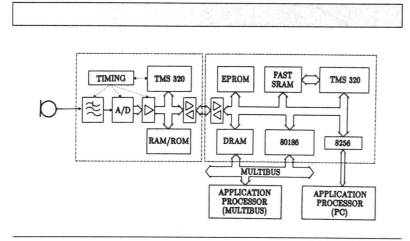

Figure 10. Block diagram of the coprocessor board. A/D: analog-to-digital converter. TMS320: Texas Instruments 32010 signal processor chip. RAM/ROM: 4K-word random-access memory, 256-word programmable read-only memory. EPROM: 64K-byte electrically erasable read-only memory. DRAM: 512K-byte dual-port random-access memory. SRAM: 96K-byte paged dual-port random-access memory. 80186: Intel microprocessor CPU. 8256: parallel interface.

As a complete speech recognition device, our system can be made to operate in either of two modes: (1) transcribing dictation of *unlimited* text, whereby the words (at least in some common idioms) can be connected, since similar rules are applicable for the editing of spaces between the words (at present short pauses are needed to insert spaces); and (2) isolated-word recognition from a large vocabulary.

In isolated-word recognition we first use the phonotopic map and its segmentation algorithm to produce a raw phonemic transcription of the uttered word. Then this transcription is compared with reference transcriptions earlier collected from a great many words. Comparison of partly erroneous symbolic expressions (strings) can be related to many standard similarity criteria. Rapid prescreening and spotting of the closest candidates can again be performed by associative or hash-coding methods; we have introduced a very effective error-tolerant searching scheme called *redundant hash addressing*, by which a small number of the best candidates, selected from vocabularies of thousands of items, can be located in a few hundred milliseconds (on a personal computer). After that, the more accurate final comparison between the much smaller number of candidates can be made by the best statistical methods.

Hardware implementations and performance

The system's neural network could, in principle, be built up of parallel hardware components that behave according to Equations 5 and 6. For the time being, no such components have been developed. On the other hand, for many applications the equivalent functions from Equations 7a and 7b are readily computable by fast digital signal processor chips; in that case the various neurons only exist *virtually*, as the signal processors are able to solve their equations by a timesharing principle. Even this operation, however, can be performed in real time, especially in speech processing.

The most central neural hardware of our system is contained on the coprocessor board shown in Figure 9. Its block diagram is shown in Figure 10. Only two signal processors have been necessary: one for the acoustic preprocessor that produces the input pattern vectors x, and another for timeshared computation of the responses from the neural network. For the time being, the self-organized computation of the templates m_i, or "learning," is made in an IBM PC AT-compatible host processor, and the transmittance parameters (synaptic transmittances) are loaded onto the coprocessor board. Newer designs are intended to operate as stand-alone systems. A standard microprocessor CPU chip on our board takes care of overall control and data routing and performs some preprocessing operations after FFT (such as logarithmization and normalization), as well as segmenting the quasiphoneme strings and deciding whether the auxiliary transient maps are to be used. Although the 80186 is a not-so-effective CPU, it still has extra capacity for postprocessing operations: it can be programmed to apply the context-sensitive grammar for unlimited text or to perform the isolated-word recognition operations.

The personal computer has been used during experimentation for all postprocessing operations. Nonetheless, the overall recognition operations take place in near real time. In the intended mode of operation the speech recognizer will only assist the keyboard operations and communicate with the CPU through the same channel.

One of the most serious problems with this system, as well as with any existing speech recognizer, is recognition accuracy, especially for an arbitrary speaker. After postprocessing, the present transcription accuracy varies between 92 and 97 percent, depending on speaker and difficulty of text. We performed most of the experiments reported here with half a dozen male speakers, using office text, names, and the most frequent words of the language. The number of tests performed over the years is inestimable. Typically, thousands of words have been involved in a particular series of tests. Enrollment of a new speaker requires dictation of 100 words, and the learning processes can proceed concurrently with dictation. The total learning time on the PC is less than 10 minutes. During learning, the template vectors of the phonotopic map are tuned to the new samples.

Isolated-word recognition from a 1000-word vocabulary is possible with an accuracy of 96 to 98 percent. Since the recognition system forms an intermediate symbolic transcription that can be compared with any standard reference tran-

scriptions, the vocabulary or its active subsets can be defined in written form and changed dynamically during use, without the need of speaking any samples of these words.

All output, for unlimited text as well as for isolated words, is produced in near real time: the mean delay is on the order of 250 milliseconds per word. It should be noticed that contemporary microprocessors already have much higher speeds (typically five times higher) than the chips used in our design.

To the best of our knowledge, this system is the only existing complete speech recognizer that employs neural computing principles and has been brought to a commercial stage, verified by extensive tests. Of course, it still falls somewhat short of expectations; obviously some kind of linguistic postprocessing model would improve its performance. On the other hand, our principal aim was to demonstrate the highly adaptive properties of neural networks, which allow a very accurate, nonlinear statistical analysis of real signals. These properties ought to be a goal of all practical "neurocomputers." □

References

1. W.A. Lea, ed., *Trends in Speech Recognition*, Prentice-Hall, Englewood Cliffs, N.J., 1980.

2. S.E. Levinson, L.R. Rabiner, and M.M. Sondhi, "An Introduction to the Application of the Theory of Probabilistic Functions of a Markov Process to Automatic Speech Recognition," *Bell Syst. Tech. J.*, Apr. 1983, pp. 1035-1073.

3. P.A. Devijver and J. Kittler, *Pattern Recognition: A Statistical Approach*, Prentice-Hall, London, 1982.

4. D.H. Klatt, "Review of the ARPA Speech Understanding Project," *J. Acoust. Soc. Amer.*, Dec. 1977, pp. 1345-1366.

5. R. Reddy and V. Zue, "Recognizing Continuous Speech Remains an Elusive Goal," *IEEE Spectrum*, Nov. 1983, pp. 84-87.

6. P. Petre, "Speak, Master: Typewriters That Take Dictation," *Fortune*, Jan. 7, 1985, pp. 56-60.

7. M.R. Schroeder and J.L. Hall, "Model for Mechanical to Neural Transduction in the Auditory Receptor," *J. Acoust. Soc. Am.*, May 1974, pp. 1055-1060.

8. R. Meddis, "Simulation of Mechanical to Neural Transduction in the Auditory Receptor," *J. Acoust. Soc. Am.*, Mar. 1986, pp. 703-711.

9. T. Kohonen, *Self-Organization and Associative Memory*, Series in Information Sciences, Vol. 8, Springer-Verlag, Berlin-Heidelberg-New York-Tokyo, 1984; 2nd ed. 1988.

10. J. Makhoul, S. Roucos, and H. Gish, "Vector Quantization in Speech Coding," *Proc. IEEE*, Nov. 1985, pp. 1551-1588.

11. D.E. Rumelhart, G.E. Hinton, and R.J. Williams, "Learning Internal Representations by Error Propagation," in *Parallel Distributed Processing, Explorations in the Microstructure of Cognition, Volume 1: Foundations*, ed. by David E. Rumelhart, James L. McClelland, and the PDP Research Group, MIT Press, Cambridge, Mass., 1986, pp. 318-362.

12. T. Kohonen, "Dynamically Expanding Context, with Application to the Correction of Symbol Strings in the Recognition of Continuous Speech," *Proc. Eighth Int'l Conf. Pattern Recognition*, IEEE Computer Society, Washington, D.C., 1986, pp. 1148-1151.

Teuvo Kohonen is a professor on the Faculty of Information Sciences of Helsinki University of Technology, Finland. He is also a research professor of the Academy of Finland, a member of the Finnish Academy of Sciences, and a member of the Finnish Academy of Engineering Sciences. He received his D.Eng. degree in physics from Helsinki University of Technology in 1962. His scientific interests are neural computers and pattern recognition.

Kohonen has written four textbooks, of which *Content-Addressable Memories* (Springer, 1987) and *Self-Organization and Associative Memory* (Springer, 1988) are best known. He was the first vice chairman of the International Neural Network Society. Kohonen is a senior member of the IEEE. He was awarded the Eemil Aaltonen Honorary Prize in 1983 and the Cultural Prize of Finnish Commercial Television in 1984.

Kohonen's address is Helsinki University of Technology, Laboratory of Computer and Information Science, Rakentajanaukio 2 C, SF-02150 Espoo, Finland.

39
Introduction

(1988)
Halbert White

Economic prediction using neural networks: the case of IBM daily stock returns
Proceedings of the IEE International Conference on Neural Netorks, San Diego, 1988,
pp. II-451 – II-459

Few applications of a predictive algorithm are of more general interest than financial prediction. One of us (Anderson) remembers a recent talk at a conference where the speaker was discussing the use of a neural network to predict future values of a chaotic function. One could almost see a stir of excitement moving across the audience as the same thought occurred to the listeners almost simultaneously: "My God, maybe we can use this thing to predict the stock market . . ."

The same thought occurred to Halbert White, an economist with expertise in statistical methods, financial prediction, and neural networks. There is a long, colorful and largely unsuccessful history of attempts to predict future stock prices, and techniques of varying usefulness and sophistication have been suggested by everyone from respectable academics to con artists. The basic problem seems to be that there is good evidence that, for actively traded stocks, the stock market is *efficient*. According to White, this means that "asset prices follow a random walk . . . the movement of an asset's price is completely unpredictable from publicly available information." New public information that genuinely changed the value of the stock would be immediately reflected in the price. Potential Gordon Geckos (of the movie *Wall Street*'s "Greed is good" fame) are acutely aware that insider information can give genuine profit possibilities because this private information will not be incorporated in the stock price, which is set by public information.

White used neural networks as a method for the technical analysis of the prices of IBM stock. Technical analysis uses only the past history of price movements to predict future movements. It does not incorporate other information about the world or the company. White started by performing a simple linear autoregressive analysis on the historical record of IBM prices. The results suggest strongly that the market is indeed efficient and not predictable. However, neural networks are supposed to be nonlinear and to be able to integrate very large amounts of information. So perhaps they could do better. Certainly some of the hype for the field has infused networks with a little bit of magic.

The most popular nonlinear network learning algorithm is backpropagation (papers 41 and 42 in *Neurocomputing: Foundations of Research*), and White used it for his simulation. The network was trained using a nonlinear least squares technique that should give the same asymptotic results as true backpropagation because standard backpropagation was excessively slow. The training set was 1,000 days of IBM stock price *returns*, a ratio derived from price movements and dividends that is independent of the absolute price of the stock. (Fortunately for investors, for most stocks there is a slow upward average movement of the price.)

The backpropagation network predicted the training set considerably better than did the linear autoregressive model. Alas when it was tested against new sets of IBM return data taken from times before and after those used for the training set, the network performed at the chance level. The better fit to the training set seemed to be due to the ability of the network to learn some specific large price movements that occurred during the training period. The tendency of neural networks to learn specific instances from the training set, especially ones that are somehow unusual, is well known.

This simulation suggests that there is no easy road to riches in the stock market by using neural nets as a predictor of prices. However, it is possible that by incorporating additional large amounts of information about the economy, about interest rates, about the weather, as well as other significant economic indicators such as the length of skirts or whether a former AFC or NFL team wins the Superbowl, it would be possible for a network to do better than chance. It might be worth a try. . . .

(1988)
Halbert White

Economic prediction using neural networks: the case of IBM daily stock returns
Proceedings of the IEEE International Conference on Neural Networks, San Diego, 1988,
pp. II-451 – II-459

Abstract

This paper reports some results of an on-going project using neural network modelling and learning techniques to search for and decode nonlinear regularities in asset price movements. We focus here on the case of IBM common stock daily returns. Having to deal with the salient features of economic data highlights the role to be played by statistical inference and requires modifications to standard learning techniques which may prove useful in other contexts.

I. Introduction

The value of neural network modelling techniques in performing complicated pattern recognition and nonlinear forecasting tasks has now been demonstrated across an impressive spectrum of applications. Two particularly interesting recent examples are those of Lapedes and Farber who in [1987a] apply neural networks to decoding genetic protein sequences, and in [1987b] demonstrate that neural networks are capable of decoding deterministic chaos. Given these successes, it is natural to ask whether such techniques can be of use in extracting nonlinear regularities from economic time series. Not surprisingly, especially strong interest attaches to the possibility of decoding previously undetected regularities in asset price movements, such as the minute-to-minute or day-to-day fluctuations of common stock prices. Such regularities, if found, could be the key to great wealth.

Against the optimistic hope that neural network methods can unlock the mysteries of the stock market is the pessimistic received wisdom (at least among academics) of the "efficient markets hypothesis." In its simplest form, this hypothesis asserts that asset prices follow a random walk (e.g. Malkiel [1985]). That is, apart from a possible constant expected appreciation (a risk-free return plus a premium for holding a risky asset), the movement of an asset's price is completely unpredictable from publicly available information such as the price and volume history for the asset itself or that of any other asset. (Note that predictability from publicly unavailable (insider) information is not ruled out.) The justification for the absence of predictability is akin to the reason that there are so few $100 bills lying on the ground. Apart from the fact that they aren't often

dropped, they tend to be picked up very rapidly. The same is held to be true of predictable profit opportunities in asset markets: they are exploited a soon a they arise. In the case of a strongly expected price increase, market participants go long (buy), driving up the price to its expected level, thus quickly wiping out the profit opportunity which existed only moments ago. Given the human and financial resources devoted to the attempt to detect and exploit such opportunities, the efficient markets hypothesis is indeed an attractive one. It also appears to be one of the few well documented empirical successes of modern economic theory. Numerous studies have found little evidence against the simple efficient markets hypothesis just described, although mixed results have been obtained using some of its more sophisticated variants (see e.g. Baillie [1988], Lo and MacKinley [1988], Malkiel [1985] and Shiller [1981]).

Despite the strength of the simple efficient markets hypothesis, it is still only a theory, and any theory can be refuted with appropriate evidence. It may be that techniques capable of finding such evidence have not yet been applied. Furthermore, the theory is realistically mitigated by bounded rationality arguments (Simon [1955, 1982]). Such arguments hold that humans are inherently limited in their ability to process information, so that efficiency can hold only to the limits of human information processing. If a new technology (such a neural network methods) suddenly becomes available for processing available information, then profit opportunities to the possessor of that technology may arise. The technology effectively allows creation of a form of inside information. However, the efficient markets hypothesis implies that as the new technology becomes publicly available, these advantages will dwindle (rapidly) and ultimately disappear.

In view of the relative novelty of neural network methods and the implications of bounded rationality, it is at least conceivable that previously undetected regularities exist in historical asset price data, and that such regularities may yet persist. The purpose of this paper is to illustrate how the search for such regularities using neural network methods might proceed, using the case of IBM daily common stock returns as an example. The necessity of dealing with the salient features of economic time series highlights the role to be played by methods of statistical inference and also requires modifications of neural network learning methods which may prove useful in general contexts.

II. Data, Models, Methods and Results

The target variable of interest in the present study is r_t, the one day rate of return to holding IBM common stock on day t, as reported in the Center for Research in Security Price's security price data file ("the CRSP file"). The one day return is defined as $r_t = (p_t - p_{t-1} + d_t)/p_{t-1}$, where p_t is the closing price on day t and d_t the dividend paid on day t. The one-day return r_t is also adjusted for stock splits if any. Of the available 5000 days of returns data, we select a sample of 1000 days for training purposes, together with samples of 500 days before and after the training period which we use for evaluating whatever knowledge our networks have acquired. The training sample covers trading days during the period 1974:II through 1978:I. The evaluation periods cover 1972:II through 1974:I and 1978:II through 1980:I. The training set is depicted in Figure 1.

Stated formally, the simple efficient markets hypothesis asserts that $E(r_t|I_{t-1}) = r^*$, where $E(r_t|I_{t-1})$ denotes the conditional expectation of r_t given publicly available information at time $t-1$, I_{t-1} (formally I_{t-1} is the σ-field generated by publicly available information), and r^* is a constant (which may be unknown) consisting of the risk free return plus a risk premium. Because I_{t-1} includes the previous IBM price history, the force of the simple efficient markets hypothesis is that this history is of no use in forecasting r_t.

In the economics literature, a standard way of testing this form of the efficient markets hypothesis begins by embedding it as a special case in a linear autoregressive model for asset returns of the form

$$r_t = w_0 + w_1 r_{t-1} + \cdots + w_p r_{t-p} + \varepsilon_t, \ t = 1,2,\ldots,$$

where $\underline{w} = (w_0, w_1, \ldots, w_p)'$ is an unknown column vector of weights, p is a positive integer determining the order of the autoregression, and ε_t is a stochastic error assumed to be such that $E(\varepsilon_t|I_{t-1}) = 0$.

The efficient markets hypothesis implies the restriction that $w_1 = \cdots = w_p = 0$ Thus, any empirical evidence that $w_1 \neq 0$ or $w_2 \neq 0 \ldots$ or $w_p \neq 0$ is evidence against the efficient markets hypothesis. On the other hand, empirical evidence that $w_1 = \cdots = w_p = 0$, while not refuting the efficient markets hypothesis, does not confirm it; numerous instances of deterministic nonlinear processes with no linear structure whatsoever are now well known (e.g. Sarkai and Tokumaru [1980]; see also Eckmann and Ruelle [1985]). The finding that $w_1 = \cdots = w_p = 0$ is consistent with either the efficient markets hypothesis or the presence of linearly undetectable nonlinear regularities.

An equivalent implication of the simple efficient markets hypothesis that will primarily concern us here is that $var\ r_t = var\ \varepsilon_t$, where var denotes the variance of the indicated random variable. Equivalently,

$$R^2 \equiv 1 - var\ \varepsilon/var\ r_t = 0$$

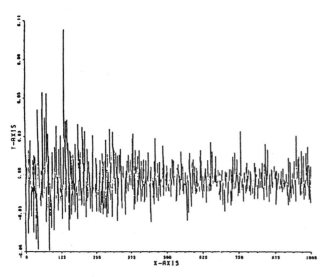

Figure 1

under the simple efficient market hypothesis. Thus, empirical evidence that $R^2 \neq 0$ is evidence against the simple efficient markets hypothesis, while empirical evidence that $R^2 = 0$ is consistent with either the efficient markets hypothesis or the existence of nonlinear structure.

Thus, as a first step, we examine the empirical evidence against the simple efficient markets hypothesis using the linear model posited above. The linear autoregressive model of order p ($AR(p)$ model) corresponds to a very simple two layer linear feedforward network. Given inputs $r_{t-1}, \ldots, r_{t-p}$ the network output is given as $\hat{r}_t = \hat{w}_0 + \hat{w}_1 r_{t-1} + \cdots + \hat{w}_p r_{t-p}$, where $\hat{w}_0 \hat{w}_1, \ldots \hat{w}_p$ are the network weights arrived at by a suitable learning procedure. Our interest then attaches to an empirical estimate of R^2, computed in the standard way (e.g. Theil [1971, p. 176]) as $\hat{R}^2 \equiv 1 - \hat{var}\,\varepsilon_t / \hat{var}\,r_t$, where

$$\hat{var}\,\varepsilon_t \equiv n^{-1}\sum_{t=1}^{n}(r_t - \hat{r}_t)^2,$$

$$\hat{var}\,r_t \equiv n^{-1}\sum_{t=1}^{n}(r_t - \bar{r})^2,$$

$$\bar{r} \equiv n^{-1}\sum_{t=1}^{n}r_t,$$

and n is the number of training observations. Here $n = 1000$.

These quantities are readily determined once we have arrived at suitable values for the network weights. A variety of learning procedures is available. A common learning method for linear networks is the delta method

$$\underline{w}_{t+1} = \underline{w}_t - \eta \underline{x}'_t(r_t - \underline{x}_t \underline{w}_t) \quad t = 1, \ldots, 1000$$

where $\underline{w}_t$ is the $(p+1) \times 1$ weight vector after presentation of $t - 1$ target/input pairs, η is the learning rate, and $\underline{x}_t$ is the $1 \times (p + 1)$ vector of inputs $\underline{x} = (1, r_{t-1}, \ldots, r_{t-p})$. A major defect of this method is that because of the constant learning rate and the presence of a random component ε_t in r_t, this method will never converge to a useful set of weight values, but is doomed to wander eternally in the netherworld of suboptimality.

A theoretical solution to this problem lies in allowing η to depend on t. As shown by White [1987a, b] an optimal choice is $\eta_t \alpha t^{-1}$. Nevertheless, this method yields very slow convergence. A very satisfactory computational solution is to dispense with recursive learning methods altogether, and simply apply the method of ordinary least squares (OLS). This gives weights by solving the problem

$$\min_{\underline{w}} \sum_{t=1}^{n}(r_t - \underline{x}_t\underline{w})^2.$$

The solution is given analytically as

$$\underline{w} = (X'X)^{-1}X'r,$$

where X is the $1000 \times (p+1)$ matrix with rows $\underline{x}_t$, r is the 1000×1 vector with elements r_t, and the -1 superscript denotes matrix inversion.

Network learning by OLS is unlikely as a biological mechanism; however, our interest is not on learning per se, but on the results of learning. We are interested in the performance of "mature" networks. Furthermore, White [1987a, b] proves that as $n - \infty$ both OLS and the delta method with $\eta_t \alpha t^{-1}$ converge stochastically to identical limits. Thus, nothing is lost and much computational effort is saved by using OLS.

When OLS is applied to the linear network with $p = 5$, we obtain $\hat{R}^2 = .0079$. By construction, $\hat{R}^2$ must lie between zero and one. The fact that $\hat{R}^2$ is so low suggests little evidence against the simple efficient markets hypothesis. In fact, under some statistical regularity conditions, $n\hat{R}^2$ is distributed approximately as χ_p^2 when $w_1 = \cdots = w_p = 0$. In our case, $n\hat{R}^2 = 7.9$, so we have evidence against $w_1 = \cdots = w_p = 0$ at less than the 10% level, which is below usual levels considered to be statistically significant. The plot of $\hat{r}_t$ also reveals the virtual absence of any relation between $\hat{r}_t$ and r_t. (See Figure 2.)

Thus, standard methods yield standard conclusions, although nonlinear regularities are not ruled out. To investigate the possibility that neural network methods can detect nonlinear regularities inconsistent with the simple efficient markets hypothesis, we trained a three layer feedforward network with the same five inputs and five hidden units over the same training period. The choice of five hidden units is not entirely ad hoc, as it represents a compromise between the necessity to include enough hidden units so that at least simple nonlinear regularities can be detected by the network (Lapedes and Farber [1987b] detected the deterministic chaos of the logistic map using five hidden units with tanh squashing functions; we use logistic squashes, but performance in that case at least is comparable, even with only three or even two hidden units) and the necessity to avoid including so many hidden units that the network is capable of "memorizing" the entire training sequence. It is our view that this latter requirement is extremely important if one wishes to obtain a network which has any hope at all of being able to generalize adequately in an environment in which the output is not some exact function of the input, but exhibits random variation around some average value determined by the inputs. Recent results in the statistics literature for the method of sieves (e.g. Grenander [1981], Geman and Hwang [1982]) suggest that with a fixed number of inputs and outputs, the number of hidden units should grow only

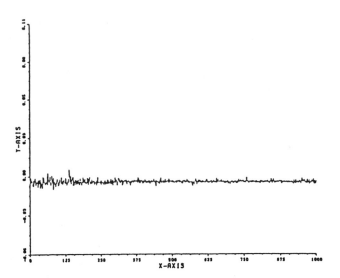

Figure 2

as some small power of the number of training observations. Over-elaborate networks are capable of data-mining as enthusiastically as any young graduate student.

The network achitecture used in the present exercise is the standard single hidden layer architecture, with inputs $\underline{x}_t$ passed to a hidden layer (with full interconnections) and then with hidden layer activations passed to the output unit. Our analysis was conducted with and without a logistic squash at the output; results were comparable, so we discuss the results without an output squash.

The output of this network is given by

$$\tilde{r}_t = \hat{\beta}_0 + \sum_{j=1}^{5} \Psi(\underline{x}_t \hat{\underline{\gamma}}_j)\hat{\beta}_j \equiv f(\underline{x}_t, \hat{\underline{\theta}})$$

where $\hat{\beta}_0, \hat{\beta}_1, \ldots, \hat{\beta}_5)$ are a bias and weights from the hidden units to the output and $\hat{\underline{\gamma}} \equiv (\hat{\underline{\gamma}}_1, \ldots, \hat{\underline{\gamma}}_5)$ are weights from the input units, both after a suitable training procedure; and Ψ is the logistic squashing function. The function f summarizes the dependence of the output on the input $\underline{x}_t$ and the vector of all connection strengths, $\hat{\underline{\theta}}$.

As with the preceding linear network, the efficient markets hypothesis implies that $\tilde{R}^2 \equiv 1 - v\hat{a}r\ \tilde{\varepsilon}_t/v\hat{a}r\ r_t$ should be approximately zero, where now

$$v\hat{a}r\tilde{\varepsilon}_t \equiv n^{-1}\sum_{t=1}^{n}(r_t - \tilde{r}_t)2$$

and

$$v\hat{a}r\ r_t = n^{-1}\sum_{t=1}^{n}n(r_t - \bar{r})^2$$

as before. This result will be associated with values for $\hat{\beta}_1, \ldots, \hat{\beta}_5$ close to zero, and random values for $\hat{\gamma}_j$. A value for $\tilde{R}^2$ close to zero will reflect the inability of the network to extract nonlinear regularities from the training set.

As with the linear network, a variety of training procedures is available. One popular method is the method of back propagation (Parker [1982], Rumelhart et. al. [1986]). In our notation, it can be represented as

$$\underline{\theta}_{t+1} = \underline{\theta}_t - \eta_t \nabla_\theta f(\underline{x}_t, \underline{\theta}_t)'(r_t - f(\underline{x}_t, \underline{\theta}_t))$$

where $\underline{\theta}_t$ is the vector of all connection strengths after $t-1$ training observations have been presented, η_t is the learning rate (now explicitly dependent on t) ∇_θ represents the gradient with respect to $\underline{\theta}$ (a row vector) and the other notation is as before.

Back propagation shares the drawbacks of the delta method previously discussed. With η_t a constant, it fails to converge, while with $\eta_t \alpha t^{-1}$, it converges (in theory) to a local minimum. Unfortunately, the random component of r_t renders convergence extremely difficult to obtain in practice. In fact, running on an IBM RT at well over 4 mips, convergence was not achieved after 36 hours of computation.

Rather quick convergence was obtained using a variant of the method of nonlinear least squares described in White [1988]. The method of nonlinear least squares (NLS) uses standard iterative numerical methods such a Newton-Raphson and Davidson-Fletcher-Powell (see e.g. Dennis [1983]) to solve the problem

$$\min_{\underline{\theta}} \sum_{t=1}^{n} (r_t - f(\underline{x}_1, \underline{\theta}))^2 \, .$$

Under general condition, both NLS and back-propagation with $\eta_t \alpha t^{-1}$ convergence stochastically to the same limit, as shown by White [1987a, b].

Our nonlinear least squares method yields connection strengths $\hat{\theta}$ which imply $\tilde{R}^2 = .175$. At least superficially, this is a surprisingly good fit, apparently inconsistent with the efficient markets hypothesis and consistent with the presence of nonlinear regularities. Furthermore, the plot of fitted $(\tilde{r}_t)$ values shows some very impressive hits. (See Figure 3.)

If for the moment we imagine that $\hat{\gamma}$ is given, and not the result of an optimization procedure, then $n\tilde{R}^2 = 175$ is χ_5^2 under the simple efficient markets hypothesis, a highly significant result by any standards. Unfortunately, $\hat{\gamma}$ is the result of an optimization procedure, not given *a priori*. For this reason $n\tilde{R}^2$ is in fact not χ_5^2; indeed, its distribution is a complicated non-standard distribution. The present situation is similar to that considered by Davies [1977, 1987] in which certain parameters (γ here) are not identified under the null hypothesis. A theory applicable in the present context has not yet been developed and constitutes an important area for further research.

Given the unknown distribution for $n\tilde{R}^2$, we must be cautious in claiming that the simple efficient markets hypothesis has been statistically refuted. We need further evidence. One way to obtain this evidence is to conduct out-of-sample forecasting experiments. Under the efficient markets hypothesis, the out-of-sample correlation between r_t and $\tilde{r}_t$ (or $\hat{r}_t$), where $\tilde{r}_t(\hat{r}_t)$ is computed using weights determined during the training (sample) period and inputs from the evaluation (out-of-sample) period, should be close to zero. If, contrary to the simple efficient markets hypothesis, our three layer network has detected nonlinear structure, we should observe significant positive correlation between r_t and $\tilde{r}_t$.

This exercise was carried out for a post sample period of 500 days, and a pre-sample period of 500 days. For the post-sample period we observe a correlation of $-.0699$; for the pre-sample period, it is $.0751$ (for comparison, the linear model gives post-sample correlation of $-.207$ and pre-sample correlation of $.0996$). Such results do not constitute convincing statistical evidence against the efficient markets hypothesis. The in-sample (training period) results are now seen to be over-optimistic, being either the result of over-fitting (random fluctuations recognized incorrectly as nonlinearities) or of learning evanescent features (features which are indeed present during the training period, but which subsequently disappear). In either case the implication is the same: the present neural network is not a money machine.

III. Concluding Remarks

Although some might be disappointed by the failure of the simple network considered here to find evidence against the simple efficient markets hypothesis, the present exercise suggests some valuable insights: (1) finding evidence

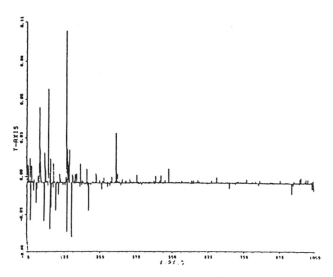

Figure 3

against efficient markets with such simple networks is not going to be easy; (2) even simple networks are capable of misleadingly overfitting an asset price series with as many as 1,000 observations; (3) on the positive side, such simple networks are capable of extremely rich dynamic behavior, a evidenced by time-series plots of $\tilde{r}_t$ (Figure 3).

The present exercise yields practical benefits by fostering the development of computationally efficient methods for obtaining mature networks (White [1988]). It also highlights the role to be played by statistical inference in evaluating the performance of neural network models, and in fact suggests some interesting new statistical problems (finding the distribution of $n\tilde{R}^2$). Solution of the latter problem will yield statistical methods for deciding on the inclusion or exclusion of additional hidden units to a given network.

Of course, the scope of the present exercise is very limited; indeed, it is intended primarily as a vehicle for presenting the relevant issues in a relatively uncomplicated setting, and for illustrating relevant approaches. Expanding the scope of the search for evidence against the efficient markets hypothesis is a high priority. This can be done by elaborating the network to allow additional inputs (e.g., volume, other stock prices and volume, leading indicators, macroeconomic data, etc.) and by permitting recurrent connections of the sort discussed by Jordan [1986]. Any of these elaborations must be supported with massive infusions of data for the training period: the more connections, the greater the danger of overfitting. There may also be useful insights gained by permitting additional network outputs, for example, returns over several different horizons (two day, three day, etc.) or prices of other assets over several different horizons, as well as by using within rather than between day data.

Another important limitation of the present exercise is that the optimization methods used here are essentially local. Although the final weight values were determined as giving the best performance over a range of different starting values for our iterations, there is no guarantee that a global maximum was found. A global optimization method such as simulated annealing or the genetic algorithm would be preferable.

Finally, it is extremely important to point out that while the method of least squares (equivalently, back-propagation) is adequate for testing the efficient markets hypothesis, it is not necessarily the method that one should use if interest attaches to building a network for market trading purposes. Such networks should be evaluated and trained using profit and loss in dollars from generated trades, not squared forecast error. Learning methods for this criterion are under development by the author.

References

Baillie, R.T. [1986]: "Econometric Tests of Rationality and Market Efficiency," Michigan State University Department of Economics Working Paper.

Davies, R.B. [1977]: "Hypothesis Testing When a Nuisance Parameter is Present Only Under the Alternative," *Biometrika* 64, 247-54.

Davies, R.B. [1987]: "Hypothesis Testing When a Nuisance Parameter is Present Only Under the Alternative," *Biometrika* 74, 33-43.

Dennis, J.E. [1983]: Numerical Methods for Unconstrained Optimization and Nonlinear Equations. Englewood Cliffs: Prentice-Hall.

Eckmann, J.-P. and D. Ruelle [1985]: "Ergodic Theory of Chaos and Strange Attractors," *Review of Modern Physics* 57, 617-656.

Geman, S. and C.H. Hwang [1982]: "Nonparametric Maximum Likelihood Estimation by the Method of Sieves," *Annals of Statistics* 70, 401-414.

Grenander, U. [1981]: *Abstract Inference.* New York: Wiley.

Jordan, M. [1986], "Serial Order: A Parallel Distributed Processing Approach," UCSD Institute of Cognitive Science Report 86-04.

Lapedes, A. and R. Farber [1987a]: "Genetic Data Base Analysis with Neural Nets," paper presented to the IEEE conference on Neural Information Processing Systems-Natural and Synthetic.

Lapedes, A. and R. Farber [1987b]: "Nonlinear Signal Processing Using Neural Networks," paper presented to the IEEE Conference on Neural Information Processing System-Natural and Synthetic.

Lo, A. and A.C. MacKinley [1988]: "Stock Market Prices do not Follow Random Walks: Evidence From a Simple Specification Test," *Review of Financial Studies* (forthcoming).

Malkiel, B.G. [1985]: *A Random Walk Down Wall Street.* New York: Norton.

Parker, D.B. [1982[: "Learning Logic," Invention Report, S81-64, File 1, Office of Technology Licensing, Stanford University.

Rumelhart, D.E., G.E. Hinton and R.J. Williams [1986]: "Learning Internal Representations by Error Propagation," in D.E. Rumelhart and J.L. McClelland eds., *Parallel Distributed Processing: Explorations in the Microstructures of Cognition,* Vol. 1, Cambridge: MIT Press, 318-362.

Sakai, H. and H. Tokumaru [1980]: "Autocorrelations of a Certain Chaos," *IEEE Transactions on Acoustics, Speech and Signal Processing* ASSP-28, 588-590.

Shiller, R.J. [1981]: "The Use of Volatility Measures in Assessing Market Efficiency," *Journal of Finance* 36, 291-304.

Simon, H. [1955]: "A Behavioral Model of Rational Choice," *Quarterly Journal of Economics* 69, 99-118.

Simon, H. [1982]: *Models of Bounded Rationality* (2 vols). Cambridge: MIT Press.

Theil, H. [1971]: *Principles of Econometrics.* New York: Wiley.

White, H. [1987a]: "Some Asymptotic Results for Learning in Single Hidden Layer Feedforward Network Models," UCSD Department of Economics Discussion Paper 87-13.

White, H. [1987b]: "Some Asymptotic Results for Back-Propagation," *Proceedings of the First Annual IEEE Conference on Neural Networks.*

White, H. [1988]: "A Performance Comparison for some On-Line and Off-Line Learning Methods for Single Hidden Layer Feedforward Nets," UCSD Department of Economics Discussion Paper.

Introduction

(1988)
Ning Qian and Terrence J. Sejnowski

Predicting the secondary structure of globular proteins using neural network models
Journal of Molecular Biology 202: 865–884

This paper applies a neural network to an important and difficult problem in biochemistry: predicting the shapes of protein molecules. Proteins are involved in every aspect of biological structure and function. Enzymes catalyze most biochemical reactions, and the bulk of tissue itself is largely composed of protein: Perhaps 75 percent of the dry weight of animal tissue is protein. There are many thousands of different kinds of protein molecules.

Proteins are put together from a small set of different components. There are about 21 different amino acids. To form a protein, a long chain of amino acids is connected together in a specific order. Proteins are large molecules, and a chain can contain hundreds of amino acids. As a point of terminology, when the chemical reaction occurs that actually links the amino acids, the resulting reacted, joined amino acids are called *amino acid residues*, or *residues*, a term that appears several times in this paper and its tables. The order in which the amino acids are joined to form a particular protein is determined by the sequence of base pairs on a segment of a DNA molecule in the genetic apparatus. Heredity is largely concerned with the passing of information about the details of protein construction from generation to generation.

The order of the amino acids used in the chain determines the shape of the molecule. Shape is critical. If a protein is to be used as an enzyme, the detailed shape determines its catalytic function: For example, bumps and grooves in the protein molecule can hold other molecules in the right orientation so chemical reactions can occur.

Protein chemists define several types of structure in protein molecules. Because amino acids in a chain can and do interact with each other, the protein molecule twists itself up to form its final complex shape. Instead of a long chain, the final shape of many proteins is *globular*, which really means ellipsoidal or compact, with a major to minor axis of ten or less. The bonds responsible for the major twists that turn the molecule back on itself are chemical bonds, but much of the local structure, which the neural network will try to predict, is due to weaker hydrogen bonding. An enzyme catalyzing a chemical reaction is something like a self-assembling molecular machine tool, a convenient device to have.

In describing proteins and their shape, the *primary* structure is the sequence of amino acids, and the *secondary* structure is the form of the local structure on the chain. *Tertiary* structure is the large-scale folding of the chain, and if one protein molecule fits together with others in a larger structure, it is called a *subunit* and is part of *quaternary* structure.

This paper constructs a neural network that tries to determine which form of *secondary* structure is present, when it is given a local sequence of amino acids. Qian and Sejnowski use a three-layer backpropagation algorithm, very similar to the one used by Sejnowski and Rosenberg in the famous text-to-speech simulation, NETtalk (paper 40 in *Neurocomputing: Foundations of Research*).

The input to the network is a "window" that looks at 13 contiguous amino acids. Each amino acid is coded by one active unit out of 21 possible units representing each position in the molecule, for a total of 273 input units. The number of units in the hidden layer ranged in number from 0 to 40. The effect of changing the number of hidden units was a parameter that Qian and Sejnowski studied carefully, because of its theoretical and practical importance.

There are three possible secondary structure configurations: α-helix, β-sheet, and coil. In the network, activity of one of three output units corresponds to one of these three states.

Qian and Sejnowski paid considerable attention to the construction of the training and testing sets. Very large numbers of proteins have had their amino acid sequence determined. Many of them are sufficiently well characterized so the details of their secondary structure are known and they can be used to construct a network training set. However, many proteins are very similar in sequence; that is, they are *homologous* proteins, where the exact sequence is varied somewhat to change function, or perhaps simply because of random variation from species to species. Natural variation is one of the essential mechanisms used by evolution (see papers 17, 18, and 19 for the use of selection and variation in neural networks).

The proteins used for most of the training and testing sets for the simulations were chosen to have sequences dissimilar from each other. However, proteins similar to proteins in the training set were used in a later test to see if the network could learn the peculiarities of one protein and apply it to a protein with a similar sequence.

During training the window of 13 amino acids was passed over the sequence, and the experimentally determined secondary structure at the location of the amino acid in the middle of the window was used as the desired output for the backpropagation algorithm. There were about 100 proteins in the training set, which gives rise to thousands of different sequence windows, as the window moves across the protein.

When the neural network was applied to real proteins, the results were far above the chance value of 33 percent but well below perfection: Results hovered around 63 percent for most network variants. This is good prediction and is somewhat better than previous statistical techniques. Qian and Sejnowski looked at many aspects of the resulting networks. For example, most of the information about secondary structure was coming from the amino acid in the middle of the window. The network also did the best predictions in the region of the protein near the ends, probably because there is less interference there from higher-level structure than in the middle of the chain.

Qian and Sejnowski's theoretically most significant results concerned manipulation of the number of hidden units. Hidden units are traditionally considered to be the place where higher-order correlations and some kinds of non-linearities make their effect felt on the network. Qian and Sejnowski found that with their simple grandmother cell input and output representations, accuracy was independent of the number of hidden units: That is, the hidden units were contributing *nothing* to the classification power of the network. A two-layer network worked just as well as a three-layer network. Building more data into the representation—some information on biophysical properties of the training set, or encoding information about pairs of amino acids—did nothing to improve performance. Changes in network architecture did not help either.

However, when the network was tested with homologous proteins, the situation changed. The reason seems clear. If there are large numbers of hidden units, it has often been observed that individual hidden units will learn particular examples. Obviously, if there are enough hidden units so that every member of the training set can be assigned its own unit, then the network will make no errors on the training set. But it is also observed that the resulting network will not generalize well to new data. However, if some of the test items are very similar to members of the training set, as they will be if they are homologous, then accuracy should go up as the network learns the peculiarities (as opposed to the generalities!) of the training set. And the more hidden units that are present, the higher the accuracy on the homologous training set should become. This is exactly what was found in the simulation.

A good deal of discussion is devoted to arguing that *any* method using strictly local features for predicting secondary structure will not do any better than the network. Therefore, the authors argue, it seems that building in some kind of input representing longer-range structure will be necessary to improve accuracy beyond what was obtained.

This paper describes a particularly satisfying set of simulations. First, Qian and Sejnowski are concerned with a very hard, real problem that has been attempted with other techniques so comparisons can be made. Second, the network did as well or better than previous attempts at prediction. It is not clear that any statistical method, using the data given, could have done better. Third, the response of the network to manipulations of structure and representation was not the result of magic. Instead the network responded in a systematic way, according to principles we are starting to understand.

(1988)

Ning Qian and Terrence J. Sejnowski

Predicting the secondary structure of globular proteins using neural network models

Journal of Molecular Biology 202: 865–884

We present a new method for predicting the secondary structure of globular proteins based on non-linear neural network models. Network models learn from existing protein structures how to predict the secondary structure of local sequences of amino acids. The average success rate of our method on a testing set of proteins non-homologous with the corresponding training set was 64·3% on three types of secondary structure (α-helix, β-sheet, and coil), with correlation coefficients of $C_\alpha = 0·41$, $C_\beta = 0·31$ and $C_{\text{coil}} = 0·41$. These quality indices are all higher than those of previous methods. The prediction accuracy for the first 25 residues of the N-terminal sequence was significantly better. We conclude from computational experiments on real and artificial structures that no method based solely on local information in the protein sequence is likely to produce significantly better results for non-homologous proteins. The performance of our method of homologous proteins is much better than for non-homologous proteins, but is not as good as simply assuming that homologous sequences have identical structures.

1. Introduction

Most of our knowledge of protein structure comes from the X-ray diffraction patterns of crystallized proteins. This method can be very accurate, but many steps are uncertain and the procedure is time-consuming. Recent developments in genetic engineering have vastly increased the number of known protein sequences. In addition, it is now possible to selectively alter protein sequences by site-directed mutagenesis. But to take full advantage of these techniques it would be helpful if one could predict the structure of a protein from its primary sequence of amino acids. The general problem of predicting the tertiary structure of folded proteins is unsolved.

Information about the secondary structure of a protein can be helpful in determining its structural properties. The best way to predict the structure of a new protein is to find a homologous protein whose structure has been determined. Even if only limited regions of conserved sequences can be found, then template matching methods are applicable (Taylor, 1986). If no homologous protein with a known structure is found, existing methods for predicting secondary structures can be used but are not always reliable. Three of the most commonly used methods are those of Robson (Robson & Pain, 1971; Garnier *et al.*, 1978), of Chou & Fasman (1978), and Lim (1974). These methods primarily exploit, in

different ways, the correlations between amino acids and the local secondary structure. By local, we mean an influence on the secondary structure of an amino acid by others that are no more than about ten residues away. These methods were based on the protein structures available in the 1970s. The average success rate of these methods on more recently determined structures is 50 to 53% on three types of secondary structure (α-helix, β-sheet, and coil: Nishikawa, 1983; Kabsch & Sander, 1983a).

In this paper, we have applied a new method for discovering regular patterns in data that is based on neural network models. The brain has highly developed pattern matching abilities and neural network models are designed to mimic them. This study was inspired by a previous application of network learning to the problem of text-to-speech. In the NETtalk system (Sejnowski & Rosenberg, 1987), the input to the network is strings of letters representing words and the output is strings of phonemes representing the corresponding speech sounds. Predicting the secondary structure of a protein is a similar problem, in which the input symbols analogous to letters are amino acids and the output symbols analogous to phonemes are the secondary structures.

The goal of the method introduced here is to use the available information in the database of known protein structures to help predict the secondary structure of proteins for which no homologous structures are available. The known structures implicitly contain information about the biophysical properties of amino acids and their interactions. This approach is not meant to be an alternative to other methods that have been developed to study protein folding that take biophysical properties explicitly into account, such as the methods of free energy minimization (Scheraga, 1985) and integration of the dynamical equations of motion (Karplus, 1985; Levitt, 1983). Rather, our method provides additional constraints to reduce the search space for these other methods. For example, a good prediction for the secondary structure could be used as the initial conditions for energy minimization, or as the first step in other predictive techniques (Webster et al., 1987).

2. Methods

(a) Database

Proteins with known structures were obtained from the Brookhaven National Laboratory. Secondary structure assignments based on the atomic co-ordinates were assigned by the method of Kabsch & Sander (1983b). We

selected a representative sample of proteins from the database that limited the number of almost identical sequences, such as the similar types of haemoglobin. Table 1 contains a listing of the 106 proteins that were used in our study. A subset of these proteins were taken out for testing and the remaining proteins used for the training set. Our results were highly sensitive to homologies between proteins in the testing and training sets, so homologies were exhaustively searched using diagon plots for all pairs of proteins (Staden, 1982). One of our 2 testing sets, listed in Table 2A, had practically no homologies in the training set. (α-Lytic protease in the testing set has very weak homologies with proteinase A in the training set but was included in the testing set to balance the proportion of residues with β-sheet structure. The inclusion of this protein reduced the overall testing accuracy, because β-sheet was the most difficult structure to predict.) A 2nd testing set with homologies is listed in Table 3A. The 6 proteins in the 2nd testing set had an average homology of 73% with 6 proteins in the corresponding training set, but little or no homology with the other training proteins, which were greatly in the majority. Special care was taken to balance the overall frequencies of α-helix, β-sheet and coil in the training and testing sets, as shown in Tables 2 and 3. The sequence of amino acids and secondary structures were concatenated to form 2 separate long strings for each of the training and testing sets, with spacers between the proteins to separate them during training.

Table 1
All proteins used to train and test networks

Code	Protein name	N	n_i	h	e	—
1abp	1-Arabinose-binding protein	1	All	106	18	182
1acx	Actinoxanthin	1	All	0	47	61
1apr	Acid protease	1	All	11	39	274
1aza	Azurin	2	1	13	43	73
1azu	Azurin	1	All	14	34	77
1bp2	Phospholipase A2	1	All	54	8	61
1cac	Carbonic anhydrase form c	1	All	18	68	170
1cc5	Cytochrome $c5$ (oxidized)	1	All	39	0	44
1ccr	Cytochrome c (rice)	1	All	44	0	67
1cpv	Calcium-binding parvalbumin b	1	All	52	6	50
1crn	Crambin	1	All	19	4	23
1ctx	α-Cobratoxin	1	All	4	16	51
1cy3	Cytochrome $c3$	1	All	16	0	102
1cyc	Ferrocytochrome c	1	All	35	0	68
1ecd	Haemoglobin (deoxy)	1	All	97	0	39
1est	Tosyl-elastase	1	All	13	82	145
1fc2	Immunoglobulin FC-Frag B complex	2	All	36	91	125
1fdh	Haemoglobin (deoxy, human fetal)	2	All	192	0	96
1fdx	Ferredoxin	1	All	5	4	45
1fx1	Flavodoxin	1	All	43	32	72
1gcn	Glucagon (pH 6-pH 7 form)	1	All	14	0	15
1gcr	γ-Crystallin	1	All	5	77	92
1gf1	Insulin-like growth factor	1	All	20	0	50
1gf2	Insulin-like growth factor	1	All	20	4	43
1gp1	Glutathione peroxidase	4	1,2	39	29	117
1hds	Haemoglobin (sickle cell)	4	1,2	152	0	135
1hip	High potential iron protein	1	All	10	9	66
1hmq	haemerythrin (met)	4	1	73	0	40
1ig2	Immunoglobunlin G1	2	All	15	186	255
1ige	Fc fragment (model)	2	1	16	121	185
1ins	Insulin	4	1,2	22	3	27
1ldx	Lactate dehydrogenase	1	All	114	45	170
1lz1	Lysozyme	1	All	39	10	81
1lzm	Lysozyme	1	All	83	14	67
1lzt	Lysozyme, triclinic crystal form	1	All	42	8	79
1mbd	Myoglobin (deoxy, pH 8·4)	1	All	113	0	40

Table 1 *(continued)*

Code	Protein name	N	n_i	h	e	–
1mbs	Myoglobin (met)	1	All	111	0	42
1mlt	Melittin	2	1	22	0	4
1nxb	Neutrotoxin b	1	All	0	26	36
1p2p	Phospholipase A2	1	All	45	6	73
1pfc	Fragment of IgG	1	All	4	34	73
1ppd	2-hydroxyethylthiopapain d	1	All	49	36	127
1ppt	Avian pancreatic polypeptide	1	All	18	0	18
1pyp	Inorganic pyrophosphatase	1	All	36	28	217
1rei	Immunoglobulin B-J fragment V	2	1	0	51	56
1rhd	Rhodanese	1	All	81	32	180
1rn3	Ribonuclease A	1	All	22	43	59
1sn3	Scorpion neurotoxin (variant 3)	1	All	8	12	45
1tim	Triose phosphate isomerase	2	1	106	42	99
1tgs	Trypsinogen complex	2	All	25	96	161
2act	Actinidin (sulphhydryl proteinase)	1	All	56	40	122
2adk	Adenylate kinase	1	All	108	22	64
2alp	α-Lytic protease	1	All	8	104	86
2ape	Acid proteinase, endothiapepsin	1	All	9	102	197
2app	Acid proteinase, penicillopepsin	1	All	30	147	146
2b5c	Cytochrome $b5$ (oxidized)	1	All	21	21	43
2cab	Carbonic anhydrase form b	1	All	17	77	162
2ccy	Cytochrome c (prime)	2	1	90	0	37
2cdv	Cytochrome $c3$	1	All	27	10	70
2cyp	Cytochrome c peroxidase	1	All	134	16	143
2dhb	Haemoglobin (horse, deoxy)	2	All	172	0	116
2fdl	Ferredoxin	1	All	0	0	106
2gch	γ-Chymotrypsin a	3	All	14	78	147
2gn5	Gene 5/DNA binding protein	1	All	0	4	83
2grs	Glutathione reductase	1	All	125	86	250
2icb	Calcium-binding protein	1	All	47	0	28
2kai	Kallikrein a	3	All	17	86	188
2lh1	Leghaemoglobin (acetate, met)	1	All	107	0	46
2lhb	Haemoglobin V (cyano, met)	1	All	100	0	49
2mcp	Ig Fab mcpc603/phosphocholine	2	All	8	211	224
2mdh	Cytoplasmic malate dehydrogenase	2	All	213	110	327
2mt2	Cd, Zn metallothionein	1	All	0	0	61
2pab	Prealbumin (human plasma)	2	1	8	59	47
2rhe	Immunoglobulin B-J fragment V-MN	1	All	0	49	65
2sbt	Subtilisin novo	2	All	59	38	179
2sga	Proteinase A	1	All	12	98	71
2sns	Staphylococcal nuclease complex	1	All	26	28	87
2sod	Cu,Zn superoxide dismutase	4	1	0	58	93
2ssi	*Streptomyces* subtilisin inhibito	1	All	17	26	64
2stv	Satellite tobacco necrosis virus	1	All	18	82	84
2taa	Taka-amylase a	1	All	99	69	310
2tbv	Tomato bushy stunt virus	6	1,2,5	8	164	321
3c2c	Cytochrome $c2$ (reduced)	1	All	44	0	68
3cna	Concanavalin A	1	All	0	96	141
3fxc	Ferredoxin	1	All	7	15	76
3gpd	Glyceraldehyde-3-P-dehydrogenase	2	1	85	70	179
3hhb	Haemoglobin (deoxy)	2	All	196	0	92
3pcy	Plastocyanin (Hg^{2+} substituted)	1	All	4	35	60
3pgk	Phosphoglycerate kinase complex	1	All	143	46	226
3pgm	Phosphoglycerate mutase	1	All	69	15	146
3rp2	Rat mast cell protease	2	1	12	83	129
3sgb	Proteinase B	2	All	22	107	107
3tln	Thermolysin	1	All	118	52	146
451c	Cytochrome $c551$ (reduced)	1	All	38	0	44
4cts	Citrate synthase complex	2	1	223	18	196
4dfr	Dihydrofolate reductase	2	1	33	49	77
4fxn	Flavodoxin (semiquinone form)	1	All	47	29	62
4sbv	Southern bean mosaic virus coat protein	3	1,3	56	142	224
5atc	Aspartate carbamoyltransferase	4	1,2	134	62	268
5cpa	Carboxypeptidase	1	All	108	50	149
5ldh	Lactate dehydrogenase complex	1	All	124	31	178
5pti	Trypsin inhibitor	1	All	8	14	36
5rxn	Rubredoxin (oxidized)	1	All	0	8	46
6adh	Alcohol dehydrogenase complex	2	1	58	72	244
6api	Modified α-1-antitrypsin	2	All	109	124	142
8cat	Catalase	2	1	137	77	284

N, total number of subunit chains in the protein; n_i, subunit numbers used in this study; h, α-helix; e, β-sheet; –, coil.

Table 2
Proteins in testing and training set 1

A. *Testing set proteins with no homology with corresponding training set*

Code	Protein name
1abp	L-Arabinose-binding protein
1acx	Actinoxanthin
1hmq	Haemerythrin (met)
1ige	Fc fragment (model)
1nxb	Neurotoxin B
1ppd	2-Hydroxyethylthiopapain d
1pyp	Inorganic pyrophosphatase
2act	Actinidin (sulphhydryl proteinase)
2alp	α-Lytic protease
2cdv	Cytochrome c3
2grs	Glutathione reductase
2lhb	Haemoglobin V (cyano,met)
2sbt	Subtilisin novo
3gpd	Glyceraldehyde-3-P-dehydrogenase
6api	Modified α-1-antitrypsin

Total number of residues: 3520

Amino acid fractions

A : 0·090	C : 0·012	D : 0·055	E : 0·051	F : 0·038
G : 0·091	H : 0·024	I : 0·055	K : 0·068	L : 0·066
M : 0·019	N : 0·045	P : 0·046	Q : 0·035	R : 0·032
S : 0·072	T : 0·070	V : 0·079	W : 0·014	Y : 0·033

Secondary structure fractions

h, 0·241   e, 0·213   –, 0·547

B. *The training set*

Training set proteins: proteins in Table 1 minus Table 2A

Total number of residues: 18105

Amino acid fractions

A : 0·087	C : 0·015	D : 0·056	E : 0·048	F : 0·038
G : 0·086	H : 0·024	I : 0·045	K : 0·067	L : 0·083
M : 0·015	N : 0·048	P : 0·045	Q : 0·036	R : 0·034
S : 0·077	T : 0·064	V : 0·074	W : 0·015	Y : 0·035

Secondary structure fractions

h, 0·254   e, 0·201   –, 0·546

Table 3
Proteins in testing and training set 2

A. *Testing set proteins with homology with corresponding training set*

Code	Protein name
1p2p	Phospholipase A2
2ape	Acid proteinase, endothiapepsin
2rhe	Immunoglobulin B-J fragment V-MN
2sga	Proteinase A
3hhb	Haemoglobin (deoxy)
5ldh	Lactate dehydrogenase complex

Total number of residues: 1357

Amino acid fractions

A : 0·101	C : 0·012	D : 0·051	E : 0·032	F : 0·034
G : 0·103	H : 0·026	I : 0·041	K : 0·047	L : 0·091
M : 0·012	N : 0·054	P : 0·036	Q : 0·033	R : 0·021
S : 0·096	T : 0·070	V : 0·084	W : 0·012	Y : 0·035

Secondary structure fractions

h, 0·292   e, 0·211   –, 0·498

B. *The training set*

Training set proteins: proteins in Table 1 minus Table 3A

Total number of residues: 20268

Amino acid fractions

A : 0·087	C : 0·015	D : 0·056	E : 0·049	F : 0·038
G : 0·086	H : 0·024	I : 0·047	K : 0·068	L : 0·080
M : 0·016	N : 0·047	P : 0·046	Q : 0·036	R : 0·034
S : 0·075	T : 0·064	V : 0·074	W : 0·015	Y : 0·035

Secondary structure fractions

h, 0·249   e, 0·202   –, 0·549

overall success rate of network models during learning, although it is not as good an indicator as the individual correlation coefficients.

(c) *Neural networks and their properties*

The neural network models used in this study are based on a class of supervised learning algorithms first developed by Rosenblatt (1959) and Widrow & Hoff (1960). These are networks of non-linear processing units that have adjustable connection strengths, or weights between them, and learning consists in altering the values of the weights in response to a "teaching" signal that provides information about the correct classification in input patterns. In the present study, the teacher was the secondary structure assignments of Kabsch & Sander (1983b) based on the Brookhaven databank of protein structures. In this section, we give a brief introduction to feedforward neural networks and the back-propagation learning algorithm used in this study. Further details can be found in Rumelhart et al. (1986) and Sejnowski & Rosenberg (1987).

A feedforward network is composed of 2 or more layers of processing units. The first is the input layer, the last is the output layer, and all the other layers between are termed hidden layers. There are feedforward connections from all the units in one layer to those on the next layer, as shown in Fig. 1. The strength of the connection from unit j to unit i, called a weight, is represented by a real number, w_{ij}. The state of each unit, s_i, has a real value in the range between 0 and 1. The states of all the input

(b) *Performance measures*

There are many ways to assess the performance of a method for predicting secondary structures. The most commonly used measure is a simple success rate, or Q_3, which is the percentage of correctly predicted residues on all 3 types of secondary structure:

$$Q_3 = \frac{P_\alpha + P_\beta + P_{coil}}{N}, \quad (1)$$

where N is the total number of predicted residues and P_α is the number of correctly predicted secondary structures of type a. The correlation coefficient (Mathews, 1975) is another useful measure, defined here for the α-helix:

$$C_\alpha = \frac{(p_\alpha n_\alpha) - (u_\alpha o_\alpha)}{\sqrt{(n_\alpha + u_\alpha)(n_\alpha + o_\alpha)(p_\alpha + u_\alpha)(p_\alpha + o_\alpha)}}, \quad (2)$$

where p_α is the number of positive cases that were correctly predicted, n_α is the number of negative cases that were correctly rejected, o_α is the number of over-predicted cases (false positives), and u_α is the number of underpredicted cases (misses). Similar expressions hold for C_β and C_{coil}. The Q_3 measure will be used to assay the

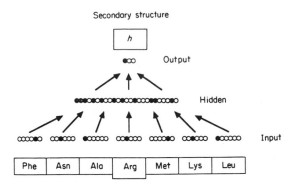

Sequence of amino acids

Figure 1. A diagram of network architecture. The standard network had 13 input groups, with 21 units/group, representing a stretch of 13 contiguous amino acids (only 7 input groups and 7 units/group are illustrated). Information from the input layer is transformed by an intermediate layer of "hidden" units to produce a pattern of activity in 3 output units, which represent the secondary structure prediction for the central amino acid.

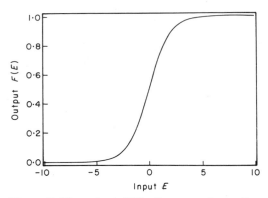

Figure 2. The output $F(E)$ of a processing unit as a function of the sum E of its inputs.

units that form an input vector are determined by an input window of amino acid residues (typically 13) through an input coding scheme (see the next section). Starting from the 1st hidden layer and moving toward the output layer, the state of each unit i in the network is determined by:

$$s_i = F(E_i) = \frac{1}{1 + e^{-E_i}}. \qquad (3)$$

where the total input E_i to unit i is:

$$E_i = \sum_j w_{ij} s_j + b_i \qquad (4)$$

and b_i is the bias of the unit, as shown in Fig. 2.

The goal of this network is to carry out a desired input–output mapping. For our problem, the mapping is from amino acid sequences to secondary structures (as explained in detail in the next section). The back-propagation learning algorithm can be used in networks with hidden layers to find a set of weights that performs the correct mapping between sequences and structures. Starting with an initial set of randomly assigned numbers, the weights are altered by gradient descent to minimize the error between the desired and the actual output vectors.

A network with a single layer of modifiable weights (i.e. no hidden layers), called a "perceptron" (Rosenblatt, 1959), has been analysed extensively by Minsky & Papert (1969). An important concept introduced by them is the order of a mapping, defined as the smallest number n such that the mapping can be achieved by a perceptron whose input have supports equal to or smaller than n. The support of an input unit is the number of elements in the input array that are encoded by the input unit. For example, most of our networks use a local coding scheme in which the input units have a support of 1, since each of them codes only a single amino acid. We have also used 2nd order conjunctive encodings in which an input unit encodes combinations of 2 amino acids, and thus has a support of 2. By definition, if a mapping can be

performed by a perceptron with the support of all of its input units equal to 1, then the order of this mapping is 1. Minsky & Papert (1969) showed very elegantly that many interesting mappings are of very high order and cannot be performed by a perceptron that does not have any input units with support larger than 1.

For the convenience of description, we define nth order perceptrons as those whose input units have size of support up to and including n. According to the above discussion, a 1st order perceptron can perform only a limited part of a higher order mapping correctly. In this paper, we define the 1st order features of a mapping as the part of the mapping that can be predicted by any 1st order perceptron, and the 2nd order features as the additional part of the mapping that can be performed by any 2nd order perceptron, and so on. With regard to the problem of predicting secondary structure of proteins, the 1st order features are the part of the mapping that can be predicted by each individual amino acid in the input window, and the 2nd order features are the part determined by all pairs of amino acids.

In principle, networks with hidden layers can extract higher-order features even when all of their input units have a support of 1. Learning algorithms for networks with more than one layer of modifiable weights have been introduced only recently (Ackley et al., 1985; Rumelhart et al., 1986). Not all of the information available may be extractable with a particular learning algorithm. An example is given in Results, section (a), where the back-propagation learning algorithm fails to recover a small amount of the 1st order features available to a 1st order perceptron.

A 1st order feature as defined above is stronger than the 1st order statistics used in standard statistical treatments. (We thank Dr Richard Durbin for pointing this out to us.) We illustrate the difference in the following example. Consider 2 sets of input–output mappings in Table 4. Define $P(I_i, O)$ as the joint probability that the ith $(=1, 2, 3, 4)$ input unit is equal to I_i $(=0, 1)$ and the output unit is equal to O $(=0, 1)$. The joint probabilities are identical for both sets of mappings as shown in Table 5. Therefore, these 2 sets have the same 1st order statistics. However, these 2 sets can be learned by 2 different 1st order perceptrons with the weights given in Table 6. These 1st order perceptrons, therefore, have extracted more information than 1st order statistics. This observation will be used to explain why the neural network method yields better results than

Table 4

Two sets of mappings with identical first order statistics

	Set 1				Set 2			
	Input			Output	Input			Output
0	0	1	0	1	0	0	1	0	0
0	0	0	1	0	0	0	0	1	1
0	1	1	0	0	1	0	1	0	1
1	0	0	1	1	0	1	0	1	0

Table 6

Weights for the two mappings in Table 4

	Input position i			
Set	1	2	3	4
1	2	-2	1	-1
2	2	2	-1	1

Two sets of weights for the 2 single-layer networks that perform the mappings in Table 4. The biases of all the units are 0.

the information theory method of Robson & Suzuki (1976).

(d) Network design

The network design used in this study is similar to the NETtalk system (Sejnowski & Rosenberg, 1987). The network maps sequences of input symbols onto sequences of output symbols. Here, the input symbols are the 20 amino acids and a special spacer symbol for regions between proteins; the output symbols correspond to the 3 types of secondary structures: α-helix, β-sheet and coil.

A diagram of the basic network is shown in Fig. 1. The processing units are arranged in layers, with the input units shown on the bottom and output units shown at the top. The units on the input layer have connections to the units on the intermediate layer of "hidden" units, which in turn have connections to the units on the output layer. In networks with a single layer of modifiable weights (perceptrons), there are no hidden units, in which case the input units are connected directly to the output layer.

The network is given a contiguous sequence of, typically, 13 amino acids. The goal of the network is to correctly predict the secondary structure for the middle amino acid. The network can be considered a "window" with 13 positions that moves through the protein, 1 amino acid at a time.

The input layer is arranged in 13 groups. Each group has 21 units, each unit representing 1 of the amino acids (or spacer). For a local encoding of the input sequence, 1 and only 1 input unit in each group, corresponding to the appropriate amino acid at each position, is given a value 1, and the rest are set to 0. This is called a local coding scheme, because each unit encodes a single item, in

Table 5

First order statistics for the two mappings in Table 4

$P(I_i, O=0)$

I_i	Input position i			
	1	2	3	4
0	0·5	0·25	0·25	0·25
1	0·	0·25	0·25	0·25

$P(I_i, O=1)$

I_i	In position i			
	1	2	3	4
0	0·25	0·5	0·25	0·25
1	0·25	0	0·25	0·25

contrast with a distributed coding scheme in which each unit participates in representing several items. In some experiments, we used distributed codings in which units represented biophysical properties of residues, such as their hydrophobicity. Another coding scheme that we used was the 2nd order conjunctive encoding, in which each unit represented a pair of residues, 1 residue from the middle position and a 2nd residue at another position. Many more units are needed to represent a string of amino acids with conjunctive encoding, but this form of encording makes explicit information about the 2nd order features.

In the basic network, the output group has 3 units, each representing one of the possible secondary structures for the centre amino acid. In other versions, more output units were used to represent a larger number of possible secondary structures, or several groups of output units were used to represent a sequence of secondary structures. See Results for more details. For a given input and set of weights, the output of the network will be a set of numbers between 0 and 1. The secondary structure chosen was the output unit that had the highest activity level; this was equivalent to choosing the output unit that had the least mean-square error with the target outputs.

Based on the discussions in section (c), above, a network with a single layer of modifiable weights and using a local coding scheme for the amino acid sequence is a 1st order perceptron and so can detect only 1st order features, i.e. the independent contributions of each amino acid to the secondary structure. However, a network can extract higher order features, such as correlations between pairs of amino acids and the secondary structure, if conjunctive input coding schemes are used to construct higher-order perceptrons or "hidden" processing units are introduced between the input and output layers.

(e) Network training procedure

Initially, the weights in the network were assigned randomly with values uniformly distributed in the range $[-0·3, 0·3]$. The initial success rate was at chance level, around 33%. The performance was gradually improved by changing the weights using the back-propagation learning algorithm (Rumelhart et al., 1986). During the training, the output values are compared with the desired values, and the weights in the network are altered by gradient descent to minimize the error. Details about our implementation of the learning procedure can be found in Sejnowski & Rosenberg (1987). A diffent random position in the concatenated training sequence of amino acids (see section (a), above) was chosen as the centre position of the input window at each training step. The surrounding amino acids were then used to clamp the input units in the window. All the amino acids in the training set were sampled once before starting again. This random sampling procedure was adopted to prevent erratic oscillations in the performance that occurred when the amino acids were sequentially sampled. The performance of the network on the testing set was monitored frequently during training and the set of weights was kept that achieved the best average success rate on the testing set. The training time of a network with 13 input groups and 40 hidden units was approx. 1 h of Ridge 32 time (equivalent to a VAX 780 FPA) per 10,000 residues.

The performance of the network on the training and testing sets depends on many variables, including the number of training examples, the number of hidden units, and the amount of homology between the training and testing sets. If there are too few training examples, the network can "memorize" all of the correct outputs because of the large capacity of the weights. The resulting network is accurate on the training set but makes poor predictions on the testing set. When the number of training examples is large, the learning procedure finds common features amongst the examples in the training set that enable the network to correctly predict the secondary structure of testing proteins that were not included in the training set. The ability of a network to extract higher order features from the training set depends on the layer of hidden units and the types of input encoding. A significant amount of information about homologies between proteins is contained in their higher-order features (see below).

3. Results

(a) Artificial structures

Before training networks on the database of known protein structures, we first tested the method on artificial structures with known input–output relations. The results of these experiments helped in interpreting the results of training on real proteins whose statistics are not known *a priori*.

(i) Generation of first order artificial structures

Amino acid sequences were chosen either from real proteins in the training set or generated from the statistics of those proteins. The first step in the latter method was to measure the frequency of occurrence of each amino acid in the database, as given in Table 2. Amino acids were chosen randomly with the same frequencies and assembled into a long sequence. Once the primary amino acid sequences were determined, the secondary structures were then assigned to each amino acid according to the information given in Tables 1, 2 and 4 of Garnier *et al.* (1978), which were based on the statistics of real proteins. These Tables were used by Robson and co-workers to predict secondary structures, but here we used them to generate artificial secondary structures.

Each amino acid in a window of 17 amino acids, eight on either side of the central residue, independently contributed toward an information measure for the type of secondary structures S:

$$I(s_i = S | R_{i-8}, \cdots R_i, \cdots R_{i+8}) = \sum_{j=-8}^{8} I(s_i = S | R_{i+j}), \quad (5)$$

where $I(s_i = S | R_k)$ represents the contribution from the kth position to the secondary structure s_i of R_i, which ranges over $S = \alpha$, β, coil. The secondary structure with the largest information measure was assigned to the central amino acid, and the process was repeated for each position in the sequence. This is a first order mapping.

(ii) Prediction of secondary structure

A network with 17 input groups having 21 units per group, 40 hidden units and three output units was trained on the training set of artificial structures. The learning curves shown in Figure 3 rose quickly for both the training set and a testing set of artificial structures. The learning algorithm is capable of discovering the "rules" that were used to generate the artificial structures and to predict with high accuracy the secondary structure of "novel" artificial structures that were not in the training set. Similar results were obtained when a network with one layer of weights and a local coding scheme was used. This was expected since, by construction, there were only first order features in the data.

The central amino acid has the largest influence on the secondary structure in the artificial structures, based on Robson's information tables. This should be reflected in the sizes of the weights from the input groups. The average magnitude of the weights from each input group is plotted in Figure 4 for a network at different stages of training. The average magnitude of the weights generally increased with time, but those at the centre more quickly than those near the ends of the window.

(iii) Effects of noise in the data

The long-range effects on the secondary structure would effectively add noise to the short-range effects that could be captured in a short window. In an effort to mimic these effects, we generated a new set of artificial structures that included a 30% random component to the rules used above. The networks with 40 hidden units and a local coding

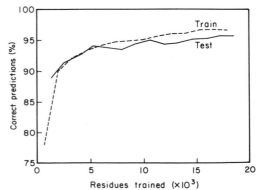

Figure 3. Learning curves for artificial structures. The percentage of correct predicted secondary structure is plotted as a function of the number of amino acids presented during training for both the training and testing sets.

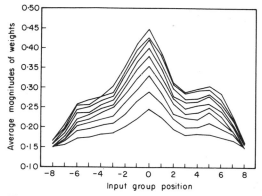

Figure 4. Values of the average magnitude of the weights from each weight group shown at several times during training on artificial structures. The lowest curve represents the averaged weights early in training.

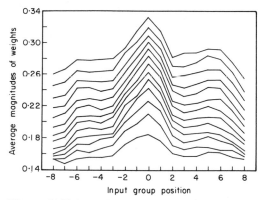

Figure 6. Values of the average magnitude of the weights from each weight group shown at several times during training on artificial structures with 30% noise added to the secondary structures. The lowest curve represents the averaged weights early in training.

scheme trained on proteins with 30% noise were able to learn the training, though not as well as the training set without noise, as shown in Figure 5. The performance on the testing set reached 63%, close to the theoretical limit of 70%. When a network with one layer of weights and a local coding scheme was used, both learning and training performances were about 63%. This indicates that the learning algorithm can extract 90% (63/70) of all the first order features. The noise had an interesting effect on the weights, as shown in Figure 6. The central weights were larger in magnitude, as before, but now even the weights from the end groups continue to increase with time. The ratio of the average magnitude of weights from the central group to the average magnitude of weights from the end groups was much smaller when noise was added to the training set.

(iv) *Effects of irrelevant weights*

Networks were trained having either 17 input groups or 21 input groups, but the secondary

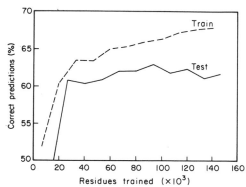

Figure 5. Learning curve for artificial structures with 30% noise added to the secondary structures. The percentage of correctly predicted secondary structures is plotted as a function of the number of amino acids presented during training for both the training and testing sets.

structures were generated from a group of size 17. The larger network was trained to determine the effect of the extra weights to inputs that could not contain any information about the secondary structure. The success rate of the network with 21 input groups was consistently lower than the network with 17 groups by about 1 to 2%. Thus, irrelevant weights can interfere with the performance of the network. The time evolution of the weights was different in the network with 21 input groups for the weights outside the middle window of 17 input groups. These weights fluctuated around 0·15, close to their initial, randomly generated values, compared with weights in the central groups that tended to increase with time.

(v) *Second order artificial structures*

The first order common features of artificial structures were learned very quickly by a network with one layer of weights. We generated a new set of artificial structures with both first order and second order features to determine how well a network with hidden units could learn the higher order common features.

The second order contribution of the residue at R_{i+j} to the secondary structure of the residue at R_i depends jointly on the identity of both residues. We generalized the first order information measure given by Garnier *et al.* (1978) given in equation (5) to include this second order contribution:

$$I(s_i = S | R_{i-8}, \ldots R_i, \ldots R_{i+8})$$
$$= \sum_{j=-8}^{8} I(s_i = S | R_i, R_{i+j}) + B_S, \qquad (6)$$

where B_S are constant biases used to match the relative proportion of secondary structures ($S = \alpha$, β, coil), to those of real proteins ($B_\alpha = 0$, $B_\beta = -55$, $B_{coil} = 150$), and:

$$I(s_i = S | R_i, R_{i+j}) = I(s_i = S | R_{i+j}) + A(S, R_i, R_{i+j}, j),$$
$$(7)$$

where $A(S, R_i, R_{i+j}, j)$ for each possible combination of (S, R_i, R_{i+j}, j) is a random (but fixed) number taken from a uniform distribution in the range $[-a, a]$. The magnitude of a determines the amount of second order features added into the original first order features. We chose $a = 100$ to match the fraction of first order features observed in real proteins.

When the local coding scheme for the inputs was used to train a network with one layer of modifiable weights (first order perceptron), the maximum testing success rate was 63%. This represents the amount of structure that can be predicted solely from the first order features. When a network with 80 hidden units and the same input coding scheme was used, the learning was much slower and the success rate was 65% and climbing very slowly after 70,000 training examples.

Improved performance was obtained using a second order conjunctive coding scheme for the inputs as described in Methods. This coding scheme makes it possible for a network with only one layer of weights to have access to second order features for the inputs. When such a network was trained on the artificial second order structures, the learning was much faster and the testing success rate was 85%. The dependence of the asymptotic success rate on the size of the training set is shown in Figure 7.

(b) Real proteins

(i) Testing with non-homologous proteins

We trained standard networks (13 input groups, local coding scheme, and 3 output units) with either 0 or 40 hidden units. The learning curves for the training and testing sets are shown in Figure 8. In all cases, the percentage of correctly predicted structures for both the training and testing sets rose quickly from the chance level of 33% to around 60%. Further training improved the performance of the networks with hidden units on the training set, but performance on the testing set did not improve but tended to decrease. This behaviour is an indication that memorization of the details of

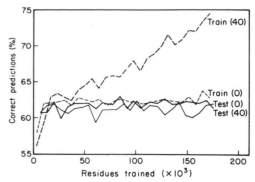

Figure 8. Learning curves for real proteins with testing on non-homologous proteins. Results for 2 networks are shown, one with no hidden units (direct connections between input and output units) and another with 40 hidden units. The percentage of correctly predicted secondary structure is plotted as a function of the number of amino acids presented during training.

the training set is interfering with the ability of the network to generalize. The peak performance for a network with 40 hidden units was $Q_3 = 62.7\%$, with the corresponding $C_\alpha = 0.35$, $C_\beta = 0.29$ and $C_{coil} = 0.38$. The performance with no hidden units is similar, as shown in Figure 8 and indicated in section (b) (iii), below.

The values of the weights for the network with no hidden units are given in Tables 13, 14 and 15 in the Appendix, and a graphical representation of these weights, called a Hinton diagram, is shown in Figure 9. The relative contribution to the secondary structure made by each amino acid at each position is apparent in this diagram. Physical properties of the amino acids can be correlated with their contributions to each form of secondary structure; in this way, hypotheses can be generated concerning the physical basis for secondary structure formation (see Fig. 9).

(ii) Change of the weights in the network during training

The average magnitude of the weights from each input group is plotted as a function of the input group and of time in Figure 10. The network had 17 input groups and 40 hidden units. The weights are largest in the centre and are approximately symmetric around the centre group. Over time, both the central peak and the flanks increase in size. This behaviour is similar to the previous experiments on artificial structures to which noise had been added to the data (Fig. 6) but unlike the behaviour of the weights when noise was not present (Fig. 4). This suggests that the weights from groups more than about eight residues from the central amino acid may not contribute information to the prediction of the secondary structure, even though the weights to these distant groups are large and increase with time during training. This conjecture was tested by varying the number of input groups and the results are reported below.

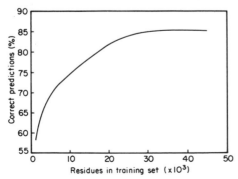

Figure 7. Dependence of the success rate for 2nd order artificial structures as a function of the training set size. The input encoding was a 2nd order conjunctive scheme.

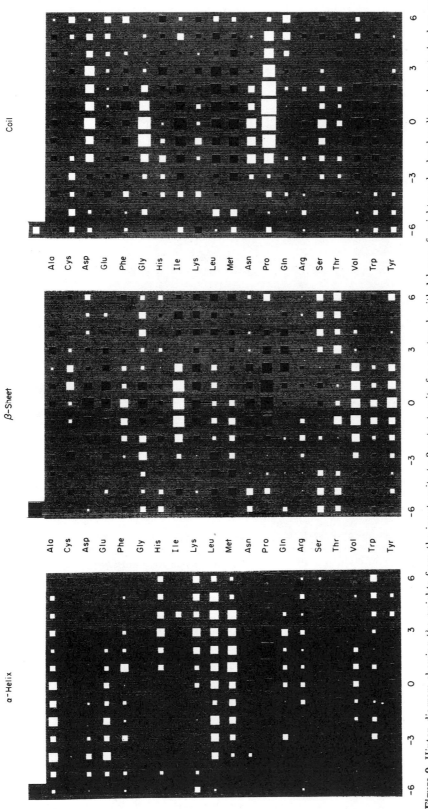

Figure 9. Hinton diagram showing the weights from the input units to 3 output units for a network with 1 layer of weights and a local coding scheme trained on real proteins. Three grey rectangular blocks show the weights to the 3 output units, each representing 1 of the 3 possible secondary structures associated with the centre amino acid. A weight is represented by a white square if the weight is positive (excitatory) and a black square if it is negative (inhibitory), with the area of the square proportional to the value of the weight. The 20 amino acid types are arranged vertically and the position of each of them in the 13-residue input window is represented horizontally and is numbered relative to the centre position. The weight in the upper left-hand corner of each large rectangle represents the bias of the output unit in eqn (4). The contribution to each type of secondary structure by amino acids at each position is apparent in this diagram. For example, proline is a strong α-helix breaker, while alanine, leucine and methionine are strong helix formers, especially when they are on the C-terminal side. Two basic amino acids, lysine and arginine, are helix formers when they are on the C-terminal side, while glutamate, an acidic amino acid, supports helical structure when it is on the N-terminal side. Isoleucine, valine, tryptophan and tyrosine are strong β-sheet formers and show no preferences toward the C-terminal or N-terminal side.

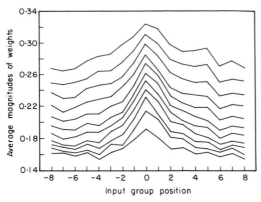

Figure 10. Values of the average magnitude of the weights from each weight group shown at several times during training on real proteins. The lowest curve represents the average magnitudes of the weights early in training.

Based on the observations with artificial structures that small randomly fluctuating weights were useless and could even interfere with the performance of the network, we systematically pruned small weights in one experiment. In a network with 17 input groups, 40 hidden units and 1 output group, we set all of the weights smaller than 0·15 to zero after every 12,000 amino acids were presented during training. We found that at the end of training, 60% of the weights were zero and the performance was slightly improved.

(iii) *Dependence on the number of hidden units*

Table 7 shows the surprising result that the peak performance on the testing set was almost independent of the number of hidden units although the learning rates of the training set (not shown) became slower as the number of hidden units decreased. Even more surprising, the testing success rate of a network with no hidden units was about the same as one with 40 hidden units, as shown in Figure 8. Furthermore, the training and

Table 7
Dependence of testing success rate on hidden units

Hidden units	$Q_3(\%)$
0	62·5
3	62·5
5	61·6
7	62·2
10	61·5
15	62·6
20	62·3
30	62·5
40	62·7
60	61·4

Dependence of the performance of the non-homologous testing set on the number of hidden units.

Table 8
Dependence of testing success rate on window size

Window size	$Q_3(\%)$	MC_α	MC_β	MC_{coil}
21	61·6	0·33	0·27	0·32
17	61·5	0·33	0·27	0·37
15	62·2	0·35	0·31	0·38
13	62·7	0·35	0·29	0·38
11	62·1	0·36	0·29	0·38
9	62·3	0·33	0·28	0·38
7	61·9	0·32	0·28	0·39
5	60·5	0·28	0·26	0·37
3	57·7	0·22	0·20	0·30
1	53·9	0·11	0·14	0·17

Dependence of the performance of the non-homologous testing set on number of input groups. MC_α, MC_β and MC_{coil} are the maximum correlation coefficients during training, which may occur at different stages.

testing performances of the network with no hidden units were indistinguishable.

These results suggest that the common features in the training and testing proteins are all first order features and that all of the first order features learned from the training set that we used were common features. The higher order features (the information due to interactions between 2 or more residues) learned by the network were specific to each individual protein, at least for the proteins that were used. In a later section, we show that if the training set is too small then not all the first order features learned during training are common features.

(iv) *Dependence on the number of input groups*

We studied the dependence of testing success rate on the size of the input window using a standard network with 40 hidden units. The results shown in Table 8 indicate that when the size of the window was small the performance on the testing set was reduced, probably because information outside the window is not available for the prediction of the secondary structure. When the size of the window was increased, the performance reached a maximum at around 13 groups (6 on either size of the centre residue). For larger window sizes, the performance deteriorated, probably for the reason given in section (a) (iv), above. Similar results were obtained for networks without hidden units.

(v) *Dependence on size of the training set*

A standard network with 13 input groups and no hidden units was trained on training sets with different numbers of amino acids in them. The maximum performance of the network as a function of the training set size is presented in Figure 11. The maximum occurred after different training times in the different networks.

The maximum performance on the training set decreases with the number of amino acids in the training set because more information is being

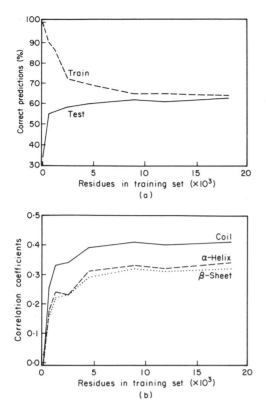

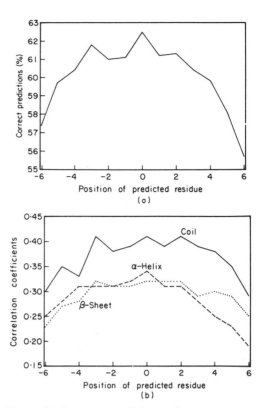

Figure 11. Dependence of the prediction accuracy on the size of the training set of non-homologous proteins. (a) Percentage correct for the training and testing sets. (b) Correlation coefficients for the testing set.

Figure 12. Dependence of the prediction accuracy on the position within a window of 13 amino acids. The position is indicated relative to the centre of the window, so that −2 refers to a network that is attempting to predict the secondary structure of the amino acid 2 positions toward the N-terminal from the central residue. (a) Success rate as a function of position. (b) Correlation coefficients as a function of position.

encoded in a fixed set of weights. The testing success rate, on the other hand, increases with size because the larger the training set, the better the network is able to generalize. When the training set is small, the network is able to "memorize" the details, but this strategy is not possible when the training set is large. Another conclusion from Figure 11 is that a further increase of the data set is unlikely to improve the performance of the network on the testing set.

(vi) *Relative importance of information on the N and C-terminal sides*

We trained a network with no hidden units and a window size of 13 to predict the secondary structure of the amino acid m positions away from the centre. There are 13 values of m ranging from −6 to 6, where a negative value indicates a position to the N-terminal side of centre. The maximum testing success rate and maximum correlation coefficients are shown in Figure 12. All curves are approximately symmetric around the centre and have broad maxima between −3 and +3. This result is consistent with about equal contributions from the information in the N-terminal and C-terminal sequences.

(vii) *Prediction near the N terminus*

Other methods for predicting the secondary structure are more accurate near the N terminus of most proteins (Argos *et al.*, 1976). In Table 9 the success rate for our method on the 25 amino acid N-terminal sequence is compared with the average success rate. The performance of our method on this segment is significantly higher, consistent with previous findings. Our method considers only local interactions, which suggests that local interactions are more important in determining the secondary structure at the N terminus of globular proteins, as proposed by other authors.

(viii) *Cascaded networks improve performance*

For a given input sequence, the output of the network is a three-dimensional vector whose components have values between 0 and 1. The secondary structure for the above networks was predicted by choosing the output unit with the largest value, as mentioned in Methods. However, information about the certainty of the prediction is

Table 9

Prediction of a short segment at the N-terminal end

Segment	$Q_3(\%)$	C_α	C_β	C_{coil}
1st 20 residues	73·8	0·45 (62)	0·45 (69)	0·54 (209)
1st 25 residues	72·2	0·46 (91)	0·45 (84)	0·52 (250)
1st 30 residues	68·0	0·41 (117)	0·39 (111)	0·48 (282)
1st 40 residues	63·4	0·33 (167)	0·35 (156)	0·43 (352)
All but 1st 25	61·3	0·34 (758)	0·27 (664)	0·36 (1675)

The numbers in parentheses are the numbers of residues in the testing sets.

not exploited by this procedure. Neither is the information available in the correlations between neighbouring secondary structure assignments, since predictions are made one residue at a time. However, we can take advantage of this additional information by designing a second network.

The inputs to the second network were sequences of outputs from the first network, trained as described above. Hence, the input layer of the second network contained 13 groups with three units per group, each group representing the complete information about the secondary structure assignment derived from the first network. The first network was fixed while the second network was trained on the same set of training proteins as the first network. The average performance for two cascaded networks was $Q_3 = 64\cdot3\%$, $C_\alpha = 0\cdot41$, $C_\beta = 0\cdot31$ and $C_{\text{coil}} = 0\cdot41$ with 40 hidden units in both nets. This was our best result on the testing set of non-homologous proteins. Performance on each of the non-homologous proteins in the training set is given in Table 10. The weights for a second network without hidden units (whose input is from the first network in Tables 13 to 15) is given in Table 16.

The improvement provided by the second network is apparent in Figure 13, which compares

the predictions made by the first and seco[ ] networks. The second network "cleans up" t[ ] predictions of the first by joining short fragments [ ] secondary structure and eliminating isolated assig[ ] ments. The improvement was mainly in the regio[ ] of α-helix and coil, but not in regions of β-sheet.

(ix) *Methods that did not improve performance*

We experimented with many variations of th[ ] basic network, but none of them helped improv[ ] the performance on the testing set. The following methods were of little or no help (less than 1%):

(ix)(a) *Modification of the input representations*

The local input representation of the amino acids we used contains no information about their bio-physical properties. We tried using distributed coding schemes representing charge, size, hydro-phobicities, and other detailed information about the conformation of the side groups. In another attempt, we used the information measures of Robson (Garnier *et al.*, 1978) as part of the input representations. A second order conjunctive encoding was also used. We experimented with varying the input representations during the learning without success.

These physical properties are of known bio-physical importance for determining the secondary structure. The failure to improve performance does not necessarily imply that the network is not capable of taking advantage of these properties; an alternative interpretation is that the network is already extracting all of the relevant information available from these properties. The failure of the second order conjunctive encoding proves that no second order common features about the secondary structure are present locally.

(ix)(b) *Modifications to the network architecture*

We examined a number of variations of the standard network architecture. We studied net-works with up to seven output groups corre-sponding to a secondary structure prediction of up to seven contiguous amino acids. All sets of output for a given amino acid were averaged before making a prediction.

Many networks were studied that had altered connectivities: networks with two hidden layers; networks with direct connections between the input and output layers as well as through a layer of

Table 10

Results on non-homologous testing proteins

Protein	C_α	C_β	C_{coil}	$Q_3(\%)$
1abp	0·33	0·31	0·23	61
1acx	—	0·28	0·28	65
1hmq	0·46	—	0·49	72
1ige	0·18	0·42	0·50	68
1nxb	—	0·49	0·43	71
1ppd	0·39	0·24	0·49	66
1pyp	0·32	0·34	0·48	73
2act	0·40	0·36	0·35	64
2alp	0·30	0·32	0·29	57
2cdv	0·47	0·25	0·38	71
2grs	0·41	0·30	0·44	64
2lhb	0·50	—	0·58	74
2sbt	0·26	0·36	0·34	66
3gpd	0·40	0·25	0·45	64
6api	0·34	0·27	0·32	52
Weighted average	0·41	0·31	0·41	64·3

Results of a 2-network cascade with 40 hidden units each for non-homologous testing set of proteins (Table 2).

α-Lytic protease

```
ANIVGGIEYSINNASLCSVGFSVTRGATKGFVTAGHCGTVNATARIGGAVVGTFAARVFPGNDRAWVSLT sequence
_____e_e_____eee__eee_____eeeee_____e___eh__eeeheeh_e_____eeeee_ 1st net
_____eee_____eeee_eee_____eeeee_____ee__eeehhhe_____eeeeh 2nd net
_eeee__eeee___eeee__eeeee__eeeee_____eeee__eeeeeeeeee__eeeeeee_ real


SAQTLLPRVANGSSFVTVRGSTEAAVGAAVCRSGRTTGYQCGTITAKNVTANYAEGAVRGLTQGNACMGR
_h_____ee_____eeeee___hh_hhehe_____e__ee__e_h_eh__hh_____ee__ 1st net
h_____ee_____eeeee___hhhhhhe_____e__ee_____hhhhhhhh_____ee__ 2nd net
___eeeeeee__eeee_____eeeee___eeeeeeeeeeeeeee__eeeeeeee_____ real


GDSGGSWITSAGQAQGVMSGGNVQSNGNNCGIPASQRSSLFERLQPILSQYGLSLVTG
_____eeeee_____eee_____h__hh_eehe__ee___ 1st net
_____eeee_____eeee_____h___hhhhh__eeee__ 2nd net
_____eee_____eeeeeee_____eeeeehhhhhhhh__ee___ real
```

Haemoglobin V (cyano, met)

```
PIVDTGSVAPLSAAEKTKIRSAWAPVYSTYETSGVDILVKFFTSTPAAQEFFPKFKGLTTADELKKSADV sequence
_____hhhhhhh_____ee_____eeeee_____hh_____hhhhh____h 1st net
_____hhhhhhhhh_____ee_____eeeeee_____hh_____hhhhhhhhhhh 2nd net
_____hhhhhhhhhhhhhhhhh_hhhhhhhhhhhhhhhh_____hhhhh__hhh real


RWHAERIINAVDDAVASMDDTEKMSMKLRNLSGKHAKSFQVDPEYFKVLAAVIADTVAAGDAGFEKLMSM
hhhhh_eee___hhh_____hhhhhhhhh__h__h___e__hhhhhhheh_hhh_____hhhhhhhh 1st net
hhhhhhhhhh__hhhh_____hhhhhhhhhhhh_____hhhhhhhhhhhhhh____hhhhhhhhh 2nd net
hhhhhhhhhhhhhhhhh____hhhhhhhhhhhhhhhhhh_____hhhhhhhhhhhhh___hhhhhhhh real


ICILLRSAY
heeehh___
hhhhhh___
hhhhhh___
```

Figure 13. Comparison of the predictions for the secondary structure of haemoglobin V (21hb) and a α-lytic protease (2alp). The results are shown for 1 network and 2 cascaded networks. The 2nd network improved on the prediction of the 1st network for haemoglobin V, which was rich in α-helix, but slightly decreased the accuracy of the prediction for α-lytic protease, which contained a high proportion of β-sheet structure.

hidden units; recursive networks, in which the previous outputs were fed back to serve as extra input units.

Multiplicative synaptic weights were used that depended quadratically on pairs of input units. In particular, we used multiplicative units to represent global variables such as the position of the amino acid in the protein and the average hydrophobicity of the protein.

(ix)(c) *More detailed secondary structure predictions*

Kabsch & Sander (1983b) distinguish three types of helices, two types of β-structures and two types of turns, as well as the coil. We attempted to train a network on this finer classification scheme first, and then to collapse the assignments into the three final states.

(x) *Comparison with other methods*

The performance of our method for secondary structure prediction is compared with those of Robson and co-workers (Garnier *et al.*, 1978), Chou & Fasman (1978) and Lim (1974) in Table 11. The original measures of accuracy reported by these authors were based in part on the same proteins from which they derived their methods, and these proteins are equivalent to our training set. The performance of our networks with hidden units on the training set was as high as $Q_3 = 95\%$ after sufficiently long training. However, these methods should be compared on proteins with structures that were not used in or homologous with those in the training set. The results of testing these three methods on novel proteins is reported in Table V of

Table 11

Comparison of methods

Method		$Q_3(\%)$	C_α	C_β	C_{coil}
Robson		53	0·31	0·24	0·24
Chou–Fasman		50	0·25	0·19	0·24
Lim		50	0·35	0·21	0·20
Neural	1 net	62·7	0·35	0·29	0·38
Network	2 nets	64·3	0·41	0·31	0·41

Comparison with other methods for predicting secondary structure on a non-homologous testing set of proteins (Table 2). Q_3 is the average success rate on 3 types of secondary structure and C_α, C_β and C_{coil} are the corresponding correlation coefficients for the α-helix, β-sheet and coil, respectively. Results are shown for a single network (1 net) or a 2-network cascade (2 nets).

Nishikawa (1983) and are listed in Table 11 with the performance of our networks on the non-homologous testing set of proteins.

The correlation coefficient introduced by Mathews (1975) is another measure of the quality of a prediction, one that takes into account over-prediction as well as underprediction. These parameters have been calculated by Nishikawa (1983) for previous methods and are listed in Table 11 with the correlation coefficients of our method. Our predictions are better than all previous methods for all secondary structure predictions. Our method has a success rate that is an absolute improvement of 11% and a relative improvement of 21% over the method of Robson et al. (Garnier et al., 1978), which is the most reliable of other existing methods. The correlation coefficients of our method have a relative improvement of 32%, 29% and 41% for the α-helix, β-sheet and coil, respectively.

Our training and testing sets of proteins were different from those used to construct and test the previous methods. To determine how much of our improvement was due to this difference, we trained a new network using 22 of the 25 proteins found in Robson & Suzuki (1976) as the training set for a network. (Three of the proteins were missing from our database: carp myoglobin, horse cytochrome c, and adenylate cyclase. Deleting these proteins from our training set would decrease slightly the performance of the network, as indicated in Fig. 11.) Our testing set was a subset of those found in Table V of Nishikawa (1983). (The following 10 testing proteins were in our database: citrate synthease, erabutoxin B, prealbumin, γ-crystallin II, protease B, subtilisin inhibitor, phospholipase A_2, glutathione peroxidase, rhodanese and alcohol dehydrogenase.) The testing success rate of Robson's method on these ten proteins was 51·2% compared with 61·9% for our method with two cascaded networks. Thus, less than 1% of the 11% improvement in Table 11 can be attributed to differences in the training sets. The relatively small effect of the larger database available to use is consistent with the asymptotic slope of the dependence on training set size shown in Figure 11.

The improvement of our method over that of Robson et al. may seem puzzling, since they also use one layer of weights. The difference in performance can be attributed to the observation at the end of Methods, section (c), that first order features are stronger than first order statistics. The information measure in Robson's method depends only on the first order statistics. Therefore, exactly the same information measures would be obtained through the probabilities in Table 5 for the two sets of mappings shown in Table 4. However, two different sets of weights would be obtained by training two first order perceptrons on the two mappings separately. Thus, neural networks can distinguish mappings with same first order statistics but different first order features.

Levin et al. (1986) proposed an algorithm for determining secondary structures based on sequence similarity (We thank one of the referees for bringing this paper to our attention). In Table 3 of that paper, they showed that the prediction success rate for nine new proteins (corresponding to our testing proteins) is 63·4%. However, as pointed out by these authors, four out of their nine testing proteins had homologous counterparts in their database (corresponding to our training proteins), and these should be treated separately when the prediction accuracy of the method is assessed. The prediction success rate for these four proteins after the corresponding homologous proteins are removed from the database were given in the legend of their Table 3. The recalculated total success rate for the nine testing proteins falls to 59·7%, which is about 4·6% less than the success rate for our non-homologous testing set. However, this comparison may not be accurate, because the β-sheet content of their nine new proteins is about 17%, while it is 21% in our non-homologous testing set. Because β-sheet is the most difficult part of the structure to predict, we expect that the 4·6% improvement for our method is probably an underestimate. We cannot conduct a better-controlled comparison, as we did with Robson's method in the last section, because we do not have six of the nine proteins they used for testing (we used 6 homologous proteins in our database to estimate the proportion of the β-sheet in their testing proteins shown above). Another observation is that our method should be faster, because a set of weights obtained through training can be used for predicting secondary structures for all new proteins. The method of Levin et al. (1986), on the other hand, requires an exhaustive search of the whole database for every seven-amino acid sequence in the new protein.

(xi) *Testing with homologous proteins*

In all of the experiments described above, the testing set was carefully chosen not to have any homology with the proteins in the training set. The results were significantly different when homologies were present, as shown in Figure 14, in comparison with the results from the non-homologous testing set shown in Figure 8. The main difference is that, for the network with 40 hidden units, the performance on the testing set continued to

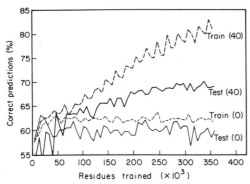

Figure 14. Learning curves for real proteins with testing on homologous proteins using the training and testing sets in Table 3. Results for 2 networks are shown, one with no hidden units (direct connections between input and output units) and another with 40 hidden units. The percentage of correctly predicted secondary structure is plotted as a function of the number of amino acids presented during training.

improve up to about $Q_3 = 70\%$, about 10% better than the network with no hidden units. With two cascaded networks, $Q_3 = 74\cdot4\%$. The hidden units were evidently able to exploit the additional information present in the homologous proteins.

We varied the composition of the training set and found that in most cases the best performance was obtained when the training set consisted only of proteins that had homologies with the testing protein. The results for 12 pairs of homologous proteins are shown in Table 12. For each pair of homologous proteins p_a and p_b, we trained a network on p_a and tested it on p_b. The testing success rate was almost always between the sequence homology and the structure homology.

However, this is less than the success rate that is obtained by aligning the two proteins and assigning to the amino acids of p_b the corresponding secondary structures in p_a.

When the sequence homology between p_a and p_b is below 65%, the testing success rate can often be improved by adding other unrelated proteins to the training set, but the best result is still not as high as the structure homology.

We attempted to improve on our results for homologous proteins by using different input coding schemes. None of the coding schemes based on the physical properties of amino acids, on Robson's information measures, or on conjunctive encodings, were more effective than the simple local coding scheme with hidden units. Second order conjunctive encoding without hidden units gave results that were similar to a network with local input encoding and 40 hidden units.

4. Discussion

The new method for predicting the secondary structure of globular proteins presented here is a significant improvement over existing methods for non-homologous proteins and should have many applications. We have emphasized the distinction between training and testing sets, between homologous and non-homologous testing sets, and the balance of the relative amount of each type of secondary structure in assessing the accuracy of our method, and have provided objective measures of performance that can be compared with other methods. Tables 13 to 16 in the Appendix contain all the information needed to program our method.

However, the absolute level of performance achieved by our method is still disappointingly low. Perhaps the most surprising result was the conclusion that further improvement in local

Table 12
Results on homologous testing proteins

| Homologous pairs | | Number of | Sequence | Structural | |
Test	Train	residues	homology(%)	homology(%)	$Q_3(\%)$
1azu	1aza	125	69	84	78
1lzt	1lzl	129	65	96	83
1pfc	1fc2	111	66	62	63
1ppd	2act	212	54	93	83
2gch	1tgs	237	46	87	70
1gfl	1fr2	70	71	94	99
1p2p	1bp2	124	83	91	90
2ape	2app	318	67	80	61
2rhe	1ig2	114	77	92	77
2sga	3sgb	181	65	91	76
3hhb	2dhb	287	85	91	89
5ldh	1ldx	333	71	86	68
Weighted average			68	87	76

Results of networks with hidden units on homologous proteins. The overall weighted correlation coefficients corresponding to $Q_3 = 76\%$ were $C_\alpha = 0\cdot70$, $C_\beta = 0\cdot58$ and $C_{coil} = 0\cdot54$. The sequence and structural homologies, defined as the percentage of identical amino acids or secondary structures between 2 proteins, were estimated by manual inspection.

methods for predicting the secondary structure of non-homologous proteins is unlikely, based on known structures. The fact that networks with no hidden units performed as well as networks with hidden units on the non-homologous training set suggests that there are little or no second or higher order features locally available in the training set to guide the prediction of secondary structure. Could this be due to a database of insufficient size or failure of the network to detect higher order common features?

Two lines of evidence argue against these possible explanations. First, the dependence of the performance on the size of the training set suggests that the addition of more protein structures to the training set will not significantly improve the method for non-homologous proteins. Second, we can definitively conclude that no second order features are present in the database from our experiments with conjunctive input representations of the amino acids (which make 2nd order features available as 1st order features to the output layer). The use of hidden units, which are capable of exploiting higher order features in the data, did not improve the performance either. Experiments with second order artificial structures suggests that our method was capable of detecting second order features. All of these experiments are consistent with the hypothesis that little or no information is available in the data beyond the first order features that have been extracted.

However, it is still possible that our method may not extract all of the information available as first order features from the training set. An estimate for the maximum obtainable accuracy of local methods such as ours can be obtained from our study of artificial structures. We stochastically generated artificial structures that had only information in the first order statistics, as estimated by Garnier et al. (1978) from real proteins. The profile of the magnitudes of the weights from different input groups and the increase in the size of the weights was similar to that observed for real proteins, but only when 30% noise was added to artificial structures. This suggests that a theoretical limit of 70% can be obtained with local methods, which is close to our present performance of 64·3%. The pattern recognition method that we used is not effective when the information contained in the statistics of the training set is global. If further statistical analysis of the database of protein structures confirms our results, then a significant fraction of the local secondary structure depends on influences outside the local neighbourhood of an amino acid and significant improvements for non-homologous proteins would require better methods for taking into account these long-range effects.

The prediction accuracy of networks tested with homologous proteins is much better than that for non-homologous proteins. Other methods are also much better when tested with homologous proteins. For a highly homologous testing protein, our best results were obtained by training a network solely with the homologous protein, but the success rate is almost always less than the structure homology. This is not surprising, since a single protein contains little information about amino acid substitutions that do not alter the secondary structure. With a much larger database of homologous proteins, it should be possible for a network to discover the equivalence classes of amino acids in different contexts.

Appendix

The weights in Tables 13 to 15 can be used to program a network that predicts the secondary structure for globular proteins. Each row represents one of the input groups, and each column represents one of the amino acids. There are no hidden units in the network, so each weight is for a connection from one of the 273 input units to one of the three output units. Note that a separate unit in each group is dedicated to the spacer (which appears in the

Table 13
Weights for α-helix

Amino acid	Window position												
	−6			−3			0			3			6
Ala	0·12	0·26	0·64	0·29	0·68	0·34	0·57	0·33	0·13	0·31	0·21	0·18	−0·08
Cys	−0·25	−0·15	0·03	−0·05	−0·15	−0·18	−0·15	−0·03	−0·09	−0·26	−0·12	−0·29	−0·25
Asp	0·01	0·15	0·33	0·11	−0·02	0·06	−0·46	−0·44	−0·71	−0·81	−0·58	−0·32	−0·24
Glu	−0·02	0·21	0·51	0·28	0·44	0·20	0·26	0·21	0·13	−0·06	−0·23	−0·25	−0·19
Phe	0·05	0·12	−0·03	0·24	0·06	0·15	0·03	0·48	0·15	0·10	−0·06	0·05	0·00
Gly	−0·02	−0·37	−0·09	−0·67	−0·73	−0·88	−0·71	−0·46	−0·39	−0·42	−0·15	−0·40	−0·10
His	−0·06	0·10	−0·23	−0·26	−0·14	−0·09	−0·05	0·27	0·32	0·51	0·37	0·28	0·29
Ile	−0·07	−0·03	−0·22	0·00	−0·08	−0·03	0·00	−0·33	0·00	−0·15	0·31	−0·03	−0·01
Lys	0·26	0·12	−0·17	−0·19	0·03	−0·11	0·16	0·23	0·37	0·47	0·28	0·41	0·45
Leu	0·05	−0·02	0·41	0·47	0·61	0·20	0·48	0·57	0·50	0·56	0·70	0·62	0·28
Met	0·00	0·00	0·13	0·27	0·39	0·43	0·41	0·79	0·63	0·58	0·61	0·21	0·11
Asn	−0·10	−0·03	0·09	−0·04	−0·09	−0·33	−0·36	−0·19	−0·07	−0·10	−0·04	−0·03	−0·08
Pro	−0·19	−0·08	−0·43	−0·34	−0·76	−0·81	−1·12	−1·86	−1·40	−1·33	−1·03	−0·84	−0·42
Gln	−0·03	−0·13	−0·23	0·26	−0·15	0·01	0·15	0·19	0·12	0·41	0·13	−0·27	−0·28
Arg	0·04	−0·14	−0·10	−0·03	−0·22	0·22	0·23	0·10	0·08	0·18	0·07	0·21	0·05
Ser	−0·19	0·01	−0·10	0·17	−0·26	−0·35	−0·47	−0·23	−0·28	−0·49	−0·28	−0·05	0·07
Thr	−0·04	−0·34	−0·07	−0·20	−0·10	−0·37	−0·54	−033	−0·21	−0·44	−0·25	−0·16	−0·33
Val	−0·03	0·02	−0·01	−0·01	0·12	0·13	0·31	0·24	0·17	−0·01	0·00	0·06	−0·13
Trp	−0·06	−0·01	−0·02	0·25	0·20	0·07	−0·10	0·15	0·02	0·14	0·21	0·32	0·36
Tyr	−0·14	−0·29	−0·38	−0·30	−0·04	−0·31	−0·35	−0·19	−0·10	−0·08	0·16	0·11	0·00
—	−0·12	−0·15	−0·52	−0·58	−0·64	−0·37	−0·03	−0·47	−0·77	−0·66	−0·56	−0·22	0·24

Tables 13 to 15 show weights for a 1st network without hidden units that predicts secondary structure. Sequences of 13 amino acids are inputs and the structure of the centre residue is the output. The biases for the output units are −1·08 for α-helix −1·50 for β-sheet and 0·41 for coil.

Table 14
Weights for β-sheet

Amino acid	Window position												
	−6			−3			0			3			6
Ala	−0·18	−0·01	−0·19	−0·14	−0·31	−0·10	−0·25	−0·26	0·05	−0·44	−0·31	−0·02	−0·06
Cys	−0·26	−0·27	−0·29	−0·64	−0·06	0·13	0·13	0·47	0·36	0·13	−0·11	−0·02	−0·19
Asp	0·05	−0·09	−0·06	−0·10	−0·54	−0·89	−1·01	−0·55	−0·11	−0·20	0·13	0·11	0·24
Glu	·0·06	0·09	−0·10	−0·39	−0·52	−0·34	−0·62	−0·75	−0·35	−0·28	−0·05	0·10	−0·04
Phe	−0·18	−0·12	−0·32	0·08	0·24	0·36	0·48	0·20	0·20	−0·13	−0·04	−0·03	−0·33
Gly	0·23	0·13	0·19	0·46	0·37	−0·45	−0·72	−0·56	0·14	0·08	0·45	0·38	0·17
His	0·24	0·22	−0·16	−0·04	−0·32	−0·34	−0·16	−0·04	0·02	0·09	−0·06	−0·09	0·19
Ile	−0·42	−0·27	−0·08	0·16	0·57	0·95	1·10	0·94	0·47	−0·04	−0·25	−0·48	−0·20
Lys	0·03	0·08	−0·09	0·04	−0·29	−0·46	−0·59	−0·55	−0·51	−0·33	−0·44	−0·39	−0·43
Leu	−0·23	−0·25	−0·42	−0·57	0·09	0·32	0·23	0·25	0·32	−0·12	−0·44	−0·26	−0·46
Met	−0·42	−0·57	−0·38	0·24	0·29	0·43	0·32	−0·05	−0·10	−0·21	−0·28	−0·14	−0·52
Asn	0·28	0·41	0·02	−0·27	−0·53	−0·89	−0·77	−0·34	−0·40	0·05	0·06	0·03	0·10
Pro	−0·13	0·26	0·05	0·02	−0·31	−0·91	−1·24	−1·28	−0·79	−0·48	−0·29	−0·04	0·37
Gln	0·21	0·01	0·02	−0·11	0·07	−0·04	−0·12	−0·33	−0·67	−0·58	−0·47	−0·17	−0·04
Arg	−0·13	0·02	0·03	0·14	0·25	0·19	−0·02	−0·09	−0·11	−0·13	−0·10	0·04	0·02
Ser	0·41	0·44	0·25	−0·12	0·11	−0·12	−0·31	−0·28	0·03	0·27	0·34	0·41	0·43
Thr	0·33	0·35	0·22	0·00	0·03	0·49	0·17	0·08	−0·15	0·47	0·27	0·36	0·50
Val	−0·07	−0·09	−0·15	0·29	0·48	0·76	0·69	0·67	0·58	0·06	0·11	−0·18	0·00
Trp	−0·10	−0·15	−0·19	−0·10	0·15	0·34	0·45	0·22	0·09	−0·22	−0·08	−0·01	−0·32
Tyr	−0·10	0·15	0·05	0·18	0·29	0·42	0·77	0·53	0·34	−0·11	0·06	−0·08	0·35
—	0·21	−0·23	−0·32	−0·50	−0·71	−0·61	0·03	−0·58	−0·32	−0·10	0·06	−0·25	−0·12

See Table 13.

Table 15
Weights for coil

Amino acid	\-6			\-3			0			3			6
Ala	-0·05	-0·19	-0·43	-0·19	-0·25	-0·27	-0·42	-0·24	-0·14	0·01	-0·30	-0·23	0·08
Cys	0·30	0·41	0·19	0·42	0·18	0·00	-0·18	-0·38	-0·09	-0·31	0·03	0·19	0·37
Asp	0·15	0·09	-0·31	-0·27	0·60	0·54	0·95	0·65	0·66	0·78	0·44	0·34	0·04
Glu	-0·02	-0·20	-0·41	-0·22	-0·12	-0·12	-0·09	0·07	0·06	0·09	0·18	0·28	0·36
Phe	0·09	0·07	0·25	-0·31	-0·29	-0·47	-0·39	-0·61	-0·25	-0·20	0·11	-0·02	0·34
Gly	-0·14	0·28	-0·21	0·17	0·09	1·14	1·24	0·85	0·36	0·14	-0·12	0·14	-0·02
His	-0·07	-0·19	0·21	0·17	0·42	0·18	0·05	-0·21	-0·31	-0·56	-0·20	-0·22	-0·45
Ile	0·26	-0·06	0·29	-0·34	-0·54	-0·74	-1·17	-0·65	-0·51	-0·09	-0·07	0·42	0·09
Lys	-0·42	-0·20	0·33	0·00	0·14	0·45	0·09	0·17	-0·14	-0·43	0·06	-0·15	-0·27
Leu	0·04	0·34	-0·10	-0·22	-0·55	-0·54	-0·69	-0·80	-0·80	-0·81	-0·18	-0·36	0·24
Met	0·25	0·45	-0·01	-0·53	-0·47	-0·76	-0·86	-0·71	-0·56	-0·49	-0·44	-0·19	0·16
Asn	0·00	-0·38	0·00	0·17	0·61	0·71	0·81	0·45	0·35	-0·11	-0·12	0·06	-0·06
Pro	0·31	0·04	0·28	0·14	0·89	1·40	1·77	2·27	1·59	1·14	0·77	0·78	0·16
Gln	-0·08	0·04	0·14	-0·29	0·09	-0·08	-0·01	0·01	;·11	-0·13	0·24	0·47	0·48
Arg	0·06	0·17	0·06	-0·07	0·12	-0·40	-0·23	-0·04	0·21	-0·13	-0·09	-0·20	-0·01
Ser	-0·11	-0·23	-0·23	0·22	0·24	0·40	0·63	0·33	0·32	0·13	-0·09	-0·29	-0·35
Thr	-0·06	-0·02	-0·26	0·10	0·16	-0·10	0·29	0·13	0·21	-0·02	-0·27	-0·30	-0·04
Val	0·04	0·05	-0·10	-0·33	-0·45	-0·86	-1·32	-0·99	-0·70	-0·11	-0·06	0·29	0·18
Trp	0·19	0·16	0·15	-0·15	-0·44	-0·46	-0·37	-0·44	-0·17	-0·20	-0·09	-0·18	-0·06
Tyr	0·33	0·22	0·09	-0·02	-0·19	-0·05	-0·41	-0·49	-0·35	0·10	-0·25	0·07	-0·20
—	-0·33	0·01	0·54	1·00	1·04	0·76	-0·21	0·84	1·05	0·41	0·49	0·24	-0·20

See Table 13.

Table 16
Weights in the second network

α	\-6			\-3			0			3			6
h	0·09	0·04	0·52	0·36	0·30	0·35	0·73	0·60	0·33	0·57	0·09	0·29	0·12
e	-0·04	-0·11	-0·26	-0·32	-0·30	-0·73	-0·81	-0·50	-0·55	-0·46	-0·24	0·13	-0·19
—	0·19	-0·03	0·10	-0·09	-0·19	-0·48	-0·97	-0·49	-0·21	0·12	0·16	0·12	-0·20

β	\-6			\-3			0			3			6
h	-0·56	-0·33	-0·09	-0·11	-0·51	-0·73	-0·50	-0·39	-0·10	-0·18	0·02	-0·25	-0·37
e	0·09	-0·08	0·42	0·44	0·64	1·15	1·58	0·78	0·46	0·08	-0·03	0·01	0·28
—	0·11	0·15	0·07	-0·01	-0·02	-0·28	-1·12	-0·56	-0·20	-0·10	0·13	-0·06	0·11

Coil	\-6			\-3			0			3			6
h	0·04	0·15	-0·32	-0·33	-0·02	-0·15	-0·58	-0·53	-0·36	-0·37	-0·17	-0·08	-0·04
e	-0·03	0·17	-0·27	-0·17	-0·36	-0·83	-1·40	-0·60	0·02	0·31	0·09	-0·08	0·02
—	-0·23	0·14	-0·09	-0·18	0·09	0·60	1·42	0·60	0·28	0·08	-0·37	-0·05	0·17

Weights for 2nd network without hidden units in a 2-network cascade. The sequence of 13 outputs from the 1st network are inputs to the 2nd network, whose output is the corrected secondary structure of the centre amino acid. The biases for the output are $-0·19$ for the α-helix, $-0·73$ for the β-sheet and $-0·04$ for the coil. Performance of the network on the testing set of non-homologous proteins (Table 2) was $Q_3 = 64 °C\%$, where $C_\alpha = 0·36$, $C_\beta = 0·31$ and $C_{coil} = 0·42$.

window only when the leading or trailing edge of the protein is present).

The weights in Table 16 can be used to program the second network in a two-network cascade. The input to the second network is the value of the three output units from the first network given in Tables 13 to 15. The overall performance of these cascaded networks is $Q_3 = 64\%$, 0·3% less than the figure quoted in Table 11, which was based on networks that had 40 hidden units.

We thank Dr Kevin Ullmer for helping with the database and for many discussions during the course of the research. Drs Carl Pabo and Richard Durbin suggested important improvements in the presentation. Drs Warner Love, Richard Cone and Evangelos

Moudrianakis provided helpful advice on many aspects of protein structure. We are grateful to Paul Kienker for discussions and the use of his network simulator. T.J.S. was supported by a Presidential Young Investigator Award (NSF BNS-83-51331).

References

Ackley, D. H., Hinton, G. E. & Sejnowski, T. J. (1985). *Cong. Sci.* **9**, 147–169.

Argos, P., Schwartz, J. & Schwarz, J. (1976). *Biochim. Biophys. Acta*, **439**, 261–273.

Chou, P. Y. & Fasman, G. D. (1978). *Advan. Enzymol.* **47**, 45–148.

Garnier, J., Osguthorpe, D. J. & Robson, B. (1978). *J. Mol. Biol.* **120**, 97–120.

Kabsch, W. & Sander, C. (1983a). *FEBS Letters*, **155**, 179–182.

Kabsch, W. & Sander, C. (1983b). *Biopolymers*, **22**, 2577–2637.

Karplus, M. (1985). *Ann. N.Y. Acad. Sci.* **439**, 107–123.

Levin, J. M., Robson, B. & Garnier, J. (1986). *FEBS Letters*, **205**, 303–308.

Levitt, M. (1983). *Cold Spring Harbor Symp. Quant. Biol.* **47**, 251–262.

Lim, V. I. (1974). *J. Mol. Biol.* **88**, 873–894.

Mathews, B. W. (1975). *Biochim. Biophys. Acta*, **405**, 442–451.

Minsky, M. & Papert, S. (1969). *Perceptrons*, MIT Press, Cambridge MA.

Nishikawa, K. (1983). *Biochim. Biophys. Acta*, **748**, 285–299.

Robson, B. & Pain, R. H. (1971). *J. Mol. Biol.* **58**, 237–259.

Robson, B. & Suzuki, E. (1976). *J. Mol. Biol.* **107**, 327–356.

Rosenblatt, F. (1959). In *Mechanisation of Thought Processes*, vol. 1, pp. 421–456, HM Stationery Office, London.

Rumelhart, D. E., Hinton, G. E. & Williams, R. J. (1986). In *Parallel Distributed Processing*, vol. 1, pp. 318–362, MIT Press, Cambridge, MA.

Scheraga, H. A. (1985). *Ann. N. Y. Acad. Sci.* 439, 170–194.

Sejnowski, T. J. & Rosenberg, R. R. (1987). *Compl. Syst.* **1**, 145–168.

Staden, R. (1982). *Nucl. Acids Res.* **10**, 2951–2961.

Taylor, W. R. (1986). *J. Mol. Biol.* **188**, 233–258.

Webster, T. A., Lathrop, R. H., & Smith, T. F. (1987). *Biochemistry*, **26**, 6950–6957.

Widrow, R. M. & Hoff, M. E. (1960). In *Institute of Radio Engineers, Western Electronic Show and Convention, Convention Record*, part 4, pp. 96–104. IRE, New York.

Edited by S. Brenner

41
Introduction

(1990)
James A. Anderson, Michael L. Rossen, Susan R. Viscuso, and Margaret E. Sereno

Experiments with representation in neural networks: object motion, speech, and arithmetic
Synergetics of Cognition, H. Haken and M. Stadler (Eds.) Berlin: Springer

[Comments by *Anderson*] One of the perks of being an editor of a reprint volume is having the final say. *Neurocomputing: Foundations of Research* ended with an afterword, giving some conclusions about the state of neural network research in 1987. The paper we present here, which describes the Ph.D. thesis research of three recent graduates from Brown University, suggests one future path for the development of neural networks: toward very large, rather simple networks performing clear-cut and modest computations. Neural network power is due to size and precisely designed function rather than to sophisticated and elaborate learning algorithms that may not scale well.

Neural network research is developing in at least two separate streams: In the first are engineers and computer scientists who are often interested in small systems that often function as adaptive pattern classifiers. Although neural networks may not work any better than traditional pattern classifiers, they are often much easier to use and train, which gives them important practical advantages. Small systems are worth studying because they are adequate for many problems and because current VLSI technology simply does not allow large systems to be built economically.

In the second stream there is a deliberate attempt to understand psychology or physiology with ideas taken from neural network theory. For purely practical reasons simulations in these areas also involve small systems. In some cases this is entirely appropriate, for example, trying to model a small part of the nervous system of an invertebrate. In other cases, particularly in attempts to model the higher levels of cognition in humans, this may be a serious mistake. One fact haunts me: Why do we have 10 billion neurons? We must need them all! Neurons are biologically expensive: They use lots of fuel, they are damage prone, and they are mechanically delicate. There is no free lunch for neurons.

Although these two groups have been growing apart recently, we suggest that they will soon start to come together again. Neural networks are a technology-driven field. In the 1960s one reason symbol processing artificial intelligence (AI) was so effective at suppressing neural net research was that *small* AI systems work well. On even a small computer, given human difficulties with abstract reasoning, a little bit of symbol manipulation looks brilliant. The real problems usually come at the level of getting data into and out of the symbol manipulator—connecting the abstract symbol manipulation to the messy real world. It was possible to ignore these problems at first because we, as humans, are not consciously aware of how hard they are. We have a great deal of painfully evolved special-purpose hardware that lets us do them without effort. But before these perceptual problems became apparent, AI was impressive. Neural networks simply could not compete.

To do much that is significant, neural networks must be larger than a certain size. How large is large? This is not clear, but except for some special applications, not much interesting happens with less than a hundred or so units. It is no accident that the first really impressive neural net demonstration was NETtalk, which used several hundred units (paper 40 in *Neurocomputing: Foundations of Research*). By contrast, symbol processing AI tends to deteriorate with increased size, because large symbol systems break down in combinatorial explosions.

Now that powerful workstations and supercomputers are easily available, it is possible to run neural networks of a reasonable size. But even supercomputers are not large enough for important applications. The systems described in this paper are unusually large and were all run on supercomputers or minisupercomputers. But even so they use only a few thousand elements at most, four or five orders of magnitude smaller than the biological system they are trying to model. Along with other implications, the two papers from Gerald Edelman's laboratory (papers 18 and 19) suggest that many interesting effects do not even begin to appear until the systems are large, complex, and contain a good deal of essential intrinsic variability.

Although neurons and synapses are compact and impressive devices, they still take up space and energy. Let us make the assumption, made by all biologists, that biological hardware design is optimized. This suggests a strategy: We should look carefully at the details of the biology because it is telling us how to organize large groups of units efficiently.

The three Ph.D. theses summarized here provide early examples of the results of this approach. All are based to some degree on computational strategies arising from biology. All work best when there are many elements involved. In fact both the arithmetic simulation and the object motion simulation could not be tested full scale, but had to use reduced systems. However, scaling the simulations up in size is straightforward because the networks are simple. In particular the object motion simulation tests one module of a highly modular system.

The first project described here, deriving global object motion from local edge motion, is taken from the thesis of Margaret Sereno (Sereno 1989, Sereno in press). It is a good example of a perceptual problem that is often not even seen as a problem. Neurons in the early part of our visual system only look at a small part of the visual field. Therefore a moving object is seen by many receptors. Motion sensors with small fields show what is called the *aperture problem*. All the motion sensor can detect is the component of motion of an edge perpendicular to that edge. This means many possible object motions can give rise to a particular edge motion; that is, the sensor is ambiguous with respect to object motion. Physiology and psychophysics show clearly that the earliest stages of vision are subject to the aperture problem in that they respond to edge motion and not to overall object motion. Somehow many individually ambiguous motion signals are put together to form an unambiguous and quite accurate computation of object motion. The visual system seems to do this in the pattern of connections between the primary visual cortical area, V1, and an area of cortex called MT, part of the motion processing channel in the cortex. The problem is well defined, and a solution for a simple network with only two unit layers and one layer of modifiable connections can be found in two ways: First, the solution can be *guessed* based on the geometry of the computation, and, second, perhaps the simplest learning network, the linear associator, can be used to *learn* the transformation (papers 14 and 15 in *Neurocomputing: Foundations of Research*). The learned transformation and the guessed solution are similar. The distributed representation used is based on the kinds of cell selectivities seen in the visual cortex. Although the simulations involve thousands of units, they actually model only one module of an object motion system. A large number of psychophysical predictions and illusions also follow from the model, which are described in detail in the references.

The second project briefly describes a speech recognition system developed by Michael Rossen (1989). It is somewhat removed from physiology, but it does make use of a number of ideas taken from auditory system physiology. Speech recognition is an important practical problem and is also of considerable scientific interest because it can help in the understanding of the human speech system.

Speech has proved to be a difficult network problem for a number of reasons, not least because it involves analysis of a signal that changes in time. Neural networks at this point have technical difficulty in handling information that is intrinsically in the time domain. Many attempts to do this have involved such "hacks" as turning a temporal problem into a spatial problem.

In Rossen's speech model information is fed continuously into the network as it is received by the system. Time integration from different, successively presented frames of input data is performed by a simple dynamical system, an attractor model called the BSB model (paper 22 in *Neurocomputing: Foundations of Research*) operating on the output layer of a partially connected backpropagation network (paper 41 in *Neurocomputing: Foundations of Research*).

The data representation used was directly suggested by properties of units in the auditory cortex. Although it is sometimes assumed that the auditory system only responds selectively to the frequency components of the input signal like a narrow band filter, the reality is more complex. Some cortical auditory units respond most strongly to a best frequency at a best amplitude, that is, they are responding to a region in a two-dimensional frequency intensity space. Signals that are *either* too weak *or* too strong will cause the cell to cease firing. The representation used in the simulations used units responding like this:

Results from the system were good, getting over 95 percent correct with simple consonant-vowel monosyllables. The data representation used was sufficiently good so that complete removal of the hidden layer still obtained recognition accuracies of over 90 percent. (For a description of other neural network speech recognition systems, see the review by Lippman (1989).)

The third simulation, on arithmetic learning, was part of the thesis research of Susan Viscuso (see Viscuso, Anderson, and Spoehr 1989, Viscuso 1989) and was much more speculative. It is surprising that humans have so much trouble learning simple arithmetic, when they seem to effortlessly pick up the complex regularities involved in syntax and language. We were interested in seeing if neural networks would have difficulties learning arithmetic and, more important, if some insight could be gained into the way humans do arithmetic. There is compelling experimental evidence that humans do not view arithmetic and numbers as mere abstract relationships and entities, but that we seem to think of numbers as having "sensory" components. Creative mathematics done by professional mathematicians is remarkably intuitive, with visualization and even kinesthesis playing a major role in the *understanding* of mathematics (see Hadamard 1949).

This simulation describes a hybrid system capable of learning (poorly) the multiplication tables. It contains both a symbolic part (number names) and a sensory part (position on a topographic bar code). Although such a system learns with difficulty, the resulting network, when it does make errors, makes "reasonable" errors, in that the errors are close to the correct answers. The network has developed a kind of mechanical intuition. A modest speculative leap suggests that such techniques may be used to develop systems with "common sense," probably the most difficult thing for a traditional AI system to develop. In humans these "intuitive" techniques can be checked, complemented, and extended with abstract reasoning. The resulting hybrid processor, even though it may not reason or do arithmetic very well, *can do it*, and that seems to be part of the reason for our species' recent spectacular evolutionary success.

The representation techniques used in all three problems are similar. All make extensive use of the topographic maps that are ubiquitous in cerebral cortex. Maps seem to "waste" many units. For example, a position in two-dimensional space could be coded by graded activities of two units or by position of an active region on a topographic map of thousands of units. The second choice seems to be a common biological choice for sensory data representation. It seems that the properties of redundancy, generalization, distribution, and computational efficiency require the maps.

Note by the way that the single units used in the topographic representations in all three simulations are nonlinear *and* nonmonotonic, referred to the input parameters. Increases in a parameter (say, object speed, intensity of a frequency, or arithmetic magnitude) will cause a particular unit responding to that parameter to first increase in activity and then decrease in activity. Simple neural networks using a large number of units, combined with well-defined but nonlinear initial representations of the data, can produce well-behaved and quite functional systems.

References

J. Hadamard (1949), *The Psychology of Invention in the Mathematical Field*. Princeton, NJ: Princeton University Press.

R. Lippman (1989), Review of neural networks for speech recognition. *Neural Computation* 1: 1–38.

M.L. Rossen (1989), Speech syllable recognition with a neural network. Ph.D. thesis, Department of Psychology, Brown University, Providence, RI.

M.E. Sereno (1989), A neural network model of visual motion processing. Ph.D. thesis, Department of Psychology, Brown University, Providence, RI.

M.E. Sereno (in press), *A Neural Network Model of Visual Motion Processing*. Cambridge, MA: MIT Press.

S.R. Viscuso (1989), Memory for arithmetic facts: A perspective gained from two methodologies. Ph.D. thesis, Department of Psychology, Brown University.

S.R. Viscuso, J.A. Anderson, and K.T. Spoehr (1989), Representing simple arithmetic in neural networks. In G. Tiberghien (Ed.), *Advanced Cognitive Science: Theory and Applications*. Cambridge, England: Horwoods.

(1990)

James A. Anderson, Michael L. Rossen, Susan R. Viscuso, and Margaret E. Sereno

Experiments with representation in neural networks: object motion, speech, and arithmetic

Synergetics of Cognition, H. Haken and M. Stadler (Eds.), Berlin: Springer

Abstract

Simple network models for object motion, perception of spoken syllables, and learning of simple arithmetic are discussed. Many of the same data representation techniques can be used for all three of these highly dissimilar tasks.

1. Introduction

Neural networks are composed of large numbers of simple, 'neuron like' computing elements connected together with connections of varying strengths. The architecture of the networks is highly parallel. Most of them are capable of learning from experience and effective learning algorithms are known for adjusting connection strengths between units to give appropriate outputs. Since the networks are highly parallel, they can be extremely fast. Since they are built from many identical processing elements, they are not difficult to implement in special purpose hardware. However, neural networks are not magic and they have severe performance limitations, along with their strengths. It is usually difficult to represent a problem for a network so that the network will perform the task reliably. The "software" aspects of neural networks will prove to be far more difficult (and less glamorous) than building special purpose hardware or studying the dynamics of abstract networks.

In neural networks, information is represented as distributed patterns of activity on the computing elements, the model neurons. These activity patterns are represented as state vectors. The evolution of the state vectors with time represents the computations done by the network. For an introduction to neural networks see, for example, Anderson and Rosenfeld (1988), McClelland and Rumelhart (1986), Rumelhart and McClelland (1986), or Hinton and Anderson (1981, 9)

It might be worth mentioning our general philosophy toward using neural networks. Human cerebral cortex contains billions of neurons. The cortex is a layered two dimensional system which is divided up into a moderate number of subregions. The subregions project to other subregions over pathways that are physically parallel. One large group of neurons projects to another large group of neurons. Much of what we can perceive depends on the details of the way the nervous system converts information from the physical world into discharges of nerve cells. The neurons in a real brain, though sometimes capable of a degree of modifiability, respond selectively to specific aspects of the environment. The selectivities they show are those needed to perform the behaviors that allow them to survive and reproduce. The brain is in no sense a general purpose computing device. Only in our own brains has sufficient flexibility developed that such an idea could even be contemplated.

Much, perhaps most, of the computational power of the brain is in the details of the neural codes, that is, the biologically developed representation of the stimulus. Perhaps the brain does little clever computation but, instead, does powerful, brute force operations on information that has been so highly processed that little needs to be done to it. Given good preprocessing and huge numbers of cells, the power of the system becomes great. Since neurons have a large biological overhead, the huge numbers of cells in the mammalian nervous system must be earning their keep. Perhaps lots of cells are required to get analytical power and flexibilty, proper generalization to new situations, and good learning. The brain is telling us that we should look at information representation that intrinsically requires large numbers of computing elements rather than clever and subtle architectures.

We feel that the same considerations are true of neural networks that we want to use for practical tasks. Our own experience in a number of areas has been that representing the data for the network, i.e., deciding the information content of the elements of the state vector in the first place, is what gives the system the ability to generalize properly, to learn, and to show the proper noise and damage immunity. Also, experimentation with representations may give a good deal of insight into the operation of the human cognitive system. Although some neural networks form interesting representations as part of their learning process, the representations so formed are extremely dependent on the details of the training set, the connectivity, and the initial data representation and are nowhere near as general as one might expect.

We will sketch three, seemingly quite different applications of neural networks: (1) a network for determining large scale object motion from small scale local motion signals (the "aperture problem"), (2) a speech syllable recognition system, and (3) a neural net that learns to do the multiplication tables badly. These networks represent information in almost the same way.

1. The Aperture Problem

Single units early in the visual system have small receptive fields, that is, they generally see small parts of the visual field, somewhat like looking at the visual world through a bunch of straws. Somehow the visual system puts together information from many sensors to give rise to perception of the large scale structure in the visual world. Determination of object motion from local motion signals is one well studied example of such a computation. This work is described in detail in a recent thesis (Sereno, 1989).

Moving objects are patterns that can contain line elements that move with the same velocity as the object. If considered in isolation, however, the true motion of a single component line segment cannot be determined. As a demonstration, one can isolate a single featureless line segment by moving it behind a circular aperture. If the line is moved in different directions while its orientation is held constant, it will always appear to move in a direction perpendicular to its orientation. The task of detecting the true motion of an oriented line segment is known as the *aperture* problem. It is possible to determine the true motion of the line, and the object containing that element, only if the motion of several lines of different orientation belonging to the same object are observed at the same time. A simple neural net can combine local information about edge movements to determine larger scale object motion.

An attempt was made to take account of the structure of the visual system in constructing a parallel network to estimate object velocity from local motion signals. An analysis of the connectivity developed by the system suggests how the solution to the aperture problem may be implemented in the real neural networks of visual cortex.

The model sets out to solve the aperture problem for rigid translational motion in the plane. Henceforth, local, one-dimensional (1-D), or component motion refers to the motion of 1-D lines, or edges, while 2-D or pattern motion refers to the actual motion of the object, which is to be determined. In Figure 1, a simple two-dimensional (2-D) pattern consisting of two oriented contours moves rightward with a speed and direction indicated by the the arrow located at the corner of the pattern. At each contour, local movement detectors, represented by circular aper-

tures, measure only the perpendicular component of motion, represented by the thick vectors.

A family of possible pattern motions consistent with the perpendicular motion is represented by vectors whose tips lie along the *constraint line*. The length of each vector specifies speed and its angle specifies direction.

Both psychophysical and physiological studies suggest that the solution to the aperture problem is at least a two stage process. The first stage extracts perpendicular components of motion while the second stage combines these local motion measurements to compute pattern motion. (Adelson and Movshon, 1982; Albright, 1984; Hildreth, 1984; Movshon et al., 1985).

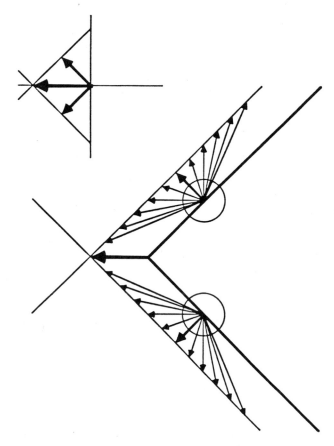

Figure 1 The *aperture problem*. A simple 2-dimensional pattern consisting of two oriented contours moves rightward with a speed and direction indicated by the arrow located at the corner of the pattern. At each local contour, local motion detectors (represented by circular apertures) measure only the perpendicular component of motion. A family of possible pattern motions consistent with the observed motion is represented by vectors whose tips lie along a *constraint line*. The inset figure presents the *velocity space* solution: the correct answer is the common vector between the two families generated by the constraint lines.

A simple formal solution to the aperture problem that accurately predicts the perceived motion of patterns, given local information is also shown in Figure 1. (Fennema and Thompson, 1979; Adelson and Movshon, 1982). At each contour, the constraint lines indicate the family of global pattern velocities consistent with the locally measured component velocity vector. When we compare at least two, non-parallel moving contours belonging to the same pattern, we find that only one vector is common to both 1-D families. This common vector describes the motion of the entire pattern. This vector is the point in velocity space at which the constraint lines intersect.

It is possible to construct a simple network model that learns to approximate this intersection of constraint lines solution. (See Van Essen, 1985; Maunsell and Newsome, 1987 for relevant physiology.) Some neurons in area V1 (striate cortex), are selective for orientation, speed, and direction of edges. However, these neurons respond only to the component of motion perpendicular to the preferred orientation of the unit, that is, they are subject to the aperture problem. Area MT, an area involved in motion analysis, receives a direct topographic projection from V1 and is selective for the direction and speed of motion of an object, while having little selectivity for spatial structure. Area MT is also characterized by larger excitatory receptive fields than V1, suggesting converging inputs from V1 units sampling adjacent areas of space. Moreover, 25% of MT units exhibit pattern direction selectivity, that is, they are selective for the motion of the pattern as a whole. (Movshon et al., 1985).

A simple formal solution to the aperture problem by constraint line satisfaction could be implemented neurophysiologically if each unit in the input layer projects to the family of pattern velocities in the output layer that describes all of the possible true physical motions underlying its response.

A single component motion neuron projects to the family of possible pattern velocities consistent with its velocity. With such a connectivity, when a number of differently oriented line segments belonging to a translating pattern stimulate the input layer units, the activity of the output units describing the overall pattern motion is selectively enhanced, because only those motion units receive a common activation from all of the active input units. This connection scheme is a description of an input layer neuron's *projective field*. Such a scheme can also be represented in terms of an output layer neuron *receptive field*. In this case, each output layer unit receives input from all the possible component motions of a pattern moving with the preferred velocity of the output unit. Figure 2 presents the receptive field of an MT cell. It is receives inputs from the

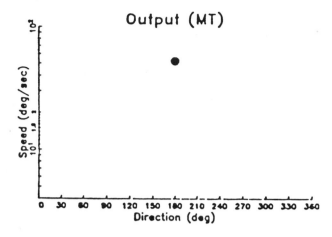

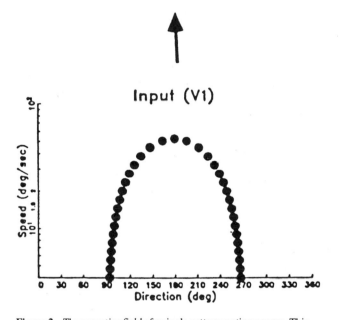

Figure 2 The *receptive field* of a single pattern motion neuron. This neuron has a preferred direction of 180 degrees and speed of 64 degrees/second. It receives inputs from units with component velocities that may be contained in a pattern moving with the velocity of the pattern motion unit.

V1 model neurons that are consistent with the MT unit's speed sensitivity and direction.

A network was constructed with an input layer of component selective V1 neurons and an output layer of pattern selective MT neurons. Because the units have overlapping tuning functions, velocity is represented as a distributed pattern of activity across the units. In addition, multiple sets of V1 units with adjacent receptive fields project to one set of MT units at one position. In Figure 3, a number of groups of neurons form the input layer. The individual units are the circles within each cluster. The input layer, modelled after area V neurons, has component motion units selective for velocities perpendicular to their preferred orientation (D1, D2 , . . . Dy) and speed (S1, S2, . . . or Sx) Each cluster of input units has units tuned to a complete spectrum of directions and speeds. Different clusters respond to different regions of the visual field, that is, a cluster has X and Y coordinates ($X1, Y1, X2, Y2, ... Xn, Yn$). The output layer, modelled after area MT neurons, has pattern motion units selective for different directions and speeds. Note the spatial resolution of the output layer is poor because it is integrating information from a number of different input locations. The overall response of each unit is the multipli-

cation of its individual responses to direction and speed. The units are broadly tuned so that a single unit responds to a wide range of speeds, and a single speed is represented by several active units. (See Figure 4.)

We used a linear associator, one of the simplest neural networks, with error correction training, to see if it was possible to learn a good solution to the aperture problem from a training set, by adjusting the set of weights between the V1 and the MT units. (Anderson, 1983; Kersten et al., 1987). The network was presented with a large number of input patterns. For each pattern, activity in the input layer is propagated linearly to the output layer:

$$g'_i = A f_i$$

where g'_i is the vector of output layer neuron activities resulting when a pattern f_i is input to the system, and A is a matrix of connection strengths between input and output layers. Actual output (g') is compared to correct output (g) for that pattern, and all weights in the system are then adjusted to reduce error between actual and correct output using the vector form of the Widrow Hoff learning rule:

$$A_{i=1} = A_i + \eta(g_i - g'_i) f_i^T$$

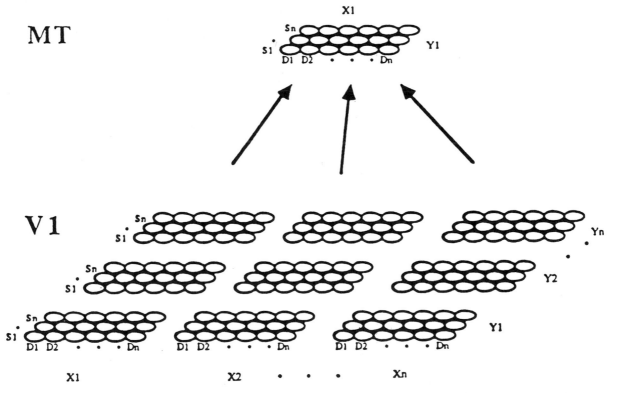

Figure 3 Network model of the aperture problem. There are 2 layers of units. The input layer has component motion units with different preferred directions, and speeds. There are a number of different spatial locations, each with a full complement of receptor speeds and directions. The output layer, modelled after MT neurons, has pattern motion units selective for different directions and speeds of pattern motion.

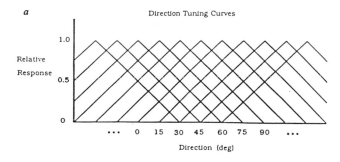

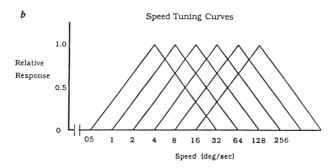

Figure 4 Direction and speed tuning functions used in the model. (a) Direction tuning curves with one-half response bandwidths of 60 degrees and peaks at 15 degree intervals. (b) Speed tuning curves range from 4 to 128 degrees per second on a log scale. These ranges and bandwidths are consistent with neurophysiological data.

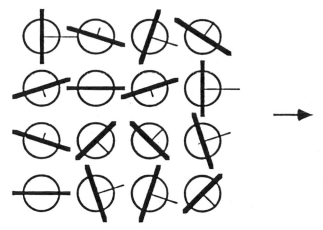

Figure 5 Example pattern used to train the system. Each open circle represents a set of 144 V1 units tuned to different speeds and locations at one retinal location. The motion of the pattern is rightward and the component motion of each element is represented by the length and orientation of the thin lines.

where f_i is the vector of input layer activities representing component velocities for the ith pattern, g_i is the vector of output layer neuron activities representing pattern velocities for the ith pattern, and η is a learning constant.

A representative simulation uses units having 24 direction tuning curves, spanning 360 degrees with peaks at 15 degree intervals, and half response widths of 60 degrees, and with six speed tuning curves, spanning 128 degrees/second with peaks at one octave intervals and half response widths of 3 octaves. Since each unit is sensitive to a different combination of preferred speed and direction, a total of 144 units are available for each spatial location. The model uses 16 sets of V1 units, that is, 16 locations, and one set of MT units. The system is trained on 360 patterns and tested on the same pattern, plus 360 new ones. The patterns are textures composed of 16 line segments— one line segment per V1 location. Figure 5 provides an example of a pattern used to train the system. Each open circle represents a set of 144 V1 units tuned to different speeds and directions at one retinotopic location out of 16 possible locations. The pattern is a texture composed of 16 oriented line segments—1 line segment per location. The motion of the example pattern is rightward, represented by the thick arrow, and the component motion of each texture

element is represented by the length and orientation of the attached thin lines.

After 15 passes through the training set, performance reached a plateau. When activity across the output layer produced by a moving pattern was represented as a vector whose elements were the activity strength of each unit, the mean cosine of the angle between the correct output vector and the actual output vector that the system produced was 0.98; the mean cosine of new, non-associated vectors was 0.93. This represents good performance, and demonstrates that the system generalizes well to stimuli it has never seen. The weights were examined to determine whether the solution developed by the system to solve the aperture problem resembled the velocity space solution. Figure 6 shows the weights between a complete set of 144 V1 units at one location and a single MT unit. Each circle represents the weight between a V1 unit and MT unit: the V1 unit's direction and speed is determined by its x and y coordinate, the strength of connection by the size of the circle, and the type of connection (positive or negative) by whether the circle is filled or open, respectively. If the system implements the velocity space solution, the MT unit's receptive field should be similar to the one illustrated in Figure 2.

The chevron pattern of large weights in the graph confirms this prediction. Thus, the MT unit has strong positive weights to V1 units with component motions possible in any pattern moving with the velocity of the MT unit. The MT unit is strongly connected to the V1 units with the same preferred speed and direction. As speed decreases, the strongest connections are to units with directions increasingly dissimilar to the MT unit's direction. At the lowest

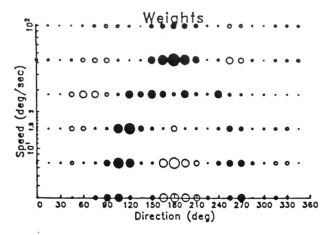

Figure 6 Receptive field of a single pattern motion unit. Note the similarity of this set of weights derived from learning in a network to the set of weights suggested in Figure 2.

speed, the strongest connection is to V1 units with directions nearly perpendicular to that of the MT unit.

These results demonstrate that a perceptual solution to the aperture problem can be realized in a two-layer neural-like network. The specific implementation predicts how component selective V1 neurons project to pattern selective MT neurons transforming the response from selectivity to 1-D motion to selectivity for 2-D motion. The projection produces MT units with a wider range and higher cutoff of preferred speeds than V1 units, a finding consistent with neurophysiological data. The model suggests that 2-D motion measurements result from integration of 1-D motion measurements over an area instead of along connected contours.

The computation performed is a rapid parallel disambiguation given simultaneous input information from adjacent portions of the velocity field. Networks, even simple ones, are effective at disambiguation. (See Kawamoto and Anderson, 1985; Kawamoto, 1986) A similar feedforward operation may be implemented in the real visual system.

2. Speech Recognition

The speech recognition system we have developed recognizes consonant-vowel (CV) tokens from the set /b,d,g,p,t,k/x/a,i,u/ when preceded by noise and when information on syllable start and end points is not supplied during testing. Examples of stimuli are /ba/, /tu/ and so on. Presently our best two-speaker systems perform with about a 3% phoneme error rate. (The error rate falls to 1.3% when test token end points are supplied to the system.) We also have implemented a 4-speaker system (2 male, 2 female) using the stop consonants, /b,d,g,p,t,k/ in the three vowel contexts. This 4-speaker system performed with 5% error rate on consonants and 11% on the vowels. (The relatively poor vowel accuracy is due to the shortness of the speech segment that we were forced to use due to computer limitations. Generally, vowels are much easier to recognize than stop consonants.) Systems of this architecture may be useful in more general signal processing functions as well. More details and references are available in Rossen, 1989.

In most models for speech recognition using neural networks, (for example, Kohonen (1988); Landauer, Kamm and Singhal (1988); Waibel (1988)) a nearly direct representation of the power spectrum of the speech signal is used, sometimes with simple extensions involving the time domain. The speech waveform is sampled (with a window) at one or more locations in the speech signal, an FFT is performed on the contents of the window and a state vector is constructed which contains the amplitudes of the spectral components. Perhaps 20 or 30 elements are required for such a spectral representation. This state vector might be interpreted as a list of the filter outputs from a filter bank at a moment in time. Sometime changes with time of the spectra are represented more or less explicitly. Time domain techniques are used effectively by Waibel, for example.

The system as implemented is highly modular, as shown in Figure 7. It consists of a layer of input units, a layer of hidden units, and an output layer, which contains auto associative feedback, based on the BSB model, an energy minimizing categorization algorithm. (Anderson, Silverstein, Ritz, and Jones, 1977; Anderson, 1983) The input layer contains several representations of the input signal. We have found that no one of the input representations that we considered works as well as several of them used together. In particular, a topographic, two-dimensional intensity map, of several alternative signal representations, provides the best recognition accuracy. Presently, we have 682 input units, 100 hidden units, and 36 output units in the

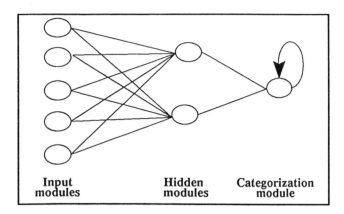

Figure 7 Each circle represents a module of elementary units, coding one aspect of the input acoustic data. Information is continuously fed to the input module, and the output module decides upon the final phonetic classification. Note the autoassociative feedback present in the output module.

network. The coding of the output units is distributed, so that several output elements correspond to a single output phoneme. The input representation is suffiently rich, so that the hidden layer seems to add rather little power to the classification ability of the system, though its use does improve overall recognition accuracy by 5% or so, roughly from 90% to 95%. The coding in the output module is distributed: when phonemes are present in a signal four units are active in one pattern; when phonemes are not present, these four units are active in another pattern. Addition of autoassociative feedback at the output layer improves classification by a few percent and never hurts.

We have not segmented the speech stream. This was because we wanted to use co-articulation information in the most effective way, by allowing associations to be formed between the proper CV output and the partial information about the vowel contained in the consonant, and vice versa. However, the structure of our neural network can easily produce segmentation at the output layer as part of its natural time evolution. The BSB dynamics that we incorporate in the output layer forms a dynamical system with stable attractors. As speech input is presented to the system, one way for the output to function would be to move from attractor to attractor, each attractor representing a segment, under the influence of inputs and past state of the system. We have looked at multistability in the BSB system in relation to the Necker Cube in vision (Kawamoto and Anderson, 1985) and linguistic disambiguation (Kawamoto, 1985). In that case, it was easy to set up the network to give multistable behavior by adjusting a couple of parameters and incorporating a decay term involving Hebbian antilearning in the feedback matrix. The output of such a system would provide a segmented output stream, where, if properly adjusted, each segment might corresponds roughly to a phoneme. Output segmentation might be of value to feed a higher, more traditional speech system, such a hidden Markov Model (HMM) in a practical system. Such hybrid speech recognition systems show considerable promise. (Lippman, 1989).

Since our ultimate aim is to recognize continuous speech, we do not want to tell the system where the start of the utterance is. Target segments are fuzzy entities embedded in a continuous input stream. In our system, each token is preceded by a few milliseconds of white noise. Sometimes these frames are used for noise rejection training, that is, deliberately training the model not to recognize noise frames as phonemes. In the continuous speech context, there are two classes of errors: *omission* where the network fails to recognize a phoneme that is present, and *confusion* where a phoneme is inaccurately classified.

The "Standard" representation in Table 1 has three two dimensional representations: frequency-intensity, time difference-intensity, and a frequency discriminator-intensity. (See Figure 5.) The "1-D Standard" has the three one dimensional representations corresponding to the 2-D ones used by the standard system. The "1-D Full" has, in addition to the 1-D standard representations information about cepstrum, frequency modulation, and spectral slope.

We have looked at, and incorporated into the initial represention, information on spectral time differences (i.e.

the spectrum at one moment in time subtracted from the spectrum a number of milliseconds in the past), the cepstrum, and information that could be interpreted as information on frequency modulation, i.e. how rapidly strong frequency components in the spectrum are changing with time. The frequency modulation information adds significantly to the information in the raw spectral data and improves classification accuracy markedly.

We try to model our representation on the kinds of analysis that seem to be performed by the neurons in the auditory system. There is general agreement that a crude kind of spectral analysis is performed at a low level in the auditory system, though simple spectral analysis overlooks the important phase information contained in the firing patterns of eighth nerve units. We achieved a marked increase in the accuracy of our speech system by using a representation that was suggested by neurons seen in cortical area AI. (Brugge and Reale, 1985). Units in the eighth nerve tend to respond monotonically to intensity, that is, if a unit responds to a particular frequency it will continue to respond to that frequency if the intensity of the tone is increased. The dynamic range of such units is often small, perhaps 10 or 15 db, but response is montonic with intensity.

In cortex one sees non-monotonic units. That is, a cell will respond to increased amplitude of a tone with an increase in firing rate up to a point, and then will respond to a further increase of amplitude with a decrease in rate. It is as if the cell is representing a point in a two dimensional frequency-intensity surface. The spectral representation of a waveform then corresponds to a graph drawn on this two dimensional surface: auditory recognition becomes like a pattern recognition problem in vision. Figure 8 shows the representation of speech signals used in the standard system for two frames of data.

Low amplitude components are represented not as low values of a particular frequency unit, but as a particular active region of frequency-intensity space. That means low values of spectral intensity have as much activity associated with them as high values of spectral intensity, it is just located in a different place. This is a non-linear

coding technique since input amplitude change produces a complex spatial pattern of shifts of element activities. (Notice that the same is true of the speed-orientation units used for the aperture problem.) The price that has to be paid, is the use of more units to code the information. Topographic representations are highly effective ways of representing continuous information, both in the speech system and are ubiquitous in the nervous system. Though our representation in this case was suggested by auditory physiology, it is also consistent with a simplified version of a pattern recognition technique called 'Radial Basis Functions' which suggests that a useful way to represent information is as little bumps of response in state space. (Niranjan and Fallside, 1988)

3. Arithmetic Learning: Multiplication with a Neural Network

We have recently looked at learning simple arithmetic with a neural network (Viscuso, Anderson and Spoehr, 1988). We might expect neural networks to perform arithmetic poorly, because humans find it hard. Arithmetic is learned with considerable difficulty in elementary school. This is curious, because arithmetic and related simple logic and mathematics are about the simplest rule governed behavior possible. These tasks are certainly far less complicated than the language 'rules' we apply in milliseconds when we speak.

Arithmetic learning has been studied for many years. It can be viewed as simply a set of relations between symbols, such as the memorization of flashcard information. But there are clearly richer meanings attached to the numbers that are being added or multiplied. At least part of a representation of number is symbolic, but another part reflects its magnitude and other formally redundant information. A large series of experiments indicates that humans possess an internal representation of numbers related to their magnitudes. (See Moyer and Landauer, 1967) Experiments involving arithmetic magnitude comparisons (i.e. "Which is greater—17 or 85?" or "Which is greater—74 or 73?") show consistently that people answer the second question more slowly than the first. Comparison times betwen a two digit number and a standard decreases as a function of the absolute difference between the quantities. It is as if people have an internal representation of number that acts like a weight, or a light intensity. Magnitude estimates seem to suggest a logarithm or (more precisely) a power law relation in the way we code numerical magnitude. Intervals between numbers at the 'small' end of the scale are larger than between numbers at the 'large' end of the scale.

But there must be a symbolic relationship as well in mathematics. The symbolic aspects of mathematics are

Table 1 Manipulations of the Input Representation (2-speaker system)

	Consonant Errors	Vowel Errors	Mean Errors
Standard System	4.8	5.4	5.1
1-D Full	9.7	7.2	8.4
2-D Spectrum Only	18.1	8.9	13.5
1-D Standard	31.1	14.6	22.9

often emphasized in teaching. (Overemphasized in the opinion of many. See Davis and Anderson, 1979, for a spirited discussion of the devastating effects of excessive rigor and emphasis on the linguistic aspects of proof on the teaching of mathematics. Also see Hadamard, 1946, for a fascinating discussion of how 'real' mathematicians think.) The name of the number is clearly a more abstract entity than its 'weight' or magnitude.

We tried three coding strategies to represent arithmetical information for our simulations. A symbolic code representation, that is, simply associating arbitrary letter strings, resulted in poor simulation performance, because of the powerful interference between digits and answers (i.e. 6x1 = 6, 6x2 = 12, etc. has '6' associated with many different answers). Interestingly, the trickiest mathemtical concept in simple arithmetic involves 'zero', yet, viewed strictly as associations, learning the zero times tables is trivial for children because there is no interference. Our simulations show that neural networks easily learn the zero times table. Associating magnitudes works, but the model also makes many errors, particularly for larger numbers. By far the best simulation results were obtained with hybrid codes, partly continuous and partly abstract. For the symbolic part, we simply used number names, represented as character

/BA/ TOKEN, INPUT REPRESENTATION

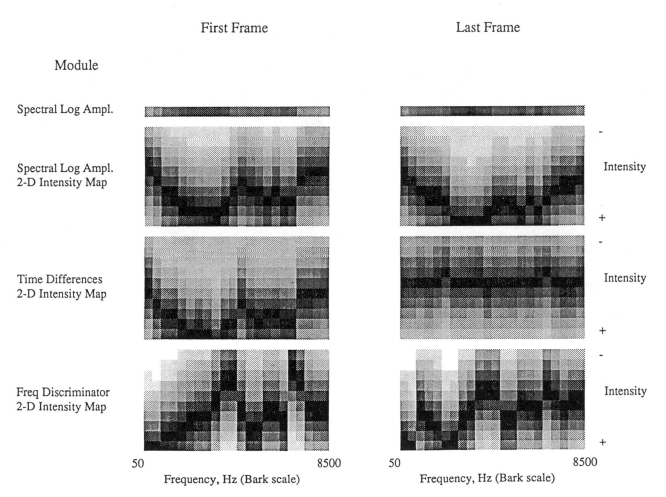

Figure 8 Representation of two frames of auditory data for the standard system. After initial normalization, the spectrum is represented by a group of units. The one dimensional strip is the one dimensional spectral data, with the darkness of the box representing the intensity. The three larger boxes represent (1) a two dimensional frequency-intensity plot, (2) a time difference representation, where a frequency-intensity plot two frames in the past is subtracted from the current frequency-intensity plot and (3) a frequency discriminator-intensity map. This coding tends to respond to derivatives of the spectrum.

strings. For the 'analog' part, we used the bar codes that have been so valuable in other contexts. The resulting code seems to have the strengths of both approaches. The simulations show that the model estimates values that it has not learned, showing signs of a rudimentary 'intuition' process. But the model can also learn arbitrary relations between names.

Table 2 shows examples of the hybrid code used in the simulations. The character strings represent a particular product. The number names are used as the arbitrary associative coding. The magnitude information is represented by the position of the bar of '++++'. Larger numbers move the bar to the right. Blank is also a character, so these state vectors contain no zero elements but are all plus or minus ones. Even with access to supercomputers, we were not able to simulate learning of the entire times table. We were forced to use approximations to many values. For these large simulations, the system used roughly 1000 elements. We approximated the times table, so 9 times 9 was assumed to be 80, 2 times 2 was assumed to be 5, and so on. Some example products are given in Table 3.

After learning the state vectors, the resulting system obtained about 70% correct answers when given two integers to multiply. It may seem remarkable to spend hours of supercomputer time to obtain the wrong answers to simple arithmetic, but that is cognitive science. The initial codings for the integers are used for the test state vector and the answer is replaced with zeros. The energy minimizing BSB dynamics replaces the zeros with the answer. (See Anderson, 1986) When the system makes errors, the errors tend to be 'close' to correct answers. Some typical errors are shown in Table 4. For convenience in interpretation, the state vectors are broken into three segments, one per line: the two integers and the product. The product line was orginally all zeros.

Table 2 Examples of State-Vector Codings

A two++++	*B two++++	= five++++
Athree ++++	*B two++++	= five++++
A four ++++	*B five ++++	= twenty ++++

Table 3 Examples of the Qualitative Multiplication Tables

$0 \times 2 = 0$	$1 \times 2 = 1$	$2 \times 2 = 5$	$7 \times 7 = 50$
$0 \times 3 = 0$	$1 \times 3 = 5$	$2 \times 3 = 5$	$7 \times 8 = 60$
$0 \times 4 = 0$	$1 \times 4 = 5$	$2 \times 4 = 10$	$7 \times 9 = 60$

Table 4 Examples of Errors

Output Vector			Correct Product
A two		*	
Bseven	++++		15
=	ten ++++		
A five	++++	*	
Bseven	++++		40
+	fifty	++++	

There is a great deal of data on human error patterns in arithmetic learning. Most errors are similar in magnitude to the correct answers. Errors observed in the simulations showed a similar pattern. The analog portion of the number code makes errors 'close' to the correct answers and the errors are not random, as might be suggested by an associative system with a purely symbolic representation.

We can look at more subtle aspects of arithmetic learning as well. (For more details and other predictions, see Viscuso, Anderson, and Spoehr, 1988.) Humans have difficulty rejecting false products when they are close to the correct product, but they can easily reject wrong answers when the incorrect answer is far away. For example, it is more difficult to verify the accuracy of '8 ∗ 7 = 63' than '8 ∗ 7 = 12.' Plausible nearby but incorrect answers show long reaction times, and high error rates. The computer simulations mimic this pattern easily. When given a false product at the opposite end of the scale (i.e. a state vector representing 9 ∗ 9 = 5) the model immediately rejects the input by changing the output to the correct answer (9 ∗ 9 = 80), by overwriting the incorrect answer. When the model is given a false product that is close to a correct product (i.e., 2 ∗ 2 = 10), the error is accepted and is not overwritten. Tables 5 and 6 present several examples of both of these results.

Table 5 Answers to False Products Near Correct Answer

Vector			False Product	Correct Product
A two++++		*	10	5
B two++++				
=	ten ++++			
Aseven	++++	*	70	60
B nine	++++			
=	seventy	++++		

Table 6 Answers to False Products That are Very Different in Magnitude from Correct Products

Vector			False Product	Correct Product
A three ++++		*	80	5
B two++++				
= five				
A nine	++++*		5	70
B eight	++++			
= seventy		++++		

It is also possible to model some other common effects seen in arithmetic learning (See Viscuso, et al, 1989, and Viscuso, 1989).

4. Conclusions

We have tried to show in these three very different examples that some principles used to represent information in simple neural networks may be useful when applied to real problems. First, the use of topographic maps with localized activities to code a continuous magnitude is effective. It allows natural generalization and estimation. They also require very large numbers of units. These representations are also highly non-linear, *relative to the input stimulus dimensions*. Perhaps it makes more sense to have a highly nonlinear representation combined with a linear or simple non-linear network than to represent stimulus magnitudes directly and place all the significant non-linear operations in the network. Second, simple neural networks can make effective use of very large amounts of learned information. The computations can be truly consensual and cooperative. This result should bode well for the functioning of extremely large simple nets. Notice that more complex multilayer nets may not have this desirable scaling property. *If* the representation of the data (or the problem) can be made good enough to avoid the use of the more complex networks, very large, and potentially usable, nets can be constructed. Use of very large nets can be particularly effective in neural network signal processing. One thing we know from biology is that biological maps are often extremely distorted if it is helpful in doing the necessary computation. A particularly good example is the highly distorted representation of frequency on the cortex of the mustache bat (Suga and Jen, 1976). There is an enormous amount of cortex devoted to frequencies around 60 kHz, because processing the Doppler shifted return echo requires careful analysis to extract target velocity information with satisfactory resolution. A general rule seems to be that, to a first approximation, the relative importance of different subparts of a modality in a sensory or motor system is a function of the number of cells devoted to it. We feel that

we see some common strategies emerging that will allow useful applications of neural nets to both engineering and cognitive science. What, after all, is the brain but an engineering solution to problems posed by the environment.

References

Adelson, E.H. and Movshon, J.A.(1982), Phenomenal coherence of moving visual patterns, *Nature, 300,* 523-525.

Albright, T.D. (1984), Direction and orientation selective of neurons in visual area MT of the Macaque, *Journal of Neurophysiology, 52,* 1106-1130.

Anderson, J.A. (1983), Neural models for cognitive computation. *IEEE Transactions: Systems, Man, and Cybernetics, SMC-13,* 799-815.

Anderson, J.A. (1986), Cognitive Capabilities of a Parallel System. In E. Bienenstock, F. Foglemann, and G. Weisbuch, (Eds.) *Disordered Systems and Biological Organization,* Berlin: Springer.

Anderson, J.A. and Rosenfeld, E., Eds. (1988) Neurocomputing: Foundations of Research, Cambridge, MA: MIT Press.

Anderson, J.A., Silverstein, J.W, Ritz, S.A., and Jones, R.S., Distinctive features, categorical perception, and probability learning: Some applications of a neural model, *Psychological Review, 84,* 413-451.

Brugge, J.F. and Reale, R. A. (1985), Auditory cortex, In A. Peters and E.G. Jones, *Cerebral Cortex, Volume 4, Association and Auditory Cortices,* New York: Plenum Press.

Davis, P.J. and Anderson, J.A., (1979), Nonanalytic aspects of mathematics and their implication for research and education, *SIAM Review, 21,* 112-127.

Fennema, C.L. and Thompson, W.B. (1979), Velocity determination in scenes containing multiple moving objects, *Computer Graphics and Image Processing,* 9, 301-315.

Hadamard, J. (1945) *The Psychology of Invention in the Mathematical Field,* Princeton, NJ: Princeton University Press.

Harrison, T.D. and Fallside, F. (1988), A connectionist structure for phoneme recognition, Technical Report CUED/F-INFENG/TR.15 from Cambridge University Engineering Department.

Hildreth, E.C. (1984), *The Measurement of Visual Motion,* Cambridge, MA: MIT Press.

Hinton, G.E. and Anderson, J.A., Eds. (1981,1989), *Parallel Models of Associative Memory,* (Revised edition, 1989) Hillsdale, NJ: Erlbaum.

Kersten, D., O'Toole, A.J., Sereno, M.E., Knill, D.C. and Anderson, J.A. (1987), Associative learning of scene parameters from images, *Applied Optics, 26,* 4999-5006.

Kawamoto, A.H. (1985), Dynamic Processes in the (Re)solution of lexical ambiguity, Ph.D. dissertation, Brown University, Providence, RI.

Kawamoto, A.H. and Anderson, J.A. (1985), A neural network model of multistable perception. *Acta Psychologica,* 59, 35-65.

Kohonen, T. (1988), The 'neural' phonetic typewriter, *Computer, 21* (March), 11-22.

Landauer, T.K., Kamm, C.A., and Singhal, S. (1988) Teaching a minimally structured back-propagation to recognize speech sounds, In *Proceedings of the Cognitive Science Society. 9th Annual Meeting,* 531-536, Seattle, WA.

Lippman, R.P. (1989) Review of neural networks for speech recognition, *Neural Computation,* 1, 1-39.

McClelland, J.L. and Rumelhart, D.E., Eds. (1986), *Parallel, Distributed Processing, Volume 2*, Cambridge, MA: MIT Press.

Maunsell, J.H.R. and Newsome, W.T. (1987), Visual processing in monkey extrastriate cortex, *Annual Review of Neuroscience*, 10, 363-401.

Movshon, J.A., Adelson, E.H., Gizzi, M.S. and Newsome, W.T. (1985), The analysis of moving visual patterns, in C. Chagas, R. Gattas, and C.G. Gross (Eds.), *Pattern Recognition Mechanisms*, Rome: Vatican Press.

Moyer, R.S. and Landauer, T.K. (1967), Time required for judgement of numerical inequality, *Nature, 215*, 1519-1520.

Niranjan, M. and Fallside, F. (1988), Neural networks and radial basis functions in classifying static speech patterns, Technical Report CUED/F-INFENG/TR-22 from Department of Engineering, Cambridge University.

Rossen, M.L. (1989), Speech syllable recognition with a neural network, Ph.D. thesis, Department of Psychology, Brown University, Providence, RI.

Rumelhart, D.E. and McClelland, J.L., Eds. (1986), *Parallel, Distributed Processing, Volume 1*, Cambridge, MA: MIT Press.

Sereno, M.E. (1989), A neural network model of visual motion processing, Ph.D. thesis, Department of Psychology, Brown University, Providence, RI.

Suga, N. and Jen, P.H.S. (1976), Disproportionate tonotopic representation for processing CF-FM sonar signals in the mustache bat auditory complex, *Science, 194*, 542-544.

Van Essen, D.C. (1985), Functional organization of primary visual cortex, In A. Peters and E.G. Jones (Eds.) *Cerebral Cortex, Volume 3: Visual Cortex*, New York: Plenum.

Viscuso, S.R. (1989), Memory for arithmetic facts: A perspective gained from two methodologies, Ph.D. thesis, Department of Psychology, Brown University, Providence, RI.

Viscuso, S.R., Anderson, J.A. and Spoehr, K.T., (1989) Representing simple arithmetic in neural networks, Technical Report 88-01 from Brown University Department of Cognitive and Linguistic Sciences, also in G. Tiberghien, Ed., *Advanced Cognitive Science: Theory and Applications*, Cambridge: Horwoods.

Waibel, A. (1988), Modular construction of phonetic neural networks, ATR Workshop on Neural Networks and Parallel Distributed Processing, July, 1988, Osaka, Japan.

Watrous, R.L. and Shastri, L. (1987), Learning acoustic features from speech data using connectionist networks, *Proceedings of the Ninth Annual Cognitive Science Society Meeting, Seattle, Washington*, Hillsdale, NJ: Erlbaum.

Name Index

Italicized page numbers indicate papers appearing in this volume.

Ackley, D. H., 548, 571, 684
Adrian, E. D., 218, 219, 221, 241
Ahn, S. M., 394
Aitkin, L. M., 428
Albano, S., 424
Albright, T. D., 425, 431
Amari, S. I., 123–124, *135–145*, 147, 298, 351, 380, 500
Anderson, J. A., 46, 74–78, *80–86*, 148, 249, 295, 395, 396, 502, 701–704, *705–716*
Anderson, R. A., 433, *440–446*
Andrew, A., 204
Apter, J. T., 125
Arbib, M. A., 135, 380, 403, 603
Argos, P., 691
Aristotle, 1–3, *5–10*
Ashby, W. R., 404
Atkinson, K. E., 573
Atkinson, R. C., 119
Auslander, D., 401

Babloyantz, A., 391, 399, 410
Bachmann, C. M., 509, 512
Bahadur, R. R., 468, 469
Baillie, R. T., 671
Baird, B., 388, 390
Baldi, P., 47, 544, *570–575*
Ballard, D. H., 395, 605, 632
Bard, P., 219
Barlow, H. B., 161, 204, 207, 208, 215–217, *218–234*, 386, 537
Barna, G., *516–523*
Barnden, J. A., 399–400, 409–411
Baron, R. J., *102–121*
Barrett, T. W., 112, 115
Bartlett, F. C., 24
Barto, A. G., 500
Batchelor, B. G., 149, *489–496*
Bateson, G., 22, 25, 305
Baum, E. B., 648, 651
Beazely, L., 126
Becker, S., 650
Benevento, L. A., 114
Bertolotti, R., 312
Beurle, R. L., 102, 114
Bickford, R. G., 411
Bickley, W. G., 352
Bienenstock, E. L., 46, 217
Bigelow, J., 15, 16
Bindman, L., 312
Bishop, P. O., 117, 225
Blakemore, C., 223, 224
Bliss, T. V. P., 451
Bobrowski, L., 500
Boole, G., 229
Boring, E. G., 229

Boser, B., *648–652*
Bottou, L.-Y., 650, 652
Boudreau, J. C., 429
Bourlard, H., 571
Bower, G. H., 631
Boycott, B. B., 116
Brain, A. E., 468, 469
Bransford, J. D., 501
Breiman, L., 388
Bressler, S., 394
Brooks, L., 501
Brown, P. B., 427, 434
Brown, R., 400–401, 481
Brown, T. H., *451–455*
Bullock, T. H., 161, 241, 386, 433
Burckhardt, C. B., 102
Burns, B. D., 222, 389
Bush, V., 15, 20
Buskirk, D. R., 312

Caianiello, E. R., 45–47, *48–64*
Caldwell, S., 16
Calford, M. B., 429
Cameron, S. H., 481
Camhi, J. M., 199
Campbell, F., 117, 221, 397
Cannon, W., 14
Cant, N. B., 427
Carnevali, P., 648
Carpenter, G., 147–150, *151–163*
Carroll, L., 40
Cattel, M., 241
Cavanagh, J. P., 102, 113, 114
Chan-Palay, V., 312
Changeux, J. P., 295–299, *300–307*
Chapman, C., 249
Chapman, P. F., *451–455*
Chay, T. R., 404
Chomsky, N., 199, 309, 623
Chou, P. Y., 680, 693, 694
Chow, K. L., 102, 114, 115
Chrisely, R., *516–523*
Chuong, C. M., 312
Churchland, P. M., 603
Churchland, P. S., 603
Cohan, C. S., 404
Cohen, M. A., 148
Colburn, H. S., 426
Coles, R. B., 426
Collier, R. J., 102, 106
Collins, D., 148
Conrad, M., 393
Constantine-Paton, M., 328
Cooper, G. F., 223
Cooper, L., 148, 217, 497–499, *500–506*, *509–512*
Cottrell, G. W., 47, 541–545, *546–569*, 571

Cover, T. M., 149, 481, *482–488*
Cowan, W. M., 309, 311, 328
Cragg, B. G., 224
Craik, J. W., 229
Creutzfeldt, O. D., 114
Crick, F., 46, 232
Cronholm, B., 318

Daniel, P. M., 242, 246, 346, 347
Darwin, C., 296, 300, 309
Davies, R. B., 675
Davis, H., 219
Davis, T. L., 505
Dean, A. F., 505
Dembo, A., *509–512*
Denker, J. S., *648–652*
de No, L., 319
Deschenes, M., 321, 346
Destexhe, A., 391
de Valois, R. L., 221
Devijver, P. A., 516
Devor, M., 319, 348
Dewson, J. H., III, 115
De Yoe, E. A., 255
Dodt, H., 394
Dostrovsky, J. O., 348
Dow, B. M., 324
Dowling, J. E., 103, 116
Dreyfus, H. L., 229, 399
Dreyfus, S., 395
Duda, R. O., 469, 502
duLac, S., *424–436*
Durlach, N. I., 426
Dykes, R. W., 328, 336

Earle, D. C., 400, 407
Edelman, G. M., 46, 125, 295–299, 303, *308–334*, 309–314, *335–348*, 702
Efron, B., 481
Eggers, M. D., 348
Einstein, A., 352
Elbaum, C., 148, *500–506*
Ellias, S. A., 402
Ellman, J. L., 571
Engle, J., 115
Enroth-Cugell, C., 116
Erickson, R. P., 219, 240
Ermentrout, B., 397
Esterly, S. D., *424–436*
Ewart, J. P., 199, 219

Fahlman, S. E., 603, 627
Fairen, A., 320
Fallside, F., 519
Farber, R., 671, 673
Farhat, N. J., 101
Fasman, G. D., 680, 693, 694
Fawcett, J. W., 123
Feldman, J. A., 395, 605, 627, 631
Feyerabend, P., 406
Finkel, L. H., 125, 297, *308–334*, *335–348*
Fiorentini, A., 117
Fischer, G. L., Jr., 469
Fisher, R. A., 18, 468
Fitzhugh, R., 204
Fix, E., 483
Fodor, J. A., 216, *603–636*
Foldiak, P., 217
Franks, J. J., 501

Fraser, S. E., 348
Freeman, R., 224
Freeman, W. J., 355, 383–386, *386–415*, 387, 388, 389, 390
Fujisawa, H. N., 327
Fukuda, Y., 245
Fukushima, K., 649

Gabor, D., 99, 104, 231
Galambos, R., 102, 219
Ganchrow, J. R., 219
Garfinkel, A., 399, 401, 407, 412
Garnier, J., 680, 686, 692, 693, 694, 696
Gately, M. T., 148
Gauld, A., 399
Gaze, R. M., 129, 135, 141, 211
Geman, S., 137, 673
Gerstein, G. L., 404
Gibson, R. E., 352
Gilbert, C. D., 321
Glass, L., 401
Gleick, J., 384
Glezer, V. D., 117
Goldberg, J. M., 239, 240, 249
Goldscheider, A., 102
Gonzales, R. C., 550, 552
Goodman, J. W., 102
Graf, H. P., *643–647*
Grajski, K., 388, 389
Granit, R., 219
Grassberger, P., 390
Gray, C. M., 389, 393
Green, D. M., 221, 222
Grenander, U., 673
Gross, C. G., 220, 225
Grossberg, S., 147–150, *151–163*, 165, 166, 168, 171, 172, 396, 402, 412, 500
Grusser, O. J., 219
Grusser-Comehls, U., 219
Guckenheimer, J., 401, 404
Guyon, I., *643–647*

Haas, H. L., 433
Hadamard, J., 703
Hammond, P., 116
Hand, P. J., 328
Harley, T., 468
Harrison, T. D., 519
Hart, P. E., 149, *482–488*, 501
Hartline, H. K., 202, 205, 207, 208
Hatfield, G., 603, 631
Haussler, D., 648
Hawkins, J., 468
Hawkins, R. D., 348
Hay, G. E., 352
Hebb, D., 46, 127, 297, 301, 302, 329, 331, 346, 385, 451, 454, 530–533
Hecht, S., 222
Heidmann, T., *300–307*
Henderson, D., *648–652*
Henry, G. H., 117
Highleyman, W. H., 481
Hill, K. G., 219
Hillis, D., 629
Hinton, G., 11, 395, 404, 518, 519, 546, 567, 568, 627, 628
Hirsch, H. V. B., 222, 431
Hodges, J. L., 483
Hoeltzell, P. B., 328
Hoff, M. E., 683
Hoffman, K. P., 117

Hoffman, S., 311
Holden, A. V., 407
Holmes, P., 405
Hope, R. A., 135
Hopfield, J. J., 163, 164, 305, 396, 403, 404, 509, 516, 533
Hornik, K., 47, 544, *570–575*
Horridge, G. A., 386
Horton, L. H., 102
Howard, R. E., *648–652*
Huang, J. J., 553
Huang, W. Y., 517
Hubbard, W., *648–652*
Hubel, D. H., 76, 103, 116, 118, 215, 220–225, 239, 240, 245–246, 305,
   328, 425, 433, 538, 651
Hunt, R. K., 348
Hurvich, L. M., 221
Hwang, C. H., 673

Irvine, D. R. F., 430
Ito, M., 114
Ivanoff, V. A., 117

Jackel, L. D., 643–647, *648–652*
James, W., 2, 88, 147, 148, 300, 453
Jameson, D., 221
Jeffries, J. G. R., 433
Jenkins, W. M., 346
John, E. R., 80
Johns, M. V., 483
Jones, E. G., 320, 322
Jones, R. S., 396
Jordan, M., 676
Joseph, R. D., 481
Julesz, B., 114, 395
Juola, J. F., 119

Kaas, J. H., 335, 336
Kabrisky, M., 103
Kabsch, W., 680, 681, 683, 693
Kaczmarek, L. K., 410
Kairiss, E. W., *451–455*
Kamback, M. C., 118
Kanal, L. N., 468, 483
Kandel, E. R., 75, 348
Kanerva, P., 177–179, *180–196*
Karplus, M., 681
Katz, J. J., 404, 612
Kawamoto, A. H., 46, 631
Kay, D. C., 352
Keating, M. J., 135
Keele, S. W., 501
Keenan, C. L., *451–455*
Kelso, S. R., 452
Kelly, D. G., 336
Killacky, H. P., 348
King, A. J., 430
Kishimoto, K., 135, 137
Kittler, L., 516
Knapp, A. G., 76
Knudsen, E. I., 421–423, *424–436*
Koerner, F., 247
Koford, J., 481
Kogh, C., 505
Kohonen, T., 5, 145, 147, 166, 168, 351, 396, 500, 502, 509, *516–523*,
   538
Kolmogoroff, A. N., 18
Kosko, B., 147, 163–164, *165–176*
Kosslyn, S., 2, 603, 631
Kraft, M. S., 102

Kubovy, M., 308
Kuffler, S. W., 116, 204, 220
Kuhl, P. K., 433
Kuhn, G. F., 427

Lakoff, G., 603
Landry, P., 328, 331
Lapedes, A., 671, 673
Lashley, K. S., 76, 99, 100, 102
Laskin, S. E., 321
Lauria, F., 64
LeCun, Y., *648–652*
Lee, C., 237
Lee, J. R., 116, 117
Lee, Y. W., 15, 21, 81
Lehky, S. R., 441
Leon, M., 404
Lettvin, J. Y., 12, 20, 33, 76, 199, *202–213*, 219
LeVay, S., 431
Levick, W. R., 219, 225
Levin, J. M., 694
Levine, D. S., 403, 412, 413
Levitt, M., 681
Levy, H., 24
Levy, S., 199
Lewin, K., 22
Lewis, P. M., 468, 469
Leyton, A. S. F., 335
Liberman, A., 426, 433
Lim, V. I., 680, 693
Linsker, R., 47, 217, 525–527, *528–540*, 541, 542, 571
Lippmann, R., 517, 518
Lippold, O., 312
Livingstone, M. S., 215
Llinas, R., 47, 330, 352–355, *356–382*
Loeb, J., 102
Loeve, M., 24
Loftsgaarden, D. O., 483
Lund, J. S., 328

MacArthur, R. H., 326
MacColl, L., 17, 22
Mackey, M., 401
MacKinley, A. C., 671
Maffei, L., 117
Makhoul, J., 520
Malkiel, B. G., 671
Manabe, T., 272, 275
Mandelbrot, B., 404
Mandell, A. J., 404
Manley, J. A., 429
Margoliash, D., 424
Marr, D., 127, 401, 537
Marshall, W. H., 219
Martinez, D. M., 394
Mason, C. J. W., 493
Mathews, B. W., 694
Maturana, H. R., *202–213*, 406
Maunsell, J. H. R., 431
Max, J., 553
May, R. M., 326, 404
Mayr, E., 309, 311
McClelland, J. M., 604, 612, 628, 631, 634, 635
McCulloch, W. S., 11, 12, 19, 22, 23, 38, 45, 47, 54, 199, *202–213*, 222
McDermott, E., 631
McIlwain, J. T., 123, 235–238, *239–253*
Mead, M., 22, 25
Medin, D. L., 501
Meinhardt, H., 346

Melzack, M., 240
Merzenich, M. M., 297, 308, 315, 316, 331, 336, 345, 346, 347
Middlebrooks, J. C., 431
Miller, R. G., 469
Minsky, M., 182–184, 546, 579–582, *583–597*, 674
Misgeld, U., 394
Mitchell, D. E., 224
Moiseff, A., 429
Moore, G. P., 404
Morrison, R., 23
Moudrianakis, E., 698–699
Moulton, D. G., 387
Mountcastle, V. B., 103, 126, 221, 318, 328, 335
Moyer, R. S., 118
Mozer, M. C., 551, 649
Müller, J., 240–241
Munro, P. W., 47, 217, 505, 543–544, *546–569*

Nakano, K., *90–98*
Nance, D. M., 348
Nass, M., 502
Neisser, U., 118
Nelson, R. J., 348
Newberry, N., 394
Newsome, W. T., 441
Nicoll, R., 394
Nillsson, N., *464–481*
Nishikawa, K., 680, 694
Noest, A. J., 399, 409, 410
Norton, T. T., 102
Nuwer, M., *102–121*

Ochs, M. T., 348
Oja, E., 145, 573
Olsen, J. F., 287, 289
Olsen, R. W., 348
O'Neill, W. E., 281, 286, 426
Oster, G., 397

Packard, D., 401
Pain, R. H., 680
Palmer, A. R., 430
Pao, Y.-H., 462
Papert, S., 182–184, 546, 579–582, *583–597*, 633, 684
Parker, D. P., 518, 674
Parnas, H., 329
Patrick, E. A., 489, 496, 516
Patte, P., 295–299, *300–307*
Pearson, J. C., 297–298, *335–349*, 433
Pellionisz, A., 47, 352–355, *356–381*
Pennington, K. S., 102, 106
Penz, P. A., 148
Perkel, D. H., 241, 386, 403, 410, 411
Peters, A., 320
Pettigrew, J. D., 220, 224
Pfaffman, C., 219
Phelps, R. W., 114
Piske, V. A., 481
Pitts, W. H., 11, 12, 45, 199, *202–213*
Poggio, G. F., 321, 505
Pollen, D. A., 116, 117
Polyak, S., 239
Pomerantz, J. R., 30
Postal, P., 612
Potter, T. W., 509
Powell, T. P. S., 320
Prager, R. W., 519
Prestige, M. C., 127, 135
Preston, K., Jr., 107

Pribram, K. H., 102, *102–121*
Procaccia, I., 390
Psaltis, D., 101
Pylyshyn, Z., 216, 386, *603–637*

Quesenberry, C. P., 483
Quian, N., *680–699*

Rakic, P., 319, 629
Ramon Y Cajal, P., 203, 211, 394
Rao, C. R., 468
Rasmusson, D. D., 348
Ratliff, F., 103, 116
Rayleigh, J., 406
Reeke, G. N., Jr., 309, 310, 331, 337, 338
Reilly, D. L., 148, *500–506*
Richards, W., 117
Rieger, P., 247
Rinzel, J., 404
Ritz, S. A., 396
Robson, B., 680, 686, 692, 694
Robson, J. G., 116, 221
Rockland, K. S., 328
Rodieck, R., 103, 116
Roeder, K. D., 257
Rohrer, W. H., 237
Rose, D., 505
Rose, J. E., 126, 426
Rosenberg, C., 680, 683, 685
Rosenblatt, F., 102, 584, 586, 587, 683, 684
Rosenblueth, A., 14–17, 19–22
Rosenfeld, E., 705
Rosenfeld, R., 404, 412, 413
Rosenzweig, M., 115
Rossen, M. L., 701–704, *705–716*
Rossler, O. E., 390
Rothbard, J. B., 312
Roucoux, A., 424
Ruelle, D., 405
Rumelhart, D. E., 12, 147, 396, 518, 546, 548, 549, 583, 604, 605, 607, 613, 628, 634, 635, 648, 674, 683, 684, 685

Sakit, B., 222, 223
Sampath, G., 404
Sander, C., 680, 681, 683, 693
Schaffer, M., 501
Scheibel, M. E., A. B., 427
Scheraga, H., 681
Schiller, P. H., 247, 431
Schmidt, J. T., 313, 348
Schmitt, E., 65–66, *67–74*
Schneider, W. S., 388, 414, 603
Schultheiss, P. M., 553
Schwartz, E. L., 257
Searle, J. R., 426
Sebestyen, G. S., 468, 493–494
Segel, L. A., 329
Sejnowski, T., 449, 519, 548, 603, *680–699*
Sekuler, R., 241
Selfridge, O., 11, 21, 27, 33
Semple, M. N., 428
Sereno, M. E., 701–704, *705–716*
Shannon, C. E., 227
Sharma, S. C., 135
Shaw, G. L., 404
Shepherd, G. M., 46, 320
Sherrington, C. S., 231, 404
Shlaer, R., 223
Shotter, J., 399

Silverman, D. J., 404
Singleton, R. C., 481
Skarda, C., 12, 355, 383–386, *386–415*
Skinner, B., 393
Skolnik, M. I., 255
Slansky, J., 462
Smolensky, P., 605, 612, 624, 627
Somogyi, P., 320
Sorabji, R., 1, 3
Sparks, D. C., 426
Sparks, D. L., 238
Spencer, W. A., 321
Sperry, R., 135, 211
Spinelli, D. N., 103, 116, 118, 119
Spitzberg, R., 117
Srihari, S. N., 648
Srinivasan, S. K., 404
Stanfill, C., 462
Stein, L., 426
Steinbuch, K., 65–66, *67–74*
Stemberg, S., 119
Stone, J., 245
Stone, S., 220
Stroke, G. W., 102, 108
Stryker, M. P., 431
Suga, N., 255–258, *259–294*, 433
Sullivan, R. M., 404, 427
Sur, M., 328, 347
Svaetichin, G., 116, 219, 221
Swets, J. A., 81, 222
Swigert, C. J., 112
Szentagothai, J., 114, 320

Takahashi, T. T., 427
Takens, F., 391
Takeuchi, A., 135, 136, 145
Talbot, S. A., 103, 126
Talbot, W. H., 221
Tank, D. W., 403
Tanner, W. P., 222
Thom, R., 303, 405, 410, 414
Tippet, J. T., 108
Tishby, N., 648
Touretsky, D., 404, 634
Trabasso, T., 118
Turin, G. L., 113
Turing, A. M., 31, 346, 603, 604, 616

Udin, S. B., 123
Ullmer, K., 698

Vanderburgh, A., 108
Van der Loos, H., 348
Van Dijk, B., 395
Van Essen, D. C., 255, 431
van Heerden, P. J., 102, 108
Varela, F. J., 406
Vernon, M. D., 308
Viana Di Prisco, G., 387, 389, 392, 393
Viscuso, S. R., 701–704, *705–716*
von Bekesy, G., 116
von Bonin, B., 22
von der Malsburg, C., 46, 123–125, *126–134*, 135, 136, 147, 217, 298, 328, 351
von Neumann, J., 20, 603, 604, 616
Voss, J. F., 118

Waddington, C. H., 406
Wagner, H. G., 221, 428

Wall, P. D., 319, 348
Waltz, D. L., 462
Wang, C. H., 648
Warren, S., 349
Wassel, G. N., 462
Watanabe, A., 433
Watson, J., 232
Weaver, W., 21, 227
Webster, T. A., 681
Weiss, P., 102, 126
Wenstrup, J. J., 424, 429
Werblin, F. S., 103
Werner, G., 103, 407
Westlake, P. R., 102, 112
White, E. L., 320, 505
White, H., *671–676*
Whitelaw, A., 328
Whitsel, B. L., 336
Whitteridge, D., 126, 242, 246, 347
Widrow, R. M., 683
Wiener, N., 11–13, *14–44*, 46, 63
Wiesel, T. N., 76, 103, 116, 118, 220–225, 239, 240, 245–246, 305, 328, 346, 425, 538, 651
Wigstrom, H., 337
Williams, R. J., 518
Willshaw, D. J., *126–134*
Wilson, H. R., 145
Winder, R. O., 481
Wise, L. Z., 430
Wohlgemuth, A., 222
Wong, D., 430
Woodrow, B., 227
Woolsey, C., 126, 322, 348
Wurtz, R. H., 239, 240, 249, 424

Yin, T. C. T., 428
Yoon, M., 136

Zangwill, O. L., 231
Zeeman, C., 135, 145
Zeki, S. M., 424
Zipser, D., 47, 147, *440–446*, 571
Zotterman, Y., 219

Subject Index

Abstraction, 59
Acoustic signals, and stored information, 284
Action potential, 529
Activity loops, 47
Activity patterns, distributed, 177
Adaptation, 46
Adaptive pattern classification, 459
Adaptive resonance theory (ART), 147–149, 151–163, 402
Adaptive signal processing, 535
Adaptive systems, models of, 65–66, 67–74
Adiabatic Learning Hypothesis, 45, 50, 54, 62
Adjustable Transformation Unit, 68
Algorithm performance, comparative, 513
Algorithms, substitutes for, 581
Amino acid residues, 667
Antibody synthesis, 300
Aplysia, 75–76, 303, 323
Arborization, 321
Artificial intelligence, 88, 589, 600
Association, 83–84
    and cognition, 599
    problems with, 600
Associationists, views of, 600
Associative mapping, optional, 509
Associatron, model of associative memory, 90–98
    computer simulation, 94–96
    properties of, 92
"Atomic facts," 88
Attractor basin, 149
Attractors, 148, 384, 405
Auditory cortex, bat, 254–258, 259–293
    representation in, 259
Auditory information, and vocalization system, 289
Auditory space representation, 282
Auditory system, peripheral, 257
Autoassociation, 87–88
Autocorrelation, 87–88

Babies, "prewiring" in, 148
Back propagation, 515, 518–519, 542, 570, 678
Backpropagation network, 516, 544, 641, 669
Bat cry portions, 256
Bat targets, characteristics of, 281
Bats, anatomy of, 259, 269, 291
Bayes classifier, 314, 460, 482, 484, 516, 521
Behavior
    epileptic, 57
    instinctive vs. intelligent, 52
    and single cells, 216
Benchmarking studies, 516–523
Best match problem, 177–179, 187, 190–192
Bidirectional associative memories, 163–164
Bifurcation theory, 404
Binary prediction, 72–74
Biological computation, 77

Biological memory, 11
Bisonar information, representation of, 259–261, 264, 284–287
Boltzmann machines, 516–517, 519
Brain
    adult learning in, 301, 304
    anatomical model of, 49
    as computer, 301, 309
    mammalian, 218
    as network, 594
    organization of, and engineering, 199
    single units of, 215–217, 218–232
    somatotopically organized layers of, 135
    vs. thinking machine, 52
Brain metaphors, 99
    traditional, 404
Brainstem, 215
Brain theory, 135, 386
"Bubble" activity region, 654
"Bug" detectors, 201

Categorization, context dependent, 309
Category formation, 147
Category stability, 147
Cell death, 312
Cells
    center surround, 531
    complex, 117
    computer simulation of, 129–131
    correlation of, 655
    cortical, 217, 529
    feature-analyzing, 528
    ganglion, 116
    orientation selective, 531
    pyramidal, 320
    retinal, 529
    simple, 117
    selectivity of, 217
    variance of, 526
    visual, 526
Central nervous system, and tensor network theory, 356–371
Cerebellar networks, 370
    essential, 361
Cerebellum
    and sensorimotor transformations, 357
    tensor model of, 360
Chaos, 386–417
    and "noise," 390–391
    and odor recognition, 393
    roles of, 396
    virtues of, 401
Circuitry, neural, large scale, 403
Classification algorithms, 497
    testing of, 513
Classification problem, description of, 482
Coarse coding, 11, 235

Codes, sensory, self-organization of, 402
Cognition, 406, 602
   systematicity of, 620–622
Cognitive architecture, 603
Cognitivism, 386, 406
Colliculus, superior, 235, 247
Color blob cells, 215
Command neurons, 76, 216
Component analysis, principal, 534, 571–575
Computation
   biological, 77
   and cognition, 579–580
   parallel, 583, 629
Computational ability, and neural network models, 579–597, 599–602,
     603–636
Computational flexibility, 599–600
Computational parameter. *See* Maps
Computer memory, 177
Concepts, 75
Conditioning, classical, 303
Connection strengths, 447, 529
   template of, 497
Connectionism
   vs. classical theories of mental structure, 605
   and cognitive architecture, 599–602, 603–636
   inefficiency of for computation, 599
   "lure" of, 627–628
   and neural dynamics, 397
   role of labels in, 610
   vs. symbolism, 594–596
   as theory of implementation, 634–635
Connectionist models, 403, 590. *See also* Networks
   and cognitive architecture, 606–607, 633
   and cognitivism, 408
   vs. digital computer as brain model, 400
   and graph structures, 610–611
   as neural abstractions, 404–405
   and neuroscience, 632
   popularity of, 603
   and psychologists, 603
   recent vs. early, 386–387
   and "scaling" problems in, 590–591
Convergence processes, retinal, 242
Correlational synapses, 526
Cortical analyzers, 236
Cortical inhibition, 46
Cortical layers, sequential scanning in, 12
Cortical maps, adult, plasticity in, 335–349
Cybernetics, 11–13

Darwinian selection, 304
Data classification, problem of, 468
Data representation, effective, 642
Data sorting, 464
Decision equations, 63
Decision regions, 499
Decision surfaces, 465, 470, 481
   quadric, 475–477
Decorrelation process, 217
Degeneracy, anatomical, 302
Dendritic fields
   and afferent maps, 242
   dimensions, 243
Depression, long term, 449
Digit recognition, handwritten, 639–652
Digital computer, as model for brain function, 386
Discriminant functions, 466–467, 469, 473, 476–480, 516
   linear, 469

Distributed storage, 187–190, 192–194
   and brain damage, 196
Diversity, neuronal, 311
DNA, 304
Doppler radar signal processing, 256
Doppler shift compensation, 260–264, 268, 272
Doppler sonar, 256

Echo delay, 276
Economic prediction, 671
EEG recordings, 386–392
   background activity in, 389
Efficient markets hypothesis, 675–676
Eigenvectors, 543
Electro-olfactogram, 387
Electrophysiology, 239
Energy function, 507
Energy landscape, 462
Energy minima, 507
Ensemble codes, 236, 241
Ensemble coding hypothesis, 2
Environment, features of, 528
Epigenesis, 305
Evolution equations, 63
Evolution, theory of, 539
   applications to learning and brain organization, 297–299, 593
   complexity and variability in, 296
   designer in, 296
   selection processes in, 297
Eye movement, 235, 237
Eyes, in vertebrates, 235

Feature analysis, 528, 542
Feature detector hypothesis, 240
Feature detectors, 386
Feature maps, 641–642
Feedback, 13
   and ART models, 148
   and connectionist models, 396, 604
Frog, visual system of, 200–201, 203–213

Gated dipole fields, 148
Generalization mechanisms, 460
Generalizations, 596
Genes, number in genome, 304
Genetic algorithm, 581
Geometry, functional, and brain function, 356–371, 375
Globular proteins, secondary structure of, 680–699
Grandmother cells, 76, 216
Group competition, 318, 324
Group confinement, 318, 319, 321
Group selection, 318, 321, 322–324

Hebb connectivity matrix, 47
Hebb rule, 302, 329, 410, 448, 451, 507, 526, 530–533, 654
   optimization properties of, 532
Hebb synapses, 45, 302, 318, 329, 526, 527
   self-organization in, 527
Hebbian modification, 449
Hidden units, 544
High density storage model, 509
"Hill climbing," 580, 587–588
Hippocampus, 448–450
Holographic theory, 100–101
Holographic transformations, 118
Homunculus, problem of, 309
Hopfield network, 533
Hopfield relaxation model, 509

Hypercolumns, 245–246
Hyperplane geometry, 472
Hyperspaces, metaorganization of, 378

Ideas, as patterns, 48
Image compression, 548–569
Images, basis, 552
In vitro technology, 454
Inference, 507, 541, 542, 625–626, 672
Information bearing parameters (IBPs), 259, 290
Information preservation, 536–537
Information processing, 289–290, 529
    and Connectionism, 603
    and symbolic representation, 400–401
Information representation, 217
Information storage, 80
    and activity loops, 447
Information theory, 535
Information, visual, 529
Informax principle, 537–539
Input patterns, 459
Invertebrates, and physiologists, 75

Karhunen-Loeve expansion, 541

Language, and logical syntax, 601
Large scale system behavior
    centrality of, 47
Lateral inhibition, 655
Learning
    adult, critical periods of, 306
    algorithm, 640
    back propagation, 570
    and connection strengths, 46
    from examples, 570–573
    "Generalized Delta Rule," 586–589
    and mismatch sensitivity, 159
    rapid, in mammals, 451
    by repetition, 58
    as slow process, 48
    by selection, 300–306
Learning matrix, 65, 71
    neuron in, 65
Learning matrix dipole, 66, 70
Learning matrix systems, 67
Learning rules, "real," 450
Learning Vector Quantization, 514, 516, 519–522
Linear machines, 470
LTP, 448–450, 451–455. See also Synaptic potentiation
    varieties of, 451–452

Maps
    movement in, 325
    ordered topographic (cortical), 314–318, 335–349
    plasticity and population variables in, 336
Matching functions, 597
Mathematical structures, as neural metaphors, 40
McCulloch-Pitts neuron, 45
Memory
    activity loops in, 447
    control functions of, 119
    genetic, 52
Memory capacity, 194–196
Memory model
    relaxation model for, 509–511
    and spatial correlation functions, 75–78
    sparse distributed, 177–179
    and synaptic strength, 447
Memory retrieval, 533

Memory storage, 76, 80–86, 118, 447
Memory traces, 80, 118–119
Mental objects, 301
Metaorganization principle, 362. See also Tensor theory
Mind
    abstraction in, 59
    classical models of, 603
    "Representationalist" vs. "Eliminativist" theories of, 605
Minima, local and global, 581
Minimum distance classifiers, 470
Mnemonic equations, 45, 50–52, 56, 61, 63
Modification threshold, 449
Motor action, geometry of, 351–352
Motor apparatus, 365
Motor neuron output, 352
Motor proprioception, 352
Motor system, complexity of, 351
Multilayer nets, 498
    middle layer units of, 541
Muscles, 351

"Nearest neighbor," 641
    algorithms, 513
    categorizers, 461
    classifiers, 460–461, 482
    error probability, 481
    rule, 482
Nerve fields, topographic organization of, 135
Nervous system
    balance of, 217
    internal loop of, 353
    mapping relations in, 421–423
    vertebrate, 135
Network architecture, 237
Network models
    non-linear, 544
    standard, 46
    and system energy functions, 507
Network oscillations, 47, 384
Network stability, importance of, 147
Networks, layered self-adaptive, 529–532
Networks, connectionist. See also Neural networks
    and linear networks, 565
    and principal component analysis (PCA), 541–545, 561–569
Networks, tectal metric type, 376
Neural adhesion, 311
Neural circuitry, development of, 528
Neural circuits, redundant, 296–297
Neural computation, simple distributed, 235
Neural dynamics, 399
Neural field theory, 135–136
Neural nets
    economic, 671–676
    as predictors, 670
    re: protein molecule shapes, 677–690
Neural networks. See also Network models; Networks
    and Bayes classifiers, 460–461
    computational abilities of, 579, 599
    and connection strengths, 447
    and decision making accuracy, 516
    as decoders, 671
    vs. human cognition, 579–580
    optical realizations of, 100–102
    parallel, 251
    and pattern classification, 450–460
    resonance models, 147
    simplicity vs. detail in, 13
    statistical inference in, 541
    uses of, 599

Neural networks (cont.)
    Winner-take-all, 148
Neural representations, 301–302. *See also* Representations
Neurobiology, 75
Neurocomputer, and "real problem" solving, 250
Neuroethology, 199
Neuronal assemblies, and thought 45, 55
Neuronal group, definition of, 318
Neuronal group selection, 125, 295–296, 297–299, 309–311, 338–342
Neuronal representations, covariant and contravariant, 357–360
Neuronal variation, 313
Neuronic equations, 45, 49, 51, 55, 63
Neuron-neuron adhesion, developmental, 311–312
Neurons
    auditory, specialized, 289–290
    large field, 239–240
Neurophysiology
    routines of, 215
NMDA synapse, 46, 448–450
Non-linear dynamics, 386

Oculomotor system, 248
Odotopic representation, 277, 280, 287
Olfaction, information processing in, 387
Olfactory bulb, 383–384
    learning in, 395
Olfactory discrimination, 394–395, 399
Output categories, 459
Output code, distributed, 237
Overlapping categories, 514

Pandemonium model, 462
"Parallel-hierarchical" processing, 287–289
Parallel networks, programming of by example, 547
Parallel processing
    advantages of, 596
    paradox of, 596
Parzen windows, 462
Pattern analysis, learned, 60
Pattern Classification, 459–523, 465–481, 482–487, 489–496
    linear, 471
    practical, 459
Pattern Classifiers
    neural networks as, 459–463
    static, 459
Pattern recognition, statistical, 516, 523
Pavlovian conditioning, 403, 451
Perception, 386, 533
Perceptrons, 580, 587
    limitations of, 584–585
Perceptual network, self-organization in, 528–540
Physiologists, 407
Point images, 236, 243–244
"Pontifical" neuron, 216
Postsynaptic activity, 448
Postsynaptic receptor, 302
Potential function classifiers, 507–508
Predictive algorithm, 669–670
Prepyriform cortex, 383–384
Prerepresentations, 302–303
Presynaptic activity, 448
Primary percepts, 301
Programming, extensional, 567–568
Psychopathology, 12
Pulse compression, 255
Pulsed radar, 255

Quadric decision surfaces, 475
Quadric discriminant functions, 475–476

Quantizer, 552–553

Reasoning, by past example, 462
Recall, perfect, 509
Receptive field overlap, 326
Receptive fields, neuronal, increases in, 249
Receptor desensitization, 303
Receptor mosaic, 239
Recognition, 77, 81–82
Recognition threshold, 119
Recollection, 2–3
Reconstruction, 82–83
Representations,
    compositionality of, 622–625
    distributed, 596–597, 604, 611–615
    vs. local, 217
    stored, 391
Resonance, concept of, 303
Retina, 235
    convergence processes in, 242
Reverberations, neuronic, 54–55

Self-organizing systems, 525
    constraints of, 398
    nonbiological, 398
Semantic content, 608
Sensation, 386
Sensorimotor systems, tensorial scheme of, 374
Sensorimotor transformations, 377
Sensory systems, peripheral, 386
Signal processing, 255
Simulation, importance of, 408
Single cell development, 537–539. *See also* Cells
Single units, importance of, 12, 215
Sodium channels, 448
Speech recognition, 462, 515, 516–523
State vectors, 177, 351
Statistical pattern recognition, 516–523
Stereotaxic atlas, 215
Stripes, 328
Subjective perception, 216
Symbol manipulation, 407
Symbol systems, need for, 618–620
Symbols
    and behavior, 409
    and sub-symbols, 605
Synapses,
    excitatory, 393
    selective stabilization of, 302–304
Synaptic model, with group selection, 329
Synaptic modification, 46, 135–138, 447
Synaptic potentiation, long term, 447–450, 451–455
Synaptic strength
    and ion flow, 448
    and memory storage, 447
Syntax, 626

Tensor theory, 352
    and metric tensor, 354
    and summation convention, 355
    and vector components, 352–353
Thalamus, 56, 239
Thinking machines, 45–47
    criteria of stability in, 57
Thought
    definition of, 53
    language of, 603
Thought processes, theory of, 48–64
Threshold Logic Unit (TLU), 460, 471–473

Tonotopic representation, 265–268
Topographic maps, 257
Trainable pattern classifier, 467–468
Tremors, 363, 379
Typewriter, neural phonetic, 653–666

"Units," in connectionist networks, 604
"Unlearning," 509

Visual grasp reflex, 236
Visual neurons, 239
Visual system
    large receptive fields in, 239–249
    mammalian, 249, 257, 525
Visualization, as computational tool, 2
Vocalization system (in bats), 289

"Weights," in connectionist networks, 604